ADMINISTRATIVE LAW AND POLITICS

OPP

ADMINISTRATIVE LAW AND POLITICS: CASES AND COMMENTS

FOURTH EDITION

CHRISTINE B. HARRINGTON
New York University

LIEF H. CARTER
Colorado College

CQ PRESS

A DIVISION OF SAGE
WASHINGTON, D.C.

CQ Press
2300 N Street, NW, Suite 800
Washington, DC 20037

Phone: 202-729-1900; toll-free, 1-866-4CQ-PRESS (1-866-427-7737)

Web: www.cqpress.com

Cover design: designfarm
Composition: Marcie Pottern

∞ The paper used in this publication exceeds the requirements of the American National Standard for Information Sciences—Permanence of Paper for Printed Library Materials, ANSI Z39.48-1992.

Printed and bound in the United States of America

12   11   10   09   08   1   2   3   4   5

Library of Congress Cataloging-in-Publication Data

Harrington, Christine B.
    Administrative law and politics : cases and comments /
Christine B. Harrington, Lief H. Carter.— 4th ed.
        p. cm.
    Authors' names appear in different order in previous ed.;
    Carter, Lief H. name appears first.
    Includes bibliographical references and indexes.
    ISBN 978-0-87289-934-6 (alk. paper)
  1. Administrative law—United States. I. Carter, Lief H. II. Title.

KF5402.C37 2009
342.73'06—DC22

                                        2008048858

To my wonderful sons, Peter McCusker Brigham-Hill
and Atticus Harrington Brigham.
C.B.H.

For Plummy Jean Carter and Lillian Frances Carter.
L.H.C.

CONTENTS

FIGURES AND TABLES

PREFACE

Administrative law is a vitally important part of our legal and political systems. It affects us all, not just lawyers and judges. This book opens the doors of administrative law for students, business people, and public servants—the non-lawyers whose lives are influenced by government and law every day.

For liberal arts students we hope this book does two things. It should alert them to the tremendous scope and power of administrative government, and it should illuminate how the legal system shapes administrative procedure and practice. For students of business the book provides a guide to the features of a legal and political process that can often seem like an impenetrable morass of rules and regulations. And for readers who now practice or are training to work as public administrators, we hope this book will help them navigate the treacherous reefs of administrative law and procedure, rather than run aground through poor legal navigation or, worse, remain at anchor, paralyzed by legal uncertainties. We hope, in other words, to help people aspiring to work (or already working) in government and the private sector acquire knowledge for effective decision making, so they will know when they need to send an S.O.S. to a lawyer asking for professional help.

We have tried for the most part to write about administrative law as clearly as possible for non-law students. Part I presents a working definition of administrative law and introduces a theoretical framework for evaluating modern administrative law. Part II reviews some of the major issues in the field, and Part III illustrates these issues in action. Part IV draws upon the knowledge readers have gained in the first three parts to evaluate the politics of contemporary administrative law issues, such as privatization and outsourcing of government services.

None of us can make much conceptual sense of law and politics until we are able to fit what we see into some theoretical structure. Therefore, this book emphasizes more than other texts what the rule of law means in administrative governance. We believe this focus will aid practitioner and academician alike. You will find our approach introduced and sketched in Part I, referred to in passing in Parts II and III, and fully defended in Part IV.

Judged by the theories of law and politics presented in this book, we believe that administrative law today lacks a unifying philosophical basis. Some may count the field's lack of a clear normative voice as a virtue on the ground that it permits a more fluid, pragmatic, and incremental evolution of policy. We disagree. This book, in other words, does take sides. At least users who disagree with our positions will have what we hope are evaluative standards to argue against (e.g., fairness and equality in the rule of law, transparency, and accountability).

The hardest part of developing this book was deciding what to leave out. We are writing here for non-lawyers about a murky, sprawling, and arguably underdeveloped branch of law, one rich with issues about which law professors and judges abidingly disagree, and rife with topics that have a reputation for being (next to "estates in land") some of the most highly technical material taught in law school. Thus, much has been omitted. Teachers and readers with strong administrative law backgrounds will have to accept that many of the more interesting legal puzzles—the *Wyman-Gordon* problem for example, and the Administrative Procedure Act's labyrinthine definitions of rules and rulemaking, orders, and adjudication—do not appear here, precisely because they are so interesting to law professors. Given those objectives, we have de-emphasized some classic cases like *Crowell v. Benson* because the complicated contexts from which they arise are likely to confuse non-lawyers, and because the law they represent has little practical significance in the present day. We have tried to include cases easily digested by readers who lack formal legal training. And we have tried to present cases featuring a diverse array of the federal and state agencies whose work those cases reveal in order to expand students' appreciation for the complexities of the administrative process.

A few practical suggestions for learning and teaching from this book may be helpful. First, do not be surprised if the material as organized by chapter is not in the end so neatly divided as it appears from the table of contents. In part, this intersection and overlapping of topics follows from the nature of administrative law itself. Thus, when you reach chapter 9 you will find material on administrative enforcement that recalls the discussion of administrative information-gathering found in chapter 5.

Second, because of the richness and diversity of administrative law, teachers are often tempted to focus on the many extant exceptions and qualifications to more generally accepted rules. This approach can create a choppy text, and a discontinuous course of study that students may find difficult to follow. We have tried to avoid this by placing some of the contradictory but nevertheless important material in the "Exercises" sections at the end of each chapter. We hope the chapter-end exercises and questions stimulate and aid effective teaching. Please be aware, however, that some of these sections make points that teachers and students will not want to neglect and which they will not find in the body of the book.

Third, we have organized Part II roughly to follow the steps of an actual contested administrative action, from information gathering to judicial review. College students and graduate students in masters of public administration programs much appreciate this sequence. However, teachers who put judicial review at the theoretical front of their courses, in the manner of Gellhorn, Byse, Strauss, Rakoff, and Schotland, for example, may prefer that students at least skim chapter 10 as they read chapters 2, 3, and 4. As we move through the steps of the administrative process, we included in chapter 3 material on the current status of the "regulatory takings" doctrine, such as state legislative actions following the Supreme Court's decision in *Kelo* (2005) and research on the ideologies and institutions of the private property movement. Chapter 4 looks beyond the era of administrative discretion to the post-*Chevron* legal developments.

Fourth, throughout this new edition we give concrete examples of non-enforcement and government inaction in such areas as environmental regulation, consumer protection, and occupational-health-and-safety rulemaking. Specifically, chapters 5, 6, 9, and 10 have been revised significantly to reflect the increasing role of the executive branch in establishing informal policy groups, such as former Vice President Cheney's National Energy Policy Development Group, that come under the rules of informal administrative policy making. Related to this trend, we discuss the shift toward executive inaction and the struggle by states (*Massachusetts v. EPA*, 2007) as well as public interest groups to judicially mandate that the government enforce its own rules. We ask readers to consider such government inaction as an affirmative exercise of executive powers, rather than as merely neglect. This perspective enables us to see beyond the particular policy preferences of any one presidential administration to the fundamental role of executive power in administrative policymaking and law.

Finally, as this edition of our book goes to press, the free-market regulatory paradigm of the last thirty years is not only falling out of favor with American voters but also with the automobile, banking, and insurance industries that have long advocated for deregulation. Major corporations from these same industries are seeking—and receiving—government financial bailouts. Will President Barack Obama's administration reverse the course of this economic solution by, for example, proposing large-scale employment programs similar to those introduced during the New Deal? Given recent evidence of structural shortcomings in the free-market economy, readers may find especially topical our emphasis on cases that exemplify the pitfalls of protecting private property rights at the expense of public interest values. For example, we highlight a growing trend by states to institute stricter pollution controls than those imposed under federal law, and the persistent efforts by public interest organizations to encourage government compliance with the law, both through agency and court actions. Chapter 14 has completely new material to help students learn and think about policy outcomes, such as privatization of prisons and outsourcing of government services, that have been institutionalized under the rubric of free market economic self-regulation. In short, our focus in this edition is to prepare students for a new era of administrative law disputes, and their attendant legal interpretations, during a time of political change.

Acknowledgments

This new edition builds on the talents of those colleagues who worked with us over the years to construct a sound text. We remain thankful to them for their efforts. They are Professors Alfred C. Aman, Jr., Suffolk University Law School; John Brigham, University of Massachusetts, Amherst; James Colvin, University of Colorado at Colorado Springs; Chris Eisgruber, Princeton University; Carolyn Long, Washington State University Vancouver; Albert R. Matheny, University of Florida; Charles Nobel, California State University, Long Beach; Roger Richman, Old Dominion University; James S. Robert, University of Nevada, Reno; Steven Seitz, University of Illinois; Martin Shapiro, University of California-Berkeley; Sally Jo Vasicko, Ball State University; George Warp, University of Minnesota; and and Peter Woll, Brandeis University.

Political scientists and law professors who approach administrative law with an eye toward strengthening democratic governance also inspired this book. While we are mindful that the debate persists whether doctrinal materials are properly part of an administrative law text or belong, rather, to the agendas of public-interest law, we are grateful that Professors David Fellman, David Trubek, and Louise Trubek, University of Wisconsin, Madison, and Joel Handler, University of California, Los Angeles, urged us to ask how administrative law may or may not advance social justice in a liberal democracy. We also want to acknowledge scholars in law and social science whose empirical research on comparative practices and transnational institutions contributed to this new edition: Professors Renee Cramer, Drake University; Simon Halliday, University of Strathclyde, Scotland; Laura Hatcher, Southern Illinois University-Carbondale; Bronwen Morgan, University of Bristol, UK; and Patrick Schmidt, Macalester College. Our students' reactions to earlier editions and their labor as research assistants were essential in producing a book we hope will enliven the classroom. This new edition benefited greatly from the research assistance of Ziya Umut Turem, PhD candidate, Law and Society Program, New York University, who also used the previous edition in his undergraduate administrative law course. We acknowledge and thank graduate teaching assistants Gabrielle Clark and Leila Kawar of New York University, who provided invaluable feedback on what works and doesn't in the classroom. Undergraduates also had a hand in shaping this text and we are grateful for their assistance: Stuart Address, Rutgers University, New Brunswick; Peter Brigham, Lake Forest College; and Sipoura Barzideh, Nina Berman, Sarah Fritz-Randolph Brown, Hayley Campbell, Sarah Lensing, Filip Mardjokic, Ryan P. McCarthy, Larry Shapiro, Thais-Lyn Trayer, and Catherine Zack, New York University.

Finally, we have worked with several great editors over the course of writing this book. First, John Covell, now at Yale University Press, but previously at Little, Brown, encouraged us to do the second edition, which we did with the support of two editorial groups and two publishing houses over the course of a corporate buy-out: Richard Welna at Scott Foresman and Company and Lauren Silverman, Catherine Woods, and Michael Weinstein at HarperCollins. The third edition was placed in the trusty hands of Eric Stano, Acquisitions Editor, Political Science, and his staff at Addison Wesley Longman shortly after they purchased the college division of HarperCollins.

This new edition is the result of the exceptionally talented team of people at CQ Press. In particular, Charisse Kiino, Chief Acquisitions Editor, understands where administrative law fits alongside the study of politics and public administration. Her wise counsel, encouraging hand, and ability to get things done exemplify the highest standards in publishing. We owe her a great debt for her patience and a big thank you for all her support. Allison McKay, Assistant Editor, diligently and very competently transmitted our manuscript into the capable hands of copyeditor and lawyer Michael Coffino. He has been sim-

ply brilliant in his capacity to find better ways of communicating the legal language of administrative politics. We value the careful production work of Anne Stewart and her coordination of the composition process. Thanks to Steve Pazdan, Managing Editor, for shepherding the manuscript from final draft to published book. Bonnie Moore, the proofreader, and Enid Zafran, who prepared the index, also deserve our thanks and appreciation. Christopher O'Brien and Erin Snow, Marketing Manager and Associate Marketing Manager, have done a fine job in getting the word out about this edition. In the end, of course, we assume responsibility for the text, but all of these people helped us realize what an administrative law and politics book could be, and we acknowledge them with gratitude.

Christine B. Harrington and Lief H. Carter
November 2008

CHAPTER 1
WHY ADMINISTRATIVE LAW?

This book introduces you to one of the most important and far-reaching fields in American law and politics. From a local zoning board that decides whether a tall apartment building can go up across the street and obstruct our lovely view, to the large federal agencies that tax us and regulate the safety of the air we breathe and the airplanes we fly on, unelected public administrators make and enforce the vast majority of rulings that govern our lives. We may think of politics as elections, fights in Congress and declarations of policy from the White House, but the real muscle of government resides in bureaucrats and bureaucracies.

Because we live in a liberal democratic political system, "we, the people" are empowered to question how government uses its muscle. We do that in large part by insisting that government justify its uses of power in terms of legal rules and procedures. The principles of administrative law you are about to explore describe the legal tools that government uses to defend its bureaucratic power and that aggrieved parties use to attack that power.

Administrative law has political consequences for all citizens, but it has even more immediate consequences for people who deal with government on a daily basis. Students of business know they will contend in their professional lives with much governmental control of their efforts. They want to know what protections the law affords them in this process. Students who now work or plan to work in public careers have an equally pragmatic

reason for studying administrative law. They need a road map to help them find their way through the maze of rules and procedures they may confront on the job. This book teaches both the practical aspects of administrative law and the important political theories that underlie them.

The themes raised in this book touch central problems in American politics—how we came to have our present political system, how that system may fail to achieve the ends we expect of it, and what we may be able to do about such failures. Here, in a nutshell, are the five major themes of this book.

FIVE THEMES

1. Bureaucratic government has existed in varying degrees in nearly all organized political systems. Modern American bureaucratic government has been shaped by a belief that the dominant free market economic system cannot meet certain important social needs. Administrative power grew to offset the tremendous economic, social, and political power that another form of organization—large private business enterprises—accumulated in the nineteenth century.

2. Today the effects of administrative government influence us literally every moment of our lives. Understanding the character of administrative regulation, as well as its scope, is critical for understanding the development of the modern state. The initial motivation—to counter the power of large business enterprises—remains, but the authority of administrative government

today includes goals like regulating technology and protecting people from major unforeseeable and/or uncontrollable modern risks, such as natural disasters, global warming or chemical/biological hazards.

3. Bureaucratic government has provided no utopian cure for the shortcomings of capitalism. Nor have the policies and technologies to protect people from risks in modern life produced a worry-free environment. In fact, the bureaucratic state has built-in tendencies that can lead it to treat individuals unfairly and to produce arbitrary and unjustifiable policies.

4. Administrative law seeks to reduce the tendency toward arbitrariness and unfairness in bureaucratic government. It is part of a political culture that values placing controls on the use of power, thus keeping exercise of power within democratic boundaries.

5. Administrative law is a relatively new and open-ended field of law. This book reviews the key ethical issues in administrative law: Does administrative law actually improve the quality of our lives? If not, how must it change in order to do so?

The remainder of this chapter elaborates the first three stage-setting themes. The last two themes will introduce administrative law itself in chapter 2.

THEME ONE: A BRIEF HISTORY OF THE ADMINISTRATIVE STATE

Political leaders from the beginning of recorded history have controlled their subjects through rules and government enforcement of rules. Most aspects of life have been regulated at some time in history and some public concerns have been regulated since ancient times. For example, regulation of ferryboat operators trace back to 1900 BC. In 1901, archeologists working in what is now Iraq discovered ancient stone inscriptions now known as the Code of Hammurabi, king of Babylon. The code, a record of the legal rulings the king had made during his reign, contained 280 entries, carefully organized by subject matter. Twenty-five sections regulated a variety of professionals, among whom were ferrymen. Similarly, in the eighteenth century, one of the Maryland state legislature's first statutes authorized county judges to set the

maximum prices that could be charged by those ferrying passengers and cargo across the state's waterways. In 1838, after one-too-many explosions of steamboat boilers, Congress created an agency to inspect steamboats for safety. Today, if you travel across the northwestern part of Washington state, you will cross Puget Sound by a state-operated ferry.

Surely, if a phenomenon such as governmental control of the ferry business occurs throughout human history, good reasons for it must exist. Public safety is one obvious reason. Another, which applies equally to ancient Babylon, eighteenth-century Baltimore and twentieth-century Bremerton, Washington, is perhaps less obvious: Once a society begins to follow the principle of the division of labor, some people will develop monopolies. The person who controls the land where people find it safe to cross a river, or the person who has obtained the privilege of ferrying people across for a fee, possesses a natural monopoly. He can charge not only his operational costs plus a reasonable profit, but whatever the customer is willing to pay, which may be much more. Farmers in ancient and modern times alike resent losing part of the value of their crop to such a monopolist, and they complain to their king or their government when they believe someone gouges them. The ferrying business, in other words, is an ancient example of a natural monopoly and hence of a free market failure.

But why should powerful kings listen to ordinary citizens? Honoring the claims of such citizens often means ruling against the interests of the wealthy and powerful. What political advantage does a king gain by siding with the powerless? How can we explain the existence of regulation in the public interest? This is one of the great, fundamental questions of politics in general, and one to which we can suggest the beginnings of an answer. Some rulers are truly altruistic. Others try to remain popular to prevent uprisings that could remove them from power by force. Furthermore, rulers throughout history have had to build and maintain the power to fight—to defend territory against outsiders at the very least and wage effective territorial conquests at best. History rather clearly indicates that rulers, while they may win battles, do not win wars when the bulk of the citizenry resists them or stops caring about the outcome. Thucydides's history of the losses of Athens to Sparta teaches this lesson. So does the United States' defeat in Vietnam and its failures in Iraq.[1] To maintain political popularity and military strength, rulers must please not just those few with wealth and power, but also the less wealthy majority that constitutes the political base and on whose morale the war effort depends. This, in fact, is the most significant aspect of "democracy" as a political system: it gives people a tangible resource—the right to vote—to make sure that rulers in a democracy, the politicians, are forced to "please" them.

Today we use words like *liberty*, *equality*, and *individual dignity* in our discussions of public policy. We want to believe that government serves all social interests. These values are indeed noble, but we must recognize that governments honor them partly for reasons of self-preservation.

Administrative Government in the United States

Recall the Maryland statute allowing county judges to regulate ferry charges. Why would judges rather than administrators perform such tasks? The early authors of regulations—Hammurabi or the Maryland legislature—had no grand scheme of administrative government plotted out for the future. In Maryland, county judges were mainly responsible for governing their counties. The legislature simply added the setting of ferry rates to their list of duties.

Congress's early efforts to create administrative agencies had no grand design either. The first Congress of 1789 faced two problems for which the expedient solution at the time rather obviously seemed an office or agency. The first problem was to establish a way of estimating the duties that importers should pay on goods they obtained in foreign countries. The second task was to organize a response to claims for pensions filed by soldiers "wounded and disabled during the late war."

1. On a smaller but more dramatic scale, so does the American film *On the Waterfront* (1954), which depicts the breakdown of an organized crime syndicate.

Congress created two agencies to solve those problems, presumably because each problem would last for the foreseeable future and because some expertise and consistency from case to case would be desirable. Both organizations continue to this day.

In one sense these early agencies had very modest aims. They resulted not from any monumental political battles between the wealthy and the common man, but rather from a basic need to serve widely recognized public interests. Notice also how both these tasks fit squarely into the age-old reasons for government to protect "us" (domestic producers, in this case) against "them" (foreign competition) and to encourage, in the case of veterans' claims, the willingness to fight in defense of country.

The expansion of administrative government in the United States since 1789 did not follow anyone's plan. One relatively minor contemporary indication of this fact is that the various names of government offices—*Agency, Board, Commission, Administration, Bureau*, and so forth—tell you absolutely nothing about the office to which they attach.

Understanding the growth of administrative government, particularly in the twentieth century, requires review of some economic history. The producer of, say, Flemish harpsichords in Antwerp in the seventeenth century, would have belonged to a guild. The agreements and customs of the guild controlled most aspects of the harpsichord trade: who could work, how many units per year they could produce, prices, wages, and the like. The introduction of so-called free competition would only upset this balance. By the end of the eighteenth century, however, the concept of free and unlimited competition had been elevated from something devilish to something holy. In no small part because of Adam Smith's widely read *The Wealth of Nations* (1776), people in power began to undo self-imposed restrictions on who could produce how many of which goods. Freedom to compete was also the freedom to specialize, and in specializing and dividing labor lay the key to increasing the productivity of labor.

This idea seemed particularly benign in America, where the losers in the competitive game could simply "go

West" rather than starve. *Laissez faire*[2] ruled, so that the major nineteenth-century manufacturing, banking, and transportation businesses operated with near-complete freedom from either governmental or guild-imposed regulations. If anything, by the last half of the century, government actively promoted business. Government promotion of business and protection of private property rights is itself a form of regulation, although we do not commonly use the term regulation in this sense. The economic theory of *laissez faire* favors open competition among capitalists over government control of the economy, but it also relies on the state to protect private property rights and to enforce private business agreements such as contracts. Even Adam Smith recognized that the state played an important role in policing and maintaining order *for* the "free market."

Business bought some of this support with outright bribes. Standard Oil, a common joke of the times put it, did everything to the Ohio legislature except refine it. Yet even without bribes the government would have assisted railroad and lumber and cattle interests with huge grants of land. It would have maintained high tariffs, an anti-competitive policy disguised as promoting competition. Local police and the National Guard supported management with physical force in the 1892 Homestead Steel Strike. Facing a devastating labor strike in 1894, the Pullman Company bypassed the more progressive state government in Illinois and took its case straight to President Grover Cleveland, who sent in the Army to break up the strike.

For the bulk of the century, these forces converged to produce a remarkably unrestrained economy: mushrooming industrial technology that climaxed in the electrification of America; tremendously abundant natural resources easily exploited by well-capitalized large corporations; a thoroughly pro-business attitude by government; and a theory of *laissez faire* to call upon for support.

Well before the end of the century, however, this burst of economic freedom, this exception to the more usual course of economic history, began to die. The more successful businesses engaged in powerful domination of the less successful. And when economic panics (recessions or depressions we would call them today) struck, as they have throughout economic history, even more monopolizing occurred as investors created trusts to restore the blessed protection of the guilds.

Before the end of the century this unrestrained power had begun to impose such crushing costs on the average citizen that democratic politics mobilized to check it. Here, for example, is the farmer's point of view in 1891:

Farmers are passing through the "valley and shadow of death"; farming as a business is profitless; values of farm products have fallen 50 per cent since the great war, and farm values have depreciated 25 to 50 per cent during the last ten years; farmers are overwhelmed with debts secured by mortgages on their homes, unable in many instances to pay even the interest as it falls due, and unable to renew the loans because securities are weakening by reason of the general depression; many farmers are losing their homes under this dreadful blight, and the mortgage mill still grinds. We are in the hands of a merciless power; the people's homes are at stake. . . .

From this array of testimony the reader need have no difficulty in determining for himself "how we got here." The hand of the money changer is upon us. Money dictates our financial policy; money controls the business of the country; money is despoiling the people. . . . These men of Wall Street . . . hold the bonds of nearly every state, county, city and township in the Union; every railroad owes them more than it is worth. Corners in grain and other products of toil are the legitimate fruits of Wall Street methods. Every trust and combine made to rob the people had its origin in the example of Wall Street dealers. . . . This dangerous power which money gives is fast undermining the liberties of the people. It now has the control of nearly half their homes, and is reaching out its clutching hands for the rest. This is the power we have to deal with.[3]

After the close of the Civil War, government was caught between popular cries like Mr. Peffer's and the appeal of the theory of free competition. The wealthy and influential supporters of free competition gained further strength because *laissez faire* appeared to fit so neatly into

2. *Laissez faire* is a French term that literally means "let do." It became an important slogan in France in the 18th century among people who wanted to eliminate trade restrictions imposed by the French government. Later, it came to represent "a doctrine opposing governmental interference in economic affairs beyond the minimum necessary for the maintenance of peace and property rights," in the words of Merriam-Webster's dictionary.

3. W. A. Peffer, *The Farmer's Side* (New York: D. Appleton & Co., 1891), 42.

Darwin's theory of evolution. To many, Herbert Spencer's *Social Statics* established the scientific justification for free competition. (Indeed the term *survival of the fittest* was first Spencer's, later appropriated by Darwinians.[4])

But this allegedly virtuous logic bringing together social Darwinism and free competition suffers from a terminal defect. The laws of supply and demand produce the greatest good for the greatest number only when laborers, farmers, businessmen, and financiers can easily and quickly enter any market which promises them a better return than they currently get. It works only in the absence of monopolies. The lawyers, railroad owners, industrialists, and bankers who busily constructed trusts and monopolies defended their right to eliminate competition by invoking the rhetoric of free enterprise itself! It is surprising how few people appreciated this inconsistency at the time.

Caught in this ideological squeeze, state and federal governments wriggled inconclusively for decades before breaking free of the unworkable ideology. Between 1870 and 1874 four midwestern states, responding to strong pressure from their voting farmers, passed laws—the "Granger" laws—regulating the prices railroads, warehouses, and grain elevators could charge. In 1877 the United States Supreme Court upheld the constitutionality of these laws,[5] but within a decade the Court began to shift gears. Any time a state attempted to pass a law regulating charges for freight traveling through more than one state, the Court struck it down on the grounds that only Congress could regulate interstate commerce. While its motives were political, the Court's move actually made economic sense, since a multitude of inconsistent state regulations was practically unworkable for something as complex as interstate railroad traffic.

In 1886 the Supreme Court ruled that state regulation of interstate railroad traffic was unconstitutional. Congress in 1887 responded by creating the Interstate Commerce Commission (ICC), the first modern federal regulatory agency. The Interstate Commerce Act prohibited a variety of discriminatory and unfair pricing practices. It required railroads to make their rates public and report them to the five-person agency. It required that rates be "reasonable and just," but did not grant to the ICC power to set railroad rates in so many words. The ICC was granted this power in 1906.

This is unfortunate because by the end of the century the *laissez faire* philosophy dominated the political values of the justices on the Supreme Court. Having told the states that only Congress could regulate interstate rail rates, they then announced that Congress hadn't.[6] When the ICC issued a cease and desist order requiring railroads to lower rates, the railroads refused. The ICC possessed no enforcement power of its own, so it had to go to the courts to seek a judicially enforceable order. The courts did not cooperate. Of the first sixteen cases to reach the Supreme Court, the railroads won fifteen. In 1890 Congress passed the Sherman Antitrust Act with virtually no party opposition. The Supreme Court promptly ruled that it didn't apply to any of the oil, steel, sugar, or other manufacturing monopolies because manufacturing was not part of the "commerce" that Congress had constitutional power to control.

Why Modern Bureaucracy?

Why, given our present day understanding, was the Supreme Court wrong? What shortcomings in unregulated markets did the Court blindly fail to appreciate? Markets contain within them forces that tend toward collusion, toward eliminating or reducing competition, toward monopoly. The conditions of the economists' perfect market—many buyers and sellers, ability to enter and exit a market rapidly, and complete information about market conditions available at all times to each buyer and seller—do not occur very often in the real world. The trade in farm products through futures trading is often cited as an example of something close to a perfect market, but neither entering and leaving the business itself nor purchasing and selling farm land and machinery are rapid or easy. As we know, the spike in oil prices in 2008 was due in part to speculative "free trade"

---

4. John C. Grene, *The Death of Adam* (New York: Mentor, 1961), 295.
5. *Munn v. Illinois*, 94 U.S. 113 (1876).

6. *Cincinnati, New Orleans and Texas Pacific Railway Co. v. ICC*, 162 U.S. 184 (1896).

gambles, with negative results on, among other things, the cost of food. Agricultural prices can fluctuate wildly, often with such potentially ruinous consequences for farmers that the United States government instituted policies designed to control farm prices during most of the twentieth century.

The key to understanding the shortcomings of free markets lies in the fact that "free" markets do not necessarily possess the characteristics of perfect markets. A free market is simply a private, unregulated market. The real-world imperfections of such markets lead some companies (such as Microsoft in the late 1990s) to grow significantly stronger than their competitors. Once a firm holds a position of market dominance, it can wield its power to increase its share of the business in that market, often in collusion with other businesses.

Other market shortcomings also deserve an explanation. Because free markets seem in economic history to go through boom and bust business cycles, modern government takes administrative steps to smooth the cycles out. Most modern central banking regulations, to say nothing of other monetary and fiscal policies, exist for this purpose alone. Furthermore, free markets have no mechanism that requires producers of goods to pay for the indirect costs of production, for example, the costs imposed by air and water pollution. There is no incentive to control pollution because producers can sell a product for less if they do not have to recover pollution control costs as part of the selling price of their products. Hence the creation of the Environmental Protection Agency (EPA).

Even when we imagine markets without tendencies to monopolize, and production techniques that do not impose significant and unrecovered indirect costs, we still can identify evils that may call for regulation. To name the most obvious, people have a tendency to cheat. Commodities sellers in Medieval markets were tempted to use false weights. Promoters of new corporate schemes tend to overstate the prospects of their new venture and minimize its risks when they try to convince people to buy stock in the company. Hence the existence of the Securities and Exchange Commission (SEC). The sudden collapse of the economies of Southeast Asia in 1998 can be directly attributed to the fact that these countries, and

indeed Japan, did not have regulatory mechanisms like the SEC to check private greed. A more vigilant SEC and Federal Exchange Board could, during President George W. Bush's second term, have regulated the markets in mortgage financing so as to prevent the inflation and subsequent collapse of housing values.

None of these descriptions of free market shortcomings should surprise a reader familiar with basic economics. Three other, and deeper, dimensions to the free market problem, however, may not be so obvious or familiar. First, in the United States, the administrative process plays a major role because of increasing technological complexity. We live our lives surrounded by very dangerous things—elevators, cars, airplanes, industrial wastes and chemical products, radioactivity, and genetically engineered DNA. Such technological complexity and dangers associated with it impact even the remotest areas on the globe. Global warming is one such man-made problem. To be sure, we are safer and better cared for than those who lived and died before the advent of modern medicine. Centuries ago people perceived many of the sources of insecurity to rest in the hands of the gods. People who view their lives theologically would more likely support the church than lobby to create regulatory agencies. Today people believe that, while they cannot control the safety of the things around them, somebody else—experts—can, and this explains much of the support for new governmental programs and agencies.

In a world defined by increasing interconnectedness (what is commonly referred to as globalization) such calls for expert regulation frequently issue beyond the boundaries of a particular country—and this constitutes the second, deeper dimension to the market problem. In general there is very little empirical data about what a market is or how it works. As Douglass North, the 1993 Nobel Prize winner in economics, has summarized it: "It is a peculiar fact that the literature on economics . . . contains so little discussion of the central institution that underlies neoclassical economics—the market."[7] This lack of clear understanding is not just an academic puzzle, and it has

7. Cited in Michel Callon, ed., *The Laws of the Markets* (London: Blackwell, 1998), 1.

become even more problematic in the process of globalization. As the movement of money and goods have speeded up enormously, the neat view of a "national" market can no longer be taken for granted. Market failures are now much more complex and multi-dimensional, and a market failure in one part of the world can pose significant risks even for far away nations.

The third deeper dimension to the market problem is political. Markets do not fail or succeed in the abstract. Like almost anything else in life, failure and success exist only in relation to standards. The standards by which the political culture of the United States judges the effectiveness of free markets have shifted considerably with increased *democracy*. Note the small *d*. In the past century American society has increasingly accepted the validity of the claims of average citizens, of workers, women, blacks, the poor, and other classes previously excluded from voting. The spread of the franchise to these classes has increased the responsiveness of government to their claims, and these groups most keenly feel the effects of all of the free market's evils. Welfare programs, public education, and consumer protection all seek to promote the interests of those who feel the exploitative effects of business entrepreneurial efforts most directly. The labor movement and the agencies like the National Labor Relations Board (NLRB) and state worker compensation commissions that support the labor movement fit the same category. In short, our commitment to equality of opportunity, coupled with an electorate containing many voters whose self-interest supports programs and candidates that favor those who cannot help themselves, has created a standard of free markets which makes their failures stand out in stronger relief than ever before.

It took the first forty years of the twentieth century for the political process, with the courts very much at the rear, to work free of the impasse between economic fact and free enterprise ideology. The move started with Theodore Roosevelt's presidency, during which Congress gave the ICC the specific power to regulate rates it had lacked. A year later, in 1907, Congress created the second major national regulatory agency, the Food and Drug Administration (FDA). In 1982 President Reagan urged a shift from national to state regulatory power, but there is little reason to believe that the amount of bureaucratic power in government will dramatically lessen, even if its locus shifts to the states.

On the surface this history seems a fairly simple story. Powerful government has been the norm during the development of civilization throughout the world. *Laissez faire* flourished only when an educated and industrious people seemed able to combine abundant natural resources with new technologies, and new corporate business forms to accumulate capital and thus produce unlimited wealth without creating problems that required governmental solutions. The problems appeared in due course, and government predictably reasserted its usual control, this time propelled by truly democratic forces.

But this history does not yet fully account for the creation of such a large bureaucracy. Why could the three traditional branches of government not handle the job? The Congress is not structured to do so. Members of Congress are essentially ombudspeople who try to help constituents with problems. When the problems seem serious enough, Congress passes laws dealing with them. These functions don't leave any time for processing large volumes of routine claims, nor for elected officials is there much payoff for doing so. State legislatures, most of which still meet only a few weeks per year, have much less capacity to administer than does Congress.

The executive branch, of course, does contain the large majority of administrative employees, people who work in the regular chain of command in a department headed by a cabinet official. But Congress has often worried that partisan presidential politics and the tremendous presidential powers to exploit the office could seep into regulation of sensitive areas like transportation and communications. Besides, presidents come and go quite frequently, and with them their cabinet appointees. Coping with technologically complex problems needs continuing expertise and leadership.

Why not, then, leave the problems in the hands of the courts? While all federal judges serve for life, only 3 states have lifetime appointments—MA, NH, and RI. Both federal and state legislatures can create more judgeships any time they wish. Yet for a mix of reasons judges do not make good administrators. We have already seen how, at the very time the need for regulation became clear to the politicians at all levels, the courts resisted. Moreover, our judicial system, unlike the French legal system, in which judges have played a strong regulatory role, works in ways not well suited to regulation. Our judicial system specializes in resolving disputes between people or organizations *fairly*. It stresses the requirement that judges remain aloof and impartial. The laws of evidence strictly prohibit judges and juries from considering much potentially useful information. Our idea of "due process of law" drastically limits the way judges can communicate with the parties involved. The judge cannot call someone on the phone from his chambers and ask for the missing evidence in the case. Most important, judges cannot initiate investigations. They can constitutionally act only when an injured party files a lawsuit, thus bringing a case to the court. The mechanics of our common law system require people with the best of legal claims to invest considerable money in litigation that often takes years to complete. The farmer, nickle-and-dimed to death by high railroad rates, was in no position to gain judicial help even if the courts had been more sympathetic. Finally, courts cannot effectively cope with the volume of regulatory work. The volume of administrative problems is so unpredictable, and the nature of abuses so potentially complex, that a static body of judges unable to specialize can deal neither efficiently nor effectively with regulatory problems.

Consider by contrast the administrative capacity that something as simple as a family or a small sorority needs in order to solve problems. Even simple problem-solving groups must be able to specialize, divide the labor, budget how to spend their limited resources, and set priorities accordingly. Their members do not want to get bogged down in the formalities of the rules of evidence. They want to be able to meet, haggle, compromise, experiment with a policy, and quickly reject it if it fails. The communications network in any effective problem-solving group must not squelch feedback to policymakers from the field.

In other words, despite the curses leveled at "faceless bureaucracies" in political speeches, bureaucratic organizations have certain characteristics that are functional to the needs of government. They have *continuity* that outlasts the political two- and four-year cycles. And unlike legislatures they have *memories* that allow them to apply information from past experiences to new situations. Unlike courts, agencies routinely *divide labor* into more efficient specialities. They work, as courts do not and legislatures only partially do, with fairly fixed budgetary limits which require *priority setting and judicious compromising*. Finally, unlike courts, they are *proactive*. They have the *capacity to take sides*, to accept a mission, and to battle in the political arena to complete the mission successfully. Consider how necessary these administrative qualities are to the pursuit of consumer product safety, an area in which the free market has not performed very well.

In 1970, the National Commission on Product Safety, reported to Congress some chilling facts about accidental deaths. Over 30,000 people, it reported, were killed and over one-half million were injured annually from accidents around the home. At least 150,000 were seriously cut by broken glass alone, mainly from windows and doors. Congress concluded that this problem required a publicly funded administrative solution.

In order to cope with problems, such as product safety for example, an agency must have the authority to initiate investigations to develop a clear idea of the greatest sources of actual harm around the home. It would need power to initiate specific investigations of suspicious products like rotary lawnmowers, not merely to show that they are dangerous, but also to devise the least costly design changes to reduce the danger. A governing agency needs the flexibility to negotiate and make some compromises with manufacturers if it is to accommodate competing interests satisfactorily. At the same time, however, it must develop a staff sufficiently independent from, yet familiar with, the businesses regulated to decide whether the information is reliable when provided by an industry presumably reluctant to be regulated.

Administrative government, like private business, exists to accomplish results. Both need the resources to do it. The legal system and the judicial process, on the other hand, exist primarily to preserve fairness. Fairness and efficiency, or getting on with the job, often collide with each other. This, as we have seen, is the main reason courts cannot assume the administrative burden directly.

The political debates over regulation are not simple either. It is important not to reduce the differences of opinion about regulation into pro and con positions toward government regulation of the economy. In addition, debates over regulation concern the provision of government benefits or entitlements. Administrative law therefore indirectly but powerfully shapes the role of government regulation of business and the scope and nature of the state. The historical record shows that a multiplicity of interests demanded regulation at the turn of the century, and regulation has served conflicting sets of interests ever since. Two models of regulation which have been in competition with each other are the *public interest model* and the *capture model.* Neither model entirely opposes government regulation. Rather, each provides political justifications for a particular theory of government regulation. As you study the political debates about the purpose and goals of administrative law, you will see that these models, at their core, prescribe who regulates the regulated—officials from within the regulated industries and interests, or public officials who respond to elections and use public procedures of adjudication and rule making.

An Overview of Theme One

The next section will give specific examples of modern regulatory government. Before turning there, one central point deserves repeating: The scope of public regulation has broadened, yet its emphasis today remains primarily where it was when the Congress founded the Interstate Commerce Commission over a century ago. This emphasis focuses, now as then, on private economic power. Just as the ICC sought to offset the monopoly price-setting power of railroads, at its inception in the mid-1970s the Occupational Safety and Health Administration (OSHA) sought to correct a tendency among businesses to maintain unsafe workplaces, so today's Environmental Protection Agency (EPA) deals primarily with industrial pollution, both from factories and the automobiles and other machines factories produce, so today's Consumer Product Safety Commission (CPSC) seeks to force businesses to produce safer and more reliable products. And as the functions of agencies are eliminated from the national policy agenda, so too are the agencies themselves. In 1995, Congress, perceiving that truckers and airlines created free market competition with the railroads, abolished the ICC by unanimous vote.

In comparing older regulations with newer kinds of regulation like OSHA and EPA, however, Alan Stone argues that the goals have changed somewhat.[8] Older regulation was premised on economic performance goals, such as price, costs, and profits, while post–New Deal regulation addresses intangible costs, such as pain and suffering—costs that Stone equates with social performance goals. The distinction between economic and social regulation captures the changing political orientations of the regulatory state. While the distinction can be helpful, it is important not to overstate the difference between the two. We will see in later chapters how the contemporary debate over the use of a cost-benefit analysis in regulation is essentially a struggle over the weight that should be given to economic and social goals when regulating economic power.[9]

THEME TWO: THE BROAD REACH OF ADMINISTRATIVE ACTION AND POWER

Just as Charles Dickens begins *A Christmas Carol* by telling his readers that they must accept that Marley was "dead as a doornail" in order to appreciate his story, you must believe in (and understand well) the tremendous reach and power of bureaucratic government in order to appreciate the importance of the study of administrative law. Here are just a few bits of data that document the twentieth-century administrative explosion.

• The federal bureaucracy now issues approximately seven thousand rules and policy statements a year, two thousand of which legally bind the citizenry. By law, agencies must publish these actions in the *Federal Register*. The Federal Register, which was created in 1935, occupies

---

8. See Alan Stone, *Regulation and Its Alternatives* (Washington, D.C.: CQ Press, 1982).
9. See Richard A. Harris and Sidney M. Milkis, *The Politics of Regulatory Change*, 2nd ed. (New York: Oxford University Press, 1996).

more library shelf space than all the laws passed by Congress since it first met in 1789. In just the first four months of 2008, 24,850 pages were published in the Federal Register.[10]

• Annually the Social Security Administration (SSA) alone processes 9 million applications for Social Security benefits.[11] Most of these raise no legal problems, yet the small fraction that does is twenty times greater in number than all of the civil and criminal lawsuits heard in the regular federal courts each year with the exception of bankruptcy cases.

• There are now approximately 646 federal trial judges in the U.S.,[12] but there are over 1,400 federal administrative law judges,[13] 79% (n=1,100) of whom work for the Social Security Administration.[14]

• Of the 153.8 million Americans in the civilian (non-farm) labor force,[15] about 2.7 million work for the federal government[16] and over 19.2 million for state and local governments.[17]

How broad is the reach of regulatory government? Consider these typical news stories, all from the *New York Times*:

• *March 30, 2006.* The Transportation Department announced new fuel economy standards for sport utility vehicles, pickup trucks and minivans that will make some

of them go farther on a gallon of gasoline than the average car does, and will apply to many of the biggest S.U.V.'s for the first time.

• *April 20, 2006.* The Food and Drug Administration announced, contradicting a 1999 review by a panel of highly regarded scientists, that "no scientific studies" supported the medical use of marijuana.

• *March 13, 2008.* The Environmental Protection Agency announced a modest tightening of the smog standard from 84 parts per billion to 75 (overruling the unanimous advice of its scientific advisory council for a more protective standard of 60 to 70 parts per billion).

• *March 20, 2008.* The Federal Communications Commission unanimously approved a rule banning exclusive telephone service agreements between apartment building owners and carriers, giving tenants their pick of providers.

In just one week—June 3 to June 10, 1998—the *New York Times* reported that the Department of Health and Human Services announced its intention to change the rules that determine which, of the tens of thousands of patients who require an organ transplant to stay alive, will get the first chance at available organs; the Food and Drug Administration authorized the first full testing of an HIV vaccine; the Federal Trade Commission filed an antitrust suit against the Intel Corporation for allegedly trying to coerce computer manufacturers to drop their disputes about patent rights against Intel; the Food and Drug Administration challenged as "an illegal and unapproved drug" an over-the-counter remedy for reduction of cholesterol that consists of pulverized rice fermented in red yeast. The substance has been used in Chinese cooking for over 2,000 years.

Figure 1.1 displays the simple number of main federal government agencies. It is awesome, but would be even more so if the chart included all state and local agencies as well.

There are three basic types of federal administrative agencies: (1) independent regulatory commissions; (2) agencies housed within a cabinet level department; and (3) agencies outside the formal structure of a cabinet department. Figure 1.2 on page 12 shows the structure of

10. The Federal Register is now also published online and the entire content of the volumes 59–73 (1994–2008) can be viewed/searched at http://www.gpoaccess.gov/fr/index.html.

11. Social Security Administration, "The Fiscal Year 2008 Budget Press Release," February 5, 2007. See also "Fast Facts and Figures about Social Security" (Washington, D.C.: Social Security Administration, Office of Research, Evaluation, and Statistics Publications, 2007).

12. PL 101–650, December 1990.

13. See Statement of Linda M. Springer, Director, U.S. Office of Personnel Management, on Administrative Law Judges at the Social Security Administration before the Subcommittee on Social Security, Committee on Ways and Means, U.S. House of Representatives (May 1, 2007).

14. Ibid. Note, however, that, on February 26, 2008, the Social Security Administration announced that the agency had begun making offers to 144 of the 175 new Administrative Law Judges it will hire in the 2008 fiscal year. See SSA Press Office, "News Release: Social Security Offers Positions to 144 Administrative Law Judges. New Hires a Key Step in Reducing Agency's Backlog of Disability Cases," February 26, 2008. These new hires will increase the number of administrative law judges.

15. *Monthly Labor Review* (Washington, D.C.: U.S. Dept. of Labor, Bureau of Labor Statistics, March 2008).

16. Ibid.

17. Ibid.

Figure 1.1 The Government of the United States

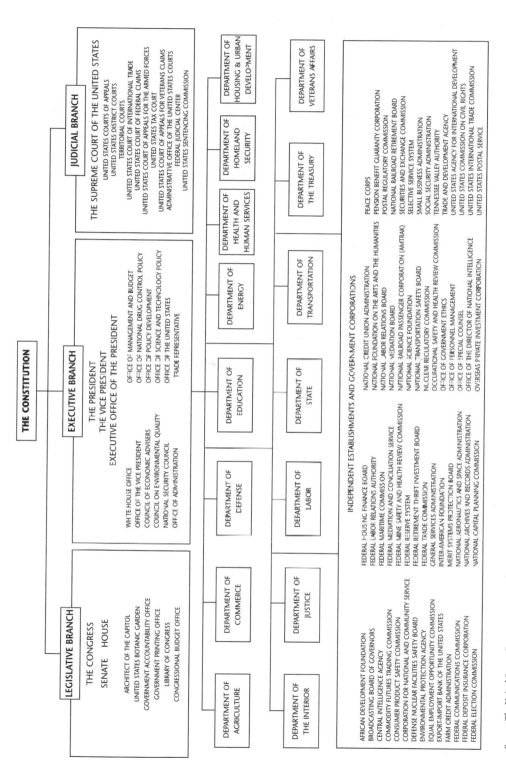

THE CONSTITUTION

LEGISLATIVE BRANCH

THE CONGRESS
SENATE   HOUSE

ARCHITECT OF THE CAPITOL
UNITED STATES BOTANIC GARDEN
GOVERNMENT ACCOUNTABILITY OFFICE
GOVERNMENT PRINTING OFFICE
LIBRARY OF CONGRESS
CONGRESSIONAL BUDGET OFFICE

EXECUTIVE BRANCH

THE PRESIDENT
THE VICE PRESIDENT
EXECUTIVE OFFICE OF THE PRESIDENT

WHITE HOUSE OFFICE
OFFICE OF THE VICE PRESIDENT
COUNCIL OF ECONOMIC ADVISERS
COUNCIL ON ENVIRONMENTAL QUALITY
NATIONAL SECURITY COUNCIL
OFFICE OF ADMINISTRATION

OFFICE OF MANAGEMENT AND BUDGET
OFFICE OF NATIONAL DRUG CONTROL POLICY
OFFICE OF POLICY DEVELOPMENT
OFFICE OF SCIENCE AND TECHNOLOGY POLICY
OFFICE OF THE UNITED STATES
TRADE REPRESENTATIVE

JUDICIAL BRANCH

THE SUPREME COURT OF THE UNITED STATES

UNITED STATES COURTS OF APPEALS
UNITED STATES DISTRICT COURTS
TERRITORIAL COURTS
UNITED STATES COURT OF INTERNATIONAL TRADE
UNITED STATES COURT OF FEDERAL CLAIMS
UNITED STATES COURT OF APPEALS FOR THE ARMED FORCES
UNITED STATES TAX COURT
UNITED STATES COURT OF APPEALS FOR VETERANS CLAIMS
ADMINISTRATIVE OFFICE OF THE UNITED STATES COURTS
FEDERAL JUDICIAL CENTER
UNITED STATES SENTENCING COMMISSION

DEPARTMENT OF AGRICULTURE
DEPARTMENT OF COMMERCE
DEPARTMENT OF DEFENSE
DEPARTMENT OF EDUCATION
DEPARTMENT OF ENERGY
DEPARTMENT OF HEALTH AND HUMAN SERVICES
DEPARTMENT OF HOMELAND SECURITY
DEPARTMENT OF HOUSING & URBAN DEVELOPMENT

DEPARTMENT OF THE INTERIOR
DEPARTMENT OF JUSTICE
DEPARTMENT OF LABOR
DEPARTMENT OF STATE
DEPARTMENT OF TRANSPORTATION
DEPARTMENT OF THE TREASURY
DEPARTMENT OF VETERANS AFFAIRS

INDEPENDENT ESTABLISHMENTS AND GOVERNMENT CORPORATIONS

AFRICAN DEVELOPMENT FOUNDATION
BROADCASTING BOARD OF GOVERNORS
CENTRAL INTELLIGENCE AGENCY
COMMODITY FUTURES TRADING COMMISSION
CONSUMER PRODUCT SAFETY COMMISSION
CORPORATION FOR NATIONAL AND COMMUNITY SERVICE
DEFENSE NUCLEAR FACILITIES SAFETY BOARD
ENVIRONMENTAL PROTECTION AGENCY
EQUAL EMPLOYMENT OPPORTUNITY COMMISSION
EXPORT-IMPORT BANK OF THE UNITED STATES
FARM CREDIT ADMINISTRATION
FEDERAL COMMUNICATIONS COMMISSION
FEDERAL DEPOSIT INSURANCE CORPORATION
FEDERAL ELECTION COMMISSION

FEDERAL HOUSING FINANCE BOARD
FEDERAL LABOR RELATIONS AUTHORITY
FEDERAL MARITIME COMMISSION
FEDERAL MEDIATION AND CONCILIATION SERVICE
FEDERAL MINE SAFETY AND HEALTH REVIEW COMMISSION
FEDERAL RESERVE SYSTEM
FEDERAL RETIREMENT THRIFT INVESTMENT BOARD
FEDERAL TRADE COMMISSION
GENERAL SERVICES ADMINISTRATION
INTER-AMERICAN FOUNDATION
MERIT SYSTEMS PROTECTION BOARD
NATIONAL AERONAUTICS AND SPACE ADMINISTRATION
NATIONAL ARCHIVES AND RECORDS ADMINISTRATION
NATIONAL CAPITAL PLANNING COMMISSION

NATIONAL CREDIT UNION ADMINISTRATION
NATIONAL FOUNDATION ON THE ARTS AND THE HUMANITIES
NATIONAL LABOR RELATIONS BOARD
NATIONAL MEDIATION BOARD
NATIONAL RAILROAD PASSENGER CORPORATION (AMTRAK)
NATIONAL SCIENCE FOUNDATION
NATIONAL TRANSPORTATION SAFETY BOARD
NUCLEAR REGULATORY COMMISSION
OCCUPATIONAL SAFETY AND HEALTH REVIEW COMMISSION
OFFICE OF GOVERNMENT ETHICS
OFFICE OF PERSONNEL MANAGEMENT
OFFICE OF SPECIAL COUNSEL
OFFICE OF THE DIRECTOR OF NATIONAL INTELLIGENCE
OVERSEAS PRIVATE INVESTMENT CORPORATION

PEACE CORPS
PENSION BENEFIT GUARANTY CORPORATION
POSTAL REGULATORY COMMISSION
NATIONAL RAILROAD RETIREMENT BOARD
SECURITIES AND EXCHANGE COMMISSION
SELECTIVE SERVICE SYSTEM
SMALL BUSINESS ADMINISTRATION
SOCIAL SECURITY ADMINISTRATION
TENNESSE VALLEY AUTHORITY
TRADE AND DEVELOPMENT AGENCY
UNITED STATES AGENCY FOR INTERNATIONAL DEVELOPMENT
UNITED STATES COMMISSION ON CIVIL RIGHTS
UNITED STATES INTERNATIONAL TRADE COMMISSION
UNITED STATES POSTAL SERVICE

Source: The United States Government Manual 2007/08 (Washington, D.C.: Government Printing Office, 2008), 21.

Figure 1.2 The Federal Trade Commission (FTC)

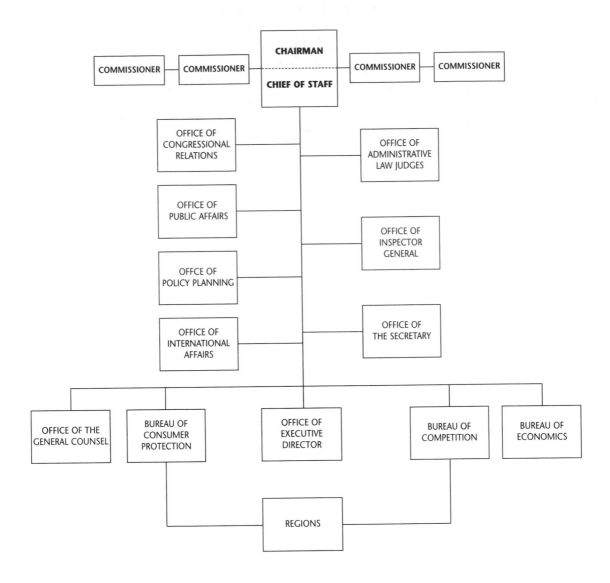

Source: The United States Government Manual 2007/08 (Washington, D.C.: Government Printing Office, 2008), 426.

Figure 1.3 Cabinet Level Agency (OSHA in the Department of Labor)

DEPARTMENT OF LABOR

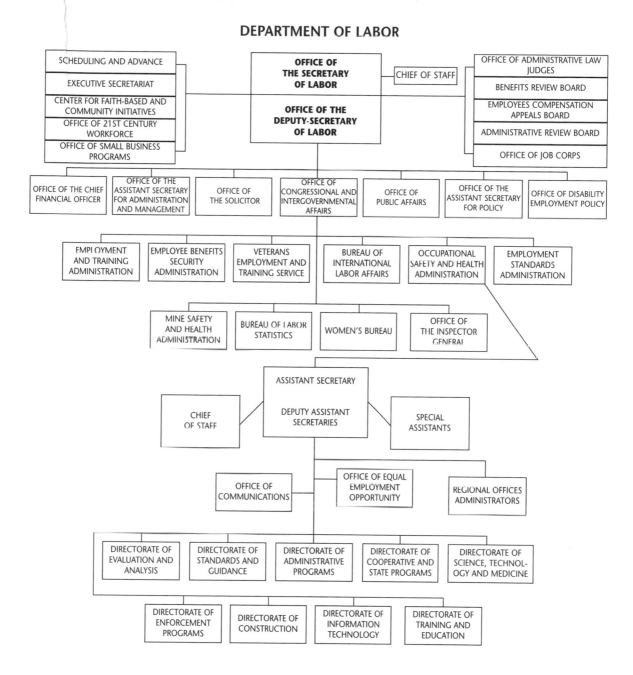

*Source: The United States Government Manual 2007/0*8 (Washington, D.C.: Government Printing Office, 2008), 281.

Figure 1.4 The Environmental Protection Agency (EPA)

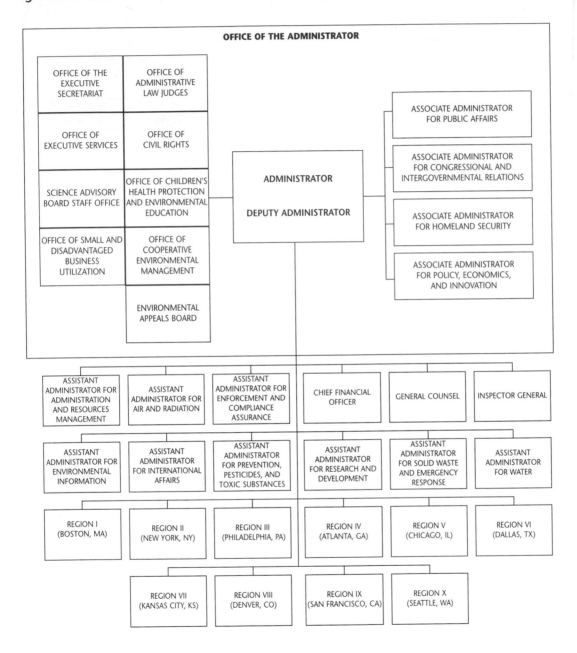

one independent regulatory commission, the FTC. Following the creation of an independent commission by Congress, five or more commissioners are appointed by the president with the advice and consent of the Senate for staggered terms. One commissioner serves as the chair. Although commissions (e.g., FTC, NRC, FCC, SEC, EEOC, etc.) are technically within the executive branch of government, they can act more independently from presidential policy programs than officials in other types of agencies primarily because the president cannot remove commissioners without cause, whereas the president may remove heads of other agencies at his discretion. Figure 1.3 on page 13 shows the structure of an agency, OSHA, that is within a cabinet level department, the Department of Labor. You will note that in addition to OSHA, the Department of Labor houses several other agencies, such as the Mine Safety and Health Administration, and Employee Benefits Security Administration. Figure 1.4 on page 14 shows the organization of the Environmental Protection Agency, an agency outside the formal structure of a cabinet department.

Before we move on to the third theme, we would like to draw your attention to the relative fluidity of administrative structures. The figure presenting different types of federal government agencies and the figures of OSHA, FTC, or EPA are snapshots and, as such, change quite frequently. Reorganization is one of the recurring themes in administrative government. With a desire to achieve various goals, including reducing costs, increasing efficiency, scientific management, increasing democratic participation, etc., administrative units are fused, separated, and ultimately reorganized. The Environmental Protection Agency, for instance, was established with Reorganization Plan No. 3, by President Nixon. A large number of functions and duties were transferred to EPA from the Departments of Interior; Health, Education and Welfare; Agriculture; Atomic Energy Commission; Federal Radiation Council; and Council on Environmental Quality. The most recent major example of such reorganization is the creation of the Department of Homeland Security (DHS).

The Department of Homeland Security was established in 2002 by bringing together 22 different agencies under one roof. Below, Figure 1.5 shows the flow of departments from within agencies to the newly created Department of Homeland Security. Figure 1.6 displays the structural elements of DHS.

THEME THREE: THE SHORTCOMINGS OF REGULATORY GOVERNMENT

The third and final stage-setting theme discussed in this chapter explores and begins to explain what every reader already knows: Human beings run the government, and human beings everywhere sometimes "screw up." Regulatory government has not satisfactorily resolved all of the problems created by modern, highly technological economies. Worse, some reasonably successful solutions have simultaneously created other problems of their own. For example, the Social Security system has successfully created a support system for millions of retired, disabled, and otherwise disadvantaged citizens. Yet the system lends itself to abuse by citizens who present false claims and by administrators who may arbitrarily withhold benefits recipients are entitled to.

Some shortcomings in regulatory government will never disappear. Probably the most obvious of these results from inevitable economic change. An administrative program, structured and constrained by legislative mandates and its own goals and procedures, does not automatically adjust to technological advances and changes in competition. The regulation of transportation began when railroads had a near monopoly on long-distance carrying of people and cargo. Many of the practices of transport regulation were carried over into the trucking and airline markets and remained there long after economists and businesspeople realized that trucks, buses, trains, and airlines had created a much more competitive and self-regulating market than regulatory policy admitted. Under President Carter in the late 1970s deregulation of transportation began.

Figure 1.5 The Creation of the Department of Homeland Security

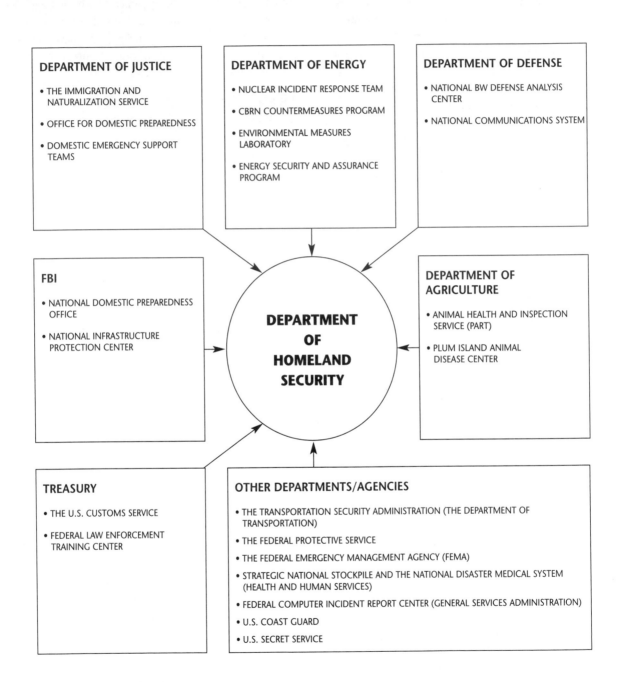

DEPARTMENT OF JUSTICE

- THE IMMIGRATION AND NATURALIZATION SERVICE
- OFFICE FOR DOMESTIC PREPAREDNESS
- DOMESTIC EMERGENCY SUPPORT TEAMS

DEPARTMENT OF ENERGY

- NUCLEAR INCIDENT RESPONSE TEAM
- CBRN COUNTERMEASURES PROGRAM
- ENVIRONMENTAL MEASURES LABORATORY
- ENERGY SECURITY AND ASSURANCE PROGRAM

DEPARTMENT OF DEFENSE

- NATIONAL BW DEFENSE ANALYSIS CENTER
- NATIONAL COMMUNICATIONS SYSTEM

FBI

- NATIONAL DOMESTIC PREPAREDNESS OFFICE
- NATIONAL INFRASTRUCTURE PROTECTION CENTER

DEPARTMENT OF HOMELAND SECURITY

DEPARTMENT OF AGRICULTURE

- ANIMAL HEALTH AND INSPECTION SERVICE (PART)
- PLUM ISLAND ANIMAL DISEASE CENTER

TREASURY

- THE U.S. CUSTOMS SERVICE
- FEDERAL LAW ENFORCEMENT TRAINING CENTER

OTHER DEPARTMENTS/AGENCIES

- THE TRANSPORTATION SECURITY ADMINISTRATION (THE DEPARTMENT OF TRANSPORTATION)
- THE FEDERAL PROTECTIVE SERVICE
- THE FEDERAL EMERGENCY MANAGEMENT AGENCY (FEMA)
- STRATEGIC NATIONAL STOCKPILE AND THE NATIONAL DISASTER MEDICAL SYSTEM (HEALTH AND HUMAN SERVICES)
- FEDERAL COMPUTER INCIDENT REPORT CENTER (GENERAL SERVICES ADMINISTRATION)
- U.S. COAST GUARD
- U.S. SECRET SERVICE

Source: Created by Ziya Umut Turem in 2008, based on information from www.dhs.gov/xabout/history/editorial_0133.shtm

Figure 1.6 The Department of Homeland Security

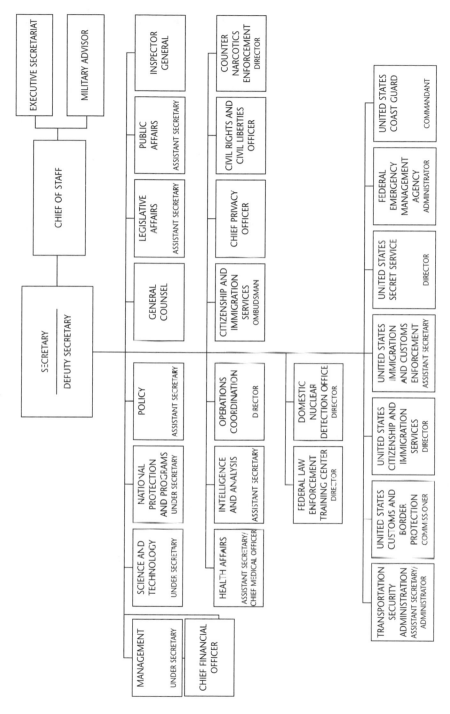

Source: The United States Government Manual 2007/08 (Washington, D.C.: Government Printing Office, 2008), 234.

The Dilemmas of Goal Attainment

Another and subtler inescapable shortcoming is the elusiveness of organizational goals. It may help to possess a mental picture of the objectives of administration, but it is essential to understand that goals are, more often than not, the innocent-looking tip of a very extensive iceberg. Americans, with their "can-do" pragmatism are tempted to expect government simply to figure out what needs doing and do it. In this view administration, either public or private, amounts to formulating goals, choosing the means that will achieve the goals, and then getting on with the job. But several harsh realities make that approach naive. The first harsh reality we may call the *level of goal formation* problem.

Promoting any good—the cleanliness of air, fair wages and healthy working conditions, the nutritional value of granola, television programming that informs and entertains without corrupting—can constitute an administrative goal. So can the prevention of evils: blocking monopolistic mergers, deterring consumer fraud, minimizing traffic fatalities, and so forth. Conceived this way administrative policy goals are too numerous to count. Virtually every statute creating a federal or state administrative body sets forth, usually in flowery and imprecise language, the agency's mission.

Some analysts prefer to collapse all these goals into one goal: elected and appointed government officials alike should foster the public good. Unfortunately, people cannot agree what constitutes the public good or the "public interest." Which serves the public good: building nuclear power plants to free ourselves from dependence on foreign energy sources? Or not building nuclear power plants to avoid both the risks of radiation damage and the tremendous expenses of such plants?

At this general level we encounter the second harsh reality. Broadly stated goals prevent us from seeing the trade-offs inherent in policy choices. A trade-off exists whenever people must sacrifice one good to attain another. Trade-offs contrast rather sharply with "good investments." A good investment of time or money can achieve several goals simultaneously. For example, if a university diverts money from non-revenue sports to add seats to the football stadium, it may in the short term hurt the university's cross-country or tennis programs. But if the university soon recovers its construction costs by selling tickets for the new seats, and then uses the added revenue to increase support for unprofitable programs, no real trade-off occurs. Both goods benefit in the long run. A trade-off, on the other hand, exists when one good is permanently lost, as in the trade-off between energy self-sufficiency and radiation safety. Thus one of the irksome things about goals is that they tend to fool us into thinking we live in a world without trade-offs, a world where we can have everything. In fact useful administrators earn their pay because they must make difficult decisions about which good things we must sacrifice, and how much of them to sacrifice, in order to achieve other good things.

Goals also present themselves at different moral levels. Sometimes national security is not a controversial goal. Without giving it much thought most people would agree that the United States fought for just causes in World War II. But national security did *not* justify the steps taken by the West Coast military commander to relocate Japanese-American *citizens* in something close to concentration camps. Did national security justify U.S. intervention in Vietnam? In Iraq? Can we justify, by referring to "national security" alone, the extralegal interrogation methods employed at Guantanamo Bay in the aftermath of the September 11, 2001, terrorist attacks? A statement of goals alone does not resolve disagreements about values. Goals are merely an expression of values.

Hugh Heclo, in his excellent descriptive study of middle- and upper-level federal administrators, lists the normative contradictions in government. For Heclo the unresolvable tensions—between the norm of nonpartisanship and the norm of being responsive to citizen needs, between the obligation to behave in a legal and orderly fashion on one hand and to be creative and innovative on the other, and between the human instinct to be cooperative and loyal and at the same time not become corrupted—call for powerful leadership. His book describes how the current system fails to produce such leadership.[18]

18. Hugh Heclo, *A Government of Strangers* (Washington, D.C.: Brooking, 1977), 103, 111.

Jerry Mashaw notes similar normative contradictions among three administrative models: bureaucratic efficiency, professional judgment, and fairness to clients and citizens.[19] Mashaw explained how the Social Security Administration's management efforts to limit the compensation awards made by administrative law judges ran into resistance from the judges because management valued efficiency while the judges valued professional independence and fairness.

Consider now the human side of bureaucratic life. Our culture encourages us to develop and pursue our own personal goals: career advancement, good pay, and so forth. Much effort in any organization, be it a private corporation or an administrative agency, goes into keeping its workers happy by meeting as best it can their personal goals. Doing so not only consumes resources, it requires compromising some aspects of the organization's mission. For example, many public defenders in our major population centers are recent graduates of law schools who seek trial experience. Because their superiors generally know this, they may discourage new public defenders from settling cases with plea bargains and encourage them instead to take their clients' cases to trial, even where the chances of a conviction are high, so the lawyer gets the trial experience he or she seeks. Personnel training may undercut the value of fair prosecution or it may add additional—avoidable—costs to the administrative process.

Bureaucratic Pathologies

The psychological reality of a front-lines human service agency or a school or a police department is that it contains high levels of stress. Such stress is one example of a bureaucratic pathology. Charles Goodsell's description of the reaction to stress in an Appalachian county welfare agency illustrates the problem:

The concept of compression . . . refers to the stress of "heat" faced by service delivery workers. The manifestations of such stress are now being widely discussed around the country under the rubric of "burnout." In the department studied perhaps a fifth of the workers exhibited symptoms associated with this syndrome, such as disillusionment, weariness, frustration, and demoralization.

When the subject of personal stress was explored in interviews with workers several factors surfaced. One universally identified by respondents is the activity known pejoratively as "paperwork." The completion of forms, the preparation of reports, and the arrangement for documentation involve an enormous amount of tedious clerical work, taking half or more of the worker's on-duty time. (When inventoried, no less than 65 forms were found to be in use for financial assistance processing alone.)

A second origin of stress is clearly related, namely escalating caseloads. In recent years they have grown dramatically as a combined consequence of new programs, added accountability requirements, successful outreach activities, and only modest staff growth. Mandated deadlines for acting on benefit applications (ranging from 48 hours to 45 days) increase the pressure to produce. No overtime pay is available in the office to ease the time-bind. Low salaries generally (some receptionists and clerks are themselves eligible for the Food Stamps they issue) offer little compensation for the pressures, and staff turnover is quite high.

To compound matters, some workers complain that in addition to enduring strains of time-crowded routine, they must live with the anxiety of being ready to face the unusual "incident." This is shouted verbal abuse at the office, tire slashings on home visits, or threatening phone calls at home. Drunks, armed men, and distraught or even deranged individuals must occasionally be dealt with. Personnel are cautioned to take no more chances than necessary, yet at the same time departmental norms forbid answering unpleasantness in kind—workers must simply "take it."[20]

Another illustration of a bureaucratic pathology that need not inevitably occur concerns the tendency of people in all sorts of settings, public and private, to advance their self-interest at the expense of organizational needs. This reality can take the form of outright bribery and other forms of corruption. Far more prevalent and perhaps even more difficult to redress is the phenomenon of *agency capture*. In the process of governing, officials find themselves acting to protect or advance the interests of

19. Jerry L. Mashaw, "Conflict and Compromise Among Models of Administrative Justice," *Duke Law Journal* (1981): 181.

20. Charles Goodsell, "Looking Once Again at Human Service Bureaucracy," *Journal of Politics* 43 (1981): 770, 771, footnotes omitted. For an excellent and disturbing book-length treatment of the problem, see Michael Lipsky, *Street Level Bureaucracy* (New York: Russell Sage, 1980).

those they govern. Capture differs from deliberate promotion, that is, when Congress by law authorizes an agency to protect and promote an industry as well as regulate it. The old Atomic Energy Commission operated under the mandate to promote the use of nuclear energy as well as to regulate it, a goal conflict that finally prompted the creation of the Nuclear Regulatory Commission (NRC) that, underfunded though it was, did not suffer from a split administrative personality.

Capture occurs when agencies informally promote the very interests they are officially responsible for regulating. A. Lee Fritschler's study, *Smoking and Politics*, describes why the FDA did not follow through on the Surgeon General's determination that smoking correlated with a variety of illnesses this way:

The Food and Drug Administration, the agency that the surgeon general suggested as the proper regulator of warning requirements, had demonstrated even less interest in the smoking and health issue than its sister agency, the PHS. The FDA's reluctance is due, according to Senator Neuberger's book, *Smoke Screen: Tobacco and the Public Welfare*, to a late Victorian episode in congressional politics. She claims that the item "tobacco" appeared in the 1890 edition of the *U.S. Pharmacopoeia*, an official listing of drugs published by the government. It did not appear in the 1905 or later editions, according to the senator, because the removal of tobacco from the *Pharmacopoeia* was the price that had to be paid to get the support of tobacco state legislators for the Food and Drug Act of 1906. The elimination of the word tobacco automatically removed the leaf from FDA supervision.

The FDA was given what appeared to be another opportunity to concern itself with cigarette smoking when the Hazardous Substances Labeling Act was passed in 1960. It empowered the FDA to control the sale of substances which, among other things, had the capacity to produce illness to man through inhalation. Secretary Celebrezze suggested in a letter to the Senate that the act could be interpreted to cover cigarettes as "hazardous substances." In what had become characteristic behavior of HEW, however, the secretary went on to argue that it would be better to wait and let Congress amend the act to make it more explicit and thereby avoid controversy. Subsequently, Congress rejected such an amendment.

The reluctance of the FDA could be traced to still other factors. During the early 1960s, the agency was having serious problems of its own. It suffered through some devastating investigations conducted by late Senator Estes Kefauver (D.-Tennessee). The hearings dealt with the pricing practices, safety, and monopoly aspects of the drug industry. One of the alarming revelations to emerge from the hearings was the extent to which the FDA was dominated and supported by that sector of the business community it was supposed to regulate, i.e., drug manufacturers and distributors. In what might have been simple reflex action, the FDA found it easier to keep quiet and follow Secretary Celebrezze's lead to continue to protect its good standing in the business community. The FDA found it expedient to ignore the cigarette health issue even though scientific indictments mounted in the early 1960s and other agencies began to take some action.[21]

Fritschler's fascinating study contrasts the FDA's refusal to tackle the tobacco health hazard with the willingness of the FTC to do so. It is remarkable how the differences in the effectiveness of agencies, including their susceptibility to capture, depend on the unique and often idiosyncratic combination of political forces, personalities and leadership that characterize different agencies. In 1990 President George H. W. Bush appointed Dr. David Kessler, who held both a law degree and an M.D., to head the Food and Drug Administration. When he retired in late 1996, he was praised for "revitalizing a moribund agency." Even though the FDA's efforts to regulate tobacco products were effectively halted by the Supreme Court in *FDA v. Brown and Williamson Tobacco Inc.* 529 U.S. 120 (2000) (see case on p. 119,), Kessler's aggressive move to initiate regulating tobacco products as a drug was a critical step in the dramatic collapse of the tobacco industry's political defense against public regulation in the last half of the 1990s. Kessler's revitalized FDA also took on misleading food labels and accelerated the process of approving new drugs and medical devices. He inevitably made a number of political enemies.[22] To repeat a point made earlier, agencies may employ professional experts and Congress may label them "independent," but they are all deeply enmeshed in the political process.

A recent position taken by the EPA on the issue of global warming provides yet another stark view of expertise deeply enmeshed in politics. The *New York Times*

21. A. Lee Fritschler, *Smoking and Politics*, 2nd ed. (Englewood Cliffs, N.J.: Prentice-Hall, 1975), 34–35.

22. "FDA Commissioner Is Resigning after Six Hectic Years in Office," *New York Times*, November 26, 1996.

reported that during 2002 and 2003, Philip Cooney, the Chief of Staff to President George W. Bush's Council on Environmental Quality, altered or rewrote reports by federal agencies on various aspects of climate change, so that the reports reflected greater uncertainty in the scientific community about global warming than the studies in fact showed. Even more interesting was the fact that Mr. Cooney had been a former lobbyist for the American Petroleum Institute and that, upon resigning after these revelations, he was immediately hired by Exxon Mobil.[23]

SETTING THE STAGE FOR THE STUDY OF ADMINISTRATIVE LAW

This chapter has emphasized the tremendous scope and power of administrative agencies of government. These agencies combine legislative, executive and judicial functions. We ask for and expect extraordinary accomplishments from government. We expect it to protect our personal safety. Obviously police and other law enforcement agencies do that, but so does the national defense establishment, the biggest single consumer of citizens' tax dollars. So does the Environmental Protection Agency, the Federal Aviation Agency (FAA), and the Occupational Safety and Health Administration. We expect government to assure social and economic justice, to protect small businesses from domination by larger ones, and to protect consumers, for whom the costs of gathering information are very high, against the tendency of businesses large and small to provide misleading information about their products. We expect welfare agencies to provide for the poor. We expect the Internal Revenue Service and state and local tax boards to collect tax money fairly. We expect the Federal Communications Commission (FCC) to fairly allocate the limited number of bands in the spectrum of receivable radio waves. We expect the National Science Foundation (NSF) to promote the acquisition of knowledge and the National Endowment for the Humanities (NEH) to promote the liberal arts. And on and on.

This chapter has also discussed certain potential and real imperfections in the administrative process. These failings, which we will look at more closely in the following chapters, fall roughly into four categories. First, agencies charged with protecting the general public by preventing certain monopolies from overcharging for their services have ended up promoting rather than regulating the same monopolies. Second, administrative decisions may be procedurally unfair. We will meet an FTC chairman who gave speeches condemning a business while he sat in administrative judgment of that same business. Third, administration may be inefficient. And, fourth, we shall meet the beleaguered NRC, which, despite the best of intentions and the most efficient possible use of its resources, still scares some people because they fear it is ineffective.

These imperfections as well as the others mentioned in this section are all embedded in a deeper political and legal structure that you will increasingly come to know as you progress through this book. Agencies exist because, for a variety of reasons, legislatures delegate powers to administrative bodies for the purpose of creating and enforcing specific policies. However, if they choose to, politicians can retain considerable influence in the bureaucratic process. Policy is often forged by interest groups, agencies and legislators within the so-called iron triangle of compromise. Agencies often act cautiously, as the FDA did in response to growing evidence of the dangers of smoking. And agencies jockey for position among themselves for both authority and secure funding from year to year. Thus it is a mistake to assume that "bureaucracy" is a monolith, immune from political or legal influence. The real problem may arise not because agencies are relatively unresponsive to public claims, but because some organized interest groups sometimes speak much louder than the public at large. You must judge by the end of this book the seriousness of the iron triangle's threat.

This chapter has opened up an immense terrain, but we do not want to lose sight of administrative law's big picture. So we conclude this chapter by returning to its beginning. We need administrative law to check regulatory government. It is a basic tenet of our political theory that perverse things can happen when government operations are hidden from public scrutiny. In March 1998, the files of a

23. Andrew C. Revkin, "Bush Aide Edited Climate Reports," *New York Times*, June 8, 2005; and Andrew C. Revkin, "Ex Bush Aide Who Edited Climate Reports to Join Exxon Mobil," *New York Times*, June 15, 2005.

public agency in the State of Mississippi were opened to the public for the first time. We reprint the first portion of the *New York Times* report, followed by an excerpt from the files.[24] The key question to ask about this agency, the Mississippi State Sovereignty Commission, is *not* whether it violated the law. From our perspective, it surely did. Rather we should ask whether, if proponents of racial justice had been able to use the tools of administrative law which the chapters to come describe, would the commission have been able to do its sinister work at all?

Mississippi Reveals Dark Secrets of a Racist Time

KEVIN SACK

Jackson, Miss., March 17—After a 21-year court fight, the state of Mississippi today unsealed more than 124,000 pages of secret files from a state agency that used spy tactics, intimidation, false imprisonment, jury tampering and other illegal methods to thwart the activities of civil rights workers during the 1950s, 60s and early 70s.

Like an eerie journey into a shadowy past, the files of the agency, the Mississippi State Sovereignty Commission, provided a profoundly unsettling reminder of the state's determination to maintain Jim Crow segregation, as reporters and individuals named in the commission's files began to review the computerized records.

While some of the commission's methods have been known for years, the full files released today demonstrated the scope of its work. Investigators made note of the skin color, associations, religious beliefs and sexual proclivities of the civil rights workers they tracked. They jotted down the license plate numbers of cars parked at civil rights meetings and peeked into bank accounts. Informants, many of them black Mississippians, reported to the commission about plans for marches and boycotts.

In some cases, the potential for using violence against civil rights workers is discussed in commission memorandums. Although none of the documents reviewed to date show a direct state hand in the numerous deaths of rights advocates in Mississippi in those years, they clear-

24. Kevin Sack, "Mississippi Reveals Dark Secrets of a Racist Time," *New York Times*, March 18, 1998.

ly reflect the mindset of the state's white supremacists: to maintain segregation at all costs.

In one 1959 memorandum, for example, Zack J. VanLandingham, a commission investigator, tells of a conversation he had with a Hattiesburg lawyer, Dudley Connor, about Clyde Kennard, a black man who tried to desegregate Mississippi Southern College in Hattiesburg in the late 1950s.

"If the Sovereignty Commission wanted that Negro out of the community and out of the state they would take care of the situation," Mr. VanLandingham quoted Mr. Connor as saying. "And when asked what he meant by that, Mr. Connor stated that Kennard's car could be hit by a train or he could have some accident on the highway and nobody would ever know the difference."

In another memo, this one written by Mr. VanLandingham to Gov. J. P. Coleman in 1959, the investigator related a conversation he had with John Reiter, a campus police officer.

"Reiter had several weeks ago told me that when Kennard was attempting to enter Mississippi Southern College in December, 1958, that he had been approached by individuals with possible plans to prevent Kennard's going through with his attempt," he wrote. "One of the plans was to put dynamite to the starter of Kennard's Mercury. Another plan was to have some liquor planted in Kennard's car and then he would be arrested."

On Sept. 15, 1959, Kennard was in fact arrested on charges of illegal possession of whisky, after police officers claimed to have found five half-pints of whisky and other liquor under the front seat of his car. . . .

Excerpts from Mississippi File on a Black

The New York Times

Jackson, Miss., March 17—Following are excerpts from a 1958 report to the Mississippi Sovereignty Commission about Clyde Kennard, a black man who was trying to become the first black student at what was then called Mississippi Southern College, now the University of Southern Mississippi, in Hattiesburg. The report was written by a commission investigator, Zack J. VanLandingham, and was also filed to the Governor and the Attorney General of Mississippi.

After contacting a black preacher and three black school principals in the Hattiesburg area on Dec. 9 and 10, Mr. VanLandingham reported:

It was suggested to these individuals that since they were leaders of their race in the community and since they were in favor
of maintaining segregated schools, that it might serve a useful
purpose if they would constitute themselves as a committee to
call on Clyde Kennard and persuade him that it was for the best
interest of all concerned that he withdraw and desist from filing
an application for admission to Mississippi Southern College. . . .

It was interesting to note, however, that all three of the
Negro educators when interviewed on separate occasions
brought into the conversation their need for a Negro junior college in that area. The inference was inescapable that they were
attempting to bargain in a subtle manner. They were merely
told that their desire and need for a junior college would be
called to the attention of the Governor. . . .

Gov. J. P. Coleman telephonically contacted Dr. McCain [W.
D. McCain, president of Mississippi Southern College] of the
college with reference to this conference. Dr. McCain advised
that he had given Kennard a conference and had attempted to
persuade Kennard that he should enroll at some other school in
the North to continue his education. However, Kennard had
said that he did not want to go to any other school than
Mississippi Southern.

J. H. White, the president of another all-white college,
Mississippi Vocational College in Itta Bena, suggested that Dr.
McCain get Kennard and bring him to Jackson, Miss., in his car
. . . and while Kennard is there, Governor Coleman will drop in
as if by accident at the meeting, and talk to Kennard, showing
him he is taking the wrong course and the ill will, tensions and
the like he will engender between the races should he continue his efforts to enter Mississippi Southern; also the fact he
would have on his shoulders the responsibility of causing possibly Mississippi Southern College to close and maybe other
educational institutions by his actions. . . .

It might be pointed out that White during his conversation
brought up the fact that the Negroes in Hattiesburg were
greatly desirous of getting a Negro junior college for that area.
Undoubtedly this is a bargaining point which they would try to
present at such a conference as outlined above.

In conclusion of this section, VanLandingham promises:

Will through the State Banking Department get access to and
examine the bank account of Clyde Kennard at Citizens
National Bank, Hattiesburg, Miss. An attempt was made to
examine this bank account during the period of this investigation; however, the President of the bank, Mr. Brett, declined to
exhibit this account, stating that there was a law which prohibited him from doing so. The records of this account may reflect
the source of some of Kennard's money and also to whom he
has been paying out money.

In the United States, law plays a key role in determining both the process and substance of government. The
concept that government must operate within legal limits
is the core of our constitution itself, a document that
structures and limits government and calls itself "the
supreme law of the land." Administrative law matters
because a system that adheres to the concept of the rule of
law employs the courts and the constitutional and statutory principles courts enforce to check the shortcomings
of government. Administrative law is not the only mechanism we have for coping with the bureaucratic shortcomings this chapter has described, but it has become
one of the most significant of those mechanisms. This is
why administrative law matters. Now the stage is set to
introduce administrative law. Chapter 2 proceeds to
explain more precisely what administrative law and the
rule of law mean and how they operate.

EXERCISES AND QUESTIONS FOR FURTHER THOUGHT

1. Shortly after his inauguration as president, Ronald Reagan sought to kill the Department of Energy's (DOE) proposed rules setting minimum standards for energy efficiency for home appliances, including air-conditioning units. One argument for doing so was that the free market would solve the problem, i.e., that consumers would naturally buy the most efficient unit over the long run. But officials of the Carrier Corporation, a well-known manufacturer of air-conditioning systems, argued that every apartment house owner and every new home builder would have only an incentive to buy the lowest priced unit regardless of operating costs because the tenants or buyers, not the owners or builders, would pay the energy bills. What potential weakness in the free market system discussed above does this illustrate? What self-interested reasons might a corporation like Carrier have for supporting these rules? See "A Tale of Regulation," *Newsweek*, March 2, 1981, p. 31.

2. Reflect on the nature of political power. What do the powerful have that the less powerful lack? It is often said that the most powerful are those who possess the most political resources. These resources include the capacity to use superior physical force on others, the capacity to coerce others, high status, legitimacy prestige, money, and finally, information. How might such a power model explain how the Mississippi State Sovereignty Commission got away for so long with what it did? In terms of this power model, what qualities of "acting in the name of the law" empower otherwise weak people and interests?

3. What justifications for robust administrative regulation does the following story support?

According to the *New York Times* (February 2, 2008) the Humane Society, a non-governmental organization (NGO), sued the U.S. Agriculture Department contending that it created a "loophole" in violation of its own procedural requirements that gave the beef industry financial incentives to permit potentially sick cows into the food supply. As evidence, the Humane Society cited a widely publicized undercover videotape of workers at the Westland/Hallmark Meat Company in Chino, Calif., abusing cows that appeared unable to walk. The lawyers for the Humane Society said that when the agency relaxed the ban, it "did so without really telling people that that's what they were going to do and without explaining how this complies with their obligation to protect consumers and ensure humane treatment."

4. This chapter has stressed the linkage between monopolistic power and the growth of government, but you should not neglect the reality that the profit motive in business leads some people, in both competitive and noncompetitive businesses, to cheat. How, for example, should government respond, if it all, to the case of the "University of Central Arizona," a two-person mail order house selling doctoral degree certificates to anyone who wanted to buy one? Is it significant that some people, especially in public education, increase their potential for job advancement if they can claim a graduate degree?

Or take the problem of the fraudulent sale of over-the-counter dietary supplements. Suppose I package a mixture of sugar and cornstarch dyed green in a capsule, and sell it as a valuable aid to reducing cholesterol levels in the blood. Can we count on an unregulated private market to discover such a fraud? Note that the fraud does not merely take a few dollars from someone under false pretenses. The consumer may forgo using a product that would actually improve health by lowering blood cholesterol.

5. We hope that by the end of this chapter you do not hold the view that government by administrative agency is a means of escaping from politics. Politics can be good or evil, but it is always with us, and agencies always operate in sensitive political environments. The real question is whether the political environment threatens to cause a violation of basic legal commands. Here are two stories from the *New York Times*. Does either of these situations ring your legal danger bell? What other information might you need to answer that question move confidently? The first story is headlined: "U.S. Documents Said to Show Endowment Bowed to Pressure" (September 18, 1991, p. B1). It continues:

Government documents released yesterday show that the National Endowment for the Arts yielded to political pressure last year in overturning grant recommendations for four sexually explicit performance artists, said spokesmen for a coalition of civil rights groups that obtained the documents. . . . In one of the documents, the transcript of a closed meeting of a grant-recommending panel in May 1990, John E. Frohnmayer, chairman of the arts endowment, is quoted as asking members "if in the very short political run," it is more important to support the controversial performers or to save the endowment "in some sort of recognizable form."

The second story reports on the nomination of Judge Stephen Breyer in 1994 to the U.S. Supreme Court. The *New York Times* described how Judge Breyer had very specific ideas about regulatory government and practical political experience with implementing them. Does this article reveal anything politically objectionable?[25]

Judge Breyer, who is the Chief Judge of the United States Court of Appeals for the First Circuit, in Boston, has outlined his theories of regulation in two books, the most recent published last year. And as a senior Congressional aide in the 1970s he was able to see his theories put into practice when he was the principal architect of deregulating the nation's airlines. Airline deregulation was a bold policy experiment that continues to provoke heated debate, both from scholars and from ordinary air travelers befuddled by ever-changing and incomprehensible fare schedules.

Quick to Question Priorities

In his 1993 book, *Breaking the Vicious Circle, Toward Effective Risk Regulation* (Harvard University Press), Judge Breyer painted a portrait of Federal regulators and Congress continually wasting resources because of distorted priorities in areas like toxic dumps and dangerous food additives. The regulators and lawmakers devote resources to the wrong problems, Judge Breyer wrote, because they are too sensitive to public opinion.

Many of the situations he cites in his book are from court cases in which judges ruled on Federal agencies' regulations. Judge Breyer argued that exaggerated public fears about the potential damage of breathing asbestos, for example, have produced an unwise and costly rush to clean up asbestos in buildings.

In a 1992 case he cites with approval, the Fifth Circuit Court of Appeals struck down an ambitious plan by the Environmental Protection Agency to remove asbestos. The agency wanted to spend a quarter billion dollars in hopes of saving an estimated seven or eight lives over a 13-year period. The court said the nation could expect that many deaths from individuals swallowing toothpicks.

Regulators, he wrote, will pay extra attention to risks that come to the public's attention and, he noted, "Study after study shows that the public's evaluation of risk problems differs radically from any consensus of experts."

Ralph Nader, the public interest lobbyist, who is one of Judge Breyer's most vocal critics, has depicted him as instinctively distrustful of all government regulation and a servant of corporate interests. . . .

25. "For This Court Choice, Policy is Passion," *New York Times*, July 11, 1994 .

CHAPTER 2

THE ORIGINS AND MEANING
OF ADMINISTRATIVE LAW

So far we have said surprisingly little about the subjects administrative law addresses. This is because administrative law operates within such a complex political and economic context that it makes little sense to explain the law without first having some idea of the setting in which it operates. The three themes of Chapter 1 examined aspects of this context. We now turn to two main themes of administrative law itself. The bulk of this chapter defines administrative law and illustrates it in action.

Administrative law is a mechanism designed to control and correct administrative government. Political checks exercised in legislatures and executive offices are another such mechanism. Administrative law, however, not only limits the authority of bureaucratic government; it also gives legitimacy and authority to state actions. Therefore, as we describe administrative law, think about the ways in which this body of law both *limits* administrative discretion and *empowers* administrative government.

The description of administrative law begins with a sketch of the legal process in general. It proceeds to show how administrative law differs from other branches of law and offers a brief history of administrative law in the 20th and early 21st centuries. This part of the chapter will distinguish, more particularly, between regulatory law and administrative law. Regulatory law includes such things as antitrust statutes and environmental protection policy. It is part of the machinery of governmental power. Administrative law, by contrast, creates rules and proce-

dures for controlling that power. Administrative law regulates the regulators. It also empowers administrators to act. Administrative law is not the actual rules, decisions, and policies that administrators make. We often refer to these substantive rules as *regulatory laws.* Administrative law deals not primarily with the substance, or content, of policy outcomes but with the process of making policies. Administrative law focuses on the procedural problems of *fairness and accuracy* in governmental decision making. Distinctions between administrative law and regulatory law, and between making public policy and the substance of those policies may be analytically useful at times, but in fact, particular procedures may or may not lead to certain substantive outcomes. In other words, the process may affect or even determine the kind of regulatory policies agencies like the Occupational Safety and Health Administration (OSHA) make and enforce. One cannot understand the significance of procedural requirements or principles of administrative law apart from the substantive responsibilities of particular agencies and the means available to agencies for accomplishing their goals.

This chapter's final section tackles theme five, the ethical issue that lurks in any administrative law case. Starting on page 47, we examine a variety of ethical models for shaping and evaluating administrative law. Notwithstanding the merits of the first six approaches, we develop our own, seventh, approach and explain why we do not altogether agree with the previous models. You should study this section carefully as these ethical issues will present themselves in every administrative law case you encounter.

Before turning to the description of administrative law itself, let us alert you to the philosophical debate toward which our description points. In America, we often say ours is a government of laws, not of men. The concept of the *rule of law* expresses this idea more formally. The rule of law means that government in the United States must operate within limits created and policed by law. In its most familiar form the rule of law idea specifies that the government should not have too much power, that the bulk of human activity should remain in non-governmental hands, that we should avoid a totalitarian police state. There are, however, applications of the rule of law concept that do not narrow power so much as they clarify and rationalize the use of power. The rule of law tries to keep the use of power open to participation by the governed. It seeks to call the use of power to public account and thus prevent the emergence of the unresponsive and unfathomable bureaucracies found in Franz Kafka's[1] literary nightmares.

Administrative law refers to the way that judges, like referees and umpires in sports, translate the theory of the rule of law into controls on bureaucratic power. But while American political philosophy rejects the idea of totalitarian, unresponsive government, the slogan that we are a government of laws, not of men, is a misleading oversimplification. Individual men and women, after all, make and enforce the laws. Furthermore, the laws they make and enforce are not always crystal clear. Unlike the rules of sports like baseball, vague or ambiguous laws leave room for human discretion. Law does not act "alone" but in relation to political, social, and economic choices and policies of the legislators and judges who make and enforce the law. The judicial opinions you read in this book might look at first like mechanical and inevitable constructions, like making a cake from a recipe. But as you learn more about the politics of administrative law you will see how the individual judges in administrative law cases must often search for or even create theories

about fairness, equality, and democracy to arrive at what they believe is a just solution. How can we evaluate the wisdom of these theories? That is the crucial ethical question in administrative law. It is the most important question in this book.

WHAT IS LAW?

Law is one of several techniques people use to prevent or resolve conflicts. Unlike fighting or going to a counselor, law is a process that starts by referring to governmental rules and practices. The United States political system makes legal rules in four kinds of ways. Each of the four kinds of law contains both substantive and procedural rules.

1. *Statutes.* State legislatures and the Congress of the United States pass laws after gathering information, debating the meaning of the evidence and the wording of the bill, and, in most cases, after compromising differing political interests in the final product. A *statute* is simply a law established by an act of a legislature. Statutes may address social conditions and problems, for example, the threat of a business monopoly, the need to prevent fraudulent advertising, or the desire to create and fund an agency charged with giving emergency assistance to people whose homes and livelihoods have been wiped out by natural disasters. Statutes speak for the future. Because legislators cannot tell precisely what shape the problem will take in the future, or predict what new methods of monopolizing trade or what new consumer fraud schemes people will dream up, statutes must address the future in language that is general and flexible enough to be adapted to new conditions. Since general and flexible statutory language cannot resolve specific cases (and because people deliberately violate clear rules), the courts exist to interpret the meaning of statutes when they are applied to human activities.

2. *Common Law.* In the old English legal system judges decided conflicts between citizens without the benefit of statutes. If someone damaged your water wheel by banging it with his boat, if someone agreed to buy your cow and then broke her promise, if three of your pigs wandered into a neighbor's field and he refused to return

1. See Franz Kafka, "Before the Law," *The Penal Colony, Stories and Short Pieces* (New York: Schocken Books, 1972), 148–150.

them, your only legal recourse would be to ask a judge to resolve the conflict. No formal, written body of law governed the judge's decision. But as time went on, the judicial decisions themselves came to constitute a body of *precedent* to which other judges would refer in deciding similar cases that came before them. Rules that emerged from earlier cases provided the authority a judge needed to decide a particular case. The aggregation of such rules and principles eventually constituted the common law of a variety of discrete legal subfields, such as torts, contracts, property, and so on.

Today in the United States, if your dog gets loose and digs up the prizewinning flowers in your neighbor's garden, or if you agree to perform a service for someone and then break your promise, or if you keep a package of valuable silver delivered to your home by mistake, a judge will determine your legal responsibility, if any, and decide what you must do to correct any harm. Unless a statute clearly indicates what the outcome should be, the judge's decision will often be based on common-law principles that resemble the judge-made law that prevailed in England centuries ago. This is also sometimes referred to as "case law," as distinguished from "statutory law."

Statutes are especially important in administrative law because agencies are created by statutes and derive their powers from legislatures. Common law, or case law, nevertheless has special significance for our purposes because it rests on the questionable assumption that judges decide cases correctly even in the absence of clear direction from the legislature.

3. *Constitutions.* Constitutions state the underlying rules for the operation of a political system. They create and govern the government. When it became clear that the original Articles of Confederation did not establish an effective form of government, the representatives from the colonies met in Philadelphia to create a new constitution. Gatherings of political leaders in the territories similarly drafted constitutions as these territories sought admission to the Union. Legislatures update constitutions by amendment. In some states this process is almost as simple as legislating. In the case of the national government, however, amendments must win approval from the Senate, the House of Representatives, and three-fourths of the states before they become part of the constitution.

Constitutional provisions also regulate the citizenry directly. This occurred with the prohibition amendment, and amendments to state constitutions do so more often. However, the bulk of constitutional law clearly defines not what citizens can and cannot do but what powers the government may or may not exercise. The first three articles of the United States Constitution, for example, prescribe a general structure for the three branches of government. They also detail some of the powers those branches may exercise: "Congress shall have power . . . to regulate commerce . . . among the several states," or "The President shall be Commander in Chief of the Army and Navy of the United States." You may already discern that if we care about limiting the power of bureaucratic government, and if the Constitution is the law that governs the government, then the Constitution must play a central role in administrative law.

4. *Regulatory Law.* Congress makes statutes, judges create common law, constitutional conventions and the amendment process develop constitutions. The fourth and final kind of law takes an interesting twist. Administrative agencies also make law. The Federal Communications Commission (FCC), by rule, limits the number of commercial broadcasting stations a company may own. The Internal Revenue Service (IRS), by rule, decides which groups qualify as "charities" and therefore need not pay taxes. The IRS creates tax law. The Federal Drug Administration (FDA) decides whether to classify red yeast rice as a "drug," a designation that makes it legally available only by prescription. These laws regulate citizens. So do environmental law, antitrust law, and consumer protection law. Books have been written about each one of these fields of substantive law made by bureaucrats. *Administrative law, on the other hand, governs the bureaucrats themselves.* It focuses on matters of procedural law in contrast to substantive law. Yet, as we noted above, these two kinds of law may affect each other in important ways over time.

Administrative law applies legal principles from each of the four basic kinds of law. Thus administrative law tries to insure that agencies operate within their statutory limits. Its equally important mission, however, is to apply the Constitution to the administrative process. Therefore we must take a second look at constitutional law.

Americans have long accepted the legal authority of the Constitution. Therefore let us agree that when the United States Constitution or the constitution of any state prohibits the government from doing something, it becomes just as illegal for the government to go ahead and do it as it is for a person to rob a bank in violation of the criminal law. No law means very much, however, if courts do not try to follow its meaning when making legal decisions. All law—statutory law, common law, constitutional law, and regulatory law—depends for legal force on the willingness of judges to make its provisions (or what judges believe are its provisions) stick. Therefore, when a constitution prohibits the government from depriving any person "of life, liberty, or property, without due process" as do the Fifth and Fourteenth amendments to the Constitution, courts must enforce this provision. Courts do so when presented with lawsuits claiming that some governmental action violates this or that constitutional provision. This, in a nutshell, is the rule of law. If governments, including their administrative agencies, remained free to step beyond their legal boundaries whenever they wish, free of judicial interference, the rule of law itself would evaporate.

Unfortunately this description may mislead you. Constitutional law is not as straightforward. Does it, for example, violate "due process" to hold an accused person in jail simply because he is too poor to pay the bail money? Does government violate the equal protection rights of same-sex couples if it passes a law prohibiting such couples from adopting children? Judges must *choose* or interpret what the vague, general and ambiguous words in the Constitution mean. Judges cannot avoid making up the law, or at least filling in the holes and clarifying the uncertainties, as they go along. Lawyers also supply judges with arguments why one particular interpretation of the Constitution is better than another; they, too, actively participate in the lawmaking. The following chapters spend a great deal of time studying what judges have to say about administrative law but much less time on the words of the Constitution itself. The classic ques-

tion in political philosophy, "Who polices the policeman?", continues to stir political controversy. In administrative law, as elsewhere in law, social scientists claim that judges and lawyers *are* the police. This observation has provoked considerable debate about the power of judges and lawyers in a democratic society.

A First Look at the Development of Administrative Law

At the end of this book you will be in a better position to decide how satisfactorily the administrative law that courts have created polices bureaucratic power. Bear in mind, however, that administrative law is a remarkably new field. Courts in the United States have had little more than a century to come to grips with the reality of bureaucratic power, so the presence of unsolved problems and confusing legal doctrines should not surprise us. Furthermore, we have seen that administrative agencies exist, in part, because courts are not well structured to make and implement administrative policy.

The legal profession has come to occupy a prominent role in regulatory politics and administrative lawmaking despite these differences. It is still puzzling how lawyers and judges acquired this position. The field of government administration originally presumed that public policy and administrative practices had to be free from the constraints of procedural legality. Indeed during the late nineteenth and early twentieth centuries, *non-lawyers* such as traffic engineers, city planners, and businessmen practiced administrative law.[2] Also during the early period, the leadership of the American Bar Association (ABA), a private organization of lawyers established in 1879, raised questions about the constitutionality of administrative agencies. Their claim was based on the assertion that Congress had unconstitutionally delegated its legislative authority to agencies and that these same agencies violated the principles of due process by adjudicating conflicts involving their own rules and regulations. By the early 1930s, the private bar lobbied Congress for a

2. See Louis L. Jaffe, "Law Making by Private Groups," *Harvard Law Review* 51 (1937): 201; and Louis L. Jaffe, "Invective and Investigation in Administrative Law," *Harvard Law Review* 52 (1939): 1201.

statute that would impose legal procedures on administrative agencies.[3] The politics of the ABA's design for administrative agencies emphasized the common-law view of fairness. The common-law definition of procedural fairness to the client was the main argument put forward by the private bar. It argued that agencies should be allowed to proceed, for example, to order rate reductions or cease and desist orders, only after following many of the judicial characteristics of a hearing. If agencies departed from the lawyers' model, as one did in the *Morgan* case reported later in this chapter, judges should strike down the agency's decision.

At the same time these debates were going on, a new flow of judicial blood came to the Supreme Court. William O. Douglas, a former chairman of the Securities and Exchange Commission (SEC), and Felix Frankfurter, both former law professors who had specialized in administrative problems and who had actively helped design the New Deal's response to the Great Depression, joined the Court. As President Franklin Roosevelt's appointees to the Court, they argued that the courts needed to give agencies greater freedom to make decisions based on their own expertise, and they encouraged courts to defer to agencies' expertise in policymaking.

Along with FDR's new appointments to the Supreme Court, a "new breed of lawyers" went to Washington to work for the government. Jerold S. Auerbach, a legal historian, argues that these lawyers were not from the same ethnic or racial backgrounds as traditional private lawyers who represented corporations.[4] New Deal agencies provided openings for black and Jewish lawyers who had not found opportunities in private practice. Women lawyers were less active in government agencies in part because law schools and the legal profession discriminated against women. The number of women lawyers did not increase significantly until the 1970s, with substantial pressure placed on law schools to admit qualified women.

Today women comprise between 40–50 percent of entering law school classes. Auerbach's studies were of men, since they predominated. And despite differences in their class backgrounds and political orientations, Auerbach suggests that after the novelty of being a government lawyer wore off, the professional training and professional bonds between lawyers on both sides prevailed and a consensus on administrative procedure began to form.[5]

While some politicians and administrators agreed that a general administrative procedure statute might be useful, they disagreed over the extent to which the legislation should force agencies to act like courts. The ABA, having not fully endorsed the New Deal, pushed for the creation of an administrative law court to which all final contested administrative decisions would go. Congress did not buy that idea, but it did pass the Walter-Logan Bill in 1940. This bill required the agencies to follow court-like procedures for nearly all administrative policymaking, thus formalizing much that agencies had informally done in the past. The bill also authorized the regular courts to review all agencies' decisions. Peter Woll describes the bill this way:

The Walter-Logan bill provides an interesting example of the extent to which the legal profession was willing to go in forcing the administrative process into a judicial mold. With respect to the rule-making (legislative) functions of administrative agencies, the bill provided that "hereafter administrative rules and all amendments or modifications or supplements of existing rules implementing or filling in the details of any statute affecting the rights of persons or property shall be issued . . . only after publication of notice and public hearings." In addition to this extreme provision regarding rule-making, the bill provided that any "substantially interested" person could, within a three-year period, petition the agency for a reconsideration of any rule, and could furthermore demand a hearing. In this manner the bill attempted to enforce common-law due process, applicable only to adjudication, upon the legislative process of administrative agencies. It would have been equally appropriate to enforce judicial procedure upon Congress![6]

President Roosevelt successfully vetoed the bill. However, in 1946 Congress passed a more modest version

3. See Louis G. Caldwell, "A Federal Administrative Court," *University of Pennsylvania Law Review* 84 (1936): 966.

4. Jerold S. Auerbach, *Unequal Justice* (New York: Oxford University Press, 1976). See also Fritz Morstein Marx, "The Lawyer's Role in Public Administration," *Yale Law Journal* 55 (1946): 498; and Peter H. Irons, *The New Deal Lawyers* (Princeton, N.J.: Princeton University Press, 1982).

5. Auerbach, *Unequal Justice*, 215.

6. Peter Woll, *Administrative Law. The Informal Process* (Berkeley: University of California Press, 1963), 18–19.

with the backing and support of the ABA—the Administrative Procedure Act (APA).[7] The act did not judicialize administrative action as thoroughly as did Walter-Logan. The APA (sec. 554) requires agencies to follow court-like hearings only when the legislation creating the agency expressly requires the agency to hold hearings. The APA also does not authorize judicial review of anything and everything the agency does (sec. 701a). This was a prudent move in light of the fact that the legislation creating some agencies specifically forbade judicial review and/or explicitly permitted the agencies to take certain steps at their own discretion.

Nonetheless, as Martin Shapiro points out, "American administrative procedures had been proceeding for 150 years without such a statute," which "fact is crucial to understanding the qualities of American administrative law that place it so firmly in the *intermediate realm.*"[8] Shapiro uses the phrase "intermediate realm" to convey the idea that administrative law requires both constitutional and statutory interpretation. The passage of the APA in 1946 does not remove administrative law from this realm. Indeed, according to Shapiro, the APA "in theory does [not] provide a complete set of procedures adequate to the needs of each agency and its clients. Instead it establishes a kind of residual body of procedural rules that come into play if the rules particular to any given agency are insufficient."[9]

Although the APA is but one source of administrative law, it has become an important document, like the U.S. Constitution, for administrative agencies. You will read cases that address specific portions of the APA, but by way of introducing you to the document let us mention four important areas of administration it governs: (1) *adjudication*, which deals with the process for hearing and deciding controversies; (2) *rulemaking*, which concerns the procedures for developing and amending regulatory rules; (3) *discretion of administrative agencies*, which

is defined in the statute that creates an agency (i.e., the organic act) and reviewing courts must defer to the statute; and (4) *judicial review*, which establishes the standards that courts must apply when reviewing agency actions.

As you proceed through this book, particularly through the chapters that describe the law regulating formal adjudication and semi-formal rulemaking, keep in mind that in many circumstances the APA permits agencies to act informally without following any prescribed due process. Before cases reach the formal stage, many attempts to resolve them informally have usually occurred. Indeed, the vast majority of cases never reach formal administrative decision levels at all.

In its short history, administrative law has developed along four tracks: administrative, judicial, constitutional, and statutory. The administrative track developed first out of procedures originating within the agencies. The APA gave statutory authority to these existing agency-made procedures. The judicial track depends on how judges interpret agency procedures. In the 1960s and 1970s nearly all of the current rules for notice and comment rulemaking were created in the common-law manner by court decisions not based on the wording of statutes or past procedural practices of agencies. The constitutional track has also depended primarily on the judicial applications of the due process clauses that apply to all agencies at all levels of government. Much administrative law labors to articulate the circumstances in which agency procedures do or do not "deprive citizens of life, liberty, or property without due process of law." The statutory track is somewhat more complicated. It includes judicial interpretations of the provisions in statutes that grant agency powers. For example, does the Federal Power Act require the Federal Power Commission to eliminate racial discrimination by producers of electricity and natural gas? The statutory track also includes the generic administrative procedure acts at the national and state levels. These acts specify certain procedures that apply to many agencies, not just one.

At this point, students new to the field may be confused about the definition of administrative law. It is not regulatory law itself, but what is it? The next section

---

7. See Appendix B. On April 6, 1982 the Senate approved, 94–0 the first substantial revision of the APA. More will be said of this bill later.

8. Martin Shapiro, "The Supreme Court's 'Return' to Economic Regulation," *Studies in American Political Development* 1 (1986): 102.

9. Ibid. See also Martin Shapiro, *Who Guards the Guardians? Judicial Control of Administration* (Athens, Ga.: University of Georgia Press, 1988).

provides three administrative law cases. All three involve the constitutional track of administrative law. You should study them with several goals in mind. First, familiarize yourself with the format and style of judicial opinions in general. Second, develop your skill in extracting the important points and conclusions from these cases. Third, think about the issues themselves. We say relatively little about the administrative law issues in these cases so that you can focus on the mechanics of analyzing cases. You can be sure, however, that these important questions of law will come up in many contexts in later chapters. Finally, as you read, begin to evaluate the role of the courts in governing the government.

ADJUDICATION AND THE BASICS OF DUE PROCESS: THREE ILLUSTRATIONS

Adjudication is the focal point in any study of either the constitutional or statutory track of administrative law. This is so because laws so often contain uncertainties that courts ultimately must determine and announce what the laws mean. Having declared what the law means, the courts proceed to enforce their declarations. Fortunately, judges in our system have traditionally given reasons for their decisions. In this book you will find many references to judicial opinions giving reasons for their interpretations of constitutions and of the national and state administrative procedure statutes mentioned above. These statutes, like constitutions, govern how bureaucrats regulate us, and the courts have much to say about their meaning.

If you have not studied law by the *case method* before, you may still struggle with some of the technical terms and concepts of legal analysis. The most important of these is the concept of *precedent*. Each judicial decision tries to justify itself by showing that it is consistent with published judicial decisions that preceded it. Each new decision also speaks to the future. To read a judicial opinion is therefore to read the law, just as much as reading a statutory clause. Students of cases need a method of abstracting and summarizing cases. We recommend the following: 1. Read the entire case through; 2. Reread the case noting in the following order as you read: (a) the key

facts in the case, (b) the primary legal questions in the case, (c) the court's answer(s) to the question(s) ("holdings"), (d) the court's reasons for the holdings and, (e) the arguments of a dissenting opinion (if we include one). You will soon discover that the process of reasoning from precedents in law is not mechanical. The key to understanding holdings is to discover the normative, or value, judgments the judges make about the facts surrounding the case.

Morgan v. United States

304 U.S. 1 (1938) 6-1
+ *Hughes, McReynolds, Brandeis, Butler, Stone, Roberts*
– *Black*
NP *Cardozo, Reed*

[In *Morgan* we have a complex set of facts that lead up to a legal dispute over whether regulated parties, in this case stockyard operators, were treated fairly by government administrators. In 1921, Congress authorized the secretary of agriculture to specify maximum "just and reasonable" charges that stockyard operators could set for their services. In the Packers and Stockyards Act of 1921, Congress instructed the secretary to do so only after a "full hearing." In 1930 the department notified Morgan and other stockyard operators to appear for a hearing concerning their prices. The hearing, which had to be held twice due to the rapidly changing conditions in the Depression, took many months and accumulated a 10,000-page transcript of oral testimony and another 1,000 pages of statistical exhibits. Initially the secretary of agriculture did not personally review the hearing at all. He delegated to subordinates the job of listening to the oral arguments based on the hearing. In an earlier case involving Morgan the stockyard operators appealed to the Supreme Court claiming that they did not have a full or fair hearing because the decider had not reviewed the evidence. The Court agreed and sent the case back to the Department of Agriculture to try again.

Before the completion of the next round a new Secretary was appointed. He did receive and review a list of 180 hearing findings organized by the department's Bureau of Animal Industries. The secretary made a few minor changes in the findings but otherwise approved them and ordered the stockyards to lower their prices. This time when the Court heard the case the stockyard operators had a new set of complaints. The Bureau of Animal Industries had been, in effect, the prosecutor in the case. For the secretary to rely only on its assessment of the issues seemed unfair to the stockyard operators. Also, the operators were not allowed to see the tentative report of the examiner in the hearing, so they had no basis for defining and making their final arguments, nor were they allowed to see the bureau's findings. The department, in effect, left them punching the air. Indeed, from the very beginning of the case, the department never formulated a specific complaint against the prices the stockyards charged.

The opinion of the Court that follows properly insists on basic administrative fairness. *Morgan* was one of the Court's first serious efforts to define administrative fairness in a modern administrative setting. In fact, the case had to go back twice more to the Court before the dust finally settled. As you read this first example of administrative law in action, try to imagine some additional potential defects in a hearing that would make it unfair.]

Mr. Chief Justice Hughes delivered the opinion of the Court

The first question goes to the very foundation of the action of administrative agencies entrusted by the Congress with broad control over activities which in their detail cannot be dealt with directly by the Legislature. The vast expansion of this field of administrative regulation in response to the pressure of social needs is made possible under our system of adherence to the basic principles that the Legislature shall appropriately determine the standards of administrative action and that in administrative proceedings of a quasi-judicial character the liberty and property of the citizen shall be protected by the rudimentary requirements of fair play. These demand "a fair and open hearing," essential alike to the legal validity of the administrative regulation and to the maintenance of public confidence in the value and soundness of this important governmental process. Such a hearing has been described as an "inexorable safeguard." *St. Joseph Stock Yards Co. v. United States,* 298 U.S. 38. [Other citations omitted] And in equipping the Secretary of Agriculture with extraordinary powers under the Packers and Stockyards Act, the Congress explicitly recognized and emphasized this recruitment by making his action depend upon a "full hearing."...

No opportunity was afforded to appellants for the examination of the findings . . . prepared in the Bureau of Animal Industry until they were served with the order. Appellants sought a rehearing by the Secretary, but their application was denied on July 6, 1933, and these suits followed.

The part taken by the Secretary himself in the departmental proceedings is shown by his full and candid testimony. . . . He did not hear the oral argument. The bulky record was placed upon his desk and he dipped into it from time to time to get its drift. He decided that probably the essence of the evidence was contained in appellants' briefs. These, together with the transcript of the oral argument, he took home with him and read. He had several conferences with the Solicitor of the Department and with the officials in the Bureau of Animal Industry, and discussed the proposed findings. He testified that he considered the evidence before signing the order. The substance of his action is stated in his answer to the question whether the order represented his independent conclusion, as follows: "My answer to the question would be that that very definitely was my independent conclusion as based on the findings of the men in the Bureau of Animal Industry. I would say, I will try to put it as accurately as possible, that it represented my own independent reactions to the findings of the men in the Bureau of Animal Industry."

Save for certain rate alterations, he "accepted the findings."

In the light of this testimony there is no occasion to discuss the extent to which the Secretary examined the evidence, and we agree with the Government's contention that it was not the function of the court to probe the mental processes of the Secretary in reaching his conclusions if he gave the hearing which the law required. The Secretary read the summary presented by appellants' briefs and he conferred with his subordinates who had sifted and analyzed the evidence. We assume that the Secretary sufficiently understood its purport. But a "full hearing"—a fair and open hearing—requires more than that. The right to a hearing embraces not only the right to present evidence, but also a reasonable opportunity to know the claims of the opposing party and to meet them. The right to submit argument implies that opportunity; otherwise the right may be but a barren one. Those who are brought into contest with the Government in a quasi-judicial proceeding aimed at the control of their activities are entitled to be fairly advised of what the Government proposes and to be heard upon its proposals before it issues its final command.

No such reasonable opportunity was accorded appellants. The administrative proceeding was initiated by a notice of inquiry into the reasonableness of appellants' rates. No specific complaint was formulated and, in a proceeding thus begun by the Secretary on his own initiative, none was required. Thus, in the absence of any definite complaint and in a sweeping investigation, thousands of pages of testimony were taken by the examiner and numerous complicated exhibits were introduced bearing upon all phases of the broad subject of the conduct of the market agencies. In the absence of any report by the examiner or any findings proposed by the Government, and thus without any concrete statement of the Government's claims, the parties approached the oral argument.

Nor did the oral argument reveal these claims in any appropriate manner. The discussion by counsel for the Government was "very general," as he said, in order not to take up "too much time." It dealt with generalities both as to principles and procedure. . . .

Congress, in requiring a "full hearing," had regard to judicial standards—not in any technical sense but with respect to those fundamental requirements of fairness which are of the essence of due process in a proceeding of a judicial nature. If in an equity cause, a special master or the trial judge permitted the plaintiff's attorney to formulate the findings upon the evidence, conferred ex parte with the plaintiff's attorney regarding them, and then adopted his proposals without affording an opportunity to his opponent to know their contents and present objections, there would be no hesitation in setting aside the report or decree as having been made without a fair hearing. The requirements of fairness are not exhausted in the taking or consideration of evidence, but extend to the concluding parts of the procedure as well as to the beginning and intermediate steps.

The answer that the proceeding before the Secretary was not of an adversary character, as it was not upon complaint but was initiated as a general inquiry, is futile. It has regard to the mere form of the proceeding and ignores realities. In all substantial respects, the Government acting through the Bureau of Animal Industry of the Department was prosecuting the proceeding against the owners of the market agencies. The proceeding had all the essential elements of contested litigation, with the Government and its counsel on the one side and the appellants and their counsel on the other. . . .

Again, the evidence being in, the Secretary might receive the proposed findings of both parties, each being notified of the proposals of the other, hear argument thereon, and make his own findings. But what would not be essential to the adequacy of the hearing if the Secretary himself makes the findings is not a criterion for a case in which the Secretary accepts and makes as his own the findings which have been prepared by the active prosecutors for the Government, after an ex parte discussion with them and without according any reasonable opportunity to the respondents in the proceeding to know the claims thus presented and to contest them. That is more than an irregularity in practice; it is a vital defect.

The maintenance of proper standards on the part of administrative agencies in the performance of their quasi-judicial functions is of the highest importance and in no way cripples or embarrasses the exercise of their appropriate authority. On the contrary, it is in their manifest interest. For, as we said at the outset, if these multiplying agencies deemed to be necessary in our complex society are to serve the purposes for which they are created and endowed with vast powers, they must accredit themselves by acting in accordance with the cherished judicial tradition embodying the basic concepts of fair play.

As the hearing was fatally defective, the order of the Secretary was invalid. In this view, we express no opinion upon the merits. The decree of the District Court is reversed. . . .

[Justice Black's dissenting opinion is omitted]

When they finally finished in 1941, the *Morgan* cases had consumed nearly a decade of litigation. Indeed, two decades had passed since Congress enacted the Packers and Stockyards Act, and by the early 1940s wartime conditions and the programs to deal with them made the act obsolete. One complaint aimed at the administrative process is that its cumbersome machinery allows wealthy interests with clever lawyers to delay the implementation of important policies for years. Against such tactics, scholars and practitioners of administrative law suggested a flexible discretionary space for administrative agencies, allowing them to ignore certain individual complaints and focus on efficiency and public interest instead. But how far can a bureaucracy go in the name of efficiency without denying a citizen due process of law? How close can an agency come to shooting first and asking questions later? Suppose a state welfare agency receives information that a certain welfare recipient is a drug addict. Can the agency cut off the recipient's payments until he agrees to accept counseling and rehabilitation for drug addiction? A number of people imprisoned at Guantanamo Bay, Cuba, made just this claim, that they were innocent bystanders, rounded up by mistake by U.S. forces seeking to defeat the Taliban. What if the recipient insists he does not use drugs, that the agency has made a mistake? Should courts interpret the due process clause so as to give the welfare recipient a hearing at which the agency would have the burden of proving its claim that he or she is a drug user? If so, must the agency offer the hearing *before* it stops sending the checks? *Goldberg v. Kelly* (1970), the next case, addressed this last question.

While *Morgan* involved a federal statute and federal administration, *Goldberg* is a state case. Nevertheless, the Constitution and federal law still govern. That is because the Fourteenth Amendment, which requires due process of law in state government, is part of the Constitution. And the case reached the Supreme Court of the United States, not merely a state supreme court, because Article III of the Constitution gives the Supreme Court power to decide cases arising under the Constitution. There is further federal involvement: Because Congress has authorized the expenditure of federal funds to supplement state welfare programs, the federal government could impose conditions on how states administer the federal money. Prior to *Goldberg*, the Department of Health, Education, and Welfare already required states to offer hearings. Whether these hearings had to precede termination as a constitutional matter remained, however, in doubt. Before *Goldberg*, the due process requirements of a fair termination hearing were also uncertain. Chapter 7 will cover the components of fair hearings more thoroughly,

but a careful reading of both *Morgan* and *Goldberg* will allow you to anticipate many of these components.

Goldberg also illustrates several characteristics of the judicial machinery that you need to master. First, recall that the *Morgan* opinion closed with the sentence, "The decree of the District Court is reversed." What is the "District Court" and how does it differ from the Supreme Court? Both federal and state legal systems are hierarchies. Figure 2.1 shows the United States court system and paths of appeals from federal trial courts (United States District Courts), federal administrative agencies, and state courts to the appellate courts (state appellate courts, state supreme courts, United States courts of appeals, and the United States Supreme Court). Lawsuits usually begin in trial courts, where judges preside over a process of fact finding. Trials in our legal system try to find out who did what to whom—or, rather, what can be *proved* to have happened. Decisions about the meaning of law often enter the picture only at the edges, either because both sides agree about the meaning of the law or because the trial judge makes rather quick decisions about the law to keep the fact-finding process moving. The federal system refers to its trial courts as "district courts." Hence the Supreme Court, which disagreed with the trial result in *Morgan*, "reversed" the district court. In *Goldberg* the Supreme Court agreed with the trial court and "affirmed" its results in the case.

Second, if a party believes the trial judge applied the law incorrectly, that party can appeal to a higher appellate court. Appellate courts do not hold new trials. They accept as true the facts as the trial determined them. But they do resolve legal questions, sometimes affirming the trial court's legal decisions, sometimes reversing them. The United States Courts of Appeals hear most of the appeals from administrative agencies, although this was not the case in *Goldberg*.[10] Figure 2.2 is a map of the twelve regional U.S. Courts of Appeals, which are sometimes called *circuit* courts. The District of Columbia Court of Appeals decides a disproportionately high number of

10. See Woodford J. Howard, *Courts of Appeals in the Federal Judicial System: A Study of the Second, Fifth, and District of Columbia Circuits* (Princeton, N.J.: Princeton University Press, 1981).

Figure 2.1 The United States Court System

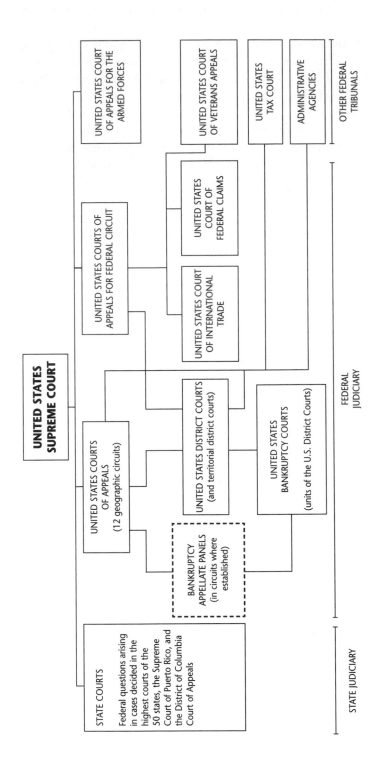

Source: The United States Courts: Their Jurisdiction and Work (Washington, D.C.: U.S. Administrative Office of the United States Courts, 1989), 3.

Figure 2.2 Number and Composition of Federal Judicial Circuits

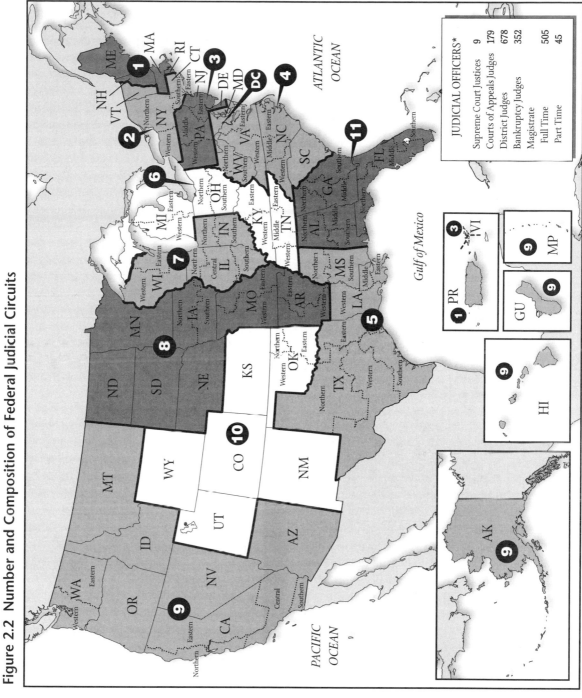

Sources: Understanding Federal Courts (Washington, D.C.: Administrative Office of the U.S. Courts, 2003), 11. *Box: *Judicial Business of the United States Courts* (Washington, D.C.: U.S. Government Printing Office, 2008), 41–43.

Table 2.1 Disposition of Administrative Appeals in the U.S. Court of Appeals, 1945–2005

Year	Total Cases Disposed	Without Hearing	With Hearing	Affirmed		Reversed		Dismissed	
1945	566	185	381	297	(78%)	81	(21%)	3	(1%)
1950	541	169	372	273	(74%)	77	(21%)	15	(4%)
1955	523	150	373	247	(66%)	107	(29%)	13	(3%)
1960	660	299	361	258	(71%)	91	(25%)	4	(1%)
1965	866	377	489	367	(75 %)	95	(19%)	7	(1%)
1970	1248	584	664	527	(79%)	103	(16%)	16	(2%)
1975	1553	874	679	474	(70%)	146	(22%)	37	(5%)
1980	2210	1217	993	662	(67%)	222	(22%)	53	(5%)
1985	2485	1229	1256	953	(76%)	141	(11%)	57	(5%)
1990	2868	1026	1159	841	(73%)	148	(13%)	54	(5%)
1995	3264	1405	1585	1042	(66%)	168	(11%)	232	(15%)
2000	3764		1455	706	(54%)	102	(7%)	397	(27%)
2005	10960		4421	2439	(55%)	293	(7%)	792	(18%)

Sources: Christine B. Harrington, "Regulatory Reform: Creating Gaps and Making Markets," *Law and Policy* 10 (1988): 305. Data derived from U.S. Administrative Office of the United States Courts, Annual Reports. A few cases categorized as "other" have been excluded from this table. The data for 1990 is from *Federal Judicial Workload Statistics,* December 31, 1990 [published 1991] (Washington D.C.: Administrative Office of the United States Courts, Statistical Analysis and Reports Division.) For 1995, 2000, and 2005 data is derived from *Judicial Business of the United States Courts 1995, 2000, and 2005, Report of the Director* respectively (Washington D.C.: Administrative Office of the United States Courts, Statistical Analysis and Reports Division).

agency cases. Almost half of its docket is made up of appeals from regulatory agencies. The United States Court of Appeals for the Ninth Circuit also hears a substantial percentage of administrative appeals.[11] The circuit courts tend to affirm nearly three-quarters of the agency cases they hear. Table 2.1 shows the disposition of administrative appeals in the circuit courts for 1945–2005.

Third, unlike the *Morgan* excerpt above, the *Goldberg* opinion refers favorably to ideas it attributes to opinions in other cases. This reasoning from the example of other cases—precedents—is an important part of legal reasoning. It is a habit inherited from common law. Remember that in common law, judges make decisions without referring to statutes at all. They try to keep their decisions consistent by making their results agree with results in similar

cases. The reasons they give in their opinions become part of, and build up further, the body of common law. In many of the cases in this book you will see citations to other opinions.[12]

Goldberg v. Kelly

397 U.S. 254 (1970) 6-3
+ *Douglas, Harlan, Brennan, White, Marshall, Blackmun*
– *Black, Stewart, Burger*

[Several residents of New York City, Kelly among them, received welfare payments under the federally assisted Aid to Families with Dependent Children program or the state's Home Relief program. They brought suit to pre-

11. See Christine B. Harrington, "Regulatory Reform: Creating Gaps and Making Markets," *Law & Policy* 10 (1988): 300.

12. Lief Carter and Thomas Burke's *Reason in Law,* 8th ed. (New York: Longman, 2009) explores the complexities of legal reasoning in much more detail.

vent the termination of their welfare payments before a hearing had taken place. New York law did, however, allow an oral hearing before an independent state hearing officer *after* termination, at which time the recipient could offer oral evidence, cross-examine witnesses and have a record made of the hearing. If the recipient wins at this hearing he or she receives all the funds erroneously withheld.[13]]

Mr. Justice Brennan delivered the opinion of the Court

[T]he State Department of Social Services Official Regulations . . . require that local social services officials proposing to discontinue or suspend a recipient's financial aid do so according to a procedure [which] . . . must include the giving of notice to the recipient of the reasons for a proposed discontinuance or suspension at least seven days prior to its effective date, with notice also that upon request the recipient may have the proposal reviewed by a local welfare official holding a position superior to that of the supervisor who approved the proposed discontinuance or suspension, and, further, that the recipient may submit, for purposes of the review, a written statement to demonstrate why his grant should not be discontinued or suspended. The decision by the reviewing official whether to discontinue or suspend aid must be made expeditiously, with written notice of the decision to the recipient. The section further expressly provides that "[a]ssistance shall not be discontinued or suspended prior to the date such notice or decision is sent to the recipient and his representative, if any, or prior to the proposed effective date of discontinuance or suspension, whichever occurs later." . . . [T]he New York City Department of Social Services promulgated Procedure No. 68-18. A caseworker who has doubts about the recipient's continued eligibility must first discuss them with the recipient. If the caseworker concludes that the

recipient is no longer eligible, he recommends termination of aid to a unit supervisor. If the latter concurs, he sends the recipient a letter stating the reasons for proposing to terminate aid and notifying him that within seven days he may request that a higher official review the record, and may support the request with a written statement prepared personally or with the aid of an attorney or other person. If the reviewing official affirms the determination of ineligibility, aid is stopped immediately and the recipient is informed by letter of the reasons for the action. Appellees' challenge to this procedure emphasizes the absence of any provisions for the personal appearance of the recipient before the reviewing official, for oral presentation of evidence, and for confrontation and cross-examination of adverse witnesses. . . .

The constitutional issue to be decided, therefore, is the narrow one whether the Due Process Clause requires that the recipient be afforded an evidentiary hearing *before* the termination of benefits. The District Court held that only a pre-termination evidentiary hearing would satisfy the constitutional command, and rejected the argument of the state and city officials that the combination of the post-termination "fair hearing" with the informal pre-termination review disposed of all due process claims.

For qualified recipients, welfare provides the means to obtain essential food, clothing, housing, and medical care. . . . [T]hus the crucial factor in this context—a factor not present in the case of the black-listed government contractor, the discharged government employee, the taxpayer denied a tax exemption, or virtually anyone else whose governmental largesse is ended—is that termination of aid pending resolution of a controversy over eligibility may deprive an eligible recipient of the very means by which to live while he waits. Since he lacks independent resources, his situation becomes immediately desperate. His need to concentrate upon finding the means of daily subsistence, in turn, adversely affects his ability to seek redress from the welfare bureaucracy.

Moreover, important governmental interests are promoted by affording recipients a pre-termination evidentiary hearing. From its founding the nation's basic commitment has been to foster the dignity and well-being of all persons within its borders. We have come to recognize that forces not within the control of the poor contribute to their poverty. This perception, against the background of our traditions, has significantly influenced the development of the

---

13. It is now possible to locate the published opinions in virtually every federal court case on the World Wide Web. If your school or public library subscribes to Lexis/Nexus "UNIVerse," you will find hyperlink connections to many of the cases cited in those opinions. "Findlaw" (www.findlaw.com/) is a free service that includes all U.S. Supreme Court decisions. Some of the more famous U.S. Supreme Court decisions even have the recorded oral arguments of the lawyers available on the Web via RealAudio. For this unrestricted service, contact http://oyez.nwu.edu./ Oral arguments in both *Goldberg* and *Mathews* (the next case in this chapter) can be heard with RealAudio at this site.

contemporary public assistance system. Welfare, by meeting the basic demands of subsistence, can help bring within the reach of the poor the same opportunities that are available to others to participate meaningfully in the life of the community. At the same time, welfare guards against the societal malaise that may flow from a widespread sense of unjustified frustration and insecurity. Public assistance, then, is not mere charity, but a means to "promote the general Welfare, and secure the Blessings of Liberty to ourselves and our Posterity." The same governmental interests which counsel the provision of welfare, counsel as well its uninterrupted provision to those eligible to receive it; pre-termination evidentiary hearings are indispensable to that end.

Appellant does not challenge the force of these considerations but argues that they are outweighed by countervailing governmental interests in conserving fiscal and administrative resources. These interests, the argument goes, justify the delay of any evidentiary hearing until after discontinuance of the grants. Summary adjudication protects the public by stopping payments promptly upon discovery of reason to believe that a recipient is no longer eligible. Since most terminations are accepted without challenge, summary adjudication also conserves both the fiscal and administrative time and energy by reducing the number of evidentiary hearings actually held.

We agree with the District Court, however, that these governmental interests are not overriding in the welfare context. The requirements of a prior hearing doubtless involve some greater expense, and the benefits paid to ineligible recipients pending decisions at the hearing probably cannot be recouped, since these recipients are likely to be judgment-proof. But the State is not without weapons to minimize these increased costs. Much of the drain on fiscal and administrative resources can be reduced by developing procedures for prompt pre-termination hearings and by skillful use of personnel and facilities. Indeed, the very provision for post-termination evidentiary hearing in New York's Home Relief program is itself cogent evidence that the State recognizes the primacy of the public interest in correct eligibility determinations and therefore in the provision of procedural safeguards. Thus, the interest of the eligible recipient in uninterrupted receipt of public assistance, coupled with the State's interest that his payments not be erroneously terminated, clearly outweighs the State's competing concern to prevent any increase in its fiscal and administrative burdens. . . .

We also agree with the District Court, however, that the pre-termination hearing need not take the form of a judicial or quasi-judicial trial. We bear in mind that the statutory "fair hearing" will provide the recipient with a full administrative review. Accordingly, the pre-termination hearing has one function only: to produce an initial determination of the validity of the welfare department's grounds for discontinuance of payments in order to protect a recipient against an erroneous termination of his benefits. . . . Thus, a complete record and a comprehensive opinion, which would serve primarily to facilitate judicial review and to guide future decisions, need not be provided at the pre-termination stage. We recognize, too, that both welfare authorities and recipients have an interest in relatively speedy resolution of questions of eligibility, that they are used to dealing with one another informally, and that some welfare departments have very burdensome caseloads. These considerations justify the limitation of the pre-termination hearing to minimum procedural safeguards, adapted to the particular characteristics of welfare recipients, and to the limited nature of the controversies to be resolved. We wish to add that we, no less than the dissenters, recognize the importance of not imposing upon the States or the Federal Government in this developing field of law any procedural requirements beyond those demanded by rudimentary due process.

"The fundamental requisite of due process of law is the opportunity to be heard." *Grannis v. Ordean*, 234 U.S. 385, 394 (1914). The hearing must be "at a meaningful time and in a meaningful manner." *Armstrong v. Manzo*, 380 U.S. 545, 552 (1965). In the present context these principles require that a recipient have timely and adequate notice detailing the reasons for a proposed termination, and an effective opportunity to defend by confronting any adverse witnesses and by presenting his own arguments and evidence orally. These rights are important in cases such as those before us, where recipients have challenged proposed terminations as resting on incorrect or misleading factual premises or on misapplication of rules or policies to the facts of particular cases.

We are not prepared to say that the seven-day notice currently provided by New York City is constitutionally insufficient per se, although there may be cases where fairness would require that a longer time be given. Nor do we see any constitutional deficiency in the content or form of the notice. New York employs both a letter and a personal conference with a caseworker to inform a recipient of the precise questions raised about his continued eligibility. Evidently the recipient is told the legal and factual bases for the Department's doubts. This combination is probably the most effective method of communicating with recipients.

The city's procedures presently do not permit recipients to appear personally with or without counsel before the official who finally determines continued eligibility. Thus a recipient is not permitted to present evidence to that official orally, or to confront or cross-examine adverse witnesses. These omissions are fatal to the constitutional adequacy of the procedures.

The opportunity to be heard must be tailored to the capacities and circumstances of those who are to be heard. It is not enough that a welfare recipient may present his position to the decision maker in writing or second-hand through his caseworker. Written submissions are an unrealistic option for most recipients, who lack the educational attainment necessary to write effectively and who cannot obtain professional assistance. Moreover, written submissions do not afford the flexibility of oral presentations; they do not permit the recipient to mold his argument to the issues the decision maker appears to regard as important. Particularly where credibility and veracity are at issue, as they must be in many termination proceedings, written submissions are a wholly unsatisfactory basis for decision. The second-hand presentation to the decision maker by the caseworker has its own deficiencies; since the caseworker usually gathers the facts upon which the charge of ineligibility rests, the presentation of the recipient's side of the controversy cannot safely be left to him. Therefore a recipient must be allowed to state his position orally. Informal procedures will suffice; in this context due process does not require a particular order of proof or mode of offering evidence. . . .

In almost every setting where important decisions turn on questions of fact, due process requires an opportunity to confront and cross-examine adverse witnesses. . . .

. . . What we said in *Greene v. McElroy*, 360 U.S. 474, 496–497 (1959) is particularly pertinent here:

Certain principles have remained relatively immutable in our jurisprudence. One of these is that where governmental action seriously injures an individual, and the reasonableness of the

action depends on fact finding, the evidence used to prove the Government's case must be disclosed to the individual so that he has an opportunity to show that it is untrue. While this is important in the case of documentary evidence, it is even more important where evidence consists of the testimony of individuals whose memory might be faulty or who, in fact, might be perjurers or persons motivated by malice, vindictiveness, intolerance, prejudice, or jealousy. We have formalized these protections in the requirements of confrontation and cross-examination. . . .

Welfare recipients must therefore be given an opportunity to confront and cross-examine the witnesses relied on by the department.

"The right to be heard would be, in many cases, of little avail if it did not comprehend the right to be heard by counsel." *Powell v. Alabama*, 287 U.S. 45, 68–69 (1932). We do not say that counsel must be provided at the pre-termination hearing, but only that the recipient must be allowed to retain an attorney if he so desires. . . .

Finally, the decision maker's conclusion as to a recipient's eligibility must rest solely on the legal rules and evidence adduced at the hearing. *Ohio Bell Tel. Co. v. PUC*, 301 U.S. 292 (1937). . . . To demonstrate compliance with this elementary requirement, the decision maker should state the reasons for his determination and indicate the evidence he relied on, cf. *Wichita R.R. & Light* Co. v. *PUC*, 260 U.S. 48, 57–59 (1922), though his statement need not amount to a full opinion or even formal findings of fact and conclusions of law. And, of course, an impartial decision maker is essential. Cf. *In re Murchison*, 349 U.S. 133 (1955); *Wong Yang Sung v. McGrath*, 330 U.S. 33, 45–46 (1950). We agree with the District Court that prior involvement in some aspects of a case will not necessarily bar a welfare official from acting as a decision maker. He should not, however, have participated in making the determination under review.

Affirmed.

Goldberg's extension of the due process requirement of an evidentiary hearing to routine state administrative matters initiated a dramatic change in administrative law, one which later chapters analyze in depth. One very significant aspect of such change is the re-conceptualization of the link between citizens in need and the state. Justice Brennan's majority opinion put forward a very significant argument about welfare and welfare beneficiaries:

Brennan argued, citing eminent legal scholars of his day, that welfare benefits must be treated and protected as "property." In the famous footnote -8- to his decision, Justice Brennan explained:

It may be realistic today to regard welfare entitlements as more like "property" than a "gratuity." Much of the existing wealth in this country takes the form of rights that do not fall within traditional common-law concepts of property. It has been aptly noted that "[s]ociety today is built around entitlement. The automobile dealer has his franchise, the doctor and lawyer their professional licenses, the worker his union membership, contract, and pension rights, the executive his contract and stock options; all are devices to aid security and independence. Many of the most important of these entitlements now flow from government: subsidies to farmers and businessmen, routes for airlines and channels for television stations; long term contracts for defense, space, and education; social security pensions for individuals. Such sources of security, whether private or public, are no longer regarded as luxuries or gratuities; to the recipients they are essentials, fully deserved, and in no sense a form of charity. It is only the poor whose entitlements, although recognized by public policy, have not been effectively enforced." Reich, Individual Rights and Social Welfare: The Emerging Legal Issues, 74 *Yale L. J.* 1245, 1255 (1965). See also Reich, The New Property, 73 *Yale L. J.* 733 (1964).

A close reading of *Goldberg*, however, shows that the Court neglected to answer perhaps the most important question of all: *In what circumstances* does the due process clause require an evidentiary hearing? The next case did address the issue. Here the Court *denied* the recipient's claim to a pre-termination hearing. You should use the techniques of case analysis discussed above to dig out the reasons for this denial.

Mathews v. Eldridge

424 U.S. 319 (1976) 6-2
+ *Burger, Stewart, White, Blackmun, Powell, Rehnquist*
– *Brennan, Marshall*
NP Stevens

[Eldridge had received Social Security benefits because he claimed he was completely disabled. The Social Security Administration determined after some years that Eldridge had recovered sufficiently to hold a job. It there-fore terminated his Social Security benefit checks without holding an oral hearing. The details are reported in the opinion.]

Mr. Justice Powell delivered the opinion of the Court

The issue in this case is whether the Due Process Clause of the Fifth Amendment requires that prior to the termination of Social Security disability benefit payments the recipient be afforded an opportunity for an evidentiary hearing.
. . .

Cash benefits are provided to workers during periods in which they are completely disabled under the disability insurance benefits program created by the 1956 amendments to . . . the Social Security Act. . . . Eldridge was first awarded benefits in June 1968. In March 1972, he received a questionnaire from the state agency charged with monitoring his medical condition. Eldridge completed the questionnaire, indicating that his condition had not improved and identifying the medical sources, including physicians, from whom he had received treatment recently. The state agency then obtained reports from his physician and psychiatric consultant. After considering these reports and other information in his file the agency informed Eldridge by letter that it had made a tentative determination that his disability had ceased in May 1972. The letter included a statement of reasons for the proposed termination of benefits, and advised Eldridge that he might request reasonable time in which to obtain and submit additional information pertaining to his condition.

In his written response, Eldridge disputed one characterization of his medical condition and indicated that the agency already had enough evidence to establish his disability. The state agency then made a final determination that he had ceased to be disabled in May 1972. This determination was accepted by the Social Security Administration (SSA), which notified Eldridge in July that his benefits would terminate after that month. The notification also advised him of his rights to seek reconsideration by the state agency of this initial determination within six months.

Instead of requesting reconsideration Eldridge commenced this action challenging the constitutional validity of the administrative procedures established by the Secretary of Health, Education, and Welfare for assessing whether there exists a continuing disability. He sought an immediate reinstatement of benefits pending a hearing on the issue of his disability. . . . The Secretary moved to dismiss on the grounds that Eldridge's benefits had been terminated in accordance with valid administrative regulations and procedures and that he had failed to exhaust available remedies. . . .

. . . [The] District Court held that prior to termination of benefits Eldridge had to be afforded an evidentiary hearing of the type required for welfare beneficiaries under . . . the Social Security Act. . . . [T]he Court of Appeals for the Fourth Circuit affirmed. . . . We reverse. . . .

Procedural due process imposes constraints on governmental decisions which deprive individuals of "liberty" or "property" interests within the meaning of the Due Process Clause of the Fifth or Fourteenth Amendment. The Secretary does not contend that procedural due process is inapplicable to terminations of Social Security disability benefits. He recognizes, as has been implicit in our prior decisions, . . . that the interest of an individual in continued receipt of these benefits is a statutorily created "property" interest protected by the Fifth Amendment. . . . Rather, the Secretary contends that the existing administrative procedures . . . provide all the process that is constitutionally due before a recipient can be deprived of that interest.

This Court consistently has held that some form of hearing is required before an individual is finally deprived of a property interest. . . . the "right to be heard before being condemned to suffer grievous loss of any kind, even though it may not involve the stigma and hardships of a criminal conviction, is a principle basic to our society." . . . The fundamental requirement of due process is the opportunity to be heard "at a meaningful time and in a meaningful manner." Eldridge agrees that the review procedures available to a claimant before the initial determination of ineligibility becomes final would be adequate if disability benefits were not terminated until after the evidentiary hearing stage of the administrative process. The dispute centers upon what process is due prior to the initial termination of benefits, pending review.

In recent years this Court increasingly has had occasion to consider the extent to which due process requires an evidentiary hearing prior to the deprivation of some type of property interest even if such a hearing is provided thereafter. In only one case, *Goldberg v. Kelly*, . . . has the Court held that a hearing closely approximating a judicial trial is necessary. In other cases requiring some type of pre-termination hearing as a matter of constitutional right the Court has spoken sparingly about the requisite procedures. . . .

These decisions underscore the truism that "'[d]ue process, unlike some legal rules, is not a technical conception with a fixed content unrelated to time, place, and circumstances.'" . . . "[D]ue process is flexible and calls for such procedural protections as the particular situation demands." . . . Accordingly, resolution of the issue whether the administrative procedures provided here are constitutionally sufficient requires analysis of the governmental and private interests that are affected. . . . More precisely, our prior decisions indicate that identification of the specific dictates of due process generally requires consideration of three distinct factors: first, the private interest that will be affected by the official action; second, the risk of an erroneous deprivation of such interest through the procedures used, and the probable value, if any, of additional or substitute procedural safeguards; and finally, the Government's interest, including the function involved and the fiscal and administrative burdens that the additional or substitute procedural requirement would entail. . . .

Despite the elaborate character of the administrative procedures provided by the Secretary, the courts below held them to be constitutionally inadequate concluding that due process requires an evidentiary hearing prior to termination. In light of the private and governmental interests at stake here and the nature of the existing procedures, we think this was an error.

Since a recipient whose benefits are terminated is awarded full retroactive relief if he ultimately prevails, his sole interest is in the uninterrupted receipt of this source of income pending final administrative decision on his claim. . . .

Only in *Goldberg* has the Court held that due process requires an evidentiary hearing prior to a temporary deprivation. It was emphasized there that welfare assistance is given to persons on the very margin of subsistence. . . . Eligibility for disability benefits, in contrast, is not based upon financial need. Indeed, it is wholly unrelated to the worker's income or support from many other sources, such as earnings of other family members, workmen's compensation awards, tort claims awards, savings, private insurance, public or private pensions, veterans' benefits, food stamps, public assistance, or the "many other important programs, both public and private, which contain provisions for disability payments affecting a substantial portion of the work force. . . ."

As *Goldberg* illustrates, the degree of potential deprivation that may be created by a particular decision is a factor to be considered in assessing the validity of any administrative decision-making process. . . . The potential deprivation here is generally likely to be less than in *Goldberg*, although the degree of difference can be overstated. . . . [T]o remain eligible for benefits a recipient must be "unable to engage in substantial gainful activity.". . .

As we recognized last Term, ". . . the possible length of wrongful deprivation of . . . benefits [also] is an important factor in assessing the impact of official action on the private interests." The Secretary concedes that the delay between a request for a hearing before an administrative law judge and a decision on the claim is currently between 10 and 11 months. Since a terminated recipient must first obtain a reconsideration decision as a prerequisite to invoking his right to an evidentiary hearing, the delay between the actual cutoff of benefits and final decision after a hearing exceeds one year.

In view of the torpidity of this administrative review process, . . . and the typically modest resources of the family unit of the physically disabled worker, the hardship imposed upon the erroneously terminated disability recipient may be significant. Still, the disabled worker's need is likely to be less than that of a welfare recipient. In addition to the possibility of access to private resources, other forms of government assistance will become available where the termination of disability benefits places a worker or his family below the subsistence level. . . . In view of these potential sources of temporary income, there is less reason here than in *Goldberg* to depart from the ordinary principle, established by our decisions, that something less than an evidentiary hearing is sufficient prior to adverse administrative action. . . .

An additional factor to be considered here is the fairness and reliability of the existing pre-termination procedures, and the probable value, if any, of additional procedural safeguards. Central to the evaluation of any administrative process is the nature of the relevant inquiry. . . . In order to remain eligible for benefits the disabled worker must demonstrate by means of "medically acceptable clinical and laboratory diagnostic techniques" . . . that he is unable to

"engage in any substantial gainful activity by reason of any *medically determinable* physical or mental impairment . . . " [emphasis supplied]. In short, a medical assessment of the worker's physical or mental condition is required. This is a more sharply focused and easily documented decision than the typical determination of welfare entitlement. In the latter case, a wide variety of information may be deemed relevant, and issues of witness credibility and veracity often are critical to the decision-making process. . . .

By contrast, the decision whether to discontinue disability benefits will turn, in most cases, upon "routine, standard, and unbiased medical reports by physician specialists," . . . concerning a subject whom they have personally examined. . . . To be sure, credibility and veracity may be a factor in the ultimate disability assessment in some cases. But procedural due process rules are shaped by the risk of error inherent in the truthfinding process as applied to the generality of cases, not the rare exceptions. The potential value of an evidentiary hearing, or even oral presentation to the decision maker, is substantially less in this context than in *Goldberg*. . . .

A further safeguard against mistake is the policy of allowing the disability recipient's representative full access to all information relied upon by the state agency. In addition, prior to the cutoff of benefits the agency informs the recipients of its tentative assessment, the reasons therefore, and provides a summary of the evidence that it considers most relevant. Opportunity is then afforded the recipient to submit additional evidence or arguments, enabling him to challenge directly the accuracy of information in his file as well as the correctness of the agency's tentative conclusions. These procedures . . . enable the recipient to "mold" his argument to respond to the precise issues which the decision maker regards as crucial. . . .

In striking the appropriate due process balance the final factor to be assessed is the public interest. This includes the administrative burden and other societal costs that would be associated with requiring, as a matter of constitutional right, an evidentiary hearing upon demand in all cases prior to the termination of disability benefits. The most visible burden would be the incremental costs resulting from the increased number of hearings and the expense of providing benefits to ineligible recipients pending decision. No one can predict the extent of the increase, but the fact that full benefits would continue until after such hearings would assure the exhaustion in most cases of this attractive option. Nor would the theoretical right of the Secretary to recover undeserved benefits result, as a practical matter, in any substantial offset to the added outlay of public funds. . . . [E]xperience with the constitutionalizing of government procedures suggests that the ultimate additional costs in terms of money and administrative burden would not be insubstantial.

Financial cost alone is not a controlling weight in determining whether due process requires a particular procedural safeguard prior to some administrative decision. But the Government's interest, and hence that of the public, in conserving scarce fiscal and administrative resources, is a factor that must be weighed. At some point the benefit of an additional safeguard to the individual affected by the administrative action and to society, in terms of increased assurance that the action is just, may be outweighed by the cost. Significantly, the cost of protecting those whom the preliminary administrative process has identified as likely to be found undeserving may in the end come out of the pockets of the deserving since resources available for any particular program of social welfare are not unlimited. . . .

But more is implicated in cases of this type than ad hoc weighing of fiscal and administrative burdens against the interest of a particular category of claimants. The ultimate balance involves a determination as to when, under our constitutional system, judicial-type procedures must be imposed upon administrative action to assure fairness. We reiterate the wise admonishment of Mr. Justice Frankfurter that differences in the origin and function of administrative agencies "preclude wholesale transplantation of the rules of procedure, trial, and review which have evolved from the history and experience of courts." . . . The judicial model of an evidentiary hearing is neither a required, nor even the most effective, method of decision making in all circumstances. The essence of due process is the requirement that "a person in jeopardy of serious loss [be given] notice of the case against him and opportunity to meet it" . . . All that is necessary is that the procedures be tailored, in light of the decision to be made, to "the capacities and circumstances of those who are to be heard," . . . to insure that they are given a meaningful opportunity to present their case. In assessing what process is due in this case, substantial weight must be given to the good-faith judgments of the individuals charged by Congress with the administration of

social welfare programs that the procedures they have provided assure fair consideration of the entitlement claims of individuals.

. . . This is especially so where, as here, the prescribed procedures not only provide the claimant with an effective process for asserting his claim prior to any administrative action, but also assure a right to an evidentiary hearing, as well as to subsequent judicial review, before the denial of his claim becomes final. . . .

We conclude that an evidentiary hearing is not required prior to the termination of disability benefits and that the present administrative procedures fully comport with due process. . . .

Reversed.

Mr. Justice Brennan with whom Mr. Justice Marshall concurs, dissenting

. . . I agree with the District Court and the Court of Appeals that, prior to termination of benefits, Eldridge must be afforded an evidentiary hearing of the type required for welfare beneficiaries. . . . I would add that the Court's consideration that a discontinuance of disability benefits may cause the recipient to suffer only a limited deprivation is no argument. It is speculative. Moreover, the very legislative determination to provide disability benefits, without any prerequisite determination of need in fact, presumes a need by the recipient which is not this Court's function to denigrate. Indeed, in the present case, it is indicated that because disability benefits were terminated there was a foreclosure upon the Eldridge home and the family's furniture was repossessed, forcing Eldridge, his wife and children to sleep in one bed. . . . Finally, it is also no argument that a worker, who has been placed in the untenable position of having been denied disability benefits, may still seek other forms of public assistance.*

The central legal issues in these three cases concern the rule of law itself, which we shall address shortly. To complete this chapter's descriptive theme, consider three background aspects of the legal process reflected in these cases. First, readers may wonder why these cases do not

* Eldridge, a truck driver, claimed in a post-termination hearing that his bad back prevented him from working. The administrative law judge ruled in his favor. Eldridge recovered "back" benefits in both senses!

draw upon the requirements stated in *any* administrative procedure act. The answer regarding *Morgan* is simple. The Court decided the case before the federal APA was passed in 1946. As to the relatively recent cases, the APA does not apply because by its own words it does not cover welfare payment programs.

Second, students who have studied the legal process may wonder about the applicability of the doctrine of *stare decisis.* This doctrine encourages courts to follow the precedents in previous cases that *control,* that is, are factually similar to, the case in question. Thus one might expect *Goldberg* to control or dictate the result in *Mathews* and to suspect the Court of employing devious reasoning to reach the *Mathews* result. However, a careful reading of *Mathews* shows that the Court believed the case did not factually resemble *Goldberg.* The conclusion—that Eldridge did not deserve an oral pre-termination hearing because, he, unlike Kelly, could obtain other forms of public assistance while awaiting a post-termination hearing—is a choice on the part of the six-member majority to narrowly distinguish the two cases. Courts use judicial discretion to decide whether previous cases do or do not factually resemble the one before them.

Finally, recall the earlier point that regulatory law in large part responds to perceived shortcomings in the private economic system. You may ask yourself what welfare cases have to do with the shortcomings of free markets. An important, if not obvious, linkage exists, however. Welfare programs exist *because* society has come to accept a public obligation to support those whom the private system does not, for a variety of reasons, support. For better or worse, once the obligation to provide relief becomes by political agreement a public responsibility, the Due Process Clause and the rule of law do affect how government carries the programs out.

THEME FOUR: WHAT IS ADMINISTRATIVE LAW?

The agencies themselves, with varying degrees of legal help from legislatures, create regulatory law. Administrative law, by contrast, comes primarily from judicial interpretations of legal statements setting forth the *procedures* agencies must follow. These come mainly from due process clauses in federal and state constitutions, from administrative procedure statutes when they apply, and from the occasional clause within a statute creating an agency. It was in this last category that the "full hearing" requirement adjudicated in *Morgan* originated. Regulatory law governs the citizenry; administrative law governs the government. We might say that administrative law governs the bureaucracy as other constitutional provisions govern the judicial, legislative and presidential powers in government. Together with constitutional law, administrative law operationalizes the framework of political commitment to the rule of law.

THEME FIVE: THE ETHICS OF THE RULE OF LAW IN BUREAUCRATIC GOVERNMENT

The philosophical concept of the rule of law plays a central role in administrative law because it has been a part of our liberal-legal political tradition since the founding of the nation and the adoption of our national constitution. It is a command to those who govern to obey the law and a command to all citizens to respect the law. Abraham Lincoln, in a speech he delivered as a young man, said:

[L]et every man remember that to violate the law, is to trample on the blood of his father, and to tear the charter of his own, and his children's liberty. Let reverence for the laws be breathed by every American mother, to the lisping babe, that prattles on her lap; let it be taught in schools, in seminaries, and in colleges; let it be written in primers, spelling books, and in almanacs: let it be preached from the pulpit, proclaimed in legislative halls, and enforced in courts of justice. And, in short, let it become the political religion of the nation. . . . Reason, cold, calculating, unimpassioned reason, must furnish all the materials for our future support and defense. Let those materials be moulded into general intelligence, sound morality and, in particular, a reverence for the Constitution and laws. . . .[14]

In spite of Lincoln's appeal and Americans' general agreement with the principle of the rule of law, no single operational definition of the concept has won general

---

14. Abraham Lincoln, "Address to the Young Men's Lyceum of Springfield, Illinois," January 27, 1838, from T. Harry Williams, ed., *Abraham Lincoln: Selected Speeches, Messages, and Letters* (New York: Rinehart and Co., 1957), 10, 14.

acceptance, either among scholars or the public. This book adopts one of several definitions of the ethical meaning of the rule of law. On this definition rests this book's most important assessments and conclusions about modern administrative law. Therefore let us make this definition as clear as possible by contrasting it with the definitions we reject.

Before describing the various concepts of the rule of law, one further point needs coverage. While the rule of law as a philosophical matter urges all citizens to obey and respect the law, in practical terms the concept applies primarily to courts. The courts in our constitutional scheme have primary responsibility for deciding what laws mean as they decide concrete cases. The rule of law commands judges to play an impartial role in this process, just as the rules of football or baseball specify roles of impartiality for referees and umpires. But just what law do judges apply and how do they do so impartially? The answers to this question provide various ethical, or normative, models of the rule of law. This book endorses the last of these models.

1. *Constitutions are the supreme law in the U.S.; the rule of law therefore requires courts to follow the constitution.* The difficulty with this view is that a constitution's words are often so broad, general, and ambiguous that they provide in themselves no limit on judicial discretion. To cite a due process requirement does not really constrain a judge or help define impartiality because a judge can assert that whatever he or she wishes to accomplish is or isn't due process. This pattern occurred during that point in our economic history when judges struck down a wide variety of social programs regulating business simply by asserting that they violated due process. To extend the analogy to referees, constitutions often say nothing more specific than would a basketball rule that commanded referees "to call a foul whenever a player does something dirty." Such a rule would leave referees free to define "dirty" as they choose.

2. *The rule of law requires judges to enforce statutes as written.* Some legislative language is concrete and clear, but very often it is no less general or ambiguous than the language of constitutions. In fact, statutory imprecision

pops up particularly often in administrative law for the simple reason that if Congress could make clear law on a subject, it would not need to create a regulatory body in the first place. Part II of this book will reveal instances in which Congress has merely commanded agencies "to regulate in the public interest." Also, the phrase *full bearing* is not much clearer than *due process.* In such circumstances judges are just as free under statutes as they are under constitutions to draw on their personal biases. And, if you criticize this argument by citing statutes that do state concrete and unambiguous provisions, you must recall that cases involving these statutes usually do not reach the appellate courts precisely because the law is clear. Parties do not routinely invest tens of thousands of dollars of legal fees in cases they expect to lose. For both parties to carry a suit forward, they must be able to predict, or strongly believe, that the law in question is uncertain enough to take a shot at winning their claims.

3. *The rule of law requires judges to follow precedents.* This more limited formulation of the rule of law recognizes that judges simply draw on their biases in deciding cases otherwise. The restraint of law arises merely in the obligation to follow these decisions in future similar cases. The trouble here is that, as we saw in *Mathews*'s treatment of *Goldberg*, judges are free to say a case is factually different from a previous case and hence escape the restraining influence of prior law.

4. *The rule of law refers to a philosophy of justice, not a concept of "following the law."* If we seek a test of judicial impartiality but cannot find it in the black and white letters of society's rules, a philosophy of justice may offer the only alternative. But which philosophy should judges choose? Should they attempt to articulate prevailing social customs? Marxism? A natural law theory? We are on the right track but have yet to get on the proper philosophical train.

5. *The rule of law is a philosophy of compromising and balancing among social interests.* This statement pinpoints a common political as well as judicial approach to constitutional and administrative law problems. The Supreme Court selected this very test in its decision in *Mathews.* It said the costs in *Goldberg* of denying a hearing were greater than in *Mathews* because Eldridge could get wel-

fare payments while he waited, but Kelly could not. Many administrative law cases use the language of "balancing interests" because it conveys some idea of weighing interest and producing a fair outcome. But the balancing test usually leaves judges free to define the balance any way they wish, and the "public" interest almost always outweighs one individual person's problem. To be sure, not all disabled recipients depend on the checks. But most do, and Eldridge certainly did. Being deprived of a hearing may be less costly to him than it was to Kelly, but is the difference *enough* to justify the Court's decision against him? Balancing will play a part in the judicial administrative law role, but it does not fully satisfy the obligation to the rule of law.

6. *The rule of law seeks to achieve fairness, rationality, and social equality by promoting public participation in decision making.* Return to the Supreme Court's reasoning in *Morgan* and *Goldberg*. The requirements the cases call for do not leap out of the phrases *full hearing* or *due process of law.* These two opinions call for a set of procedures—confrontation, cross-examination, and so forth—designed to minimize the likelihood that a secretary of agriculture or a welfare supervisor will make the wrong decision in a case. They hope to offset the chances that laziness, the desire to preserve pride, loyalty to one party, biased views toward the facts or the parties, or any other common human failing will produce an irrational decision, that is, a decision not justified by the facts and the law. Legal disputes may be framed in certain ways so as to call for different judicial solutions. In *Mathews*, for example, the Court was concerned with balancing costs and benefits, which is very different from its approach in *Goldberg*. This perspective on the rule of law provides students of American politics and public administration with a guide for interpreting and evaluating the role of judges in administrative law. You will need to study several cases in the following chapters before you begin to feel comfortable with this approach.

This sixth ethical model for administrative law holds that governmental decisions must take place through an open and public process—open at least to the participation of those immediately affected, open at most to observation by the whole community. *Open* and *public* are not

mere ideals. They rest on the demonstrated fact that when decision makers must decide and/or defend their decision in front of potential critics, they are less likely to commit the kind of errors that result from laziness, bias, and other sources of arbitrariness. Appellate courts attempt to meet this test by writing opinions that justify their rulings, exposing their reasoning to professional criticism. Public elections seek to push the legislative process toward openness. Two of the three cases above promoted openness in government. When the Court forbade the Secretary of Agriculture from meeting in private with the Bureau of Animal Industry, or when the Court told a welfare office not to deny a recipient access to his or her only funds with which to finance a protest, the Court pushed the administrative decisionmaking process toward publicness.

Note here one critically important aspect of this definition of the rule of law. It does *not* ask the courts themselves to inquire so deeply into decision making as to *guarantee* that the administrator reached a correct decision on the facts. The courts are usually in a poorer position than the parties to judge what is substantively best. The courts' role is instead predominantly procedural. From this perspective, administrative law assumes that open participation will minimize arbitrariness in administrative decisionmaking.

7. *The rule of law checks and shapes the power of government by seeking the maximum feasible reduction of arbitrariness.* Our sixth ethical model for administrative law certainly appeals to our democratic political values. What could be more right and fair than insisting on full and open participation? Did we not see in chapter 1 that such openness might have prevented the evils perpetrated by the Mississippi State Sovereignty Commission? How could we reject this democratic model?

We don't actually reject it, but the participation model is not by itself a solution. To achieve full participation in every case costs too much time and money. Worse, practical experience with administrative politics teaches that those who resist new regulatory programs will convert their opportunity to participate into delaying tactics, dragging out the processes and preventing, sometimes for many years, the implementation of new rules. We thus believe that the ethical demand that administrative law must meet is to articulate for different situations different mixes of participation, on one hand, and rapid policy response (for example, to the unique problems faced by residents of New Orleans after Hurricane Katrina) on the other. The overall goal is not participation per se, but something more like "common sense in the circumstances."[15]

To refine the concept, consider the definition of the "ideal of legality" offered by Philippe Nonet and Philip Selznick:

But the ideal of legality should not be confused with the paraphernalia of legalization—the proliferation of rules and procedural formalities. The bureaucratic patterns that pass for due process (understood as an "obstacle course") or for accountability (understood as compliance with official rules) are alien to responsive law. The ideal of legality needs to be conceived more generally and to be cured of formalism. In a purposive system

legality is the progressive reduction of arbitrariness in positive law and its administration. To press for a maximum feasible reduction of arbitrariness is to demand a system of law that is capable of reaching beyond formal regularity and procedural fairness to substantive justice. That achievement, in turn, requires institutions that are competent as well as legitimate.[16]

The precise nature of legal rationality in administrative law will emerge through the pages of this book. While readers may disagree with each other and with us about the components of rationality, administrative law boils down to a dialogue or political debate about just what is procedurally fair in modern politics and government. Debates have more than one side, however. This book takes a position in the debate, but in the end you must develop the analytical skills to make reasoned judgments for yourself. Every case you read in this book is, either implicitly or explicitly, a comment upon the nature of legal rationality and arbitrariness in government.

15. See Phillip K. Howard, *The Death of Common Sense* (New York: Random House, 1994).

16. *Law and Society in Transition: Toward Responsive Law* (New York: Harper Colophon, 1978), 107–108.

EXERCISES AND QUESTIONS FOR FURTHER THOUGHT

1. The space limits of this book prevent it from covering all aspects of the administrative process itself. There are, however, some general categories of administrative agencies and classifications of their tasks that may help you decipher the facts and issues in cases to follow. It is useful to differentiate the major *values* that drive administrative policies. These include (a) promoting personal safety, (b) assuring social and economic justice, and (c) reallocating wealth. Think of an agency or program in government that illustrates each of these values. Where, for example, does OSHA's regulation of toxic substances in the workplace fit in this scheme? Which of these values figure in the government programs in the three cases in this chapter?

Next, consider the *tools* of administration. The main administrative task is to shape events and influence behavior. In this regard, the bureaucrat and the busi-

nessperson, the parent and the football coach, share the same task. How do any of us influence events and behavior? The most common way to control something is to claim ownership. Feudalism was a system of government built upon this idea. Kings claimed they and those beneath them literally possessed their kingdoms just as we possess automobiles and homes, at least once we pay off the loan. Today public or governmental ownership plays a less significant role than it once did, at least in Western civilization. But public ownership and management nevertheless remain important governmental tools. Governments build and manage many things. The Tennessee Valley Authority, for example, controls flooding and produces energy by owning and managing resources.

The second main tool of government is regulation. Parents do not own their children, but they do regulate their behavior. The administrator may work with a more complex set of problems than the parent, but when they regulate, both will resort to one or a combination of these factors they hope will influence behavior: *prescription, promotion, permission*, and *prohibition*. The Federal Communications Commission *prescribes* that station operators must provide the FCC routinely with logs and other information about their daily programming. The National Science Foundation *promotes* scholarly research by giving money to the best research proposals. The Nuclear Regulatory Commission *permits* a nuclear power plant to begin operation if it has passed its safety tests. The FCC *prohibits* any company from owning more than the maximum number of station outlets promulgated in FCC rules. Think of others.

Is it not true that each public agency is a mix of values and tools but that the mix varies from agency to agency? What, for example, is the mix of values and tools in Amtrak? The Environmental Protection Agency? The Food Stamp program? Can you think of other mixes of values and tools in "real world" administrative agencies? Which mixes characterize the agencies in this chapter's three cases?

2. Scholars of regulation have argued for at least the last two decades that prohibitions and penalties, what are commonly known as "command and control" techniques, are poor tools of regulatory governance in many circumstances. They argue that an ongoing relationship between regulators and regulatees requires a more flexible and sometimes informal set of tools. Do you agree? How would you define "better outcomes"? For example, think about what type of regulatory tool would more likely reduce carbon emissions from automobiles, trucks, etc. If the EPA decides to regulate such emissions, what outcomes should be considered? Air quality? Global warming? Profit margins of the automobile companies?

3. Suppose an elected county "commission" creates and funds a "County Health Department." The commissioners appoint a department head who in turn employs various subordinates, each with responsibility for a different kind of health problem. One such division is called the "Division of Animal and Livestock Diseases." The head of this division decides to issue the following rule, which the division head has published in the legal notice section of the local paper: "The maintaining of any pen or lot for the keeping of swine within 200 feet of any dwelling or potable water supply shall not be permitted."

A parent living in that town gives his son a pet piglet for Christmas. When the pig gets too smelly and unmanageable to live in its cardboard box in the house—that is, about December 26—the boy moves the pig under the house, where it lives in the crawlspace running the entire length of the house. Assume the family lets the pig out to play from time to time, and a cranky neighbor becomes offended by the sight. Assume also the pig badly startles more than one jogger trotting down the street late on winter afternoons.

Pigs are one of nature's most efficient converters of grain into meat, and this pig soon becomes equal in size, footspeed and friendliness to a St. Bernard dog. The neighbor complains to the Health Department and, one March afternoon, a Ms. South, of the Animal and Livestock Disease Division, appears at the door. She informs the family that the pig must go because, she says, "You can't keep pigs in the county. It's against the law."

When the parent reads the rule in question she immediately sees she can make at least three arguments that the rule does not apply to her son's pig:

(i) The crawlspace under the house is not a pen or lot for the keeping of swine.

(ii) "Swine" is a plural word and does not cover keeping one pet pig.

(iii) The purpose of the rule is clearly to prevent noise and nose pollution, water pollution, and so on, and one pet pig simply cannot do the harm the act seeks to prevent. Therefore the rule does not apply.

List separately all the questions of (a) regulatory law and (b) administrative law this story might raise. Invent further facts if they will help.

4. After you have mastered the Court's handling of the legal questions in this chapter's three cases, try to identify how each majority opinion defines the problem of arbitrariness in public administration. Is there a difference in emphasis, particularly between *Mathews*, on one hand, and its two predecessors, on the other? Is it fair to say that *Mathews* is more concerned about the trade-off between fairness to the individual and cost to society? Is it not true that courts must consider this trade-off to avoid arbitrariness—that we cannot afford complete and total fairness to individuals at all times regardless of cost?

5. The three cases in this chapter all involve decisions about an individual's or a business enterprise's specific claims, rights, and interests. Where administrators decide the fortunes of an individual on the unique facts of his, her, or its case, they resemble judges. As you may have guessed by now, the degree to which these administrators must operate like actual judges in the legal system is one of the most common problems in the field. Think of other instances in which public officials act like judges. Does a teacher who assigns a grade in a class do so? Does a police officer who issues a speeding ticket do so? How far would such decisions about the individuals be formalized? Also, you should anticipate that agencies often act like legislatures, that is, they may promulgate rules covering entire industries. Start thinking about the legal limits, if any, that the ideal of legality which Nonet and Selznick discuss should call for in administrative rulemaking.

CHAPTER 3
THE CONSTITUTIONAL
AUTHORITY OF AGENCIES

The sequence of the next seven chapters roughly follows the sequence of steps that end in a final agency decision. Beginning students have no reason to know this pattern beforehand, so let us explain it here. Any agency action begins with a constitutionally valid authorizing rule from an elected body. Usually this is a congressional statute, occasionally an executive order. Agencies have no constitutional status unless and until this statutory language creates them. This chapter explores the significance of constitutional law for agency authority. The next chapter then turns to the statutory language and authority for agency decision making. Chapter 5 addresses the next step—the gathering of information about problems needing administrative attention. Once an agency recognizes that a problem exists, it may resolve it by informal means. Chapter 6 describes these informal procedures and in doing so introduces by comparison formal adjudication (chapter 7) and formal rulemaking (chapter 8). The next step, enforcement (chapter 9), prepares the way for judicial intervention, judicial review of administrative actions (chapter 10). Not all cases actually follow this sequence because courts review only a tiny fraction of administrative decisions, and sometimes the courts review early in the process. But it is a rough approximation.

THE CONSTITUTIONAL FRAMEWORK FOR ADMINISTRATIVE GOVERNMENT

Constitutions state the law that governs the government. We often say that we have a government of "limit-ed powers." Limits that constitutions place on governmental power and the willingness of courts to enforce them make limited government a reality. Indeed, liberty and limited government are two sides of the same coin. Thus the same restrictions that limit the power of the police to torture someone on the often misguided belief that torture will extract information limit public administrators from doing so, and when such limits do not apply, abuses like those at Abu Ghraib prison in Iraq will happen. The Bill of Rights expresses our basic liberties, which include freedom of religion, speech, press, and assembly (First Amendment), freedom from unreasonable searches and seizures (Fourth Amendment), freedom against self-incrimination (Fifth Amendment), freedom against having our property taken for public use without just compensation (Fifth Amendment), right to the assistance of counsel (Sixth Amendment), and so on. The famous "due process clause" of the Fourteenth Amendment applies virtually all of the important limitations on the power of government expressed in the original Bill of Rights as limitations on the powers of state and local governments as well. This means that federal cases imposing constitutional limits on a U.S. agency presumably impose the same restriction on state and local administrative bodies. Close analysis of these substantive limitations on government power belongs in courses on constitutional law, but students of administration must know these limitations exist. We will illustrate some examples applying these limitations.

• In the early 1990s, an artist named Michael Lebron, was hired by the National Railroad Passenger Corporation (Amtrak) to create a billboard about public issues in New York City's Pennsylvania Station. The area for display was 103 feet wide by 10 feet high, and was known as "The Spectacular." But when Lebron's design showed a Coors Light beer container blazing out of the sky and threatening to destroy some innocent peasant villagers, Amtrak refused to allow the artwork because is was too explicitly political. Lebron sued. Congress had declared in the statute creating Amtrak that Amtrak would "not be an agency or establishment of the United States Government." However, the Supreme Court (8-1) pointed out that Amtrak is controlled by the government, and held that Amtrak was therefore bound by the First Amendment's protections for free speech.[1] In 1998, however, the Court upheld the statutory power of the National Endowment for the Arts (NEA) to deny funding to art projects found to be "indecent." The lower court had found this term unconstitutionally vague, and Justice David Souter's lone dissent pointed out that "indecency" of expression does not generally allow the government to censor or punish expression under the First Amendment. But the majority held that, since the NEA gave only a limited number of awards on a competitive basis, contemporary standards of decency were a permissible measure of a project's worthiness. Justice Antonin Scalia, concurring with the majority opinion, noted that artists were still free to pursue funding from other sources, so there was no constitutional "abridgment" of artists' rights.[2]

• During George W. Bush's presidency, between 2000 and 2008, the Federal Communications Commission (FCC), increased its efforts to regulate what it deemed to be "vulgarities" on broadcast TV stations. It all began with the FCC's indecency finding against NBC for vulgar utterances by the singer Bono. In what were called "indecency rulings" the FCC tried to penalize NBC, Fox, CBS or any station using public airwaves for the use of a "fleeting expletive" by celebrities such as Paris Hilton, Cher, or Nicole Richie. Reed Hundt, a former chairman of the FCC (1993–1997) argued that "the Federal Communication Commission's recent crackdown on television indecency poses a significant threat to First Amendment protections by (1) limiting television viewers' freedom of choice and (2) implying the possibility of punishment for failure to cooperate with the political objectives of the governing party."[3] In 2007, the United States Court of Appeals for the Second Circuit decided in *Fox v. FCC* (06-1760) that the FCC acted in an arbitrary and capricious manner in penalizing Fox and others for the use of fleeting expletives by celebrities. The Court reasoned that: "As NBC illustrates in its brief, in recent times even the top leaders of our government have used variants of these expletives in a manner that no reasonable person would believe referenced sexual or excretory organs or activities." (See Br. of Intervenor NBC at 31-32 & n.3, citing President Bush's remark to British Prime Minister Tony Blair that the United Nations needed to "get Syria to get Hezbollah to stop doing this shit," and Vice President Cheney's widely-reported "fuck yourself" comment to Senator Patrick Leahy on the floor of the U.S. Senate.) The Court added, however, that even if the FCC could come up with a reasoned, non-arbitrary, rationale for the fines, it is still doubtful whether such a rationale could survive First Amendment analysis.

• In addition to guaranteeing liberties, the Constitution, through the "equal protection clause" of the Fourteenth Amendment, protects against discrimination on the basis of race. In the 1990s, affirmative action policies came under increasing attack as unconstitutional acts of "reverse discrimination." The affirmative action debate—which often gets heated—revolves around the meaning of the Supreme Court's "strict scrutiny test" for determining permissible discrimination according to race. In a nutshell,

1. *Lebron v. National Railroad Passenger Corp.*, 513 U.S. 374 (1995). The Supreme Court reversed and remanded the case to the U.S. Court of Appeals for the Second Circuit, where a divided three-judge panel ruled in favor of Amtrak based on the First Amendment, finding that Amtrak had followed a generic policy against explicitly political statements on "The Spectacular," and had not singled out and rejected Mr. Lebron's artwork because of its message. See 69 F.3d 650 (1995). Like the lone dissenting judge on the Second Circuit, we question the majority's reasoning.
2. See *National Endowment for the Arts v. Finley*, 524 U.S. 569 (1998). Respondent Karen Finley did continue to perform her one-woman feminist review, "The Chocolate Smeared Woman," and "Return of the Chocolate Smeared Woman." For a description of respondent's show, see "There's Still No Vanilla in a Finley Encounter," *New York Times*, June 24, 1998.

3. Reed Hundt, "Regulating Indecency: The Federal Communication Commission's Threat to the First Amendment," *Duke Law and Technology Review* 13 (2005).

this test permits discrimination by racial categories only when such discrimination is essential to achieving some very important public goal. In 1998, a three-judge panel of the United States Court of Appeals for the District of Columbia used the test to strike down a decades-long policy of the FCC. The FCC had for many years required that broadcasters, as a condition of keeping their broadcasting licenses, prove by documentary evidence that they had tried to hire numbers of women and minorities that were in rough proportion to the population as a whole. Perhaps as a result, the percentage of minorities permanently employed in broadcasting had risen from 9.1% to virtually 20% between 1971 and 1997. The FCC imposed a $25,000 fine on a radio broadcast operation of the Lutheran Church–Missouri Synod (which featured religious and classical music programming) after concluding that the station had not made a genuine attempt to recruit minorities. The Church sued the FCC and the National Association for the Advancement of Colored People (NAACP), which had separately sued the FCC seeking to have the FCC revoke the Church's broadcast license, and won. The judges unanimously held that the FCC had failed to show that racial balance on the radio station's staff was essential (or even related at all) to the quality of programming policies of the station.[4]

From a normative standpoint, if we are to preserve liberties and limited government, it is obviously essential that courts apply civil liberties protections in administrative and regulatory contexts. That said, however, no provisions in the U.S. Constitution have had more of a historical impact on administrative power than the clauses protecting property. These are: (1) the due process clause's stipulation that the government may not deprive a person of property without due process of law; and (2) the "takings" clause of the Fifth Amendment, which says "nor shall private property be taken for public use, without just compensation." These limitations apply to state and local governments through the Fourteenth Amendment.

For over half a century, from the 1870s to the 1930s, in a wave of enthusiasm for unfettered (read "monopoly") capitalism and the ruthless theory of "social Darwinism," the U.S. Supreme Court waged war against the very regulations of wealth and property that chapters 1 and 2 have described as integral to effective government. In 1893, Justice David Brewer, in a speech to the New York Bar Association, stated:

. . . the permanence of government of and by the people rests upon the independence and vigor of the judiciary, to restrain the greedy hand of the many from filching from the few that which they have honestly acquired.[5]

History records that the presidency of Franklin Roosevelt ultimately engineered the defeat of fundamentalist defenders of property like Justice Brewer. However, this historical political battle is a key to understanding not only that period in our history but also the nature of cultural resistance to government power today. We therefore reproduce at some length the contending arguments in one of the great constitutional debates over the protection of property.

Note, however, that the case below and other contemporary cases, had not solely been decided on property interests. In fact, as Howard Gillman, a political scientist, argues, the police power jurisprudence of the Supreme Court in the second half of the 19th century played a significant role in shaping the outcome of the following case and the like cases. According to Gillman:

Police powers jurisprudence during the *Lochner* era had its origins in the founders' desire to delegitimize "factional politics," attempts by competing classes to use public power to gain unfair or unnatural advantages over their market adversaries. The object of this agenda was not to promote the value of market liberty per se, nor to reduce government intervention in the market to a bare minimum; rather, the goal was to prohibit the government from passing laws designed merely to promote the interests of certain classes at the expense of their competitors, to impose special burdens and benefits on particular groups without linking these burdens and benefits to the welfare of the community as a whole.[6]

---

4. *Lutheran Church–Missouri Synod v. FCC,* 141 F.3d 344 (1998). The opinion cited the important 1995 Supreme Court case constricting the scope of permissible affirmative action policies, *Adarand Constructors v. Peña,* 515 U.S. 200. It also cited the *Federal Power Commission* case presented in chapter 4.

5. *Proceedings of the New York State Bar Association* (1893), 37.
6. See Howard Gillman, *The Constitution Beseiged: The Rise and Demise of* Lochner *Era Police Power Jurisprudence* (Durham and London: Duke University Press, 1993), 61.

Certainly, such jurisprudence and the society it envisioned had a particular view of property ownership. As Gillman states:

The legitimacy of this vision rested on the assumption that market relations in the new American Republic (with its vast frontier) are essentially liberty loving and harmonious and did not pose a threat to any citizen's republican independence—the condition whereby one did not depend on another for his well-being.[7]

In other words, the ideal of a factionless society could be realized if every (white) man was to own sufficient property—in this case land—which would ensure that he was independent from others. Economic independence, in turn, was considered to be a prerequisite of civic and political virtue. This vision was considered possible, for the white man of course, in the early days of the republic, most notably because of the possibility of westward expansion. As the limits of territorial expansion were reached at the end of the 19th century and a new economy arose based on large-scale industrialization, such a vision began to lose its relevance, and reality.

The next two cases you are going to read are decided against such a historical background and they roughly follow the historical change. As you read these cases, notice the evolution of the argument in the dissenting opinion in *Munn v. Illinois* (1877) into the argument of the majority opinion in *Lochner v. New York* (1905), something we will elaborate on in the following pages.

Munn v. Illinois

94 U.S. 113 (1876) 7-2
+ *Waite, Clifford, Swayne, Miller, Davis, Bradley, Hunt*
– *Field, Strong*

[Article XIII of the Illinois Constitution, adopted in 1870, declared grain elevators[8] to be "public warehouses" and gave the general assembly the power to pass legislation relating to the storage of grain. In 1871, the

assembly passed an act creating a state commission for the purposes of establishing rates which warehouse owners could charge, requiring licenses to operate a warehouse, and other regulations governing the conduct of warehouse owners and operators. Munn and Scott, managers and proprietors of a grain warehouse in Chicago, were convicted and fined $100 for operating a warehouse without a license and for charging farmers, whose grain they stored, prices higher than those specified by the commission. They sought review in the U.S. Supreme Court on a writ of error after failing to reverse this conviction in the Illinois Supreme Court.]

Chief Justice Waite delivered the opinion of the Court

The question to be determined in this case is whether the general assembly of Illinois can, under the limitations upon the legislative power of the States imposed by the Constitution of the United States, fix by law the maximum of charges for the storage of grain in warehouses at Chicago and other places in the State having not less than one hundred thousand inhabitants, "in which grain is stored in bulk, and in which the grain of different owners is mixed together, or in which grain is stored in such a manner that the identity of different lots or parcels cannot be accurately preserved."

It is claimed that such a law is repugnant—

1. To that part of sect. 8, art. 1, of the Constitution of the United States which confers upon Congress the power "to regulate commerce with foreign nations and among the several States;"

2. To that part of sect. 9 of the same article which provides that "no preference shall be given by any regulation of commerce or revenue to the ports of one State over those of another;" and

3. To that part of amendment 14 which ordains that no State shall "deprive any person of life, liberty, or property, without due process of law, nor deny to any person within its jurisdiction the equal protection of the laws."

We will consider the last of these objections first. . . .

The Constitution contains no definition of the word "deprive," as used in the Fourteenth Amendment. To determine its signification, therefore, it is necessary to ascertain the effect which usage has given it, when employed in the same or a like connection.

---

7. Ibid., 62.

8. The grain elevator, which was invented in 1842 by Joseph Dart, mechanized the process of handling grain. A steam-powered mechanism "elevated" the grain and transfered it to tall bins for storage until it was shipped out.

While this provision of the amendment is new in the Constitution of the United States, as a limitation upon the powers of the States, it is old as a principle of civilized government. It is found in Magna Charta, and, in substance if not in form, in nearly or quite all the constitutions that have been from time to time adopted by the several States of the Union. By the Fifth Amendment, it was introduced into the Constitution of the United States as a limitation upon the powers of the national government, and by the Fourteenth, as a guaranty against any encroachment upon an acknowledged right of citizenship by the legislatures of the States. . . .

When one becomes a member of society, he necessarily parts with some rights or privileges which, as an individual not affected by his relations to others, he might retain. "A body politic," as aptly defined in the preamble of the Constitution of Massachusetts, "is a social compact by which the whole people covenants with each citizen, and each citizen with the whole people, that all shall be governed by certain laws for the common good." This does not confer power upon the whole people to control rights which are purely and exclusively private, . . . but it does authorize the establishment of laws requiring each citizen to so conduct himself, and so use his own property, as not unnecessarily to injure another. This is the very essence of government, and has found expression in the maxim *sic utere tuo ut alienum non laedas* (so use your own as not to injure others). From this source come the police powers, which, as was said by Mr. Chief Justice Taney in the *License Cases,* . . . "are nothing more or less than powers of government inherent in every sovereignty, . . . that is to say, . . . the power to govern men and things." Under these powers the government regulates the conduct of its citizens one towards another, and the manner in which each shall use his own property, when such regulation becomes necessary for the public good. In their exercise it has been customary in England from time immemorial, and in this country from its first colonization to regulate ferries, common carriers, hackmen, bakers, millers, wharfingers, innkeepers, &c., and in so doing to fix a maximum of charge to be made for services rendered, accommodations furnished, and articles sold. To this day, statutes are to be found in many of the States upon some or all these subjects; and we think it has never yet been successfully contended that such legislation came within any of the constitutional prohibitions against interference with private property. With the Fifth Amendment in force, Congress, in 1820, conferred power upon the city of Washington "to regulate . . . the rates of wharfage at private wharves, . . . the sweeping of chimneys, and to fix the rates of fees therefore, . . . and the weight and quality of bread," . . . and, in 1848, "to make all necessary regulations respecting hackney carriages and the rates of fare of the same, and the rates of hauling by cartmen, wagoners, carmen, and draymen, and the rates of commission of auctioneers." . . .

From this it is apparent that, down to the time of the adoption of the Fourteenth Amendment, it was not supposed that statutes regulating the use, or even the price of the use, of private property necessarily deprived an owner of his property without due process of law. Under some circumstances they may, but not under all. The amendment does not change the law in this particular: it simply prevents the States from doing that which will operate as such a deprivation.

This brings us to inquire as to the principles upon which this power of regulation rests, in order that we may determine what is within and what without its operative effect. Looking, then, to the common law, from whence came the right which the Constitution protects, we find that when private property is "affected with a public interest, it ceases to be *juris privati* only." This was said by Lord Chief Justice Hale more than two hundred years ago, in his treatise *De Portibus Maris,* . . . and has been accepted without objection as an essential element in the law of property ever since. Property does become clothed with a public interest when used in a manner to make it of public consequence, and affect the community at large. When, therefore, one devotes his property to a use in which the public has an interest, he, in effect, grants to the public an interest in that use, and must submit to be controlled by the public for the common good, to the extent of the interest he has thus created. He may withdraw his grant by discontinuing the use; but, so long as he maintains the use, he must submit to the control. . . .

We . . . quote . . . the words of . . . eminent expounders of the common law, because, as we think, we find in them the principle which supports the legislation we are now examining. Of Lord Hale it was once said by a learned American judge,—

"In England, even on rights of prerogative, they scan his words with as much care as if they had been found in Magna Charta; and the meaning once ascertained, they do not trouble themselves to search any further." . . .

In later times, the same principle came under consideration in the Supreme Court of Alabama. That court was called upon in 1841, to decide whether the power granted to the city of Mobile to regulate the weight and price of bread was unconstitutional, and it was contended that "it would interfere with the right of the citizen to pursue his lawful trade or calling in the mode his judgment might dictate;" but the court said, "there is no motive . . . for this interference on the part of the legislature with the lawful actions of individuals, or the mode in which private property shall be enjoyed, unless such calling affects the public interest, or private property is employed in a manner which directly affects the body of the people. Upon this principle, in this State, tavernkeepers are licensed; . . . and the County Court is required, at least once a year, to settle the rates of innkeepers. Upon the same principle is founded the control which the legislature has always exercised in the establishment and regulation of mills, ferries, bridges, turnpike roads, and other kindred subjects." *Mobile v. Yuille*, 3 Ala. N. S. 140.

From the same source comes the power to regulate the charges of common carriers, . . . [who] exercise a sort of public office, and have duties to perform in which the public is interested. . . . Their business is, therefore, "affected with a public interest," within the meaning of the doctrine which Lord Hale has so forcibly stated.

. . . Enough has already been said to show that, when private property is devoted to a public use, it is subject to public regulation. It remains only to ascertain whether the warehouses of these plaintiffs in error, and the business which is carried on there, come within the operation of this principle.

For this purpose we accept as true the statements of fact contained in the elaborate brief of one of the counsel of the plaintiffs in error. From these it appears that

"the great producing region of the West and North-west sends its grain by water and rail to Chicago, where the greater part of it is shipped by vessel for transportation to the seaboard by the Great Lakes, and some of it is forwarded by railway to the Eastern ports. . . . Vessels, to some extent, are loaded in the Chicago harbor, and sailed through the St. Lawrence, directly to Europe. . . . The quantity [of grain] received in Chicago has made it the greatest grain market in the world. This business has created a demand for means by which the immense quantity of grain can be handled or stored, and these have been found in grain warehouses, which are commonly called elevators, because the grain is elevated from the boat or car, by machinery operated by steam, into the bins prepared for its reception, and elevated from the bins, by a like process, into the vessel or car which is to carry it on. . . . In this way the largest traffic between the citizens of the country north and west of Chicago and the citizens of the country lying on the Atlantic coast north of Washington is in grain which passes through the elevators of Chicago. In this way the trade in grain is carried on by the inhabitants of seven or eight of the great States of the West with four or five of the States lying on the sea-shore, and forms the largest part of interstate commerce in these States. The grain warehouses or elevators in Chicago are immense structures, holding from 300,000 to 1,000,000 bushels at one time, according to size. They are divided into bins of large capacity and great strength. . . . They are located with the river harbor on one side and the railway tracks on the other; and the grain is run through them from car to vessel, or boat to car, as may be demanded in the course of business. It has been found impossible to preserve each owner's grain separate, and this has given rise to a system of inspection and grading, by which the grain of different owners is mixed, and receipts issued for the number of bushels which are negotiable, and redeemable in like kind, upon demand. This mode of conducting the business was inaugurated more than twenty years ago, and has grown to immense proportions. The railways have found it impracticable to own such elevators, and public policy forbids the transaction of such business by the carrier, the ownership has, therefore, been by private individuals, who have embarked their capital and devoted their industry to such business as a private pursuit."

In this connection it must also be borne in mind that, although in 1874 there were in Chicago fourteen warehouses adapted to this particular business, and owned by about thirty persons, nine business firms controlled them, and that the prices charged and received for storage were such "as have been from year to year agreed upon and established by the different elevators or warehouses in the city of Chicago, and which rates have been annually published in one or more newspapers printed in said city, in the month of January in each year, as the established rates for the year then next ensuing such publication." Thus it is apparent that all the elevating facilities through which these vast productions "of seven or eight great States of the West" must pass on the way "to four or five of the States on the seashore" may be a "virtual" monopoly.

Under such circumstances it is difficult to see why, if the common carrier, or the miller, or the ferryman, or the innkeeper, or the wharfinger, or the baker, or the cartman, or the hackney-coachman, pursues a public employment and exercise "a sort of public office," these plaintiffs in error do not. They stand, to use again the language of their counsel, in the very "gateway of commerce," and take toll from all who pass. Their business most certainly "tends to a common charge, and is become a thing of public interest and use." Every bushel of grain for its passage "pays a toll, which is a common charge," and, therefore, according to Lord Hale, every such warehouseman "ought to be under public regulation, viz., that he . . . take but reasonable toll." Certainly, if any business can be clothed "with a public interest, and cease to be *juris privati* only," this has been. It may not be made so by the operation of the Constitution of Illinois or this statute, but it is by the facts.

We also are not permitted to overlook the fact that, for some reason, the people of Illinois, when they revised their Constitution in 1870, saw fit to make it the duty of the general assembly to pass laws "for the protection of producers, shippers, and receivers of grain and produce." . . . This indicates very clearly that during the twenty years in which this peculiar business had been assuming its present "immense proportions," something had occurred which led the whole body of the people to suppose that remedies such as are usually employed to prevent abuses by virtual monopolies might not be inappropriate here. For our purposes we must assume that, if a state of facts could exist that would justify such legislation, it actually did exist when the statute now under consideration was passed, for us the question is one of power, not of expediency. If no state of circumstances could exist to justify such a statute, then we may declare this one void, because in excess of the legislative power of the State. But if it could, we must presume it did. Of the propriety of legislative interference within the scope of legislative power, the legislature is the exclusive judge.

Neither is it a matter of any moment that no precedent can be found for a statute precisely like this. It is conceded that the business is one of recent origin, that its growth has been rapid, and that it is already of great importance. And it must also be conceded that it is a business in which the whole public has a direct and positive interest. It presents, therefore, a case for the application of a long-known and well-established principle in social science, and this statute simply extends the law so as to meet this new development of commercial progress. There is no attempt to compel

these owners to grant the public an interest in their property, but to declare their obligations, if they use it in this particular manner. . . .

It is insisted, however, that the owner of property is entitled to a reasonable compensation for its use, even though it be clothed with a public interest, and that what is reasonable is a judicial and not a legislative question.

As has already been shown, the practice has been otherwise. In countries where the common law prevails, it has been customary from time immemorial for the legislature to declare what shall be a reasonable compensation under such circumstances, or, perhaps more properly speaking, to fix a maximum beyond which any charge made would be unreasonable. Undoubtedly, in mere private contracts, relating to matters in which the public has no interest, what is reasonable must be ascertained judicially. But this is because the legislature has no control over such a contract. So, too, in matters which do affect the public interest, and as to which legislative control may be exercised, if there are no statutory regulations upon the subject, the courts must determine what is reasonable. The controlling fact is the power to regulate at all. If that exists, the right to establish the maximum of charge, as one of the means of regulation, is implied. In fact, the common-law rule, which requires the charge to be reasonable, is itself a regulation as to price. Without it the owner could make his rates at will, and compel the public to yield to his terms, or forego the use.

But a mere common-law regulation of trade or business may be changed by statute. A person has no property, no vested interest, in any rule of the common law. That is only one of the forms of municipal law, and is no more sacred than any other. Rights of property which have been created by the common law cannot be taken away without due process; but the law itself, as a rule of conduct, may be changed at the will, or even at the whim, of the legislature, unless prevented by constitutional limitations. Indeed, the great office of statutes is to remedy defects in the common law as they are developed, and to adapt it to the changes of time and circumstances. To limit the rate of charge for services rendered in a public employment, or for the use of property in which the public has an interest, is only changing a regulation which existed before. It establishes no new principle in the law, but only gives a new effect to an old one.

We know that this is a power which may be abused but that is no argument against its existence. For protection against abuses by legislatures the people must resort to the polls, not to the courts. . . .

Judgment affirmed.

Justice Field and Justice Strong dissented

Justice Field . . . The principle upon which the opinion of the majority proceeds is, in my judgment, subversive of the rights of private property, heretofore believed to be protected by constitutional guaranties against legislative interference, and is in conflict with the authorities cited in its support. . . .

The declaration of the Constitution of 1870, that private buildings used for private purposes shall be deemed public institutions, does not make them so. The receipt and storage of grain in a building erected by private means for that purpose does not constitute the building a public warehouse. There is no magic in the language, though used by a constitutional convention, which can change a private business into a public one, or alter the character of the building in which the business is transacted. A tailor's or a shoemaker's shop would still retain its private character, even though the assembled wisdom of the State should declare, by organic act or legislative ordinance, that such a place was a public workshop, and that the workmen were public tailors or public shoemakers. One might as well attempt to change the nature of colors, by giving them a new designation. The defendants were no more public warehousemen, as justly observed by counsel, than the merchant who sells his merchandise to the public is a public merchant, or the blacksmith who shoes horses for the public is a public blacksmith; and it was a strange notion that by calling them so they would be brought under legislative control. . . .

The doctrine declared is that property "becomes clothed with a public interest when used in a manner to make it of public consequence, and affect the community at large;" and from such clothing the right of the legislature is deduced to control the use of the property, and to determine the compensation which the owner may receive for it. When Sir Matthew Hale, and the sages of the law in his day, spoke of property as affected by a public interest, and ceasing from that cause to be *juris privati* solely, that is, ceasing

to be held merely in private right, they referred to property dedicated by the owner to public uses, or to property the use of which was granted by the government, or in connection with which special privileges were conferred. Unless the property was thus dedicated, or some right bestowed by the government was held with the property, either by specific grant or by prescription of so long a time as to imply a grant originally, the property was not accepted by any public interest so as to be taken out of the category of property held in private right But it is not in any such sense that the terms "clothing property with a public interest" are used in this case. From the nature of the business under consideration—the storage of grain—which, in any sense in which the words can be used, is a private business, in which the public are interested only as they are interested in the storage of other products of the soil, or in articles of manufacture, it is clear that the court intended to declare that, whenever one devotes his property to a business which is useful to the public—"affects the community at large,"—the legislature can regulate the compensation which the owner may receive for its use, and for his own services in connection with it. . . .

The public has no greater interest in the use of buildings for the storage of grain than it has in the use of buildings for the residences of families, nor, indeed, any thing like so great an interest; and, according to the doctrine announced, the legislature may fix the rent of all tenements used for residences, without reference to the cost of their erection. If the owner does not like the rates prescribed, he may cease renting his houses. He has granted to the public, says the court, an interest in the use of the buildings, and "he may withdraw his grant by discontinuing the use; but, so long as he maintains the use, he must submit to the control." The public is interested in the manufacture of cotton, woollen, and silken fabrics, in the construction of machinery, in the printing and publication of books and periodicals, and in the making of utensils of every variety, useful and ornamental; indeed, there is hardly an enterprise or business engaging the attention and labor of any considerable portion of the community, in which the public has not an interest in the sense in which that term is used by the court in its opinion; and the doctrine which allows the legislature to interfere with and regulate the charges which the owners of property thus employed shall make for its use, that is, the rates at which all these different kinds of business shall be carried on, has never before been asserted, so far as I am aware, by any judicial tribunal in the United States. . . .

If the constitutional guaranty extends no further than to prevent a deprivation of title and possession, and allows a deprivation of use, and the fruits of that use, it does not merit the encomiums it has received. Unless I have misread the history of the provision now incorporated into all our State constitutions, and by the Fifth and Fourteenth Amendments into our Federal Constitution, and have misunderstood the interpretation it has received, it is not thus limited in its scope, and thus impotent for good. It has a much more extended operation than either court, State, or Federal has given to it. The provision, it is to be observed, places property under the same protection as life and liberty. Except by due process of law, no State can deprive any person of either. The provision has been supposed to secure to every individual the essential conditions for the pursuit of happiness; and for that reason has not been heretofore, and should never be, construed in any narrow or restricted sense.

No State "shall deprive any person of life, liberty, or property without due process of law," says the Fourteenth Amendment to the Constitution. . . .

By the term "liberty," as used in the provision, something more is meant than mere freedom from physical restraint or the bounds of a prison. It means freedom to go where one may choose, and to act in such manner, not inconsistent with the equal rights of others, as his judgment may dictate for the promotion of his happiness; that is, to pursue such callings and avocations as may be most suitable to develop his capacities, and give to them their highest enjoyment.

The same liberal construction which is required for the protection of life and liberty, in all particulars in which life and liberty are of any value, should be applied to the protection of private property. If the legislature of a State, under pretence of providing for the public good, or for any other reason, can determine, against the consent of the owner, the uses to which private property shall be devoted, or the prices which the owner shall receive for its uses, it can deprive him of the property as completely as by a special act for its confiscation or destruction. . . . The power of the State over the property of the citizen under the constitutional guaranty is well defined. The State may take his property for public uses, upon just compensation being made therefore. It may take a portion of his property by way of taxation for the support

of the government. It may control the use and possession of his property, so far as may be necessary for the protection of the rights of others, and to secure to them the equal use and enjoyment of their property. The doctrine that each one must so use his own as not to injure his neighbor—*sic utere tuo ut alienum non laedas*—is the rule by which every member of society must possess and enjoy his property, and all legislation essential to secure this common and equal enjoyment is a legitimate exercise of State authority. Except in cases where property may be destroyed to arrest a conflagration or the ravages of pestilence, or be taken under the pressure of an immediate and overwhelming necessity to prevent a public calamity, the power of the State over the property of the citizen does not extend beyond such limits. . . .

There is nothing in the character of the business of the defendants as warehousemen which called for the interference complained of in this case. Their buildings are not nuisances; their occupation of receiving and storing grain infringes upon no rights of others, disturbs no neighborhood, infects not the air, and in no respect prevents others from using and enjoying their property as to them may seem best. The legislation in question is nothing less than a bold assertion of absolute power by the State to control at its discretion the property and business of the citizen, and fix the compensation he shall receive. The will of the legislature is made the condition upon which the owner shall receive the fruits of his property and the just reward of his labor, industry, and enterprise. "That government," says Story, "can scarcely be deemed to be free where the rights of property are left solely dependent upon the will of a legislative body without any restraint. The fundamental maxims of a free government seem to require that the rights of personal liberty and private property should be held sacred." . . . The decision of the court in this case gives unrestrained license to legislative will. . . .

I am of opinion that the judgment of the Supreme Court of Illinois should be reversed.

Justice Strong concurred with Justice Field's dissent.

The political perspective advocated by Justice Field in his famous dissent in *Munn* had become the Supreme Court's majority view on regulation by the late nineteenth century. With the appointment of six new justices to the Court between 1880 and 1890, and an aggressive effort by lawyers who represented business interests before the Court, *laissez faire* dominated judicial ideology.[9] Justice Field's dissent in *Munn* states this ideology clearly: "If a monopoly results [from the absence of state regulation] it is an outgrowth of 'entrepreneurial talent,' and such 'talent' should be protected by the judiciary." The Court's shift away from the majority in *Munn* meant (and dealt) a serious blow to the view that government should protect the public from unfair business practices, such as monopolies which deprive consumers of market choices.

In *Chicago, Milwaukee and St. Paul R.R. Co. v. Minnesota* (1890),[10] several railroads challenged the constitutionality of an 1887 Minnesota statute regulating railroad rates. The Minnesota State Supreme Court upheld the statute based on the Court's reasoning in *Munn*. On appeal, the U.S. Supreme Court overturned the statute, arguing that it stripped the power of a court to "stay the hands of the commission, if it [the commission] chooses to establish rates that are unequal and unreasonable." The Court not only objected to the commission's power to establish fair rates for privately owned railroads, but the Court also emphatically established the judiciary's authority to decide what constitutes a fair market rate. Thus regulatory schemes were attacked by industrial capitalists and the federal judges during the period when *laissez faire* economics influenced the judiciary's legal and political views on regulation (1890–1930s).

Why is it important for students of administrative law to know the early twentieth-century story of the rise and fall of the due process clause as a tool used for the benefit of propertied interests? One simple answer is that this story is endlessly repeated in the political and legal debates on the character and scope of regulation. Additionally, in our constitutional democracy, wherein the protection of property rights and the general welfare are governmental responsibilities, political struggles to define both responsibilities take place in legal institutions, such as the United States Supreme Court. There,

justices develop and employ legal theories about individual rights (property and liberty for example) and interpret the meaning of constitutional authority to protect them, as well as the authority delegated to Congress to legislate in the interest of the general welfare.

As you read these early cases, it is important for you to identify the reasons the Court gives to strike down or uphold policy decisions made by democratically elected politicians. On what grounds do the Justices in the Court's majority and minority opinions base their opinions?

Lochner v. New York

198 U.S. 45 (1905) 5-4
+ *Peckham, Brown, White, Fuller, Brewer*
– *Harlan, Holmes, White, Day*

[In this case the Supreme Court reviewed the constitutionality of a New York state statute passed in 1897 that prohibited employment in a bakery for more than sixty hours a week or ten hours a day. Lochner, an employer, repeatedly violated this statute. He was convicted and the highest court in New York affirmed the conviction. He then appealed his conviction to the U.S. Supreme Court, arguing that the labor statute denied him "property" (i.e., profits made from the labor of workers he employed in his bakery) without due process of law. Further he maintained that state regulation of working hours interfered with his "freedom of contract," allegedly protected under the Constitution. A five-member majority of the Court agreed with Lochner and struck down the New York labor law.

Lochner is a classic example of the influence of laissez-faire economic thought on judicial philosophy. The Court treated workers and bosses as if they were both equally free to make choices regarding how long they wanted to work and under what conditions. In this sense the case is often cited as an example of "legal formalism"—the school of jurisprudence that ignores the impact of economic and social inequalities on the "freedom" of individuals or groups. The dissenting opinions in this case, however, sharply dispute the validity of *laissez-faire* assumptions and their social Darwinian implications for the role of government in protecting the public interest.]

9. See Benjamin Twiss, *Lawyers and the Constitution* (Princeton, N.J.: Princeton University Press, 1942).

10. 134 U.S. 418.

Justice Peckham delivered the opinion of the Court

[. . .]

The question whether this act is valid as a labor law, pure and simple, may be dismissed in a few words. There is no reasonable ground for interfering with the liberty of person or the right of free contract, by determining the hours of labor in the occupation of a baker. There is no contention that bakers as a class are not equal in intelligence and capacity to men in other trades or manual occupations, or that they are not able to assert their rights and care for themselves without the protecting arm of the State, interfering with their independence of judgment and of action. They are in no sense wards of the State. Viewed in the light of a purely labor law, with no reference whatever to the question of health, we think that a law like the one before us involves neither the safety, the morals nor the welfare of the public, and that the interest of the public is not in the slightest degree affected by such an act. The law must be upheld, if at all, as a law pertaining to the health of the individual engaged in the occupation of a baker. It does not affect any other portion of the public than those who are engaged in that occupation. Clean and wholesome bread does not depend upon whether the baker works but ten hours per day or only sixty hours a week. The limitation of the hours of labor does not come within the police power on that ground.

It is a question of which of two powers or rights shall prevail—the power of the State to legislate or the right of the individual to liberty of person and freedom of contract. The mere assertion that the subject relates though but in a remote degree to the public health does not necessarily render the enactment valid. The act must have a more direct relation, as a means to an end, and the end itself must be appropriate and legitimate, before an act can be held to be valid which interferes with the general right of an individual to be free in his person and in his power to contract in relation to his own labor. . . .

We think that there can be no fair doubt that the trade of a baker, in and of itself, is not an unhealthy one to that degree which would authorize the legislature to interfere with the right to labor, and with the right of free contract on the part of the individual, either as employer or employee. In looking through statistics regarding all trades and occupations, it may be true that the trade of a baker does not appear to be as healthy as some other trades, and is also vastly more healthy than still others. To the common understanding the trade of a baker has never been regarded as an unhealthy one. Very likely physicians would not recommend the exercise of that or of any other trade as a remedy for ill health. Some occupations are more healthy than others, but we think there are none which might not come under the power of the legislature to supervise and control the hours of working therein, if the mere fact that the occupation is not absolutely and perfectly healthy is to confer that right upon the legislative department of the Government. It might be safely affirmed that almost all occupations more or less affect the health. There must be more than the mere fact of the possible existence of some small amount of unhealthiness to warrant legislative interference with liberty. It is unfortunately true that labor, even in any department, may possibly carry with it the seeds of unhealthiness. But are we all, on that account, at the mercy of legislative majorities? A printer, a tinsmith, a locksmith, a carpenter, a cabinetmaker, a dry goods clerk, a bank's, a lawyer's or a physician's clerk, or a clerk in almost any kind of business, would all come under the power of the legislature, on this assumption. No trade, no occupation, no mode of earning one's living, could escape this all-pervading power, and the acts of the legislature in limiting the hours of labor in all employments would be valid, although such limitation might seriously cripple the ability of the laborer to support himself and his family. In our large cities there are many buildings into which the sun penetrates for but a short time in each day, and these buildings are occupied by people carrying on the business of bankers, brokers, lawyers, real estate, and many other kinds of business, aided by many clerks, messengers, and other employees. Upon the assumption of the validity of this act under review, it is not possible to say that an act, prohibiting lawyers' or bank clerks, or others, from contracting to labor for their employers more than eight hours a day, would be invalid. It might be said that it is unhealthy to work more than that number of hours in an apartment lighted by artificial light during the working hours of the day; that the occupation of the bank clerk, the lawyer's clerk, the real estate clerk, or the broker's clerk in such offices is therefore unhealthy, and the legislature in its paternal wisdom must, therefore, have the right to legislate on the subject of and to limit the hours for such labor, and if it exercises that power and its validity be questioned, it is sufficient to say, it has reference to the public health; it has reference to the health of the employees condemned to labor day after day in buildings where the sun never shines; it is a health law, and therefore it is valid, and cannot be questioned by the courts. . . .

The act is not, within any fair meaning of the term, a health law, but is an illegal interference with the rights of individuals, both employers and employees, to make contracts regarding labor upon such terms as they may think best, or which they may agree upon with other parties to such contracts. Statutes of the nature of that under review, limiting the hours in which grown and intelligent men may labor to earn their living, are mere meddlesome interferences with the rights of the individual, and they are not saved from condemnation by the claim that they are passed in the exercise of the police power and upon the subject of the health of the individual whose rights are interfered with, unless there be some fair ground, reasonable in and of itself, to say that there is material danger to the public health or to the health of the employees, if the hours of labor are not curtailed. . . .

This interference on the part of the legislatures of the several States with the ordinary trades and occupations of the people seems to be on the increase. . . .

It is impossible for us to shut our eyes to the fact that many of the laws of this chapter, while passed under what is claimed to be the police power for the purpose of protecting the public health or welfare, are, in reality, passed from other motives. We are justified in saying so when, from the character of the law and the subject upon which it legislates, it is apparent that the public health or welfare bears but the most remote relation to the law. The purpose of a statute must be determined from the natural and legal effect of the language employed; and whether it is or is not repugnant to the Constitution of the United States must be determined from the natural effect of such statutes when put into operation, and not from their proclaimed purpose. . . .

It seems to us that the real object and purpose were simply to regulate the hours of labor between the master and his employees (all being men, *sui juris*), in a private business, not dangerous in any degree to morals or in any real and substantial degree, to the health of the employees. Under such circumstances the freedom of master and employee to contract with each other in relation to their employment, and in defining the same, cannot be prohibited or interfered with, without violating the Federal Constitution.

The judgment of the Court of Appeals of New York as well as that of the Supreme Court and of the County Court of Oneida County must be reversed and the case remanded to the County Court for further proceedings not inconsistent with this opinion.
Reversed.

Justice Harlan, with whom Justice White and Justice Day concurred, dissenting

It is plain that this statute was enacted in order to protect the physical well-being of those who work in bakery and confectionery establishments. It may be that the statute had its origin, in part, in the belief that employers and employees in such establishments were not upon an equal footing, and that the necessities of the latter often compelled them to submit to such exactions as unduly taxed their strength. Be this as it may, the statute must be taken as expressing the belief of the people of New York that, as a general rule, and in the case of the average man, labor in excess of sixty hours during a week in such establishments may endanger the health of those who thus labor. Whether or not this be wise legislation it is not the province of the court to inquire. Under our systems of government the courts are not concerned with the wisdom or policy of legislation. So that in determining the question of power to interfere with liberty of contract, the court may inquire whether the means devised by the State are germane to an end which may be lawfully accomplished and have a real or substantial relation to the protection of health, as involved in the daily work of the persons, male and female, engaged in bakery and confectionery establishments. But when this inquiry is entered upon I find it impossible, in view of common experience, to say that there is here no real or substantial relation between the means employed by the State and the end sought to be accomplished by its legislation. . . . Nor can I say that the statute has no appropriate or direct connection with that protection to health which each State owes to her citizens. . . . or that it is not promotive of health of the employees in question, . . . or that the regulation prescribed by the State is utterly unreasonable and extravagant or wholly arbitrary. . . . Still less can I say that the statute is, beyond question, a plain, palpable invasion of rights secured by the fundamental law. . . . Therefore I submit that this court will transcend its functions if it assumes to annul the statute of New York. It must be remembered that this statute does not apply to all kinds of business. It applies only to work in bakery and confectionery establishments, in which, as all know, the air constantly breathed by workmen is not as pure and healthful as that to be found in some other establishments or out of doors.

Professor Hut in his treatise on the "Diseases of the Workers" has said: "The labor of the bakers is among the hardest and most laborious imaginable, because it has to be performed under conditions injurious to the health of those engaged in it. It is hard, very hard work, not only because it requires a great deal of physical exertion in an overheated workshop and during unreasonably long hours, but more so because of the erratic demands of the public, compelling the baker to perform the greater part of his work at night, thus depriving him of an opportunity to enjoy the necessary rest and sleep, a fact which is highly injurious to his health." Another writer says: "The constant inhaling of flour dust causes inflammation of the lungs and of the bronchial tubes. The eyes also suffer through this dust, which is responsible for the many cases of running eyes among the bakers. The long hours of toil to which all bakers are subjected produce rheumatism, cramps and swollen legs. The intense heat in the workshops induces the workers to resort to cooling drinks, which together with their habit of exposing the greater part of their bodies to the change in the atmosphere, is another source of a number of diseases of various organs. Nearly all bakers are pale-faced and of more delicate health than the workers of other crafts, which is chiefly due to their hard work and their irregular and unnatural mode of living, whereby the power of resistance against disease is greatly diminished. The average age of a baker is below that of other workmen; they seldom live over their fiftieth year, most of them dying between the ages of forty and fifty. During periods of epidemic diseases the bakers are generally the first to succumb to the disease, and the number swept away during such periods far exceeds the number of other crafts in comparison to the men employed in the respective industries. When, in 1720, the plague visited the city of Marseilles, France, every baker in the city succumbed to the epidemic, which caused considerable excite-

ment in the neighboring cities and resulted in measures for the sanitary protection of the bakers."

In the Eighteenth Annual Report by the New York Bureau of Statistics of Labor it is stated that among the occupations involving exposure to conditions that interfere with nutrition is that of a baker. . . . In that Report it is also stated that "from a social point of view, production will be increased by any change in industrial organization which diminishes the number of idlers, paupers and criminals. Shorter hours of work, by allowing higher standards of comfort and purer family life, promise to enhance the industrial efficiency of the wage-working class—improved health, longer life, more content and greater intelligence and inventiveness." . . .

Statistics show that the average daily working time among workingmen in different countries is, in Australia, 8 hours; in Great Britain, 9; in the United States, 9 3/4; in Denmark, 9 3/4; in Norway, 10; Sweden, France and Switzerland, 10 1/2; Germany, 10 1/4; Belgium, Italy and Austria, 11; and in Russia, 12 hours.

We judicially know that the question of the number of hours during which a workman should continuously labor has been, for a long period, and is yet, a subject of serious consideration among civilized peoples, and by those having special knowledge of the laws of health. Suppose the statute prohibited labor in bakery and confectionery establishments in excess of eighteen hours each day. No one, I take it, could dispute the power of the State to enact such a statute. But the statute before us does not embrace extreme or exceptional cases. . . .

Justice Holmes dissenting

This case is decided upon an economic theory which a large part of the country does not entertain. If it were a question whether I agreed with that theory, I should desire to study it further and long before making up my mind. But I do not conceive that to be my duty, because I strongly believe that my agreement or disagreement has nothing to do with the right of a majority to embody their opinions in law. It is settled by various decisions of this court that state constitutions and state laws may regulate life in many ways which we as legislators might think as injudicious or if you like as tyrannical as this, and which equally with this interfere with the liberty to contract. Sunday laws and usury laws are ancient examples. A more modern one is the prohibition of lotteries. The liberty of the citizen to do as he likes so long as he does not interfere with the liberty of others to do the same, which has been a shibboleth for some well-known writers, is interfered with by school laws, by the Post Office, by every state or municipal institution which takes his money for purposes thought desirable, whether he likes it or not. The Fourteenth Amendment does not enact Mr. Herbert Spencer's Social Statics. The other day we sustained the Massachusetts vaccination law. *Jacobson v. Massachusetts.* 197 U.S. . . . Two years ago we upheld the prohibition of sales of stock on margins or for future delivery in the constitution of California. *Otis v. Parker*, 187 U.S. 606. The decision sustaining an eight hour law for miners is still recent. *Holden v. Hardy*, 169 U.S. 366. Some of these laws embody convictions or prejudices which judges are likely to share. Some may not. But a constitution is not intended to embody a particular economic theory, whether of paternalism and the organic relation of the citizen to the State or of *laissez faire*. It is made for people of fundamentally differing views, and the accident of our finding certain opinions natural and familiar or novel and even shocking ought not to conclude our judgment upon the question whether statutes embodying them conflict with the Constitution of the United States. . . .

I think that the word liberty in the Fourteenth Amendment is perverted when it is held to prevent the natural outcome of a dominant opinion, unless it can be said that a rational and fair man necessarily would admit that the statute proposed would infringe fundamental principles as they have been understood by the traditions of our people and our law. It does not need research to show that no such sweeping condemnation can be passed upon the statute before us. A reasonable man might think it a proper measure on the score of health. Men whom I certainly could not pronounce unreasonable would uphold it as a first installment of a general regulation of the hours of work. Whether in the latter aspect it would be open to the charge of inequality I think it unnecessary to discuss.

11. See James Weinstein, *The Corporate Ideal in the Liberal State, 1900–1918* (Boston: Beacon Press, 1968). See Thomas McCraw's discussion of the capture thesis, "Regulation in America: A Review Article," *Business History Review* 49 (1975): 159. See also Gillman, *The Constitution Besieged.*

In *Lochner* the Court gave private property interests priority over what a state legislature had defined as the public interest. The political and economic battle between these two sets of interests were at the core of the legal debate over regulation in the early twentieth century and continue to play an important role in today's debates. This debate did not consider replacing private property with state-owned industries, as in socialist countries. Rather the form of public regulation emerging at this time merely placed certain conditions (e.g., licensing, inspection, etc.) on industries affected by a public interest. Thus capitalism and state regulation were not fundamentally at odds with one another. As James Weinstein argues, some corporate capitalists supported, if they did not initiate, regulatory programs in order to represent and legitimate private economic and political interest as the "public interest," hence securing the long-term future of capitalism.[11] This position, of course, was not shared by all business groups. Indeed, while big business tended to provide the leadership for reform, forming associations that lobbied to create regulatory agencies such as the case of the Federal Trade Commission (1914), the National Manufacturers Association, which represented small manufacturers, "dragged its feet until its membership was gradually converted to support" regulatory reforms.[12]

In addition to offering a crystallized example of the clash between public interest and private property, *Lochner* is also a landmark case standing on the transitional territory between the ideal of faction-free republic and the reality of industrialized America. It is true, as the political scientist Howard Gillman points out, that the Supreme Court did not decide the case out of sheer regard for the rights of property owners. Rather, it was a logical extension of existing police power jurisprudence that emphasized the illegitimacy of "class-" or "faction"-based legislation. Only three years later, in *Muller v. Oregon* (1908),[13] the Court upheld a state's restrictions on the working hours of women as promoting the special state interest in protecting women's health. The rationale, according to Gillman, was that since women were

12. Weinstein, *The Corporate Ideal in the Liberal State*, 92.
13. 208 U.S. 412.

important to the well being of society as a whole, any legislation about their health could not be considered "class" politics.

However, in hindsight, what made a majority of Supreme Court justices friends/defenders of the propertied interests was their perhaps conscious decision to close their eyes to the dramatic changes that had taken place in the society and to ignore the discrepancy between the faction-free republic ideal and the harsh realities of industrialization. By 1905, rapid industrialization in the second half of the nineteenth century had created a society riven by deep inequalities and a social environment that highlighted the oppressive character of the market machine. The "entrepreneurial talent" once championed by Justice Field in his *Munn* dissent, turned into a mechanism of oppression preventing many landless workers from enjoying the benefits of the republican ideals. With the concentration of capital and land in the hands of the few, it was no longer possible for individual men to be "independent." The divide between propertyless labor and capital grew exponentially, making it practically impossible to imagine a public interest beyond factions.

Nevertheless, the Court's approach to property cases remained unchanged and *Lochner* was decided accordingly. In fact, as we will see briefly, the Court did not alter its position on property regulation and the rise of the administrative state in general until 1937. Despite the emergence of various movements in the legal academy, such as the Sociological Jurisprudence of Roscoe Pound and the Legal Realists who advocated for the use of the law to solve social problems, the Court remained a strong supporter of the powerful until late in the New Deal years.

Although administrative law combines many different legal traditions (constitutional, statutory, and judge-made law) whose own origins predate the twentieth century, with the development of the modern state administrative law came into its own. Prior to the 1930s major policy areas were ignored, were left entirely to the states, or were only marginally provided for by the federal government. The legal historian Harry Scheiber notes that in 1929 national government expenditures ($2.6 billion) were one-third the amount spent by state and local governments. Ten years later, national spending had risen to

$9 billion and surpassed state and local spending of $8.5 billion in 1939.[14]

Increased federal spending in this decade had both *quantitative* and *qualitative* results. The New Deal put into place a modern state, beginning with the 1933 Agricultural Adjustment Act and the National Industry Recovery Act. Until the Supreme Court struck them down in 1935, these two pieces of legislation brought agriculture and manufacturing within the scope of federal regulatory power. Other programs, however, survived judicial review by the conservative, *laissez faire* Supreme Court: in 1933 the Tennessee Valley Authority instituted the first natural resource and regional land management program under the federal government; the Social Security Act of 1935, the first national social entitlement program; the Works Progress Administration, created to provide government-financed employment programs administered by the states; and other areas of federal activity and regulation discussed in chapter 2.

In *National Labor Relations Board v. Jones & Laughlin Steel Corp.* (1937), the Supreme Court upheld the Wagner Act, which established the National Labor Relations Board (NLRB). Chief Justice Hughes's opinion for a five-member majority offers a legal solution to the political and economic debate over regulation—a solution that combines private property rights and public rights to protect the general health and welfare of society. Karl Klare, a law professor, argues that the Court's solution was to "update legal consciousness and to make it more responsive to contemporary social exigencies—that is, to give a new life to the liberal legal order—while at the same time preserving its contradictions and mystification" about the relationship between capitalism and democracy.[15] Chief Justice Hughes's New Deal jurisprudence combines protection for private and public rights and serves as a justification for an administrative process.

14. Harry N. Scheiber, "From the New Deal to the New Federalism, 1933–1983" (proceedings of a Conference at Boalt Hall School of Law, University of California, Berkeley, April 16, 1983), 2–4.

15. Karl Klare "Judicial Deradicalizaton of the Wagner Act and the Origins of Modern Legal Consciousness, 1937–1941,"*Minnesota Law Review* 62 (1978): 2806. Also see William E. Forbath, "The Shaping of the American Labor Movement," *Harvard Law Review* 102 (1989): 1109.

At the same time, Hughes carved out a supervisory role for judiciary in administrative law.

National Labor Relations Board v. Jones & Laughlin Steel Corporation

301 U.S. 1 (1937) 5-4
+ Hughes, Stone, Brandeis, Roberts, Cardozo
– Sutherland, Van Devanter, McReynolds, Butler

Chief Justice Hughes delivered the opinion of the Court

In a proceeding under the National Labor Relations Act of 1935, the National Labor Relations Board found that the respondent, Jones & Laughlin Steel Corporation, had violated the Act by engaging in unfair labor practices affecting commerce. The proceeding was instituted by the Beaver Valley Lodge No. 200, affiliated with the Amalgamated Association of Iron Steel and Tin Workers of America, a labor organization. The unfair labor practices charged were that the corporation was discriminating against members of the union with regard to hire and tenure of employment, and was coercing and intimidating its employees in order to interfere with their self-organization. The discriminatory and coercive action alleged was the discharge of certain employees.

The National Labor Relations Board, sustaining the charge, ordered the corporation to cease and desist from such discrimination and coercion, to offer reinstatement to ten of the employees named, to make good their losses in pay, and to post for thirty days notices that the corporation would not discharge or discriminate against members, or those desiring to become members, of the labor union. As the corporation failed to comply, the Board petitioned the Circuit Court of Appeals to enforce the order. The court denied the petition, holding that the order lay beyond the range of federal power. . . . We granted certiorari.

The scheme of the National Labor Relations Act—which is too long to be quoted in full—may be briefly stated. The first section sets forth findings with respect to the injury to commerce resulting from the denial by employers of the right of employees to organize and from the refusal of employers to accept the procedure of collective bargaining.

There follows a declaration that it is the policy of the United States to eliminate these causes of obstruction to the free flow of commerce. The Act then defines the terms it uses, including the terms "commerce" and "affecting commerce." It creates the National Labor Relations Board and prescribes its organization. It sets forth the right of employees to self-organization and to bargain collectively through representatives of their own choosing. It defines "unfair labor practices." It lays down rules as to the representation of employees for the purpose of collective bargaining. . . .

As an affirmative defense respondent challenged the constitutional validity of the statute and its applicability in the instant case. Notice of hearing was given and respondent appeared by counsel. The board first took up the issue of jurisdiction and evidence was presented by both the Board and the respondent. Respondent then moved to dismiss the complaint for lack of jurisdiction; and, on denial of that motion, respondent in accordance with its special appearance withdrew from further participation in the hearing. The Board received evidence upon the merits and at its close made its findings and order.

Contesting the ruling of the Board, the respondent argues (1) that the Act is in reality a regulation of labor relations and not of interstate commerce; (2) that the Act can have no application to the respondent's relations with its production employees because they are not subject to regulation by the federal government; and (3) that the provisions of the Act violate § 2 of Article III and the Fifth and Seventh Amendments of the Constitution of the United States. . . .

Summarizing the operations [of Jones & Laughlin Steel Corporation], the Labor Board concluded that the works in Pittsburgh and Aliquippa "might be likened to the heart of a self-contained, highly integrated body. They draw in the raw materials from Michigan, Minnesota, West Virginia, Pennsylvania in part through arteries and by means controlled by the respondent; they transform the materials and then pump them out to all parts of the nation through the vast mechanism which the respondent has elaborated."

To carry on the activities of the entire steel industry, 33,000 men mine ore, 44,000 men mine coal, 4,000 men quarry limestone, 16,000 men manufacture coke, 343,000 men manufacture steel, and 83,000 men transport its product. Respondent has about 10,000 employees in its

Aliquippa plant which is located in a community of about 30,000 persons. . . .

These employees were active leaders in the labor union. Several were officers and others were leaders of particular groups. Two of the employees were motor inspectors; one was a tractor driver, three were crane operators; one was a washer in the coke plant; and three were laborers. Three other employees were mentioned in the complaint but it was withdrawn as to one of them and no evidence was heard on the action taken with respect to the other two.

While respondent criticizes the evidence and the attitude of the Board, which is described as being hostile toward employers and particularly toward those who insisted upon their constitutional rights, respondent did not take advantage of its opportunity to present evidence to refute that which was offered to show discrimination and coercion. In this situation, the record presents no ground for setting aside the order of the Board so far as the facts pertaining to the circumstances and purpose of the discharge of the employees are concerned. . . . We turn to the questions of law which respondent urges in contesting the validity and application of the Act.

First. The scope of the Act.—The Act is challenged in its entirety as an attempt to regulate all industry, thus invading the reserved powers of the States over their local concerns. . . .

We think it clear that the National Labor Relations Act may be construed so as to operate within the sphere of constitutional authority. The jurisdiction conferred upon the Board, and invoked in this instance, is found in s 10 (a), which provides:

"SEC. 10 (a). The Board is empowered, as hereinafter provided, to prevent any person from engaging in any unfair labor practice (listed in section 8) affecting commerce." . . .

There can be no question that the commerce thus contemplated by the Act (aside from that within a Territory or the District of Columbia) is interstate and foreign commerce in the constitutional sense. . . .

The grant of authority to the Board does not purport to extend to the relationship between all industrial employees and employers. Its terms do not impose collective bargaining upon all industry regardless of effects upon interstate or foreign commerce. It purports to reach only what may be

deemed to burden or obstruct that commerce and, thus qualified, it must be construed as contemplating the exercise of control within constitutional bounds. . . . Whether or not particular action does affect commerce in such a close and intimate fashion as to be subject to federal control, and hence to lie within the authority conferred upon the Board, is left by the statute to be determined as individual cases arise. We are thus to inquire whether in the instant case the constitutional boundary has been passed.

Second. The unfair labor practices in question.—The unfair labor practices found by the Board are those defined in §8, subdivisions (1) and (3). These provide:

Sec. 8. It shall be unfair labor practice for an employer—

"(1) To interfere with, restrain, or coerce employees in the exercise of the rights guaranteed in section 7."

"(3) By discrimination in regard to hire or tenure of employment or any term or condition of employment to encourage or discourage membership in any labor organization: . . ."

Section 8, subdivision (1), refers to §7, which is as follows:

"Sec. 7. Employees shall have the right to self-organization, form, join, or assist labor organizations, to bargain collectively through representatives of their own choosing, and to engage in concerted activities, for the purpose of collective bargaining or other mutual aid or protection."

Thus in its present application, the statute goes no further than to safeguard the right of employees to self-organization and to select representatives of their own choosing for collective bargaining or other mutual protection without restraint or coercion by their employer.

That is a fundamental right. Employees have as clear a right to organize and select their representatives for lawful purposes as the respondent has to organize its business and select its own officers and agents. Discrimination and coercion to prevent the free exercise of the right of employees to self-organization and representation is a proper subject for condemnation by competent legislative authority. Long ago we stated the reason for labor organizations. We said that they were organized out of the necessities of the situation; that a single employee was helpless in dealing with an employer; that he was dependent ordinarily on his daily wage for the maintenance of himself and family; that if the employer refused to pay him the wages that he thought fair, he was nevertheless unable to leave the employ and resist arbitrary and unfair treatment; that union was essential to give laborers opportunity to deal on an equality with their employer." . . . Fully recognizing the legality of collective action on the part of employees in order to safeguard their proper interests, we said that Congress was not required to ignore this right but could safeguard it. Congress could seek to make appropriate collective action of employees an instrument of peace rather than of strife. We said that such collective action would be a mockery if representation were made futile by interference with freedom of choice. . . .

Third. The application of the Act to employees engaged in production.—The principle involved.— Respondent says that whatever may be said of employees engaged in interstate commerce, the industrial relations and activities in the manufacturing department of respondent's enterprise are not subject to federal regulation. The argument rests upon the proposition that manufacturing in itself is not commerce. . . .

Fourth. Effects of the unfair labor practice in respondent's enterprise. . . . It is obvious that it would be immediate and might be catastrophic. We are asked to shut our eyes to the plainest facts of our national life and to deal with the question of direct and indirect effects in an intellectual vacuum. Because there may be but indirect and remote effects upon interstate commerce in connection with a host of local enterprises throughout the country, it does not follow that other industrial activities do not have such a close and intimate relation to interstate commerce as to make the presence of industrial strife a matter of the most urgent national concern. When industries organize themselves on a national scale, making their relation to interstate commerce the dominant factor in their activities, how can it be maintained that their industrial labor relations constitute a forbidden field into which Congress may not enter when it is necessary to protect interstate commerce from the paralyzing consequences of industrial war? We have often said that interstate commerce itself is a practical conception. It is equally true that interferences with that commerce must be appraised by a judgment that does not ignore actual experience.

Experience has abundantly demonstrated that the recognition of the right of employees to self-organization and to have representatives of their own choosing for the

purpose of collective bargaining is often an essential condition of industrial peace. Refusal to confer and negotiate has been one of the most prolific causes of strife. This is such an outstanding fact in the history of labor disturbances that it is a proper subject of judicial notice and requires no citation of instances. . . .

Fifth. The means which the Act employs.—Questions under the due process clause and other constitutional restrictions.— Respondent asserts its right to conduct its business in an orderly manner without being subjected to arbitrary restraints. What we have said points to the fallacy in the argument. Employees have their correlative right to organize for the purpose of securing the redress of grievances and to promote agreements with employers relating to rates of pay and conditions of work. . . . Restraint for the purpose of preventing an unjust interference with that right cannot be considered arbitrary or capricious. . . .

The Act does not compel agreements between employers and employees. It does not compel any agreement whatever. It does not prevent the employer "from refusing to make a collective contract and hiring individuals on whatever terms" the employer "may by unilateral action determine." The Act expressly provides in §9 (a) that any individual employee or a group of employees shall have the right at any time to present grievances to their employer. The theory of the Act is that free opportunity for negotiation with accredited representatives of employees is likely to promote industrial peace and may bring about the adjustments and agreements which the Act in itself does not attempt to compel. . . . The employer may not, under cover of that right, intimidate or coerce its employees with respect to their self-organization and representation, and, on the other hand, the Board is not entitled to make its authority a pretext for interference with the right of discharge when that right is exercised for other reasons than such intimidation and coercion. The true purpose is the subject of investigation with full opportunity to show the facts. It would seem that when employers freely recognize the right of their employees to their own organizations and their unrestricted right of representation there will be much less occasion for controversy in respect to the free and appropriate exercise of the right of selection and discharge.

The Act has been criticized as one-sided in its application; that it subjects the employer to supervision and restraint and leaves untouched the abuses for which employees may be responsible; that it fails to provide a more comprehensive plan,—with better assurances of fairness to both sides and with increased chances of success in bringing about, if not compelling, equitable solutions of industrial disputes affecting interstate commerce. But we are dealing with the power of Congress, not with a particular policy or with the extent to which policy should go. We have frequently said that the legislative authority, exerted within its proper field, need not embrace all the evils within its reach. The Constitution does not forbid "cautious advance, step by step," in dealing with the evils which are exhibited in activities within the range, of legislative power. . . . The question in such cases is whether the legislature, in what it does prescribe, has gone beyond constitutional limits. . . .

Our conclusion is that the order of the Board was within its competency and that the Act is valid as here applied. The judgment of the Circuit Court of Appeals is reversed and the cause is remanded for further proceedings in conformity with this opinion.

Reversed.

Justice McReynolds delivered the following dissenting opinion in the cases preceding

Mr. Justice Van Devanter, Mr. Justice Sutherland, Mr. Justice Butler and I are unable to agree with the decisions just announced. . . .

We are told that Congress may protect the "stream of commerce" and that one who buys raw material without the state, manufacturers it therein, and ships the output to another state is in that stream. Therefore it is said he may be prevented from doing anything which may interfere with its flow.

This, too, goes beyond the constitutional limitations heretofore enforced. If a man raises cattle and regularly delivers "them to a carrier for interstate shipment, may Congress prescribe the conditions under which he may employ or discharge helpers on the ranch? The products of a mine pass daily into interstate commerce; many things are brought to it from other states. Are the owners and the miners within the power of Congress in respect of the miners' tenure and discharge? . . .

Whatever effect any cause of discontent may ultimately have upon commerce is far too indirect to justify Congres-

sional regulation. Almost anything—marriage, birth, death—may in some fashion affect commerce. . . .

The right to contract is fundamental and includes the privilege of selecting those with whom one is willing to assume contractual relations. This right is unduly abridged by the Act now upheld. A private owner is deprived of power to manage his own property by freely selecting those to whom his manufacturing operations are to be entrusted. We think this cannot lawfully be done in circumstances like those here disclosed.

It seems clear to us that Congress has transcended the powers granted.

Jones & Laughlin and its jurisprudential philosophy did not, however, end the tension between private property rights and the government's right to protect the general health and welfare of society. A close reading of the opinions in *Munn* reveals an interesting legal wrinkle. What appeared to bother Justice Field, in his dissent, was that the ceilings on the charges grain elevators could exact from farmers through their mini-monopoly of the business took the elevator operators' property from them "without just compensation." The question, therefore, is not just whether property could be taken from its owner for a public goal. At least in theory, this power is undisputed. What is disputed, as in the case of *Munn v. Illinois*, is what counts as "property" and when a regulation can be classified as a "taking" of property. This problem—or, rather, "problematization"—of regulatory takings was revived in the Reagan-Bush era. We conclude this section with two takings cases.

The "takings" problem illustrates the political values that affect how lines are drawn in law. On one side of the line, we know that if we own a house or a farm, and the state highway commission wants to put a road through our property, they must pay us. If we don't like the price the highway authorities offer, we can initiate administrative and then judicial proceedings to challenge it. On the other side of the legal line, suppose I buy a large house in an un-zoned area, hoping to convert it into a duplex or a set of apartments, and before I get the money together, the city zones my area "single-family dwelling." I've lost a part of the value of my property, just as I would if the city built a road through my farm. Here, I get no "just compensation." I must accept losing the potential rental value of my property.

Now imagine a case in between. Suppose I own a small home on a Pacific Ocean beach in Southern California. I apply for a building permit to expand my home. No zoning law prohibits it, but the building authorities insist that to get a building permit I must allow a strip of my land to be used as an easement on which the public can travel from the road to the beach. In 1987, in *Nollan v. California Coastal Commission*, 483 U.S. 825, the Supreme Court held that this governmental coercion amounted to an unconstitutional taking. The next case continues this discussion. Do you see any similarities between Justice John Paul Stevens's dissent and the majority opinion in *Munn*, decided over a century earlier? Does the majority here tilt back toward the era of *Lochner*?

Dolan v. City of Tigard

512 U.S. 374 (1994) 5-4
+ *Rehnquist, Scalia, Kennedy, O'Connor, Thomas*
– *Stevens, Blackmun, Ginsburg, Souter*

[The Tigard, Oregon, City Planning Commission conditioned approval of petitioner Florence Dolan's application to expand her store and pave her parking lot upon her compliance with dedication of land (1) for a public greenway along Fanno Creek to minimize flooding that would be exacerbated by the increases in impervious surfaces associated with her development, and (2) for a pedestrian/bicycle pathway intended to relieve traffic congestion in the city's Central Business District. She appealed the commission's denial of her request for variances from these standards to the Land Use Board of Appeals (LUBA), alleging that the land dedication requirements were not related to the proposed development and therefore constituted an uncompensated taking of her property under the Fifth Amendment. LUBA found a reasonable relationship between (1) the development and the requirement to dedicate land for a greenway, since the larger building and paved lot would increase the impervious surfaces and thus the runoff into the creek, and (2) alleviating the impact of increased traffic from the development and facilitating the provision of

a pathway as an alternative means of transportation. Oregon's Court of Appeals and the Oregon Supreme Court affirmed.]

Chief Justice Rehnquist delivered the opinion of the Court

We granted certiorari to resolve a question left open by our decision in *Nollan v. California Coastal Comm'n*, 483 U.S. 825 (1987), of what is the required degree of connection between the exactions imposed by the city and the projected impacts of the proposed development.

The Commission made a series of findings concerning the relationship between the dedicated conditions and the projected impacts of petitioner's project. First, the Commission noted that "it is reasonable to assume that customers and employees of the future uses of this site could utilize a pedestrian/bicycle pathway adjacent to this development for their transportation and recreational needs." The Commission noted that the site plan has provided for bicycle parking in a rack in front of the proposed building and "it is reasonable to expect that some of the users of the bicycle parking provided for by the site plan will use the pathway adjacent to Fanno Creek if it is constructed." In addition, the Commission found that creation of a convenient, safe pedestrian/bicycle pathway system as an alternative means of transportation "could offset some of the traffic demand on [nearby] streets and lessen the increase in traffic congestion."

Petitioner appealed to the Land Use Board of Appeals (LUBA) on the ground that the city's dedication requirements were not related to the proposed development, and, therefore, those requirements constituted an uncompensated taking of their property under the Fifth Amendment.

The Takings Clause of the Fifth Amendment of the United States Constitution, made applicable to the States through the Fourteenth Amendment, *Chicago, B. & Q. R. Co. v. Chicago*, 166 U.S. 226 (1897), provides: "Nor shall private property be taken for public use, without just compensation." One of the principal purposes of the Takings Clause is "to bar Government from forcing some people alone to bear public burdens which, in all fairness and justice, should be borne by the public as a whole." *Armstrong v. United States*, 364 U.S. 40 (1960). Without question, had the city simply required petitioner to dedicate a strip of land along

Fanno Creek for public use, rather than conditioning the grant of her permit to redevelop her property on such a dedication, a taking would have occurred. Such public access would deprive petitioner of the right to exclude others, "one of the most essential sticks in the bundle of rights that are commonly characterized as property." *Kaiser Aetna v. United States*, 444 U.S. 164 (1979).

On the other side of the ledger, the authority of state and local governments to engage in land-use planning has been sustained against constitutional challenge as long ago as our decision in *Euclid v. Ambler Realty Co.*, 212 U.S. 365 (1926). The sort of land-use regulations . . . differ in two relevant particulars from the present case. First, they involved essentially legislative determinations classifying entire areas of the city, whereas here the city made an adjudicative decision to condition petitioner's application for a building permit on an individual parcel. Second, the conditions imposed were not simply a limitation on the use petitioner might make of her own parcel, but a requirement that she deed portions of the property to the city. In *Nollan*, we held that governmental authority to exact such a condition was circumscribed by the Fifth and Fourteenth Amendments. Under the well-settled doctrine of "unconstitutional conditions," the government may not require a person to give up a constitutional right—here the right to receive just compensation when property is taken for a public use—in exchange for a discretionary benefit conferred by the government where the property sought has little or no relationship to the benefit.

In evaluating petitioner's claim, we must first determine whether the "essential nexus" exists between the "legitimate state interest" and the permit condition exacted by the city. *Nollan.* If we find that a nexus exists, we must then decide the required degree of connection between the exactions and the projected impact of the proposed development. We were not required to reach this question in *Nollan*, because we concluded that the connection did not meet even the loosest standard. Here, however, we must decide this question.

Undoubtedly, the prevention of flooding along Fanno Creek and the reduction of traffic congestion in the Central Business District qualify as the type of legitimate public purposes we have upheld. It seems equally obvious that a nexus exists between preventing flooding along Fanno Creek and limiting development within the creek's 100-year floodplain. Petitioner proposes to double the size of her retail store and to pave her now gravel parking lot, thereby expanding the impervious surface on the property and increasing the amount of stormwater runoff into Fanno Creek. The same may be said for the city's attempt to reduce traffic congestion by providing for alternative means of transportation.

The second part of our analysis requires us to determine whether the degree of the exactions demanded by the city's permit conditions bear the required relationship to the projected impact of petitioner's proposed development. Here the Oregon Supreme Court deferred to what it termed the "city's unchallenged factual findings" supporting the dedication conditions and found them to be reasonably related to the impact of the expansion of petitioner's business.

The city required that petitioner dedicate "to the city as Greenway all portions of the site that fall within the existing 10-year floodplain [of Fanno Creek] and all property 15 feet above [the flood-plain] boundary." In addition, the city demanded that the retail store be designed so as not to intrude into the greenway area. The city relies on the Commission's rather tentative findings that increased stormwater flow from petitioner's property "can only add to the public need to manage the (floodplain] for drainage purposes" to support its conclusion that the "requirement of dedication of the floodplain area on the site is related to the applicant's plan to intensify development on the site."

The question for us is whether these findings are constitutionally sufficient to justify the conditions imposed by the city on petitioner's building permit. Since state courts have been dealing with this question a good deal longer than we have, we turn to representative decisions made by them. . . .

We think the "reasonable relationship" test adopted by a majority of the state courts is closer to the federal constitutional norm than either of those previously discussed. But we do not adopt it as such. We think a term such as "rough proportionality" best encapsulates what we hold to be the requirement of the Fifth Amendment. No precise mathematical calculation is required, but the city must make some sort of individualized determination that the required dedication is related both in nature and extent to the impact of the proposed development.

If petitioner's proposed development had somehow encroached on existing greenway space in the city, it would have been reasonable to require petitioner to provide some alternative greenway space for the public either on her property or elsewhere. But that is not the case here. We conclude that the findings upon which the city relies do not show the required reasonable relationship between the flood-plain easement and the petitioner's proposed new building. With respect to the pedestrian/bicycle pathway, we have no doubt that the city was correct in finding that the larger retail sales facility proposed by petitioner will increase traffic on the streets of the Central Business District. The city estimates that the proposed development would generate roughly 435 additional trips per day. . . . But on the record before us, the city has not met its burden of demonstrating that the additional number of vehicle and bicycle trips generated by the petitioner's development reasonably relate to the city's requirement for a dedication of the pedestrian/ bicycle pathway easement. The city simply found that the creation of the pathway "could offset some of the traffic demand and lessen the increase in traffic congestion."

No precise mathematical calculation is required, but the city must make some effort to quantify its findings in support of the dedication for the pedestrian/bicycle pathway beyond the conclusory statement that it could effect some of the traffic demand generated. The city's goals of reducing flooding hazards and traffic congestion, and providing for public greenways, are laudable, but there are outer limits to how this may be done.

Justice Stevens, with whom Justice Blackmun and Justice Ginsburg join, dissenting

The Court is correct in concluding that the city may not attach arbitrary conditions to a building permit or to a variance even when it can rightfully deny the application outright. I also agree that state court decisions dealing with ordinances that govern municipal development plans provide useful guidance in a case of this kind. Yet the Court's description of the doctrinal underpinnings of its decision, the phrasing of its fledgling test of "rough proportionality," and the application of that test to this case run contrary to the traditional treatment of these cases and break considerable and unpropitious new ground. . . .

It is not merely state cases, but our own cases as well, that require the analysis to focus on the impact of the city's action on the entire parcel of private property. In *Penn Central Transportation Co. v. New York City*, 438 U.S. 104 (1978), we stated that takings jurisprudence "does not divide a single parcel into discrete segments and attempt to determine whether rights in a particular segment have been entirely abrogated." Instead, this Court focuses "both on the character of the action and on the nature and extent of the interference with rights in the parcel as a whole." *Andrus v. Allard*, 444 U.S. 51 (1979), reaffirmed the nondivisibility principle outlined in *Penn Central*, stating that "at least where an owner possesses a full 'bundle' of property rights, the destruction of one 'strand' of the bundle is not a taking, because the aggregate must be viewed in its entirety."

The Court has made a serious error by abandoning the traditional presumption of constitutionality and imposing a novel burden of proof on a city implementing an admittedly valid comprehensive land use plan. Even more consequential than its incorrect disposition of this case, however, is the Court's resurrection of a species of substantive due process analysis that it firmly rejected decades ago.

The Court begins its constitutional analysis by citing *Chicago, B. & Q. R. Co. v. Chicago*, 166 U.S. 226 (1897), for the proposition that the Takings Clause of the Fifth Amendment is "applicable to the States through the Fourteenth Amendment." That opinion, however, contains no mention of either the Takings Clause or the Fifth Amendment; it held that the protection afforded by the Due Process Clause of the Fourteenth Amendment extends to matters of substance as well as procedure, and that the substance of "the due process of law enjoined by the Fourteenth Amendment requires compensation to be made or adequately secured to the owner of private property taken for public use under the authority of a State." *Chicago, B. & Q. R. Co.* It applied the same kind of substantive due process analysis more frequently identified with a better known case that accorded similar substantive protection to a baker's liberty interest in working 60 hours a week and 10 hours a day. See *Lochner v. New York*, 198 U.S. 45 (1905).

Later cases have interpreted the Fourteenth Amendment's substantive protection against uncompensated deprivations of private property by the States as though it incorporated the text of the Fifth Amendment's Takings Clause. There was nothing problematic about that interpretation in cases enforcing the Fourteenth Amendment against state action that involved the actual physical invasion of private property. Justice Holmes charted a significant new course, however, when he opined that a state law making it "commercially impracticable to mine certain coal" had "very nearly the same effect for constitutional purposes as appropriating or destroying it." *Pennsylvania Coal Co. v. Mahon*, 260 U.S. 393 (1922). The so-called "regulatory takings" doctrine that the Holmes dictum kindled has an obvious kinship with the line of substantive due process cases that *Lochner* exemplified. Besides having similar ancestry, both doctrines are potentially open-ended sources of judicial power to invalidate state economic regulations that Members of this Court view as unwise or unfair.

This case inaugurates an even more recent judicial innovation than the regulatory takings doctrine: the application of the "unconstitutional conditions" label to a mutually beneficial transaction between a property owner and a city. The Court tells us that the city's refusal to grant Dolan a discretionary benefit infringes her right to receive just compensation for the property interests that she has refused to dedicate to the city "where the property sought has little or no relationship to the benefit." Although it is well settled that a government cannot deny a benefit on a basis that infringes constitutionally protected interests—"especially [one's] interest in freedom of speech," *Perry v. Sindermann*, 408 U.S. 593 (1972)—the "unconstitutional conditions" doctrine provides an inadequate framework in which to analyze this case.

Dolan has no right to be compensated for a taking unless the city acquires the property interests that she has refused to surrender. Since no taking has yet occurred, there has not been any infringement of her constitutional right to compensation. . . .

In our changing world one thing is certain: uncertainty will characterize predictions about the impact of new urban developments on the risks of floods, earthquakes, traffic congestion, or environmental harms. When there is doubt concerning the magnitude of those impacts, the public interest in averting them must outweigh the private interest of the commercial entrepreneur. If the government can demonstrate that the conditions it has imposed in a land-use permit are rational, impartial and conducive to fulfilling the aims of a valid land-use plan, a strong presumption of validity should attach to those conditions. The burden of demonstrating that those conditions have unreasonably impaired the economic value of the proposed improvement belongs squarely on the shoulders of the party challenging the state action's constitutionality. That allocation of burdens has served us well in the past. The Court has stumbled badly today by reversing it.

Justice Stevens's dissent points to one major justification for the administrative state: we need a sufficiently strong bureaucratic organization with broad outreach (vision) and necessary powers (over private property rights, among others), if we want to manage risks and problems associated with modern society. In other words, we need a government where various kinds of expertise are concentrated to make sure that we can rationally plan the future.

The problem, however, is always more than a technical question of "rationalizing" government and planning the future through expertise. The idea, until recently, has been that as long as it is within the limits of Constitutional powers, the government, as the elected representative of the people, can order taking of property for a justified future goal. The courts, thus, had given more or less latitude to legislative regulation of business and economic matters, until the recent shift back to defending private property rights as you have just read. The struggle between property interests and states' regulatory actions continue in the state and federal courts—with a significant twist. Now, imagine a scenario which is even more explicitly political than regulating space for future flood dynamics: taking private property from its owners for future "economic development." State governments, as well as municipalities, can take private property for public use in an effort to stimulate economic development, through job development, more tourism, construction of low-income housing, etc. What constitutes "economic development"—a wonderfully imprecise term—is something the government has asserted the right to decide in "the public interest." The twist in this scenario is that businesses, in this case developers, are *for* the taking of private property, rather than against it (as long as the property is not theirs of course), since such takings undoubtedly generate large profits for these developers. In the next case and the immediate paragraphs following it, you will see that the line between regulation *of* businesses and regulation *for* businesses gets quite blurry.

Kelo v. City of New London

545 U.S. 469 (2005) 5-4
+ *Stevens, Kennedy, Souter, Ginsburg, Breyer*
- *Rehnquist, O'Connor, Scalia, Thomas*

Justice Stevens delivered the opinion of the Court

In 2000, the city of New London approved a development plan that, in the words of the Supreme Court of Connecticut, was "projected to create in excess of 1,000 jobs, to increase tax and other revenues, and to revitalize an economically distressed city, including its downtown and waterfront areas." In assembling the land needed for this project, the city's development agent has purchased property from willing sellers and proposes to use the power of eminent domain to acquire the remainder of the property from unwilling owners in exchange for just compensation.

We granted certiorari to determine whether a city's decision to take property for the purpose of economic development satisfies the "public use" requirement of the Fifth Amendment.

Two polar propositions are perfectly clear. On the one hand, it has long been accepted that the sovereign may not take the property of A for the sole purpose of transferring it to another private party B, even though A is paid just compensation. On the other hand, it is equally clear that a State may transfer property from one private party to another if future "use by the public" is the purpose of the taking; the condemnation of land for a railroad with common-carrier duties is a familiar example. Neither of these propositions, however, determines the disposition of this case.

As for the first proposition, the City would no doubt be forbidden from taking petitioners' land for the purpose of conferring a private benefit on a particular private party. Nor would the City be allowed to take property under the mere pretext of a public purpose, when its actual purpose was to bestow a private benefit. The takings before us, however,

would be executed pursuant to a "carefully considered" development plan. The trial judge and all the members of the Supreme Court of Connecticut agreed that there was no evidence of an illegitimate purpose in this case.

On the other hand, this is not a case in which the City is planning to open the condemned land—at least not in its entirety—to use by the general public. Nor will the private lessees of the land in any sense be required to operate like common carriers, making their services available to all comers. But although such a projected use would be sufficient to satisfy the public use requirement, this "Court long ago rejected any literal requirement that condemned property be put into use for the general public." Indeed, while many state courts in the mid-19th century endorsed "use by the public" as the proper definition of public use, that narrow view steadily eroded over time. Not only was the "use by the public" test difficult to administer (e.g., what proportion of the public need have access to the property? at what price?), but it proved to be impractical given the diverse and always evolving needs of society. Accordingly, when this Court began applying the Fifth Amendment to the States at the close of the 19th century, it embraced the broader and more natural interpretation of public use as "public purpose." See, e.g., *Fallbrook Irrigation Dist. v. Bradley*, 164 U.S. 112, 158-164 (1896). Thus, in a case upholding a mining company's use of an aerial bucket line to transport ore over property it did not own, Justice Holmes' opinion for the Court stressed "the inadequacy of use by the general public as a universal test." We have repeatedly and consistently rejected that narrow test ever since.

The disposition of this case therefore turns on the question whether the City's development plan serves a "public purpose." Without exception, our cases have defined that concept broadly, reflecting our longstanding policy of deference to legislative judgments in this field.

In *Berman v. Parker*, 348 U.S. 26, 75 (1954), this Court upheld a redevelopment plan targeting a blighted area of Washington, D.C., in which most of the housing for the area's 5,000 inhabitants was beyond repair. Under the plan, the area would be condemned and part of it utilized for the construction of streets, schools, and other public facilities. The remainder of the land would be leased or sold to private parties for the purpose of redevelopment, including the construction of low-cost housing. . . .

In *Hawaii Housing Authority v. Midkiff*, 467 U.S. 229 (1984), the Court considered a Hawaii statute whereby fee title was taken from lessors and transferred to lessees (for just compensation) in order to reduce the concentration of land ownership. We unanimously upheld the statute and rejected the Ninth Circuit's view that it was "a naked attempt on the part of the state of Hawaii to take the property of A and transfer it to B solely for B's private use and benefit." Reaffirming *Berman's* deferential approach to legislative judgments in this field, we concluded that the State's purpose of eliminating the "social and economic evils of a land oligopoly" qualified as a valid public use. Our opinion also rejected the contention that the mere fact that the State immediately transferred the properties to private individuals upon condemnation somehow diminished the public character of the taking. "[I]t is only the taking's purpose, and not its mechanics," we explained, that matters in determining public use.

In that same Term we decided another public use case that arose in a purely economic context. In *Ruckelshaus v. Monsanto, Co.*, 467 U.S. 986 (1984), the Court dealt with provisions of the Federal Insecticide, Fungicide, and Rodenticide Act under which the Environmental Protection Agency could consider the data (including trade secrets) submitted by a prior pesticide applicant in evaluating a subsequent application, so long as the second applicant paid just compensation for the data. We acknowledged that the "most direct beneficiaries" of these provisions were the subsequent applicants, but we nevertheless upheld the statute under *Berman* and *Midkiff*. We found sufficient Congress' belief that sparing applicants the cost of time-consuming research eliminated a significant barrier to entry in the pesticide market and thereby enhanced competition.

Viewed as a whole, our jurisprudence has recognized that the needs of society have varied between different parts of the Nation, just as they have evolved over time in response to changed circumstances. Our earliest cases in particular embodied a strong theme of federalism, emphasizing the "great respect" that we owe to state legislatures and state courts in discerning local public needs. For more than a century, our public use jurisprudence has wisely eschewed rigid formulas and intrusive scrutiny in favor of affording legislatures broad latitude in determining what public needs justify the use of the takings power. . . .

Those who govern the City were not confronted with the need to remove blight in the Fort Trumbull area, but their determination that the area was sufficiently distressed to justify a program of economic rejuvenation is entitled to our deference. The City has carefully formulated an economic development plan that it believes will provide appreciable benefits to the community, including—but by no means limited to—new jobs and increased tax revenue. As with other exercises in urban planning and development, the City is endeavoring to coordinate a variety of commercial, residential, and recreational uses of land, with the hope that they will form a whole greater than the sum of its parts. To effectuate this plan, the City has invoked a state statute that specifically authorizes the use of eminent domain to promote economic development. Given the comprehensive character of the plan, the thorough deliberation that preceded its adoption, and the limited scope of our review, it is appropriate for us, as it was in *Berman*, to resolve the challenges of the individual owners, not on a piecemeal basis, but rather in light of the entire plan. Because that plan unquestionably serves a public purpose, the takings challenged here satisfy the public use requirement of the Fifth Amendment.

To avoid this result, petitioners urge us to adopt a new bright-line rule that economic development does not qualify as a public use. . . . [N]either precedent nor logic supports petitioners' proposal. Promoting economic development is a traditional and long accepted function of government. There is, moreover, no principled way of distinguishing economic development from the other public purposes that we have recognized. In our cases upholding takings that facilitated agriculture and mining, for example, we emphasized the importance of those industries to the welfare of the States in question, see, e.g., *Strickley*, 200 U.S. 527; in *Berman*, we endorsed the purpose of transforming a blighted area into a "well-balanced" community through redevelopment, 348 U.S., at 33. It would be incongruous to hold that the City's interest in the economic benefits to be derived from the development of the Fort Trumbull area has less of a public character than any of those other interests. Clearly, there is no basis for exempting economic development from our traditionally broad understanding of public purpose.

Petitioners contend that using eminent domain for economic development impermissibly blurs the boundary between public and private takings. Again, our cases foreclose this objection. Quite simply, the government's pursuit of a public purpose will often benefit individual private parties. For example, in *Midkiff*, the forced transfer of property conferred a direct and significant benefit on those lessees who were previously unable to purchase their homes. . . .

It is further argued that without a bright-line rule nothing would stop a city from transferring citizen A's property to citizen B for the sole reason that citizen B will put the property to a more productive use and thus pay more taxes. Such a one-to-one transfer of property, executed outside the confines of an integrated development plan, is not presented in this case. While such an unusual exercise of government power would certainly raise a suspicion that a private purpose was afoot, the hypothetical cases posited by petitioners can be confronted if and when they arise. . . .

Alternatively, petitioners maintain that for takings of this kind we should require a "reasonable certainty" that the expected public benefits will actually accrue. Such a rule, however, would represent an even greater departure from our precedent. "When the legislature's purpose is legitimate and its means are not irrational, our cases make clear that empirical debates over the wisdom of takings—no less than debates over the wisdom of other kinds of socioeconomic legislation—are not to be carried out in the federal courts." *Midkiff*, 467 U.S., at 242. The disadvantages of a heightened form of review are especially pronounced in this type of case. Orderly implementation of a comprehensive redevelopment plan obviously requires that the legal rights of all interested parties be established before new construction can be commenced. A constitutional rule that required postponement of the judicial approval of every condemnation until the likelihood of success of the plan had been assured would unquestionably impose a significant impediment to the successful consummation of many such plans.

In affirming the City's authority to take petitioners' properties, we do not minimize the hardship that condemnations may entail, notwithstanding the payment of just compensation. We emphasize that nothing in our opinion precludes any State from placing further restrictions on its exercise of the takings power. Indeed, many States already impose "public use" requirements that are stricter than the federal baseline. Some of these requirements have been established as a matter of state constitutional law, while others are expressed in state eminent domain statutes that carefully limit the grounds upon which takings may be exer-

cised. As the submissions of the parties and their *amici* make clear, the necessity and wisdom of using eminent domain to promote economic development are certainly matters of legitimate public debate. This Court's authority, however, extends only to determining whether the City's proposed condemnations are for a "public use" within the meaning of the Fifth Amendment to the Federal Constitution. Because over a century of our case law interpreting that provision dictates an affirmative answer to that question, we may not grant petitioners the relief that they seek.

The judgment of the Supreme Court of Connecticut is affirmed.

Justice O'Connor, dissenting

Today the Court abandons this long-held, basic limitation on government power. Under the banner of economic development, all private property is now vulnerable to being taken and transferred to another private owner, so long as it might be upgraded—i.e., given to an owner who will use it in a way that the legislature deems more beneficial to the public—in the process. To reason, as the Court does, that the incidental public benefits resulting from the subsequent ordinary use of private property render economic development takings "for public use" is to wash out any distinction between private and public use of property—and thereby effectively to delete the words "for public use" from the Takings Clause of the Fifth Amendment. Accordingly I respectfully dissent.

This case returns us for the first time in over 20 years to the hard question of when a purportedly "public purpose" taking meets the public use requirement. It presents an issue of first impression: Are economic development takings constitutional? I would hold that they are not.

"A purely private taking could not withstand the scrutiny of the public use requirement; it would serve no legitimate purpose of government and would thus be void." *Midkiff*, 467 U.S., at 245. To protect that principle, those decisions reserved "a role for courts to play in reviewing a legislature's judgment of what constitutes a public use . . . [though] the Court in *Berman* made clear that it is 'an extremely narrow' one."

The Court's holdings in *Berman* and *Midkiff* were true to the principle underlying the Public Use Clause. In both those cases, the extraordinary, precondemnation use of the targeted property inflicted affirmative harm on society—in *Berman* through blight resulting from extreme poverty and in *Midkiff* through oligopoly resulting from extreme wealth. And in both cases, the relevant legislative body had found that eliminating the existing property use was necessary to remedy the harm. Thus a public purpose was realized when the harmful use was eliminated. Because each taking *directly* achieved a public benefit, it did not matter that the property was turned over to private use. Here, in contrast, New London does not claim that Susette Kelo's and Wilhelmina Dery's well-maintained homes are the source of any social harm. Indeed it could not so claim without adopting the absurd argument that any single-family home that might be razed to make way for an apartment building, or any church that might be replaced with a retail store, or any small business that might be more lucrative if it were instead part of a national franchise, is inherently harmful to society and thus within the government's power to condemn.

In moving away from our decisions sanctioning the condemnation of harmful property use, the Court today significantly expands the meaning of public use. It holds that the sovereign may take private property currently put to ordinary private use, and give it over for new, ordinary private use, so long as the new use is predicted to generate some secondary benefit for the public—such as increased tax revenue, more jobs, maybe even aesthetic pleasure. But nearly any lawful use of real private property can be said to generate some incidental benefit to the public. . . .

Any property may now be taken for the benefit of another private party, but the fallout from this decision will not be random. The beneficiaries are likely to be those citizens with disproportionate influence and power in the political process, including large corporations and development firms. As for the victims, the government now has license to transfer property from those with fewer resources to those with more. The Founders cannot have intended this perverse result. "That alone is a *just* government," wrote James Madison, "which *impartially* secures to every man, whatever is his *own*."

I would hold that the takings in both Parcel 3 and Parcel 4A are unconstitutional, reverse the judgment of the Supreme Court of Connecticut, and remand for further proceedings.

Justice Thomas, dissenting

. . . In my view, it is "imperative that the Court maintain absolute fidelity to" the Clause's express limit on the power of the government over the individual, no less than with every other liberty expressly enumerated in the Fifth Amendment or the Bill of Rights more generally. . . .

The consequences of today's decision are not difficult to predict, and promise to be harmful. So-called "urban renewal" programs provide some compensation for the properties they take, but no compensation is possible for the subjective value of these lands to the individuals displaced and the indignity inflicted by uprooting them from their homes. Allowing the government to take property solely for public purposes is bad enough, but extending the concept of public purpose to encompass any economically beneficial goal guarantees that these losses will fall disproportionately on poor communities. Those communities are not only systematically less likely to put their lands to the highest and best social use, but are also the least politically powerful. If ever there were justification for intrusive judicial review of constitutional provisions that protect "discrete and insular minorities," *United States v. Carolene Products Co.*, 304 U.S. 144 (1938), surely that principle would apply with great force to the powerless groups and individuals the Public Use Clause protects.

Those incentives have made the legacy of this Court's "public purpose" test an unhappy one. In the 1950's, no doubt emboldened in part by the expansive understanding of "public use" this Court adopted in *Berman*, cities "rushed to draw plans" for downtown development. B. Frieden & L. Sagalayn, *Downtown, Inc. How America Rebuilds Cities* 17 (1989). "Of all the families displaced by urban renewal from 1949 through 1963, 63 percent of those whose race was known were nonwhite, and of these families, 56 percent of nonwhites and 38 percent of whites had incomes low enough to qualify for public housing, which, however, was seldom available to them." Public works projects in the 1950's and 1960's destroyed predominantly minority communities in St. Paul, Minnesota, and Baltimore, Maryland. In 1981, urban planners in Detroit, Michigan, uprooted the largely "lower-income and elderly" Poletown neighborhood for the benefit of the General Motors Corporation. J. Wylie, *Poletown: Community Betrayed* 58 (1989). Urban renewal projects have long been associated with the displacement of blacks; "in cities across the country, urban renewal came to be known as 'Negro removal.' " Pritchett, The "Public Menace" of Blight: Urban Renewal and the Private Uses of Eminent Domain, 21 *Yale L. & Pol'y Rev.* 1, 47 (2003). Over 97 percent of the individuals forcibly removed from their homes by the "slum-clearance" project upheld by this Court in *Berman* were black. Regrettably, the predictable consequence of the Court's decision will be to exacerbate these effects.

When faced with a clash of constitutional principle and a line of unreasoned cases wholly divorced from the text, history, and structure of our founding document, we should not hesitate to resolve the tension in favor of the Constitution's original meaning. . . ."

The majority opinion in *Kelo* turned out to be very controversial. Even though "it was a modest decision [that] simply applied existing law and deferred to the judgments of local officials," as Adam Liptak wrote in *The Nation*, "[it] provoked outrage from Democrats and Republicans, liberals and libertarians, and everyone betwixt and between."[16] The decision triggered a massive wave of legislation in the State legislatures: 42 states have passed legislation that narrows the language of *Kelo*. Meanwhile, even though there has been, as yet, no Supreme Court decision on takings since *Kelo*, there is a developing concurring jurisprudence in the Federal Appellate and District Courts. To make things even more interesting, at the local level, many municipalities support the *Kelo* decision. National League of Cities which represents 1600 U.S. cities and towns lobbied Congress not to restrict the outcome of the *Kelo* decision.

How can we understand the complex politics of the *Kelo* decision, and the takings doctrine in general? It is too early to discern, with perfect accuracy, the political coalitions behind this struggle between defenders of property rights and governmental regulatory powers. To understand what exactly is taking place students of administrative law should watch the debate unfold in concrete locations, such as courts and legislatures. Meanwhile, in the following excerpt, political scientist Laura Hatcher situ-

16. Adam Liptak, "Case Won on Appeal (to Public)," *The Nation*, July 30, 2006.

ates current debates in an analysis of the politics of property we have just encountered in the *Kelo* decision.

"Economic Libertarians, Property, and Institutions: Linking Activism, Ideas, and Identities among Property Rights Advocates"
LAURA HATCHER

in The Worlds Cause Lawyers Make: Structure and Agency in Legal Practice, *ed. Austin Sarat and Stuart Scheingold (Stanford University Press, 2005), 112.*

[. . .]

The Heart of Laissez Faire

Lawyers of the last half of the past century were focused on encouraging economic growth, clearly believing that it and the ability of individuals to own property were the only ways to ensure individual liberty. They displayed a remarkable ability to translate economic theory as well as political and legal philosophy into legal terms and constitutional devices for their own ends. As Twiss argues . . . *laissez faire* lawyers were able to develop a constitutional doctrine of economic liberty that . . . did have an impact on society . . . and certainly is still available as a tradition within constitutional law on which today's property rights advocates are able to draw. . . .

[L]aissez-faire tradition is actually a set of arguments concerning the importance of the individual, free competition, and the state's appropriate role in economic regulation. . . . [C]ertain legal thinkers were extremely influential in shaping the various positions of the period. One such individual was Thomas M. Cooley who . . . argued that the Constitution is clear in that the Fifth Amendment constrains the federal government from depriving individuals of property without compensation, and that the Fourteenth Amendment supplements the Fifth by providing that no state can take property without due process of the law. . . .

Furthermore, Cooley felt very strongly that all "class legislation" was undemocratic. . . . [H]e argued that any legislation that seem to favor one class over another was unconstitutional, whether it was favoring the rich over the poor or the poor over the rich. This notion of equality before the law was very much a part of the legal landscape by the 1880s. It required that the government exercise a peculiar kind of neutrality where economic issues are involved, refraining from interfering on any-one's behalf regardless of the merits of their claims or the issues of social justice that develop when economic activities are structured in particular ways. . . . Moving these ideas into the law, however, took well over a decade and required . . . highly skilled lawyers. . . .

Twiss suggests that the fine art of persuasion was very much alive in the nineteenth century, as lawyers' pocketbooks, social standings, and clients all benefited from the development of *laissez-faire* jurisprudence. . . . These lawyers were quite often among the best lawyers in the profession and . . . they were [often] also businessmen and politicians, and many helped organize the bar associations in their states or were leaders in pushing for the adoption of the Langdellian case law method in a newly structured law curriculum. Such men included John Archibald Campbell . . . who served on the U.S. Supreme Court from 1853 through 1861 before setting up private practice in New Orleans. . . .

Not only were [Campbell] arguments in the *Slaughterhouse Cases* critical in the late nineteenth century to the development of a *laissez-faire* legal theory, but economic libertarians use these arguments today when promoting their interpretation of the Fourteenth Amendment. In the *Slaughterhouse Cases* he [argued] that the Constitution, particularly the thirteenth and fourteenth amendments, required the federal court to curb Louisiana's regulatory powers. His arguments [put forward] that "citizens" referred to in the fourteenth amendment are all of the citizens of the United States and not only the former slaves. Campbell's argument was at least in part an argument against redistribution of wealth by the governments. Though the U.S. Supreme Court ultimately rejected this claim, Campbell's argument has been resurrected in recent years as a means for protecting small-business owners and other individuals against various types of regulatory actions and as an argument against contemporary redistributive policies. Today, the Institute for Justice makes this claim the most strongly. . . .

Campbell's argument and arguments made by Justice Stephen Field [in *Munn v. Illinois*] provided another attorney, William Evarts, known as the "Prince of the American Bar," strong grounds on which to build work on behalf of corporate clients in cases such as *Munn v. Illinois* (1877). Evarts's significance may have . . . to do with his other professional activities . . . [such as] changes to the legal curriculum as well as the mobilization of bar associations.

It is no coincidence that the ability to make particular types of arguments became a critical aspect of legal education in this period. . . . Law schools became an important training ground for lawyers in "legal science," an ideological activity in which lawyers attempted to regularize legal decisionmaking and argument by a theoretical framework. The importance of this activity for liberal thought, as Gordon explains: "lies in the realm of personal and property rights, which define how far one may go in exercising one's liberty and where one must stop to avoid infringing upon that of others. The state is instituted to define and enforce rights; its medium of rights-definition is law, which both facilitates liberty as freedom of action and protects liberty as security, including security against the state itself."

The *laissez-faire* lawyers of the period hoped to convince judges that the law required them to strike down legislation not conforming to their theory that the state should not interfere with the economic rights of individuals. This theory . . . became part of the jurisprudence of the Supreme Court, despite the Court's initial resistance. . . . But both the initial resistance and its later adoption can be understood as aspects of the legal process—not merely judges who had decided to "switch sides" or whose politics became the only means by which they decided their cases. Rather, through the manipulation of the principles of reasoned argument, *laissez-faire* lawyers were able to gain legal ground.

There were, of course, other things happening in the period that enabled the adoption of these views. Bar associations, often organized by the most conservative lawyers, were developed to maintain the ethnic and class makeup of the bar. . . . Much of this was tied to [the lawyers'] own sense of upward mobility and the belief that if the profession became overrun by "undesirables," it would not be distinctive enough. . . . This suggests that for conservative lawyers, political and economic interests and their legal theories were informing one another in ways that shaped their ideology.

The restrictive membership requirements . . . also provided lawyers with a safe haven where they could discuss their ideas and a platform from which to argue for their world view. By excluding diverse opinions or interests, the lawyers were able to find a consensus based upon similar understandings of the world. . . . These lawyers included many of the same individuals working on behalf of the railroads and other corporate interests, and so they also had powerful connections to business and society. Through their various activities they were able to change the legal landscape over the course of the last two decades of the nineteenth century.

[These] [l]awyers at the time were aided by their ability to be autonomous from the state through the development of lawyering as a "profession," while simultaneously being allied with the state . . . through the judicial process and their relationship with judges. . . . Today's right-wing activists are able to use many of the same means to advance their position, though changes in society and the growth of the legal profession have made it necessary for them to blend old and new strategies.

Those new strategies include lawyering in nonprofit legal foundations and law firms. This form of lawyering . . . have developed in the very late nineteenth century and throughout the twentieth, coinciding with the democratization process, the rise of legal realism, and the growth of the legal profession itself. At its inception, it was connected to the lawyers discussed above, who, concerned with the status of immigrants entering this country, established organizations that later became the models for public-interest lawyering. We often connect such activities in the United States to groups such as the NAACP and the ACLU. However, their strategies became the basis for other groups, including conservatives responding to what they perceive to be a very powerful means of influencing the public's views about what is in its best interest.

Conservatives and the Construction of an "Alternative" Public Interest

The broader conservative movement . . . diminished to some extent during the Progressive Era, but began to gain ground once again . . . after World War II. The Cold War, along with a swiftly changing economy that brought with it many societal changes, provided the basis for the development of the conservative movement that gained momentum throughout the 1960s and swept the political scene in the 1980s. . . .

In the 1940s and 1950s, the differences among the economic libertarians and the "traditional" conservatives were so deep that speaking of a conservative movement was difficult. . . .

Beginning in the mid-1950s, what conservative historian George Nash refers to as "the great fusion" took place. This was a sort of rapprochement among various actors on the right side of the political spectrum. . . .

The Pacific Legal Foundation

The Pacific Legal Foundation (PLF) . . . represents the beginning of nonprofit law firms devoted to right wing

causes and remains one of the most active conservative groups. It has worked in the area of property rights protection for nearly three decades. . . .

In 1973, the PLF was founded in California, during the governorship of Ronald Reagan by two members of his administration, Ronald Zumbrun and Raymond Momboisse. They, along with the California State Chamber of Commerce and other Reagan staffers. . . . hoped to provide a conservative answer to liberal activity by providing the courts with an alternative view of the public interest which would "combat" the Liberals' use of the court. According to the PLF, its founders wanted "to preserve the basic freedoms set out by the U.S. Constitution and reverse the growing trend toward greater government control and influence in American lives."

. . .

The PLF was just the beginning. . . . After . . . its leadership . . . contemplated the possibility of a wider conservative legal movement . . . the National Legal Center for the Public Interest (NLCPI) opened in 1975. The NLCPI was instrumental in establishing a group of public interest law foundations throughout the United States including organizations such as the Mountain States Legal Foundation and the Southeastern Legal Foundation. . . . Today, over a dozen conservative and economic libertarian organizations form a nationwide network of nonprofit organizations litigating "in the public interest" on behalf of property interests as well as in other issue areas.

The Institute for Justice

William Mellor and Clint Bolick, both of whom formerly held positions in President Reagan's administration, founded the Institute for Justice (IJ) in 1991. The IJ claims to be the only true libertarian law group and . . . the best defender of civil rights and liberties. . . . Today, IJ plays an increasingly important role in litigation concerning the Fifth Amendment's takings clause and conservative litigation more generally. Its goal . . . is to "advance a rule of law in which individuals control their destinies as free and responsible members of society." This is strikingly similar to the desires for a regularized legal process where outcomes are predictable that was so salient among *laissez-faire* lawyers . . . and seems to be a characteristic of liberal legal theory.

IJ openly advocates judicial activism, maintaining that the inconsistent record of the legislative and executive branches in protecting essential rights and liberties requires the judiciary to "serve as the bulwark of liberty." An underlying assumption is that the judicial branch must thwart any legislative action that contradicts the Constitution. . . .

Litigation . . . is fundamental to IJ's strategy and the importance of argumentation is key here. Moreover, like the lawyers of 100 years ago, they emphasize having a theory that guides which cases they should take and which arguments they will make. . . .

Among their strategies, the IJ [pursues] various other means for achieving their ends includ[ing] active grass-roots campaign[s] in areas of the country where they are litigating, hoping to "build" public support and foster an ethos of "economic liberty."

The IJ also files *amicus* briefs in major Supreme Court cases . . . and Richard Epstein, a University of Chicago Law School professor, is a frequent co-author of these . . . . His scholarly work undergirds much of this group's property theory. . . . Epstein's briefs are sometimes published and the Institute makes many of their legal documents available online. Through disseminating their ideas in these forms, their theories of property and the individual are presented to a wider audience of legal academics and lawyers.

Other conservative groups, including the PLF . . . appear to understand the role of judges and courts in different ways. The PLF has not always advocated judge made law, but instead argued that judges should show restraint and act as interpreters of the laws legislators make. This tends toward a more traditional conservative theory of judicial decision making. . . .

Among conservatives working to advance property rights, the ideology underpinning beliefs concerning the roles of judges and lawyers as well as the "public interest" is largely the same today as it was in the nineteenth century, despite other shifts in the social context. Thus, their arguments are strikingly similar in both periods. But with the rise of the public interest law practice in the twentieth century, today's lawyers make one tactical move that sets them apart from their nineteenth century predecessors: they do not openly work on behalf of large corporations as the *laissez-faire* lawyers . . . did, but rather position themselves as seeking justice for the "little guy"—quite often, small businesses and private property owners fighting state regulations. The advent of the public interest lawyer in society, then, provides these lawyers with a legal forum that advances their ideology while appearing to work on behalf of disadvantaged individuals. This results in an odd mixture of ideals and language from both centuries. In order to produce this mixture . . . conservative lawyers have formed spaces within the legal academy to develop their theories.

Intellectuals, Property Rights, and the Creation of Safe Havens

As Kalman explains, in the late 1970s and early 1980s, concerns about the lack of conservatives in the legal academy led conservative legalists to call for the creation of spaces that would encourage and support law students interested in pursuing conservative jurisprudence. Quickly thereafter, the Federalist Society took shape as a debating society at Yale Law School, the University of Chicago School of Law, and Harvard Law School, and within a few years, chapters sprang up throughout the country . . . [A]lso an important place for conservative legal scholars . . . was the development of the law and economics movement.

Although both law and economics and the Federalist Society have been linked to conservative political agendas, the law and economics movement . . . is most often considered an "academic movement." . . . There are significant differences in organizational and structural elements; for our purposes . . . the most important aspect of both groups . . . is the way they function as spaces where legal ideology can be formed by conservative lawyers and scholars.

By focusing our attention here, we can see the importance of professional competition in the creation of legal ideologies while exploring the way in which ideas are developed before being implemented through legal advocacy. . . . moreover, we can see that the conditions of it in the legal academy and in this movement of property rights advocates produce certain idioms. It is their potential for elaboration that enables transformation and sustenance for conservative lawyers as these legal ideologies take shape.

Epstein and Posner: Law, Economics, and Utility

In the 1970s, Richard Epstein, now active with the IJ, . . . spent time examining economic analysis of Law. . . . His work eventually led him to critique the concept of utilitarianism as used by Judge Posner and some of the other scholars in the law and economics movement. . . . At the same time . . . he was working out a property theory and an interpretation of the takings clause of the Fifth Amendment that has become critical to many of the rights claims made by lawyers in libertarian cases. . . .

Epstein's critique of utilitarianism and wealth maximization was grounded in his interest in developing a theory of takings that would require compensation by the government for nearly all takings and severely limit eminent domain powers . . . he argues that utilitarianism, when applied to takings issues, would bring about "perverse" results because of the "leaps of faith required."

. . .

Epstein sees this perversity as occurring largely because the state cannot be trusted to make the correct calculations and protect individual rights since ultimately it would always work to protect its own interests. . . .

The more interesting . . . angle in Epstein's argument has to do with the appropriate relationship between the individual and the state. He argued from an almost Hobbesian perspective . . . that in [the] state of nature there were two major failures: the first was to protect against private aggression; and the second was that individuals would not voluntarily work to create a centralized power to combat private aggression. . . . [T]he state was created to rectify both of these problems—but this is really the only purpose of the state. Its work is not to redistribute income or ensure that distributive justice will be done. . . .

Posner took exception to much of Epstein's argument . . . [arguing] . . . that the line between regulation and redistribution is "too uncertain to support the structure of permissions and prohibitions that Epstein erects on it." Posner went on to explain that there were times when we might see rich people hurting . . . poor people and determine that redistribution would be the best form of redress for this situation. . . . But perhaps . . . Posner's most stinging criticism in a community seeking more democratic jurisprudence is that Epstein's theory would, when taken to its final conclusion, prove to be anti democratic. . . .

[T]he disagreement here is over what is truly conservative and what is truly the best form of democratic government. It turns on an epistemological debate: . . . do we find it through philosophical inquiry into natural rights? Or do we find it through the precise evaluation performed through objective criteria? Yet, throughout this debate, there is no doubt that each individual is libertarian at heart . . . Posner and Epstein . . . regard each other as fellow conservatives while simultaneously distinguishing their separate positions. They are, according to each other, libertarians of different stripes. . . .

The Federalist Society: Critiquing and Changing the Legal Academy

Founded in 1982 by five law students, the Federalist Society attracted the most important conservative law scholars, judges, and lawyers to their national meetings. Their mission statement explicitly states their goal as reforming the current legal order: "we are committed to the principles that the state exists to preserve freedom, that the separation of governmental powers is central to our constitution. . . . The Society seeks to promote the awareness of these principles and to further their application through its activities" (Federalist Society 2001a).

. . .

Very shortly after its establishment, luminaries no less prominent than President Ronald Reagan and Attorney General Edwin Meese were among the speakers at Federalist Society meetings, encouraging the development of the organization while also allowing their political views to be aired. By 1985, just three years after the organization was created, Edwin Meese used its meetings as a forum for critiquing the U.S. Supreme Court justices. . . . His use of the meeting as a platform for a critique of the judiciary has been repeated dozens of times over the last two decades. . . .

[T]he society is very action oriented. The practice groups have the continued training of legal professionals at the heart of their activity. The law school debates have the training and development of future lawyers in mind. And the newest division for faculty has the further development of their ideas and careers as an important goal. . . .

In their mission statement, the Federalist Society states that it is "empathically the duty of the judiciary to say what the law is, not what it should be" (Federalist Society 2001a). Given the source of the statement, it would be easy to associate it with the advocacy of original intent. Yet in making this connection, there is a risk of overemphasizing originalism as the only domain of the conservative. . . . As Keith Whittington (1999: 167) has pointed out . . . "a truly conservative approach to judicial interpretation would focus not only a relatively neutral methodology such as originalism but would embrace a more explicitly substantive vision of constitutional meaning that brought it into line with conservative policymaking."

. . .

Since many conservatives agreed that the state exists to protect the individual and therefore [it] should be as small as possible with a free market leading to free people, it is easy to see these differences [between conservatives] as very small ones. Although this might not seem very important, it can mean more statist approaches among traditional conservatives that directly conflict with the right libertarian anti statist approach.

Conclusion: Shifting Strategies in Shifting Contexts

Conservative legal activism did not spontaneously erupt . . . in the 1970s and 1980s. Rather, this activism appears to be part of conservatism and right-wing activity that stretches far back into our history. One issue investigated here is the connection property rights advocates have to the history of *laissez-faire* and its development as an ideology underpinning nineteenth century jurisprudence—not only during the *Lochner* era in Supreme Court history, but also through the development of professional bar associations, changes in law school curriculum, and the development of the legal profession in its modern form. My argument is that these last developments are part of the ideological construction of *laissez-faire* along with the legal academy, and they serve to shape some of the ideas fueling today's conservative legal activism and legal ideology. . . .

Once we move to the last half of the twentieth century we find that in both contexts, the state is attempting to adapt to shifts in capitalism and the economy. In the late twentieth century, some of these changes result in a reaction to the changing structure of property relations occurring through environmental law. Increased environmental protections during the Cold War and increased concern regarding pollution have had the effect of changing relations between landowners, their land, and the state. Conservatives, always concerned with the connection between property and liberty, have mobilized in order to strengthen the due compensation requirements of the takings clause. Against this backdrop and in discussions among lawyers concerning correct interpretation of the property guarantees in the Fifth Amendment, issues arise regarding the rule of law and the appropriate role of the legal profession. The point here is that conservatives are active in both periods in part as a reaction to what they see as expanding regulations that would encroach on individual liberty; and, in both periods we find disagreements among conservatives concerning the role of the state in protecting economic liberties. . . .

Like their nineteenth century counterparts, the right-wing activists I describe rely on the importance of private property and the clear distinction between the public and private spheres to ground their arguments. Individual liberty is seen as a means for ensuring upward economic and social mobility. Equality is defined as the law's neutrality to social differences. And, like their nineteenth century counterparts, they also see the courts as a place to go when others are interfering with individual liberties. . . .

AUERBACH, J. *Unequal Justice.* New York: Oxford University Press, 1975.

ARON, N. *With Liberty and Justice for All: Public Interest in the 1980s and Beyond.* Boulder: Westview Press, 1989.

CAIN, MAUREEN, AND HARRINGTON, CHRISTINE, eds. *Lawyers in a Postmodern World: Translation and Transgression.* New York University Press, 1994.

CONNOR, W. *John Archibald Campbell: Associate Justice of the United States Supreme Court, 1853–1961.* Boston and New York: Houghton Mifflin Company, 1920.

CUSHMAN, B. *Rethinking the New Deal Court: The Structure of a Constitutional Revolution.* Oxford, Miss.: Oxford University Press, 1998.

EPSTEIN, L. *Conservatives in Court.* Knoxville: University of Tennessee Press, 1985.

EPSTEIN, L. "Nuisance Law: Corrective Justice and Its Utilitarian Constraints." *Journal of Legal Studies* 8(3): 477-504.

EPSTEIN, R. *Takings: Private Power and the Power of Eminent Domain.* Cambridge: Harvard University Press, 1985.

FEDERALIST SOCIETY. "Mission Statement." Federalist Society Webpage www.fed-soc.org. Retrieved April 15, 2001.

GILLMAN, H. *The Constitution Besieged: The Rise and Demise of Lochner Era Police Powers Jurisprudence.* Duke University Press, 1993.

GORDON, R. "Legal Thought and Legal Practice in the Age of American Enterprise, 1870–1920." In *Professions and Professional Ideologies in America,* edited by G. Geison. Chapel Hill: University of North Carolina Press, 1983.

HALIDAY, TERRENCE, AND KARPIK, LUCIEN,, eds. *Lawyers and the Rise of Western Political Liberalism.* Oxford and New York: Clarendon Press, 1997.

Institute for Justice website. www.ij.org

KALMAN, L. *Legal Realism at Yale, 1927–1960.* Chapel Hill: University of North Carolina Press, 1986.

MINDA, G. *Postmodern Legal Movements: Law and Jurisprudence at Century's End.* New York: New York University Press, 1995.

NASH, G. H. *The Conservative Intellectual Movement in America Since 1945.* New York: Basic Books, 1996.

O'CONNOR, KAREN, AND EPSTEIN, LEE. "The Rise of Conservative Interest Group Litigation." *Journal of Politics* 45 (1983): 479–489;

POSNER, RICHARD. *The Problems of Jurisprudence.* Cambridge: Harvard University Press, 1993.

POWELL, M. *From Patrician to Professional Elite: The Transformation of the New York City Bar Association.* New York: Russell Sage Foundation, 1988.

TWISS, BENJAMIN. *Lawyers and the Constitution: How Laissez Faire Came to the Supreme Court.* Princeton, N.J.: Princeton University Press, 1942.

WHITTINGTON, KEITH. *Constitutional Interpretation: Textual Meaning, Original Intent and Judicial Review.* Lawrence: University Press of Kansas, 1999.

THE DELEGATION DOCTRINE

Can Congress delegate its legislative powers to administrative agencies? A strict reading of Article I of the Constitution and the principle of separation of powers establishes the doctrine that Congress may not delegate away the legislative powers that have been delegated to it by the Constitution: "All legislative powers herein granted shall be vested in the Congress of the United States." The Latin phrase *delegata potestas non potest delegari* means that no delegated powers can be further delegated. Applied to American politics, it signifies that powers delegated to Congress by the Constitution may not be redelegated. This is what we call the *nondelegation doctrine.*

However, the constitutional provision that all legislative powers shall be vested in the Congress does not forbid every form of delegation by Congress. Legislative powers granted to Congress also include the "implied powers" of Article I, section 8, which give Congress the necessary resources of flexibility and practicality to perform its legislative functions. The constitutional problem of delegation is therefore part of the Constitution itself. Our concern with delegation focuses on three questions:

1. Does Congress in fact possess the particular power that it purports to delegate? This question refers to the constitutionality of acts that delegate powers to other branches of government. Congress must first have the power before it can delegate it to another branch.

2. What are the conditions or guidelines for delegation?

3. Do the actions of those officials to whom power is delegated fall within the scope of the statute which delegates authority?

We can begin to understand how the courts have addressed these questions, and hence given constitutional support for delegating authority to administrative agencies, by turning to an early case from 1892, *Field v. Clark*.[17] In this case, an exporting company challenged the constitutionality of the Reciprocal Tariff Act passed by Congress in 1890, on the grounds that it unconstitutionally delegated legislative powers to another branch of government. The act granted the president the authority to transfer certain articles (tea and sugar) from the duty-free list to the duty list if other countries were treating U.S. exports "unequally." The Supreme Court upheld the statute while reaffirming the nondelegation doctrine. The Court reasoned that Congress itself had said what duties would be charged to what products and thus it had established the policy which the president was to merely execute. The president's authority to make such determinations, the Court argued, did not delegate legislative power, but rather supplied *factual details* to activate an already established legislative policy.

Within twenty years of the *Field v. Clark* cases, the Supreme Court unanimously held in *United States v. Grimaud* (1911)[18] that officials may lawfully be given far greater authority than the power to recognize factual details which may be the triggering conditions for executing legislative policy. The Court admitted that it was difficult to define the line between legislative power to make laws and administrative authority to make regulations: "There is no analytical difference, no difference in kind, between the legislative function—of prescribing rules for the future that is exercised by the legislature or by the agency implementing the authority conferred by the legislature."[19] The Court concluded that the problem of distinguishing legislative policymaking from administrative duties could only be resolved by placing clear *limits* on the powers that are delegated to agencies.

In *Hampton & Co. v. United States* (1928)[20] the Supreme Court formulated a general rule for placing such limits on administration. The Court said that when reviewing challenges to statutory delegation, delegation should be upheld where Congress has provided agencies with an *intelligible principle* to follow. The intelligible principle standard gave broad powers of delegation to Congress, while at the same time seeming to serve as a limit on administrative authority. The Court justified broad delegation on the grounds that there were practical limits on

17. 143 U.S. 649.

18. 220 U.S. 506.
19. Ibid.
20. 276 U.S. 394.

legislative time and expertise, thus delegation was a "necessity" of modern government.

The necessity argument for delegation became central to the architects of the New Deal. Indeed, Congress's strategy for recovering from the Great Depression took the argument for broad regulation to its extreme when it authorized the president to approve codes of "fair competition" established by *private* trade associations and business executives. According to Section 3 of the National Industrial Recovery Act (NIRA), these private groups were to be "truly representative" of their industry, and the codes could not, at least on their face, work to put smaller operators out of business. Once final, the codes bound businesses with the force of law, and fines could be imposed on those who violated the codes. In *Schechter Poultry Corp. v. United States* (1935) the Supreme Court held this delegation unconstitutional.[21] The NIRA, it said, set no limits or standards for the kinds of things the codes would cover. Worse, the statute prescribed no detailed procedures for actually making the codes. The act amounted to a legislative delegation of the entire process of making laws in this emergency to the executive and private enterprise. Such total delegation violates the constitutional requirement that Congress make the laws.

Since *Schechter*, opponents of bureaucratic power have often argued that if an authorizing statute was so broad and standardless that it fell afoul of the Constitution. Yet the courts have, with a few state court exceptions, upheld all statutes against the charge of overbroad delegation. The Supreme Court has approved Congress's turning over to the secretary of the interior the job of determining how the competing states of Arizona and California should share the scarce waters of the Colorado River.[22] It upheld President Nixon's sudden imposition of wage and price controls in 1971.[23]

In theory, the line the courts have drawn between *Schechter* and the permissible delegations makes sense. The delegation must be specific enough to allow the courts to discern the statute's limits and tell when the agencies have gone too far. Courts allow agencies to make law within these limits. Thus in the wage and price control case cited a moment ago, the late (and great) Judge Harold Leventhal stated:

The key question is not answered by noting that the authority delegation is broad. . . . The issue is whether the legislative description of the task assigned sufficiently marks the field within which the Administrator is to act so that it may be known whether he has kept within it in compliance with the legislative will. . . . The principle permitting a delegation of legislative power, if there has been sufficient demarcation of the field to permit a judgment whether the agency has kept within the legislative will, establishes a principle of accountability under which compatibility with the legislative design may be ascertained not only by Congress but by the courts and the public.[24]

Given the practical limits on legislative time and expertise, the courts really have no choice but to grant legislatures broad delegative authority. Most statutes meet the delegation test by defining a general area of policy concern—the regulation of broadcasting or interstate transportation, for example—and requiring the agency to do what is "reasonably necessary in the public interest." In practice, then, the delegations in *Schechter* and in *Arizona v. California* differ in degree more than kind, and not much in degree at that.[25]

Louis Jaffe, a Harvard law professor and an influential scholar in administrative law reform, discusses the concept of administration under the broad delegation model in the following essay.

---

21. 295 U.S. 495.
22. *Arizona v. California*, 373 U.S. 546 (1963).
23. *Amalgamated Meat Cutters etc. v. Connally*, 337 F. Supp. 737 (1971).

24. Ibid. at 737, 746.
25. State administrative law generally follows federal law on this matter. See *Chartiers Valley Joint Schools v. Allegheny Co. Board of School Directors*, 418 Pa. 520 (1965). In criminal law, which is based mostly on state law, a variation of the delegation doctrine retains some validity. The variation, called the vagueness doctrine, prevents legislatures from authorizing police to arrest people under loosely drawn vagrancy statutes. See *Papachristou v. City of Jacksonville*, 405 U.S. 156 (1972). The courts do not require that agencies, as a matter of internal operations, adopt a separation of powers model. Thus in *Withrow v. Larkin*, 421 U.S. 35 (1975), the Supreme Court ruled that a state board charged with the task of licensing physicians could investigate charges, adjudicate them, and order suspensions of licenses all in one process involving the same personnel. See chapter 12.

The Illusion of the Ideal Administration

LOUIS L. JAFFE

Harvard Law Review 86 (1973): 1183

It is once again fashionable to advocate what may be called the "broad delegation model" of administrative agencies, as both a description of what agencies are and a prescription of what they ought to be. Professor Kenneth Davis, for example, believes that an administrator is to be given broad jurisdiction over a field; preferably, as a matter of principle the ends and means should not be highly defined by the legislature. The agency then proceeds to "regulate" in the "public interest"—to reach decisions on the major policy questions for which Congress "was neither equipped nor willing" to supply clear answers. At the same time, the theory goes, the administrator has the power and the *duty* continuously to evolve rules—partly as a way of doing a job, partly as a way of providing due process for affected interests. The emphasis here is on an administration as a ready, all-purpose, efficient mechanism, which legitimizes itself by reducing its discretion and power potential through rulemaking.

This concept of administration provides a fertile ground in which criticisms of administrative agencies readily take root. The broader the power defined as appropriate for exercise by an agency, the greater the frustration of the critic who finds that the state of the regulated world is not to his tastes. The assumption that a vague delegation to regulate in the public interest yields a standard which is readily discoverable by an administrator provokes objection when results do not comport with one or another individual's concept of what the "public interest" requires. Thus, paradoxically, the more vague a delegation, the more likely the charge that an agency has failed to fulfill its congressional mandate.

To my mind, the broad delegation model is subject to numerous objections. It does not adequately or accurately describe the variety of processes which characterize administration. More important, it permits false implications and creates damaging expectations with respect to those agencies it does purport to describe. It assumes that "to regulate" has some meaning apart from the specific purposes of Congress, and that an objective has been established that is capable of disinterested and nonpolitical administration and amplification by a body variously denominated as "independent," "expert," or "neutral." In my opinion, these assumptions . . . lead to ill-founded and futile criticisms of the administrative process. . . .

In a classic article published in 1887, Woodrow Wilson found that "large powers and unhampered discretion," which seemed to him to be "the indispensable conditions of responsibility,"[26] are the essence of administration. "There is not danger in power, if only it be not irresponsible. If it be divided, dealt out in shares to many, it is obscured; and if it be obscured, it is made irresponsible." In Wilson's view, the greater the power delegated the less likely it is that an administrative official will abuse it.[27]

It may be that if the delegate is highly visible, as is the President, broad powers promote responsibility. But especially in the inordinately complex administration of our day, visibility is low and constituencies ill-defined, so that our experience does not confirm Wilson's analysis.

A view almost totally opposed to Wilson's was advanced by Ernst Freund, a professor who did not aspire to power and did not become Governor of New Jersey and President of the United States. In his opinion, "with regard to major matters the appropriate sphere of delegated authority is where there are no controversial issues of policy or of opinion."[28] Thus, a liberal delegation to regulate safety, a matter which is "purely technical," is permissible, though even here "direct statutory regulation may be preferred."[29]

Freund's model of administration may be seen as peculiarly reflecting a *laissez-faire* role for government. Freund believed that broad administrative powers would invariably be manipulated in one direction or another—in his time, he believed that it would in the direction of the wage earner, the consumer, the passenger who "will frankly and sincerely claim that his interest is identical with the public welfare."[30] Though he would have preferred legislative solutions of such conflicts of interest, Freund recognized that administrative experiments were inevitable. His preference as to the character of such administration was much influenced by continental scholarship, with its concepts of administrative law and law in general. His ideal can be seen as equivalent to that of Max Weber[31]—the rational bureaucracy as a more or less insu-

26. Woodrow Wilson, "The Study of Administration," *Political Science Quarterly* 2 (1887): 197, 213; reprinted in *Political Science Quarterly* 56 (1941): 481.

27. Ibid. at 214.

28. Ernst Freund, *Administrative Powers over Persons and Property* (University of Chicago Press, 1928), 218.

29. Ibid. See also Ibid. at 221 (delegated rulemaking "ought to be confined to noncontroversial matter of a technical character").

30. Ibid. at 31.

31. See, e.g. Max Weber, *The Theory of Social and Economic Organization*, ed. Talcott Parsons (Glencoe, Ill.: Free Press, 1964), 324–423.

lated, nonpolitical, expert hierarchy acting pursuant to an authoritative statement of ends and means. . . .

Freund's concept of administration seems to me very ill-conceived, given the degree of government involvement in the highly complex conditions of our own time. Lawmaking may appropriately take place in a variety of contexts—legislative, administrative, and judicial—each of which, by its structure or way of dealing with a problem, may have something to contribute. Freund's rigid limitation of policymaking to the legislature would make modern government impossible and would deprive us of many fruitful solutions.

The Depression and the collapse of confidence in *laissez-faire* and in minimum government triggered a rebirth of the Wilsonian notion of salvation by open-ended administration. Dean Landis' famous lectures, *The Administrative Process*,[32] espoused a paradigm of broad delegation which was the icon of the New Deal. His model was an organization with all the powers of government—legislative, executive, judicial—to make decisions in a field as the problems arose. The objectives were loosely defined; solutions were to be evolved by presumed experts. The assumed predicates were a body of technology relevant to the solution of problems in the field and a consequent self-sufficiency or autonomy, implying an immunity from the political process. While reminiscent of the Weberian model of a bureaucracy thoroughly motored and controlled by rational elaboration, Landis' model administration derived its content and its authority, not from legislative or imperial dictates, but from an assumed comprehensive body of expertise available for the implementation of legislative grants of authority. One suspects that the description, coming as it did in the heyday of the New Deal from one of its most important intellectuals, included the subconscious assumption of an expertise informed by the values of the New Deal. As long as New Dealers were in control and a powerful public opinion supported them, the new agencies performed very well as judged by those who created them.[33]

But we came to see that the Landis model, if taken as generalization valid for all administrative agencies at all times, makes certain untenable assumptions: the existence in each case of relevant, value-free concepts, and an administration located at any given moment of time

outside the political process, that is to say, outside or insulated from the power structure. It is ironic that two of the agencies so much relied on by Landis, the Federal Trade Commission and the Interstate Commerce Commission, were even when he wrote proving to be ineffective; indeed, the ICC was actually destructive of the economic health of the transportation industry.

Because these and other agencies did not keep pace with the demands made for progressive adaptation, the Landis theory gave ground to the "capture theory," which asserts that agencies become the captives of the industries which they are charged to regulate. This theory . . . grossly exaggerat[es] the germ of truth which it does indeed embody. The regulated—their interests and the pressures they exert—are very significant components in the power complex, but the theory focuses on them to the exclusion of other components. It ignores as well as the truth in the Landis thesis that there are significant inputs from a bureaucracy as such: expertness, tradition, stability, and an organization one of whose values is the rationalized exercise of power. And so, a return to the classic Landis model of broad delegation has taken place.

. . . I would propose a view of administration which recognizes the peculiar political process which provides the milieu and defines the operation of each agency. The elements of this political process are common to all potential lawmaking activity—the intensity of a given problem, the degree to which it is felt throughout an organized and stable constituency, and the representation (or lack thereof) of varying interests within and without the lawmaking body. The significance of each of these elements and the manner of their interaction are unpredictable, and likely to vary with each successive problem. Often the outcome will be determined not by the abstracted merits of a situation, but by the character of certain interests which are cohesive and vociferous. The more important point . . . is that the extent to which an agency is open—influenced by and responsive to a political process—is determined by the definiteness and specificity of the congressional expression of the agency's methods and objectives.

Taking the highly articulated scheme for tax administration as polar, one can proceed through a spectrum of agencies whose ends and means are less well defined and which, as a consequence, are to a greater or lesser extent centrally positioned in the uncertainties and structural deficiencies of the political process. Where the ends and means of an agency's role are highly defined, elaborately rationalized—as is the case with tax or social

32. James Landis, *The Administrative Process* (New Haven: Yale University Press, 1938).

33. Indeed, Landis recognized the role of favorable public opinion. See Ibid. at 61 ("The agency must have friends, friends who can give it substantial political assistance. . . .").

security—the effects of the political process on the agency are marginal, though rationalization could never go so far as totally to exclude political choice. In such agencies, the bureaucratic virtues and vices are predominant; highly rationalized administrations embody the advantages of stability, equality of treatment, order, comprehensibility and predictability, and the defects of rigidity and displacement of objectives by bureaucratic routine. Such agencies are to be judged in terms of their fair, uniform, and zealous application of well-articulated law; the very precision of the law may help to reduce pressures from the regulated. . . .

On the other hand, where in form or in substance the legislative design is incomplete, uncertain, or inchoate, a political process will take place in and around the agency, with the likely outcome a function of the usual variables which determine the product of lawmaking institutions. Each agency functions in a political milieu peculiar to itself, and reflects in its own way the virtues and vices or, if you will, the potential and limitations of a bureaucratic process. To the extent that an administration is an open one, it will have some potential for change and for meeting problems difficult to resolve or not yet ready to be resolved at other levels. To round out the portrait, it should be noted that the political framework in which the agency is situated is the primary, but not the only, factor determining the likelihood and nature of its action. Also relevant are technical elements—the state of information and the maturity of thinking on a given problem, and the rate of change in the area as it bears on the possibility of a stable solution. Finally, the potential for action may be greater or less, depending on the competence and political character of the agency's leadership, the talents and depth of its staff, and the esprit de corps, as it were, of the entire operation.

This analysis of agencies in terms of the political factors surrounding and affecting them leads me to question the notion that broad delegation is inherently preferable. It does not make sense to say that the burdens of the congressional workload and the pressure exerted by opposing political forces preclude a detailed legislative solution to a given problem, so that vague, general delegation is the better or the only alternative. The monumental detail of the tax code suggests that Congress can, and does, legislate with great specificity when it regards a matter as sufficiently important. Nor can a political conflict be avoided by relegating a problem to the care of an agency and invoking the talisman of "expertise." The effect of such a transfer of function is simply to shift the legislative process to a different level, and there is no reason to believe that the agency will be able to rise above power conflicts to achieve solutions that the legislature itself cannot or does not choose to provide. . . .

. . . The action or inaction of an agency acting under a broad delegation is often the result of the political process operating on the agency, and is, after all, all that can be expected. Indeed, the criticisms of administration must be recognized as themselves a component of the political process, and critics' invocation of the "public interest" as a standard with readily discoverable content should be viewed as but a useful tactic in the political debate.

Jaffe's essay cogently reminds us that *all* administrative decision making has very significant political consequences. He raises the distinct possibility that few "hedgerow" guidelines from Congress, combined with a reliance upon special administrative "expertise," do *not* automatically justify broad and unchecked delegation of policymaking power to agencies.[34] As you read the *Mistretta* case, ask yourself whether you believe that this delegation maximizes the feasible reduction of arbitrariness of policy in the area of criminal sentencing.

Mistretta v. United States

488 U.S. 361 (1989) 8-1
+ *Blackmun, Rehnquist, White, Marshall, Stevens,*
  O'Connor, Kennedy
+/– *Brennan*
– *Scalia*

[Congress passed the Sentencing Reform Act of 1984 to correct disparities in criminal sentences imposed by federal judges on similarly situated offenders, and to resolve persistent uncertainties about an offender's prison release date. The Act created the United States Sentencing Commission as an independent body within the Judicial Branch with power to promulgate mandatory sentencing guidelines containing a range of sentences

34. Theodore Lowi's *The End of Liberalism* (New York: Norton, 1979) makes this argument more passionately.

for all categories of federal offenses and defendants according to specific and detailed factors. The trial court upheld the constitutionality of the sentencing guidelines against claims by Mistretta, who was charged with selling cocaine, that the Commission was constituted in violation of the separation-of-powers principle, and that Congress had delegated excessive authority to the Commission to create the guidelines.]

Justice Blackmun delivered the opinion of the Court

Petitioner argues that in delegating the power to promulgate sentencing guidelines for every federal criminal offense to an independent Sentencing Commission, Congress has granted the Commission excessive legislative discretion in violation of the constitutionally based nondelegation doctrine. We do not agree.

The nondelegation doctrine is rooted in the principle of separation of powers that underlies our tripartite system of government. . . . In a passage now enshrined in our jurisprudence, Chief Justice Taft, writing for the Court, explained our approach to such co-operative ventures: "In determining what [Congress] may do in seeking assistance from another branch, the extent and character of that assistance must be fixed according to common sense and the inherent necessities of the government co-ordination." *J. W. Hampton, Jr., & Co. v. United States* (1928). So long as Congress "shall lay down by legislative act an intelligible principle to which the person or body authorized to [exercise the delegated authority] is directed to conform, such legislative action is not a forbidden delegation of legislative power."

Applying this "intelligible principle" test to congressional delegations, our jurisprudence has been driven by a practical understanding that in our increasingly complex society, replete with ever changing and more technical problems, Congress simply cannot do its job absent an ability to delegate power under broad general directives. Accordingly, this Court has deemed it "constitutionally sufficient if Congress clearly delineates the general policy, the public agency which is to apply it, and the boundaries of this delegated authority."

Until 1935, this Court never struck down a challenged statute on delegation grounds. After invalidating in 1935 two statutes as excessive delegations, see *A.L.A. Schechter Poultry Corp. v. United States* (1935), and *Panama Refining Co.*

v. Ryan [1935], we have upheld, again without deviation, Congress' ability to delegate power under broad standards.

In light of our approval of these broad delegations, we harbor no doubt that Congress' delegation of authority to the sentencing Commission is sufficiently specific and detailed to meet constitutional requirements. Congress charged the Commission with three goals: to "assure the meeting of the purposes of sentencing as set forth" in the Act; to "provide certainty and fairness in meeting the purposes of sentencing, avoiding unwarranted sentencing disparities among defendants with similar records while maintaining sufficient flexibility to permit individualized sentences," where appropriate; and to "reflect to the extent practicable, advancement in knowledge of human behavior as it relates to the criminal justice process." Congress further specified four "purposes" of sentencing that the Commission must pursue in carrying out its mandate: "to reflect the seriousness of the offense, to promote respect for the law, and to provide just punishment for the offense"; "to afford adequate deterrence to criminal conduct"; "to protect the public from further crimes of the defendant"; and "to provide the defendant with needed correctional treatment."

In addition, Congress prescribed the specific tool—the guidelines system—for the Commission to use in regulating sentencing. More particularly, Congress directed the Commission to develop a system of "sentencing ranges" applicable "for each category of offense involving each category of defendant."[35]

Congress instructed the Commission that these sentencing ranges must be consistent with pertinent provisions of Title 18 of the United States Code and could not include sentences in excess of the statutory maxima. Congress also required that for sentences of imprisonment, "the maximum of the range established for such a term shall not exceed the minimum of that range by more than the

---

35. Congress mandated that the guidelines include:
     (A) a determination whether to impose a sentence to probation, a fine, or a term of imprisonment;
     (B) a determination as to the appropriate amount of a fine or the appropriate length of a term of probation or a term of imprisonment;
     (C) a determination whether a sentence to a term of imprisonment should include a requirement that the defendant be placed on a term of supervised release after imprisonment, and, if so, the appropriate length of such a term; and
     (D) a determination whether multiple sentences to terms of imprisonment should be ordered to run concurrently or consecutively. 28 U.S.C. §994(a)(1).

greater of 25 percent or 6 months, except that, if the minimum term of the range is 30 years or more, the maximum may be life imprisonment." Moreover, Congress directed the Commission to use current average sentences "as a starting point" for its structuring of the sentencing ranges.

To guide the Commission in its formulation of offense categories, Congress directed it to consider seven factors: the grade of the offense; the aggravating and mitigating circumstances of the crime; the nature and degree of the harm caused by the crime; the community view of the gravity of the offense; the public concern generated by the crime; the deterrent effect that a particular sentence may have on others; and the current incidence of the offense. Congress set forth 11 factors for the Commission to consider in establishing categories of defendants. These include the offender's age, education, vocational skills, mental and emotional condition, physical condition (including drug dependence), previous employment record, family ties and responsibilities, community ties, role in the offense, criminal history, and degree of dependence upon crime for a livelihood.[36] Congress also prohibited the Commission from considering the "race, sex, national origin, creed, and socio-economic status of offenders," and instructed that the guidelines should reflect the "general inappropriateness" of considering certain other factors, such as current unemployment, that might serve as proxies for forbidden factors.

In addition to these overarching constraints, Congress provided even more detailed guidance to the Commission about categories of offenses and offender characteristics. Congress directed that guidelines require a term of confinement at or near the statutory maximum for certain crimes of violence and for drug offenses, particularly when committed by recidivists. Congress further directed that the Commission assure a substantial term of imprisonment for an offense constituting a third felony conviction, for a career felon, for one convicted of a managerial role in a racketeering enterprise, for a crime of violence by an offender on release from a prior felony conviction, and for an offense involving a substantial quantity of narcotics. Congress also instructed "that the guidelines reflect the general appropriateness of imposing a term of imprisonment" for a crime of violence that resulted in serious bodily injury. On the other hand, Congress direct-

ed that guidelines reflect the general inappropriateness of imposing a sentence of imprisonment "in cases in which the defendant is a first offender who has not been convicted of a crime of violence or an otherwise serious offense." Congress also enumerated various aggravating and mitigating circumstances, such as, respectively, multiple offenses or substantial assistance to the Government, to be reflected in the guidelines. In other words, although Congress granted the Commission substantial discretion in formulating guidelines, in actuality it legislated a full hierarchy of punishment—from near maximum imprisonment, to substantial imprisonment, to some imprisonment, to alternatives—and stipulated the most important offense and offender characteristics to place defendants within these categories.

We cannot dispute petitioner's contention that the Commission enjoys significant discretion in formulating guidelines. The Commission does have discretionary authority to determine the relative severity of federal crimes and to assess the relative weight of the offender characteristics that Congress listed for the Commission to consider. (Commission instructed to consider enumerated factors as it deems them to be relevant.) The Commission also has significant discretion to determine which crimes have been punished too leniently, and which too severely. Congress has called upon the Commission to exercise its judgment about which types of crimes and which types of criminals are to be considered similar for the purposes of sentencing.[37] Our cases do not at all suggest that delegations of this type may not carry with them the need to exercise judgment on matters of policy.

Developing proportionate penalties for hundreds of different crimes by a virtually limitless array of offenders is precisely the sort of intricate, labor intensive task for which delegation to an expert body is especially appropriate. Although Congress has delegated significant discretion to the Commission to draw judgments from its analysis of existing sentencing practice and alternative sentencing models, "Congress is not confined to that method of executing its policy which involves the least possible delegation of discretion to administrative officers." We have no doubt that in the hands of the Commission "the criteria which

36. Again, the legislative history provides additional guidance for the Commission's consideration of the statutory factors.

37. Petitioner argues that the excessive breadth of Congress's delegation to the Commission is particularly apparent in the Commission's considering whether to "reinstate" the death penalty for some or all of those crimes for which capital punishment is still authorized in the Federal Criminal code.

Congress has supplied are wholly adequate for carrying out the general policy and purpose" of the Act.

Having determined that Congress has set forth sufficient standards for the exercise of the Commission's delegated authority, we turn to Mistretta's claim that the Act violates the constitutional principle of separation of powers.

Mistretta argues that the Act suffers from each of these constitutional infirmities. He argues that Congress, in constituting the Commission as it did, effected an unconstitutional accumulation of power within the Judicial Branch while at the same time undermining the Judiciary's independence and integrity. Specifically, petitioner claims that in delegating to an independent agency within the Judicial Branch the power to promulgate sentencing guidelines, Congress unconstitutionally has required the Branch, and individual Article III judges, to exercise not only their judicial authority, but legislative authority—the making of sentencing policy—as well. Such rulemaking authority, petitioner contends, may be exercised by Congress, or delegated by Congress to the Executive, but may not be delegated to or exercised by the Judiciary.

According to petitioner, Congress, consistent with the separation of powers, may not upset the balance among the Branches by co-opting federal judges into the quintessentially political work of establishing sentencing guidelines, by subjecting those judges to the political whims of the Chief Executive, and by forcing judges to share their power with nonjudges.

Although the unique composition and responsibilities of the Sentencing Commission give rise to serious concerns about a disruption of the appropriate balance of governmental power among the coordinate Branches, we conclude, upon close inspection, that petitioner's fears for the fundamental structural protection of the Constitution prove, at least in this case, to be "more smoke than fire," and do not compel us to invalidate Congress' considered scheme for resolving the seemingly intractable dilemma of excessive disparity in criminal sentencing.

We conclude that in creating the Sentencing Commission—an unusual hybrid in structure and authority—Congress neither delegated excessive legislative power nor upset the constitutionally mandated balance of powers among the coordinate Branches. The Constitution's structural protections do not prohibit Congress from delegating to an expert body located within the Judicial Branch the intricate task of formulating sentencing guidelines consistent with such significant statutory direction as is present here. Nor does our system of checked and balanced authority prohibit Congress from calling upon the accumulated wisdom and experience of the Judicial Branch in creating policy on a matter uniquely within the ken of judges. Accordingly, we hold that the Act is constitutional.

Justice Scalia, dissenting

While the products of the Sentencing Commission's labors have been given the modest name "Guidelines," they have the force and effect of laws, prescribing the sentences criminal defendants are to receive. A judge who disregards them will be reversed. I dissent from today's decision because I can find no place within our constitutional system for an agency created by Congress to exercise no governmental power other than the making of laws.

It should be apparent from the above that the decisions made by the Commission are far from technical, but are heavily laden (or ought to be) with value judgments and policy assessments.

The whole theory of *lawful* congressional "delegation" is not that Congress is sometimes too busy or too divided and can therefore assign its responsibility of making law to someone else; but rather that a certain degree of discretion, and thus of law-making, *inheres* in most executive or judicial action, and it is up to Congress, by the relative specificity or generality of its statutory commands, to determine—up to a point—how small or how large that degree shall be . . . to take examples closer to the case before us: Trial judges could be given the power to determine what factors justify a greater or lesser sentence within the statutorily prescribed limits because that was ancillary to their exercise of the judicial power of pronouncing sentence upon individual defendants. And the President, through the Parole Commission subject to his appointment and removal, could be given the power to issue Guidelines specifying when parole would be available, because that was ancillary to the President's exercise of the executive power to hold and release federal prisoners. . . .

The situation is no different in principle from what would exist if Congress gave the same power of writing sentencing laws to a congressional agency such as the General Accounting Office, or to members of its staff.

The delegation of lawmaking authority to the Commission is, in short, unsupported by any legitimating theory to explain why it is not a delegation of legislative power. To disregard structural legitimacy is wrong in itself—but since structure has purpose, the disregard also has adverse practical consequences. In this case, as suggested earlier, the consequence is to facilitate and encourage judicially uncontrollable delegation.

By reason of today's decision, I anticipate that Congress will find delegation of its lawmaking powers much more attractive in the future. If rulemaking can be entirely unrelated to the exercise of judicial or executive powers, I foresee all manner of "expert" bodies, insulated from the political process, to which Congress will delegate various portions of its lawmaking responsibility. How tempting to create an expert Medical Commission (mostly MDs, with perhaps a few PhDs in moral philosophy) to dispose of such thorny, "no-win" political issues as the withholding of life-support systems in federally funded hospitals, or the use of fetal tissue for research. This is an undemocratic precedent that we set—not because of the scope of the delegated power, but because its recipient is not one of the three Branches of Government. The only governmental power the Commission possesses is the power to make law; and it is not the Congress.

Since *Mistretta* the Supreme Court has not changed its approach to cases involving challenges to the delegation of powers to administrative agencies. The "ghost of delegation," briefly revived in *Whitman v. American Trucking Associations, Inc. et al.*, 531 U.S. 457 (2001), was immediately "exorcised"[38] by a unanimous Supreme Court decision reversing the D.C. Circuit's judgment that EPA's application of Section 109 (b)(1) of the Clean Air Act violated the delegation doctrine. Justice Scalia's opinion, stressing once again that the Court has "almost never felt qualified to second guess Congress regarding the permissible degree of policy judgment that can be left to those executing or applying," has added renewed strength to already strong precedent for non-intervention by the Court in matters of delegation to administrative agencies.

We would like to end this chapter with a reminder: While the "doctrine of nondelegation" strictly defined applies only to delegation of legislative power to administrative agencies by the Congress, other forms of delegation deserve attention as well. While not an administrative agency like the EPA or the FCC, the Office of Attorney General of the United States nevertheless has been at the center of debates and lawsuits about delegation. The most recent of these cases, *Gonzales v. Oregon*, 546 U.S. 243 (2006) centered around the question of whether the United States Attorney General's delegated powers allow him to enforce the Controlled Substances Act against physicians who prescribe drugs for assisted suicide, a lawful practice under the recently accepted laws of the state of Oregon. In a 6-3 opinion, the Supreme Court answered this question in the negative, ruling that the Controlled Substances Act did not authorize the Attorney General to declare illegal a medical practice that is authorized by state law.

Thus expanded, the question of delegation intersects with recent political trends, particularly globalization and privatization, to generate a new set of questions about minimizing the level of arbitrariness in government. On one hand, the increasingly globalized nature of certain problems, notably environmental issues, generates the need for policy responses coordinated at the international level. Domestic application of such policy responses raises questions about the constitutionality of those policies, challenging the relatively neat distinction of national and international lawmaking. In a recent case, *Natural Resources Defense Council v. EPA* (2006),[39] the D.C. Circuit Court confronted the question whether Congress can delegate lawmaking power to an international treaty-making body. The Natural Resources Defense Council in this case argued that EPA had violated a provision of the Clean Air Act that requires EPA to abide by the Montreal Protocol. The alleged violation, however, occurred as a result of violation of a post-ratification agreement to implement the Protocol. The question therefore was whether such a post-ratification agreement implemented by an international body constitutes "law," in which case the Congress would have improperly granted its lawmaking power to

38. See Craig Oren, "Whitman v. American Trucking Associations—The Ghost of Delegation Revived . . . and Exorcised," in *Administrative Law Stories*, ed. Peter Strauss (New York: Foundation Press, 2006), 7–44.

39. 464 F.3d 1.

an international body. In an exercise of judicial restraint, the judges hearing the case in the United States Court of Appeals for the District of Columbia Circuit declined to resolve the issue on the grounds that doing so would raise serious constitutional questions.

On the other hand, privatization of state services and increasing contracting out of governmental programs, i.e., the delegation of governmental functions to private agencies, raise questions about the constitutionality of such delegations. While here the question is not one of "lawmaking" power, the provision of governmental services such as welfare, prison, or schools, raises serious constitutional questions, notably about due process.

EXERCISES AND QUESTIONS FOR FURTHER THOUGHT

1. Surely limited government, the main theme of this chapter, can hardly be taken for granted, as the dramatic story of Abner Louima illustrates. In 1997, two uniformed police officers brutally sodomized Louima with a stick in a Brooklyn, New York, police station, acting on the mistaken belief that Louima had punched one of the officers on the street some time earlier. Louima was hospitalized for several months and nearly died from the injuries. Police witnesses testified that one of the defendants brandished the feces-stained stick and bragged about getting even. In a political culture committed to limited government, such a violation of law would be unthinkable. Sadly, in our culture Louima's case seemed exceptional because the witnesses were willing to limit the power of one of their own. They overcame the normal impulse of a person not to "rat" on his or her colleagues. Administrative law cases are rarely so dramatic. However, we urge you to keep in mind that the fundamental reason for caring about administrative law is that it, like laws against police brutality, is the primary cultural tool we possess that distinguishes us from an authoritarian police state so vividly illustrated by Louima's tormentors and, at virtually the same time, by Slobodan Milosevic's Serbia in the 1999 Balkan War.[40]

2. How is the "freedom of contract" limitation on regulatory power under the due process clause similar to and different from the "takings clause" limitation on regulatory power?

3. This chapter reviewed the rise and fall of the due process protection of property rights starting over 100 years ago and ending in FDR's New Deal in the 1930s. It also suggested that the recent "takings clause" cases awarding money compensation for regulatory limits on the use of real estate may indicate a conservative swing back in the pro-property direction. Is this a desirable development? If the courts used a case like *Dolan* as a model for all administrative law decisions, how might administrative policymaking change? Might it become more cumbersome and costly to taxpayers, for example? Justice Stevens's dissent will help you think about this question. Similarly, how might the recent "takings" jurisprudence impact the "public right doctrine" articulated in *NLRB v. Jones & Laughlin Steel*, 301 U.S. (1937).

4. The Iowa "Freedom to Farm" statute takes away the ability of neighbors of hog farmers to recover damages in a lawsuit when they are offended by the noise and smells from the hog farms next door. Make the argument that this law is an illegal taking of property rights under the takings clause.

5. Justice Scalia's dissent in *Mistretta v. United States* mounts a sophisticated political argument. Be sure to study it closely. Would the late professor Jaffe have agreed with Scalia? What, exactly, is it that makes this delegation excessive in Scalia's eyes? What does he mean by this sentence: "The power to make law at issue here . . . is not ancillary but quite naked"? Is Scalia worried that, while most institutions in government that make law simultaneously have feedback loops that tell them when their rules work well and when they need changing, there is no such loop in this case? Do you agree with Scalia that the Sentencing Commission's rules should fail because the Commission lacks such a feedback loop? Or is Judge Levanthal's formula for acceptable delegation quoted in this chapter adequate justification for the *Mistretta* majority's position?

40. See "Officer Guilty of Helping Torture Immigrant," *New York Times*, June 9, 1999.

CHAPTER 4
THE STATUTORY AUTHORITY
OF AGENCIES

In the last chapter we discussed court decisions about the limits of *what* administrative government can do. In this chapter we turn to the question of *who*, under the authority of statutes, may make decisions. As we saw in the last chapter, the answer to this question is more than a matter of line-drawing; it involves the political and legal craft of interpreting rights and responsibilities in a constitutional democracy.

THE LAW OF SEPARATION OF POWERS

Most high school graduates know that the U.S. Constitution separates the government into three branches: legislative, executive, and judicial. By common agreement there are clear outer limits on what each branch may and may not do. The judicial branch is restricted to deciding legal cases. (Chapter 10 describes what counts as a "legal case.") The Congress can enact statutory law (with the president's signature or over presidential veto), but presumably it cannot hear ordinary lawsuits. The executive branch, at least in domestic affairs, can issue orders implementing ("executing") valid statutes, but cannot just announce new law on its own.

As might be expected in a political system that values checks and balances among the branches, a good deal of overlapping power occurs. Sometimes the branches deliberately step on each other's toes. More commonly, however, the search for accommodation and compromise (or sometimes just passing the buck) creates practical arrangements for solving problems where the legislative,

executive, and judicial functions get blurry. But are such arrangements constitutional? Two lines of cases have developed in the Supreme Court, one a series of separation-of-powers cases, and the other a series of delegation cases, as discussed in chapter 3. This body of constitutional law can be perplexing because the separation-of-powers cases tend to draw clear, inflexible lines, while the delegation cases seem to let stand virtually any delegation of power from Congress to an executive or independent regulatory agency. The law today thus presents the anomaly that while Congress cannot reserve for itself a "legislative veto" of administrative actions (the *Chadha* case, below), it can abdicate to an administrative agency the entire question of what sentences should attach to federal crimes (*Mistretta*, in chapter 3).

In actual practice, the allocation of government lawmaking power is not as simple as the tripartite model would have it. Courts order school desegregation; presidents order troops into combat in foreign countries; administrators make rules about environmental safety—all without clear statutory authorization or even political approval. Justice Robert Jackson once described administrative agencies in the following way:

[Administrative agencies] have become a veritable fourth branch of Government, which has deranged our three-branch legal theories much as the concept of a fourth dimension unsettles our three-dimensional thinking. Courts have differed in assigning a place to these seemingly necessary bodies in our constitutional system. Administrative agencies have been called quasi-legislative, quasi-executive or quasi-judicial, as the occasion required, in order to validate their functions within the separation-of-powers scheme of the Constitution. The mere retreat to the qualifying "quasi" is implicit with confession that all recognized classifications have broken down, and "quasi" is a smooth cover which we draw over our confusion as we might use a counterpane to conceal a disordered bed.[1]

Justice Jackson's words remain apt. This chapter describes what remains of the statutory linkage between elected legislators and appointed administrators. Later chapters will illustrate the political negotiations that take place between legislatures and agencies.

As a reminder, let us go over the basic *ideals* of administrative government once again. Most of the time, administrative agencies are created through acts of Congress. Agencies are thus expected to be the agents that will implement, or execute, the goals set for them by the representatives of the people, i.e., the Congress. In the traditional model of administrative law, agencies are conceived as "a mere transmission belt for implementing legislative directives in particular cases."[2] As Justice Jackson points out, however, the reality is much more complex.

Richard Stewart has explained why the simple separation model fails, and his description is worth digesting before turning to the details.[3] The fact is, many statutes simply do not prescribe specific policies for the agencies to execute in the first place. Some legislation explicitly confers on agencies the discretion to make up its own policies. Other legislation may attempt to articulate general policy preferences in vague, general, or ambiguous language that does not translate directly into specific decisions. This statutory nondirection can occur for several reasons. Not all problems have solutions. The political pressures on elected officials to do something about a problem are hard to resist, but when legislators don't have a solution, they tend to appoint a bureaucracy to find one. On the more pragmatic political side, a majority may agree a problem exists, but factions withing the majority may want different solutions. The legislative

compromise may omit a specific solution and establish general, vague, and even ambiguous goals and guidelines. Finally, in the press of other business, legislators may simply not have the time or motivation to hammer out specifics on many issues. Instead, Congress tends to pass vague statutes and then monitor what the agencies do with them case by case.

Congress has developed a number of devices for monitoring agency decisions. One example is the National Environmental Policy Act (NEPA), which since 1969 has required that certain agencies provide environmental impact statements to identify and analyze the likely impact of their decisions on the environment. Environmental impact statements are important in helping Congress refashion its policy goals and amend statutes. A more direct mechanism for monitoring agency actions is the *legislative veto*. A legislative veto is a statutory provision that allows Congress to nullify decisions made by administrators. The first legislative veto provision Congress enacted was in 1932. Between 1932 and 1983, it is estimated that Congress inserted 295 veto-type procedures in 196 different statutes. In 1983, the Supreme Court addressed the constitutionality of the legislative veto in *Immigration and Naturalization Service v. Chadha*.

Immigration and Naturalization Service v. Chadha

462 U.S. 919 (1983) 7-2
+ *Burger, Brennan, Marshall, Blackmun, Powell, Stevens, O'Connor*
– *White, Rehnquist*

[Jagdish Rai Chadha, an East Indian who held a British passport, came to the United States in 1966 on a non-immigrant student visa. When his visa expired in 1972, he was required by the Immigration and Naturalization Service (INS) to demonstrate why he should not be deported for having "remained in the United States for a longer time than permitted." An immigration judge ordered that Chadha's deportation be suspended and that he be allowed to remain in the United States as a permanent resident alien. According to the Immigration and Nationality Act, the Attorney General must provide

---

1. *FTC v. Ruberoid Co.*, 343 U.S. 470, 487–488 (1952).
2. Richard Stewart, "The Reformation of American Administrative Law," *Harvard Law Review* 88 (1975): 1669–1675.
3. Ibid. at 1669.

Congress with a "detailed statement of the facts and pertinent provisions of law" in all cases where the Attorney General recommends suspension of deportation. Though it delegated enforcement power to the Attorney General in immigration matters, Congress reserved veto power over the Attorney General's decisions. In 1975 Representative Eilberg, chair of the House of Representatives Judiciary Subcommittee on Immigration, Citizenship, and International Law, introduced a resolution to overturn the Attorney General's decision in the Chadha case. Chadha challenged the constitutionality of the resolution. Seven members of the Supreme Court agreed with Chadha and ruled that the legislative veto was unconstitutional. Justice White's dissent supports the veto as a legitimate and necessary check on administrative discretion.]

Chief Justice Burger delivered the opinion of the Court

[. . .]

The decision to provide the President with a limited and qualified power to nullify proposed legislation by veto was based on the profound conviction of the Framers that the powers conferred on Congress were the powers to be most carefully circumscribed. It is beyond doubt that lawmaking was a power to be shared by both Houses and the President. In The Federalist No. 73 (H. Lodge ed. 1888), Hamilton focused on the President's role in making laws:

"If even no propensity had ever discovered itself in the legislation body to invade the rights of the Executive, the rules of just reasoning and theoretic propriety would of themselves teach us that the one ought not to be left to the mercy of the other, but ought to possess a constitutional and effectual power of self-defence."

See also The Federalist No. 51.

The President's role in the lawmaking process also reflects the Framers' careful efforts to check whatever propensity a particular Congress might have to enact oppressive, improvident, or ill-considered measures. . . .

The bicameral requirement of Art. I, §§ 1, 7, was of scarcely less concern to the Framers than was the Presidential veto and indeed the two concepts are interdependent. By providing that no law could take effect without the concurrence of the prescribed majority of the Members of both Houses, the Framers reemphasized their belief,

already remarked upon in connection with the Presentment Clauses, that legislation should not be enacted unless it has been carefully and fully considered by the Nation's elected officials. In the Constitutional Convention debates on the need for a bicameral legislature, James Wilson, later to become a Justice of this Court, commented:

"Despotism comes on mankind in different shapes, sometimes in an Executive, sometimes in a military, one. Is there danger of a Legislative depotism? Theory & practice both proclaim it. If the Legislative authority be not restrained, there can be neither liberty nor stability; and it can only be restrained by dividing it within itself, into distinct and independent branches. In a single house there is no check, but the inadequate one, of the virtue & good sense of those who compose it." 1 Farrand 254.

These observations are consistent with what many of the Framers expressed, none more cogently than Madison in pointing up the need to divide and disperse power in order to protect liberty:

"In republican government, the legislative authority necessarily predominates. The remedy for this inconveniency is to divide the legislature into different branches; and to render them, by different modes of election and different principles of action, as little connected with each other as the nature of their common functions and their common dependence on the society will admit." The Federalist No. 51, p 324. (H. Lodge ed. 1888).

See also The Federalist No. 62. . . .

The Constitution sought to divide the delegated powers of the new Federal Government into three defined categories, Legislative, Executive, and Judicial, to assure, as nearly as possible, that each branch of government would confine itself to its assigned responsibility. The hydraulic pressure inherent within each of the separate Branches to exceed the outer limits of its power, even to accomplish desirable objectives, must be resisted.

Although not "hermetically" sealed from one another, *Buckley v. Valeo*, 424 U.S., at 121, the powers delegated to the three Branches are functionally identifiable. When any Branch acts, it is presumptively exercising the power the Constitution has delegated to it. See *J. W. Hampton & Co. v. United States*, 276 U.S. 394, 406 (1928). When the Executive acts, he presumptively acts in an executive or administrative capacity as defined in Art. II. And when, as here, one House of Congress purports to act, it is presumptively acting within its assigned sphere.

Beginning with this presumption, we must nevertheless establish that the challenged action under §244(c)(2) is of the kind to which the procedural requirements of Art. 1, §7, apply. Not every action taken by either House is subject to the bicameralism and presentment requirements of Art. I. Whether actions taken by either House are, in law and fact, an exercise of legislative power depends not on their form but upon "whether they contain matter which is properly to be regarded as legislative in its character and effect." S. Rep. No. 1335, 54th Cong., 2d Sess., 8 (1897).

Examination of the action taken here by one House pursuant to §244(c)(2) reveals that it was essentially legislative in purpose and effect. In purporting to exercise power defined in Art. 1, §8, cl. 4, to "establish an uniform Rule of Naturalization," the House took action that had the purpose and effect of altering the legal rights, duties, and relations of persons, including the Attorney General, Executive Branch officials and Chadha, all outside the Legislative Branch. Section 244(c)(2) purports to authorize one House of Congress to require the Attorney General to deport an individual alien whose deportation otherwise would be canceled under §244. The one-House veto operated in these cases to overrule the Attorney General and mandate Chadha's deportation; absent the House action, Chadha would remain in the United States. Congress has *acted* and its action has altered Chadha's status.

The legislative character of the one-house veto in these cases is confirmed by the character of the congressional action it supplants. Neither the House of Representatives not the Senate contends that, absent the veto provision in §244(c)(2), either of them, or both of them acting together, could effectively require the Attorney General to deport an alien once the Attorney General, in the exercise of legislatively delegated authority, had determined the alien should remain in the United States.

The nature of the decision implemented by the one-House veto in these cases further manifests its legislative character. After long experience with the clumsy, time-consuming private bill procedure, Congress made a deliberate choice to delegate to the Executive Branch, and specifically to the Attorney General, the authority to allow deportable aliens to remain in this country in certain specified circumstances. It is not disputed that this choice to delegate authority is precisely the kind of decision that can be imple-

mented only in accordance with the procedures set out in Art. I. Disagreement with the Attorney General's decision on Chadha's deportation—that is, Congress' decision to deport Chadha—no less than Congress' original choice to delegate to the Attorney General the authority to make that decision, involves determinations of policy that Congress can implement in only one way; bicameral passage followed by presentment to the President. Congress must abide by its delegation of authority until that delegation is legislatively altered or revoked.[4]

Finally, we see that when the Framers intended to authorize either House of Congress to act alone and outside of its prescribed bicameral legislative role, they narrowly and precisely defined the procedure for such action. There are four provisions in the Constitution, explicit and unambiguous, by which one House may act alone with the unreviewable force of law, not subject to the President's veto:

(1) The House of Representatives alone was given the power to initiate impeachments. Art. I, §2, cl. 5;

(2) The Senate alone was given the power to conduct trials following impeachment on charges initiated by the House and to convict following trial. Art. I, §3, cl. 6;

(3) The Senate alone was given unreviewable power to approve or to disapprove Presidential appointments. Art. II, §2, cl. 2;

(4) The Senate alone was given unreviewable power to ratify treaties negotiated by the President. Art. II, §2, cl. 2

Clearly, when the Draftsmen sought to confer special powers on one House, independent of the other House, or of the President, they did so in explicit, unambiguous terms.

The bicameral requirement, the Presentment Clauses, the President's veto, and Congress' power to override a veto were intended to erect enduring checks on each Branch and to protect the people from the improvident exercise of

---

4. This does not mean that Congress is required to accede to "the accretion of policy control by forces outside its chambers." See Javits and Klein, "Congressional Oversight and the Legislative Veto: A Constitutional Analysis," *NYU Law Review* 52 (1977): 455, 462. The Constitution provides Congress with abundant means to oversee and control its administrative creatures. Beyond the obvious fact that Congress ultimately controls administrative agencies in the legislation that creates them, other means of control, such as durational limits on authorizations and formal reporting requirements, lie well within Congress's constitutional power. See Ibid., at 460–461; Kaiser, "Congressional Action to Overturn Agency Rules; Alternatives to the 'Legislative Veto,'" *Administrative Law Review* 32 (1980): 667.

power by mandating certain prescribed steps. To preserve those checks, and maintain the separation of powers, the carefully defined limits on the power of each Branch must not be eroded. To accomplish what has been attempted by one House of Congress in this case requires action in conformity with the express procedures of the Constitution's prescription for legislative action: passage by a majority of both Houses and presentment to the President.

The veto authorized by §244(c)(2) doubtless has been in many respects a convenient shortcut; the "sharing" with the Executive by Congress of its authority over aliens in this manner is, on its face, an appealing compromise. In purely practical terms, it is obviously easier for action to be taken by one House without submission to the President; but it is crystal clear from the records of the Convention, contemporaneous writings and debates, that the Framers ranked other values higher than efficiency.

With all the obvious flaws of delay, untidiness, and potential for abuse, we have not yet found a better way to preserve freedom than by making the exercise of power subject to the carefully crafted restraints spelled out in the Constitution. . . .

We hold that the congressional veto provision in §244(c)(2) is severable from the Act and that it is unconstitutional. Accordingly, the judgment of the Court of Appeals is Affirmed.

Justice White, dissenting

Today the Court not only invalidates §244(c)(2) of the Immigration and Nationality Act, but also sounds the death knell for nearly 200 other statutory provisions in which Congress has reserved a "legislative veto." For this reason, the Court's decision is of surpassing importance. And it is for this reason that the Court would have been well advised to decide the cases, if possible, on the narrower grounds of separation of powers, leaving for full consideration the constitutionality of other congressional review statutes operating on such varied matters as war powers and agency rulemaking, some of which concern the independent regulatory agencies.

The legislative veto developed initially in response to the problems of reorganizing the sprawling Government structure was created in response to the Depression. The Reorganization Acts established the chief model for the

legislative veto. When President Hoover requested authority to reorganize the Government in 1929, he coupled his request that the "Congress be willing to delegate its authority over the problem (subject to defined principles) to the Executive" with a proposal for legislative review. He proposed that the Executive "should act upon approval of a joint committee of Congress or with the reservation of power of revision by Congress within some limited period adequate for its consideration." Public Papers of the Presidents, Herbert Hoover, 1929, p. 432 (1974). Congress followed President Hoover's suggestion and authorized reorganization subject to legislative review. Although the reorganization authority reenacted in 1933 did not contain a legislative veto provision, the provision returned during the Roosevelt administration and has since been renewed numerous times. Over the years, the provision was used extensively. Presidents submitted 115 Reorganization Plans to Congress of which 23 were disapproved by Congress pursuant to legislative veto provisions.

Shortly after adoption of the Reorganization Act of 1939, Congress and the President applied the legislative veto procedure to resolve the delegation problem for national security and foreign affairs. World War II occasioned the need to transfer greater authority to the President in these areas. The legislative veto offered the means by which Congress could confer additional authority while preserving its own constitutional role. During World War II, Congress enacted over 30 statutes conferring powers on the Executive with legislative veto provisions. President Roosevelt accepted the veto as the necessary price for obtaining exceptional authority.

Over the quarter century following World War II, Presidents continued to accept legislative vetos by one or both Houses as constitutional, while regularly denouncing provisions by which congressional Committees reviewed Executive activity.[5] The legislative veto balanced delegations of statutory authority in new areas of governmental involvement: for the space program, international agreements on

5. Presidential objections to the veto, until the veto by president Nixon of the War Powers Resolution, principally concerned bills authorizing committee vetoes. As the Senate Subcommittee on Separation of Powers found in 1969, "an accommodation was reached years ago on legislative vetoes exercised by the entire Congress or by one House, [while] disputes have continued to arise over the committee form of the veto." S. Rep. No. 91–549, p. 14 (1969).

nuclear energy, tariff arrangements, and adjustment of federal pay rates.

During the 1970's the legislative veto was important in resolving a series of major constitutional disputes between the President and Congress over claims of the President to broad impoundment, war, and national emergency powers. The key provision of the War Power Resolution, authorizes the termination by concurrent resolution of the use of armed forces in hostilities. A similar measure resolved the problem posed by Presidential claims of inherent power to impound appropriations in the Congressional Budget and Impoundment Control Act of 1974. In conference, a compromise was achieved under which permanent impoundments, termed "rescissions," would require approval through enactment of legislation. In contrast, temporary impoundments, or "deferrals," would become effective unless disapproved by one House. This compromise provided the President with flexibility, while preserving ultimate congressional control over the budget.[6]

In the energy field, the legislative veto served to balance broad delegations in legislation emerging from the energy crisis of the 1970's.[7]

It is an important if not indispensable political invention that allows the President and Congress to resolve major constitutional and policy differences, assures the accountability of independent regulatory agencies, and preserves Congress' control over lawmaking. Perhaps there are other means of accommodation and accountability, but the increasing reliance of Congress upon the legislative veto suggests that the alternatives to which Congress must now turn are not entirely satisfactory.[8]

The history of the legislative veto also makes clear that it has not been a sword with which Congress has struck out

6. The Impoundment Control Act's provision for legislative review have been used extensively. Presidents have submitted hundreds of proposed budget deferrals, of which 65 have been disapproved by resolutions of the House or Senate with no protest by the Executive.

7. The veto appears in a host of broad statutory delegations concerning energy rationing, contingency plans, strategic oil reserves, allocation of energy production materials, oil exports and naval petroleum reserve production.

8. While Congress could write certain statutes with greater specificity, it is doubtful that this is a realistic or even desirable substitute for the legislative veto. The controversial nature of many issues would prevent Congress from reaching agreement on many major problems if specificity were required in their enactments.

to aggrandize itself at the expense of the other branches—the concerns of Madison and Hamilton. Rather, the veto has been a means of defense, a reservation of ultimate authority necessary if Congress is to fulfill its designated role under Art. I as the Nation's lawmaker. While the President has often objected to particular legislative vetoes, generally those left in the hands of congressional Committees, the Executive has more often agreed to legislative review as the price for a broad delegation of authority. To be sure, the President may have preferred unrestricted power, but that could be precisely why Congress thought it essential to retain a check on the exercise of delegated authority.

If the legislative veto were as plainly unconstitutional as the Court strives to suggest, its broad ruling today would be more comprehensible. But, the constitutionality of the legislative veto is anything but clear-cut. The issue divides scholars, courts, Attorneys General, and the two other branches of the National Government. . . .

The Court's holding today that all legislative-type action must be enacted through the lawmaking process ignores that legislative authority is routinely delegated to the Executive Branch, to the independent regulatory agencies, and to private individuals and groups.

The wisdom and the constitutionality of these broad delegations are matters that still have not been put to rest. But for present purposes, these cases establish that by virtue of congressional delegation, legislative power can be exercised by independent agencies and Executive departments without the passage of new legislation. For some time, the sheer amount of law—the substantive rules that regulate private conduct and direct the operation of government—made by the agencies has far outnumbered the lawmaking engaged in by Congress through the traditional process. There is no question but that agency rulemaking is lawmaking in any functional or realistic sense of the term. . . .

[T]he history of the separation-of-powers doctrine is also a history of accommodation and practicality. Apprehensions of an overly powerful branch have not led to undue prophylactic measures that handicap the effective working of the National Government as a whole. The Constitution does not contemplate total separation of the three branches of Government. *Buckley v. Valeo*, 424 U.S. 1, 121 (1976).

I do not suggest that all legislative vetoes are necessarily consistent with separation-of-powers principles. A legislative check on an inherently executive function, for example, that of initiating prosecutions, poses an entirely different question. But the legislative veto device here—and in many other settings—is far from an instance of legislative tyranny over the Executive. It is a necessary check on the unavoidably expanding power of the agencies, both Executive and independent, as they engage in exercising authority delegated by Congress.

I regret that I am in disagreement with my colleagues on the fundamental questions that these cases present. But even more I regret the destructive scope of the Court's holding. It reflects a profoundly different conception of the Constitution than that held by the courts which sanctioned the modern administrative state. Today's decision strikes down in one fell swoop provisions in more laws enacted by Congress than the Court has cumulatively invalidated in its history. I fear it will now be more difficult to "insur[e] that the fundamental policy decisions in our society will be made not by an appointed official but by the body immediately responsible to the people," *Arizona v. California*, 373 U.S. 546, 626 (1963) (Harlan, J., dissenting in part). I must dissent.[9]

Legislative veto was just one example of various devices Congress could employ to monitor agency decision making. Although legislative veto provisions in Congressional statutes did not totally disappear after *Chadha*, alternative monitoring mechanisms gained significance with the Court's ruling in this case. One notable example is the Congressional Review Act of 1996 (Public Law No. 104-121). According to the Act (Sec. 801), "before a rule can take effect, the Federal agency promulgating such rule shall submit to each House of the Congress and to the Comptroller General a report containing-

(i) a copy of the rule;

(ii) a concise general statement relating to the rule, including whether it is a major rule; and

(iii) the proposed effective date of the rule."

9. For a penetrating analysis of how easily Congress adjusted to the *Chadha* decision, and how little the decision actually affected congressional oversight of policy, see Jessica Korn, *The Power of Separation* (Princeton: Princeton University Press, 1996).

The Comptroller General then, in fifteen days, shall submit a report concerning the proposed rule to each House of the Congress. If the Congress disapproves of a proposed rule, under this Act, both houses can pass a joint resolution, which would effectively invalidate the rule. Under this Act, for instance, Congress has passed, and the President has signed, Public Law 107-5, a resolution of disapproval of OSHA's final Ergonomics Program Standard.

STATUTORY LIMITS ON AGENCY DISCRETION

We now turn to the more common problem of figuring out what a statute actually commands an agency to do. Congress may grant broad power to agencies, but the agency must have some principles, guidelines, etc. telling it what to do. The Sentencing Commission may have broad leeway to establish criminal sentences, but it does not have the statutory power to make it a crime to fail to brush our teeth twice a day. As you read the next case, note how, even in this relatively simple case, the meaning of the statute is not immediately obvious. As the later cases in this section show, the problems for courts and agencies do *not* usually arise because the authorizing statute violates separation of powers or delegation rules or other constitutional provisions. The most common problem in this field is simply that no one can tell for sure what the statute means in the first place. Sometimes confusion about a statute arises from congressional sloppiness (or perhaps from the knowledge that if the statute is confusing enough, constituents won't get too upset about it). Often, though, statutory confusion simply can't be helped. For example, if we want the Food and Drug Administration (FDA) to have power to regulate the testing and safety of prescription drugs, is there really any way to define what is and is not a "drug"? The line between Prozac and St. John's Wort (or red yeast rice), and the lines between medicinal marijuana, nicotine, alcohol, and caffeine are not objectively discernible. The FDA and the courts and Congress will all work on drawing and redrawing those lines in the process we call "politics."

Agencies of course have primary responsibility for determining their own statutory limits and acting within them. Because of political pressures, many agencies choose not to exercise all the powers that courts might have ruled that their authorizing statutes permit. The Federal Trade Commission, for example, chose not to exercise its rule-making powers for the first half-century of its existence, even though the statute authorized it to "prevent" certain evils, and that arguably requires making rules to prevent harm before it happens. In the following case the agency in question interpreted its authority a certain way and the courts upheld that interpretation. It is an example of how the Court has upheld agency authority to make substantive decisions within the scope of delegated authority.

NAACP et al. v. Federal Power Commission

425 U.S. 662 (1976) 8-0

+ Brennan, Stewart, White, Blackmun, Powell, Rehnquist, Stevens, Marshall

NP Burger

[In 1972 the National Association for the Advancement of Colored People (NAACP) and several other organizations petitioned the Federal Power Commission (FPC) to issue a rule "requiring equal employment opportunity and nondiscrimination in the employment practices of its regulatees." The Federal Power Act, as amended by the Natural Gas Act, charges the FPC with responsibility to set just and reasonable prices for the sale of electricity and natural gas. Its regulations must, by statute, "serve the public interest." The petitioners claimed that racial discrimination was a costly practice and that the statutes therefore authorized the FPC to prevent it as part of its rate-controlling power. They also claimed that racial discrimination contradicted the public interest, whether it added to the cost of energy or not, and therefore that the commission possessed statutory authority to prevent it. The FPC refused the request, and the plaintiffs went to court to compel such a rule.]

Justice Stewart delivered the opinion of the Court

The question presented is not whether the elimination of discrimination from our society is an important national goal.

It clearly is. The question is not whether Congress could authorize the Federal Power Commission to combat such discrimination. It clearly could. The question is simply whether or to what extent Congress did grant the Commission such authority. Two possible statutory bases have been advanced to justify the conclusion that the Commission can or must concern itself with discriminatory employment practices on the part of the companies it regulates.

Without necessarily endorsing the specific identification of the costs "arguably within" the Commission's "range of concern," we agree with the basic conclusion of the Court of Appeals on this branch of the case. The Commission clearly has the duty to prevent its regulatees from charging rates based upon illegal, duplicative, or unnecessary labor costs. To the extent that such costs are demonstrably the product of a regulatee's discriminatory employment practices, the Commission should disallow them. For example, when a company complies with a backpay award resulting from a finding of employment discrimination in violation of Title VII of the Civil Rights Act of 1964, 42 U.S.C. §2000 et seq., it pays twice for work that was performed only once. The amount of the backpay award, therefore, can and should be disallowed as an unnecessary cost in a ratemaking proceeding.

To the extent that these and other similar costs, such as attorney's fees, can be or have been demonstrably quantified by judicial decree or the final action of an administrative agency charged with consideration of such matters, the Commission clearly should treat these costs as it treats any other illegal, unnecessary, or duplicative costs. We were told by counsel during oral argument that the Commission would routinely disallow the costs of a backpay award resulting from an order of the National Labor Relations Board or the decree of a court based upon a finding of an unfair labor practice. The governing principle is no different in the area of discriminatory employment practices.

As a general proposition it is clear that the Commission has the discretion to decide whether to approach these problems through the process of rulemaking, individual adjudication, or a combination of the two procedures. SEC v. Chenery Corp., 332 U.S. 194, 202–203. The present Commission practice, we are told, is to consider such questions only in individual ratemaking proceedings, under its detailed accounting procedures. Assuming that the Commission continues that practice, it has ample authority to consider whatever evidence and make whatever inquiries are necessary of illegitimate costs because of racially discriminatory employment practices.

The Court of Appeals rejected the broader argument based upon the statutory criterion of "public interest," and we hold that it was correct in doing so. This Court's cases have consistently held that the use of the words "public interest" in a regulatory statute is not a broad license to promote the general public welfare. Rather, the words take meaning from the purposes of the regulatory legislation.

Thus, in order to give content and meaning to the words "public interest" as used in the Power and Gas Acts, it is necessary to look to the purposes for which the Acts were adopted. In the case of the Power and Gas Acts it is clear that the principal purpose of those Acts was to encourage the orderly development of plentiful supplies of electricity and natural gas at reasonable prices. While there are undoubtedly other subsidiary purposes contained in these Acts, the parties point to nothing in the Acts or their legislative histories to indicate that the elimination of employment discrimination was one of the purposes that Congress had in mind when it enacted this legislation. The use of the words "public interest" in the Gas and Power Acts is not a directive to the Commission to seek to eradicate discrimination, but, rather, is a charge to promote the orderly production of plentiful supplies of electric energy and natural gas at just and reasonable rates.

It is useful again to draw on the analogy of federal labor law. No less than in the federal legislation defining the national interest in ending employment discrimination, Congress in its earlier labor legislation unmistakably defined the national interest in free collective bargaining. Yet it could hardly be supposed that in directing the Federal Power Commission to be guided by the "public interest," Congress thereby instructed it to take original jurisdiction over the processing of charges of unfair labor practices on the parts of its regulatees.

We agree, in short, with the Court of Appeals that the Federal Power Commission is authorized to consider the consequences of discriminatory employment practices on the part of its regulatees only insofar as such consequences are directly related to the Commission's establishment of just and reasonable rates in the public interest. Accordingly, we affirm the judgment before us.

It is ordered.

The difficulties in statutory interpretation are particularly evident in regulatory cases involving scientific research and conflicting data on the subject under regulation.[10] Saccharin, asbestos, benzene, radiation, and other substances have appeared in news reports in association with various diseases. When such research findings appear, environmental groups, health organizations, and members of Congress instruct agencies to take steps to minimize the danger. The problem is perplexing because while data may establish an association, it often cannot distinguish between safe and unsafe levels of exposure. (For example, salt is highly toxic if one consumes too much of it.) As a result, Congress's statutory instructions to agencies may be highly uncertain, so uncertain as to amount to no more than an instruction to the agencies to *do something*, the something being unspecified.

A command to do something about a health problem does not violate the delegation doctrine because the Congress does create limits to the action of the agencies involved. The Food and Drug Administration and the Occupational Safety and Health Administration (OSHA) are limited by statute in the sense they cannot regulate airline safety or safety in the home. They do not have the carte blanche power the Court rejected in *Schechter*. The problem lies in choosing between playing it safe and prohibiting exposures that are suspected but not proven to cause problems, on the one hand, and insisting on proof before forcing businesses to make costly changes on the other. In the statute creating OSHA, Congress waffled on this choice. We have included portions of the OSHA statute in Appendix D so that you can get an idea of what statutes look like and begin to comprehend the kind of issues agencies and courts face when interpreting a statute. The statutory language of the OSHA statute

10. For an overview of theories of statutory interpretations, see Cass R. Sunstein, "Interpreting Statutes in the Regulatory State," *Harvard Law Review* 103 (1989): 405.

leaves the choice open, so open it is hard to tell if any statutory command exists it all.

How should the courts interpret such statutory "guidelines"? Leave all issues to the discretionary judgment of administrative officials, or insist on rational proof? These questions have become all the more pressing with the passage of social and economic regulatory statutes in the 1960s and 1970s. Statutes passed during these decades have been characterized as having very broadly stated goals—"to provide safe and healthful employment," alongside very specific but incomplete standards and criteria—a "standard which most adequately assures, to the extent feasible, on the basis of the best available evidence." Neither regulatory agencies nor courts have settled on a formula for interpreting statutes.

The majority and dissenting opinions in the following cases reveal how divided the Court is in its response to these questions. In addition, the disputes and the disputants in these cases provide insight into the role of administrative agencies in political controversy over regulation during the Reagan administration. That agencies, such as OSHA and Environmental Protection Agency (EPA), are now under attack by public interest groups, representatives of labor, and environmental coalitions signifies how important politics is in determining administrative practices. Broad delegation may lead to very different regulatory policies depending on whether New Deal politics and welfare-state building are on the national agenda, or whether deregulation and efforts to dismantle the welfare state guide the exercise of delegated powers.

Industrial Union Department v. American Petroleum Institute

448 U.S. 607 (1980) 5-4

+ *Burger, Stewart, Stevens*
+/– *Powell, Rehnquist*
– *Brennan, White, Marshall, Blackmun*

[The Occupational Safety and Health Act of 1970 delegates broad authority to the secretary of labor to promulgate standards to ensure safe working conditions for the nation's workers. Section 3 of the act defines an "occupational safety and health standard" as a standard that is "reasonably necessary or appropriate to provide safe and healthful employment." Where toxic materials or harmful physical agents are concerned, a standard must also comply with section 6(b)(5), which directs the secretary to "set the standard which most adequately assures, to the extent feasible, on the basis of the best available evidence, that no employee will suffer material impairment of health or functional capacity." When the toxic material or harmful physical agent is a carcinogen, the secretary has taken the position that no safe exposure level can be determined and that section 6(b)(5) requires him to set an exposure limit at the lowest technologically feasible level that will not impair the viability of the industries involved.

Benzene, a known carcinogen, had previously been permitted in the air of a work place at a concentration not to exceed 10 parts per million (ppm). OSHA lowered the allowed concentration to 1 ppm in the belief that this would lead to a lower incidence of leukemia. In doing so OSHA acted on the assumption that its authorizing statute directed the substance should be set at a safe level or at the lowest level feasible if a safe level could not be determined. The American Petroleum Institute (API) brought suit challenging both OSHA's interpretation of the statute and its factual basis for the reduction in concentration. The appellate court held for the API. OSHA then brought its case to the Supreme Court.]

Justice Stevens delivered the opinion of the Court

The critical issue at this point in the litigation is whether the Court of Appeals was correct in refusing to enforce the 1 ppm exposure limit on the ground that it was not supported by appropriate fundings.

Any discussion of the 1 ppm exposure limit must, of course, begin with the Agency's rationale for imposing that limit.

The evidence in the administrative record of adverse effects of benzene exposure at 10 ppm is sketchy at best. . . . The Agency made no finding that . . . any . . . empirical evidence, or any opinion testimony demonstrated that exposure to benzene at or below the 10 ppm level had ever in fact caused leukemia.

In the end OSHA's rationale for lowering the permissible exposure limit to 1 ppm was based not on any finding that leukemia has ever been caused by exposure to 10 ppm of benzene and that it will not be caused by exposure to 1 ppm, but rather on a series of assumptions indicating that some leukemias might result from exposure to 10 ppm and that the number of cases might be reduced by reducing the exposure level to 1 ppm. In reaching the result, the Agency first unequivocally concluded that benzene is a human carcinogen. Second, it concluded that industry had failed to prove that there is a safe threshold level of exposure to benzene below which no excess leukemia cases would occur. In reaching this conclusion OSHA rejected industry contentions that certain epidemiological studies indicating no excess risk of leukemia among workers exposed at levels below 10 ppm were sufficient to establish that the threshold level of safe exposure was at or above 10 ppm. It also rejected an industry witness' testimony that a dose-response curve could be constructed on the basis of the reported epidemiological studies and that this curve indicated that reducing the permissible exposure limit from 10 to 1 ppm would prevent at most one leukemia and one other cancer death every six years.

Third, the Agency applied its standard policy with respect to carcinogens, concluding that, in the absence of definitive proof of a safe level, it must be assumed that any level above zero presents some increased risk of cancer. As the federal parties point out in their brief, there are a number of scientists and public health specialists who subscribe to this view, theorizing that a susceptible person may contract cancer from the absorption of even one molecule of a carcinogen like benzene.

Fourth, the Agency reiterated its view of the Act, stating that it was required by §6(b)(5) to set the standard either at the level that has been demonstrated to be safe or at the lowest level feasible, whichever is higher. If no safe level is established, as in this case, the Secretary's interpretation of the statute automatically leads to the selection of an exposure limit that is the lowest feasible. Because of benzene's importance to the economy, no one has ever suggested that it would be feasible to eliminate its use entirely, or to try to limit exposures to the small amounts that are omnipresent. Rather, the Agency selected 1 ppm as a workable exposure level . . . and then determined that compliance with that level was technologically feasible and that "the economic impact of . . . [compliance] will not be such as to threaten

the financial welfare of the affected firms or the general economy." It therefore held that 1 ppm was the minimum feasible exposure level within the meaning of §6(b)(5) of the Act.

Finally, although the Agency did not refer in its discussion of the pertinent legal authority to any duty to identify the anticipated benefits of the new standard, it did conclude that some benefits were likely to result from reducing the exposure limit from 10 ppm to 1 ppm. This conclusion was based, again, not on evidence, but rather on the assumption that the risk of leukemia will decrease as exposure levels decrease.

It is noteworthy that at no point in its lengthy explanation did the Agency quote or even cite §3(8) of the Act. It made no finding that any of the provisions of the new standard were "reasonably necessary or appropriate to provide safe or healthful employment and places of employment." Nor did it allude to the possibility that any such finding might have been appropriate. . . .

But we think it clear that the statute was not designed to require employers to provide absolutely risk-free workplaces whenever it is technologically feasible to do so, so long as the cost is not great enough to destroy an entire industry. Rather, both the language and structure of the Act, as well as its legislative history, indicate that it was intended to require the elimination, as far as feasible, of significant risks of harm.

By empowering the Secretary to promulgate standards that are "reasonably necessary or appropriate to provide safe or healthful employment and places of employment," the Act implies that, before promulgating any standard, the Secretary must make a finding that the workplaces in question are not safe. But "safe" is not the equivalent of "risk-free." There are many activities that we engage in every day—such as driving a car or even breathing city air—that entail some risk of accident or material health impairment; nevertheless, few people would consider these activities "unsafe." Similarly, a workplace can hardly be considered "unsafe" unless it threatens the workers with a significant risk of harm.

Therefore, before he can promulgate *any* permanent health or safety standard, the Secretary is required to make a threshold finding that a place of employment is unsafe—in the sense that significant risks are present and can be eliminated or lessened by a change in practices. . . .

In the absence of a clear mandate in the Act, it is unreasonable to assume that Congress intended to give the

Secretary the unprecedented power over American industry that would result from the Government's view of §§3(8) and 6(b)(5), coupled with OSHA's cancer policy. Expert testimony that a substance is probably a human carcinogen—either because it has caused cancer in animals or because individuals have contracted cancer following extremely high exposures—would justify the conclusion that the substance poses some risk of serious harm no matter how minute the exposure and no matter how many experts testified that they regarded the risk as insignificant. That conclusion would in turn justify pervasive regulation limited only by the constraint of feasibility. In light of the fact that there are literally thousands of substances used in the workplace that have been identified as carcinogens or suspect carcinogens, the Government's theory would give OSHA power to impose enormous costs that might produce little, if any, discernible benefit. . . .

The legislative history also supports the conclusion that Congress was concerned, not with absolute safety, but with the elimination of significant harm. . . .

Contrary to the Government's contentions, imposing a burden on the Agency of demonstrating a significant risk of harm will not strip it of its ability to regulate carcinogens, nor will it require the Agency to wait for deaths to occur before taking any action. First, the requirement that a "significant" risk be identified is not a mathematical straitjacket. It is the Agency's responsibility to determine, in the first instance, what it considers to be a "significant" risk. Some risks are plainly acceptable and others are plainly unacceptable. If, for example, the odds are one in a billion that a person will die from cancer by taking a drink of chlorinated water, the risk clearly could not be considered significant. On the other hand, if the odds are one in a thousand that regular inhalation of gasoline vapors that are 2% benzene will be fatal, a reasonable person might well consider the risk significant and take appropriate steps to decrease or eliminate it. Although the Agency has no duty to calculate the exact probability of harm, it does have an obligation to find that a significant risk is present before it can characterize a place of employment as "unsafe."

Thus, so long as they are supported by a body of reputable scientific thought, the Agency is free to use conservative assumptions in interpreting the data with respect to carcinogens, risking error on the side of overprotection rather than underprotection.

Justice Marshall, with whom Justice Brennan, Justice White, and Justice Blackmun join, dissenting

In cases of statutory construction, this Court's authority is limited. If the statutory language and legislative intent are plain, the judicial inquiry is at an end. Under our jurisprudence, it is presumed that ill-considered or unwise legislation will be corrected through the democratic process; a court is not permitted to distort a statute's meaning in order to make it conform with the Justices' own views of sound social policy.

Today's decision flagrantly disregards these restrictions on judicial authority. The plurality ignores the plain meaning of the Occupational Safety and Health Act of 1970 in order to bring the authority of the Secretary of Labor in line with the plurality's own views of proper regulatory policy. The unfortunate consequence is that the Federal Government's efforts to protect American workers from cancer and other crippling diseases may be substantially impaired.

In this case the Secretary of Labor found, on the basis of substantial evidence, that (1) exposure to benzene creates a risk of cancer, chromosomal damage, and a variety of nonmalignant but potentially fatal blood disorders, even at the level of 1 ppm; (2) no safe level of exposure has been shown; (3) benefits in the form of saved lives would be derived from the permanent standard; (4) the number of lives that would be saved could turn out to be either substantial or relatively small; (5) under the present state of scientific knowledge, it is impossible to calculate even in a rough way the number of lives that would be saved, at least without making assumptions that would appear absurd to much of the medical community; and (6) the standard would not materially harm the financial condition of the covered industries. The Court does not set aside any of these findings. Thus, it could not be plainer that the Secretary's decision was fully in accord with his statutory mandate "most adequately [to] assur[e] that no employee will suffer material impairment of health or functional capacity."

The plurality's conclusion to the contrary is based on its interpretation of 29 U.S.C. §652(8), which defines an occupational safety and health standard as one "which requires conditions reasonably necessary or appropriate to provide safe or healthful employment." According to the plurality, a standard is not "reasonably necessary or appropriate" unless the Secretary is able to show that it is "at least more likely than not," that the risk he seeks to regulate is a "significant" one. Nothing in the statute's language or legislative history, however, indicates that the "reasonably necessary or appropriate" language should be given this meaning. Indeed, both demonstrate that the plurality's standard bears no connection with the acts or intentions of Congress and is based only on the plurality's solicitude for the welfare of regulated industries. And the plurality uses this standard to evaluate not the agency's decision in this case, but a strawman of its own creation.

Unlike the plurality, I do not purport to know whether the actions taken by Congress and its delegates to ensure occupational safety represent sound or unsound regulatory policy. The critical problem in cases like the ones at bar is scientific uncertainty. While science has determined that exposure to benzene at levels above 1 ppm creates a definite risk of health impairment, the magnitude of the risk cannot be quantified at the present time. The risk at issue has hardly been shown to be insignificant; indeed, future research may reveal that the risk is in fact considerable. But the existing evidence may frequently be inadequate to enable the Secretary to make the threshold finding of "significance" that the Court requires today. If so, the consequence of the plurality's approach would be to subject American workers to a continuing risk of cancer and other fatal diseases, and to render the Federal Government powerless to take protective action on their behalf. Such an approach would place the burden of medical uncertainty squarely on the shoulders of the American worker, the intended beneficiary of the Occupational Safety and Health Act.

Because today's holding has no basis in the Act, and because the Court has no authority to impose its own regulatory policies on the Nation, I dissent.

Congress enacted the Occupational Safety and Health Act as a response to what was characterized as "the grim history of our failure to heed the occupational health needs of our workers."[11] The failure of voluntary action and legislation at the state level . . . had resulted in a "bleak" and "worsening" situation in which 14,500 persons had died

11. Foreword by Sen. Williams, "Legislative History of the Occupational Safety and Health Act of 1970" (Committee Print compiled for the Senate Committee on Labor and Public Welfare 1971), iii.

annually as a result of conditions in the workplace. In the four years preceding the Act's passage, more Americans were killed in the workplace than in the contemporaneous Vietnam War. The Act was designed as "a safety bill of rights for close to 60 million workers." Its stated purpose is "to assure so far as possible every working man and woman in the Nation safe and healthful working conditions and to preserve our human resources."

The Act is enforced primarily through two provisions. First, a "general duty" is imposed upon employers to furnish employment and places of employment "free from recognized hazards that are causing or are likely to cause death or serious physical harm." Second, the Secretary of Labor is authorized to set "occupational safety and health standards," defined as standards requiring "conditions, or the adoption or use of one or more practices, means, methods, operations, or processes, reasonably necessary or appropriate to provide safe or healthful employment and places of employment."

The legislative history of the Act reveals Congress' particular concern for health hazards of "unprecedented complexity" that had resulted from chemicals whose toxic effects "are only now being discovered." "Recent scientific knowledge points to hitherto unsuspected cause-and-effect relationships between occupational exposures and many of the so-called chronic diseases—cancer, respiratory ailments, allergies, heart disease, and others." Members of Congress made repeated references to the dangers posed by carcinogens and to the defects in our knowledge of their operation and effect. One of the primary purposes of the Act was to ensure regulation of these "insidious 'silent' killers."

The authority conferred by §655(b)(5), however, is not absolute. The subsection itself contains two primary limitations. The requirement of "material" impairment was designed to prohibit the Secretary from regulating substances that create a trivial hazard to affected employees. Moreover, all standards promulgated under the subsection must be "feasible." During the floor debates Congress expressed concern that a prior version of the bill, not clearly embodying the feasibility requirement, would require the Secretary to close down whole industries in order to eliminate risks of impairment. This standard was criticized as unrealistic. The feasibility requirement was imposed as an affirmative limit on the standard-setting power.

The remainder of §655(b)(5), applicable to all safety and health standards, requires the Secretary to base his standards "upon research, demonstrations, experiments, and such other information as may be appropriate." In setting standards, the Secretary is directed to consider "the attainment of the highest degree of health and safety protection for the employee" and also "the latest available scientific data in the field, the feasibility of the standards, and experience gained under this and other health and safety laws."

The Act makes provision for judicial review of occupational safety and health standards promulgated pursuant to §655(b)(5). The reviewing court must uphold the Secretary's determinations if they are supported by "substantial evidence in the record considered as a whole." It is to that evidence that I now turn.

The plurality's discussion of the record in this case is both extraordinarily arrogant and extraordinarily unfair. It is arrogant because the plurality presumes to make its own factual findings with respect to a variety of disputed issues relating to carcinogen regulation. . . . It should not be necessary to remind the Members of this Court that they were not appointed to undertake independent review of adequately supported scientific findings made by a technically expert agency. And the plurality's discussion is unfair because its characterization of the Secretary's report bears practically no resemblance to what the Secretary actually did in this case. Contrary to the plurality's suggestion, the Secretary did not rely blindly on some Draconian carcinogen "policy." If he had, it would have been sufficient for him to have observed that benzene is a carcinogen, a proposition respondents do not dispute. Instead, the Secretary gathered over 50 volumes of exhibits and testimony and offered a detailed and evenhanded discussion of the relationship between exposure to benzene at all recorded exposure levels and chromosomal damage, aplastic anemia, and leukemia. In that discussion he evaluated, and took seriously, respondents' evidence of a safe exposure level. . . .

The plurality is insensitive to three factors which, in my view, make judicial review of occupational safety and health standards under the substantial evidence test particularly difficult. First, the issues often reach a high level of technical complexity. In such circumstances the courts are required to immerse themselves in matters to which they are unaccustomed by training or experience. Second, the

factual issues with which the Secretary must deal are frequently not subject to any definitive resolution. . . . Causal connections and theoretical extrapolations may be uncertain. Third, when the question involves determination of the acceptable level of risk, the ultimate decision must necessarily be based on considerations of policy as well as empirically verifiable facts. Factual determinations can at most define the risk in some statistical way; the judgment whether that risk is tolerable cannot be based solely on a resolution of the facts.

The decision to take action in conditions of uncertainty bears little resemblance to the sort of empirically verifiable factual conclusions to which the substantial evidence test is normally applied. Such decisions were not intended to be unreviewable; they too must be scrutinized to ensure that the Secretary has acted reasonably and within the boundaries set by Congress. But a reviewing court must be mindful of the limited nature of its role. See *Vermont Yankee Nuclear Power Corp. v. NRDC*, 435 U.S. 519 (1978). It must recognize that the ultimate decision cannot be based solely on determinations of fact, and that those factual conclusions that have been reached are ones which the courts are ill-equipped to resolve on their own.

The plurality avoids this conclusion through reasoning that may charitably be described as obscure. According to the plurality, the definition of occupational safety and health standards as those "reasonably necessary or appropriate to provide safe or healthful . . . working conditions" requires the Secretary to show that it is "more likely than not" that the risk he seeks to regulate is a "significant" one.

The plurality suggests that under the "reasonably necessary" clause, a workplace is not "unsafe" unless the Secretary is able to convince a reviewing court that a "significant" risk is at issue. That approach is particularly embarrassing in this case, for it is contradicted by the plain language of the Act. The plurality's interpretation renders utterly superfluous the first sequence of §655(b)(5), which, as noted above, requires the Secretary to set the standard "which most adequately assures . . . that no employee will suffer material impairment of health." Indeed, the plurality's interpretation reads that sentence out of the Act. By so doing, the plurality makes the test for standards regulating toxic substances and harmful physical agents substantially identical to the test for standards generally—plainly the opposite of what Congress intended. And it is an odd canon of construction that would insert in a vague and general definitional clause a threshold requirement that overcomes the specific language placed in a standard-setting provision. The most elementary principles of statutory construction demonstrate that precisely the opposite interpretation is appropriate. . . . In short, Congress could have provided that the Secretary may not take regulatory action until the existing scientific evidence proves the risk at issue to be "significant," but it chose not to do so.

The plurality's interpretation of the "reasonably necessary or appropriate" clause is also conclusively refuted by the legislative history. While the standard-setting provision that the plurality ignores received extensive legislative attention, the definitional clause received *none at all.* An earlier version of the Act, did not embody a clear feasibility constraint and was not restricted to toxic substances or to "material" impairments. The "reasonably necessary or appropriate" clause was contained in this prior version of the bill, as it was at all relevant times. In debating this version, Members of Congress repeatedly expressed concern that it would require a risk-free universe. The definitional clause was not mentioned at all, an omission that would be incomprehensible if Congress intended by that clause to require the Secretary to quantify the risk he sought to regulate in order to demonstrate that it was "significant."

The plurality ignores applicable canons of construction, apparently because it finds their existence inconvenient. But as we stated quite recently, the inquiry into statutory purposes should be "informed by an awareness that the regulation is entitled to deference unless it can be said not to be a reasoned and supportable interpretation of the Act." *Whirlpool Corp. v. Marshall,* 445 U.S. 1, 11 (1980). Can it honestly be said that the Secretary's interpretation of the Act is "unreasoned" or "unsupportable"? And as we stated in the same case, "safety legislation is to be liberally construed to effectuate the congressional purpose." . . . The plurality's disregard of these principles gives credence to the frequently voiced criticism that they are honored only when the Court finds itself in substantive agreement with the agency action at issue.

In short, today's decision represents a usurpation of decisionmaking authority that has been exercised by and properly belongs with Congress and its authorized representa-

tives. The plurality's construction has no support in the statute's language, structure, or legislative history. The threshold finding that the plurality requires is the plurality's own invention. It bears no relationship to the acts or intentions of Congress, and it can be understood only as reflecting the personal views of the plurality as to the proper allocation of resources for safety in the American workplace.

In recent years there has been increasing recognition that the products of technological development may have harmful effects whose incidence and severity cannot be predicted with certainty. The responsibility to regulate such products has fallen to administrative agencies. Their task is not an enviable one. Frequently no clear causal link can be established between the regulated substance and the harm to be averted. Risks of harm are often uncertain, but inaction has considerable costs of its own. The agency must decide whether to take regulatory action against possibly substantial risks or to wait until more definitive information becomes available—a judgment which by its very nature cannot be based solely on determinations of fact.

Those delegations, in turn, have been made on the understanding that judicial review would be available to ensure that the agency's determinations are supported by substantial evidence and that its actions do not exceed the limits set by Congress. In the Occupational Safety and Health Act, Congress expressed confidence that the courts would carry out this important responsibility. But in these cases the plurality has far exceeded its authority. The plurality's "threshold finding" requirement is nowhere to be found in the Act and is antithetical to its basic purposes. "The fundamental policy questions appropriately resolved in Congress . . . are *not* subject to re-examination in the federal courts under the guise of judicial review of agency action." *Vermont Yankee Nuclear Power Corp. v. NRDC,* 435 U.S. (emphasis in original). Surely this is no less true of the decision to ensure safety for the American worker than the decision to proceed with nuclear power.

Because the approach taken by the plurality is so plainly irreconcilable with the Court's proper institutional role, I am certain that it will not stand the test of time. In all likelihood, today's decision will come to be regarded as an extreme reaction to a regulatory scheme that, as the Members of the plurality perceived it, imposed an unduly harsh burden on regulated industries. But as the Constitution "does not enact Mr. Herbert Spencer's *Social Statics,*" *Lochner v. New York,* 198 U.S. 45, 75 (1905) (Holmes, J., dissenting), so the responsibility to scrutinize federal administrative action does not authorize this Court to strike its own balance between the costs and benefits of occupational safety standards. I am confident that the approach taken by the plurality today, like that in *Lochner* itself, will eventually be abandoned, and that the representative branches of government will once again be allowed to determine the level of safety and health protection to be accorded to the American worker.

American Textile Manufacturers Institute v. Donovan

452 U.S. 490 (1981) 5-3

+ *Brennan, White, Marshall, Blackmun, Stevens*

– *Stewart, Burger, Rehnquist*

NP *Powell*

[In this case, the issues and facts are similar to those of the benzene case but revolve on a slightly different point. The concentration of cotton dust, which causes byssinosis, was set at a limit held by OSHA to be as safe for textile workers as was technologically feasible—a requirement of the Occupational Safety and Health Act. The textile industry challenged the rule based on its belief that the word *feasible* required a cost-benefit analysis the results of which would dictate a different outcome than a standard based solely on concerns about workers' health. In a word, the issue was whether *feasible* meant "within the realm of possibility" or "within the realm of economic practicality."]

Justice Brennan delivered the opinion of the Court

The principal question presented in this case is whether the Occupational Safety and Health Act requires the Secretary, in promulgating a standard, . . . to determine that the costs of the standard bear a reasonable relationship to its benefits. Petitioners urge not only that OSHA must show that a standard addresses a significant risk of material health impairment, . . . but also that OSHA must demonstrate that the reduction in risk of material health impairment is significant in light of the costs of attaining that

reduction. . . . Respondents on the other hand contend that the Act requires OSHA to promulgate standards that eliminate or reduce such risks "to the extent such protection is technologically and economically feasible." . . . To resolve this debate, we must turn to the language, structure, and legislative history of the Occupational Safety and Health Act.

The starting point of our analysis is the language of the statute itself. Section 6(b)(5) of the Act, 29 U.S.C. §655(b)(5) (emphasis added), provides: "The Secretary, in promulgating standards dealing with toxic materials or harmful physical agents under this subsection, shall set the standard which most adequately assures, to the extent feasible," on the basis of the best available evidence that no employee will suffer material impairment of health or functional capacity even if such employee has regular exposure to the hazard dealt with by such standard for the period of his working life."

Although their interpretations differ, all parties agree that the phrase "to the extent feasible" contains the critical language in §6(b)(5) for purposes of this case.

The plain meaning of the word "feasible" supports respondents' interpretation of the statute. According to Webster's Third New International Dictionary of the English Language, "feasible" means "capable of being done, executed, or effected." Id., at 831 (1976). Accord, The Oxford English Dictionary 116 (1933) ("Capable of being done, accomplished or carried out"); Funk & Wagnalls New "Standard" Dictionary of the English Language 903 (1957) ("That may be done, performed or effected"). Thus, §6(b)(5) directs the Secretary to issue the standard that "most adequately assures . . . that no employee will suffer material impairment of health," limited only by the extent to which this is "capable of being done." In effect then, as the Court of Appeals held, Congress itself defined the basic relationship between costs and benefits, by placing the "benefit" of worker health above all other considerations save those making attainment of this "benefit" unachievable. Any standard based on a balancing of costs and benefits by the Secretary that strikes a different balance than that struck by Congress would be inconsistent with the command set forth in §6(b)(5). Thus, cost-benefit analysis by OSHA is not required by the statute because feasibility analysis is.

Even though the plain language of §6(b)(5) supports this construction, we must still decide whether §3(8), the general definition of an occupational safety and health standard, either alone or in tandem with §6(b)(5), incorporates a cost-benefit requirement for standards dealing with toxic materials or harmful physical agents. Section 3(8) of the Act, 29 U.S.C. §652(8) (emphasis added), provides: "The term 'occupational safety and health standard' means a standard which requires conditions, or the adoption or use of one or more practices, means, methods, operations, or processes, reasonably necessary or appropriate to provide safe or healthful employment and places of employment."

Taken alone, the phrase "reasonably necessary or appropriate" might be construed to contemplate some balancing of the costs and benefits of a standard. Petitioners urge that, so construed, §3(8) engrafts a cost benefit analysis requirement on the issuance of §6(b)(5) standards, even if §6(b)(5) itself does not authorize such analysis. We need not decide whether §3(8), standing alone, would contemplate some form of cost-benefit analysis. For even if it does, Congress specifically chose in §6(b)(5) to impose separate and additional requirements for issuance of a subcategory of occupational safety and health standards dealing with toxic materials and harmful physical agents: it required that those standards be issued to prevent material impairment of health to the extent feasible. Congress could reasonably have concluded that health standards should be subjected to different criteria than safety standards because of the special problems presented in regulating them.

Agreement with petitioners' argument that §3(8) imposes an additional and overriding requirement of cost-benefit analysis on the issuance of §6(b)(5) standards would eviscerate the "to the extent feasible" requirement. Standards would inevitably be set at the level indicated by cost-benefit analysis, and not at the level specified by §6(b)(5). We cannot believe that Congress intended the general terms of §3(8) to countermand the specific feasibility requirement of §6(b)(5). Adoption of petitioners' interpretation would effectively write §6(b)(5) out of the Act. We decline to render Congress's decision to include a feasibility requirement nugatory, thereby offending the well-settled rule that all parts of a statute, if possible, are to be given effect. Congress did not contemplate any further balancing by the agency for toxic material and harmful physical agents standards, and we should not "impute to Congress a purpose to paralyze with one hand what it sought to promote with the other."

The legislative history of the Act, while concededly not crystal clear, provides general support for respondents' interpretation of the Act. The Congressional reports and debates certainly confirm that Congress meant "feasible" and nothing else in using that term.

Not only does the legislative history confirm that Congress meant "feasible" rather than "cost-benefit" when it used the former term, but it also shows the Congress understood that the Act would create substantial costs for employers, yet intended to impose such costs when necessary to create a safe and healthful working environment. Congress viewed the costs of health and safety as a cost of doing business.

Section 6(f) of the Act provides that "[t]he determinations of the Secretary shall be conclusive if supported by substantial evidence in the record considered as a whole." 29 U.S.C. §655(f) Petitioners contend that the Secretary's determination that the Cotton Dust Standard is "economically feasible" is not supported by substantial evidence in the record considered as a whole. In particular, they claim (1) that OSHA underestimated the financial costs necessary to meet the Standard's requirements; and (2) that OSHA incorrectly found that the Standard would not threaten the economic viability of the cotton industry.

In statutes with provisions virtually identical to §6(f) of the Act, we have defined substantial evidence as "such relevant evidence as a reasonable mind might accept as adequate to support a conclusion." . . . The reviewing court must take into account contradictory evidence in the record . . . , but "the possibility of drawing two inconsistent conclusions from the evidence does not prevent an administrative agency's finding from being supported by substantial evidence." . . . Therefore, our inquiry is not to determine whether we, in the first instance, would find OSHA's findings supported by substantial evidence. Instead we turn to OSHA's findings and the record upon which they were based to decide whether the Court of Appeals "misapprehended or grossly misapplied" the substantial evidence test. . . .

After estimating the cost of compliance with the Cotton Dust Standard, OSHA analyzed whether it was "economically feasible" for the cotton industry to bear this cost. OSHA concluded that it was, finding that "although some marginal employers may shut down rather than comply, the industry as a whole will not be threatened by the capital requirements of the regulation." . . . In reaching this conclusion on the Standard's economic impact, OSHA made specific findings with respect to employment, energy consumption, capital financing availability, and profitability. . . . To support its findings, the agency relied primarily on RTTs comprehensive investigation of the Standard's economic impact.

The Court of Appeals found that the agency "explained the economic impact it projected for the textile industry," and that OSHA has "substantial support in the record for its . . . findings of economic feasibility for the textile industry." . . . On the basis of the whole record, we cannot conclude that the Court of Appeals "misapprehended or grossly misapplied" the substantial evidence test.

When Congress passed the Occupational Safety and Health Act in 1970, it chose to place pre-eminent value on assuring employees a safe and healthful working environment, limited only by the feasibility of achieving such an environment. We must measure the validity of the Secretary's actions against the requirements of that Act. For "[t]he judicial function does not extend to substantive revision of regulatory policy. That function lies elsewhere—in Congressional and Executive oversight or amendatory legislation."

Accordingly, the judgment of the Court of Appeals is affirmed.

Justice Stewart, dissenting

Because I believe that OSHA failed to justify its estimate of the cost of the Cotton Dust Standard on the basis of substantial evidence, I would reverse the judgment before us without reaching the question whether the Act requires that a standard, beyond being economically feasible, must meet the demands of a cost-benefit examination.

The simple truth about OSHA's assessment of the cost of the Cotton Dust Standard is that the agency never relied on any study or report purporting to predict the cost to industry of the Standard finally adopted by the agency. OSHA did have before it one cost analysis, . . . which attempted to predict the cost of the final Standard. However, as recognized by the Court, the agency flatly rejected that prediction as a gross overestimate. The only other estimate OSHA had, the Hocutt-Thomas estimate prepared by industry researchers, was not designed to predict the cost of the final OSHA Standard. Rather, it assumed a far less stringent and inevitably far less costly standard for all phases of cotton

production except roving. The agency examined the Hocutt-Thomas study, and concluded that it too was an overestimate of the costs of the less stringent standard it was addressing. I am willing to defer to OSHA's determination that the Hocutt-Thomas study was such an overestimate, conceding that such subtle financial and technical matters lie within the discretion and skill of the agency. But in a remarkable non sequitur, the agency decided that because the Hocutt-Thomas study was an overestimate of the cost of a less stringent standard, it could be treated as a reliable estimate for the more costly final Standard actually promulgated, never rationally explaining how it came to this happy conclusion. This is not substantial evidence. It is unsupported speculation.

The benzene and cotton dust cases exposed a major practical problem in the relations between courts and agencies. If statutes are, in fact, unclear and reasonable people can disagree about their meaning, the courts could be drawn into an endless debate with agencies about what the statutes mean. The *Chevron* case below is widely hailed as one of the most important developments in administrative law in the last part of the twentieth century. In this case the Court seemed to retreat from the claim that it should impose its own statutory interpretations on agencies. As long as the agency's interpretation of the statute is "reasonable," that should end the matter.

Chevron v. Natural Resources Defense Council Inc. et al.

467 U.S. 837 (1984) 6-0
+ Brennan, White, Burger, Blackmun, Powell, Stevens
NP Marshall, Rehnquist, O'Connor

[The Clean Air Act Amendments of 1977 required states that had not met national air quality standards to establish a permit program regulating "new or modified major stationary sources" of air pollution. In 1981, the EPA created regulations on how to implement the permit requirement, allowing a state to adopt a definition of the term "stationary source." This meant that plants with several pollution-emitting devices could modify just one piece of equipment without meeting the permit conditions if the modification did not increase total emissions from the plant. Such an interpretation allowed a state to treat all of the pollution-emitting devices within the same industrial grouping as though they were encased within a single "bubble."

The Natural Resources Defense Council, a national environmental public interest organization, challenged EPA's "bubble concept," asserting it was contrary to what Congress envisioned as a "stationary source" in its amendments to the Clean Air Act.]

Justice Stevens delivered the opinion of the Court

II

When a court reviews an agency's construction of the statute which it administers, it is confronted with two questions. First, always, is the question whether Congress has directly spoken to the precise question at issue. If the intent of Congress is clear, that is the end of the matter; for the court as well as the agency, must give effect to the unambiguously expressed intent of Congress. If, however, the court determines Congress has not directly addressed the precise question at issue, the court does not simply impose its own construction on the statute, as would be necessary in the absence of an administrative interpretation. Rather, if the statute is silent or ambiguous with respect to the specific issue, the question for the court is whether the agency's answer is based on a permissible construction of the statute.

If Congress has explicitly left a gap for the agency to fill, there is an express delegation of authority to the agency to elucidate a specific provision of the statute by regulation. Such legislative regulations are given controlling weight unless they are arbitrary, capricious, or manifestly contrary to the statute. Sometimes the legislative delegation to an agency on a particular question is implicit rather than explicit. In such a case, a court may not substitute its own construction of a statutory provision for a reasonable interpretation made by the administration of an agency.

We have long recognized that considerable weight should be accorded to an executive department's construction of a statutory scheme it is entrusted to administer, and the principle of deference to administrative interpretations.

In light of these well-settled principles it is clear that the Court of Appeals misconceived the nature of its role in reviewing the regulations at issue. Once it determined, after its own examination of the legislation, that Congress did not actually have an intent regarding the applicability of the bubble concept to the permit program, the question before it was not whether in its view the concept is "inappropriate" in the general context of a program designed to improve air quality, but whether the Administrator's view that it is appropriate in the context of this particular program is a reasonable one. Based on the examination of the legislation and its history which follows, we agree with the Court of Appeals that Congress did not have a specific intention on the applicability of the bubble concept in these cases, and conclude that the EPA's use of that concept here is a reasonable policy choice for the agency to make.

III

In the 1950's and the 1960's Congress enacted a series of statutes designed to encourage and to assist the States in curtailing air pollution. . . . The Clean Air Amendments of 1970, . . . "sharply increased federal authority and responsibility in the continuing effort to combat air pollution," . . . but continued to assign "primary responsibility for assuring air quality" to the several States. . . . Section 109 of the 1970 Amendments directed the EPA to promulgate National Ambient Air Quality Standards (NAAQS's) and §110 directed the States to develop plans (SIP's) to implement the standards within specified deadlines. In addition, §111 provided that major new sources of pollution would be required to conform to technology-based performance standards; the EPA was directed to publish a list of categories of sources of pollution and to establish new source performance standards (NSPS) for each. Section 111(e) prohibited the operation of any new source in violation of a performance standard.

Section 111 (a) defined the terms that are to be used in setting and enforcing standards of performance for new stationary sources. It provided:

"For purposes of this selection:

"(3) The term 'stationary source' means any building, structure, facility, or installation which emits or may emit any air pollutant."

In the 1970 Amendments that definition was not only applicable to the NSPS program required by §111, but also was made applicable to a requirement, of §110 that each state implementation plan contain a procedure for reviewing the location of any proposed new source and preventing its construction if it would preclude the attainment or maintenance of national air quality standards.

In due course, the EPA promulgated NAAQS's, approved SIP's, and adopted detailed regulations governing NSPS's for various categories of equipment. In one of its programs, the EPA used a plantwide definition of the term "stationary source." In 1974, it issued NSPS's for the nonferrous smelting industry that provided that the standards would not apply to the modification of major smelting units if their increased emissions were offset by reductions in other portions of the same plant.

The 1970 legislation provided for the attainment of primary NAAQS's by 1975. In many areas of the country, particularly the most industrialized States, the statutory goals were not attained. In 1976, the 94th Congress was confronted with this fundamental problem, as well as many others respecting pollution control. As always in this area, the legislative struggle was basically between interests seeking strict schemes to reduce pollution rapidly to eliminate its social costs and interests advancing the economic concern that strict schemes would retard industrial development with attendant social costs. The 94th Congress, confronting these competing interests, was unable to agree on what response was in the public interest: legislative proposals to deal with nonattainment failed to command the necessary consensus.

In light of this situation, the EPA published an Emissions Offset Interpretative Ruling in December 1976, . . . to "fill the gap," as respondents put it, until Congress acted. The Ruling stated that it was intended to address "the issue of whether and to what extent national air quality standards established under the Clean Air Act may restrict or prohibit growth of major new or expanded stationary air pollution sources." . . . In general, the Ruling provided that "a major new source may locate in an area with air quality worse than a national standard only if stringent conditions can be met." The Ruling gave primary emphasis to the rapid attainment of the statute's environmental goals. Consistent with that emphasis, the construction of every new source in nonattainment areas had to meet the "lowest achievable emission rate" under the current state of the art for that type of facil-

ity. . . . The 1976 Ruling did not, however, explicitly adopt or reject the "bubble concept."

IV

The Clean Air Act Amendments of 1977 are a lengthy, detailed, technical, complex, and comprehensive response to a major social issue. A small portion of the statute expressly deals with nonattainment areas. The focal point of this controversy is one phrase in that portion of the Amendments.

Basically, the statute required each State in a nonattainment area to prepare and obtain approval of a new SIP by July 1,1979.

Most significantly for our purposes, the statute provided that each plan shall

"(6) require permits for the construction and operation of new or modified major stationary sources in accordance with section 173."

Before issuing a permit, §173 requires (1) the state agency to determine that there will be sufficient emissions reductions in the region to offset the emissions from the new source and also to allow for reasonable further progress toward attainment, or that the increased emissions will not exceed an allowance for growth established pursuant to §172(b)(5); (2) the applicant to certify that his other sources in the State are in compliance with the SIP, (3) the agency to determine that the applicable SIP is otherwise being implemented, and (4) the proposed source to comply with the lowest achievable emission rate (LAER).

The 1977 Amendments contain no specific reference to the "bubble concept." Nor do they contain a specific definition of the term "stationary source," though they do not disturb the definition of "stationary source" contained in §111 (a)(3), applicable by the terms of the Act to the NSPS program. Section 302(j), however, defines the term "major stationary source" as follows:

"(j) Except as otherwise expressly provided, the terms 'major stationary source' and 'major emitting facility' mean any stationary facility or source of air pollutants which directly emits, or has the potential to emit, one hundred tons per year or more of any air pollutant (including any major emitting facility or source of fugitive emissions of any such pollutant, as determined by rule by the Administrator)."

V

The legislative history of the portion of the 1977 Amendments dealing with nonattainment areas does not contain any specific comment on the "bubble concept" or the question whether a plantwide definition of a stationary source is permissible under the permit program. It does, however, plainly disclose that in the permit program Congress sought to accommodate the conflict between the economic interest in permitting capital improvements to continue and the environmental interest in improving air quality. Indeed, the House Committee Report identified the economic interest as one of the "two main purposes" of this section of the bill. . . .

The portion of the Senate Committee Report dealing with nonattainment areas states generally that it was intended to "supersede the EPA administrative approach," and that expansion should be permitted if a State could "demonstrate that these facilities can be accommodated within its overall plan to provide for attainment of air quality standards." . . .

The Senate Report notes the value of "case-by-case review of each new or modified major source of pollution that seeks to locate in a region exceeding an ambient standard," explaining that such a review "requires matching reductions from existing sources against emissions expected from the new source in order to assure that introduction of the new source will not prevent attainment of the applicable standard by the statutory deadline." . . . This description of a case-by-case approach to plant additions, which emphasizes the net consequences of the construction or modification of a new source, as well as its impact on the overall achievement of the national standards, was not, however, addressed to the precise issue raised by these cases.

VI

As previously noted, prior to the 1977 Amendments, the EPA had adhered to a plantwide definition of the term "source" under a NSPS program. After adoption of the 1977 Amendments, proposals for a plantwide definition were considered in at least three formal proceedings.

In January 1979, the EPA considered the question whether the same restriction on new construction in nonattainment areas that had been included in its December 1976 Ruling should be required in the revised SIP's that were scheduled to go into effect in July 1979. After noting that the 1976 Ruling was ambiguous on the question

"whether a plant with a number of different processes and emission points would be considered a single source," . . . the EPA, in effect, provided a bifurcated answer to that question. In those areas that did not have a revised SIP in effect by July 1979, the EPA rejected the plantwide definition; on the other hand, it expressly concluded that the plantwide approach would be permissible in certain circumstances if authorized by an approved SIP. . . .

In April, again in September 1979, the EPA published additional comments in which it indicated that revised SIP's could adopt the plantwide definition of source in nonattainment areas in certain circumstances. . . . On the latter occasion, the EPA made a formal rulemaking proposal that would have permitted the use of the "bubble concept" for new installations within a plant as well as for modifications of existing units. It explained:

" 'Bubble' Exemption: The use of offsets inside the same source is called the 'bubble.' EPA proposes use of the definition of 'source' (see above) to limit the use of the bubble under nonattainment requirements."

Significantly, the EPA expressly noted that the word "source" might be given a plantwide definition for some purposes and a narrower definition for other purposes.

"Source means any building structure, facility, or installation which emits or may emit any regulated pollutant. 'Building, structure, facility or installation' means plant in PSD areas and in nonattainment areas except where the growth prohibitions would apply or where no adequate SIP exists or is being carried out."

The EPA's summary of its proposed Ruling discloses a flexible rather than rigid definition of the term "source" to implement various policies and programs.

In August 1980, however, the EPA adopted a regulation that, in essence, applied the basic reasoning of the Court of Appeals in these cases. The EPA took particular note of the two then-recent Court of Appeals decisions, which had created the bright-line rule that the "bubble concept" should be employed in a program designed to maintain air quality but not in one designed to enhance air quality. Relying heavily on those cases, EPA adopted a dual definition of "source" for nonattainment areas that required a permit whenever a change in either the entire plant, or one of its components, would result in a significant increase in emissions even if the increase was completely offset by reductions elsewhere in the plant. The EPA expressed the opinion that this interpretation was "more consistent with congressional intent" than the plantwide definition because it "would bring in more sources or modifications for review," but its primary legal analysis was predicated on the two Court of Appeals decisions.

In 1981 a new administration took office and initiated a "Government-wide reexamination of regulatory burdens and complexities." In the context of that review, the EPA reevaluated the various arguments that had been advanced in connection with the proper definition of the term "source" and concluded that the term should be given the same definition in both nonattainment areas and PSD areas.

In explaining its conclusion, the EPA first noted that the definitional issue was not squarely addressed in either the statute or its legislative history and therefore that the issue involved an agency "judgment as how to best carry out the Act." It then set forth several reasons for concluding that the plantwide definition was more appropriate. It pointed out that the dual definition "can act as a disincentive to new investment and modernization by discouraging modifications to existing facilities" and "can actually retard progress in air pollution control by discouraging replacement of older, dirtier processes or pieces of equipment with new, cleaner ones." Moreover, the new definition "would simplify EPA's rules by using the same definition of 'source' for PSD, nonattainment new source review and the construction moratorium. This reduces confusion and inconsistency." Finally, the agency explained that additional requirements that remained in place would accomplish the fundamental purposes of achieving attainment with NAAQS's as expeditiously as possible. These conclusions were expressed in a proposed rulemaking in August 1981.

VII

We are not persuaded that parsing of general terms in the text of the statute will reveal an actual intent of Congress. We know full well that this language is not dispositive; the terms are overlapping and the language is not precisely directed to the question of the applicability of a given term in the context of a larger operation. To the extent any congressional "intent" can be discerned from this language, it would appear that the listing of overlapping, illustrative terms was intended to enlarge, rather than to confine, the scope of the agency's power to regulate particular sources in order to effectuate the policies of the Act.

More importantly, that history plainly identifies the policy concerns that motivated the enactment; the plantwide definition is fully consistent with one of those concerns—the allowance of reasonable economic growth—and, whether or not we believe it most effectively implements the other, we must recognize that the EPA has advanced a reasonable explanation for its conclusion that the regulations serve the environmental objectives as well.

Our review of the EPA's varying interpretations of the word "source"—both before and after the 1977 Amendments—convinces us that the agency primarily responsible for administering this important legislation has consistently interpreted it flexibly—not in a sterile textual vacuum, but in the context of implementing policy decisions in a technical and complex arena. The fact that the agency has from time to time changed its interpretation of the term "source" does not, as respondents argue, lead us to conclude that no deference should be accorded the agency's interpretation of the statute. An initial agency interpretation is not instantly carved in stone. On the contrary, the agency, to engage in informed rulemaking, must consider varying interpretations and the wisdom of its policy on a continuing basis. Moreover, the fact that the agency has adopted different definitions in different contexts adds force to the argument that the definition itself is flexible, particularly since Congress has never indicated any disapproval of a flexible reading of the statute.

Significantly, it was not the agency in 1980, but rather the Court of Appeals that read the statute inflexibly to command a plantwide definition for programs designed to maintain clean air and to forbid such a definition for programs designed to improve air quality. The distinction the court drew may well be a sensible one, but our labored review of the problem has surely disclosed that it is not a distinction that Congress ever articulated itself, or one that the EPA found in the statute before the courts began to review the legislative work product. We conclude that it was the Court of Appeals, rather than Congress or any of the decisionmakers who are authorized by Congress to administer this legislation, that was primarily responsible for the 1980 position taken by the agency.

The arguments over the policy that are advanced in the parties' briefs create the impression that respondents are now waging in a judicial forum a specific policy battle which they ultimately lost in the agency and in the 32 jurisdictions opting for the "bubble concept," but one which was never waged in Congress. Such policy arguments are more properly addressed to legislators or administrators, not to judges.

In these cases, the Administrator's interpretation represents a reasonable accommodation of manifestly competing interests and is entitled to deference: the regulatory scheme is technical and complex, the agency considered the matter in a detailed and reasoned fashion, and the decision involves reconciling conflicting policies. Congress intended to accommodate both interests, but did not do so itself on the level of specificity presented by these cases. Perhaps that body consciously desired the Administrator to strike the balance at this level, thinking that those with great expertise and charged with responsibility for administering the provision would be in a better position to do so; perhaps it simply did not consider the question at this level; and perhaps Congress was unable to forge a coalition on either side of the question, and those on each side decided to take their chances with the scheme devised by the agency. For judicial purposes, it matters not which of these things occurred.

Judges are not experts in the field, and are not part of either political branch of the Government. Courts must, in some cases, reconcile competing political interests, but not on the basis of the judges' personal policy preferences. In contrast, an agency to which Congress has delegated policymaking responsibilities may, within the limits of that delegation, properly rely upon the incumbent administration's views of wise policy to inform its judgments. While agencies are not directly accountable to the people, the Chief Executive is, and it is entirely appropriate for this political branch of the Government to make such policy choices— resolving the competing interest which Congress itself either inadvertently did not resolve, or intentionally left to be resolved by the agency charged with the administration of the statute in light of everyday realities.

When a challenge to an agency construction of a statutory provision, fairly conceptualized, really centers on the wisdom of the agency's policy, rather than whether it is a reasonable choice within a gap left open by Congress, the challenge must fail. In such a case, federal judges—who have no constituency—have a duty to respect legitimate policy choices made by those who do. The responsibilities for assessing the wisdom of such policy choices and resolving the struggle between competing views of the public interest are not judicial ones: "Our Constitution vests such responsibilities in the political branches."

We hold that the EPA's definition of the term "source" is a permissible construction of the statute which seeks to accommodate progress in reducing air pollution with economic growth.

The judgment of the Court of Appeals is reversed. It is so ordered.

Over the years, *Chevron* came to be perceived as the "Supreme Court's leading statement about the division of authority between agencies and courts in interpreting statutes."[12] It became one of the most cited Supreme Court cases in history, definitely the most cited administrative law case of all time. Interestingly, nonetheless, the case in its initial years was far from being a landmark, leading Thomas Merrill, a law professor at Columbia University, to label the story of *Chevron* as "the making of an accidental landmark." According to Merrill, "there is nothing in the [parties'] petitions suggesting that the parties were asking the Court to reconsider basic questions of administrative law."[13] The transcript of the oral argument similarly does not reveal any substantial discussion of significance, nor do Justice Blackmun's notes suggest a heated discussion about basic questions of administrative law. The case revolved around the question of the meaning and applicability of the "bubble concept." Justice Stevens, "when asked about his most famous opinion . . . would respond that he regarded it as simply a restatement of existing law. . . ."[14] Yet despite such modest beginnings, *Chevron* and the two-step framework it established became nothing short of revolutionary. "Beginning with the 1985–86 Term, *Chevron* began to appear with increasing frequency in the Court's opinions. Six cases applied the *Chevron* framework in 1985–86, two the next

12. Thomas Merrill, "The Story of *Chevron*: The Making of an Accidental Landmark," in *Administrative Law Stories*, ed. Peter Strauss (New York: Foundation Press, 2006).
13. Ibid. at 398.
14. Ibid. at 420.

term, and five the term following that. By the end of the 1980s, the percentage of deference cases in the Supreme Court adopting the *Chevron* framework had risen to around 40%; by the early 1990s it was up to around 60%. Soon the Court began to debate, in the course of resolving particular stationary questions, whether the *Chevron* approach should apply or not. . . . Eventually, the Court was granting certiorari and devoting entire cases to questions about the scope of 'the *Chevron* doctrine.' . . ." [15]

There is no single explanation why *Chevron* became the landmark case it is. Thomas Merrill, however, suggests two possibilities. On the one hand, "*Chevron* was regarded as a godsend by executive branch lawyers charged with writing briefs defending agency interpretations of law. Not only did the two-step standard provide an effective organizing principle for busy brief writers, the opinion seemed to say that deference was the default rule in any case where Congress has not spoken. . . ." This led to an aggressive promotion of the decision by executive branch lawyers. On the other hand, Merrill posits that "*Chevron* became a leading case initially in the D.C. Circuit, and then migrated back to the Supreme Court along with personnel who had previously served in the D.C. Circuit," [16] such as law clerks or Justices, notably Antonin Scalia.

The partisan political aspects of the *Chevron* case have been much debated. [17] Some commented that the Court's approval of the pro-business "bubble" rule coincided with the fact that both the Supreme Court and the EPA were, under the influence of the Reagan administration, moving in conservative policy directions. Over time, however, the *Chevron* doctrine has not generated any obvious partisan outcomes. In 1990, for example, the Court implicitly pulled back from the broadest implications of *Chevron* in a decision that overturned a pro-business decision of the White House Office of Management and Budget (OMB). The case, involving then Secretary of Labor Elizabeth Dole, challenged an interpretation by OMB of the Paperwork Reduction Act of 1980. The act required, among other things, that in order to reduce the paperwork burden on the public of supplying information to the government, agencies initiating "information collection requests" from the public had to win OMB approval first. Under OSHA, the Department of Labor (DOL) issued rules requiring employers to communicate, *not to the government but to their employees*, any hazards to employees from chemicals in the workplace. Manufacturers had to label hazardous chemical containers, conduct training on the dangers of specific chemicals, and make available to employees safety data sheets on chemicals. OMB refused to authorize the regulations, and DOL complied, but the steelworkers' union sued successfully to have OMB's interpretation of its statute overturned. We might think that politically conservative justices would draw on *Chevron* to approve OMB's move, but the Supreme Court ruled, 7-2, that the statute plainly covered only the paperwork burden imposed on people supplying information to the government. [18]

The *Dole* case illustrates an important move that judges can always make when they do not like the results that *Chevron*'s analysis produces. That is, judges can always say that the statute is not ambiguous in the first place. Judicial deference to the agency comes into play only when the statute is not clear, so judges can say the statute *is* clear, and then decline to review the reasonableness of the agency's decision.

In fact, as the doctrine aged, this discretionary power in the hands of judges, what some scholars call, "*Chevron* step zero," [19] was subject to further critical scrutiny by the Supreme Court. Along with the solidification of *Chevron* as a doctrine, [20] came the need for further accuracy about what the doctrine stood for. The aura and strength of the *Chevron* revolution, for a considerable time, led to the belief that *Chevron* applied to most, if not all, administrative decision making where the Congress has not clearly spoken on the issue at hand.

15. Ibid. at 421–422.

16. Ibid. at 426.

17. See particularly the discussion in Richard Harris and Sidney Milkis, *The Politics of Regulatory Change*, 2nd ed. (New York: Oxford University Press, 1996).

18. *Dole v. United Steelworkers of America*, 494 U.S. 26 (1990).

19. See Thomas Merrill and Kristine Hickman, "*Chevron*'s Domain," *Georgia Law Journal*, 89 (2001): 833.

20. See Mark J. Richards, Joseph L. Smith, and Herbert M. Kritzer, "Does *Chevron* Matter?" *Law & Policy* 28 (2006): 444.

In the next two cases, you will see how the Supreme Court shapes the scope of the *Chevron* doctrine. In the first case, *FDA v. Brown & Williamson*, 529 U.S. 120 (2000), the question of "step-zero" is not explicitly discussed. The Court suggests that *Chevron* applies whenever there is a statutory interpretation case like the one in *FDA v. Brown & Williamson*. However, the Court finds this statute unambiguous and does not defer to the agency. Instead, the Court reasons that deference is not due when a "major question" is involved, and that "Congress should not be taken to have asked agencies to resolve those questions."[21] This effectively means that *Chevron* (deference) does not always apply when significant, and contested, policy issues are at stake. In the second case, *U.S. v. Mead Corporation*, 533 U.S. 218 (2001), the Court is more explicit about what it regards as the boundaries of *Chevron*. Here, the Court simply states that certain agency actions are not entitled to *Chevron* deference.

FDA v. Brown & Williamson

529 U.S. 120 (2000) 5-4
+ *Rehnquist, O'Connor, Scalia, Kennedy, Thomas*
− *Breyer, Stevens, Souter, Ginsburg*

[After having declined since its inception to assert jurisdiction over the regulation of tobacco products, the Food and Drug Administration (FDA) finally did so in 1996. To combat the harmful and costly effects of tobacco consumption by minors, a population targeted by cigarette advertising, the FDA issued "Regulations Restricting the Sale and Distribution of Cigarettes and Smokeless Tobacco to Protect Children and Adolescents." Critical to the FDA's regulatory approach was its assertion that nicotine is a "drug" and cigarettes "devices" to deliver that drug, thus authorizing the FDA to regulate tobacco within the meaning of the Food, Drug, and Cosmetic Act (FDCA). The United States District Court for the Middle District of North Carolina ruled in favor of the FDA and its access and labeling regulations. The United States Court of Appeals for the Fourth Circuit reversed, holding that Congress did not grant the FDA jurisdiction to regulate tobacco products.

21. Cass Sunstein, *"Chevron Step Zero"* (working paper no. 91, Public Law and Legal Theory, University of Chicago Law School, 2005).

The Supreme Court's opinion below is perceived by many scholars in the field as a move toward weakening the authority of the *Chevron* framework. The case is significant on other levels, too. You will read a very convincing majority opinion, only to be equally convinced by the dissent later on. As you read the case, consider the larger question of how, through statutory interpretation, the Court can avoid making a decision on a contentious issue of economic and social policy.]

Justice O'Connor delivered the opinion of the Court

[. . .]

Regardless of how serious the problem an administrative agency seeks to address . . . it may not exercise its authority "in a manner that is inconsistent with the administrative structure that Congress enacted into law." *FTSI Pipeline Project v. Missouri*, 484 U.S. 495, 517 (1988). And although agencies are generally entitled to deference in the interpretation of statutes that they administer, a reviewing "court, as well as the agency, must give effect to the unambiguously expressed intent of Congress." *Chevron U.S.A. Inc. v. Natural Resources Defense Council, Inc.*, 467 U.S. 837, 842-843 (1984). In this case, we believe that Congress has clearly precluded the FDA from asserting jurisdiction to regulate tobacco products. Such authority is inconsistent with the intent that Congress has expressed in the FDCA's overall regulatory scheme and in the tobacco-specific legislation that it has enacted subsequent to the FDCA. In light of this clear intent, the FDA's assertion of jurisdiction is impermissible.

II

The FDA's assertion of jurisdiction to regulate tobacco products is founded on its conclusions that nicotine is a "drug" and that cigarettes and smokeless tobacco are "drug delivery devices." Again, the FDA found that tobacco products are "intended" to deliver the pharmacological effects of satisfying addiction, stimulation and tranquilization, and weight control because those effects are foreseeable to any reasonable manufacturer, consumers use tobacco products to obtain those effects, and tobacco manufacturers have designed their products to produce those effects. 61 Fed. Reg. 44632-44633 (1996). As an initial matter, respondents take issue with the FDA's reading of "intended," arguing that it is a term of art that refers exclusively to claims made by the manufacturer or vendor about the product . . . We need not resolve this question, however, because . . . the FDA's claim to jurisdiction contravenes the clear intent of Congress.

Because this case involves an administrative agency's construction of a statute that it administers, our analysis is governed by *Chevron U. S. A. Inc. v. Natural Resources Defense Council, Inc.,* 467 U.S. 837 (1984). . . . In determining whether Congress has specifically addressed the question at issue, a reviewing court should not confine itself to examining a particular statutory provision in isolation. The meaning—or ambiguity—of certain words or phrases may only become evident when placed in context. . . . Similarly, the meaning of one statute may be affected by other Acts, particularly where Congress has spoken subsequently and more specifically to the topic at hand. . . . See *United States v. Estate of Romani,* 523 U.S. 517, 530-531 (1998); *United States v. Fausto,* 484 U.S. 439, 453 (1988). In addition, we must be guided to a degree by common sense as to the manner in which Congress is likely to delegate a policy decision of such economic and political magnitude to an administrative agency. Cf. *MCI Telecommunications Corp. v. American Telephone & Telegraph Co. ,* 512 U.S. 218, 231 (1994).

With these principles in mind, we find that Congress has directly spoken to the issue here and precluded the FDA's jurisdiction to regulate tobacco products.

A

Viewing the FDCA as a whole, it is evident that one of the Act's core objectives is to ensure that any product regulated by the FDA is "safe" and "effective" for its intended use. See 21 U. S. C. §393(b)(2) (1994 ed., Supp. III) (defining the FDA's mission) . . . This essential purpose pervades the FDCA. For instance, 21 U. S. C. §393(b)(2) (1994 ed., Supp. III) defines the FDA's "mission" to include "protect[ing] the public health by ensuring that . . . drugs are safe and effective" and that "there is reasonable assurance of the safety and effectiveness of devices intended for human use." . . . In its rulemaking proceeding, the FDA quite exhaustively documented that "tobacco products are unsafe," "dangerous," and "cause great pain and suffering from illness." 61 Fed. Reg. 44412 (1996). It found that the consumption of tobacco products "presents extraordinary health risks," and that "tobacco use is the single leading cause of preventable death in the United States." Id., at 44398. . . . These findings

logically imply that, if tobacco products were "devices" under the FDCA, the FDA would be required to remove them from the market. . . .

In fact, based on [misbranding and device classification provisions], the FDA itself has previously taken the position that if tobacco products were within its jurisdiction, "they would have to be removed from the market because it would be impossible to prove they were safe for their intended us[e]." Public Health Cigarette Amendments of 1971: Hearings before the Commerce Subcommittee on S. 1454, 92d Cong., 2d Sess., 239 (1972) (hereinafter 1972 Hearings) (statement of FDA Commissioner Charles Edwards). Congress, however, has foreclosed the removal of tobacco products from the market. A provision of the United States Code currently in force states that "[t]he marketing of tobacco constitutes one of the greatest basic industries of the United States with ramifying activities which directly affect interstate and foreign commerce at every point, and stable conditions therein are necessary to the general welfare." 7 U. S. C. §1311(a). More importantly, Congress has directly addressed the problem of tobacco and health through legislation on six occasions since 1965. See Federal Cigarette Labeling and Advertising Act (FCLAA), Pub. L. 89-92, 79 Stat. 282; Public Health Cigarette Smoking Act of 1969, Pub. L. 91-222, 84 Stat. 87; Alcohol and Drug Abuse Amendments of 1983, Pub. L. 98-24, 97 Stat. 175; Comprehensive Smoking Education Act, Pub. L. 98-474, 98 Stat. 2200; Comprehensive Smokeless Tobacco Health Education Act of 1986, Pub. L. 99-252, 100 Stat. 30; Alcohol, Drug Abuse, and Mental Health Administration Reorganization Act, Pub. L. 102-321, §202, 106 Stat. 394. When Congress enacted these statutes, the adverse health consequences of tobacco use were well known, as were nicotine's pharmacological effects. . . . Nonetheless, Congress stopped well short of ordering a ban. Instead, it has generally regulated the labeling and advertisement of tobacco products, expressly providing that it is the policy of Congress that "commerce and the national economy may be . . . protected to the maximum extent consistent with" consumers "be[ing] adequately informed about any adverse health effects." 15 U. S. C. §1331. . . . A ban of tobacco products by the FDA would therefore plainly contradict congressional policy.

The FDA apparently recognized this dilemma and concluded, somewhat ironically, that tobacco products are actually "safe" within the meaning of the FDCA. . . . [T]he FDA reasoned that, in determining whether a device is safe under the Act, it must consider "not only the risks presented by a product but also any of the countervailing effects of use of that product, including the consequences of not permitting the product to be marketed." Id., at 44412-44413. Applying this standard, the FDA found that, because of the high level of addiction among tobacco users, a ban would likely be "dangerous." Id., at 44413. In particular, current tobacco users could suffer from extreme withdrawal, the health care system and available pharmaceuticals might not be able to meet the treatment demands of those suffering from withdrawal, and a black market offering cigarettes even more dangerous than those currently sold legally would likely develop. Ibid. . . .

It may well be, as the FDA asserts, that "these factors must be considered when developing a regulatory scheme that achieves the best public health result for these products." Id., at 44413. But . . . [s]everal provisions in the Act require the FDA to determine that the product itself is safe as used by consumers. That is, the product's probable therapeutic benefits must outweigh its risk of harm. . . . [A]lthough the FDA has concluded that a ban would be "dangerous," it has not concluded that tobacco products are "safe" as that term is used throughout the Act. . . .

Although banning a particular product might be detrimental to public health in aggregate, the product could still be "dangerous to health" when used as directed. . . .

Consequently, the analogy made by the FDA and the dissent to highly toxic drugs used in the treatment of various cancers is unpersuasive. See 61 Fed. Reg. 44413 (1996); post, at 17 (opinion of Breyer, J.). . . . Consequently, if tobacco products were within the FDA's jurisdiction, the Act would require the FDA to remove them from the market entirely. But a ban would contradict Congress' clear intent as expressed in its more recent, tobacco-specific legislation. The inescapable conclusion is that there is no room for tobacco products within the FDCA's regulatory scheme. . . .

B

In determining whether Congress has spoken directly to the FDA's authority to regulate tobacco, we must also consider in greater detail the tobacco-specific legislation that Congress has enacted over the past 35 years. Congress has enacted six separate pieces of legislation since 1965 addressing the problem of tobacco use and human health. See supra, at 14. Those statutes, among other things, require that health warnings appear on all packaging and in all print and outdoor advertisements, see 15 U. S. C. §§1331, 1333, 4402; prohibit the advertisement of tobacco products through "any medium of electronic communication" subject to regulation by the Federal Communications Commission (FCC), see §§1335, 4402(f); require the Secretary of Health and Human Services (HHS) to report every three years to Congress on research findings concerning "the addictive property of tobacco," 42 U. S. C. §290aa-2(b)(2); and make States' receipt of certain federal block grants contingent on their making it unlawful "for any manufacturer, retailer, or distributor of tobacco products to sell or distribute any such product to any individual under the age of 18," §300x-26(a)(1).

In adopting each statute, Congress has acted against the backdrop of the FDA's consistent and repeated statements that it lacked authority under the FDCA to regulate tobacco absent claims of therapeutic benefit by the manufacturer. In fact, on several occasions over this period, and after the health consequences of tobacco use and nicotine's pharmacological effects had become well known, Congress considered and rejected bills that would have granted the FDA such jurisdiction. Under these circumstances, it is evident that Congress' tobacco-specific statutes have effectively ratified the FDA's long-held position that it lacks jurisdiction under the FDCA to regulate tobacco products. Congress has created a distinct regulatory scheme to address the problem of tobacco and health, and that scheme, as presently constructed, precludes any role for the FDA. . . .

The dissent . . . argues that, even if Congress' subsequent tobacco-specific legislation did, in fact, ratify the FDA's position, that position was merely a contingent disavowal of jurisdiction. Specifically, the dissent contends that "the FDA's traditional view was largely premised on a perceived inability to prove the necessary statutory `intent' requirement." Post, at 30. A fair reading of the FDA's representations prior to 1995, however, demonstrates that the agency's position was essentially unconditional. . . . To the extent the agency's position could be characterized as equivocal, it was only with respect to the well-established exception of when the manufacturer makes express claims of therapeutic benefit. See, e.g. , 1965 Hearings 193 (statement of Deputy Commissioner Rankin) ("The Food and Drug Administration has no jurisdiction under the Food, Drug, and Cosmetic Act over tobacco, unless it bears drug claims"); Letter to ASH Executive Director Banzhaf from FDA Commissioner Kennedy (Dec. 5, 1977), App. 47 ("The interpretation of the Act by FDA consistently has been that cigarettes are not a drug unless health claims are made by the vendors"). . . . Thus, what Congress ratified was the FDA's plain and resolute position that the FDCA gives the agency no authority to regulate tobacco products as customarily marketed.

C

Finally, our inquiry into whether Congress has directly spoken to the precise question at issue is shaped, at least in some measure, by the nature of the question presented. Deference under *Chevron* to an agency's construction of a statute that it administers is premised on the theory that a statute's ambiguity constitutes an implicit delegation from Congress to the agency to fill in the statutory gaps. See *Chevron* , 467 U. S., at 844. In extraordinary cases, however, there may be reason to hesitate before concluding that Congress has intended such an implicit delegation. Cf. Breyer, Judicial Review of Questions of Law and Policy, 38 Admin. L. Rev. 363, 370 (1986). . . .

This is hardly an ordinary case. Contrary to its representations to Congress since 1914, the FDA has now asserted jurisdiction to regulate an industry constituting a significant portion of the American economy. . . . Owing to its unique place in American history and society, tobacco has its own unique political history. Congress, for better or for worse, has created a distinct regulatory scheme for tobacco products, squarely rejected proposals to give the FDA jurisdiction over tobacco, and repeatedly acted to preclude any agency from exercising significant policymaking authority in the area. Given this history and the breadth of the authority that the FDA has asserted, we are obliged to defer not to the agency's expansive construction of the statute, but to Congress' consistent judgment to deny the FDA this power.

In reasoning even more apt here, we concluded [in *MCI Telecommunications Corp. v. American Telephone & Telegraph Co.*, 512 U.S. 218 (1994)] that "[i]t is highly unlikely that Congress would leave the determination of whether an industry will be entirely, or even substantially, rate-regulat-

ed to agency discretion—and even more unlikely that it would achieve that through such a subtle device as permission to `modify' rate-filing requirements." Id., at 231.

As in *MCI* , we are confident that Congress could not have intended to delegate a decision of such economic and political significance to an agency in so cryptic a fashion. . . . By no means do we question the seriousness of the problem that the FDA has sought to address. . . . Nonetheless, no matter how "important, conspicuous, and controversial" the issue, and regardless of how likely the public is to hold the Executive Branch politically accountable, post , at 31, an administrative agency's power to regulate in the public interest must always be grounded in a valid grant of authority from Congress. . . . Reading the FDCA as a whole, as well as in conjunction with Congress' subsequent tobacco-specific legislation, it is plain that Congress has not given the FDA the authority that it seeks to exercise here. For these reasons, the judgment of the Court of Appeals for the Fourth Circuit is affirmed.

It is so ordered.

Justice Breyer, with whom Justice Stevens, Justice Souter, and Justice Ginsburg join, dissenting

The Food and Drug Administration (FDA) has the authority to regulate "articles (other than food) intended to affect the structure or any function of the body. . . ." Federal Food, Drug and Cosmetic Act (FDCA), 21 U. S. C. §321(g)(1)(C). Unlike the majority, I believe that tobacco products fit within this statutory language.

In its own interpretation, the majority nowhere denies the following two salient points. First, tobacco products (including cigarettes) fall within the scope of this statutory definition, read literally. . . . Second, the statute's basic purpose—the protection of public health—supports the inclusion of cigarettes within its scope. See *United States v. Article of Drug Bacto-Unidisk*, 394 U.S. 784, 798 (1969) (FDCA "is to be given a liberal construction consistent with [its] overriding purpose to protect the public health" [emphasis added]). Unregulated tobacco use causes "[m]ore than 400,000 people [to] die each year from tobacco-related illnesses, such as cancer, respiratory illnesses, and heart disease." 61 Fed. Reg. 44398 (1996). . . .

Despite the FDCA's literal language and general purpose . . . , the majority nonetheless reads the statute as excluding tobacco products for two basic reasons:

(1) the FDCA does not "fit" the case of tobacco because the statute requires the FDA to prohibit dangerous drugs or devices (like cigarettes) outright . . .

(2) Congress has enacted other statutes, which . . . demonstrate that Congress did not intend for the FDA to exercise jurisdiction over tobacco, ante, at 33–34.

In my view, neither of these propositions is valid. . . .

I

Before 1938, the federal Pure Food and Drug Act contained only two jurisdictional definitions of "drug."

. . .

In 1938, Congress added a third definition, relevant here:

"(3) articles (other than food) intended to affect the structure or any function of the body. . . . " Act of June 25, 1938, ch. 675, §201(g), 52 Stat. 1041 (codified at 21 U. S. C. §321(g)(1)(C)).

[T]he literal language of the third definition and the FDCA's general purpose both strongly support a projurisdiction reading of the statute. See supra, at 1–2.

The statute's history offers further support. The FDA drafted the new language, and it testified before Congress that the third definition would expand the FDCA's jurisdictional scope significantly. See Hearings on S. 1944 before a Subcommittee of the Senate Committee on Commerce, 73d Cong., 2d Sess., 15-16 (1933), . . . (hereinafter Leg. Hist.). Indeed, "[t]he purpose" of the new definition was to "make possible the regulation of a great many products that have been found on the market that cannot be alleged to be treatments for diseased conditions." Id., at 108. This Court, too, has said that the

"historical expansion of the definition of drug, and the creation of a parallel concept of devices, clearly show . . . that Congress fully intended that the Act's coverage be as broad as its literal language indicates—and equally clearly, broader than any strict medical definition might otherwise allow." *Bacto-Unidisk*, 394 U.S., at 798.

That Congress would grant the FDA such broad jurisdictional authority should surprise no one. In 1938, the President and much of Congress believed that federal administrative agencies needed broad authority and would

exercise that authority wisely—a view embodied in much Second New Deal legislation. . . .

Nor is it surprising that such a statutory delegation of power could lead after many years to an assertion of jurisdiction that the 1938 legislators might not have expected. Such a possibility is inherent in the very nature of a broad delegation. . . .

[I now turn to] several specific arguments in support of one basic contention: even if the statutory delegation is broad, it is not broad enough to include tobacco . . .

II

A

The statute defines "device," for example, as "an instrument, apparatus, implement, machine, contrivance, implant, in vitro reagent, or other similar or related article . . . intended to affect the structure or any function of the body. . . ." 21 U. S. C. §321(h). Taken literally, [the tobacco companies contend] this definition might include everything from room air conditioners to thermal pajamas. [T]o avoid such a result, the meaning of "drug" or "device" should be confined to medical or therapeutic products, narrowly defined. See Brief for Respondent United States Tobacco Co. 8-9. . . .

I do not agree that we must accept their proposed limitation. For one thing, such a cramped reading contravenes the established purpose of the statutory language. . . .

Most importantly, the statute's language itself supplies a different, more suitable, limitation: that a "drug" must be a chemical agent. The FDCA's "device" definition states that an article which affects the structure or function of the body is a "device" only if it "does not achieve its primary intended purposes through chemical action within . . . the body," and "is not dependent upon being metabolized for the achievement of its primary intended purposes." §321(h) (emphasis added). One can readily infer from this language that at least an article that does achieve its primary purpose through chemical action within the body and that is dependent upon being metabolized is a "drug," provided that it otherwise falls within the scope of the "drug" definition. . . . [T]he FDA has determined that once nicotine enters the body, the blood carries it almost immediately to the brain. See 61 Fed. Reg. 44698-44699 (1966). Nicotine then binds to receptors on the surface of brain cells, setting off a series of chemical reactions that alter one's mood and produce feelings of sedation and stimulation. See id., at 44699, 44739. . . . And nicotine stimulates the transmission of a natural chemical that "rewards" the body with pleasurable sensations (dopamine), causing nicotine addiction. See id., at 44700, 44721-44722.The upshot is that nicotine stabilizes mood, suppresses appetite, tranquilizes, and satisfies a physical craving that nicotine itself has helped to create—all through chemical action within the body after being metabolized. . . .

B

The tobacco companies' . . . assert that the statutory word "intended" means that the product's maker has made an express claim about the effect that its product will have on the body. . . . The FDCA, however, does not use the word "claimed"; it uses the word "intended." And the FDA long ago issued regulations that say the relevant "intent" can be shown not only by a manufacturer's "expressions," but also "by the circumstances surrounding the distribution of the article." 41 Fed. Reg. 6896 (1976) (codified at 21 CFR §801.4 [1999]); . . . Thus, even in the absence of express claims, the FDA has regulated products that affect the body if the manufacturer wants, and knows, that consumers so use the product. See, e.g., 60 Fed. Reg. 41527-41531 (1995). . . . The companies also cannot deny that the evidence of their intent is sufficient to satisfy the statutory word "intended" as the FDA long has interpreted it. In the first place, there was once a time when they actually did make express advertising claims regarding tobacco's mood-stabilizing and weight-reducing properties— and historical representations can portend present expectations. In the late 1920's, for example, the American Tobacco Company urged weight-conscious smokers to "'Reach for a Lucky instead of a sweet.' " Kluger, Ashes to Ashes, at 77–78. The advertisements of R J Reynolds (RJR) emphasized mood stability by depicting a pilot remarking that " 'It Takes Steady Nerves To Fly the Mail At Night . . . That's why I smoke Camels. And I smoke plenty!' " Id., at 86. . . . Although in recent decades cigarette manufacturers have stopped making express health claims in their advertising, consumers have come to understand what the companies no longer need to express—that through chemical action cigarettes stabilize mood, sedate, stimulate, and help suppress appetite.

Second, even though the companies refused to acknowledge publicly (until only very recently) that the nicotine in cigarettes has chemically induced, and habit-forming, effects . . . the FDA recently has gained access to solid, documentary evidence proving that cigarette manufacturers have long known tobacco produces these effects within the body through the metabolizing of chemicals, and that they have long wanted their products to produce those effects in this way.

For example, in 1972, a tobacco-industry scientist explained that " '[s]moke is beyond question the most optimized vehicle of nicotine,' " and " 'the cigarette is the most optimized dispenser of smoke.' " 61 Fed. Reg. 44856 (1996). That same scientist urged company executives to

" '[t]hink of the cigarette pack as a storage container for a day's supply of nicotine . . . Think of the cigarette as a dispenser for a dose unit of nicotine [and] [t]hink of a puff of smoke as a vehicle of nicotine.' " Ibid. (Philip Morris).

That same year, other tobacco industry researchers told their superiors that

" 'in different situations and at different dose levels, nicotine appears to act as a stimulant, depressant, tranquilizer, psychic energizer, appetite reducer, anti-fatigue agent, or energizer . . . Therefore, [tobacco] products may, in a sense, compete with a variety of other products with certain types of drug action.' " Id., at 44669 (RJR).

[. . .]

With such evidence, the FDA has more than sufficiently established that the companies "intend" their products to "affect" the body within the meaning of the FDCA.

C

The majority nonetheless reaches the "inescapable conclusion" that the language and structure of the FDCA as a whole "simply do not fit" the kind of public health problem that tobacco creates. Ante, at 20. That is because, in the majority's view, the FDCA requires the FDA to ban outright "dangerous" drugs or devices (such as cigarettes); yet, the FDA concedes that an immediate and total cigarette-sale ban is inappropriate. Ibid.

This argument is curious because it leads with similarly "inescapable" force to precisely the opposite conclusion, namely, that the FDA does have jurisdiction but that it must ban cigarettes. . . . First, the statute's language does not restrict the FDA's remedial powers in this way. The FDCA permits the FDA to regulate a "combination product"—i.e., a "device" (such as a cigarette) that contains a "drug" (such as nicotine)—under its "device" provisions. 21 U. S. C. §353(g)(1). And the FDCA's "device" provisions explicitly grant the FDA wide remedial discretion. . . .

[T]he statutory section that most clearly addresses the FDA's power to ban (entitled "Banned devices") says that, where a device presents "an unreasonable and substantial risk of illness or injury," the Secretary "may"—not must—"initiate a proceeding . . . to make such device a banned device." §360f(a) (emphasis added).

[. . .]

The statute's language . . . permits the agency to choose remedies consistent with its basic purpose—the overall protection of public health.

The second reason the FDCA does not require the FDA to select the more dangerous remedy, see supra, at 14, is that, despite the majority's assertions to the contrary, the statute does not distinguish among the kinds of health effects that the agency may take into account when assessing safety. The Court insists that the statute only permits the agency to take into account the health risks and benefits of the "product itself" as used by individual consumers. . . . But the FDCA expressly permits the FDA to take account of comparative safety . . . See, e.g., 21 U. S. C. §360h(e)(2)(B)(i)(II) (no device recall if "risk of recal[l]" presents "a greater health risk than" no recall); §360h(a) (notification "unless" notification "would present a greater danger" than "no such notification").

Moreover, one cannot distinguish in this context between a "specific" health risk incurred by an individual and an "aggregate" risk to a group. All relevant risk is, at bottom, risk to an individual; all relevant risk attaches to "the product itself"; and all relevant risk is "aggregate" in the sense that the agency aggregates health effects in order to determine risk to the individual consumer. . . . A "specific" risk to an individual consumer and "aggregate" risks are two sides of the same coin; each calls attention to the same set of facts. . . .

[. . .]

[T]he view the Court advances undermines the FDCA's overall health-protecting purpose by placing the FDA in the strange dilemma of either banning completely a potentially dangerous drug or device or doing nothing at all. . . .

In my view, where linguistically permissible, we should interpret the FDCA in light of Congress' overall desire to protect health. That purpose requires a flexible interpretation that both permits the FDA to take into account the realities of human behavior and allows it, in appropriate cases, to choose from its arsenal of statutory remedies. A statute so interpreted easily "fit[s]" this, and other, drug- and device-related health problems.

III

In the majority's view, laws enacted since 1965 require us to deny jurisdiction, whatever the FDCA might mean in their absence. But why? Do those laws contain language barring FDA jurisdiction? The majority must concede that they do not. Do they contain provisions that are inconsistent with the FDA's exercise of jurisdiction? With one exception, see infra, at 24, the majority points to no such provision. Do they somehow repeal the principles of law (discussed in Part II, supra) that otherwise would lead to the conclusion that the FDA has jurisdiction in this area? The companies themselves deny making any such claim. See Tr. of Oral Arg. 27 (denying reliance on doctrine of "partial repeal"). Perhaps the later laws "shape" and "focus" what the 1938 Congress meant a generation earlier. Ante, at 20. But this Court has warned against using the views of a later Congress to construe a statute enacted many years before. See *Pension Benefit Guaranty Corporation v. LTV Corp.*, 496 U.S. 633, 650 (1990). . . .

Regardless, the later statutes do not support the majority's conclusion. That is because, whatever individual Members of Congress after 1964 may have assumed about the FDA's jurisdiction, the laws they enacted did not embody any such "no jurisdiction" assumption. And one cannot automatically infer an antijurisdiction intent, as the majority does, for the later statutes are both (and similarly) consistent with quite a different congressional desire, namely, the intent to proceed without interfering with whatever authority the FDA otherwise may have possessed. See, e.g., Cigarette Labeling and Advertising—1965: Hearings on H. R. 2248 et al. before the House Committee on Interstate and Foreign Commerce, 89th Cong., 1st Sess., 19 (1965) (hereinafter 1965 Hearings) . . . [T]he subsequent legislative history is critically ambivalent, . . . [thus it] prevents the majority from drawing from the later statutes the firm, antijurisdiction implication that it needs. . . .

Congress both failed to grant express authority to the FDA when the FDA denied it had jurisdiction over tobacco and failed to take that authority expressly away when the agency later asserted jurisdiction. See, e.g., S. 1262, 104th Cong., 1st Sess., §906 (1995) (failed bill seeking to amend FDCA to say that "[n]othing in this Act or any other Act shall provide the [FDA] with any authority to regulate in any manner tobacco or tobacco products"). . . . Consequently, the defeat of various different proposed jurisdictional changes proves nothing. This history shows only that Congress could not muster the votes necessary either to grant or to deny the FDA the relevant authority. It neither favors nor disfavors the majority's position. . . .

In addition, at least one post-1938 statute reveals quite a different congressional intent than the majority infers. See Note following 21 U. S. C. §321 (1994 ed., Supp. III) (FDA Modernization Act of 1997) (law "shall [not] be construed to affect the question of whether the [FDA] has any authority to regulate any tobacco product," and "[s]uch authority, if any, shall be exercised under the [FDCA] as in effect on the day before the date of [this] enactment"). . . .

[Thus] the majority's conclusion that Congress clearly intended for its tobacco-related statutes to be the exclusive "response" to "the problem of tobacco and health," ante, at 35, is based on legislative silence. . . .

IV

I now turn to . . . the FDA's former denials of its tobacco-related authority.

Until the early 1990's, the FDA expressly maintained that the 1938 statute did not give it the power that it now seeks to assert. It then changed its mind. The majority agrees with me that the FDA's change of positions does not make a significant legal difference. . . . Nevertheless, it labels those denials "important context" for drawing an inference about Congress' intent. Ante, at 34. In my view, the FDA's change of policy, like the subsequent statutes themselves, does nothing to advance the majority's position.

When it denied jurisdiction to regulate cigarettes, the FDA consistently stated why that was so. In 1963, for example, FDA administrators wrote that cigarettes did not satisfy the relevant FDCA definitions—in particular, the "intent" requirement—because cigarette makers did not sell their product with accompanying "therapeutic

claims." Letter to Directors of Bureaus, Divisions and Directors of Districts from FDA Bureau of Enforcement (May 24, 1963), in Public Health Cigarette Amendments of 1971: Hearings on S. 1454 before the Consumer Subcommittee of the Senate Committee on Commerce, 92d Cong., 2d Sess., 240 (1972) (hereinafter FDA Enforcement Letter). And subsequent FDA Commissioners made roughly the same assertion. . . .

Other agency statements occasionally referred to additional problems . . . [b]ut a fair reading of the FDA's denials suggests that the overwhelming problem was one of proving the requisite manufacturer intent. See Action on Smoking and Health v. Harris, 655 F. 2d 236, 238-239 (CADC 1980) (FDA "comments" reveal its "understanding" that "the crux of FDA jurisdiction over drugs lay in manufacturers' representations as revelatory of their intent").

What changed? For one thing, the FDA obtained evidence sufficient to prove the necessary "intent" despite the absence of specific "claims." See supra, at 12-14. This evidence, which first became available in the early 1990's, permitted the agency to demonstrate that the tobacco companies knew nicotine achieved appetite-suppressing, mood-stabilizing, and habituating effects through chemical (not psychological) means, even at a time when the companies were publicly denying such knowledge.

Moreover, scientific evidence of adverse health effects mounted, until, in the late 1980's, a consensus on the seriousness of the matter became firm. That is not to say that concern about smoking's adverse health effects is a new phenomenon. . . . It is to say, however, that convincing epidemiological evidence began to appear mid-20th century; that the First Surgeon General's Report documenting the adverse health effects appeared in 1964; and that the Surgeon General's Report establishing nicotine's addictive effects appeared in 1988. . . .

Nothing in the law prevents the FDA from changing its policy for such reasons. . . .

V

One might nonetheless claim that, even if my interpretation of the FDCA and later statutes gets the words right, it lacks a sense of their "music." See *Helvering v. Gregory*, 69 F. 2d 809, 810-811 (CA2 1934) (L. Hand, J.) ("[T]he meaning of a [statute] may be more than that of the separate words, as a melody is more than the notes. . .").

[O]ne might claim that courts, when interpreting statutes, should assume in close cases that a decision with "enormous social consequences," 1994 Hearings 69, should be made by democratically elected Members of Congress rather than by unelected agency administrators. . . .

If there is such a background canon of interpretation, however, I do not believe it controls the outcome here.

Insofar as the decision to regulate tobacco reflects the policy of an administration, it is a decision for which that administration, and those politically elected officials who support it, must (and will) take responsibility. And the very importance of the decision taken here, as well as its attendant publicity, means that the public is likely to be aware of it and to hold those officials politically accountable. Presidents, just like Members of Congress, are elected by the public. Indeed, the President and Vice President are the only public officials whom the entire Nation elects. I do not believe that an administrative agency decision of this magnitude—one that is important, conspicuous, and controversial—can escape the kind of public scrutiny that is essential in any democracy. . . .

The upshot is that the Court today holds that a regulatory statute aimed at unsafe drugs and devices does not authorize regulation of a drug (nicotine) and a device (a cigarette) that the Court itself finds unsafe. Far more than most, this particular drug and device risks the life-threatening harms that administrative regulation seeks to rectify. The majority's conclusion is counter-intuitive. And, for the reasons set forth, I believe that the law does not require it.

Consequently, I dissent.

United States v. Mead Corporation

533 U.S. 218 (2001) 8-1
+ *Rehnquist, Stevens, O'Connor, Kennedy, Souter, Thomas, Ginsburg, Breyer*
– *Scalia*

[In this case, the Supreme Court addressed whether a tariff classification ruling by the United States Customs Service deserves "*Chevron* deference" by the courts. Respondent, the Mead Corporation, was an importer of dayplanners, three-ring binders with pages having room for notes of daily schedules and phone numbers and addresses, together with a calendar. Between 1989 and 1993, dayplanners were exempted from tariff duty. The controversy arose when, in 1993, the Customs Service decided to change, through a ruling letter, Mead's dayplanners' classification as "bound diaries," subjecting them to a 4% customs duty. After unsuccessfully challenging the new rule in the Customs Headquarters and Court of International Trade, Mead appealed to the United States Court of Appeals for the Federal Circuit, which reversed the Court of International Trade's decision. The Federal Circuit argued that planners were not diaries, because they had no space for "relatively extensive notations about demands, observations, feelings, or thoughts" in the past. The Federal Circuit also held that ring-fastened diaries cannot be considered "bound." Based on these rulings, the Federal Circuit argued that the customs ruling in question, classifying dayplanners as bound diaries, was not entitled to judicial deference. The Supreme Court, in its own words, "granted certiorari in order to consider the limits of *Chevron* deference owed to administrative practice in applying a statute."][22]

Justice Souter delivered the opinion of the Court

[. . .]

I

A

Imports are taxed under the Harmonized Tariff Schedule of the United States (HTSUS), 19 U. S. C. §1202. Title 19 U. S. C. §1500(b) provides that Customs "shall, under rules and regulations prescribed by the Secretary [of the Treasury] . . . fix the final classification and rate of duty applicable to . . . merchandise" under the HTSUS.

The Secretary provides for tariff rulings before the entry of goods by regulations authorizing "ruling letters" setting

22. The majority opinion rests heavily on claims to have read the "intent of the legislature" behind the statute. Note how this concept, as applied here, allows the majority to ignore the actual words of the law. For an extensive critique of the notion that judges can, or ought to, try to determine what a legislature was actually thinking when it passed a statute, see Lief Carter and Thomas Burke, *Reason in Law*, 8th ed. (New York: Longman, 2009).

tariff classifications for particular imports. 19 CFR §177.8 (2000). A ruling letter

"represents the official position of the Customs Service with respect to the particular transaction or issue described therein and is binding on all Customs Service personnel. . . . In the absence of a change of practice or other modification or revocation which affects the principle of the ruling set forth in the ruling letter, that principle may be cited as authority in the disposition of transactions involving the same circumstances." §177.9(a).

After the transaction that gives it birth, a ruling letter is to "be applied only with respect to transactions involving articles identical to the sample submitted with the ruling request or to articles whose description is identical to the description set forth in the ruling letter." §177.9(b)(2). As a general matter, such a letter is "subject to modification or revocation without notice to any person, except the person to whom the letter was addressed," §177.9(c). . . . Since ruling letters respond to transactions of the moment, they are not subject to notice and comment before being issued, may be published but need only be made "available for public inspection," 19 U. S. C. §1625(a), and, at the time this action arose, could be modified without notice and comment under most circumstances, 19 CFR §177.10(c) (2000). A broader notice-and-comment requirement for modification of prior rulings was added by statute in 1993, Pub. L. 103-182 §623, 107 Stat. 2186, codified at 19 U. S. C. §1625(c), and took effect after this case arose.

Any of the 46 port-of-entry Customs offices may issue ruling letters, and so may the Customs Headquarters Office, in providing "[a]dvice or guidance as to the interpretation or proper application of the Customs and related laws. . . . Most ruling letters contain little or no reasoning, but simply describe goods and state the appropriate category and tariff.

B

The tariff schedule on point falls under the HTSUS heading for "[r]egisters, account books, notebooks, order books, receipt books, letter pads, memorandum pads, diaries and similar articles," HTSUS subheading 4820.10, which comprises two subcategories. Items in the first, "[d]iaries, notebooks and address books, bound; memorandum pads, letter pads and similar articles," were subject to a tariff of 4.0%

at the time in controversy. 185 F. 3d 1304, 1305 (CA Fed. 1999). Objects in the second, covering "[o]ther" items, were free of duty. HTSUS subheading 4820.10.40; see also App. to Pet. for Cert. 46a.

We hold that administrative implementation of a particular statutory provision qualifies for *Chevron* deference when it appears that Congress delegated authority to the agency generally to make rules carrying the force of law, and that the agency interpretation claiming deference was promulgated in the exercise of that authority. . . . The Customs ruling at issue here fails to qualify, although the possibility that it deserves some deference under *Skidmore* leads us to vacate and remand.

II

A

When Congress has "explicitly left a gap for an agency to fill, there is an express delegation of authority to the agency to elucidate a specific provision of the statute by regulation," *Chevron,* 467 U.S., at 843-844, and any ensuing regulation is binding in the courts unless procedurally defective, arbitrary or capricious in substance, or manifestly contrary to the statute. . . . But whether or not they enjoy any express delegation of authority on a particular question, agencies charged with applying a statute necessarily make all sorts of interpretive choices, and while not all of those choices bind judges to follow them, they certainly may influence courts facing questions the agencies have already answered. "[T]he well-reasoned views of the agencies implementing a statute 'constitute a body of experience and informed judgment to which courts and litigants may properly resort for guidance,' " *Bragdon v. Abbott,* 524 U.S. 624, 642 (1998) (quoting *Skidmore,* 323 U.S., at 139-140), and "[w]e have long recognized that considerable weight should be accorded to an executive department's construction of a statutory scheme it is entrusted to administer . . ." *Chevron,* supra, at 844 (footnote omitted). The fair measure of deference to an agency administering its own statute has been understood to vary with circumstances, and courts have looked to the degree of the agency's care, its consistency, formality, and relative expertness, and to the persuasiveness of the agency's position, see *Skidmore,* supra, at 139–140. The approach has produced a spectrum of judicial responses, from great respect at one end to near indifference at the other. Justice Jackson summed things up in *Skidmore v. Swift & Co.*:

"The weight [accorded to an administrative] judgment in a particular case will depend upon the thoroughness evident in its consideration, the validity of its reasoning, its consistency with earlier and later pronouncements, and all those factors which give it power to persuade, if lacking power to control." 323 U. S., at 140.

Since 1984, we have identified a category of interpretive choices distinguished by an additional reason for judicial deference. This Court in *Chevron* recognized that Congress not only engages in express delegation of specific interpretive authority, but that "[s]ometimes the legislative delegation to an agency on a particular question is implicit." 467 U.S., at 844. When circumstances implying such an [implicit delegation] exist, a reviewing court has no business rejecting an agency's exercise of its generally conferred authority to resolve a particular statutory ambiguity simply because the agency's chosen resolution seems unwise, see id., at 845–846, but is obliged to accept the agency's position if Congress has not previously spoken to the point at issue and the agency's interpretation is reasonable, see id., at 842–845; cf. 5 U. S. C. §706(2). We have recognized a very good indicator of delegation meriting *Chevron* treatment in express congressional authorizations to engage in the process of rulemaking or adjudication that produces regulations or rulings for which deference is claimed. See, e.g., EEOC v. Arabian American Oil Co., 499 U.S. 244, 257 (1991) (no *Chevron* deference to agency guideline where congressional delegation did not include the power to " 'promulgate rules or regulations'" (quoting General Elec. Co. v. Gilbert, 429 U.S. 125, 141 [1976]); see also Christensen v. Harris County, 529 U.S. 576, 596–597 (2000) (Breyer, J., dissenting) (where it is in doubt that Congress actually intended to delegate particular interpretive authority to an agency, *Chevron* is "inapplicable"). It is fair to assume generally that Congress contemplates administrative action with the effect of law when it provides for a relatively formal administrative procedure tending to foster the fairness and deliberation that should underlie a pronouncement of such force. Thus, the overwhelming number of our cases applying *Chevron* deference have reviewed the fruits of notice-and-comment rulemaking or formal adjudication That

said, and as significant as notice-and-comment is in pointing to *Chevron* authority, the want of that procedure here does not decide the case, for we have sometimes found reasons for *Chevron* deference even when no such administrative formality was required and none was afforded, see, e.g., *NationsBank of N. C., N. A. v. Variable Annuity Life Ins. Co.*, 513 U.S. 251, 256–257, 263 (1995). The fact that the tariff classification here was not a product of such formal process does not alone, therefore, bar the application of *Chevron*.

There are, nonetheless, ample reasons to deny *Chevron* deference here. The authorization for classification rulings, and Customs's practice in making them, present a case far removed not only from notice-and-comment process, but from any other circumstances reasonably suggesting that Congress ever thought of classification rulings as deserving the deference claimed for them here.

B

No matter which angle we choose for viewing the Customs ruling letter in this case, it fails to qualify under *Chevron*. On the face of the statute, to begin with, the terms of the congressional delegation give no indication that Congress meant to delegate authority to Customs to issue classification rulings with the force of law. It is true that Congress had classification rulings in mind when it explicitly authorized, in a parenthetical, the issuance of "regulations establishing procedures for the issuance of binding rulings prior to the entry of the merchandise concerned," 19 U. S. C. §1502(a). The reference to binding classifications does not, however, bespeak the legislative type of activity that would naturally bind more than the parties to the ruling, once the goods classified are admitted into this country. And though the statute's direction to disseminate "information" necessary to "secure" uniformity, 19 U. S. C. §1502(a), seems to assume that a ruling may be precedent in later transactions, precedential value alone does not add up to *Chevron* entitlement . . . It is difficult, in fact, to see in the agency practice itself any indication that Customs ever set out with a lawmaking pretense in mind when it undertook to make classifications like these. Customs does not generally engage in notice-and-comment practice when issuing them, and their treatment by the agency makes it clear that a letter's binding character as a ruling stops short of third parties; Customs has regarded a classification as conclusive only as between itself and the importer to whom it was issued, 19 CFR §177.9(c) (2000), and even then only until Customs has given advance notice of intended change, §§177.9(a), (c). Other importers are in fact warned against assuming any right of detrimental reliance. §177.9(c).

Indeed, to claim that classifications have legal force is to ignore the reality that 46 different Customs offices issue 10,000 to 15,000 of them each year, see Brief for Respondent 5; . . . Any suggestion that rulings intended to have the force of law are being churned out at a rate of 10,000 a year at an agency's 46 scattered offices is simply self-refuting. Although the circumstances are less startling here, with a Headquarters letter in issue, none of the relevant statutes recognizes this category of rulings as separate or different from others. . . .

Nor do the amendments to the statute made effective after this case arose disturb our conclusion. . . . The statutory changes reveal no new congressional objective of treating classification decisions generally as rulemaking with force of law, nor do they suggest any intent to create a *Chevron* patchwork of classification rulings, some with force of law, some without.

In sum, classification rulings are best treated like "interpretations contained in policy statements, agency manuals, and enforcement guidelines." Christensen, 529 U.S., at 587. They are beyond the *Chevron* pale.

C

To agree with the Court of Appeals that Customs ruling letters do not fall within *Chevron* is not, however, to place them outside the pale of any deference whatever. *Chevron* did nothing to eliminate *Skidmore*'s holding that an agency's interpretation may merit some deference whatever its form, given the "specialized experience and broader investigations and information" available to the agency, 323 U.S., at 139, and given the value of uniformity in its administrative and judicial understandings of what a national law requires, id., at 140.

There is room at least to raise a *Skidmore* claim here, where the regulatory scheme is highly detailed, and Customs can bring the benefit of specialized experience to

bear on the subtle questions in this case: whether the daily planner with room for brief daily entries falls under "diaries," when diaries are grouped with "notebooks and address books, bound; memorandum pads, letter pads and similar articles," HTSUS subheading 4820.10.20; and whether a planner with a ring binding should qualify as "bound," when a binding may be typified by a book, but also may have "reinforcements or fittings of metal, plastics, etc.," Harmonized Commodity Description and Coding System Explanatory Notes to Heading 4820, p. 687 (cited in Customs Headquarters letter, App. to Pet. for Cert. 45a). A classification ruling in this situation may therefore at least seek a respect proportional to its "power to persuade," *Skidmore*, supra, at 140. Such a ruling may surely claim the merit of its writer's thoroughness, logic and expertness, its fit with prior interpretations, and any other sources of weight.

D

Underlying the position we take here . . . is a choice about the best way to deal with an inescapable feature of the body of congressional legislation authorizing administrative action. That feature is the great variety of ways in which the laws invest the Government's administrative arms with discretion, and with procedures for exercising it, in giving meaning to Acts of Congress.

Although we all accept the position that the Judiciary should defer to at least some of this multifarious administrative action, we have to decide how to take account of the great range of its variety. . . . If . . . it is simply implausible that Congress intended such a broad range of statutory authority to produce only two varieties of administrative action, demanding either *Chevron* deference or none at all, then the breadth of the spectrum of possible agency action must be taken into account. Justice Scalia's first priority over the years has been to limit and simplify. The Court's choice has been to tailor deference to variety. This acceptance of the range of statutory variation has led the Court to recognize more than one variety of judicial deference, just as the Court has recognized a variety of indicators that Congress would expect *Chevron* deference.

Our respective choices are repeated today. Justice Scalia would pose the question of deference as an either-or choice. On his view that *Chevron* rendered *Skidmore* anachronistic, when courts owe any deference it is *Chevron* deference that they owe, post, at 9–10.

The Court, on the other hand, said nothing in *Chevron* to eliminate *Skidmore*'s recognition of various justifications for deference depending on statutory circumstances and agency action; *Chevron* was simply a case recognizing that even without express authority to fill a specific statutory gap, circumstances pointing to implicit congressional delegation present a particularly insistent call for deference. We think, in sum . . . that judicial responses to administrative action must continue to differentiate between *Chevron* and *Skidmore*, and that continued recognition of *Skidmore* is necessary for just the reasons Justice Jackson gave when that case was decided. . . .

Since the *Skidmore* assessment called for here ought to be made in the first instance by the Court of Appeals for the Federal Circuit or the Court of International Trade, we go no further than to vacate the judgment and remand the case for further proceedings consistent with this opinion.

It is so ordered.

Justice Scalia, dissenting

Today's opinion makes an avulsive change in judicial review of federal administrative action. Whereas previously a reasonable agency application of an ambiguous statutory provision had to be sustained so long as it represented the agency's authoritative interpretation, henceforth such an application can be set aside unless "it appears that Congress delegated authority to the agency generally to make rules carrying the force of law," as by giving an agency "power to engage in adjudication or notice-and-comment rulemaking, or . . . some other [procedure] indicati[ng] comparable congressional intent," and "the agency interpretation claiming deference was promulgated in the exercise of that authority." Ante, at 6–7.1. What was previously a general presumption of authority in agencies to resolve ambiguity in the statutes they have been authorized to enforce has been changed to a presumption of no such authority, which must be overcome by affirmative legislative intent to the contrary. And whereas previously, when agency authority to resolve ambiguity did not exist the court was free to give the statute what it considered the best interpretation, henceforth the court must supposedly give the agency view

some indeterminate amount of so-called *Skidmore* deference. We will be sorting out the consequences of the Mead doctrine, which has today replaced the *Chevron* doctrine, for years to come. . . .

I

Only five years ago, the Court described the *Chevron* doctrine as follows: "We accord deference to agencies under *Chevron* . . . because of a presumption that Congress, when it left ambiguity in a statute meant for implementation by an agency, understood that the ambiguity would be resolved, first and foremost, by the agency, and desired the agency (rather than the courts) to possess whatever degree of discretion the ambiguity allows," Smiley v. Citibank (South Dakota), N. A., 517 U. S. 735, 740-741 (1996) (citing *Chevron U. S. A. Inc. v. Natural Resources Defense Council, Inc.*, 467 U. S. 837, 843-844 [1984]). Today the Court collapses this doctrine, announcing instead a presumption that agency discretion does not exist unless the statute, expressly or impliedly, says so. [T]he Court . . . asserts that "a very good indicator [is] express congressional authorizations to engage in the process of rulemaking or adjudication that produces regulations or rulings for which deference is claimed," ante, at 10. Only when agencies act through "adjudication[,] notice-and-comment rulemaking, or . . . some other [procedure] indicati[ng] comparable congressional intent" is *Chevron* deference applicable—because these "relatively formal administrative procedure[s] [designed] to foster . . . fairness and deliberation" bespeak (according to the Court) congressional willingness to have the agency, rather than the courts, resolve statutory ambiguities. Ante, at 7, 10. Once it is determined that *Chevron* deference is not in order, the uncertainty is not at an end—and indeed is just beginning. Litigants cannot then assume that the statutory question is one for the courts to determine, according to traditional interpretive principles and by their own judicial lights. No, the Court now resurrects, in full force, the pre-*Chevron* doctrine of *Skidmore* deference . . . The Court has largely replaced *Chevron*, in other words, with that test most beloved by a court unwilling to be held to rules (and most feared by litigants who want to know what to expect): the ol' "totality of the circumstances" test.

The Court's new doctrine is neither sound in principle nor sustainable in practice.

A

As to principle: The doctrine of *Chevron*—that all authoritative agency interpretations of statutes they are charged with administering deserve deference—was rooted in a legal presumption of congressional intent, important to the division of powers between the Second and Third Branches. When, *Chevron* said, Congress leaves an ambiguity in a statute that is to be done by an executive agency, it is presumed that Congress meant to give the agency discretion, within the limits of reasonable interpretation, as to how the ambiguity is to be resolved. By committing enforcement of the statute to an agency rather than the courts, Congress committed its initial and primary interpretation to that branch as well. . . .

Statutory ambiguities, in other words, were left to reasonable resolution by the Executive.

The basis in principle for today's new doctrine can be described as follows: The background rule is that ambiguity in legislative instructions to agencies is to be resolved not by the agencies but by the judges. Specific congressional intent to depart from this rule must be found—and while there is no single touchstone for such intent it can generally be found when Congress has authorized the agency to act through (what the Court says is) relatively formal procedures such as informal rulemaking and formal (and informal?) adjudication, and when the agency in fact employs such procedures. . . . [T]he Court's principal criterion of congressional intent to supplant its background rule seems to me quite implausible. There is no necessary connection between the formality of procedure and the power of the entity administering the procedure to resolve authoritatively questions of law. The most formal of the procedures the Court refers to—formal adjudication—is modeled after the process used in trial courts. . . . The purpose of such a procedure is to produce a closed record for determination and review of the facts—which implies nothing about the power of the agency subjected to the procedure to resolve authoritatively questions of law.

As for informal rulemaking: While formal adjudication procedures are prescribed (either by statute or by the Constitution), see 5 U. S. C. §§554, 556; *Wong Yang Sung v. McGrath*, 339 U.S. 33, 50 (1950), informal rulemaking is more typically authorized but not required. Agencies with such authority are free to give guidance through rulemak-

ing, but they may proceed to administer their statute case-by-case, "making law" as they implement their program (not necessarily through formal adjudication). See *NLRB v. Bell Aerospace Co.*, 416 U.S. 267, 290-295 (1974); *SEC v. Chenery Corp.*, 332 U.S. 194, 202-203 (1947). Is it likely—or indeed even plausible—that Congress meant, when such an agency chooses rulemaking, to accord the administrators of that agency, and their successors, the flexibility of interpreting the ambiguous statute now one way, and later another; but, when such an agency chooses case-by-case administration, to eliminate all future agency discretion by having that same ambiguity resolved authoritatively (and forever) by the courts? Surely that makes no sense . . .

B

As for the practical effects of the new rule:

(1) The principal effect will be protracted confusion. As noted above, the one test for *Chevron* deference that the Court enunciates is wonderfully imprecise: whether "Congress delegated authority to the agency generally to make rules carrying the force of law . . . as by . . . adjudication[,] notice-and-comment rulemaking, or . . . some other [procedure] indicati[ng] comparable congressional intent." But even this description does not do justice to the utter flabbiness of the Court's criterion, since, in order to maintain the fiction that the new test is really just the old one, applied consistently throughout our case law, the Court must make a virtually open-ended exception to its already imprecise guidance: In the present case, it tells us, the absence of notice-and-comment rulemaking . . . is not enough to decide the question of *Chevron* deference, "for we have sometimes found reasons for *Chevron* deference even when no such administrative formality was required and none was afforded." Ante, at 7, 11. The opinion then goes on to consider a grab bag of other factors—including the factor that used to be the sole criterion for *Chevron* deference: whether the interpretation represented the authoritative position of the agency, see ante, at 13–15. It is hard to know what the lower courts are to make of today's guidance.

(2) Another practical effect of today's opinion will be an artificially induced increase in informal rulemaking. . . . Since informal rulemaking and formal adjudication are the

only more-or-less safe harbors from the storm that the Court has unleashed; and since formal adjudication is not an option but must be mandated by statute or constitutional command; informal rulemaking—which the Court was once careful to make voluntary unless required by statute, see Bell Aerospace, supra, and Chenery, supra—will now become a virtual necessity . . .

(3) Worst of all, the majority's approach will lead to the ossification of large portions of our statutory law. Where Chevron applies, statutory ambiguities remain ambiguities subject to the agency's ongoing clarification. They create a space, so to speak, for the exercise of continuing agency discretion. As Chevron itself held, the Environmental Protection Agency can interpret "stationary source" to mean a single smokestack, can later replace that interpretation with the "bubble concept" embracing an entire plant, and if that proves undesirable can return again to the original interpretation. 467 U.S., at 853-859, 865-866. For the indeterminately large number of statutes taken out of Chevron by today's decision, however, ambiguity (and hence flexibility) will cease with the first judicial resolution. Skidmore deference gives the agency's current position some vague and uncertain amount of respect, but it does not, like Chevron, leave the matter within the control of the Executive Branch for the future. Once the court has spoken, it becomes unlawful for the agency to take a contradictory position; the statute now says what the court has prescribed.

I know of no case, in the entire history of the federal courts, in which we have allowed a judicial interpretation of a statute to be set aside by an agency—or have allowed a lower court to render an interpretation of a statute subject to correction by an agency. As recently as 1996, we rejected an attempt to do precisely that. [See] Chapman v. United States, 500 U.S. 453 (1991).

There is, in short, no way to avoid the ossification of federal law that today's opinion sets in motion. What a court says is the law after according Skidmore deference will be the law forever, beyond the power of the agency to change even through rulemaking.

(4) And finally, the majority's approach compounds the confusion it creates by breathing new life into the anachronism of Skidmore, which sets forth a sliding scale of deference owed an agency's interpretation of a statute that is

dependent "upon the thoroughness evident in [the agency's] consideration, the validity of its reasoning, its consistency with earlier and later pronouncements, and all those factors which give it power to persuade, if lacking power to control"; in this way, the appropriate measure of deference will be accorded the "body of experience and informed judgment" that such interpretations often embody, 323 U.S., at 140. Justice Jackson's eloquence notwithstanding, the rule of Skidmore deference is an empty truism and a trifling statement of the obvious: A judge should take into account the well-considered views of expert observers.

It was possible to live with the indeterminacy of Skidmore deference in earlier times. But in an era when federal statutory law administered by federal agencies is pervasive, and when the ambiguities (intended or unintended) that those statutes contain are innumerable, totality-of-the-circumstances Skidmore deference is a recipe for uncertainty, unpredictability, and endless litigation. . . .

II

The Court's pretense that today's opinion is nothing more than application of our prior case law does not withstand analysis.

The principles central to today's opinion have no antecedent in our jurisprudence. Chevron, the case that the opinion purportedly explicates, made no mention of the "relatively formal administrative procedure[s]," ante, at 10, that the Court today finds the best indication of an affirmative intent by Congress to have ambiguities resolved by the administering agency. Which is not so remarkable, since Chevron made no mention of any need to find such an affirmative intent; it said that in the event of statutory ambiguity agency authority to clarify was to be presumed. And our cases have followed that prescription.

Six years ago, we unanimously accorded Chevron deference to an interpretation of the National Bank Act, 12 U. S. C. §24 Seventh (1988 ed. and Supp. V), contained in a letter to a private party from a Senior Deputy Comptroller of the Currency. See NationsBank of N. C., N. A. v. Variable Annuity Life Ins. Co., 513 U.S. 251, 255, 257 (1995). We did so because the letter represented (and no one contested) that it set forth the official position of the Comptroller of the Currency, see id., at 263. . . .

I could continue to enumerate cases according *Chevron* deference to agency interpretations not arrived at through formal proceedings . . . but [s]uffice it to say that many cases flatly contradict the theory of *Chevron* set forth in today's opinion, and with one exception not a single case can be found with language that supports the theory. . . .

For the reasons stated, I respectfully dissent from the Court's judgment. . . . I dissent even more vigorously from the reasoning that produces the Court's judgment, and that makes today's decision one of the most significant opinions ever rendered by the Court dealing with the judicial review of administrative action. Its consequences will be enormous, and almost uniformly bad.

At issue in *Mead* and in the general debates around *Chevron* deference, is whether and how much courts should have a role in shaping the way agencies interpret their statutory authority. Justice Scalia argues that *Chevron* provided a much sought for uniformity by making deference the default rule, yet the decision in *Mead* is considered to have moved away from this. The problem with *Mead* is that the Court's ruling is not specific enough about "when to defer" and "when not to defer." Initial evidence post-*Mead* suggests that the appellate courts support Justice Scalia's position and acknowledge that *Mead* created a new ambiguity and ambivalence about how courts should intervene in agency interpretations of law.

This chapter has explored how constitutional and statutory language shapes and limits administrative action. But by now it should be obvious that what really shapes administrative action is not the language of legal rules itself, but what the courts say the language means. Charles Evans Hughes once said that "We are under a Constitution—but the Constitution is what the judges say it is." He was not wrong. The story of administrative law throughout this book is largely a story of the commands that the courts impose on administrators by reading the law a certain way.

We wish to conclude this chapter with a cautionary note. People often react with concern to the discovery that the courts make law. Federal judges serve for life, and many state judges, while officially elected, are insulated from ordinary political pressures. (Surely they are insulated from political reactions to things as "boring" as administrative law rulings!) The concern that courts are not democratic often leads to calls for judicial self-restraint. We encourage you to treat such calls with skepticism. In our common law system, every published decision by an appellate court makes law, no matter who wins and who loses. Was it "active" that the Court stopped the OMB from policing private paperwork? Would not the opposite decision have appeared more politically driven and less "impartial"? The proper question is not: "Should the courts be active?" but, rather: "In what circumstances do courts advance the cause of reducing arbitrariness by staying out of the way of agencies?" and "In what circumstances do courts reduce arbitrariness by intervening to question administrative decisions?" That question occupies us for the rest of this book.

EXERCISES AND QUESTIONS FOR FURTHER THOUGHT

1. Suppose the Surgeon General of the United States announced that it would be a federal offense for people not to brush their teeth at least twice a day. Trace the constitutional and statutory steps the courts would have to take to find such a ruling valid. Under current law, by the way, it is virtually certain that the courts would strike down such an order. What legal changes would have to happen before the courts might uphold it?

2. The story of the FDA's concern with over-the-counter herbal remedies is told in "A Surge in Herbal Remedies Pulls Drug Regulators' Gaze," *New York Times*, June 8, 1998. In that story a deputy commissioner of the FDA is quoted as saying: "If companies that would have tested their products and sold them as drugs are now going to not test them and sell them as dietary supplements, then we have lost information about the safety and efficacy of these products." Do you agree with him? Do you think courts can better draw the line between "drugs" and "dietary supplements" than members of the FDA?

3. It is often said "there are two things people should not see being made: sausages and laws." Legislatures occasionally make laws in strange ways. For example, in 1995 Missouri Senator Christopher Bond introduced two sentences, hidden in a huge spending bill, that would have stripped the Environmental Protection Agency of its power to review Army Corps of Engineers decisions about wetlands development. Since many of the construction and development projects that could threaten wetlands require Army Corps of Engineers review and approval, these two sentences would have deprived the EPA of its primary tool for protecting wetlands. The story made the front page of the *New York Times*, and the provisions did not ultimately become law. But if they had become law, the courts would not have questioned their validity. Except when a violation of the Constitution is raised, courts never question the validity of a law passed by Congress. Congress could pass laws by flipping coins and the courts would not care. If this is so, why should courts care about and review how agencies make rules?

4. One of the difficulties in environmental protection is to decide how much of a bad thing is enough to worry about. The Resource Conservation and Recovery Act of 1976 forbade the use of landfills for disposing of toxic waste. However, the ash produced by burning household waste (in part to generate electricity) was deemed not a toxic waste. The City of Chicago burned household and industrial garbage. The EPA, after waffling on the question of whether this ash could be put in landfills, decided that it could. The Environmental Defense Fund brought suit. How do you think this case would come out under *Chevron*? In *Chicago v. Environmental Defense Fund*, 511 U.S. 328 (1994), the Supreme Court, 7-2, ignored the EPA's decision and required Chicago to treat the ash as a toxic waste. The dissent by Justice Stevens, joined by Justice O'Connor, argues for deference. What might explain why Justice Scalia, for the majority, ignored *Chevron*?

5. Is Justice Marshall right when he says the Supreme Court's ruling in *Industrial Union Department v. American Petroleum Institute* "flagrantly disregards . . . restrictions on judicial authority"? Is it fair to compare the Court's opinion in this case with the Court's perspective on regulation in *Lochner*? In his dissent, Justice Marshall suggests they are similar. Why?[23]

6. The Federal Trade Commission Act empowers the FTC to "prevent unfair methods of competition in commerce, and unfair or deceptive acts or practices in commerce." In 1971 the FTC published a "trade regulation rule" in the Federal Register announcing that failure to post gasoline octane ratings at service stations was an unfair method of competition and an unfair and deceptive act or practice under the statute. Do you think the statute delegated authority to the FTC to announce such a specific rule? See *National Petroleum Refiners Association v. Federal Trade Commission*, 482 F.2d 672 (1973), for the opinion. Since you have presumably noticed the stickers announcing octane ratings today on pumps, you know how the case came out. The word *prevent* is the key statutory word here. Why?

7. In the continuing struggle to make sense of the concept of "separation of powers," the Supreme Court in 1998 struck down the "line-item veto." The line-item

---

23. For a description of the politics of OSHA see Charles Noble, *Liberalism at Work: The Rise and Fall of OSHA* (Philadelphia: Temple University Press, 1986).

veto allows the executive to strike down funding for specific projects in appropriations bills. Presumably this allows cutting down on pure "pork-barrel" expenditures. Representatives can go back to their constituents and say they pushed for the local dam or highway improvement, but the nasty president (or governor) thwarted them. Under the old system, the president had to either approve or veto the entire bill, which might contain thousands of projects. Opponents, however, worry that line-item veto power gives presidents the power to pressure legislators on unrelated matters. ("Vote for my judicial nominee or I'll veto your district's dam.") In spite of the fact that only seven out of the 50 state's governors do *not* have the line-item veto, and in spite of the fact that Congress passed the statute granting the president this power (and the president signed it), the Court struck it down. President Clinton had used the veto eight times since it became effective on January 1, 1997. Here are two excerpts, one from Stevens's majority opinion and one from Scalia's dissent. Do you agree with one over the other? Why?

In both legal and practical effect, the President has amended . . . Acts of Congress by repealing a portion of each. "[R]epeal of statutes, no less than enactment, must conform with Art. 1." There is no provision in the Constitution that authorizes the President to enact, to amend, or to repeal statutes. (Justice Stevens)

Insofar as the degree of political, "lawmaking" power conferred upon the Executive is concerned, there is not a dime's worth of difference between Congress's authorizing the President to *cancel* a spending item, and Congress's authorizing money to be spent on a particular item at the President's discretion. And the latter has been done since the founding of the nation. (Justice Scalia)

Justice Scalia's opinion continues to note the same inconsistency described at the beginning of this chapter between the delegation cases and the separation of powers cases.[24]

24. *Clinton v. City of New York*, 524 U.S. 417 (1998).

Chapter 5
Information and Administration

Once Congress creates an agency and sets forth that agency's responsibilities in a statute, the agency must begin to gain power over the environment it seeks to influence. Knowledge is power, says the adage. This chapter reviews some of the more common methods government officials use to obtain power over their environment by gathering information about it. However, the adage cuts two ways. In order for the concept of checks and balances on government power to have effect, citizens first need information about the operations of their government. Administrative law therefore includes controls on the flow of information to the government. These policies include methods of investigation and compulsion of testimony to obtain vital information. At the same time, another set of policies, through sunshine laws (laws requiring political decisions to be made in public) and freedom of information statutes, channels information to the governed.

INVESTIGATIONS

Most government information is acquired from the regulated industries themselves or the individuals who receive government benefits. Regulators talk to the regulated in order to learn about what the latter are doing. For example, the government collects information on industrial practices and keeps records on the medical status of people receiving Medicare. Sometimes information is communicated in an informal manner and on a voluntary basis. At other points in the regulatory process, the sub-

mission of written materials may be required. Regulators mix with the regulated in order to know enough to make short-term decisions and long-range policies. Herein lie potential sources of conflict. Does the government depend too heavily on those whom it is supposed to regulate? In the process of giving information to the government, are trade secrets jeopardized?[1] To what extent do individuals incriminate themselves when they provide information to the government?

The basic rules for administrative investigations have the same constitutional origin as do the more familiar rules governing police searches, seizures, and interrogations. The Fourth Amendment prohibits "unreasonable searches and seizures," and the Fifth Amendment prohibits government from compelling people to give evidence against themselves. In one of the earlier cases on the subject, *FTC v. American Tobacco Co.*, the Supreme Court denied the Federal Trade Commission (FTC) broad "fishing expedition" powers.[2] The FTC had ordered two tobacco companies to produce "all letters and telegrams received by the Company from, or sent by it to, all of its" customers throughout the year 1921. The agency had no specific knowledge that the papers would reveal evidence of wrongdoing. The Court's opinion held that the Fourth Amendment prohibited the government from forcing a

---

1. See *Ruckelshaus, Administrator, U.S. EPA v. Monsanto Co.*, 467 U.S. 986 (1984).
2. 264 U.S. 298 (1924).

business at any time to produce anything merely on the suspicion that this might reveal something amiss. Speaking for the Court, Justice Holmes referred to such acts on the part of agencies as "fishing expeditions" in violation of the constitutional protection against "unreasonable searches and seizures."

There are, however, important differences between a police search triggered by suspicion that a crime occurred which might lead to an arrest, and an administrative investigation initiated by the desire to foster cooperation between a regulated industry and a regulating agency. Thus the inspection of a meatpacking plant's sanitary and safety conditions is not done to send the packers to jail for a violation but rather, at least initially, to suggest steps the plant must take to improve sanitation and safety. The Internal Revenue Service audit, though it contains many anxious and aggravating moments, rarely produces a civil or criminal charge; it merely requires the taxpayer to document and support the claims on the tax return and to pay up when his documentation fails.

Because of these differences, courts have backed away from *American Tobacco*'s implication that the strict rules of criminal investigation apply to agencies. Businesses are not specifically protected by the Fifth Amendment's self-incrimination provisions regarding, for example, allegations of unfair labor practices.[3] Regarding the entry of government officials onto private property without permission or warrant, however, the Fourth Amendment influence is evident.

On-site inspections authorized by law cover hundreds of kinds of business operations. City housing inspectors may seek to enter an apartment building to see if the number of tenants exceeds the maximum permitted by the building's occupancy permit. Firefighters inspect schools and office buildings to assure compliance with fire codes. Welfare officials visit the homes of welfare recipients to see if those drawing welfare checks actually live in poverty. Health inspectors visit restaurant kitchens to ensure that food is being stored and prepared in accordance with the law. The four cases reported next describe

the basic principles of the law of administrative inspections. Keep in mind the concept of limited government. The general requirement that a government official must get a search warrant based on probable cause before invading a person's privacy is fundamental to the concept of limited government. However, in the first of these two cases, an exception is made. The Court holds that the government need not get a warrant before invading a person's privacy. As you read these two cases, compare the political status and clout of the person that the Court protects in the second case with that of the party the Court declines to protect in the first case.

Wyman v. James

400 U.S. 309 (1971) 6-3
+ *Burger, Black, Harlan, Stewart, White, Blackmun*
− *Douglas, Brennan, Marshall*

[James was a recipient of Aid for Families with Dependent Children (AFDC) for her son and herself. The New York Department of Social Services customarily had a caseworker visit the homes of the AFDC recipients to make determinations about the continued eligibility of the recipient and about the need for other available services. Upon being informed by mail of an impending visit, James notified the department that she would provide information, but would not allow a home visit. In a pre-termination hearing James and her attorney reiterated their stand. A notice of termination was subsequently issued. James brought suit to continue her eligibility on the Fourth Amendment grounds that a home visit is a search without a warrant. She prevailed in the lower courts. Please note the special meaning of the word *reasonable* in the context of search and seizure law. It is not synonymous with *rationality*.]

Justice Blackmun delivered the opinion of the Court

When a case involves a home and some type of official intrusion into that home, as this case appears to do, an immediate and natural reaction is one of concern about Fourth Amendment rights and the protection which that Amendment is intended to afford. Its emphasis indeed is

3. *Oklahoma Press Co. v. Walling*, 327 U.S. 186 (1946).

upon one of the most precious aspects of personal security in the home: "The right of the people to be secure in their persons, houses, papers, and effects. . . ." This Court has characterized that right as "basic to a free society."

In *Camara* Mr. Justice White, after noting that the "translation of the abstract prohibition against 'unreasonable searches and seizures' into workable guidelines for the decision of particular cases is a difficult task," went on to observe: "Nevertheless, one governing principle, justified by history and by current experience, has consistently been followed: except in certain carefully defined classes of cases, a search of private property without proper consent is 'unreasonable' unless it has been authorized by a valid search warrant." 387 U.S., at 528–529.

If we were to assume that a caseworker's home visit, before or subsequent to the beneficiary's initial qualification for benefits, somehow (perhaps because the average beneficiary might feel she is in no position to refuse consent to the visit), and despite its interview nature, does possess some of the characteristics of a search in the traditional sense, we nevertheless conclude that the visit does not fall within the Fourth Amendment's proscription. This is because it does not descend to the level of unreasonableness. It is unreasonableness which is the Fourth Amendment's standard.

There are a number of factors that compel us to conclude that the home visit proposed for Mrs. James is not unreasonable:

1. The public's interest in this particular segment of the area of assistance to the unfortunate is protection and aid for the dependent child whose family requires such aid for that child. The focus is on the *child* and, further, it is on the child who is *dependent*. There is no more worthy object of the public's concern.

2. The agency, with tax funds provided from federal as well as from state sources, is fulfilling a public trust. The State, working through its qualified welfare agency, has appropriate and paramount interest and concern in seeing and assuring that the intended and proper objects of that tax-produced assistance are the ones who benefit from the aid it dispenses.

3. One who dispenses purely private charity naturally has an interest in and expects to know how his charitable funds are utilized and put to work. The public, when it is the

provider, rightly expects the same. It might well expect more, because of the trust aspect of public funds, and the recipient, as well as the caseworker, has not only an interest but an obligation.

4. The emphasis of the New York statutes and regulations is upon the home, upon "close contact" with the beneficiary, upon restoring the aid recipient "to a condition of self-support," and upon the relief of his distress. The federal emphasis is no different. It is upon "assistance and rehabilitation," upon maintaining and strengthening family life, and upon "maximum self-support and personal independence consistent with the maintenance of continuing parental care and protection."

5. The home visit, it is true, is not required by federal statute or regulation. But it has been noted that the visit is "the heart of welfare administration"; that it affords "a personal, rehabilitative orientation, unlike that of most federal programs"; and that the "more pronounced service orientation" effected by Congress with the 1956 amendments to the Social Security Act "gave redoubled importance to the practice of home visiting." Note, Rehabilitation, Investigation and Welfare Home Visit, 79 *Yale L.J.* 746, 748 (1970). The home visit is an established routine in states besides New York.

6. The means employed by the New York agency are significant. Mrs. James received written notice several days in advance of the intended home visit. The date was specified, Section 134a of the New York Social Services Law, effective April, 1967 . . . sets the . . . tone. Privacy is emphasized. The applicant-recipient is made the primary source of information as to eligibility. Outside informational sources, other than public records, are to be consulted only with the beneficiary's consent. Forcible entry or entry under false pretenses or visitation outside working hours or snooping in the home are forbidden.

7. Mrs. James, in fact, on this record presents no specific complaint of any unreasonable intrusion of her home and nothing that supports an inference that the desired home visit had as its purpose the obtaining of information as to criminal activity. She complains of no proposed visitation at an awkward or retirement hour. She suggests no forcible entry. She refers to no snooping. She describes no impolite or reprehensible conduct of any kind. She alleges only, in general and nonspecific terms, that on previous visits and,

on information and belief, on visitation at the home of other aid recipients, "questions concerning personal relationships, beliefs and behavior are raised and pressed which are unnecessary for a determination of continuing eligibility." Paradoxically, this same complaint could be made of a conference held elsewhere than in the home, and yet this is what is sought by Mrs. James.

8. We are not persuaded, as Mrs: James would have us be, that all information pertinent to the issue of eligibility can be obtained by the agency through an interview at a place other than the home, or as the District Court majority suggested, by examining a lease or a birth certificate, or by periodic medical examinations, or by interviews with school personnel.

9. The visit is not one by police or uniformed authority. It is made by a caseworker of some training whose primary objective is, or should be, the welfare, not the prosecution, of the aid recipient for whom the worker has profound responsibility.

10. The home visit is not a criminal investigation, does not equate with a criminal investigation, and despite the announced fears of Mrs. James and those who would join her, is not in aid of any criminal proceeding. If the visitation serves to discourage misrepresentation of fraud, such a byproduct of that visit does not impress upon the visit itself a dominant criminal investigative aspect. And if the visit should, by chance, lead to the discovery of fraud and a criminal prosecution should follow, then, even assuming that the evidence discovered upon the home visitation is admissible, an issue upon which we express no opinion, that is a routine and expected fact of life and a consequence no greater than that which necessarily ensues upon any other discovery by a citizen of criminal conduct.

It seems to us that the situation is akin to that where an Internal Revenue Service agent, in making a routine civil audit of a taxpayer's income tax return, asks that the taxpayer produce for the agent's review some proof of a deduction the taxpayer has asserted to his benefit in the computation of his tax. If the taxpayer refuses, there is, absent fraud, only a disallowance of the claimed deduction and a consequent additional tax. The taxpayer is fully within his "rights" in refusing to produce the proof, but in maintaining and asserting those rights a tax detriment results and it is a detriment of the taxpayer's own making. So here Mrs. James has the "right" to refuse the home visit, but a consequence in the form of cessation of aid, similar to the taxpayer's resultant additional tax, flows from the refusal. The choice is entirely hers, and nothing of constitutional magnitude is involved.

Camara v. Municipal Court, 387 U.S. 523 (1967), and its companion case, *See v. City of Seattle*, 387 U.S. 541 (1967), both by a divided Court, are not inconsistent with our result here. Those cases concerned, respectively, a refusal of entry to city housing inspectors checking for a violation of a building's occupancy permit, and a refusal of entry to a fire department representative interested in compliance with a city's fire code. In each case a majority of this Court held that the Fourth Amendment barred prosecution for refusal to permit the desired warrantless inspection. *Frank v. Maryland*, 359 U.S. 360 (1959), a case that reached an opposing result and that concerned a request by a health officer for entry in order to check the source of rat infestation, was *pro tanto* overruled. Both *Frank* and *Camara* involved dwelling quarters. *See* had to do with a commercial warehouse.

But the facts of the three cases are significantly different from those before us. Each concerned a true search for violations. *Frank* was a criminal prosecution for the owner's refusal to permit entry. So, too, was *See. Camara* had to do with a writ of prohibition sought to prevent an already pending criminal prosecution. The community welfare aspects, of course, were highly important, but each case arose in a criminal context where a genuine search was denied and prosecution followed.

In contrast, Mrs. James is not being prosecuted for her refusal to permit the home visit and is not about to be so prosecuted. The only consequence of her refusal is that the payment of benefits ceases. Important and serious as this is, the situation is no different than if she had exercised a similar negative choice initially and refrained from applying for AFDC benefits.

Reversed.

Justice Douglas, dissenting

[T]he right of privacy which the Fourth protects is perhaps as vivid in our lives as the rights of expression sponsored by the First. If the regime under which Barbara James lives were enterprise capitalism as, for example, if she ran a small factory geared into the Pentagon's procurement program, she certainly would have a right to deny inspectors access to her home unless they came with a warrant.

Is a search of her home without a warrant made "reasonable" merely because she is dependent on government largesse?

Judge Skelly Wright has stated the problem succinctly:

Welfare has long been considered the equivalent of charity and its recipients have been subjected to all kinds of dehumanizing experiences in the government's effort to police its welfare payments. In fact, over half a billion dollars are expended annually for administration and policing in connection with the Aid to Families with Dependent Children program. Why such large sums are necessary for administration and policing has never been adequately explained. No such sums are spent policing for the government subsidies granted to farmers, airlines, steamship companies, and junk mail dealers, to name but a few. The truth is that in this subsidy area society has simply adopted a double standard, one for aid to business and the farmer and a different one for welfare. Poverty, Minorities, and Respect for Law, 1970 Duke L.J. 425, 437–438.

If the welfare recipient was not Barbara James but a prominent, affluent cotton or wheat farmer receiving benefit payments for not growing crops, would not the approach be different? Welfare in aid of dependent children, like social security and unemployment benefits, has an aura of suspicion. There doubtless are frauds in every sector of public welfare whether the recipient be a Barbara James or someone who is prominent or influential. But constitutional rights—here the privacy of the *home*—are obviously not dependent on the poverty or on the affluence of the beneficiary.

It may be that in some tenements one baby will do service to several women and call each one "mom." It may be that other frauds, less obvious, will be perpetrated. But if inspectors want to enter the precincts of the home against the wishes of the lady of the house, they must get a warrant. The need for exigent action as in cases of "hot pursuit" is not present for the lady will not disappear; nor will the baby.

I would place the same restrictions on inspectors entering the *homes* of welfare beneficiaries as are on inspectors entering the *homes* of those on the payroll of government, or the *homes* of those who contract with the government, or the *homes* of those who work for those having government contracts. The values of the *home* protected by the Fourth Amendment are not peculiar to capitalism as we have known it; they are equally relevant to the new form of socialism which we are entering. Moreover, as the numbers of functionaries and inspectors multiply, the need for protection of the individual becomes indeed more essential if the values of a free society are to remain.

What Lord Acton wrote Bishop Creighton about the corruption of power is increasingly pertinent today: "I cannot accept your canon that we are to judge Pope and King unlike other men, with a favourable presumption that they did no wrong. If there is any presumption it is the other way against holders of power, increasing as the power increases. Historic responsibility has to make up for the want of legal responsibility. Power tends to corrupt and absolute power corrupts absolutely. Great men are almost always bad men, even when they exercise influence and not authority: still more when you superadd the tendency or the certainty of corruption by authority."

The bureaucracy of modern government is not only slow, lumbering, and oppressive; it is omnipresent. It touches everyone's life at numerous points. It pries more and more into private affairs, breaking down the barriers that individuals erect to give them some insulation from the intrigues and harassments of modern life. Isolation is not a constitutional guarantee; but the sanctity of the sanctuary of the *home* is such—as marked and defined by the Fourth Amendment, *McDonald v. United States*, 335 U.S. 451, 453. What we do today is to depreciate it.

I would sustain the judgement of the three-judge court in the present case.

Prior to the decision in *Wyman* the Court had moved to narrow the range of permissible warrantless inspections. Note that *Frank*, *Camara*, and *See* all involved some form of criminal prosecution for refusal. In *Wyman* the private citizen did not run the risk of prosecution merely for refusing entry, and in this case the Court approves a warrantless inspection. Ask yourself whether this distinction is so important. What if the inspection uncovers evidence of a regulatory violation or criminal activity? Are the inspectors forbidden from acting on what they see or reporting it to others?

Almost 35 years after *Wyman*, warrantless home visits have become more expansive. For example, in *Sanchez v. San Diego*, 464 F.3d 916 (2006), the United States Court of Appeals for the Ninth Circuit upheld the constitutionality of a San Diego County policy requiring a warrantless home visit to establish welfare *eligibility*. The San Diego County District Attorney had initiated a program called "Project 100%," which made a home visit mandatory for all welfare applicants and included a "walk through" in the residence for the purpose of gathering eligibility information.

Relying on *Wyman*, a three-judge panel of the Ninth Circuit upheld the constitutionality of the program. The dissenting opinion by Judge Fisher, however, pointed out that the home visit in *Sanchez* was conducted by welfare fraud investigators from the District Attorney's Office, not the welfare agency, as in *Wyman*. Judge Fisher argued that the goals of the program were primarily to prevent welfare fraud, not to further the interests articulated in *Wyman*. Although the majority opinion noted that "investigators [would] report any evidence of criminal activity for potential prosecution," this was not a basis for finding the warrantless home visit provision of the program unconstitutional. An appeal for the case to be re-heard before the Ninth Circuit's full *en banc* panel of 15 judges was denied.[4] A writ of certiorari submitted by the American Civil Liberties Union (ACLU) to the Supreme Court was also denied.

Constitutional protections for what Yale law professor Charles Reich called "new property"[5] were embraced by the Court in *Goldberg v. Kelly*,[6] but have not yet acquired the same level of protection afforded to the traditional property interests. Basically, both *Wyman* and *Sanchez* conceptualized welfare benefits not as an "entitlement"[7] but as a privilege that required beneficiaries to surrender their constitutional right to privacy as a condition of receiving benefits. Some argue that this approach to regulating welfare reflects the neoliberal political values that "ended welfare as we know it" by employing a criminal justice approach to regulating social welfare.[8]

In the next case, *Marshall v. Barlow's Inc.* (1978), the Court addresses the issue whether the Occupational Health and Safety Administration (OSHA) may carry out

4. See *Sanchez v. County of San Diego*, 483 F.3d 965 (2007).
5. See Charles A. Reich, "New Property," *Yale Law Journal* 72 (1964): 733.
6. 397 U.S. 254 (1970); infra., chapter 2.
7. See John Brigham, *Property and Politics of Entitlement* (Philadelphia: Temple University Press, 1990); and Joel F. Handler, *The Poverty of Welfare Reform* (New Haven, Conn.: Yale University Press, 1995).
8. For an analysis of this regulatory approach, see Jonathan Simon, *Governing through Crime: How the War on Crime Transformed American Democracy and Created a Culture of Fear* (New York: Oxford University Press, 2007).

warrantless searches of *private businesses*. The Court rules against OSHA and in so doing further narrows the authority of administrative agencies to carry out certain types of warrantless searches. Compare how the Court treats Fourth Amendment issues in the context of inspecting business premises versus a welfare recipient's home. Why is the state's authority greater in the area of welfare regulation? Should businesses be subject to on-site inspections without notice or warrants in order to protect the safety and health of the workers they employ?

Marshall v. Barlow's, Inc.

436 U.S. 307 (1978) 5-3
+ Burger, Stewart, White, Marshall, Powell
− Blackmun, Rehnquist, Stevens
NP Brennan

[The Occupational Safety and Health Act of 1970 empowers agency officials to carry out warrantless searches for safety hazards and other violations at any employment facility within OSHA's jurisdiction. An OSHA inspector went to the customer service area of Barlow's Inc., an electrical and plumbing company in Pocatello, Idaho, and informed the president and general manager that their company had "turned up in the agency's selection process." Although no specific complaint had been received by OSHA indicating that Barlow's Inc. had violated OSHA regulations, the inspector asked to enter the business area. After Mr. Barlow refused OSHA's request, a federal district court ordered that Barlow admit the inspector. Barlow refused and sought injunctive relief against the warrantless search.]

Justice White delivered the opinion of the Court

I

The Secretary urges that warrantless inspections to enforce OSHA are reasonable within the meaning of the Fourth Amendment. Among other things, he relies on §8 (a) of the Act, 29 U. S. C. §657 (a), which authorizes inspection of business premises without a warrant and which the Secretary urges represents a congressional construction of the Fourth Amendment that the courts should not reject. Regrettably, we are unable to agree.

The Warrant Clause of the Fourth Amendment protects commercial buildings as well as private homes. To hold otherwise would belie the origin of that Amendment, and the American colonial experience. An important forerunner of the first 10 Amendments to the United States Constitution, the Virginia Bill of Rights, specifically opposed "general warrants, whereby an officer or messenger may be commanded to search suspected places without evidence of a fact committed." The general warrant was a recurring point of contention in the Colonies immediately preceding the Revolution. The particular offensiveness it engendered was acutely felt by the merchants and businessmen whose premises and products were inspected for compliance with the several parliamentary revenue measures that most irritated the colonists.

This Court has already held that warrantless searches are generally unreasonable, and that this rule applies to commercial premises as well as homes. In *Camara v. Municipal Court*, 387 U.S. 523 (1967), we held: "[E]xcept in certain carefully defined classes of cases, a search of private property without proper consent is 'unreasonable' unless it has been authorized by a valid search warrant."

On the same day, we also ruled: "As we explained in *Camara*, a search of private houses is presumptively unreasonable if conducted without a warrant. The businessman, like the occupant of a residence, has a constitutional right to go about his business free from unreasonable official entries upon his private commercial property. The businessman, too, has that right placed in jeopardy if the decision to enter and inspect for violation of regulatory laws can be made and enforced by the inspector in the field without official authority evidenced by a warrant." *See v. City of Seattle*, 387 U.S. 541 (1967).

These same cases also held that the Fourth Amendment prohibition against unreasonable searches protects against warrantless intrusions during civil as well as criminal investigations. . . . The reason is found in the "basic purpose of this Amendment . . . [which] is to safeguard the privacy and security of individuals against arbitrary invasions by governmental officials." *Camara, supra*, at 528. If the government intrudes on a person's property, the privacy interest suffers whether the government's motivation is to investigate violations of criminal laws or breaches of other statutory or regulatory standards. It therefore appears that unless some recognized exception to the warrant requirement applies, *See v. Seattle* would require a warrant to conduct the inspection sought in this case.

The Secretary urges that an exception from the search warrant requirement has been recognized for "pervasively regulated business[es]," *United States v. Biswell*, 406 U.S. 311, 316 (1972), and for "closely regulated" industries "long subject to close supervision and inspection." *Colonnade Catering Corp. v. United States*, 397 U.S. 72, 74, 77 (1970). These cases are indeed exceptions, but they represent responses to relatively unique circumstances. Certain industries have such a history of government oversight that no reasonable expectation of privacy, see *Katz v. United States*, 389 U.S. 347, 351–352 (1967), could exist for a proprietor over the stock of such an enterprise. Liquor (*Colonnade*) and firearms (*Biswell*) are industries of this type; when an entrepreneur embarks upon such a business, he has voluntarily chosen to subject himself to a full arsenal of governmental regulation.

"A central difference between those cases [*Colonnade* and *Biswell*] and this one is that businessmen engaged in such federally licensed and regulated enterprises accept the burdens as well as the benefits of their trade, whereas the petitioner here was not engaged in any regulated or licensed business. The businessman in a regulated industry in effect consents to the restrictions placed upon him." *Almeida-Sanchez v. United States*, 413 U.S. 266, 271 (1973).

[T]he Secretary attempts to support a conclusion that all businesses involved in interstate commerce have long been subjected to close supervision of employee safety and health conditions. But the degree of federal involvement in employee working circumstances has never been of the order of specificity and pervasiveness that OSHA mandates. It is quite unconvincing to argue that the imposition of minimum wages and maximum hours on employers who contracted with the Government . . . prepared the entirety of American interstate commerce for regulation of working conditions to the minutest detail. Nor can any but the most fictional sense of voluntary consent to later searches be found in the single fact that one conducts a business affecting interstate commerce; under current practice and law, few businesses can be conducted without having some effect on interstate commerce.

The critical fact in this case is that entry over Mr. Barlow's objection is being sought by a Government agent. Employees are not being prohibited from reporting OSHA violations. What they observe in their daily functions is undoubtedly beyond the employer's reasonable expectation of privacy. The Government inspector, however, is not an employee. Without a warrant he stands in no better position than a member of the public. What is observable by the public is observable, without a warrant, by the Government inspector as well. The owner of a business has not, by the necessary utilization of employees in his operation, thrown open the areas where employees alone are permitted to the warrantless scrutiny of Government agents. That an employee is free to report, and the Government is free to use, any evidence of noncompliance with OSHA that the employee observes furnishes no justification for federal agents to enter a place of business from which the public is restricted and to conduct their own warrantless search.

II

Because "reasonableness is still the ultimate standard," *Camara v. Municipal Court*, the Secretary suggests that the Court decide whether a warrant is needed by arriving at a sensible balance between the administrative necessities of OSHA inspections and the incremental protection of privacy of business owners a warrant would afford.

The Secretary submits that warrantless inspections are essential to the proper enforcement of OSHA because they afford the opportunity to inspect without prior notice and hence to preserve the advantages of surprise. While the dangerous conditions outlawed by the Act include structural defects that cannot be quickly hidden or remedied, the Act also regulates a myriad of safety details that may be amenable to speedy alteration or disguise. The risk is that during the interval between an inspector's initial request to search a plant and his procuring a warrant following the owner's refusal of permission, violations of this latter type could be corrected and thus escape the inspector's notice.

We are unconvinced, however, that requiring warrants to inspect will impose serious burdens on the inspection system or the courts, will prevent inspections necessary to enforce the statute, or will make them less effective. In the first place, the great majority of businessmen can be expected in normal course to consent to inspection without

warrant; the Secretary has not brought to this Court's attention any widespread pattern of refusal.

Whether the Secretary proceeds to secure a warrant or other process, with or without prior notice, his entitlement to inspect will not depend on his demonstrating probable cause to believe that conditions in violation of OSHA exist on the premises. Probable cause in the criminal law sense is not required. For purposes of an administrative search such as this, probable cause justifying the issuance of a warrant may be based not only on specific evidence of an existing violation but also on a showing that "reasonable legislative or administrative standards for conducting an inspection are satisfied with respect to a particular [establishment]." *Camara v Municipal Court*. A warrant showing that a specific business has been chosen for an OSHA search on the basis of a general administrative plan for the enforcement of the Act derived from neutral sources such as, for example, dispersion of employees in various types of industries across a given area, and the desired frequency of searches in any of the lesser divisions of the area, would protect an employer's Fourth Amendment rights. We doubt that the consumption of enforcement energies in the obtaining of such warrants will exceed manageable proportions.

Nor do we agree that the incremental protections afforded the employer's privacy by a warrant are so marginal that they fail to justify the administrative burdens that may be entailed. The authority to make warrantless searches devolves almost unbridled discretion upon executive and administrative officers, particularly those in the field, as to when to search and whom to search. A warrant, by contrast, would provide assurances from a neutral officer that the inspection is reasonable under the Constitution, is authorized by statute, and is pursuant to an administrative plan containing specific neutral criteria. These are important functions for a warrant to perform, functions which underlie the Court's prior decisions that the Warrant Clause applies to inspections for compliance with regulatory statutes.

III

We hold that Barlow's was entitled to a declaratory judgement that the Act is unconstitutional insofar as it purports to authorize inspections without warrant or its equivalent and to an injunction enjoining the Act's enforcement to that extent. The judgment of the District Court is therefore affirmed. So ordered.

Justice Stevens, with whom Justice Blackmun and Justice Rehnquist join, dissenting

The Fourth Amendment contains two separate Clauses, each flatly prohibiting a category of governmental conduct.

In cases involving the investigation of criminal activity, the Court has held that the reasonableness of a search generally depends upon whether it was conducted pursuant to a valid warrant. . . . There is, however, also a category of searches which are reasonable within the meaning of the first Clause even though the probable-cause requirement of the Warrant Clause cannot be satisfied. The regulatory inspection program challenged in this case, in my judgement, falls within this category.

The routine OSHA inspections are, by definition, not based on cause to believe there is a violation on the premises to be inspected. Hence, if the inspections were measured against the requirements of the Warrant Clause, they would be automatically and unequivocally unreasonable.

The Court's approach disregards the plain language of the Warrant Clause and is unfaithful to the balance struck by the Framers of the Fourth Amendment—"the one procedural safeguard in the Constitution that grew directly out of the events which immediately preceded the revolutionary struggle with England." This preconstitutional history includes the controversy in England over the issuance of general warrants to aid enforcement of the seditious libel laws and the colonial experience with writs of assistance issued to facilitate collection of the various import duties imposed by Parliament. The Framers' familiarity with the abuses attending the issuance of such general warrants provided the principal stimulus for the restraints on arbitrary governmental intrusions embodied in the Fourth Amendment.

Fidelity to the original understanding of the Fourth Amendment, therefore, leads to the conclusion that the Warrant Clause has no application to routine, regulatory inspections of commercial premises. If such inspections are valid, it is because they comport with the ultimate reasonableness standard of the Fourth Amendment.

Even if a warrant issued without probable cause were faithful to the Warrant Clause, I could not accept the Court's holding that the Government's inspection program is constitutionally unreasonable because it fails to require such a warrant procedure. In determining whether a warrant is a necessary safeguard in a given class of cases, "the Court has weighed the public interest against the Fourth Amendment

interest of the individual." *United States v. Martìnez-Fuete*, 428 U.S., at 555. Several considerations persuade me that this balance should be struck in favor of the routine inspections authorized by Congress.

Congress has determined that regulation and supervision of safety in the workplace furthers an important public interest and that the power to conduct warrantless searches is necessary to accomplish the safety goals of the legislation. In assessing the public interest side of the Fourth Amendment balance, however, the Court today substitutes its judgement for that of Congress on the question of what inspection authority is needed to effectuate the purposes of the Act.

The Court's analysis does not persuade me that Congress' determination that the warrantless-inspection power as a necessary adjunct of the exercise of the regulatory power is unreasonable. It was surely not unreasonable to conclude that the rate at which employers deny entry to inspectors would increase if covered businesses, which may have safety violations on their premises, have a right to deny warrantless entry to a compliance inspector. [E]ven if it were true that many employers would not exercise their right to demand a warrant, it would provide little solace to those charged with administration of OSHA; faced with an increase in the rate of refusals and the added costs generated by futile trips to inspection sites where entry is denied, officials may be compelled to adopt a general practice of obtaining warrants in advance.

Finally, the Court would distinguish the respect accorded Congress' judgement in *Colonnade* and *Biswell* on the ground that businesses engaged in the liquor and firearms industry " 'accept the burdens as well as the benefits of their trade.' " In the Court's view, such businesses consent to the restrictions placed upon them, while it would be fiction to conclude that a businessman subject to OSHA consented to routine safety inspection. In fact, however, consent is fictional in both contexts. Here, as well as in *Biswell*, businesses are required to be aware of and comply with regulations governing their business activities. In both situations, the validity of the regulations depends not upon the consent of those regulated, but on the existence of a federal statute embodying a congressional determination that the public interest in the health of the Nation's work force or the limitation of illegal firearms traffic outweighs the businessman's interest in preventing a Government inspector from viewing those areas of his premises which relate to the subject matter of the regulation.

I respectfully dissent.

The courts have held that evidence obtained by government officials in violation of the Fourth Amendment or other constitutional rights may not be used in criminal proceedings. This is called the *exclusionary rule.* Since the 1960s, when the Supreme Court applied the exclusionary rule to state criminal proceedings in *Mapp v. Ohio*[9] and *Miranda v. Arizona*,[10] the courts have carved out a number of significant exceptions to the rule. These exceptions bother civil libertarians, who argue that the exceptions have eroded the principle of limited government. Political conservatives, on the other hand, argue that exceptions are desirable to give law enforcement officials the flexibility they need in apprehending criminal suspects.

In the field of administrative law, the question of what evidence can be obtained and used for purposes of enforcing regulatory rules is equally controversial. The next two cases provide you with a background on the constitutional issues surrounding the gathering of evidence by inspectors. These cases also demonstrate how divided the Supreme Court is over the question of applying the exclusionary rule to administrative proceedings.

Dow Chemical Company
v. United States

476 U.S. 227 (1986) 5-4
+ *Burger, White, Rehnquist, Stevens, O'Connor*
–/+ *Brennan, Marshall, Blackmun and Powell concurred with the majority in Part III and filed a dissenting opinion*

[In 1978, officials with the Environmental Protection Agency (EPA) made an on-site visit to a 2,000-acre chemical manufacturing plant in Midland, Michigan owned by Dow Chemical Company. The company consented to the EPA inspection. However, a subsequent inspection request was denied. EPA did not seek an administrative

9. 367 U.S. 643 (1961).
10. 384 U.S. 436 (1966).

search warrant, but hired a commercial aerial photographer who took pictures of the facility while flying in lawful navigable airspace. When Dow Chemical Company found out about the photographs, it filed a lawsuit alleging that the EPA had violated its Fourth Amendment rights and had exceeded its statutory investigative authority. The U.S. Court of Appeals for the Sixth Circuit upheld EPA's actions, and Dow Chemical appealed this ruling to the U.S. Supreme Court.]

Chief Justice Burger delivered the opinion of the Court

II

The photographs at issue in this case are essentially like those commonly used in map-making. Any person with an airplane and an aerial camera could readily duplicate them. In common with much else, the technology of photography has changed in this century. These developments have enhanced industrial processes, and indeed all areas of life; they have also enhanced law enforcement techniques. Whether they may be employed by competitors to penetrate trade secrets is not a question presented in this case. Governments do not generally seek to appropriate trade secrets of the private sector, and the right to be free of appropriation of trade secrets is protected by law.

Dow nevertheless relies heavily on its claim that trade secret laws protect it from any aerial photography of this industrial complex by its competitors, and that this protection is relevant to our analysis of such photography under the Fourth Amendment. That such photography might be barred by state law with regard to competitors, however, is irrelevant to the questions presented here. State tort law governing unfair competition does not define the limits of the Fourth Amendment. . . . The Government is seeking these photographs in order to regulate, not to compete with, Dow. If the Government were to use the photographs to compete with Dow, Dow might have a Fifth Amendment "taking" claim. . . . Hence, there is no prohibition of photographs taken by a casual passenger on an airliner, or those taken by a company producing maps for its map-making purposes.

III

Congress has vested in EPA certain investigatory and enforcement authority, without spelling out precisely how this authority was to be exercised in all the myriad circumstances that might arise in monitoring matters relating to clean air and water standards. When Congress invests an agency with enforcement and investigatory authority, it is not necessary to identify explicitly each and every technique that may be used in the course of executing the statutory mission. Aerial observation authority, for example, is not usually expressly extended to police for traffic control, but it could hardly be thought necessary for a legislative body to tell police that aerial observation could be employed for traffic control of a metropolitan area, or to expressly authorize police to send messages to ground highway patrols that a particular over-the-road truck was traveling in excess of 55 miles per hour. Common sense and ordinary human experience teaches that traffic violators are apprehended by observation.

Regulatory or enforcement authority generally carries with it all the modes of inquiry and investigation traditionally employed or useful to execute the authority granted. Environmental standards such as clean air and clean water cannot be enforced only in libraries and laboratories, helpful as those institutions may be.

Under §144(a)(2), the Clean Air Act provides that "upon presentation of credentials," EPA has a "right of entry to, upon, or through any premises." 42 U.S.C. §7414(a)(2)(A). Dow argues this limited grant of authority to enter does not authorize any aerial observation. In particular, Dow argues that unannounced aerial observation deprives Dow of its right to be informed that an inspection will be made or has occurred, and its right to claim confidentiality of the information contained in the places to be photographed, as provided in §114(a) and (c), 42 U.S.C. §7414(a),(c). It is not claimed that EPA has disclosed any of the photographs outside the agency.

Section 114(a), however, appears to expand, not restrict, EPA's general powers to investigate. Nor is there any suggestion in the statute that the powers conferred by this section are intended to be exclusive. There is no claim that EPA is prohibited from taking photographs from a ground-level location accessible to the general public. The EPA, as a regulatory and enforcement agency, needs no explicit statutory provision to employ methods of observation commonly available to the public at large: we hold that the use of aerial observation and photography is within the EPA's statutory authority.

IV

We turn now to Dow's contention that taking aerial photographs constituted a search without a warrant, thereby violating Dow's rights under the Fourth Amendment.

Plainly a business establishment or an industrial or commercial facility enjoys certain protections under the Fourth Amendment. See *Marshall v. Barlow's, Inc.*, 436 U.S. 307 (1978); *See v. City of Seattle*, 387 U.S. 541 (1967).

[T]he Court has drawn a line as to what expectations are reasonable in the open areas beyond the curtilage of a dwelling; "open fields do not provide the setting for those intimate activities that the [Fourth] Amendment is intended to shelter from governmental interference or surveillance." In *Oliver*, we held that "an individual may not legitimately demand privacy for activities out of doors in fields, except in the area immediately surrounding the home." . . . To fall within the open fields doctrine the area "need be neither 'open' nor a 'field' as those terms are used in common speech."

Dow plainly has a reasonable, legitimate, and objective expectation of privacy within the interior of its covered buildings, and it is equally clear that expectation is one society is prepared to observe. . . . Moreover, it could hardly be expected that Dow would erect a huge cover over a 2,000-acre tract. In contending that its entire enclosed plant complex is an "industrial curtilage," Dow argues that its exposed manufacturing facilities are analogous to the curtilage surrounding a home because it has taken every possible step to bar access from ground level.

The intimate activities associated with family privacy and the home and its curtilage simply do not reach the outdoor areas or spaces between structures and buildings of a manufacturing plant.

Admittedly, Dow's enclosed plant complex, like the area in *Oliver*, does not fall precisely within the "open fields" doctrine. The area at issue here can perhaps be seen as falling somewhere between "open fields" and curtilage, but lacking some of the critical characteristics of both.

We pointed out in *Donovan v. Dewey*, 452 U.S. 594 (1981), that the Government has "greater latitude to conduct warrantless inspections of commercial property" because "the expectation of privacy that the owner of commercial property enjoys in such property differs significantly from the sanctity accorded an individual's home." We emphasized that unlike a homeowner's interest in his dwelling, "[t]he interest of the owner of commercial property is not one in being free from any inspections." . . . And with regard to regulatory inspections, we have held that "[w]hat is observable by the public is observable without a warrant, by the Government inspector as well." *Marshall v. Barlow's, Inc.* . . .

Here, EPA was not employing some unique sensory device that, for example, could penetrate the walls of buildings and record conversations in Dow's plants, offices or laboratories, but rather a conventional, albeit precise, commercial camera commonly used in map-making.

It may well be, as the Government concedes, that surveillance of private property by using highly sophisticated surveillance equipment not generally available to the public, such as satellite technology, might be constitutionally proscribed absent a warrant. But the photographs here are not so revealing of intimate details as to raise constitutional concerns. Although they undoubtedly give EPA more detailed information than naked-eye views, they remain limited to an outline of the facility's buildings and equipment. The mere fact that human vision is enhanced somewhat, at least to the degree here, does not give rise to constitutional problems. An electronic device to penetrate walls or windows so as to hear and record confidential discussions of chemical formulae or other trade secrets would raise very different and far more serious questions.

We hold that the taking of aerial photographs of an industrial plant complex from navigable airspace is not a search prohibited by the Fourth Amendment.

Affirmed.

Justice Powell, with whom Justice Brennan, Justice Marshall, and Justice Blackmun join, concurring in Part III, and dissenting

The Fourth Amendment protects private citizens from arbitrary surveillance by their Government. For nearly twenty years, this Court has adhered to a standard that ensured that Fourth Amendment rights would retain their vitality as technology expanded the Government's capacity to commit unsuspected intrusions into private areas and activities. Today, in the context of administrative aerial photography of commercial premises, the Court retreats from that standard. Such an inquiry will not protect Fourth Amendment rights, but rather will permit their gradual decay as technological advances.

Fourth Amendment protection of privacy interests in business premises "is based upon societal expectations that have deep roots in the history of the Amendment." *Oliver v. United States*, 466 U.S. 170 (1984). In *Marshall v. Barlow's, Inc.*, 436 U.S. 307 (1978), we observed that the "particular offensiveness" of the general warrant and writ of assistance, so despised by the Framers of the Constitution, "was acutely felt by the merchants and businessmen whose premises and products were inspected" under their authority. . . . Against that history, "it is untenable that the ban on warrantless searches was not intended to shield places of business as well as of residence." Our precedents therefore leave no doubt that proprietors of commercial premises, including corporations, have the right to conduct their business free from unreasonable official intrusion.

[W]here Congress has made a reasonable determination that a system of warrantless inspections is necessary to enforce its regulatory purpose, and where "the federal regulatory presence is sufficiently comprehensive and defined that the owner of commercial property cannot help but be aware that his property will be subject to periodic inspections," warrantless inspections may be permitted.

This exception does not apply here. The Government does not contend, nor does the Court hold, that the Clean Air Act authorizes a warrantless inspection program that adequately protects the privacy interests of those whose premises are subject to inspection.

The exception we have recognized for warrantless inspections, limited to pervasively regulated businesses, see *Donovan v. Dewey, United States v. Biswell*, 406 U.S. 311 (1972); *Colonnade Catering Corp. v. United States*, 397 U.S. 72 (1970), is not founded solely on the differences between the premises occupied by such businesses and homes, or on a conclusion that administrative inspections do not intrude on protected privacy interests and therefore do not implicate Fourth Amendment concerns. Rather, the exception is based on a determination that the reasonable expectation of privacy that the owner of a business does enjoy may be adequately protected by the regulatory scheme itself.

III

Since our decision in *Katz v. United States*, the question whether particular governmental conduct constitutes a Fourth Amendment "search" has turned on whether that conduct intruded on a constitutionally protected expectation of privacy.

An expectation of privacy is reasonable for Fourth Amendment purposes if it is rooted in a "source outside of the Fourth Amendment, either by reference to concepts of real or personal property law or to understandings that are recognized and permitted by society." *Rakas v. Illinois*, 439 U.S. 128 (1978). Dow argues that, by enacting trade secret laws, society has recognized that it has a legitimate interest in preserving the privacy of the relevant portions of its open-air plants. As long as Dow takes reasonable steps to protect its secrets, the law should enforce its right against theft or disclosure of those secrets.

Accordingly, Dow has a reasonable expectation of privacy in its commercial facility in the sense required by the Fourth Amendment. EPA's conduct in this case intruded on that expectation because the aerial photography captured information that Dow had taken reasonable steps to preserve as private.

The basic contours of the Supreme Court's jurisprudence concerning searches and inspections of the workplace have not changed significantly since *Dow Chemical*. In *Riverdale Mills Corp. v. Pimpare*, 392 F.3d 55 (1st Cir. 2004), for instance, the Court of Appeals for the First Circuit held that EPA agents' sampling of wastewater from a sewer underneath a manhole located on a firm's property was not a "search." The firm, the Court concluded, did not have a reasonable expectation of privacy in the water that was in the sewer, despite that the sewer was located on its property. A similar case, *Lakeland Enterprises of Rhinelander, Inc. v. Chao*, 402 F.3d 739 (7th Circuit, 2005), concerned an impromptu inspection by an OSHA agent of an excavation project to install sewer and water lines on a public street in Marshfield, Wisconsin. Chad Greenwood, the OSHA agent, happened to pass by the worksite one summer day in 2002, and he stepped out of his car and started videotaping the excavation, which appeared to be in violation of OSHA standards. Greenwood later introduced himself as an OSHA agent and workers let him take measurements which were the basis of a fine levied against the corporation for violation of OSHA regulations. The Corporation argued that the agent's actions constituted a

search and the evidence collected during that search should have been suppressed. Citing *Lopez-Mendoza* (below), the Court disagreed. It decided that there is no reasonable expectation of privacy in the open trench on a public roadway.

Immigration and Naturalization Service v. Lopez-Mendoza et al.

468 U.S. 1032 (1984) 5-4
+ *O'Connor, Burger, Blackmun, Powell, Rehnquist*
– *Brennan, White, Marshall, Stevens*

[The question in this case is whether evidence obtained during an unlawful arrest can be used in a civil deportation hearing. Immigration and Naturalization Service (INS) agents arrested Adan Lopez-Mendoza in 1976 at a transmission repair shop in San Mateo, California, where he worked. The INS agents did not have a warrant to search the premise or to arrest any individuals. Over the objection of the proprietor, the agents spoke with Lopez-Mendoza. He gave his name, said he was from Mexico, and indicated that he did not have close ties in the United States. The agents arrested him and initiated deportation proceeding. Another worker, Sandoval-Sanchez, was also arrested on the premises. At the deportation hearing Sandoval-Sanchez contended that he was not aware that he had a right to remain silent. The immigration judge found both individuals deportable and ruled that the legality of the arrests was not relevant to a deportation proceeding. Lopez-Mendoza and Sandoval-Sanchez appealed the ruling to the Ninth Circuit U.S. Court of Appeals, which vacated the orders of deportation and remanded the case to a lower court to determine if their Fourth Amendment rights had been violated by the arrest and whether the evidence obtained was admissible in the deportation proceeding.]

Justice O'Connor delivered the opinion of the Court

II

A deportation proceeding is a purely civil action to determine eligibility to remain in this country, not to punish an unlawful entry, though entering or remaining unlawfully in this country is itself a crime. . . . The deportation hearing looks prospectively to the respondent's right to remain in this country in the future. Past conduct is relevant only insofar as it may shed light on the respondent's right to remain.

A deportation hearing is held before an immigration judge. The judge's sole power is to order deportation; the judge cannot adjudicate guilt or punish the respondent for any crime related to unlawful entry into or presence in this country. Consistent with the civil nature of the proceeding, various protections that apply in the context of a criminal trial do not apply in a deportation hearing. The respondent must be given "a reasonable opportunity to be present at [the] proceeding," but if the respondent fails to avail himself of that opportunity the hearing may proceed in his absence. In many deportation cases the INS must show only identity and alienage; the burden then shifts to respondent to prove the time, place, and manner of his entry. A decision of deportability need be based only on "reasonable, substantial, and probative evidence." required only "clear, unequivocal and convincing" evidence of the respondent's deportability, not proof beyond a reasonable doubt. In short, a deportation hearing is intended to provide a streamlined determination of eligibility to remain in this country, nothing more. The purpose of deportation is not to punish past transgressions but rather to put an end to a continuing violation of the immigration laws.

III

The "body" or identity of a defendant or respondent in a criminal or civil proceeding is never itself suppressible as a fruit of an unlawful arrest, even if it is conceded that an unlawful arrest, search, or interrogation occurred. See *Gerstein v. Pugh*, 420 U.S. 103, 119 (1975). . . . A similar rule applies in forfeiture proceedings directed against contraband or forfeitable property.

On this basis alone the Court of Appeals' decision as to respondent Lopez-Mendoza must be reversed. At his deportation hearing Lopez-Mendoza objected only to the fact that he had been summoned to a deportation hearing following an unlawful arrest; he entered no objection to the evidence offered against him.

IV

Respondent Sandoval-Sanchez has a more substantial claim. He objected not to his compelled presence at a

deportation proceeding, but to evidence offered at that proceeding. The general rule in a criminal proceeding is that statements and other evidence obtained as a result of an unlawful, warrantless arrest are suppressible if the link between the evidence and the unlawful conduct is not too attenuated. *Wong Sun v. United States*, 371 U.S. 471 (1963). The reach of the exclusionary rule beyond the context of a criminal prosecution, however, is less clear. Although this Court has once stated in dictum that "[i]t may be assumed that evidence obtained by the [Labor] Department through an illegal search and seizure cannot be made the basis of a finding in deportation proceedings," *United States ex rel. Bilokumsky v. Tod*, 263 U.S. 149 (1923), the Court has never squarely addressed the question before.

In *United States v. Janis*, 428 U.S. 433 (1976), this Court set forth a framework for deciding in what types of proceeding application of the exclusionary rule is appropriate. Imprecise as the exercise may be, the Court recognized in *Janis* that there is no choice but to weigh the likely social benefits of excluding unlawfully seized evidence against the likely costs. On the benefit side of the balance "the 'prime purpose' of the [exclusionary] rule, if not the sole one, 'is to deter future unlawful police conduct,'" quoting *United States v. Calandra*, 414 U.S. 338, 347 (1974). On the cost side there is the loss of often probative evidence and all of the secondary costs that flow from the less accurate or more cumbersome adjudication that therefore occurs.

At stake in *Janis* was application of the exclusionary rule in a federal civil tax assessment proceeding following the unlawful seizure of evidence by state, not federal, officials. The Court noted at the outset that "[i]n the complex and turbulent history of the rule, the Court never has applied it to exclude evidence from a civil proceeding, federal or state." Two factors in *Janis* suggested that the deterrence value of the exclusionary rule in the context of that case was slight. First, the state law enforcement officials were already "punished" by the exclusion of the evidence in the state criminal trial as a result of the same conduct. Second, the evidence was also excludable in any federal criminal trial that might be held. Both factors suggested that further application of the exclusionary rule in the federal civil proceeding would contribute little more to the deterrence of unlawful conduct by state officials. On the cost side of the balance, *Janis* focused simply on the loss of "concededly relevant and reliable evidence." . . . The Court concluded that, on balance, this cost outweighed the likely social benefits achievable through application of the exclusionary rule in the federal civil proceeding.

The likely deterrence value of the exclusionary rule in deportation proceedings is difficult to assess. On the one hand, a civil deportation proceeding is a civil complement to a possible criminal prosecution, and to this extent it resembles the civil proceeding under review in *Janis*. The INS does not suggest that the exclusionary rule should not continue to apply in criminal proceedings against an alien who unlawfully enters or remains in this country, and the prospect of losing evidence that might otherwise be used in a criminal prosecution undoubtedly supplies some residual deterrent to unlawful conduct by INS officials. But it must be acknowledged that only a very small percentage of arrests of aliens are intended or expected to lead to criminal prosecutions. Thus the arresting officer's primary objective, in practice, will be to use evidence in the civil deportation proceeding. Moreover, here, in contrast to *Janis*, the agency officials who effect the unlawful arrest are the same officials who subsequently bring the deportation action. As recognized in *Janis*, the exclusionary rule is likely to be most effective when applied to such "intrasovereign" violations.

Nonetheless, several other factors significantly reduce the likely deterrent value of the exclusionary rule in a civil deportation proceeding. First, regardless of how the arrest is effected, deportation will still be possible when evidence not derived directly from the arrest is sufficient to support deportation. As the BIA has recognized, in many deportation proceedings "the sole matters necessary for the Government to establish are the respondent's identity and alienage—at which point the burden shifts to the respondent to prove the time, place and manner of entry." . . . Since the person and identity of the respondent are not themselves suppressible, the INS must prove only alienage, and that will sometimes be possible using evidence gathered independently of, or sufficiently attenuated from, the original arrest . . . . The INS's task is simplified in this regard by the civil nature of the proceeding. As Justice Brandeis stated: "Silence is often evidence of the most persuasive character. . . . [T]here is no rule of law which prohibits officers charged with the administration of the immigration law from drawing an inference from the silence of one who is called upon to speak. . . . A person arrested on the preliminary warrant is not protected by a presumption of citizen-

ship comparable to the presumption of innocence in a criminal case. There is no provision which forbids drawing an adverse inference from the fact of standing mute." *United States ex rel. Bilokumsky v. Tod*, 263 U.S., at 153–154.

The second factor is a practical one. In the course of a year the average INS agent arrests almost 500 illegal aliens. Brief for Petitioner 38. Over 97.5% apparently agree to voluntary deportation without a formal hearing. . . . Among the remainder who do request a formal hearing (apparently a dozen or so in all, per officer, per year) very few challenge the circumstances of their arrests. As noted by the Court of Appeals, "the BIA was able to find only two reported immigration cases since 1899 in which the [exclusionary] rule was applied to bar unlawfully seized evidence, only one other case in which the rule's application was specifically addressed, and fewer than fifty BIA proceedings since 1952 in which a Fourth Amendment challenge to the introduction of evidence was even raised." . . . Every INS agent knows, therefore, that it is highly unlikely that any particular arrestee will end up challenging the lawfulness of his arrest in a formal deportation proceeding. When an occasional challenge is brought, the consequences from the point of view of the officer's overall arrest and deportation record will be trivial. In these circumstances, the arresting officer is most unlikely to shape his conduct in anticipation of the exclusion of evidence at a formal deportation hearing.

Third, and perhaps most important, the INS has its own comprehensive scheme for deterring Fourth Amendment violations by its officers. Most arrests of illegal aliens away from the border occur during farm, factory, and other workplace surveys. Large numbers of illegal aliens are often arrested at one time, and conditions are understandably chaotic. . . . To safeguard the rights of those who are lawfully present at inspected workplaces the INS has developed rules restricting stop, interrogation, and arrest practices. . . . These regulations require that no one be detained without reasonable suspicion of illegal alienage, and that no one be arrested unless there is an admission of illegal alienage or other strong evidence thereof. New immigration officers receive instruction and examination in Fourth Amendment law, and others receive periodic refresher courses in law. . . . Evidence seized through intentionally unlawful conduct is excluded by Department of Justice policy from the proceeding for which it was obtained. See Memorandum from Benjamin R. Civiletti to Heads of Offices, Boards, Bureaus and Divisions, Violations of Search and Seizure Law (Jan. 16, 1981). The INS also has in place a procedure for investigating and punishing immigration officers who commit Fourth Amendment violations. See Office of General Counsel, INS, U. S. Dept. of Justice, The Law of Arrest, Search, and Seizure for Immigration Officers 35 (Jan. 1983). The INS's attention to Fourth Amendment interests cannot guarantee that constitutional violations will not occur, but it does reduce the likely deterrent value of the exclusionary rule. Deterrence must be measured at the margin.

Finally, the deterrent value of the exclusionary rule in deportation proceedings is undermined by the availability of alternative remedies for institutional practices by the INS that might violate Fourth Amendment rights. The INS is a single agency, under central federal control, and engaged in operations of broad scope but highly repetitive character. The possibility of declaratory relief against the agency thus offers a means for challenging the validity of INS practices, when standing requirements for bringing such an action can be met. . . .

On the other side of the scale, the social costs of applying the exclusionary rule in deportation proceedings are both unusual and significant. The first cost is one that is unique to continuing violations of the law.

Presumably no one would argue that the exclusionary rule should be invoked to prevent an agency from ordering corrective action at a leaking hazardous waste dump if the evidence underlying the order had been improperly obtained, or to compel police to return contraband explosives or drugs to their owner if the contraband had been unlawfully seized. Sandoval-Sanchez is a person whose unregistered presence in this country, without more, constitutes a crime. His release within our borders would immediately subject him to criminal penalties. His release would clearly frustrate the express public policy against an alien's unregistered presence in this country. Even the objective of deterring Fourth Amendment violations should not require such a result. The constable's blunder may allow the criminal to go free, but we have never suggested that it allows the criminal to continue in the commission of an ongoing crime. When the crime in question involves unlawful presence in this country, criminals may go free, but he should not go free within our borders.

Other factors also weigh against applying the exclusionary rule in deportation proceedings.

The average immigration judge handles about six deportation hearings per day. . . . Neither the hearing officers nor the attorneys participating in those hearings are likely to be well versed in the intricacies of Fourth Amendment law. The prospect of even occasional invocation of the exclusionary rule might significantly change and complicate the character of these proceedings. . . . This sober assessment of the exclusionary rule's likely costs, by the agency that would have to administer the rule in at least the administrative tiers of its application, cannot be brushed off lightly.

The BIA's concerns are reinforced by the staggering dimension of the problem that the INS confronts. Immigration officers apprehend over one million deportable aliens in this country every year. . . . A single agent may arrest many illegal aliens every day. Although the investigatory burden does not justify the commission of constitutional violations, the officers cannot be expected to compile elaborate, contemporaneous, written reports detailing the circumstances of every arrest. Fourth Amendment suppression hearings would undoubtedly require considerably more, and the likely burden on the administration of the immigration laws would be correspondingly severe.

Finally, the INS advances the credible argument that applying the exclusionary rule to deportation proceedings might well result in the suppression of large amounts of information that had been obtained entirely lawfully. INS arrests occur in crowded and confused circumstances. Though the INS agents are instructed to follow procedures that adequately protect Fourth Amendment interests, agents will usually be able to testify only to the fact that they followed INS rules. The demand for a precise account of exactly what happened in each particular arrest would plainly preclude mass arrests, even when the INS is confronted, as it often is, with massed numbers of ascertainably illegal aliens, and even when the arrests can be and are conducted in full compliance with all Fourth Amendment requirements.

In these circumstances we are persuaded that the *Janis* balance between costs and benefits comes out against applying the exclusionary rule in civil deportation hearings held by the INS. By all appearances the INS has already taken sensible and reasonable steps to deter Fourth Amendment violations by its officers, and this makes the likely additional deterrent value of the exclusionary rule small. The costs of applying the exclusionary rule in the context of civil deportation hearings are high. In particular, application of the exclusionary rule in cases such as San-doval-Sanchez', would compel the courts to release from custody persons who would then immediately resume their commission of a crime through their continuing, unlawful presence in this country. "There comes a point at which courts, consistent with their duty to administer the law, cannot continue to create barriers to law enforcement in the pursuit of a supervisory role that is properly the duty of the Executive and Legislative Branches." *United States v. Janis*, 428 U.S., at 459. That point has been reached here.

V

We do not condone any violations of the Fourth Amendment that may have occurred in the arrests of respondents Lopez-Mendoza or Sandoval-Sanchez. . . . Our conclusions concerning the exclusionary rule's value might change, if there developed good reason to believe that Fourth Amendment violations by INS officers were widespread. . . . Finally, we do not deal here with egregious violations of Fourth Amendment or other liberties that might transgress notions of fundamental fairness and undermine the probative value of the evidence obtained. . . . At issue here is the exclusion of credible evidence gathered in connection with peaceful arrests by INS officers. We hold that evidence derived from such arrests need not be suppressed in an INS civil deportation hearing.

The judgment of the Court of Appeals is therefore Reversed.

Justice Brennan, dissenting

[. . .]

I believe the basis for the exclusionary rule does not derive from its effectiveness as a deterrent, but is instead found in the requirements of the Fourth Amendment itself. My view of the exclusionary rule would, of course, require affirmance of the Court of Appeals. In this case, federal law enforcement officers arrested respondents Sandoval-Sanchez and Lopez-Mendoza in violation of their Fourth Amendment rights. The subsequent admission of any evidence secured pursuant to these unlawful arrests in civil deportation preceedings would, in my view, also infringe those rights. The Government of the United States bears an obligation to obey the Fourth Amendment; that obligation is not lifted simply because the law enforcement officers were agents of the Immigration and Naturalization Service, nor because the evidence obtained by those officers was to be used in civil deportation proceedings.

Justice White, dissenting

[T]here is no principled basis for distinguishing between the deterrent effect of the rule in criminal cases and in civil deportation proceedings. The majority attempts to justify the distinction by asserting that deportation will still be possible when evidence not derived from the illegal search or seizure is independently sufficient. However, that is no less true in criminal cases. The suppression of some evidence does not bar prosecution for the crime, and in many cases even though some evidence is suppressed a conviction will nonetheless be obtained.

The majority also suggests that the fact that most aliens elect voluntary departure dilutes the deterrent effect of the exclusionary rule. However, that fact no more diminishes the importance of the exclusionary sanction than the fact that many criminal defendants plead guilty dilutes the rule's deterrent effect in criminal cases. The possibility of exclusion of evidence quite obviously plays a part in the decision whether to contest either civil deportation or criminal prosecution. Moreover, in concentrating on the incentives under which the individual agent operates to the exclusion of the incentives under which the agency as a whole operates neglects the "systemic" deterrent effect that may lead the agency to adopt policies and procedures that conform to Fourth Amendment standards.

The majority believes "perhaps most important" the fact that the INS has a "comprehensive scheme" in place for deterring Fourth Amendment violations by punishing agents who commit such violations. . . . Since the deterrent function of the rule is furthered if it alters either "the behavior of individual law enforcement officers or the policies of their departments," it seems likely that it was the rule's deterrent effect that led to the programs to which the Court now points for its assertion that the rule would have no deterrent effect.

The suggestion that alternative remedies, such as civil suits, provide adequate protection is unrealistic. Contrary to the situation in criminal cases, once the Government has improperly obtained evidence against an illegal alien, he is removed from the country and is therefore in no position to file civil actions in federal courts. Moreover, those who are legally in the country but are nonetheless subjected to illegal searches and seizures are likely to be poor and uneducated, and many will not speak English. It is doubtful that the threat of civil suits by these persons will strike fear into the hearts of those who enforce the Nation's immigration laws.

It is also my belief that the majority exaggerates the costs associated with applying the exclusionary rule in this context. Evidence obtained through violation of the Fourth Amendment is not automatically suppressed, and any inquiry into the burdens associated with application of the exclusionary rule must take that fact into account.

Finally, the majority suggests that application of the exclusionary rule might well result in the suppression of large amounts of information legally obtained because of the "crowded and confused circumstances" surrounding mass arrests. Rather than constituting a rejection of the application of the exclusionary rule in civil deportation proceedings, however, this argument amounts to a rejection of the application of the Fourth Amendment to the activities of INS agents. . . . The Court may be willing to throw up its hands in dismay because it is administratively inconvenient to determine whether constitutional rights have been violated, but we neglect our duty when we subordinate constitutional rights to expediency in such a manner. Particularly is this so when, as here, there is but a weak showing that administrative efficiency will be seriously compromised.

In sum, I believe that the costs and benefits of applying the exclusionary rule in civil deportation proceedings do not differ in any significant way from the costs and benefits of applying the rule in ordinary criminal proceedings. Accordingly, I dissent.

[Justice Stevens's dissenting opinion omitted.]

Cost-benefit tests in law, including the one established in *Lopez-Mendoza*, have a reassuring ring of objectivity.[11] However, a number of cogent criticisms can and have

been made of this approach. First, in criminal cases, it is often too easy for a court to conclude that the interest of the state in enforcing its laws outweighs the right of individuals to be free from the government intrusion complained of. Judges at all levels of the justice system may find it difficult to apply the exclusionary rule in a principled way where that would mean throwing out incriminating evidence in cases of drug smuggling, violence, or theft. Second, there is nothing scientific in choosing what counts as a cost and what counts as a benefit. If judges are left to their own devices to decide how to measure costs and benefits, they can easily manipulate the outcome by simply selecting the "costs" and "benefits" needed to obtain the desired result. Such economic-sounding analysis can make it easier for courts to avoid such difficult questions as that in *Lopez-Mendoza*, which asked, essentially, whether certain constitutional protections apply to non-citizens.

The rule that illegally seized evidence may be used in administrative cases was relied upon by a New York appellate court in 1993. In that case, a bag of marijuana was obtained during an unlawful search of a police officer's car, and the court ruled that, in disciplinary action against the officer, the cost-benefit calculation properly tipped toward protecting the public.[12]

Occasionally, however, judges do tip the balance the other way and apply the exclusionary rule to agency proceedings in order to discourage future unlawful searches. They can do so precisely because the cost-benefit rubric is in fact predicated on values rather than simple math. In 1996, a different New York state appellate court concluded that if an agency were to use evidence that had been obtained illegally by an entity separate from the agency prosecutiong the violation, that might be acceptable. But where "the party responsible for the illegal search is the same party offering the evidence, the deterrence factor is compelling and far outweighs the benefit to be gained by using the evidence."[13]

In a 5-4 ruling in 1998, the U.S. Supreme Court underscored the position it took in *Lopez-Mendoza* that certain

11. For an overview and discussion of cost-benefit analysis, see Richard Revesz and Michael Livermore, *Retaking Rationality: How Cost Benefit Analysis Can Better Protect the Environment and Our Health* (New York: Oxford University Press, 2008).

12. *Boyd v. Constantine*, 81 N.Y. 2d 189 (1993).
13. *In re Juan C.*, 223 A.D. 2d 126.

classes of individuals in society do not enjoy the full protections of the Fourth Amendment. Since the exclusionary rule's primary purpose is to deter law enforcement officers from violating the constitutional rights of the people they investigate, you might imagine that evidence seized by parole officers who unlawfully entered the home of a parolee's mother could not be used to revoke the defendant's parole and return him to prison. But the Court, in an opinion authored by Justice Clarence Thomas, reasoned that a parolee's due process rights at a parole hearing (held to determine if he or she violated conditions of parole) are not the same as those in a criminal proceeding. Since parole revocation hearings are informal and partially non-adversarial proceedings, the exclusionary rule did not apply.[14]

Immigration issues are at center stage in current discussions about administrative searches and the Fourth Amendment. Whether non-citizens enjoy the same constitutional rights and protections as citizens has been debated for a long time with no clear answer. It is usually accepted that certain rights, such as habeas corpus, are available to non-citizens while others, such as the right to bear arms, may not be. Since the terrorist attacks of September 11, 2001, however, national security objectives have exerted greater control over administrative practices, including searches conducted by the Immigration and Customs Enforcement (ICE) branch of the Department of Homeland Security, which replaced the INS. David Harris observes that "the immigrant question," once concerned with the impact of country quotas on jobs and the economy, is now processed through the lens of "national security" and the "war on terrorism."[15]

Since 2006 ICE has significantly increased the number and scope of "immigration raids," in communities, county jails, and businesses. "Fear has gripped immigrant families across the country," wrote Juliana Barbassa of the Associated Press, "as federal agents raid neighborhoods, work sites and jails in a nationwide crackdown on illegal immigration. Tens of thousands of people have been rounded up over the past several months, and many more are afraid to leave home, answer a knock on the door or leave their children alone in fear they might be next."[16] Emblematic of this trend was a 2006 immigration raid conducted by ICE at six meatpacking plants in the Midwest owned by Swift & Co., one of the largest meat processing corporations in the world. As a result of the raid, 1,282 workers were arrested on immigration violations or existing criminal warrants in the largest such enforcement action in U.S. history. ICE did obtain civil search warrants before the raid, which "allowed them to search for and apprehend any undocumented worker."[17] According to witnesses, however, the process of finding out who, among the detained workers, was and was not undocumented resembled a "fishing expedition." A federal lawsuit was filed in September 2007 against the Department of Homeland Security and ICE by the United Food and Commercial Worker's Union on behalf of eight plaintiffs, six of them U.S. citizens, who claimed they were subjected to unreasonable searches and seizures during the raids.

Under the *Lopez-Mendoza* framework, it is likely that the court will apply a "balancing test" to weigh the workers' expectation of privacy against the declared "public interest" of the government to identify and deport illegal immigrants. What needs to be emphasized is that the balancing test itself is not as neutral an analytic tool as it might appear to be. Rather, the application of this test in law tends to be shaped by the politics of the day. An unfortunate result of the prevailing concern in the country about foreign-sponsored terrorism (as well as a perceived loss of jobs to immigrants) is that Fourth Amendment protections against unreasonable government searches and seizures may be diluted for all people, citizens, and non-citizens alike. Throughout our history, threats that are more apparent than real have undermined reasoned analysis and contributed a measure of irrationality to the outcome of political controversies and

14. *Pennsylvania Board of Probation and Parole v. Scott*, 524 U.S. 357 (1998).

15. David Harris, "The War on Terror, Local Police, and Immigration Enforcement: A Curious Tale of Police Power in Post 9/11 America," *Rutgers Law Journal* 38 (2006): 1.

16. Juliana Barbassa, "High Profile Raids Leave Immigrants in Fear Nationwide," *Associated Press*, February 18, 2007.

17. See Raquel Aldana, "Of Katz and 'Aliens': Privacy Expectations and Immigration Raids," *UC Davis Law Review* 41 (2008): 1081, 1092.

the balancing tests applied by courts to adjudicate competing interests.

A recent, and alarming, example of this trend can be seen in the National Security Agency (NSA) warrantless eavesdropping controversy. On December 16, 2005, in an exclusive news story that made the controversy public for the first time, the *New York Times* reported that "[u]nder a presidential order signed in 2002, the intelligence agency has monitored the international telephone calls and international e-mail messages of hundreds, perhaps thousands, of people inside the United States without warrants over the past three years in an effort to track possible 'dirty numbers' linked to Al Qaeda . . . ." The story instantly generated a major controversy. Even though the Bush Administration maintained that the surveillance program was justified as part of an ongoing "war," the fact that NSA was conducting domestic intelligence operations was highly controversial. Likewise, many legal scholars argued that the government needed to first obtain a warrant under the Foreign Intelligence Surveillance Act (FISA) if it wanted to eavesdrop within the United States.

The American Civil Liberties Union (ACLU) filed a lawsuit challenging the constitutionality of the so-called "Terrorist Surveillance Program" that allowed NSA to track communications without warrant. Although a federal trial court ruled that the program was unconstitutional, the United States Court of Appeals for the Ninth Circuit reversed on the narrow procedural ground that the ACLU lacked standing to bring the lawsuit, thus avoiding the question whether the program was in fact a violation of the Constitution. In February 2008, the U.S. Supreme Court declined to hear the case, letting stand the decision of the lower court.

For administrative law scholars, the crucial issue at stake has both practical and normative dimensions. Practically speaking, the question is whether the costs to political liberty of such programs are justified by their results. To the frustration of an administrative law student, unfortunately, the data that might help answer that question is kept hidden from the public eye on the grounds that disclosure could assist "our enemies."

From a normative perspective the issue is even more complex and so far, there are only questions without answers. How much further are citizens willing to sacrifice their constitutional rights in the name of national security? It is now well known that big Internet companies, notably Google, and large communications companies, such as AT&T, are sharing information about their clients with the federal government. Richard Posner, a federal appeals court judge on the Seventh Circuit U.S. Court of Appeals in Chicago, argued in a newspaper column[18] that such large-scale "data collection" does not invade privacy. "Because of their volume," he wrote, "the data are first sifted by computers, which search for names, addresses, phone numbers, etc., that may have intelligence value. This initial sifting, far from invading privacy (a computer is not a sentient being), keeps most private data from being read by any intelligence officer."

Despite Judge Posner's endorsement, critics argue that constitutional rights must be guarded by the judiciary when they are most vulnerable. Just as the privacy rights of welfare recipients must be guarded even more vigilantly because the poor are more vulnerable to having those rights violated (as Justice Brennan argued for the majority in *Goldberg v. Kelly*), constitutional privacy rights should be guarded all the more jealously when the government seems most intent on taking them away.

So far, however, it seems that the courts, the Supreme Court in particular, are trying to avoid taking a stance on the issue. As we saw in the *ACLU v. NSA* case, the Court of Appeals declined to rule on the merits of the constitutionality of the Terrorist Surveillance Program, and instead decided the case on an issue having to do with the standing, or right, of the plaintiff to sue at all. Similarly, the Supreme Court declined to rule on the question by denying to hear the case. Thus can courts avoid reaching the merits of the cases that come before them and thereby avoid taking a stand on the issue. Any lower trial or appellate court can theoretically find that the plantiffs do not have standing to sue. And the Supreme Court, which has discretionary jurisdiction, can simply decline to hear a case without even stating its reasons. It is important as students of law and politics to be aware that any action a

18. Richard Posner, "Our Domestic Intelligence Crisis," *Washington Post*, December 21, 2005.

court takes, be it a decision or a decision not to decide, it is a political action.[19] In this regard, for instance, the Supreme Court decision not to hear the appeal from the ACLU, may be viewed as a tacit approval of the Court of Appeals' decision and of the government's policy of domestic intelligence gathering. On the other hand, there are many non-political reasons why the Court may decline to hear a case. The issue may not involve a significant constitutional question, or may not provide the court with the factual pattern necessary to resolve a conflict in the lower courts. Also, to grant review of a lower court decision, at least four justices must agree to hear the case.

ACCESS TO INFORMATION HELD BY GOVERNMENT

The regulation literature regularly confirms the sobering reality that government agencies are often held captive by the powerful industries they regulate. In part this is due to the fact that citizens have little access to, or information about, a regulatory process characterized by informal negotiations between agencies and the industries.[20] Recognition of the vast power that private interests exercise over public policy prompted a wave of reforms in the mid-1960s and '70s—what we might call *counter-capture reforms*. Public interest advocates, such as Ralph Nader,[21] organized a citizens' movement—*the public interest movement*—which continues today to support efforts to expand public access and participation in the regulatory process as an antidote to corporate capture.[22]

Courts play a role in this process by broadening standing to sue, expanding notice and comment periods, and

by requiring that agencies record all the facts used in making an agency decision (see chapter 10).[23] Congress has imposed additional reforms limiting the extent to which agencies and interested parties can engage in private decision making by requiring agencies to hold meetings in public (the Government Sunshine Act 1976), by prohibiting ex parte decisions (Administrative Procedure Act 1976), and by increasing access to information (the Freedom of Information Act 1966). These reforms, coupled with procedural due process expansions during the early 1970s, seek to expand citizen participation in decision making and reduce the influence of regulated industries over administrative discretion.

The Freedom of Information Act (FOIA)[24] is the most significant law for expanding access to information about the government. This statute allows citizens to request copies of documents held by the government. Unless provisions of the act expressly exempt the document, it must be released. A version of the present law was added to the Administrative Procedure Act (APA). Initially the act required no specific deadlines for compliance through disclosure, and this toothless law was rarely enforced.[25] In 1974, however, Congress amended the act to require the agency to decide within ten days whether to comply. If the agency refuses, the petitioner can now take the issue directly to court.

In 2005, President George W. Bush signed Executive Order 13,392, emphasizing the importance of FOIA and a well-informed citizenry to the constitutional democracy of the United States. The Order, however, stated that "[information] requesters are *seeking a service* from the Federal Government and should be treated as such. Accordingly, in responding to a FOIA request, agencies shall respond courteously and appropriately." (Emphasis added.) To this end, the Order charged executive agencies with the task of designating a chief FOIA officer to facilitate and monitor FOIA-related activities within

19. See Peter Bachrach and Morton S. Baratz, "Power and Its Two Faces Revisited: A Reply to Geoffrey Debnam," *American Political Science Review* 69 no. 3 (1975): 900.
20. See Samuel Huntington, "The Marasmus of the ICC: The Commission, the Railroad and the Public Interest," *Yale Law Journal* 61 (1952): 467; M. H. Bernstein, *Regulating Business by Independent Commission* (Princeton, N.J.: Princeton University Press, 1955); and Grant McConnel, *Private Power and American Democracy* (New York: Vintage Books, 1966).
21. See Ralph Nader, *Public Interest Perspective: The Next Four Years* (Washington, D.C.: Public Citizen, 1977).
22. See Joel F. Handler, *Social Movements and the Legal System* (New York: Academic Press, 1978); David Vogel, "Promoting Pluralism: The Politics of the Public Interest Movement," *Political Science Quarterly* 95 (1981): 608; and Michael W. McCann, *Taking Reform Seriously: Perspectives on Public Interest Liberalism* (Ithaca, N.Y.: Cornell University Press, 1986).

23. See J. Delong, "Informal Rulemaking and the Integration of Law and Policy," *Virginia Law Review* 65 (1979): 257.
24. See Appendix B, the Administrative Procedure Act, Sec. 552. p. 551.
25. See Ralph Nader, "Freedom From Information: The Act and the Agencies," *Harvard Civil Rights-Civil Liberties Law Review* 5 (1970): 1.

agencies.[26] The latest major amendment to the FOIA, the "Openness Promotes Effectiveness in Our National Government Act of 2007" (Open Government Act), codified several provisions of the Executive Order 13,392.[27]

A fairly typical use of FOIA occurred when Procter and Gamble demanded about 20,000 documents from the Centers for Disease Control. These documents are part of Procter and Gamble's strategy to exonerate itself from liability for deaths and illness caused by toxic shock syndrome allegedly related to use of a Procter and Gamble product known as the Rely tampon. The effort to obtain the documents through FOIA cost the company over one million dollars.[28]

The Freedom of Information Act lists nine categories of documents exempt from the disclosure requirement:

1. Information "specifically authorized under criteria established by an Executive order to be kept secret in the interest of national defense or foreign policy"

2. Internal personnel rules and practices

3. Material specifically exempted by other statutory provisions

4. Trade secrets and business information deemed confidential or privileged

5. Inter- and intra-agency memoranda

6. Personnel and medical files

7. Law enforcement records

8. Banking records

9. Geological and geophysical data concerning mineral wealth

Exemption number 3 is open ended, leaving to Congress the statutory authority to regulate the scope of government information sharing. If Congress decides that information should not be shared with the public, it can exempt it from FOIA requirements. Indeed, this is

exactly what happened right after the September 11, 2001 attacks. When Congress wrote and approved the Homeland Security Act of 2002,[29] it created a new exemption from FOIA, relying on the 3rd category:

"critical infrastructure information (including the identity of the submitting person or entity) that is voluntarily submitted to a covered Federal agency for use by that agency regarding the security of critical infrastructure and protected systems, analysis, warning, interdependency study, recovery, reconstitution, or other informational purpose, when accompanied by an express statement"[30] shall be exempt from disclosure under FOIA.

"Critical infrastructure" includes physical- and cyber-based systems and services essential to the national defense, government, or economy of the United States, such as systems essential for telecommunications, electrical power, gas and oil storage and transportation, banking and finance, water supply, etc.

There is a considerable amount of litigation over the meaning and scope of these nine exemptions. FOIA case law has become an important area of federal administrative law practice. In particular, three exemptions (2, 5, and 6) are regularly the subject of litigation. These exemptions are often used by agencies when they deny access to government documents. Agencies claim that protecting the public's right to information under FOIA must be balanced against an individual's right to privacy.[31] In other words, agencies sometimes use an individual's right to privacy in order to shield the government from having to release documents about its own activities. This occurred in the next case, *Department of the Air Force v. Rose* (1976). The government claimed that it did not have to release materials because they fell within exemptions 2 and 6. The case following *Rose* wrestles with the protection of privacy. Both cases are good examples of the kind of arguments agencies use to avoid disclosing government documents.

26. Executive Order no. 13392, 70, *Federal Register* 75373 (Dec. 19, 2005).

27. Openness Promotes Effectiveness in our National Government Act of 2007 (signed by the president on December 31, 2007).

28. "Rely Counterattack," *Wall Street Journal*, June 26, 1981. The average citizen or small business does not have Procter and Gamble's financial capacity to pay for reproduction of large quantities of government documents. Standards and procedures for fee waivers are discussed by John E. Bonine, "Public Interest Fee Waivers Under the Freedom of Information Act," *Duke Law Journal* (1981): 213.

29. Public Law 107-296 (codified at 6 U.S.C. §133(a)(1)(A)).

30. Ibid.

31. The Privacy Act of 1974 prohibits disclosure of any kind of retrievable information about an individual such as a name or other means of identification. Exemption 6 of the FOIA is not as restrictive.

II

Congress exempted nine categories of documents from the FOIA's broad disclosure requirements. Three of those exemptions are arguably relevant to this case. Exemption 3 applies to documents that are specifically exempted from disclosure by another statute. §552(b)(3). Exemption 6 protects "personnel and medical files and similar files the disclosure of which would constitute a clearly unwarranted invasion of personal privacy." §552(b)(6). Exemption 7(C) excludes records or information compiled for law enforcement purposes, "but only to the extent that the production of such [materials] . . . could reasonably be expected to constitute an unwarranted invasion of personal privacy." §552(b)(7)(C).

Exemption 7(C)'s privacy language is broader than the comparable language in Exemption 6 in two respects. First, whereas Exemption 6 requires that the invasion of privacy be "clearly unwarranted," the adverb "clearly" is omitted from Exemption 7(C). This omission is the product of a 1974 amendment adopted in response to concerns expressed by the president. Second, whereas Exemption 6 refers to disclosures that "would constitute" an invasion of privacy, Exemption 7(C) encompasses any disclosure that "could reasonably be expected to constitute" such an invasion. This difference is also the product of a specific amendment. Thus, the standard for evaluating a threatened invasion of privacy interests resulting from the disclosure of records compiled for law enforcement purposes is somewhat broader than the standard applicable to personnel, medical, and similar files.

III

This case arises out of requests made by a CBS news correspondent and the Reporters Committee for Freedom of the Press (respondents) for information concerning the criminal records of four members of the Medico family. The Pennsylvania Crime Commission had identified the family's company, Medico Industries, as a legitimate business dominated by organized crime figures. Moreover, the company allegedly had obtained a number of defense contracts as a result of an improper arrangement with a corrupt Congressman.

The FOIA requests sought disclosure of any arrests, indictments, acquittals, convictions, and sentences of any of the four Medicos. Although the FBI originally denied the requests, it provided the requested data concerning three of the Medicos after their deaths. In their complaint in the District Court, respondents sought the rap sheet for the fourth, Charles Medico (Medico), insofar as it contained "matters of public record."

The parties filed cross-motions for summary judgment. Respondents urged that any information regarding "a record of bribery, embezzlement or other financial crime" would potentially be a matter of special public interest. In answer to that argument, the Department advised respondents and the District Court that it had no record of any financial crimes concerning Medico, but the Department continued to refuse to confirm or deny whether it had any information concerning nonfinancial crimes. Thus, the issue was narrowed to Medico's nonfinancial-crime history insofar as it is a matter of public record.

The District Court granted the Department's motion for summary judgment . . . .

The Court of Appeals reversed. It held that an individual's privacy interest in criminal-history information that is a matter of public record was minimal at best. Noting the absence of any statutory standards by which to judge the public interest in disclosure, the Court of Appeals concluded that it should be bound by the state and local determinations that such information should be made available to the general public.

IV

Exemption 7(C) requires us to balance the privacy interest in maintaining, as the Government puts it, the "practical obscurity" of the rap sheets against the public interest in their release.

The preliminary question is whether Medico's interest in the nondisclosure of any rap sheet the FBI might have on him is the sort of "personal privacy" interest that Congress intended Exemption 7(C) to protect. As we have pointed out before, "[t]he cases sometimes characterized as protecting 'privacy' have in fact involved at least two different kinds of interests. One is the individual interest in avoiding disclosure of personal matters, and another is the interest in independence in making certain kinds of important decisions." Whalen v. Roe, 429 U.S. 589, 598–600, 97 S.Ct. 869, 875–877, 51 L.Ed.2d 64 (1977). Here, the former interest, "in avoiding disclosure of personal matters," is implicated. Because events summarized in a rap sheet have been previously disclosed to the public, respondents contend that Medico's privacy interest in avoiding disclosure of a federal compilation of these events approaches zero. We reject respondents' cramped notion of personal privacy.

To begin with, both the common law and the literal understandings of privacy encompass the individual's control of information concerning his or her person. In an organized society, there are few facts that are not at one time or another divulged to another. Thus the extent of the protection accorded a privacy right at common law rested in part on the degree of dissemination of the allegedly private fact and the extent to which the passage of time rendered it private. According to Webster's initial definition, information may be classified as "private" if it is "intended for or restricted to the use of a particular person or group or class of persons: not freely available to the public." Recognition of this attribute of a privacy interest supports the distinction, in terms of personal privacy, between scattered disclosure of the bits of information contained in a rap sheet and revelation of the rap sheet as a whole. The very fact that federal funds have been spent to prepare, index, and maintain these criminal-history files demonstrates that the individual items of information in the summaries would not otherwise be "freely available" either to the officials who have access to the underlying files or to the general public. Indeed, if the summaries were "freely available," there would be no reason to invoke the FOIA to obtain access to the information they contain. Granted, in many contexts the fact that information is not freely available is no reason to exempt that information from a statute generally requiring its dissemination. But the issue here is whether the compilation of otherwise hard-to-obtain information alters the privacy interest implicated by disclosure of that information. Plainly there is a vast difference between the public records that might be found after a diligent search of courthouse files, county archives, and local police stations throughout the country and a computerized summary located in a single clearinghouse of information.

This conclusion is supported by the web of federal statutory and regulatory provisions that limits the disclosure of rap-sheet information. That is, Congress has authorized rap-sheet dissemination to banks, local licensing officials, the securities industry, the nuclear-power industry, and other law enforcement agencies. Further, the FBI has permitted such disclosure to the subject of the rap sheet and, more generally, to assist in the apprehension of wanted persons or fugitives. Finally, the FBI's exchange of rap-sheet information "is subject to cancellation if dissemination is made outside the receiving departments or related agencies." 28 U.S.C. §534(b). This careful and limited pattern of authorized rap-sheet disclosure fits the dictionary definition of privacy as involving a restriction of information "to the use of a particular person or group or class of persons." Moreover, although perhaps not specific enough to constitute a statutory exemption under FOIA Exemption 3, these statutes and regulations, taken as a whole, evidence a congressional intent to protect the privacy of rap-sheet subjects, and a concomitant recognition of the power of compilations to affect personal privacy that outstrips the combined power of the bits of information contained within.

Other portions of the FOIA itself bolster the conclusion that disclosure of records regarding private citizens, identifiable by name, is not what the framers of the FOIA had in mind. Specifically, the FOIA provides that "[t]o the extent required to prevent a clearly unwarranted invasion of personal privacy, an agency may delete identifying details when it makes available or publishes an opinion, statement of policy, interpretation, or staff manual or instruction." 5 U.S.C. §552(a)(2). Additionally, the FOIA assures that "[a]ny reasonably segregable portion of a record shall be provided to any person requesting such record after deletion of the portions which are exempt under [§(b)]." 5 U.S.C. §552(b). These provisions, for deletion of identifying references and disclosure of segregable portions of records with exempt information deleted, reflect a congressional understanding that disclosure of records containing personal details about private citizens can infringe significant privacy interests.

Also supporting our conclusion that a strong privacy interest inheres in the nondisclosure of compiled computerized information is the Privacy Act of 1974, codified at 5 U.S.C. §552a. The Privacy Act was passed largely out of concern over "the impact of computer data banks on individual privacy." The Privacy Act provides generally that "[n]o agency shall disclose any record which is contained in a system of records . . . except pursuant to a written request by, or with the prior written consent of, the individual to whom the record pertains." 5 U.S.C. §552a(b). Although the Privacy Act contains a variety of exceptions to this rule, including an exemption for information required to be disclosed under the FOIA, Congress' basic policy concern regarding the implications of computerized data banks for personal privacy is certainly relevant in our consideration of the privacy interest affected by dissemination of rap sheets from the FBI computer.

Given this level of federal concern over centralized data bases, the fact that most States deny the general public access to their criminal-history summaries should not be surprising. As we have pointed out, in 47 States nonconviction data from criminal-history summaries are not available at all, and even conviction data are "generally unavailable to the public." State policies, of course, do not determine the meaning of a federal statute, but they provide evidence that the law enforcement profession generally assumes—as has the Department of Justice—that individual subjects have a significant privacy interest in their criminal histories. It is reasonable to presume that Congress legislated with an understanding of this professional point of view.

V

Exemption 7(C), by its terms, permits an agency to withhold a document only when revelation "could reasonably be expected to constitute an unwarranted invasion of personal privacy." We must next address what factors might warrant an invasion of the interest described in Part IV, supra.

In this case—and presumably in the typical case in which one private citizen is seeking information about another—the requester does not intend to discover anything about the conduct of the agency that has possession of the requested records. Indeed, response to this request would not shed any light on the conduct of any Government agency or official.

Respondents argue that there is a two-fold public interest in learning about Medico's past arrests or convictions: He allegedly had improper dealings with a corrupt Congressman, and he is an officer of a corporation with defense contracts. But if Medico has, in fact, been arrested or convicted of certain crimes, that information would neither aggravate nor mitigate his allegedly improper relationship with the Congressman; more specifically, it would tell us nothing directly about the character of the Con-

gressman's behavior. Nor would it tell us anything about the conduct of the Department of Defense (DOD) in awarding one or more contracts to the Medico Company. Arguably a FOIA request to the DOD for records relating to those contracts, or for documents describing the agency's procedures, if any, for determining whether officers of a prospective contractor have criminal records, would constitute an appropriate request for "official information." Conceivably Medico's rap sheet would provide details to include in a news story, but, in itself, this is not the kind of public interest for which Congress enacted the FOIA. In other words, although there is undoubtedly some public interest in anyone's criminal history, especially if the history is in some way related to the subject's dealing with a public official or agency, the FOIA's central purpose is to ensure that the Government's activities be opened to the sharp eye of public scrutiny, not that information about private citizens that happens to be in the warehouse of the Government be so disclosed. Thus, it should come as no surprise that in none of our cases construing the FOIA have we found it appropriate to order a Government agency to honor a FOIA request for information about a particular private citizen.

What we have said should make clear that the public interest in the release of any rap sheet on Medico that may exist is not the type of interest protected by the FOIA. Medico may or may not be one of the 24 million persons for whom the FBI has a rap sheet. If respondents are entitled to have the FBI tell them what it knows about Medico's criminal history, any other member of the public is entitled to the same disclosure—whether for writing a news story, for deciding whether to employ Medico, to rent a house to him, to extend credit to him, or simply to confirm or deny a suspicion. There is, unquestionably, some public interest in providing interested citizens with answers to their questions about Medico. But that interest falls outside the ambit of the public interest that the FOIA was enacted to serve.

The privacy interest in maintaining the practical obscurity of rap-sheet information will always be high. When the subject of such a rap sheet is a private citizen and when the information is in the Government's control as a compilation, rather than as a record of "what the Government is up to," the privacy interest protected by Exemption 7(C) is in fact at its apex while the FOIA-based public interest in disclosure is at its nadir. Such a disparity on the scales of justice holds for a class of cases without regard to individual circumstances; the standard virtues of bright-line rules are thus present, and the difficulties attendant to ad hoc adjudication may be avoided. Accordingly, we hold as a categorical matter that a third party's request for law enforcement records or information about a private citizen can reasonably be expected to invade that citizen's privacy, and that when the request seeks no "official information" about a Government agency, but merely records that the Government happens to be storing, the invasion of privacy is "unwarranted." The judgment of the Court of Appeals is reversed.

It is so ordered.

Several other serious problems in the interpretation of the nine exemptions have also arisen. For example, section 6(b)(1) of the Consumer Product Safety Act specifies that thirty days before the Consumer Product Safety Commission makes public information concerning a product defect, it must supply such information to the manufacturer or private labeler of the product and give it a chance to respond. What if, under the FOIA, citizens petitioned for the release of information and the CPSC agrees to do so? Does 6(b)(1) qualify as an exemption from FOIA under the third FOIA exception listed above? If it does, would the manufacturers of the products have legal authority to sue to prevent the commission from releasing the information? The Court in 1980 answered both questions in the affirmative.[32]

The bulk of comment upon and analysis of the FOIA has been decidedly critical. FBI Director William Webster complained in the late 1970s that the act was too strong, requiring expenditure of millions of dollars annually. The FBI alone employs over 200 people to process FOIA requests.[33]

These FOIA complications, when combined with the debate whether the act is too strong or too weak, compel the conclusion that Congress has not fine-tuned its information policy. Information is not a thing that belongs in a policy class by itself. Information is content, facts, and ideas about government programs as complex and varied as the myriad of government programs themselves.

A host of new concerns about access to government information and privacy emerge as the government creates databases on the Internet. The Clinton administration, for example, created the largest government Internet database in 1998, making available all U.S. patents since 1976 and trademark text and images since the end of the nineteenth century. This decision was the result of "fierce debate that has gone on for years between public interest advocates who argue that Government information should routinely be made available on the Internet and companies that purchase the data from Government agencies to resell."[34] The Patent and Trademark Office's decision to post patent and trademark documents on this Web site is one aspect of automating the nation's patent system by 2003.

The 1996 amendments to FOIA define "record" to include electronic formats and require agencies to make an electronic index of available records by the end of 1999. Subsection (a) affirmatively grants a right of access and affirmatively imposes a duty for government agencies to publish certain information. Further, and importantly for public-interest advocates, anyone has standing to request agency records without showing a particular interest. However, international public-access law recognizes that a state may have a "legitimate interest" in denying access to certain classes of information, such as the enumerated exceptions in FOIA. Indeed, in 1998 D.C. Circuit Judge Karen LeCraft Henderson held that requests by researchers, scholars, organizers, and journalists under FOIA to compel disclosure of Internet addresses and programming material generated by the United States Information Agency (USIA) were exempt from disclosure

---

32. *CPSC v. GTE Sylvania, Inc.* 447 U.S. 102 (1980). See also *Chrysler Corp. v. Brown*, 441 U.S. 281 (1979).

33. See James Reston Jr., "The Jonestown Papers," *New Republic*, April 25, 1981.

34. "U.S. to Release Patent Data on a World Wide Web Site," *New York Times*, July 25, 1998.

pursuant to the Smith-Mundt Act, which prohibits USIA from disseminating information within the U.S.[35]

We turn now to a more general category of openness known as *sunshine laws.* These laws, more informatively called *public meeting laws,* rest on the assumption that so-called executive sessions, study sessions, and closed sessions of agency members produce results more self-interested than informed citizens would easily accept. Interesting issues arise where, as usual, the general statute does not anticipate the specific case.

Chapter 2 concluded with seven different ways of defining "the rule of law." The sixth of these equated the rule of law with public participation. The "sunshine" reform movement has sought to achieve this goal very explicitly. This movement to require open meetings began at the state level in the early 1960s. It was not until 1976 that Congress passed the federal Sunshine Act,[36] which requires that multimember federal agencies open their meetings to the public. The act defines "meetings" as deliberations of at least a quorum, which must be open to the public if the deliberations will affect agency policy. However, there are ten exemptions to the Sunshine Act, seven of which are similar to the FOIA exemptions. If a majority of the officials at a meeting vote in favor of closing a meeting for one of the following reasons, the public will be excluded:

1. Meeting concerns information that is vital to the national defense or foreign policy

2. Meeting concerns internal personnel rules and practices

3. Material discussed is specifically exempted by other statutory provisions

4. Trade secrets and business information deemed confidential or privileged

5. Matters discussed involve accusing a person of a crime or formally censuring a person

6. Meeting would invade personal privacy

7. Meeting concerns law enforcement records

8. Meeting concerns banking records

9. Open meeting would frustrate implementation of a proposed agency action if prematurely known

10. Meeting concerns the agency's participation in formal rulemaking or litigation

Just as litigation over the meaning of FOIA exemptions raises the issues of public access, government secrecy, and personal privacy, so too does the litigation over the meaning of the Sunshine Act exemptions. Although important decisions that influence the direction of government policy are not always made in formal meetings, we know that one way of checking the informal power structure is to make officials accountable for their decisions in a public setting. This is the philosophy of the public interest movement, and thus we find that often those who challenge closed meetings are public interest groups, such as Common Cause. In the next case, *Nuclear Regulatory Commission v. Common Cause* (1982), Circuit Court Judge Skelly Wright rejects efforts by the NRC to close its meetings under Exemption 9. Judge Wright describes the theory of democratic participation that underlies the Sunshine Act, and he gives judicial supports for this theory in his interpretation of Exemption 9.

Nuclear Regulatory Commission v. Common Cause

674 F.2D 921, U.S.C.A., D.C. CIR. (1982) 3-0

[This case involves three separate cases that were consolidated on appeal. In each case the Nuclear Regulatory Commission (NRC) closed to the public its meetings to discuss the agency's budget proposal. The NRC relied mainly on Exemption 9 of the Sunshine Act, which permits closing of meetings if the agency decides that premature disclosure would be "likely to significantly frustrate implementation of a proposed agency action," but also cited Exemptions 2 and 6. Common Cause, a public interest consumer organization, filed suit seeking a declaratory judgment that closure of the meetings had violated the Sunshine Act. It asked for an injunction ordering the release of the transcripts of each meeting and an order to the NRC to permit Common Cause to attend future Commission meetings "that are similar in nature."]

---

35. *Essential Information, Inc., et al. v. USIA* 134 F.3d 1165 (1998).
36. 5 U.S.C. §552b.

J. Skelly Wright, Circuit Judge

In these cases we must decide an important unresolved issue: whether any of the statutory exemptions from the Sunshine Act apply to agency budget deliberations. Interpreting the statutory language in light of the legislative history and underlying policies of the Act, we conclude that there is no blanket exemption for agency meetings at any stage of the budget preparation process. The availability of exemptions for specific portions of budgetary discussions must be determined upon the facts of each case.

We strike down the District Court's injunction of July 2, 1981 because it is too vague to satisfy the standards of Rule 65(d) [of the Federal Rules of Civil Procedure].[37] Reaching the substantive Sunshine Act issues, we conclude that none of the exemptions to the Sunshine Act provides any blanket exception for budget discussion at any stage—preliminary staff budget briefings, markup/reclama meetings, or meetings to prepare reclama to OMB. On the basis of our inspection of the transcripts of the Commission's two closed meetings, we decide that no portion of either meeting is exempt from disclosure, and we therefore order that the full transcripts be released.

III. Sunshine Act and the Budget Process

A. THE PURPOSES OF THE SUNSHINE ACT

Congress enacted the Sunshine Act to open the deliberations of multi-member federal agencies to public view. It believed that increased openness would enhance citizen confidence in government, encourage higher quality work by government officials, stimulate well-informed public debate about government programs and policies, and promote cooperation between citizens and government. In short, it sought to make government more fully accountable to the people. In keeping with the premise that "government should conduct the public's business in public," the Act established a general presumption that agency meetings should be held in the open. Once a person has challenged an agency's decision to close a meeting, the

agency bears the burden of proof. Even if exempt subjects are discussed in one portion of a meeting, the remainder of the meeting must be held in open session.

The Act went farther than any previous federal legislation in requiring openness in government. In general the Sunshine Act's exemptions parallel those in the Freedom of Information Act (FOIA), but there is an important difference. Unlike FOIA, which specifically exempts "predecisional" memoranda and other documents on the premise that government cannot "operate in a fishbowl," the Sunshine Act was designed to open the predecisional process in multi-member agencies to the public. During the legislative process a number of federal agencies specifically objected to the Sunshine Act's omission of an exemption for predecisional deliberations. Congress deliberately chose to forego the claimed advantages of confidential discussions among agency heads at agency meetings.

Express language in the Sunshine Act also demonstrates that Congress did not intend to follow the FOIA pattern for predecisional discussions at agency meetings.

Notwithstanding the omission of a deliberative process privilege from the Sunshine Act, the Commission asks us to hold that the deliberative process leading to formulation of an agency's budget request is exempt from the Sunshine Act. To resolve this question, we must examine the statutory underpinnings of the budget process and the specific exemptions from the Sunshine Act which the Commission invokes.

B. THE BUDGET AND ACCOUNTING ACT OF 1921

The Budget and Accounting Act, 42 Stat. 21 (1921), was designed to centralize formulation of the Executive Branch budget. . . .

The Commission contends that the Budget and Accounting Act mandates secrecy in the budget formulation process, and that the Sunshine Act must therefore be construed to permit closing of agency budget meetings. We find this statutory argument unpersuasive.

The Commission first relies on the President's authority, under the Budget and Accounting Act, to prescribe rules and regulations for preparation of the budget, 31 U.S.C. §16 (1976), and on the "longstanding practice of confidentiality for Executive Branch discussions leading to the formu-

---

37. Rule 65(d) requires: "Every order granting an injunction and every restraining order shall set forth the reasons for its issuance; shall be specific in terms; shall describe in reasonable detail, and not by reference to the complaint or other document, the act or acts sought to be restrained. . . ."

lation of the President's Budget." The statute, however, makes no reference to confidentiality, nor does it authorize the President to prescribe budgetary rules and regulations without regard to the requirements of other federal statutes. The President's rulemaking authority under 31 U.S.C. §16 is therefore subject to the specific requirements of the Sunshine Act. . . .

Second, the Commission reasons that the congressional goal of centralized budget formulation cannot be achieved without secrecy. If the proposals of individual agencies must be adopted in public, it suggests, development of the presidential budget would be "fragmented" and the President's discretion to choose among alternatives would be impaired. . . . This contention reads too much into the 1921 Act, which simply requires that the President submit a single, unified Executive Branch budget proposal to Congress for consideration. It does not prescribe any method by which he must develop the consolidated budget figures which he submits. Nor does it require that the President's proposals be the only budgetary information available to the public. Even if agencies discuss their budget proposals at public sessions, the President remains capable of revising agency requests and combining them into a unified budget.

Indeed, the Sunshine Act itself affords persuasive evidence that Congress did not intend to allow presidential claims of confidentiality under the Budget and Accounting Act to override the Sunshine Act's specific provisions regarding openness and secrecy. Exemption 3, a provision which received extensive consideration in both houses, allows closing of a meeting or portion of a meeting which would "disclose matters specifically exempted from disclosure by statute," provided that such statute

(A) requires that matters be withheld from the public in such a manner as to leave no discretion on the issue, or (B) establishes particular criteria for withholding or refers to particular types of matters to be withheld.

5 U.S.C. §552b(c)(3)(1976). The Budget and Accounting Act of 1921, which contains no explicit references to confidentiality, does not qualify under the strict requirements of Exemption 3.

Therefore, the budget process is exempt from the open meeting requirement, in whole or in part, only if it fits within the terms of other specific Sunshine Act exemptions. . . .

The budget deliberation process is of exceptional importance in agency policymaking. The agency heads must review the entire range of agency programs and responsibilities in order to establish priorities According to the Commission, a budget meeting "candidly consider[s] the merits and efficiencies of on-going or expected regulatory programs or projects" and then "decides upon the level of regulatory activities it proposes to pursue." These decisions, the government contends, have a significant impact on "the Commission's ability to marshal regulatory powers in a manner which insures the greatest protection of the public health and safety with the most economical use of its limited resources."

D. PARTICULARIZED EXEMPTIONS

The Sunshine Act contains no express exemption for budget deliberations as a whole, and we do not read such an exemption into Exemption 9(B). We recognize, nevertheless, that specific items discussed at Commission budget meetings might be exempt from the open meetings requirement of the Act, and might justify closing portions of Commission meetings on an individual and particularized basis. After examining the transcripts of the Commission's closed meetings of July 27, 1981 and October 15, 1981, however, we conclude that none of the subject matter discussed at either meeting comes within any of the exemptions cited by the Commission. The Commission must therefore release the full transcripts of these meetings to the public.

Our *in camera* inspection of the transcripts of the July 27, 1981 and October 15, 1981 Commission meetings leads us to conclude that Exemption 9(B) does not support withholding of any portion of the transcripts.

2. Exemption 2.

The Commission also relies on Exemption 2—matters that "relate solely to the internal personnel rules and practices of an agency[,]" 5 U.S.C. §552b(c)(2)(1976)—to justify closing portions of budget meetings. Under the Commission's interpretation, Exemption 2 includes discussions of allocation of personnel among programs, evaluations of the performance of offices and projects within the Commission, and consideration of more economical schemes of "internal management." This construction is belied by the statutory language and legislative history of Exemption 2.

The language in Exemption 2 to the Government in the Sunshine Act is virtually identical with that in Exemption 2 to the Freedom of Information Act. 5 U.S.C. §552(b)(2) (1976). The conference report on the Sunshine Act expressly adopts the standards of *Dep't of Air Force v. Rose, 425 U.S. 352* (1976), the leading Supreme Court decision interpreting Exemption 2 of FOIA. Under this standard, personnel-related discussions at budget meetings fall squarely outside the scope of the exemption.

Budget allocations inevitably impinge on personnel matters, because government cannot implement programs without personnel. Salaries and wages are a sizable proportion of the Commission's budget. But budget decisions regarding personnel cutbacks, and evaluations of the prior performance of offices and programs, do not relate *solely* to "internal personnel rules and procedures." Discussions of possible administrative cost savings through adoption of new "internal management" techniques also fall beyond the narrow confines of Exemption 2, because they deal with the impact of budget cuts on the Commission's ability to carry out its responsibilities.

3. Exemption 6.

The government invoked Exemption 6 to justify its decisions to close both meetings at issue; it no longer claims that the exemption protects any of the deliberations at the October 15 meeting. Exemption 6 protects information of a personal nature whose disclosure would constitute "an unwarranted invasion of personal privacy[.]" 5 U.S.C. §552b(c)(6) (1976). The agency contends that this exemption protects discussion of "an individual manager's particular qualifications, characteristics and professional competence in connection with a budget request for that particular manager's program." This contention is unsupported by the legislative history of the Sunshine Act.

Exemption 6 applies to information of a personal nature, including discussions of a person's health, drinking habits, or financial circumstances. It provides greater protection to private individuals, including applicants for federal grants and officials of regulated private companies, and to low-level government employees, than to government officials with executive responsibilities. It was not intended to shelter substandard performance by government executives. The Senate report expressly noted that "if the discussion centered on the alleged incompetence with which a

Government official has carried out his duties it might well be appropriate to keep the meeting open, since in that case the public has a special interest in knowing how well agency employees are carrying out their public responsibilities." Exemption 6, the report added, "must not be used by an agency to shield itself from political controversy involving the agency and its employees about which the public should be informed." These policy considerations apply *a fortiori* in the budget process, in which the performance of individual executives may affect the Commission's willingness to allocate budgetary resources to particular regulatory programs.

Given the narrow scope of Exemption 6 as applied to managerial officials, we hold that no portion of the discussion at the July 27, 1981 meeting was covered by Exemption 6. The Commission's discussion of individual performance was limited to managerial officials with executive responsibility.

E. COMPLIANCE WITH THE SUNSHINE ACT

Our *in camera* inspection of the transcripts of the July 27, 1981 and October 15, 1981 Commission meetings does not show that any portion of either meeting may be withheld from the public under any of the asserted exemptions to the Sunshine Act. We therefore order the Commission to release the transcripts to the public. 5 U.S.C. §552b(f)(2) (1976). The transcripts shall be made available in a place readily accessible to the public, and copies shall be furnished to any person at the actual cost of duplication. *Id.*

If in the future the Commission wishes to close all or any portion of a budget meeting, the statute requires it to announce its intention and to give a brief statement of its reasons. If any person objects to closing of the meeting, he may file a civil action in the District Court to compel the Commission to comply with the statute. He may include an application for interlocutory relief in his complaint, if the meeting has not yet been held. The District Court should act promptly on any motion for interim relief to avoid frustration of the purposes of the Sunshine Act through delay. In its decision on the merits the District Court may examine *in camera* the transcripts of closed agency meetings and may issue such relief as it deems appropriate, with due regard for orderly administration and the public interest.

IV. Conclusion

For the reasons stated in this opinion the District Court's injunction issued July 2, 1981 and its contempt finding made on September 9, 1981 are vacated. Because the Commission has not carried its burden of proving that the July 27, 1981 and October 15, 1981 meetings were lawfully closed, the Commission shall release the transcripts of those meetings to the public forthwith.

So ordered.

Consider finally the operation of the Privacy Act (1974) which, like FOIA, is part of the Administrative Procedure Act. The statute's title can mislead. It does *not* prevent the government from gathering information about people and thereby invading their privacy. It seeks instead to allow a citizen to learn what the government knows about his private life (see *Department of the Air Force v. Rose, supra,* at p.159).

As you might guess, criminal investigations, Central Intelligence Agency records, and other similarly sensitive materials are exempted from the Privacy Act. Unless exempted, an agency must provide a method for citizens to inspect records, e.g., about their financial affairs, and correct any demonstrable errors therein. It also requires the agency not to use the information for other than stated purposes and prohibits it from providing the information to others without the citizen's consent. See section 552a of the APA in Appendix B.

Before ending this chapter, we would like to point to a (rather big) elephant sitting in the living room of our constitutional democracy. This book focuses on federal administrative agencies and as such does not explore in great detail how the powers of the executive branch and the Office of the President in particular is to be checked either by law or by other branches. Recent years, however, have seen dramatic battles over obtaining information from the executive branch and these battles highlighted problems of transparency that have significant implications for the administrative state. The problem, in fact, was so deep, that "the tenure of the Bush Administration," wrote T. J. Halstead in 2003, "has thus far been characterized by an orchestrated policy of restricting congressional and public access to information from executive agencies and the White House."[38]

In what turned out to be the most controversial of such actions, Vice President Dick Cheney refused to supply the comptroller general, David Walker, with information regarding the activities of the National Energy Policy Development Group (NEPDG). This group was established on January 29, 2001 by President George W. Bush via presidential memorandum, and Cheney was directed to serve as the chair of the group. All the other members of the group were federal government officers such as the secretary of treasury, secretary of interior, or the secretary of commerce. The goal of NEPDG was to set forth "a recommended national energy policy designed to help the private sector, and as necessary and appropriate State and local governments, promote dependable, affordable, and environmentally sound production and distribution of energy for the future."

Upon the request of Representatives Henry Waxman (D-Cal.) and John Dingell (D-Mich.), the Government Accounting Office (GAO) initiated an investigation about the NEPDG and asked the vice president on several occasions to provide the names and titles of individuals present at NEPDG meetings. The rumor was that top-level managers of various large energy and oil companies had been frequent participants in NEPDG meetings and the representatives wanted to know whether these allegations were true. Arguing that the investigation by the GAO, itself part of the legislative branch, is in violation of constitutional separation of powers, the Office of the Vice President consistently refused to provide all the information requested by the GAO.

The GAO decided to postpone its request in the immediate aftermath of the September 11th attacks but finally, when the controversy surfaced once again in January 2002 as the Enron Corporation was declared bankrupt, the comptroller general decided to sue the Office of the Vice President in order to be able to access the information he requested. It was alleged that top-level managers

38. T. J. Halstead, "The Law: *Walker v. Cheney:* Legal Insulation of the Vice President from GAO Investigations," *Presidential Studies Quarterly* 33 (2003): 635-648.

of Enron were among those who contributed significantly to the drafting of energy policy of the United States. In *Walker v. Cheney*, 230 F.Supp. 2d 51 (D.D.C. 2002), however, the District Court for the District of Columbia, dismissed the case, arguing that the comptroller general did not have standing to sue. The court apparently did not want to be part of a potentially problematic constitutional question of separation of powers and decided as it did. This decision meant, nevertheless, that even the Congress was unable to access information it needed regarding the executive branch activities.

Comptroller General David Walker decided not to appeal the case and it was briefly closed. In a case which started in parallel to *Walker v. Cheney* but reached all the way to the Supreme Court, this time, environmental groups, and outside groups sued. After the NEPDG published its recommendations, Judicial Watch, a government watchdog, and the Sierra Club, an environmental non-governmental organization (NGO), filed suit alleging that the advisory group violated the Federal Advisory Committee Act (FACA) by not disclosing all the relevant committee meeting memos. Normally, FACA does not apply to committees composed only of federal officials. The plaintiffs, however, argued that lobbyists regularly attended NEPDG meetings, therefore the exemption in the FACA should not apply. In order to find out whether the allegations were true, the District Court allowed a dis-

covery process and requested documents from the Office of the Vice President. Cheney appealed this decision to the Supreme Court. In *Cheney v. United States District Court for the District of Columbia*, 542 U.S. 367 (2004), the vice president asked the Supreme Court to order the District Court to stop its discovery process. The Court, in a 7–2 opinion, did just that. On separation of powers grounds, the Court held the discovery processes, "by virtue of their overbreadth," had the potential of interfering with presidential activity. With this case, yet another attempt to obtain information about an important governmental policy, allegedly related to various other significant issues from Enron bankruptcy to the governing of Iraqi oil, failed.

We have told this long story to demonstrate a real problem in the administrative state, one that surfaced most pointedly in recent years. An important administrative law rule is that no one in the government is immune from lawful accountability requests and everyone is subject to the laws and the constitutional norms including checks and balances. But how can you make an official subject to the rule of law if he or she does not even want to tell you who he has met with in the formation of a policy? And if the only way to hold someone accountable is to discover through the force of law, whether he is telling the truth and if that avenue is closed by the courts themselves, is that not a dead end where the rule of law ceases to exist?

EXERCISES AND QUESTIONS FOR FURTHER THOUGHT

1. How valid is Justice Douglas's point, dissenting in *Wyman*, that our legal system grants a weaker presumption of innocence to the poor than to those believed by some to be more respectable citizens? If some inequity exists, is this a valid basis for Douglas's legal conclusion in *Wyman?* Why or why not? How do you think the controversy in *Sanchez v. County of San Diego* proves or challenges Justice Douglas's point?

2. The dissenting judge in the *Sanchez v. County of San Diego* case said that just as the IRS is not likely to go to people's homes to check on the number of dependents claimed in tax filings, so too state officials should not make

house visits to check on whether recipients are eligible for welfare. Do you agree? What kind of similarities, and differences, exist between the two possible "searches"?

3. Investigations for administrative purposes occasionally raise problems of entrapment. In 1981, IRS agents seized eight boxes of books and records from the home of Mr. and Mrs. William Jones after obtaining a search warrant issued by a judge acting on information that had been gathered in the following manner:

The IRS had instituted an undercover "Business Opportunities Project" targeting businesses that keep two sets of books, one reflecting *reported* income and another reflecting *real* income, which included cash earnings on which the business sought to avoid paying taxes. Agents posed as prospective buyers of businesses with high cash flows and indicated their interest in profit skimming. They tried to win the seller's confidence so they would be shown the second set of books. Caught in one such trap, the Joneses revealed to an IRS agent documents showing an additional $25,000 in unreported annual income.

Defense attorneys for the Joneses claim that the IRS's tactics amount to illegal entrapment. Comment on the legal and ethical implications of this practice.[39]

4. Justices on the U.S. Supreme Court and other courts of appeals deliberate in secret when they meet to decide legal cases. Why should the meetings of agencies, commissioners, and other decision-making bodies covered by "sunshine laws" be treated differently and with less trust than the courts?

5. In 1995 the *New York Times* reported that, starting as early as the 1940s, Federal Bureau of Investigations (FBI) director J. Edgar Hoover ordered the FBI to monitor and report on the classical music composer and conductor Leonard Bernstein. According to the story, when Bernstein held a fund-raising party for the Black Panthers at his New York apartment in 1970, "the FBI went beyond intelligence-gathering and schemed to undermine him with damaging news leaks." The story reported that agents routinely went through the trash of people suspected of being Communist sympathizers. The *Times* gained this information because the Southern California office of the ACLU filed a FOIA request in 1990 for the bureau's files on Bernstein. The materials, with parts of the files blacked out, were turned over in 1995.[40] What arguments would the ACLU have had to make to gain release of this information?

(On December 16, 1995 the *Denver Post* reported that a federal trial judge had ordered the FBI to reveal the names and activities of agents who had shadowed John Lennon in the 1970s. Biographers of Lennon believe that the government was seeking to deport Lennon because of his opposition to the Vietnam War. Without FOIA, such information would probably never have been made public.)

6. As you read the freedom of information material, it may have occurred to you that in many political situations, time is of the essence. Thus, an agency may force a person to go to court to get information they are legally entitled to, knowing that by the time the court orders it released the political damage will have been avoided. We know of an instance where a concerned parent wanted to get a copy of the proposed budget for her school district. The budget called for a tax increase to purchase a large number of new computers. The district reassured the parent, and the voters generally, that it would buy computers for student use, but the district refused to let the parent see the budget. The budget and the tax increase passed, and only later did it turn out that the budgeted computers were for administrators only. Can you imagine any judicial remedy that could prevent such abuse of the spirit, if not the letter, of freedom of information laws?

7. The average e-mail user spends many hours a day online. Do e-mail exchanges among government officials have to comply with sunshine laws? In "Behind Closed E-Mail," the *New York Times* on April 1, 1999 called this the "politician's nightmare." According to most sunshine laws, officials cannot meet to discuss public business without notifying the public of the meeting in advance. In the case of Spokane County, Washington, there are only three county commissioners, so any communication between any two of them is automatically a policy-making majority. A reporter for the local paper asked the commissioners to release all their e-mail over the past two months concerning county business. Assume that you are the attorney general in your state in charge of sunshine law enforcement. Given the political objectives of sunshine laws, how will you advise public officials to handle their e-mail?

8. Some legal scholars have argued that NSA's power to eavesdrop on international communications without a warrant does not violate the Fourth Amendment even though one of the parties may be within the United States. The rationale is that communications outside the United States are akin to searches of "border areas," which have long been considered special places where the requirements of the Fourth Amendment do not strictly apply. Do you agree with this analogy? What kind of dangers might result from this position concerning the rule of law and administrative limits?

39. See *Wall Street Journal*, December 23, 1981.
40. "Bernstein Was Monitored as Late as '70's," *New York Times*, May 17, 1995. Leonard Bernstein died in 1990.

CHAPTER 6
INFORMALITY AND FORMALITY
IN ADMINISTRATIVE LAW

Chapters 6–8 teach what is initially the most challenging side of administrative law to master. Before you panic, however, let us assure you that there is light at the end of this tunnel. In fact, once you begin to think through the character of administrative decision making, as opposed to judicial or legislative decision making, you will come to appreciate the *range* of options available to those who participate in administrative processes.

These three chapters review the legal procedures required to adjudicate (the judicial side of public administration) and to make administrative rules (the legislative side of administration). These procedures are the most familiar aspects of administrative law. Most judicial opinions in administrative law focus on legal controls and requirements that govern these two processes. Students who only learn administrative law from cases tend to think that these two processes occupy the bulk of administrators' time, that they are the main thing public administration is "about."

But administrators do much more than adjudicate controversies and make rules to guide their future behavior. While the formal procedures for adjudication and rulemaking are better documented, a host of less familiar *informal procedures* make up the daily activities of administrators. The best way to appreciate the full range of administrative procedures is to imagine where its various examples are found on a continuum of legal formality. The least formal procedures are those that administrators

can undertake with the least concern for legal rules, that is, with the most discretion. The most formal are those decisions that must conform to the detailed procedural requirements prescribed by statutes and the courts. In everyday practice administrators make most of their decisions informally, without significant legal constraints on what to decide or how to decide it.

So why is this material sometimes difficult for nonlawyers? One reason is that both adjudication and rulemaking, the staples of administrative law, can fall *anywhere* on the informality-formality continuum. Since the distinction between rulemaking and adjudication is often more apparent than real, the trick is to identify what formalities the law requires in a given set of circumstances, regardless whether the law labels the problem rulemaking or adjudication.

Legal constraints on the raw exercise of political power, of course, are a relatively recent historical development. Just as legal systems in Western societies came to predominate and grow more complex, the evolution of administrative law has seen an increase in administrative formalities. To appreciate the development of formality within administrative law, it is best to understand the primordial political soup from which this new life form emerged.

To help you pull these materials together we have illustrated an administrative law formality continuum in Appendix A, page 431. The illustration may help you put in perspective the court cases discussed in the chapters.

We wish to emphasize that the type of administrative procedures used is not always an apolitical or value-free decision. You will see that normative concerns and cost-benefit determinations play a role in determining the type of procedure used.

The next section gives some examples of informal administration. Studying this kind of unrestrained decision making might seem out of place in a book on administrative law. But there is an important connection between apparently informal administrative decisions and more formal procedures, since the availability of a formal procedure with a more predictable outcome greatly influences the results obtained through less formal means. To take an example from criminal law, while most criminal cases are settled through plea bargains and prosecutorial discretion, the established rules of criminal law provide a source of authority for *bargaining in the shadow of the law*. This close connection between the formal and informal is also apparent in administrative law.

Perhaps 80 percent or more of the daily activity of administrators takes place on the informal side of the continuum.[1] But the existence of a body of authority and formal procedures that may be invoked where necessary shapes informal practices, even as they reside in the background as a kind of "brooding omnipresence in the sky," to quote Chief Justice Oliver Wendell Holmes. At the same time, when courts affirm the authority of agencies to make informal decisions or use informal procedure, such as mediation, they are putting a stamp of approval on the informal dimensions of administration. Whether and to what extent an informal process should be formalized has been an issue in nearly every case thus far reported in this book. For example, the Department of Agriculture acted less formally before *Morgan* than afterward. And the welfare recipient facing a loss of his benefits had no pretermination hearing right before *Goldberg*, but he has one now.

1. James O. Freedman, *Crisis and Legitimacy* (New York: Columbia University Press, 1978), 10.

EXAMPLES OF INFORMAL ADMINISTRATION

1. The commissioners of the Federal Trade Commission (FTC) decide to eliminate abuses in the undertaking business. They may proceed either by charging individual violators with unfair business practices through lawsuits (an adjudication strategy), or by writing rules and applying them to all undertakers (a rulemaking strategy). In the case of the FTC, at least, the *choice* between the two is entirely at the discretion of the commissioners.

2. A hospital reports to a state health agency that a patient has suffered from the toxic poisoning known as botulism. The hospital has traced the offending organism to a certain brand of canned meat. The health agency, without further investigation, orders all grocers to pull the brand from their shelves immediately.

3. Officials at the Internal Revenue Service (IRS) decide to audit all returns in which the taxpayer claims the costs of operating a yacht as a deductible business expense. They also decide to shift personnel from the review of estate tax returns to the review of income tax returns. Both IRS decisions are discretionary.

4. The Christian Coalition, headed by Pat Robertson, petitioned the Internal Revenue Service throughout the 1990s to grant it tax-exempt status. To qualify an organization must not engage in substantial political activities. According to the IRS, this prohibits supporting political parties or candidates. But Pat Robertson himself had run for the Republican presidential nomination in 1988, and the Coalition visibly supported Oliver North in his Senate race against Charles Robb in 1994. After many informal exchanges with the IRS, the Coalition finally announced that it was withdrawing its application because it knew it would not be approved.

5. After a female administrator in the U.S. Department of Justice reports to the head of her division that she has been sexually harassed by her male supervisor, the division head tells her "not to worry about it" because he will speak to her supervisor informally about the matter. The division head goes to the supervisor's office and discusses the complaint against him confidentially. The male supervisor agrees to stop the behavior in

question. The division head's decision not to advise a federal employee of her rights under Title VII of the Civil Rights Act of 1964 to bring legal actions against her supervisor and the Department of Justice, and his decision to talk informally to the male supervisor about the complaint, are both exercises in administrative discretion.

In all five examples administrators made decisions not to apply formal rules or enforce written regulations. Yet in each instance the administrator acted in the capacity of a government official.

INFORMAL ADMINISTRATION IN RULEMAKING AND ADJUDICATION

The journey out of this morass of specific instances starts with a very important step. When an agency *adjudicates* an issue, the courts have often stated that the United States Constitution does impose some legal formalities. When an agency makes rules, however, the Constitution does not necessarily require any legal procedures, and the Administrative Procedure Act (APA) in section 553, exempts some classes of rulemaking from its legal requirements. In adjudication, court rulings that seem to deny a person's claim for legal formalities on closer inspection usually say that the person has a proper claim, but not yet, not this early in the game.[2] This is the gist of *Mathews v. Eldridge* and *Wyman v. James.* But in rulemaking situations, in the absence of statutory legal requirements, courts may approve discretionary agency decisions now and forever.

Thus the first step is to distinguish rulemaking and adjudication. To help clarify the distinction, begin by thinking of the difference between the legal outputs of legislatures and of courts. Legislatures make statutes—rulemaking—that speak to a general class of citizens, often to all adults. Courts, on the other hand, make judgments—adjudication—that resolve the interests of specific parties by assessing a set of facts unique to them and their dispute. The following case, *Bi-Metallic Investment*

2. Courts also deny claims for adjudication when they conclude that the claimant has no legal interest that merits protection. The personnel cases discussed in Chapter 13 illustrate this point.

Co. v. State Board of Equalization of Colorado (1915), is the Supreme Court's classic case distinguishing rulemaking and adjudication. Although this case is pre-APA, it provides a good example of the Court's understanding of the difference between rulemaking and adjudication even after passage of the APA.

Bi-Metallic Investment Co. v. State Board of Equalization of Colorado

239 U.S. 441 (1915) 9-0
+ White, McKenna, Holmes, Day, Hughes, Van Devanter,
– Lamar, Pitney, McReynolds

[The Supreme Court of Colorado had upheld the order of the State Board of Equalization raising the tax valuation of all taxable property in Denver by an across-the-board forty percent. The decision by the board was unilateral and without any prior hearings where those adversely affected could present their case. The petitioner, a property owner in Denver, brought this lawsuit claiming he had suffered loss of property through increased taxation without an opportunity to be heard. He asserted that this constituted a deprivation of property without due process of law in violation of the Fourteenth Amendment, and asked that the board's order be set aside.]

Justice Oliver Wendell Holmes Jr. delivered the opinion of the Court

For the purposes of decision we assume that the constitutional question is presented in the baldest way—that neither the plaintiff nor the assessor of Denver, who presents a brief on the plaintiff's side, nor any representative of the city and county, was given an opportunity to be heard, other than such as they may have had by reason of the fact that the time of meeting of the boards is fixed by law. On this assumption it is obvious that injustice may be suffered if some property in the county already has been valued at its full worth. But if certain property has been valued at a rate different from that generally prevailing in the county the owner has had his opportunity to protest and appeal as usual in our system of taxation. *Hagar v. Reclamation District,* 111 U.S. 701, 709, 710, so that it must be assumed that the property owners in the county all stand alike. The question then is whether all individuals have a constitutional right to be heard before a matter can be decided in which all are equally concerned—here, for instance, before a superior board decides that the local taxing officers have adopted a system of underevaluation throughout a county, as notoriously often has been the case. The answer of this court in the *State Railroad Tax Cases*, 92 U.S. 575, at least as to any further notice, was that it was hard to believe that the proposition was seriously made.

Where a rule of conduct applies to more than a few people it is impracticable that every one should have a direct voice in its adoption. The Constitution does not require all public acts to be done in town meeting or an assembly of the whole. General statutes within the state power are passed that affect the person or property of individuals, sometimes to the point of ruin, without giving them a chance to be heard. Their rights are protected in the only way that they can be in a complex society, by their power, immediate or remote, over those who make the rule. If the result in this case had been reached as it might have been by the State's doubling the rate of taxation, no one would suggest that the Fourteenth Amendment was violated unless every person affected had been allowed an opportunity to raise his voice against it before the body entrusted by the state constitution with the power. In considering this case in this court we must assume that the proper state machinery has been used, and the question is whether, if the state constitution had declared that Denver had been undervalued as compared with the rest of the State and had decreed that for the current year the valuation should be forty percent higher, the objection now urged could prevail. It appears to us that to put the question is to answer it. There must be a limit to individual argument in such matters if government is to go on. In *Londoner v. Denver*, 210 U.S. 373, 385, a local board had to determine "whether, in what amount, and upon whom" a tax for paving a street should be levied for special benefits. A relatively small number of persons were concerned, who were exceptionally affected, in each case upon individual grounds, and it was held that they had a right to a hearing. But that decision is far from reaching a general determination dealing only with the principle upon which all the assessments in a county had been laid.

In due course we will see that the line between adjudication and rulemaking becomes more blurred the closer we study it. Nevertheless the classic *Bi-Metallic* case states two critical distinguishing factors. First, does the agency action affect a small specifically identified number of people whom the agency can feasibly hear without sinking under this burden? Second, does the agency decision depend at least in part on facts about specific people and their cases such that an individual, if given some right to be heard, might show the agency it made a factual mistake in his case? Note how the decision to cut off an individual's welfare payments on the basis of some facts about the individual falls in the adjudication category. On the other side, an IRS decision to audit the tax returns of all taxpayers in a certain category, e.g., people who claim deductions for operating yachts, falls in the rulemaking category. The IRS cannot possibly hear all potentially interested yacht owners, and no one yacht owner possesses the facts that might prove that auditing *all* yacht owners is a bad policy. The decision to raise all property values an equal amount falls in this same rulemaking category.

ADJUDICATION AT THE INFORMAL END OF THE CONTINUUM

The more formal adjudication becomes, the more it resembles trial procedures before an impartial judge. For both historical and practical reasons agencies have never used lay juries, but in most other respects a formal administrative "trial" resembles a trial before a judge in the judicial system. Sections 554, 556, and 557 of the APA prescribe the features of a hearing at the federal level, procedures that agencies must sometimes follow in rulemaking as well as adjudication if statutes require. However, many decisions regarding the interests of specific parties in concrete fact situations do not require a formal trial. The constitutional due process requirements of *Goldberg v. Kelly* together with the statutory requirements of the APA mark the formal end of our continuum. The next few pages show that courts often permit much less formality than *Goldberg* seems to require, and sometimes none at all.

Goldberg remains the Supreme Court's most complete statement of the Constitution's due process requirements for adjudication. It has triggered much comment and research, including Dean Paul Verkuil's careful review of the nature of informal adjudication in just a few agencies in the federal government. We reproduce much of it here not merely to show how much informal adjudication takes place but to give beginning students a sense of the vastness of federal activity. The article also teaches that the bureaucratic world hardly marches in lockstep with the occasional pronouncements of the Supreme Court. Despite its density, the article is therefore worth reading. Veteran students of public affairs may wish to skim parts of this study. Do, however, take note of Verkuil's list of the ten *Goldberg* ingredients. Chapter 7 will explain each in more detail.

A Study of Informal Adjudication Procedures

PAUL VERKUIL
University of Chicago Law Review 43 (1976): 739, 757–771

Since there are so many different ways the federal government adjudicates informally, the study, conducted in the summer of 1975, was designed to reduce the observation process to manageable size. In order to establish a controlled setting, four agencies were selected for study in terms of four typical informal adjudication categories. The agencies selected were the Departments of Agriculture (USDA), Commerce, Housing and Urban Development (HUD), and the Interior. The categories selected were: (1) grants, benefits, loans, and subsidies; (2) licensing, authorizing, and accrediting; (3) inspecting, grading, and auditing; and (4) planning, policymaking, and economic development. The resulting "four-by-four" study was intended to permit comparison of intra- and interagency behavior in informal adjudication.

The study focused on forty-two individual programs in the four categories, with the bulk of the programs falling in the first two categories. The study of each program involved direct contact by the author with responsible agency personnel, usually government lawyers with backgrounds in the particular programs and their attendant procedures. Each contact person was provided with a written request for information (a procedural "checklist") that was further explained in follow-ups both in person and by telephone. As the data requested were

received, they were compiled according to the checklist paragraphs. From these compilations summaries by program and by agency were produced.

One goal of this empirical phase was to determine how much impact emerging notions of procedural due process were having upon the process of informal adjudication. To measure this awareness more precisely, the individual procedural ingredients mandated in *Goldberg* were isolated and tabulated with respect to each of the programs studied. *Goldberg* has been described as requiring the following ten ingredients:

1. timely and adequate notice;
2. confronting adverse witnesses;
3. oral presentation of arguments;
4. oral presentation of evidence;
5. cross-examination of adverse witnesses;
6. disclosure to the claimant of opposing evidence;
7. the right to retain an attorney;
8. a determination on the record of the hearing;
9. a statement of reasons for the determination and an indication of the evidence relied on; and
10. an impartial decision maker.*

The survey data will be presented first by program in descending order of the number of *Goldberg* ingredients; then, after noting some significant procedural innovations and other practices worthy of comment, the data will be summarized and cross-tabulated.

A. Presentation by Ingredients

The ten *Goldberg* procedural ingredients were present in their entirety in only two of the forty-two programs

---

*See *Goldberg v. Kelly*, 397 U.S. 254, 267–71 (1970). The ten ingredients extracted from *Goldberg* are substantially as identified by Professor Davis. See K. Davis (*Administrative Law*, 5th ed. [St. Paul: West Publishing Co., 1973]) at 288. Their enumeration is not uncontroversial, however. Professor Clark Byse, in discussions with the author, has interpreted ingredient 6 to be of no independent vitality (a discovery device) but rather to be only the inevitable consequence of providing ingredients 3, 4, and 5. He would, therefore, find only nine *Goldberg* ingredients. This survey, however, proceeds on the assumption that ingredient 6 has separate meaning as a discovery device, and agency procedures will be measured against its requirements. For a quick overview, the following statistical summary should be helpful. Of the forty-two programs studied, two provided all ten *Goldberg* ingredients, five provided nine, two provided eight, four provided seven, one provided six, one provided five, nine provided four, thirteen provided three, three provided two, and two provided none. These totals were taken from operative procedural regulations, which do not exist for the last two programs. . . . Alternatively stated, the summary by ingredient shows forty of the functions provided ingredient 1, ten ingredient 2, twenty-one ingredient 3, twelve ingredient 4, nine ingredient 5, ten ingredient 6, sixteen ingredient 7, eight ingredient 8, thirty-seven ingredient 9, and thirty-eight ingredient 10.

studied. Both of these programs are administered by the Department of Agriculture, and involve category one (grants, benefits, loans, and subsidies). They are disqualification of recipients under the food stamp program, and establishment of agricultural marketing quotas. Since the food stamp program has social goals similar to the welfare program, it is not surprising that the full *Goldberg* ingredients should be provided. On the other hand, the other USDA program presents an unexpectedly elaborate procedural mechanism. USDA currently sets quotas for support payments to farmers who produce tobacco, peanuts, and extra-long staple cotton. These quotas are set initially by local county committees. Upon receiving notification of his quota, a dissatisfied farmer has fifteen days to apply for review before the local review committee, which is composed of three farmers appointed from the farmer's locality by the Secretary of Agriculture. The hearing before this committee contains the full *Goldberg* ingredients. Judicial review of the committee's decision, based upon the substantial evidence test, may be had within fifteen days in the United States district court or a state court of record.

Four programs, all administered by the Department of Agriculture, have procedures containing nine of the ten *Goldberg* ingredients. Two of the programs have every ingredient by number 8 (a determination resting solely on the record of the hearing): reparations proceedings under the Packers and Stockyards Act (PSA) and under the Perishable Agricultural Commodities Act (PACA). Both resist classification within the four categories of informal adjudication established at the outset. Essentially, the Department of Agriculture exacts reparations for farmers injured by the unfair conduct of packers, stockyards, and dealers in perishable agricultural commodities (fresh fruits and vegetables). The informal adjudication procedures established by the Department for making these reparations decisions offer useful insights into the informal adjudication process. Of particular interest is the fact that the reparation proceedings under both acts provide for a *Goldberg*-type (nine ingredient) oral hearing and a shortened procedure which is much more summary in form. In addition the Department engages in an informal settlement stage before either procedural route is undertaken. Attorneys in the Department's Office of General Counsel are responsible for administering the reparation proceedings. They first investigate all claims, conduct the oral or shortened hearings at field offices, and prepare recommended decisions for the judicial officer, who reviews the transcript of the record and renders the final agency decision. There does not appear to be any articulated policy for excluding the *Goldberg* requirement for a determination on the record from the otherwise elaborate oral hearings, unless it is that the judicial officer who renders the final decision is not the hearing officer and that the order itself is not directly reviewable.

The two other Department of Agriculture programs that provide nine of the *Goldberg* ingredients are in the licensing and inspection categories; revocation or suspension of veterinary accreditations and withdrawal of approval of markets or facilities under the animal quarantine laws. In both cases the missing procedural ingredient is number six, disclosure to claimant of opposing evidence, which is precluded by explicit department policy.

There were two programs with eight *Goldberg* ingredients: debarring of "responsibility connected" employees of licensees who violate the Perishable Agricultural Commodities Act from future employment with PACA licensees, a procedure that omits ingredients 2 (confrontation) and 5 (cross-examination); and issuing permits under the Offshore Shrimp Fisheries Act, a Commerce program that omits ingredients 6 (disclosure of opposing evidence) and 8 (determination on the record). The "responsibly connected" debarment determination has for a long time been made by the Chief of the Regulatory Branch of the Fruit and Vegetable Division, USDA, without any established procedural regulations. Nonetheless, in the cases where the initial determination is questioned, the division provides the debarred employee with an informal hearing containing each of the *Goldberg* ingredients except confrontation and cross-examination. Recently, however, the division's procedures for determining who is a "responsible employee" have come under judicial scrutiny, and significant changes may be necessary in the future.

Four programs operated under procedures with seven of the *Goldberg* ingredients: removal of grain inspectors' licenses under the United States Grain Standards Act (a USDA function); debarment of lender-builders, appraisers, and attorneys under the Federal Housing Administration (HUD); issuance of permits under the Antiquity Act (Interior); and grants and loans by the Bureau of Indian Affairs (Interior). The first program fails to provide ingredients 3 (oral argument), 6 (disclosure of opposing evidence), and 10 (impartial decision maker); the second fails to provide 2 (confrontation), 5 (cross-examination), and 6 (disclosure of opposing evidence); the third also omits ingredients 2, 5, and 8; and the fourth omits ingredients, 2, 4 (oral presentation of evidence), and 5.

One program has procedures with six *Goldberg* ingredients. Retailer disqualification under the food stamp program is a USDA function that omits ingredients 2 (confrontation), 4 (oral presentation of evidence), 5 (cross-examination), and 8 (determination on the record). Retailers may be disqualified under the Food Stamp Act for irregularities such as selling ineligible items or discounting stamps for cash. The disqualification can be for up to three years. It should be noted that the procedures for retailer disqualifications are considerably less formal than for disqualifications of food stamp recipients. The decisions are made by a single official (the Chief, Retailer-Wholesaler Branch, Food Stamp Division) in an effort, according to USDA, to obtain uniformity of treatment for retailers throughout the nation. This official reviews case summaries from local officials who collect information, issue notices of charges, and allow the retailer and his counsel to make an oral and written explanation of the charge. The retailer is entitled to administrative review of any order of disqualification. Approximately 49 percent of the retailers seek this review, which represents the final agency decision. In the last five years 182 retailers have sought judicial review.

One program had five *Goldberg* ingredients; leasing of oil, gas, and coal deposits. The program is in the Department of the Interior and has an informal procedure with ingredients, 1, 6, 7, 9, and 10.

Over one-half of the forty-two programs studied (twenty-two) provided procedures with either four or three of the *Goldberg* ingredients. Of the nine programs with four ingredients, all but one had ingredients 1, 3, 9, and 10; of the thirteen programs with three ingredients, all had ingredients 1, 9, and 10. Thus the distinction between eight of the nine four-ingredient programs and the thirteen three-ingredient programs is the addition of oral argument (ingredient 3) to the minimal adversary informal procedures of notice, a statement of reasons, and an impartial decision maker. The eight four-ingredient programs are: loans by the Farmers Home Administration (USDA); public works grants, business development loans, and technical assistance grants by the Economic Development Administration (Commerce); financial guarantees to developers of new communities (HUD); establishment of estuarine sanctuaries (Commerce); master planning for new parks (Interior); and planning for outer continental shelf oil and gas leasing (Interior). The thirteen three-ingredient programs include seven programs within the Department of Commerce; three within the Department of Interior; and three within HUD.

The preponderance of these three- and four-ingredient programs is in the categories of grants and benefits or planning and policymaking. Each of the four agencies studied has programs within these classifications, with Commerce the leader at eleven programs.

Three programs surveyed provided procedures with two of the *Goldberg* ingredients; in each case those ingredients are 1 (notice) and 10 (impartial decision maker). These programs are auditing of money grants for outdoor recreation (Interior); voluntary inspection of fish products (Commerce); and inspection for lead base paint and structural defects on public housing (HUD). Since each program involves inspections, it is not surprising that the adversary procedural ingredients are held to a minimum.

The two remaining programs have no designated procedures, and for the purposes of this study they are categorized as having none of the *Goldberg* ingredients. Both these programs are in the Department of Agriculture: meat and poultry inspections and plant quarantine certifications. . . .

Let us highlight four implications of Verkuil's study. First, the survey reveals a range of administrative adjudicatory formality that is all the more surprising because the study involves only a small minority of federal programs and agencies. Second, most of these procedures have been adopted by the agencies at their own discretion. They are not the results of court orders or statutory prescriptions. Third, please be reassured that this chapter only introduces the ten *Goldberg* ingredients. You *should* at this point feel some frustration about the terminology Verkuil uses, for example, the meaning of a *determination on the record or an impartial decision maker*. The next chapters will flesh out these concepts.

The fourth and most important implication is a particularly important principle of modern administrative law raised by the survey. How, you may have asked, can agencies get away with adjudications less formal than *Goldberg* requires? The answer is that the courts have not only used the so-called balancing test to decide whether, at a given point, any hearing is legally necessary. They have also said that the circumstances of many types of adjudication permit use of fewer than all ten ingredients, even when some hearing is required. This form of balancing is less explicitly cost-benefit than the *Mathews* analysis. The how-many-ingredients balance tries to assess which ingredients are suited to the needs of the parties in the situation.[3]

Thus in *Goss v. Lopez*, 419 U.S. 565 (1975), students were suspended from school for allegedly disrupting classes and fighting. They received no hearing prior to their suspension. The Supreme Court ruled that the school administration erred by failing to allow the students at least to tell their side in an informal give-and-take with school officials. The Court in effect required an approximation of the first four ingredients but no more. Note that the Court did not require an impartial decision-maker. It did, however, state that the minimal hearing was suitable in education because hearings could have educational value for students regardless of their outcomes.

Hence the *Goldberg* decision has not produced a single set of criteria that all adjudication must meet. In fact, when all ten elements are present, an agency is very close to the formal end of the continuum. The Supreme Court seems to have concluded that the Constitution demands varying amounts of formality depending on the nature of the problem, and no single set of criteria will necessarily ever be applied. The next case shows just how informal adjudication can become.

Board of Curators of the University of Missouri et al. v. Horowitz

435 U.S. 78 (1978) 5-4
+ *Burger, Stewart, Powell, Rehnquist, Stevens*
+/– *Brennan, White, Marshall, Blackmun*

[Horowitz, a medical student, was placed on academic probation at the end of her first year in medical school for poor clinical performance and a deficiency in personal hygiene. The same situation existed at the end of her second year and she was dropped from school. She

---

3. "Without saying so directly, the Court set *Goldberg*'s rigid model aside and replaced it with an admittedly vague procedural balancing test." Paul Verkuil, "The Emerging Concept of Administrative Procedure," *Columbia Law Review* 78 (1978): 258, 288.

brought suit claiming procedural due process had not been afforded her since she had been given no opportunity to rebut the evidence against her at a hearing. The Eighth Circuit Court of Appeals, reversing the district court, held this procedure violated due process.]

Justice Rehnquist delivered the opinion of the Court

We granted certiorari to consider what procedures must be accorded to a student at a state educational institution whose dismissal may constitute a deprivation of "liberty" or "property" within the meaning of the Fourteenth Amendment. We reverse the judgment of the Court of Appeals. . . .

Respondent was admitted with advanced standing to the Medical School in the fall of 1971. During the final years of a student's education at the school, the student is required to pursue in "rotational units" academic and clinical studies pertaining to various medical disciplines such as obstetrics-gynecology, pediatrics, and surgery. Each student's academic performance at the School is evaluated on a periodic basis by the Council on Evaluation, a body composed of both faculty and students, which can recommend various actions including probation and dismissal. The recommendations of the Council are reviewed by the Coordinating Committee, a body composed solely of faculty members, and must ultimately be approved by the Dean. Students are not typically allowed to appear before either the Council or the Coordinating Committee on the occasion of their review of the student's academic performance.

In the spring of respondent's first year of study, several faculty members expressed dissatisfaction with her clinical performance during a pediatrics rotation. The faculty members noted respondent's "performance was below that of her peers in all clinical patient-oriented settings," that she was erratic in her attendance at clinical sessions, and that she lacked a critical concern for personal hygiene. Upon the recommendation of the Council on Evaluation, respondent was advanced to her second and final year on a probationary basis.

Faculty dissatisfaction with respondent's clinical performance continued during the following year. For example, respondent's docent, or faculty adviser, rated her clinical skills as "unsatisfactory." In the middle of the year, the

Council again reviewed respondent's academic progress and concluded that respondent should not be considered for graduation in June of that year; furthermore, the Council recommended that, absent "radical improvement," respondent be dropped from the school.

Respondent was permitted to take a set of oral and practical examinations as an "appeal" of the decision not to permit her to graduate. Pursuant to this "appeal," respondent spent a substantial portion of time with seven practicing physicians in the area who enjoyed a good reputation among their peers. The physicians were asked to recommend whether respondent should be allowed to graduate on schedule, and, if not, whether she should be dropped immediately or allowed to remain on probation. Only two of the doctors recommended that respondent be graduated on schedule. Of the other five, two recommended that she be immediately dropped from the school. The remaining three recommended that she not be allowed to graduate in June and be continued on probation pending further reports on her clinical progress. Upon receipt of these recommendations, the Council on Evaluation reaffirmed its prior position.

The Council met again in mid-May to consider whether respondent should be allowed to remain in school beyond June of that year. Noting that the report on respondent's recent surgery rotation rated her performance as "low-satisfactory," the Council unanimously recommended that "barring receipt of any reports that Miss Horowitz has improved radically, [she] not be allowed to re-enroll in the . . . School of Medicine." The Council delayed making its recommendation official until receiving reports on other rotations; when a report on respondent's emergency rotation also turned out to be negative, the Council unanimously reaffirmed its recommendation that respondent be dropped from the school. The Coordinating Committee and the Dean approved the recommendation and notified respondent, who appealed the decision in writing to the University's Provost for Health Sciences. The Provost sustained the school's actions after reviewing the record compiled during the earlier proceedings. . . .

In *Goss v. Lopez*, 419 U.S. 565 (1975), we held that due process requires, in connection with the suspension of a student from public school for disciplinary reasons, "that the student be given oral or written notice of the charges against him, and if he denies them, an explanation of the evidence the authorities have and an opportunity to present his side of the story." Id., at 581. The Court of Appeals apparently read *Goss* as requiring some type of formal hearing at which respondent could defend her academic ability and performance. All that *Goss* required was an "informal give-and-take" between the student and the administrative body dismissing him that would, at least, give the student "the opportunity to characterize his conduct and put it in what he deems the proper context." But we have frequently emphasized that "[t]he very nature of due process negates any concept of inflexible procedures universally applicable to every imaginable situation." *Cafeteria Workers v. McElroy*, 367 U.S. 886, 895 (1961). The need for flexibility is well illustrated by the significant difference between the failure of a student to meet academic standards and the violation by a student of valid rules of conduct. This difference calls for far less stringent procedural requirements in the case of an academic dismissal.

Since the issue first arose 50 years ago, state and lower federal courts have recognized that there are distinct differences between decisions to suspend or dismiss a student for disciplinary purposes and similar actions taken for academic reasons which may call for hearings in connection with the former but not the latter. Thus, in *Barnard v. Inhabitants of Shelburne*, 216 Mass. 19, 102 N.E. 1095 (1913), the Supreme Judicial Court of Massachusetts rejected an argument, based on several earlier decisions requiring a hearing in disciplinary contexts, that school officials must also grant a hearing before excluding a student on academic grounds. According to the court, disciplinary cases have "no application. . . . Misconduct is a very different matter from failure to attain a standard of excellence in studies. A determination as to the fact involves investigation of a quite different kind. A public hearing may be regarded as helpful to the ascertainment of misconduct and useless or harmful in finding out the truth as to scholarship. . . ."

Reason, furthermore, clearly supports the perception of these decisions. A school is an academic institution, not a courtroom or administrative hearing room. In Goss, this Court felt that suspensions of students for disciplinary reasons have a sufficient resemblance to traditional judicial and administrative factfinding to call for a "hearing" before the relevant school authority. While recognizing that school authorities must be afforded the necessary tools to maintain discipline, the Court concluded:

[I]t would be a strange disciplinary system in an educational institution if no communication was sought by the disciplinarian with the student in an effort to inform him of his dereliction and to let him tell his side of the story in order to make sure that an injustice is not done. . . .

[R]equiring effective notice and informal hearing permitting the student to give his version of the events will provide a meaningful hedge against erroneous action. At least the disciplinarian will be alerted to the existence of disputes about facts and arguments about cause and effect. 419 U.S., at 580, 583–584.

Even in the context of a school disciplinary proceeding, however, the Court stopped short of requiring a formal hearing since "further formalizing the suspension process and escalating its formality and adversary nature may not only make it too costly as a regular disciplinary tool but also destroy its effectiveness as a part of the teaching process." Id., at 583.

Academic evaluations of a student, in contrast to disciplinary determinations, bear little resemblance to the judicial and administrative factfinding proceedings to which we have traditionally attached a full-hearing requirement. In Goss, the school's decision to suspend the students rested on factual conclusions that the individual students had participated in demonstrations that had disrupted classes, attacked a police officer, or caused physical damage to school property. The requirement of a hearing, where the student could present his side of the factual issue, could under such circumstances "provide a meaningful hedge against erroneous action." Ibid. The decision to dismiss respondent, by comparison, rested on the academic judgment of school officials that she did not have the necessary clinical ability to perform adequately as a medical doctor and was making insufficient progress toward that goal. Such a judgment is by its nature more subjective and evaluative than the typical factual questions presented in the average disciplinary decision. Like the decision of an individual professor as to the proper grade for a student in his course, the determination whether to dismiss a student for academic reasons requires an expert evaluation of cumulative information and is not readily adapted to the procedural tools of judicial or administrative decisionmaking.

Under such circumstances, we decline to ignore the historic judgment of educators and thereby formalize the academic dismissal process by requiring a hearing. The educational process is not by nature adversary; instead it centers around a continuing relationship between faculty and students, "one in which the teacher must occupy many roles—educator, adviser, friend, and, at times, parent-substitute," Goss v. Lopez, 419 U.S., at 594 (Powell, J., dissenting). This is especially true as one advances through the varying regimes of the educational system, and the instruction becomes both more individualized and more specialized. In Goss, this Court concluded that the value of some form of hearing in a disciplinary context outweighs any resulting harm to the academic environment. Influencing this conclusion was clearly the belief that disciplinary proceedings, in which the teacher must decide whether to punish a student for disruptive or insubordinate behavior, may automatically bring an adversary flavor to the normal student-teacher relationship. The same conclusion does not follow in the academic context. . . .

The judgment of the Court of Appeals is therefore reversed.

Justice Powell, concurring

I join the Court's opinion because I read it as upholding the District Court's view that respondent was dismissed for academic deficiencies rather than for unsatisfactory personal conduct, and that in these circumstances she was accorded due process.

In the numerous meetings and discussions respondent had with her teachers and advisers, . . . culminating in the special clinical examination administered by seven physicians . . . respondent was warned of her clinical deficiencies and given every opportunity to demonstrate improvement or question the evaluations. The primary focus of these discussions and examinations was on respondent's competence as a physician. . . .

It is well to bear in mind that respondent was attending a medical school where competence in clinical courses is as much of a prerequisite to graduation as satisfactory grades in other courses. Respondent was dismissed because she was as deficient in her clinical work as she was proficient in the "book-learning" portion of the curriculum. Evaluation of her performance in the former area is no less an "academic" judgment because it involves observation of her skills and techniques in actual conditions of practice, rather than assigning a grade to her written answers on an essay question.

Because it is clear from the findings of fact by the District Court that respondent was dismissed solely on academic grounds, and because the standards of procedural due process were abundantly met before dismissal occurred, I join the Court's opinion.

Justice White, concurring in part and concurring in the judgment

I join Parts I, II-A, and III of the Court's opinion and concur in the judgment.

I agree with my Brother Blackmun that it is unnecessary to decide whether respondent had a constitutionally protected property or liberty interest or precisely what minimum procedures were required to divest her of that interest if it is assumed she had one. Whatever that minimum is, the procedures accorded her satisfied or exceeded that minimum.

The Court nevertheless assumes the existence of a protected interest, proceeds to classify respondent's expulsion as an "academic dismissal," and concludes that no hearing of any kind or any opportunity to respond is required in connection with such an action. Because I disagree with this conclusion, I feel constrained to say so and to concur only in the judgment.

As I see it, assuming a protected interest, respondent was at the minimum entitled to be informed of the reasons for her dismissal and to an opportunity personally to state her side of the story. Of course, she had all this, and more. I also suspect that expelled graduate or college students normally have the opportunity to talk with their expellers and that this sort of minimum requirement will impose no burden that is not already being shouldered and discharged by responsible institutions.

Justice Marshall, concurring in part and dissenting in part

I agree with the Court that, "[a]ssuming the existence of a liberty or property interest, respondent has been awarded at least as much due process as the Fourteenth Amendment requires." . . . I cannot join the Court's opinion, however, because it contains dictum suggesting that respondent was

entitled to even less procedural protection than she received. I also differ from the Court in its assumption that characterization of the reasons for a dismissal as "academic" or "disciplinary" is relevant to resolution of the question of what procedures are required by the Due Process Clause. Finally, I disagree with the Court's decision not to remand to the Court of Appeals for consideration of respondent's substantive due process claim.

We held in *Goss v. Lopez*, 419 U.S. 565 (1975), that "due process requires, in connection with a suspension of 10 days or less, that the student be given oral or written notice of the charges against him and, if he denies them, an explanation of the evidence the authorities have and an opportunity to present his side of the story." *Id.*, at 581. There is no question that respondent received these protections, and more. . . .

[The] meetings and letters plainly gave respondent all that *Goss* requires: several notices and explanations, and at least three opportunities "to present [her] side of the story." 419 U.S., at 581. I do not read the Court's opinion to disagree with this conclusion. Hence I do not understand why the Court indicates that even the "informal give-and-take" mandated by *Goss, id.* at 584, need not have been provided here. . . . This case simply provides no legitimate opportunity to consider whether "far less stringent procedural requirements," . . . than those required in *Goss* are appropriate in school contexts. While I disagree with the Court's conclusion that "far less" is adequate, as discussed *infra*, it is equally disturbing that the Court decides an issue not presented by the case before us. As Mr. Justice Brandeis warned over 40 years ago, the " 'great gravity and delicacy' " of our task in constitutional cases should cause us to " 'shrink' " from " 'anticipa[ting] a question of constitutional law in advance of the necessity of deciding it,' " and from " 'formulat[ing] a rule of constitutional law broader than is required by the precise facts to which it is to be applied.' " *Ashwander, v. TVA*, 297 U.S. 288, 345–347 (1936) (concurring opinion).

In the view of the Court's dictum to the effect that even the minimum procedures required in *Goss* need not have been provided to respondent, I feel compelled to comment on the extent of procedural protection mandated here. I do so within a framework largely ignored by the Court, a framework derived from our traditional approach to these problems. According to our prior decisions, as summarized in *Mathews v. Eldridge*, 424 U.S. 319 (1976), three factors are of principal relevance in determining what process is due:

First, the private interest that will be affected by the official action; second, the risk of an erroneous deprivation of such interest through the procedures used, and the probable value, if any, of additional or substitute procedural safeguards; and finally, the Government's interest, including the function involved and the fiscal and administrative burdens that the additional or substitute procedural requirement would entail. *Id.*, at 335. . . .

Neither of the other two factors mentioned in *Mathews* justifies moving from a high level to the lower level of protection involved in *Goss*. There was at least some risk of error inherent in the evidence on which the Dean relied in his meetings with and letters to respondent; faculty evaluations of such matters as personal hygiene and patient and peer rapport are neither as "sharply focused" nor as "easily documented" as was, *e.g.*, the disability determination involved in *Mathews, supra*, at 343. See *Goss v. Lopez*, 419 U.S., at 580 (when decisionmakers "act[s] on the reports and advice of others . . . [t]he risk of error is not at all trivial").

Nor can it be said that the university had any greater interest in summary proceedings here than did the school in *Goss*. Certainly the allegedly disruptive and disobedient students involved there, . . . posed more of an immediate threat to orderly school administration than did respondent. As we noted in *Goss*, moreover, "it deserves . . . the interest of the State if [the student's] suspension is in fact unwarranted." . . . Under these circumstances—with respondent having much more at stake than did the students in *Goss*, the administration at best having no more at stake, and the meetings between respondent and the Dean leaving some possibility of erroneous dismissal—I believe that respondent was entitled to more procedural protection than is provided by "informal give-and-take" before the school could dismiss her.

The contours of the additional procedural protection to which respondent was entitled need not be defined in terms of the traditional adversary system so familiar to lawyers and judges. . . . We have emphasized many times that "[t]he very nature of due process negates any concept of inflexible procedures universally applicable to every imaginable situation." *Cafeteria Workers v. McElroy*, 367 U.S. 886, 895 (1961). . . . In other words, what process is due

will vary "according to specific factual contexts." *Hannah v. Larche*, 363 U.S. 420, 442 (1960). . . .

Justice Blackmun, with whom Justice Brennan joins, concurring in part and dissenting in part

The Court's opinion, and that of Justice Marshall, together demonstrate conclusively that, assuming the existence of a liberty or property interest, respondent received all the procedural process that was due her under the Fourteenth Amendment. That, for me, disposes of this case, and compels the reversal of the judgment of the Court of Appeals.

I find it unnecessary, therefore, to indulge in the arguments and counterarguments contained in the two opinions as to the extent or type of procedural protection that the Fourteenth Amendment requires in the graduate-school-dismissal situation. Similarly, I also find it unnecessary to choose between the arguments as to whether respondent's dismissal was for academic or disciplinary reasons (or, indeed, whether such a distinction is relevant). I do agree with Justice Marshall, however, that we should leave to the District Court and to the Court of Appeals in the first instance the resolution of respondent's substantive due process claim and of any other claim presented to, but not denied by, those courts.

Accordingly, I, too, would reverse the judgment of the Court of Appeals and remand the case for further proceedings.

How many of the *Goldberg* ingredients did the medical school include in its recipe for handling Horowitz? Since she had no hearing, many of the ten did not even potentially come into play. Presumably she had notice that something was wrong and was given a chance to correct it but not through any trial-like proceedings. You should at this point begin to speculate on the practical reasons for holding hearings. What good would a hearing have done Horowitz? What would it cost the school? Are you satisfied that being expelled from medical school for academic reason deserves any less protection than having welfare benefits cut off pending a formal hearing? It may strike you that Ms. Horowitz suffered more long-term harm than the welfare recipient and therefore that she deserves greater protection. On the other hand, Horowitz's performance did receive very extensive scrutiny over many months, and the Court assumes that she had ample chance to correct her shortcomings. This differs from the situation where a faceless bureaucracy cuts off a person's livelihood through the mail. Nevertheless, the concern lingers that she might have been judged on irrelevant grounds. Just what was her personal hygiene problem? Is this relevant to medical practice? Might a more formal hearing avoid judging on irrelevant bases? How might formality affect the relevance of the criteria used in judging cases?

Recall the various sources of error that may affect an administrative decision. The hearing required in *Goss* would allow an open-minded administrator to correct an honest mistake of fact. It is not clear the *Horowitz* requirement even goes this far. Neither case prescribes a procedure that would alter the decision of a lazy or harried administrator or an administrator whose mind was made up or whose ego and credibility were at stake. More disturbing, perhaps, is Justice Rehnquist's distinction between factual and adversarial situations on one hand and evaluative, subjective, and nonadversarial situations on the other. The benefits of a hearing, at least of *Goss*'s informal give-and-take hearing, can occur equally in adversarial and nonadversarial settings. Parents and children, teachers and students, policemen and suspects can all find themselves in disagreement about the factual aspects of a problem. Justice Rehnquist's distinctions have a glib and unconvincing quality that imply a retreat from *Goldberg* and *Goss*.[4]

The bottom line in informal adjudication is that *Horowitz* marks a substantial Supreme Court retreat from *Goldberg*. It now appears ready to articulate constitutional standards on a case-by-case basis. In school discipline the decision may require only informal give and take. For academic dismissals the Court requires no more than giving the student a fair chance to succeed. The ambiguity in this area is frustrating, but administrators must learn to live with it, partly because informal adjudication is at the heart of the administrative law of personnel. Chapter 12 reviews the implications of *Horowitz* for personnel law in more detail.

In fact, there is a larger historical background to post-*Goldberg* debates about due process and necessary formalities. According to Verkuil, "once it understood the revolutionary potential of *Goldberg*, the Court began to ameliorate its impact," starting with the balancing test of *Matthews*. Case by case analysis and the balancing test are not the only ways to narrow the scope of *Goldberg*-style formalities, however. According to Verkuil, due process determinations initially necessitate deciding that a "state action" exists. Over the years, courts have narrowed the definition of "state action" so that certain acts would not be required to follow certain formalities. In *Jackson v. Metropolitan Edison, Co.*, 419 U.S. 345 (1974), which involved the termination of a customer's utility service, "the Court found no state action despite the fact that the private utility was regulated by the state as a natural monopoly." Such blurring of what constitutes "state action" becomes all the more relevant as we are now living in an age of public-private partnerships. Even welfare programs and the provision of other social services have been delegated to private, non-governmental firms. The case law about such blurring has not been settled. We urge you to watch future developments in this area of law with an eye on how public policy disputes are solved on the formality-informality continuum.

Before going on to informal rulemaking, we would like to remind you that adjudication is not always about individuals seeking to enforce their rights, as in *Horowitz*. Sometimes larger groups also go through the process of administrative adjudication. The federal government's recognition of Native American tribes, which is termed federal acknowledgment, is a notable example. The process not only involves a group, not merely individuals, but also the process itself contains a continuum of informality-formality. The process of federal acknowledgment starts with an Indian tribe petitioning the Assistant Secretary for Indian Affairs for federal recognition. If the tribe's application it found to meet the criteria set forth in

---

4. See "Due Process, Due Politics and Due Respect: Three Models of Legitimate School Governance," *Harvard Law Review* 94 (1981): 1109.

the relevant statute, the process is straightforward: the Assistant Secretary, after evaluating the evidence, publishes the proposed findings in the *Federal Register* and, after a brief period for comment, the Assistant Secretary publishes the agency's final decision in the *Federal Register.* If a case is deemed to be more complicated, however, the tribe does not automatically gain Indian identity. If the evidence is weak or if there are groups challenging the tribe's application, the level of formality increases and the Assistant Secretary may order hearings before an administrative law judge where cross examination is possible. A tribe whose application is rejected may request a reconsideration, which usually involves more formalized administrative actions, hearings, etc.[5]

This process of federal acknowledgment points to yet another crucial, but underexplored, aspect of administrative law. Administrative actions and processes at various times go beyond being a mere instrument of securing material rights. As Renee Cramer demonstrates, the process as well as the end result of federal acknowledgment involves officialization, and in many ways the (re)production of an "Indian" identity. Not only does a tribe become "Indian" in the process of trying to put together the required historical and social evidence, but also upon being "acknowledged by the federal government as an Indian tribe, a group of people then has access to particular rights reserved for native populations.[6]

INFORMAL RULEMAKING

We have already seen that, when agencies make rules, courts may require no legal formalities whatsoever, except, of course, that the agency must act within the limits of its authority as prescribed in the statute that created it. As the examples of informal administration listed at the start of the chapter suggest, agencies do a great many things that resemble policymaking apart from adjudication. Some policies, however, are not exempt from some legal formalities. APA section 553 is the starting place for

distinguishing the degrees of formality required in rulemaking:

553. Rulemaking

(a) This section applies, according to the provisions thereof, except to the extent that there is involved—

(1) a military or foreign affairs function of the United States; or

(2) a matter relating to agency management or personnel or to public property, loans, grants, benefits, or contracts.

(b) General notice of proposed rule making shall be published in the Federal Register, unless persons subject thereto are named and either personally served or otherwise have actual notice thereof in accordance with law. The notice shall include—

(1) a statement of the time, place, and nature of public rule making proceedings;

(2) reference to the legal authority under which the rule is proposed; and

(3) either the terms or substance of the proposed rule or a description of the subjects and issues involved.

Except when notice or hearing is required by statute, this subsection does not apply

(a) to interpretative rules, general statements of policy, or rules of agency organization, procedure, or practice; or

(b) when the agency for good cause finds (and incorporates the finding and a brief statement of reasons therefore in the rules issued) that notice and public procedure thereon are impracticable, unnecessary, or contrary to the public interest.

(c) After notice required by this section, the agency shall give interested persons an opportunity to participate in the rule making through submission of written data, views, or arguments with or without opportunity for oral presentation. After consideration of the relevant matter presented, the agency shall incorporate in the rules adopted a concise general statement of their basis and purpose. When rules are required by statute to be made on the record after opportunity for an agency hearing, sections 556 and 557 of this title apply instead of this subsection.

5. See Roberto Iraola, "The Administrative Tribal Recognition Process and the Courts," *Akron Law Review* 38 (2005): 867

6. Renee Cramer, *Cash, Color, and Colonialism: The Politics of Tribal Acknowledgment* (Norman: University of Oklahoma Press, 2005).

(d) The required publication or service of a substantive rule shall be made not less than 30 days before its effective date, except—

(1) a substantive rule which grants or recognizes an exemption or relieves a restriction;

(2) interpretative rules and statements of policy; or

(3) as otherwise provided by the agency for good cause found and published with the rule.

(e) Each agency shall give an interested person the right to petition for the issuance, amendment, or repeal of a rule.

The section is well salted with exceptions to the requirement of notice and comment, and we shall discuss these exceptions momentarily. Before doing so, however, a bit more background is necessary. First, some statutes creating or defining agency responsibilities create their own rulemaking procedures, which preempt the APA. The most prominent of these today is the Federal Trade Commission Improvement Act of 1975. Occasionally a statute requires a full trial-type hearing for rulemaking. This brings into play the provisions of APA sections 554, 556, and 557. These rules primarily govern formal adjudication and are described in this chapter. Second, you should be aware that the Model State Administrative Procedure Act, included in Appendix C, particularly sections 3–7, states fewer exceptions than the federal act and seems to give citizens somewhat greater voice in the making of such rules. Finally, chapter 7 of this book will discuss what section 553 of the APA does require, plus extra requirements that some courts have added for constitutional reasons in rulemaking proceedings.

Some of section 553's exceptions hardly surprise us. Section (a)(1)'s military and diplomatic affairs may require such speed and secrecy that the advance notice and comments gathering process could devastate the policy's effectiveness. Other exceptions are less obvious and will benefit from some illustrations.

1. *Section (a)(2): Matter Relating to Public Property.* The Bureau of Reclamation, which operated a federal hydroelectric dam and sold the power at low rates, decided to reallocate the electricity. A city cut off from this low-cost power supply sued claiming that the bureau should have held a 553-type hearing. The Court denied the claim because the dam and the power were federal public property.[7]

2. *Section (a)(2): Matter Relating to Grants.* Without following 553 procedures, the Federal Highway Administration set standards that states must meet to receive federal highway funds. Since these funds are grants, the Court approved the agency's action.[8]

3. *Section (b)(A): Notice and Hearing Not Required for Interpretative Rules.* A hospital that was trying to recover from bankruptcy assumed that the Medicare payments due from the Department of Health and Human Services (HHS) would be paid to them under "generally accepted accounting principles." HHS, however, with no notice and comment, issued regulations that it would not pay the benefits in one lump, but spread them over a longer period of time, thus making it harder for the hospital to get back on its feet. The Supreme Court, 5-4, ruled that the regulations merely interpreted more general rules for reimbursement, and did not require notice and comment. Justice O'Connor, dissenting, wrote:

Unlike the Court, I believe that general Medicare reporting and reimbursement regulations require provider costs to be treated according to "generally accepted accounting principles." As a result, I would hold that contrary guidelines issued by the Secretary of Health and Human Services in an informal policy manual and applied to determine the timing of reimbursement in this case are invalid for failure to comply with the notice and comment procedures established by the Administrative Procedure Act, 5 U. S. C. §553.[9]

4. *Section (b)(B): Notice Not Required When Contrary to the Public Interest.* During President Nixon's wage and price freeze, announced on August 15, 1971, the White House and the Cost of Living Council issued many executive orders and regulations regarding wages and prices. Some businesses who raised prices in the face of these rules claimed that the rules had no legal effect because no advance notice had been given. Courts held that the delay

---

7. *City of Santa Clara v. Kleppe*, 418 F. Supp. 1243 (1976). And see *Lodge 1647 and Lodge 1904, American Federation of Government Employees v. McNamara*, 291 F. Supp. 286 (1968), describing a federal personnel matter exempt from 553.

8. *Center for Auto Safety v. Cox*, 580 F.2d 689 (1978).

9. See *Shalala v. Guernsey Memorial Hospital*, 514 U.S. 87 (1995).

required by 553 would encourage businesses to raise their prices in advance of the effective date of the freeze and that 553 procedures would therefore hurt the public interest.[10]

These examples show that the APA leaves much room for discretionary administrative policymaking. Indeed, these exceptions seem potentially elastic enough to allow agencies to avoid 553 whenever they so desire. Agencies could do this by simply calling any rule an interpretation of its authorizing statute, or a statement of general policy, or by claiming that notice would hurt the national interest. Courts have resisted such stretching of these words. Especially where the "interpretative rule" loophole threatens to expand, courts have insisted either that the agency be interpreting specific legislative language, or that it follow notice and comment proceedings whenever the rule has a substantial negative impact on specific interests.[11]

LEGAL PROBLEMS IN INFORMAL ADMINISTRATION

In a sense every legal issue in administrative law wrestles with the question, "How much formality is enough?" This was, after all, the problem in *Morgan*, *Goldberg*, and *Horowitz*. A few issues do, however, arise out of informality itself, and this chapter concludes by examining one of the more perplexing of these, the problem of administrative *estoppel*. What if an agency official gives a person informal advice that turns out to violate official policy? Or what if an agency simply reneges on its advice, even though it was accurate when given? Can the disappointed citizen require an administrative agency to act consistently with its informal advice, even if that advice is mistaken or superseded? Does giving incorrect advice informally "estop," that is, preclude, the government from enforcing its actual policies upon the misinformed citizen? This raises the related question of when an agency becomes legally obligated to follow its own informal decisions.

10. See *DeRieux v. Five Smiths, Inc.*, 499 F.2d 1321 (1974).
11. See *Chrysler Corp. v. Brown*, 441 U.S. 281 (1979).

Federal Crop Insurance Corp. v. Merrill

332 U.S. 380 (1947) 5-4
+ *Vinson, Reed, Frankfurter, Murphy, Burton*
– *Black, Rutledge, Jackson, Douglas*

[Merrill had inquired of the Federal Crop Insurance Corporation, which is completely government-owned, whether spring wheat planted on land that had grown winter wheat was insurable under the Federal Crop Insurance Act. After being assured that it was, Merrill planted the spring wheat, which was subsequently destroyed by drought. The corporation refused to pay since its regulations prohibited the insuring of reseeded crops. Merrill brought a lawsuit seeking to enforce his insurance coverage, claiming he had been misled by the government. The Idaho courts agreed with Merrill's contention.]

Justice Frankfurter delivered the opinion of the Court

We brought this case here because it involves a question of importance in the administration of the Federal Crop Insurance Act. . . .

The case no doubt presents phases of hardship. We take for granted that, on the basis of what they were told by the Corporation's local agent, the respondents reasonably believed that their entire crop was covered by petitioner's insurance. And so we assume that recovery could be had against a private insurance company. But the Corporation is not a private insurance company. It is too late in the day to urge that the Government is just another private litigant, for purposes of charging it with liability, whenever it takes over a business theretofore conducted by private enterprise or engages in competition with private ventures. Government is not partly public or partly private, depending upon the governmental pedigree of the type of particular activity or the manner in which the Government conducts it. The Government may carry on its operations through conventional executive agencies or through corporate forms especially created for defined ends. *See Keifer & Keifer v. Reconstruction Finance Corp.*, 306 U.S. 381, 390. Whatever the form in which the Government functions, anyone entering into an arrangement with the Government takes the risk of having accurately ascertained that he who purports to act for the Government stays within the bounds of his authority. The scope of this authority may be explicitly defined legislation, properly exercised through the rule-making power. And this is so even though, as here, the agent himself may have been unaware of the limitations upon his authority. . . .

If the Federal Crop Insurance Act had by explicit language prohibited the insurance of spring wheat which is reseeded on winter wheat acreage, the ignorance of such a restriction, either by the respondents or the Corporation's agent, would be immaterial and recovery could not be had against the Corporation for loss of such reseeded wheat. Congress could hardly define the multitudinous details appropriate for the business of crop insurance when the Government entered it. Inevitably "the terms and conditions" upon which valid governmental insurance can be had must be defined by the agency acting for the Government. And so Congress had legislated in this instance, as in modern regulatory enactments it so often does, by conferring the rule-making power upon the agency created for carrying out its policy. . . .

Accordingly, the Wheat Crop Insurance Regulations were binding on all who sought to come within the Federal Crop Insurance Act, regardless of actual knowledge of what is in the Regulations or of the hardship resulting from innocent ignorance. The oft-quoted observation in *Rock Island, Arkansas & Louisiana R. Co. v. United States*, 254 U.S. 141, 143, that "Men must turn square corners when they deal with the Government," does not reflect a callous outlook. It merely expresses the duty of all courts to observe the conditions defined by Congress for charging the public treasury. The "terms and conditions" defined by the Corporation, under authority of Congress, for creating liability on the part of the Government preclude recovery for the loss of the reseeded wheat no matter with what good reason the respondents thought they had obtained insurance from the Government. Indeed, not only do the wheat regulations limit the liability of the Government as if they had been enacted by Congress directly, but they were in fact incorporated by reference in the application, as specifically required by the Regulations.

We have thus far assumed, as did the parties here and the courts below, that the controlling regulation in fact precluded insurance coverage for spring wheat reseeded on winter wheat acreage. It explicitly states that the term "wheat crop shall not include . . . winter wheat in the 1945 crop year, and spring wheat which has been reseeded on winter wheat acreage in the 1945 crop year." Sec. 414–37 (v) of Wheat Crop Insurance Regulations, 10 F.R. 1591. The circumstances of this case tempt one to read the regulation, since it is for us to read it, with charitable laxity. But not even the temptations of a hard case can elude the clear meaning of the regulation. It precludes recovery for "spring wheat which has been reseeded on winter wheat acreage in the 1945 crop year." Concerning the validity of the regulation, as "not inconsistent with the provisions" of the Federal Crop Insurance Act, no question has been raised.

The Judgment is reversed and the cause remanded for further proceedings not inconsistent with this opinion.

Reversed.

Justice Black and Justice Rutledge, dissent; Justice Jackson, dissenting

It was early discovered that fair dealing in the insurance business required that the entire contract between the policyholder and the insurance company be embodied in the writings which passed between the parties, namely the written application, if any, and the policy issued. It may be well enough to make some types of contracts with the Government subject to long and involved regulations published in the Federal Register. To my mind, it is an absurdity to hold that every farmer who insures his crops knows what the Federal Register contains or even knows that there is such a publication. If he were to peruse this voluminous and dull publication as it is issued from time to time in order to make sure whether anything has been promulgated that affects his rights, he would never need crop insurance, for he would never get time to plant any crops. Nor am I convinced that a reading of technically-worded regulations would enlighten him much in any event. . . .

It is very well to say that those who deal with the Government should turn square corners. But there is no reason why the square corners should constitute a one-way street.

Justice Douglas joins in this opinion.

Estoppel cases like *Merrill* raise the ancient problem expressed in the maxim "Ignorance of the law excuses no man." If one need not turn square corners, then farmers who lose uninsured crops can falsely claim that someone on the phone told them they had insurance and succeed. The opposite result from the one reached in *Merrill* thus could encourage fraud. However, other cases arise in which estoppel seems manifestly unfair to the aggrieved person. The farmers in *Merrill* presumably would have planted anyway and taken their chances, so their losses are not altogether in the hands of the government. But what if a government official explains the law accurately to a client and then says, "but we will waive the law in your case"? Following the decision in *Heckler v. Community Health Services*, 467 U.S. 51 (1984), some commentators

see a small relaxation in the standard. Steven J. Cann says that, as long as (a) the party is actually made worse off because he or she relied on government advice, and (b) the party did not act simply out of ignorance of the legal rules applicable to the case, then the party may recover.[12]

Is it possible that courts, perhaps because they are part of "the government," become protective of the government in cases where people claim the government erred? The cases in chapter 11 outlining the law allowing tort suits against the government suggest that the answer may be, Yes. Note particularly in that chapter the 1998 decision *Gebser v. Lago Vista Independent School District* exempting school districts from liability for employee behavior (in this case, sexual exploitation of students) except in rare circumstances.

EXERCISES AND QUESTIONS FOR FURTHER THOUGHT

1. Review the Model State APA rulemaking provisions in Appendix C. If they had been in effect when the *Bi-Metallic* case arose, would the Colorado board have had to follow a different course from the one they actually used in this situation?

2. Suppose that a state law providing for the licensing of race horse trainers states that the license of any trainer will be immediately suspended if, following a race, a urine test on a horse under his care shows that the horse was drugged. Suppose a suspended trainer sues to have his license reinstated, at least pending a hearing on the merits of the case in which he presents his side of the story. He cites *Goldberg*. What result would the court reach? See *Barry v. Barchi*, 443 U.S. 55 (1979).

3. In the years since it was decided, *Mathews v. Eldridge*'s balancing test (presented in chapter 2) has shaped many court decisions that shift between formality and informality. In one such case, Connecticut law allowed a plaintiff to "attach," which means gain a legal claim to, a defendant's real estate before the actual trial

and without any hearing. All the plaintiff had to do was file an affidavit stating in a few sentences why the plaintiff expected to win the suit. In this case, which arose out of a fistfight, the first time the defendant heard about the attachment was when the sheriff attached his property. Although the defendant would have a "post attachment" hearing, he instead sued, claiming a due process right to a pre-attachment hearing. He won. You should be able to construct the winning argument based on *Mathews*.[13]

In 1996, however, the United States Court of Appeals for the Sixth Circuit used *Mathews* to deny the right of a social security claimant to oral cross examination of a doctor whose evidence reduced the award the claimant received. The claimant was allowed to examine the doctor through written questions ("interrogatories"). The court held that Social Security claims are in part "non-adversarial" and that the massive number of such claims tips the balance in favor of the efficiency of interrogatories. Do you agree? Does such a ruling raise the same worries as those in the *Horowitz* case?[14]

---

12. See Steven Cann, *Administrative Law* (Thousand Oaks, Calif.: Sage Publications, 1995), 196–202.

13. *Connecticut v. Doehr*, 501 U.S. 1 (1991).

14. *Flatford v. Charter*, 93 F.3d 1296 (1996).

4. The *Mathews* test, over time, has also been used in contexts that fall outside of the administrative realm. Courts have relied on the balancing test to decide how much formality is required in a range of circumstances. In *Hamdi v. Rumsfeld*, 542 U.S. 507 (2004), the Court held that the importance of providing the right of *habeas corpus* to a person captured in Afghanistan in the immediate aftermath of the September 11th attacks outweighed the cost of detaining him without charges. In other words, the Court held that a minimum degree of formality should be provided for Yasser Hamdi, a U.S. citizen whom the Bush Administration asserted was an "enemy combatant" because they claimed he was fighting against U.S. soldiers in Afghanistan. In his dissenting opinion, Justice Antonin Scalia, joined by Justice John Paul Stevens, argued that a cost-benefit analysis is not constitutionally permissible in this case because Hamdi is a U.S. citizen and he had to be given *habeas corpus* rights unless the Congress specifically instructed the Courts not to do so. Only Justice Clarence Thomas, in his dissent, agreed with the government's claim that the balance fell in its favor. Do you agree with Justice Scalia, or Justice Thomas, or the majority opinion? What factors should be taken into account when deciding on the scope of legal formalities? (Speaking of informality, Hamdi was later released to Saudi Arabia, on the condition that he relinquish his U.S. citizenship!)

5. The next two chapters will further clarify the elements of adjudication and rulemaking and articulate the differences and similarities more fully. You should note here, however, that, when requiring a hearing, courts do not consider the costs an administrative action may impose. The *Bi-Metallic* tax decision imposed a much greater cost on people than did the tax decision in *Londoner v. Denver*, cited by Justice Holmes in *Bi-Metallic*, yet the Court required a hearing only in *Londoner*. Is it wise for courts to ignore this difference? Why or why not?

6. Suppose a grade-school principal adopts a policy that allows spanking a student with a wooden paddle for violations of certain school rules. Assume that the principal communicates the paddling policy in advance to students and their parents. A student was paddled after being accused of violating a school rule. No hearing was provided prior to the paddling. Through his parents, the student sued, claiming, for himself and other students who might receive future paddlings, that due process required a hearing with at least some of the *Goldberg* ingredients before execution of punishment. Should their view prevail? In *Ingraham v. Wright*, 430 U.S. 651 (1977), it did not. A student paddled without justification can at common law bring a tort action against the school for assault and battery. Does this fact affect your analysis in *Ingraham*? Why or why not?

7. Sometimes what appear to be mundane interpretations of when notice and comment rulemaking is required in fact have major political implications. For example, in 1988, under the presidency of Ronald Reagan, the Department of Health and Human Services (HHS) issued directives that strictly prohibited government-funded health programs from advising or counseling about abortion. In 1991, President George H. W. Bush, concerned that the original rule interfered with the physician-patient relationship, directed HHS to implement the rules in a way that would not "prevent a woman from receiving complete medical information about her condition from a physician." President Bush also directed that physicians refer women to whatever health care service was appropriate to her, "even if the ultimate result may be the termination of her pregnancy." HHS implemented Bush's orders without a hearing. A group of plaintiffs, who included nurses who were excluded from Bush's order, sued to have Bush's order, and by implication the entire set of regulations, set aside. They claimed that the rules both violated the Constitution and were invalid because HHS had not held notice and comment proceedings before issuing them. The Court did not address the constitutional question. It could have called these interpretive rules, but instead determined that the rules made new policy and required 553 procedures. The election of President Clinton on the same day this opinion was issued effectively terminated this dispute.[15]

8. *Gratz v. Bollinger*, 539 U.S. 244 (2003), a Supreme Court case dealing with the constitutionality of affirmative action in undergraduate admissions, offers interesting insights about the choice of formal and informal procedures in the context of higher education. In *Gratz*, two students sued the university after they were denied

---

15. *National Family Planning and Reproductive Health Association v. Sullivan*, 979 F.2d 227 (1992).

admission, claiming that the university's admissions policy favored racial minorities and therefore violated their equal protection rights. They argued that the university's goal of promoting racial diversity in the student body was not a compelling interest, and that even if it were, the means the university chose to achieve that goal was not "narrowly tailored." In a 6-3 opinion, the Court agreed with the petitioners and held that the University of Michigan's system of evaluating applications was unconstitutional. By striking down an affirmative action plan whose explicit goal was to promote racial diversity, the Court in effect was saying that "you may engage in affirmative action but doing it openly may make it unconstitutional." As Justice David Souter cautioned in his dissent:

Without recourse to such plans, institutions of higher education may resort to camouflage. For example, schools may encourage applicants to write of their cultural traditions in the essays they submit, or to indicate whether English is their second language. Seeking to improve their chances for admission, applicants may highlight the minority group associations to which they belong, or the Hispanic surnames of their mothers or grandparents. In turn, teachers' recommendations may emphasize who a student is as much as what he or she has accomplished.... If honesty is the best policy, surely Michigan's accurately described, fully disclosed College affirmative action program is preferable to achieving similar numbers through winks, nods, and disguises.

Do you agree with Justice Souter? Do you prefer bold and formal statements of policy expressed in statutes or governing orders, or more informal, camouflaged criteria? Do you think that such camouflage could have any value at all? What benefits or harms might result from a policy of addressing contentious issues without identifying them as such?

CHAPTER 7
ELEMENTS OF AN
ADMINISTRATIVE HEARING

T he time has come to halt the journey into the forest of administrative law long enough to look at a map of the terrain. The first six chapters have described a great variety of administrative actions. Each time an agency acts, we try to discover the various ways law controls the decision-making process. In previous chapters we have said that there are at least four *sources* of administrative law (administrative, judicial, constitutional, and statutory). Here we want to discuss three *kinds* of laws that may control any given action, whether it be action taken by an agency or a court.

CONTROLLING LAW

Constitutional Due Process

Both the federal government, through the Fifth Amendment, and the state governments, through the Fourteenth Amendment, must afford their citizens *due process of law*. If the courts decide that an agency action falls in the rulemaking category, then, under *Bi-Metallic*'s reasoning, the due process clause does not come into play. Agencies may, as far as the Constitution goes, simply announce rules following whatever discretionary informal procedure they wish. Such instances mark the informal end of our legal continuum. If, on the other hand, a court feels an agency action has some of the qualities of adjudication—that it speaks to a relatively manageable group of people whose participation might improve the quality of the decision-making process—the courts say

due process requires agencies to do something to insure fairness to the person or people affected. We have seen that this something may, depending on the judicial analysis of the specific situation, require a formal hearing in which the agency observes the *Goldberg* conditions. But we have also seen how courts have applied *Goldberg* quite narrowly and that the Supreme Court has permitted some very informal adjudicatory procedures, particularly in the school discipline cases of *Goss* and *Horowitz*. This due process law of administration frustrates beginning and expert students of administrative law alike. The case-by-case analysis does not give administrators clear guidance across the full range of adjudicative problems.

The Supreme Court's failure, at the present point in the development of administrative law, to articulate clear constitutional principles to guide adjudication raises a suspicion that the justices have no philosophy of administrative due process at all. The suspicion grows when we ask whether the degree of informality the Court may permit at the informal end of the continuum adequately protects the interests of citizens. Before condemning the Court on such grounds, however, we must recognize that the Court is made up of nine people with strong but divergent views on legal issues who often must modulate their views to win adherents to a majority opinion. Individual justices may have detailed and precise administrative law philosophies, such as Justice White's theory of administration articulated in his lengthy dissenting opinion in *INS v. Chadha*. However, as in the *Chadha* case, such philosophies do not necessarily produce majority opinions that state any one of them. None of the justices who decided *Goldberg* remain on the Court, but their replacements, under the leadership of three conservative chief justices, Warren Burger, William Rehnquist, and John Roberts, have not yet managed to hammer out a strong consensus on detailed constitutional principles of administrative law. In this period of groping uncertainty and disagreement, legal ambiguity may be unavoidable.

Two administrative law specialists currently on the Supreme Court, Justices Stephen Breyer and Antonin Scalia, have written articles and books outlining their legal philosophies.[1] While they are leading figures on how to interpret the law of administration, neither of their competing philosophies has established a solid majority on the Court thus far.

The Statutes Creating and Authorizing Agencies to Act

Any time a legislature creates an agency by statute, and any time it chooses to amend agency power by statute, that legislature can prescribe both what the agency does and how it shall do it. Legislatures need not pay attention to the due process distinction between rulemaking and adjudication as long as they do not prescribe *less* than due process requires. In other words, legislatures may require fully formal hearings for rulemaking, or perhaps something in the middle of the continuum, as Congress did for the Federal Trade Commission (FTC) in the Federal Trade Commission Improvement Act. The same statutes may specify adjudicatory procedures. If the agency's statute requires a formal hearing for either rulemaking or adjudication, then the agency must follow the Administrative Procedure Act's (APA) formal hearing requirements, to which we turn in a moment. Before doing so, however, please recall another entirely separate point about creating and authorizing statutes: These statutes, but not the

Constitution or the APA, define what the agency may do as well as how it proceeds. Courts may step in, as chapter 4 showed, to overrule agency action that does not fit within the power delegated to the agency by statute.

The Administrative Procedure Act

The APA uses the rulemaking/adjudication distinction, but on close inspection this is not the APA's most important contribution. The APA does not so much distinguish rulemaking and adjudication as it defines the elements of a hearing when it is required. Section 556, for example, defines some procedural elements of a formal hearing that apply to *both* rulemaking and adjudication whenever the authorizing statute calls for a hearing "on the record" (section 554[a]). If the agency authorizing statute does not call for "adjudication . . . to be determined on the record after opportunity for an agency hearing" (section 554[a]), then the APA has little influence on the agency's adjudication and we fall back on the vague constitutional due process tests.[2] By contrast, the APA *does* require a rulemaking procedure when the agency's authorizing statute is silent. Section 553 states the nature of such "notice and comment" hearings along with the exceptions (see chapter 6) where agencies need not follow notice and comment procedures. The 553 machinery is much less formal than that of a formal hearing.

In summary, each of these three kinds of laws (constitutional, statutory, and the APA) may prescribe that an agency follow one or more procedural elements, regardless of the rulemaking or adjudicative character of the administrative action. This chapter makes little effort to teach you how to tell *when* any given element is legally necessary. Instead it describes what each element means when, for whatever reason, the law does require it or an agency voluntarily adopts the element on its own. For example, both kinds of APA hearings, "notice and comment" and "formal," require *notice*, and this chapter reports what notice means in both contexts.

1. See Antonin Scalia and Amy Guttman, eds., *A Matter of Interpretation* (Princeton: Princeton University Press, 1997); Stephen Breyer, *Active Liberty: Interpreting Our Democratic Constitution* (New York: Vintage Books, 2006).

2. Compare section 1(2) and section 9 of the Model State APA (Appendix C) to the federal APA (Appendix B).

A Threshold Question: What Triggers Formal Adjudication under the APA?

We have seen that, for the formal hearing provisions of the APA to come into play, an agency's authorizing statute must require it. More specifically, section 554(a) "applies . . . in every case of adjudication required by statute to be determined *on the record* after opportunity for an agency hearing . . ." (emphasis added). What if the authorizing statute calls for a hearing but fails to state explicitly that the hearing must be on the record? In some case, courts will refuse to decide simply on the basis of the presence or absence of the magic words *on the record* in the authorizing statute. In *U.S. v. Florida East Coast Railway, Inc.*, 410 U.S. 224 (1973) (see chapter 8), the Court held that even if the word "hearing" is spelled out clearly in a statute, that does not mean an agency needs to conduct a trial-type formal hearing. With this level of open endedness, courts may look to the legislative history of the statute in order to determine if formal adjudication is required.[3] Judges do not require that the statute literally express the "magic words." Here is a 1996 summary of the case law by a federal trial judge, who in this case granted farmers a right to a 554 hearing when they disputed terms of a government farm loan: "Although Section 554 specifies that the governing statute must satisfy the 'on the record' requirement, those three magic words need not appear for a court to determine that formal hearings are required. It is enough that Congress clearly indicate its intent to trigger the formal, on-the-record hearing provisions of the APA."[4]

Marathon Oil Co. v. Environmental Protection Agency

564 F.2D 1253, United States Court of Appeals for the Ninth Circuit (1977) 3-0

[Marathon Oil claimed that an Environmental Protection Agency (EPA) regulation on effluent limits for the transfer of oil was defective since it resulted from a hearing in which rulemaking standards were used. Marathon claimed that the adverse impact suffered, coupled with the disputable nature of the facts justifying the rule, made the hearing adjudicatory and, thus, called for fuller protections than those available in a rulemaking setting.]

Judge Joseph Sneed delivered the opinion of the court

In setting out procedures that an agency must follow in making "adjudicatory" determinations, Congress recognized that certain administrative decisions closely resemble judicial determinations and, in the interest of fairness, require similar procedural protections. These "quasi-judicial" proceedings determine the specific rights of particular individuals or entities. And, like judicial proceedings, the ultimate decision often turns, in large part, on sharply-disputed factual issues. As a result, such APA procedures as cross-examination of key witnesses are needed both for the protection of affected parties and to help achieve reasoned decisionmaking. At the opposite end of the pole are agency determinations that depend less on the resolution of factual disputes and more on the drawing of policy: such "rulemaking" decisions must by necessity be guided by more informal procedures. See *Bi-Metallic Investment Co. v. State Board of Equalization*, 239 U.S. 441 (1915). According to the Attorney General's Manual on the APA, issued shortly after the APA was passed,

the entire act is based upon [this] dichotomy between rule making and adjudication. . . . Rule making . . . is essentially legislative in nature, not only because it operates in the future but also because it is primarily concerned with policy consideration. . . . Typically, the issues relate not to the evidentiary facts, as to which the veracity and demeanor of witnesses would often be important, but rather to the policymaking conclusions to be drawn from the facts. . . . Conversely, adjudication is concerned with the determination of past and present rights and liabilities. . . . In such proceedings, the issues of fact are often sharply controverted. (Attorney General's Manual on the Administrative Procedure Act, at 14–15 [1947].)

Working from this basic dichotomy, the setting of effluent limitations under section 402 of the Control Act is clearly "adjudicatory" in nature and requires the special protections of sections 554, 556 and 557 of the APA. Unlike, for example, section 304 proceedings which lead to the promulgation of industry-wide effluent limitation guidelines

---

3. See *United States v. Independent Bulk Transport Co.*, 480 F. Supp. 474 (1979).

4. *Lane v. Department of Agriculture*, 929 F. Supp. 1290 (1996).

and which are in large measure policy-making, section 402 proceedings focus on whether particular effluent limitations are currently practicable for individual point sources. As the instant proceeding well demonstrates, the factual questions involved in the issuance of section 402 permits will frequently be sharply disputed. Adversarial hearings will be helpful, therefore, in guaranteeing both reasoned decision-making and meaningful judicial review. In summary, the proceedings were conducted in order "to adjudicate disputed facts in particular cases," not "for the purpose of promulgating policy-type rules or standards." The protections of sections 554, 556 and 557 of the APA are therefore particularly appropriate. . . .

Moreover, whether the formal adjudicatory hearing provisions of the APA apply to specific administrative processes does not rest on the presence or absence of the magical phrase "on the record." Absent congressional intent to the contrary, it rests on the substantive character of the proceedings involved. The 79th Congress' purpose in limiting the APA provisions to determinations made "on the record" after opportunity for a hearing was not to provide future Congresses with a talisman that they would use to signify whether or not sections 554, 556 and 557 of the APA should apply. It was to limit the sections' applications to those types of adjudications, discussed above, needing special procedural safeguards. The APA defines "adjudication" broadly as an agency process leading to a final disposition "other than rulemaking." 5 U.S.C. §§551(6)—(7) (1970). But not all "non-rulemakings" are "adjudications" of the nature outlined above and calling for special protective proceedings. Thus, Congress inserted section 554's prefatory language cited by the EPA to exclude from the residual definition of adjudication "governmental functions, such as the administration of loan programs, which traditionally have never been regarded as adjudicative in nature and as a rule have never been exercised through other than business procedures." Attorney General's Manual, supra, at 40. . . .

In summary, the crucial question is not whether particular talismanic language was used but whether the proceedings under review fall within that category of quasi-judicial proceedings deserving of special procedural protections. . . . "[I]t would be a disservice to our form of government and to the administrative process itself if the courts should fail, so far as the terms of the Act warrant, to give effect to its

remedial purposes where the evils it aimed at appear." *Wong Yang Surg v. McGrath* (339 U.S. 33 [1950]). . . .
Remanded.

The *Marathon Oil* case gives us a good idea when the APA's formal adjudication requirements come into the picture. Most of the time, however, statutes are quite ambiguous and cases are seldom as clear as *Marathon Oil*. There has been controversy and uncertainty over what triggers formal adjudication. Historically, courts have used three approaches:

1. If the statute is ambiguous, there should be formal adjudication;

2. If there is ambiguity, there is no need for formality; and

3. If there is ambiguity, *Chevron* deference should apply if the agency provides a reasonable interpretation of the statute.

In the recent years, the trend is toward endorsing the third approach. Courts are leaving the issue to agency interpretation, and not surprisingly agencies tend to favor informal, or less formal, means. The First Circuit Court of Appeals, for instance, recently abandoned its approach in favor of greater formality and stated that it should uphold agency interpretations of choice of procedures under the *Chevron* precedent.[5] This development could pose problems of agency accountability. If courts defer to the informality agencies are inclined to practice, then who will ensure that agency procedures are fair?[6]

THE COMPONENTS OF A HEARING

We shall follow Paul Verkuil's list of the *Goldberg* ingredients (see chapter 6) as a means to structure this section. Since you are familiar with the components of due process as described in *Goldberg*, we draw on them to review the comparable APA requirements.

5. See *Citizens Awareness Network v. United States*, 391 F.3d 338 (2004) and *Dominion Energy Brayton Point v. Johnson*, 443 F.3d 12 (2006).
6. See Melissa M. Berry, "Beyond *Chevron*'s Domain: Agency Interpretations of Statutory Procedural Provisions," *Seattle University Law Review* 30 (2007):541.

Timely and Adequate Notice

Providing advance notice to potentially affected parties lies at the heart of the problem of fairness of any judging situation. Individuals and organizations subject to government regulation want to know in advance what rules the government will apply to them. Both APA hearing procedures, section 553(b) and section 554(b), stress adequate notice, and even the most informal constitutional adjudications, for example, that of *Horowitz* and *Goss*, presume that the citizen knows what the government claims he or she did wrong and knows it in time to do something about it if he or she wishes. You will note that the APA provisions insure that the citizen learns the mechanics of the hearing in their case—for instance when and where they will be heard. But the essence of fair notice has to do with substance, the terms of the proposed rule, and the matters of fact and law asserted in adjudication.

Disclosure of Opposing Evidence and Opportunity to Confront Adverse Witnesses

The second, fifth, and sixth items on the *Goldberg* list are closely related to each other. These requirements deal not with the charge of wrongdoing but with proof of wrongdoing. Under the conventional theory of rulemaking, of course, no charge of wrongdoing arises, therefore section 553 does not on its face provide any opportunity to challenge the evidence on the side one opposes. This conventional theory is under attack, and we shall examine that attack in chapter 8. For now, consider how important these three elements are in a case judging a person's security clearance, a prerequisite for working for a private company that produced goods for the armed forces. In *Greene v. McElroy* (1959), the Defense Department withdrew the plaintiff Greene's security clearance based on "confidential information" which it refused to provide him.[7] Although the case was decided on narrower grounds, Chief Justice Earl Warren in his opinion for the Court stated:

Certain principles have remained relatively immutable in our jurisprudence. One of these is that where governmental action seriously injures an individual, and the reasonableness of the action depends on fact findings, the evidence used to prove the Government's case must be disclosed to the individual so that he has an opportunity to show that it is untrue. While this is important in the case of documentary evidence, it is even more important where the evidence consists of the testimony of individuals whose memories might be faulty or who, in fact, might be perjurers or persons motivated by malice, vindictiveness, intolerance, prejudice, or jealousy. We have formalized these protections in the requirements of confrontation and cross-examination. They have ancient roots. They find expression in the Sixth Amendment which provides that in all criminal cases the accused shall enjoy the right "to be confronted with the witnesses against him." This Court has been zealous to protect these rights from erosion. It has spoken out not only in criminal cases, ... but also in all types of cases where administrative and regulatory action were under scrutiny.... Nor, as it has been pointed out, has Congress ignored these fundamental requirements in enacting regulatory legislation. ...

Greene was not an APA-based decision. Given Chief Justice Earl Warren's ringing statement, we might expect the APA emphatically to require these elements in formal hearings. In fact the APA speaks to this issue with a curiously soft voice, saying merely in section 556(d): "A party is entitled to present his case or defense by oral or documentary evidence, to submit rebuttal evidence, and to conduct such cross-examination as may be required for a full and true disclosure of the facts." While under this provision administrative law judges have considerable control over rebuttal and cross-examination, the custom has been to afford ample opportunity in formal hearings to cross-examine and rebut. Also, section 556(e) says that "When an agency decision rests on official notice of a material fact not appearing in the evidence in the record, a party is entitled, on timely request, to an opportunity to show the contrary." The implication is that the agency would allow the same opportunity regarding facts in the record as in fact they customarily do.

Oral Presentation of Arguments and Evidence

The APA itself, as the excerpt from 556(d) shows, does not necessarily permit claimants to present their position orally before the agency. The result is that when a person

---

7. 360 U.S. 474. Recall that the Court quoted this passage approvingly in the *Goldberg* case, at page 41.

claims a right to be heard orally, courts will fall back on the due process analysis of *Goldberg*. However, formal hearings generally do allow ample oral presentations if the parties insist. Furthermore, the APA unambiguously protects the opportunity to present one's case in writing. This forms the *comment* part of the notice and comment requirements for rulemaking; in many rulemaking situations the comments of interested parties run many hundreds of pages. In formal hearings written submission of evidence accomplishes in most cases the same result as oral presentation. Through written depositions, a questionnaire version of examination, and cross-examination of witnesses, parties can usually introduce the same information as they do via oral presentations.

The Right to Retain an Attorney

Unlike in criminal cases, where the government must provide lawyers for people who cannot afford them, the right to an attorney in administrative proceedings only covers the right to hire and pay for legal assistance.[8] When the federal government regulates private business activities we need not worry that a party may not be able to afford a lawyer. But in precisely the situation described by *Goldberg*—welfare cases—parties will not usually be able to afford counsel, and therefore the "right" to hire an attorney does little good. There is no right to appointed counsel for indigent people involved in administrative hearings even when those involve decisions by the administrative personnel of probation offices, or parole boards about whether to reincarcerate a convict after a parole violation.[9]

The right to hire and pay for attorneys can, of course, only be exercised by those who have sufficient economic resources. The majority of Americans cannot easily afford representation of their interests by attorneys in administrative processes. Interest groups litigating in the public interest, such as the National Resources Defense Council (NRDC) and the Environmental Defense Fund (EDF), provide legal representation for citizens concerned about cleaning up and protecting the environment. These non-

profit organizations rely on contributions from the public for some of their expenses, but they depend more heavily on court-awarded attorneys' fees to cover their litigation costs. The following article by political scientists Karen O'Connor and Lee Epstein describes public policy changes in awarding attorneys' fees. The article also discusses different interest group theories that political scientists have developed to explain interest-group behavior and politics.

Bridging the Gap between Congress and the Supreme Court: Interest Groups and the Erosion of the American Rule Governing Awards of Attorneys' Fees

KAREN O'CONNOR AND LEE EPSTEIN
Western Political Quarterly 38 (1985): 238

Erosion of the American rule governing awards of attorneys' fees is an important legal-political development. For more than 170 years, Congress and the Supreme Court clung to the view that prevailing parties were not entitled to recover their costs or attorneys' fees when they successfully advanced their claims on the merits. In 1964 this situation changed dramatically; passage of Title II of the Civil Rights Act coupled with a subsequent expansive Supreme Court interpretation of that provision, quickly led to erosion of the rule. . . .

The Evolution of the American Rule

Either by statute or in equity, English courts traditionally have awarded litigation costs to prevailing parties. American courts and legislatures, however, did not follow suit. In fact, in the United States, "the litigant, win, lose, or draw, [paid] his own lawyer" (Derfner 1980: 15). Rejection of this tradition stands in sharp contrast to the colonists' adoption of most other English common law traditions (Newberg 1980: 15–17). Yet, many theories have been offered to explain rejection of "attorney subsidies." Some, for example, have pointed to the prevalent distrust of lawyers noting that attorneys symbolized the worst facets of British rule (Falcon 1973: 379–81; *Yale Law Journal* 1940: 699–701). Thus, it was not surprising that the colonies and subsequently the states, drafted laws that severely limited fee awards . . . . While this is the most widely

8. APA, Section 555(b).
9. See *Gagnon v. Scarpelli*, 411 U.S. 778 (1973).

accepted explanation for the rejection of the English rule, others have posited that colonists believed that the rule was "undemocratic" because it limited the poor's access to the courts as they could not risk liability for attorneys' fees (*Hastings Law Journal* 1973: 733). Still, another reason offered was that early fee legislation specified the exact dollar amount of awards that soon became meaningless as a result of inflation (Ehrenzweig 1966: 792; McCormick 1931: 619).

Regardless of the reasons why the English rule was not adopted, the "American rule" as it has come to be known generally has stood as a bar to recovery of plaintiffs' costs in litigation. Thus, as historically applied, the American rule prohibits the recovery of attorneys' fees unless there is a specific statute empowering the courts to make such an award.

Since 1796 when the Supreme Court first examined the attorneys' fees issue in *Arcambel v. Wiseman*, it consistently has enforced the view that in the absence of specific statutory provisions, the federal courts would not award attorneys' fees to prevailing plaintiffs. In response to this judicial interpretation, Congress periodically has provided for awards of attorneys' fees in specific pieces of legislation. Until the 1960s, however, the vast majority of these allowed for recovery to the prevailing party in only highly technical areas of economic relations. These provisions varied; some required the courts to award attorneys' fees while others left awards to the discretion of the presiding judge.

In the 1960s, a major change occurred in congressional policy toward attorneys' fees. Recognition of the fact that the resources of the federal government would be inadequate to enforce fully the provisions contained in sections of the Civil Rights Act of 1964, Congress, at the urgings of the NAACP, the ACLU, the National Lawyers Guild, and other organizations, voted to include specific authorizations for awards of attorneys' fees. Specifically, Title II of the Act stated that: "In any action pursuant to this title, the court, in its discretion may allow the prevailing party other than the United States a reasonable attorney's fee as part of the costs. . . ." Congress' inclusion of that attorneys' fees provision thus institutionalized the notion that private enforcement of civil rights laws was necessary because the U.S. government lacked the resources to pursue the problem adequately. This is known as the private attorney general concept.

The full import of the private attorney general concept was realized in *Newman v. Piggie Park Enterprises, Inc.*

in 1968. *Newman* was a lawsuit filed under Title II of the Civil Rights Act of 1964 by the NAACP Legal Defense Fund (LDF) to enjoin the actions of five drive-in restaurants and a sandwich shop that refused to serve black patrons. After a U.S. Court of Appeals enjoined the practice, the LDF sought a writ of certiorari to the U.S. Supreme Court on the question of the proper construction of Title II's attorneys' fees authorization. In a per curiam opinion, the Court, following the lead of Congress, endorsed the private attorney general concept. The Court stressed that:

When the Civil Rights Act of 1964 was passed, it was evident that enforcement would prove difficult and that the nation would have to rely in part upon private litigation as a means of securing broad compliance with the law.

When a plaintiff brings an action under that Title [II], he cannot recover damages. If he obtains an injunction, he does so not for himself alone but also as a "private attorney general," vindicating a policy that Congress considered of the highest priority (390 U.S. at 401–402).

Thus, according to the Court, those who sued on behalf of others and not simply as individuals could recover the cost of their attorney's fees from the private party found guilty of discrimination prohibited by the act.

This ruling immediately was hailed by civil rights leaders as a major victory and viewed as one that would facilitate litigation brought in the public interest. According to Roy Wilkins, then Executive Director of the NAACP, *Newman* would make "it possible for poor persons denied services to file suit without fear of having to pay legal fees beyond their means" (*New York Times* 1968: 30).

Even more important, perhaps, was that *Newman* was partially responsible for the proliferation of liberal interest groups dedicated to securing policy change through litigation. The Ford Foundation, for example, recognizing the potential of *Newman*, began to provide seed money for the establishment of diverse kinds of interest groups dedicated to using the courts as well as for the creation of litigating arms within "traditional" interest groups (McKay 1977) with the expectation that they would contribute to and increase their own budgets through recovery of attorneys' fees. . . . This attitude led to the phenomenal growth of these kinds of interest groups. Following *Newman* through 1974, more than 50 new groups were created to litigate on behalf of the public interest.

Not only did the number of these groups increase, but as Ford expected, so did the proportion of their annual operating budgets derived from attorneys' fees awards. Between 1972 and 1975, attorneys' fees as a source of funding increased almost fourfold. By 1975, the NAACP LDF, for example, received $550,000 of its 3 million dollar operating budget from attorneys' fees (Settle and Weisbrod 1978: 534–36).

The proliferation of these firms and the expectation that they could recover their operating expenses subsequently led to a dramatic increase in litigation being initiated by "private attorneys general." And, even though *Newman* involved fee recovery for race discrimination litigation, most interpreted the decision to apply to all areas of public interest law. Buttressing this assumption was the fact that Congress was beginning to include specific authorizations providing for attorneys' fees recovery in most major pieces of legislation of interest to existing groups. For example, most environmental laws passed since 1970 included provisions allowing the court to award reasonable attorneys' fees to prevailing parties. Thus, in the period after *Newman*, it appeared that the vitality of the American rule was seriously in doubt; Congress, the Court, and various interest groups accepted the private attorney general interpretation.

In 1975, the Supreme Court, however, severed this alliance and dealt litigating groups, whose coffers by this time were extremely dependent on fee awards (Witt 1975), a severe blow in *Alyeska Pipeline Service Co. v. Wilderness Society.* In *Alyeska*, the Wilderness Society, the Environmental Defense Fund (EDF), and the Friends of the Earth, represented by the Center for Law and Social Policy (CLSP), a D.C. based public interest law firm, had successfully sued to stop the Secretary of the Interior from issuing permits necessary for the construction of the trans-Alaska pipeline. Litigation on the merits, however, was terminated after Congress amended the Mineral Leasing Act to allow issuance of the permit. After passage of that amendment, the CLSP attempted to recoup its attorneys' fees from the Pipeline Company. Its lawyers argued that they had acted as private attorneys general, litigating on behalf of the public interest. The Court of Appeals accepted this argument and allowed the CLSP to recover one-half of the fees to which it was entitled, over $100,000 for more than 4,000 hours of legal work. In its opinion, the Court of Appeals held that:

. . . respondents had acted to vindicate "important statutory rights of all citizens . . . ," had ensured that the governmental system functioned properly, and were entitled to attorneys' fees

lest the great cost of litigation of this kind, particularly against well-financed defendants such as Alyeska, deter private parties desiring to see the laws protecting the environment properly enforced (495 F.2d 1029).

The Court further noted that:

It may well be that counsel serve organizations like [respondents] for compensation below that obtainable in the market because they believe the organizations further a public interest. Litigation of this sort should not have to rely on the charity of counsel any more than it should rely on the charity of parties volunteering to serve as private attorneys general. The attorneys who worked on this case should be reimbursed the reasonable value of their services, despite the absence of any obligations on the part of [respondents] to pay attorneys' fees (495 F.2d 1037).

In a 5-2 decision, the U.S. Supreme Court rejected this reasoning. Writing for the Court, Justice Byron White presented a lengthy history of the relations between Congress and the courts on the issue of attorneys' fees provisions. On the basis of that analysis, Justice White concluded that attorneys' fees were not recoverable absent specific statutory authorization. Thus, since Congress had not included specific provisions allowing for recovery in any of the statutes relied on by CLSP, the Court of Appeals award was reversed.

The reaction from interest groups was immediate; organizations throughout the country claimed that *Alyeska* had sounded the death knell for public interest law. As noted by Charles Halpern, a founder of CLSP, "Until *Alyeska* . . . I would have probably said that attorneys' fee awards were the number one factor in the future of public interest law financing" (Quote in Witt 1975: 35).

Other public interest lawyers were less pessimistic about the decision, realizing that there was still one institution potentially sympathetic to their cause—Congress. According to Bruce Terris, a D.C. based, public interest attorney:

Perhaps now the issue will be so squarely focused before Congress that it will act. . . . I don't think this ruling was the most devastating thing in the world. It did halt a trend, but it's best to go through Congress, not the courts, to establish attorneys' fee awards. I'm hopeful that since Congress has been challenged by the courts to make clear what it wants, that's what it will do. (Quoted in Witt 1975: 35–38.)

Unwilling to rely on Congress to accept the Court's cue, however, leaders of these organizations immediately went to Congress to ask for a more favorable policy proclamation. After hearings early in 1976, where numerous groups including the National Organization for Women, the Consumers Union of the United States, the Consumer Federation of America, the Center for National Policy Review, several Nader groups, the Mental Health Law Project, and the Southern Poverty Law Center testified or submitted statements, Congress passed the Civil Rights Attorneys' Fees Awards Act of 1976. The Act provided for awards of attorneys' fees at a court's discretion to participants bringing actions under all civil rights legislation passed since 1876. Under the terms of this Act, plaintiffs could recover fees from the states as well as from private parties. And, even though this Act failed to permit prevailing plaintiffs to recover their fees from the federal government, Congress still claimed that the purpose of the Act was "to remedy anomalous gaps in our civil rights laws created by the U.S. Supreme Court's recent decision in *Alyeska* and to achieve consistency in our civil rights laws."

During the period from 1976 to 1980, however, interest groups and environmentalists in particular were able to convince Congress to add such provisions to legislation allowing for recovery from the U.S. government on a piecemeal basis. The 1976 Toxic Substance Control Act, for example, allows the party challenging the federal government to recover fees whether or not they actually win the entire suit. Finally in 1980, Congress succumbed to the wishes of interest groups and passed the all encompassing Equal Access to Justice Act, which "authorizes the federal government to pay attorneys' fees for individual and small businesses that defend themselves against 'overreaching' government actions" (Jackson 1982: 680).

Since passage of the Civil Rights Attorneys' Fees Awards and Equal Access to Justice Acts, interest groups have taken full advantage of their provisions. Some groups claim to derive up to 50 percent of their operating budgets from these awards. In fact, in some instances, groups that have lost most of the major issues in a case on the merits have been able to recoup their costs in later attorneys' fees proceedings. Groups that have been able to do so, even though they lost the case in principle, have considered these "wins" in the final analysis because no money was lost (Sherwood 1981).

Yet, the success of these groups in translating adverse judicial decisions into favorable congressional legislation has prompted some members of the Reagan administration to seek to limit recovery of fees against the federal government.

Analysis

There is no question that the demise of the American rule has acted as an incentive for groups to deepen their involvement in the judicial process. Even several justices of the U.S. Supreme Court have noted this trend.* One justice, in particular, noted that the Court is literally "swamped" by these kinds of suits and that there is a "ceiling on how much time [the Court] can give to these issues."

Yet beyond the readily observable implications of the importance of the fee shifting issue, is that it provides support for key elements of several theories that have been offered to explain interest group behavior. E. E. Schattschneider (1935, 1960), for example, argued that pressure groups attempt to achieve their goals by expanding or contracting what he termed the scope of conflict. According to Schattschneider, different kinds of groups attempt to meet this challenge in different ways. "The most powerful special interests" (1960: 40) want to keep the scope of conflict private, that is, they know they will fare best, given their resources when government is excluded from the conflict. In contrast, "losers in the private conflict involve public authority in the struggle" (1960: 40). In Schattschneider's terms, these "weak" groups must "socialize conflict" before they can achieve their goals. To accomplish socialization, weak groups must enlarge the scope of the conflict by bringing other, likeminded groups into the fray so that they can alter the bias of the political system in their favor.

Schattschneider's theory, then, provides a powerful lens for viewing policy changes in the awards of attorneys' fees. Groups initially desiring such awards could be classified as "losers" because of their very nature: the ideas to which they adhere ("equality, consistency, equal protection of the laws, justice, liberty" . . . (1960: 7)— and their continual inability to convince the judiciary to award them these fees. Thus, to succeed, these weak groups were forced to socialize the issue of attorneys' fees by mobilizing to pressure Congress for change. There, they could take advantage of a bias in the political system, a bias that favors groups who retain lobbyists in Washington, D.C. (1935: 164–84). Those groups who early on fought for inclusion of an attorneys' fees provision in the Civil Rights Act of 1964 well fit this description in that they could call on their experienced lobbyists to attend congressional hearings, an activity

* Interviews were conducted by the authors with five Supreme Court justices during the 1983–84 academic year.

that Schattschneider has noted as inherently biased toward groups with these resources.

Once the rule was initially altered, "weak" groups continued to socialize the conflict. This task was clearly facilitated by the fact that the alteration in the rule itself had led to the creation of more groups, which in turn further expanded the scope of the conflict. In fact, by the time Congress passed the Civil Rights Attorneys' Fees Awards Act of 1976, the scope of the conflict had been sufficiently enlarged so as to realter the "balance of forces." This, in turn, led to continued policy change.

While elements of Schattschneider's theory well explain how liberal groups expanded the scope of the conflict to create policy change, David Truman's (1951) "disturbance theory" provides a useful perspective for framing the current struggle in this area. Truman's theory suggests that groups will form to dissipate societal disturbances in order to restore equilibrium. Truman, for example, claimed that employer associations formed to restore the equilibrium that had been unbalanced after unions began to become a power force in society. Currently, a new set of organizations, formed to "restore" a balance in the field of public interest law, has vowed to support plans limiting fee awards. Many of these conservative firms are "frustrated," believing that liberals have benefited far too much from the legislation they so ably urged. Thus, just as Truman predicted, a new wave of organizations arose to fight what they view as a political inequity.

Our findings in this study also provide support for the notions enunciated by scholars examining issues of group maintenance. More specifically, as Jeffrey M. Berry (1977) and Jack Walker (1983) have both noted, public interest groups depend upon outside sources to maintain themselves. By seeking such support, public interest groups overcome the "free rider" problem inherent in the economic groups discussed by Mancur Olson (1965). As Walker has noted, "during recent years group leaders learned how to cope with the public goods dilemma not by inducing large numbers of new members to join their groups through the manipulation of selective benefits, but by locating important new sources of funding outside the immediate membership" (1983: 397). Once again, our findings lend support to this idea. As liberal groups pushed for further alteration in the American rule, the Ford Foundation entered the conflict as the political patron of these groups: it began to provide seed money for public interest law firms with the expectation that they would contribute to their own maintenance through the recovery of attorneys' fees.

In sum, the importance of the fee shifting issue goes beyond immediate appearances: it provides an interesting lens by which to view and then bridge existing theories of interest group behavior. Clearly, as Schattschneider predicted, policy change came about when affected groups sought to expand the scope of the conflict. Their ability to obtain their goals in such short order was largely determined by their success in socializing the conflict, e.g., an ever growing number of groups repeatedly pressured Congress. In other words, numbers count for something in the political process: the more groups that can be brought in on one side of a conflict, the greater the chances are for their success.

This task was facilitated by the fact that political patrons such as the Ford Foundation saw the utility in providing funding for organizations that could help to maintain themselves by pursuing the activity for which they were created in the first instance. Thus, a combination of theories help to explain how and why these groups succeeded.

Truman's disturbance theory, however, would lead us to expect that these groups may not continue to enjoy further expansions of the rule. Conservatives, perceiving an imbalance in the process, are leading efforts to modify the rule. If these new forces can unite in numbers, as did their liberal counterparts, then they too may be able to force change. Any diminution in attorneys' fee recovery provisions in turn would lead to reprivatization of the scope of the conflict, and the cycle would start anew.

Cases

Alyeska Pipeline Service Co. v. Wilderness Society, 421 U. S. 240 (1975)

Arcambel v. Wiseman, 3 U.S. (3 Dall.) 306 (1796)

Hensley v. Eckerhart, 461 U.S. 424 (1983)

Mills v. Electric-Auto Lite Co., 396 U.S. 375 (1970)

Newman v. Piggie Park Enterprises, Inc., 390 U.S. 400 (1968)

Ruckelshaus v. Sierra Club, 463 U.S. 680 (1983)

Trustees v. Greenough, 307 U.S. 161 (1882)

Vaughan v. Atkinson, 369 U.S. 527 (1962)

References

J.M. Berry, *Lobbying for the People* (Princeton: Princeton University Press, 1977).

M.F. Derfner, "The Civil Rights Attorneys' Fees Awards Act of 1976," in *Public Interest Practice and Fee Awards,* ed. H. Newberg (New York: Practising Law Institute, 1980).

A. Ehrenzweig, "Reimbursement of Counsel Fees and the Great Society" *California Law Review* 54 (1966): 1619.

R. Falcon, "Award of Attorneys' Fees in Civil Rights and

Constitutional Litigation," *Maryland Law Review* 33 (1973): 379.

Ford Foundation, *The Public Interest Law Firm: New Voices for New Constituencies* (New York: Ford Foundation, 1973).

H. Handler, "The Public Interest Law Industry," in *Public Interest Law,* ed. B. Weisbrod, et al. (Berkeley: University of California Press, 1978), 50.

"Awarding Attorneys' Fees to the 'Private Attorney General': Judicial Green Light to Private Litigation in the Public Interest," *Hastings Law Journal* 24 (1973): 733.

Interview conducted in Washington, D.C. with M. Horowitz, 1983.

D. Jackson, "Paying Lawyers to Sue the Government—An Expense that OMB Could Do Without," *National Journal,* April 17, 1982, 680.

D. McCormick, "Counsel Fees and Other Expenses of Litigation as an Element of Damages," *Minnesota Law Review* 15 (1931): 619.

R. McKay, *Nine for Equality Under Law: Civil Rights Litigation* (New York: Ford Foundation, 1977).

Interview with R. Momboisse, Managing Attorney, Pacific Legal Foundation in Washington, D.C., 1982.

"High Court Orders Defendants to Pay Rights Case Fees," *New York Times,* March 19, 1968.

H. Newberg, *Public Interest Practice and Fee Awards* (New York: Practising Law Institute, 1980).

K. O'Connnor and L. Eptsein, "The Rise of Conservative Interest Group Litigation," *Journal of Politics* 45 (1983): 479.

M. Olson, *The Logic of Collective Action* (Cambridge: Harvard University Press, 1965).

Interview with D. Popeo, General Counsel, Washington Legal Foundation in Washington, D.C., 1982.

E.E. Schattschneider, *Politics, Pressures and the Tariff* (New York: Prentice-Hall, 1960.); *The Semi-Sovereign People* (New York: Holt, Rinehart, and Winston, 1975).

R. Settle and A. Weisbrod, "Financing Public Interest Law: An Evaluation of Alternative Financing Arrangements," in *Public Interest Law,* ed. B. Weisbrod, et al. (Berkeley: University of California Press, 1979), 534.

Interview with P. Sherwood, Staff Attorney, NAACP Legal Defense Fund in New York City, N.Y., 1981.

D.B. Truman, *The Governmental Process* (New York: Knopf, 1951).

J. Walker, "The Origins and Maintenance of Interest Groups in America," *American Political Science Review* 77 (1983): 390.

E. Witt, "After Alyeska: Can the Contender Survive," *Juris Doctor* (1975): 35.

"Distribution of Legal Expense Among Litigants," *Yale Law Journal* 49 (1940): 699.

The contemporary political struggle over whether the state and private parties should pay attorneys' fees to prevailing parties in public interest litigation takes place in the courtroom and in legislative halls. The possibility of awarding attorneys' fees and other expenses to the prevailing party in a civil/administrative suit against the government is a significant instrument of accountability in the administrative state. Normatively speaking, the attorneys' fees are a means of preventing arbitrary administrative action and providing accountability. If administra-

tors know that the government, and indeed taxpayers, might lose money if they commit malfeasance, they may be more careful about their work. With the permanent enactment of the Equal Access to Justice Act in 1985, this mechanism of oversight and accountability has been institutionalized. The Act provides that if a claimant prevails in a civil action against the United States, he or she can be awarded attorneys' fees and other expenses. Reasonable fees will be awarded unless the government demonstrates special circumstances, or provides a substantial justification why they should not be awarded.

What if, as a citizen, you applied for attorneys' fees in a timely and adequate manner, but forgot to use specific language citing the government's inability to demonstrate substantial justification for its position? Would you still be able to recover your expenses? In *Scarborough v. Principi*, 541 U.S. 401 (2004), this was the question before the Supreme Court. Randall Scarborough, a former Navy serviceman, claimed disability benefits from the Department of Veterans Affairs arguing that his disability was a result of his service in the armed forces. A local office of Veterans Affairs denied his request and the Board of Veterans' Appeals affirmed the rejection. Then Scarborough went to the Court of Appeals for Veteran Claims (CAVC) and in July 1999, the Court of Appeals for Veteran Claims reversed. Scarborough's lawyer then filed an application for attorneys' fees. The content of the application satisfied the Equal Access to Justice Act requirements with the exception that it did not explicitly state that the position of the United States was unjustified. Recognizing this only after the filing deadline had passed, the lawyer amended his application to include the required language. The CAVC dismissed the fee application on the grounds that it was jurisdictionally deficient. The Court of Appeals for the Federal Circuit affirmed the CAVC holding. But on May 3, 2004, the Supreme Court reversed the decision of the Court of Appeals. Writing for the 7-2 majority, Justice Ruth Bader Ginsburg argued that since the required statement—that the government was unable to substantially justify its position—imposed no burden of proof on the fee applicant, it was "nothing more than an allegation or pleading requirement." Despite the dissenting opinion of Justice Clarence Thomas, who was joined by Antonin Scalia, the

Court in effect concluded that legislative purpose should prevail over a plain language approach.

The economics of funding public interest litigation does require mobilizing support for the political values at stake in litigation. The next case, *Walters v. National Association of Radiation Survivors* (1985), illustrates how the Supreme Court has responded to the issues of access to litigation and litigation resources, such as attorneys' fee reimbursement, in administrative law. In this case the Court rejected the right to have counsel appointed at Veterans Administration hearings for disabilities caused by exposure to radiation during atomic bomb tests.

Walters v. National Association of Radiation Survivors

475 U.S. 305 (1985) 6-3

+ *Burger, White, Blackmun, Powell, Rehnquist, O'Connor*
– *Brennan, Marshall, Stevens*

[Veterans' organizations, veterans and a veteran's widow brought action challenging the constitutionality of a statutory provision that imposed a $10 maximum fee to be paid an attorney or agent who represents a veteran before the Veterans Administration (VA) seeking benefits for service-connected death or disability. The plaintiffs claimed that the fee limitation denied them any "realistic opportunity" to obtain legal representation in presenting their claims to the VA and hence violated their rights under the due process clause of the Fifth Amendment and the freedom of speech clause of the First Amendment. The United States District Court for the Northern District of California agreed and issued a nationwide "preliminary injunction" prohibiting the enforcement of the fee limitation. The Administrator of Veterans Affairs appealed.]

Justice Rehnquist delivered the opinion of the Court

I

Congress has by statute established an administrative system for granting service-connected death or disability benefits to veterans . . . . The amount of the benefit award is not based upon need, but upon service connection—that is, whether the disability is causally related to an injury sustained in the service—and the degree of incapacity caused by the disability.

Appellees here are two veterans' organizations, three individual veterans, and a veteran's widow. The two veterans' organizations are the National Association of Radiation Survivors, an organization principally concerned with obtaining compensation for its members for injuries resulting from atomic bomb tests, and Swords to Plowshares Veterans Rights Organization, an organization particularly devoted to the concerns of Vietnam veterans. The complaint contains no further allegation with respect to the numbers of members in either organization who are veteran claimants. Appellees did not seek class certification . . . .

To understand fully the posture in which the case reaches us it is necessary to discuss the administrative scheme in some detail.

Congress began providing veterans pensions in early 1789, and after every conflict in which the nation has been involved Congress has, in the words of Abraham Lincoln, "provided for him who has borne the battle, and his widow and his orphan." The VA was created by Congress in 1930, and since that time has been responsible for administering the congressional program for veterans' benefits. In 1978, the year covered by the report of the Legal Services Corporation to Congress that was introduced into evidence in the District Court, approximately 800,000 claims for service-connected disability or death and pensions were decided by the 58 regional offices of the VA. Slightly more than half of these were claims for service-connected disability or death, and the remainder were pension claims. Of the 800,000 total claims in 1978, more than 400,000 were allowed, and some 379,000 were denied. Sixty-six thousand of these denials were contested at the regional level; about a quarter of these contests were dropped, 15% prevailed on reconsideration at the local level, and the remaining 36,000 were appealed to the [Board of Veterans' Appeals] BVA. At that level some 4,500, or 12%, prevailed, and another 13% won a remand for further proceedings. Although these figures are from 1978, the statistics in evidence indicate that the figures remain fairly constant from year to year.

As might be expected in a system which processes such a large number of claims each year, the process prescribed by Congress for obtaining disability benefits does not contemplate the adversary mode of dispute resolution utilized by courts in this country. It is commenced by the submission of a claim form to the local veterans agency, which form is provided by the VA either upon request or upon receipt of notice of the death of a veteran. Upon application a claim generally is first reviewed by a three-person "rating board" of the VA regional office—consisting of a medical specialist, a legal specialist, and an "occupational specialist." A claimant is "entitled to a hearing at any time on any issue involved in a claim. . . ." 38 CFR §3.103(c) (1984). Proceedings in front of the rating board "are ex parte in nature," §3.103(a); no Government official appears in opposition. The principal issues are the extent of the claimant's disability and whether it is service connected. The board is required by regulation "to assist a claimant in developing the facts pertinent to his claim," §3.103(a), and to consider any evidence offered by the claimant. See §3.103(b). In deciding the claim the board generally will request the applicant's Armed Service and medical records, and will order a medical examination by a VA hospital. Moreover, the board is directed by regulation to resolve all reasonable doubts in favor of the claimant. §3.102.

After reviewing the evidence the board renders a decision either denying the claim or assigning a disability "rating" pursuant to detailed regulations developed for assessing various disabilities. Money benefits are calculated based on the rating. The claimant is notified of the board's decision and its reasons, and the claimant may then initiate an appeal by filing a "notice of disagreement" with the local agency. If the local agency adheres to its original decision it must then provide the claimant with a "statement of the case"—a written description of the facts and applicable law upon which the board based its determination—so that the claimant may adequately present his appeal to the BVA. Hearings in front of the BVA are subject to the same rules as local agency hearings—they are ex parte, there is no formal questioning or cross-examination, and no formal rules of evidence apply. . . . The BVA's decision is not subject to judicial review. . . .

The process is designed to function throughout with a high degree of informality and solicitude for the claimant.

There is no statute of limitations, and a denial of benefits has no formal res judicata effect; a claimant may resubmit as long as he presents new facts not previously forwarded. . . . Perhaps more importantly for present purposes, however, various veterans' organizations across the country make available trained service agents, free of charge, to assist claimants in developing and presenting their claims. These service representatives are contemplated by the VA statute, 38 U.S.C. §3402, and they are recognized as an important part of the administrative scheme. . . .

III

We think that the District Court went seriously awry in assessing the constitutionality of §3404.

Appellees' first claim, accepted by the District Court, is that the statutory fee limitation, as it bears on the administrative scheme in operation, deprives a rejected claimant or recipient of "life, liberty or property, without due process of law" . . . by depriving him of representation by expert legal counsel. Our decisions establish that "due process" is a flexible concept—that the processes required by the Clause with respect to the termination of a protected interest will vary depending upon the importance attached to the interest and the particular circumstances under which the deprivation may occur. See *Mathews, supra*, 424 U.S., at 334. . . . (1972). In defining the process necessary to ensure "fundamental fairness" we have recognized that the Clause does not require that "the procedures used to guard against an erroneous deprivation . . . be so comprehensive as to preclude any possibility of error," *Mackey v. Montrym*, 443 U.S. 1 (1979), and in addition we have emphasized that the marginal gains from affording an additional procedural safeguard often may be outweighed by the societal cost of providing such a safeguard. See *Mathews*, 424 U.S., at 348. . . .

. . . While Congress has recently considered proposals to modify the fee limitation in some respects, a Senate Committee Report in 1982 highlighted the body's concern that "any changes relating to attorneys' fees be made carefully so as not to induce unnecessary retention of attorneys by VA claimants and not to disrupt unnecessarily the very effective network of nonattorney resources that has evolved in the absence of significant attorney involvement in VA claims matters." S.Rep. No. 97–466, p. 49 (1982). Although this same Report professed the Senate's belief that the original stated interest in protecting veterans from unscrupulous lawyers was "no longer tenable," the Senate nevertheless concluded that the fee limitation should with a limited exception remain in effect, in order to "protect claimants' benefits" from being unnecessarily diverted to lawyers. . . .

There can be little doubt that invalidation of the fee limitation would seriously frustrate the oftrepeated congressional purpose for enacting it. Attorneys would be freely employable by claimants to veterans' benefits, and the claimant would as a result end up paying part of the award, or its equivalent, to an attorney. But this would not be the only consequence of striking down the fee limitation that would be deleterious to the congressional plan.

A necessary concomitant of Congress' desire that a veteran not need a representative to assist him in making his claim was that the system should be as informal and nonadversarial as possible. This is not to say that complicated factual inquiries may be rendered simple by the expedient of informality, but surely Congress desired that the proceedings be as informal and nonadversarial as possible. The regular introduction of lawyers into the proceedings would be quite unlikely to further this goal. . . .

As indicated by the statistics set out earlier in this opinion, more than half of the 800,000 claims processed annually by the VA result in benefit awards at the regional level. An additional 10,000 claims succeed on request for reconsideration at the regional level, and of those that do not, 36,000 are appealed to the BVA. Of these, approximately 16% succeed before the BVA. It is simply not possible to determine on this record whether any of the claims of the named plaintiffs, or of other declarants who are not parties to the action, were wrongfully rejected at the regional level or by the BVA, nor is it possible to quantify the "erroneous deprivations" among the general class of rejected claimants. If one regards the decision of the BVA as the "correct" result in every case, it follows that the regional determination against the claimant is "wrong" in the 16% of the cases that are reversed by the Board.

Passing the problems with quantifying the likelihood of an erroneous deprivation, however, under Mathews we must also ask what value the proposed additional procedure may have in reducing such error. In this case we are fortunate to have statistics that bear directly on this question, which statistics were addressed by the District Court. These unchallenged statistics chronicle the success rates before the BVA depending on the type of representation of the claimant, and are summarized in the following figures taken from the record.

Ultimate Success Rates before the Board of Veterans' Appeals by Mode of Representation

American Legion	16.2%
American Red Cross	16.8%
Disabled American Veterans	16.6%
Veterans of Foreign Wars	16.7%
Other nonattorney	15.8%
No representation	15.2%
Attorney/Agent	18.3%

The District Court opined that these statistics were not helpful, because in its view lawyers were retained so infrequently that no body of lawyers with an expertise in VA practice had developed, and lawyers who represented veterans regularly might do better than lawyers who represented them only pro bono on a sporadic basis. The District Court felt that a more reliable index of the effect lawyers would have on the proceedings was a statistical study showing success of various representatives in appeals to discharge review boards in the uniformed services—statistics that showed a significantly higher success rate for those claimants represented by lawyers as compared to those claimants not so represented.

We think the District Court's analysis of this issue totally unconvincing, and quite lacking in the deference which ought to be shown by a federal court in evaluating the constitutionality of an Act of Congress. We have the most serious doubt whether a competent lawyer taking a veteran's case on a pro bono basis would give less than his best effort, and we see no reason why experience in developing facts as to causation in the numerous other areas of the law where it is relevant would not be readily transferable to proceedings before the VA. Nor do we think that lawyers' success rates in proceedings before military boards to upgrade discharges—proceedings which are not even conducted before the VA, but before military boards of the uniformed services—are to be preferred to the BVA statistics which show reliable success by mode of representation in the very type of proceeding to which the litigation is devoted.

The District Court also concluded, apparently independently of its ill-founded analysis of the claim statistics, (1) that the VA processes are procedurally, factually, and legally complex, and (2) that the VA system presently does not work as designed, particularly in terms of the representation afforded by VA personnel and service representatives, and that these representatives are "unable to perform all of the services which might be performed by a claimant's own paid attorney" . . . . Unfortunately the court's findings on "complexity" are based almost entirely on a description of the plan for administering benefits in the abstract, together with references to "complex" cases involving exposure to radiation or agent orange, or post-traumatic stress syndrome. The court did not attempt to state even approximately how often procedural or substantive complexities arise in the run-of-the-mill case, or even in the unusual cases. The VA procedures cited by the court do permit a claimant to prejudice his rights by failing to respond in a timely manner to an agency notice of denial of an initial claim, but despite this possibility there is nothing in the District Court's opinion indicating that these procedural requirements have led to an unintended forfeiture on the part of a diligent claimant. On the face of the procedures, the process described by the District Court does not seem burdensome: one year would in the judgment of most be ample time to allow a claimant to respond to notice requesting a response. In addition, the VA is required to read any submission in the light most favorable to the claimant, and service representatives are available to see that various procedural steps are complied with. It may be that the service representative cannot, as the District Court hypothesized, provide all the services that a lawyer could, but there is no evidence in the record that they cannot or do not provide advice about time limits.

The District Court's opinion is similarly short on definition or quantification of "complex" cases. If this term be understood to include all cases in which the claimant asserts injury from exposure to radiation or agent orange, only approximately 3 in 1,000 of the claims at the regional level and 2% of the appeals to the BVA involve such claims. Nor does it appear that all such claims would be complex by any fair definition of that term: at least 25% of all agent orange cases and 30% of the radiation cases, for example, are disposed of because the medical examination reveals no disability. What evidence does appear in the record indicates that the great majority of claims involve simple questions of fact, or medical questions relating to the degree of a claimant's disability; the record also indicates that only the rare case turns on a question of law. There are undoubtedly "complex" cases pending before the VA, and they are undoubtedly a tiny fraction of the total cases pending. Neither the District Court's opinion nor any matter in the record to which our attention has been directed tells us more than this. . . .

[W]here, as here, the only interest protected by the Due Process Clause is a property interest in the continued receipt of Government benefits, which interest is conferred and terminated in a nonadversary proceeding, these precedents are of only tangential relevance. Appellees rely on *Goldberg v. Kelly*, 397 U.S. 254 . . . (1970), in which the . . . Court said that "counsel can help delineate the issues, present the factual contentions in an orderly manner, conduct cross-examination, and generally safeguard the interests of the recipient." *Id.*, at 270–271. . . . But in defining the process required the Court also observed that "the crucial factor in this context . . . is that termination of aid pending resolution of a controversy over eligibility may deprive an *eligible* recipient of the very means by which to live while he waits. . . . His need to concentrate upon finding the means for daily subsistence, in turn, adversely affects his ability to seek redress from the welfare bureaucracy." *Id.*, at 264 . . . (emphasis in original).

We think that the benefits at stake in VA proceedings, which are not granted on the basis of need, are more akin to the Social Security benefits involved in *Mathews* than they are to the welfare payments upon which the recipients in *Goldberg* depended for their daily subsistence. Just as this factor was dispositive in *Mathews* in the Court's determination that no evidentiary hearing was required prior to a temporary deprivation of benefits, 424 U.S., at 342–343, so we think it is here determinative of the right to employ counsel. Indeed, there appears to have been no stated policy on the part of New York in *Goldberg* against permitting an applicant to divide up his welfare check with an attorney who had represented him in the proceeding; the procedures there simply prohibited personal appearance of the recipient with or without counsel and regardless of whether counsel was compensated, and in reaching its conclusion the Court relied on agency regulations allowing recipients to be represented by counsel under some circumstances. . . .

This case is further distinguishable from our prior decisions because the process here is not designed to operate adversarially. While counsel may well be needed to respond to opposing counsel or other forms of adversary in a trial-type proceeding, where as here no such adversary appears, and in addition a claimant or recipient is provided with substitute safeguards such as a competent representative, a decision-maker whose duty it is to aid the claimant, and significant concessions with respect to the claimant's burden of proof, the need for counsel is considerably diminished. We have expressed similar concerns in other cases holding that counsel is not required in various proceedings that do not approximate trials, but instead are more informal and nonadversary. . . .

IV

Finally, we must address appellees' suggestion that the fee limitation violates their First Amendment rights. . . .

[A]ppellees' First Amendment arguments, at base, are really inseparable from their due process claims. The thrust is that they have been denied "meaningful access to the courts" to present their claims. This must be based in some notion that VA claimants, who presently are allowed to speak in court, and to have someone speak for them, also have a First Amendment right to pay their surrogate speaker, beyond that questionable proposition, however, even as framed appellees' argument recognizes that such a First Amendment interest would attach only in the absence of a "meaningful" alternative. . . . [W]e concluded that appellees had such an opportunity under the present claims process, and that significant Government interests favored the limitation on "speech" that appellees attack. Under those circumstances appellees' First Amendment claim has no independent significance. The decision of the District Court is accordingly reversed.

[Dissenting opinions by Justice O'Connor and Justice Brennan omitted.]

Justice Stevens, with whom Justice Brennan and Justice Marshall join, dissenting

The Court does not appreciate the value of individual liberty. It may well be true that in the vast majority of cases a veteran does not need to employ a lawyer . . . and that the system of processing veterans benefit claims, by and large,

functions fairly and effectively without the participation of retained counsel. . . . Everyone agrees, however, that there are at least some complicated cases in which the services of a lawyer would be useful to the veteran and, indeed, would simplify the work of the agency by helping to organize the relevant facts and to identify the controlling issues. . . . What is the reason for denying the veteran the right to counsel of his choice in such cases? The Court gives us two answers: First, the paternalistic interest in protecting the veteran from the consequences of his own improvidence . . . and second, the bureaucratic interest in minimizing the cost of administering the benefit program. . . . I agree that both interests are legitimate, but neither provides an adequate justification for the restraint on liberty imposed by the $10-fee limitation. . . .

The language in §3405, particularly the use of the words "directly or indirectly," apparently would apply to consultations between a veteran and a lawyer concerning a claim that is ultimately allowed, as well as to an appearance before the agency itself. In today's market, the reasonable fee for even the briefest conference would surely exceed $10. Thus, the law that was enacted in 1864 to protect veterans from unscrupulous lawyers—those who charge excessive fees—effectively denies today's veteran access to *all* lawyers who charge reasonable fees for their services . . . .

In my opinion, the bureaucratic interest in minimizing the cost of administration is nothing but a red herring. Congress has not prohibited lawyers from participating in the processing of claims for benefits and there is no reason why it should. The complexity of the agency procedures can be regulated by limiting the number of hearings, the time for argument, the length of written submissions, and in other ways, but there is no reason to believe that the *agency's* cost of administration will be increased because a claimant is represented by counsel instead of appearing *pro se.* The informality that the Court emphasizes is desirable because it no doubt enables many veterans, or their lay representatives, to handle their claims without the assistance of counsel. But there is no reason to assume that lawyers would add confusion rather than clarity to the proceedings. As a profession, lawyers are skilled communicators dedicated to the service of their clients. Only if it is assumed that the average lawyer is incompetent or unscrupulous can one rationally conclude that the efficiency of the agency's work would be undermined by allowing counsel to participate whenever a veteran is willing to pay for his services. I categorically reject any such assumption.

The fact that a lawyer's services are unnecessary in most cases, and might even be counterproductive in a few, does not justify a total prohibition on their participation in all pension claim proceedings . . . .

The paternalistic interest in protecting the veteran from his own improvidence would unquestionably justify a rule that simply prevented lawyers from overcharging their clients. Most appropriately, such a rule might require agency approval, or perhaps judicial review, of counsel fees. It might also establish a reasonable ceiling, subject to exceptions for especially complicated cases. In fact, I assume that the $10-fee limitation was justified by this interest when it was first enacted in 1864. But time has brought changes in the value of the dollar, in the character of the legal profession, in agency procedures, and in the ability of the veteran to proceed without the assistance of counsel . . . .

It is evident from what I have written that I regard the fee limitation as unwise and an insult to the legal profession. It does not follow, however, that it is unconstitutional. The Court correctly notes that the presumption of constitutionality that attaches to every Act of Congress requires the challenger to bear the burden of demonstrating its invalidity . . . .

The fact that the $10-fee limitation has been on the books since 1864 does not, in my opinion, add any force at all to the presumption of validity. Surely the age of the *de jure* segregation at issue in *Brown v. Board of Education*, 347 U.S. 483 (1954), or the age of the gerrymandered voting districts at issue in *Baker v. Carr*, 369 U.S. 186 (1962), provided no legitimate support for those rules. In this case, the passage of time, instead of providing support for the fee limitation, has effectively eroded the one legitimate justification that formerly made the legislation rational. The age of the statute cuts against, not in favor of, its validity.

It is true that the statute that was incorrectly invalidated in *Lochner* provided protection for a group of workers, but that protection was a response to the assumed disparity in the bargaining power of employers and employees, and was justified by the interest in protecting the health and welfare of the protected group. It is rather misleading to imply that a rejection of the *Lochner* holding is an endorsement of rational paternalism as a legitimate legislative goal . . . . But in any event, the kind of paternalism reflected in this statute as it operates today is irrational. It purports to protect the veteran who has little or no need for protection, and it actually denies him assistance in cases in which the help of his own lawyer may be of critical importance.

But the statute is unconstitutional for a reason that is more fundamental than its apparent irrationality. What is at stake is the right of an individual to consult an attorney of his choice in connection with a controversy with the Government. In my opinion that right is firmly protected by the Due Process Clause of the Fifth Amendment and by the First Amendment . . . .

The fundamental error in the Court's analysis is its assumption that the individual's right to employ counsel of his choice in a contest with his sovereign is a kind of second-class interest that can be assigned a material value and balanced on a utilitarian scale of costs and benefits . . . .

Unfortunately, the reason for the court's mistake today is all too obvious. It does not appreciate the value of individual liberty.

I respectfully dissent.

The question of the right to retain an attorney in the VA proceedings continued to present political questions for the veterans' organizations, as well as Congress. On May 2, 2006, the "Veteran's Choice of Representation and Benefits Enhancement Act of 2006" was submitted to the Congress. One goal of the bill was to remove the limitations for hiring legal counsel. The bill, even though it was passed in the Senate, never became law because two years after its introduction, it still had not been voted on in the House. Throughout the debates about the bill in the Senate, opponents repeated the criticism voiced by the Court in the *Walters* case, that encouraging lawyers to participate in VA hearings would create an adversarial system in a setting that should be as non-confrontational as possible.

A DETERMINATION ON THE RECORD AND STATEMENT OF REASONS

The eighth and ninth *Goldberg* ingredients (discussed now) plus the final ingredient in the next subsection, focus our attention on the process by which agencies actually reach decisions. You will recall that the APA distinguishes between its two main forms of hearings in terms of the presence or absence of the on-the-record requirement. Section 553 imposes no obligation on the agency to decide one way rather than another. After gathering comments and making its decision the agency must "adopt a concise general statement of their basis and purpose" (553)(d), but it need not show that it reached the decision on the basis of the comments.

In formal trial-type hearings, however, agencies must satisfy courts that they have reached any given result on the basis of information formally presented on the record. The opportunity to appear, give arguments, cross-examine opposing witnesses and so forth does not suffice. After those things have taken place and some person or group has analyzed what it means, the agency must show that its decision is based on the evidence in the case itself, rather than a secret or off-the-record reason. This issue of course was central in *Morgan*, where communications between the Bureau of Animal Industries and the secretary of agriculture were not on the record.

These findings requirements are often called the *substantial evidence* test. It is a test of reasonableness. If the decision maker's conclusions necessarily require facts X, Y, and Z to be true, then the record of the hearing must contain credible (that is, believable) evidence that X, Y, and Z are in fact true. Note that this test requires a lesser degree of certainty than the proof of guilt "beyond a reasonable doubt" standard in criminal cases. It is also weaker than the "preponderance of the evidence" standard applied in civil cases. The following law review article describes some of the philosophy underlying the findings requirements. As you read it, think about how professors grading student papers might grade more fairly if they heeded its advice.

Note: Administrative Findings under Section 8(c)

VIRGINIA LAW REVIEW 51 (1965): 459, 462

The most obvious reason for requiring findings is that government should not operate in secret. The acts of the sovereign should be done in the open, subject to comment and criticism. Of course, the lack of findings to support an administrative act does not make the effects of the act any less discoverable, but the process by which the decision was reached is part of the process of government, and a basic premise of the APA is that insofar as possible the entire process of government should be revealed.

The parties, and losing parties especially, have a right to know as fully as possible the grounds upon which their case was decided . . . . The parties need to know the basis of a decision if they are to prepare intelligently for agency review of the decision of a subordinate officer, or for reconsideration by the agency of its own decision, or for judicial review.

Findings are the essential basis of proper judicial review of administrative action. The respective roles of agency and court have ever been hard to define, but the court is responsible at least for seeing that the agency acts within its discretion and not arbitrarily or capriciously. Before the court can do this it must know the basis for the administrative decision . . . .

Another reason for requiring findings is that the doctrines of *stare decisis*, *res judicata*, and law of the case depend on the clarity of previous decisions . . . . Only adequate findings will reveal whether a decision was on the merits, what issues were actually decided, and what policies were involved.

Practically, additional benefits will result from an agency's explication of its decisions, particularly of important policy decisions. When the parties dealing with an agency know exactly what it has decided and why, there is likely to be less duplicative litigation on the same point. Often adjudication could be avoided if the agency initially would make clear its position. While abbreviated findings might seem expedient to the overworked agency at the moment, they may create greater workloads in the long run.

Finally, it should be recognized that inadequate disclosure and careless writing of opinions, possible indicia of a careless decision, will hardly engender in the public mind confidence in the studied competence and expertise which supposedly justify the relaxed procedures and wide discretion allowed administrative agencies . . . .

While disclosure is the basis of the foregoing considerations, another broad policy underlies the findings requirement which does not directly involve disclosure— the policy of insuring thorough consideration by the agency of its decisions. Anyone is less likely to act arbitrarily or capriciously if he is required to set down with some particularity the reasons for his action. It is all too easy to be arbitrary through mere inadvertence because the thought given to the action was insufficient to uncover all the factors involved. Requiring the agency to publish its reasoning fully not only decreases the likelihood that issues will be neglected: it may also prompt a reexamination of assumptions essential to the rationale which are overlooked until it is reduced to writing. The reasons for requiring findings may thus be classed under two main headings: the policy of disclosure and the policy of insuring thorough agency consideration.

Before going further we must clarify a critical point. The APA itself leaves agencies some flexibility in structuring the outlines of the formal hearing process. Section 557(b) permits agencies to use an administrative law judge to conduct the initial hearing and to make findings and potentially final decisions. But the agency members themselves may also conduct this trial-type hearing. And in some instances the agency members may conduct a second hearing in the process of reviewing the decision of the administrative law judge. In these formal procedures both the judge and the agency itself must comply with the APA.

Most federal formal trial-type hearings do begin with an administrative law judge. States, operating under due process requirements and their own constitutions and administrative procedure acts, also frequently use this division of labor. The relationship between the initial fact finder and the final decision maker has posed one of the most controversial legal issues surrounding the "on the record" requirement. Obviously a decider cannot, after the hearing but before the decision, get on the phone and consult anybody he or she wishes about the issues. In fact the APA, section 557, now quite strictly prohibits all forms of off-the-record *ex parte* communications in for-

mal hearings. But what if the decider does some independent reading? What if the decider looks up past similar cases for ideas and approaches that might tip the balance? What if the final decider sits down with the initial fact finder and discusses the case, not to review new or secret facts but simply to develop wise solutions? We never forbid conventional judges from doing library research or discussing cases with their clerks or even having clerks author opinions for them. Are these practices unacceptable just because they take place in the context of administrative law? The following case discusses the reasoning for prohibiting *ex parte* communications in the administrative process.

Mazza v. Cavicchia

SUPREME COURT OF NEW JERSEY, 15 N.J. 498 (1954) 5-2

[Mazza operated a hotel and restaurant with a license allowing liquor to be consumed on the premises. The license was revoked because Mazza allowed lewd activity and the sale of contraceptives to take place at the business. Both acts violated state rules governing the operation of businesses authorized to sell liquor by the drink. A hearing before the Division on Alcoholic Beverage Control was held and Mazza's license was suspended for 180 days on the basis of the record developed at the hearing. However, Mazza was not provided a copy of the proceedings that was used as the basis of the decision. The lower court upheld the decision and Mazza appealed to the state supreme court.]

Chief Justice Vanderbilt delivered the opinion of the court

Mazza appeals here asserting that his constitutional rights have been infringed, N.J. Const. 1947, Art. VI, Sec. V, par. 1, clause (a), in that he was denied due process and a fair hearing before the Division [of Alcohol Beverage Control]. It is unnecessary for us to determine each of the points raised because we are of the opinion that by reason of the failure to supply the appellant with a copy of the hearer's secret report to the Director [of the Division] the appellant was deprived of his right to due process and a fair hearing before the administrative tribunal . . . .

The crucial point in the pending appeal is whether the failure to supply the appellant with a copy of the hearer's secret report to the Director constitutes reversible error.

It was conceded at the oral argument in the [lower court] as well as in this court that "The hearer in fact files a report of his conclusions with the Director, although there is no official and public rule which requires it, and no notice of the submission of the report is given to the affected licensee."

It is argued in the brief of the respondent Director that his determination was made "upon the basis of his own independent findings and not by a subordinate." This, however, is not saying that the hearer's report was not used by him in the process of deciding the case. Nowhere in the record before us is it stated that he failed to read and otherwise utilize the hearer's confidential report. Every inference is entirely to the contrary. The respondent's brief concedes that hearers' reports have been consistently used since the inception of the agency in 1933. Is it not inconceivable that the Director should have insisted on having hearer's reports for 21 years and yet not used them in preparing his decisions? Is it reasonable to suppose that they merely served the function speciously assigned to them in the respondent's brief:

"The hearer's report serves merely to save the Director the time-consuming effort involved in the mechanical task of dictating his decision. The report has neither official status nor binding force. While it normally accompanies the record submitted to the Director for decision, the preparation of the report, so far as its place in the determinative action of the Director is concerned, could well await the Director's determination made after examination of the complete record."

What possible purpose could the consistent submission of such reports for 21 years have served, but to furnish the Director a key to the facts and the law of each case? . . .

In any proceeding that is judicial in nature, whether in a court or in an administrative agency, the process of decision must be governed by the basic principle of the exclusiveness of the record. "Where a hearing is prescribed by statute, nothing must be taken into account by the administrative tribunal in arriving at its determination that has not been introduced in some manner into the record of the hearing." . . . Unless this principle is observed, the right to a hearing itself becomes meaningless. Of what real worth is

the right to present evidence and to argue its significance at a formal hearing, if the one who decides the case may stray at will from the record in reaching his decision? Or consult another's findings of fact, or conclusions of law, or recommendations or even hold conferences with him? . . .

It should be borne in mind that the danger of unfairness in this type of procedure is particularly great in an agency in which there is such a high degree of concentration of prosecuting and judicial functions in the one agency . . . .

It is as much to the advantage of the Division as to private parties before it that the public have confidence in the fairness of its procedure. Whatever inconvenience the agency may suffer in modifying its practice (and one wonders how great it will really be) will be more than offset by the increased trust which the public will have in the justness of its procedure . . . .

Justice Jacobs, with whom Justice Burling agrees, dissenting

In the proper discharge of our function of judicial review we should examine the proceedings with full recognition that the Division of Alcoholic Beverage Control is part of a coordinate branch of government and that its administrator has the same capacity for the wholesome administration of justice in his lawful sphere as judges have in theirs. Thus viewed, the record leaves little room for doubt that the appellant was fairly charged, tried and found guilty on the basis of compelling evidence, and that his liquor license was justly suspended in strict compliance with all statutory and constitutional requirements . . . .

. . . [N]o request was ever made on the licensee's behalf to examine the hearer's analysis and recommendation and, in any event, the Director did not rely upon them. The record may be searched in vain for any suggestion to the contrary and the Director's opinion states unequivocally that he had "examined and reexamined the entire record" before him and that, having done so he was "thoroughly convinced that a careful reading of the testimony and evidence could lead any dispassionate, discerning person to but one conclusion, namely, that the testimony of the Division's agent truthfully represents the facts in all material and probative respects." Further on, he states that "on the basis of the full testimonial record, revealingly corroborated by all of the attendant circumstances, I am convinced that the violations were committed as charged herein." There is no contention advanced by the licensee that the Director did not personally study all of the testimony and evidence as he says he did . . . .

[I]n the first Morgan case . . . Chief Justice Hughes took pains to point out that evidence may be taken by an examiner and "may be sifted and analyzed by competent subordinates." . . .

It would seem that the majority have mistakenly dealt with the instant proceeding as one in which the Director went beyond the strict record. Even in that situation, however, this court recently held that the administrative determination will not be upset in the absence of a showing of prejudice. [T]he setting aside of the licensee's suspension disregards the essential justice of the proceeding and the important public interests involved, and tends to impose upon the Director, though the legislature has declined to do so, rigid judicial notions as to the precise form of procedural routine to be followed by him . . . .

Both *Mazza*, as an illustration of state law, and the federal APA take a very tough stance against *ex parte* influences. One reason to forbid such off-the-record influences on decision makers is that officials can easily claim to have based a decision on facts contained in the record when in fact it is based on something else.

The Impartial Decision Maker

At first glance you might expect this last category of legal formality to pose the fewest legal puzzles of any issue in this chapter. After all, the very essence of judging is impartiality. But on closer look we see that partiality and bias take several forms. Some biases are unavoidable. Some—the Environmental Protection Agency's statutory obligation to protect the environment, for example—are required by law. Congress delegates powers to agencies so that they may implement and enforce legislative policies that are meant to serve a particular mission.

Judges, like most people, hold certain values about policy that merge into their views about law. The Warren Court judges shared values about the moral rightness of treating citizens equally without regard to race. These

beliefs—so different from those at the end of the previous century—caused them to forbid school segregation under the Equal Protection Clause in *Brown v. Board of Education*, 347 U.S. 484 (1954). As a democratic society brings new values to bear on political and legal questions, it is desirable that law adapt and change. In the administrative world the "rightness" of some values is every bit as strong as it is in our conventional courts. For example, Congress created the EPA to protect the environment. We can hardly expect people who work in that agency to have no interest in protecting the environment.

But there are specific types of bias that administrative law seeks to prevent. The following cases describe two kinds of improper bias. The first is called *prejudgment*. Someone prejudges a case when he or she reaches a decision in the case before hearing the facts. This accusation is less often leveled at administrative law judges in the federal system than at the politically appointed members of the agency themselves.

The second form of bias is called *improper interest in the result*. Do we suspect that the decider stands to gain in any systematic way—perhaps financially or politically—by deciding a certain way? Unlike the prejudgment problem, which depends on evidence in the case itself, improper interest occurs when the judge is in a position to benefit from the outcome. In a classic case in this area the Supreme Court held that a mayor in charge of a small town's financial fortunes could not sit as traffic judge if the fines in traffic court supported the town's budget.[10] *Gibson v. Berryhill* treats the same problem.

Gibson v. Berryhill

411 U.S. 564 (1973) 9-0
+ Burger, Douglas, Brennan, Stewart, White, Marshall, Blackmun, Powell, Rehnquist

[An Alabama statute was repealed that had allowed private companies to practice optometry by employing optometrists. One of the affected companies, Lee Optical, continued to employ its optometrists in the practice of optometry. The Alabama Optometric

10. *Ward v. Village of Monroeville*, 409 U.S. 57 (1972).

Association, made up of optometrists in private practice, filed charges with the Alabama Board of Optometry—also composed solely of optometrists in private practice—asking that the licenses of optometrists employed by Lee Optical be revoked for unprofessional conduct. After a delay in which the board successfully sought court enforcement to stop the company from operating, the board prepared to hear the charges. The affected optometrists sued in federal district court to restrain the board from acting, since its composition indicated a bias that could deny the affected optometrists a fair hearing. The trial court agreed with their contention.]

Justice White delivered the opinion of the Court

The District Court thought the Board to be impermissibly biased for two reasons. First, the Board had filed a complaint in state court alleging . . . charges . . . substantially similar to those pending against appellees before the Board . . . .

Secondly, the District court determined that the aim of the Board was to revoke the licenses of all optometrists in the State who were employed by business corporations such as Lee, and that these optometrists accounted for nearly half of all the optometrists practicing in Alabama. Because the Board of Optometry was composed solely of optometrists in private practice for their own account, the District Court concluded that success in the Board's efforts would possibly redound to the personal benefit of members of the Board, sufficiently so that . . . the Board was constitutionally disqualified from hearing the charges filed against the appellees.

The District Court apparently considered either source of possible bias—prejudgment of the facts or personal interest—sufficient to disqualify the members of the Board. Arguably, the District Court was right on both scores, but we need reach, and we affirm, only on the latter ground of possible personal interest.

It is sufficiently clear from our cases that those with substantial pecuniary interest in legal proceedings should not adjudicate these disputes. *Tumey v. Ohio*, 273 U.S. 510 (1927). And *Ward v. Village of Monroeville*, 409 U.S. 57 (1972), indicates that the financial stake need not be as direct or positive as it appeared to be in *Tumey*. It has also come to be the prevailing view that "[m]ost of the law con-

cerning disqualification because of interest applies with equal force to . . . administrative adjudicators." K. Davis, Administrative Law Text §12.04, p. 250 (1972), and cases cited. The District Court proceeded on this basis and, applying the standards taken from our cases, concluded that the pecuniary interest of the members of the Board of Optometry had sufficient substance to disqualify them, given the context in which this case arose. As remote as we are from the local realities underlying this case and it being very likely that the District Court has a firmer grasp of the facts and of their significance to the issues presented, we have no good reason on this record to overturn its conclusion and we affirm it . . . .

The next case raises the important due process issue whether an agency can ignore an administrative law judge's decision, and if so, on what basis. *Cinderella Career and Finishing Schools, Inc. v. FTC* (1970) is a good illustration of the two-level federal processes mentioned in section 557 of the APA. Agencies generally retain the power to make the final decision. It need not agree with the administrative law judge's decision.

Cinderella Career and Finishing Schools, Inc. v. Federal Trade Commission

425 F.2D 583, UNITED STATES DISTRICT COURT FOR THE DISTRICT OF COLUMBIA CIRCUIT (1970) 3-0

[Cinderella, a private vocational school, was charged by the Federal Trade Commission (FTC) with making exaggerated claims in advertisements about the career benefits to be gained by attending its courses. After an in-depth hearing (50 witnesses, 200 exhibits) contained in 1,810 pages of testimony, the hearing examiner (now called an *administrative law judge*) ruled in favor of Cinderella. The FTC reversed the hearing examiner on some of the charges, and in so doing ignored all the testimony and relied completely on its own evaluation of the advertisements. Additionally, the chairman of the FTC made a speech during the commission's review of the case implying that he had already made up his mind that Cinderella was in the wrong. Cinderella brought suit challenging the decision for lack of due process in the consideration of the evidence and for possible prejudgment on the part of the chairman. All emphases in the material were added by Judge Tamm.]

Judge Tamm delivered the opinion of the court

We are faced with two principal issues on this appeal: whether the action of the Commission in reversing the hearing examiner comports with standards of due process, and whether then Chairman Paul Rand Dixon should have recused himself from participation in the review of the initial decision due to public statements he had previously made which allegedly indicated pre-judgment of the case on his part . . . .

In their final decision the Commissioners first criticized the hearing examiner for his handling of some of the testimony, stating that "[f]rom the initial decision it appears that the examiner ignored some of this testimony and some of it was given little or no weight because the examiner either questioned the credibility of the witness or considered their testimony hearsay." . . . The Commissioners themselves then proceeded to ignore all testimony completely: "[I]n view of our decision to independently analyze—and without assistance from consumer or other witnesses—the challenged advertisements and their impact . . . *it becomes unnecessary to review the testimony of these expert and consumer witnesses.*" . . . Later in the opinion they again noted that "for the reasons stated above *the Commission will rely on its own reading and study of the advertisements to determine whether the questioned representation has the capacity to deceive.*" . . . The hearing examiner in a Federal Trade Commission proceeding has both the right and duty to make determinations concerning the credibility of witnesses and the exclusion of hearsay evidence; while the Commissioners may review those determinations on appeal, in light of the record, they may not choose to ignore completely the testimony adduced at the hearing.

A further example of the Commissioners' determination to make a de novo review of the advertisements rather than considering the record as developed during the hearing is the statement that: "A review of the examiner's initial decision has persuaded the members of the Commission *to examine firsthand and independently* the challenged representations contained in respondents' advertisements rather than relying on the analysis thereof contained in the initial decision."

. . . Not only do we find this conduct on the part of the Commissioners a violation of their own rules and hence of due process, but we also seriously question their ability to make the determination called for without the aid of the testimony in the record . . . . "The Commission, as stated in its opinion . . . *evaluated Cinderella's advertising entirely on the basis of its own study of the material. It found no need to resolve the conflicting expert and consumer testimony in the record* bearing upon the meaning of the advertisements."

. . . We are unable to find any authority for their proposition—that a sixteen-day hearing may be completely ignored if the Commissioners are dissatisfied with the result reached by their hearing examiner . . . .

We think it as preposterous for the Commission to claim a right to ignore that evidence and, with more daring than prudence, to decide a case de novo as it would be for this court to claim a right to ignore the findings of fact and conclusions of law of a district in a proceeding here, substituting the judgment of this court on a cold record for that of the finder of the fact below . . . .

[W]hile the appeal from the examiner's decision was pending before him, Chairman [of the Commission] Dixon made a speech . . . in which he stated:

. . . *What about carrying ads that offer college educations in five weeks,* fortunes by raising mushrooms in the basement, getting rid of pimples with a magic lotion, *or becoming an airline hostess by attending a charm school? . . . Granted that newspapers are not in the advertising policing business, their advertising managers are savvy enough to smell deception when the odor is strong enough . . . .*

[T]here is in fact and law authority in the Commission, acting in the public interest, to alert the public to *suspected violations* of the law by *factual press releases* whenever the Commission shall have reason to believe that a respondent is engaged in activities made unlawful by the Act . . . . This does not give individual Commissioners license to prejudge cases or to make speeches which give the appearance that the case has been prejudged. Conduct such as this may have the effect of entrenching a Commissioner in a position which he has publicly stated, making it difficult, if not impossible, for him to reach a different conclusion in the event he deems it necessary to do so after consideration of the record. There is a marked difference between the issuance of a press release which states that the Commission has filed a complaint because it has "reason to believe" that there have been violations, and statements by a Commissioner after an appeal has been filed which give the appearance that he has already prejudged the case and that the ultimate determination of the merits will move in pre-destined grooves. While these two situations—Commission press releases and a Commissioner's pre-decision public statements—are similar in appearance, they are obviously of a different order of merit.

Chairman Dixon, sensitive to theory but insensitive to reality, made the following statement in declining to recuse himself from this case after petitioner requested that he withdraw:

As . . . I have stated . . . this principle "is not a rigid command of the law, compelling disqualification for trifling causes, but a consideration addressed to the discretion and sound judgment of the administrator himself in determining whether, irrespective of the law's requirements, he should disqualify himself."

. . . If this is a question of "discretion and judgment," Commissioner Dixon has exercised questionable discretion and very poor judgment indeed, in directing his shafts and squibs at a case awaiting his official action. We can use his own words in telling Commissioner Dixon that he has acted "irrespective of the law's requirements." . . .

The test for disqualification has been succinctly stated as being whether "a disinterested observer may conclude that [the agency] has in some measure adjudged the facts as well as the law of a particular case in advance of hearing it." . . .

[T]he Sixth Circuit was required to reverse a decision of the FTC because Chairman Dixon refused to recuse himself from the case even though he had served as Chief Counsel and Staff Director to the Senate Subcommittee which made the initial investigation into the production and sale of the "wonder drug" tetracycline . . . . Incredible though it may seem, the court was compelled to note in that case that:

[T]he Commission is a fact-finding body. As Chairman, Mr. Dixon sat with the other members as triers of the facts and *joined in making the factual determination* upon which the order of the Commission is based. *As counsel for the Senate Subcommittee, he had investigated and developed many of these same facts. [American Cyanamid Co. v. F.T.C., 363 F.2d 757 (1966) at 767.]*

. . . It is appalling to witness such insensitivity to the requirements of due process; it is even more remarkable to find ourselves once again confronted with a situation in which Mr. Dixon, pouncing on the most convenient victim, has determined either to distort the holdings in the cited cases beyond all reasonable interpretation or to ignore them altogether. We are constrained to this harshness of language because of Mr. Dixon's flagrant disregard of prior decisions.

The rationale for remanding the case despite the fact that former Chairman Dixon's vote was not necessary for a majority is well established. Litigants are entitled to an impartial tribunal whether it consists of one man or twenty and there is no way which we know of whereby the influence of one upon the others can be quantitatively measured. [W]e vacate the order of the Commission and remand with instructions that the Commissioners consider the record and evidence in reviewing the initial decision, without the participation of Commissioner Dixon . . . .

Who actually makes the decision in a formal adjudication? Before the passage of the Administrative Procedure Act in 1946, a staff member who presided at agency hearings was variously referred to as a "hearing examiner," "trial examiner," "referee," "presiding officer," "district engineer, "deputy commission," or "register."[11] This person was responsible for collecting information, producing a report and making a recommendation. By 1941, however, considerable controversy developed over the propriety of combining the two roles of prosecutor and judge into the duties on one decision maker. The Attorney General's Committee on Administrative Procedure convened to address this matter and to address concerns that there was a lack of uniformity in examiners' decisions. In response, the APA instituted the requirement of an "internal separation" of functions. Agency investigations are now performed by inspectors, while agency hearings are conducted by independent administrative law judges (ALJs). Neither inspectors nor agency employees investigating or prosecuting a case may participate in the decision except as counsel in public proceedings or as witnesses.

Under the APA, ALJs are appointed by various agencies but are all subject to the APA formal hearing requirements. The Office of Personnel and Management (formerly the

11. Bernard Schwartz, "Adjudication and the Administrative Procedure Act," *Tulsa Law Journal* 32 (1996): 203.

Civil Service Commission) has the authority to determine their qualifications and salary. Through its Office of Administrative Law Judges, ALJs are recruited and hired. The minimum criteria to be an ALJ is that one must be an attorney with seven or more years of "qualifying experience" (i.e., court experience, such as representing clients at trial or on appeal).[12] In 2007 there were 1,343 ALJs; 84% (1,095) worked in the Social Security Administration. Indeed, as Jeffrey S. Lubbers describes in the following essay, growth in the number of ALJs has been in the Social Security Administration. Table 7.1 lists the number of ALJs by agency for 2007. This should give you some idea about the distribution of ALJs among federal agencies.

Deregulation, the dominant regulatory approach in the U.S. from the late 1970s to the present, brought with it two developments that reopened concerns about the impartiality of agency decision makers. One, discussed in the next essay by Jeffrey Lubbers, concerns the "drift away from APA-ALJs." Lubbers, along with other administrative law scholars, questions the wisdom of non-ALJs conducting federal agencies outside the APA requirements. Bernard Schwartz documents that we now have twice as many non-APA "administrative judges" than APA-ALJs. They are deciding 83 different categories of cases totaling 350,000 individual cases a year, with the largest number of non-ALJs serving as "immigration judges" in the Department of Justice. With this kind of outsourcing, are people in these cases

12. Jeffrey Lubbers, "Federal Administrative Law Judges: A Focus on Our Invisible Judiciary," *Administrative Law Review* 33 (1981): 109.

Table 7.1 Number of Administrative Law Judges by Agency, 2007 (December)

Commodity Futures Trading Commission	2
Department of Agriculture	3
Department of Education	1
Department of Homeland Security / U.S. Coast Guard	7
Department of Housing and Urban Development	1
Department of Justice / Drug Enforcement Administration	2
Department of Justice / Executive Office for Immigration Review	1
Department of Labor	41
Department of the Interior	11
Department of Transportation / Office of the Secretary	3
DHHS / Department Appeals Board	7
DHHS / Food and Drug Administration	1
DHHS / Office of Medicare Hearings and Appeals	65
Environmental Protection Agency	4
Federal Communications Commission	2
Federal Energy Regulatory Commission	14
Federal Labor Relations Authority	4
Federal Maritime Commission	1
Federal Mine Safety and Health Review Commission	9
Federal Trade Commission	1
International Trade Commission	4
National Labor Relations Board	41
National Transportation Safety Board	4
Occupational Safety and Health Review Commission	12
Office of Financial Institution Adjudication	1
Securities and Exchange Commission	4
Small Business Administration	1
Social Security Administration	1095
United States Postal Service	1
TOTAL	1343

Source: Correspondence with the Office of Personnel and Management, June 25, 2008.

receiving "second-class administrative justice?"[13] A second development that was especially problematic during the Ronald Reagan and George H.W. Bush administrations is the extent to which agencies impose subtle incentives on ALJs hearing social security claims cases to deny benefits. The Association of Administrative Law Judges, a national organization, said the Social Security Administration "imposes a monthly quota of cases and retaliates against those who do not meet it."[14] *Ventura v. Shalala* (1995), a U.S. Court of Appeals case, discusses the right a claimant has to an unbiased ALJ. In this case the plaintiffs were seeking disability insurance benefits under the Social Security Administration.

APA-Adjudication: Is the Quest for Uniformity Faltering?

JEFFREY S. LUBBERS

10 *Administrative Law Journal American University* 65 (1996)

. . . A look at the number of ALJs in the federal government shows a tremendous increase since 1947—from 196 to 1,333 in March 1996. Most of this increase, however, occurred between 1947 and October 1982, when the number was 1,183. Since then, the number has increased only 11.3% in 14 years. Moreover, all of the growth has been in the Social Security Administration. In 1947, only 13 of 196 (6.6%) were in the SSA. In 1978, the number had jumped to 660 of 1,071 (61.6%); in 1984, 760 of 1,121 (67.8%); and today, 1,060 of 1,333 (79.5%). Since 1978, in fact, there has been a steady decline in the number of non-SSA ALJs—from 410 to 361 in 1984 and 273 in 1996. Factor in the other two largest employers of ALJs, the NLRB and the Department of Labor, and the decline of the government-wide use of ALJs is even more apparent. Apart from the big three agencies, there were 170 ALJs in other agencies in 1984; now there are 155. And as of March 1996, the number of ALJs working for economic regulatory agencies had declined to 3.3 percent.

To some extent, of course, this decrease reflects the effect of deregulation—the elimination of agencies like the CAB and ICC. But the number of agencies and departments employing ALJs has stayed about the same (approximately 30) since 1978. What is striking is how few ALJs are employed by most administrative and regulatory agencies. For example, the Departments of Agriculture, Commerce, Education, HUD, and Justice have only four, one, one, five, and six ALJs, respectively. The Departments of Defense, State, and Veterans Affairs have none. The five bank regulatory agencies share two; major adjudicatory and enforcement agencies like the CFTC, FTC, ITC, MSPB, and SBA have one or two each; and the CPSC, EEOC, NRC, and Postal Rate Commission have none.

This is not because agencies have stopped adjudicating. They have just limited their reliance on ALJs. "Non-ALJ adjudicators" are sprouting faster than tulips in Holland. Nearly three thousand such officials are deciding cases every day, and the number is growing. John Frye's study, using 1989 data gathered by the Administrative Conference,* identified 2,692 non-ALJ adjudicators along with others not counted.

Their numbers have surely grown since then with the rapid growth in immigration and asylum judges and the Agriculture Department's newly created National Appeals Division (NAD). The Department of Justice now relies on about 200 immigration judges and 260 asylum officers, and the NAD is staffed with about 80 "hearing officers" across the country to hear appeals from departmental actions.

In addition, there are numerous other large groupings of "administrative judges" (AJs). There are about 80 AJs who serve on Boards of Contract Appeals in about a dozen agencies. The Department of Commerce employs over 50 administrative patent judges and administrative trademark judges; the Defense Department uses hundreds of hearing officers (but no ALJs); and the Department of Veterans Affairs has a 55-member Board of Veterans Appeals (but no ALJs). The MSPB has 55 administrative judges that hear federal employee appeals (and one ALJ); the EEOC uses some 95 to 100 AJs (but no ALJs); and the NRC uses 11 full-time and 22 part-time Atomic and Safety Licensing Board members (and, currently, no ALJs).

---

* John H. Frye III, "Survey of Non-ALJ Hearing Programs in the Federal Government," *Administrative Law Review* 44 (1992): 261.

* William F. Funk, "Close Enough for Government Work? Using Informal Procedures for Imposing Administrative Penalties," *Seton Hall Law Review* 24 (1993): 1.

---

13. Schwartz, "Adjudication and the Administrative Procedure Act."

14. "Judges Who Decide Social Security Claims Say Agency Goads Them to Deny Benefits," *New York Times*, January 8, 1989.

Congress has even gone so far as to approve the use of non-ALJ adjudicators and non-APA procedures in the assessment of agency civil penalties.* Debarment and suspension of government contractors and grantees also continue to be heard and decided by non-ALJ adjudicators.*

In short, the initial trial level in federal agency adjudication is becoming almost as variegated as the agency appellate structures—which have always been "unregulated" by the APA.

Reasons for the Drift

Why has this occurred? Why have most agencies (with congressional endorsement) voted with their feet by running away from the ALJ program? In my opinion, it is because of a perception that, compared to non-ALJ adjudicators, ALJs are less desirable because of their cost, restrictions on their selection, and their effective immunity from performance management.

A. Cost Considerations

ALJs' salaries range from $75,205 to $115,700 but, after six years, most have reached the level of $104,130. On the other hand, most AJs are paid in the GS-12 to GS-15 range ($41,104 to $88,326).

B. Selection Difficulties

It is very difficult for agencies to hire the applicant (or even the type of applicant) they want for an ALJ position. The strict provisions of the competitive civil service, as historically applied to ALJ hiring, require agencies to select from a register of candidates served up by the Office of Personnel Management (OPM). The ranking process for the register highly values litigating experience (without sufficiently distinguishing between types of litigators) and service as a veteran, while giving short shrift to special expertise and diversity values. This means that an agency seeking a judge with an economics or social services background, for example, cannot hire one from the register unless such a person happens to be at the top of the list. It also means that women (who tend to lack veterans' preference points) have become very underrepresented in the ALJ corps.* Contrast these hurdles with the ease with which an

agency can typically hire lawyers—including lawyers who serve as non-ALJ adjudicators. Because lawyers are in the "excepted" service, they can be hired by agencies almost as readily as they are by private-sector firms.

C. Management Issues

ALJs are exempt by statute and by OPM regulation from both the first-year probationary period and the performance ratings that are applied to most other federal employees. AJs, on the other hand, typically can be made subject to performance measures. Although the APA does provide a process for disciplining or removing ALJs "for cause," a series of decisions by the MSPB makes it difficult for agencies to successfully bring complaints against ALJs for lack of productivity.

Agency managers obviously have great incentive to opt for using hearing officers who can be selected strategically, who are easier to manage, and who can be procured at bargain rates. Is it any wonder that the ALJ (outside of the SSA with its burgeoning caseload due to the graying of America) is becoming an endangered species? And what is the outlook for the 80% of the ALJs at the SSA? Already there are indications that the new SSA is looking for ways to reduce its dependence on ALJs.*

The Need to Redirect Reform Efforts

Surprisingly little attention is being paid to the issues of whether, and to what extent, this tide of balkanization and antipathy toward using ALJs should be stemmed. Unlike the last major legislative attempt to amend the APA that occurred from 1979 to 1981, none of the leading regulatory reform bills addresses agency adjudication. Various bills address the particular wish lists of specific groups of non-ALJ adjudicators. Immigration judges, MSPB AJs, and DVA AJs have all promoted legislation to increase their pay and status (although none of these bills has proposed making them ALJs). But the only major legislation to address ALJs and APA adjudication in recent years is the "ALJ Corps" bill that (in various iterations) has received serious consideration for over 15 years.

This legislation would extract the ALJs out of their employing agencies and locate them in a new agency

---

* Brian D. Shannon, "Debarment and Suspension Revisited: Fewer Eggs in the Basket?" *Catholic University Law Review* 44 (1995): 363.

* Paul R. Verkuil et al., "The Federal Administrative Judiciary," *ACUS Recommendations & Reports 770*, 1992, 960–64. See also Ann Crittenden, Op-Ed, "Quotas for Good Old Boys," *Wall Street Journal*, June 14, 1995.

* See Social Security Administration, Pub. No. 01–005, *Plan for a New Disability Claim Process* (September 1994). The description of the proposed new "administrative appeals process" (at 33–34) includes the use of an "adjudication officer" who will handle the initial aspects of the case for the ALJ and who will have full authority to grant (but not deny) claims. While apparently intended to be a subordinate assistant to the ALJ, it is not difficult to envision that greater reliance on adjudication officers might reduce the number of ALJs at the SSA.

that would be headed by a presidentially appointed Chief ALJ. Agencies that need an ALJ would have one assigned by the Corps. The newer versions of the bill have sought to address agency concerns by dividing the Corps into specialized panels, creating a complaint handling board, allowing the Chief ALJ to be selected from managerial ranks, and capping the Corps's budget. Nevertheless, the bill remains controversial and has its fervent supporters and detractors.*

While I see some merit in the latest versions of the proposal and believe that the model has worked well in some states, I do not think the legislation is the answer to the problems sketched out above. For one thing, the sponsors have never come to grips with the reality that 80% of the Corps would serve in the SSA panel. And SSA benefit cases—typically brief, nonadversarial hearings without government counsel involved—are distinctly different from most of the other cases that would be heard by the Corps.

More fundamentally, enactment of the Corps bill would make agencies even less inclined to go the APA/ALJ route. At least agencies now know that cases assigned to ALJs are assigned to their own ALJs—who are presumably expert in the agency's programs. If agencies had less confidence in the expertise of Corps ALJs and even less say in their selection than they do now, wouldn't agencies also tend to work harder to avoid APA/ALJ hearings than they do under the current flawed system?

Therefore, I do not believe the Corps bill is the cure for what ails the current federal administrative adjudicative system. Rather I would suggest a new reform agenda designed to return to a more ordered and consistent approach to formal administrative adjudication across the government.

Agenda for Reform

The basic purpose of the following proposals is to reinvigorate the demand among agencies and their congressional overseers and patrons for using ALJs. This

requires making ALJs more cost-effective by reducing their monetary and managerial costs and by increasing the perceived value of their work product. I am pursuing this because I think highly skilled, independent, bureaucratically separate, specialized, highly regarded administrative judges are a crucial linchpin of our system of administration. I believe the 1941 Attorney General's Committee's vision of a uniform professional cadre of such officers was a good one and I would like to see us return to it. To those ends, I suggest the following steps be taken.

A. Establish an Administrative Office for Agency Adjudication

Such an office—similar to the Administrative Office of the U.S. Courts and to the original Attorney General's Committee proposal for an Office of Fair Administrative Procedure—would bring a higher level of attention to the ALJ system than has been possible through the years by the chronically understaffed, low-profile Office of Administrative Law Judges in OPM.

B. Return to a Multitiered Corps of ALJs

The Attorney General's Committee originally suggested a two-level structure, allowing agencies with a high volume of small cases to seek permission from the Office of Fair Administrative Procedure to use the lower salary level. The APA's implementation went even further. As then-Professor Scalia pointed out in 1979, "As late as 1953, the 294 APA hearing examiners were distributed broadly among five grade levels from GS-11 to GS-15." He went on to call "for a return to a multi-grade structure."

Instead the ALJ organizations persuaded Congress to go the other way and do away with the remaining two-step (GS-15/GS-16) division between "benefits" judges (primarily SSA judges) and the other "regulatory" judges. The current salary provisions retain this unitary model by providing for automatic step increases for seniority and a higher grade only for chief judges. I agree with Justice Scalia, and would reverse this trend. I would permit agencies the leeway to seek permission to create categories of ALJs on a much wider salary range—say from GS-12 to the SES. The title of ALJ (along with the protections and status it affords) would continue, and the wider salary range would afford agencies and applicants more flexibility while also creating a real career path for aspiring administrative judges.

---

* Indeed, there is now division within the ranks of the Federal Administrative Law Judges Conference (FALJC), which in prior years had been in the forefront of support for the Corps bill. In 1994, the Executive Committee of the FALJC voted not to endorse S. 486, which had passed the Senate in 1993. H. R. 1802, as introduced in the 104th Congress, was identical to S. 486. See Letter from William Pope, President, FALJC, to FALJC membership (July 24, 1995) (on file with author). The main points of disagreement were with (1) the selection process for the chief and division chief judges, (2) the chief judge's power to order transfers and reductions in force, and (3) the restrictive appropriations cap.

C. Introduce More Flexibility into the Selection Process

Ideally, the hiring process for ALJs should be removed from the tight strictures of the civil service selection process, as is the current process for hiring federal lawyers, now generally applicable to non-lawyers, so that a more flexible system of merit selection can be devised. I would retain a screening step (perhaps by the new Administrative Office) but would allow agencies much greater leeway to choose from among prescreened qualified applicants. If the current basic system is maintained, the certificates presented to agencies should be enlarged, veterans preference for this position should be reduced or eliminated, and the ranking process should give greater weight to specialized experience. A probationary period should also be considered.

D. Allow Peer-Review-Based Evaluation

As I have suggested before, the current prohibitions of performance appraisals and ratings should be eliminated and a system of peer review, supervised by chief ALJs, should be established. Many federal and state courts have established judicial evaluation programs, and ALJs in a large number of states are also subject to performance evaluation. Such a system should be feasible and consistent with judicial independence values in the federal ALJ program as well.

E. Maintain Other Key APA Protections of ALJ Independence

ALJs should continue to be located in organizationally distinct offices; they should not be assigned any extrajudicial duties; and the "for cause" disciplinary hearing process at MSPB should be retained.

F. Encourage Experimentation with Pools or "Minicorps"

One of the attractive arguments for the ALJ Corps bill is its potential to introduce economies of scale into programs with a small number of ALJs. The banking agencies have already established such a pool, and there are other agencies (i.e., trade agencies, business-related agencies) that might benefit from such an arrangement.

G. Give ALJs More Authority

Agency heads should be encouraged to delegate more decisional authority to ALJs—through self- or legislatively imposed limitations on agency review. The need for political control of agency adjudication diminishes in high-volume, fact-based enforcement and benefit adjudications. ALJ decisions should ordinarily speak for the agency, except in rare cases where a new major policy issue is involved or where the ALJ's fealty to established law and policy is questioned.

More courtroom authority is also needed. In this day of metal detectors in courtrooms, ALJs need more authority to control hearings. This should include more power to sanction disruptive or frivolous behavior and more authority to reject duplicative or irrelevant evidence.

H. Increase Opportunities for Training and Continuing Legal Education

A professional group of judges requires initial and periodic training in legal, technical, and information resources management issues. Few agencies can afford either initial or periodic training at present. This is pennywise and pound-foolish.

I. Enlarge the Role of ALJs in ADR

A few years ago, we used to say that Alternative Dispute Resolution [ADR] was the "wave of the future." But it is here today, and many agencies have developed ADR programs using mediators and other outside "neutrals."* With appropriate safeguards, ALJs can and should serve as neutrals in settlement judge programs, minitrials, and even negotiated rulemaking.

J. Mandate the Use of ALJs

The Administrative Conference has already suggested that, even under current circumstances, Congress should take pains to ensure that certain types of cases be heard by ALJs.* If all or most of the foregoing nine recommendations are acted upon, it will be feasible for Congress to mandate that most agency formal hearings be conducted by ALJs. This would mean converting many of the current AJ positions to ALJ positions.

---

* Admin. Conf. of the U.S., "Toward Improved Agency Dispute Resolution: Implementing the ADR Act," February 1995.

* These include those cases likely to involve:
  a. substantial impact on personal liberties or freedom;
  b. orders that carry with them a finding of criminal-like culpability;
  c. imposition of sanctions with substantial economic effect; or
  d. determination of discrimination under civil rights or other analogous laws.

ACUS Recommendation 92–7, supra note 65, at pt. I.

Conclusion

The current decline in agency use of administrative law judges to conduct formal adjudications poses a threat to the uniformity and consistency of administrative decisionmaking procedure envisioned by the framers of the APA. To reverse this trend, regulatory reformers need to refocus their attention on the issue and sponsor a series of interrelated improvements to the ALJ program.

Despite the need for reform we see a continuing trend towards reducing ALJ oversight The Office of Personnel Management, responsible for maintaining the ALJ program and keeping a register of qualified applicants, closed its Office of Administrative Law Judges in 2003. In 2005, the American Bar Association adopted a recommendation "encourage[ing] Congress to establish The Administrative Law Judge Conference of the United States as an independent agency to assume the responsibility of the United States Office of Personnel Management with respect to Administrative Law Judges including their testing, selection, and appointment."[15]

And some substantive decisions of ALJ hearings have also received criticism. ALJs, particularly in the Social Security Administration, regularly exercise discretion when interpreting (medical) evidence and make innumerable credibility determinations. Even though there are broad rules to direct their exercise of discretion, the possibility of "bias" creeping in is high. The absence of a code of conduct or a code of judicial ethics for administrative law judges are considered to be quite problematic.[16]

The next case gives you a glimpse at the actual workings of an administrative law hearing. Here the claimant argues that the ALJ was biased. Note that the court in this case did not employ technical definitions of "prejudgment" and "improper interest." The court simply concluded that the judge did not treat this claimant fairly. Do we believe that other ALJs prone to abusive behavior will pay attention to this kind of appellate court response and

---

15. See "Recommendation" adopted by the House of Delegates, American Bar Association (August 8–9, 2005).

16. Jason D. Vendel, "General Bias and Administrative Law Judges: Is There a Remedy for Social Security Disability Claimants?" *Cornell Law Review* 90 (2005): 769.

reform themselves without policing from the courts? It is a sad but indisputable fact that most people cannot afford to litigate such cases, and the courts do not have time to review in detail every administrative result.

Ventura v. Shalala

55 F.3D 900, UNITED STATES COURT OF APPEALS FOR THE THIRD CIRCUIT (1995)

[In this unusual opinion, the court voided the results of a hearing on a social security claim before an ALJ on the basis that the ALJ was not impartial. The evidence for his partiality is contained in the excerpts from the transcript. We have omitted without ellipses the profusion of citations to the transcript of the administrative hearing.]

Circuit Judge H. Lee Sarokin delivered the opinion of the court

Applicants for social security disability payments, most of whom are truly ill or disabled, are entitled to be treated with respect and dignity no matter what the merits of their respective claims. This is especially so at a time they are most vulnerable when representing themselves or being represented by lay-persons. Notwithstanding and recognizing the time pressures imposed upon those hearing the huge volume of such claims, rudeness, impatience, or outright bias cannot be tolerated. We hold that claimant in the instant case did not receive the full and fair hearing to which he was entitled. Accordingly, we remand the case for a new hearing before another administrative law judge.

I

Stephen Ventura ("claimant") applied for disability insurance benefits under Title II of the Social Security Act, alleging disability because of back injuries. The state agency handling claimant's application denied his claim initially and upon reconsideration. Claimant requested a hearing before an administrative law judge ("ALJ"). The ALJ issued a decision finding claimant able to work. The Appeals Council, however, vacated the decision of the ALJ and remanded the case for a new hearing because the ALJ had taken the testimony of a medical expert and a vocational expert outside the presence of claimant. After holding a new hearing, the

record fully and fairly and to consider seriously the findings of a treating physician. Importantly, the representative had already provided the ALJ with information concerning claimant's visits to the veterans' hospital and had agreed to provide any additional information requested by the ALJ.

IV

We now turn to the question of whether claimant is entitled to a new hearing because of the ALJ's conduct. We hold that the ALJ's offensive conduct prevented claimant from receiving a full and fair hearing and, therefore, a new hearing must be held before another ALJ to determine whether claimant is entitled to disability benefits.

The district court's decision in *Rosa v. Bowen*, 677 F. Supp. 782 (D.N.J. 1988), is instructive. There, the district court addressed the issue of whether a disability claimant was accorded a full and fair hearing. Upon reviewing the transcript of the hearing, the court found that claimant's hearing "was shameful in its atmosphere of alternating indifference, personal musings, impatience and condescension." . . .

V

Because of the ALJ's offensive and unprofessional conduct, claimant in the instant case did not receive the full and fair hearing to which he was entitled. We hold, therefore, that claimant is entitled to a new hearing before another ALJ. In light of our disposition of this case, we need not reach the merits of the other issues raised on appeal. Accordingly, we reverse the district court's grant of summary judgment in favor of the Secretary and remand the case for further proceedings consistent with this opinion.

Unfortunately, the judge's conduct in *Ventura v. Shalala* is not an isolated incident. Over the years, questions of bias by ALJ's in social security disability hearings have raised a serious problem.[17] It is relatively easy to prove bias if a hearing officer or an ALJ has a stake in the outcome of the case. But what if the bias is less easily identifiable? What if an ALJ loses his or her objectivity because of his or her own perceptions about the disability claimant? This was the allegation in *Pronti v.*

17. Ibid.

Barnhart, 339 F. Supp.2d 480 (2004). In this case, ALJ Franklin Russell had made some inflammatory comments in cases in which he rejected disability claims, but did nothing as egregious as the ALJ in the *Shalala* case. Anne Pronti alleged that he was biased, in part because he regularly attacked the credibility of the claimants and was alleged to have dismissed the opinions of the claimants' physicians. How could one prove such a "hidden" bias? Pronti filed "numerous affidavits from lawyers who practice before ALJ Russell"[18] asserting his bias. Similarly Pronti documented the rate at which Judge Russell had denied benefits. According to the lawyers who supported Pronti's case with affidavits, Judge Russell had an exceptionally high rate of denial: His 63% denial rate was well above 43% denial rate of the judges in his region and almost double the 34% denial rate in the country as a whole! The district court in the case sided with Pronti and remanded the case back to the Social Security Administration with specific instructions for the agency.

ANOTHER VIEW OF INFORMALITY AND FORMALITY IN ADMINISTRATIVE HEARINGS

Rarely in administrative practice do claimants go to a formal hearing without first trying, and failing, to settle the issue informally. We conclude this chapter on the elements of hearings with an example of an official policy, in this case dealing with the problem of sexual harassment, that provides for both less and more formal ways of making complaints and resolving them. The time frame within which this policy evolved is suggestive. Congress passed Title VII of the Civil Rights Act in 1964. In the 1970s the women's movement successfully lobbied to classify sexual harassment as a form of sex discrimination prohibited in Title VII.[19] In 1980, in the last months of the Carter Administration, the Equal Employment Opportunity Commission (EEOC) published its first guidelines on sexual harassment. Note that it took well into the

18. Ibid.
19. See Catharine A. MacKinnon, *Sexual Harassment of Working Women* (New Haven, Conn.: Yale University Press, 1979).

1980s before even progressive institutions like the University of Massachusetts adopted the kind of policy reproduced here.

EEOC Guidelines on Discrimination Because of Sex[20]

§1604. 11 Sexual harassment.

a. Harassment on the basis of sex is a violation of Sec. 703 of Title VII.* Unwelcome sexual advances, requests for sexual favors, and other verbal or physical conduct of a sexual nature constitute sexual harassment when (1) submission to such conduct is made either explicitly or implicitly a term or condition of an individual's employment, (2) submission to or rejection of such conduct by an individual is used as the basis for employment decisions affecting such individual, or (3) such conduct has the purpose or effect of unreasonably interfering with an individual's work performance or creating an intimidating, hostile, or offensive working environment.

b. In determining whether alleged conduct constitutes sexual harassment, the Commission will look at the record as a whole and at the totality of the circumstances, such as the nature of the sexual advances and the context in which the alleged incidents occurred. The determination of the legality of a particular action will be made from the facts, on a case by case basis.

c. Applying general Title VII principles, an employer, employment agency, joint apprenticeship committee or labor organization (hereinafter collectively referred to as "employer") is responsible for its acts and those of its agents and supervisory employees with respect to sexual harassment regardless of whether the specific acts complained of were authorized or even forbidden by the employer and regardless of whether the employer knew or should have known of their occurrence. The Commission will examine the circumstances of the particular employment relationship and the job functions performed by the individual in determining whether an individual acts in either a supervisory or agency capacity.

d. With respect to conduct between fellow employees, an employer is responsible for acts of sexual harassment in the workplace where the employer (or its agents or supervisory employees) knows or should have known of the conduct, unless it can show that it took immediate and appropriate corrective action.

e. An employer may also be responsible for the acts of nonemployees, with respect to sexual harassment of employees in the workplace, where the employer (or its agents or supervisory employees) knows or should have known of the conduct and fails to take immediate and appropriate corrective action. In reviewing these cases the Commission will consider the extent of the employer's control and any other legal responsibility which the employer may have with respect to the conduct of such non-employees.

f. Prevention is the best tool for the elimination of sexual harassment. An employer should take all steps necessary to prevent sexual harassment from occurring, such as affirmatively raising the subject, expressing strong disapproval, developing appropriate sanctions, informing employees of their right to raise and how to raise the issue of harassment under Title VII, and developing methods to sensitize all concerned.

g. Other related practices: Where employment opportunities or benefits are granted because of an individual's submission to the employer's sexual advances or requests for sexual favors, the employer may be held liable for unlawful sex discrimination against other persons who were qualified for but denied that employment opportunity or benefit.

As you read the University of Massachusetts at Amherst Sexual Harassment Policy, below, consider the following questions. Does this University's procedure satisfy the EEOC Guidelines? If so, why? If not, why not? What impact does the informal process have on the formal procedures? The University of Massachusetts's policy states that there are two modes of resolution for formal complaints—mediation and a hearing. How is mediation different from a hearing in this context? And finally, think about what impact mediation, an informal procedure, has on the formal hearing process.

---

20. See Billie Wright and Linda Weiner, *The Lecherous Professor* (Boston: Beacon Press, 1984), 189–193.

* The principles involved here continue to apply to race, color, religion, or other origin.

University of Massachusetts at Amherst Sexual Harassment Policy (October 2004)

POLICY

The University of Massachusetts Amherst is committed to providing faculty, staff and students with an environment where they may pursue their careers or studies without being sexually harassed. Sexual harassment of or by any member of the University community is unacceptable and will not be tolerated. It is illegal and constitutes a violation of Title VII of the Civil Rights Act of 1964, Title IX of the Education Amendments of 1972, and Massachusetts G.L.c.151B and 151C.

For the purposes of this policy, it is defined as follows:

Unwelcomed sexual advances, requests for sexual favors, and other verbal or physical conduct of a sexual nature constitute sexual harassment when: 1) submission to or rejection of such conduct is made either explicitly or implicitly a term or condition of an individual's employment or academic work; or 2) submission to or rejection of such conduct by an individual is used as the basis for employment or academic decisions affecting such individual; or 3) such conduct has the purpose or effect of unreasonably interfering with an individual's performance or creating an intimidating, hostile or sexually offensive working or academic environment.

Examples of sexual harassment include, but are not limited to the following:

repeated unwanted sexual flirtations, advances or propositions;

continued or repeated verbal abuse or innuendo of a sexual nature;

uninvited physical contact such as touching, hugging, patting, brushing or pinching;

verbal comments of a sexual nature about an individual's body or sexual terms used to describe an individual;

display of pictures, posters or cartoons that a reasonable person would find offensive or sexually suggestive;

continued or repeated jokes, language, epithets or remarks of a sexual nature;

prolonged staring or leering;

making obscene gestures or suggestive or insulting sounds;

demand for sexual favors accompanied by an implied or overt threat concerning an individual's employment or academic status or promises of preferential treatment; indecent exposure.

In determining whether an alleged incident constitutes sexual harassment, those entrusted with administering this policy will look at the totality of the circumstances, such as the nature of the sexual advances and the context in which the alleged incidents occurred. The final decision regarding a suitable penalty will be made from the finding of fact on a case-by-case basis and from any record of previous sexual harassment by the Respondent.

The Equal Opportunity and Diversity Office, . . . will be responsible for administering this policy and its procedures. The Associate Chancellor for Equal Opportunity and Diversity will serve as Chair of the Sexual Harassment Board . . . but may delegate all or part of this role to a designee. In such instances, overall decision making authority for matters related to this policy and procedures will continue to rest with the Associate Chancellor. The Equal Opportunity and Diversity Office, in concert with the Chancellor, the Deputy Chancellor, and Vice Chancellors will see that all supervisors on the Amherst campus receive information and training concerning sexual harassment and the responsibilities of supervisors when complaints are received.

PROCEDURES

I. Purpose and Scope

This grievance procedure is intended to provide a fair, prompt and reliable determination about whether the University's sexual harassment policy has been violated. Anyone who, at the time of the alleged harassment, was either employed by or enrolled at the University of Massachusetts Amherst may file a complaint alleging violation of this policy . . . . No University employee or student is exempt from the jurisdiction of this policy.

In most instances, complaints will be initiated by the target of the alleged harassment. However, the University reserves the right to initiate a formal grievance . . . when, in the opinion of the Chair of the Sexual Harassment Board, it is appropriate to do so . . .

As in any grievance procedure justice requires that the legal rights, as well as the right to academic freedom, of the Complainant and the Respondent be fully assured. The University will make every effort to protect these rights and will knowingly undertake no action that threatens or compromises them. Notwithstanding, nothing in these procedures is intended to prevent the University administration from taking appropriate interim measures to protect one or more of the parties until such time final adjudication regarding the complaint has been reached.

This procedure is not intended to impair or limit the right of anyone to seek a remedy available under state or federal law. A Complainant may file a complaint with an external agency to meet state and federal agency deadlines without jeopardizing his or her right to a University hearing . . . Upon official notification that an individual has filed with an external agency, the University will inquire if the Complainant wishes to continue with the internal grievance process. Should the Complainant seek to discontinue the internal process, the University will nonetheless continue to fact find and take appropriate measures.

When the Respondent in a formal grievance is an undergraduate student, the Complainant should contact the Dean of Students Office, . . . all such complaints will be handled in accordance with procedures as described in the Code of Student Conduct. When the Respondent is a graduate student, the Complainant will be referred to the Dean of the Graduate School . . . (In instances in which a Respondent is both a student and an employee, the Chair of the Sexual Harassment Board shall review the circumstances of the case and determine which grievance procedure is appropriate.)

II. Confidentiality

All parties involved in any aspect of this process will act at all times to preserve the confidentiality of these proceedings. Information will be shared with those individuals who have a legitimate and operational need to be informed, and to the extent that it is necessary to maintain the effectiveness of this process. Individuals found to have violated the confidentiality of this process may be subject to disciplinary proceedings consistent with the provisions of their collective bargaining agreement or other applicable administrative rules and regulations.

III. Deadlines

A Complainant will have twelve months following an incident to initiate a complaint under this policy and procedures unless he or she can show good reason for having that deadline waived . . . Legal counsel may be consulted in making this determination.

. . .

IV. Requirements for Participation & Withdrawals

If a Respondent fails to answer a charge or to participate in this process, the Chair of the Sexual Harassment Board will notify his or her Vice Chancellor of that fact.

Failure to respond to a claim or to appear at a hearing will be considered a breach of responsibility and could result in disciplinary action. Furthermore, a Respondent will not prevent this process from proceeding by his or her silence or absence; failure to respond to a complaint or to appear at a hearing may result in the process proceeding solely on the basis of the Complainant's testimony and evidence.

A Complainant may request to withdraw a formal grievance after it has been filed by submitting written reasons for the withdrawal to the Chair of the Sexual Harassment Board. The Chair will be responsible for notifying the Respondent of the request to withdraw. The Respondent must provide written agreement to the withdrawal before the charges are dropped. A Respondent who does not agree to the withdrawal request must provide written reasons to the Chair of the Sexual Harassment Board who, after consultation with appropriate administrators including, where necessary, legal counsel, will issue a written determination to the parties regarding the status of the claim. A Complainant may not interrupt the process simply by failing to appear at the hearing or other required meetings. Failure to appear may result in the hearing proceeding solely on the basis of the Respondent's testimony and evidence.

None of the above actions should be construed to impinge upon the right of the University to initiate or continue a claim in spite of a request to withdraw when, in the opinion of the Chair of the Sexual Harassment Board, the allegations are sufficiently egregious to merit further action on the part of the University. The alleged victim will be relied upon to serve as a witness under these circumstances.

V. Retaliation

No individual shall be retaliated or discriminated against for participating in these procedures. Any act of retaliation directed against person(s) participating in these procedures is illegal. Complaints of retaliation should be addressed to the Associate Chancellor for Equal Opportunity & Diversity who will determine the appropriate action.

VI. Penalties

The penalties for those found to have violated this policy may include, but will not be limited to, any one or combination of the following: verbal admonition, written warning placed in the personnel file, probation, suspension without pay, demotion, removal from administrative duties, and dismissal. Any disciplinary measures imposed

will be consistent with applicable union contractual provisions.

VII. Filing Sexual Harassment Complaints

The University recognizes that it has a responsibility
to provide a procedure for rapid and equitable resolution of all sexual harassment complaints. In many
instances, resolution can be reached without the need
for formal measures. The goal in all instances is to ensure
that inappropriate and offensive behavior is stopped. To
assist Complainants in resolving sexual harassment complaints, the University has established both informal and
formal procedures, and has identified a group of individuals, "Complaint Handlers" (see Appendix A [omitted]),
who can advise parties of appropriate options and procedures. In addition, the University has identified volun-
teers from the University community who are willing to
serve as "Support and Referral Contacts" (see Appendix
B [omitted]); Support and Referral Contacts, who can
serve the needs of either Complainants or Respondents,
are available to accompany participants to meetings or
formal hearings and can provide support throughout
the process.

VII.A. Initiating a Complaint

Complainants may initially consult with a Support and
Referral Contact . . . who can provide information
about the complaint handling system and options available for resolution. Individuals may alternatively initiate
discussions regarding a potential complaint directly with
their departmental supervisor; department head or chair;
or similarly situated administrator with line authority
(these individuals may collectively be referred to as
"Complaint Handlers" . . .); or Complainants may
directly contact the Equal Opportunity & Diversity Office
(EO&D). [Note: The Appendices referred to in this paragraph will be updated annually and widely published.]
All of the above-named individuals can provide advice
regarding available options and procedures, and assist in
determining how to proceed with the complaint (i.e.,
informally or formally).

The Complaint Handler (initial intake person as identified in the preceding paragraph) will assess the matter;
determine what immediate action must be taken; and
advise the Complainant about how to proceed—informally, using one of the methods described in Section
VII.B.1-3 or formally, using the methods described in
Sections VII.C and VIII.

The Complaint Handler may also consult with the
Chair of the Sexual Harassment Board to determine the
appropriateness of proceeding under these procedures.

The Chair of the Sexual Harassment Board has the
authority to discontinue processing a complaint. This
decision is final and not subject to appeal.

The Complaint Handler, in consultation with the
Chair of the Sexual Harassment Board, will identify the
appropriate fact finding mechanism. Fact-finding will be
done either internally (by a University staff member) or
externally (by a person whose services will be retained
specifically for this purpose). When fact-finding results in
a written report, this report will be forwarded to the
Chair of the Sexual Harassment Board and may later be
introduced into the record during a formal hearing
process.

Complaint Handlers must file a written report of all
complaints, regardless of their disposition, with the Equal
Opportunity and Diversity Office who will maintain a
record of all informal complaints and formal grievances.
Such record will include Complainants' and Respondents' names and the outcome of proceedings, including
sanctions imposed if any. At the end of every academic
year the EO&D Office will prepare an annual report of
statistics and relevant commentary for the Chancellor.
The annual report will be available to faculty, staff and
students upon written request to the Equal Opportunity
and Diversity Office. The annual report will not contain
names, but may contain other relevant statistical data
including, but not limited to, status of the parties (e.g.,
undergraduate or graduate student; classified or professional staff; or faculty); department or other campus affiliation; nature of the complaint; and outcome.

VII.B. Informal Resolution

In some circumstances informal resolution of a complaint prior to or instead of initiating the formal process
may be more satisfactory than directly proceeding to a
formal grievance. Informal resolution options include,
but are not limited to, self-help; consultation and action
at the department level; or mediation through the
Ombuds Office . . . .

VII.B.1 Self-Help

The goal in any complaint process is to stop the
harassing behavior. If a Complainant believes he or she is
experiencing inappropriate conduct and can comfortably confront the individual responsible for the inappropriate conduct, then the following steps may be taken:

confront the person(s) promptly;
inform the person(s) that the conduct is offensive,
intimidating, or embarrassing;
describe the affect of this behavior;
request that the behavior stop immediately.

The Complainant should have the above conversation with a witness present who can corroborate the exchange. If this is not possible or practical, the Complainant may write a letter incorporating the above points and give it to the person in front of a witness. The Complainant should retain a copy of this letter.

In all instances, the Complainant should document the event(s), including dates, times, places and witnesses.

If this action fails to provide the Complainant with the appropriate relief, or as an alternative to using this approach, the measures described below may be considered.

. . .

VII.B.3 Mediation

It is sometimes the case that the issue under contention can be resolved through mediation. The Ombuds Office, located in . . . , is available to provide mediation services. Ombuds Office is also prepared to provide referrals for more formal measures when circumstances warrant it.

VII.C. Formal Resolution (Filing a Formal Grievance)

Complainants who are dissatisfied with or do not wish to utilize informal resolution should consult directly with the EO&D Office to determine the appropriateness of filing a formal grievance. Although informal resolution attempts are not required prior to filing a formal grievance, they are nonetheless encouraged.

Any individual who chooses to file a formal sexual harassment grievance may do so immediately following the incident giving rise to the complaint, or following efforts to reach an informal settlement. In no event will it be filed greater than twelve months following the incident which gave rise to the complaint unless the provisions of Section III have been met. After initially meeting with the Complainant to assess the complaint, including the appropriateness of the complaint being filed under this Policy and Procedures (see Section VII.A.), the EO&D Office will advise the Complainant of appropriate next steps.

VIII. Formal Grievance Procedure

Following appropriate initial consultation with the EO&D Office, the grievance must be submitted in writing to the Chair of the Sexual Harassment Board on an official grievance form (obtainable from the EO&D Office). The grievance must clearly and concisely state a description of the matter being complained about; it may also indicate any remedy sought. The complaint form must be signed and dated by the Complainant. The Chair of the Sexual Harassment Board will provide the Respondent and the Respondent's Vice Chancellor with a copy of the complaint in a timely manner.

. . .

The fact-finder will conduct a thorough investigation and forward a written report to the Chair of the Sexual Harassment Board as quickly as possible. The Chair of the Sexual Harassment Board will review the report to determine next steps.

When a hearing is to be held, it will be conducted in accordance with the procedures outlined below.

If, consistent with Section VII.A (paragraph 3), the Chair of the Sexual Harassment Board determines that the complaint should be dismissed and a hearing should not be held, the Chair will provide written notification of this decision to the Complainant, the Respondent, and the Respondent's Vice Chancellor. This decision is final and not subject to appeal under these procedures.

The Chair of the Sexual Harassment Board will provide copies of the fact-finder's report to the Complainant and the Respondent.

VIII.A. The Sexual Harassment Board

The Sexual Harassment Board consists of fifty members of the University community, appointed by the Chancellor, each for a term of three years, which may be renewed. Every effort will be made to ensure a widely representative and diverse group. The Board will include at least eight members from each of the campus' five constituent groups, namely classified employees, faculty, graduate students, professional staff, and undergraduate students. The Chancellor will appoint remaining Board members without regard to constituent group.

Following their appointment, Board members will participate in a workshop designed to educate them about sexual harassment as well as the procedures for conducting a sexual harassment hearing.

VIII.B. The Hearing Panel

When a hearing is to be held, the Chair of the Sexual Harassment Board will appoint a three member Hearing Panel. At least one member of each Hearing Panel will be drawn from the Complainant's and Respondent's respective constituencies (that is, classified employee, faculty member, graduate or undergraduate student, or professional staff). The Chair will designate one member to serve as the Presiding Officer.

Prior to their participation in a hearing, the Chair of the Sexual Harassment Board will meet with the Hearing Panel to review sexual harassment issues and the hearing procedures.

Before the hearing is convened, the parties will receive written notification of the Panel's appointment from the Chair of the Sexual Harassment Board. Each party to the proceeding will have the right to object to the appointment of any panel member on the grounds that that member's participation would jeopardize the party's right to a fair and reliable hearing. All objections must be submitted in writing to the Chair of the Sexual Harassment Board. The Chair of the Sexual Harassment Board will determine whether objections have merit; will judge whether a panel member will be seated; and will provide the objecting party with a written decision. This decision will be final.

The Hearing Panel will hear testimony and consider evidence related to the complaint, including the written findings of fact as prepared by the fact-finder. (These findings will be provided to the Panel along with copies of the complaint and the response prior to the hearing.) The Panel will, on the basis of all relevant information and testimony before them, make a determination about whether the University policy on sexual harassment has been violated and, if so, will submit a recommendation for appropriate penalty and relief to the Chair of the Sexual Harassment Board. The Chair will review the Panel's recommendation and forward it, along with appropriate commentary, to the Respondent's Vice Chancellor.

Duties and Powers of the Presiding Officer and the Hearing Panel

The Presiding Officer will:

1. ensure an orderly presentation of all evidence;

2. ensure that the proceedings are accurately recorded; and

3. see that a fair and impartial decision based on the issues and evidence presented at the hearing is issued by the Hearing Panel.

The Hearing Panel will:

1. define issues of contention;

2. conduct a fair and impartial hearing which ensures the rights of all parties involved;

3. receive and consider all relevant evidence which reasonable people customarily rely upon in the conduct of serious business;

4. ensure that the Complainant and Respondent have full opportunity to present their positions and to present witnesses and evidence which support their positions; further, the Hearing Panel may also name individuals to appear as witnesses;

5. ask relevant questions of the Complainant, Respondent, and witnesses to elicit information which may assist the Hearing Panel in making a decision; members of the University community have a responsibility to fully cooperate with this process;

6. continue the hearing to a subsequent date if necessary to permit either party or the Panel to produce additional evidence, witnesses, or other relevant materials;

7. change the date, time or place of the hearing on its own motion or for good reason shown by either party, and with due notice to all parties;

8. permit both parties to submit written arguments following the conclusion of the hearing;

9. rule by majority vote on all questions of fact, interpretations of rules, regulations and policies, recommendations for penalties and relief, and any requests that are made during the hearing.

The Hearing Panel may consult with or have the assistance of University Legal Counsel throughout this process.

VIII.C. The Hearing

The Hearing is intended to provide a forum within which a panel of peers determines whether University policy has been violated. Both parties will be given a full and fair hearing. The proceeding, although formal, is not a court proceeding and the Hearing Panel will not be bound by the procedures and rules of evidence of a court of law. In most instances, Complainants and Respondents will be expected to speak for themselves. The Hearing Panel will hear and admit evidence which it believes is pertinent to the case.

The Hearing Panel will conduct the hearing by the following procedures:

The Chair of the Sexual Harassment Board will initially provide the Hearing Panel with copies of the complaint, the response, and the fact-finder's report; the Chair will also work with the Hearing Panel and the parties to coordinate the scheduling of the hearing. A closed hearing will be held as soon as possible following the final appointment of the Hearing Panel. The Complainant and the Respondent must submit all documents they intend to introduce at the hearing, as well as the names and affiliations of their witnesses and advocates (see Section VIII.C.5) in reasonable advance of the hearing date. Actual deadlines for submissions of these materials will be established once a hearing date has been set. The Chair of the Sexual Harassment Board will ensure that the parties and the Hearing Panel receive copies of all submitted materials. Documents not submitted in advance of the hearing may be introduced into the record on the day of the hearing provided all parties and the Panel are accorded sufficient time to review the documents and respond accordingly. In this case, the party submitting the documents must provide sufficient copies for all relevant parties.

The Hearing Panel will convene prior to the hearing date to review the complaint, the response, the fact-finder's report and all materials submitted by the parties. The Panel may, upon review of materials and witness lists submitted by the parties, identify additional witnesses they wish to call on the day of the hearing or request that the parties provide additional materials. The Presiding Officer will provide the parties with the names of additional witnesses and copies of all additional materials requested by the Panel as far in advance of the hearing as possible.

The Presiding Officer may meet with the parties prior to the hearing to review hearing procedures and to respond to any procedural matters that have arisen.

The Complainant and Respondent will have the opportunity to hear and respond to all testimony, to examine all evidence, and to present evidence and witnesses which advance arguments relevant to the issues in contention.

Each party will have the right to be accompanied and advised by two people at any stage of the proceedings. Advisors are not restricted to Support and Referral Contacts. Either one of the advisors may be an attorney. In most instances, Complainants and Respondents will be expected to speak for themselves. Advisors, including legal counsel, will not address the Hearing Panel directly except with the permission of the Panel.

The Chair of the Sexual Harassment Board must be advised as soon as possible, but in no event less than five working days in advance of the hearing date if either party will be accompanied by an attorney.

Each of the parties is responsible for informing their respective advocates and witnesses of the date, time, and place of the hearing.

If either party is a member of a collective bargaining unit, the advisors mentioned above may, upon the request of the party, be representatives of his or her union. However, neither party will be required to be advised by a union representative. When there is no request for union representation, the Chair of the Sexual Harassment Board will notify the appropriate union in writing that a hearing has been scheduled; the union will be allowed to send an observer.

The hearing will be recorded on tape by the Hearing Panel and the tapes will become the property of the University. Following the completion of the hearing, either party may have supervised access to the tapes by submitting a written request to the Chair of the Sexual Harassment Board.

The proceedings before the Hearing Panel will be as follows:

Following opening remarks, the Presiding Officer will summarize the charge(s) and ask the Respondent to either admit or challenge the allegation(s).

The Complainant will present a brief opening statement, followed by the same from the Respondent. Each party will then present their evidence and witnesses, followed by witnesses called by the Hearing Panel. Questions may be posed at any stage of the proceedings consistent with the protocol established by the Presiding Officer at the onset of the hearing process. Each party may make a brief concluding statement to the Hearing Panel.

Either party may submit a written argument following the hearing, provided he or she notifies the Presiding Officer no later than two working days after the hearing. The written argument may not introduce new information, but rather must be a summary of the information already introduced and presented. The Parties will have ten working days to submit written arguments to the Presiding Officer. The Presiding Officer will send copies of written arguments to each party.

A Hearing Panel, by a majority vote of its members, may make other rules concerning the procedure of a hearing which it deems appropriate and consistent with this Sexual Harassment Policy.

VIII.D. Decision of the Hearing Panel

Following the hearing and submission of written arguments, if any, the Hearing Panel will convene for private deliberations to determine whether the University's policy on sexual harassment has been violated. The Panel will prepare a detailed report noting its conclusion; this report will clearly state the facts of the case and the supporting evidence; the conclusion must be fully supported by the evidence elicited at the hearing. The decision of the Hearing Panel will be submitted to the Chair of the Sexual Harassment Board as soon as possible following the completion of the Panel's deliberations.

. . .

When the Panel finds a violation of the Sexual Harassment Policy has occurred, the Hearing Panel will recommend a penalty for the Respondent and relief for the Complainant if appropriate. The Chair of the Sexual Harassment Board will review the Panel's decision and provide appropriate commentary to the Vice Chancellor. This commentary may include an adjustment to the recommended penalty if, upon review of University records, it is determined that there have been past violations of this Policy by the Respondent; specific written reasons for the adjusted penalty must be provided. The Chair will subsequently forward the Hearing Panel's report, the complete record of the hearing, and appropriate commentary to the Respondent's Vice Chancellor.

The Vice Chancellor will render his or her decision in writing directly to the Complainant, the Respondent, and the Chair of the Sexual Harassment Board immediately following review of all of the materials noted above. When a violation has been found, the Vice Chancellor will be responsible for determining and implementing both the penalty and relief. The Vice Chancellor's determination of penalty and relief (including the dates by which each will be implemented) will be included in the written decision submitted to the Complainant, the Respondent, and the Chair of the Sexual Harassment Board. The Chair will notify the Hearing Panel of the final decision.

Following receipt of the Vice Chancellor's decision, the parties may request copies of any written record. Requests must be submitted in writing to the Chair of the Sexual Harassment Board.

VIII.E. Review

Within thirty days after receiving a written copy of the Vice Chancellor's decision, the Respondent, the Complainant, or the Chair of the Sexual Harassment Board may request a review by submitting a written petition to the Chancellor (who may appoint a designee to handle the review). The petition for review will set forth in detail the specific grounds upon which review is sought. The Chancellor will ensure that the Respondent's Vice Chancellor, Chair of the Sexual Harassment Board, the Hearing Panel, and the parties receive a copy of the petition. The Chancellor will review the record of the case, which includes the taped record of the hearing; documents considered by the Panel; the Panel's findings and recommendations; and any record of previous offenses. Based upon this review, the Chancellor may modify or vacate a Vice Chancellor's decision. The Chancellor may, for example, decide that the Panel's findings are unsupported by a preponderance of evidence, or that some aspect of the process violated an individual's legal rights, academic freedom, or these procedures.

The Chancellor or designee may: a) affirm or revise the decision of the Vice Chancellor; b) request specific findings from the Panel; or c) remand the case to the Chair of the Sexual Harassment Board for a new hearing before a new Hearing Panel. In the course of review, the Chancellor may consult with University Legal Counsel who will have access to the complete record of the case.

The Chancellor or designee will render a written decision in as timely a manner as possible following receipt of the petition for review and all materials relating to the grievance. The Chancellor's decision will be sent to the Respondent's Vice Chancellor, the Complainant, the Respondent, the Hearing Panel, and the Chair of the Sexual Harassment Board. The Chancellor's decision will constitute final University disposition of the matter.

IX. Records

Records of all proceedings under this Policy will be kept by the Equal Opportunity and Diversity Office and may be accessible to authorized staff as necessary. For example, records may be accessed when determining an appropriate penalty for a subsequent sexual harassment complaint; when a complaint of retaliation is made; when a decision is reviewed; or when a Respondent is a candidate for a supervisory position.

X. Standard of Proof

A violation of this Sexual Harassment Policy will be found only where there is a preponderance of evidence that a violation has occurred. The Hearing Panel, the Vice Chancellors, the Deputy Chancellor and the Chancellor will be bound to make their determinations based on this standard of proof.

Though focused on sexual harassment complaints in particular, the policy you just read has basic features of a *generic grievance procedure*: (1) it defines what type of behaviors and actors come within its jurisdiction—who may bring complaints against whom and for what reasons; (2) it describes a process for collecting evidence and filing a complaint—confidentially, records, deadlines; (3) it describes options parties may (and may not) pursue—self-help, informal resolution, mediation, formal hearing; and (4) it articulates the rights and duties of disputing parties, the role of the organization in decision making, and the relationship of the organization's internal procedure to external legal actions parties initiate in state and/or federal courts.

EXERCISES AND QUESTIONS FOR FURTHER THOUGHT

1. After the Supreme Court announced its opinion in the *Morgan* case the secretary of agriculture was so incensed that he wrote a letter to the *New York Times* publicly criticizing the Court's position. The same secretary then had to reconsider the case after the Supreme Court remanded it. Should his letter disqualify him from reconsidering the issues? See *United States v. Morgan*, 313 U.S. 409 (1941).

2. The question of bias is not specific to administrative agencies and judges of course. Recently, in *Cheney v. United States District Court for the District of Columbia*, 541 U.S. 913 (2004), Justice Antonin Scalia was asked to recuse himself by the Sierra Club, one of the parties in the case. The reason cited was that three weeks *after* the Supreme Court agreed to hear the case, Justice Scalia went on a duck-hunting trip to Louisiana with the opposing party in the case, Vice President Dick Cheney, traveling to Louisiana on Cheney's private jet. Justice Scalia declined to recuse himself and wrote in response, "if it is reasonable to think that a Supreme Court Justice can be bought so cheap, the Nation is in deeper trouble than I had imagined." He also pointed out that if he were to recuse himself, the remaining eight justices might split 4-4, resulting in a tie that would be more damaging than anything else. Who do you agree with, Scalia or the Sierra Club? Do you think Justice Scalia could be biased in the case? Or do you think, as he said, that he could not be bought so cheap? Is it really a question of bribery, or a larger question of improper influence? In any case, do you think it is ethical for a judge to have a close personal relationship with someone who happens to be defending himself and his actions in that judge's court?

3. The Employment Standards Administration (ESA) imposes and collects civil fines from those who illegally employ child laborers. Federal law requires that the fines thus collected be turned over to the administration to help reimburse its enforcement costs. Is this legally permissible? What if the fines collected amount to less than one percent of the ESA's annual budget? What if in an average year the ESA underspends its budget so that it refunds to the Treasury at the end of the year an average of five percent of its budget authorization? See *Marshall v. Jerrico, Inc.*, 446 U.S. 238 (1980).

4. Review APA section 554(d)'s restrictions on *ex parte* communications in formal hearings. At first glance the section seems to write the *Morgan* result into law. It prevents the administrative law judge from consulting others about the facts of the case off the record without giving the parties a chance to rebut, and it prohibits the investigator or prosecutor from influencing the final decision. Note, however, that the politically appointed members of the agencies, who make the final decisions, are exempted from 554(d).

5. One of the attractions of working for the government is that it provides good training for future private careers. Part of the reason private employers like to hire former government employees is because those employees are personally acquainted with agency personnel who remain at the agency. Should there be limits on the extent to which former government employees may participate in actions involving the government? See the 1978 Ethics in Government Act as described in Thomas D. Morgan, "Appropriate Limits on Participation by a Former Agency Official in Matters Before an Agency," *Duke Law Journal* 1980: 1. Note this matter is not confined to adjudication. Why?

6. Administrative law judges, like trial judges sitting without juries in complex cases, write opinions explaining and justifying their findings. So do the members of the administrative boards themselves who make final decisions. These written opinions create a body of precedent that agencies could theoretically follow, just as common law courts follow judicial precedents. In administrative adjudication agencies may decide a case by citing "rules," which consist of principles announced in previous adjudications. Throughout its history the National Labor Relations Board (NLRB) has made labor law in just this way. Is this just, particularly in cases where such rules are applied retroactively? See *Brooks v. NLRB*, 348 U.S. 96 (1954). Once the decision has been announced, should courts *require* agencies to follow these principles in the future under the common law doctrine of *stare decisis*, or should agencies have the flexibility to change their "common law"? See *Office of Communications of the United Church of Christ v. FCC*, 590 F.2d 1062 (1978).

7. Accusations of bias are often raised in immigration cases. A built-in problem with immigration hearings is that Congress has authorized immigration judges to occupy the dual role of prosecutor and judge. Deborah Anker reported on research into more than 200 asylum hearings, where refugees must show a likelihood of persecution in their home country because of their race, religion, political activities, or other protected categories. She reports that "asylum claimants are often required to meet an excessively high standard of proof, contrary to U.S. Supreme Court precedent and international requirements; standards and rules are not clearly stated; inconsistent legal principles are applied; objective human rights assessments are discounted; restrictive evidentiary rules, not provided by regulation, are applied; and adequate interpretation is not available."[21]

Judge Richard Posner of the 7th Circuit U.S. Court of Appeals, in his dissent in an asylum case, *Apouviepseakoda v. Gonzales*, 475 F.3d. 881 (2007), identifies reasons for bias by immigration judges: immigration judges too often judge social conditions in the refugee's home country through an American lens, downplaying the likelihood of prosecution. Similarly, immigration judges' perceptions about the credibility of asylees may be colored by the culturally specific mannerisms and speech of the applicant, both of which are likely alien to the immigration judge. Such judgments are perilous, since facial expressions may mean different things in different cultures. Judge Posner points out that denying asylum in a meritorious case may literally doom the applicant.

But why should we be concerned with deciding asylum cases correctly? There are always costs and benefits associated with improving administrative action. Finding administrative law judges who are sensitive to cultural differences would be difficult and costly. Where should we draw the line? At present there is a huge backlog of disability cases in the Social Security Administration and a need to hire more judges to decide them, without which fair and timely adjudications may never resume. Which of these areas should have priority, reforming Social Security adjudications or reforming asylum hearings? Why?

21. Deborah Anker, "Determining Asylum Claims in the United States: Summary Report of an Empirical Study of the Adjudication of Asylum Claims Before the Immigration Court," *International Journal of Refugee Law* 2 (1990): 252.

CHAPTER 8
AMBIGUITIES IN RULEMAKING PROCEDURES

Chapters 6 and 7 provided a general outline of the law of administrative procedures. When we analyze procedures for rulemaking, at first blush the procedure looks quite simple. The Constitution itself would seem to require no particular process, since when an agency makes a rule it simply acts on behalf of the legislature, and legislatures have no constitutional obligation to hold hearings or provide interested citizens a chance to comment on proposed laws. According to this interpretation, the law of rulemaking is whatever the statutes call for. If authorizing statutes call for a full hearing, then the agency must follow the formal hearing requirements discussed in the last chapter. If a statute calls for something more than notice and comment but less than a formal hearing, as does legislation governing the Federal Trade Commission (FTC), then the agency must do whatever the statute requires.[1] And if the authorizing statute is silent, then the agency must follow the Administrative Procedure Act (APA) section 553 notice and comment requirements unless one of the exceptions applies.

This chapter introduces a serious complication to that simple scheme. It can be boiled down to a single question. Since agencies can follow *either* the rulemaking *or* the adjudication route, should an agency be permitted to escape the formalities of a hearing by simply changing the name they give to what they do? Consider the following.

What if, instead of investigating the allegations against the Cinderella Finishing School (p. 215) through a trial-type hearing, the FTC simply listed all the charges against Cinderella and, after notice and written comment, issued a rule prohibiting any "finishing school" from doing any of these things? The rule would be general—it would apply to all finishing schools—and it would impose no legal liability (at that point, anyway) on Cinderella. But would that be fair to Cinderella? If Cinderella persisted in those practices, the cards would then be stacked against it at the hearing since it would be in violation of the new FTC rule. Cinderella would not have the opportunity to show the administrative law judge that its practices were not deceptive.

This chapter deals with the basic problem we have just illustrated. Unlike the past two chapters, which drew a large map of the law in this field, this chapter explores one dark jungle on the map.

IS RULEMAKING A DESIRABLE ADMINISTRATIVE STRATEGY?

Professor Kenneth C. Davis has called simple notice and comment rulemaking "perhaps one of the greatest inventions of modern government."[2] These procedures

---

1. Thus in the proceeding to regulate children's advertising on television under the "Magnuson-Moss Act" the plaintiffs won a court order to disqualify the Chairman of the FTC. The court held the chairman, Michael Pertschuk, had prejudged the issue very much as his predecessor had done in *Cinderella Association of National Advertisers v. FTC*, 460 F. Supp. 996 (1978). An appellate court reversed, but Pertschuk recused himself anyway.

2. Kenneth Davis, *Administrative Law* (St. Paul: West Publishing Co., 1973), 243.

permit agencies to gather and examine any information they wish. Their judgment need not depend on the information generated by contending parties on the record of a hearing. Any and all citizens and groups are free to submit evidence. Furthermore, the agency can seek out what it feels is useful information, either from experts on its own staff or from specialists elsewhere. Because no lengthy trial occurs, agencies reach decisions quickly— that is, in a matter of months rather than years. And in one sense such decisions are fairer because they hold no one at fault for past practices. They work toward the future and allow those whom the rule governs to conform to it without paying the costs of elaborate legal proceedings.

The power of agencies to issue rules, however, has led some to fear that agencies will usurp legislative power. During the New Deal, which laid the foundation for modern administration, politicians expressed concern that agencies with legislative rulemaking authority could become far too powerful. You will recall that the Walter-Logan bill, sponsored by the American Bar Association, required a much more formal public hearing than does the APA. The simple analogy that agencies need no rulemaking limits because they act in a legislative manner breaks down because legislators submit directly to elections but bureaucrats do not. The accountability link between the public and the bureaucrats appears too remote to be meaningful. By the 1960s, however, fear of administrative dictatorships was replaced by concern about administrative ineffectiveness. The possibility that administrators would become all-powerful was no doubt exaggerated from the beginning. After all, adjudication in agencies duplicates to a large extent the work of courts. Many agencies were created with implied rulemaking power *because* case-by-case judicial adjudication, as in antitrust law, failed to solve the social problem. The judicial move to acknowledge and encourage administration through rulemaking rather than adjudication gathered strength in the 1960s. Rulemaking received a major boost in 1973 in the following landmark case.

United States v. Florida East Coast Railway, Inc.

410 U.S. 224 (1973) 6-2
+ Burger, Brennan, White, Marshall, Blackmun, Rehnquist
– Douglas, Stewart
NP Powell

[In the 1960s the Interstate Commerce Commission (ICC) became concerned about a shortage of railroad freight cars. To encourage railroad corporations to buy more cars for their own use (as opposed to leasing them from other lines), the ICC adopted "incentive per diem rates" that one railroad line would have to pay a fee to use another line's rolling stock. The ICC tried to set these rates high enough that it would be more economical to simply buy new cars than lease those belonging to someone else. However, the Interstate Commerce Act, section 1 (14)(a), said the ICC could make such rules only "after hearing." In past cases the ICC had followed formal trial-type procedures. Thus the issue was whether the words "after hearing" required a formal hearing or only notice and comment under section 553.]

Justice Rehnquist delivered the opinion of the Court

We here decide that the Commission's proceeding was governed only by § 553 . . . and that appellees received the "hearing" required by §1 (14)(a) of the Interstate Commerce Act.

. . . Here, the Commission promulgated a tentative draft of an order, and accorded all interested parties 60 days in which to file statements of position, submissions of evidence, and other relevant observations. The parties had fair notice of exactly what the Commission proposed to do, and were given an opportunity to comment, to object, or to make some other form of written submission. The final order of the Commission indicates that it gave consideration to the statements of the two appellees here. Given the "open-ended" nature of the proceedings, and the Commission's announced willingness to consider proposals for modification after operating experience had been acquired, we think the hearing requirement of § 1 (14)(a) of the Act was met.

Appellee railroads cite a number of our previous decisions dealing in some manner with right to a hearing in an administrative proceeding. Although appellees have asserted no claim of constitutional deprivation in this proceeding, some of the cases they rely upon expressly speak in constitutional terms, while others are less than clear as to whether they depend upon the Due Process Clause of the Fifth and Fourteenth Amendments to the Constitution, or upon generalized principles of administrative law formulated prior to the adoption of the Administrative Procedure Act.

Morgan v. United States, 304 U.S. 1 (1938), is cited in support of appellees' contention that the Commission's proceedings were fatally deficient. That opinion describes the proceedings there involved as "quasi-judicial," id., at 14, and thus presumably distinct from a rulemaking proceeding such as that engaged in by the Commission here. But since the order of the Secretary of Agriculture there challenged did involve a form of ratemaking, the case bears enough resemblance to the facts of this case to warrant further examination of appellees' contention. The administrative procedure in *Morgan* was held to be defective primarily because the persons who were to be affected by the Secretary's order were found not to have been adequately apprised of what the Secretary proposed to do prior to the time that he actually did it. Illustrative of the Court's reasoning is the following passage from the opinion:

The right to a hearing embraces not only the right to present evidence but also a reasonable opportunity to know the claims of the opposing party and to meet them. The right to submit argument implies that opportunity; otherwise the right may be but a barren one. Those who are brought into contest with the Government in a quasi-judicial proceeding aimed at the control of their activities are entitled to be fairly advised of what the Government proposes and to be heard upon its proposals before it issues its final command . . .

The proceedings before the Secretary of Agriculture had been initiated by a notice of inquiry into the reasonableness of the rates in question, and the individuals being regulated suffered throughout the proceeding from its essential formlessness. The Court concluded that this formlessness denied the individuals subject to regulation the "full hearing" that the statute had provided.

Assuming, arguendo, that the statutory term "full hearing" does not differ significantly from the hearing requirement of § 1 (14)(a), we do not believe that the proceedings

of the Interstate Commerce Commission before us suffer from the defect found to be fatal in *Morgan.* Though the initial notice of the proceeding by no means set out in detail what the Commission proposed to do, its tentative conclusions and order of December 1969 could scarcely have been more explicit or detailed. All interested parties were given 60 days following the issuance of these tentative findings and order in which to make appropriate objections. Appellees were "fairly advised" of exactly what the Commission proposed to do sufficiently in advance of the entry of the final order to give them adequate time to formulate and to present objections to the Commission's proposal. *Morgan*, therefore, does not aid appellees . . .

The basic distinction between rulemaking and adjudication is illustrated by this Court's treatment of two related cases under the Due Process Clause of the Fourteenth Amendment. In *Londoner v. Denver*, cited in oral argument by appellees, 210 U.S. 373 (1908), the Court held that due process had not been accorded a landowner who objected to the amount assessed against his land as its share of the benefit resulting from the paving of a street. Local procedure had accorded him the right to file a written complaint and objection, but not to be heard orally. This Court held that due process of law required that he "have the right to support his allegations by argument however brief, and, if need be, by proof, however informal." Id., at 386. But in the later case of *Bi-Metallic Investment Co. v. State Board of Equalization*, 239 U.S. 441 (1915), the Court held that no hearing at all was constitutionally required prior to a decision by state tax officers in Colorado to increase the valuation of all taxable property in Denver by a substantial percentage. The Court distinguished *Londoner* by stating that there a small number of persons "were exceptionally affected, in each case upon individual grounds." . . .

Later decisions have continued to observe the distinction adverted to in *Bi-Metallic Investment Co.*, supra. In *Ohio Bell Telephone Co. v. Public Utilities Comm'n*, 301 U.S. 292, 304–305 (1937), the Court noted the fact that the administrative proceeding there involved was designed to require the utility to refund previously collected rate charges. The Court held that in such a proceeding the agency could not, consistently with due process, act on the basis of undisclosed evidence that was never made a part of the record before the agency. The case is thus more akin to *Louisville &*

Nashville R. Co., 227 U.S. 88 (1913) than it is to this case. *FCC v. WJR,* 337 U.S. 265 (1949), established that there was no across-the-board constitutional right to oral argument in every administrative proceeding regardless of its nature. While the line dividing them may not always be a bright one, these decisions represent a recognized distinction in administrative law between proceedings for the purpose of promulgating policy-type rules or standards, on the one hand, and proceedings designed to adjudicate disputed facts in particular cases on the other.

Here, the incentive payments proposed by the Commission in its tentative order, and later adopted in its final order, were applicable across the board to all of the common carriers by railroad subject to the Interstate Commerce Act. No effort was made to single out any particular railroad for special consideration based on its own peculiar circumstances. Indeed, one of the objections of appellee Florida East Coast was that it and other terminating carriers should have been treated differently from the generality of the railroads. But the fact that the order may in its effects have been thought more disadvantageous by some railroads than by others does not change its generalized nature. Though the Commission obviously relied on factual inferences as a basis for its order, the source of these factual inferences was apparent to anyone who read the order of December 1969. The factual inferences were used in the formulation of a basically legislative-type judgment, for prospective application only, rather than in adjudicating a particular set of disputed facts.

The Commission's procedure satisfied both the provisions of § 1 (14)(a) of the Interstate Commerce Act and of the Administrative Procedure Act, and were not inconsistent with prior decisions of this Court. We, therefore, reverse the judgment of the District Court, and remand the case so that it may consider those contentions of the parties that are not disposed of by this opinion.

It is so ordered.

Justice Douglas, with whom Justice Stewart concurs, dissenting

The present decision makes a sharp break with traditional concepts of procedural due process. The Commission order under attack is tantamount to a rate order. Charges are fixed that nonowning railroads must pay owning railroads for boxcars of the latter that are on the tracks of the former. . . . This is the imposition on carriers by administrative fiat of a new financial liability. I do not believe it is within our traditional concepts of due process to allow an administrative agency to saddle anyone with a new rate, charge, or fee without a full hearing that includes the right to present oral testimony, cross-examine witnesses, and present oral argument. That is required by the Administrative Procedure Act, 5 U.S.C. § 556 (d); § 556 (a) states that § 556 applies to hearings required by § 553. Section 553 (c) provides that § 556 applies "[w]hen rules are required by statute to be made on the record after opportunity for an agency hearing." A hearing under § 1 (14)(a) of the Interstate Commerce Act fixing rates, charges, or fees is certainly adjudicatory, not legislative in the customary sense.

The question is whether the Interstate Commerce Commission procedures used in this rate case "for the submission of . . . evidence in written form" avoided prejudice to the appellees so as to comport with the requirements of the Administrative Procedure Act. . . .

The more exacting hearing provisions of the Administrative Procedure Act, 5 U.S.C. §§ 556–557, are only applicable, of course, if the "rules are required by statute to be made on the record after opportunity for an agency hearing." *Id.,* § 553 (c).

. . . The rules in question here established "incentive" per diem charges to spur the prompt return of existing cars to make the acquisition of new cars financially attractive to the railroads. Unlike those we considered in *Allegheny-Ludlum,* these rules involved the creation of a new financial liability. Although quasi-legislative, they are also adjudicatory in the sense that they determine the measure of the financial responsibility of one road for its use of the rolling stock of another road. The Commission's power to promulgate these rules pursuant to § 1 (14)(a) is conditioned on the preliminary *finding* that the supply of freight cars to which the rules apply is inadequate. Moreover, in fixing incentive compensation once this threshold finding has been made, the Commission "shall give consideration to the national level of ownership of such type of freight car and to other factors affecting the adequacy of the national freight car supply. . . ."

I . . . find a clear mandate that where, as here, ratemaking must be based on evidential facts, § 1 (14)(a) requires that full hearing which due process normally entails. . . .

Accordingly, I would hold that appellees were not afforded the hearing guaranteed by § 1 (14)(a) of the Interstate Commerce Act and 5 U.S.C. §§ 553, 556, and 557, and would affirm the decision of the District Court.

LEGISLATIVE AND ADJUDICATIVE RULEMAKING

Today courts, scholars, politicians and agencies themselves widely approve the idea of administration through rulemaking and this makes informal rulemaking the most frequently used administrative tool. The ambiguities and criticisms arise in the practical implementation of section 553. You can appreciate the problem better by reviewing all the formalities described in chapter 7 which section 553 does *not* require. It does not, above all, require a decision "on the record." This means that, to suppose an extreme case, an agency could ignore all submitted comments. It could allow an interested party to appear at a secret session in the agency conference room and decide only on the basis of this information. Or the Office of Management and Budget could call and threaten to cut the agency's recommended appropriation for the next fiscal year unless the agency reached a decision the White House desired.

Recall that the opinion in *Morgan* condemned *ex parte*, off-the-record fact finding. The potential unfairness of *ex parte* communications lies at the heart of the rulemaking jungle. Despite the *Bi-Metallic* principle and despite the fact that section 553 imposes no such limit on rulemaking, some courts have imposed fairness requirements on rulemaking.

One of the first cases to do so was *Sangamon Valley Television Corp. v. United States*, decided in 1959.[3] Appreciation of this case requires some background knowledge of the work of the FCC. Whenever two or more companies competed for the right to operate a television channel in a certain location, the FCC would hold a hearing. In deciding which channels should operate in which cities (based in part on technical data about interference among stations), however, the FCC did not hold hearings. Rather, it announced its decisions after informal rulemaking proceedings in its "Table of Television Channel Assignments." At the beginning of this story Sangamon was competing with another company for the license to operate VHF Channel 2 in Springfield, Illinois. Another company, headed by Mr. Tenenbaum, owned a much less potentially profitable UHF channel in St. Louis. Because St. Louis had the larger potential audience, the FCC was persuaded to consider switching the UHF channel to Springfield and moving Channel 2 to St. Louis. Both before and after the notice of this proposed rule was published, Tenenbaum repeatedly visited the FCC commissioners in their offices to urge that the channels be switched. Since he would lose the UHF channel he felt he would have the inside track to getting the license for the more profitable Channel 2 once it was transferred to St. Louis. Tenenbaum did not stop there. He sent each commissioner Thanksgiving and Christmas turkeys. Both he and his attorney privately sent letters to the FCC with information about the proposed rule.

Now consider the case from Sangamon's perspective. The rulemaking process blocked them from their opportunity to operate a profitable VHF station, Channel 2, and there was certainly reason to believe that a hidden, off-the-record process which they could not examine or influence could have affected the outcome. The FCC had, in effect, managed to employ a rulemaking proceeding to accomplish an adjudicatory result. Sangamon sued to set aside the reassignment of Channel 2 to St. Louis. The Supreme Court agreed with Sangamon.

It held that "whatever the proceeding may be called it involved not only allocation of TV channels among communities but also resolution of conflicting private claims to a valuable privilege . . . [Therefore] basic fairness requires such a proceeding be carried out in the open."[4]

---

3. 269 F.2d 221.

4. Ibid. at 224. On remand from the appellate court Tenenbaum was vindicated. See L. Jaffe and N. Nathanson, *Administrative Law* (Boston: Little, Brown & Co., 1961), 684–685.

The opinion thus helped create a distinction between purely legislative rulemaking and rulemaking with adjudicatory overtones.

Since it was decided, courts have sometimes extended the rule of *Sangamon* and other times limited it. In the most expansionary decision of all, *Home Box Office, Inc. v. FCC*, 567 F.2d 9 (1977), the Court of Appeals for the District of Columbia ruled that, regardless of the legislative character of rulemaking, all *ex parte* communication must cease once the notice of rulemaking is published.[5] *Home Box Office* got generally poor reviews by the legal critics. Nathaniel Nathanson, reporting to the Administrative Conference, said the decision "carries the concept of improper *ex parte* communications far beyond that previously entertained by the Congress, the courts and most of the federal administrative agencies."[6] *Home Box Office*'s position was undercut in what is today the Supreme Court's most powerful statement on the problem of rulemaking, the *Vermont Yankee* case. The case does not directly involve *ex parte* communications, but rather the extent to which courts can require agencies to supplement section 553 with other due process requirements.

From the mid-1960s into the 1970s, a new judicial consciousness about administrative policymaking emerged called *hybrid rulemaking*. The philosophy of hybrid rulemaking is that courts should require agencies to develop an evidentiary basis for a decision that is less formal than a full-fledged trial-type hearing but more substantial than traditional notice and comment requirements. By increasing transparency of rulemaking through the use of courts, it becomes possible to render administrative agencies more accountable. The potential of such hybrid rulemaking was particularly attractive to the public inter-

est movement of the 1960s, as the movement sought to prevent "capture" of administrative agencies by regulated industries.

Judge David Bazelon's decision for the U.S. Court of Appeals for the District of Columbia Circuit in *Natural Resources Defense Council v. Nuclear Regulatory Commission* (1976) is a classic endorsement of hybrid rulemaking. His decision was overturned by the U.S. Supreme Court in *Vermont Yankee Nuclear Power Corp. v. Natural Resources Defense Council* (1978). Since that Supreme Court decision it appears that hybrid rulemaking has come under attack, resulting in a judicial preference for the less formal mode of rulemaking. These two opinions, however, represent divergent legal responses to the question of how formal agency rulemaking should be. These two opinions also reflect an underlying political debate about agency rulemaking. How much authority should administrative "experts" have over policymaking in a democratic society? How shall we hold agencies accountable for their decisions? To what extent do formal or informal procedures for agency rulemaking insure that participation by interested parties, such as public interest groups, is meaningful?

We address these important questions by examining both the legal and political dimensions of rulemaking. We compare the legal and political perspectives offered by Judge Bazelon to the Supreme Court's unanimous opinion written by Justice Rehnquist in the *Vermont Yankee* cases. We then analyze agency rulemaking as a framework for developing policy preferences.

Natural Resources Defense Council v. Vermont Yankee Nuclear Power Corp.

547 F.2D 633 (1976) UNITED STATES COURT OF APPEALS FOR THE DISTRICT OF COLUMBIA CIRCUIT 3-0

[This case involves one of the most controversial areas of public policy today—the safety of nuclear power plants. The Atomic Energy Commission (AEC) (now the Nuclear Regulatory Commission) may grant operating licenses to nuclear plants only if safe operation is assured.

---

5. John Robert Long, "Comment: Ex Parte Contacts in Informal Rule Making: The Bread and Butter of Administrative Procedure," *Emory Law Journal* 27 (1978): 293, 303–304.

6. "Report to the Select Committee on Ex Parte Communications in Informal Rulemaking Proceedings," *Administrative Law Review* 30 (1978): 377, 379. See also generally, Paul Verkuil, "The Emerging Concept of Administrative Procedure," *Columbia Law Review* 78 (1978): 258; Long, "Ex Parte Contacts in Informal Rule Making;" and Glenn T. Carberry, "*Ex Parte* Communications in Off-the-Record Administrative Proceedings: A Proposed Limitation on Judicial Innovation," *Duke Law Review* 1980: 65.

The Commission, of course, must insure the safe construction of the plants themselves, but the waste products from nuclear power generation also create public risks. When the Vermont Yankee Nuclear Power Corp. sought an operating license, no plan existed for disposal of nuclear waste. Through rulemaking, the AEC finessed the problem. Relying on vague promises that scientists would find a solution to the waste problem the AEC's "spent fuel cycle rule" announced that the nuclear waste safety problem would not itself prevent the AEC from issuing operating licenses to plants.

The National Resources Defense Council, sought to discover the full range of evidence the AEC possessed about the waste disposal safety problem. It also sought to cross-examine witnesses and otherwise challenge the evidence before the AEC. The AEC refused.]

Chief Judge David Bazelon
delivered the opinion of the court

It is undisputed that a reactor licensing is a "major Federal action significantly affecting the quality of the human environment" which requires a "detailed" environmental impact statement under § 102(2)(c) of NEPA, [National Environmental Policy Act], 42 U.S.C. § 4332(2)(C). That section requires an impact statement to consider, inter *alia*,

(ii) any adverse environmental effects which cannot be avoided should the proposal be implemented, . . .

(v) any irreversible and irretrievable commitments of resources which would be involved in the proposed action should it be implemented.

The plain meaning of this language encompasses radioactive wastes generated by the operations of a nuclear power station, just as it does the stack gases produced by a coal-burning power plant.

Nor are the wastes generated by the subject reactor *de minimis*. We were informed at argument that the Vermont Yankee plant will produce approximately 160 pounds of plutonium wastes annually during its 40-year life span. Plutonium is generally accepted as among the most toxic substances known; inhalation of a single microscopic particle is thought to be sufficient to cause cancer. Moreover, with a half-life of 25,000 years, plutonium must be isolated from the environment for 250,000 years before it becomes

harmless. Operation of the facility in question will also produce substantial quantities of other "high-level" radioactive wastes in the form of strontium-90 and cesium-137 which, with their shorter, 30-year half-lives, must be isolated from the environment for "only" 600 to 1000 years. . . .

The Board agreed that "there will be an incremental environmental effect ultimately resulting from the operation of this reactor as the result of the operation of whatever reprocessing and disposal grounds may from time to time be used during the life of the plant." In its opinion, however, these effects were too "contingent and presently indefinable" to be evaluated at the time of licensing in view of the 40-year expected life of the reactor. The Board wrote:

. . . The possibility that improved technology may be developed during the 40-year life span of a reactor does not render consideration of environmental issues too speculative, as the Board appears to suggest. NEPA's requirement for forecasting environmental consequences far into the future implies the need for predictions based on existing technology and those developments which can be extrapolated from it. . . .

The second argument advanced by the Board is that licensing proceedings for reprocessing plants are a more "appropriate proceeding" in which to weigh the environmental effects of reprocessing and waste disposal. . . . Licensing of a reprocessing plant or waste disposal facility is itself a "major Federal action" affecting the environment which requires a NEPA statement. The real question posed by the Board's opinion is whether the environmental effects of the wastes produced by a nuclear reactor may be ignored in deciding whether to build it because they will later be considered when a plant is proposed to deal with them. To answer this question any way but in the negative would be to misconstrue the fundamental purpose of NEPA. Once a series of reactors is operating, it is too late to consider whether the wastes they generate should have been produced, no matter how costly and impractical reprocessing and waste disposal turn out to be; all that remain are engineering details to make the best of the situation which has been created. NEPA's purpose was to break the cycle of such incremental decision-making. . . .

The order granting a full-term license for the Vermont Yankee plant is hereby remanded to await the outcome of further proceedings in the rulemaking, discussed hereafter. . . .

An "informal rulemaking hearing" of the "legislative-type" was scheduled [by the NRC] to receive comments in the form of "oral or written statements." By subsequent notice, the Commission designated a three-member hearing board to preside, and reiterated, "The procedural format for the hearing will follow the legislative pattern, and no discovery or cross-examination will be utilized." 38 Fed. Reg. 49 (Jan. 3, 1973).

The primary argument advanced by the public interest intervenors is that the decision to preclude "discovery or cross-examination" denied them a meaningful opportunity to participate in the proceedings as guaranteed by due process. They do not question the Commission's authority to proceed by informal rulemaking, as opposed to adjudication. They rely instead on the line of cases indicating that in particular circumstances procedures in excess of the bare minima prescribed by the Administrative Procedure Act, 5 U.S.C. § 553, may be required.

The Government concedes that "basic considerations of fairness may under exceptional circumstances" require additional procedures in "legislative-type proceedings," but contends that the procedures here were more than adequate. Thus, we are called upon to decide whether the procedures provided by the agency were sufficient to ventilate the issues.

A few general observations are in order concerning the role of a court in this area. Absent extraordinary circumstances, it is not proper for a reviewing court to prescribe the procedural format which an agency must use to explore a given set of issues. Unless there are statutory directives to the contrary, an agency has discretion to select procedures which it deems best to compile a record illuminating the issues. Courts are no more expert at fashioning administrative procedures than they are in the substantive areas of responsibility which are left to agency discretion. What a reviewing court can do, however, is scrutinize the record as a whole to insure that genuine opportunities to participate in a meaningful way were provided, and that the agency has taken a good, hard look at the major questions before it.

We have sometimes suggested that elucidation of certain types of issues, by their very nature, might require particular procedures, including cross-examination. In fact, we have been more concerned with making sure that the record developed by agency procedures discloses a thorough ventilation of the issues than with what devices the agency used to create the dialogue. . . .

A reviewing court must assure itself not only that a diversity of informed opinion was heard, but that it was genuinely considered. . . . Since a reviewing court is incapable of making a penetrating analysis of highly scientific or technical subject matter on its own, it must depend on the agency's expertise, as reflected in the statement of basis and purpose, to organize the record, to distill the major issues which were ventilated and to articulate its reasoning with regard to each of them.

An agency need not respond to frivolous or repetitive comments it receives. However, where apparently significant information has been brought to its attention, or substantial issues of policy or gaps in its reasoning raised, the statement of basis and purpose must indicate why the agency decided the criticisms were invalid. Boilerplate generalities brushing aside detailed criticism on the basis of agency "judgment" or "expertise" avail nothing; what is required is a reasoned response, in which the agency points to particulars in the record which, when coupled with its reservoir of expertise, support its resolution of the controversy. An agency may abuse its discretion by proceeding to a decision which the record before it will not sustain, in the sense that it raises fundamental questions for which the agency has adduced no reasoned answers.

With these observations in mind, we turn to our examination of this record. . . .

The only discussion of high-level waste disposal techniques was supplied by a 20-page statement by Dr. Frank K. Pittman, Director of the AEC's Division of Waste Management and Transportation. This statement, delivered during the oral hearings, was then incorporated, often verbatim, into the revised version of the Environmental Survey published after the comment period. . . .

Dr. Pittman proceeded to describe for the first time in public the "design concepts" for a federal surface repository for retrievable storage of high-level waste. This is essentially a warehouse in which sealed canisters containing cylinders of solidified nuclear wastes can be stored in water-filled basins recessed into the ground on a temporary basis (up to 100 years), until such time as a permanent waste disposal scheme is devised, when they can be removed. While the "intended life" of the facility is only 100 years, some high-level wastes must be isolated for up to 250,000 years. . . . Therefore, the Environmental Survey states, without further explanation, that in the future a "permanent" Federal repository for "geologic storage of high-level wastes" will be established and that the "Federal government will have the obligation to maintain control over the site *in perpetuity.*" . . .

Until recently the AEC planned to dispose of wastes by burying them deep inside abandoned salt mines. These plans were postponed indefinitely after a series of technical difficulties, including the discovery the salt mines might be susceptible to underground flooding. The Revised Environmental Survey devotes two sentences to recounting how prior waste disposal plans fared:

It was planned to construct a Federal repository in a salt mine for long-term geological storage of solid high-level wastes by the mid 1970's. However, subsequent events have deferred the site selection and construction of such a facility. . . .

Dr. Pittman's description of the new plan—now also postponed indefinitely—to build a surface storage facility can only fairly be described as vague, but glowing. . . . In less than two pages, he set out a very general description of what the facility is supposed to do, accompanied by several schematic drawings. . . .

[W]ithout benefit of details, Dr. Pittman offers conclusory reassurances that the proposed facility will be designed so that the possibility of a "melt-down" can be dismissed as "incredible." . . .

There is no discussion of how "adequate human surveillance and maintenance" can be assured for the periods involved, nor what the long-term costs of such a commitment are, nor of the dangers if surveillance is not maintained. Nor is any explanation offered for Dr. Pittman's optimism regarding bedded salt as a disposal method, since the problems which have surfaced and delayed that program are not mentioned. Nor does the statement anywhere describe what "other acceptable geologic disposal concepts" are under consideration.

Based on Dr. Pittman's statement, the Revised Environmental Survey concludes that the resources consumed in waste storage will be minimal, that "under normal conditions" no radioactivity will be released, and that the possibility of a serious accident is "incredible." In short, based on the information in Dr. Pittman's statement, the Commission con-

cluded that the future environmental effects from the disposal of high-level nuclear wastes are negligible. . . .

We do not dispute these conclusions. We may not uphold them, however, lacking a thorough explanation and a meaningful opportunity to challenge the judgments underlying them. Our duty is to insure that the reasoning on which such judgments depend, and the data supporting them, are spread out in detail on the public record. Society must depend largely on oversight by the technically-trained members of the agency and the scientific community at large to monitor technical decisions. The problem with the conclusory quality of Dr. Pittman's statement—and the complete absence of any probing of its underlying basis—is that it frustrates oversight by anyone: Commission, intervenors, court, legislature or public . . .

Although the vagueness of the presentation regarding waste disposal made detailed criticism of its specifics impossible, . . . the public interest inter-venors did offer a number of more general comments concerning the Commission's approach. They criticized the Commission for a general "failure to distinguish between design objectives on the one hand and performance on the other," . . . noting that no consideration had been given actual experience with storage of wastes generated by weapons production. . . . They also questioned confident assertions by the AEC that long-term waste management is feasible, laying particular stress on the immense time periods involved which mock human institutions: . . .

They reiterated repeatedly that the problems involved are not merely technical, but involve basic philosophical issues concerning man's ability to make commitments which will require stable social structures for unprecedented periods.

The intervenors pointed out that storing wastes aboveground places a premium on stable human institutions for monitoring and surveillance, . . . that until plans for long-term disposal in the salt beds at Lyons, Kansas fell through, . . . , the agency had itself rejected the idea of surface storage because of the surveillance problems. . . .

. . . The Commission disposed of these issues summarily in its statement of basis and purpose accompanying the promulgation of the rule without attempting to articulate responses to any of the points which had been raised regarding waste disposal. . . .

Not only were the generalities relied on in this case not subject to rigorous probing—in any form—but when apparently substantial criticisms were brought to the Commission's attention, it simply ignored them or brushed them aside without answer. Without a thorough exploration of the problems involved in waste disposal, including past mistakes, and a forthright assessment of the uncertainties and differences in expert opinion, this type of agency action cannot pass muster as reasoned decisionmaking.

Many procedural devices for creating a genuine dialogue on these issues were available to the agency—including informal conferences between intervenors and staff, document discovery, interrogatories, technical advisory committees comprised of outside experts with differing perspectives, limited cross-examination, funding independent research by intervenors, detailed annotation of technical reports, surveys of existing literature, memoranda explaining methodology. We do not presume to intrude on the agency's province by dictating to it which, if any, of these devices it must adopt to flesh out the record. It may be that no combination of the procedures mentioned above will prove adequate, and the agency will be required to develop new procedures to accomplish the innovative task of implementing NEPA through rulemaking. On the other hand, the procedures the agency adopted in this case, if administered in a more sensitive, deliberate manner, might suffice. Whatever techniques the Commission adopts, before it promulgates a rule limiting further consideration of waste disposal and reprocessing issues, it must in one way or another generate a record in which the factual issues are fully developed.

. . . NEPA does not guarantee a particular outcome on the merits; rather, the statute mandates only a "careful and informed decisionmaking process" to enlighten the decisionmaker and the public. In the rulemaking context, that requires the Commission to identify and address information contrary to its own position, to articulate its reasoning and to specify the evidence on which it relies. The Commission may well reach the same conclusion on remand. But if it does so on such a record, the Congress, the courts, and the public will all know where we stand.

It has become commonplace among proponents of nuclear power to lament public ignorance. The public—the "guinea pigs" who will bear the consequences of either res-olution of the nuclear controversy—is apprehensive. But public concern will not be quieted by proceedings like the present . . .

Separate Statement of Chief Judge Bazelon:

I add a word of my own on some of the broader implications of Judge Tamm's concurrence.

I agree that courts should be reluctant to impose particular procedures on an agency. For example, requiring cross-examination in a rulemaking proceeding is radical therapy, which may cause the patient to suffer a slow, painful death. . . . But I reject the implication that any techniques beyond rudimentary notice and comment are needless "over-formalization" of informal rulemaking. . . . Unhappily, no such bright line can be drawn between rulemaking and adjudicatory proceedings.

The purpose of rulemaking was to allow public input on policy, whereas adjudication was designed to resolve disputed facts. . . . However, in response to the "paralysis" of the administrative process in the last decade, rulemaking has been expanded into fact-intensive areas previously thought to require adjudicatory procedures. Administrative proceedings are now common which do not fit neatly into either the rulemaking or adjudicatory category. These new proceedings are "hybrids" in the sense that involve issues of general applicability which can be treated efficiently only in generic proceedings, but nonetheless involve factual components of such relative importance that a greater assurance of accuracy is required than that which accompanies notice and comment procedures."*

The need for reliable fact-finding does not necessarily imply transplanting trial-type procedures. Factual issues in hybrid proceedings tend to be complex scientific or technical ones involving mathematical or experimental data, or other "legislative facts" peculiarly inappropriate for trial-type procedures. Agencies should innovate procedural for-

---

*The development of scientific or technical standards is a prime example. These decisions may involve both assessing scientific evidence, and also a "legislative" or policy component as to what level of risk is "safe," and how uncertainties are to be valued. See Handler, "A Rebuttal: The Need for a Sufficient Scientific Base for Governmental Regulation," *George Washington Law Review* 43 (1975): 808, 809.

mats responsive to the new problems created by hybrid rulemaking. . . .

Of course, important differences remain *from the standpoint of a reviewing court.* I am convinced that in highly technical areas, where judges are institutionally incompetent to weigh evidence for themselves, a focus on agency procedures will prove less intrusive, and more likely to improve the quality of decisionmaking, than judges "steeping" themselves "in technical matters to determine whether the agency has exercised a reasoned discretion." See *Ethyl Corp. v. EPA*, 176 U.S.App.D.C. 373, 541 F.2d 1, No. 73–2205 (1976) (en banc) (Bazelon, C.J., concurring), cert. denied, 526 U.S. 941 (1976).

Tamm, Circuit Judge, separate statement concurring in result

[T]he inadequacy of the record demands that we remand this case to the Commission in order to ensure that it has taken a hard look at the waste storage issue. I cannot, however, without qualification, endorse the approach the majority has taken to reach this result or its suggested disposition on remand.

The majority appears to require the Commission to institute further procedures of a more adversarial nature than those customarily required for informal rulemaking by the Administrative Procedure Act, 5 U.S.C. § 553 (1970). The Commission chose to proceed by "hybrid" rulemaking below, allowing petitioners to present oral arguments before the Commission and subjecting participants to questions, but not permitting participants to cross-examine. . . . By so proceeding the Commission exceeded the minimum procedural requirements of section 553. In my view, the deficiency is not with the *type* of proceeding below, but with the completeness of the record generated. More procedure will not, in this case, guarantee a better record, and a better record can be generated without reopening the oral proceeding at this time. . . .

I am also troubled by two other aspects of the majority opinion. First, I am distressed because I believe the majority opinion fails to inform the Commission in precise terms what it must do in order to comply with the court's ad hoc standard of review. The majority sends the waste storage issue back to the Commission for a "thorough ventilation."

This language, of course, means very little in procedural terms. In order to aid the Commission in filling in the gaps in the record, the majority enumerates a number of procedural alternatives in varying degrees of formality, some less intrusive into agency prerogatives than others . . . The Commission is thus left to decide which to adopt, further confused by the majority's statement. . . . I believe it almost inevitable that, after fully considering the problems and alternative methods of waste disposal and storage, the Commission will reach the same conclusion and therefore see little to be gained other than delay from imposing increased adversarial procedures in excess of those customarily required.

This brings me to my second, related concern with the majority's approach. I believe the majority's insistence upon increased adversariness and procedural rigidity, uneasily combined with its non-direction toward any specific procedures, continues a distressing trend toward over-formalization of the administrative decisionmaking process which ultimately will impair its utility. As Judge Wright has recently noted, the administrative response to overuse of judicial imposition of such ad hoc procedural refinements is easily foreseeable. Fearing reversal, administrators will tend to overformalize, clothing their actions "in the full wardrobe of adjudicatory procedures," until the advantages of informal rulemaking as an administrative tool are lost in a heap of judicially imposed procedure. Wright, *The Courts and the Rule-making Process: The Limits of Judicial Review*, 59 Cornell L Rev. 375, 387–88 (1974). The majority's reliance upon the so-called "hybrid rulemaking" cases for its conclusion that the procedures prescribed by section 553 are inadequate for resolution of the complex issues involved in this case and its insistence that the Commission adopt more formal adversary procedures are, I believe, misplaced. . . .

Vermont Yankee Nuclear Power Corp. v. Natural Resources Defense Council, Inc.

435 U.S. 519 (1978) 7–0
+ *Burger, Brennan, Stewart, White, Marshall, Rehnquist, Stevens*
NP Blackmun, Powell

Justice Rehnquist delivered the opinion of the Court

In 1946, Congress enacted the Administrative Procedure Act, which as we have noted elsewhere was not only "a new basic and comprehensive regulation of procedures in many agencies," *Wong Yang Sung v. McGrath*, 339 U.S. 33 (1950), but was also a legislative enactment which settled "long-continued and hard-fought contentions, and enacts a formula upon which opposing social and political forces have come to rest." Section 553 of the Act, dealing with rulemaking, requires that ". . . notice of proposed rulemaking shall be published in the Federal Register . . . ," describes the contents of that notice, and goes on to require in subsection (c) that after the notice the agency "shall give interested persons an opportunity to participate in the rulemaking through submission of written data, views, or arguments with or without opportunity for oral presentation. After consideration of the relevant matter presented, the agency shall incorporate in the rules adopted a concise general statement of their basis and purpose." 5 U.S.C.A. § 553. Interpreting this provision of the Act in *United States v. Allegheny Ludhum Steel, Corp.* 406 U.S. 742 (1972), and *United States v. Florida East Coast Railroad* Co., 410 U.S. 224 (1973), we held that generally speaking this section of the Act established the maximum procedural requirements which Congress was willing to have the courts impose upon agencies in conducting rule-making procedures. Agencies are free to grant additional procedural rights in the exercise of their discretion, but reviewing courts are generally not free to impose them if the agencies have not chosen to grant them. This is not to say necessarily that there are no circumstances which would ever justify a court in overturning agency action because of a failure to employ procedures beyond those required by the statute. But such circumstances, if they exist, are extremely rare. . . .

It is in the light of this background of statutory and decisional law that we granted certiorari to review two judgments of the Court of Appeals for the District of Columbia Circuit because of our concern that they had seriously misread or misapplied this statutory and decisional law cautioning reviewing courts against engrafting their own notions of proper procedures upon agencies entrusted with substantive functions of Congress. . . .

[B]efore determining whether the Court of Appeals reached a permissible result, we must determine exactly what result it did reach, and in this case that is no mean feat. Vermont Yankee argues that the court invalidated the rule because of the inadequacy of the procedures employed in the proceedings. Respondent NRDC, on the other hand, labeling petitioner's view of the decision a "straw man," argues to this Court that the court merely held that the record was inadequate to enable the reviewing court to determine whether the agency had fulfilled its statutory obligation. . . .

After a thorough examination of the opinion itself, we conclude that while the matter is not entirely free from doubt, the majority of the Court of Appeals struck down the rule because of the perceived inadequacies of the procedures employed in the rulemaking proceedings. The court first determined the intervenors' primary argument to be "that the decision to preclude 'discovery or cross-examination' denied them a meaningful opportunity to participate in the proceedings as guaranteed by due process" . . . The court also refrained from actually ordering the agency to follow any specific procedures, but there is little doubt in our minds that the ineluctable mandate of the court's decision is that the procedures afforded during the hearings were inadequate. This conclusion is particularly buttressed by the fact that after the court examined the record, . . . and declared it insufficient, the court proceeded to discuss at some length the necessity for further procedural devices or a more "sensitive" application of those devices employed during the proceedings. . . .

In prior opinions we have intimated that even in a rulemaking proceeding when an agency is making a " 'quasi-judicial' " determination by which a very small number of persons are " 'exceptionally affected, in each case upon individual grounds,' " in some circumstances additional procedures may be required in order to afford the aggrieved individuals due process. *United States v. Florida East Coast R.* Co., 410 U.S. 224, 242–245, quoting from *Bi-Metallic Investment* Co. *v. State Board of Equalization*, 239 U.S. 441, 446 (1915). It might also be true, although we do not think the issue is presented in this case and accordingly do not decide it, that a totally unjustified departure from well settled agency procedures of long standing might require judicial correction.

But this much is absolutely clear. Absent constitutional constraints or extremely compelling circumstances "the administrative agencies should be free to fashion their own rules of procedure and to pursue method of inquiry capable of permitting them to discharge their multitudinous duties."

Respondent NRDC argues that § 553 of the Administrative Procedure Act merely establishes lower procedural bounds and that a court may routinely require more than the minimum when an agency's proposed rule addresses complex or technical factual issues or "issues of great public import." We have, however, previously shown that our decisions reject this view.

We also think the legislative history, even the part which it cites, does not bear out its contention. ... Congress intended that the discretion of the agencies and not that of the courts be exercised in determining when extra procedural devices should be employed.

There are compelling reasons for construing § 553 in this manner. In the first place, if courts continually review agency proceedings to determine whether the agency employed procedures which were, in the court's opinion, perfectly tailored to reach what the court perceives to be the "best" or "correct" result, judicial review would be totally unpredictable. And the agencies, operating under this vague injunction to employ the "best" procedures and facing the threat of reversal if they did not, would undoubtedly adopt full adjudicatory procedures in every instance. Not only would this totally disrupt the statutory scheme, through which Congress enacted "a formula upon which opposing social and political forces have come to rest," *Wong Yang Sung v. McGrath, supra*, at 40, but all the inherent advantages of informal rulemaking would be totally lost.

Secondly, it is obvious that the court in this case reviewed the agency's choice of procedures on the basis of the record actually produced at the hearing, and not on the basis of the information available to the agency when it made the decision to structure the proceedings in a certain way. This sort of Monday morning quarterbacking not only encourages but almost compels the agency to conduct all rulemaking proceedings with the full panoply of procedural devices normally associated only with adjudicatory hearings.

Finally, and perhaps most importantly, this sort of review fundamentally misconceives the nature of the standard for judicial review of an agency rule. The court below uncritically assumed that additional procedures will automatically result in a more adequate record because it will give interested parties more of an opportunity to participate and contribute to the proceedings. But informal rulemaking need not be based solely on the transcript of a hearing held before an agency. Indeed, the agency need not even hold a formal hearing. See 5 U.S.C.A., § 553(c). Thus, the adequacy of the "record" in this type of proceeding is not correlated directly to the type of procedural devices employed, but rather turns on whether the agency has followed the statutory mandate of the Administrative Procedure Act or other relevant statutes. If the agency is compelled to support the rule which it ultimately adopts with the type of record produced only after a full adjudicatory hearing, it simply will have no choice but to conduct a full adjudicatory hearing prior to promulgating every rule. In sum, this sort of unwarranted judicial examination of perceived procedural shortcomings of a rulemaking proceeding can do nothing but seriously interfere with that process prescribed by Congress ...

Reversed and remanded.

Justice Rehnquist's opinion does not officially shut the door on the power of the courts to supplement section 553 with due process requirements, like the opportunity to cross-examine or the prohibition against *ex parte* communications, in adjudicatory-like rulemaking. His language does preserve the distinction between legislative and adjudicative rulemaking. Nevertheless the opinion dramatically narrows the door's opening. This is because Rehnquist implies that adjudicatory rulemaking requiring constitutional as well as section 553 standards is rare in administrative action. In fact, as the *Sangamon* decision defined it, adjudicative rulemaking is very common. Most administrative rules, at least those that section 553 does not itself exempt, do depend on factual considerations on which reasonable people disagree and which an adversary process might illuminate. More important, most rules resolve "conflicting private claims to a valuable privilege." What if the AEC had announced a rule refusing to license further nuclear power plants until the spent fuel problem had been solved? What if it had followed the *same* procedure on the same issue but decided differently? We can imagine that Vermont Yankee's lawyers would try to invoke the *Sangamon* doctrine precisely because the rule would deny them their valuable privilege of operating their power plant.

So far you have seen that agencies do not make a simple choice between adjudication or rulemaking when they make policy. Both rulemaking and adjudication vary in formality. Judge Bazelon argues that the NRC should be required to carry out a more formal rulemaking process (i.e., hybrid rulemaking) than the NRC and the Supreme Court support. Hence the decision about which administrative procedure to use for making policy cannot be resolved abstractly.

Indeed, the most significant issue in this policy dispute is the fact that, thirty years after *Vermont Yankee*, the problem of nuclear waste disposal has still not been solved. Currently, the federal government is trying to build a central permanent site to store spent nuclear reactor fuel in Yucca Mountain, Nevada. But on January 9, 2008 the *New York Times* reported that the "Energy Department official in charge of the [ongoing] project has projected 2017 as the earliest the site could open, with a price tag now topping $77 billion."[7] Besides questions about its scientific and economic feasibility, the Yucca Mountain project from the start has faced opposition from various environmental groups. A basic question, of course, concerns the shipment of used nuclear fuel from plants located around the country to a central storage facility. Another is about the site. Nevadans are not particularly enthused about having a radioactive storage facility in their state. Not surprisingly, courts have been part of the politics of nuclear waste. In *Nuclear Energy Institute v. EPA*, 373 F.3d 1251 (2004), the Court of Appeals for the D.C. Circuit rejected an EPA rule limiting the radiation standards in the area until 10,000 years after the facility is closed. EPA, on remand, revised the standard to be effective for a million, years after the site is closed.

Meanwhile, the license of the Vermont Yankee Nuclear Power Plant needs to be renewed as it expires in 2012 and, not surprisingly, one of the most hotly debated issues around this renewal is the safe storage of used fuel.[8]

The same reasons that make rulemaking less formal and visible (and hence more efficient) than adjudication also make rulemaking a prime target for political manipulation from the White House, Congress, and powerful interest groups. The remaining materials in this chapter discuss several of these influences. For example, the Office of Management and Budget (OMB), the protagonist in the *State Farm* case, on page 259, was used by the Reagan administration to overturn anti-business regulatory policies. OMB once successfully forced the EPA to withdraw a rule requiring air polluting industries to notify the public when they knew their emissions exceeded air pollution emission standards.

More than 20 years after President Reagan left office, OMB continues to put significant institutional leverage in the hand of the executive. The Executive Order dealing with the regulatory process, E.O. 13422 (amending previous E.O. 12866), is a case in point. E.O. 13422 orders each agency to have a regulatory policy officer appointed by the president to supervise the development of rules. Even though the Bush administration says that this order has not targeted any specific agency, the *New York Times* reports that the administration's concern with the EPA and the Occupational Safety and Health Administration is the prime motive behind this executive order.[9] The concern of the administration with the so-called "social regulations" is indeed reflected in the new Executive Order. In the words of OMB Watch, a nonprofit think tank closely following the OMB, "the executive order shifts the criterion for promulgating regulations from the identification of a problem like public health or environmental protec-

---

7. "A Shift at Yucca Mountain," *New York Times*, January 9, 2008.

8. In May 2006, for instance, the Vermont State Legislature passed "An Act Relating to a Certificate of Public Good for Extending the Operating License of a Nuclear Power Plant" to make sure that the General Assembly of the Vermont State Legislature has the power to decide whether the Vermont Yankee Power Plant may continue beyond its current license, which expires in 2012.

9. "Bush Directive Increases Sway on Regulation," *New York Times*, January 30, 2007.

tion to the identification of a 'specific market failure' (such as externalities, market power, lack of information) . . . that warrant new agency action."[10]

Such struggles to gain power through the regulatory process are better understood when viewed in their larger historical and political framework. The development of negotiated rulemaking in the 1980s, which led to the passage of the Negotiated Rulemaking Act of 1990, may only provide another avenue by which the best-funded interest groups—usually representatives of commercial interests—out-muscle the less well-funded consumer, social, and environmental groups.[11] Again, the critical questions in administrative law are: (1) How can courts effectively determine when political influences like these do and do not lead to arbitrary and irrational decisions; and (2) When decisions are arbitrary and irrational, what can courts do to correct them?

The most ambitious effort currently underway to reform agency rulemaking is called *regulatory negotiation*. In the article below, Professor Harrington describes regulatory negotiation and examines its political implications. Regulatory negotiation is an informal process that uses private mediators to resolve conflicts between parties *before* an agency gives "notice and comment" in the *Federal Register* on a proposed rule. Regulatory negotiation has been promoted by reformers who find fault with more formal rulemaking processes, like hybrid rulemaking, and who want to reduce legal challenges to administrative rules. They maintain that one way to achieve this is to establish a consensus among "interested parties" before announcing a proposed rule. Professor Harrington's article questions the extent to which regulatory negotiation privatizes the rulemaking process and signifies a return to the model of interest group liberalism, which Theodore Lowi so aptly criticized three decades ago.

10. "A Failure to Govern: Bush's Attack on the Regulatory Process," *OMB Watch Report*, March 2007.

11. Cornelius Kerwin surveyed the many political influences on rulemaking in his *Rulemaking: How Government Agencies Write Law and Make Policy* (Washington, D.C.: CQ Press, 1994). The classic critique of regulatory failure to meet the requirements of democratic government is Theodore Lowi, *The End of Liberalism*, 2nd ed. (New York: W.W. Norton & Co., 1979).

Regulatory Reform: Creating Gaps and Making Markets

CHRISTINE B. HARRINGTON
Law & Policy 10 (1988): 293

. . . Alternative dispute resolution techniques, such as mediation and arbitration, have been proposed for courts, in part, as a response to the perceived dispute resolution "crisis" of the courts. Informal dispute resolution is said to be a less adversarial and hence more effective method for resolving a range of disputes. . . .

. . . Facilitators, or mediators, are selected from outside the agency to help the parties reach an agreement on a rule. Once a consensus is reached, the rule will be published in the Federal Register and a period for public notice and comment is set. Examples of federal agency negotiated rulemaking are: Environmental Protection Agency penalties for heavy engine manufacturers who fail to comply with the requirement of the Clean Air Act, exemptions from pesticide licensing regulations, rules governing the removal of asbestos in public schools, and standards for residential woodburning stoves; Federal Aviation Administration regulations dealing with maximum flight time and minimum rest period for pilots; and Occupational Safety and Health Administration standards governing exposure to benzene and methylenedianiline.

The use of private mediators in the regulatory rulemaking process raises many questions about the influence of private interests on public policy. Questions of this sort have already been raised in the debates over civil settlement. Political scientists and legal scholars have taken issue with the new claim that private settlement is always a desirable alternative to public adjudication (Resnik, 1982; Fiss, 1984; Provine, 1986; Kritzer, 1986). In the case of civil settlement, and the legal process more generally, this debate is over whether the judiciary should be in the business of making public policy. There is less attention to this element of formalism in the area of administrative regulation. Indeed, given the history of regulation, the shift to informal negotiation is a curious development because the regulatory process is much less clearly associated with the ideals of formalism than the civil courts. Even the so-called "judicialization" of the administrative process, following the passage of the Administrative Procedure Act in 1946 (Seidman and Gilmour, 1986) and during the early 1970s (Funston, 1974), did not seek to replicate the adversarial nature of the judicial process. Despite differences between the role of agencies and courts in shaping public policy, administrative capacity like court capacity is a current focus of scholarly attention and reform. . . .

This is appropriate to examine the conceptualization of state-market relations embedded in this reform. In this sense . . . reforms tell us about the role of law in organizing state-market relations. Dispute processes, such as regulatory negotiation, not only serve political and economic interests, they also help constitute those interests. . . .

II. Reforming Regulation through Dispute Processing

. . . A fundamental premise of the alternative dispute resolution movement is that there is a "gap" between the promise and the capacity of formal justice. This perceived gap is the product of an idealized conception of formal justice. Used as the standard for evaluating institutional practices, this ideal becomes the criterion for judging institutional capacity. The ideal itself is treated as nonproblematic, separate from its social meaning and its historic functions. Locating the limits of legalism in an idealized conception of formal justice creates a gap which then underlies the claim for alternative dispute resolution. The reform then seeks to reduce the "gap" by using law (i.e., legal institutions and legal processes) as a tool for social change. . . .

A. Conventional Regulatory Rulemaking

Despite a [1960s–1970s] trend towards the judicialization of the administrative process, the relative informality of administrative regulation remains. Agencies, such as the Environmental Protection Agency, bargain regularly with affected parties. In fact, before the EPA publishes a proposed rule which it believes will be controversial, EPA officials notify Congress, industry, environmentalists, and state and local officials. For some time the agency has operated on the belief that informal discussions with affected parties will help resolve controversy (Comment, 1981).

The informal character of administrative regulation is also found in the image of agency capture . . . The capture thesis focuses on informal negotiations between regulator and regulated because it is believed that informal bargaining enhances the power of private interests over public policy.

The capture thesis prompted a wave of reforms in the 1970s—what we might call counter-capture reforms. . . .

. . . [C]hanges in the approach to agency policymaking came about in the 1970s as a response to a particular type of regulation—social regulation. The rise of social regulation, such as environmental, consumer, health and safety regulation, expanded the scope of regulation from one industry to many. Unlike the economic regulation of the New Deal agencies, social regulation is generic. It mandates that agencies regulate the conduct of firms across industrial sectors instead of within a specific industry. Consequently agencies engaged in social regulation often use rulemaking instead of adjudication in order to establish a uniform rule and "economize on decision costs" (Diver, 1981).

Rulemaking institutionalized greater interest group and citizen participation than adjudication. Citizens and groups could comment on a proposed rule made through the rulemaking process whereas participation in adjudication was limited to those who challenged an agency decision. At the same time that agencies were shifting to a rulemaking approach the public interest law movement sought to expand the impact of participation in rulemaking by demanding that agencies do more than afford interested parties the opportunity to be heard. They sought to require that agencies engage in a more probing fact-finding process and establish a record responding to alternative policy proposals. . . .

Where public interest reforms expanded the right of direct participation in the rulemaking process these reforms challenged the New Deal model of administrative expertise by transforming the agency from protector of the public interest to umpire assessing competing claims. Informal agreement on an agency rule has less chance of being established in the case of social regulation, it is argued, because a rule, for example on exposure to toxic substances in the work place affects many industries, and the procedures are too adversarial. Today, this approach to regulatory decisionmaking is criticized for promoting "costly litigation because it decreases the opportunity for the development of long-term continuing relationships between regulator and regulated" (Stewart, 1985: 655).

Efforts to reduce agency capture have been somewhat successful where regulatory practices have created an unfriendly environment for the development of long-term continuing relationships. Yet, advocates of regulatory negotiation maintain that the economic and social costs of litigation are too high a price to pay for regulating private interests. They say that by "encouraging and empowering regulatees to challenge agency decision making in an effort to enhance the political legitimacy of the rule-making process, Congress and the courts have increased the complexity, cost, and time it takes to generate rules that can be implemented" (Susskind and McMahon, 1985: 136). A debilitating complexity is the linchpin to the ideology of this reform.

B. Negotiated Rulemaking

According to ACUS [the Administrative Conference of the U.S.] recommendations, regulatory negotiation may be initiated by either an agency or one of its constituencies. The agency designates a "neutral convenor," a private mediator or facilitator, whose job is to identify the interested parties and relevant issues. First the convenor undertakes a "feasibility analysis" to establish whether or not the parties, including agency actors, will agree to negotiate a rule. In a number of cases the agency will empanel the interested parties as an advisory committee under authority from the Federal Advisory Committee Act of 1976 (FACA). If negotiations produce agreement between parties, a rule will be announced in the Federal Register.

As with other proposals for alternative dispute resolution, the advocates are very enthusiastic about the advantages of rulemaking by negotiation. They see the following advantages: (1) negotiated rulemaking offers the parties direct participation in the process; (2) the mediator is more active in "outreach" to the parties affected by the regulation than in the "customary rule-making route" (Harter, 1984:4); (3) the parties will be engaged in direct substantive decisions rather than appearing as expert witnesses providing testimony before the agency; (4) the costs of participation are reduced because the parties need not prepare "defensive research" (Harter, 1982); and (5) the quality of participation is richer because the parties are in a setting that provides incentives to rank their concerns. . . .

The emphasis on increased participation through a negotiation process appears to respond to the age-old criticism about the failure of a responsive bureaucracy in a democratic policy. . . .

[Yet] it is significant that those who criticize the expansion of party participation under the public interest law reforms in the 1970s are now calling for regulatory negotiation as a way of enhancing party involvement in the regulatory process. This fact suggests that participation alone is not the central value, but rather the form of participation is the pivotal point of debate. Thus, the parties to negotiated rulemaking, including the state, become

the "experts" who exercise regulatory discretion.

Regulatory negotiation turns away from traditional measures for restricting agency discretion, such as more stringent due process requirements, and instead brings a private mediator/facilitator into the process. Harter explains that an outside mediator "enhances the appearance of neutrality and has control over the calendar and the ability to move in ways that may be different for an insider" (1984:4). A private nonpartisan convenor, it is argued, is preferable to the sponsoring agency who will be viewed as "suspect by the potential participants" (Susskind and McMahon, 1985: 163). Here, the process blunts the power of traditional public authority in the name of neutrality. Yet, advocates deny that regulatory negotiation delegates public authority to private parties. They claim that agencies participate in the process and have the equivalent of a veto over a "consensus." Here, the state becomes simply one of the participants. Its veto is not special. It is in this sense that regulatory negotiation shares a market conception with deregulation, an issue we will address later.

Still, many questions about delegating public authority remain. Will negotiations be open to the public? Regulatory negotiation groups constituted as advisory committees under the FACA are required to hold their plenary meetings in public, but caucuses and work group sessions may be held privately. A related question concerns the scope of judicial review for negotiated regulation. Advocates propose a less stringent standard of review, one which narrowly focuses on the process of negotiation, rather than the adequacy of the substantive rule. Judicial review is valued only in so far as it may "enhance the efficiency and perceived legitimacy of the rulemaking process" (Ibid., 165). . . .

III. The "Crisis" of Regulatory Litigation

. . . My study of regulatory litigation rates is based on data collected from the Annual Report of the Administrative Office of the U.S., which started categorizing administrative appeals in 1937. . . .

Figure 8.1 shows cases filed in the U.S. Circuit Courts of Appeals per 100,000 people from 1945–1985. Overall the trend is toward an increase in appellate case filing since 1960. Administrative appeals, however, do not increase at the same pace as other appellate litigation, particularly private civil and U.S. civil cases where over time the increases are most dramatic A comparison of the percent change in filings per 100,000 people shows

Figure 8.1 Cases Filed in the U.S. Court of Appeals per 100,000 People, 1945–1985

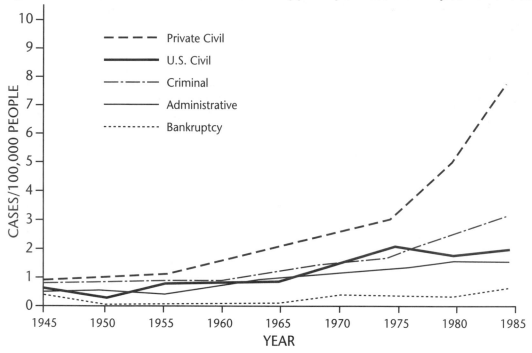

Source: Data derived from the Administrative Office of the United States, 1945–1985.

that between 1960 and 1965, when the trend upward begins, administrative appeals increase by 39% whereas other kinds of appellate litigation increases from 57% (bankruptcy) to 85% (criminal) (see Table 8.1). Although there is considerable fluctuation in bankruptcy and criminal appellate cases from 1960 to 1980, there is a steady increase in administrative, private civil, and U.S. civil filings in this period. Administrative appeals increase slightly faster (39.5%) than private civil (27.5%) and U.S. civil (30.2%) filings between 1970–1975.* Private civil, U.S. civil, and bankruptcy filings outpace administrative appeals from 1975 to 1985.

Over the past fifteen years, when reformers claim there has been significant increase in regulatory litiga-

*The growth in administrative appeals between 1970 and 1975 might be attributed to the establishment of new regulatory agencies such as the EPA and OSHA in this period. Initial challenges of agency authority and decisionmaking procedures are common ways of shaping agency practices (Shapiro, 1968). Thus, following the creation of new agencies, such as those in the 1970s, we would expect an increase in legal activity. The Administrative Office data categorizes appeals from these new agencies as "other" until 1976.

tion, the smallest increase in appellate filing has been in administrative appeals. Administrative appeals increased 75% from 1970 to 1985, compared with a 340% increase in bankruptcy; 199% increase in private civil; 166% increase in U.S. civil; and 79% increase in criminal appeals. Low as the increase was during these years, it begins to level off almost entirely between 1980 and 1985 with a growth rate that constitutes the smallest increase in appellate filings of any category (2%). . . .

Rather than sharp increases in regulatory litigation there appears to be a redistribution of cases within the circuit courts and a concentration of regulatory litigation in one particular circuit—the D.C. Circuit. Procedural changes in agency rulemaking and judicial review are less likely explanations for this shift, however, than are jurisdictional changes or changes in the organization of the regulatory bar.

Over the past fifteen years regulatory litigation has actually declined as a percentage of cases filed in the U.S. Courts of Appeals (see Figure 8.2). In 1940, administrative appeals constituted 23% of the cases filed in the circuit courts; in 1985, administrative appeals constitute

Table 8.1 Variability of Filings in the U.S. Court of Appeals, 1945–1985 (% Change in Filings per 100,000 people)

	Administrative	Private Civil	Criminal	U.S. Civil	Bankruptcy
1945–1950	−15.8	+28.1	−44.4	−6.1	−52.9
1950–1955	+9.4	4.1	+105.0	−6.5	+12.5
1955–1960	+17.1	+11.8	−17.1	−10.2	−22.2
1960–1965	+39.0	+62.4	+85.3	+61.4	+57.1
1965–1970	+33.0	+71.0	+106.3	+49.3	−9.1
1970–1975	+39.5	+27.5	+49.2	+30.2	+10.0
1975–1980	+22.6	+48.8	−0.5	+47.8	+54.5
1980–1985	+2.3	+57.4	+8.3	+38.2	+158.8

Source: Data derived from the *Annual Reports of the Administrative Office of the United States and the Statistical Abstract of the United States.*

10% of the cases filed. From 1955 to 1960, administrative appeals increased slightly from 16% to 19%; then, by 1965 they dropped back to 16% of the circuit court's docket. Since 1960 a slow decline continues in administrative appeals as a percentage of the total appellate courts' filings. . . .

Has judicial support for agency decision weakened over the past fifteen years? Are the courts reversing more agency decisions and thus perhaps encouraging more appeals? We do not have data on the percentage of agency decisions appealed, but we do have data on how the circuit courts treat those cases that are appealed. Table 8.1 shows the disposition of administrative appeals in the U.S. Courts of Appeals, 1945–1985. On the average, the circuit courts affirm 73% of agency decisions during this forty year period. The highest level of support for agency decision was in 1970 (79%); the lowest level of support was in 1955 (66%). The range of fluctuation in support levels over this period is not great, and certainly there appears to be no significant deviation from the norm or average over the past fifteen years. . . . Here we also find that the circuit courts provide stability if not legitimacy for agency rules.

IV. The Political Economy of Regulatory Negotiation

The contemporary reform movement creates a picture of regulatory litigation that is not supported by an empirical study of litigation rates. The pace of regulatory litigation has not increased sharply in the last fifteen years nor has judicial support for agency rules weakened. These findings provide us with a sociolegal context for analyzing the construction of a regulatory litigation "crisis" and the constitution of new regulatory relations through dispute processing reform. That is, rather than conclude that these findings identify a fundamental flaw in the logic of regulatory negotiation, I argue that from the empirical study of regulatory litigation we identify the conception of law which underlies this reform. The "crisis" in regulatory litigation is constructed from a formalist conception of law which, in this instance, equates conventional rulemaking with the rule of law. . . .

A. Communication in the Market

Why does this anti-adversarial campaign persist in the face of regulatory politics that call for a turn away from an expansionist state through deregulation? On the one hand, anti-adversarial processes for administrative rulemaking and deregulation both minimize state intervention. Yet, attacks on regulatory litigation focus on the

Figure 8.2 Administrative Appeals as Percentage of All Cases Filed in the U.S. Court of Appeals, 1940–1985

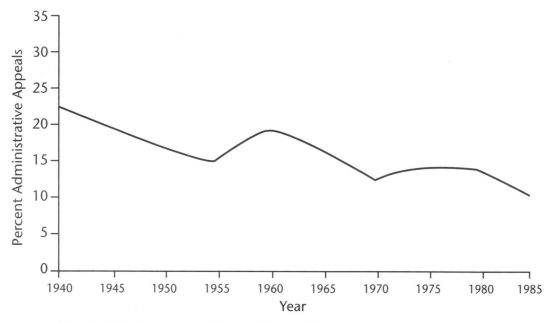

Source: Data derived from the Administrative Office of the United States, 1940–1985.

need for more direct participation by interested parties. Traditional rulemaking came under attack in the late 1970s. The attack focused on social regulation and targeted "its economic inefficiency in failing to discriminate between low-cost and high-cost compliance activity" (Rabin, 1986: 1318; also see Breyer, 1982; Derthick and Quirk, 1985). Advocates of regulatory negotiation built on this critique, but emphasized procedural inefficiencies accompanying social regulation rather than the substance of what was being regulated. The anti-regulation mood of the late 1970s was directed at administrative activity that went beyond the policing model. If deregulation is no more than a "preference for the less intrusive of the two mainstream approaches that characterize the American regulatory tradition—a preference for a ubiquitous but relatively narrow policing model of regulation over a mixed policing-cartelization system of administrative governance" (Rabin, 1986: 1318–19), then how might we characterize the political economy of regulatory negotiation?

The market created by regulatory negotiation is not an "alternative" to regulation; rather it applies a very traditional view of regulation to new regulatory relations—

social regulation. There are many points in the conventional regulatory process where negotiation takes place, linking tradition to the reform. We know that parties create opportunities for negotiation by challenging a regulation and then offering to withdraw their challenge in exchange for a more acceptable rule that the agency will agree to publish as their proposed rule. This type of negotiation, called "sequential negotiation," has been characterized as more adversarial than regulatory negotiation. Regulatory negotiation is bargaining that is explicitly structured to work toward accommodating differences before a formal rule challenge is made. Regulatory negotiation may complement existing rulemaking practices by emphasizing negotiation prior to setting an agency rule, but does it change the political philosophy of agency regulation?

Underlying the argument for regulatory negotiation is an old image of the market. That image is one of the state withdrawing from its regulatory role as a welfare state so that the self-balancing market system can reassert itself. Rather than speak directly about markets, however, the language of regulatory negotiation is about communications between the parties. The market-place of ideas, as it were, malfunctions in an adversarial rule-making setting because it produces distorted dialogue—dialogue between lawyers who make "flat arguments for extreme positions based on defensive research" (Harter, 1982: 22). The adversarial process is criticized for not giving the parties an opportunity to communicate directly with one another.

B. Rulemaking in the Minimalist State

The vision of state-market relations is one in which self-balancing incentives operate to express and accommodate conflict and overcome private and public coercion. Voluntary compliance is the primary goal to be strengthened with this regulatory reform. The state becomes one of the interested parties in regulatory negotiation because it is seen as being too biased to police effectively the market and achieve high levels of voluntary compliance. A private mediator, instead, plays the policing role of facilitating a consensus among the parties—a consensus on voluntary compliance.

Regulatory negotiation may not articulate a strong anti-statist stance, but elements of anti-statism are evident in the negotiator's role. The traditional model of regulation is concerned with controlling agency discretion and protecting private interests from unwarranted government intrusion. Regulatory negotiation appears to be a strategy of this sort. Yet, once an agency commits itself to the negotiation process, its role changes from "umpire" to interested party and the state's role in the process also changes. From the point negotiations begin, political legitimacy derives not from the accountability of public authorities or even from the publicness of the process; instead, the process of sharing in making the "ultimate judgment" about the rules is said to provide political legitimacy to regulatory negotiation. . . .

The minimalist state and interest group theory are familiar combinations in American politics. Together they constitute a laissez-faire theory of the economy and a pluralist image of politics. In regulatory negotiation, groups advance their claims not only to the state but to all other groups participating in rulemaking. This produces a notion of "balancing interests" that is very similar to the market notion of economic exchange—each group receives some of what it wants in negotiation (win-win outcome), but no group receives everything (win-lose outcome). Interest representation has long been part of the politics of dispute processing reform and American politics. Theodore Lowi described "interest group liberalism" as a theory of interest representation in

his analysis of post-New Deal public philosophy (1979). Lowi argued that the model of interest group liberalism rested on the following assumptions: 1) all interests are organized; 2) organized interests have representatives who answer and check other organized groups; and 3) the state insures access to organized groups and ratifies the "agreements and adjustments worked out among the competing leaders" (Ibid., 51). He further noted that interest group liberalism resembled the pluralist model of modern political science. The assumptions of this model have been subject to considerable criticism within political science over the past two decades. Most significantly, critics of pluralism argue that organized groups do not compete among themselves, as assumed by the market theory of the economy. Instead, the most powerful groups have institutionalized their interests by forming a partnership with the state (Kariel, 1961; McDonnell, 1966; Lowi, 1979).

Social movement litigation strategies were employed by public interest law reformers in the 1970s to remedy "institutionalized pluralism" (Handler, 1978). Advocacy representation was the principal method they adopted for redistributing resources to social-reform groups. This method was used in the regulatory arena as well as the courts. Although reformers such as Ralph Nader criticized regulatory capture for resembling institutionalized pluralism, the political philosophy of interest representation was retained by the public interest law movement. Law reformers sought to use legal advocacy in effect to make pluralism work.

Regulatory negotiation is another interest representation approach to making pluralism work. It differs from the social-reform litigation approach in its return to the informal bargaining style of interest group liberalism. Regulatory negotiation seems to reproduce what Lowi and others so forcefully criticized interest group liberalism for—substituting an informal process for meaningful political debate over the values of regulation. . . .

Regulatory negotiation does not, however, replicate all aspects of interest group liberalism. It cannot be said of this reform, as Lowi said of interest group liberalism, that "the role of government is one of insuring access to the most effectively organized, and of ratifying the agreements and adjustments worked out among the competing leaders" (1979: 51). The repudiation of New Deal regulation during the Public Interest era may have transformed the role of agencies from "expert" to umpire. However, regulatory negotiation does not simply shift the role of agencies as third party intervener from umpire to facilitator, it puts a private party into what was formerly a public position. Under this arrangement, the state relinquishes the more direct policing role of interest group liberalism. The parties, including the state, become the "experts" controlling regulatory discretion over public policy.

Regulatory negotiation reconstitutes the public philosophy of interest group liberalism in a theory of political legitimacy associated with a minimalist state. . . .

References

ADMINISTRATIVE OFFICE OF THE UNITED STATES: *Reports of the Annual Meetings* (various years). Washington, D.C.

BREYER, S. *Regulation and Its Reform.* Cambridge: Harvard University Press, 1982.

COMMENT "Rethinking Regulation: Negotiation as an Alternative to Traditional Rulemaking," *Harvard Law Review* 99 (1981): 1871.

DERTHICK, M. AND P. J. QUIRK. *The Politics of Deregulation.* Washington, D.C.: The Brookings Institution, 1985.

DIVER, C. S. "Policymaking Paradigms in Administrative Law," *Harvard Law Review* 95 (1981): 393.

FISS, O. "Against Settlement," *Yale Law Journal* 93 (1984): 1073.

FUNSTON, R. "Judicialization of the Administrative Process," *American Politics Quarterly* 2 (1974): 38.

HANDLER, J. F. 1978. *Social Movements and the Legal System.* New York: Academic Press.

HARTER, P. J. 1982. "Negotiating Regulations: A Cure for Malaise," *Georgetown Law Journal* 71: 1.

HARTER, P. J. "Status Report on Project on 'The Uses of Alternative Means of Dispute Resolution in the Administrative Process,' " Memorandum to Committee on Administration of the Administrative Conference of the U.S., Washington, D.C., November 19, 1984.

KARIEL, H. S. *The Decline of American Pluralism.* Stanford: Stanford University Press, 1961.

KRITZER, H. M. "Adjudication to Settlement: Shading in the Gray," *Judicature* 70 (1986): 161.

LOWI, T. J. *The End of Liberalism.* 2nd ed. New York: W.W. Norton & Company, 1979.

MCCANN, M. W. *Taking Reform Seriously: Perspectives on Public Interest Liberalism.* Ithaca: Cornell University Press, 1986.

McDONNELL, G. *Private Power and American Democracy.* New York: Vintage Books, 1966.

PROVINE, M. D. "Managing Negotiated Justice: Settlement Procedures in the Courts," prepared for the Conference on Judicial Administration Research Rockefeller College, State University of New York at Albany, June 16–18, 1986.

RABIN, R. L. "Federal Regulation in Historical Perspective," *Stanford Law Review* 38 (1986): 1189.

RESNIK, J. "Managerial Judges," *Harvard Law Review* 96 (1982): 374.

SEIDMAN, H. AND R. GILMOUR. *Politics, Position, and Power: from the Positive to the Regulatory State.* 4th ed. New York: Oxford University Press, 1986.

SHAPIRO, M. *The Supreme Court and Administrative Agencies.* New York: Free Press, 1968.

STEWART, R. B. "The Discontents of Legalism: Interest Group Relations in Administrative Regulation. *Wisconsin Law Review* 1985: 655.

SUSSKIND, L. AND G. MCMAHON. "The Theory and Practice of Negotiated Rulemaking," *The Yale Journal of Regulation* 3 (1985): 133.

WALD, P. M. "Negotiation of Environmental Disputes: A New Role for the Courts." *Columbia Journal of Environmental Law* 10 (1985): 1.

Professor Cary Coglianese came up with some surprising findings in his empirical study of negotiated rulemaking:

Over its thirteen-year history, the negotiated rulemaking process has yielded only thirty-five final administrative rules. By comparison, the federal government publishes over 3,000 final rules each year through the ordinary notice-and-comment process. Why have federal agencies relied so little on negotiated rulemaking? I examine this question by assessing the impact of negotiating rulemaking on its two major purposes: (1) reducing rulemaking time; and (2) decreasing the amount of litigation over agency rules. My analysis suggests that the asserted problems used to justify negotiated rulemaking have been overstated and that the limitations of negotiated rulemaking have been understated. Negotiated rulemaking by all accounts consumes more resources for agencies and stakeholders than does notice-and-comment rulemaking, yet it fails to yield any significant impact on the levels of litigation or controversy which normal rulemaking occasionally engenders. Indeed, six out of the 12 negotiated rules adopted by the U.S. Environmental Protection Agency (EPA) have resulted in court challenges, a litigation rate higher than the overall rate for EPA rules. My findings draw into question the growing call among scholars and policymakers for reforming the regulatory process to rely more extensively on formal negotiated rulemaking, suggesting that formal negotiation can actually expand the range of potential conflicts in the regulatory process rather than reduce them.[12]

Christine Harrington has confirmed in a joint research project, the results of the research done by Coglianese. Harrington and Turem find that negotiated rulemaking as practiced by agencies and checked by the courts decreases, rather than increases, accountability of administrative agencies. One of the major problems with negotiated rulemaking is that the selection of those at the table is opaque, and the decisions by the agency about who will

12. See "Assessing Consensus: The Promise and Performance of Negotiated Rulemaking," *Duke Law Journal* 46 (1997): 1021.

be at the table cannot be challenged in courts.[13] Danielle Holley-Walker, who teaches at the University of South Carolina School of Law, echoes this concern in her research on the "No Child Left Behind Act." She argues that even when one is successful in getting to the negotiation table, chances are still high that the oppositional voices will be silenced by the agency, in this case the Department of Education, through various tactics. Walker argues that the negotiated rulemaking procedure is one of the major reasons why the "No Child Left Behind Act" has failed to achieve its objectives.[14]

Will the recent political shift toward deregulation change the law governing administrative procedure? We conclude this chapter by discussing the effect of deregulation on agency rulemaking procedures. Under the Reagan administration we witnessed several efforts by federal regulatory agencies to implement the philosophy of deregulation. In *Motor Vehicles Manufacturers Assn. v. State Farm Mutual Automobile Ins. Co.* (1983), the Supreme Court held that the National Highway Traffic Safety Administration (NHTSA) could not carry out its policy agenda of deregulation by discarding rules it had made requiring vehicle manufacturers to install air bags without going through a rulemaking process. This case demonstrates how changing political perspectives on regulation can affect agency rulemaking procedures. After you read *Motor Vehicles Manufacturers Assn. v. State Farm Mutual Automobile Ins. Co.*, you will have been exposed to a wide array of political perspectives on agency rulemaking procedures—from the public interest movement's push for hybrid rulemaking to the Reagan administration's efforts to rescind rules in order to implement such new policies as deregulation. All these cases and commentary on the legal and political dimensions of the administrative policy-making process implicitly ask: how does agency rulemaking function to democratize the regulatory process? If a political party comes to power in

Washington and advocates deregulation, should administrative procedures conform to those policy goals?

Motor Vehicles Manufacturers Association v. State Farm Mutual Automobile Insurance Co.

463 U.S. 29 (1983) 5-4

+ *Brennan, White, Marshall, Blackmun, Stevens*

+/– *Burger, Powell, Rehnquist, O'Connor*

[The National Highway Traffic Safety Act of 1966 directs the Secretary of Transportation to issue motor vehicle safety standards that "shall be practicable, shall meet the need for motor vehicle safety, and shall be stated in objective terms." After numerous rulemaking notices, NHTSA established a rule requiring new motor vehicles produced after September 1982 to be equipped with "passive restraints," such as seatbelts. In 1981, NHTSA rescinded the requirement. Insurance companies petitioned for review of the rescinding order.]

Justice White delivered the opinion of the Court

The development of the automobile gave Americans unprecedented freedom to travel, but exacted a high price for enhanced mobility. Since 1929, motor vehicles have been the leading cause of accidental deaths and injuries in the United States. In 1982, 46,300 Americans died in motor vehicle accidents and hundreds of thousands more were maimed and injured. While a consensus exists that the current loss of life on our highways is unacceptably high, improving safety does not admit to easy solution. In 1966, Congress decided that at least part of the answer lies in improving the design and safety features of the vehicle itself. But much of the technology for building safer cars was undeveloped or untested. . . . This task called for considerable expertise and Congress responded by enacting the National Traffic and Motor Vehicle Safety Act of 1966 (Act). . . . The Act, created for the purpose of "reduc[ing] traffic accidents and deaths and injuries to persons resulting from traffic accidents." . . .

The Act . . . authorizes judicial review under the previsions of the Administrative Procedure Act (APA) . . . of all

---

13. See Christine B. Harrington and Z. Umut Turem, "Accounting for Accountability in the Neoliberal Regulatory Regimes," *Public Accountability: Designs, Dilemmas and Experiences* (Cambridge: Cambridge University Press, 2006), 195–220.

14. "The Importance of Negotiated Rulemaking to the No Child Left Behind Act," *Nebraska Law Review* 85 (2007): 1015.

"orders establishing, amending, or revoking a Federal motor vehicle safety standard." . . . Under this authority, we review today whether NHTSA acted arbitrarily and capriciously in revoking the requirement in Motor Vehicle Standard 208 that new motor vehicles produced after September 1982 be equipped with passive restraints to protect the safety of the occupants of the vehicle in the event of a collision. Briefly summarized, we hold that the agency failed to present an adequate basis and explanation for rescinding the passive restraint requirement and that the agency must either consider the matter further or adhere to or amend Standard 208 along lines which its analysis supports.

I

The regulation whose rescission is at issue bears a complex and convoluted history. Over the course of approximately 60 rulemaking notices, the requirement has been imposed, amended, rescinded, reimposed, and now rescinded again.

As originally issued by the Department of Transportation in 1967, Standard 208 simply required the installation of seatbelts in all automobiles. . . . It soon became apparent that the level of seatbelt use was too low to reduce traffic injuries to an acceptable level. The Department therefore began consideration of "passive occupant restraint systems"—devices that do not depend for their effectiveness upon any action taken by the occupant except that necessary to operate the vehicle. Two types of automatic crash protection emerged: automatic seatbelts and airbags. The automatic seatbelt is a traditional safety belt, which when fastened to the interior of the door remains attached without impeding entry or exit from the vehicle, and deploys automatically without any action on the part of the passenger. The airbag is an inflatable device concealed in the dashboard and steering column. It automatically inflates when a sensor indicates that deceleration forces from an accident have exceeded a preset minimum, then rapidly deflates to dissipate those forces. The life-saving potential of these devices was immediately recognized, and in 1977, after substantial on-the-road experience with both devices, it was estimated by NHTSA that passive restraints could prevent approximately 12,000 deaths and over 100,000 serious injuries annually. . . .

In 1969, the Department formally imposed a standard requiring the installation of passive restraints, . . . thereby commencing a lengthy series of proceedings. In 1970, the agency revised Standard 208 to include passive protection requirements, and in 1972, the agency amended the Standard to require full passive protection for all front seat occupants of vehicles manufactured after August 15, 1975. . . . On review, the agency's decision to require passive restraints was found to be supported by "substantial evidence" and upheld. *Chrysler Corp. v. Department of Transportation*, 472 F.2d 659 (CA6 1972).

In preparing for the upcoming model year, most cars makers chose the "ignition interlock" option, a decision which was highly unpopular, and led Congress to amend the Act to prohibit a motor vehicle safety standard from requiring or permitting compliance by means of an ignition interlock or a continuous buzzer designed to indicate that safety belts were not in use. . . . The 1974 Amendments also provided that any safety standard that could be satisfied by a system other than seatbelts would have to be submitted to Congress where it could be vetoed by concurrent resolution of both Houses. . . .

The effective date for mandatory passive restraint systems was extended for a year until August 31, 1976. . . . But in June 1976, Secretary of Transportation William T. Coleman Jr. initiated a new rulemaking on the issue. . . . After hearing testimony and reviewing written comments, Coleman extended the optional alternatives indefinitely and suspended the passive restraint requirement. Although he found passive restraints technologically and economically feasible, the Secretary based his decision on the expectation that there would be widespread public resistance to the new systems. He instead proposed a demonstration project involving up to 500,000 cars installed with passive restraints, in order to smooth the way for public acceptance of mandatory passive restraints at a later date. . . .

Coleman's successor as Secretary of Transportation disagreed. Within months of assuming office, Secretary Brock Adams decided that the demonstration project was unnecessary. He issued a new mandatory passive restraint regulation, known as Modified Standard 208 [1977]. . . . The Modified Standard mandated the phasing in of passive restraints beginning with large cars in model year 1982 and extending to all cars by model year 1984. The two principal systems that would satisfy the Standard were airbags and passive belts; the choice of which system to install was left to the manufacturers. . . . The Standard also survived scrutiny by Congress, which did not exercise its authority under the legislative veto provision of the 1974 Amendments.

Over the next several years, the automobile industry geared up to comply with Modified Standard 208. . . .

In February 1981, however, Secretary of Transportation Andrew Lewis reopened the rulemaking due to changed economic circumstances and, in particular, the difficulties of the automobile industry. . . . Two months later, the agency ordered a one-year delay in the application of the Standard to large cars, extending the deadline to September 1982, . . . and at the same time, proposed the possible rescission of the entire Standard. . . . After receiving written comments and holding public hearings, NHTSA issued a final rule (Notice 25) that rescinded the passive restraint requirement contained in Modified Standard 208.

II

In a statement explaining the rescission, NHTSA maintained that it was no longer able to find, as it had in 1977, that the automatic restraint requirement would produce significant safety benefits. . . . This judgment reflected not a change of opinion on the effectiveness of the technology, but a change in plans by the automobile industry. In 1977, the agency had assumed that airbags would be installed in 60% of all new cars and automatic seatbelts in 40%. By 1981 it became apparent that automobile manufacturers planned to install the automatic seatbelts in approximately 99% of the new cars. For this reason, the lifesaving potential of airbags would not be realized. Moreover, it now appeared that the overwhelming majority of passive belts planned to be installed by manufacturers could be detached easily and left that way permanently. . . .

State Farm Mutual Automobile Insurance Co. and the National Association of Independent Insurers filed petitions for review of NHTSA's rescission of the passive restraint Standard. The United States Court of Appeals for the District of Columbia Circuit held that the agency's rescission of the passive restraint requirement was arbitrary and capricious. . . . 680 F.2d 206 (1982). While observing that rescission is not unrelated to an agency's refusal to take action in the first instance, the court concluded that, in this case, NHTSA's discretion to rescind the passive restraint requirement had been restricted by various forms of congressional "reaction" to the passive restraint issue. . . .

III

Unlike the Court of Appeals, we do not find the appropriate scope of judicial review to be the "most troublesome question" in these cases. Both the Act and the 1974 Amendments concerning occupant crash protection standards indicate that motor vehicle safety standards are to be promulgated under the informal rulemaking procedures of the Administrative Procedure Act. 5 U.S.C. § 553. The agency's action in promulgating such standards therefore may be set aside if found to be "arbitrary, capricious, an abuse of discretion, or otherwise not in accordance with law." . . . *Citizens to Preserve Overton Park v. Volpe* 401 U.S. 402. . . . (1971). . . . We believe that the rescission or modification of an occupant-protection standard is subject to the same test. . . .

Petitioner Motor Vehicle Manufacturers Association (MVMA) disagrees, contending that the rescission of an agency rule should be judged by the same standard a court could use to judge an agency's refusal to promulgate a rule in the first place—a standard petitioner believes considerably narrower than the traditional arbitrary-and-capricious test. We reject this view. The Act expressly equates orders "revoking" and "establishing" safety standards; neither that Act nor the APA suggests that revocations are to be treated as refusals to promulgate standards. Petitioner's view would render meaningless Congress' authorization for judicial review of orders revoking safety rules. Moreover, the revocation of an extant regulation is substantially different than a failure to act. Revocation constitutes a reversal of the agency's former views as to the proper course. . . . Accordingly, an agency changing its course by rescinding a rule is obligated to supply a reasoned analysis for the change beyond that which may be required when an agency does not act in the first instance.

In so holding, we fully recognize that "[r]egulatory agencies do not establish rules of conduct to last forever," *American Trucking Assns., Inc. v. Atchison, T. & S.F.R. Co.,* 387 U.S. 397 . . . (1967), and that an agency must be given ample latitude to "adapt their rules and policies to the demands of changing circumstances." *Permian Basin Area Rate Cases*, 390 U.S. 747. . . . But the forces of change do not always or necessarily point in the direction of deregulation. In the abstract, there is no more reason to presume that changing circumstances require the rescission of prior action, instead of a revision in or even the extension of current regulation. If Congress established a presumption from which judicial review should start, that presumption—contrary to petitioners' views—is not *against* safety regulation, but *against* changes in current policy that are not justified by the rulemaking record. . . .

. . . Normally, an agency rule would be arbitrary and capricious if the agency has relied on factors which Congress has not intended it to consider, entirely failed to consider an important aspect of the problem, offered an explanation for its decision that runs counter to the evidence before the agency, or is so implausible that it could not be ascribed to a difference in view or the product of agency expertise. The reviewing court should not attempt itself to make up for such deficiencies; we may not supply a reasoned basis for the agency's action that the agency itself has not given. . . . For purposes of these cases, it is also relevant that Congress required a record of the rulemaking proceedings to be compiled and submitted to a reviewing court, . . . and intended that agency findings under the Act would be supported by "substantial evidence on the record considered as a whole." . . .

IV

The Court of Appeals correctly found that the arbitrary-and-capricious test applied to rescissions of prior agency regulations, but then erred in intensifying the scope of its review based upon its reading of legislative events. It held that congressional reaction to various versions of Standard 208 "raise[d] doubts" that NHTSA's rescission "necessarily demonstrates an effort to fulfill its statutory mandate," and therefore the agency was obligated to provide "increasingly clear and convincing reasons" for its action. . . .

This path of analysis was misguided and the inferences it produced are questionable. . . . While an agency's interpretation of a statute may be confirmed or ratified by subsequent congressional failure to change that interpretation, . . . in the cases before us, even an unequivocal ratification—short of statutory incorporation—of the passive restraint standard would not connote approval or disapproval of an agency's later decision to rescind the regulation. That decision remains subject to the arbitrary-and-capricious standard. . . .

V

. . . The first and most obvious reason for finding the rescission arbitrary and capricious is that NHTSA apparently gave no consideration whatever to modifying the Standard to require that airbag technology be utilized. . . . Automatic belts were added as a means of complying with the Standard because they were believed to be as effective as airbags in achieving the goal of occupant crash protection. . . .

The agency has now determined that the detachable automatic belts will not attain anticipated safety benefits because so many individuals will detach the mechanism. Even if this conclusion were acceptable in its entirety, . . . standing alone it would not justify any more than an amendment of Standard 208 to disallow compliance by means of the one technology which will not provide effective passenger protection. It does not cast doubt on the need for a passive restraint standard or upon the efficacy of airbag technology. . . .

At the very least this alternative way of achieving the objectives of the Act should have been addressed and adequate reasons given for its abandonment. But the agency not only did not require compliance through airbags, it also did not even consider the possibility in its 1981 rulemaking. Not one sentence of its rulemaking statement discusses the airbags-only option. . . . We have frequently reiterated that an agency must cogently explain why it has exercised its discretion in a given manner, and we reaffirm this principle again today.

The automobile industry has opted for the passive belt over the airbag, but surely it is not enough that the regulated industry has eschewed a given safety device. For nearly a decade, the automobile industry waged the regulatory equivalent of war against the airbag and lost—the inflatable restraint was proved sufficiently effective. Now the automobile industry has decided to employ a seatbelt system which will not meet the safety objectives of Standard 208. This hardly constitutes cause to revoke the Standard itself. Indeed, the Act was necessary because the industry was not sufficiently responsive to safety concerns. The Act intended that safety standards not depend on current technology and could be "technology-forcing" in the sense of inducing the development of superior safety design. . . .

Petitioners also invoke our decision in *Vermont Yankee Nuclear Power Corp. v. Natural Resources Defense Council, Inc.*, 435 U.S. 519 . . . (1978), as though it were a talisman under which any agency decision is by definition unimpeachable. Specifically, it is submitted that to require an agency to consider an airbags-only alternative is, in essence, to dictate to the agency the procedures it is to follow. Petitioners both misread *Vermont Yankee* and misconstrue the nature of the remand that is in order. In *Vermont Yankee*, we held that a court may not impose additional procedural requirements upon an agency. We do not require today any specific procedures which NHTSA must follow. Nor do we broadly require an agency to consider all policy alternatives in reaching decision. It is true that rule-making "cannot be found wanting simply because the agency failed to include every alternative device and thought conceivable by the mind of man . . . regardless of how uncommon or unknown that alternative may have been. . . . " *Id.*, at 551. . . . But the airbag is more than a policy alternative to the passive restraint Standard; it is a technological alternative within the ambit of the existing Standard. We hold only that given the judgment made in 1977 that airbags are an effective and cost-beneficial life-saving technology, the mandatory passive restraint rule may not be abandoned without any consideration whatsoever of an airbags-only requirement. . . .

In these cases, the agency's explanation for rescission of the passive restraint requirement is *not* sufficient to enable us to conclude that the rescission was the product of reasoned decisionmaking. To reach this conclusion, we do not upset the agency's view of the facts, but we do appreciate the limitations of this record in supporting the agency's decision. We start with the accepted ground that if used, seatbelts unquestionably would save many thousands of lives and would prevent tens of thousands of crippling injuries. Unlike recent regulatory decisions we have reviewed, *Industrial Union Dept. v. American Petroleum Institute*, 448 U.S. 607 . . . (1980); *American Textile Mfrs. Institute, Inc. v. Donovan*, 452 U.S. 490 . . . (1981), the safety benefits of wearing seat-belts are not in doubt, and it is not challenged that were those benefits to accrue, the monetary costs of implementing the Standard would be easily

justified. We move next to the fact that there is no direct evidence in support of the agency's finding that detachable automatic belts cannot be predicted to yield a substantial increase in usage. The empirical evidence on the record, consisting of surveys of drivers of automobiles equipped with passive belts, reveals more than a doubling of the usage rate experienced with manual belts. Much of the agency's rulemaking statement—and much of the controversy in these cases—centers on the conclusions that should be drawn from these studies. The agency maintained that the doubling of seatbelt usage in these studies could not be extrapolated to an across-the-board mandatory standard because the passive seatbelts were guarded by ignition interlocks and purchasers of the tested cars are somewhat atypical. Respondents insist these studies demonstrate that Modified Standard 208 will substantially increase seatbelt usage. We believe that it is within the agency's discretion to pass upon the generalizability of these field studies. This is precisely the type of issue which rests within the expertise of NHTSA, and upon which a reviewing court must be most hesitant to intrude.

But accepting the agency's view of the field tests on passive restraints indicates only that there is no reliable real-world experience that usage rates will substantially increase. . . .

The agency is correct to look at the costs as well as the benefits of Standard 208. The agency's conclusion that the incremental costs of the requirements were no longer reasonable was predicated on its prediction that the safety benefits of the regulation might be minimal. Specifically, the agency's fears that the public may resent paying more for the automatic belt systems is expressly dependent on the assumption that detachable automatic belts will not produce more than "negligible safety benefits." *Id.*, at 53424. When the agency reexamines its findings as to the likely increase in seatbelt usage, it must also reconsider its judgment of the reasonableness of the monetary and other costs associated with the Standard. In reaching its judgment, NHTSA should bear in mind that Congress intended safety to be the preeminent factor under the Act. . . .

By failing to analyze the continuous seatbelts option in its own right, the agency has failed to offer the rational connection between facts and judgment required to pass muster under the arbitrary-and-capricious standard. . . . While the agency is entitled to change its view on the acceptability of continuous passive belts, it is obligated to explain its reasons for doing so.

. . . Accordingly, we vacate the judgment of the Court of Appeals and remand the case to that court with directions to remand the matter to the NHTSA for further consideration consistent with this opinion.

So ordered.

Justice Rehnquist, with whom the Chief Justice Burger, Justice Powell, and Justice O'Connor join, concurring in part and dissenting in part

I join Parts I, II, III, IV, and V-A of the Court's opinion. In particular, I agree that, since the airbag and continuous spool automatic seatbelt were explicitly approved in the Standard the agency was rescinding, the agency should explain why it declined to leave those requirements intact. In this case, the agency gave no explanation at all. Of course, if the agency can provide a rational explanation, it may adhere to its decision to rescind the entire Standard.

I do not believe, however, that NHTSA's view of detachable automatic seatbelts was arbitrary and capricious. The agency adequately explained its decision to rescind the Standard insofar as it was satisfied by detachable belts. . . .

. . . The agency chose not to rely on a study showing a substantial increase in seatbelt usage in cars equipped with automatic seatbelts *and* an ignition interlock to prevent the car from being operated when the belts were not in place *and* which were voluntarily purchased with this equipment by consumers. . . . It is reasonable for the agency to decide that this study does not support any conclusion concerning the effect of automatic seatbelts that are installed in all cars whether the consumer wants them or not and are not linked to an ignition interlock system. . . .

The agency's changed view of the standard seems to be related to the election of a new President [Reagan] of a different political party [Republican]. It is readily apparent that the responsible members of one administration may consider public resistance and uncertainties to be more important than do their counterparts in a previous administration. A change in administration brought about by the people casting their votes is a perfectly reasonable basis for an executive agency's reappraisal of the costs and benefits of its programs and regulations. As long as the agency remains within the bounds established by Congress,* it is entitled to assess administrative records and evaluate priorities in light of the philosophy of the administration.

The *Chevron* case, reported in chapter 4 and decided only a year after *State Farm*, did not overrule *State Farm*, but the philosophies behind them are quite different. Both remain on the books as precedents authorizing more or less active judicial oversight of agency action. The Court seems ready to accept informalities in rulemaking. In 2005, however, the Court took this philosophy to a new level. It held, in *National Cable & Telecommunications Association, et al. v. Brand X Internet Services, et al.*[15] that "a court's prior construction of a statute trumps an agency construction . . . only if the prior court decision holds that its construction follows from the unambiguous terms of the statute and thus leaves no room for agency discretion." The Court, in effect, said that "*Chevron* . . . would trump *stare decisis*; an interpretation of an ambiguous statute that ordinarily would be entitled to deference under *Chevron* would still receive that deference—and an agency would be permitted to revise a prior statutory interpretation—irrespective of anything that a court had ever said on the subject."[16]

---

* Of course, a new administration may not choose not to enforce laws of which it does not approve, or to ignore statutory standards in carrying out its regulatory functions. But in this case, as the Court correctly concludes, *ante*, at 2867–2668, Congress has not required the agency to require passive restraints.

15. 545 U.S. 967 (2005).

16. Jonathan Masur, "Judicial Deference and the Credibility of Agency Commitments," *Vanderbilt Law Review* 60 (2007): 1021.

EXERCISES AND QUESTIONS FOR FURTHER THOUGHT

1. Review one more time the *Morgan* case in chapter 2. Suppose the case arose under the modern APA but the other statutory law was the same. Suppose further that the Secretary of Agriculture announced a new set of prices after section 553 notice and comment hearings only. If the packers challenged the procedure, how would Justice Rehnquist rule? Does his statement in the rail car leasing case necessarily reveal how he would decide that issue, particularly after his opinion in *Vermont Yankee*?

2. Suppose a state liquor agency determined by rule that no liquor store could remain open after 10 p.m. in any town with a public college, junior college, or university. Suppose this state to be covered by the Model State Administrative Procedure Act in Appendix C. In what circumstances would ex parte communication be forbidden in this rulemaking? Start with section 13 and work back through the definitions you will need to solve this puzzle.

3. Consider the political characteristics and implications of Justice Rehnquist's positions in *Vermont Yankee* and his dissent in *Motor Vehicles Manufacturers Assn. v. State Farm Mutual Automobile Ins. Co.* Justice Rehnquist is generally regarded as a proponent of judicial self-restraint, and both of these decisions seek to reduce the oversight of the courts in the administrative process. But he is also by reputation a conservative, an Arizona Republican appointed by President Nixon. Is it not fair to say that both these decisions are pro-government? Can we best explain Justice Rehnquist's position by pointing out that free enterprise benefited by the policies he allows the agencies to pursue, or are other, less ideological factors, at work?

4. By statute the Federal Aviation Administration (FAA) may suspend the license of any commercial airline pilot for safety's sake. The statute gives the pilot an opportunity to be heard first. The FAA also has power to issue "reasonable rules . . . to provide adequately for national security and safety in air commerce." Following only section 553 rulemaking proceedings the Administrator, the one-man head of the FAA, issued a rule that automatically terminated the licenses of commercial pilots at the age of 60. The pilots brought suit claiming they had been denied their opportunity to be heard. The Administrator stated that the age of 60 was as defensible a cut-off as any and that the FAA did not have the resources to evaluate the health of every pilot frequently enough to catch the many health problems that crop up past that age. What decision should a court reach in this lawsuit?[17]

5. A basic legal precept holds that new legislation is not applied retroactively to actions that took place prior to its passage. Should administrative rules be applied retroactively by the agencies that create them? Courts have justified some retroactive applications of new legislation where the benefits outweigh the costs. See *Tennessee Gas Pipeline Co. v. Federal Energy Regulation Commission*, 606 F.2d 1094 (1979).

6. Do you agree with the Supreme Court's *Brand X* decision holding that agency interpretations of statutes should trump conflicting interpretations by the courts? What are the potential benefits and costs of such an approach?

---

17. See *Airline Pilots Association v. Quesada*, 276 F.2d 892 (1960).

CHAPTER 9
ENFORCEMENT OF ADMINISTRATIVE POLICY

This chapter completes the book's description of the actions and processes common to administrative governance. Enforcement is the last step an agency can take to achieve its policy goals. Any remaining changes in policy or action will occur in the courts in the course of judicial review of agency action, discussed in the next chapter. This chapter does not limit itself to a single focal point or theme. Some of the issues raised here have appeared with varying specificity in earlier chapters, and some, particularly enforcement through revocation and threat of revocation of licenses, will appear again in chapter 12. This chapter seeks primarily to fill in descriptive details so students will be familiar with the routines of administrative action.

ADMINISTRATIVE LAW AND THE PROBLEM OF COMPLIANCE

The word *enforcement* evokes images of police officers with guns drawn using force to apprehend law violators and by this example to deter others from violating the law in the future. Yet use of physical force represents but a small fraction of the enforcement activities the legal system uses to ensure compliance with law. To illustrate a few of the many types of administrative enforcement, consider the following news stories from the *New York Times* reported during the first half of 2008:

• "Would You Like Sick Cow With Those Fries?"—After a Humane Society video revealed shocking treatment of sick cows at a California factory, the Department of Agriculture (USDA)

ordered the factory closed. California law requires that sick animals who are unable to stand be humanely euthanized and their carcasses destroyed, rather than sold as food. The video showed sick animals being beaten, shocked or abused before being slaughtered along with healthy animals. Despite immediate action by the USDA, the agency's spotty record in identifying "non-ambulatory" cows led to various initiatives to prevent sick cows being slaughtered. New York City school officials refused to accept 300,000 hamburger patties produced by the California factory, and McDonalds took steps to make sure their meat came from secure sources. Several states passed laws to punish animal abuse more severely. (February 15, 2008).

• "President Appears to Seek a Warming Legacy."—The president of the United States is sometimes referred to as the chief enforcer of laws in the country. After being criticized for failing to act during his first seven years in office on scientific findings that point to human-caused climate change, President George Bush decided to take action during his last year in office. Facing a potential regulatory nightmare on the issue, Bush, decided to move the administration and the Republican party closer to the center by making international deals with European leaders that included a promise to reduce carbon emissions if China and India agreed to do the same. (April 14, 2008).

In administrative law we must begin by broadening the concept of enforcement to include the full array of administrative actions that encourage compliance with the Constitution, compliance with statutory policy created by the legislature, compliance with rules made by agencies, and compliance with adjudicatory outcomes directed at individual parties. These levels of compliance tend to succeed one another. For example, to the extent statutory policy or administrative rules are clear and are abided by, adjudication (itself an enforcement process) becomes less likely. Thus the best introduction to enforcement begins with a brief review of compliance itself.

Compliance occurs when actions are consistent with legal commands. If a rule speaks generally or ambiguously in a policy area—and we have seen how and why many statutes are general and ambiguous—it is not realistic to expect compliance because the rule provides no clear standard by which to measure compliance. This is particularly true in much of the regulatory policy that delegates to agencies the obligation to develop rules of conduct specific enough to command compliance. Thus in administrative law, just as in criminal law or any body of rules, government policies can change social practices. The question naturally arises: Which kinds of policies are best at ensuring compliance? The answer depends on a number of social factors (i.e., legal, political, and economic) that can vary from one regulatory context to another.[1] Here, in summary form, is a list of conditions we often associate with different degrees of regulatory compliance. In some settings the significance of one condition, such as the economic and political power of the regulated parties, may be more important than the severity of the sanction in determining whether regulatory compliance will be high or low. As you read this list, think about the relationship between these conditions and consider the extent to which they may impact differently on different regulatory contexts.

1. *Rules.* Compliance varies with the following characteristics of rules:

a. the clarity with which a rule describes the people covered by it;

b. the clarity with which the rule assigns responsibility to specific individuals to enforce the rule;

c. the clarity of the sanction imposed for noncompliance;

d. the severity of the sanction.

2. *Enforcers.* Compliance varies with the following characteristics of those who enforce or implement a rule or policy:

a. the extent to which enforcers in fact know it is their responsibility to enforce;

b. the extent to which enforcers feel the command to enforce is legitimate and proper;

c. the extent to which enforcers believe the command to enforce is consistent with their operational objectives as well as their personal objectives and ambitions;

d. the capacity of enforcers to devote resources to the enforcement task.

3. *Beneficiaries.* Beneficiaries include consumers of products of regulated businesses. Often the general public benefits, as in the case of reduced air and water pollution. Compliance varies with the following characteristics of the beneficiaries of public policy:

a. the extent to which beneficiaries perceive the benefits they receive and the amount of value they put on them;

b. the resources beneficiaries possess to promote the enforcement process;

c. the extent to which beneficiaries believe enforcers will listen to their specific complaints about instances of noncompliance.

4. *Regulated Parties.* Compliance varies with the following characteristics of those whose behavior the rule or policy seeks to affect:

a. the extent to which the regulated perceive a command that requires or proscribes specific behaviors;

b. the extent to which the regulated define the command as legitimate and proper;

c. the extent to which the regulated lack resources to prevent detection and/or block enforcement;

d. the benefits to the regulated of noncompliance relative to the cost of the sanction if imposed;

e. the extent to which the regulated believe that a sanction will be applied once noncompliance has been detected.

1. For a good introduction to the different perspectives on regulatory compliance, see Deborah A. Stone, *Policy Paradox and Political Reason* (Glenview, Ill.: Scott, Foresman/Little, Brown, 1988). For work that addresses particular regulatory compliance problems, see Eugene Bardach and Robert A. Kagan, eds., *Social Regulation: Strategies for Reform* (San Francisco: Institute for Contemporary Studies, 1982).

These categories hardly exhaust the problem of enforcement and compliance.[2] They do, however, explain a large proportion of the legal and illegal practices we observe in society. This compliance model helps us understand many of the phenomena we have already uncovered in administrative government. The Federal Trade Commission (FTC) delayed for decades regulating through rulemaking because it doubted the legitimacy of the process (2b) and because consumer group beneficiaries were poorly organized (3a and 3b). You can explain the Nuclear Regulatory Commission (NRC)'s failure to police the South Texas Nuclear Project in terms of its resource shortages (2d and 4c & d), and so on.

You should remember at this point that "regulation," as a mode of governance, is distinct because of its flexibility and adaptability; and this is what makes rulemaking one of the greatest inventions of modern government. Sharing this belief in the efficacy of regulation, many foreign countries have recently begun to insert more flexibility in their governance structures. Regulation is "going global," so to speak. Enforcement of rules created through the regulatory process is no exception to the in-built flexibility of the system of regulation. Bronwen Morgan and Karen Yeung, regulation scholars from the United Kingdom, emphasize that a regulatory system must have at least three components: a capacity for standard setting, a capacity for information gathering and monitoring, and a capacity for behavior modification.[3] Regulation is a mix of these capacities and yet there is no pre-defined formula for the mix. Decisions about which component to emphasize are made on a case-by-case basis. Regulation consists in the art of obtaining results. Rigid enforcement regimes are hardly useful in achieving that goal.

The rest of this chapter focuses on three specific characteristics of enforcement implicit in the compliance model. These are the nature of sanctions (costs) that administrators can impose, the devices administrators may use short of formal adjudication or criminal prosecution to pressure people to comply, and the role of citizens in enforcing government policies through litigation.

THE NATURE OF ADMINISTRATIVE SANCTIONS

A sanction is a cost imposed for noncompliance. Section 551 (10) of the Administrative Procedure Act (APA) defines sanctions to include:

(A) prohibition, requirement, limitation, or other condition affecting the freedom of a person;

(B) withholding of relief;

(C) imposition of penalty or fine;

(D) destruction, taking, seizure, or withholding of property;

(E) assessment of damages, reimbursement, restitution, compensation, costs, charges, or fees;

(F) requirement, revocation, or suspension of a license; or

(G) taking other compulsory or restrictive action.

As the compliance model indicates, the effectiveness of sanctions depends not so much on the label we use for it as it does on the likelihood of the sanction being imposed and the degree of hardship it causes the sanctioned party. Here are some illustrations of administrative sanctions.

Cutting Funds or Other Financial Aids

Cutting funds has been a major enforcement tool in areas, particularly education, that have grown to depend on federal support. Desegregation in many parts of the country, for example, occurred less because of Supreme Court rulings than because of the threat to withdraw educational funds.[4] In 1982 the Environmental Protection Agency (EPA) threatened to cut off hundreds of millions of dollars of federal aid after finding that a dozen major U.S. cities had failed to comply with clean air laws. The cutoffs took place through withholding future federal grants for construction of highways and sewers in

2. For an exhaustive treatment, see F. Zimring and G. Hawkins, *Deterrence* (Chicago: University of Chicago Press, 1973).

3. Bronwen Morgan and Karen Yeung, *An Introduction to Law and Regulation* (New York: Cambridge University Press, 2007), 3.

4. See Rodgers and Bullock, *Coercion to Compliance* (Lexington, Mass.: Lexington Books, 1976).

Pittsburgh, Chicago, Houston, and other major cities. This was not the first time such a major cutoff occurred to enforce environmental rules. In 1980 the Carter administration cut off $850 million for eight communities that failed to create mandatory inspection programs for automobile pollution-control equipment.[5]

Loss of License

This sanction raises such a serious threat that it is covered in a separate chapter. Licenses range from the driver's permit, with which we are all familiar, to occupational, professional, and other business licenses. To operate without a license exposes the citizen in most cases to immediate criminal liability, which makes the sanction potentially effective *if*, as the compliance model suggests, the perceived risks of detection are reasonably high.

Administrative Fines

Administrative fines can be a serious financial threat. For example, in 1983 the NRC, with Congress's permission, sought to increase nuclear safety by levying six-figure fines.[6] Forfeiture of property is another type of administrative fine. A forfeiture action can be taken as a civil action following a criminal conviction. This is not considered double jeopardy if the money or goods were obtained in the commission of the criminal offense. Generally, forfeitures are used to sanction drug traffickers and people who evade taxes. However, the Excessive Fines clause of the Eighth Amendment may act as a limitation on the government's power to exact fines. *U.S. v. Bajakajian* (1998)[7] illustrates this point. Bajakajian boarded an international flight with $357,144 in cash and was charged with attempting to leave the country without reporting that he was transporting more than $10,000 in United States currency, which is required by law. The government wanted to punish him by having him forfeit the entire amount. The District Court found that although all $357,144 was "involved in" the crime of not reporting, the money was not gained through the commission of a crime, and therefore forfeiture of the entire amount was "excessive" under the Eighth Amendment. On appeal, the United States Court of Appeals for the Ninth Circuit affirmed and laid out two conditions required to avoid the Excessive Fines limitation: first, the forfeiture has to be an "instrumentality" of the crime, and in this case the $357,144 was not instrumental to Bajakajian's failure to report; and second, the value of the forfeiture must be proportional to the crime, and in this case the court held it was excessive. The Supreme Court affirmed.

Criminal Sanctions

While agency actions rarely impose criminal penalties, these penalties always loom as a background threat. Even if an agency has no direct authority to seek criminal penalties in court, courts have the authority to fine or jail those who refuse a court order to obey an agency. In some areas of policy the authorizing statutes prescribe criminal penalties for violations. This is true of one of our oldest regulatory policies, antitrust law, though the Federal Trade Commission (FTC) and the Justice Department usually prefer to exercise their option of proceeding civilly in such cases. Similarly, most readers know that the Internal Revenue Service (IRS) can seek criminal penalties for tax fraud, as do the taxing authorities in the states. No agency can impose and enforce criminal penalties alone. Criminal penalties result only from proceedings in the regular courts.[8] After a major financial scandal at Houston, Texas-based Enron Corporation, for instance, several executives at the company received prison sentences for deceiving analysts and investors about the true financial condition of the company. Jeffrey Skilling, the Chief Executive Officer of Enron, began serving a 24-year sentence in 2006. The Securities and Exchange Commission (SEC) participated in the investigation right from the start.

5. "EPA Threatens Cutoff of Road, Sewer Aid . . ." *Wall Street Journal*, April 5, 1982.
6. "NRG Staff Proposes Boston Edison Pay Record $550,000 for Alleged Violations," *Wall Street Journal*, January 20, 1982.
7. 524 U.S. 321.
8. For a discussion of the political barriers to imposing criminal penalties against corporations, see Marshall B. Clinard and Peter C. Yeager, *Corporate Crime* (New York: Free Press, 1980).

Economic Sanctions

In addition to the other sanctions listed in the APA, agencies whose programs involve financial decisions can use economic sanctions to achieve policy aims. Thus the Carter administration made procurement policies a part of its inflation-reduction strategy. Agencies were encouraged not to purchase from those who had significantly raised prices. The former Department of Health, Education, and Welfare often made minority participation a prerequisite for receiving various community development funds. Finally, the IRS has denied tax-exempt status to certain institutions, schools primarily, that practice racial segregation or otherwise offend public policy goals.

ADMINISTRATIVE ENFORCEMENT TECHNIQUES

The detailed techniques of enforcement vary from agency to agency. To describe them in combination with all the available sanctions would require a book exclusively on enforcement. This description outlines the five most common forms.[9]

1. Consent Settlements

Prior to formal adjudication, and usually with the threat of adjudication looming, the parties negotiate a consent settlement. In a large agency such as the FTC, where the five commissioners do not themselves do the negotiating, the agency head or heads will review and tentatively accept, reject, or modify the settlement. The settlement is then communicated to all interested parties who have an opportunity to react informally to the tentative agreement. After a specified period the agreement becomes effective. At this point the agreement has all the legal effect of a formal order arising from adjudication. If a party to the agreement violates it in the future, the agency may seek summarily to impose penalties for violations.

Agencies benefit from consent settlements because they avoid the time and expense of adjudication but produce a legally binding result. The private parties also save

time and money. Additionally they make no admission of formal violation and avoid the possible embarrassment of being found in violation after a formal hearing.

2. Advisory Opinions

When a party seeks information regarding the lawfulness of a proposed action, advisory opinions are used. Under certain conditions agencies adopt internal procedures for issuing advisory opinions. In such circumstances agencies routinely honor their advisory opinions.

3. Industry Guides

To develop guidelines dealing with either problematic practices in a variety of business contexts or a practice in a specific industry, agencies use industry guides. These guides have no force of law and therefore do not necessarily follow APA notice and comment procedures. The FTC has, however, normally invited comment, and has even sponsored "trade practice conferences" in which industry representatives meet and try to agree on a voluntary code to deal with a problem. The commission might, for example, seek a conference to develop voluntary standards for the use of the descriptive term "light" in reference to lower-calorie beer and wine.

4. Cease and Desist Orders

Adjudication, unless it entirely exonerates the position of the citizen in question, results in an order. In fact, section 551(7) defines adjudication in these terms: " 'adjudication' means agency process for the formulation of an order." Section 551(6) defines *order* as "the whole or a part of a final disposition, whether affirmative, negative, injunctive, or declaratory in form, of an agency in a matter other than rule-making but including licensing." Not all orders are cease and desist orders. An order can impose any of the sanctions listed in section 551(10) above. A cease and desist order specifies certain actions which the party must not take in the future. It is therefore sometimes called a *negative* order. The effect of this order imposes no punishment for any prior illegal practice and, except for the added costs of the hearing, produces the same sanctions as a consent decree.

5. Affirmative Disclosure and Other Corrective Orders

When an agency believes that a business has actively misled its customers, through advertising or other pro-

9. This section is based on the more detailed review of FTC enforcement in G. Robinson, W. Gellhorn, and C. Bruff, *The Administrative Process* (St. Paul: West Publishing, 1980), 544–607.

motional materials, it can by order require the business to correct the misinformation. In *J. B. Williams Co. v. FTC*, 381 F.2d 884 (1967), the appellate court upheld an FTC order requiring Geritol commercials to disclose that most fatigue does not result from iron deficiency anemia, the only cause that Geritol plausibly could alleviate. And in *Warner-Lambert Co. v. FTC*, 562 F.2d 749 (1977), the appellate court required the makers of Listerine to state that their product would not prevent colds or sore throats or lessen their severity. The FTC had also ordered Warner-Lambert to state in their advertisement that this disclaimer was "contrary to prior advertising." The court modified the FTC's order by removing this corrective statement. It held the corrective statement was punitive. Punitive sanctions are appropriate in cases of deliberate deception and bad faith. However, the court noted that Listerine had been promoted for a hundred years as a cold preventative or remedy and that for the bulk of that time the claim was, at least according to the facts on the record of the hearing, made in good faith. Listerine was required to spend as much money advertising that the product did not prevent colds as it spent, between April 1962 and March 1972, on its advertisement that Listerine did prevent or alleviate colds.

ENFORCEMENT AND POLITICAL RESISTANCE

When administrative action poses an immediate threat, through the enforcement of sanctions, to citizens' economic or personal interests, private citizens and groups are most likely to seek political support in Congress to block action. The pattern of lobbying Congress to block enforcement of certain programs has increased significantly since 1970. Since 1975 and particularly in the late 1990s, Congress and individual legislators have, by attaching amendments to appropriations bills and by threatening to reduce the IRS's own appropriations, curtailed national enforcement of several IRS policies designed to reduce tax avoidance and evasion. Some of Congress's meddling with the IRS raises serious constitutional questions. However, few if any administrative agencies are powerful enough to bring lawsuits to test

Congress's power to intervene without increasing legislative ire.[10]

CITIZEN INITIATION OF AGENCY ENFORCEMENT

Private citizens and interest groups have the right to bring their own actions in court to enforce statutory policies for which administrative agencies are responsible. Enforcement suits that citizens initiate differ somewhat from suits which challenge the orders or rules of an agency.[11] In the next case, *Environmental Defense Fund v. Ruckelshaus* (1971), an environmental organization brought a suit against the secretary of agriculture for failing to take actions authorized by Congress. Citizen suits to enforce governmental policy are an outgrowth of the public interest movement and its efforts to monitor agency decisions and *nondecisions*. However, citizens may sue private parties as well. For example, in *Gwaltney of Smithfield v. Chesapeake Bay Foundation, Inc. and Natural Resources Defense Council* (1987), two environmental organizations filed suit against a meat-packing company for violating pollution regulations of the Clean Water Act. While Congress delegated the responsibility for enforcing the Clean Water Act to the EPA, many environmental groups have argued that the EPA, particularly under the direction of the Reagan and George H.W. Bush administrations, has failed to prosecute violators and hence has contributed to the noncompliance problem. Finally, states may also try to initiate agency enforcement through courts. As we will see, in *Massachusetts v. EPA* a number of states sued the EPA to regulate carbon emissions.

Although it is important to consider citizen suits as one method of enforcing governmental policy, we also need to be aware of how citizen groups have used litigation to enforce policy. What kind of sanctions did the citizen organizations in these cases seek to impose against those who failed to comply with governmental policies? In what sense are citizen suits more powerful as agents of political

10. See Archie Parnell, "Congressional Interference in Agency Enforcement: The IRS Experience," *Yale Law Journal* 89 (1980): 1360.
11. See "Comment: Private Enforcement and Rulemaking Under the Federal Trade Commission Act," *Northwestern Law Review* 69 (1974): 462.

mobilization (i.e., arousing public awareness of regulatory noncompliance) than as tools of regulatory enforcement? Because the courts have been involved in interpreting legislation that grants citizens the authority to bring such suits, the answers to these questions in part turn on legal opinions about citizens' suits. In the next two cases you have an opportunity to examine, once again, how the politics of administrative law are shaped by the legal ideology of courts.

Environmental Defense Fund v. Ruckelshaus

439 F.2D 584, UNITED STATES DISTRICT COURT FOR THE DISTRICT OF COLUMBIA CIRCUIT (1971) 2-1

[The Federal Insecticide, Fungicide, and Rodenticide Act (FIFRA) provides that certain pesticides must be registered with the Secretary of Agriculture and that they must conform to the statutory standards of product safety, which requires that they "not cause unreasonable adverse effects on the environment." The act also provides for a trial-type adjudication process for removing pesticides that fail to conform to the standards. In addition, the act authorizes the Secretary to suspend registration when "necessary to prevent imminent hazard to the public." The Environmental Defense Fund submitted a petition to the Secretary in 1969 to do just that with the pesticide DDT. The Secretary refused to suspend the federal registration of DDT, and no action was taken. The Environmental Defense Fund challenged the Secretary's decision.]

Chief Judge David Bazelon

This is a petition for review of an order of the Secretary of Agriculture, refusing to suspend the federal registration of the pesticide DDT or to commence the formal administrative procedures that could terminate that registration. We conclude that the order was based on an incorrect interpretation of the controlling statute, and accordingly remand the case for further proceedings.

I

At the outset, we reject respondents' contention that this court lacks jurisdiction to entertain the petition. . . . In

the ordinary case, the administrative process begins when the Secretary issues a notice of cancellation to the registrant. The matter may then be referred, at the request of the registrant, to a scientific advisory committee, and to a public hearing, before the Secretary issues the order that effectively cancels or continues the registration. Instead of issuing a notice of cancellation, the Secretary may alternatively initiate the process by summarily suspending a registration, when "necessary to prevent imminent hazard to the public" . . . The suspension order thus operates to afford interim relief during the course of the lengthy administrative proceedings. . . .

On May 28, 1970, this court concluded that the Secretary's silence on the request for suspension was equivalent to a denial of that request, and that the denial was reviewable as a final order, because of its immediate impact on the parties.* The court remanded the case to the Secretary for a fresh determination on the question of suspension and for a statement of the reasons for his decision. With respect to the request for cancellation notices, we similarly remanded for a decision on the record or for a statement of reasons for deferring the decision, but we reserved judgment on the question whether there was presently a decision ripe for review in this court. We rejected the suggestion that petitioners lack standing to seek review of the action of the Secretary, and that the decisions with respect to suspension and cancellation are committed by law to the unreviewable discretion of the Secretary.

II

We do not find in the FIFRA any conclusive indication that Congress intended to limit review to those orders made after advisory committee proceedings and a public hearing. . . . In the first place, statutory review is available to persons other than the manufacturer, who may have no right to call for advisory committee proceedings or a public hearing. In the second place, the manufacturer himself may in some circumstances be entitled to judicial review of an administrative determination that is not subject to further consideration in subsequent administrative proceedings. In either case, the lack of a committee report and a hearing record may limit the scope of review, but it does not preclude review entirely.

*EDF v. Hardin, 428 F.2d 1098.

Nor can we find in the statutory scheme any support for the *Nor-Am* distinction between orders granting and denying suspension. For the administrative proceedings that follow suspension are equally available after a refusal to suspend. If the Secretary orders suspension, the proceedings are expedited; otherwise they may follow in due course after he issues cancellation notices. In either event, there is a prospect of further administrative action, but that prospect does not resolve for us the question of reviewability. The subsequent proceedings are designed solely to resolve the ultimate question whether cancellation is warranted, and not to shed any further light on the question whether there is a sufficient threat of "imminent hazard" to warrant suspension in the interim. . . .

III

[. . .]

[A] decision of the Secretary to issue cancellation notices is not reviewable, because it merely sets in motion the administrative process that terminates in a reviewable final order. An unqualified refusal to issue notices, on the other hand, operates with finality as an administrative rejection of the claim that cancellation is required.

If the Secretary had simply refused to issue the requested notices of cancellation, we would have no difficulty concluding that his order was a final order, ripe for review in this court in accordance with the FIFRA. Here, however, the Secretary has taken the position that investigations are still in progress, that final determinations have not yet been made concerning the uses for which cancellation notices have not yet issued. Therefore, with respect to the cancellation notices, we treat the petition as a request for relief in the nature of mandamus, to compel the Secretary to issue notices as required by statute.

The FIFRA . . . language vests discretion in the Secretary to determine whether an article is in compliance with the act, and to decide what action should be taken with respect to a nonconforming article. Nevertheless, his decisions are reviewable for abuse of discretion. . . .

The stated purpose of the amendment was to protect the public by removing from the market any product whose safety or effectiveness was doubted by the Secretary. The legislative history supports the conclusion that Congress intended any substantial question of safety to trigger the

issuance of cancellation notices, shifting to the manufacturer the burden of proving the safety of his product. . . .

[W]hen Congress creates a procedure that gives the public a role in deciding important questions of public policy, that procedure may not lightly be sidestepped by administrators. The cancellation decision does not turn on a scientific assessment of hazard alone. The statute leaves room to balance the benefits of a pesticide against its risks. The process is a delicate one, in which greater weight should be accorded the value of a pesticide for the control of disease, and less weight should be accorded its value for the protection of a commercial crop. The statutory scheme contemplates that these questions will be explored in the full light of a public hearing and not resolved behind the closed doors of the Secretary. There may well be countervailing factors that would justify an administrative decision, after committee consideration and a public hearing, to continue a registration despite a substantial degree of risk, but those factors cannot justify a refusal to issue the notices that trigger the administrative process.

In this case the Secretary has made a number of findings with respect to DDT. On the basis of the available scientific evidence he has concluded that (1) DDT in large doses has produced cancer in test animals and various injuries in man, but in small doses its effect on man is unknown; (2) DDT is toxic to certain birds, bees, and fish, but there is no evidence of harm to the vast majority of species of nontarget organisms; (3) DDT has important beneficial uses in connection with disease control and protection of various crops. These and other findings led the Secretary to conclude "[t]hat the use of DDT should continue to be reduced in an orderly, practicable manner which will not deprive mankind of uses which are essential to the public health and welfare. To this end there should be continuation of the comprehensive study of essentiality of particular uses and evaluations of potential substitutes." . . .

[W]hen [the Secretary] reaches the conclusion that there is a substantial question about the safety of a registered item, he is obliged to initiate the statutory procedure that results in referring the matter first to a scientific advisory committee and then to a public hearing. We recognize, of course, that one important function of that procedure is to afford the registrant an opportunity to challenge the initial decision of the Secretary. But the hearing, in particular, serves other functions as well. Public hearings bring the public into the decision-making process, and create a record that facilitates judicial review. If hearings are held only after the Secretary is convinced beyond a doubt that cancellation is necessary, then they will be held too seldom and too late in the process to serve either of those functions effectively. . . .

IV

[. . .]

Petitioners do not challenge the Secretary's determination of the kinds of harm that may be associated with DDT. They argue that his estimate of the probability that harm will occur is too low, in light of available reports of scientific studies. They also argue that he has set the standard of proof too high, in light of the clear legislative purpose. On the first point, we think it appropriate in the circumstances of this case to defer to the administrative judgment. We have neither an evidentiary record, nor the scientific expertise, that would permit us to review the Secretary's findings with respect to the probability of harm. We have found no error of law that infects the Secretary's inferences from the scientific data. And we have recognized that it is particularly appropriate to defer to administrative findings of fact in reviewing a decision on a question of interim relief.

The second part of the petitioners' challenge, however, is entirely appropriate for judicial consideration at this time. The formulation of standards for suspension is entrusted to the Secretary in the first instance, but the court has an obligation to ensure that the administrative standards conform to the legislative purpose, and that they are uniformly applied in individual cases. . . .

We stand on the threshold of a new era in the history of the long and fruitful collaboration of administrative agencies and reviewing courts. For many years, courts have treated administrative policy decisions with great deference, confining judicial attention primarily to matters of procedure. On matters of substance, the courts regularly upheld agency action, with a nod in the direction of the "substantial evidence" test, and a bow to the mysteries of administrative expertise. Courts occasionally asserted, but less often exercised, the power to set aside agency action on the ground that an impermissible factor had entered into the decision, or a crucial factor had not been considered.

Gradually, however, that power has come into more frequent use, and with it, the requirement that administrators articulate the factors on which they base their decisions.

Strict adherence to that requirement is especially important now that the character of administrative litigation is changing. As a result of expanding doctrines of standing and reviewability, and new statutory causes of action, courts are increasingly asked to review administrative action that touches on fundamental personal interests in life, health, and liberty. These interests have always had a special claim to judicial protection, in comparison with the economic interests at stake in a ratemaking or licensing proceeding.

To protect these interests from administrative arbitrariness, it is necessary, but not sufficient, to insist on strict judicial scrutiny of administrative action. For judicial review alone can correct only the most egregious abuses. Judicial review must operate to ensure that the administrative process itself will confine and control the exercise of discretion. Courts should require administrative officers to articulate the standards and principles that govern their discretionary decisions in as much detail as possible. Rules and regulations should be freely formulated by administrators, and revised when necessary. Discretionary decisions should more often be supported with findings of fact and reasoned opinions. When administrators provide a framework for principled decision-making, the result will be to diminish the importance of judicial review by enhancing the integrity of the administrative process, and to improve the quality of judicial review in those cases where judicial review is sought.

Remanded for further proceedings consistent with this opinion.

Robb, Circuit Judge, dissenting

In my view the majority opinion substitutes the judgment of this court for the judgment of the Secretary in a matter committed to his discretion by law. This action is taken without the benefit of any administrative hearing in which the validity of the petitioner's forebodings and the soundness of the Secretary's discretionary action might be tested. In effect, the court is undertaking to manage the Department of Agriculture. Finding nothing in the statutes that gives us such authority I respectfully dissent.

Gwaltney of Smithfield v. Chesapeake Bay Foundation, Inc. and Natural Resources Defense Council

484 U.S. 49 (1987) 6-3

+ *Burger, Brennan, White, Marshall, Rehnquist, Blackmun*
+/– *Stevens, Scalia, O'Connor*

[The Clean Water Act of 1972 lets citizens bring lawsuits to enforce the provisions of the act. A meat-packing company in Virginia called Gwaltney of Smithfield repeatedly violated the conditions of a pollutant discharge permit issued pursuant to the act. Two environmental groups filed suit in district court alleging that the company had violated and would continue to violate the act. The company moved for the dismissal of the action for want of subject-matter jurisdiction, but the district court ruled that citizens could bring enforcement actions on the basis of past violations under the act. The United States Court of Appeals for the Fourth Circuit affirmed this ruling. The U.S. Supreme Court granted review.]

Justice Marshall delivered the opinion of the Court

In this case, we must decide whether § 505(a) of the Clean Water Act, also known as the Federal Water Pollution Control Act . . . confers federal jurisdiction over citizen suits for wholly past violations.

I

The Clean Water Act . . . was enacted in 1972 "to restore and maintain the chemical, physical, and biological integrity of the Nation's waters." . . . In order to achieve these goals . . . the Act makes unlawful the discharge of any pollutant into navigable waters except as authorized by specified sections of the Act. . . .

One of these specified sections . . . is § 402, which establishes the National Pollutant Discharge Elimination System (NPDES). . . . Pursuant to it . . . the Administrator of the Environmental Protection Agency (EPA) may issue permits authorizing the discharge of pollutants in accordance with specified conditions . . . each State may establish and administer its own permit program if the program conforms to federal guidelines and is approved by the Administrator. . . .

The holder of a federal NPDES permit is subject to enforcement action by the Administrator for failure to comply with the conditions of the permit. The Administrator's enforcement arsenal includes administrative, civil, and criminal sanctions. . . . The holder of a state NPDES permit is subject to both federal and state enforcement action for failure to comply. . . . In the absence of federal or state enforcement, private citizens may commence civil actions against any person "alleged to be in violation of" the conditions of either a federal or state NPDES permit. . . . If the citizen prevails in such an action, the court may order injunctive relief and/or impose civil penalties payable to the United States Treasury. . . .

The Commonwealth of Virginia established a federally approved state NPDES program administered by the Virginia State Water Control Board (Board). . . . In 1974, the Board issued an NPDES permit to ITT-Gwaltney authorizing the discharge of seven pollutants from the company's meat-packing plant on the Pagan River in Smithfield, Virginia. The permit, which was reissued in 1979 and modified in 1980, established effluent limitations, monitoring requirements, and other conditions of discharge. In 1981, petitioner Gwaltney of Smithfield acquired the assets of ITT-Gwaltney and assumed obligations under the permit.

Between 1981 and 1984, petitioner repeatedly violated the conditions of the permit by exceeding effluent limitations on five of the seven pollutants covered. These violations are chronicled in the Discharge Monitoring Reports (DMRs) that the permit required petitioner to maintain. . . . The most substantial of the violations concerned the pollutants fecal coliform, chlorine, and total Kjeldahl nitrogen (TKN). Between October 27, 1981, and August 30, 1984, petitioner violated its TKN limitation 87 times, its chlorine limitation 34 times, and its fecal coliform limitation 31 times. . . . Petitioner installed new equipment to improve its chlorination system in March 1982, and its last reported chlorine violation occurred in October 1982. . . . Petitioner installed an upgraded wastewater treatment system in October 1983, and its last reported TKN violated occurred on May 15, 1984. . . .

Respondents Chesapeake Bay Foundation and Natural Resources Defense Council, two nonprofit corporations dedicated to the protection of natural resources, sent notice in February 1984, to Gwaltney, the Administrator of EPA, and the Virginia State Water Control Board, indicating respondents' intention to commence a citizen suit under the Act based on petitioner's violations of its permit conditions. Respondents proceeded to file this suit in June 1984. . . .

II

A

It is well settled that "the starting point for interpreting a statute is the language of the statute itself." . . . The Court of Appeals concluded that the "to be in violation" language of § 505 is ambiguous, whereas petitioner asserts that it plainly precludes the construction adopted below. We must agree with the Court of Appeals that § 505 is not a provision in which Congress' limpid prose puts an end to all dispute. But to acknowledge ambiguity is not to conclude that all interpretations are equally plausible. The most natural reading of "to be in violation" is a requirement that citizen-plaintiffs allege a state of either continuous or intermittent violation—that is, a reasonable likelihood that a past polluter will continue to pollute in the future. Congress could have phrased its requirement in language that looked to the past ("to have violated"), but it did not choose this readily available option.

Respondents urge that the choice of the phrase "to be in violation," rather than phrasing more clearly directed to the past, is a "careless accident," the result of a "debatable lapse of syntactical precision." . . . But the prospective orientation of that phrase could not have escaped Congress' attention. Congress used identical language in the citizen suit provisions of several other environmental statutes that authorize only prospective relief. . . .

Respondents seek to counter this reasoning by observing that Congress also used the phrase "is in violation" in § 309(a) of the Act, which authorizes the Administrator of EPA to issue compliance orders. . . . That language is incorporated by reference in § 309(b), which authorizes the Administrator to bring civil enforcement actions. Because it is little questioned that the Administrator may bring enforcement actions to recover civil penalties for wholly past violations, respondents contend, the parallel language of § 309(a) and § 505(a) must mean that citizens, too, may maintain such actions.

Although this argument has some initial plausibility, it cannot withstand close scrutiny and comparison of the two statutory provisions. The Administrator's ability to seek civil penalties is not discussed in either § 309(a) or § 309(b); civil penalties are not mentioned until § 309(d), which does not contain the "is in violation" language. . . . The citizen suit provision suggests a connection between injunctive relief and civil penalties that is noticeably absent from the provision authorizing agency enforcement. A comparison of § 309 and § 505 thus supports rather than refutes our conclusion that citizens, unlike the Administrator, may seek civil penalties only in a suit brought to enjoin or otherwise abate an ongoing violation.

B

Our reading of the "to be in violation" language of § 505(a) is bolstered by the language and structure of the rest of the citizen suit provisions in § 505 of the Act. These provisions together make plain that the interest of the citizen-plaintiff is primarily forward-looking.

One of the most striking indicia of the prospective orientation of the citizen suit is the pervasive use of the present tense throughout § 505. A citizen suit may be brought only for violation of a permit limitation "which is in effect" under the Act. . . . Citizen-plaintiffs must give notice to the alleged violator, the Administrator of EPA, and the State in which the alleged violation "occurs." . . . A Governor of a State may sue as a citizen when the Administrator fails to enforce an effluent limitation "the violation of which is occurring in another State and is causing an adverse effect on the public health or welfare in his State." . . . The most telling use of the present tense is in the definition of "citizen" as "a person . . . having an interest which is or may be adversely affected" by the defendant's violations of the Act. . . . This definition makes plain what the undeviating use of the present tense strongly suggests: the harm sought to be addressed by the citizen suit lies in the present or the future, not in the past. . . .

Adopting respondent's interpretation of § 505's jurisdictional grant would create a . . . disturbing anomaly. The bar on citizen suits when governmental enforcement action is under way suggests that the citizen suit is meant to supplement rather than to supplant governmental action. The legislative history of the Act reinforces this view of the role of the citizen suit. The Senate Report noted that "[t]he Committee intends the great volume of enforcement actions [to] be brought by the State," and that citizen suits are proper only "if the Federal, State, and local agencies fail to exercise their enforcement responsibility." S Rep No. 92–414, p 64 (1971). . . . Permitting citizen suits for wholly past violations of the Act could undermine the supplementary role envisioned for the citizen suit. This danger is best illustrated by an example. Suppose that the Administrator identified a violator of the Act and issued a compliance order under § 309(a). Suppose further that the Administrator agreed not to assess or otherwise seek civil penalties on the condition that the violator take some extreme corrective action, such as to install particularly effective but expensive machinery, that it otherwise would not be obliged to take. If citizens could file suit, months or years later, in order to seek the civil penalties that the Administrator chose to forgo, then the Administrator's discretion to enforce the Act in the public interest would be curtailed considerably. The same might be said of the discretion of state enforcement authorities. Respondents' interpretation of the scope of the citizen suit would change the nature of the citizens' role from interstitial to potentially intrusive. We cannot agree that Congress intended such a result.

C

The legislative history of the Act provides additional support for our reading of § 505. Members of Congress frequently characterized the citizen suit provisions as "abatement" provisions or as injunctive measures. . . .

Moreover, both the Senate and House Reports explicitly connected § 505 to the citizen suit provisions authorized by the Clean Air Act, which are wholly injunctive in nature . . . .

III

Our conclusion that § 505 does not permit citizen suits for wholly past violations does not necessarily dispose of this lawsuit, as both lower courts recognized. The District Court found persuasive the fact that "[respondents] allegation in the complaint, that Gwaltney was continuing to violate its NPDES permit when plaintiffs filed suit[,] appears to have been made fully in good faith." On this basis, the District Court explicitly held, albeit in a footnote, that "even if Gwaltney were correct that a district court has no jurisdiction over citizen suits based entirely on unlawful conduct that occurred entirely in the past, the Court would still have jurisdiction here." The Court of Appeals acknowledged, also

in a footnote, that "[a] very sound argument can be made that [respondents'] allegations of continuing violations were made in good faith," but expressly declined to rule on this alternative holding. Because we agree that § 505 confers jurisdiction over citizen suits when the citizen-plaintiffs make a good-faith allegation of continuous or intermittent violation, we remand the case to the Court of Appeals for further consideration.

Petitioner argues that citizen-plaintiffs must prove their allegations of ongoing noncompliance before jurisdiction attaches under § 505. . . .

We cannot agree. The statute does not require that a defendant "be in violation" of the Act at the commencement of suit; rather, the statute requires that a defendant be "*alleged* to be in violation." . . . Our acknowledgement that Congress intended a good-faith allegation to suffice for jurisdictional purposes, however, does not give litigants license to flood the courts with suits premised on baseless allegations. Rule 11 of the Federal Rules of Civil Procedure, which requires pleadings to be based on good-faith belief, formed after reasonable inquiry, that they are "well grounded in fact," adequately protects defendants from frivolous allegations.

Petitioner contends that failure to require proof of allegations under § 505 would permit plaintiffs whose allegations of ongoing violation are reasonable but untrue to maintain suit in federal court even though they lack constitutional standing. Petitioner reasons that if a defendant is in complete compliance with the Act at the time of suit, plaintiffs have suffered no injury remediable by the citizen suit provisions of the Act. Petitioner, however, fails to recognize that our standing cases uniformly recognize that allegations of injury are sufficient to invoke the jurisdiction of a court. In *Warth v. Seldin*, 422 US 490 (1975), for example, we made clear that a suit will not be dismissed for lack of standing if there are sufficient "allegations of fact"—not proof—in the complaint or supporting affidavits. This is not to say, however, that such allegations may not be challenged. In *United States v. SCRAP*, 412 US 699 (1973), we noted that if the plaintiffs' "allegations [of standing] were in fact untrue, then the [defendants] should have moved for summary judgment on the standing issue and demonstrated to the District Court that the allegations were sham and raised no genuine issue of fact." If the defendant fails to make such a showing after the plaintiff offers evidence to support the allegation, the case proceeds to trial on the merits, where the plaintiff must prove the allegations in order to prevail. But the Constitution does not require that the plaintiff offer this proof as a threshold matter in order to invoke the District Court's jurisdiction.

Petitioner also worries that our construction of § 505 would permit citizen-plaintiffs, if their allegations of ongoing noncompliance become false at some later point in the litigation because the defendant begins to comply with the Act, to continue nonetheless to press their suit to conclusion. According to petitioner, such a result would contravene both the prospective purpose of the citizen suit provisions and the "case or controversy" requirement of Article III. Longstanding principles of mootness, however, prevent the maintenance of suit when "there is no reasonable expectation that the wrong will be repeated." . . . In seeking to have a case dismissed as moot, however, the defendant's burden "is a heavy one." . . . The defendant must demonstrate that it is *absolutely clear* that the allegedly wrongful behavior could not reasonably be expected to recur." . . . (emphasis added). Mootness doctrine thus protects defendants from the maintenance of suit under the Clean Water Act based solely on violations wholly unconnected to any present or future wrongdoing, while it also protects plaintiffs from defendants who seek to evade sanction by predictable "protestations of repentance and reform." [. . .]

Because the court below erroneously concluded that respondents could maintain an action based on wholly past violations of the Act, it declined to decide whether respondents' complaint contained a good-faith allegation of ongoing violation by petitioner. We therefore remand the case for consideration of this question. The judgment of the Court of Appeals is vacated, and the case is remanded for further proceedings consistent with this opinion.

It is so ordered.

Justice Scalia, with whom Justice Stevens and Justice O'Connor join, concurring in part and concurring in the judgment

I join Parts I and II of the Court's opinion. I cannot join Part III because I believe it misreads the statute to create a peculiar new form of subject matter jurisdiction.

The Court concludes that subject matter jurisdiction exists under § 505 if there is good-faith allegation that the defendant is "in violation." Thereafter, according to the Court's interpretation, the plaintiff can never be called on to prove that jurisdictional allegation. . . . This creates a regime that is not only extraordinary, but to my knowledge utterly unique. I can think of no other context in which, in order to carry a lawsuit to judgment, allegations are necessary but proof of those allegations (if they are contested) is not. The Court thinks it necessary to find that Congress produced this jurisprudential anomaly because any other conclusion, in its view, would read the word "alleged" out of § 505. It seems to me that, quite to the contrary, it is the Court's interpretation that ignores the words of the statute.

Section 505(a) states that "any citizen may *commence* a civil action on his own behalf . . . against any person . . . who is alleged to be in violation . . ." (emphasis added). There is of course nothing unusual in the proposition that only an allegation is required to *commence* a lawsuit. Proof is never required, and could not practically be required, at that stage. From this clear and unexceptionable language of the statute, one of two further inferences can be made: (1) The inference the Court chooses, that the requirement for commencing a suit is the same as the requirement for maintaining it, or (2) the inference that, in order to maintain a suit the allegations that are required to commence it must, if contested, be proven. It seems to me that to favor the first inference over the second is to prefer the eccentric to the routine. It is well ingrained in the law that subject matter jurisdiction can be called into question *either* by challenging the sufficiency of the allegation *or* by challenging the accuracy of the jurisdictional facts alleged. . . . Had Congress intended us to eliminate the second form of challenge, and to create an extraordinary regime in which the jurisdictional fact consists of a good-faith belief, it seems to me it would have delivered those instructions in more clear fashion than merely specifying how a lawsuit can be commenced.

In my view, therefore, the issue to be resolved by the Court of Appeals on remand of this suit is not whether the allegation of a continuing violation on the day suit was brought was made in good faith after reasonable inquiry, but whether the petitioner was in fact "in violation" on the date suit was brought. . . .

Even if the Court were correct that no evidence of a state of noncompliance has to be produced to survive a motion for dismissal on grounds of subject matter jurisdiction, such evidence would still be required in order to establish the plaintiff's standing. While Gwaltney did not seek certiorari (or even appeal to the Circuit Court) on the denial of its motion to dismiss for lack of standing, it did raise the standing issue before us here . . . and we in any event have an independent obligation to inquire into standing where it is doubtful . . . . If it is undisputed that the defendant was in a state of compliance when this suit was filed, the plaintiff would have been suffering no remediable injury in fact that could support suit. The constitutional requirement for such injury is reflected in the statute itself, which defines "citizen" as one who has "an interest which is or may be adversely affected." [. . .]

What if a state, in addition to private citizens and environmental organizations, wants to force an agency to take action against a problem that is causing injury for that state? Does the state have a different status than private citizens or should it be treated just like a private citizen? *Massachusetts v. EPA*, 549 U.S. 497 (2007), addressed exactly this question. When reading, pay close attention to the question of "standing" which is at the heart of the case. We will go back to the doctrine(s) of standing in the next chapter when we analyze judicial review of agency decisions.

Massachusetts v. EPA

549 U.S. 497 (2007) 5-4
+ *Stevens, Kennedy, Souter, Ginsburg, Breyer*
+/– *Roberts, Scalia, Thomas, Alito*

[In 1999, Massachusetts and several other states petitioned the EPA to regulate carbon dioxide (and other greenhouse gas) emissions from new motor vehicles, which they argued were among the significant causes of global warming. The EPA, according to petitioners, had the authority to regulate under the Clean Air Act, Article 202. After seeking public comments, the EPA denied the petition in 2003, arguing that the Clean Air Act did not authorize the agency to regulate greenhouse gases as air pollutants. Even if it did, the EPA argued it had the legal discretion not to regulate and did not do so. A divided Court of Appeals deferred to the EPA's judgment, ruling at the same time that the petitioners had no standing to sue. The Supreme Court granted certiorari.]

Justice Stevens delivered the opinion of the Court

[P]etitioners asked us to answer two questions concerning the meaning of §202(a)(1) of the Act: whether EPA has the statutory authority to regulate greenhouse gas emissions from new motor vehicles; and if so, whether its stated reasons for refusing to do so are consistent with the statute. . . .

I

Section 202(a)(1) of the Clean Air Act . . . provides:

"The [EPA] Administrator shall by regulation prescribe (and from time to time revise) in accordance with the provisions of this section, standards applicable to the emission of any air pollutant from any class or classes of new motor vehicles or new motor vehicle engines, which in his judgment cause, or contribute to, air pollution which may reasonably be anticipated to endanger public health or welfare. . . ."

The Act defines "air pollutant" to include "any air pollution agent or combination of such agents, including any physical, chemical, biological, radioactive . . . substance or matter which is emitted into or otherwise enters the ambient air." §7602(g). "Welfare" is also defined broadly: among other things, it includes "effects on . . . weather . . . and climate." §7602(h) . . .

IV

Article III of the Constitution limits federal-court jurisdiction to "Cases" and "Controversies." Those two words confine "the business of federal courts to questions presented in an adversary context and in a form historically viewed as capable of resolution through the judicial process." *Flast v. Cohen*, 392 U. S. 83, 95 (1968).

The parties' dispute turns on the proper construction of a congressional statute, a question eminently suitable to resolution in federal court. Congress has moreover authorized this type of challenge to EPA action. That authorization is of critical importance to the standing inquiry: "Congress has the power to define injuries and articulate chains of causation that will give rise to a case or controversy where none existed before" . . . .

EPA maintains that because greenhouse gas emissions inflict widespread harm, the doctrine of standing presents an insuperable jurisdictional obstacle. We do not agree . . . As Justice Kennedy explained in his *Lujan* concurrence:

"While it does not matter how many persons have been injured by the challenged action, the party bringing suit must show that the action injures him in a concrete and personal way . . . "

To ensure the proper adversarial presentation . . . a litigant must demonstrate that it has suffered a concrete and particularized injury that is either actual or imminent, that the injury is fairly traceable to the defendant, and that it is likely that a favorable decision will redress that injury. . . . However, a litigant to whom Congress has "accorded a procedural right to protect his concrete interests . . . can assert that right without meeting all the normal standards for redressability and immediacy." When a litigant is vested with a procedural right, that litigant has standing if there is some possibility that the requested relief will prompt the injury-causing party to reconsider the decision that allegedly harmed the litigant. It is of considerable relevance that the party seeking review here is a sovereign State and not, as it was in *Lujan*, a private individual.

Well before the creation of the modern administrative state, we recognized that States are not normal litigants for the purposes of invoking federal jurisdiction. As Justice Holmes explained in *Georgia v. Tennessee Copper Co.*, 206 U.S. 230, 237 (1907), a case in which Georgia sought to protect its citizens from air pollution originating outside its borders:

" . . . This is a suit by a State for an injury to it in its capacity of quasi-sovereign. In that capacity the State has an interest independent of and behind the titles of its citizens, in all the earth and air within its domain. . . ."

Just as Georgia's "independent interest . . . in all the earth and air within its domain" supported federal jurisdiction a century ago, so too does Massachusetts' well-founded desire to preserve its sovereign territory today. . . . That Massachusetts does in fact own a great deal of the "territory alleged to be affected" only reinforces the conclusion that its stake in the outcome of this case is sufficiently concrete to warrant the exercise of federal judicial power.

When a State enters the Union, it surrenders certain sovereign prerogatives. Massachusetts . . . cannot negotiate an emissions treaty with China or India. . . . These sovereign prerogatives are now lodged in the Federal Government, and Congress has ordered EPA to protect Massachusetts (among others) by prescribing standards applicable to the "emission of any air pollutant from any class or classes of new motor vehicle engines, which in [the Administrator's] judgment cause, or contribute to, air pollution which may reasonably be anticipated to endanger public health or welfare." Congress has moreover recognized a concomitant procedural right to challenge the rejection of its rulemaking petition as arbitrary and capricious. Given that procedural right and Massachusetts' stake in protecting its quasi-sovereign interests, the Commonwealth is entitled to special solicitude in our standing analysis.

With that in mind, it is clear that petitioners' submissions as they pertain to Massachusetts have satisfied the most demanding standards of the adversarial process. EPA's steadfast refusal to regulate greenhouse gas emissions presents a risk of harm to Massachusetts that is both "actual" and "imminent." . . .

The Injury

The harms associated with climate change are serious and well recognized. . . . Petitioners allege that this only hints at the environmental damage yet to come. According to the climate scientist Michael MacCracken, "qualified scientific experts involved in climate change research" have reached a "strong consensus" that global warming threatens (among other things) a precipitate rise in sea levels by the end of the century, MacCracken Decl. ¶15, Stdg. App. 207 . . . .

That these climate-change risks are "widely shared" does not minimize Massachusetts' interest in the outcome of this litigation. According to petitioners' unchallenged affidavits, global sea levels rose somewhere between 10 and 20 centimeters over the 20th century as a result of global warming. These rising seas have already begun to swallow Massachusetts' coastal land. Because the Commonwealth "owns a substantial portion of the state's coastal property," id., at 171 (declaration of Karst R. Hoogeboom ¶4),19 it has alleged a particularized injury in its capacity as a landowner. The severity of that injury will only increase over the course of the next century. . . .

Causation

EPA does not dispute the existence of a causal connection between man-made greenhouse gas emissions and global warming. . . .

EPA nevertheless maintains that its decision not to regulate greenhouse gas emissions from new motor vehicles contributes so insignificantly to petitioners' injuries that the agency cannot be haled into federal court to answer for them. For the same reason, EPA does not believe that any realistic possibility exists that the relief petitioners seek would mitigate global climate change and remedy their injuries. That is especially so because predicted increases in greenhouse gas emissions from developing nations, particularly China and India, are likely to offset any marginal domestic decrease.

But EPA overstates its case. . . . Even leaving aside the other greenhouse gases, the United States transportation sector emits an enormous quantity of carbon dioxide into the atmosphere . . . more than 6% of worldwide carbon dioxide emissions. Considering just emissions from the transportation sector, which represent less than one-third of this country's total carbon dioxide emissions, the United States would still rank as the third-largest emitter of carbon dioxide in the world, outpaced only by the European Union and China. . . .

The Remedy

While it may be true that regulating motor-vehicle emissions will not by itself reverse global warming, it by no means follows that we lack jurisdiction to decide whether EPA has a duty to take steps to slow or reduce it. . . .

In sum—at least according to petitioners' uncontested affidavits—the rise in sea levels associated with global warming has already harmed and will continue to harm Massachusetts. The risk of catastrophic harm, though remote, is nevertheless real. That risk would be reduced to some extent if petitioners received the relief they seek. We therefore hold that petitioners have standing to challenge the EPA's denial of their rulemaking petition.

V

The scope of our review of the merits of the statutory issues is narrow. [A]n agency has broad discretion to choose how best to marshal its limited resources and personnel to carry out its delegated responsibilities. See *Chevron U. S. A. Inc. v. Natural Resources Defense Council, Inc.,* 467 U. S. 837, 842-845 (1984). That discretion is at its height when the agency decides not to bring an enforcement action [and] agency's refusal to initiate enforcement proceedings is not ordinarily subject to judicial review. In contrast . . . agency refusals to initiate rulemaking "are less frequent, more apt to involve legal as opposed to factual analysis, and subject to special formalities, including a public explanation." They moreover arise out of denials of petitions for rulemaking which (at least in the circumstances here) the affected party had an undoubted procedural right to file in the first instance. Refusals to promulgate rules are thus susceptible to judicial review, though such review is "extremely limited" and "highly deferential." . . .

EPA concluded . . . that it lacked authority . . . to regulate new vehicle emissions because carbon dioxide is not an "air pollutant" as that term is defined in §7602. [E]ven if it possessed authority, it would decline to do so because regulation would conflict with other administration priorities. As discussed earlier, the Clean Air Act expressly permits review of such an action. §7607(b)(1). We therefore "may reverse any such action found to be . . . arbitrary, capricious, an abuse of discretion, or otherwise not in accordance with law." §7607(d)(9).

VI

On the merits, the first question is whether §202(a)(1) of the Clean Air Act authorizes EPA to regulate greenhouse gas emissions from new motor vehicles in the event that it forms a "judgment" that such emissions contribute to climate change. . . . [I]t does. In relevant part, §202(a)(1) provides that EPA "shall by regulation prescribe . . . standards applicable to the emission of any air pollutant from any class or classes of new motor vehicles or new motor vehicle engines, which in [the Administrator's] judgment cause, or contribute to, air pollution which may reasonably be anticipated to endanger public health or welfare." Because EPA believes that Congress did not intend it to regulate substances that contribute to climate change, the agency maintains that carbon dioxide is not an "air pollutant" within the meaning of the provision.

The statutory text forecloses EPA's reading. The Clean Air Act's sweeping definition of "air pollutant" includes "any air pollution agent or combination of such agents, including *any* physical, chemical . . . substance or matter which is emitted into or otherwise enters the ambient air . . . " The statute is unambiguous.26

EPA's reliance on *Brown & Williamson Tobacco Corp.*, 529 U. S. 120, is similarly misplaced. In . . . that [case] . . . we found critical at least two considerations that have no counterpart in this case.

First, we thought it unlikely that Congress meant to ban tobacco products. . . . Here, in contrast, EPA jurisdiction would lead to no such extreme measures. EPA would only *regulate* emissions. . . . Second . . . we pointed to an unbroken series of congressional enactments that made sense only if adopted "against the backdrop of the FDA's . . . repeated statements that it lacked authority . . . to regulate tobacco." We can point to no such enactments here: EPA has not identified any congressional action that conflicts in any way with the regulation of greenhouse gases from new motor vehicles. . . .

[T]he Congresses that drafted §202(a)(1) . . . did understand that without regulatory flexibility, changing circumstances and scientific developments would soon render the Clean Air Act obsolete. The broad language of §202(a)(1) reflects an intentional effort to confer the flexibility necessary to forestall such obsolescence. . . . Because greenhouse gases fit well within the Clean Air Act's capacious definition of "air pollutant," we hold that EPA has the statutory authority to regulate the emission of such gases from new motor vehicles.

VII

The alternative basis for EPA's decision—that even if it does have statutory authority to regulate greenhouse gases, it would be unwise to do so at this time—rests on reasoning divorced from the statutory text. While the statute does condition the exercise of EPA's authority on its formation of a "judgment," that judgment must relate to whether an air pollutant "cause[s], or contribute[s] to, air pollution which may reasonably be anticipated to endanger public health or welfare." Put another way, the use of the word "judgment" is not a roving license to ignore the statutory text. It is but a direction to exercise discretion within defined statutory limits.

If EPA makes a finding of endangerment, the Clean Air Act requires the agency to regulate emissions of the deleterious pollutant from new motor vehicles. . . . [O]nce EPA has responded to a petition for rulemaking, its reasons for action or inaction must conform to the authorizing statute. Under the clear terms of the Clean Air Act, EPA can avoid taking further action only if it determines that greenhouse gases do not contribute to climate change or if it provides some reasonable explanation as to why it cannot or will not exercise its discretion to determine whether they do. . . .

EPA has refused to comply with this clear statutory command. Instead, it has offered a laundry list of reasons not to regulate. . . .

Although we have neither the expertise nor the authority to evaluate these policy judgments, it is evident they have nothing to do with whether greenhouse gas emissions contribute to climate change. Still less do they amount to a reasoned justification for declining to form a scientific judgment. . . .

Nor can EPA avoid its statutory obligation by noting the uncertainty surrounding various features of climate change. . . . If the scientific uncertainty is so profound that it precludes EPA from making a reasoned judgment as to whether greenhouse gases contribute to global warming, EPA must say so. That EPA would prefer not to regulate greenhouse gases because of some residual uncertainty . . . is irrelevant. The statutory question is whether sufficient information exists to make an endangerment finding.

In short, EPA has offered no reasoned explanation for its refusal to decide whether greenhouse gases cause or contribute to climate change. Its action was therefore "arbitrary, capricious . . . or otherwise not in accordance with law." We need not and do not reach the question whether on remand EPA must make an endangerment finding. . . . We hold only that EPA must ground its reasons for action or inaction in the statute.

VIII

The judgment of the Court of Appeals is reversed, and the case is remanded for further proceedings consistent with this opinion.

It is so ordered.

Chief Justice Roberts, with whom
Justice Scalia, Justice Thomas,
and Justice Alito join, dissenting

. . .

I

[. . .]

Our modern framework for addressing standing is familiar: "A plaintiff must allege personal injury fairly traceable to
the defendant's allegedly unlawful conduct and likely to be
redressed by the requested relief.". . . Applying that standard here, petitioners bear the burden of alleging an injury
that is fairly traceable to the Environmental Protection
Agency's failure to promulgate new motor vehicle greenhouse gas emission standards, and that is likely to be
redressed by the prospective issuance of such standards.

Before determining whether petitioners can meet this
familiar test, however, the Court . . . asserts that "States are
not normal litigants for the purposes of invoking federal
jurisdiction," and that given "Massachusetts' stake in protecting its quasi-sovereign interests, the Commonwealth is
entitled to special solicitude in our standing analysis" . . .
(emphasis added).

Relaxing Article III standing requirements because asserted injuries are pressed by a State, however, has no basis in
our jurisprudence, and support for any such "special solicitude" is conspicuously absent from the Court's opinion. The
general judicial review provision cited by the Court, 42 U. S.
C. §7607(b)(1), affords States no special rights or status. . . .
Congress knows how to do that when it wants to . . . but it
has done nothing of the sort here. . . .

Nor does the case law cited by the Court provide any
support for the notion that Article III somehow implicitly
treats public and private litigants differently. . . . The
Court's analysis hinges on *Georgia v. Tennessee Copper Co.*,
206 U. S. 230 (1907)—a case that did indeed draw a distinction between a State and private litigants, but solely
with respect to available remedies. . . .

In contrast to the present case, there was no question in
Tennessee Copper about Article III injury. There was certainly
no suggestion that the State could show standing where
the private parties could not. . . .

What is more, the Court's reasoning falters on its own
terms. The Court asserts that Massachusetts is entitled to

"special solicitude" due to its "quasi-sovereign interests,"
but then applies our Article III standing test to the asserted
injury of the State's loss of coastal property. . . .

On top of everything else, the Court overlooks the fact
that our cases cast significant doubt on a State's standing to
assert a quasi-sovereign interest—as opposed to a direct
injury—against the Federal Government. As a general rule,
we have held that while a State might assert a quasi-sovereign right as *parens patriae* "for the protection of its citizens,
it is no part of its duty or power to enforce their rights in
respect of their relations with the Federal Government. . . .

II

[. . .] [T]he status of Massachusetts as a State cannot
compensate for petitioners' failure to demonstrate injury in
fact, causation, and redressability.

When the Court actually applies the three-part test, it
focuses . . . on the State's asserted loss of coastal land as the
injury in fact. If petitioners rely on loss of land as the Article
III injury, however, they must ground the rest of the standing analysis in that specific injury. That alleged injury must
be "concrete and particularized," *Defenders of Wildlife*, 504
U. S., at 560, and "distinct and palpable," *Allen*, 468 U. S.,
at 751. Central to this concept of "particularized" injury is
the requirement that a plaintiff be affected in a "personal
and individual way," and seek relief that "directly and tan-
gibly benefits him" in a manner distinct from its impact on
"the public at large," . . .

The very concept of global warming seems inconsistent
with this particularization requirement. Global warming is a
phenomenon "harmful to humanity at large," . . . If petitioners' particularized injury is loss of coastal land, it is also
that injury that must be "actual or imminent, not conjectur-
al or hypothetical," . . . "real and immediate," . . . and
"certainly impending." . . .

As to "actual" injury, the Court observes that "global sea
levels rose somewhere between 10 and 20 centimeters over
the 20th century as a result of global warming" and that
"[t]hese rising seas have already begun to swallow
Massachusetts' coastal land." But none of petitioners' declarations supports that connection. [A]side from a single
conclusory statement, there is nothing in petitioners' 43
standing declarations and accompanying exhibits to support an inference of actual loss of Massachusetts coastal

land from 20th century global sea level increases. It is pure conjecture.

The Court's attempts to identify "imminent" or "certainly impending" loss of Massachusetts coastal land fares no better. . . . One of petitioners' declarants predicts global warming will cause sea level to rise by 20 to 70 centimeters *by the year 2100.* . . . Allegations of possible future injury do not satisfy the requirements of Art. III. A threatened injury must be *certainly impending* to constitute injury in fact.

III

[. . .] To establish standing, petitioners must show a causal connection between th[e] specific injury and the lack of new motor vehicle greenhouse gas emission standards, and that the promulgation of such standards would likely redress that injury. As is often the case, the questions of causation and redressability overlap.

Petitioners view the relationship between their injuries and EPA's failure to promulgate new motor vehicle greenhouse gas emission standards as simple and direct: Domestic motor vehicles emit carbon dioxide and other greenhouse gases. Worldwide emissions of greenhouse gases contribute to global warming and therefore also to petitioners' alleged injuries. . . .

The Court ignores the complexities of global warming. . . . First . . . [b]ecause local greenhouse gas emissions disperse throughout the atmosphere and remain there for anywhere from 50 to 200 years, it is global emissions data that are relevant. According to one of petitioners' declarations, domestic motor vehicles contribute about 6 percent of global carbon dioxide emissions and 4 percent of global greenhouse gas emissions. The amount of global emissions at issue here is smaller still; §202(a)(1) of the Clean Air Act covers only *new* motor vehicles and *new* motor vehicle engines, so petitioners' desired emission standards might reduce only a fraction of 4 percent of global emissions.

This gets us only to the relevant greenhouse gas emissions; linking them to global warming and ultimately to petitioners' alleged injuries next requires consideration of further complexities. . . .

Petitioners are never able to trace their alleged injuries back through this complex web to the fractional amount of global emissions that might have been limited with EPA standards. . . .

IV

Redressability is even more problematic. To the tenuous link between petitioners' alleged injury and the indeterminate fractional domestic emissions at issue here, add the fact that petitioners cannot meaningfully predict what will come of the 80 percent of global greenhouse gas emissions that originate outside the United States. . . .

No matter, the Court reasons, because *any* decrease in domestic emissions will "slow the pace of global emissions increases, no matter what happens elsewhere." Every little bit helps, so Massachusetts can sue over any little bit. . . .

[E]ven if regulation *does* reduce emissions—to some indeterminate degree—the Court never explains why that makes it *likely* that the injury in fact—the loss of land—will be redressed. . . . The realities make it pure conjecture to suppose that EPA regulation of new automobile emissions will *likely* prevent the loss of Massachusetts coastal land.

V

[. . .] [T]he Court's self-professed relaxation of [the] Article III requirements has caused us to transgress "the proper—and properly limited—role of the courts in a democratic society." *Allen>/I>, 468 U. S., at 750 (internal quotation marks omitted).*

I respectfully dissent.

*Justice Scalia, with whom
The Chief Justice, Justice Thomas,
and Justice Alito join, dissenting*

I

A

. . . As the Court recognizes, the statute "condition[s] the exercise of EPA's authority on its formation of a 'judgment.' " There is no dispute that the Administrator has made no such judgment in this case. . . . The question thus arises: Does anything *require* the Administrator to make a "judgment" whenever a petition for rulemaking is filed? . . . [T]he Court says yes. Why is that so? When Congress wishes to make private action force an agency's hand, it knows how to do so. . . . Where does the CAA say that the EPA Administrator is required to come to a decision on this question whenever a rulemaking petition is filed? The Court points to no such provision because none exists. . . . I am willing to assume, for the sake of argument, that the Administrator's discretion in this regard is not entirely unbounded—that if he has no reasonable basis for deferring judgment he must grasp the nettle at once. The Court, however . . . rejects all of EPA's stated "policy judgments" as not "amount[ing] to a reasoned justification." . . . Judgment can be delayed [according to the Court] *only* if the Administrator concludes that "the scientific uncertainty is [too] profound." [O]ther reasons—perfectly valid reasons—were set forth in the agency's statement.

"We do not believe . . . that it would be either effective or appropriate for EPA to establish [greenhouse gas] standards for motor vehicles at this time. As described in detail below, the President has laid out a comprehensive approach to climate change that calls for near-term voluntary actions and incentives along with programs aimed at reducing scientific uncertainties and encouraging technological development so that the government may effectively and efficiently address the climate change issue over the long term.

. . .

"[E]stablishing [greenhouse gas] emission standards for U. S. motor vehicles at this time would . . . result in an inefficient, piecemeal approach to addressing the climate change issue." . . .

"Unilateral EPA regulation of motor vehicle [greenhouse gas] emissions could also weaken U. S. efforts to persuade developing countries to reduce the [greenhouse gas] intensity of their economies. . . .

The Court dismisses this analysis as "rest[ing] on reasoning divorced from the statutory text. While the statute does condition the exercise of EPA's authority on its formation of a 'judgment,' " [it] says *nothing at all* about the reasons for which the Administrator may *defer* making a judgment. . . . Thus, the various "policy" rationales that the Court criticizes are not "divorced from the statutory text," except in the sense that the statutory text is silent, as texts are often silent about permissible reasons for the exercise of agency discretion. . . .

B

Even on the Court's own terms, however, the same conclusion follows. . . . [T]he Court gives EPA the option of determining that the science is too uncertain to allow it to form a "judgment" as to whether greenhouse gases endan-

ger public welfare. . . . "If," the Court says, "the scientific uncertainty is so profound that it precludes EPA from making a reasoned judgment as to whether greenhouse gases contribute to global warming, EPA must say so." But EPA *has* said precisely that—and at great length, based on information contained in a 2001 report by the National Research Council (NRC) entitled Climate Change Science: An Analysis of Some Key Questions:

"The [NRC] state[s] . . . that '[b]ecause of the large and still uncertain level of natural variability inherent in the climate record and the uncertainties in the time histories of the various forcing agents (and particularly aerosols), a [causal] linkage between the buildup of greenhouse gases in the atmosphere and the observed climate changes during the 20th century cannot be unequivocally established . . .

"The science of climate change is extraordinarily complex and still evolving. Although there have been substantial advances in climate change science, there continue to be important uncertainties in our understanding of the factors that may affect future climate change and how it should be addressed. . . . I simply cannot conceive of what else the Court would like EPA to say.

II

[. . .]

B

Using (as we ought to) EPA's interpretation of the definition of "air pollutant," we must next determine whether greenhouse gases are "agent[s]" of "air pollution." If so, the statute would authorize regulation; if not, EPA would lack authority.

. . . [T]he term "air pollution" is not itself defined by the CAA; thus, once again we must accept EPA's interpretation of that ambiguous term, provided its interpretation is a "permissible construction of the statute." *Chevron*, 467 U. S., at 843. . . . [I]n deciding whether it had authority to regulate, EPA had to determine whether the concentration of greenhouse gases assuredly responsible for "global climate change" qualifies as "air pollution." EPA began with the commonsense observation that the "[p]roblems associated with atmospheric concentrations of CO2," id., at 52927, bear little resemblance to what would naturally be termed "air pollution":

"EPA's prior use of the CAA's general regulatory provisions provides an important context. Since the inception of the Act, EPA has used these provisions to address air pollution problems that occur primarily at ground level or near the surface of the earth . . . CO2, by contrast, is fairly consistent in concentration throughout the world's atmosphere up to approximately the lower stratosphere."

In other words, regulating the buildup of CO2 and other greenhouse gases in the upper reaches of the atmosphere, which is alleged to be causing global climate change, is not akin to regulating the concentration of some substance that is *polluting* the *air*.

We need look no further than the dictionary for confirmation that this interpretation of "air pollution" is eminently reasonable. . . .

In the end, EPA concluded that since "CAA authorization to regulate is generally based on a finding that an air pollutant causes or contributes to air pollution," 68 Fed. Reg. 52928, the concentrations of CO2 and other greenhouse gases allegedly affecting the global climate are beyond the scope of CAA's authorization to regulate. "[T]he term 'air pollution' as used in the regulatory provisions cannot be interpreted to encompass global climate change."

[. . .]

The Court's alarm over global warming may or may not be justified, but it ought not distort the outcome of this litigation. . . . No matter how important the underlying policy issues at stake, this Court has no business substituting its own desired outcome for the reasoned judgment of the responsible agency.

The Court decision was a major victory for the environmentalist groups and petitioner states because it had the potential to force the EPA to regulate greenhouse gases. Enforcement of the laws is never so straight, however. After the case was sent back to the EPA for an endangerment finding, the agency reached the conclusion that greenhouse gases were air pollutants that must be regulated, estimating that the regulation of motor vehicle emissions might "produce $500 billion to $2 trillion in economic benefits over the next 32 years." In response, the White House first pressured the EPA to eliminate certain parts of the report, but in a more awkward move, the White House and the Office of Management and Budget simply refused to open the e-mail from the EPA, that contained the final report![12] This rather strange "inaction" shows, yet again, that enforcement can be extremely problematic when the executive branch is unwilling to act.

We conclude the chapter with an article by four sociologists who seek to identify what compliance depends on and how laws regulating organizations can most effectively obtain compliance. They isolate this large problem by focusing on compliance efforts by affirmative action officers. As you read their study, consider other administrative contexts and whether these sociologists have identified an approach to compliance that might apply more broadly. Also, what might be some possible links between our previous discussion of compliance and the following study of compliance officers' "dilemma"?[13]

Legal Ambiguity and the Politics of Compliance: Affirmative Action Officers' Dilemma

Lauren B. Edelman, Stephen Petterson, Elizabeth Chambliss, and Howard S. Erlanger
Law & Policy 73 (1991)

Equal employment opportunity and affirmative action (EEO/AA) mandates, like many other laws regulating organizations, do not clearly define what constitutes compliance. Thus, compliance depends largely on the initiative and agenda of those persons within organizations who are charged with managing the compliance effort: in the case of civil rights, "affirmative action officers." We argue that the political climate within which affirmative action officers work, together with the officers' interpretations of the law, their role conceptions, and their profes-

---

12. "White House Refused to Open Pollutants Email," *New York Times*, June 25, 2008.

13. For additional discussion of regulatory enforcement, see Suzanne Weaver, *Decision to Prosecute: Organization and Public Policy in the Antitrust Division* (Cambridge: MIT Press, 1977); Eugene Bardach and Robert A. Kagan, *Going by the Book: The Problem of Regulatory Unreasonableness* (Philadelphia: Temple University Press, A Twentieth Century Fund Report, 1982); and R. Shep Melnick, *Regulation and the Courts: The Case of the Clean Air Act* (Washington, D.C.: Brookings Institution, 1983), especially chapter 7.

sional aspirations have important implications for the nature and extent of organizational compliance with law.

The literature on regulation and on organizational behavior tends to emphasize the capacity of organizations to resist compliance with law. This is especially true for studies of regulatory agencies, which overwhelmingly emphasize noncompliance . . . . In explaining noncompliance, these accounts tell us that resources for enforcement are inadequate . . . and that regulatory agencies . . . negotiate the meaning of compliance with, or succumb to pressure or "capture" by, the organizations they regulate. . . .

Studies of organizations subject to regulation show how organizational structure encourages inattention to legal requirements . . . and how the internal normative environment of organizations often encourages individuals to place organizational goals over legal goals when the two conflict (Vaughan, 1983). . . .

While we do not take issue with the literature on organizational compliance with law, we seek to shift the focus of inquiry from the existence or nonexistence of compliance to the *process* of compliance. Much of the regulation literature treats law as a clear mandate to which organizations either comply or fail to comply. In contrast, we suggest that compliance is a social and political process that evolves over time. Our view of compliance builds upon institutional analyses of organizations, which emphasize that organizations must be understood as emergent and dynamic institutions that are responsive to both internal and environmental normative pressures. . . .

Edelman (1992) shows that in response to the vague prohibition against discrimination, organizations often create "symbolic structures" such as special affirmative action officers, anti-discrimination rules, and affirmative action officer positions. Given ambiguity in the law, legal provisions that emphasize procedural rather than substantive compliance, and weak enforcement mechanisms, it is unclear what organizations must do to comply with law. Edelman argues that this poses a dilemma to organizations: they must appear attentive to law in order to gain legitimacy and public resources and, at the same time, seek to minimize law's constraints on traditional managerial prerogatives. Organizations respond to this dilemma by creating symbolic structures, which serve as visible efforts to comply with law. Edelman points out that because the normative value of these structures does not depend on their effectiveness, they do not guarantee substantive change in the employment status of minorities and women.

However, the creation of symbolic structures is only the first stage of organizational response to law. Once in place, structures within organizations tend to develop a life of their own (Selznick, 1949). To understand the role that symbolic structures play in the construction of compliance, then, it is important to study the evolution of such structures within organizations. This paper focuses on the developing character of one such structure: the position of the affirmative action officer* . . . .

EEO/AA Law and Its Implementation by Affirmative Action Officers

Title VII of the 1964 Civil Rights Act, § 703(a)(1) states that:

It shall be an unlawful employment practice for an employer: to fail or refuse to hire or to discharge any individual, or otherwise to discriminate against any individual with respect to his compensation, terms, conditions, or privileges of employment, because of such individual's race, color, religion, sex, or national origin. (42 U.S.C. § 2000e-2)

While seemingly specific, the meaning of such phrases as "because of such individual's race, color, religion, sex, or national origin" is unclear. This ambiguity has engendered debate over two basic interpretations of EEO/AA law: a "procedural interpretation" and a "substantive interpretation." The procedural interpretation defines equality in terms of equal treatment in employment decision-making. The substantive interpretation defines equality in terms of the substantive outcome of organizational practices. Procedural equality does not guarantee substantive equality, because the former perpetuates existing inequalities that are the result of past discrimination. . . .

This ambiguity in EEO/AA law affects affirmative action officers in three ways. First, affirmative action officers must construct the law in shaping their organizations' compliance programs. Officers' constructions of law critically affect the form, strength and comprehensiveness of their organizations' responses to law. Several factors may influence how an affirmative action officer constructs EEO/AA law. Public opinion is one factor: the public and legal debate over whether the law requires or permits special compensatory treatment of minorities

---

*Although the term "affirmative action officer" is used rather broadly to refer to heads of affirmative action offices, other staff members of those offices, or functionaries with responsibility for handling EEO/AA-related complaints, we use the term to refer to the organizational personnel who have principal responsibility for handling EEO/AA mandates.

and women feeds into affirmative action officers' constructions of law. Judicial decisions are another: they affect affirmative action officers' constructions of law by legitimating or rejecting practices that develop within organizations.

Secondly, ambiguity in EEO/AA law allows multiple "clienteles," often with competing interests, to make legitimate claims to the loyalties of affirmative action officers. Affirmative action officers must often negotiate among the demands of women and minorities who claim a protected legal status; white and male employees who worry about "reverse discrimination", and community members who claim that the organization discriminates in hiring. These competing claims flow directly from the conflict between the procedural and substantive interpretations of civil rights law . . .

An even deeper source of conflict for the affirmative action officer is the structural dilemma that arises from the constraints that EEO/AA law imposes upon traditional managerial prerogatives. . . .

Affirmative action officers vary significantly in how they resolve these contradictory claims to their services, adopting either a partisan or neutral strategy in response to claims from competing clienteles (Larson, 1977). A partisan affirmative action officer may favor either the administration's interest in minimal restriction or the interests of previously disenfranchised employees to special treatment. A neutral client orientation may be conciliatory, involving an active attempt to mediate among conflicting interests, or it may be indifferent, reflecting a passive lack of attention to competing interests.

The third way that legal ambiguity affects affirmative action officers is that it allows professionals within organizations to gain power through the assertion of expertise regarding what constitutes compliance. How professionals use that power depends in part on their professional interests and expectations. Larson (1977) suggests that professionals may use their expertise either to claim power within the bureaucratic hierarchy or to claim countervailing power vis-à-vis the bureaucratic hierarchy. She argues that power within the bureaucratic hierarchy yields participation and integration in administrative decision-making while power vis-à-vis the bureaucratic hierarchy yields autonomy from the administration. In general, professionals who strive to move up the bureaucratic hierarchy will claim power within that hierarchy while professionals whose status derives from external sources (such as educational credentials) will claim power to act autonomously.

Structural conflict in affirmative action officers' roles, then, forces them to make choices about constructions of law, client interests, and professional orientations. These three dimensions are not independent. Orientation to the administration as client or to success in the bureaucratic hierarchy will tend to be associated with the procedural interpretation of EEO/AA law, while orientation to underrepresented interests and to recognition outside the organization will tend to be associated with the substantive interpretation of the law. Affirmative action officers' resolution of role conflict will have major ramifications for the type of compliance that affirmative action officers seek and achieve. . . .

Data and Methods

To explore the politics of the compliance process, we conducted three case studies of the implementation of EEO/AA policies. Because we wanted access to organizational personnel and documents, all three are public or educational organizations, where we found it easier to secure access. We recognize that the response to EEO/AA law in these organizations is likely to be unrepresentative of for-profit firms in the private sector. For this and all the usual reasons relating to small, ad hoc samples, our findings must be considered suggestive and tentative.

Each case study consisted of in-depth interviews with principal actors on the organizations' response to and implementation of EEO/AA policies. We also relied on a variety of secondary materials, such as internal documents, affirmative action plans, newspaper accounts, and press releases.

The first case is a medium-sized eastern city, which made its first serious effort to introduce affirmative action policies in 1978. The second case is a small liberal arts college and its decision to hire an affirmative action officer in 1988. Our third study is of the local government of a midwest city with a population of about 175,000. Because the first case study involves three different affirmative action officers, these three cases yield five examples of the interaction between affirmative action officers and their employing organizations.

Officers' Responses to Structural Contradictions

. . . Four strategies for handling structural contradictions could be discerned from the interviews we conducted. We do not claim that these are the only types of response to EEO/AA law: clearly there may be other strategies, especially in private organizations, but the responses we observed show that different strategies for responding to competing interests can result in very different forms of compliance. For heuristic purposes, we characterize the four strategies we observed as: the Advocate, the Team Player, the Professional, and the Technician.

A. The Advocate

One strategy is to adopt a strong substantive construction of the law and therefore to pursue minorities' and women's interests aggressively. This strategy requires that the affirmative action officer place the interests of the minority and female employees clearly above any conflicting interests of the administration. We refer to this as the "Advocate" strategy. The Advocate strategy is the most likely to produce significant social reform but carries high risk: advocates continuously risk failure because their role as champions of the law (and those protected by law) continuously brings them into conflict with, and evokes resistance from, organizational management. . . .

Advocates' resolution of that conflict is clear: they contend that legal requirements (as they construe them) require them to represent and advocate the interests of minority and female employees and they deny any allegiance to management. Advocates draw on their knowledge of the law, and on community and employee support, to justify and buttress their efforts to bring about changes in employment practices. Both of these factors become a source of countervailing power vis-à-vis the administration. Advocates also draw upon the symbolic value of their position; they are somewhat insulated because the public may view an attack on the affirmative action officer as an attack on civil rights.

We have two examples of Advocates in our case studies . . . our Advocates were affirmative action officers in city governments, both were public advocates of civil rights prior to their appointments, and both were appointed amidst considerable civil rights conflict. Importantly, both had short tenures due to the controversy that their actions generated.

One of these Advocates was employed in a medium-sized eastern city which did not make a serious effort to introduce affirmative action policies until 1978. This city has an unusually high poverty rate and a weak tax base, and therefore has faced considerable financial problems over the past few decades as it tried to stretch its resources to provide basic public services. The city's Hispanic population has grown dramatically, from 3.2

percent in 1970 to 12.6 percent in 1980. This rapid growth has created considerable tension between the older ethnic white population and the more recent settlers. Given these problems, the employment of minorities by the city and the creation of affirmative action structures are politically charged issues.

With heightened racial tension as the backdrop, it was community action that precipitated the development of a municipal affirmative action program. In the late 1970s, a Hispanic community group filed a complaint against the city with the Department of Housing and Urban Development (HUD) in which it alleged that the city had made itself ineligible for federal grants because of its failure to hire minorities. HUD threatened to withhold development funds if the city did not improve its minority hiring record. The city agreed to minority hiring goals and promised to create a centralized office to monitor EEO/AA in employment as well as an oversight committee of community members.

Shortly after the agreement was reached, the city hired its first affirmative action officer, Juan Martinez (a pseudonym), a Hispanic community leader. Martinez' appointment was clearly intended to appease the rapidly growing Hispanic community. But his commitment to implementing a strong form of EEO/AA law brought him into immediate conflict with the administration that hired him. Shortly after Martinez took office, a conflict arose over the role of the community oversight committee, the Equal Opportunity Council (EOC). About half of the EOC members appointed by the mayor were minorities, many of them prominent Hispanic leaders. The issue was how much oversight the EOC would have over the city's EEO/AA policy. The mayor's purpose would best be served by a visible but nonpowerful EOC, and he sought to narrow the council's powers, stating that: "[t]he EOC will not set equal opportunity policy but will instead serve as advisors to [the mayor]."

Martinez, however, supported an active role for the EOC, which could back him in foreseeable fights with the city administration. Demonstrating his willingness to challenge the mayor, Martinez was quoted in the local newspaper as saying, "[i]f the council makes a recommendation for the benefit of the community and the mayor doesn't go along with it, I will resign, because my job will be nothing more than [to occupy] a cubby hole [in the City Hall Annex]." By tying his own fate to that of the EOC, Martinez clearly established himself as an advocate of the Hispanic community, and demonstrated his commitment to strong affirmative action. . . .

Due to his advocacy of minority interests and repeated challenges to the mayor, the autonomy and authority of Martinez' position became a point of contention. Martinez proposed that his office be granted more autonomy, arguing that his ability to act as an advocate was constrained by the mayor's tight control over his job. The mayor denied this charge: "I don't control [Martinez]. I want him to do his job independently . . . I don't agree with his report, but it doesn't affect his position with me one iota."

After this contest over Martinez' autonomy, Martinez' relationship with the mayor quickly deteriorated and a few months later he resigned. In his letter of resignation, Martinez "expressed his disappointment and disgust with the unfulfilled promises . . . 'I have decided to terminate my services with your racist administration.' " In this case, then, a zealous advocate of the minority community was progressively discouraged as the administration that hired him reacted negatively to his attempts to implement a strong form of affirmative action.

Our second example of an Advocate also shows that the Advocate strategy promotes a strong form of compliance but is highly volatile. "John Brown" (pseudonym) was the affirmative action officer for a midwestern college town, which has a reputation as politically liberal. As in the previous case, the position of affirmative action officer was created amidst political controversy. Brown, an outspoken leader of the minority community, was chosen as the city's first affirmative action officer. He had been involved in city politics since his youth, and in 1969 at the age of twenty-one was elected as the city's first black alderman. During the course of his political career Brown developed a reputation as an outspoken civil rights activist.

Once appointed, Brown made it clear that even as a mayoral appointee, he saw himself as an advocate of disenfranchised groups. In a 1988 interview, he stated: "I consider it my job to oppose racism, sexism and militarism wherever it exists . . . isn't that what public officials are supposed to do?" Brown also repeatedly used the term "we" to refer to himself and the public, and "them" to refer to the city administration. For example, "[w]e're telling officials in this city we don't want any more jive, we want some action. We're telling them in no uncertain words, we want real integration, we want affirmative action." And like Martinez, Brown was willing to bring in federal and state forces to change the policies of the organization he worked for. In April 1988, Brown called for FBI and U.S. Justice Department investigations of an assault on a black woman and other racial incidents on the local college campus.

Brown's statement about "real integration" shows that he, like Martinez, constructed EEO/AA law as a substantive requirement, requiring affirmative action to effect equal treatment of minorities and women. Brown's substantive interpretation of EEO/AA law led him to become frustrated with procedural requirements when they conflicted with substantive EEO/AA goals. He repeatedly pointed out that formal procedures could be used as a substitute for, rather than a means of implementing, EEO/AA in the workplace, and announced that he hoped to expose city policies "to remove the veneer of liberalism—the facade."

Finally, as in Martinez' case, Brown was able to command power vis-à-vis the administration, at least for a time, by successfully mobilizing public support. He made his disputes with the mayor and other city officials public in order to take advantage of the fact that the city would incur a significant legitimacy cost by crushing his efforts at reform: "[h]ad I not had the ability to be heard by the public, I would have been fired long ago. The media has been my first line of defense."

Initially, the city administration tried to control Brown by redefining the chain of command. In June of 1988, the mayor proposed a reorganization of the affirmative action office that would subsume the office under the Human Resources Department, which also handled personnel and labor relations matters. Brown condemned the plan as a means of weakening the office by inserting a "manager"—another level of bureaucracy—between the Director of Affirmative Action and the mayor. . . . The mayor's response was that "[t]he Affirmative Action Office will be more effective when it's integrated into a better functioning system."

Perhaps frustrated by the structural difficulties in implementing a strong form of affirmative action, Brown became openly hostile toward the mayor and other officials. Three days after criticizing the reorganization plan, Brown shouted insults at a board member of a local technical college, calling him a coward, a racist and a liar, for reneging on his promise to vote for a black district director. This led to a written reprimand from the mayor, unfavorable press coverage of Brown, and a rapid deterioration of public support. More public confrontations followed and the mayor ultimately fired Brown, who then filed an unsuccessful lawsuit against the city for discriminatory discharge.

The Advocate strategy, then, is to take an aggressive view of what constitutes compliance, which often requires an adversarial stance against management. An obvious question is why organizations would choose Advocates rather than officers who would be less likely to challenge the existing policies. In some cases, of course, the administration may be unaware of the affirmative action officers' client orientation and construction of law. But in the two examples we observed, the Advocates were well-known public figures and were selected precisely because of their strong public stand on EEO/AA issues. The appointment of an Advocate constitutes a visible symbol of commitment to EEO/AA law and thus may represent an attempt to gain legitimacy for the organization.

For Advocates, the legitimacy they confer on organizations can be the key to their power and effectiveness within the organization. The administration always has the formal authority to replace the affirmative action officer or eliminate the position. However, organizations risk loss of legitimacy by public confrontation of affirmative action officers who adopt a strategy of advocacy. Advocates can draw upon the clientele they serve to support their actions; employee and community support for the affirmative action officer raises the cost to legitimacy that the administration would incur by exercising control. . . .

The threat of termination does not seem to deter use of the Advocate strategy. The Advocates we spoke to judge professional success on the basis of their achievement of substantive goals rather than on the basis of their position in or progression up the bureaucratic hierarchy. Since their career goals are relatively independent of any particular bureaucracy, termination is less of a threat and they are willing to risk it in order to pursue EEO/AA goals. . . .

B. The Team Player

A second strategy is to resolve the conflict inherent in the affirmative action officer role in favor of the administration. The "Team Player" views the administration as the primary client and is attentive to the threat that EEO/AA law poses to traditional managerial prerogatives. In order to protect these prerogatives, the affirmative action officer constructs EEO/AA law as a procedural requirement, requiring like treatment of all employees. This construction preserves maximum managerial freedom because it does not require—or indeed even allow—employers to take affirmative action to correct imbalances or inequities in their workforces. It could, however, require changes in formal policy if extant rules or procedures clearly discriminate on the basis of a protected status.

Affirmative action officers who use the Team Player strategy are unlikely to be seen as a threat to the organization and may therefore be granted considerable autonomy. But, for the same reason, they are unlikely to use that autonomy to challenge administration policies or practices. It is in the Team Player's career interest to resolve EEO/AA related problems efficiently (not to ignore them), but to do so in a manner that is minimally disruptive to the organization. Serious challenges to administrative policy would be inconsistent with their career goals. . . .

The Team Player strategy is likely to be used by affirmative action officers who see their position as part of the bureaucratic management structure and as a stepping stone to higher (non-EEO/AA) bureaucratic positions. When career aspirations are defined in terms of the progression up the bureaucratic hierarchy, affirmative action officers have strong motivations to use their expertise to justify participation and integration in administrative matters and are less likely to judge professional success by their achievements in reaching EEO/AA goals (Larson, 1977).

Our example of a Team Player is the affirmative action officer who was hired by the eastern city after Martinez left. The mayor appointed a hiring committee to review candidates for the position vacated by Martinez, and the committee selected and ranked three finalists. The mayor, however, "apparently ignoring the recommendations of his own interview committee," appointed a Hispanic woman, Maria Lopez (pseudonym). The appointment clearly lacked the legitimacy that Martinez' appointment had provided and alienated the Hispanic community that had supported Martinez. Lopez was especially criticized for her inability to work with the city's minority community. "The appointment of [Lopez]," said a Hispanic leader, "is geared to serve the Mayor's political interest and it is not an appointment that will prove beneficial."

Lopez demonstrated her allegiance to the city administration early in her tenure in a hiring dispute between the Board of Aldermen and the Mayor's office. Using her authority to review applications, she refused to appoint the aldermen's choice for the Assistant Director of Parks and Recreation and instead endorsed the selection of another candidate, a handicapped man, preferred by the mayor. Outraged aldermen began to call Lopez the "patronage secretary" for the mayor's administration. One alderman said "he is harsh on the [EEO/AA] office because 'the job is not being done.' "

Lopez' tenure continued to be characterized by her close relationship with the mayor and consistent support for his positions. Lopez stated that "[a]s far as the mayor is concerned and everybody else, my job is not to make policy, it's to implement policy." In her last year in office, "pundits" said the affirmative action office "is simply an instrument and extension of the mayor. . . . They charge [Lopez] with being the mayor's puppet. . . . High level public officials say privately they don't know if she is unqualified for the job or whether the mayor has tied her hands."

Whereas Martinez derived support from the EOC, Lopez came into conflict with the EOC. Lopez refused to attend EOC meetings and instead sent her assistant (who, new to his job, was unfamiliar with the agreement reached with HUD). Further, while the EOC was working on an affirmative action plan for the city, city officials disclosed as a fait accompli their own plan, which was negotiated privately with HUD over the previous six months. Stunned EOC members requested at least the opportunity to review the plan before it was implemented.

Lopez was not ineffective in implementing EEO policies. In 1985, a news article reported that the city "is in compliance with state regulations which require the proportion of minorities hired to reflect their number in the city. Last year [1984], out of the ninety-one city employees hired, twenty-two percent were minorities." But even as the city improved its minority hiring record, the Hispanic community did not rally behind Lopez or the mayor. The consensus among Hispanic activists was that the mayor was committed to affirmative action only because it brought in federal grants. In 1985, even though the mayor was reelected, minorities "turned out in unprecedented numbers to cast their vote for his challenger." After a five-year tenure, Lopez resigned at the end of 1985, not in protest, but for a better job.

Team Players' identification with administration interests, then, do not necessarily preclude implementation of EEO/AA law as long as the administration is somewhat sympathetic to the law or at least interested in complying with it. But the form of compliance they implement is likely to be of the weakest sort. . . .

Administrators are more likely to choose a Team Player when the need to control the affirmative action officer and the implementation of EEO/AA law outweighs the need to appease a threatening minority or female constituency. . . . In this case, and perhaps in others, the organization sought an officer who would be a Team Player in order to thwart an aggressive form of compliance.

C. The Professional

Whereas the Advocate and Team Player strategies involve partisan client orientations, the third strategy is to maintain a stance of detached neutrality. We refer to this strategy as the "Professional" strategy because the professional management literature advances it as the best strategy for compliance with EEO/AA law. In keeping with its neutral orientation toward parties, the Professional strategy does not embrace either the procedural or the substantive construction of EEO/AA law. Rather it circumvents the conflict between these approaches by constructing EEO/AA law as a simple matter of fairness and good personnel policy.

By equating EEO/AA requirements with those of good personnel management, Professionals reframe EEO/AA goals in terms of traditional managerial interests: efficiency and productivity. . . .

The emphasis on fairness leads to concerns both with formal personnel policy that meets legal criteria and with conflict-resolution procedures. The professional management literature emphasizes the importance of formalizing personnel policies against discrimination in hiring, placement, promotion, and discharge as a means of avoiding lawsuits. . . .

[T]he creation of structures for dispute resolution creates an aura of neutrality even though affirmative action officers of necessity confer substantive benefits on one party or the other. Dispute resolution procedures highlight impartiality in the process and create the impression that the outcome of that process must also be fair. . . .

Of course, the extent to which dispute resolution procedures seem fair depends upon the apparent impartiality of the decision-maker, who is usually the affirmative action officer. Here Professionals can draw upon their professional training and background to claim the capacity to remain neutral in a highly politicized realm. Just as lawyers and judges can use ambiguous statutes to support contradictory positions, affirmative action officers—employing the Professional strategy—can turn to broad organizational rules to legitimate their decisions. When organizational policy supports affirmative action officers' actions, even top administrators are pressed to defer to their judgment; thus the Professionals' use of expertise to claim neutrality helps them to procure power within the organizational hierarchy.

Our example of a Professional is an affirmative action officer who was hired as the first officer in a college that did not create an affirmative action office until 1988. As in the case of the two cities we discussed earlier, the college's decision to create an affirmative action office and officer position came after a series of racist incidents. But rather than turning to a local civil rights activist, the college undertook a nationwide search. Jones [pseudonym], the person eventually hired, was a black lawyer who had worked in the affirmative action and equal employment opportunity field for twenty years and had held academic and state government affirmative action officer positions.

Whereas the Advocates and Team Player we discussed defined their tasks in terms of their respective clienteles, Jones told us that her task was to implement the college's affirmative action plan and to serve as an ombudsperson who would resolve discrimination-related disputes. She argued that her position was neither structurally problematic nor politically controversial, and stated emphatically that her orientation would be one of neutrality: she would not serve as an advocate for either party in a dispute. Jones believed that the affirmative action plan constituted closure on political battles, and that "taking sides" would undermine her position. She also rejected any notion that she might need to develop a constituency to support her in her endeavors.

Jones' characterization of the affirmative action plan as a binding set of rules bolstered her claims to neutrality. As Edwards (1979) observes, formal policies tend to obscure the power and volition of officials so that the policies appear to dictate decisionmaking. To date, Jones' relationship with the administration has been largely unproblematic. She appears to have considerable autonomy and authority and has not developed either antagonistic or very close relationships with any of the parties that might make claims to her loyalty.

We saw that the Advocate strategy invites criticism from the administration while the Team Player is open to criticism from protected employees and potential employees. The Professional's stance of detached neutrality and reliance on formal rules renders this strategy far more stable than either the Advocate or the Team Player strategies because these factors help to insulate the affirmative action officer from criticism.

Perhaps for this reason, the personnel management profession is helping to institutionalize the Professional strategy as the dominant strategy for compliance with EEO/AA law. Professional networks, which provide a regular means of interaction through management journals, workshops run by organizations such as the Bureau of National Affairs, and professional conventions, strongly endorse formal EEO/AA policy and dispute resolution as key elements of compliance. Affirmative action officers participate in professional conventions and workshops as a means of acquiring and demonstrating expertise and because these activities help to create an aura of professionalism, which Professionals can then rely upon to support their claims of neutrality. These networks both diffuse and legitimate the Professional model.

D. The Technician

We have left until last a strategy that is almost a nonstrategy for handling role conflict, which is that of the "Technician." Technicians concentrate on the mundane aspects of the affirmative action officer job, such as collecting workforce statistics and completing required forms for the EEOC. Officers who adopt this strategy are largely uninvolved in creating EEO/AA policy. Like the Professional, the Technician maintains a nonpartisan client orientation. However, whereas the Professional engages in a studied neutrality, the Technician is indifferent to the political demands of various constituencies. And whereas the Professional assumes a prominent conciliatory role, the Technician either retreats from, or is barred from, any substantive role within organizations.

For our example of a Technician, we now return to the eastern city that had first hired an Advocate (Martinez, who resigned under pressure), and then a Team Player (Lopez, who left for a better job). After Lopez left and before the mayor appointed Lopez' replacement, the affirmative action office was essentially gutted. Four positions were merged into one, that of the affirmative action officer. In an interview with the current officer, Smith [pseudonym], we were told that the staff reduction was intended to weaken the office.

Comparing her tenure to that of Lopez (she was unaware of Martinez), Smith noted that the affirmative action issue has "quieted down," which, interestingly, she attributed to characteristics of the office, namely, the smaller staff, lack of resources and, consequently, her inability to act forcefully. Whereas Lopez acted as an agent of the mayor in various conflicts with the Hispanic community and the board of aldermen, Smith has not assumed a political role: "[i]t's their government," she said, "they can do as they please." She also did not dwell on her relation to the Hispanic community except to note that some persons feel she should be doing more. Although the current officer still believes she is on a "hot seat"—due to continued resistance to affirmative action in some quarters of the city government—she copes by shying away from a public role.

For the Technician, then, compliance becomes a minimalist endeavor: it consists only of filing required documents. The Technician avoids conflict by recording workforce composition rather than trying to justify or to change it. Given the ambiguity of EEO/AA law, the Technician will probably still be in compliance as long as there is no blatant exclusion of minorities and women. Unlike the other three strategies, Technicians are not likely to claim professional expertise or attempt to acquire power within the bureaucracy. They are subordinates in all respects and, therefore, tend passively to support the administration's interests.

Discussion and Implications

Of course, the Advocate, Team Player, Professional, and Technician do not exist in pure form. At times, affirmative action officers are likely to use mixtures of the strategies suggested by these types opportunistically. . . .

Although we cannot generalize on the basis of five examples, we suggest some tentative conclusions about the internal politics of compliance. First, although the Advocate strategy has the greatest potential for substantively oriented reform, that strategy is likely to be frustrated by the very factors that give it that potential: a client orientation that favors minorities and women, a substantive construction of EEO/AA law, and the use of expertise to challenge the administration. Each of these factors intensifies the threat to traditional managerial prerogatives. Organizations select Advocates as symbols of compliance, but Advocates are not likely to serve as passive symbols. Advocates tend to generate rather than quell political tension. That tension may undermine their community support and claims to professional expertise in such a way that the administration can exercise control without significant loss of legitimacy. Thus the strong form of compliance that Advocates tend to favor is unlikely to occur.

None of the other affirmative action officer types exacerbate the structural contradictions of the position as much as Advocates because they pose far less of a threat to management. Unless the administration is serious about reform, Team Players are likely to engender compliance with EEO/AA law at a minimal level; they may eliminate overt procedural discrimination but are unlikely to reduce the substantive differences in employment

status between white males and other groups. Where organizations have Technicians as affirmative action officers, the responsibility for compliance usually remains elsewhere within the administration. As with the Team Player, unless an administration strongly favors substantive change, it is unlikely to occur.

The Professional approach is likely to be the most stable and effective in producing some change. Because of their claims of neutrality, Professionals can be more effective because they are relatively insulated from serious political challenge and because they are likely to enjoy more autonomy from the administration. And, because the power and status of their profession depends upon the continued importance of EEO/AA law and their management of it, Professionals have a vested interest in instituting EEO/AA programs that are visibly effective.

Professionals' network ties are an important component of their capacity to institutionalize EEO/AA measures. In order to demonstrate and maintain their professional status, they participate in a set of institutionalized activities in which models of compliance are exchanged, negotiated, and standardized. Over time, the network connections of Professionals help to define and institutionalize formal affirmative action rules, programs and plans. As these formal structures become more prevalent, they may help to entrench EEO/AA norms into formal organizational policy.

Affirmative action officers, then, are important actors in a highly political process of compliance. As individuals, their strategies for resolving conflicting demands affect the character and agenda of their organizations' compliance programs. As a profession, they collectively construct and help to institutionalize the meaning of compliance with EEO/AA law. If the Professional strategy is in fact becoming the dominant one, two conclusions may be drawn. First, the institutionalization of formal EEO/AA policies and dispute resolution structures means that they will not be erased by the political and legal climate of the 1980s, which disfavors affirmative action. Second, since the thrust of the Professional approach is to accommodate competing interests, it is not one that will evoke striking reform.

More generally, the process of compliance we have begun to illuminate suggests that accounts that emphasize efforts by officials within organizations to mask violations . . . or to place organizational goals over legal goals . . . do not apply universally and may oversimplify the process of compliance. . . . Rather than overt noncompliance, we find that compliance is a complex process of defining a response to mandates that are often ambiguous. . . .

References

EDELMAN, LAUREN B. "Legal Ambiguity and Symbolic Structures: Organizational Mediation of Civil Rights Law." *American Journal of Sociology* 97, no. 6 (1992): 1531.

EDWARDS, RICHARD. *Contested Terrain: The Transformation of the Workplace in the Twentieth Century.* New York: Basic Books, 1979.

LARSON, MARGALI SARFATI. *The Rise of Professionalism: A Sociological Analysis.* Berkeley: University of California Press, 1977.

SELZNICK, PHILIP. *TVA and the Grass Roots: A Study in the Sociology of Formal Organization.* Berkeley: University of California Press, 1949.

VAUGHAN, DIANE. *Controlling Unlawful Organizational Behavior: Social Structure and Corporate Misconduct.* Chicago: University of Chicago Press, 1983.

EXERCISES AND QUESTIONS FOR FURTHER THOUGHT

1. Should private citizens and interest groups be granted a right of their own to bring actions in court to enforce statutory policies for which administrative agencies are responsible? On one hand, this could offset the problem of capture. On the other hand, judicial decisions might contradict or interfere with the orderly development of agency policy.

2. The model of compliance described in this chapter helps explain the dynamics of regulation. It also serves another less obvious but more important purpose, one which you should begin to think about now. The principles of administrative law announced in appellate court decisions either succeed or fail to shape administrative behavior because of the pushing and pulling of the very same forces in the compliance model that affect regulatory compliance. Think of any case covered thus far that imposes a behavioral constraint on administrators. Then speculate about the forces pushing toward and away from administrative compliance. You should differentiate the compliance of a governmental party to the case, from the extent to which other agencies similarly situated will voluntarily adopt the policies expressed in the opinion.

3. Return to the two examples of enforcement that we drew from the *New York Times* at the beginning of this chapter. Try your hand at applying the elements of this chapter's compliance model to these situations. For example, who are the beneficiaries of USDA regulations, the workers or the consumers or both? More generally, one of the strongest cases for regulatory enforcement is precisely when the beneficiaries cannot be relied upon to enforce on their own.

CHAPTER 10
JUDICIAL REVIEW

The previous chapters in this part have moved you along a path—a path that starts at the point where a constitutionally valid statute authorizes agency action. It then passes through information-gathering to informal and formal decision making and enforcement. In this chapter we arrive at the last phase of any administrative decision, which will determine its success or failure if and when courts review its legality.

Actually the path is not usually so straight. We have already studied cases where courts reviewed administrative decisions before any enforcement occurred. And some decisions—the Nuclear Regulatory Commission's green light to operate nuclear plants before the waste disposal problem was solved, for example—don't create a need to enforce anything. The result permits the agency to proceed with its plans. Nevertheless the path does end with judicial review because courts tend to have the last word. The only avenue open from the courts goes to Congress, which has only rarely set aside judicial administrative law rulings. Chapters 11 through 13, part III, do not take the path further. Instead they illustrate three important areas of administrative law that raise questions on the path we have already traveled.

Because courts potentially have the last word in all cases, this chapter is as important as any in the book. It describes the ground rules governing the process by which courts have reached all the decisions you read in this or any other legal casebook. Although constitutions, administrative procedure acts, and authorizing statutes help define administrative law, such legal pronouncements do not answer every contingency. Judges create judicial concepts and principles in the process of reviewing administrative decisions. These concepts often reappear in an agency's own justifications for its actions. In this respect administrative law resembles other sites of law where judicial pronouncements become embedded in the way institutions, such as agencies, present themselves.

This chapter covers the two major components of judicial review. One concerns the ground rules—ripeness, standing, mootness, exhaustion, and primary jurisdiction—for obtaining *access* to judicial review of agency decisions. These rules govern when courts will review agency decisions. Courts play an important role in shaping the very rules that determine when they will review agency decisions and under what circumstances. The second component, hinted at in earlier chapters, concerns the *scope* of judicial review. There is considerable disagreement about how deferential courts should be toward administrative discretion. In the *Vermont Yankee* cases you compared Judge Bazelon's opinion, calling for greater judicial scrutiny of agency rulemaking, with Justice Rehnquist's opinion, reversing the Court of Appeals decision and narrowing the scope of judicial review. The scope of judicial review is also an important issue in many judicial opinions about statutory interpretation, such as *Chevron v. NRDC* (chapter 4). This chapter articulates the various dimensions of this fundamental problem.

Here are some typical scope of review questions:

1. How much deference should courts give to an agency's interpretation of its own statutory authority?

2. When an agency, either in rulemaking or adjudication, finds certain facts and incorporates them into its decision, how willingly should judges dispute the facts the agency found? How freely should judges substitute their own interpretation of the facts for the agency's interpretation?

3. How aggressively should courts force agencies to give detailed factual justification for their decisions?

Controversy surrounds the scope of judicial review in part for historical reasons. At the time of the final political triumph of the New Deal, both lawyers and students of government agreed that administrators could cope with the problems of economic regulation better than either legislatures or courts. Administrators, they believed, could combine expert training with effective information-gathering techniques to shape wise policy closely and continuously without constant political interference. Since courts lacked these virtues, they should not actively oppose administrative choices the way they opposed so much administrative policy in the fifty years before 1937. If these assumptions about administrative superiority held true in practice, then courts should intervene only to prevent violations of the Constitution itself and to block administrative actions that lacked any legislative authorization.

The consensus that courts should defer to agency expertise, information processing and impartiality has, since the New Deal, come unglued for several reasons. Let us review them briefly. The first of these is agency capture: an industry that an agency tries to regulate so controls the flow of information and expertise to the agency and develops such close interpersonal relationships with agency staff (in no small part by offering good jobs to agency staff) that the agency in the end protects an industry more than it regulates it. The second deficiency is that many agencies have to accommodate inconsistent philosophies about the agency's mission. Some who work for the Social Security Administration feel the organization should try to ease human misfortunes, while others in the same organization place cost control at the top of their priority list. Third, we have learned that agencies cannot mechanically implement clear public policy. Much is left to discretion, and agencies do not always use it wisely. A law that calls for regulating the communications industry "in the public interest" resembles an empty balloon that the Federal Communications Commission may inflate as much as it wants without explicit legislative guidance. You can see how the extent to which we trust the administrative process to avoid these pitfalls will influence how judges should answer questions of judicial scope such as the three listed on the previous page.

Part IV will again address these problems. For this chapter's purposes, you need only appreciate that *one* plausible way to cope with increasing doubts about administrative performance is to increase judicial surveillance of it. We do not have to believe that judges are somehow magically better administrators to justify judicial review. We need merely accept the wisdom in H. L. Mencken's observation that conscience is the small voice within us that tells us that someone may be looking.

You also need to appreciate, however, that court involvement with regulatory process generates "costs." Having yet another institution, the judiciary, to check the soundness of administrative decision making is ideal, but it means more time and money spent on regulation. Administration of justice thus necessitates a middle ground between securing sound administrative performance and court surveillance. Some of the rules about access to review that we discuss below, "standing" in particular, are devices to make sure that regulatory process is not unnecessarily burdened. Of course what does it mean to *unnecessarily* burden a regulatory process is in part a question about expending judicial resources.

ACCESS TO JUDICIAL REVIEW

We turn now to the first and most general problem of judicial review. Courts, like any other branch of government, face constitutional limits on their power. Courts of course say what the law is, but they do not inevitably interpret their own powers to be as far-reaching as they might. To reduce their workload to manageable proportions, judges have often decided that they lack the power to intervene in certain situations.

Article III, section 2, of the Constitution confers on federal courts jurisdiction (power) to decide "cases" and "controversies." The courts have consistently interpreted these two jurisdiction-granting words to cover only the power to decide lawsuits. A lawsuit exists only when a plaintiff files a complaint against a defendant and the court gains jurisdictional power over the defendant to force him to answer the complaint in court. This process creates a genuine legal disagreement. We call this the *requirement of adversariness*. Where parties disagree about something they presumably will present their best evidence and their best arguments in court to demonstrate why they should win. For a court to reach out and decide a case without getting the best evidence from both sides increases the risk that courts will make mistakes.

In practice, although there are some specific exceptions in the laws of some states, judges take for granted that they may act only to resolve lawsuits. The interesting legal issues today deal not with the mere existence of a lawsuit, but with whether the suit is adversarial enough to fall within Article III's grant of power. Thus in the extreme case where two sides agree to sue each other, but both really hope for the same result, the "case and controversy" requirement is not met.[1] Other issues are not quite so obvious, and this section examines five of these.

You may initially think these five issues are mere legal technicalities, issues for lawyers to handle with no significance for administrators themselves. However, these topics—ripeness, standing, mootness, exhaustion, and primary jurisdiction—do involve important assumptions about the role of courts in modern government. A restrictive definition of ripeness or standing, for example, necessarily eliminates some occasions for judicial review. These five items primarily affect only the theoretical timing of judicial review, but in the practice of law, just as in love and politics, timing affects whether some things happen at all.

The most important reason to study these seemingly technical rules—especially the rules of standing—is that they can have significant political consequences and shape important policy results. To cite just one example, it is common knowledge that campaign financing distorts public policy. An article in the *Wall Street Journal* described the reaction of freshman Congresswoman Linda Smith (a conservative Republican from Washington state) this way:

Soon after arriving in Congress, as [Smith] tells it, she made an unsettling discovery: Republicans were just as bad as Democrats when it came to slurping up money from political-action committees and lobbyist-arranged junkets. . . .

She says she quickly discovered that it was a common practice for the GOP majority to hold up action on bills while milking interested contributors for more campaign contributions. "I said, 'We do what? Isn't that extortion?'"[2]

In theory the Federal Elections Commission (FEC) enforces the laws governing campaign fund-raising. But who has the right to challenge the FEC's decisions in court, i.e., what groups can file lawsuits against the FEC? In 1998, to the surprise of some commentators, the Supreme Court ruled, 6-3, that all voters have standing to challenge the FEC in court. While people who have no more than "generalized grievances" normally do not have standing, voters were held to have a specific enough grievance to win standing.[3] As you will see in the standing cases that follow, rulings on standing have played a central role in the politics of environmental protection.

1. Ripeness and the Presumption of Reviewability

What if a person or corporation or government agency has made a decision that will affect others when it is implemented but has not yet begun to implement it? Should courts wait until the harm has occurred before deeming the case adversarial, or should they intervene to examine whether the harm is legally permissible before it happens? If the former, how much harm must take place before the courts will step in? These questions deal with how *ripe* a dispute must be in order to merit judicial scrutiny. Judges who believe courts should avoid interfering with the administrative process will require much ripeness. Hence it is not surprising to find that one of the strongest judicial statements in favor of judicial review of administration simultaneously requires only a moderate ripening of the harm before courts can review a decision.

---

1. *Muskrat v. United States*, 219 U.S. 346 (1911).

2. "Combative Washington Conservative Rep. Smith Girds for Senate Battle by Fighting Her Own GOP," June 17, 1998.
3. *FEC v. Akins*, 524 U.S. 11 (1998).

As you read this next case try to identify the harm the drug companies will suffer if the courts refuse to intervene at this point in the proceedings. Does this harm make the issue real and substantial enough to assure a fully adversary proceeding? Also, try to articulate the ways judicial intervention at this stage might impair the regulatory process. Note the majority's argument that both sides can benefit from a ruling at this time.[4]

Abbott Laboratories, Inc. v. Gardner

387 U.S. 136 (1967) 8-0
+ Warren, Black, Douglas, Harlan, Stewart,
   Clark, White, Fortas
NP Brennan

[Congress in 1962 required manufacturers of prescription drugs to print the "established," i.e., generic, name of the drug along with the manufacturer's own proprietary brand name on drug labels, in advertisements, and in other printed materials. The commissioner of the Food and Drug Administration (FDA) required the drug manufacturers to print the generic name alongside the brand name every time the brand name appeared, not just once or at the top of the label or other material. Before the FDA made any effort to enforce this regulation, a group of thirty-seven drug manufacturers, of which Abbott Laboratories was the first alphabetically listed, asked the courts to declare the regulation void for exceeding the statutory authority granted the FDA.]

Justice Harlan delivered the opinion of the Court

The injunctive and declaratory judgment remedies are discretionary, and courts traditionally have been reluctant to apply them to administrative determinations unless these arise in the context of a controversy "ripe" for judicial resolution. Without undertaking to survey the intricacies of the ripeness doctrine it is fair to say that its basic rationale is to prevent the courts, through avoidance of premature adjudi-

4. See also *Koebring Co. v. Adams*, 605 F.2d 280 (1979), and *City of Rochester v. Bond*, 603 F.2d 927 (1979).

cation, from entangling themselves in abstract disagreements over administrative policies, and also to protect the agencies from judicial interference until an administrative decision has been formalized and its effects felt in a concrete way by the challenging parties. The problem is best seen in a twofold aspect, requiring us to evaluate both the fitness of the issues for judicial decision and the hardship to the parties of withholding court consideration.

As to the former factor, we believe the issues presented are appropriate for judicial resolution at this time. First, all parties agree that the issue tendered is a purely legal one: whether the statute was properly construed by the Commissioner to require the established name of the drug to be used every time the proprietary name is employed. Both sides moved for summary judgment in the District Court, and no claim is made here that further administrative proceedings are contemplated. It is suggested that the justification for this rule might vary with different circumstances, and that the expertise of the Commissioner is relevant to passing upon the validity of the regulation. This of course is true, but the suggestion overlooks the fact that both sides have approached this case as one purely of congressional intent, and that the Government made no effort to justify the regulation in factual terms.

Second, the regulations in issue we find to be "final agency action" within the meaning of § 10 of the Administrative Procedure Act, 5 U.S.C. § 704, as construed in judicial decisions. An "agency action" includes any "rule," defined by the Act as "an agency statement of general or particular applicability and future effect designed to implement, interpret, or prescribe law or policy," §§ 2(c), 2(g), 5 U.S.C. §§ 551(4), 551(13). The cases dealing with judicial review of administrative actions have interpreted the "finality" element in a pragmatic way. Thus in *Columbia Broadcasting System v. United States*, 316 U.S. 407, a suit under the Urgent Deficiencies Act, 38 Stat. 219, this Court held reviewable a regulation of the Federal Communications Commission setting forth certain proscribed contractual arrangements between chain broadcasters and local stations. The FCC did not have direct authority to regulate these contracts, and its rule asserted only that it would not license stations which maintained such contracts with the networks. Although no license had in fact been denied or revoked, and the FCC regulation could properly be characterized as a statement only of its intentions, the Court held that "Such regulations have the force of law before their sanctions are invoked as well as after. When as here they are promulgated by order of the Commission and the expected conformity to them causes injury cognizable by a court of equity, they are appropriately the subject of attack. . . ." 316 U.S., at 418–419. . . .

Again, in *United States v. Storer Broadcasting Co.*, 351 U.S. 192, the Court held to be a final agency action within the meaning of the Administrative Procedure Act an FCC regulation announcing a Commission policy that it would not issue a television license to an applicant already owning five such licenses, even though no specific application was before the Commission. The Court stated: "The process of rulemaking was complete. It was final agency action . . . by which Storer claimed to be 'aggrieved.' "

We find decision in the present case following a fortiori from these precedents. The regulation challenged here, promulgated in a formal manner after announcement in the Federal Register and consideration of comments by interested parties is quite clearly definitive. There is no hint that this regulation is informal, see *Helco Products Co. v. McNutt*, 78 U.S. App. D.C. 71, . . . or only the ruling of a subordinate official, see *Swift & Co. v. Wickbarm*, D.C., 230 F.Supp. 398, 409, aff'd, 2 Cir., 364 F.2d 241, or tentative. It was made effective upon publication, and the Assistant General Counsel for Food and Drugs stated in the District Court that compliance was expected. . . .

This is also a case in which the impact of the regulations upon the petitioners is sufficiently direct and immediate as to render the issue appropriate for judicial review at this stage. These regulations purport to give an authoritative interpretation of a statutory provision that has a direct effect on the day-to-day business of all prescription drug companies; its promulgation puts petitioners in a dilemma that it was the very purpose of the Declaratory Judgment Act to ameliorate. As the District Court found on the basis of uncontested allegations, "Either they must comply with the every time requirement and incur the costs of changing over their promotional material and labeling or they must follow their present course and risk prosecution." 228 F. Supp. 855, 861. The regulations are clear-cut, and were made effective immediately upon publication; as noted earlier the agency's counsel represented to the District Court that immediate compliance with their terms was expected.

If petitioners wish to comply they must change all their labels, advertisements, and promotional materials; they must destroy stocks of printed matter; and they must invest heavily in new printing type and new supplies. The alternative to compliance—continued use of material which they believe in good faith meets the statutory requirements, but which clearly does not meet the regulation of the Commissioner—may be even more costly. That course would risk serious criminal and civil penalties for the unlawful distribution of "misbranded" drugs.

It is relevant at this juncture to recognize that petitioners deal in a sensitive industry, in which public confidence in their drug products is especially important. To require them to challenge these regulations only as a defense to an action brought by the Government might harm them severely and unnecessarily. Where the legal issue presented is fit for judicial resolution, and where a regulation requires an immediate and significant change in the plaintiffs' conduct of their affairs with serious penalties attached to noncompliance, access to the courts under the Administrative Procedure Act and the Declaratory Judgment Act must be permitted, absent a statutory bar or some other unusual circumstance, neither of which appears here. . . .

The Government further contends that the threat of criminal sanctions for noncompliance with a judicially untested regulation is unrealistic; the Solicitor General has represented that if court enforcement becomes necessary, "the Department of Justice will proceed only civilly for an injunction . . . or by condemnation." We cannot accept this argument as a sufficient answer to petitioners' petition. This action at its inception was properly brought and this subsequent representation of the Department of Justice should not suffice to defeat it.

Finally, the Government urges that to permit resort to the courts in this type of case may delay or impede effective enforcement of the Act. We fully recognize the important public interest served by assuring prompt and unimpeded administration of the Pure Food, Drug, and Cosmetic Act, but we do not find the Government's argument convincing. First, in this particular case, a pre-enforcement challenge by nearly all prescription drug manufacturers is calculated to speed enforcement. If the Government prevails, a large part of the industry is bound by the decree; if the Government loses, it can more quickly revise its regulation. . . .

Lastly, although the Government presses us to reach the merits of the challenge to the regulation in the event we find the District Court properly entertained this action, we believe the better practice is to remand the case to the Court of Appeals for the Third Circuit to review the District Court's decision that the regulation was beyond the power of the Commissioner.

Reversed and remanded.

Abbott Laboratories's tilt in favor of ripeness seems both fair and practically wise. Wise because it allows administrative actions that may rest on unwarranted interpretations of the authorizing statutes, or of the Constitution, to be tested with a minimum of time and expenditure of money on litigation. Thus *Reno v. Catholic Social Services*, 509 U.S. 43 (1993) came as something of a surprise. In that case the Immigration Reform and Control Act of 1986 set up a procedure whereby people who were in the United States illegally could obtain permanent legal residence if they had "resided continuously in the United States in an unlawful status since at least January 1, 1982," and "been physically present in the United States continuously since November 6, 1986." The Immigration and Naturalization Service (INS) then issued regulations interpreting these provisions of the 1986 statute. These regulations seemed automatically to disqualify large numbers of aliens from establishing legal temporary residence. They filed class action lawsuits. Both lower courts found the regulations inconsistent with the statute. But the Supreme Court held that the cases were not ripe because no individual alien had yet been turned down. The majority distinguished *Abbott Labs* because the INS regulations did not compel the aliens in this case to make an immediate choice. Justice John Paul Stevens grumbled in dissent that the decision would only prolong uncertainty and increase litigation expenses.

In a more recent case, *National Park Hospitality Association v. Department of Interior*, 538 U.S. 803 (2003), the Supreme Court used the *Abbott Labs'* two-tiered test to guide its ripeness inquiry. A six-member majority held that a National Park Service (NPS) rule stating that NPS concession contracts are not subject to the Contract Disputes Act

was not ripe for review, since "Absent [a statutory provision providing for immediate judicial review] a regulation is not ordinarily considered the type of agency action ripe for review . . . until the scope of the controversy has been reduced to more manageable proportions, and its factual components fleshed out by some concrete action applying the regulation to the claimant's situation in a fashion that harms or threatens to harm him."

2. Standing

Professor Paul Freund once described Justice Marian's opinions as possessing the qualities of fine, well-aged wine. Marian's opinion in *Abbott Labs* makes satisfyingly clear that, despite the traditional view that courts must simply insure adversariness when they intervene, these doctrines—ripeness and presumption of reviewability—really accomplish more. They insure that the facts are fully developed and that the parties will address the applicable law, not tangential or speculative matters. The standing requirement fulfills the same objectives as does ripeness. The standing concept applies throughout the legal system, so we may begin to explore it with an example less abstract than those typical of administrative law.

Suppose a couple plans to marry. Two months before the wedding a drunk driver runs into the would-be groom in a crosswalk. He suffers such serious injuries that the couple must postpone the wedding for a year. The law recognizes the man's legal capacity to bring suit to recover from the drunk driver for his injuries, but the woman has no standing to sue because she was not injured and has no legally recognized relationship with him. Standing doctrine thus recognizes the claims of plaintiffs *directly injured* by a defendant. While the driver's action may have harmed the bride-to-be in an obvious way, she has no standing. If her fiancée earned $200,000 a year and postponing the marriage meant she lost a year of that shared income, she would suffer a real and measurable loss, but indirectly, not directly, from the defendant's negligent act.

Until 1968 the Court had consistently refused standing to taxpayer suits. In that year the Court granted limited standing to taxpayers if their suits met two requirements.

First, taxpayer-plaintiffs had to challenge a specific congressional enactment made under the taxing and spending clause of Article I, section 8, of the Constitution. Second, they had to allege that the government violated some specific constitutional limitation on its taxing and spending power. In this case, plaintiffs gained standing to challenge expenditure of tax money that aided private schools operated by religious groups.[5]

In administrative law the requirements for standing are generally not as strict as they are for constitutional claims. Section 702 of the Administrative Procedure Act (APA) grants a person standing if she has been "aggrieved by [an] agency action within the meaning of the relevant statute." In *Association of Data Processing Service Organizations, Inc. v. Camp* (1970), Justice William O. Douglas spells out the rationale for granting standing to parties before administrative tribunals if their claims are within a "zone of interest," as compared to the more narrow requirement that parties demonstrate "direct injury."

Association of Data Processing Service Organizations, Inc. v. Camp

397 U.S. 150 (1970) 7-2
+ Burger, Black, Douglas, Harlan, Stewart, Marshall, Blackmun
+/– Brennan, White

[The Association of Data Processing Service Organizations challenged a riding by the Comptroller of the Currency permitting national banks to provide data processing services as part of their banking services. The lower court dismissed the suit on the grounds that the petitioners lacked standing and the Court of Appeals affirmed.]

Justice Douglas delivered the opinion of the Court

Generalizations about standing to sue are largely worthless as such. One generalization is, however, necessary and that is that the question of standing in the federal courts is

5. *Flast v. Cohen*, 392 U.S. 83 (1968).

to be considered in the framework of Article III which restricts judicial power to "cases" and "controversies." As we recently stated in *Flast v. Cohen*, 392 U.S. 83, 101, "[I]n terms of Article III limitations on federal court jurisdiction, the question of standing is related only to whether the dispute sought to be adjudicated will be presented in an adversary context and in a form historically viewed as capable of judicial resolution." *Flast* was a *taxpayer's* suit. The present is a *competitor's* suit. And while the two have the same Article III starting point, they do not necessarily track one another.

The first question is whether the plaintiff alleges that the challenged action has caused him injury in fact, economic or otherwise. There can be no doubt but that petitioners have satisfied this test. The petitioners not only allege that competition by national banks in the business of providing data processing services might entail some future loss of profits for the petitioners, they also allege that respondent American National Bank & Trust Company was performing or preparing to perform such services for two customers for whom petitioner Data Systems, Inc. had previously agreed or negotiated to perform such services. . . .

Those tests were based on prior decisions of this Court, such as *Tennessee Power Co. v. TVA*, 306 U.S. 118, where private power companies sought to enjoin TVA from operating, claiming that the statutory plan under which it was created was unconstitutional. The court denied the competitors' standing, holding that they did not have that status "unless the right invaded is a legal right,—one of property, one arising out of contract, one protected against tortious invasion, or one founded on a statute which confers a privilege." *Id.*, at 137–138.

The "legal interest" test goes to the merits. The question of standing is different. It concerns, apart from the "case" or "controversy" test, the question whether the interest sought to be protected by the complainant is arguably within the zone of interests to be protected or regulated by the statute or constitutional guarantee in question. Thus the Administrative Procedure Act grants standing to a person "aggrieved by agency action within the meaning of a relevant statute." 5 U.S.C. § 702. That interest, at times, may reflect "aesthetic, conservational, and recreational" as well as economic values. *Scenic Hudson Preservation Conf., v. FPC*, 354 F.2d 608, 616; *Office of Communication of United Church of Christ v. FCC*, 123 U.S. App. D.C. 328, 334–340, 359 F.2d 994, 1000–1006. A person or a family may have a spiritual stake in First Amendment values sufficient to give standing to raise issues concerning the Establishment Clause and the Free Exercise Clause. *Abington School District v. Schempp*, 374 U.S. 203. We mention these noneconomic values to emphasize that standing may stem from them as well as from the economic injury on which petitioners rely here. Certainly he who is "likely to be financially" injured, *FCC v. Sanders Bros. Radio Station*, 309 U.S. 470, 477, may be a reliable private attorney general to litigate the issues of the public interest in the present case.

Apart from Article III jurisdictional questions, problems of standing, as resolved by this Court for its own governance, have involved a "rule of self-restraint." *Barrows v. Jackson*, 346 U.S. 249, 255. Congress can, of course, resolve the question one way or another, save as the requirements of Article III dictate otherwise. *Muskrat v. United States*, 219 U.S. 346.

Where statutes are concerned, the trend is toward enlargement of the class of people who may protest administrative action. The whole drive for enlarging the category of aggrieved "persons" is symptomatic of that trend. In a closely analogous case we held that an existing entrepreneur had standing to challenge the legality of the entrance of a newcomer into the business, because the established business was allegedly protected by a valid city ordinance that protected it from unlawful competition. *Chicago v. Atchison, T. & S. F. R. Co.*, 357 U.S. 77, 83–84. . . .

. . . There is great contrariety among administrative agencies created by Congress as respects "the extent to which, and the procedures by which, different measures of control afford judicial review of administrative action." *Stark v. Wickard*, 321 U.S. 288, 312 (Frankfurter, J., dissenting). The answer, of course, depends on the particular enactment under which review is sought. . . .

We read § 701 (a) as sympathetic to the issue presented in this case. As stated in the House Report:

The statutes of Congress are not merely advisory when they relate to administrative agencies, any more than in other cases. To preclude judicial review under this bill a statute, if not specific in withholding such review, must upon its face give clear and convincing evidence of an intent to withhold it. The mere failure to provide specially by statute for judicial review is certainly no evidence of intent to withhold review. H. R. Rep. No. 1980, 79th Cong., 2d Sess., 41.

There is no presumption against judicial review and in favor of administrative absolutism (see *Abbott Laboratories v. Gardner*, 387 U.S. 136, 140), unless that purpose is fairly discernible in the statutory scheme. . . .

We find no evidence that Congress in either the Bank Service Corporation Act or the National Bank Act sought to preclude judicial review of administrative rulings by the Comptroller as to the legitimate scope of activities available to national banks under those statutes. Both Acts are clearly "relevant" statutes within the meaning of § 702. The Acts do not in terms protect a specified group. But their general policy is apparent; and those whose interests are directly affected by a broad or narrow interpretation of the Acts are easily identifiable. It is clear that petitioners, as competitors of national banks which are engaging in data processing services, are within that class of "aggrieved" persons who, under § 702, are entitled to judicial review of "agency action."

Whether anything in the Bank Service Corporation Act or the National Bank Act gives petitioners a "legal interest" that protects them against violations of those Acts, and whether the actions of respondents did in fact violate either of those Acts, are questions which go to the merits and remain to be decided below.

We hold that petitioners have standing to sue and that the case should be remanded for a hearing on the merits.

Reversed and remanded.

Justice Brennan, with whom Justice White joins, concurring in the result and dissenting

I concur in the result in [this] case but dissent from the Court's treatment of the question of standing to challenge agency action.

The Court's approach to standing, set out in *Data Processing*, has two steps: (1) since "the framework of Article III . . . restricts judicial power to 'cases' and 'controversies,' " the first step is to determine "whether the plaintiff alleges that the challenged action has caused him injury in fact"; (2) if injury in fact is alleged, the relevant statute or constitutional provision is then examined to determine "whether the interest sought to be protected by the complainant is arguably within the zone of interests to be protected or regulated by the statute or constitutional guarantee in question."

My view is that the inquiry in the Court's first step is the only one that need be made to determine standing. I had thought we discarded the notion of any additional requirement when we discussed standing solely in terms of its constitutional content in *Flast v. Cohen*, 392 U.S. 83 (1968). By requiring a second, nonconstitutional step, the Court comes very close to perpetuating the discredited requirement that conditioned standing on a showing by the plaintiff that the challenged governmental action invaded one of his legally protected interests. . . .

Before the plaintiff is allowed to argue the merits, it is true that a canvass of relevant statutory materials must be made in cases challenging agency action. But the canvass is made, not to determine *standing*, but to determine an aspect of *reviewability*, that is, whether Congress meant to deny or to allow judicial review of the agency action at the instance of the plaintiff.* The Court in the present cases examines the statutory materials for just this purpose but only after making the same examination during the second step of its standing inquiry. Thus in Data Processing the Court determines that the petitioners have standing because they alleged injury in fact and because "§ 4 [of the Bank Service Corporation Act of 1962] arguably brings a competitor within the zone of interests protected by it." The Court then determines that the Comptroller's action is reviewable at the instance of the plaintiffs because "[b]oth [the Bank Service Corporation Act and the National Bank Act] are clearly 'relevant' statutes within the meaning of [the Administrative Procedure Act, 5 U.S.C. § 702 (1964 ed., Supp. IV)]. The Acts do not in terms protect a specified group. But their general policy is apparent; and those whose interests are directly affected by a broad or narrow interpretation of the Acts are easily identifiable. . . .

I submit that in making such examination of statutory materials an element in the determination of standing, the Court not only performs a useless and unnecessary exercise but also encourages badly reasoned decisions, which may well deny justice in this complex field. When agency action is challenged, standing, reviewability, and the merits pose discrete, and often complicated, issues which can best be resolved by recognizing and treating them as such.

Although *Flast v. Cohen* was not a case challenging agency action, its determination of the basis for standing should resolve that question for all cases. We there con-

firmed what we said in *Baker v. Can*, 369 U.S. 186, 204 (1962), that the "gist of the question of standing" is whether the party seeking relief has "alleged such a personal stake in the outcome of the controversy as to assure that concrete adverseness which sharpens the presentation of issues upon which the court so largely depends for illumination of difficult . . . questions." "In other words," we said in *Flast*, "when standing is placed in issue in a case, the question is whether the person whose standing is challenged is a proper party to request an adjudication of a particular issue" and not whether the controversy is otherwise justifiable, or whether, on the merits, the plaintiff has a legally protected interest that the defendant's action invaded. 392 U.S., at 99–100. The objectives of the Article III standing requirement are simple: the avoidance of any use of a "federal court as a forum [for the airing of] generalized grievances about the conduct of government," and the creation of a judicial context in which "the questions will be framed with the necessary specificity . . . the issues . . . contested with the necessary adverseness and . . . the litigation . . . pursued with the necessary vigor to assure that the . . . challenge will be made in a form traditionally thought to be capable of judicial resolution." . . .

Just two years after the *Data Processing* case, the Supreme Court in *Sierra Club v. Morton*[6] indicated that it did not intend to expand standing as far as many had thought the Court did in *Data Processing*. Instead, the Supreme Court applied the requirement of direct injury in an administrative law case. The Sierra Club complained that the United States Forest Service had violated federal rules protecting forests when it approved a Walt Disney Enterprises resort in the Mineral King Valley of California's Sierra Nevada Mountains. The Club claimed to be "adversely affected or aggrieved by agency action" under APA section 702. The Court dismissed the claim for lack of standing because "nowhere in the pleadings or affidavits did the Club state that its members use Mineral King for any purpose, much less that they use it in any way that would be significantly affected by the proposed actions of the [gov-

---

* Reviewability has often been treated as if it involved a single issue: whether agency action is conclusive and beyond judicial challenge by anyone. In reality, however, reviewability is equally concerned with a second issue: whether the *particular* plaintiff then requesting review may have it. See the Administrative Procedure Act, 5 U.S.C. §§ 701 (a) and 702 (1964 ed., Supp. IV). Both questions directly concern the extent to which persons harmed by agency action may challenge its legality.

6. 405 U.S. 727 (1972) 5-2. See Justice Douglas's and Justice Blackmun's dissenting opinions.

ernment].[7] Section 702, said the Court, requires "that the party seeking review be himself among the injured."[8]

This result might seem a setback to the ability of citizen's groups to protest governmental action, but in practice it has not been. The Sierra Club amended its suit to allege that its members used the valley and would be affected by changing it. The Disney project died.

United States v. Students Challenging Regulatory Agency Procedures

412 U.S. 669 (1973) 8-0
+ Brennan, Stewart, Blackmun
+/– Douglas, White, Marshall, Burger, Rehnquist
NP Powell

[SCRAP, a public interest group composed of five law school students with the avowed mission of improving the environment, brought suit for injunctive relief to stop the Interstate Commerce Commission from allowing increased freight charges on the nation's railroads. SCRAP claimed it had standing because the higher rates would cause its members to pay more for goods carried by the railroads and thus lead to greater use of throwaway products in place of the more expensive durable goods typically carried by railroads. This would create more litter in national parks, resulting in SCRAP members paying more taxes for cleanup. Also, they claimed, production of throwaway items would tax natural resources and harm recreational areas SCRAP members used during their outdoor pursuits. The trial court agreed with the students and enjoined the ICC from permitting the railroads to raise their rates.]

Justice Stewart delivered the opinion of the Court

The appellants challenge the appellees' standing to sue, arguing that the allegations in the pleadings as to standing were vague, unsubstantiated and insufficient under our recent decision in *Sierra Club v. Morton.* . . . The appellees

7. Ibid., at 735.
8. Ibid.

respond that unlike the petitioner in *Sierra Club*, their pleadings sufficiently alleged that they were "adversely affected" or "aggrieved" within the meaning of [Sec. 702] of the Administrative Procedure Act . . . and they point specifically to the allegations that their members used the forests, streams, mountains, and other resources in the Washington metropolitan area for camping, hiking, fishing, and sightseeing, and that this use was disturbed by the adverse environmental impact caused by the nonuse of recyclable goods brought about by a rate increase on those commodities. . . .

The petitioner in *Sierra Club*, "a large and long-established organization, with a historic commitment to the cause of protecting our Nation's natural heritage from man's depredations" . . . sought a declaratory judgment and an injunction to restrain federal officials from approving the creation of an extensive ski-resort development in the scenic Mineral King Valley of the Sequoia National Forest. The Sierra Club claimed standing to maintain its "public interest" lawsuit because it had " 'a special interest in the conservation and [the] sound maintenance of the national parks, game refuges and forests of the country . . . ' " We hold those allegations insufficient.

Relying upon our prior decisions . . . we held that [Sec. 702] of the APA . . . "injury in fact" . . . made it clear that standing was not confined to those who could show "economic harm," although both *Data Processing* and *Barlow* had involved that kind of injury. Nor, we said, could the fact that many persons shared the same injury be sufficient reason to disqualify from seeking review of an agency's action any person who had in fact suffered injury. . . .

In *Sierra Club*, though, we went on to stress the importance of demonstrating that the party seeking review be himself among the injured, for it is this requirement that gives a litigant a direct stake in the controversy and prevents the judicial process from becoming no more than a vehicle for the vindication of the value interests of concerned bystanders. No such specific injury was alleged in *Sierra Club*. In that case the asserted harm "will be felt directly only by those who use Mineral King and Sequoia National Park, and for whom the aesthetic and recreational values of the area will be lessened by the highway and ski resort," . . . yet "[t]he Sierra Club failed to allege that it or its members would be affected in any of their activities or pastimes by the . . . development" . . . Here, by contrast, the appellees claimed that the specific and allegedly illegal action of the Commission would directly harm them in their use of the natural resources of the Washington Metropolitan Area.

Unlike the specific and geographically limited federal action of which the petitioner complained in *Sierra Club*, the challenged agency action in this case is applicable to substantially all of the Nation's railroads, and thus allegedly has an adverse environmental impact on all the natural resources of the country. Rather than a limited group of persons who used a picturesque valley in California, all persons who utilize the scenic resources of the country, and indeed all who breathe its air, could claim harm similar to that alleged by the environmental groups here. But we have already made it clear that standing is not to be denied simply because many people suffer the same injury. Indeed some of the cases on which we relied in *Sierra Club* demonstrated the patent fact that persons across the Nation could be adversely affected by major governmental actions. . . . To deny standing to persons who are in fact injured simply because many others are also injured, would mean that the most injurious and widespread Government actions could be questioned by nobody. We cannot accept that conclusion.

But the injury alleged here is also very different from that at issue in *Sierra Club* because here the alleged injury to the environment is far less direct and perceptible. The petitioner there complained about the construction of a specific project that would directly affect the Mineral King Valley. Here, the Court was asked to follow a far more attenuated line of causation to the eventual injury of which the appellees complained—a general rate increase would allegedly cause increased use of nonrecyclable commodities as compared to recyclable goods, thus resulting in the need to use more natural resources to produce such goods, some of which resources might be taken from the Washington area, and resulting in more refuse that might be discarded in national parks in the Washington area. The railroads protest that the appellees could never prove that a general increase in rates would have this effect, and they contend that these allegations were a ploy to avoid the need to show some injury in fact.

Of course, pleadings must be something more than an ingenious academic exercise in the conceivable. A plaintiff must allege that he has been or will in fact be perceptibly harmed by the challenged agency action, not that he can imagine circumstances in which he could be affected by the agency's action. And it is equally clear that the allegations must be true and capable of proof at trial. But we deal here simply with the pleadings in which the appellees alleged a specific and perceptible harm that distinguished them from other citizens who had used the natural resources that were claimed to be affected. If, as the railroads now assert, these allegations were in fact untrue, then the appellants should have moved for summary judgment on the standing issue and demonstrated to the District Court that the allegations were sham and raised no genuine issue of fact. We cannot say on these pleadings that the appellees could not prove their allegations which, if proved, would place them squarely among those persons injured in fact by the Commission's action, and entitled under the clear import of *Sierra Club* to seek review. The District Court was correct in denying the appellants' motion to dismiss the complaint for failure to allege sufficient standing to bring this lawsuit. . . .

[Reversed on other grounds.]

Note the *SCRAP* opinion's assertion that standing depends on what might arguably be true. The law of standing does not require plaintiffs to prove their case in order to gain the right to prove their case. It merely gives plaintiffs a chance to prove their case, which in the end *SCRAP* did not. To gain standing, plaintiffs must show a second element in addition to direct legal injury. The injury must also be substantial. Since the harm to any single individual is not very substantial if the cost of shipping empty beer cans increases a few cents a ton, *SCRAP* establishes a precedent that expands standing for interest groups.

By the end of the 1970s, standing in administrative law seemed "well settled" in two separate senses. First, standing law seemed fairly clear. Anyone who could show direct injury (or relief from a threat of injury if their suit succeeded), and whose injury fell within the zone of interests protected by the law, had standing. In 1978 the Court granted standing to a citizens' group to challenge a $560-million limit on the damages that nuclear power companies would have to pay in the case of a nuclear accident.

The decision did not seem surprising.[9] Note that the Court had no difficulty finding the case ripe.

But since about 1980, with the rise of the "Reagan Court," standing law has undergone tumultuous shifts. We describe here three controversial cases that denied standing, and then conclude by reprinting a case that seems to tip back in favor of broader understandings both of what counts as an "injury in fact" and what falls in the zone of protected interests.

• *Standing to Challenge Racial Segregation.* In 1983 the Supreme Court upheld a decision of the Internal Revenue Service (IRS) to revoke the tax-exempt status of private schools that practiced racial segregation. A group of African-American parents sued the IRS claiming it was not systematically enforcing its own rule. The parents argued that white students who might help integrate public schools were instead being attracted to segregated, tax-exempt, private schools. The Court, 5-3, denied the parents' standing. The causal chain, said Justice Sandra Day O'Connor, was too weak.[10]

• *Standing to Protect the Environment.* The Endangered Species Act of 1973 (ESA) authorizes the Secretary of the Interior to compile and update a list of endangered species. The act then orders that each federal agency ensure that "any action authorized, funded, or carried out by that agency . . . is not likely to jeopardize the continued existence of any endangered species or any threatened species or result in the destruction or adverse modification of the habitat of such species." The Secretary issued a regulation limiting the coverage of the ESA to species endangered in the territorial United States and on the high seas. In 1992 the Court denied standing to the Defenders of Wildlife, a pro-environment lobby group that was prepared to show how activities of some agencies threaten species abroad and that the loss of a species anywhere could impact Americans. It ruled that the Defenders' claim was not in the proper zone of interests.[11]

• *Standing to Protect Jobs.* In 1993 the U.S. Postal Service used an informal rulemaking procedure to interpret recent legislation from Congress (the "Private Express Statutes") to permit using private mail companies to deliver letters destined for foreign countries to the foreign post offices. The postal workers sued. The Court admitted that they had, in losing jobs to the private companies, suffered a direct injury, but the Court insisted that jobs were not in the zone of interests protected by the Private Express Statutes.[12]

These cases, and cases like them, have raised eyebrows. After all, the primary purpose of these "technical" rules is to make sure that judges hearing cases have a fully informed and genuinely adversarial case in front of them. But it is hard to imagine that any of the plaintiffs denied standing in the cases above were halfhearted or unprepared to go to the mat on the merits of their arguments. The legal claims of each plaintiff seemed fully ripe. The case about environmental protection, *Lujan v. Defenders of Wildlife*, 504 U.S. 555 (1992) showed how standing questions may easily create deep divisions in the Supreme Court, especially in politically contested cases. Even though the case was decided against the Defenders of Wildlife, the Court in this particular case could not produce a solid majority opinion in all counts. Justice Antonin Scalia's majority opinion in this case summarized the basics of standing doctrine. Accordingly, Scalia wrote that any standing inquiry necessitates a showing that:

a) there is an injury in fact that is both concrete and particularized and actual or imminent rather than hypothetical;

b) the injury is fairly traceable to the acts of the defendant;

c) the injury will be redressed by a favorable decision to the plaintiff.[13]

In terms of redressability, the Court could not produce a majority opinion. A plurality decided that question.

9. *Duke Power Co. v. Carolina Environmental Study Group*, 438 U.S. 59 (1978).

10. *Allen v. Wright*, 468 U.S. 737 (1984).

11. *Lujan v. Defenders of Wildlife*, 504 U.S. 555 (1992).

12. *Air Courier Conference v. American Postal Workers Union*, 498 U.S. 517 (1991).

13. These points are also discussed in Chief Justice Roberts's dissenting opinion in *Massachusetts v. EPA*, which is excerpted in the previous chapter. We encourage you to go back to that case and read it again, this time focusing on the question of standing, since it is a very important case on the issue of standing.

Justice Stevens, even though he concurred with the Court about reversing, did not join the conclusion that the plaintiffs lacked standing. Justice Blackmun wrote a dissenting opinion, joined by Justice O'Connor. Justice Kennedy wrote a concurring opinion, which nevertheless weakened the majority's arguments about standing.

After this fractured decision, the Court appeared to be more united on the question of standing in *Bennett v. Spear*, 520 U.S. 154 (1997). This case revisited the standing question with regard to the Endangered Species Act. The question presented was whether under the Act, private parties who claim they have suffered economically from the enforcement of the Act have standing to sue to reverse regulation carried out under the authority of the Act. In a unanimous decision announced by Justice Scalia, the Court said yes. The court claimed that the Act required the secretary, in reaching his decision to categorize a certain site as critical habitat, needed to use the best scientific and commercial data and consider economic impact. This, according to the Court, was a sign that the Congress wanted to prevent "overenforcement." Because the secretary failed to consider economic impact and overenforced the statute, the Court concluded that the petitioners, in this case two irrigation districts in Oregon, had standing to bring a suit.

After *Lujan*, *Bennett* seemed to have broadened standing, but on closer inspection there is a significant issue: it is commercial interests, not environmental interests, that received standing in *Bennett*. Furthermore, even though the case arose out of Endangered Species Act, a very straightforward legislative directive to protect wildlife, the Court in this case sided with those who would like to see the Act *not applied*. After *Bennett*, wrote William Buzbee, "the zone of interests discussion . . . still leaves courts and litigants room to engage in outcome oriented manipulation of standing criteria." Maybe even worse, by recognizing the right of the "regulated interests" in *Bennett*, the Court tilted the language of "zone of interest" theories towards favoring not the beneficiaries of regulation, but those who are regulated by it.[14] Thus, it was not

surprising to see four justices dissenting vigorously in *Massachusetts v. EPA*, because the majority's argument recognizes standing rights for those who see benefits in regulation, such as the Commonwealth of Massachusetts.

Notably, the Court was again badly split when environmental interests were at stake in *Massachusetts v. EPA*, which you read in the previous chapter. This case was as much about standing as it was about regulatory enforcement. Despite the unanimous Court which granted standing to commercial interests in *Spear*, a four justice minority declined to recognize standing rights for environmental interests in *Massachusetts v. EPA*.

Finally, yet another case, *Hein v. Freedom from Religion Foundation*, 127 S.Ct. 166 (2007), shows that when politically charged questions are presented to the Court, the Court is deeply divided. In this case, the Court decided that citizens as taxpayers have no standing to challenge the constitutionality of expenditures by the executive branch. The case was brought by the Freedom from Religion Foundation and its individual members who argued that as federal taxpayers they could challenge President Bush's faith-based and community initiatives. They argued that such initiatives violate the First Amendment by singling out specific organizations as worthy of federal funding because of their religious orientations. The plurality opinion, written by Justice Alito and joined by Chief Justice Roberts, argued that *Flast*, relied on by the petitioners, was a very narrow exception and does not cover discretionary spending by the Executive Branch. So in effect the opinion made it very hard to claim standing based on taxpayer status. Justice Scalia, a senior judge from the Reagan court, on the other hand, argued in his concurring opinion for an overturning of *Flast*, which would make sure that taxpayer status cannot be used as a mechanism to obtain standing.

3. Mootness

A case becomes moot when the harm affecting the plaintiff somehow ceases during the course of litigation. For example, when Marco DeFunis challenged the decision of the University of Washington's law school to deny his admission even though the school admitted nonwhite students with lower numerical scores than DeFunis's, the lower court ordered DeFunis admitted to the school. By the time this reverse discrimination issue reached the United States Supreme Court, DeFunis was close to completing his final year. The law school conceded that, regardless of the Court's decision, it would grant DeFunis a degree when he completed the requirements for it. The Court found the case moot as a result.[15]

4. Exhaustion of Administrative Remedies

The ripeness doctrine and the law requiring that plaintiffs exhaust their chances for administrative remedies are sometimes virtually indistinguishable. A difference does exist, however. A case that is unripe is somehow incomplete. Further facts need to be developed or rules interpreted, and thus the Court does not have the final problem necessarily before it. Exhaustion is narrower. A decision is final. A potential or actual harm has taken clear shape. Yet the agency itself may provide relief from the harm the plaintiff fears.[16] Exhaustion is thus primarily a gatekeeping rule, one designed to avoid work for courts unless and until it becomes unavoidable.

There are, of course, some exceptions to the exhaustion doctrine. (By now you have no doubt concluded that law is never simple!) For example, an agency may provide an opportunity to appeal its decision, yet have no authority to award monetary damages. Plaintiffs who seek monetary damages in such circumstances may go directly to the courts. Also, when no statute or agency rule *requires* a claimant to exhaust appellate remedies, the Supreme Court held in 1993 that the decision of the Administrative Law Judge becomes a final agency action (APA sec. 704) and may be taken directly to the courts.[17]

5. Primary Jurisdiction

In a complex governmental bureaucracy that, like ours, has grown piecemeal, the authorities and jurisdictions of agencies overlap each other and in some cases overlap the work of the courts themselves. *Primary jurisdiction* is a traffic-light doctrine designed to steer cases in one direction. Thus if someone sued a power company alleging that the electromagnetic fields created by the company's power lines damaged them, but if the state's public utilities regulatory agency had jurisdiction to regulate and decide such matters, the court would tell the plaintiff to take the case to the public utilities agency and dismiss the suit.

However, the jurisdiction of the agency must be clear and unquestioned. In 1975 the Sunflower Electric Cooperative charged the Kansas Power and Light Company, along with several other utilities, in federal district court with conspiring to monopolize the exchange of power in violation of the Sherman Antitrust Act. The defendants asked the court, under the primary jurisdiction doctrine, to refuse to hear the case because the Federal Power Commission (FPC) had authority over rate-setting for electricity. The trial court agreed to do so because the FPC possessed special competence in the matter. The appellate court reversed. The FPC, it held, had no authority to address antitrust matters directly and had no particular experience with such matters. Besides, the FPC had no direct authority to regulate the practice of energy exchange that the plaintiffs accused the defendants of illegally monopolizing. Since courts traditionally hear antitrust cases and because an inconsistency between a judicial and an agency ruling might, but probably would not, occur, the appellate court ordered the trial court to hear the antitrust case.[18]

The rules of judicial reviewability discussed in this section may seem technical or legalistic, but they affect the openness and rationality of the bureaucratic system just as powerfully as do the principles of rulemaking and adjudication themselves. Indeed the rules of ripeness, standing, etc., at bottom form another instance of judicial bal-

15. *DeFunis v. Odegaard*, 416 U.S. 312 (1974). See *Roe v. Wade*, 410 U.S. 113 (1973), for different results regarding the mooting effect of the termination of a pregnancy on a lawsuit challenging a statute imposing criminal penalties for performing an abortion.

16. See also *Bowen v. City of New York*, 476 U.S. 467 (1986), where the Supreme Court unanimously held that the rules of exhaustion do not apply to claimants under the Social Security Administration's disability provisions if plaintiff alleges an irregularity in the agency's proceedings.

17. *Darby v. Cisneros*, 509 U.S. 137 (1993). The late Bernard Schwartz concluded that, in practice, most ALJ decisions may be taken directly to court. "Administrative Law Cases During 1996," *Administrative Law Review* 49 (1997): 519.

18. *Sunflower Electric Coop. v. Kansas Power and Light Co., et al.*, 603 F.2d 791 (1979).

ancing. The reviewability rules balance the degree of injury suffered, the obviousness of the potential administrative error, the lack of a chance to gain relief elsewhere than in the courts, and the importance of judicial intervention to clarify law for the future. As each of these factors increases in magnitude, judicial intervention becomes more appropriate.[19]

THE SCOPE OF JUDICIAL REVIEW

We now enter the legal thicket known as "scope of judicial review." Here we assume that all of the prerequisites for lawsuits described in the preceding section have been met. The case has gone to court, but how thoroughly and aggressively will courts review what administrative agencies have done? Of necessity we must leave mastery of all the intricacies to legal specialists. But as students of politics, and of the political environment with which public administrators must cope, there is still much to learn. This is because the scope of review cases actually debate two conflicting but very important political values.

On one hand we have the value of democratic fairness. When an agency acts so as to harm a person, we want that person to have a chance to claim that he or she was harmed unfairly—denied due process of law. We think it wrong if the system denies an aggrieved person a chance to get any court anywhere to review the case. As the Ninth Circuit put it in a deportation case, "agencies are run by people and people make mistakes. Review by a tribunal outside the agency helps correct these rare but tragic errors. . . . In the absence of judicial review, grave injustices could take place. . . . [Judicial review] may mean the difference between life and death; the effort is surely worth the candle."[20]

But a variety of other values push against the basic value of fairness. One is efficiency. Agencies vastly outnumber courts. Courts cannot possibly review every administrative decision. Another is respect for the competence that specialists in a field develop, a competence that judges cannot equal. And a third is the basic premise

of democracy itself: legislatures, not courts, make law and public policy. If the plain language of federal and state administrative procedure acts, or the specific language of the statutes creating and authorizing specific agencies, prohibits or drastically restricts review, what should courts do? For example, the federal APA's "Chapter 7" (Appendix B) governs judicial review. Its first section, among other things, precludes judicial review of actions "committed to agency discretion by law." What does that phrase mean?

We already encountered one facet of this problem in chapter 4. There we saw how the *Chevron* case announced great judicial deference to agency interpretations of the legal rules that apply to the cases it must resolve. But *State Farm* seemed to endorse more aggressive judicial review. And so we turn to this political debate. At the outset, we see that, when a person raises a claim that an agency has violated the Constitution itself, courts are very reluctant to deny themselves the power to review.

Can Congress erase federal court jurisdiction to hear constitutional questions themselves, including those involving important civil rights? This question has become a hotly debated political issue. Cases have tried to avoid directly confronting the problem by interpreting statutes limiting jurisdiction narrowly. Thus section 211 (a) of Title 38 of the United States Code reads: "the decisions of the Administrator [of the Veterans' Administration] of any question of law or fact under any law administered by the Veterans' Administration providing benefits for veterans . . . shall be final and conclusive and no . . . court of the United States shall have the power or jurisdiction to review such decision. . . ." When the administrator denied veterans' benefits to a conscientious objector, the conscientious objector challenged the decision in court on religious freedom grounds. The Supreme Court accepted jurisdiction by treating his claim as one *under* the Constitution and not *under* section 21 l(a) at all. The plaintiff lost on the merits.[21]

As a practical matter Congress usually says nothing about reviewability of administrative decisions in authorizing legislation. The statutory language that does exist

---

19. See Gary Cheedes, "Understanding Judicial Review of Federal Agency Action," *University of Richmond Law Review* 12 (1978): 469.

20. *Rodriguez-Roman v. INS*, 98 F.3d 416, 433 (1996).

21. *Johnson v. Robison*, 415 U.S. 361 (1974).

often reiterates APA language and/or *Abbott Labs*'s presumption of reviewability. Occasionally, however, Congress imposes specific time limits for the reviewability by courts of administrative rules. For example, the Clean Air Act Amendments of 1977 allow only sixty days from the time it becomes official to contest a rule. But what if a rule's defects and the hardship it imposes only become clear when, perhaps much later, the rule is applied and enforced? Several courts have refused to honor the statutory time limit in such instances.[22]

Reviewing Agency Action Committed to Agency Discretion

The debate over the scope of review often revolves around the meaning of Chapter 7 of the APA, which we recommend that you read before going further. This section reviews cases on both sides of the debate. To illustrate the issues involved, consider *Webster v. Doe*. This case permitted the firing of a CIA employee without judicial review. Here are the specifics.

Section 102(c) of the National Security Act of 1947 (NSA) authorizes the Director of the Central Intelligence Agency (CIA) "to terminate the employment of any CIA employee "whenever he shall deem such termination necessary or advisable in the interests of the United States." After respondent, a covert electronics technician in the CIA's employ, voluntarily informed the agency that he was a homosexual, the Director discharged him. Respondent Doe sued, alleging violations of the Administrative Procedure Act (APA), of his rights to property, liberty, and privacy under the First, Fourth, Fifth, and Ninth Amendments, and of his rights to procedural due process and equal protection of the laws under the Fifth Amendment. The District Court and Court of Appeals agreed that judicial review under the APA of petitioner's termination decisions was not precluded by the provision of the APA, 5 U.S.C. § 701(a), which renders that Act inapplicable whenever "(1) statutes preclude judicial review; or (2) agency action is committed to agency discretion by law." For the majority, Chief Justice

Rehnquist held that the APA did not permit judicial review because the statute gave the Director such complete discretion that the law simply did not contain any rule, including constitutional protections, that could serve as a test of whether the Directors acted properly.[23]

The CIA results do not sit comfortably with the philosophy that administrative law should minimize arbitrariness. Can the CIA Director fire someone for not donating a thousand dollars to the Director's favorite slush fund? But now let us turn to the older and classic case, *Overton Park*. This case interpreted provisions of APA Chapter 7 to push for some degree of judicial oversight in a case that, on the surface, looked like a typically discretionary—and very political!—decision.

Citizens to Preserve Overton Park v. Volpe

401 U.S. 402 (1971) 8-0

+ *Burger, Black, Harlan, Brennan, Stewart, White, Marshall, Blackmun*

NP Douglas

[The Department of Transportation (DOT) planned to construct a section of Interstate 40 through Overton Park in Memphis and had acquired both the right-of-way and the approval of local officials. When constructed, the interstate would effectively sever one part of the park from the other. The secretary of the DOT was authorized by statute to approve the routing of interstates through public parks only if no "feasible and prudent" alternate route existed. Further, if no "feasible and prudent" alternative could be found, the secretary was directed by statute to approve construction only if there had been every effort to plan for a minimum of harm to the park. When the secretary did approve the construction without any factual findings about possible alternatives and that harm to the park had been minimized, the citizens group brought suit. The district court entered summary judgment for the secretary and was affirmed by the appellate court.]

---

22. See Frederick Davis, "Judicial Review of Rulemaking: New Patterns and New Problems," *Duke Law Journal* (1981): 279.

23. *Webster v. Doe*, 486 U.S. 592 (1988).

Opinion of the Court by Justice Marshall, announced by Justice Stewart

The growing public concern about the quality of our natural environment has prompted Congress in recent years to enact legislation designed to curb the accelerating destruction of our country's natural beauty. We are concerned in this case with § 4 (0 of the Department of Transportation Act of 1966, as amended, and § 18 (a) of the Federal-Aid Highway Act of 1968, . . . 23 U.S.C. § 138 . . . (hereafter § 138). These statutes prohibit the Secretary of Transportation from authorizing the use of federal funds to finance the construction of highways through public parks if a "feasible and prudent" alternative route exists. If no such route is available, the statutes allow him to approve construction through parks only if there has been "all possible planning to minimize harm" to the park. . . ."

Petitioners contend that the Secretary's action is invalid without such formal findings and that the Secretary did not make an independent determination but merely relied on the judgment of the Memphis City Council. They also contend that it would be "feasible and prudent" to route I–40 around Overton Park either to the north or to the south. And they argue that if these alternative routes are not "feasible and prudent, " the present plan does not include "all possible" methods for reducing harm to the park. Petitioners claim that I–40 could be built under the park by using either of two possible tunneling methods,* and they claim that, at a minimum, by using advanced drainage techniques the expressway could be depressed below ground level along the entire route through the park including the section that crosses the small creek.

Respondents argue that it was unnecessary for the Secretary to make formal findings, and that he did, in fact, exercise his own independent judgment which was supported by the facts. In the District Court, respondents introduced affidavits, prepared specifically for this litigation, which indicated that the Secretary had made the decision and that the decision was supportable. These affidavits were contradicted by affidavits introduced by petitioners, who

---

* Petitioners argue that either a bored tunnel or a cut-and-cover tunnel, which is a fully depressed route covered after construction, could be built. Respondents contend that the construction of a tunnel by either method would greatly increase the cost of the project, would create safety hazards, and because of increases in pollution would not reduce harm to the park.

also sought to take the deposition of a former Federal Highway Administrator who had participated in the decision to route I–40 through Overton Park.

The District Court and the Court of Appeals found that formal findings by the Secretary were not necessary and refused to order the deposition of the former Federal Highway Administrator because those courts believed that probing of the mental processes of an administrative decisionmaker was prohibited. And, believing that the Secretary's authority was wide and reviewing courts' authority narrow in the approval of highway routes, the lower courts held that the affidavits contained no basis for a determination that the Secretary had exceeded his authority.

We agree that formal findings were not required. But we do not believe that in this case judicial review based solely on litigation affidavits was adequate.

A threshold question—whether petitioners are entitled to any judicial review—is easily answered. Section 701 of the Administrative Procedure Act, 5 U.S.C. § 701 . . . , provides that the action of "each authority of the Government of the United States," which includes the Department of Transportation, is subject to judicial review except where there is a statutory prohibition on review or where "agency action is committed to agency discretion by law." In this case, there is no indication that Congress sought to prohibit judicial review and there is most certainly no "showing of 'clear and convincing evidence' of a . . . legislative intent" to restrict access to judicial review. *Abbott Laboratories v. Gardner*, 387 U.S. 136, 141 (1967). . . .

Similarly, the Secretary's decision here does not fall within the exception for action "committed to agency discretion." This is a very narrow exception. Berger, "Administrative Arbitrariness and Judicial Review, " 65 *Col. L. Rev.* 55 (1965). The legislative history of the Administrative Procedure Act indicates that it is applicable in those rare instances where "statutes are drawn in such broad terms that in a given case there is no law to apply." . . .

Section 4 (f) of the Department of Transportation Act and § 138 of the Federal-Aid Highway Act are clear and specific directives. Both the Department of Transportation Act and the Federal-Aid Highway Act provided that the Secretary "shall not approve any program or project" that requires the use of any public parkland "unless (1) there is no feasible and prudent alternative to the use of such land,

and (2) such program includes all possible planning to minimize harm to such park. . . ." This language is a plain and explicit bar to the use of federal funds for construction of highways through parks—only the most unusual situations are exempted.

Despite the clarity of the statutory language, respondents argue that the Secretary has wide discretion. They recognize that the requirement that there be no "feasible" alternative route admits of little administrative discretion. For this exemption to apply the Secretary must find that as a matter of sound engineering it would not be feasible to build the highway along any other route. Respondents argue, however, that the requirement that there be no other "prudent" route requires the Secretary to engage in a wide-ranging balancing of competing interests. They contend that the Secretary should weigh the detriment resulting from the destruction of parkland against the cost of other routes, safety considerations, and other factors, and determine on the basis of the importance that he attaches to these other factors whether, on balance, alternative feasible routes would be "prudent."

But no such wide-ranging endeavor was intended. It is obvious that in most cases considerations of cost, directness of route, and community disruption will indicate that parkland should be used for highway construction whenever possible. Although it may be necessary to transfer funds from one jurisdiction to another, there will always be a smaller outlay required from the public purse when parkland is used since the public already owns the land and there will be no need to pay for right-of-way. And since people do not live or work in parks, if a highway is built on parkland no one will have to leave his home or give up his business. Such factors are common to substantially all highway construction. Thus, if Congress intended these factors to be on an equal footing with preservation of parkland there would have been no need for the statutes.

Congress clearly did not intend that cost and disruption of the community were to be ignored by the Secretary. But the very existence of the statutes indicates that protection of parkland was to be given paramount importance. The few green havens that are public parks were not to be lost unless there were truly unusual factors present in a particular case or the cost or community disruption resulting from alternative routes reached extraordinary magnitudes. If the

statutes are to have any meaning, the Secretary cannot approve the destruction of parkland unless he finds that alternative routes present unique problems.

Plainly, there is "law to apply" and thus the exemption for action "committed to agency discretion" is inapplicable. But the existence of judicial review is only the start: the standard for review must also be determined. For that we must look to § 706 of the Administrative Procedure Act, 5 U.S.C. § 706 . . . which provides that a "reviewing court shall . . . hold unlawful and set aside agency action, findings, and conclusions found" not to meet six separate standards. In all cases agency action must be set aside if the action was arbitrary, capricious, an abuse of discretion, or otherwise not in accordance with law" or if the action failed to meet statutory, procedural, or constitutional requirements. 5 U.S.C. §§ 706 (2)(A), (B), (C), (D). . . .

In certain narrow, specifically limited situations, the agency action is to be set aside if the action was not supported by "substantial evidence." And in other equally narrow circumstances the reviewing court is to engage in a *de novo* review of the action and set it aside if it was "unwarranted by the facts." 5 U.S.C. §§ 706 (2) (E), (F). . . .

Petitioners argue that the Secretary's approval of the construction of I-40 through Overton Park is subject to one or the other of these latter two standards of limited applicability. First, they contend that the "substantial evidence" standard of § 706 (2) (E) must be applied. In the alternative, they claim that § 706 (2) (F) applies and that there must be a *de novo* review to determine if the Secretary's action was "unwarranted by the facts." Neither of these standards is, however, applicable.

Review under the substantial-evidence test is authorized only when the agency action is taken pursuant to a rule-making provision of the Administrative Procedure Act itself, 5 U.S.C. § 553 . . . , or when the agency action is based on a public adjudicatory hearing. See 5 U.S.C. §§ 556, 557. . . . The Secretary's decision to allow the expenditure of federal funds to build I-40 through Overton Park was plainly not an exercise of a rulemaking function. See 1 K. Davis, Administrative Law Treatise § 5.01 (1958). And the only hearing that is required by either the Administrative Procedure Act or the statutes regulating the distribution of federal funds for highway construction is a public hearing conducted by local officials for the purpose of informing the community about the proposed project and eliciting community views on the design and route. 23 U.S.C. § 128. . . . The hearing is nonadjudicatory, quasi-legislative in nature. It is not designed to produce a record that is to be the basis of agency action—the basic requirement for substantial-evidence review. . . .

Petitioners' alternative argument also fails. *De novo* review of whether the Secretary's decision was "unwarranted by the facts" is authorized by § 706 (2)(F) in only two circumstances. First, such *de novo* review is authorized when the action is adjudicatory in nature and the agency fact-finding procedures are inadequate. And, there may be independent judicial fact-finding when issues that were not before the agency are raised in a proceeding to enforce nonadjudicatory agency action. . . . Neither situation exists here.

Even though there is no *de novo* review in this case and the Secretary's approval of the route of I-40 does not have ultimately to meet the substantial-evidence test, the generally applicable standards of § 706 require the reviewing court to engage in a substantial inquiry. Certainly, the Secretary's decision is entitled to a presumption of regularity. . . . But that presumption is not to shield his action from a thorough, probing, in-depth review.

The court is first required to decide whether the Secretary acted within the scope of his authority. . . . This determination naturally begins with a delineation of the scope of the Secretary's authority and discretion. L. Jaffe, Judicial Control of Administration Action 359 (1965). As has been shown, Congress has specified only a small range of choices that the Secretary can make. Also involved in this initial inquiry is a determination of whether on the facts the Secretary's decision can reasonably be said to be within that range. The reviewing court must consider whether the Secretary properly construed his authority to approve the use of parkland as limited to situations where there are no feasible alternative routes or where feasible alternative routes involve uniquely difficult problems. And the reviewing court must be able to find that the Secretary could have reasonably believed that in this case there are no feasible alternatives or that alternatives do involve unique problems.

Scrutiny of the facts does not end, however, with the determination that the Secretary has acted within the scope of his statutory authority. Section 706 (2)(A) requires a finding that the actual choice made was not "arbitrary," capricious, an abuse of discretion, or otherwise not in accordance with law." . . . To make this finding the court must consider whether the decision was based on a consideration of the relevant factors and whether there has been a clear error of judgment. Although this inquiry into the facts is to be searching and careful, the ultimate standard of review is a narrow one. The court is not empowered to substitute its judgment for that of the agency.

The final inquiry is whether the Secretary's action followed the necessary procedural requirements. Here the only procedural error alleged is the failure of the Secretary to make formal findings and state his reason for allowing the highway to be built through the park.

Undoubtedly, review of the Secretary's action is hampered by his failure to make such findings, but the absence of formal findings does not necessarily require that the case be remanded to the Secretary. Neither the Department of Transportation Act nor the Federal-Aid Highway Act requires such formal findings. Moreover, the Administrative Procedure Act requirements that there be formal findings in certain rulemaking and adjudicatory proceedings do not apply to the Secretary's action here. See 5 U.S.C. §§ 553 (a)(2), 554 (a) . . . [T]here is an administrative record that allows the full, prompt review of the Secretary's action that is sought without additional delay which would result from having a remand to the Secretary.

That administrative record is not, however, before us. The lower courts based their review on the litigation affidavits that were presented. These affidavits were merely "*post hoc* rationalizations," which have traditionally been found to be an inadequate basis for review. And they clearly do no constitute the "whole record" compiled by the agency: the basis for review required by § 706 of the Administrative Procedure Act. . . .

Thus it is necessary to remand this case to the District Court for plenary review of the Secretary's decision. That review is to be based on the full administrative record that was before the Secretary at the time he made his decision. But since the bare record may not disclose the factors that were considered or the Secretary's construction of the evidence it may be necessary for the District Court to require some explanation in order to determine if the Secretary acted within the scope of his authority and if the Secretary's action was justifiable under the applicable standard.

The court may require the administrative officials who participated in the decision to give testimony explaining their action. Of course, such inquiry into the mental processes of administrative decision-makers is usually to be avoided. *United States v. Morgan*, 313 U.S. 409, 422 (1941). And where there are administrative findings that were made at the same time as the decision, as was the case in *Morgan*, there must be a strong showing of bad faith or improper behavior before such inquiry may be made. But here there are no such formal findings and it may be that the only way there can be effective judicial review is by examining the decisionmakers themselves. See *Shaughnessy v. Accardi*, 349 U.S. 280 (1955).

The District Court is not, however, required to make such an inquiry. It may be that the Secretary can prepare formal findings including the information required by DOT Order 5610.1 that will provide an adequate explanation for his action. Such an explanation will, to some extent, be a "*post hoc* rationalization" and thus must be viewed critically. If the District Court decides that additional explanation is necessary, that court should consider which method will prove the most expeditious so that full review may be had as soon as possible.

Reversed and remanded.

Overton Park's insistence that the agency produce a record sufficient for the courts to review had a powerful practical result. Faced with the need to justify destroying the park to build this stretch of highway, Secretary Volpe could not, and that section of the Interstate was never built. The majority's move pursues the same philosophy that Judge Bazelon did in the first *Vermont Yankee* case. However, since *Chevron*, the balance has tipped more toward unreviewability. The next case, decided just a year later, holds agency inaction unreviewable. In announcing that the "presumption of unreviewability" applies to agency *inaction*, the Court moved further away from the jurisprudence of the hard-look standard. In an era of conservative deregulation, federal agencies appear less enthusiastic about carrying out the policy missions of regulatory statutes born in the liberal political environment of the 1960s and 1970s. These same political conditions have led to the growth of citizen suits seeking judicial intervention and review of agencies' refusals to act.[24]

Heckler v. Chaney

470 U.S. 821 (1985) 9–0
+ *Burger, Brennan, White, Marshall, Blackmun, Powell, Rehnquist, Stevens, O'Connor*

[Prison inmates convicted of capital offenses and sentenced to death by lethal injection petitioned the Food and Drug Administration (FDA), alleging that the use of drugs for these purposes violated the Federal Food, Drug, and Cosmetic Act (FDCA). They requested the FDA to enforce the act so as to prevent the use of drugs for lethal injection. The FDA refused the request, and the inmates sued in federal district court. The lower court held that "nothing in the FDCA indicated an intent to circumscribe the FDA's enforcement discretion or to make it reviewable." The United States Court of Appeals for the D.C. Circuit reversed, holding that the FDA's refusal to take enforcement action was reviewable and that their decision was an abuse of discretion. Secretary of Health and Human Services Margaret Heckler appealed this ruling to the Supreme Court.]

Justice Rehnquist delivered the opinion of the Court

I

Respondents have been sentenced to death by lethal injection under the laws of the States of Oklahoma and Texas. Those States, and several others, have recently adopted this method for carrying out the capital sentence. Respondents first petitioned the FDA, claiming that the drugs used by the states for this purpose, although approved by the FDA for the medical purposes stated on their labels, were not approved for use in human executions. They alleged that the drugs had not been tested for the purpose for which they were to be used, and that, given

24. See Barry Boyer and Errol Meidinger, "Privatizing Regulatory Enforcement: A Preliminary Assessment of Citizen Suits Under Federal Environmental Law," *Buffalo Law Review* 34 (1985): 833.

that the drugs would likely be administered by untrained personnel, it was also likely that the drugs would not induce the quick and painless death intended. They urged that use of these drugs for human execution was the "unapproved use of an approved drug" and constituted a violation of the Act's prohibitions against "misbranding."* . . . [T]hey requested the FDA to affix warnings to the labels of all the drugs stating that they were unapproved and unsafe for human execution, to send statements to the drug manufacturers and prison administrators stating that the drugs should not be so used, and to adopt procedures for seizing the drugs from state prisons and to recommend the prosecution of all those in the chain of distribution who knowingly distribute or purchase the drugs with intent to use them for human execution.

The FDA Commissioner responded, refusing to take the requested actions. The Commissioner . . . [concluded] that FDA jurisdiction in the area was generally unclear but in any event should not be exercised to interfere with this particular aspect of state criminal justice systems. . . .

II

The Court of Appeals' decision addressed three questions: (1) whether the FDA had jurisdiction to undertake the enforcement actions requested, (2) whether if it did have jurisdiction its refusal to take those actions was subject to judicial review, and (3) whether if reviewable its refusal was arbitrary, capricious, or an abuse of discretion. In reaching our conclusion that the Court of Appeals was wrong, however, we need not and do not address the thorny question of the FDA's jurisdiction. For us, this case turns on the important question of the extent to which determinations by the FDA *not to exercise* its enforcement authority over the use of drugs in interstate commerce may be judicially reviewed. That decision in turn involves the construction of two separate but necessarily interrelated statutes, the APA and the FDCA.

The APA's comprehensive provisions for judicial review of "agency actions" are contained in 5 U.S.C. §§ 701–706. Any person "adversely affected or aggrieved" by agency action, see § 702, including a "failure to act," is entitled to "judicial review thereof," as long as the action is a "final agency action for which there is no other adequate remedy

* See 21 U.S.C. § 352(f): "A drug or device shall be deemed to be misbranded . . . [u]nless its labeling bears (1) adequate directions for use. . . ."

in a court," see §§ 704. The standards to be applied on review are governed by the provisions of § 706. But before any review at all may be had, a party must first clear the hurdle of § 701 (a). That section provides that the chapter on judicial review "applies, according to the provisions thereof, except to the extent that—(1) statutes preclude judicial review; or (2) agency action is committed to agency discretion by law." Petitioner urges that the decision of the FDA to refuse enforcement is an action "committed to agency discretion by law" under § 701(a)(2).

This Court has not had occasion to interpret this second exception in § 701(a) in any great detail. On its face, the section does not obviously lend itself to any particular construction; indeed, one might wonder what difference exists between § (a)(1) and § (a)(2). The former section seems easy in application; it requires construction of the substantive statute involved to determine whether Congress intended to preclude judicial review of certain decisions. That is the approach taken with respect to § (a)(l) in cases such as *Southern R. Co., v. Seaboard Allied Miffing Corp.*, 442 U.S. 444 (1979), and *Dunlop v. Bachowski*, 421 U.S., at 567. But one could read the language "committed to agency discretion *by law*" in § (a)(2) to require a similar inquiry. In addition, commentators have pointed out that construction of § (a)(2) is further complicated by the tension between a literal reading of § (a)(2), which exempts from judicial review those decisions committed to agency "discretion," and the primary scope of review prescribed by § 706(2)(A)—whether the agency's action was "arbitrary, capricious, or an *abuse of discretion*." How is it, they ask, that an action committed to agency discretion can be unreviewable and yet courts still can review agency actions for abuse of that discretion? See 5 K. Davis, Administrative Law § 28:6 (1984) (hereafter Davis); Berger, Administrative Arbitrariness and Judicial Review, 65 *Colum. L. Rev.* 55, 58 (1965). The APA's legislative history provides little help on this score. Mindful, however, of the common-sense principle of statutory construction that sections of a statute generally should be read "to give effect, if possible, to every clause . . . , " see *United States v. Menasche*, 348 U.S. 528, 538–539 (1955), we think there is a proper construction of § (a)(2) which satisfies each of these concerns.

This Court first discussed § (a)(2) in *Citizens to Preserve Overton Park v. Volpe*, 401 U.S. 402 (1971). . . . Interested citizens challenged the Secretary's approval under the APA, arguing that he had not satisfied the substantive statute's requirements. This Court first addressed the "threshold question" of whether the agency's action was at all reviewable. After setting out the language of § 701 (a), the Court stated:

"In this case, there is no indication that Congress sought to prohibit judicial review and there is most certainly no showing of "clear and convincing evidence" of a . . . legislative intent* to restrict access to judicial review. *Abbott Laboratories v. Gardner*, 387 U.S. 136, 141 (1967). . . .

Similarly, the Secretary's decision here does not fall within the exception for action 'committed to agency discretion.' This is a very narrow exception . . . . The legislative history of the Administrative Procedure Act indicates that it is applicable in those rare instances where 'statutes are drawn in such broad terms that in a given case there is no law to apply.' S. Rep. No. 752, 79th Cong., 1st Sess., 26 (1945)." *Overton Park, supra*, at 410.

The previous quote answers several of the questions raised by the language of § 701 (a), although it raises others. First, it clearly separates the exception provided by § (a)(l) from the § (a)(2) exception. The former applies when Congress has expressed an intent to preclude judicial review. The latter applies in different circumstances; even where Congress has not affirmatively precluded review, review is not to be had if the statute is drawn so that a court would have no meaningful standard against which to judge the agency's exercise of discretion. In such a case, the statute ("law") can be taken to have "committed" the decisionmaking to the agency's judgment absolutely. This construction avoids conflict with the "abuse of discretion" standard of review in § 706—if no judicially manageable standards are available for judging how and when an agency should exercise its discretion, then it is impossible to evaluate agency action for "abuse of discretion." In addition, this construction satisfies the principle of statutory construction mentioned earlier, by identifying a separate class of cases to which § 701 (a)(2) applies.

To this point our analysis does not differ significantly from that of the Court of Appeals. That court purported to apply the "no law to apply" standard of *Overton Park*. We disagree, however, with that court's insistence that the "narrow construction" of § (a)(2) required application of a presumption of reviewability even to an agency's decision not to undertake certain enforcement actions. Here we think the

Court of Appeals broke with tradition, case law, and sound reasoning.

Overton Park did not involve an agency's refusal to take requested enforcement action. It involved an affirmative act of approval under a statute that set clear guidelines for determining when such approval should be given. Refusals to take enforcement steps generally involve precisely the opposite situation, and in that situation we think the presumption is that judicial review is not available. This Court has recognized on several occasions over many years that an agency's decision not to prosecute or enforce, whether through civil or criminal process, is a decision generally committed to an agency's absolute discretion. . . . This recognition of the existence of discretion is attributable in no small part to the general unsuitability for judicial review of agency decisions to refuse enforcement.

The reasons for this general unsuitability are many. First, an agency decision not to enforce often involves a complicated balancing of a number of factors which are peculiarly within its expertise. Thus, the agency must not only assess whether a violation has occurred, but whether agency resources are best spent on this violation or another, whether the agency is likely to succeed if it acts, whether the particular enforcement action requested best fits the agency's overall policies, and, indeed, whether the agency has enough resources to undertake the action at all. . . . The agency is far better equipped than the courts to deal with the many variables involved in the proper ordering of its priorities. Similar concerns animate the principles of administrative law that courts generally will defer to an agency's construction of the statute it is charged with implementing, and to the procedures it adopts for implementing that statute. See *Vermont Yankee Nuclear Power Corp. v. Natural Resources Defense Council, Inc.*, 435 U.S. 519 (1978); *Train v. Natural Resources Defense Council, Inc.*, 421 U.S. 60 (1975).

In addition to these administrative concerns, we note that when an agency refuses to act it generally does not exercise its *coercive* power over an individual's liberty or property rights, and thus does not infringe upon areas that courts often are called upon to protect. . . . Finally, we recognize that an agency's refusal to institute proceedings shares to some extent the characteristics of the decision of a prosecutor in the Executive Branch not to indict—a decision which has long been regarded as the special province of the Executive Branch, inasmuch as it is the Executive who is charged by the Constitution to "take Care that the Laws be faithfully executed." U.S. Const., Art. II, § 3. . . .

III

. . . Respondents nevertheless present three separate authorities that they claim provide the courts with sufficient indicia of an intent to circumscribe enforcement discretion. Two of these may be dealt with summarily. First, we reject respondents' argument that the Act's substantive prohibitions of "misbranding" and the introduction of "new drugs" absent agency approval, see 21 U.S.C. §§ 352(f)(1), 355, supply us with "law to apply." These provisions are simply irrelevant to the agency's discretion to refuse to initiate proceedings.

We also find singularly unhelpful the agency "policy statement" on which the Court of Appeals placed great reliance. We would have difficulty with this statement's vague language even if it were a properly adopted agency rule. Although the statement indicates that the agency considered itself "obligated" to take certain investigative actions, that language did not arise in the course of discussing the agency's discretion to exercise its enforcement power, but rather in the context of describing agency policy with respect to unapproved uses of approved drugs by physicians. . . .

Respondents' third argument, based upon § 306 of the FDCA, merits only slightly more consideration. That section provides:

"Nothing in this chapter shall be construed as requiring the Secretary to report for prosecution, or for the institution of libel or injunction proceedings, minor violations of this chapter whenever he believes that the public interest will be adequately served by a suitable written notice or ruling." 21 U.S.C. § 336.

Respondents seek to draw from this section the negative implication that the Secretary is required to report for prosecution all "major" violations of the Act, however those might be defined, and that it therefore supplies the needed indication of an intent to limit agency enforcement discretion. We think that this section simply does not give rise to the negative implication which respondents seek to draw from it. The section is not addressed to agency proceedings designed to discover the existence of violations, but applies only to a situation where a violation has already been estab-

lished to the satisfaction of the agency. We do not believe the section speaks to the criteria which shall be used by the agency for investigating possible violations of the Act.

. . . The fact that the drugs involved in this case are ultimately to be used in imposing the death penalty must not lead this Court or other courts to import profound differences of opinion over the meaning of the Eighth Amendment to the United States Constitution into the domain of administrative law.

The judgment of the Court of Appeals is reversed.

Justice Brennan, concurring

Today the Court holds that individual decisions of the Food and Drug Administration not to take enforcement action in response to citizen requests are presumptively not reviewable under the Administrative Procedure Act, 5 U.S.C. §§ 701–706. I concur in this decision. This general presumption is based on the view that, in the normal course of events, Congress intends to allow broad discretion for its administrative agencies to make particular enforcement decisions, and there often may not exist readily discernible "law to apply" for courts to conduct judicial review of non-enforcement decisions. See *Citizens to Preserve Overton Park v. Volpe*. . . .

I also agree that, despite this general presumption, "Congress did not set agencies free to disregard legislative direction in the statutory scheme that the agency administers." *Ante*, at 833 . . . .

Justice Marshall, concurring in the judgment

Easy cases at times produce bad law, for in the rush to reach a clearly ordained result, courts may offer up principles, doctrines, and statements that calmer reflection, and a fuller understanding of their implications in concrete settings, would eschew. In my view, the "presumption of unreviewability" announced today is a product of that lack of discipline that easy cases make all too easy. The majority, eager to reverse what it goes out of its way to label as an "implausible result," not only does reverse, as I agree it should, but along the way creates out of whole cloth the notion that agency decisions not to take "enforcement action" are unreviewable unless Congress has rather specifically indicated otherwise. Because this "presumption of unreviewability" is fundamentally at odds with rule-of-law principles firmly embedded in our jurisprudence, because it seeks to truncate an emerging line of judicial authority subjecting enforcement discretion to rational and principled constraint, and because, in the end, the presumption may well be indecipherable, one can only hope that it will come to be understood as a relic of a particular factual setting in which the full implications of such a presumption were neither confronted nor understood.

I write separately to argue for a different basis of decision: that refusals to enforce, like other agency actions, are reviewable in the absence of a "clear and convincing" congressional intent to the contrary, but that such refusals warrant deference when, as in this case, there is nothing to suggest that an agency with enforcement discretion has abused that discretion.

. . . The "tradition" of unreviewability upon which the majority relies is refuted most powerfully by a firmly entrenched body of lower court case law that holds reviewable various agency refusals to act. This case law recognizes that attempting to draw a line for purposes of judicial review between affirmative exercises of coercive agency power and negative agency refusals to act, . . . is simply untenable; one of the very purposes fueling the birth of administrative agencies was the reality that governmental refusal to act could have just as devastating an effect upon life, liberty, and the pursuit of happiness as coercive governmental action. As Justice Frankfurter, a careful and experienced student of administrative law, wrote for this Court, "any distinction, as such, between 'negative' and 'affirmative' orders, as a touchstone of jurisdiction to review [agency action] serves no useful purpose." *Rochester Telephone Corp. v. United States*, 307 U.S. 125, 143 (1939). The lower courts, facing the problem of agency inaction and its concrete effects more regularly than do we, have responded with a variety of solutions to assure administrative fidelity to congressional objectives: a demand that an agency explain its refusal to act, a demand that explanations given be further elaborated, and injunctions that action "unlawfully withheld or unreasonably delayed," 5 U.S.C. §§ 706, be taken. . . . Whatever the merits of any particular solution, one would have hoped the Court would

have acted with greater respect for these efforts by responding with a scalpel rather than a blunderbuss.

[T]he Court . . . implies far too narrow a reliance on positive law, either statutory or constitutional, . . . as the sole source of limitations on agency discretion not to enforce. In my view, enforcement discretion is also channeled by traditional background understandings against which the APA was enacted and which Congress hardly could be thought to have intended to displace in the APA . . . . Congress should not be presumed to have departed from principles of rationality and fair process in enacting the APA. Moreover, the agency may well narrow its own enforcement discretion through historical practice, from which it should arguably not depart in the absence of explanation, or through regulations and informal action. Traditional principles of rationality and fair process do offer "meaningful standards" and "law to apply" to an agency's decision not to act, and no presumption of unreviewability should be allowed to trump these principles. . . .

The problem of agency refusal to act is one of the pressing problems of the modern administrative state, given the enormous powers, for both good and ill, that agency inaction, like agency action, holds over citizens. As *Dunlop v. Bachowski*, 421 U.S. 560 (1975), recognized, the problems and dangers of agency inaction are too important, too prevalent, and too multifaceted to admit of a single facile solution under which "enforcement" decisions are "presumptively unreviewable." Over time, I believe the approach announced today will come to be understood, not as mandating that courts cover their eyes and their reasoning power when asked to review an agency's failure to act, but as recognizing that courts must approach the substantive task of reviewing such failures with appropriate deference to an agency's legitimate need to set policy through the allocation of scarce budgetary and enforcement resources. Because the Court's approach, if taken literally, would take the courts out of the role of reviewing agency inaction in far too many cases, I join only the judgment today.

It is true that courts, particularly in the post-*Chevron* period, afforded great deference to agency decisions not to act. You will recall, however, that in the *Massachusetts v. EPA* a five-justice majority ruled that the inaction of the EPA against air pollutants and carbon emissions violated the Clean Air Act. The majority argued that the discretion to be exercised by the EPA must be "within defined statutory limits." "[O]nce EPA has responded to a petition for rulemaking" read the majority opinion, "its reasons for action or inaction must conform to the authorizing statute. Under the clear terms of the Clean Air Act, EPA can avoid taking further action only if it determines that greenhouse gases do not contribute to climate change or if it provides some reasonable explanation as to why it cannot or will not exercise its discretion to determine whether they do." This stance of the court seems in some ways inconsistent with the *Heckler* decision above. You should note, however, that the critical vote in *Massachusetts v. EPA* was the vote of Justice Kennedy. Justice Kennedy's decision to go with the majority was most likely based on his previous rulings favoring states' rights.

Finally, the Court analyzed the reviewability of an agency decision to *discontinue* a program which it started at its own discretion in *Lincoln v. Vigil*. From 1978 to 1985 the Indian Health Service had funded the Indian Children's Program, which provided clinical services to handicapped Indian children in the Southwest. In 1985, the Service announced that it was discontinuing direct clinical services under the program in order to establish a nationwide treatment program. Indian children eligible to receive services under the old program sued, alleging that the decision to discontinue services violated the federal trust responsibility to Indians, the Snyder Act, the Improvement Act, the Administrative Procedure Act, and the Fifth Amendment's Due Process Clause. Both lower courts held that the decision was reviewable and that the Service had erred by not following APA sec. 553 rulemaking procedures. But the Supreme Court reversed, holding that allocations of funds from lump-sum appropriations are "committed to agency discretion by law" and therefore not subject to judicial review under sec. 701(a)(2). Again, we urge you to ponder the wisdom of this principle. On one hand, if courts could review every agency reallocation of funds, those who stood to lose from the reallocation could file a lawsuit and delay the realloca-

tion, perhaps for years. But if the Indians only claim that the Service should have followed normal rulemaking procedures, is that so time-consuming?[25]

REVIEWING QUESTIONS OF FACT AND QUESTIONS OF LAW

Section 706 (2) seems to divide the scope of review into two neat categories, review of questions of law (A–D) and review of questions of fact (E and F). We can for analytical purposes follow this formal division, but in practice the formality breaks down. Decisions, both in agencies and in courts, really occur when the decider brings together facts and law. To evaluate a decision effectively one must examine facts and law in combination, not isolation.[26]

Reviewing the Evidence

During the first part of this century, when courts actively sought to protect private economic interests against governmental interference, courts often insisted that they must exercise independent judgment about evidence in cases threatening property and related *vested* rights. To require *de novo* review in all such cases, however, would paralyze the administrative process. With the advent of administrative state courts and deregulation policies from the Carter administration through Bush II, the judiciary has been much more deferential.

This deference takes two paths. First, courts do not hold agencies to the same rules that limit the admissibility of evidence in courts. Hearsay evidence is admissible and may, depending on how convincing it is in context, rise to the level of substantial evidence.[27] Similarly, while an appellate court might require a new trial if the trial judge allowed irrelevant and immaterial evidence into the record, courts will not set aside an agency finding that does so as long as other substantial evidence supports the finding.

25. *Lincoln v. Vigil*, 508 U.S. 182 (1993).
26. Compare Section 15(g) of the Model State APA (Appendix C).
27. In *Carroll v. Knickerbocker Ice Co.*, 218 N.Y. 435, 113 N.E. 507 (1916) the court set aside a workmen's compensation award because the only evidence submitted was based on hearsay testimony. The court concluded that "there must be a residuum of legal evidence to support the claim before an award can be made." This is known as the residuum rule.

The second path considers how much freedom the courts should allow agencies in weighing the evidence. In criminal trials the jury must believe the accused's guilt beyond a reasonable doubt. In civil trials the decision is based on the preponderance of the evidence (meaning it is more likely than not that the respondent is responsible for the actions alleged)". But in administrative law substantial evidence may be considerably less. Courts will not set aside a result even though an inconsistent and inherently more convincing interpretation of the evidence could be drawn. A conclusion from the facts, in other words, may be hotly disputed without being necessarily arbitrary, unreasonable, or capricious, and courts generally let reasonable but debatable conclusions stand. This practice depends on the assumption that the agency's decision has a history of administrative expertise behind it but the judge's view of the same factual dispute does not.

Universal Camera Corp. v. National Labor Relations Board

340 U.S. 474 (1951) 7-2
+ *Vinson, Reed, Frankfurter, Jackson, Burton, Clark, Minton*
+/- *Black, Douglas*

[An employee sued his employer after he was fired from his job as a supervisor at Universal Camera. He claimed he was fired for giving testimony to the National Labor Relations Board (NLRB) favoring recognition of a new union at the plant. The company claimed he was fired for various other reasons, including insubordination and for accusing his boss of being drunk. The charges were heard in an adjudicatory hearing. The hearing examiner decided that the evidence did not show he was fired because of his testimony before the NLRB, and therefore the company did not have to reinstate him. After reviewing the record the full NLRB reached the opposite conclusion and ordered him reinstated. It is significant that the employee gave his pro-union testimony on November 30, 1943, yet the company did not finally fire him until January 24, 1944. The alleged acts of insubordination all occurred *after* November 30, 1943.]

Justice Frankfurter delivered the opinion of the Court

The essential issue raised by this case . . . is the effect of the Administrative Procedure Act and the legislation colloquially known as the Taft-Hartley Act, 5 U.S.C.A. §1001 et seq.; 29 U.S.C.A. §141 et seq., on the duty of Courts of Appeals when called upon to review orders of the National Labor Relations Board.

The Court of Appeals for the Second Circuit granted enforcement of an order directing, in the main, that petitioner reinstate with back pay an employee found to have been discharged because he gave testimony under the Wagner Act, 29 U.S.C.A. §151 et seq., and cease and desist from discriminating against any employee who files charges or gives testimony under that Act. The court below, Judge Swan dissenting, decreed full enforcement of the order. . . .

Want of certainty in judicial review of Labor Board decisions partly reflects the intractability of any formula to furnish definiteness of content for all the impalpable factors involved in judicial review. But in part doubts as to the nature of the reviewing power and uncertainties in its application derive from history, and to that extent an elucidation of this history may clear them away.

The Wagner Act provided: "The findings of the Board as to the facts, if supported by evidence, shall be conclusive" Act of July 5, 1935, §10(e), 49 Stat. 449, 454, 29 U.S.C. §160(e), 29 U.S.C.A. §160(e). This Court read "evidence" to mean "substantial evidence." *Washington. V & M. Coach Co. v. Labor Board*, 301 U.S. 142, . . . and we said that "[s]ubstantial evidence is more than a mere scintilla. It means such relevant evidence as a reasonable mind might accept as adequate to support a conclusion." *Consolidated Edison Co. v. National Labor Relations Board*, 305 U.S. 197, 229.

. . . Accordingly, it "must do more than create a suspicion of the existence of the fact to be established. . . . [I]t must be enough to justify, if the trial were to a jury, a refusal to direct a verdict when the conclusion sought to be drawn from it is one of fact for the jury." *National Labor Relations Board v. Columbian Enameling & Stamping Co.*, 306 U.S. 292, 300. . . .

The very smoothness of the "substantial evidence" formula as the standard for reviewing the evidentiary validity of the Board's findings established its currency. But the inevitably variant applications of the standard to conflicting evidence soon brought contrariety of views and in due course bred criticism. Even though the whole record may have been canvassed in order to determine whether the evidentiary foundation of a determination by the Board was "substantial," the phrasing of this Court's process of review readily lent itself to the notion that it was enough that the evidence supporting the Board's result was "substantial" when considered by itself. It is fair to say that by imperceptible steps regard for the fact-finding function of the Board led to the assumption that the requirements of the Wagner Act were met when the reviewing court could find in the record evidence which, when viewed in isolation, substantiated the Board's findings. This is not to say that every member of this Court was consciously guided by this view or that the Court ever explicitly avowed this practice as doctrine. What matters is that the belief justifiably arose that the Court had so construed the obligation to review. . . .

[In addition,] [t]he final report of the Attorney General's Committee . . . submitted in January, 1941 . . . concluded that "[d]issatisfaction with the existing standards as to the scope of judicial review derives largely from dissatisfaction with the fact-finding procedures now employed by the administrative bodies." Departure from the "substantial evidence" test, it thought, would either create unnecessary uncertainty or transfer to courts the responsibility for ascertaining and assaying matters the significance of which lies outside judicial competence. Accordingly, it recommended against legislation embodying a general scheme of judicial review.

Three members of the Committee registered a dissent. Their view was that the "present system or lack of system of judicial review" led to inconsistency and uncertainty. They reported that under a "prevalent" interpretation of the "substantial evidence" rule "if what is called 'substantial evidence' is found anywhere in the record to support conclusions of fact, the courts are said to be obliged to sustain the decision without reference to how heavily the countervailing evidence may preponderate—unless indeed the stage of arbitrary decision is reached. Under this interpretation, the courts need to read only one side of the case and, if they find any evidence there, the administrative action is to be sustained and the record to the contrary is to be ignored." Their view led them to recommend that Congress enact principles of review applicable to all agencies not excepted by unique

characteristics. One of these principles was expressed by the formula that judicial review could extend to "findings, inferences, or conclusions of fact unsupported, upon the whole record, by substantial evidence." So far as the history of this movement for enlarged review reveals, the phrase "upon the whole record" makes its first appearance in this recommendation of the minority of the Attorney General's Committee. This evidence of the close relationship between the phrase and the criticism out of which it arose is important, for the substance of this formula for judicial review found its way into the statute books when Congress with unquestioning— we might even say uncritical—unanimity enacted the Administrative Procedure Act. . . .

Similar dissatisfaction with too restricted application of the "substantial evidence" test is reflected in the legislative history of the Taft-Hartley Act. The bill as reported to the House provided that the "findings of the Board as to the facts shall be conclusive unless it is made to appear to the satisfaction of the court either (1) that the findings of the fact are against the manifest weight of the evidence, or (2) that the findings of fact are not supported by substantial evidence." The bill left the House with this provision. Early committee prints in the Senate provided for review by "weight of the evidence" or "clearly erroneous" standards. But, as the Senate Committee Report relates, "it was finally decided to conform the statute to the corresponding section of the Administrative Procedure Act where the substantial evidence test prevails. In order to clarify any ambiguity in that statute, however, the committee inserted the words 'questions of fact, if supported by substantial evidence *on the record considered as a whole. . . .*' "

This phraseology was adopted by the Senate. The House conferees agreed. They reported to the House: "It is believed that the provisions of the conference agreement relating to the courts' reviewing power will be adequate to preclude such decisions as those in *N.L.R.B. v. Nevada Consol. Copper Corp.*, 316 U.S. 105, . . . without unduly burdening the courts." The Senate version became the law.

It is fair to say that in all this Congress expressed a mood. And it expressed its mood not merely by oratory but by legislation. As legislation that mood must be respected, even though it can only serve as a standard for judgment and not as a body of rigid rules assuring sameness of application. Enforcement of such broad standards implies subtlety of mind and solidity of judgment. But it is not for us to question that Congress may assume such qualities in the federal judiciary.

From the legislative story we have summarized, two concrete conclusions do emerge. One is the identity of aim of the Administrative Procedure Act and the Taft-Hartley Act regarding the proof with which the Labor Board must support a decision. The other is that now Congress has left no room for doubt as to the kind of scrutiny which a court of appeals must give the record before the Board to satisfy itself that the Board's order rests on adequate proof.

It would be mischievous word-playing to find that the scope of review under the Taft-Hartley Act is any different from that under the Administrative Procedure Act. The Senate Committee which reported the review clause of the Taft-Hartley Act expressly indicated that the two standards were to conform in this regard, and the wording of the two Acts is for purposes of judicial administration identical. And so we hold that the standard of proof specifically required of the Labor Board by the Taft-Hartley Act is the same as that to be exacted by courts reviewing every administrative action subject to the Administrative Procedure Act.

Whether or not it was ever permissible for courts to determine the substantiality of evidence supporting a Labor Board decision merely on the basis of evidence which in and of itself justified it, without taking into account contradictory evidence or evidence from which conflicting inferences could be drawn, the new legislation definitively precludes such a theory of review and bars its practice. The substantiality of evidence must take into account whatever in the record fairly detracts from its weight. This is clearly the significance of the requirement in both statutes that courts consider the whole record. Committee reports and the adoption in the Administrative Procedure Act of the minority views of the Attorney General's Committee demonstrate that to enjoin such a duty on the reviewing court was one of the important purposes of the movement which eventuated in that enactment. . . .

We conclude, therefore, that the Administrative Procedure Act and the Taft-Hartley Act direct that courts must now assume more responsibility for the reasonableness and fairness of Labor Board decisions than some courts have shown in the past. Reviewing courts must be influenced by a feeling that they are not to abdicate the conventional judi-

cial function. Congress has imposed on them responsibility for assuring that the Board keeps within reasonable grounds. That responsibility is not less real because it is limited to enforcing the requirement that evidence appear substantial when viewed, on the record as a whole, by courts invested with the authority and enjoying the prestige of the Courts of Appeals. The Board's findings are entitled to respect; but they must nonetheless be set aside when the record before a Court of Appeals clearly precludes the Board's decision from being justified by a fair estimate of the worth of the testimony of witnesses or its informed judgment on matters within its special competence or both. . . .

The decision of the Court of Appeals is assailed on two grounds. It is said (1) that the court erred in holding that it was barred from taking into account the report of the examiner on questions of fact insofar as the report was rejected by the Board, and (2) that the Board's order was not supported by substantial evidence on the record considered as a whole, even apart from the validity of the court's refusal to consider the rejected portions of the examiner's report.

The latter contention is easily met. . . . [I]t is clear from the court's opinion in this case that it in fact did consider the "record as a whole," and did not deem itself merely the judicial echo of the Board's conclusion. . . . On such a record we could not say that it would be error to grant enforcement.

The first contention, however, raises serious questions to which we now turn. . . .

The direction in which the law moves is often a guide for decision of particular cases, and here it serves to confirm our conclusion. However halting its progress, the trend in litigation is toward a rational inquiry into truth, in which the tribunal considers everything "logically probative of some matter requiring to be proved." Thayer, A Preliminary Treatise on Evidence, 530. This Court has refused to accept assumptions of fact which are demonstrably false, even when agreed to by the parties. Machinery for discovery of evidence has been strengthened; the boundaries of judicial notice have been slowly but perceptibly enlarged. It would reverse this process for courts to deny examiners' findings the probative force they would have in the conduct of affairs outside a courtroom.

We do not require that the examiner's findings be given more weight than in reason and in the light of judicial experience they deserve. The "substantial evidence" standard is not modified in any way when the Board and its examiner disagree. We intend only to recognize that evidence supporting a conclusion may be less substantial when an impartial, experienced examiner who has observed the witnesses and lived with the case has drawn conclusions different from the Board's than when he has reached the same conclusion. The findings of the examiner are to be considered along with the consistency and inherent probability of testimony. The significance of his report, of course, depends largely on the importance of credibility in the particular case. To give it this significance does not seem to us materially more difficult than to heed the other factors which in sum determine whether evidence is "substantial."

We therefore remand the cause to the Court of Appeals. On reconsideration of the record it should accord the findings of the trial examiner the relevance that they reasonably command in answering the comprehensive question whether the evidence supporting the Board's order is substantial. But the court need not limit its reexamination of the case to the effect of that report on its decision. We leave it free to grant or deny enforcement as it thinks the principles expressed in this opinion dictate.

Judgment vacated and cause remanded.

Reviewing the Law

The Court's classic opinion in the following case, *Hearst*, shows how questions of law and fact inevitably merge. Whether newsboys are or are not independent contractors is, of course, a legal conclusion. But the conclusion in turn depends on the facts, on what newsboys do and whether their degree of economic power vis-à-vis their employers really typifies those of most independent contractors. The Hearst company refused to recognize and bargain collectively with a properly elected union representing newsboys. It insisted that newsboys were independent contractors and not "employees" at all. Therefore, they were not covered by the National Labor Relations Act. The NLRB decided that the newsboys were employees within the meaning of the act, but the lower court on review held that at common law the newsboys were independent contractors and not employees pro-

tected by the act. The question before the Supreme Court therefore was whether the agency, here the NLRB, possessed any expertise or other quality that gave its conclusions on matters of law special weight or credibility. This case arose before the adoption of the APA, but its influence is still strong.

National Labor Relations Board v. Hearst Publications, Inc.

322 U.S. 111 (1944) 8–1
+ *Stone, Black, Reed, Frankfurter, Douglas, Murphy, Jackson, Rutledge*
– *Roberts*

[The issue in this case was whether "newsboys" are independent contractors with a newspaper or are to be considered employees of the newspaper. Only employees are protected by the Wagner Act. The NLRB had found them to be employees. This finding was challenged by the newspaper.]

Justice Rutledge delivered the opinion of the Court

. . . The papers are distributed to the ultimate consumer through a variety of channels, including independent dealers and newsstands often attached to drug, grocery or confectionery stores, carriers who make home deliveries, and newsboys who sell on the streets of the city and its suburbs. Only the last of these are involved in this case.

The newsboys work under varying terms and conditions. They may be "bootjackers," selling to the general public at places other than established corners, or they may sell at fixed "spots." They may sell only casually or part-time, or full-time; and they may be employed regularly and continuously or only temporarily. The units which the Board determined to be appropriate are composed of those who sell full-time at established spots. Those vendors, misnamed boys, are generally mature men, dependent upon the proceeds of their sales for their sustenance, and frequently supporters of families. Working thus as news vendors on a regular basis, often for a number of years, they form a stable group with relatively little turnover, in contrast to schoolboys and others who sell as bootjackers, temporary and casual distributors.

Overall circulation and distribution of the papers are under the general supervision of circulation managers. But for purposes of street distribution each paper has divided metropolitan Los Angeles into geographic districts. Each district is under the direct and close supervision of a district manager. His function in the mechanics of distribution is to supply the newsboys in his district with papers which he obtains from the publisher and to turn over to the publisher the receipts which he collects from their sales, either directly or with the assistance of "checkmen" or "main spot" boys. The latter, stationed at the important corners or "spots" in the district, are newsboys who, among other things, receive delivery of the papers, redistribute them to other newsboys stationed at less important corners, and collect receipts from their sales. For that service, which occupies a minor portion of their working day, the checkmen receive a small salary from the publisher. The bulk of their day, however, they spend in hawking papers at their "spots" like other full-time newsboys. A large part of the appropriate units selected by the Board for the News and the Herald are checkmen who, in that capacity, clearly are employees of those papers.

The newsboys' compensation consists in the difference between the prices at which they sell the papers and the prices they pay for them. The former are fixed by the publishers and the latter are fixed either by the publishers or, in the case of the News, by the district manager. In practice the newsboys receive their papers on credit. They pay for those sold either sometime during or after the close of their selling day, returning for credit all unsold papers. Lost or otherwise unreturned papers, however, must be paid for as though sold. Not only is the "profit" per paper thus effectively fixed by the publisher, but substantial control of the newsboys' total "take home" can be affected through the ability to designate their sales areas and the power to determine the number of papers allocated to each. While as a practical matter this power is not exercised fully, the newsboys' "right" to decide how many papers they will take is also not absolute. In practice, the Board found, they cannot determine the size of their established order without cooperation of the district manager. And often the number of papers they must take is determined unilaterally by the district managers.

In addition to effectively fixing the compensation, respondents in a variety of ways prescribe, if not the minutiae of daily activities, at least the broad terms and conditions of work. This is accomplished largely through the supervisory efforts of the district managers, who serve as the nexus between the publishers and the newsboys. The district managers assign "spots" or corners to which the newsboys are expected to confine their selling activities. Transfers from one "spot" to another may be ordered by the district manager for reasons of discipline or efficiency or other cause. Transportation to the spots from the newspaper building is offered by each of the respondents. Hours of work on the spots are determined not by the impersonal pressures of the market, but to a real extent by explicit instructions from the district managers. Adherence to the prescribed hours is observed closely by the district managers or other supervisory agents of the publishers. Sanctions, varying in severity from reprimand to dismissal, are visited on the tardy and the delinquent. By similar supervisory controls minimum standards of diligence and good conduct while at work are sought to be enforced. However wide may be the latitude for individual initiative beyond those standards, district managers' instructions in what the publishers apparently regard as helpful sales technique are expected to be followed. Such varied items as the manner of displaying the paper, of emphasizing current features and headlines, and of placing advertising placards, or the advantages of soliciting customers at specific stores or in the traffic lanes are among the subjects of this instruction. Moreover, newsboys are furnished with sales equipment, such as racks, boxes and change aprons, and advertising placards by the publishers. In this pattern of employment the Board found that the newsboys are an integral part of the publishers' distribution system and circulation organization. And the record discloses that the newsboys and checkmen feel they are employees of the papers and respondents' supervisory employees, if not respondents themselves, regard them as such.

In addition to questioning the sufficiency of the evidence to sustain these findings, respondents point to a number of other attributes characterizing their relationship with the newsboys and urge that on the entire record the latter cannot be considered their employees. They base this conclusion on the argument that by common-law standards the extent of their control and direction of the newsboys' working activities creates no more than an "independent contractor" relationship and that common-law standards determine the "employee" relationship under the Act. . . .

The principal question is whether the newsboys are "employees." Because Congress did not explicitly define the term, respondents say its meaning must be determined by reference to common-law standards. In their view "common-law standards" are those the courts have applied in distinguishing between "employees" and "independent contractors" when working out various problems unrelated to the Wagner Act's purposes and provisions.

The argument assumes that there is some simple, uniform and easily applicable test which the courts have used, in dealing with such problems, to determine whether persons doing work for others fall in one class or the other. Unfortunately this is not true. . . . Few problems in the law have given greater variety of application and conflict in results than the cases arising in the borderland between what is clearly an employer-employee relationship and what is clearly one of independent entrepreneurial dealing. . . .

Two possible consequences could follow. One would be to refer the decision of who are employees to local state law. The alternative would be to make it turn on a sort of pervading general essence distilled from state law. Congress obviously did not intend the former result. It would introduce variations into the statute's operation as wide as the differences the forty-eight states and other local jurisdictions make in applying the distinction for wholly different purposes. Persons who might be "employees" in one state would be "independent contractors" in another. They would be within or without the statute's protection depending not on whether their situation falls factually within the ambit Congress had in mind, but upon the accidents of the location of their work and the attitude of the particular local jurisdiction in casting doubtful cases one way or the other. Persons working across state lines might fall in one class or the other, possibly both, depending on whether the Board and the courts would be required to give effect to the law of one state or of the adjoining one, or to that of each in relation to the portion of the work done within its borders.

Both the terms and the purposes of the statute, as well as the legislative history, show that Congress had in mind no such patchwork plan for securing freedom of employees' organization and of collective bargaining. The Wagner Act is federal legislation, administered by a national agency, intended to solve a national problem on a national scale. It is an Act, therefore, in reference to which it is not only proper, but necessary for us to assume, "in the absence of a plain indication to the contrary, that Congress . . . is not making the application of the federal act dependent on state law." . . .

Whether, given the intended national uniformity, the term "employee" includes such workers as these newsboys must be answered primarily from the history, terms and purposes of the legislation. . . . It will not do, for deciding this question as one of uniform national application, to import wholesale the traditional common-law conceptions or some distilled essence of their local variations as exclusively controlling limitations upon the scope of the statute's effectiveness. To do this would be merely to select some of the local, hairline variations for nation-wide application and thus to reject others for coverage under the Act. That result hardly would be consistent with the statute's broad terms and purposes. . . .

The mischief at which the Act is aimed and the remedies it offers are not confined exclusively to "employees" within the traditional legal distinctions separating them from "independent contractors." Myriad forms of service relationship, with infinite and subtle variations in the terms of employment, blanket the nation's economy. Some are within this Act, others beyond its coverage. Large numbers will fall clearly on one side or on the other, by whatever test may be applied. But intermediate there will be many, the incidents of whose employment partake in part of the one group, in part of the other, in varying proportions of weight. And consequently the legal pendulum, for purposes of applying the statute, may swing one way or the other, depending upon the weight of this balance and its relation to the special purpose at hand.

Unless the common-law tests are to be imported and made exclusively controlling, without regard to the statute's purposes, it cannot be irrelevant that the particular workers in these cases are subject, as a matter of economic fact, to the evils the statute was designated to eradicate and that the remedies it affords are appropriate for preventing them or curing their harmful effects in the special situation. . . .

It is not necessary in this case to make a completely definitive limitation around the term "employee." That task has been assigned primarily to the agency created by Congress to administer the Act. Determination of "where all the conditions of the relation require protection" involves inquiries of the Board charged with this duty. Everyday experience in the administration of the statute gives it familiarity with the circumstances and backgrounds of employment relationships in various industries, with the abilities and needs of the workers for self organization and collective action, and with the adaptability of collective bargaining for the peaceful settlement of their disputes with their employers. The experience thus acquired must be brought frequently to bear on the question who is an employee under the Act. Resolving that question, like determining whether unfair labor practices have been committed, "belongs to the usual administrative routine" of the Board. . . .

In making that body's determination as to the facts in these matters conclusive, if supported by evidence, Congress entrusted to it primarily the decision whether the evidence establishes the material facts. Hence in reviewing the Board's ultimate conclusions, it is not the court's function to substitute its own inferences of fact for the Board's, when the latter have support in the record. Undoubtedly questions of statutory interpretation, especially when arising in the first instance in judicial proceedings, are for the courts to resolve, giving appropriate weight to the judgment of those whose special duty is to administer the questioned statute. But where the question is one of specific application of a broad statutory term in a proceeding in which the agency administering the statute must determine it initially, the reviewing court's function is limited. Like the commissioner's determination under the Longshoremen's & Harbor Workers' Act, that a man is not a "member of a crew" . . . or that he was injured "in the course of his employment" . . . and the Federal Communications Commission's determination that one company is under the "control" of another . . . , the Board's determination that specified persons are "employees" under this Act is to be accepted if it has "warrant in the record" and a reasonable basis in law.

In this case the Board found that the designated newsboys work continuously and regularly, rely upon their earnings for the support of themselves and their families, and have their total wages influenced in large measure by the publishers who dictate their buying and selling prices, fix their markets and control their supply of papers. Their hours of work and their efforts on the job are supervised and to some extent prescribed by the publishers or their agents. Much of their sales equipment and advertising materials is furnished by the publishers with the intention that it be used for the publisher's benefit. Stating that "the primary consideration in the determination of the applicability of the statutory definition is whether effectuation of the declared policy and purposes of the Act comprehend securing to the individual the rights guaranteed and protection afforded by the Act," the Board concluded that the newsboys are employees. The record sustains the Board's findings and there is ample basis in the law for its conclusion. . . . Reversed and remanded.

Justice Roberts, dissenting opinion

. . . I think it plain that newsboys are not "employees" of the respondents within the meaning and intent of the National Labor Relations Act. When Congress, in § 2(3), said "The term 'employee' shall include any employee, . . ." it stated as clearly as language could do it that the provisions of the Act were to extend to those who, as a result of decades of tradition which had become part of the common understanding of our people, bear the named relationship. Clearly also Congress did not delegate to the National Labor Relations Board the function of defining the relationship of employment so as to promote what the Board understood to be the underlying purpose of the statute. The question who is an employee, so as to make the statute applicable to him, is a question of the meaning of the Act and, therefore, is a judicial and not an administrative question. . . .

In the following work Professors Mashaw and Merrill, with some assistance from the late Judge Harold Leventhal, have provided a wise analysis of the law-fact interplay.

Scope of Review: Introduction to the American Public Law System

JERRY L. MASHAW AND RICHARD A. MERRILL
St. Paul: West Publishing Co., 1975, 786–788

... [T]he law-fact distinction presents obvious conceptual difficulties. The part of administrative decision-making that seems to raise the most difficult questions for administrators and for reviewing courts—the application of law to facts—is not exclusively the decision of a question of law or the finding of facts. To take a prosaic example, reasonable men may easily agree both on the abstract definition of "negligence" (the failure to act prudently under the circumstances) as well as on the operative facts of a given case; yet they may and often do disagree about whether those facts fit the legal definition, i.e., establish negligence on the part of the defendant. Is the conclusion in a particular case that the defendant was or was not negligent a conclusion of law or of fact? Obviously, it is at once neither ... and both. Similar sorts of judgments abound in administrative decisionmaking; for example, an FTC determination that practices are "unfair or deceptive"; an NLRB determination that an employer has "interfered with," "restrained" or "coerced" employees in their exercise of collective rights; or an FCC determination that the award of a broadcast license to one of two competing applicants better serves "the public interest."

Finally, even if conceptual difficulties did not undermine the law-fact dichotomy in many situations, we would be likely to doubt that the relationship between administrative agencies that exercise widely varying administrative functions and courts that review their activities in many types of proceedings should or could be based on bipolar tests. We know that in construing statutes, courts often give significant weight to the interpretations of responsible administrators. Because the interpretation of a statute is clearly a question of law, administrators are thus conceded an important role in deciding at least some types of legal questions. Indeed, our experience with a wide range of agencies leaves no doubt that administrators may be "law determiners" as well as "fact finders." The issue for reviewing courts therefore becomes one of determining the permissible range of administrative law-making and deciding whether a particular action falls within that range.

This is not to say that the form in which a claim of administrative illegality is presented to a reviewing court has no bearing on the court's resolution of the dispute. But the formulation of the question is only one of the factors that will influence the degree to which judicial review becomes penetrating rather than perfunctory. Judicial review of administrative action may be as much art as science, as much "feel" and "flavor" as formal structure and analysis. This view was elaborated by Judge Harold Leventhal, one of the judiciary's most insightful students of administrative law, in *Greater Boston Television Corp. v. FCC*, 444 F.2d 841 [850–852] (D.C. Cir. 1970), *cert, denied*, 406 U.S. 950 (1972). The case involved review of the FCC's renewal of a broadcast license for which the appellant had been an unsuccessful competing applicant:

Approaching this case as we have with full awareness of and responsiveness to the court's "supervisory" function in review of agency decision, it may be appropriate to take note of the salient aspects of that review. It begins at the threshold, with enforcement of the requirement of reasonable procedure, with fair notice and opportunity to the parties to present their case. It continues into examination of the evidence and agency's findings of facts, for the court must be satisfied that the agency's evidentiary fact findings are supported by substantial evidence, and provide rational support for the agency's inferences of ultimate fact. Full allowance must be given not only for the opportunity of the agency ... to observe the demeanor of the witnesses, but also for the reality that agency matters typically involve a kind of expertise—sometimes technical in a scientific sense, sometimes more a matter of specialization in kinds of regulatory programs. ... A court does not depart from its proper function when it undertakes a study of the record, hopefully perceptive, even as to the evidence on technical and specialized matters, for this enables the court to penetrate to the underlying decisions of the agency, to satisfy itself that the agency has exercised a reasoned discretion, with reasons that do not deviate from or ignore the ascertainable legislative intent. ...

Assuming consistency with law and the legislative mandate, the agency has latitude not merely to find facts and make judgments, but also to select the policies deemed in the public interest. The function of the court is to assure that the agency has given reasoned consideration to all the material facts and issues. This calls for insistence that the agency articulate with reasonable clarity its reasons for decision, and identify the significance of the crucial facts, a course that tends to assure that the agency's policies effectuate general standards, applied without unreasonable discrimination. ...

Its supervisory function calls on the court to intervene not merely in case of procedural inadequacies, or bypassing of the mandate in the legislative charter, but more broadly if the court becomes aware, especially from a combination of danger signals, that the agency has not really taken a "hard look" at the salient problems, and has not genuinely engaged in reasoned decisionmaking. If the agency has not shirked this fundamental task, however, the court exercises restraint and affirms the agency's action even though the court would on its own account have made different findings or adopted different standards. . . .

The process thus combines judicial supervision with a salutary principle of judicial restraint, an awareness that agencies and courts together constitute a "partnership" in furtherance of the public interest, and are "collaborative instrumentalities of justice." The court is in a real sense part of the total administrative process, and not a hostile stranger to the office of first instance.

Finally, we would like to mention a controversial area, that includes important lessons concerning the *philosophy* of judicial review in the modern state. Treatment of detainees at the U.S. prison in Guantanamo Bay, Cuba has attracted broad attention and caused controversy. Such controversy, not surprisingly, found its way to the Supreme Court. In the first of a number of cases, *Hamdi v. Rumsfeld*, 542 U.S. 507 (2004), the Court announced, in a 5-4 decision, that the government does not have the power and authority to detain U.S. citizens indefinitely as "illegal enemy combatants." The Court reasoned that detainees who are U.S. citizens must have the right to challenge their detention before impartial judges. Next, in *Hamdan v. Rumsfeld* 548 U.S. 557 (2006), also a 5-4 decision, the Court held the military commissions set up to try the detainees in Guantanamo Bay are illegal because they do not conform to the Uniform Code of Military Justice or the Geneva Conventions. The Court once again in this case made clear that the methods used by the executive in the "war against terror" have to conform to basic rule-of-law principles. Finally, in *Boumediene v. Bush*, 553 U.S. ___ (2008), the Court decided that foreign nationals can similarly not be held indefinitely in detention without being given the right of *habeas corpus*. The Court reached this conclusion by referring to the U.S.

Constitution and announced that the suspension of *habeas corpus* by the Military Commissions Act was unconstitutional.

In the following decision, a unanimous Court of Appeals for the D.C. Circuit eloquently explains the rationale for judicial review and the judiciary's role in checking and balancing the power of the other branches of government.

Huzaifa Parhat v. Robert Gates, Secretary of Defense et al.

District of Columbia USCA (2008) 3-0
+ Sentelle, Garland, Griffith

[Huzaifa Parhat was a Chinese citizen of Uighur heritage. He fled his home in what Uighur people call the East Turkistan region of China in opposition to the policies of the Chinese government against his people. He was in Afghanistan, in an East Turkistan Islamic Movement (ETIM) camp, when the United States military retaliated against the September 11, 2001 terrorist attacks. After his camp was destroyed by an air strike, Parhat crossed the border to Pakistan, where, in December 2001, he was turned over to the U.S. military by local Pakistani officials. After considering testimony of Parhat and evidence against him, a Combatant Status Review Tribunal declared Parhat an enemy combatant, allowing the government to continue to hold him in detention without a specific charge. In December 2006 Parhat filed a petition for relief under the Detainee Treatment Act of 2005, which granted the D.C. Circuit Court of Appeals "exclusive jurisdiction" to determine the validity of any final decision of a Combatant Status Review Tribunal.]

Judge Garland delivered the opinion of the court

It is undisputed that [Parhat] is not a member of al Qaida or the Taliban, and that he has never participated in any hostile action against the United States or its allies. The Tribunal's determination that Parhat is an enemy combatant is based on its finding that he is "affiliated" with a Uighur independence group [ETIM], and the further finding that the group was "associated" with al Qaida and the Taliban.

The Tribunal's findings regarding the Uighur group rest, in key respects, on statements in classified State and Defense Department documents that provide no information regarding the sources of the reporting upon which the statements are based, and otherwise lack sufficient indicia of the statements' reliability. Parhat contends, with support of his own, that the Chinese government is the source of several of the key statements. Parhat's principal argument on this appeal is that the record before his Combatant Status Review Tribunal is insufficient to support the conclusion that he is an enemy combatant, even under the Defense Department's own definition of that term. We agree. To survive review under the Detainee Treatment Act, a Tribunal's determination of a detainee's status must be based on evidence that both the Tribunal and the court can assess for reliability. Because the evidence the government submitted to Parhat's Tribunal did not permit the Tribunal to make the necessary assessment, and because the record on review does not permit this court to do so, we cannot find that the government's designation of Parhat as an enemy combatant is supported by a "preponderance of the evidence" and "was consistent with the standards and procedures" established by the Secretary of Defense, as required by the Act.

To affirm the Tribunal's determination under such circumstances would be to place a judicial imprimatur on an act of essentially unreviewable executive discretion. That is not what Congress directed us to do when it authorized judicial review of enemy combatant determinations under the Act. Accordingly, we direct the government to release Parhat, to transfer him, or to expeditiously convene a new Combatant Status Review Tribunal to consider evidence submitted in a manner consistent with this opinion. . . .

We also deny, without prejudice, the government's motion to protect from public disclosure all nonclassified record information that it has labeled "law enforcement sensitive," as well as the names and "identifying information" of all U.S. government personnel mentioned in the record. Although we do not doubt that there is information in these categories that warrants protection, the government has proffered only a generic explanation of the need for protection, providing no rationale specific to the information actually at issue in this case.

By resting its motion on generic claims, equally applicable to all of the more than one hundred other detainee cases

now pending in this court, the government effectively "proposes unilaterally to determine whether information is 'protected.' " Bismullah v. Gates, 501 F.3d 178, 188 (D.C. Cir. 2007). Without an explanation geared to the information at issue in this case, we are left with no way to determine whether that specific information warrants protection—other than to accept the government's own designation. But as we held in Bismullah, "[i]t is the court, not the Government, that has discretion to seal a judicial record, which the public ordinarily has the right to inspect and copy." Id. (internal citations omitted). We therefore deny the government's motion and direct it to file a renewed motion, accompanied by a copy of the record identifying the specific information it seeks to designate and pleadings explaining why protecting that specific information is required.

I

. . . [In December 2004] a Combatant Status Review Tribunal determined that Parhat was an enemy combatant. It did so on the theory that he was "affiliated" with a Uighur independence group known as the East Turkistan Islamic Movement (ETIM), that ETIM was "associated" with al Qaida and the Taliban, and that ETIM is engaged in hostilities against the United States and its coalition partners. The basis for the charge of Parhat's "affiliation" with ETIM was that the Uighur camp at which he lived and received training on a rifle and pistol was run by an ETIM leader. The Tribunal acknowledged, however, that "no source document evidence was introduced to indicate . . . that the Detainee had actually joined ETIM, or that he himself had personally committed any hostile acts against the United States or its coalition partners." The grounds for the charges that ETIM was "associated" with al Qaida and the Taliban, and that it is engaged in hostilities against the United States or its coalition partners, were statements in classified documents that do not state (or, in most instances, even describe) the sources or rationales for those statements. Parhat denied knowing anything about an al Qaida or Taliban association with Uighur camps. . . .

II

The DTA grants this court jurisdiction to "determine the validity of any final decision of a Combatant Status Review Tribunal that an alien is properly detained as an enemy combatant." DTA § 1005(e)(2)(A). The scope of our review is "limited to the consideration of":

(i) whether the status determination of the [CSRT] was consistent with the standards and procedures specified by the Secretary of Defense for [CSRTs] (including the requirement that the conclusion of the Tribunal be supported by a preponderance of the evidence and allowing a rebuttable presumption in favor of the Government's evidence); and

(ii) to the extent the Constitution and laws of the United States are applicable, whether the use of such standards and procedures to make the determination is consistent with the Constitution and laws of the United States.

. . .

Each CSRT is composed of "three neutral commissioned officers." Navy Memorandum at E-1 § C(1). The Recorder, also a commissioned officer, is charged with gathering the "Government Information," which is defined as "reasonably available information in the possession of the U.S. Government bearing on the issue of whether the detainee" meets the enemy combatant criteria. The Recorder must present to the Tribunal both the "Government Evidence," defined as "such evidence in the Government Information as may be sufficient to support the detainee's classification as an enemy combatant," and any evidence in the Government Information that is exculpatory, described as "evidence to suggest that the detainee should not be designated as an enemy combatant." . . .

The CSRT must "determine whether the preponderance of the evidence supports the conclusion that [the] detainee meets the criteria to be designated as an enemy combatant." There is a rebuttable presumption that the Government Evidence is "genuine and accurate." Id. The Tribunal "may consider hearsay evidence, taking into account the reliability of such evidence in the circumstances."

An important DOD "standard" for our purposes is the definition of "enemy combatant." [T]he DOD Order and the Navy Memorandum both define an "enemy combatant" as:

an individual who was part of or supporting Taliban or al Qaida forces, or associated forces that are engaged in hostilities against the United States or its coalition partners. This includes any person who has committed a belligerent act or has directly supported hostilities in aid of enemy armed forces.

DOD Order at 1; Navy Memorandum at E-1 § B.

Parhat contends that the record before his CSRT does not support its finding that he is an enemy combatant, even under the government's own definition, and hence that the Tribunal's determination is not "consistent with the standards and procedures specified by the Secretary of Defense for Combatant Status Review Tribunals." DTA § 1005(e)(2)(C)(i) . . . .

III

[In this Part, the Court describes the evidence relevant to the CSRT's determination that Parhat is an enemy combatant and identifies deficiencies in that evidence.]
. . .

IV

As Part III indicates, the principal evidence against Parhat regarding the second and third elements of DOD's definition of enemy combatant consists of four government intelligence documents. The documents make assertions—often in haec verba—about activities undertaken by ETIM, and about that organization's relationship to al Qaida and the Taliban. The documents repeatedly describe those activities and relationships as having "reportedly" occurred, as being "said to" or "reported to" have happened, and as things that "may" be true or are "suspected of" having taken place. But in virtually every instance, the documents do not say who "reported" or "said" or "suspected" those things. Nor do they provide any of the underlying reporting upon which the documents' bottom-line assertions are founded, nor any assessment of the reliability of that reporting. Because of those omissions, the Tribunal could not and this court cannot assess the reliability of the assertions in the documents. And because of this deficiency, those bare assertions cannot sustain the determination that Parhat is an enemy combatant.

The CSRT's obligation to assess the reliability of evidence is expressly stated in the Navy Memorandum's provision on "Admissibility of Evidence." This provision states that the Tribunal may consider hearsay evidence—which the intelligence reports plainly are—but in so doing it must "tak[e] into account the reliability of such evidence in the circumstances." That obligation, and the concomitant requirement that reliability be assessable, are also inherent in the Memorandum's direction—adopted by Congress in the

DTA—that the CSRT must decide whether "a preponderance of the evidence" supports the determination that the detainee is an enemy combatant. . . . This court, in turn, has two responsibilities with respect to the reliability of the evidence presented to the CSRT. First . . . we must assure ourselves that the CSRT had the opportunity to—and did—evaluate the reliability of the evidence it considered. Second, in order to ensure, as the DTA requires, that "the conclusion of the Tribunal [is] supported by a preponderance of the evidence," allowing only a "rebuttable" presumption in favor of the Government's evidence, id., we must be able to assess the reliability of that evidence ourselves.

Insistence that the Tribunal and court have an opportunity to assess the reliability of the record evidence is not simply a theoretical exercise. Parhat contends that the ultimate source of key assertions in the four intelligence documents is the government of the People's Republic of China, and he offers substantial support for that contention. Parhat further maintains that Chinese reporting on the subject of the Uighurs cannot be regarded as objective, and offers substantial support for that proposition as well.

The CSRT's own written decision makes clear both its inability to assess the reliability of most of the evidence presented to it and the importance of its being able to do so. Although the cover sheet of the Tribunal's decision reaches the bottom-line conclusion that Parhat "is properly designated as an enemy combatant" . . . the underlying decision is considerably more qualified. It states: "The Tribunal found the Detainee to be an enemy combatant because of his apparent ETIM affiliation . . . [classified material redacted], but despite the fact that the ETIM is said to be making plans for future terrorist activities against U.S. interests, no source document evidence was introduced to indicate how this group has actually done so. . . ." It further states that the "Detainee is considered to be an enemy combatant because he is said to be affiliated with the ETIM," and that "[t]he camp at which he trained was an ETIM camp apparently funded in part by Usama bin Laden and the Taliban." . . .

Moreover, in the two instances in which the CSRT did have exogenous information with which to assess the reliability of statements made in the intelligence documents, it found sufficient discrepancies to question one statement and to "doubt the veracity" of the other. The Tribunal plainly fulfilled its obligation to evaluate the reliability of those two statements. In doing so, it performed the kind of assessment that a CSRT must make in order to determine whether a detainee has been properly classified as an enemy combatant. And yet, that is precisely the kind of assessment that the Tribunal could not make with respect to the bulk of the evidence before it.

The government . . . argues, however, that the Tribunal was able to do so here—for two reasons.

First, the government suggests that several of the assertions in the intelligence documents are reliable because they are made in at least three different documents. We are not persuaded. Lewis Carroll notwithstanding, the fact that the government has "said it thrice" does not make an allegation true. See LEWIS CARROLL, THE HUNTING OF THE SNARK 3 (1876) ("I have said it thrice: What I tell you three times is true."). In fact, we have no basis for concluding that there are independent sources for the documents' thrice-made assertions. To the contrary, as noted in Part III, many of those assertions are made in identical language, suggesting that later documents may merely be citing earlier ones, and hence that all may ultimately derive from a single source. And as we have also noted, Parhat has made a credible argument that—at least for some of the assertions—the common source is the Chinese government, which may be less than objective with respect to the Uighurs. Other assertions in the documents may ultimately rely on interview reports (not provided to the Tribunal) of Uighur detainees, who may have had no first-hand knowledge and whose speculations may have been transformed into certainties in the course of being repeated by report writers.

Second, the government insists that the statements made in the documents are reliable because the State and Defense Departments would not have put them in intelligence documents were that not the case. This comes perilously close to suggesting that whatever the government says must be treated as true, thus rendering superfluous both the role of the Tribunal and the role that Congress assigned to this court. We do not in fact know that the departments regard the statements in those documents as reliable; the repeated insertion of qualifiers indicating that events are "reported" or "said" or "suspected" to have occurred suggests at least some skepticism. Nor do we know whether the departments rely on those documents for decisionmaking purposes in the form in which they were presented to the Tribunal, or whether they supplement them with backup documentation and reliability assessments before using them to take actions of consequence.

To be clear, we do not suggest that hearsay evidence is never reliable—only that it must be presented in a form, or with sufficient additional information, that permits the Tribunal and court to assess its reliability. Nor do we suggest that the government must always submit the underlying basis for its factual assertions in order to make such an assessment possible. . . . In this opinion, we neither prescribe nor proscribe possible ways in which the government may demonstrate the reliability of its evidence. We merely reject the government's contention that it can prevail by submitting documents that read as if they were indictments or civil complaints, and that simply assert as facts the elements required to prove that a detainee falls within the definition of enemy combatant. To do otherwise would require the courts to rubber-stamp the government's charges, in contravention of our understanding that Congress intended the court "to engage in meaningful review of the record." Bismullah, 503 F.3d at 180 (emphasis added); see

Boumediene, slip op. at 49 (stating that the "DTA should be interpreted to accord some latitude to the Court of Appeals to fashion procedures necessary to make its review function a meaningful one"). . . .

So ordered. [footnotes and citations omitted]

We said at the beginning of this chapter that its topic of judicial review is the most important topic in the book. We trust that, now that you have finished it, you see why this is so. In all fields of law, not just administrative law, our common law tradition gives courts the ultimate power to declare what the law means. In a sense, every chapter in this book rests primarily on what the courts say "the law" means. While this power of judicial review seems undemocratic to some, it is inherent in the concept of limited government and the rule of law. If, as we believe, administrative law seeks the maximum feasible reduction of arbitrary, irrational, and hence unfair actions by government officials, it follows that politically independent judges must play a central role in the process.

EXERCISES AND QUESTIONS FOR FURTHER THOUGHT

1. Some of the problems of judicial review discussed in this chapter involve questions of statutory interpretation and thus extend the principles discussed in chapter 3. The main issue concerns the extent courts should defer to agency interpretations of their own statutes. Apply the principles in *Universal Camera* and *Hearst* to the benzene, cotton dust, or *Chevron v. NRDC* cases in chapter 3. Did the Court employ any of them? Should it have? Also, ask yourself whether *Overton Park* does not implicitly retreat from the principle in *Hearst*. Does *Heckler v. Chaney* affirm the principles of *Hearst*? If the NLRB was presumptively correct, why wasn't Secretary Volpe? Does the difference lie in the presence of a reviewable record in *Hearst* but not in *Overton Park*?

2. We commented that the influence of the *Hearst* decision remains strong in administrative law today. However, in 1980, the Supreme Court upheld a lower

court *reversal* of an NLRB classification of faculty members at Yeshiva University as "professional employees." The Court held that faculty members were managers, not workers, and therefore their efforts to organize were not covered by the National Labor Relations Act. The majority said the case raised a "mixed" question "of fact and law." Does this distinguish the case from *Hearst*? See *NLRB v. Yeshiva University*, 444 U.S. 672 (1980).

3. Would it have been permissible for the Supreme Court to decide George Eldridge's claim (*Mathews v. Eldridge*) against him for failure to exhaust administrative remedies? Why or why not?

4. A federal statute provides that "where the father or one or more sons or daughters of a family were killed in action or died in line of *duty* while serving in the Armed Forces . . . , the sole surviving son of such family shall not be inducted for [military] service." McKart, a sole surviving son, was called up for his preinduction military physical exam after his mother died. Selective Service had concluded that the statute did not apply in these circumstances. Without reporting for his physical and without exhausting any other administrative remedy, McKart sued to have this statutory interpretation set aside. Should courts defer to agency expertise on this matter? See *McKart v. United States*, 395 U.S. 185 (1969).

5. The courts in the early part of this century gave relatively little credence to claims of superior administrative fact-gathering capacity and expertise. As a result courts often permitted full trials in court of the issues already resolved by the agency. Only under the Roosevelt Court was begun the withdrawal of the presumption of complete, or "de novo," judicial review and the insistence upon deference to administrative findings. In this perspective Justice Frankfurter's opinion in *Universal Camera* served to further bolster the credibility of fact finding by administrative law judges. But does this opinion go too far? Is it not plausible, based on experience with many such cases and consistent with achieving the policy goals of the nation's new labor laws, that the NLRB itself might believe that the Chairman was "set up" by his superiors? Is it not plausible that experienced NLRB members might conclude that management had hounded the Chairman into taking unwise actions, or that in such uncertain cases labor law ought to presume this to be true unless the company can show it isn't? Recall that *Vermont Yankee* and the current trend in administrative law is to defer to discretionary agency actions.

6. During the New Deal, political liberals supported deference to agency decision making in part because the Court repeatedly applied the philosophy of laissez faire to strike down government regulation. Administrative agencies developed and implemented New Deal policies at a time when courts opposed these policies. Today we find that a politically conservative Supreme Court is limiting judicial review of agency actions and inactions. Hence, like the New Deal liberals, conservatives support agency discretion. Discuss this administrative law/politics paradox. Is it just simply a change in the guard—conservatives are now dominating national politics and are in the majority on the Supreme Court—which explains the current support for administrative authority? Consider the difference between Justice Rehnquist's majority opinion and Justice Marshall's concurring opinion in *Heckler v. Chaney*. In this case, conservatives and liberal justices deferred to administrative interpretation, but their reasoning for doing so differed substantially. How would you describe the difference between contemporary political liberal and conservative jurisprudence on judicial review of agency action and inaction?

7. Should agencies have standing to sue other agencies where there appears to be some conflict in the policies and operations of the two? See *Director v. Newport News Shipbuilding and Dry Dock*, 514 U.S. 122 (1995). The Court said no. Is this result consistent with the most recent cases reported in this chapter? In *Franklin v. Massachusetts*, 505 U.S. 788 (1992), state officials sued to force review of the way the Secretary of Commerce, under orders from the President, allocated to various districts for election purposes the population of Americans who in fact resided abroad. The Court held the decisions unreviewable. Indeed, it suggested that the actions of the President per se are rarely if ever final, since they will be implemented elsewhere.

CHAPTER 11
LIABILITY

T he three chapters in this part apply law to several recurring problems in public administration, describing real-world applications of the legal principles explained in prior chapters. For example, chapter 12 (on licensing issues in areas ranging from drivers' licenses to licenses for nuclear power plants), and chapter 13 (on personnel decisions), extend your appreciation for the varying requirements of a hearing. These chapters also introduce some new legal principles that students of administration need to know. Despite differences of emphasis, these chapters fit together because each describes a problem that occurs at all levels of government, from the most powerful agencies in Washington, D.C., to small towns in rural America.

RESPONSIBILITIES AND LIABILITIES IN LAW

Up to this point we have focused mainly on the legal responsibilities of administrators. These are the things administrators ought to do in a given set of circumstances: hold a trial-type hearing, publish the draft of the proposed rule in the *Federal Register*, conduct an informal give-and-take with students before expelling them, and so forth. Nearly all the cases covered thus far declared for the first time that such responsibilities existed. That is, they held that where the law in a particular area was ambiguous, "from now on the law shall require in circumstances similar to those of this case. . . ." You can finish the sentence differently to suit each case.

The issue of legal liability by agencies raises a different question. If an agency or government official has a clear legal responsibility and fails to carry it out, how shall this failure be redressed? In all cases where courts declare new responsibilities, the court simply instructs the agency to follow the court's order. No question of compensation or liability arises unless the agency refuses to comply with the order.

In other circumstances, however, courts decide that people or institutions must provide some compensation for their past wrongs. When a court finds a person liable for wrongdoing it usually requires the person to pay money damages and/or that the person take action to prevent further harm. The idea of liability is so common that lawyers and students take it for granted. The law of contract defines a legally binding agreement and provides that damages be paid to a party who breaches the contract. The tort law of negligence holds that the wrongdoer must pay for the damages he or she caused. In criminal law a convicted person may be required to compensate society itself (in addition to paying restitution to victims) through payment of fines, incarceration in a jail or prison or, in a rare case, execution by the government as punishment for his or her crime.

Public administrators and governments are in many legal respects exposed to the same legal liabilities as any private citizen. No matter how incensed Chairman Dixon may have been at the advertisements of the Cinderella Finishing School, he would face the same civil liability as a private citizen if he punched Cinderella's president in the nose, and be exposed to the same criminal penalties for that act as well.

With some important exceptions—the soldier's legal authority to kill, for example—the criminal law applies equally to all of us. On the other hand, the law of government contracting is written specifically for application to government business, and it does not follow general contract law or the Uniform Commercial Code. *Tort law* falls somewhere in between. Torts are direct harms to people and property of a civil, rather than criminal nature. They include (in addition to negligence) assault, battery, false imprisonment, libel, slander, and so forth. For curious historical reasons, courts have not held governments in the United States to ordinary tort liability, but by statute and recent court decisions the tort liability of government has expanded. In one controversial area, the responsibility to protect the civil rights of citizens, the government and its officials have an even broader liability than private citizens.

LIABILITIES AND RESPONSIBILITIES DISTINGUISHED: AN IMPORTANT ILLUSTRATION

Before turning to the main business of this chapter, we consider a celebrated legal issue that will allow you to pin down the difference between responsibility and liability. The legal issue concerns the responsibility of public officials to present testimony and other tangible evidence they possess in court when properly subpoenaed to do so. The issue, as you may already have spotted, gained its notoriety during the Watergate scandal involving the Nixon administration, and during the impeachment of President Bill Clinton.

In the course of the criminal trials resulting from the 1972 burglary of the Democratic Party offices in the Watergate complex in Washington, D.C., the trial court subpoenaed tape recordings in President Richard Nixon's possession. Nixon insisted that the tapes were protected by the doctrine of executive privilege and that he therefore had no legal responsibility to turn them over. The Supreme Court held that he was legally obligated to produce them.[1] It said in part:

However, neither the doctrine of separation of powers, nor the need for confidentiality of high level communications, without more, can sustain an absolute, unqualified presidential privilege of immunity from judicial process under all circumstances. The President's need for complete candor and objectivity from advisers calls for great deference from the courts. However, when the privilege depends solely on the broad, undifferentiated claim of public interest in the confidentiality of such conversations, a confrontation with other values arises. Absent a claim of need to protect military, diplomatic or sensitive national security secrets, we find it difficult to accept the argument that even the very important interest in confidentiality of presidential communications is significantly diminished by production of such material for *in camera* inspection with all the protection that a district court will be obliged to provide.

You might think that if a president of the United States must produce evidence in court, then everyone must do so, there being no stronger claim than that of executive privilege. In fact, there are stronger kinds of privileges recognized in law. If, for example, the president or any administrator refused to testify on the grounds that the testimony would incriminate him, the courts would generally honor the refusal. (Trial judges can, however, conduct hearings to determine the validity of a claim of privilege on this or any other ground.) President Nixon invoked no such claim, and the Supreme Court ordered him to produce the materials. He did so, and the rest is history. But what if Nixon had refused? Here the difference between responsibility and liability may be seen. In the case of a sitting president, he is only liable to impeachment and removal from office as long as he is president. Nixon's was the rare case in which the courts could impose no liability on him for refusing. Only the Congress could do so. Special Prosecutor Kenneth Starr's 1998 impeachment prosecution of President Clinton, particularly with respect to Clinton's possible perjury in a civil suit while he was president, involves the same distinction.[2]

TORT LIABILITY OF GOVERNMENT FOR ACTS OF OFFICIALS

When a court concludes that a private person or institution has committed a tort, a wrong directed against the

1. *United States v. Nixon*, 418 U.S. 683, 706 (1974).

2. For a discussion of the issues involved in compelling a president to testify in a civil case, see *Clinton v. Jones*, 520 U.S. 681 (1997).

plaintiff or the plaintiff's property, the court then normally awards some money to the plaintiff. In some instances the court simply tries to estimate the dollar value of the plaintiff's losses and orders compensation. Where, for example, the plaintiff loses property in an auto accident caused by the defendant, the damages will cover the property the plaintiff lost. In cases of personal injury, however, courts may award for pain and suffering as well as direct medical expenses, which makes ascertainment of damages less certain. Furthermore, in some cases—libel and slander for example—the plaintiff's damages are very hard to estimate. A further category of damages that a court may award called *punitive damages* (or sometimes exemplary damages) are intended to punish and deter the wrongdoer, as well as others, from doing the same thing in the future. Although punitive damages awards typically go to the injured party, the sum awarded is not directly related to the injured party's actual losses.

Tort law has two basic goals: to compensate people when they are harmed by others and to discourage people from engaging in behavior that may cause harm in the first place.[3] You might assume that government officials or the government itself should be expected to provide the same standard of care toward people as anyone else. One could argue that the state should even owe a *higher* duty of care toward its citizens than its citizens owe each other. But American law evolved in virtually the opposite direction. Borrowing from the English principle that "the king can do no wrong," the courts early on held that people could sue the government in tort only when the government by statute gave them permission to do so. This doctrine of "sovereign immunity" would seem particularly out of place in a governmental system formed in opposition to a monarchy, and whose constitution forbids titles of nobility. Nevertheless, until Congress adopted the Federal Tort Claims Act (FTCA) in 1946, tort suits against the federal government got nowhere in court. In the strictest legal sense the government simply could not commit a tort because no law recognized that possibility. Congress did pass many "private bills" to compensate victims of government torts. In fact, one purpose for Congress's adopting the FTCA was to get rid of this time-consuming duty.[4]

A number of valid arguments have been advanced for the doctrine of sovereign immunity. A lawsuit filed by one private citizen against another is a costly, time-consuming process. Often the defendant must cease pursuing some course of action until the lawsuit is resolved. But, by definition, if a government is sovereign over its citizens those citizens cannot make the functions of their government come to a grinding halt simply by filing a lawsuit.[5] Besides, lawsuits raise the possibility that the sovereign's treasury will have to pay damages, or its employees perform services—consequences that could hamper effective public administration. These arguments do have some merit. But as you read the cases below, ask yourself whether Congress and the courts have struck a wise balance between the requirements of sovereignty and the rule of law, between the need for effective administration of government and the ideal of legality. Is not the essence of democracy that law *does* limit the authority of the sovereign? Also you may note that the sovereign (in this case government and administration) is made up of actual human beings, and such human beings have a tendency to commit wrongs, whether it be on purpose, by accident, or through negligence. The king, in other words, can do wrong and rule of law and fairness requires that such wrongs be corrected.

The FTCA on first reading seems to strike a proper balance. Its most pertinent part reads: "The United States shall be liable, respecting the provisions of this title relating to tort claims, in the same manner and to the same extent as a private individual under like circumstances." Note that the act only creates liability for the government as a separate legal entity. It creates no individual liability on the part of the officials themselves. The act, at least according to one plausible reading of these words, applies the private rules of tort to public actions: If while doing your job you negligently drive a truck into someone else's

---

3. See G. Edward White, *Tort Law in America: An Intellectual History* (New York: Oxford University Press, 1980).

4. See Peter H. Schuck, *Suing Government: Citizen Remedies for Official Wrong* (New Haven, Conn.: Yale University Press, 1983).

5. See Phillip J. Cooper, "The Supreme Court on Government Liability: The Nature and Origins of Sovereign and Official Immunity," *Administration and Society* 16 (1984): 257.

truck, your company is liable to pay the damages; so too, when a soldier negligently drives one tank into another, the government must pay the damages. In *Feres v. United States*, 340 U.S. 135 (1950), one of the first judicial interpretations of the act, the Supreme Court rejected this plausible reading. It said that the act only covered the government when it did the sorts of things private people do. Since there exists no private army, navy, air force, FBI, etc., the act did not apply to the negligent acts of soldiers and police. The *Feres* doctrine has since been limited, but Congress created the tort liability of law enforcement officials only in 1974.[6]

The original FTCA contained several exceptions. The most important excludes from coverage claims "based upon the exercise or performance or the failure to exercise or perform a discretionary function or duty on the part of a federal agency or an employee of the Government, whether or not the discretion involved be abused." Three years after the Supreme Court, in *Feres*, narrowly interpreted the coverage of the FTCA, it interpreted this exception very broadly. The "accordion words" in this exception are *discretionary function* and *discretion*. Expanded to their furthest, these words could cover every choice anyone makes. We have discretion to buy peas or beans for dinner, discretion whether to drink coffee or the whiskey that might cause us to injure another negligently if we then drive a car. Interpreted this broadly, the exception would swallow up the statute. Most narrowly, we can define governmental discretion as the top level of policy-making, whether by the White House or by the regulatory commissions themselves. While officially taking a position closer to the narrow interpretation, the Court actually applied the concept far more broadly than its words suggest.

The Court took this position in *Dalehite v. United States*, 346 U.S. 15 (1953). Henry G. Dalehite and 559 other people died in a tragic waterfront explosion in Texas City, Texas while loading ammonium nitrate fertilizer being shipped to postwar France under a United States government aid program. Dalehite's heirs and others in the consolidated case filed claims for $200,000,000. In general, a person acts negligently when he or she fails to use the standard of care a reasonable and prudent person would adopt in the circumstances. Here it was alleged that the fertilizer, which had been coated with a flammable substance to prevent it from caking in the bags, had not been properly labeled so as to warn handlers of the fire danger. We can assume that a court would have found a private company that acted thusly to be negligent and liable.

However, the packaging and shipping of the fertilizer were part of a government program. The Court interpreted *discretion* to cover all the judgmental or policy decisions made by experts at a planning rather than an operational level of government. It said, "The acts found to have been negligent were thus performed under the discretion of a plan developed at a high level under a direct delegation of plan-making authority from the apex of the Executive Department. The establishment of this plan . . . clearly required the exercise of expert judgment."[7] The plaintiffs lost in court, but they eventually received some compensation by virtue of a special private bill passed by Congress to compensate them. This of course put the burden of compensation back on congressional shoulders.

The case nicely illustrates the inevitable open-endedness of legal reasoning. The judgment depends much less on formal legal analysis than on deeply ingrained judicial hunches and values. The judges in this close (4-3) majority presumably felt a primary obligation to the treasury of the United States and the taxpayers who support it. They refused to authorize the expenditure of large sums because Congress had not clearly approved their doing so. Yet judges starting with different values and hunches would likely reach the opposite result. Judges who believe that those who are injured through no fault of their own should not bear the cost of the loss because others *have* been at fault might have ordered the government to pay. Judges might further believe: (1) that making those at fault pay for losses they cause will encourage greater care and less harm in the long run; and (2) that the fairest

---

6. See Howard Ball, "The U.S. Supreme Court's Glossing of the Federal Tort Claims Act: Statutory Construction and Veterans' Tort Action," *Western Political Quarterly* 41 (1988): 529.

7. 346 U.S. 15 (1953), 39–40.

social response to catastrophic loss is to spread the loss to the entire population, either through insurance covered by many thousands of premiums or through the government supported by taxpayers. These judges might have believed the government should pay for the loss here. The fact that the decision to ship fertilizer to France was "discretionary" in this view simply does not change the reasons why the government should reimburse honest citizens for their losses in this disaster.

The question raised in many tort liability cases, therefore, is whether the agency, administration, or government employee responsible for the alleged tort acted within their discretionary authority and whether such discretionary action creates liability. In the years since *Dalehite* the pendulum has swung away from "pro-government" interpretations, but now it may be swinging back. The legal distinction remains between decisions made at the planning stage and those made at an operational level and is generally accepted. The real error in *Dalehite*, then, is that the causes of the fire, bad labeling and careless handling of the bags, really occurred at the operational, not the planning level. However, establishing a link between an alleged injury and government action requires more than sorting out the facts. Indeed, judicial interpretation of "the facts" in government tort liability cases determines whether the government has met its "duty of care" or not. As you read these cases pay close attention to the judicial process of constructing liability through the interpretation of facts. You will see how the expansion of government liability in *Indian Towing Co., Inc. v. U.S.* (1955) and *Griffin v. U.S.* (1974) rests on a welfare-state theory of the government's obligation to its citizens. According to this theory, once the state decides to become involved in certain activities, such as regulating lighthouses and inspecting vaccines, the state has an affirmative obligation to protect its citizens from negligent actions by government officials. In contrast, you will see in *Allen v. United States* (1987) and *DeShaney v. Winnebago County Social Services* (1989) how the courts have undermined this theory in recent years by reducing the scope of the state's obligation and reinstating the narrow interpretation, articulated in *Dalehite*, of citizen rights under the Federal Tort Claims Act.

Indian Towing Co., Inc. v. United States

350 U.S. 61 (1955) 5-4
+ Warren, Black, Frankfurter, Douglas, Harlan
– Reed, Burton, Clark, Minton

[A towed barge belonging to the Indian Towing Company went aground on an island in the Mississippi River and its cargo of fertilizer was damaged. The company alleged that the grounding was due solely to the failure of a Coast Guard-operated warning light on the island. The company brought suit under the Federal Tort Claims Act to recover the damages it suffered, claiming that the light's failure was due to: (1) the failure of responsible Coast Guard officials to check the light's battery and sun relay system; (2) the failure of a chief petty officer to inspect electrical connections exposed to the weather; (3) the failure to check the light for a period of 24 days before the grounding; and (4) the failure to repair the light or give warning that it wasn't working. The company alleged also that there was a loose connection that could have been discovered with a proper inspection. The district court and United State Court of Appeal for the Fifth Circuit found in favor of the government.]

Justice Frankfurter delivered the opinion of the Court

The relevant provisions of the Federal Tort Claims Act are 28 U.S.C. §§ 1346(b), 2674, and 2680(a):

§ 1346(b). ". . . the district courts . . . shall have exclusive jurisdiction of civil actions on claims against the United States, for money damages, accruing on and after January 1, 1945, for injury or loss of property, or personal injury or death caused by the negligent or wrongful act or omission of any employee of the Government while acting within the scope of his office or employment, under circumstances where the United States, if a private person, would be liable to the claimant in accordance with the law of the place where the act or omission occurred."

§ 2674. "The United States shall be liable . . . in the same manner and to the same extent as a private individual under like circumstances, but shall not be liable for interest prior to judgment or for punitive damages."

§ 2680. The provisions of this chapter and section 1346(b) of this title shall not apply to—

"(a) Any claim based upon an act or omission of an employee of the Government, exercising due care, in the execution of a statute or regulation, whether or not such statute or regulation be valid, or based upon the exercise or performance or the failure to exercise or perform a discretionary function or duty on the part of a federal agency or an employee of the Government, whether or not the discretion involved be abused."

The question is one of liability for negligence at what this Court has characterized the "operation level" of governmental activity. *Dalehite v. United States*, 346 U.S. 15, 42. The Government concedes that the exception of § 2680 relieving from liability for negligent "exercise of judgment" (which is the way the Government paraphrases a "discretionary function" in § 2680(a)) is not involved here, and it does not deny that the Federal Tort Claims Act does provide for liability in some situations on the "operational level" of its activity. But the Government contends that the language of § 2674 (and the implications of § 2680) imposing liability "in the same manner and to the same extent as a private individual under like circumstances . . ." must be read as excluding liability in the performance of activities which private persons do not perform. Thus, there would be no liability for negligent performance of "uniquely governmental functions." The Government reads the statute as if it imposed liability to the same extent as would be imposed on a private individual "under the same circumstances." But the statutory language is "under like circumstances," and it is horn-book tort law that one who undertakes to warn the public of danger and thereby induces reliance must perform his "good Samaritan" task in a careful manner.

Furthermore, the Government in effect reads the statute as imposing liability in the same manner as if it were a municipal corporation and not as if it were a private person, and it would thus push the courts into the "non-governmental"–"governmental" quagmire that has long plagued the law of municipal corporations. A comparative study of the cases in the forty-eight States will disclose an irreconcilable conflict. More than that, the decisions in each of the States are disharmonious and disclose the inevitable chaos when courts try to apply a rule of law that is inherently unsound. The fact of the matter is that the theory whereby municipalities are made amenable to liability is an endeavor, however awkward and contradictory, to escape from the basic historical doctrine of sovereign immunity. The Federal Tort Claims Act cuts the ground from under that doctrine. . . .

While the Government disavows a blanket exemption from liability for all official conduct furthering the "unique-ly governmental" activity in any way, it does claim that there can be no recovery based on the negligent performance of the activity itself, the so-called "end-objective" of the particular governmental activity. Let us suppose that the Chief Petty Officer going in a Coast Guard car to inspect the light on Chandeleur Island first negligently ran over a pedestrian; later, while he was inspecting the light, he negligently tripped over a wire and injured someone else; he then forgot to inspect an outside connection and that night the patently defective connection broke and the light failed, causing a ship to go aground and its cargo of triple super phosphate to get wet; finally the Chief Petty Officer on his way out of the lighthouse touched a key to an uninsulated wire to see that it was carrying current, and the spark he produced caused a fire which sank a nearby barge carrying triple super phosphate. Under the Government's theory, some of these acts of negligence would be actionable, and some would not. But is there a rational ground, one that would carry conviction to minds not in the grip of technical obscurities, why there should be any difference in result? The acts were different in time and place but all were done in furtherance of the officer's task of inspecting the lighthouse and in furtherance of the Coast Guard's task in operating a light on Chandeleur Island. Moreover, if the United States were to permit the operation of private lighthouses— not at all inconceivable—the Government's basis of differentiation would be gone and the negligence charged in this case would be actionable. Yet there would be no change in the character of the Government's activity in the places where it operated a lighthouse, and we would be attributing bizarre motives to Congress were we to hold that it was predicating liability on such a completely fortuitous circumstance—the presence or absence of identical private activity.

While the area of liability is circumscribed by certain provisions of the Federal Tort Claims Act, see 28 U.S.C. § 2680, all Government activity is inescapably "uniquely governmental" in that it is performed by the Government. In a case in which the Federal Crop Insurance Corporation, a wholly Government-owned enterprise, was sought to be held liable on a crop-insurance policy on the theory that a private insurance company would be liable in the same situation, this Court stated: "Government is not partly public or partly private, depending upon the governmental pedigree of the type of a particular activity or the manner in which the Government conducts it." *Federal Crop Insurance Corp. v.*

Merrill, 332 U.S. 380, 383–384. On the other hand, it is hard to think of any governmental activity on the "operational level," our present concern, which is "uniquely governmental," in the sense that its kind has not at one time or another been, or could not conceivably be, privately performed. . . .

The Coast Guard need not undertake the lighthouse service. But once it exercised its discretion to operate a light on Chandeleur Island and engendered reliance on the guidance afforded by the light, it was obligated to use due care to make certain that the light was kept in good working order; and, if the light did become extinguished, then the Coast Guard was further obligated to use due care to discover this fact and to repair the light or give warning that it was not functioning. If the Coast Guard failed in its duty and damage was thereby caused to petitioners, the United States is liable under the Tort Claims Act.

The Court of Appeals for the Firth Circuit considered *Feres v. United States*, 340 U.S. 135, and *Dalehite v. United States*, 346 U.S. 15, controlling. Neither case is applicable. *Feres* held only that "the Government is not liable under the Federal Tort Claims Act for injuries to servicemen where the injuries arise out of or are in the course of activity incident to service. Without exception, the relationship of military personnel to the Government has been governed exclusively by federal law." 340 U.S., at 146. And see *Brooks v. United States*, 337 U.S. 49. The differences between this case and *Dalehite* need not be labored. The governing factors in *Dalehite* sufficiently emerge from the opinion in that case.

Reversed.

Justice Reed, with whom Justice Burton, Justice Clark, and Justice Minton join, dissenting

The question of the liability of the United States for this negligence depends on the scope and meaning of the Federal Tort Claims Act. The history of the adoption of that Act has heretofore been thoroughly explained. Before its enactment, the immunity of the Government from such tort actions was absolute. The Act authorized suits against the Government under certain conditions. . . .

In *Feres v. United States*, 340 U.S. 135, we passed upon the applicability of the Act to claims by members of the armed services injured through the negligence of other military personnel. . . . [I]n *Feres* the Court was of the view that

the Act does not create new causes of action theretofore beyond the applicable law of torts. So, in determining whether an action for negligence in maintaining public lights is permissible, we must consider whether similar actions were allowed by the law of the place where the negligence occurred, prior to the Tort Claims Act, against public bodies otherwise subject to suit.

Dalehite v. United States, 346 U.S. 15, 42, followed the reasoning of *Feres*. . . . These two interpretive decisions have not caused Congress to amend the Federal Tort Claims Act. As a matter of fact, the catastrophe that gave rise to the *Dalehite* case was subsequently presented to Congress for legislative relief by way of compensation for the losses which resulted, as found by the trial court, partly from the negligence of the Coast Guard. Throughout the reports, discussion and enactment of the relief act, there was no effort to modify the Tort Claims Act so as to change the law, in any respect, as interpreted by this Court in *Feres* and *Dalehite*. . . . One cannot say that when a statute is interpreted by this Court we must follow that interpretation in subsequent cases unless Congress has amended the statute. . . . [W]e should continue to hold, as a matter of *stare decisis* and as the normal rule, that inaction of Congress, after a well-known and important decision of common knowledge, is "an aid in statutory construction . . . useful at times in resolving statutory ambiguities." *Helvering v. Reynolds*, 313 U.S. 428, 432. The nonaction of Congress should decide this controversy in the light of the previous rulings. The reasons which led to the conclusions against creating new and novel liabilities in the *Feres* and *Dalehite* cases retain their persuasiveness.

Griffin v. United States

500 F.2D 1059, UNITED STATES COURT
OF APPEALS FOR THE THIRD CIRCUIT (1974) 2-1

[Mrs. Griffin had become a quadriplegic as a result of a faulty lot (Lot 56) of polio vaccine. She settled out of court with the manufacturer of the vaccine but sued under the Federal Tort Claims Act charging negligence on the part of the Division of Biological Standards (DBS) of the Department of Health, Education, and Welfare, which had routinely inspected the lot and allowed it to be distributed for public use. Subsequent tests proved

Lot 56 did not meet federal standards for release to public use. The District Court awarded Mrs. Griffin damages in excess of $2,000,000.]

Rosenn, Circuit Judge

The threshold question confronting us is whether this action is barred because of the "discretionary function" exception to the Torts Claims Act. . . .

The Government contends that the decision to release Lot 56 involved the exercise of a discretionary function. It argues that the determination called for by the regulation . . . that the neurovirulence of a particular lot does not exceed that of the "reference strain" involves the exercise of judgment. It maintains that Congress intended, by the discretionary function exception, § 2680(a), to exclude all claims "arising from acts of a regulatory nature."

We believe that the construction of 2680(a) urged upon us by the Government is too broad. Activity of any consequence is rarely without its judgmental component. The effect of accepting the Government's contention would effectively immunize all Governmental activity from judicial review except the most ministerial acts. In its landmark decision, *Dalehite v. United States* . . . the Supreme Court explicitly recognized that not all activity involving judgment is necessarily encompassed within the Act's exception: "The 'discretion' protected by the section is not that of the judge—a power to decide within the limits of positive rules of law subject to judicial review. It is the discretion of the executive or the administrator to act according to one's judgment of the best course, a concept of substantial historical ancestry in American law. . . ." The decisions held discretionary in *Dalehite* involved, at minimum, some consideration as to the feasibility or practicability of Government programs. Such decisions involved considerations of public policy, calling for a balance of such factors as cost of Government programs against the potential benefit. The Court stated: "[The discretionary function] also includes determinations made by executives or administrators in establishing plans, specifications or schedules of operations. Where there is room for *policy* judgment and decision, there is discretion." [Emphasis supplied.] . . . Where decisions have not involved policy judgments as to the public interest, the courts have not held the decisions to be immune from judicial review. . . .

To determine the applicability of the discretionary function exception, therefore, we must analyze not merely whether judgment was exercised but also whether the nature of the judgment called for policy considerations. . . .

Plaintiffs, in the instant case, challenge solely the manner by which the regulation was implemented. They contend that in approving a particular lot, Lot 56, for release to the public, DBS failed to comply with the standard established by the Surgeon General.

The issue before us, therefore, is whether the implementation of regulation 73.114(b)(1)(iii) by DBS involved a "discretionary function." To decide this question we must first determine exactly what the regulation required be done in determining whether to release a particular lot.

The crucial action in approving a particular test lot for polio vaccine manufacture was the determination that the neurovirulence of the test lot "[did] not exceed" that of the NIH "reference strain." The regulation required a "comparative analysis" of the monkey neurovirulence test results of a particular test lot with the monkey neurovirulence test results of the reference strain. The regulation enumerates five criteria as evidence of neurovirulence: the number of animals showing lesions characteristic of poliovirus infection, the number of animals showing lesions other than those characteristic of poliovirus infection, the severity of the lesions, the degree of dissemination of the lesions, and the rate of occurrence of paralysis not attributable to the mechanical injury resulting from inoculation trauma.

Plaintiffs contend that the test lot could not be approved if it exceeded the reference strain with respect to any *one* of the five enumerated criteria. Under this interpretation of the regulation DBS could not approve a lot which minimally exceeded the reference strain with respect to any one criterion, even if DBS considered that criterion the poorest indicia of neurovirulence of the enumerated criteria, and even though the test lot was far superior to the reference strain with respect to the other four criteria.

We do not agree with this construction of the regulation. The regulation merely lists five criteria as evidence of neurovirulence and calls for a "comparative analysis." DBS has consistently construed the regulation as permitting it to weight the criteria in accordance with the degree to which it believed each criterion reflected neurovirulence.

The Supreme Court has stated on another occasion: "Since this involves an interpretation of an administrative regulation a court must necessarily look to the administrative construction of the regulation if the meaning of the words used is in doubt. . . . [T]he ultimate criterion is the administrative interpretation, which becomes of controlling weight unless it is plainly erroneous or inconsistent with the regulation." *Bowles v. Seminole Rock and Sand Co.*, 325 U.S. 410, 413–414 (1945). We find the DBS interpretation of the regulation to allow weighting of the five criteria of neurovirulence neither "plainly erroneous" nor "inconsistent with the regulation."

We acknowledge that under DBS' construction of the regulation, the implementation called for a judgment determination as to the degree to which each of the enumerated criteria indicated neurovirulence in monkeys. The judgment, however, was that of a professional measuring neurovirulence. It was not that of a policy-maker promulgating regulations by balancing competing policy considerations in determining the public interest. Neither was it a policy planning decision nor a determination of the feasibility or practicability of a government program. At issue was a scientific, but not policy-making, determination as to whether each of the criteria listed in the regulation was met and the extent to which each such factor accurately indicated neurovirulence. DBS' responsibility was limited to merely executing the policy judgments of the Surgeon General. It had no authority to formulate new policy in the immunization program.

Where the conduct of the Government employees in implementing agency regulations required only performance of scientific evaluation and not the formulation of policy, we do not believe that the conduct is immunized from judicial review as a "discretionary function." As Judge Waterman of the Second Circuit has stated: "The fact that judgments of government officials occur in areas requiring professional expert evaluation does not necessarily remove those judgments from the examination of courts by classifying them as discretionary functions under the Act." *Hendry v. United States*, 418 F.2d 774, 783 (2d Cir. 1969). . . .

The case will be remanded for proceedings consistent with this opinion.

The two preceding cases do not alter the immunity granted for discretionary activities. Documents uncovered in the 1990s by the President's Advisory Committee on Human Radiation Experiments established that the managers of the nuclear bomb tests in the 1950s knew of the radiation dangers of the tests, but chose to conduct them close to major population centers in order to get better information on fallout. Nevertheless, that finding would not upset the decision that all atomic testing, harmful to many civilians though it was, remained immune from tort claims. *Allen v. United States*, 816 F.2d 1417 (10th Cir., 1987) is the case in point here. We also think this case is important because it reveals the intersection between two federal statutes which enabled the Circuit Court judges to formulate their view that the U.S. government is not liable for radiation toxic torts. Congress passed the Radiation Exposure Compensation Act and it was signed by President George H. W. Bush on October 15, 1990. He stated that the legislation would establish a compensation system in the executive branch that could not otherwise be administered efficiently without the expense and delay of litigation. Plaintiffs in *Allen v. U.S.* were left with a legislative versus judicial form of recovery/compensation. The Act provides that individuals can recover $50,000 if they prove they lived downwind from the government's radiation test site in Nevada. In 1990, 100 million dollars was authorized for the trust fund; the following session, this amount was replaced with "such sums as may be necessary" (HR Conf. Rep. 101–923, 1990 WL 201558). The Fund is to operate for 22 years from the date of enactment. By the same token, while the Food and Drug Administration (FDA) knew as early as 1982 that breast implants were subject to leakage and other complications, yet took no action until 1990, the FDA had no liability in tort for its inaction.[8]

Cases litigated directly under the FTCA against the federal government arguably reach a moderate balance between the value of sovereign immunity and the value that innocent individuals should not bear the costs of harm that others, including the government, do to them. But what of actions brought against state and local

---

8. See "Breast Implant Settlement Creates a Medical Rush to Cash In," *New York Times*, September 18, 1995.

governments? Here we encounter a provision of federal law, section 1983 of Title 42 of the U.S. Code. Originally passed in 1871 during Reconstruction, 1983 reads:

Every person who, under color of any statute, ordinance, regulation, custom, or usage of any State or Territory, subjects or causes to be subjected, any citizen of the United States or other person within the jurisdiction of thereof to the deprivation of any rights, privileges, or immunities secured by the Constitution and laws, shall be liable to the party injured. . . .

While section 1983 reads as if it imposes individual liability (and would thus belong in the next section of this chapter), courts have interpreted it as imposing liability on the government itself. Most suits against state and local officials under section 1983 have claimed a violation of the due process rights of individuals injured by government action. But what, practically, counts as a violation of due process? What if government social workers ignore evidence that a child under their care is being abused, fail to remove the child from the home, and a parent inflicts permanent brain damage on the child? What if a police officer engaged in a high-speed chase negligently runs over and kills an innocent person? What if a county sheriff hires a relative of his, either knowing the person has a record of criminal violence, or simply refuses to do the usual background check, and the new deputy illegally inflicts a severe beating on a person?[9]

In each of these cases the Court has denied recovery under section 1983.

Allen v. United States

816 F.2D 1417, UNITED STATES COURT OF
APPEALS FOR THE TENTH CIRCUIT (1987) 3-0

[In a class action lawsuit against the United States, some twelve hundred named plaintiffs alleged five hundred deaths and injuries resulting from radioactive fallout from open-air atomic bomb testing in Nevada during the 1950s and 60s. The district court selected and tried twenty-four of these claims to arrive at a legal framework it could use to resolve the remaining cases. The district

court ruled against the government on nine claims and in favor of the government on fourteen claims, leaving one outstanding claim.]

Logan, Circuit Judge

In 1950 the AEC [Atomic Energy Commission] chose an area in Nevada as a testing site. The President approved this choice. Thereafter, between 1951 and 1962, eight series of open-air tests were conducted, with the President approving each series of tests. Over one hundred atomic bombs were detonated.

Each test explosion was executed according to detailed plans which the AEC officially reviewed and adopted. Separate plans for protecting the public, and for providing the public with appropriate information, were also adopted by the AEC. To actually execute the plans, however, the AEC delegated some of its authority. The AEC selected a "Test Manager" for each test series, who had some day-to-day discretion. The Test Manager could, for example, postpone a given test because of adverse weather conditions. The Test Manager in turn delegated authority to a Radiological Safety Officer (a "Radsafe Officer") who was in charge of implementing plans to avoid radiation dangers, and a Test Information Officer who was in charge of implementing plans to provide public information on the tests. Both the Radsafe Officer and the Test Information Officer also had some day-to-day discretion in performing their duties.

At trial, as a basis for government liability, plaintiffs singled out the alleged failure of the government, especially of the Radsafe Officers and the Test Information Officers, to fully monitor offsite fallout exposure and to fully provide needed public information on radioactive fallout. The district court focused on these two failures in finding government liability. . . .

The Federal Tort Claims Acts (FTCA) authorizes suits for damages against the United States

"for injury or loss of property, or personal injury or death caused by the negligent or wrongful act or omission of any employee of the Government while acting within the scope of his office or employment, under circumstances where the United States, if a private person, would be liable to the claimant in accordance with the law of the place where the act or omission occurred."

28 U.S.C. § 1346(b). In such suits, the United States is liable "in the same manner and to the same extent as a pri-

9. *Commissioners of Bryan County v. Brown*, 520 U.S. 397 (1997).

vate individual under like circumstances." 28 U.S.C. 2674. Suit is not allowed, however, for any claim

"based upon an act or omission of an employee of the Government, exercising due care, in the execution of a statute or regulation, whether or not such statute or regulation be valid or *based upon the exercise or performance or the failure to* on the part of a federal agency or an employee of the Government, *whether or not the discretion involved be abused."*

28 U.S.C. § 2680(a) (emphasis added). The key term, "discretionary function," is not defined. For over thirty-five years the federal courts have been attempting to define it.

Plaintiffs in the present case attempted to distinguish between the discretionary initiation of government programs, at the highest levels of administration, and the decisions involved in carrying out programs, at lower levels. Plaintiffs argued that while low-level decisions may involve some "judgment," they do not fall within the discretionary function exception of 2680(a). *See, e.g., Indian Towing Co. v. United States*, 350 U.S. 61 (1955) (reference to "operational level" of activity; no immunity found for government failure to operate lighthouse). The district court agreed, basing its finding of government liability squarely on a distinction between high-level and low-level governmental activity. . . .

After the district court judgment in the present case, the Supreme Court decided *United States v. S.A. Empresa de Viacao Aerea Rio Grandense (Varig Airlines)*, 467 U.S. 797 . . . (1984), in which it explicitly rejected distinctions based on the administrative level at which the challenged activity occurred. In *Varig*, various plaintiffs brought an FTCA suit against the United States, claiming that the Federal Aviation Administration (FAA) had negligently implemented plane inspection and design certification programs, allowing improper flammable materials and a defective heater system to be used to construct a specific Boeing 707 and a specific DeHavilland Dove. The planes in question caught fire and burned, killing most of those on board. The Supreme Court held, however, that the United States was immune from suit. The Court found that the contested FAA actions constituted the performance of a "discretionary function," exempt under 28 U.S.C. 2680(a) from potential FTCA liability. . . .

The plaintiffs in *Varig* focused on "low-level" decisions in their suit. They challenged the actual issuance by the FAA of design approval certificates for two plane types, the decision to enforce FAA standards with a particular "spot-check"

system, and the actual plane inspections that were and were not carried out under that system. . . . The Supreme Court found that each of these actions constituted a discretionary function, immune from suit under 2680(a). . . . The Court emphasized that it is "the nature of the conduct, rather than the status of the actor, that governs whether the discretionary function exception applies in a given case." *Varig*, 467 U.S. at 813. . . .

On appeal, plaintiffs contend that the AEC, in planning and conducting its monitoring and information programs, was not making the kind of policy judgments protected by § 2680(a). They point to the general statutory provisions instructing the AEC to consider public health and safety, and claim that these broad congressional directives leave no further room for discretion. We disagree.

In the case before us, as in *Varig*, the government actors had a general statutory duty to promote safety; this duty was broad and discretionary. In the case before us it was left to the AEC, as in *Varig* it was left to the Secretary of Transportation and the FAA, to decide exactly *how* to protect public safety. If anything, the obligation imposed on the FAA to protect public safety was greater and the discretion granted to the FAA by Congress was less, in the circumstances reviewed by *Varig*, than the comparable obligation imposed and discretion available to the AEC in the present case. . . . We cannot say that what was protected by the Supreme Court in *Varig* is now subject to liability.

Plaintiffs further contend that, even if the initial discretion granted by the AEC by statute was broad, test site personnel violated the AEC's own policy directives by failing to implement adequate protective measures. We cannot accept this argument either. Neither the plaintiffs nor the district court have been able to point to a single instance in which test site personnel ignored or failed to implement specific procedures mandated by the AEC for monitoring and informing the public. Indeed, the district court's conclusions appear to be based, at least in part, on perceived inadequacies in the AEC's radiological safety and information plans themselves. The court relied heavily on a 1954 report to the AEC by the Committee to Study Nevada Proving Grounds which was moderately critical of the measures taken up to that point to inform and warn the public. . . . The stated objective of this report, however, was "[t]o be a basis for Commission decisions on future policy." . . .

The operational plans the district court considered deficient embody those AEC policy decisions. As such, these plans clearly fall within the discretionary function exception.

Government liability cannot logically be predicated on the failure of test-site personnel to go beyond what the operational plans specifically required them to do. If, as the plaintiffs maintain, the AEC delegated "unfettered authority" to a Test Manager and his subordinates to implement public safety programs, this simply compels the conclusion that those officers exercised considerable discretion. Their actions, accordingly, also fall within the discretionary function exception.

It is irrelevant to the discretion issue whether the AEC or its employees were negligent in failing to adequately protect the public . . . When the conduct at issue involves the exercise of discretion by a government agency or employee, § 2680(a) preserves governmental immunity "whether or not the discretion involved be abused." For better or worse, plaintiffs here "obtain their 'right to sue from Congress [and] necessarily must take it subject to such restrictions as have been imposed.' " *Dalehite v. United States*, 346 U.S. 15.

. . . The *Dalehite* plaintiffs, like the present plaintiffs, were unable to point to any instances in which government employees acted negligently in performing specific, mandatory duties. The *Dalehite* plaintiffs instead argued primarily, just as the present plaintiffs argue here, that at various points the government could have made better plans, and that the government failed to fully investigate the hazards of the dangerous material involved and to fully inform and warn the nearby populace. . . .

The Supreme Court in *Dalehite* found every contested government decision, action, and omission to be the performance of a discretionary function, exempt from suit under § 2680(a): the cabinet-level decision to export the fertilizer, the lower-level failure to fully test for explosive properties, the Field Director's fertilizer production plan, the actual production of the fertilizer in accordance with the government specifications, and the specific decisions to bag the fertilizer at a certain temperature and to label the fertilizer in a certain way . . . The various actions and omissions of the Coast Guard, supervising the actual loading of the ships, were also exempted, as was the general failure to warn the nearby populace of potential dangers. . . .

. . . Given the Court's holding in *Dalehite*, reaffirmed in *Varig*, we must conclude that the government is immune from liability for the failure of the AEC administrators and employees to monitor radioactivity more extensively or to warn the public more fully than they did. . . .

Our decision here adheres to the principle enunciated by the Supreme Court of broad sovereign immunity. An inevitable consequence of that sovereign immunity is that the United States may escape legal responsibility for injuries that would be compensable if caused by a private party. There remain administrative and legislative remedies; we note the express authorization under 42 U.S.C. § 2012(i) for the government to make funds available for damages suffered by the public from nuclear incidents. Nonetheless, judicial reluctance to recognize the sometimes harsh principle of sovereign immunity explains much of the tangle of the prior FTCA cases. . . .

For the above reasons, we find all challenged actions surrounding the government atomic bomb tests in the 1950s and 1960s to be immune from suit, as the performance by a federal agency of a "discretionary function," protected by § 2680(a).

We reverse the district court's decision with regard to those nine claims in which the government was found to have liability and remand for further proceedings consistent with this opinion.

McKay, Circuit Judge, concurring: [omitted].

DeShaney v. Winnebago County Department of Social Services

489 U.S. 189 (1989) 6-3
+ *Rehnquist, White, Stevens, O'Connor, Scalia, Kennedy*
– *Brennan, Marshall, Blackmun*

[A four-year-old boy in Winnebago County, Wisconsin was severely beaten by his natural father, causing brain damage that required he live in an institution for the profoundly retarded for the rest of his life. The boy, Joshua DeShaney, and his mother, Melody DeShaney, brought suit against the County's Department of Social Services (DSS) and individual DSS employees, alleging that they failed to intervene to protect him against a known risk of violence and thus deprived him of his liberty without due process of law. The district court and the Court of Appeals for the Seventh Circuit held that a state agency's failure to render protective services to persons within its jurisdiction does not violate the due process clause of the Fourteenth Amendment. The DeShaneys appealed to the U.S. Supreme Court.]

Chief Justice Rehnquist delivered the opinion of the Court

I

The facts of this case are undeniably tragic. Petitioner Joshua DeShaney was born in 1979. In 1980, a Wyoming court granted his parents a divorce and awarded custody of Joshua to his father, Randy DeShaney. The father shortly thereafter moved to Neenah, a city located in Winnebago County, Wisconsin, taking the infant Joshua with him. There he entered into a second marriage, which also ended in divorce.

The Winnebago County authorities first learned that Joshua DeShaney might be a victim of child abuse in January 1982, when his father's second wife complained to the police, at the time of their divorce, that he had previously "hit the boy causing marks and [was] a prime case for child abuse." . . . The Winnebago County Department of Social Services (DSS) interviewed the father, but he denied the accusations, and DSS did not pursue them further. In January 1983, Joshua was admitted to a local hospital with multiple bruises and abrasions. The examining physician suspected child abuse and notified DSS, which immediately obtained an order from a Wisconsin juvenile court placing Joshua in the temporary custody of the hospital. Three days later, the county convened an ad hoc "Child Protection Team"—consisting of a pediatrician, a psychologist, a police detective, the county's lawyer, several DSS case workers, and various hospital personnel—to consider Joshua's situation. At this meeting, the Team decided that there was insufficient evidence of child abuse to retain Joshua in the custody of the court. The Team did, however, decide to recommend several measures to protect Joshua, including enrolling him in a preschool program, providing his father with certain counseling services, and encouraging his father's girlfriend to move out of the home. Randy

DeShaney entered into a voluntary agreement with DSS in which he promised to cooperate with them in accomplishing these goals.

Based on the recommendation of the Child Protection Team, the juvenile court dismissed the child protection case and returned Joshua to the custody of his father. A month later, emergency room personnel called the DSS caseworker handling Joshua's case to report that he had once again been treated for suspicious injuries. The caseworker concluded that there was no basis for action. For the next six months, the caseworker made monthly visits to the DeShaney home, during which she observed a number of suspicious injuries on Joshua's head; she also noticed that he had not been enrolled in school and that the girlfriend had not moved out. The caseworker dutifully recorded these incidents in her files, along with her continuing suspicions that someone in the DeShaney household was physically abusing Joshua, but she did nothing more. In November 1983, the emergency room notified DSS that Joshua had been treated once again for injuries that they believed to be caused by child abuse. On the caseworker's next two visits to the DeShaney home, she was told that Joshua was too ill to see her. Still DSS took no action.

In March 1984, Randy DeShaney beat 4-year-old Joshua so severely that he fell into a life-threatening coma. Emergency brain surgery revealed a series of hemorrhages caused by traumatic injuries to the head inflicted over a long period of time. Joshua did not die, but he suffered brain damage so severe that he is expected to spend the rest of his life confined to an institution for the profoundly retarded. Randy DeShaney was subsequently tried and convicted of child abuse. . . .

Because of the inconsistent approaches taken by the lower courts in determining when, if ever, the failure of a state or local governmental entity or its agents to provide an individual with adequate protective services constitutes a violation of the individual's due process rights . . . and the importance of the issue to the administration of state and local governments, we granted certiorari. . . .

II

The Due Process Clause of the Fourteenth Amendment provides that "[n]o State, shall . . . deprive any person of life, liberty, or property, without due process of law."

Petitioners contend that the State deprived Joshua of his liberty interest in "free[dom] from . . . unjustified intrusions on personal security," see *Ingraham v. Wright*, 430 US 651, 673 (1977), by failing to provide him with adequate protection against his father's violence. The claim is one invoking the substantive rather than procedural component of the Due Process Clause; petitioners do not claim that the State denied Joshua protection without according him appropriate procedural safeguards, see *Morrissey v. Brewer*, 408 US 471 (1972).*

But nothing in the language of the Due Process Clause itself requires the State to protect the life, liberty, and property of its citizens against invasion by private actors. The Clause is phrased as a limitation on the State's power to act, not as a guarantee of certain minimal levels of safety and security . . . [I]ts language cannot fairly be extended to impose an affirmative obligation on the State to ensure that those interests do not come to harm through other means. Nor does history support such an expansive reading of the constitutional text. . . . Its purpose was to protect the people from the State, not to ensure that the State protected them from each other. The Framers were content to leave the extent of governmental obligation in the latter area to the democratic political processes.

Consistent with these principles, our cases have recognized that the Due Process Clauses generally confer no affirmative right to governmental aid, even where such aid may be necessary to secure life, liberty, or property interests of which the government itself may not deprive the individual. See, e.g., *Harris v. McRae*, 448 US 297 (1980). . . . As we said in *Harris v. McRae*, "[a]lthough the liberty protected by the Due Process Clause affords protection against unwarranted government interference . . . it does not confer an entitlement to such [governmental aid] as may be necessary to realize all the advantages of that freedom." 448 US, at 317–318 . . . (emphasis added). If the Due Process Clause does not require the State to provide its citizens with partic-

ular protective services, it follows that the State cannot be held liable under the Clause for injuries that could have been averted had it chosen to provide them. As a general matter, then, we conclude that a State's failure to protect an individual against private violence simply does not constitute a violation of the Due Process Clause.

Petitioners contend, however, that even if the Due Process Clause imposes no affirmative obligation on the State to provide the general public with adequate protective services, such a duty may arise out of certain "special relationships" created or assumed by the State with respect to particular individuals. . . . Petitioners argue that such a "special relationship" existed here because the State knew that Joshua faced a special danger of abuse at his father's hands, and specifically proclaimed, by word and by deed, its intention to protect him against that danger. . . . Having actually undertaken to protect Joshua from this danger—which petitioners concede the State played no part in creating—the State acquired an affirmative "duty," enforceable through the Due Process Clause, to do so in a reasonably competent fashion. Its failure to discharge that duty, so the argument goes, was an abuse of governmental power that so "shocks the conscience," *Rochin v. California*, 342 US 165 (1952), as to constitute a substantive due process violation. . . .

We reject this argument. It is true that in certain limited circumstances the Constitution imposes upon the State affirmative duties of care and protection with respect to particular individuals. In *Estelle v. Gamble*, 429 US 97 (1976), we recognized that the Eighth Amendment's prohibition against cruel and unusual punishment Clause requires the State to provide adequate medical care to incarcerated prisoners. . . . We reasoned that because the prisoner is unable "'by reason of the deprivation of his liberty [to] care for himself,'" it is only "'just'" that the State be required to care for him. . . .

In *Youngberg v. Romeo*, 457 US 307 (1982), we extended this analysis beyond the Eighth Amendment setting, holding that the substantive component of the Fourteenth Amendment's Due Process Clause requires the State to provide involuntarily committed mental patients with such services as are necessary to ensure their "reasonable safety" from themselves and others. . . .

But these cases afford petitioners no help. Taken together, they stand only for the proposition that when the State

---

* Petitioners also argue that the Wisconsin child protection statutes gave Joshua an "entitlement" to receive protective services in accordance with the terms of the statute, an entitlement which would enjoy due process protection against state deprivation under our decision in *Board of Regents v. Roth*, 408 US 564. . . . (1972). . . . But this argument is made for the first time in petitioners' brief to this Court: it was not pleaded in the complaint, argued to the Court of Appeals as a ground for reversing the District Court, or raised in the petition for certiorari. We therefore decline to consider it here.

takes a person into its custody and holds him there against his will, the Constitution imposes upon it a corresponding duty to assume some responsibility for his safety and general well-being. . . . The rationale for this principle is simple enough: when the State by the affirmative exercise of its power so restrains an individual's liberty that it renders him unable to care for himself, and at the same time fails to provide for his basic human needs—e.g., food, clothing, shelter, medical care, and reasonable safety—it transgresses the substantive limits on state action set by the Eighth Amendment and the Due Process Clause. . . . The affirmative duty to protect arises not from the State's knowledge of the individual's predicament or from its expressions of intent to help him, but from the limitation which it has imposed on his freedom to act on his own behalf. . . .

Petitioners concede that the harms Joshua suffered did not occur while he was in the State's custody, but while he was in the custody of his natural father, who was in no sense a state actor. While the State may have been aware of the dangers that Joshua faced in the free world, it played no part in their creation, nor did it do anything to render him any more vulnerable to them. That the State once took temporary custody of Joshua does not alter the analysis, for when it returned him to his father's custody, it placed him in no worse position than that in which he would have been had it not acted at all; the State does not become the permanent guarantor of an individual's safety by having once offered him shelter. Under these circumstances, the State had no constitutional duty to protect Joshua.

It may well be that, by voluntarily undertaking to protect Joshua against a danger it concededly played no part in creating, the State acquired a duty under state tort law to provide him with adequate protection against that danger . . . But the claim here is based on the Due Process Clause of the Fourteenth Amendment, which, as we have said many times, does not transform every tort committed by a state actor into a constitutional violation. . . .

Judges and lawyers, like other humans, are moved by natural sympathy in a case like this to find a way for Joshua and his mother to receive adequate compensation for the grievous harm inflicted upon them. But before yielding to that impulse, it is well to remember once again that the harm was inflicted not by the State of Wisconsin, but by Joshua's father. The most that can be said of the state func-

tionaries in this case is that they stood by and did nothing when suspicious circumstances dictated a more active role for them. In defense of them it must also be said that had they moved too soon to take custody of the son away from the father, they would likely have been met with charges of improperly intruding into the parent-child relationship, charges based on the same Due Process Clause that forms the basis for the present charge of failure to provide adequate protection.

The people of Wisconsin may well prefer a system of liability which would place upon the State and its officials the responsibility for failure to act in situations such as the present one. They may create such a system, if they do not have it already, by changing the tort law of the State in accordance with the regular law-making process. But they should not have it thrust upon them by this Court's expansion of the Due Process Clause of the Fourteenth Amendment.

Affirmed.

Justice Brennan, with whom Justice Marshall and Justice Blackmun join, dissenting

"The most that can be said of the state functionaries in this case," the Court today concludes, "is that they stood by and did nothing when suspicious circumstances dictated a more active role for them." . . . Because I believe that this description of respondents' conduct tells only part of the story and that, accordingly, the Constitution itself "dictated a more active role" for respondents in the circumstances presented here, I cannot agree that respondents had no constitutional duty to help Joshua DeShaney.

It may well be, as the Court decides . . . that the Due Process Clause as construed by our prior cases creates no general right to basic governmental services. That, however, is not the question presented here; indeed, that question was not raised in the complaint, urged on appeal, presented in the petition for certiorari, or addressed in the briefs on the merits. No one, in short, has asked the Court to proclaim that, as a general matter, the Constitution safeguards positive as well as negative liberties.

This is more than a quibble over dicta; it is a point about perspective, having substantive ramifications. In a constitutional setting that distinguishes sharply between action and inaction, one's characterization of the misconduct alleged under § 1983 may effectively decide the case. Thus, by lead-ing off with a discussion (and rejection) of the idea that the Constitution imposes on the States an affirmative duty to take basic care of their citizens, the Court foreshadows—perhaps even preordains—its conclusion that no duty exist-ed even on the specific facts before us. This initial discussion establishes the baseline from which the Court assesses the DeShaneys' claim. . . .

The Court's baseline is the absence of positive rights in the Constitution and a concomitant suspicion of any claim that seems to depend on such rights. From this perspective, the DeShaneys' claim is first and foremost about inaction (the failure, here, of respondents to take steps to protect Joshua), and only tangentially about action (the establish-ment of a state program specifically designed to help chil-dren like Joshua). And from this perspective, holding these Wisconsin officials liable . . . would seem to punish an effort that we should seek to promote.

I would begin from the opposite direction. I would focus first on the action that Wisconsin *has* taken with respect to Joshua and children like him rather than on the actions that the State failed to take. Such a method is not new to this Court. Both *Estelle v. Gamble* and *Youngberg v. Romeo* began by emphasizing that the States had confined J. W. Gamble to prison and Nicholas Romeo to a psychiatric hospital. This initial action rendered these people helpless to help them-selves or to seek help from persons unconnected to the gov-ernment. . . . Cases from the lower courts also recognize that a State's actions can be decisive in assessing the consti-tutional significance of subsequent inaction. . . .

In striking down a filing fee as applied to divorce cases brought by indigents and in deciding that a local govern-ment could not entirely foreclose the opportunity to speak in a public forum . . . we have acknowledged that a State's actions—such as the monopolization of a particular path of relief—may impose upon the State certain positive duties. Similarly, *Shelley v. Kraemer*, 334 U.S. 1 (1948), and *Burton v. Wilmington Parking Authority*, 365 U.S. 715 (1961), sug-gest that a State may be found complicit in an injury even if it did not create the situation that caused the harm. . . .

. . . To put the point more directly, these cases signal that a State's prior actions may be decisive in analyzing the constitutional significance of its inaction. I thus would locate the DeShaneys' claims within the framework of cases like

Youngberg and *Estelle*, and more generally, *Boddie* and *Schneider*, by considering the actions that Wisconsin took with respect to Joshua.

Wisconsin has established a child-welfare system specifi-cally designed to help children like Joshua. Wisconsin law places upon the local departments of social services such as respondent . . . a duty to investigate reported instances of child abuse. . . . While other governmental bodies and pri-vate persons are largely responsible for the reporting of pos-sible cases of child abuse, . . . Wisconsin law channels all such reports to the local departments of social services for evaluation and, if necessary, further action. . . . Even when it is the sheriff's office or police department that receives a report of suspected child abuse, that report is referred to local social services departments for action, . . . the only exception to this occurs when the reporter fears for the child's *immediate* safety. . . . In this way, Wisconsin law invites—indeed, directs—citizens and other governmental entities to depend on local departments of social services such as respondent to protect children from abuse.

The specific facts before us bear out this view of Wisconsin's system of protecting children. Each time some-one voiced a suspicion that Joshua was being abused, that information was relayed to the Department for investigation and possible action. . . . (As to the extent of the social work-er's involvement in and knowledge of Joshua's predicament, her reaction to the news of Joshua's last and most devastat-ing injuries is illuminating: "I just knew the phone would ring some day and Joshua would be dead." 812 F2d 298, 300 (CA7 1987).)

Even more telling than these examples is the Department's control over the decision whether to take steps to protect a particular child from suspected abuse. While many different people contributed information and advice to this decision, it was up to the people at DSS to make the ultimate decision. . . . whether to disturb the fam-ily's current arrangements. . . . When Joshua first appeared at a local hospital with injuries signaling physical abuse, for example, it was DSS that made the decision to take him into temporary custody for the purpose of studying his situa-tion—and it was DSS, acting in conjunction with the Corporation Counsel, that returned him to his father. . . . Unfortunately for Joshua DeShaney, the buck effectively stopped with the Department. . . .

. . . Through its child-welfare program . . . the State of Wisconsin has relieved ordinary citizens and governmental bodies other than the Department of any sense of obligation to do anything more than report their suspicions of child abuse to DSS. If DSS ignores or dismisses these suspicions, no one will step in to fill the gap. Wisconsin's child-protection programs thus effectively confined Joshua DeShaney within the walls of Randy DeShaney's violent home until such time as DSS took action to remove him. Conceivably, then, children like Joshua are made worse off by the existence of this program when the persons and entities charged with carrying it out fail to do their jobs.

It simply belies reality, therefore, to contend that the State "stood by and did nothing" with respect to Joshua. . . . Through its child-protection program, the State actively intervened in Joshua's life and, by virtue of this intervention, acquired ever more certain knowledge that Joshua was in grave danger. These circumstances, in my view, plant this case solidly within the tradition of cases like *Youngberg* and *Estelle*. . . .

I would allow Joshua and his mother the opportunity to show that respondents' failure to help him arose, not out of the sound exercise of professional judgment that we recognized in *Youngberg* as sufficient to preclude liability . . . but from the kind of arbitrariness that we have in the past condemned.

. . . *Youngberg's* deference to a decisionmaker's professional judgment ensures that once a caseworker has decided, on the basis of her professional training and experience, that one course of protection is preferable for a given child, or even that no special protection is required, she will not be found liable for the harm that follows . . . . Moreover, that the Due Process Clause is not violated by merely negligent conduct . . . means that a social worker who simply makes a mistake of judgment under what are admittedly complex and difficult conditions will not find herself liable in damages under § 1983. . . .

. . . My disagreement with the Court arises from its failure to see that inaction can be every bit as abusive of power as action, that oppression can result when a State undertakes a vital duty and then ignores it. Today's opinion construes the Due Process Clause to permit a State to displace private sources of protection and then, at the critical moment, to shrug its shoulders and turn away from the harm that it has promised to try to prevent. Because I cannot agree that our Constitution is indifferent to such *indifference*, I respectfully dissent.

Justice Blackmun, dissenting

Today, the Court purports to be the dispassionate oracle of the law, unmoved by "natural sympathy." . . . But, in this pretense, the Court itself retreats into a sterile formalism which prevents it from recognizing either the facts of the case before it or the legal norms that should apply to those facts. As Justice Brennan demonstrates, the facts here involve not mere passivity, but active state intervention in the life of Joshua DeShaney—intervention that triggered a fundamental duty to aid the boy once the State learned of the severe danger to which he was exposed.

The Court fails to recognize this duty because it attempts to draw a sharp and rigid line between action and inaction. But such formalistic reasoning has no place in the interpretation of the broad and stirring clauses of the Fourteenth Amendment. Indeed, I submit that these clauses were designed, at least in part, to undo the formalistic legal reasoning that infected antebellum jurisprudence, which the late Professor Robert Cover analyzed so effectively in his significant work entitled *Justice Accused* (1975).

Like the antebellum judges who denied relief to fugitive slaves . . . the Court today claims that its decision, however harsh, is compelled by existing legal doctrine. On the contrary, the question presented by this case is an open one, and our Fourteenth Amendment precedents may be read more broadly or narrowly depending upon how one chooses to read them. Faced with the choice, I would adopt a "sympathetic" reading, one which comports with dictates of fundamental justice and recognizes that compassion need not be exiled from the province of judging. . . .

Poor Joshua! Victim of repeated attacks by an irresponsible, bullying, cowardly, and intemperate father, and abandoned by respondents who placed him in a dangerous predicament and who knew or learned what was going on, and yet did essentially nothing except, as the Court revealingly observes, "dutifully recorded these incidents in [their] files." It is a sad commentary upon American life, and constitutional principles—so full of late of patriotic fervor and proud proclamations about "liberty and justice for all," that this child, Joshua DeShaney, now is assigned to live out the remainder of his life profoundly retarded. Joshua and his mother, as petitioners here, deserve—but now are denied by this Court—the opportunity to have the facts of their case considered in the light of the constitutional protection that 42 USC § 1983 [42 USCS § 1983] is meant to provide.

County of Sacramento v. Lewis

523 U.S. 833 (1998) 9-0
+ *Souter, Rehnquist, O'Connor, Kennedy,*
  Ginsburg, Breyer, Stevens, Scalia, Thomas

[After petitioner James Smith, a county sheriff's deputy, responded to a call along with another officer, Murray Stapp, the latter returned to his patrol car and saw a motorcycle approaching at high speed, driven by Brian Willard, and carrying Philip Lewis, respondents' decedent, as a passenger. Stapp turned on his rotating lights, yelled for the cycle to stop, and pulled his car closer to Smith's in an attempt to pen the cycle in, but Willard maneuvered between the two cars and sped off. Smith immediately switched on his own emergency lights and siren and began a high-speed chase. The motorcycle eventually tipped over. Smith slammed on his brakes, but his car skidded into Lewis, causing massive injuries and death. The District Court granted summary judgment for Smith, but the Ninth Circuit reversed, holding that the appropriate degree of fault for substantive due process liability for high-speed police pursuits is deliberate indifference to, or reckless disregard for, a person's right to life and personal security.]

Justice Souter delivered the opinion of the Court

The issue in this case is whether a police officer violates the Fourteenth Amendment's guarantee of substantive due process by causing death through deliberate or reckless indifference to life in a high-speed automobile chase aimed at apprehending a suspected offender. We answer no, and hold that in such circumstances only a purpose to cause harm unrelated to the legitimate object of arrest will satisfy the element of arbitrary conduct shocking to the conscience, necessary for a due process violation.

I

On May 22, 1990, at approximately 8:30 p.m., petitioner James Everett Smith, a Sacramento County sheriff's deputy, along with another officer, Murray Stapp, responded to a call to break up a fight. Upon returning to his patrol car, Stapp saw a motorcycle approaching at high speed. It was operated by 18-year-old Brian Willard and carried Philip Lewis, respondents' 16-year-old decedent, as a passenger. Neither boy had anything to do with the fight that prompted the call to the police.

Stapp turned on his overhead rotating lights, yelled to the boys to stop, and pulled his patrol car closer to Smith's, attempting to pen the motorcycle in. Instead of pulling over in response to Stapp's warning lights and commands, Willard slowly maneuvered the cycle between the two police cars and sped off. Smith immediately switched on his own emergency lights and siren, made a quick turn, and began pursuit at high speed. For 75 seconds over a course of 1.3 miles in a residential neighborhood, the motorcycle wove in and out of oncoming traffic, forcing two cars and a bicycle to swerve off of the road. The motorcycle and patrol car reached speeds up to 100 miles an hour, with Smith following at a distance as short as 100 feet; at that speed, his car would have required 650 feet to stop.

The chase ended after the motorcycle tipped over as Willard tried a sharp left turn. By the time Smith slammed on his brakes, Willard was out of the way, but Lewis was not. The patrol car skidded into him at 40 miles an hour, propelling him some 70 feet down the road and inflicting massive injuries. Lewis was pronounced dead at the scene. . . .

The Court of Appeals for the Ninth Circuit [held] that "the appropriate degree of fault to be applied to high-speed police pursuits is deliberate indifference to, or reckless disregard for, a person's right to life and personal security," and conclud[ed] that "the law regarding police liability for death or injury caused by an officer during the course of a high-speed chase was clearly established" at the time of Philip Lewis's death. Since Smith apparently disregarded the Sacramento County Sheriff's Department's General Order on police pursuits, the Ninth Circuit found a genuine issue of material fact that might be resolved by a finding that Smith's conduct amounted to deliberate indifference:

The General Order requires an officer to communicate his intention to pursue a vehicle to the sheriff's department dispatch center. But defendants concede that Smith did not contact the dispatch center. The General Order requires an officer to consider whether the seriousness of the offense warrants a chase at speeds in excess of the posted limit. But here, the only apparent "offense" was the boys' refusal to stop when another officer told them to do so. The General Order requires an officer to consider whether the need for apprehension justifies the pursuit under existing conditions. Yet Smith apparently only "needed" to apprehend the boys because they refused to stop. The General Order requires an officer to consider whether the pursuit presents unreasonable hazards to life and property. But taking the facts here in the light most favorable to plaintiffs, there existed an unreasonable hazard to Lewis's and Willard's lives. The General Order also directs an officer to discontinue a pursuit when the hazards of continuing outweigh the benefits of immediate apprehension. But here, there was no apparent danger involved in permitting the boys to escape. There certainly was risk of harm to others in continuing the pursuit.

II

B

Since the time of our early explanations of due process, we have understood the core of the concept to be protection against arbitrary action:

The principal and true meaning of the phrase has never been more tersely or accurately stated than by Mr. Justice Johnson, in *Bank of Columbia v. Okely*, 17 U.S. 235, [(1819)]: "As to the words from Magna Charta, incorporated into the Constitution of Maryland, after volumes spoken and written with a view to their exposition, the good sense of mankind has at last settled down to this: that they were intended to secure the individual from the arbitrary exercise of the powers of government, unrestrained by the established principles of private right and distributive justice." *Hurtado v. California*, 110 U.S. 516 (1884).

It should not be surprising that the constitutional concept of conscience-shocking duplicates no traditional category of common-law fault, but rather points clearly away from liability, or clearly toward it, only at the ends of the tort law's spectrum of culpability. Thus, we have made it clear that the due process guarantee does not entail a body of constitutional law imposing liability whenever someone cloaked with state authority causes harm. In *Paul v. Davis*, 424 U.S. 693 (1976), for example, we explained that the Fourteenth Amendment is not a "font of tort law to be superimposed upon whatever systems may already be administered by the States," and in *Daniels v. Williams*, 474 U.S. at 332, we reaffirmed the point that "our Constitution deals with the large concerns of the governors and the governed, but it does not purport to supplant traditional tort law in laying down rules of conduct to regulate liability for injuries that attend living together in society." We have accordingly rejected the lowest common denominator of customary tort liability as any mark of sufficiently shocking conduct, and have held that the Constitution does not guarantee due care on the part of state officials; liability for negligently inflicted harm is categorically beneath the threshold of constitutional due process. It is, on the contrary, behavior at the other end of the culpability spectrum that would most probably support a substantive due process claim; conduct intended to injure in some way unjustifiable by any government interest is the sort of official action most likely to rise to the conscience-shocking level. See *Daniels v. Williams*, 474 U.S. at 331 ("Historically, this guarantee of due process has been applied to *deliberate* decisions of government officials to deprive a person of life, liberty, or property") (emphasis in original). . . .

But just as the description of the custodial prison situation shows how deliberate indifference can rise to a constitutionally shocking level, so too does it suggest why indifference may well not be enough for liability in the different circumstances of a case like this one. We have, indeed, found that deliberate indifference does not suffice for constitutional liability (albeit under the Eighth Amendment) even in prison circumstances when a prisoner's claim arises not from normal custody but from response to a violent disturbance. Our analysis is instructive here:

In making and carrying out decisions involving the use of force to restore order in the face of a prison disturbance, prison officials undoubtedly must take into account the very real threats the unrest presents to inmates and prison officials alike, in addition to the possible harms to inmates against whom force might be used. . . . In this setting, a deliberate indifference standard does not adequately capture the importance of such competing obligations, or convey the appropriate hesitancy to critique in hindsight decisions necessarily made in haste, under pressure, and frequently without the luxury of a second chance.

Whitley v. Albers, 475 U.S. at 320.

We accordingly held that a much higher standard of fault than deliberate indifference has to be shown for officer liability in a prison riot. In those circumstances, liability should turn on "whether force was applied in a good faith effort to maintain or restore discipline or maliciously and sadistically for the very purpose of causing harm." (internal quotation marks omitted). The analogy to sudden police chases (under the Due Process Clause) would be hard to avoid.

Like prison officials facing a riot, the police on an occasion calling for fast action have obligations that tend to tug against each other. Their duty is to restore and maintain lawful order, while not exacerbating disorder more than necessary to do their jobs. They are supposed to act decisively and to show restraint at the same moment, and their decisions have to be made "in haste, under pressure, and frequently without the luxury of a second chance." A police officer deciding whether to give chase must balance on one hand the need to stop a suspect and show that flight from the law is no way to freedom, and, on the other, the high-speed threat to everyone within stopping range, be they suspects, their passengers, other drivers, or bystanders.

To recognize a substantive due process violation in these circumstances when only mid-level fault has been shown would be to forget that liability for deliberate indifference to inmate welfare rests upon the luxury enjoyed by prison officials of having time to make unhurried judgments, upon the chance for repeated reflection, largely uncomplicated by the pulls of competing obligations. When such extended opportunities to do better are teamed with protracted failure even to care, indifference is truly shocking. But when unforeseen circumstances demand an officer's instant judgment, even precipitate recklessness fails to inch close enough to harmful purpose to spark the shock that implicates "the large concerns of the governors and the governed." *Daniels v. Williams*, 474 U.S. at 332. Just as a purpose to cause harm is needed for Eighth Amendment liability in a riot case, so it ought to be needed for Due Process liability in a pursuit case. Accordingly, we hold that high-speed chases with no intent to harm suspects physically or to worsen their legal plight do not give rise to liability under the Fourteenth Amendment, redressible by an action under § 1983. . . .

Smith was faced with a course of lawless behavior for which the police were not to blame. They had done nothing to cause Willard's high-speed driving in the first place, nothing to excuse his flouting of the commonly understood law enforcement authority to control traffic, and nothing (beyond a refusal to call off the chase) to encourage him to race through traffic at breakneck speed forcing other drivers

out of their travel lanes. Willard's outrageous behavior was practically instantaneous, and so was Smith's instinctive response. While prudence would have repressed the reaction, the officer's instinct was to do his job as a law enforcement officer, not to induce Willard's lawlessness, or to terrorize, cause harm, or kill. Prudence, that is, was subject to countervailing enforcement considerations, and while Smith exaggerated their demands, there is no reason to believe that they were tainted by an improper or malicious motive on his part.

Regardless whether Smith's behavior offended the reasonableness held up by tort law or the balance struck in law enforcement's own codes of sound practice, it does not shock the conscience, and petitioners are not called upon to answer for it under § 1983. The judgment below is accordingly reversed.

It is so ordered.

[Concurring opinions of Chief Justice Rehnquist and Justices Kennedy, O'Connor, Breyer, and Stevens omitted.]

Justice Scalia, with whom Justice Thomas joins, concurring in the judgment

Adhering to our decision in *[Washington v.] Glucksberg*, rather than ask whether the police conduct here at issue shocks my unelected conscience, I would ask whether our Nation has traditionally protected the right respondents assert. The first step of our analysis, of course, must be a "careful description" of the right asserted. Here the complaint alleges that the police officer deprived Lewis "of his Fourteenth Amendment right to life, liberty and property without due process of law when he operated his vehicle with recklessness, gross negligence and conscious disregard for his safety." I agree with the Court's conclusion that this asserts a substantive right to be free from "deliberate or reckless indifference to life in a high-speed automobile chase aimed at apprehending a suspected offender."

Respondents provide no textual or historical support for this alleged due process right, and, as in *Carlisle*, I would "decline to fashion a new due process right out of thin air." 517 U.S. at 429. Nor have respondents identified any precedential support. Indeed, precedent is to the contrary: "Historically, the guarantee of due process has been applied to *deliberate* decisions of government officials to deprive a person of life, liberty, or property." *Daniels v. Williams*, 474 U.S. 327 (1986). Though it is true, as the Court explains, that "deliberate indifference" to the medical needs of pretrial detainees, *City of Revere v. Massachusetts Gen. Hospital*, 463 U.S. 239 (1983), or of involuntarily committed mental patients, *Youngberg v. Romeo*, 457 U.S. 307 (1982), may violate substantive due process, it is not the deliberate indifference alone which is the "deprivation." Rather, it is that combined with "the State's affirmative act of restraining the individual's freedom to act on his own behalf—through incarceration, institutionalization, or other similar restraint of personal liberty," *DeShaney v. Winnebago County Dept. of Social Servs.* "When the State by the affirmative exercise of its power so restrains an individual's liberty that it renders him unable to care for himself, and *at the same time* fails to provide for his basic human needs . . . it transgresses the substantive limits on state action set by the . . . Due Process Clause." We have expressly left open whether, in a context in which the individual has *not* been deprived of the ability to care for himself in the relevant respect, "something less than intentional conduct, such as recklessness or 'gross negligence,' " can ever constitute a "deprivation" under the Due Process Clause. Needless to say, if it is an open question whether recklessness can *ever* trigger due process protections, there is no precedential support for a substantive-due-process right to be free from reckless police conduct during a car chase. . . .

If the people of the State of California would prefer a system that renders police officers liable for reckless driving during high-speed pursuits, "they may create such a system . . . by changing the tort law of the State in accordance with the regular law-making process." For now, they prefer not to hold public employees "liable for civil damages on account of personal injury to or death of any person or damage to property resulting from the operation, in the line of duty, of an authorized emergency vehicle . . . when in the immediate pursuit of an actual or suspected violator of the law." Cal. Veh. Code Ann. § 17004. It is the prerogative of a self-governing people to make that legislative choice. "Political society," as the Seventh Circuit has observed, "must consider not only the risks to passengers, pedestrians, and other drivers that high-speed chases engender, but also the fact that if police are forbidden to pursue, then many more suspects will flee—and successful flights not only reduce the number of crimes solved but also create their own risks for passengers and bystanders." *Mays v. City of East St. Louis*, 123 F.3d 999, 1003 (1997). In allocating such risks, the people of California and their elected representatives may vote their consciences. But for judges to overrule that democratically adopted policy judgment on the ground that it shocks *their* consciences is not judicial review but judicial governance.

I would reverse the judgment of the Ninth Circuit, not on the ground that petitioners have failed to shock my still, soft voice within, but on the ground that respondents offer no textual or historical support for their alleged due process right. Accordingly, I concur in the judgment of the Court.

What if police officers fail to protect someone they are supposed to protect and this failure results in a major injury to that person? Are the police officers or the township liable? We have already said that the pendulum is swinging in the direction of giving more discretionary authority to the government in cases concerning tort liability. In a case that further confirmed this direction, *Castle Rock v. Gonzales* 545 U.S. 748 (2005), the Supreme Court said, in a 7–2 decision, that police officers cannot be held liable for their inaction even if clear commands ordering them to act in specific circumstances exist. Jessica Gonzales had obtained a restraining order against her ex-husband when she got a divorce. The notice to the police on the back of the order stated that the police "shall use every reasonable means to enforce this restraining order . . . [and they] shall arrest, or . . . seek a warrant . . . when [the police] have information amounting to probable cause that the restrained person has violated th[e] order." On the evening of June 22, 1999, Jessica Gonzales learned that her ex-husband had removed their daughters from her home and she went to the police to ask for enforcement of the restraining order. The police, however, failed to act even after her repeated requests. Some hours later the ex-husband came to the police station and began shooting at the police. He was eventually killed by police gunfire. All three daughters were found dead in his truck from gunshots to the head earlier in the evening. Jessica Gonzales brought a section 1983 action, claiming that Castle Rock police had violated her rights under the Due Process Clause of the Constitution by willfully or negligently refusing to enforce her restraining order. The Court of Appeals for the Tenth Circuit agreed that she had a protected property interest in the enforcement of the terms of her restraining order and the police violated this interest. The Supreme Court reversed, however, arguing that a restraining order does not create a property interest. Even though the language seems to suggest that there is mandate to act, according to the court, police activity is indeed discretionary and thus cannot be said to create an enforceable legal right.

Where the *DeShaney* case made it more difficult for people injured by the negligence of state agencies to pursue claims against the government via the due process clause of the Constitution, *Castle Rock* made it well nigh impossible for a citizen to complain about any infringement of property rights protected by the due process clause when the government acts adversely to their interests. Equally problematic for the concept of the rule of law is the seeming impunity these cases appear to grant government actors who fail to act when they should.

These cases lead ineluctably to the conclusion that under our current law government agencies have far less tort liability than private individuals, corporations, or other non-governmental actors. In *Castle Rock v. Gonzales*, Justice Stevens underscored this fact by pointing out that if Ms. Gonzales had made a contract with a private security company to protect herself and her children, the company would unquestionably be liable had it acted the same way the police did. In practical terms, he said, a restraining order is no different than a contract between the police and Ms. Gonzales—and yet a failure to honor that contract on the part of the police did not lead to their being found legally at fault.

As if to underscore the conclusion that government is less vulnerable to tort liability, in the last week of its 1998 term, the Court decided two sexual harassment liability lawsuits. In a case brought against a private employer, the Court held that under Title VII, employers *could* be liable for sexual harassment damages if: (1) employees subjected co-workers to a sexually hostile work environment;

and (2) the employer had no grievance procedure for filing and correcting complaints. In this case, the complaining employee need not have submitted to sexual advances, nor have been in any way penalized for failing to do so.[10]

Now compare just the "syllabus" summary in the case of *Gebser v. Lago Vista Independent School District* (524 U.S. 274), announced just a few days before the private harassment case. Justice O'Connor's opinion for the five-person majority describes a protracted affair between a teacher and Ms. Gebser, beginning when she was in the eighth grade.

Petitioner Gebser, a high school student in respondent Lago Vista Independent School District, had a sexual relationship with one of her teachers. She did not report the relationship to school officials. After the couple was discovered having sex and the teacher was arrested, Lago Vista terminated his employment. During this time, the district had not distributed an official grievance procedure for lodging sexual harassment complaints or a formal antiharassment policy, as required by federal regulations. Petitioners filed suit raising, among other things, a claim for damages against Lago Vista under Title IX of the Education Amendments of 1972, which provides in pertinent part that a person cannot "be subjected to discrimination under any education program or activity receiving Federal financial assistance," 20 U.S.C. § 1681 (a). The Federal District Court granted Lago Vista summary judgment. In affirming, the Fifth Circuit held that school districts are not liable under Title IX for teacher-student sexual harassment unless an employee with supervisory power over the offending employee actually knew of the abuse, had the power to end it, and failed to do so, and ruled that petitioners could not satisfy that standard.

Held: Damages may not be recovered for teacher-student sexual harassment in an implied private action under Title IX unless a school district official who at a minimum has authority to institute corrective measures on the district's behalf has actual notice of, and is deliberately indifferent to, the teacher's misconduct.

A year after the *Gebser* decision, a 5-justice majority of the Court held that a school system may be liable for student-on-student harassment, but only where the school that receives federal funds "acts with deliberate indifference to known acts of harassment in its programs or

10. *Burlington Industries v. Ellerth*, 524 U.S. 742 (1998).

activities." In this case, *Davis v. Monroe County Board of Education*, a fifth-grade girl was repeatedly touched and molested by an elementary school boy who later pleaded guilty to sexual battery in juvenile court.[11] The plaintiffs alleged that school officials knew about the ongoing harassment and did nothing to stop it. Title IX states that "no person in the United States shall, on the basis of sex be (1) excluded from participation in, (2) be denied the benefits of, or (3) be subjected to discrimination under any education program or activity receiving Federal financial assistance." The four dissenting justices complained vigorously that basic principles of federalism forbade Congress from regulating something so parochial as the behavior of children in local schools.

A NEW LEGAL SHIELD FOR STATES

On the last day of its 1999 term, the Supreme Court issued three very surprising decisions. They prompted the *New York Times* to publish a front-page news story the following day headlined "States Are Given New Legal Shield by Supreme Court." The cases, which were ostensibly about the sovereign immunity of states, threatened to reduce Congress's power over individual states and to return regulatory politics to the early days of the New Deal that we discussed in chapter 3.

The cases themselves held that the language of the Eleventh Amendment prevented people from suing states for violating legal rights created by Congress. In one case, state probation officers who had been required to work overtime sued to recover overtime wages as provided by the national wage and hour laws. In another case a state university had violated patent rights, and in the third case the state, which had engaged in the lending business in competition with private lenders, allegedly violated lending laws. In all three cases the Supreme Court told the plaintiffs that the Eleventh Amendment prevented their lawsuits. The Amendment reads:

The judicial power of the United States shall not be construed to extend to any suit in law or equity, commenced or prosecuted against one of the United States by Citizens of another state. . . .

Since these words seem to speak to the power of the federal courts to hear such lawsuits, the narrow 5-4 majority went on to say that, because the states are "joint participants" in the federal system, the very structure of the federal system immunizes them.[12] As we will see in more detail in chapter 13, this perspective protects the states against Congress's efforts to make individual states liable in tort for violations of federal legislation such as the Americans with Disabilities Act (ADA) or the Age Discrimination in Employment Act. Pursuant to *Kimel v. Florida*, 528 U.S. 62 (2000), the Supreme Court employs a two-pronged test to determine whether Congress can make states pay damages for violating federal laws. The first prong of the test requires proof that Congress clearly intended to "abrogate" a state's sovereignty—whether, that is, it wanted to infringe a bit on the state's independent political status. If that prong is satisfied, the next prong requires a showing that the remedy is proportional to the harm sought to be redressed. The language of proportionality derives from the Fourteenth Amendment. As we will see, the requirement of proportionality provides the states with a variety of potential defenses to tort actions filed against them by individuals. The increased sovereignty of the states is consistent with the more general trend toward decreasing government liability in civil suits brought against government officials or organizations.

Finally, we urge readers (especially those interested in working for state and local government agencies) to investigate carefully the circumstances in which you, as an individual, might be found liable for legal wrongs you allegedly commit on the job. In the past, courts have often sidestepped the Eleventh Amendment and allowed lawsuits to proceed against individuals acting in their official government capacities. The law here is unsettled. But if the past is an indication of what may develop, the Supreme Court's trend toward allowing the Eleventh Amendment to provide a legal shield for the states, may well lead to an increase in lawsuits against individuals who acted on behalf of the government.

---

11. 526 U.S. 629 (1999).

12. See *Alden v. Maine* (1999); *Florida v. College Savings Bank* (1999); *College Savings Bank v. Florida* (1999).

EXERCISES AND QUESTIONS FOR FURTHER THOUGHT

1. At the turn of the millennium lawsuits seeking money damages to address major public policy problems were in the news more and more frequently. For example, in July 1999, a six-person jury in Florida found tobacco companies liable for harm that befell cigarette smokers. In a master settlement between the tobacco companies and attorney generals of 46 states, tobacco companies agreed to pay more than 200 billion to the states to compensate for healthcare expenses caused by smoking. Do you approve of using such lawsuits to make public policy? The same dynamics work in lawsuits against the government. In 1999 a jury made a $5 million award against New York City in favor of a class of 63,000 people who had been illegally strip-searched upon arrest during a ten-month period several years earlier.[13] Do you think that the same criteria for evaluating "high-stakes" lawsuits against private companies like tobacco companies and gun manufacturers should also apply to high-stakes suits against the government? Is there any difference between all taxpayers paying for big awards to a few people, and all consumers paying awards to a few?

2. In *United States v. Union Trust Co.*, 221 F.2d 62 (1954), the plaintiffs sought to recover damages suffered when two small aircraft collided while approaching a runway. The air traffic controller, a government employee, had given each pilot permission to land on the same runway at the same time. Under the law of *Feres*, what decision would the court reach? What about under *Dalehite*? Under more recent decisions? Is it appropriate to describe air traffic controllers' decisions as "discretionary"? Why or why not?

3. Not only do the recent government tort liability cases signal a movement back to the narrow view of governmental liability under the FTCA (as stated in *Dalehite*), the Supreme Court's refusal to hold officials liable for *inaction* also leads to a narrow interpretation of state power. How accurate do you find Chief Justice Rehnquist's view of state power in the *DeShaney* case? Compare his perspective on the state's obligation, subsequent to the provision of services, with Justice Brennan's dissent in that case. In what sense is the majority opinion in the *DeShaney* case similar to the Court's unanimous opinion in *Heckler v. Chaney*, 1985 (p. 315). Why do you think Justices Brennan, Marshall, and Blackmun concurred with the majority in *Heckler*, but dissented in *DeShaney*?

4. The Constitution specifically protects members of congress from lawsuits arising from anything they do in their role as lawmakers. Should the courts grant the same protection to all members of lawmaking bodies, including city councils, county commissions, and state legislatures? In *Bogan v. Scott-Harris*, 523 U.S. 44 (1998), a mayor and city council passed an ordinance eliminating Ms. Scott-Harris's job. She complained that they did so to punish her for exercising her free speech right to complain about a fellow worker. She also claimed racial discrimination. She lost. The Court created blanket immunity from tort suit for all legislative actions. Does this ruling create a loophole by which administrators can escape tort threats for making otherwise legally suspicious decisions?

5. Given the decisions in *Gebser* and *Davis* concerning school liability for failure to correct persistent, flagrant and well-known sexual harassment at the school, suppose the following problem. Officials at a public university, aware of the persistence of "date rape" (often alcohol-induced) choose not to take steps to tighten regulation of alcohol on campus for fear of destroying the school's "life-style." Suppose then that a female first-year student accuses a football player of having sex with her against her will. School administrators urge her not to file a criminal complaint but to follow internal grievance procedures. She does. The football player admits to the rape. The school suspends the football player for two semesters, but delays the suspension to the point where he graduates before the suspension takes place. She sues under Title IX. Would you say the school was "deliberately indifferent" to this sexual harassment? See *Brzonkala v. Virginia Polytechnic Institute and State University*, 132 F.3d 949 (1997) and 169 F.3d 820 (1999). In the second decision, in 1999, the full panel of the Fourth Circuit Court of Appeals overturned the original three-judge panel and held for Virginia Polytechnic. It reasoned that Congress had no power to regulate sexual harassment of this sort under the commerce clause. The majority opinion here reinforces the conclusion that conservative judges are actively trying to curb Congress's regulatory power at the turn of the millennium.

13. See "$5 Million Jury Award in Strip-Search Case," *New York Times*, May 12, 1999.

CHAPTER 12
LICENSING

The next two chapters allow you to see how administrative law principles are developed in familiar settings. Of all the governmental activities covered by administrative law, the one you have most likely experienced is the licensing process. We refer to the familiar and often nerve-wracking experience nearly all teenagers go through—getting a driver's license. Adults, too, live in varying degrees of awareness that they could lose their drivers' licenses in certain circumstances.

A license to operate a motor vehicle is the most common kind of license issued by the government. As we will see, driver's license revocation proceedings have yielded some of the most interesting materials in due process adjudication. However, it would be misleading to treat the driver's license as a model of all licensing situations or problems. Governmental licensing covers an astonishing range of issues and can serve several quite different purposes. For example, the *Vermont Yankee* case dealt with safety issues at nuclear-generated power plants that environmental groups felt should have been resolved prior to granting operating licenses. When the Federal Communications Commission (FCC) grants a rare and prized license to operate a television station or cable service in a metropolitan area it is giving the license holder a ticket to almost guaranteed profits.

THE VARIETIES OF LICENSING PROGRAMS

A license is a grant of permission from the government to do something. In most cases operating without such permission leads directly to criminal prosecution. Obviously the law governing the right to operate a citizen's band radio in a car involves issues different from those having to do with safety at a nuclear power plant. To help conceptualize the various species of licensing programs, consider the following four categories.

1. Control of Public Resources

To operate a concession stand in a public park the concessionaire must get a license. To cut timber in a national forest the logger must get permission from the U.S. Forest Service. The main reason the government requires licenses in these situations is to encourage such private parties to operate in ways that are consistent with the agency's policies. To varying degrees licensing laws provide for sanctions in the event of a violation of the licensing requirement as a means of ensuring compliance, as we discussed in chapter 9. Regulating public resources is usually the primary goal. This task concerns the allocation of public resources and sets limits for aesthetics, safety, and other reasons. For years businessmen, politicians, and even some economists believed that the market alone could not ensure safe use of the public airways by commercial airlines. Hence the Civil Aeronautics Board (CAB) issued two kinds of licenses to airlines: licenses to operate at all, and licenses to operate on specific routes. That process has ended. The CAB officially expired in 1985. Whether market forces alone have resulted in a safer commercial airline industry is questionable.

2. Fair Allocation of Limited Resources

Licensing policy must cope with the interaction between technology and natural resources. In chapter 6 Paul Verkuil mentioned in passing the government program for licensing coastal shrimp fishermen. The theory here will be familiar to recreational fishermen and hunters. Left unregulated, the sheer volume of people who hunt or fish would soon exhaust or destroy the natural resource in question. Likewise, the radio bandwidth for which it is economical to design and sell receivers is a limited resource; hence the work of the FCC. The need for fair procedure in allocating licenses is critical. If Smith gets a fishing license but Jones does not, the decision-making process must be based on considerations that are fair and reasoned, rather than arbitrary or capricious. Often such basic principles as *first come, first served* will produce fair results, but this of course depends on the subject matter. (The FCC once considered a program of awarding licenses by lottery.)[1]

3. Assurance of Competence in Complex and Dangerous Occupations

As in the first category, this type of licensing program seeks to limit the number of people in a market, but the goal is not merely to reduce the number of players. Rather, in the case of doctors, lawyers, pharmacists, and other professionals, licensing seeks to ensure their competence. Licensing is critical because incompetence in these fields can cause great harm and because most consumers lack the training necessary to judge competence themselves.[2]

4. Maintenance of Public Order

The difference between the third and fourth categories is slight. Poor automobile driving can cause as much harm as medical malpractice. So can an unregulated access to alcoholic beverages, which gave rise to laws in some states limiting the number of suppliers. The license requirement for drivers and liquor sellers, however, does not involve detailed tests and standards of performance

designed to increase the competence of the licensee. In professional licensing, by contrast, the candidate must demonstrate his or her mastery of a large quantity of complex material. Where the license seeks to maintain public order, it is the threat of losing the license that produces the greater sanctioning effect. Liquor stores refuse to sell to minors not because of professional training in a "liquor school" but because they face the threat of losing their license if caught.

LICENSING AS ADJUDICATION

Granting, denying, or revoking licenses is a form of adjudication that requires due process protections, regardless of what administrative procedure statutes or authorizing statutes may demand. But here two problems arise. First, licensing programs serve different goals and vary in complexity from nuclear energy to hot dog vendor permits. One procedure does not fit all types of licenses. Second, the degree of hardship to the licensee that may result from denying or revoking a license may vary radically from one situation to another. If a businessperson invests in the liquor business, if a restaurant is capitalized based on projected receipts from alcohol as well as food, the revocation of the license may put the person out of business altogether. But if the Nuclear Regulatory Commission (NRC) does not establish a licensing procedure for the proposed national high-level radioactive waste dump in Yucca Mountain, Nevada, the U.S. Department of Energy will not then build a repository for the existing waste generated by private nuclear power and government nuclear weapons facilities, let alone future waste. Should the due process protection for revocation be greater than the protections in initial license decisions, at least where the initial decisions are not "life or death" business matters?

The Administrative Procedure Act (APA), Section 558, requires formal adjudication for denial, termination, or revocation of licenses, but 554(d)(A) exempts initial applications for licenses from 558's hearing procedures. When a nuclear power company seeks an operating license or a broadcaster seeks a television station license, millions or even billions of dollars are at stake. Authorizing statutes

---

1. In 1982, Congress passed legislation (HR 3239-PL 97–259) authorizing the FCC to establish licensing lottery rules. The FCC declared this process "unworkable." See *Congressional Quarterly Almanac* 38 (1982): 338.

2. See Kenneth M. Meier, *Regulation: Politics, Bureaucracy, and Economics* (New York: St. Martin's Press, 1985), in particular chap. 7.

and due process requirements generally provide full-hearing protections in such cases. The interesting administrative law questions in licensing arise at the more mundane levels of auto licensing, occupational licensing, and the like. Because the majority of readers will more often deal with state and local licensing activities, the cases and discussion in this chapter focus exclusively on state licensing programs.

Hornsby v. Allen

326 F.2D 605, UNITED STATES COURT OF APPEALS
FOR THE FIFTH CIRCUIT (1964) 2-1

[Mrs. Hornsby applied for a license to operate a retail liquor store in Atlanta. Even though her background and the store's proposed location met the licensing requirements, her application was denied by the city council. No reasons were given for the denial. Mrs. Hornsby filed a lawsuit claiming that a denial without explanation constituted a violation of due process. Additionally, she claimed that her due process rights were violated because either of the two aldermen in the ward where the store was to be located could veto the application whatever its merits. The district court dismissed the case as not falling under the Fourteenth Amendment because it centered on a so-called political question concerning the motives of a legislative body, and because no charge of discrimination was made. Mrs. Hornsby appealed.]

Tuttle, Chief Judge

At the outset, we note our disagreement with the district court's classification of the challenged actions as purely those of a legislative body; we do not conceive the denial of an application for a license to be an act of legislation. Although there is disagreement on the matter, we prefer the view that licensing proper is an adjudicative process. Thus when a municipal or other governmental body grants a license it is an adjudication that the applicant has satisfactorily complied with the prescribed standards for the award of that license. Similarly the denial of a license is based on an adjudication that the applicant has not satisfied those qualifications and requirements. On the other hand, the prescription of standards which must be met to obtain a license

is legislation, since these standards are authoritative guides for future conduct derived from an assessment of the needs of the community. A government agency entrusted with the licensing power therefore functions as a legislature when it prescribes these standards, but the same agency acts as a judicial body when it makes a determination that a specific applicant has or has not satisfied them.

Since licensing consists in the determination of factual issues and the application of legal criteria to them—a judicial act—the fundamental requirements of due process are applicable to it. Due process in administrative proceedings of a judicial nature has been said generally to be conformity to fair practices of Anglo-Saxon jurisprudence, which is usually equated with adequate notice and a fair hearing. Although strict adherence to the common-law rules of evidence at the hearing is not required the parties must generally be allowed an opportunity to know the claims of the opposing party, to present evidence to support their contentions, and to cross-examine witnesses for the other side. Thus it is not proper to admit *ex parte* evidence, given by witnesses not under oath and not subject to cross-examination by the opposing party. *A fortiori*, the deciding authority may not base its decision on evidence which has not been specifically brought before it; the findings must conform to the evidence adduced at the hearing. Furthermore, the Supreme Court has said that an administrative order "cannot be upheld merely because findings might have been made and considerations disclosed which would justify its order. . . . There must be such a responsible finding." . . .

Also, the Supreme Court has held that the arbitrary refusal to grant a license or permit to one group when other groups have obtained permits under similar circumstances constitutes a denial of equal protection of the law. . . .

Neither is the assertion that liquor may be a menace to public health and welfare a sufficient answer to Mrs. Hornsby's allegations. The potential social undesirability of the product may warrant absolutely prohibiting it, or as the Aldermanic Board has done to some extent here, imposing restrictions to protect the community from its harmful influences. But the dangers do not justify depriving those who deal in liquor, or seek to deal in it, of the customary constitutional safeguards. Indeed, the great social interest in the liquor industry makes an exceptionally strong case for adherence to proper procedures and access to judicial review in licensing the retail sale of liquor . . . judications on the basis of merit. The first step toward insuring that these expectations are realized is to require adherence to the standards of due process; absolute and uncontrolled discretion invites abuse. . . .

It follows that the trial court must entertain the suit and determine the truth of the allegations. If it develops that no ascertainable standards have been established by the Board of Aldermen by which an applicant can intelligently seek to qualify for a license, then the court must enjoin the denial of licenses under the prevailing system and until a legal standard is established and procedural due process provided in the liquor store licensing field.

The judgment is reversed.

IMPARTIAL DECISION MAKERS IN LICENSING

Recall from chapter 6 that judicial impartiality has two components. Decision makers must neither prejudge the case before they hear facts presented to them on the record, nor decide cases in which they have a personal stake in the outcome. It was for the latter reason that the Supreme Court struck down a method of licensing optometrists in Alabama in *Gibson v. Berryhill*. The next case addresses both components of impartiality. Notice particularly that the same people who investigate also make an important decision about the termination of a license. This phenomenon is called *combination of functions*.

Withrow et al. v. Larkin

421 U.S. 35 (1975) 9–0
+ Burger, Douglas, Brennan, Stewart, White, Marshall, Blackmun, Powell, Rehnquist

[The state of Wisconsin passed a law specifying certain criminal offenses for which a physician could have his license suspended. Larkin was charged by the board with fee-splitting, practicing under an alias, and allowing an unlicensed physician to practice at his Milwaukee clinic. At an investigatory hearing Larkin's attorney was allowed to introduce evidence but not to cross-examine witnesses. The board then notified Larkin that it would hold a contested hearing to determine if he should have his license suspended. Larkin sought and obtained an order from the district court restraining the board from holding the hearing. However, the board held another investigatory hearing in which it found probable cause to start the process of revoking his medical license. A three-judge district court found that the procedure presented a substantial federal due process question and enjoined enforcement of the licensing statutes against Larkin. The board appealed.]

Justice White delivered the opinion of the Court

The District Court framed the constitutional issue, which it addressed as being whether "for the board temporarily to suspend Dr. Larkin's license at its own contested hearing on charges evolving from its own investigation would constitute a denial to him of his rights to procedural due process." . . . The question was initially answered affirmatively, and in its amended judgment the court asserted that there was a high probability that appellee would prevail on the question. Its opinion stated that the "state medical examining board [did] not qualify as [an independent] decisionmaker [and could not] properly rule with regard to the merits of the same charges it investigated and, as in this case, presented to the district attorney." . . . We disagree. On the present record, it is quite unlikely that appellee would ultimately prevail on the merits of the due process issue presented to the District Court, and it was an abuse of discretion to issue the preliminary injunction.

Concededly, a "fair trial in a fair tribunal is a basic requirement of due process." *In re Murchison*, 349 U.S. 133, 136 (1955). This applies to administrative agencies which adjudicate as well as to courts. *Gibson v. Berryhill*, 411 U.S. 564, 579 (1973). Not only is a biased decisionmaker constitutionally unacceptable but "our system of law has always endeavored to prevent even the probability of unfairness." . . . In pursuit of this end, various situations have been identified in which experience teaches that the probability of actual bias on the part of the judge or decisionmaker is too high to be constitutionally tolerable. Among these cases are those in which the adjudicator has a pecuniary interest in the outcome and in which he has been the target of personal abuse or criticism from the party before him.

The contention that the combination of investigative and adjudicative functions necessarily creates an unconstitutional risk of bias in administrative adjudication has a much more difficult burden of persuasion to carry. It must overcome a presumption of honesty and integrity in those serving as adjudicators; and it must convince that, under a realistic appraisal of psychological tendencies and human weakness, conferring investigative and adjudicative powers on the same individuals poses such a risk of actual bias or prejudgment that the practice must be forbidden if the guarantee of due process is to be adequately implemented.

Very similar claims have been squarely rejected in prior decisions of this Court. . . .

This Court has also ruled that a hearing examiner who has recommended findings of fact after rejecting certain evidence as not being probative was not disqualified to preside at further hearings that were required when reviewing courts held that the evidence had been erroneously excluded. . . . The Court of Appeals had decided that the examiner should not again sit because it would be unfair to require the parties to try "issues of fact to those who may have prejudged them. . . ." But this Court unanimously reversed, saying: "Certainly it is not the rule of judicial administration that, statutory requirements apart, . . . a judge is disqualified from sitting in a retrial because he was reversed on earlier rulings. We find no warrant for imposing upon administrative agencies a stiffer rule, whereby examiners would be disentitled to sit because they ruled strongly against a party in the first hearing." . . .

More recently we have sustained against due process objection a system in which a Social Security examiner has responsibility for developing the facts and making a decision as to disability claims, and observed that the challenge to this combination of functions "assumes too much and would bring down too many procedures designed, and working well, for a governmental structure of great and growing complexity." . . .

That is not to say that there is nothing to the argument that those who have investigated should not then adjudicate. The issue is substantial, it is not new, and legislators and others concerned with the operations of administrative agencies have given much attention to whether and to what extent distinctive administrative functions should be performed by the same persons. No single answer has been reached. Indeed, the growth, variety, and complexity of the administrative processes have made any one solution highly unlikely. Within the Federal Government itself, Congress has addressed the issue in several different ways, providing for varying degrees of separation from complete separation of functions to virtually none at all. For the generality of agencies, Congress has been content with § 5 of the Administrative Procedure Act, 5 U.S.C. § 554(d), which provides that no employee engaged in investigating or prosecuting may also participate or advise in the adjudicating function, but which also expressly exempts from this prohibition "the agency or a member or members of the body comprising the agency."

It is not surprising, therefore, to find that "[t]he case law, both federal and state, generally rejects the idea that the combination [of] judges [and] investigating functions is a denial of due process. . . ." 2 K. Davis, Administrative Law Treatise § 13.02, p. 175 (1958). Similarly, our cases, although they reflect the substance of the problem, offer no support for the bald proposition applied in this case by the District Court that agency members who participate in an investigation are disqualified from adjudicating. The incredible variety of administrative mechanisms in this country will not yield to any single organizing principle . . . When the Board instituted its investigative procedures, it stated only that it would investigate whether proscribed conduct had occurred. Later in noticing the adversary hearing, it asserted only that it would determine if violations had been committed which would warrant suspension of appellee's license. Without doubt, the Board then anticipated that the proceeding would eventuate in an adjudication of the issue; but there was no more evidence of bias or the risk of bias or prejudgment than inhered in the very fact that the Board had investigated and would now adjudicate. Of course, we should be alert to the possibilities of bias that may lurk in the way particular procedures actually work in practice. The processes utilized by the Board, however, do not in themselves contain an unacceptable risk of bias. The investigative proceeding had been closed to the public, but appellee and his counsel were permitted to be present throughout; counsel actually attended the hearings and knew the facts presented to the Board. No specific foundation has been presented for suspecting that the Board had been prejudiced by its investigation or would be disabled from hearing and deciding on the basis of the evidence to be presented at the contested hearing. The mere exposure to evidence presented in nonadversary investigative procedures is insufficient in itself to impugn the fairness of the Board members at a later adversary hearing. Without a showing to the contrary, state administrators "are assumed to be men of conscience and intellectual discipline, capable of judging a particular controversy fairly on the basis of its own circumstances." *United States v. Morgan*, 313 U.S. 409, 421 (1941).

We are of the view, therefore, that the District Court was in error when it entered the restraining order against the Board's contested hearing and when it granted the preliminary injunction based on the untenable view that it would be unconstitutional for the Board to suspend appellee's license "at its own contested hearing on charges evolving from its own investigation. . . ." The contested hearing should have been permitted to proceed. . . .

The judgment of the District Court is reversed and the case is remanded to that court for further proceedings consistent with this opinion. . . .

In evaluating the *Withrow* case you should consider two ways in which the procedural posture differs from that in *Cinderella* and *Gibson*. Those cases set aside *final* decisions that may have been affected by bias. By contrast, the *Withrow* decision impacted an administrative proceeding at an early stage. Second, as Justice White points out, no *specific* evidence of bias was introduced. In reasoning similar to the later *Horowitz* case, the Court presumes that "professional" decisions are impartial and valid in the absence of specific evidence to the contrary.

PROFESSIONAL STANDARDS IN LICENSING

How much deference should courts give to a licensing board just because it is made up of professionals, who are presumably fair and impartial? The next two cases show that the Supreme Court has not blindly approved all "professional" judgments.

Schware v. Board of Bar Examiners

353 U.S. 232 (1957) 8-0
+ Warren, Black, Frankfurter, Douglas, Burton, Clark, Harlan, Brennan
[NP] Whittaker

[Schware applied to take the New Mexico bar examination in 1953. His application was denied because of his prior use of aliases, his criminal record, and his membership in a subversive organization in the 1930s. Schware had not been in trouble for fifteen years and had served honorably in World War II. He received support at the hearing from a rabbi, a member of the bar, and his law school. Schware appealed the board's refusal to admit him to the state bar, arguing that it amounted to a denial of his right to due process of law under the Fourteenth Amendment, but the New Mexico Supreme Court upheld the board's decision.]

Justice Black delivered the opinion of the Court

The question presented is whether petitioner, Rudolph Schware, has been denied a license to practice law in New Mexico in violation of the Due Process Clause of the Fourteenth Amendment to the United States Constitution.

A State cannot exclude a person from the practice of law or from any other occupation in a manner or for reasons that contravene the Due Process or Equal Protection Clause of the Fourteenth Amendment. . . . A State can require high standards of qualification, such as good moral character or proficiency in its law, before it admits an applicant to the bar, but any qualification must have a rational connection with the applicant's fitness or capacity to practice law. . . . Obviously an applicant could not be excluded merely because he was a Republican or a Negro or a member of a particular church. Even in applying permissible standards, officers of a State cannot exclude an applicant when there is no basis for their finding that he fails to meet these standards, or when their action is invidiously discriminatory. . . .

Here the State concedes that Schware is fully qualified to take the examination in all respects other than good moral character. Therefore the question is whether the Supreme

Court of New Mexico on the record before us could reasonably find that he had not shown good moral character.

There is nothing in the record which suggests that Schware has engaged in any conduct during the past 15 years which reflects adversely on his character. The New Mexico Supreme Court recognizes that he "presently enjoys good repute among this teachers, his fellow students and associates and in his synagogue." . . . The undisputed evidence in the record shows Schware to be a man of high ideals with a deep sense of social justice. Not a single witness testified that he was not a man of good character. . . .

The State contends that even though the use of aliases, the arrests, and the membership in the Communist Party would not justify exclusion of petitioner from the New Mexico bar if each stood alone, when all three are combined his exclusion was not unwarranted. We cannot accept this contention. In the light of petitioner's forceful showing of good moral character, the evidence upon which the State relies—the arrests for offenses for which petitioner was neither tried nor convicted, the use of an assumed name many years ago, and membership in the Communist Party during the 1930s—cannot be said to raise substantial doubts about his present good moral character. There is no evidence in the record which rationally justifies a finding that Schware was morally unfit to practice law. . . .

Reversed.

Cord v. Gibb

SUPREME COURT OF VIRGINIA 254 S.E.2D 71 (1979) 7-0

[The background of the case is succinctly explained in this short opinion.]

Per Curiam

This is an appeal by Bonnie C. Cord . . . from an order denying her the certificate of honest demeanor or good moral character required by Code § 54–60 as a prerequisite to her right to take the bar examination conducted by the Virginia Board of Bar Examiners. . . .

Cord, a 1975 law school graduate, was admitted by examination to practice law in the District of Columbia that same year. After engaging in private practice for a period of 13 months, Cord accepted a position as an Attorney-Advisor with an agency of the federal government. She was still employed in that capacity on the date she petitioned for the required certificate. At that time Cord was a member, in good standing, of The District of Columbia Bar, The Bar Association of the District of Columbia, and the American Bar Association.

The court below, as required by the second paragraph of Code § 54–60, appointed three practicing attorneys to make an investigation of the moral character and fitness of Cord and to report their findings to the court.

In their written report, the attorneys disclosed that they had completed their investigation, which included a personal interview with Cord and contacts with her former employers. The reports also related that petitioner, in her interview, stated that she had jointly purchased a home in a rural area of Warren County with Jeffrey Blue, and that she and Blue jointly resided there. Two of the investigating attorneys reported that they were of the opinion that from the standpoint of "moral character and fitness," Cord was qualified to take the bar examination. One of the investigating attorneys, believing that Cord's living arrangement affected her character and fitness, recommended that the required certificate not be issued.

After reviewing this report, the trial court convened [a] . . . hearing to allow Cord to present further evidence in support of her petition. At this hearing four of Cord's neighbors, all of whom were aware of her living arrangement, vouched for her good moral character, integrity and acceptance in the community. All these witnesses testified that Cord's living arrangement, while generally known in the community, was not a "matter of discussion within the community" and that her admission to practice law would not reflect adversely on the organized bar.

In addition to this testimony, the court received and considered a letter written by Cord's nearest neighbor attesting to her "high character" and acceptance in the community. The court also received and considered letters from three practicing attorneys in the District of Columbia with whom Cord had been associated while in private law practice. Each of these letters vouched for Cord's professional competence, integrity and good moral character in such terms as "she is of the highest moral character both

professionally and personally" and "Bonnie, during the thirteen months that she was associated with this firm, always
demonstrated the highest possible morals, both professionally and personally."

In its order the trial court, while finding that Cord met
the statutory requirements for taking the bar examination
in all other respects, refused to issue the certificate of honest demeanor or good moral character "on the grounds
that the living arrangement of Applicant would lower the
public's opinion of the Bar as a whole." In applying this
standard in lieu of the statutory standard, the trial court
erred.

Whether a person meets the "honest demeanor, or good
moral character" standard of Code § 54–60 is, of course,
dependent upon the construction placed on those terms.
The United States Supreme Court, recognizing that a state
may require "high standards of qualification, such as good
moral character or proficiency in its law, before it admits an
applicant to the bar," has held that such qualifications, to
pass constitutional muster, must have a "rational connection with the applicant's fitness to practice law." *Schware v.
Board of Bar Examiners. . . .* Except for Cord's statement
that she and a male to whom she was not married jointly
owned and resided in the same dwelling, the record is
devoid of any evidence which would otherwise reflect unfa-
vorably on Cord's professional competence, honest
demeanor and good moral character. In fact, the evidence
of a number of responsible citizens in the community where
Cord resides establishes that she is of good character and
honest demeanor. Likewise, the letters received from Cord's
former employers vouch for her good moral character, as
well as her professional competence.

While Cord's living arrangement may be unorthodox
and unacceptable to some segments of society, this conduct
bears no rational connection to her fitness to practice law. It
cannot, therefore, serve to deny her the certificate required
by Code § 54–60.

Accordingly, we hold the trial court erred in refusing to
issue to petitioner a certificate of honest demeanor or good
moral character. The order below will be reversed and the
case will be remanded with direction that the trial court
forthwith issue the certificate requested by petitioner.

Reversed and remanded.

Schware and *Cord* both defend constitutional rights
derived from the First Amendment—freedom of political
belief and freedom of association. Since World War II the
Court has provided greater protection for these and related
freedoms than it has for the due process rights. When freedom of expression or other First Amendment rights are not
at issue in licensing cases, courts tend to give licensing
boards considerably more discretion. To this we now turn.

DISCRETIONARY ANALYSIS OF THE FACTS: THE CASE OF THE DRIVER'S LICENSE

With its 1971 decision in *Bell v. Burson* the Supreme
Court announced a significant application of *Goldberg v.
Kelly*'s due process philosophy in the licensing context.[3]
The case involved a decision by the state of Georgia to
suspend a person's driver's license because he failed to
carry liability insurance as required by Georgia law. The
Court ruled that the state was required to give the driver
a pre-suspension hearing comparable to that awarded the
welfare recipient in *Goldberg v. Kelly*. The Court rejected
the argument that a license is a privilege rather than a
right, noting that drivers have an obvious interest, often a
financial one, in their ability to drive, and that this interest qualified for constitutional protection. The additional
expense of such hearings did not justify dispensing with
due process protections.

Bell v. Burson rejected the argument that Georgia could
suspend the license without a hearing because the statute
operated automatically, that is, required no findings of
fact. The Court observed that various defenses the driver
might present at a hearing would make suspension
unnecessary, including that the license holder was not
responsible for a traffic accident and hence not liable for
damages (making liability insurance unnecessary), or a
showing that the license holder had paid off a damages
judgment resulting from an accident.

The same requirement would seem to apply to "point
system" license suspensions and revocations. While seemingly automatic in application, point system decisions

3. *Bell v. Burson*, 402 U.S. 535 (1971), opinion by Justice William
Brennan.

could involve a variety of disputed factual questions. These could include: (1) convictions mistakenly counted against a licensee because of mistaken identity; (2) clerks errors in traffic court records that erroneously assigned points to the wrong licensee; (3) improper calculation of points; or (4) failure to grant point credits properly earned. In the following case the Supreme Court refused to extend *Bell* to point system cases. The Court chose instead to rely on the hearing officials to make accurate decisions and properly exercise discretion. This may be unjust to the driver, but as you read the case, *Dixon v. Love*, try to identify what obstacles this ruling might create in the effort to improve traffic safety. Thirty-nine states have a "one strike" policy—meaning the driver's license is revoked and in some cases the automobile seized—if it is established that a person's blood alcohol content is above the legal limit, which ranges between .08 percent and .10 percent by weight of the person's total blood volume, or if a person refuses to take a Breathalyzer test. Most states allow courts to grant a temporary license for driving to and from work or school after a person convicted of driving under the influence of alcohol completes an initial mandatory suspension period.[4]

Dixon v. Love

431 U.S. 105 (1977) 8-0
+ *Burger, Stewart, White, Brennan, Marshall, Blackmun, Stevens*
[NP] *Rehnquist*

[Love, a truck driver, had his license suspended by the state of Illinois after he was convicted three times within a twelve-month period of various traffic offenses. When he was convicted a fourth time of driving with a suspended license, another suspension was imposed. Several years after both suspensions had expired, Love was convicted twice more for speeding and cited for a third speeding charge. While he was waiting to resolve the third speeding charge, Love received a notice from the state informing him that his license would be revoked for over a year if he was convicted of a third violation. As it turned out, he was convicted and his license was revoked without a hearing pursuant to Illinois law. The law as written did not provide for a hearing until after the suspension had already taken effect. Love challenged that rule and the district court agreed with him.]

Justice Blackmun delivered the opinion of the Court

The issue in this case is whether Illinois has provided constitutionally adequate procedures for suspending or revoking the license of a driver who repeatedly has been convicted of traffic offenses. The statute and administrative regulations provide for an initial summary decision based on official records, with a full administrative hearing available only after the suspension or revocation has taken effect.

The case centers on § 6–206 of the Illinois Driver Licensing Law (c. 6 of the Illinois Vehicle Code). The section is entitled "Discretionary authority to suspend or revoke license or permit." It empowers the Secretary of State to act "without preliminary hearing upon a showing by his records or other sufficient evidence" that a driver's conduct falls into any one of 18 enumerated categories. . . .

Pursuant to his rulemaking authority under this law . . . the Secretary has adopted administrative regulations that further define the bases and procedures for discretionary suspensions. These regulations generally provide for an initial summary determination based on the individual's driving record. The Secretary has established a comprehensive system of assigning "points" for various kinds of traffic offenses, depending on severity, to provide an objective means of evaluating driving records.

One of the statutorily enumerated circumstances justifying license suspension or revocation is conviction of three moving traffic offenses within a 12-month period. This is one of the instances where the Secretary, by regulation, has provided a method for determining the sanction according to the driver's accumulated "points."

Another circumstance, specified in the statute, supporting suspension or revocation is where a licensee

[h]as been repeatedly involved as a driver in motor vehicle collisions or has been repeatedly convicted of offenses against laws and

4. U.S. Department of Transportation, National Highway Traffic Safety Administration, *Traffic Safety Program* (202) 366–2672, Washington, D.C. (1997).

ordinances regulating the movement of traffic, to a degree which indicates lack of ability to exercise ordinary and reasonable care in the safe operation of a motor vehicle or disrespect for the traffic laws and the safety of other persons upon the highway. . . .

Here again the Secretary has limited his broad statutory discretion by an administrative regulation. This regulation allows suspension or revocation, where sufficient points have been accumulated to warrant a second suspension within a 5-year period. The regulation concludes flatly: "A person who has been suspended thrice within a 10-year period shall be revoked."

Section 6–206(c)(1) requires the Secretary "immediately" to provide written notice of a discretionary suspension or revocation under this statute, but no prior hearing is required. Within 20 days of his receiving a written request from the licensee, the Secretary must schedule a full evidentiary hearing for a date "as early as practical" in either Sangamon County or Cook County, as the licensee may specify. . . . The final decision of the Secretary after such hearing is subject to judicial review in the Illinois courts. . . . In addition, a person whose license is suspended or revoked may obtain a restricted permit for commercial use or in case of hardship. . . .

It is clear that the Due Process Clause applies to the deprivation of a driver's license by the State: "Suspension of issued licenses . . . involves state action that adjudicates important interests of the licensees. In such case the licenses are not to be taken away without that procedural due process required by the Fourteenth Amendment." *Bell v. Burson*, 402 U.S., at 539, 91 S.Ct., at 1589.

It is equally clear that a licensee in Illinois eventually can obtain all the safeguards procedural due process could be thought to require before a discretionary suspension or revocation becomes final. Appellee does not challenge the adequacy of the administrative hearing, noted above. . . . The only question is one of timing. This case thus presents an issue similar to that considered only last Term in *Mathews v. Eldridge*, . . . namely, "the extent to which due process requires an evidentiary hearing prior to the deprivation of some type of property interest even if such a hearing is provided thereafter." We may analyze the present case, too, in terms of the factors considered in *Eldridge*:

[I]dentification of the specific dictates of due process generally requires consideration of three distinct factors: first, the private interest that will be affected by the official action; second, the risk of an erroneous deprivation of such interest through the procedures used, and probable value, if any, of additional or substitute procedural safeguards; and finally, the Government's interest, including the function involved and the fiscal and administrative burdens that the additional or substitute procedural requirement would entail. . . .

The private interest affected by the decision here is the granted license to operate a motor vehicle. Unlike the social security recipients in *Eldridge*, who at least could obtain retroactive payments if their claims were subsequently sustained, a licensee is not made entirely whole if his suspension or revocation is later vacated. On the other hand, a driver's license may not be so vital and essential as are social insurance payments on which the recipient may depend for his very subsistence. . . . The Illinois statute includes special provisions for hardship and for holders of commercial licenses, who are those most likely to be affected by the deprival of driving privileges. . . . We therefore conclude that the nature of the private interest here is not so great as to require us "to depart from the ordinary principle, established by our decisions, that something less than an evidentiary hearing is sufficient prior to adverse administrative action." . . . Moreover, the risk of an erroneous deprivation in the absence of a prior hearing is not great. Under the Secretary's regulations, suspension and revocation decisions are largely automatic. Of course, there is the possibility of clerical error, but written objection will bring a matter of that kind to the Secretary's attention. In this case appellee had the opportunity for a full judicial hearing in connection with each of the traffic convictions on which the Secretary's decision was based. Appellee has not challenged the validity of those convictions or the adequacy of his procedural rights at the time they were determined. . . . Since appellee does not dispute the factual basis for the Secretary's decision, he is really asserting the right to appear in person only to argue that the Secretary should show leniency and depart from his own regulations. Such an appearance might make the licensee feel that he has received more personal attention, but it would not serve to protect any substantive rights. We conclude that requiring additional procedures would be unlikely to have significant value in reducing the number of erroneous deprivations.

Finally, the substantial public interest in administrative efficiency would be impeded by the availability of a pretermination hearing in every case. Giving licensees the choice thus automatically to obtain a delay in the effectiveness of a suspension or revocation would encourage drivers routinely to request full administrative hearings. . . . Far more substantial than the administrative burden, however, is the important public interest in safety on the roads and highways, and in the prompt removal of a safety hazard . . .

We conclude that the public interests present under the circumstances of this case are sufficiently visible and weighty for the State to make its summary initial decision effective without a predecision administrative hearing.

The present case is a good illustration of the fact that procedural due process in the administrative setting does not always require application of the judicial model. When a governmental official is given the power to make discretionary decisions under a broad statutory standard, case-by-case decisionmaking may not be the best way to assure fairness. Here the Secretary commendably sought to define the statutory standard narrowly by the use of his rule-making authority. The decision to use objective rules in this case provides drivers with more precise notice of what conduct will be sanctioned and promotes equality of treatment among similarly situated drivers. The approach taken by the District Court would have the contrary result of reducing the fairness of the system, by requiring a necessarily subjective inquiry in each case as to a driver's "disrespect" or "lack of ability to exercise ordinary and reasonable care."

The judgment of the District Court is reversed. It is so ordered.

Justice Stevens, Justice Marshall, and Justice Brennan, concurring [omitted]

In an article critical of the decision in *Dixon v. Love*, George D. Brandt, chief of the Adjudication Branch of the National Highway Traffic Safety Administration, argues that the best method of improving traffic safety lies in correcting the behavior of problem drivers. This, he believes, requires a highly skilled staff of traffic advisors who possess the flexibility to negotiate specific driving

limitations in individual cases. Such a program will involve discretion and therefore will necessarily need to include *Goldberg* protections. But Brandt goes further and challenges the notion that professionalism requires less due process. He believes that the *Bell* decision resulted in a gradual improvement in the training and caliber of traffic safety officers. *Dixon*, he fears, may have stopped this trend and set back traffic safety in the process.

===

Due Process and Driver Licensing Suspension Hearings: What Do the States Do after Love?

GEORGE D. BRANDT
Administrative Law Review 30 (1979): 223

Since license withdrawal is the ultimate weapon in the arsenal to deter violations and accidents, it is better used as a threat instead of being imposed. With this threat held in reserve, driver improvement efforts through probation and the issuance of restricted licenses may encourage improved driver performance. Professor John H. Reese, in his definitive study on driver licensing administration, concluded that a point system has no utility as a highway safety measure unless "beneficial effects" can be demonstrated from the remedial action taken. . . .

Since only a few states have developed an effective driver licensing agency hearing authority capability, there are not many models to discuss. New York has fourteen safety referees throughout the state. All of the referees spend two to three weeks in training before conducting any hearings. Pretermination point-system suspension hearings are tape recorded with evidence submitted formally into the record and all testimony given under oath. Considerable time is devoted by the referees in reviewing the driver's record to allow the driver to discuss or challenge it. At the end of the hearing the driver may explain his need for a license. The safety referee has considerable latitude in case disposition. He can issue a "restricted use license" to a person, such as Love, whose driver's license has been suspended and is necessary to his employment. The applicant for a "restricted use license" may be required to attend a driver rehabilitation program as a condition of issuance.

[A] NHTSA study made a number of recommendations for the upgrading of the nation's driver licensing agency hearing authority. Ten of the more significant ones are as follows:

1. That the authority to withdraw the driver license and to conduct driver license hearings be vested with the administrative agency responsible for issuing and controlling driver licenses;

2. That state legislatures delegate sufficient authority to driver licensing agencies to support their conduct of these hearings and the subsequent administrative decisions concerning license withdrawals;

3. That Administrative Procedures Acts be adopted and made applicable to driver license withdrawal proceedings;

4. That an independent unit responsible for conducting "trial-type" hearings be established;

5. That action be taken by each driver licensing agency to ensure that drivers are heard before licenses are withdrawn;

6. That formal hearing procedures be used in "trial-type" hearings involving contested facts;

7. That first appeals be made to the agency;

8. That appeals to a court of law be made on the record;

9. That trained specialists serve as hearing officers;

10. That the hearing officer position be a senior level position in the agency.

Regardless of whether the hearing officers are attorneys or trained senior licensing agency officials, the legal profession (particularly state assistant attorney generals who work or are assigned to motor vehicle departments and department counsel) has a responsibility to assist driver licensing agencies to upgrade all license suspension hearing officer activities, including point-system suspensions. This should mean, as a minimum, the creation of an independent hearing officer unit within the licensing agency. This upgrading may be difficult to accomplish in the face of bureaucratic inertia, the lack of an understanding of what needs to be done and budgetary constraints.

First, if a jurisdiction can pay a driver improvement analyst a maximum salary of $15,000 a year, why pay experienced, qualified, hearing officers as much as $25,000 a year? Second, even though courts have no interest or expertise in driver license suspension cases, some jurisdictions will continue to postpone the development of a qualified hearing officer cadre through the use of de novo court appeal. This will exacerbate current court case delay and backlog problems. Third, jurisdictions may interpret *Love* to justify continued use of point-system suspension authority without providing the problem driver with a pretermination "opportunity to be heard" and additional driver improvement benefits.

In conclusion, the effect of the U.S. Supreme Court's decision in *Love*, relying on *Mathew's* balancing of interests approach, may be to eviscerate pretermination hearing requirements in most driver licensing suspension and revocation cases. While the Court distinguished *Love* from *Bell* on the grounds that it was a point-system mandatory revocation involving limited contested facts, the reality is otherwise. The Court did not rest its decision on such narrow grounds. Instead, the Court found the interests of efficiency, highway safety effectiveness and fairness to be better served without a pretermination hearing.

The Court in *Love* stressed that a motorist faced with license suspension or revocation could rebut the agency's determination in writing. The Court held that "requiring an inquiry in each case on a driver's disrespect or lack of ability to exercise ordinary and reasonable care" would reduce fairness. The "personal attention" the court found so repugnant is the essence of state driver licensing agency action aimed at improved driver behavior and highway safety. Oral statements before an impartial hearing officer by the driver improvement analyst and the motorist on these issues are the central features of this process.

The use by the Court of "prompt removal of a safety hazard" as justification for summary suspension in Love was illusory. The Court knew that professional drivers, such as Love, were treated with leniency under the Illinois law. This lenient treatment led the Court to require "something less than an evidentiary" pretermination hearing. The Court was not aware of the body of highway safety knowledge which recommends the integration of license withdrawal action with referral to driver improvement and the issuance of hardship or restricted licenses. This integration can be accomplished both fairly and effectively through hearings conducted by an impartial hearing officer. Summary suspension or revocation action which permits only written comment is inadequate.

The Court, in backing off from the due process principles established in *Goldberg* and its progeny, such as

Bell, needs to be fully aware of the nation's current driver licensing agency hearing capability. In approximately half of the states, hearing officers have neither the authority to make a decision nor issue an order and few states have hearing officers who are properly trained. In only three out of twenty-two states with hearing officers do lawyers constitute all or most of the staff. For the Court to sanction the use of written comment only in point-system suspension or revocation cases supports the pre-Bell situation among driver licensing agencies.

The states need to develop an independent, qualified, driver licensing agency hearing officer unit with the authority to handle all hearing requirements both formal and informal. This would include rendering decisions and issuing orders in point-system and other license suspension actions. In support of this unit, states should adopt the following five-point program:

1. a notice to drivers of a pending license withdrawal action, and a statement of reasons and due process rights,

2. an opportunity to pretermination hearings in point-system suspension or revocation cases,

3. pretermination hearings before hearing officers who do not also serve as driver improvement analysts,

4. employment of hearing officers who occupy senior level positions in the driver licensing agency, and

5. hearing officer training in due process, traffic law and adjudicatory procedures, and driver behavior and highway safety.

The establishment of an independent driver licensing hearing officer unit within the agency would go a long way toward ensuring impartiality. The professionalization of hearing officers, either by employing predominately legal personnel or through training, is also impor-tant. New York has employed professional, trained, hearing officers to hear point-system suspension cases. They have the authority under an administrative point system to suspend or place drivers on restrictive status and require attendance at a driver improvement program. This combines the best features of administrative rulemaking and individual case-by-case decisionmaking that is necessary to improve driver performance. . . .

One major safety issue concerning driver's licenses has started to make itself felt, yet much more is to come. "Road safety analysts predict that by 2030, when all baby boomers are at least 65, they will be responsible for 25% of all fatal [car] crashes."[5] This is a problem not only for those elderly drivers, but also for the safety of others, as evidenced tragically when a 87-year-old driver ran his car into a farmers market in Santa Monica, Calif., killing 10 and leaving more than 70 injured.[6] As with other issues in administrative law, however, there is no easy solution or rather, the solution(s) must be sufficiently fine-tuned that a right, driving, is not arbitrarily taken away from the elderly in a discriminatory fashion. Many states now request renewal of driver's licenses and mail-in renewals are not available for senior citizens. For now, this seems to be the best solution but you should continue watching debates on this particular issue as they crystallize, in a relatively bounded issue area, various aspects of administrative law we have talked about: emergence of a societal problem and the need for regulations to ensure safety; a property right and problems of due process in its violation, discrimination against the elderly, etc.

5. "Older, Dangerous Drivers A Growing Problem," *USA Today*, May 2, 2007.

6. "Elderly Driver Who Killed 10 is Sentenced to Probation," *New York Times*, November 21, 2006.

EXERCISES AND QUESTIONS FOR FURTHER THOUGHT

1. We distinguished *Withrow v. Larkin* from *Cinderella* and *Gibson* on the basis that the latter two cases contained specific evidence of bias. What precisely was that evidence and why does it rightly call for closer judicial inspection than the Court gave Dr. Larkin's case?

2. Can the government insist that individuals receive a license before exercising First Amendment freedoms, particularly before freely exercising their religion? What if a city ordinance requiring a license for all door-to-door sales interfered with a particular religious group's belief that it needed to conduct door-to-door evangelizing accompanied by sales of the group's religious tracts? See *Jones v. Opelika*, 316 U.S. 584 (1942) and *Murdock v. Pennsylvania*, 319 U.S. 105 (1943).

3. Should a board of medical examiners that excludes chiropractors be presumed impartial in cases where chiropractors seek licenses to practice?

4. The state's power to grant and revoke licenses in order to regulate certain professions is often delegated to a "board of examiners." Suppose you were a member of a licensed profession and your profession's examining board instituted proceedings against you for "unprofessional conduct" pursuant to a statute authorizing the board to revoke licenses for such conduct. What if the statute did not specify what constitutes "unprofessional conduct"? What *constitutional* defense do you think would be helpful to your case? How would you distinguish your situation from the time-honored usage in military law of the phrase *conduct unbecoming an officer and a gentleman* or the provision in the Constitution that the president may be impeached for *high crimes and misdemeanors*? What if your state operates under an administrative procedure act that has been judicially interpreted to require agencies to make rules to flesh out legislation? How would that affect your constitutional defense or provide a statutory defense? To see how a state court handled these issues, see *Megdal v. Oregon State Board of Dental Examiners*, 605 P.2d 273 (1980).

CHAPTER 13
THE LAW OF
PUBLIC EMPLOYMENT

T hus far the presentation has centered on relationships between administrative agencies and parties outside the agency that the agency affects. These outsiders include such individuals as welfare recipients, who have a nearly client-like relationship to the agency; large regulated corporations—commercial broadcasters, for example—that often cooperate with their regulators to reap the protective benefits of regulation; and lobbying groups such as the Sierra Club or the Environmental Defense Fund that may try to block administrative actions that harm their causes.

Administrative law seeks to formulate minimum standards of accuracy, rationality and fairness in these relationships. But agencies also hold tremendous power over the employees who work within the agencies.

The law of public employment illustrates three important practical aspects of administrative law. The first, which we shall cover only briefly, is historical. Some of the first statutory efforts to control administrative practice of any kind involved personnel. The Pendleton Act of 1883, which created the United States Civil Service Commission, sought to eliminate the favoritism of the spoils system by rationalizing the appointment of employees and regulating their political obligations.

The second area of administrative law illustrated by the personnel cases deals with the constitutional requirements for hearings. We have traced the effects of *Goldberg* *and Mathews* on several welfare cases that followed it and saw its decline in the field of education, but the *Goldberg*

and Mathews "doctrine" has had an even more substantial impact on law dealing with personnel. The Administrative Procedure Act (APA) is silent on matters of internal management, including employment, so the governing law in this area is based largely on common law and constitutional law.

Finally, public employment law returns us to an issue raised briefly in Part 1. Agencies have a duty not just to comply with administrative procedure acts and employ processes that are "due," they must also avoid violating any other part of the Constitution. We shall see that the courts often tie the constitutional protections of free speech and due process together in the employment area. Also, agencies must not practice racial and sexual discrimination in personnel matters. The last section of this chapter explores this persistent issue.

THE DEVELOPMENT OF CIVIL SERVICE

American history is full of nearly forgotten stories of political courage. One of these concerns Chester A. Arthur. As head of the port of New York for many years, he openly supported the machine system of politics and its method of maintaining loyalty by distributing the spoils of political success to the faithful. He stalwartly supported one of New York's leading spoilers of the day, Senator Roscoe Conkling (R-N.Y.). Arthur became vice-president under James Garfield in 1881. Garfield soon offended the Conkling crowd by refusing to make many of the spoils appointments they recommended. Four months after the election a frustrated and presumably mad office-seeker associated with the Conkling crowd fatally shot President Garfield.

On assuming the presidency, Arthur, sincerely shocked by the assassination, turned against the spoils system, and with much general public support, promoted adoption of the Pendleton Act. Only 14,000 employees were initially covered by the act. However, through an interesting political dynamic, politicians steadily expanded its scope. This occurred because the act permitted the president by executive order to expand its coverage. As new presidents took office, they deliberately expanded the act to cover their own *political* appointees so as to freeze them in their jobs after the president's term ended.

The Pendleton Act itself provided few modern legal protections. Justice William Rehnquist, in *Arnett v. Kennedy*, noted the very limited nature of its protections:

While the Pendleton Act is regarded as the keystone in the present arch of Civil Service legislation, by present-day standards it was quite limited in its application. It dealt almost exclusively with entry into the federal service and hardly at all with tenure, promotion, removal, veterans' preference, pensions and other subjects addressed by subsequent Civil Service legislation. The Pendleton Act provided for the creation of a Classified Service, and required competitive examination for entry into that service. Its only provision with respect to separation was to prohibit removal for the failure of an employee in the classified service to contribute to a political fund or to render any political service.

For 16 years following the effective date of the Pendleton Act, this last-mentioned provision of the Act appears to have been the only statutory or regulatory limitation on the right of the Government to discharge classified employees.[1]

The first tentative move toward due process in the handling of government employees came with the Lloyd-LaFollette Act of 1913. This act gave the employee threatened with dismissal the right to respond to the charges that occasioned his dismissal. But the right to respond in a hearing was made contingent on the wishes of the superior making the removal, and the potential for arbitrariness thus remained strong.

Neither the Pendleton Act nor the Lloyd-LaFollette Act seriously addressed the full range of issues that may surround the decision to terminate an employee. This is because at common law one's possession of a job, including a job with the government, constituted a privilege, not a constitutionally protected right. For our purposes the simplest way to conceive of a legal privilege is to assume that it exists only to the extent a contract creates it. In the field of employment, a worker would have the privilege of working for the government only to the extent a legally binding contract would obligate the government to pay the employee for his or her work. For a variety of reasons employment contracts and the common law of contract on which they were based normally permitted governmental employers to fire employees on relatively short notice and without any necessary showing of cause.[2] As long as a government job remained a legal privilege, due process questions simply did not arise. And this brings us to the second and most important of this chapter's illustrations of administrative law in practice.

THE CONSTITUTIONAL REQUIREMENTS OF A TERMINATION HEARING

In 1964 Yale Law Professor Charles Reich published an article entitled "The New Property."[3] In it he insisted that post-WWII government had amassed so much financial power, particularly in its welfare aid programs, that the old legal rights/privileges distinction was no longer wise social policy. A job with the government, a welfare check, a research grant, have all replaced the forms of property, like farm land, that the Founders sought to protect through the due process clause. Reich argued that by establishing public employment, contracts, services, and so forth, the state itself created expectations that it would provide such benefits to citizens qualified to receive them. Reich reasoned that if the state denied these benefits without due process, it would violate the expectations

---

1. 416 U.S. 134 (1974). *Arnett* itself held that due process did not require a hearing prior to the employee's termination.

2. *Bailey v. Richardson*, 341 U.S. 918 (1951).
3. *Yale Law Journal* 73 (1964): 733.

it had created. Therefore due process protections belong in welfare and employment terminations. *Goldberg v. Kelly* was widely viewed as a positive legal response to Reich's call. A few years later the rights/privilege doctrine began to fade in employment termination cases. The classification of statutory entitlements as property stimulated a growing number of legal claims as the scope of governmental responsibilities expanded. The area of government employment fostered many of the early claims to entitlement.[4] The cases described here involve state but not federal action; due process clauses cover both levels of government.

In June 1972 the Supreme Court decided cases in which two college professors, neither of whom had official tenure, were fired without a hearing. In the first case, *Board of Regents v. Roth*, David Roth was hired for his first teaching job as an assistant professor of political science at Wisconsin State University at Oshkosh.[5] His contract ran for one year. The university refused to rehire him for a second year. The university gave no reasons for its decision and its own rules did not require it to do so. Roth alleged that he was not rehired because he had publicly criticized the university's administration and that its employment decision therefore violated his right to freedom of speech. The Court held that Roth had no property right to be rehired. If the university had publicly criticized Roth by stating why he was not rehired, reasons that might injure his chances for future employment, then the Court stated he would have at least a right to some of the *Goldberg* protections. Similarly he would be protected if he had some informal promise of tenure or of contract renewal. But Roth failed to meet either of these conditions and lost. The Court did not therefore thoroughly analyze his freedom of speech claim.

The second case, decided the same day and set out below, involved rather different facts. Note the importance of the interaction between free speech and due process claims.

4. For an extended description and analysis of constitutional property, see John Brigham, *Property and the Politics of Entitlement* (Philadelphia: Temple University Press, 1990).
5. 408 U.S. 564 (1972).

Perry et al. v. Sindermann

408 U.S. 593 (1972) 5–3
+ Burger, Stewart, White, Blackmun, Rehnquist
– Douglas, Brennan, Marshall
NP Powell

[Sindermann, a faculty member at Odessa (Texas) Junior College, had previously been employed at six other Texas junior colleges and for three years at Odessa pursuant to a series of one-year contracts when he came into conflict with the college's board of regents for advocating that the school become a four-year college. He actively criticized the regents, and an advertisement critical of the regents appeared in a newspaper over his name. Further, because he was the elected president of the Texas Junior College Teachers Association, he sometimes missed classes in order to testify before the state legislature. At the end of his fourth year, the regents voted not to offer him another one-year contract. The regents commented on Sindermann's alleged insubordination in a press release, but provided neither an official statement of the reason for the nonrenewal of the contract nor the opportunity of a hearing where Sindermann could try to rebut any charges. Sindermann brought suit alleging violations of his First Amendment right to free speech and his Fourteenth Amendment right to due process in the form of a hearing. The district court granted summary judgment against Sindermann, but the appellate court reversed.]

Justice Stewart delivered the opinion of the Court

The first question presented is whether the respondent's lack of a contractual or tenure right to reemployment, taken alone, defeats his claim that the nonrenewal of his contract violated the First and Fourteenth Amendments. We hold that it does not.

For at least a quarter-century, this Court has made clear that even though a person has no "right" to a valuable governmental benefit and even though the government may deny him the benefit for any number of reasons, there are some reasons upon which the government may not rely. It may not deny a benefit to a person on a basis that infringes his constitutionally protected interests—especially, his interest in freedom of speech. For if the government could deny a benefit to a person because of his constitutionally protected speech or associations, his exercise of those freedoms would in effect be penalized and inhibited. This would allow the government to "produce a result which [it] could not command directly." *Speiser v. Randall*, 357 U.S. 513, 526. Such interference with constitutional rights is impermissible. . . .

Thus, the respondent's lack of a contractual or tenure "right" to re-employment for the 1969–1970 academic year is immaterial to his free speech claim. Indeed, twice before, this Court has specifically held that the nonrenewal of a nontenured public school teacher's one-year contract may not be predicated on his exercise of First and Fourteenth Amendment rights. *Shelton v. Tucker* . . . , *Keyishian v. Board of Regents*. . . . We reaffirm those holdings here.

In this case, of course, the respondent has yet to show that the decision not to renew his contract was, in fact, made in retaliation for his exercise of the constitutional right of free speech. The District Court foreclosed any opportunity to make this showing when it granted summary judgment. Hence, we cannot now hold that the Board of Regents' action was invalid.

But we agree with the Court of Appeals that there is a genuine dispute as to "whether the college refused to renew the teaching contract on an impermissible basis—as a reprisal for the exercise of constitutionally protected rights." 430 F.2d, at 943. The respondent has alleged that his nonretention was based on his testimony before legislative committees and his other public statements critical of the Regents' policies. And he has alleged that this public criticism was within the First and Fourteenth Amendments' protection of freedom of speech. Plainly, these allegations present a bona fide constitutional claim. For this Court has held that a teacher's public criticism of his superiors on matters of public concern may be constitutionally protected and may, therefore, be an impermissible basis for termination of his employment. *Pickering v. Board of Education*. . . .

The respondent's lack of formal contractual or tenure security in continued employment at Odessa Junior College, though irrelevant to his free speech claim, is highly relevant to his procedural due process claim. But it may not be entirely dispositive.

We have held today in *Board of Regents v. Roth* . . . , that the Constitution does not require opportunity for a hearing before the nonrenewal of a nontenured teacher's contract, unless he can show that the decision not to rehire him somehow deprived him of an interest in "liberty" or that he had a "property" interest in continued employment, despite the lack of tenure or a formal contract. In *Roth* the teacher had not made a showing on either point to justify summary judgment in his favor.

Similarly, the respondent here has yet to show that he has been deprived of an interest that could invoke procedural *due process* protection. *As* in *Roth*, the mere showing that he was not rehired in one particular job, without more, did not amount to a showing of a loss of liberty. Nor did it amount to a showing of a loss of property.

But the respondent's allegations—which we must construe most favorably to the respondent at this stage of the litigation—do raise a genuine issue as to his interest in continued employment at Odessa Junior College. He alleged that this interest, though not secured by a formal contractual tenure provision, was secured by a no less binding understanding fostered by the college administration. In particular, the respondent alleged that the college had a de facto tenure program, and that he had tenure under that program. He claimed that he and others legitimately relied upon an unusual provision that had been in the college's official Faculty Guide for many years:

Teacher Tenure: Odessa College has no tenure system. The Administration of the College wishes the faculty member to feel that he has permanent tenure as long as his teaching services are satisfactory and as long as he displays a cooperative attitude toward his co-workers and his superiors, and as long as he is happy in his work.

Moreover, the respondent claimed legitimate reliance upon guidelines promulgated by the Coordinating Board of the Texas College and University System that provided that a person, like himself, who had been employed as a teacher in the state college and university system for seven years or more has some form of job tenure. Thus, the respondent offered to prove that a teacher with his long period of service at this particular State College had no less a "property" interest in continued employment than a formally tenured teacher at other colleges, and had no less a procedural due process right to a statement of reasons and a hearing before college officials upon their decision not to retain him.

We have made clear in *Roth, supra*, at 571–572, that "property" interests subject to procedural due process protection are not limited by a few rigid, technical forms. Rather, "property" denotes a broad range of interests that are secured by "existing rules or understandings." . . . A person's interest in a benefit is a "property" interest for due process purposes if there are such rules or mutually explicit understandings that support his claim of entitlement to the benefit and that he may invoke at a hearing. . . .

A written contract with an explicit tenure provision clearly is evidence of a formal understanding that supports a teacher's claim of entitlement to continued employment unless sufficient "cause" is shown. Yet absence of such an explicit contractual provision may not always foreclose the possibility that a teacher has a "property" interest in re-employment. For example, the law of contracts in most, if not all, jurisdictions long has employed a process by which agreements, though not formalized in writing, may be "implied." . . . Explicit contractual provisions may be supplemented by other agreements implied from "the promisor's words and conduct in the light of the surrounding circumstances." . . . And, "[t]he meaning of [the promisor's] words and acts is found by relating them to the usage of the past." . . .

A teacher, like the respondent, who has held his position for a number of years, might be able to show from the circumstances of this service—and from other relevant facts—that he has a legitimate claim of entitlement to job tenure. Just as this Court has found there to be a "common law of a particular industry or of a particular plant" that may supplement a collective-bargaining agreement, *Steelworkers v. Warrior & Gulf* Co., 363 U.S. 574, 579, so there may be an unwritten "common law" in a particular university that certain employees shall have the equivalent of tenure. This is particularly likely in a college or university, like Odessa Junior College, that has no explicit tenure system even for senior members of its faculty, but that nonetheless may have created such a system in practice. See C. Byse & L. Joughin, Tenure in American Higher Education 17–28 (1959).

In this case, the respondent has alleged the existence of rules and understandings, promulgated and fostered by state officials, that may justify his legitimate claim of entitlement to continued employment absent "sufficient cause." We disagree with the Court of Appeals insofar as it held that

a mere subjective "expectancy" is protected by procedural due process, but we agree that the respondent must be given an opportunity to prove the legitimacy of his claim of such entitlement in light of "the policies and practices of the institution." . . . Proof of such a property interest would not, of course, entitle him to reinstatement. But such proof would obligate college officials to grant a hearing at his request, where he could be informed of the grounds for his nonretention and challenge their sufficiency. . . .

Affirmed.

Justice Brennan, with whom Justice Douglas joins, dissenting in part [omitted]

Justice Marshall, dissenting in part

. . . I agree with Part I of the Court's opinion holding that respondent has presented a bona fide First Amendment claim that should be considered fully by the District Court. But, for the reasons stated in my dissenting opinion in *Board of Regents v. Roth*, . . . I would modify the judgment of the Court of Appeals to direct the District Court to enter summary judgment for respondent entitling him to a statement of reasons why his contract was not renewed and a hearing on disputed issues of fact.

[Portions from Justice Marshall's dissenting opinion in Board of Regents v. Roth:]

. . . This Court has long maintained that "the right to work for a living in the common occupations of the community is of the very essence of the personal freedom and opportunity that it was the purpose of the [Fourteenth] Amendment to secure." *Truax v. Raich*, 239 U.S. 33, 41 (1915) (Hughes, J.). It has also established that the fact that an employee has no contract guaranteeing work for a specific future period does not mean that as the result of action by the government he may be "discharged at any time for any reason or for no reason." *Truax v. Raich, supra*, at 38.

In my view, every citizen who applies for a government job is entitled to it unless the government can establish some reason for denying the employment. This is the "property" right that I believe is protected by the Fourteenth Amendment and that cannot be denied "without due process of law." And it is also liberty—liberty to work—which is the "very essence of the personal freedom and opportunity" secured by the Fourteenth Amendment. . . .

Employment is one of the greatest, if not the greatest, benefits that governments offer in modern-day life. When something as valuable as the opportunity to work is at stake, the government may not reward some citizens and not others without demonstrating that its actions are fair and equitable. And it is procedural due process that is our fundamental guarantee of fairness, our protection against arbitrary, capricious, and unreasonable government action. . . .

It may be argued that to provide procedural due process to all public employees or prospective employees would place an intolerable burden on the machinery of government. Cf. *Goldberg v. Kelly, supra.* The short answer to that argument is that it is not burdensome to given reasons when reasons exist. Whenever an application for employment is denied, an employee is discharged, or a decision not to rehire an employee is made, there should be some reason for the decision. It can scarcely be argued that government would be crippled by a requirement that the reason be communicated to the person most directly affected by the government's action.

Where there are numerous applicants for jobs, it is likely that few will choose to demand reasons for not being hired. But, if the demand for reasons is exceptionally great, summary procedures can be devised that would provide fair and adequate information to all persons. As long as the government has a good reason for its actions it need not fear disclosure. It is only where the government acts improperly that procedural due process is truly burdensome. And that is precisely when it is most necessary.

It might also be argued that to require a hearing and a statement of reasons is to require a useless act, because a government bent on denying employment to one or more persons will do so regardless of the procedural hurdles that are placed in its path. Perhaps this is so, but a requirement of procedural regularity at least renders arbitrary action more difficult. Moreover, proper procedures will surely eliminate some of the arbitrariness that results, not from malice, but from innocent error. "Experience teaches. . . . that the affording of procedural safeguards, which by their nature serve to illuminate the underlying facts, in itself often operates to prevent erroneous decisions on the merits from occurring." *Silver v. New York Stock Exchange,* 373 U.S. 341, 366 (1963). When the government knows it may have to justify its decisions with sound reasons, its conduct is likely to be more cautious, careful, and correct.

Professor Gellhorn put the argument well:

"In my judgment, there is no basic division of interest between the citizenry on the one hand and officialdom on the other. Both should be interested equally in the quest for procedural safeguards. I echo the late Justice Jackson in saying: 'Let it not be overlooked that due process of law is not for the sole benefit of an accused. It is the best insurance for the Government itself against those blunders which leave lasting stains on a system of justice'—blunders which are likely to occur when reasons need not be given and when the reasonableness and indeed legality of judgments need not be subjected to any appraisal other than one's own. . . ." Summary of Colloquy on Administrative Law, 6 J. Soc. Pub. Teachers of Law 70, 73 (1961).

Accordingly, I dissent.

In hindsight, the *Roth* and *Sindermann* cases look like the proverbial camel's nose under the tent. They hardly stand as a ringing endorsement of the right of due process in the employment context, but they did suggest that employees deserve protection for some constitutional rights on the job. This holding naturally steered lawyers who represented fired public workers toward the argument that the job itself is a form of property right protected by due process. In a transitional case in 1976, *Bishop v. Wood*, the Supreme Court upheld firing a police officer without a due process pretermination hearing in the following circumstances: Officer Bishop, having completed his first "probationary" year of employment for the city of Marion, North Carolina, was by Marion city ordinance considered "tenured." The ordinance stated that he could only be fired "for cause," and the causes specified in the policy all related to the failure of an employee to perform the job properly. The Court majority held that, since no public explanation for the firing was given, no hearing was necessary, but on close analysis this argument falls apart. If the city could fire him only for failing to do his job properly, then the firing itself is a public rebuke, one that would damage his liberty and property interest in gaining employment elsewhere. And if, instead, he were wrongly fired, is that not an additional reason to grant the worker some kind of due process hearing?[6]

Today the legal protections against such firings are stronger, in part because of state and federal rules and statutes protecting employees. The Civil Service Reform Act of 1978 provides an illustration of this trend. This act provides for a two-tiered hearing process if the employee requests it. Section 7513 of the act requires that an employee who is to be removed, suspended for more than fourteen days, reduced in pay or grade, or laid off for thirty days or less be provided with certain protections at the agency level. Specifically, the employee is entitled to:

1. At least thirty days advance written notice setting forth the reasons for the action. The requirement is waived if the employee is believed to have committed a crime for which imprisonment is a possible punishment.

2. Not less than seven days to answer the charges orally and/or in writing to include the submission of affidavits or other documentary evidence.

3. Representation by an attorney or other person.

4. Receipt of a written decision and the reasons for it at the earliest practicable date.

Additionally, at the discretion of the agency, the employee may be afforded a hearing in place of or in addition to provision 2.

The second tier of the process described in section 7701 of the act begins with the employee's statutorily created right to appeal the decision of the agency under the procedures listed on pp. 436–437 to the Merit System Protection Board—the employee protection arm of the federal civil service system. When this occurs the board may hear the case itself or assign the hearing to an administrative law judge or to an employee of the board. In the hearing, a transcript must be maintained and the employee may be represented by an attorney or other representative. Thus, while the courts have not mandated a hearing in all instances, the federal government has gone beyond the minimum set by the courts to afford all covered employees the opportunity for such a hearing. Further, the act provides that the decisions of the Merit System Protection Board may be judicially reviewed—in effect, a third tier of review.

In addition to these statutory protections, the Supreme Court itself has moved away from the logic of *Bishop*. Here are two cases that describe the employee's due process property right to a hearing. Pay attention to the Court's interpretations of the relationship between the substantive aspect of employment as a property right and the procedural requirements for protecting that right. Prior to *Loudermill*, the Court had reasoned that property rights are defined by and conditioned on the legislature's choice of a procedure when those rights are to be terminated. (See *Arnett v. Kennedy*, 416 U.S. 134 [1974].) In *Arnett* the Court said: "[W]here the grant of a substantive right is inextricably intertwined with the limitations on the procedures which are to be employed in determining that right, a litigant in the position of appellee must take the bitter with the sweet."[7] By linking the scope of procedural protection to the substantive nature of property interests, legislatures could erode the value of entitlements simply by specifying limited procedural protection for termination of employment. In *Loudermill* the Court majority rejects this theory and affirms a constitutional due process requirement for statutory entitlements.

Cleveland Board of Education v. Loudermill

470 U.S. 532 (1985) 7–2
+ *Burger, White, Blackmun, Powell, Stevens, O'Connor, Marshall*
+/– *Brennan*
– *Rehnquist*

[When he filled out a job application to become a security guard with the Cleveland Board of Education in 1979, James Loudermill indicated he had never been convicted of a felony. In 1981, he was fired after the Board discovered that he had been convicted of grand larceny in 1968. Loudermill was not afforded an opportunity to

6. 426 U.S. 341 (1976).

7. 416 U.S. 134, at 152–154.

respond to the charge of dishonesty or to challenge his dismissal. Loudermill filed an appeal with the Cleveland Civil Service Commission stating that he had thought his 1968 conviction was for a misdemeanor, not a felony. The hearing referee recommended he be reinstated, but after hearing argument the full commission upheld his dismissal. Loudermill filed suit in federal court alleging that the Ohio law was unconstitutional because it did not provide public employees with an opportunity to respond to charges against them prior to dismissal, and thereby deprived him of property without due process of law. The district court denied his claim; however, the Court of Appeals for the Sixth Circuit reversed. The Supreme Court granted certiorari.]

Justice White delivered the opinion of the Court

II

Property interests are not created by the Constitution, "they are created and their dimensions are defined by existing rules or understandings that stem from an independent source such as state law. . . ." *Board of Regents v. Roth* at 577. . . . The Ohio statute plainly creates such an interest. Respondents were "classified civil service employees." Ohio Rev. Code Ann. § 124.11 (1984), entitled to retain their positions "during good behavior and efficient service," who could not be dismissed "except . . . for . . . misfeasance, malfeasance, or nonfeasance in office," § 124.34.* The statute plainly supports the conclusion, reached by both lower courts, that respondents possessed property rights in continued employment. . . .

The . . . Board argues, however, that the property right is defined by, and conditioned on, the legislature's choice of procedures for its deprivation. . . . The Board stresses that in addition to specifying the grounds for termination, the statute sets out procedures by which termination may take place. The procedures were adhered to in these cases. According to petitioner, "[t]o require additional procedures

*The relevant portion of § 124.34 provides that no classified civil servant may be removed except "for incompetency, inefficiency, dishonesty, drunkenness, immoral conduct, insubordination, discourteous treatment of the public, neglect of duty, violation of such sections or the rules of the director of administrative services or the commission, or any other failure of good behavior, or any other acts of misfeasance, malfeasance, or nonfeasance in office."

would in effect expand the scope of the property interest itself." Id., at 27. . . .

This argument, which was accepted by the District Court, has its genesis in the plurality opinion in *Arnett v. Kennedy*, 416 U.S. 134 (1974). *Arnett* involved a challenge by a former federal employee to the procedures by which he was dismissed. The plurality reasoned that where the legislation conferring the substantive right also sets out the procedural mechanism for enforcing that right, the two cannot be separated:

"The employee's statutorily defined right is not a guarantee against removal without cause in the abstract, but such a guarantee as enforced by the procedures which Congress has designated for the determination of cause.

"[W]here the grant of a substantive right is inextricably intertwined with the limitations on the procedures which are to be employed in determining that right, a litigant in the position of appellee must take the bitter with the sweet." Id., at 152–154.

This view garnered three votes in *Arnett*, but was specifically rejected by the other six Justices. Since then, this theory has at times seemed to gather some additional support. See *Bishop v. Wood*, 426 U.S. 341, 355–361 (1976) (White, J., dissenting); *Goss v. Lopez*, 419 U.S., at 586–587 (Powell, J., joined by Burger, C.J., and Blackmun and Rehnquist, JJ., dissenting). More recently, however, the Court has clearly rejected it. In *Vitek v. Jones*, 445 U.S. 480, 491 (1980), we pointed out that "minimum [procedural] requirements [are] a matter of federal law, they are not diminished by the fact that the State may have specified its own procedures that it may deem adequate for determining the preconditions to adverse official action." This conclusion was reiterated in *Logan v. Zimmerman Brush Co.*, 455 U.S. 422, 432 (1982), where we reversed the lower court's holding that because the entitlement arose from a state statute, the legislature had the prerogative to define the procedures to be followed to protect entitlement.

In light of these holdings, it is settled that the "bitter with the sweet" approach misconceives the constitutional guarantee. If a clearer holding is needed, we provide it today. The point is straightforward: the Due Process clause provides that certain substantive rights—life, liberty, and property—cannot be deprived except pursuant to constitutionally adequate procedures. The categories of substance and procedure are distinct. Were the rule otherwise, the Clause would be reduced to a mere tautology. "Property" cannot be defined by the procedures provided for its deprivation any more than can life or liberty. The right to due process "is conferred, not by legislative grace, but by constitutional guarantee. While the legislature may elect not to confer a property interest in [public] employment, it may not constitutionally authorize the deprivation of such an interest, once conferred, without appropriate procedural safeguards." . . .

III

. . . The need for some form of pretermination hearing, recognized in these cases, is evident from a balancing of the competing interests at stake. These are the private interest in retaining employment, the governmental interest in the expeditious removal of unsatisfactory employees and the avoidance of administrative burdens, and the risk of an erroneous termination. See *Mathews v. Eldridge*, 424 U.S. 319, 335 (1976).

The case before us illustrates these considerations. . . . [I]n light of the referee's recommendation . . . we cannot say that a fully informed decisionmaker might not have exercised its discretion and decided not to dismiss him, notwithstanding its authority to do so. In any event, the termination involved arguable issues, and the right to a hearing does not depend on a demonstration of certain success. . . .

The governmental interest in immediate termination does not outweigh these interests. . . . [A]ffording the employee an opportunity to respond prior to termination would impose neither a significant administrative burden nor intolerable delays. Furthermore, the employer shared the employee's interest in avoiding disruption and erroneous decisions; and until the matter is settled, the employer would continue to receive the benefit of the employee's labors. It is preferable to keep a qualified employee on than to train a new one. A governmental employer also has an interest in keeping citizens usefully employed rather than taking the possibly erroneous and counterproductive step of forcing its employees onto the welfare rolls. Finally, in those situations where the employer perceives a significant hazard in keeping the employee on the job, it can avoid the problem by suspending with pay.

IV

The foregoing considerations indicate that the pretermination "hearing," though necessary, need not be elaborate.

We have pointed out that "[t]he formality and procedural requisites for the hearing can vary, depending upon the importance of the interests involved and the nature of the subsequent proceedings." *Boddie v. Connecticut*, 401 U.S., at 378. See *Cafeteria Workers v. McElroy*, 367 U.S. 886, 894–895 (1961). In general, "something less" than a full evidentiary hearing is sufficient prior to adverse administrative action. *Mathews v. Eldridge*, 424 U.S., at 343. Under state law, respondents were later entitled to a full administrative hearing and judicial review. The only question is what steps were required before the termination took effect.

In only one case, *Goldberg v. Kelly*, 397 U.S. 254 (1970), has the Court required a full adversarial evidentiary hearing prior to adverse governmental action. However, as the *Goldberg* Court itself pointed out, see *id.*, at 264, that case presented significantly different considerations than are present in the context of public employment. . . .

The essential requirements of due process, and all that respondents seek or the Court of Appeals required, are notice and an opportunity to respond. The opportunity to present reasons, either in person or in writing, why proposed action should not be taken is a fundamental due process requirement. See Friendly, "Some Kind of Hearing," 123 *U. Pa. L. Rev.* 1267, 1281 (1975). The tenured public employee is entitled to oral or written notice of the charges against him, an explanation of the employer's evidence, and an opportunity to present his side of the story. . . . To require more than this prior to termination would intrude to an unwarranted extent on the government's interest in quickly removing an unsatisfactory employee. . . .

VI

We conclude that all the process that is due is provided by a pretermination opportunity to respond, coupled with post-termination administrative procedures as provided by the Ohio statute. Because respondents allege in their complaints that they had no chance to respond, the District Court erred in dismissing for failure to state a claim. The judgment of the Court of Appeals is affirmed, and the case is remanded for further proceedings consistent with this opinion.

So ordered.

Justice Marshall, concurring in part and concurring in the judgment

I write separately . . . to reaffirm my belief that public employees who may be discharged only for cause are entitled, under the Due Process Clause of the Fourteenth Amendment, to more than respondents sought in this case. I continue to believe that *before the decision is made to terminate an employee's wages*, the employee is entitled to an opportunity to test the strength of the evidence "by confronting and cross-examining adverse witnesses and by presenting witnesses on his own behalf, whenever there are substantial disputes in testimonial evidence," *Arnett v. Kennedy*, 416 U.S. 134, 214 (1974) (Marshall, J., dissenting). Because the Court suggests that even in this situation due process requires no more than notice and an opportunity to be heard before wages are cut off, I am not able to join the Court's opinion in its entirety. . . .

. . . The opinion for the Court does not confront this reality. I cannot and will not close my eyes today—as I could not 10 years ago—to the economic situation of great numbers of public employees, and to the potentially traumatic effect of a wrongful discharge on a working person. Given that so very much is at stake, I am unable to accept the Court's narrow view of the process due to a public employee before his wages are terminated, and before he begins the long wait for a public agency to issue a final decision in his case.

Justice Brennan, concurring in part and dissenting in part

Today the Court puts to rest any remaining debate over whether public employers must provide meaningful notice and hearing procedures before discharging an employee for cause. . . .

Accordingly, I concur in Parts I–IV of the Court's opinion. I write separately to comment on two issues the Court does not resolve today, and to explain my dissent from the result in Part V of the Court's opinion.

First, the Court today does not prescribe the precise form of required pretermination procedures in cases where an employee disputes the *facts* proffered to support his discharge. . . .

Factual disputes are not involved in these cases, however, and the "very nature of due process negates any concept of inflexible procedures universally applicable to every imaginable situation." *Cafeteria Workers v. McElroy*, 367 U.S. 886, 895 (1961). . . .

The second issue not resolved today is that of administrative delay. In holding that Loudermill's administrative proceedings did not take too long, the Court plainly does *not* state a flat rule that 9-month delays in deciding discharge appeals will pass constitutional scrutiny as a matter of course. . . . The holding in Part V is merely that, in this particular case, Loudermill failed to allege facts sufficient to state a cause of action, and not that nine months can never exceed constitutional limits.

Justice Rehnquist, dissenting

In *Arnett v. Kennedy*, 416 U.S. 134 (1974), six Members of this Court agreed that a public employee could be dismissed for misconduct without a full hearing prior to termination. A plurality of Justices agreed that the employee was entitled to exactly what Congress gave him, and no more. . . .

. . . We ought to recognize the totality of the State's definition of the property right in question, and not merely seize upon one of several paragraphs in a unitary statute to proclaim that in that paragraph the State has inexorably conferred upon a civil service employee something which it is powerless under the United States Constitution to qualify in the next paragraph of the statute. This practice ignores our duty under *Roth* to rely on state law as the source of property interests for purposes of applying the Due Process Clause of the Fourteenth Amendment. While it does not impose a federal definition of property, the Court departs from the full breadth of the holding in *Roth* by its selective choice from among the sentences the Ohio Legislature chooses to use in establishing and qualifying a right.

Having concluded by this somewhat tortured reasoning that Ohio has created a property right in the respondents in these cases, the Court naturally proceeds to inquire what process is "due" before the respondents may be divested of that right. This customary "balancing" inquiry conducted by the Court in these cases reaches a result that is quite unobjectionable, but it seems to me that it is devoid of any principles which will either instruct or endure. The balance is simply an ad hoc weighing which depends to a great extent upon how the Court subjectively views the underlying interests at stake. The results in previous cases and in these cases have been quite unpredictable. To paraphrase Justice Black, today's balancing act requires a "pretermination opportunity to respond" but there is nothing that indicates what tomorrow's will be. *Goldberg v. Kelly*, 397 U.S. 254, 276 (1970) (Black, J., dissenting). The results from today's balance certainly do not jibe with the result in *Goldberg* or *Mathews v. Eldridge*, 424 U.S. 319 (1976). The lack of any principled standards in this area means that these procedural due process cases will recur time and again. Every different set of facts will present a new issue on what process was due and when. One way to avoid this subjective and varying interpretation of the Due Process Clause in cases such as these is to hold that one who avails himself of government entitlements accepts the grant of tenure along with its inherent limitations.

Because I believe that the Fourteenth Amendment of the United States Constitution does not support the conclusion that Ohio's effort to confer a limited form of tenure upon respondents resulted in the creation of a "property right" in their employment, I dissent.

Gilbert et al. v. Homar

520 U.S. 924 (1997) 9–0
+ *Scalia, Rehnquist, Stevens, O'Connor, Kennedy, Thomas, Souter, Ginsburg, Breyer*

[On August 26, 1992, while employed as a policeman at East Stroudsburg University [ESU], a Pennsylvania state institution, Richard Homar was arrested and charged with felony drug possession. ESU officials suspended him without pay, effective immediately, pending their own investigation. Although the criminal charges were dismissed on September 1, his suspension remained in effect. On September 18, Homar was provided the opportunity to tell his side of the story to ESU officials. He was then reinstated but demoted to groundskeeper. He filed a lawsuit under 42 U.S.C. § 1983, claiming that ESU President Gilbert's failure to provide him with notice and a hearing before suspending him without pay violated his constitutional due process rights.]

Justice Scalia delivered the opinion of the Court

This case presents the question whether a State violates the Due Process Clause of the Fourteenth Amendment by failing to provide notice and a hearing before suspending a tenured public employee without pay.

I

Respondent Richard J. Homar was employed as a police officer at East Stroudsburg University (ESU), a branch of Pennsylvania's State System of Higher Education. On August 26, 1992, when respondent was at the home of a family friend, he was arrested by the Pennsylvania State Police in a drug raid. Later that day, the state police filed a criminal complaint charging respondent with possession of marijuana, possession with intent to deliver, and criminal conspiracy to violate the controlled substance law, which is a felony. The state police notified respondent's supervisor, University Police Chief David Marazas, of the arrest and charges. Chief Marazas in turn informed Gerald Levanowitz, ESU's Director of Human Resources, to whom ESU President James Gilbert had delegated authority to discipline ESU employees. Levanowitz suspended respondent without pay effective immediately. Respondent failed to report to work on the day of his arrest, and learned of his suspension the next day, when he called Chief Marazas to inquire whether he had been suspended. That same day, respondent received a letter from Levanowitz confirming that he had been suspended effective August 26 pending an investigation into the criminal charges filed against him. The letter explained that any action taken by ESU would not necessarily coincide with the disposition of the criminal charges.

Although the criminal charges were dismissed on September 1, respondent's suspension remained in effect while ESU continued with its own investigation. On September 18, Levanowitz and Chief Marazas met with respondent in order to give him an opportunity to tell his side of the story. Respondent was informed at the meeting that the state police had given ESU information that was "very serious in nature," but he was not informed that that included a report of an alleged confession he had made on the day of his arrest; he was consequently unable to respond to damaging statements attributed to him in the police report.

In a letter dated September 23, Levanowitz notified respondent that he was being demoted to the position of groundskeeper effective the next day, and that he would receive backpay from the date the suspension took effect at the rate of pay of a groundskeeper. (Respondent eventually received backpay for the period of his suspension at the rate of pay of a university police officer.) The letter maintained that the demotion was being imposed "as a result of admissions made by yourself to the Pennsylvania State Police on August 26, 1992, that you maintained associations with individuals whom you knew were dealing in large quantities of marijuana and that you obtained marijuana from one of those individuals for your own use. Your actions constitute a clear and flagrant violation of Sections 200 and 200.2 of the [ESU] Police Department Manual." Upon receipt of this letter, the president of respondent's union requested a meeting with President Gilbert. The requested meeting took place on September 24, at which point respondent had received and read the police report containing the alleged confession. After providing respondent with an opportunity to respond to the charges, Gilbert sustained the demotion. . . .

II

The protections of the Due Process Clause apply to government deprivation of those perquisites of government employment in which the employee has a constitutionally protected "property" interest. Although we have previously held that public employees who can be discharged only for cause have a constitutionally protected property interest in their tenure and cannot be fired without due process, see *Board of Regents of State Colleges v. Roth*, 408 U.S. 564 (1972), *Perry v. Sindermann*, 408 U.S. 593 (1972), we have not had occasion to decide whether the protections of the Due Process Clause extend to discipline of tenured public employees short of termination. Petitioners, however, do not contest this preliminary point, and so without deciding it we will, like the District Court, "assum[e] that the suspension infringed a protected property interest," and turn at once to petitioners' contention that respondent received all the process he was due.

A

In *Cleveland Bd. of Ed. v. Loudermill*, 470 U.S. 532 (1985), we concluded that a public employee dismissible only for

cause was entitled to a very limited hearing prior to his termination, to be followed by a more comprehensive posttermination hearing. Stressing that the pretermination hearing "should be an initial check against mistaken decisions—essentially, a determination of whether there are reasonable grounds to believe that the charges against the employee are true and support the proposed action," we held that pretermination process need only include oral or written notice of the charges, an explanation of the employer's evidence, and an opportunity for the employee to tell his side of the story. In the course of our assessment of the governmental interest in immediate termination of a tenured employee, we observed that "in those situations where the employer perceives a significant hazard in keeping the employee on the job, it can avoid the problem by suspending *with pay.*"

Relying on this dictum, which it read as "strongly suggesting that suspension without pay must be preceded by notice and an opportunity to be heard *in all instances,*" and determining on its own that such a rule would be "eminently sensible," the Court of Appeals adopted a categorical prohibition: "[A] governmental employer may not suspend an employee without pay unless that suspension is preceded by some kind of pre-suspension hearing, providing the employee with notice and an opportunity to be heard." Respondent (as well as most of his *amici*) makes no attempt to defend this absolute rule, which spans all types of government employment and all types of unpaid suspensions. This is eminently wise, since under our precedents such an absolute rule is indefensible.

It is by now well established that " 'due process,' unlike some legal rules, is not a technical conception with a fixed content unrelated to time, place and circumstances." *Cafeteria & Restaurant Workers v. McElroy*, 367 U.S. 886 (1961). "Due process is flexible and calls for such procedural protections as the particular situation demands." *Morrissey v. Brewer*, 408 U.S. 471 (1972). This Court has recognized, on many occasions, that where a State must act quickly, or where it would be impractical to provide predeprivation process, postdeprivation process satisfies the requirements of the Due Process Clause. See, *e.g., . . . James Daniel Good Real Property*, 510 U.S. 43, 53 (1993). . . . And in *FDIC v. Mallen*, 486 U.S. 230 (1988), where we unanimously approved the Federal Deposit Insurance Corporation's suspension, without prior hearing, of an indicted private bank employee, we said: "An important government interest, accompanied by a substantial assurance that the deprivation is not baseless or unwarranted, may in limited cases demanding prompt action justify postponing the opportunity to be heard until after the initial deprivation."

The dictum in *Loudermill* relied upon by the Court of Appeals is of course not inconsistent with these precedents. To say that when the government employer perceives a hazard in leaving the employee on the job it "can avoid the problem by suspending with pay" is not to say that that is the only way of avoiding the problem. Whatever implication the phrase "with pay" might have conveyed is far outweighed by the clarity of our precedents which emphasize the flexibility of due process as contrasted with the sweeping and categorical rule adopted by the Court of Appeals.

B

To determine what process is constitutionally due, we have generally balanced three distinct factors:

"First, the private interest that will be affected by the official action; second, the risk of an erroneous deprivation of such interest through the procedures used, and the probable value, if any, of additional or substitute procedural safeguards; and finally, the Government's interest." *Mathews v. Eldridge*, 424 U.S. 319 (1976).

Respondent contends that he has a significant private interest in the uninterrupted receipt of his paycheck. But while our opinions have recognized the severity of depriving someone of the means of his livelihood, they have also emphasized that in determining what process is due, account must be taken of "the *length*" and "*finality* of the deprivation." Unlike the employee in *Loudermill*, who faced *termination*, respondent faced only a *temporary suspension* without pay. So long as the suspended employee receives a sufficiently prompt postsuspension hearing, the lost income is relatively insubstantial (compared with termination), and fringe benefits such as health and life insurance are often not affected at all.

On the other side of the balance, the State has a significant interest in immediately suspending, when felony charges are filed against them, employees who occupy positions of great public trust and high public visibility, such as police officers. Respondent contends that this interest in maintaining public confidence could have been accommodated by suspending him *with* pay until he had a hearing. We think, however, that the government does not have to give an employee charged with a felony a paid leave at taxpayer expense. If his services to the government are no longer useful once the felony charge has been filed, the Constitution does not require the government to bear the added expense of hiring a replacement while still paying him. ESU's interest in preserving public confidence in its police force is at least as significant as the State's interest in preserving the integrity of the sport of horse racing, see *Barry v. Barchi*, 443 U.S. at 64, an interest we "deemed sufficiently important. . . . to justify a brief period of suspension prior to affording the suspended trainer a hearing."

The last factor in the *Mathews* balancing, and the factor most important to resolution of this case, is the risk of erroneous deprivation and the likely value of any additional procedures. Petitioners argue that any pre-suspension hearing would have been worthless because pursuant to an Executive Order of the Governor of Pennsylvania a state employee is automatically to be suspended without pay "as soon as practicable after [being] formally charged with . . . a felony." According to petitioners, supervisors have no discretion under this rule, and the mandatory suspension without pay lasts until the criminal charges are finally resolved. If petitioners' interpretation of this order is correct, there is no need for any presuspension process since there would be nothing to consider at the hearing except the independently verifiable fact of whether an employee had indeed been formally charged with a felony. Respondent, however, challenges petitioners' reading of the Code, and contends that in any event an order of the Governor of Pennsylvania is a "mere directive which does not confer a legally enforceable right." We need not resolve this disputed issue of state law because even assuming the Code is only advisory (or has no application at all), the State had no constitutional obligation to provide respondent with a presuspension hearing. We noted in *Loudermill* that the purpose of a pre-*termination* hearing is to determine "whether there are reasonable grounds to believe the charges against the employee are true and support the proposed action." 470 U.S. at 545–546. By parity of reasoning, the purpose of any pre-*suspension* hearing would be to assure that there are reasonable grounds to support the suspension without pay. But here that has already been assured by the arrest and the filing of charges. . . .

C

Much of respondent's argument is dedicated to the proposition that he had a due process right to a presuspension hearing because the suspension was open-ended and he "theoretically may not have had the opportunity to be heard for weeks, months, or even years after his initial suspension without pay." But, as respondent himself asserts in his attempt to downplay the governmental interest, "because the employee is entitled, in any event, to a prompt post-suspension opportunity to be heard, the period of the suspension should be short and the amount of pay during the suspension minimal."

Whether respondent was provided an adequately prompt *post-suspension* hearing in the present case is a separate question. Although the charges against respondent were dropped on September 1 (petitioners apparently learned of this on September 2), he did not receive any sort of hearing until September 18. Once the charges were dropped, the risk of erroneous deprivation increased substantially, and, as petitioners conceded at oral argument, there was likely value in holding a prompt hearing. Because neither the Court of Appeals nor the District Court addressed whether, under the particular facts of this case, petitioners violated due process by failing to provide a sufficiently prompt post-suspension hearing, we will not consider this issue in the first instance, but remand for consideration by the Court of Appeals.

. . .

The judgment of the Court of Appeals is reversed.

OTHER PROTECTIONS FOR PUBLIC EMPLOYEES

The cases in the previous section struggle to determine when a termination requires some kind of hearing and which of the *Goldberg* ingredients such hearings should include. A major difference between due process protections and the protections of other constitutional rights is that we think of the latter as substantive rights, such as speech rights of employees, while we tend to treat the former as procedural rights. However, as we have sought to emphasize throughout this book, the process (means) shapes the substance (ends) of administrative legality.

Freedom of Political Expression

We have already seen, in *Perry* and in *Loudermill*, that the Court is only partially sensitive to the harsh reality of political life. Modern politics contains its own equivalent of killing the messenger. People who speak out against superiors are more likely to get fired. Because the First Amendment protects free speech, employees fired for exercising that right have persuaded trial courts to order their reinstatement. Courts similarly order reinstatement of those fired for discriminatory reasons, which we shall discuss shortly.

The Court's protection of political freedom reached further in *Elrod v. Burns*.[8] Here, when a Democrat defeated a Republican to be Sheriff of Cook County, Illinois, he fired all of the sheriff's deputies who refused to join the Democratic party or otherwise support the party. Citing *Perry*, among other cases, the Court struck down this practice, stating in part:

Patronage practice falls squarely within the prohibitions of . . . *Perry*. Under that practice, public employees hold their jobs on the condition that they provide, in some acceptable manner, support for the favored political party. The threat of dismissal for failure to provide that support unquestionably inhibits protected belief and association, and dismissal for failure to provide support only penalizes its exercise. The belief and association which Government may not ordain directly are achieved by indirection. And regardless of how evenhandedly these restraints may operate in the long run, after political office has changed hands several times, protected interests are still infringed and thus the violation remains.

Although the practice of patronage dismissals clearly infringes First Amendment interests, our inquiry is not at an end, for the prohibition on encroachment of First Amendment protections is not an absolute. Restraints are permitted for appropriate reasons. . . . [I]f conditioning the retention of public employment on the employee's support of the in-party is to survive constitutional challenge, it must further some vital government end by a means that is least restrictive of freedom of belief

---

8. 427 U.S. 347 (1976), reaffirmed by 5-4 vote in *Rutan et al. v. Republican Party of Illinois et al.*, 497 U.S. 62 (1990).

and association in achieving that end, and the benefit gained must outweigh the loss of constitutionally protected rights.

One interest which has been offered in justification of patronage is the need to insure effective government and the efficiency of public employees. It is argued that employees of political persuasions not the same as that of the party in control of public office will not have the incentive to work effectively and may even be motivated to subvert the incumbent administration's efforts to govern effectively. We are not persuaded. The inefficiency resulting from the wholesale replacement of large numbers of public employees every time political office changes hands belies this justification. And the prospect of dismissal after an election in which the incumbent party has lost is only a disincentive to good work. Further, it is not clear that dismissal in order to make room for a patronage appointment will result in replacement by a person more qualified to do the job since appointment often occurs in exchange for the delivery of votes, or other party service, not job capability. More fundamentally, however, the argument does not succeed because it is doubtful that the mere difference of political persuasion motivates poor performance; nor do we think it legitimately may be used as a basis for imputing such behavior. . . . At all events, less drastic means for insuring government effectiveness and employee efficiency are available to the State. Specifically, employees may always be discharged for good cause, such as insubordination or poor job performance, when those bases in fact exist. . . .

A second interest advanced in support of patronage is the need for political loyalty of employees, not to the end that effectiveness and efficiency be insured, but to the end that representative government not be undercut by tactics obstructing the implementation of policies of the new administration, policies presumably sanctioned by the electorate. The justification is not without force, but is nevertheless inadequate to validate patronage wholesale. Limiting patronage dismissals to policy-making positions is sufficient to achieve this governmental end. Nonpolicymaking individuals usually have only limited responsibility and are therefore not in a position to thwart the goals of the in-party. . . .

In 1996, in *Board of County Commissioners v. Umbehr*, the Court, 7-2, extended this protection to those who, though not employees, had contracts with the government to provide services. Mr. Umbehr, who had a contract with Wabaunsee County, Kansas, to haul trash, lost his contract. He alleged that the only reason he lost his contract was that he had vociferously criticized the County Commission in public. He filed a section 1983

action and won. Justice Antonin Scalia, joined in dissent by Justice Clarence Thomas, stated a starkly different approach to such issues:

When a practice not expressly prohibited by the text of the Bill of Rights bears the endorsement of a long tradition of open, widespread, and unchallenged use that dates back to the beginning of the Republic, we have no proper basis for striking it down. Such a venerable and accepted tradition is not to be laid on the examining table and scrutinized for its conformity to some abstract principle of First Amendment adjudication devised by this Court. To the contrary, such traditions are themselves the stuff out of which the Court's principles are to be formed. They are, in these uncertain areas, the very points of reference by which the legitimacy or illegitimacy of other practices is to be figured out. When it appears that the latest "rule," or "three-part test," or "balancing test" devised by the Court has placed us on a collision course with such a landmark practice, it is the former that must be recalculated by us, and not the latter that must be abandoned by our citizens. I know of no other way to formulate a constitutional jurisprudence that reflects, as it should, the principles adhered to, over time, by the American people, rather than those favored by the personal (and necessarily shifting) philosophical dispositions of a majority of this Court.[9]

As you can tell, this position implicitly rejects many of the premises on which contemporary administrative law rests.

The coin protecting Mr. Umbehr, so criticized by Justice Scalia, does have a flip side. Courts could, without doing violence to the dictionary, extend "freedom of speech" to protect workers who are fired for speaking out privately against their bosses, or otherwise speaking in ways that bosses find disruptive to the workplace. However, the courts have held that only on-the-job speech that addresses "matters of public concern" is protected. In *Connick v. Myers*, Sheila Myers, an assistant district attorney in New Orleans, strenuously objected to being transferred to a different division of the criminal courts and distributed a questionnaire to 15 other prosecutors about the office's transfer policy and office morale. She was told that her distribution of the questionnaire was an act of insubordination and was fired for refusing the

---

9. 518 U.S. 668 (1996). Justice Scalia's dissent begins at page 686.

transfer. The Court held that her "in-house" protest was not a matter of public concern and that her firing had not infringed upon the First Amendment's guarantee of the right to freedom of speech.[10]

The Court reached a similar result in 1994, when a nurse, Cheryl Churchill, was fired from her job in a hospital. The hospital claimed that Churchill had made highly critical remarks on the job about other workers and hospital managers. Churchill claimed that her remarks had been inaccurately reported to management, and that she only complained about how the hospital's "cross training" program was putting inadequately trained staff in life-threatening situations. The Court concluded that, regardless of what Ms. Churchill actually said, courts should uphold the firing if the hospital could show that it reasonably believed she had made the highly critical private remarks. At the same time the Court did require a hearing to investigate whether the hospital's understanding was a reasonable one.[11]

In *Garcetti v. Ceballos*, 547 U.S. 410 (2006), the Court further limited public employees' First Amendment right to freedom of speech. Prior cases held that a public employer could discipline or fire an employee for speaking out if the speech substantially impaired the efficiency of the workplace, unless the speech in question involved a matter of public concern. Until *Garcetti*, however, the Court had only addressed speech acts committed by people acting as "private citizens," rather than in their capacity as employees. The question presented in *Garcetti* was whether speech made in an employee's official capacity is protected by the First Amendment. Ceballos, a deputy district attorney in Los Angeles was denied a promotion and transferred because he complained to his superiors about inaccuracies in an affidavit that had been prepared by a deputy sheriff. Ceballos claimed that these criticisms were the reason he was denied a promotion and asked for relief under the First and Fourteenth Amendments.

In the majority opinion written by Justice Anthony Kennedy, the Court rejected Ceballos's claim and ruled

that "when public employees make statements pursuant to their official duties, the employees are not speaking as citizens for First Amendment purposes." The rule announced by the Court in *Garcetti* is that speech by government employees, even if it is about a matter of public concern, is not protected if it is deemed to be part of the employee's "official duties." To some, this ruling threatens to have a chilling effect on government employees' willingness to express criticism of office policies or engage in open dialogue about controversial topics, even where those topics are directly related to the work of the government office itself.

Right of Privacy

The Supreme Court in 1965, in *Griswold v. Connecticut*, 381 U.S. 479, suggested that the Constitution protects a "penumbra" of rights, rights implied by but not stated in the Bill of Rights itself. One of these has loosely been called the *right* of *privacy*. Should such a right prevent employers from setting standards for the dress and hair length of employees?

Kelley v. Johnson

425 U.S. 238 (1976) 6-2
+ *Burger, Stewart, White, Blackmun, Powell, Rehnquist*
– *Brennan, Marshall*
NP Stevens

[Johnson, a Suffolk County, New York, policeman brought suit against county authorities to stop them from enforcing a regulation limiting the length of a policeman's hair. His claim was that such a regulation deprived him of his liberty under the Fourteenth Amendment to regulate his own personal appearance. The district court dismissed his lawsuit but the Second Circuit reversed. In reversing the Second Circuit and rejecting Johnson's claims, the Court noted in a footnote that "[h]istory is dotted with instances of governments regulating the personal appearance of their citizens. For instance, in an effort to stimulate his countrymen to adopt a modern lifestyle, Peter the Great issued an edict in 1698 regulating the wearing of beards throughout Russia. Anyone who wanted to grow a beard had to pay

10. 461 U.S. 138 (1983).
11. *Waters v. Churchill*, 511 U.S. 661 (1994).

an annual tax of from one kopek for a peasant to one hundred rubles for a rich merchant."]

Justice Rehnquist delivered the opinion of the Court

Section 1 of the Fourteenth Amendment to the United States Constitution provides in pertinent part: "[No State] shall . . . deprive any person of life, liberty, or property, without due process of law."

This section affords not only a procedural guarantee against the deprivation of "liberty," but like-wise protects substantive aspects of liberty against unconstitutional restriction by the State.

The "liberty" interest claimed by respondent here, of course, is distinguishable from those protected by the Court in *Roe v. Wade*, 410 U.S. 113 (1973); *Eisenstadt v. Baird*, 405 U.S. 438 (1972); *Stanley v. Illinois*, 405 U.S. 645 (1972); *Griswold v. Connecticut* . . . and *Meyer v. Nebraska*, 262 U.S. 390 (1923). Each of those cases involved a substantial claim of infringement on the individual's freedom of choice with respect to certain basic matters of procreation, marriage, and family life. But whether the citizenry at large has some sort of "liberty" interest within the Fourteenth Amendment in matters of personal appearance is a question on which this Court's cases offer little, if any, guidance. We can, nevertheless, assume an affirmative answer for purposes of deciding this case, because we find that assumption insufficient to carry the day for respondent's claim.

Respondent has sought the protection of the Fourteenth Amendment not as a member of the citizenry at large, but on the contrary as an employee of the police force of Suffolk County, a subdivision of the State of New York. While the Court of Appeals made passing reference to this distinction, it was thereafter apparently ignored. We think, however, it is highly significant. In *Pickering v. Board of Education*, 391 U.S. 563, 568 (1968), after noting that state employment may not be conditioned on the relinquishment of First Amendment rights, the Court stated that "[a]t the same time it cannot be gainsaid that the State has interests as an employer in regulating the speech of its employees that differ significantly from those it possesses in connection with regulation of the speech of the citizenry in general." More recently, we have sustained comprehensive and substantial restrictions upon activities of both federal and state employees lying at the core of the First Amendment. . . . If such state regulations may survive challenges based on the explicit language of the First Amendment, there is surely even more room for restrictive regulations of state employees where the claim implicates only the more general contours of the substantive liberty interest protected by the Fourteenth Amendment. . . .

The promotion of safety of persons and property is unquestionably at the core of the State's police power, and virtually all state and local governments employ a uniform police force to aid in the accomplishment of that purpose. Choice of organization, dress, and equipment for law enforcement personnel is a decision entitled to the same sort of presumption of legislative validity as are state choices designed to promote other aims within the cognizance of the State's police power. . . . Thus the question is not, as the Court of Appeals conceived it to be, whether the State can "establish" a "genuine public need" for the specific regulation. It is whether respondent can demonstrate that there is no rational connection between the regulation, based as it is on petitioner's method of organizing its police force, and the promotion of safety of persons and property.

We think the answer here is so clear that the District Court was quite right in the first instance to have dismissed respondent's complaint. Neither this Court, the Court of Appeals, nor the District Court is in a position to weigh the policy arguments in favor of and against a rule regulating hair styles as a part of regulations governing a uniformed civilian service. The constitutional issue to be decided by these courts is whether petitioner's determination that such regulations should be enacted is so irrational that it may be branded "arbitrary," and therefore a deprivation of respondent's "liberty" interest in freedom to choose his own hair style. *Williamson v. Lee Optical Co.*, 348 U.S. 483, 487–488 (1955). The overwhelming majority of state and local police of the present day are uniformed. This fact itself testifies to the recognition by those who direct those operations, and by the people of the States and localities who directly or indirectly choose such persons, that similarity in appearance of police officers is desirable. This choice may be based on a desire to make police officers readily recognizable to the members of the public, or a desire for the *esprit de corps* which such similarity is felt to inculcate within the police force itself. Either one is a sufficiently rational justification for regulations so as to defeat respondent's claim based on the liberty guaranty of the Fourteenth Amendment. . . .

Reversed.

Justice Powell, concurring [omitted]

Justice Marshall, with whom
Justice Brennan joins, dissenting

. . . I think it clear that the Fourteenth Amendment does indeed protect against comprehensive regulation of what citizens may or may not wear. And I find that the rationales offered by the Court to justify the regulation in this case are insufficient to demonstrate its constitutionality. Accordingly, I respectfully dissent. . . .

. . . [W]e have observed that "[l]iberty under law extends to the full range of conduct which the individual is free to pursue." *Bolling v. Sharpe*, 347 U.S. 497, 499 (1954). See also *Poe v. Ullman*, 367 U.S. 497, 543 (1961) (Harlan, J., dissenting). It seems to me manifest that that "full range of conduct" must encompass one's interest in dressing according to his own taste. An individual's personal appearance may reflect, sustain, and nourish his personality and may well be used as a means of expressing his attitude and lifestyle.* In taking control over a citizen's personal appearance, the government forces him to sacrifice substantial elements of his integrity and identity as well. To say that the liberty guarantee of the Fourteenth Amendment does not encompass matters of personal appearance would be fundamentally inconsistent with the values of privacy, self-identity, autonomy, and personal integrity that I have always assumed the Constitution was designed to protect. See *Roe v. Wade*, 410 U.S. 113 (1973); *Stanley v. Georgia*, 394 U.S. 557, 564 (1969); *Griswold v. Connecticut*, 381 U.S. 479, 485 (1965); *Olmstead v. United States*, 277 U.S. 438, 478 (1928) (Brandeis, J., dissenting).

If little can be found in past cases of this Court or indeed in the Nation's history on the specific issue of a citizen's

*While the parties did not address any First Amendment issues in any detail in this Court, governmental regulation of a citizen's personal appearance may in some circumstances not only deprive him of liberty under the Fourteenth Amendment but violate his First Amendment rights as well. *Tinker v. Des Moines School Dist.*, 393 U.S. 503 (1969).

right to choose his own personal appearance, it is only because the right has been so clear as to be beyond question. When the right has been mentioned, its existence has simply been taken for granted. For instance, the assumption that the right exists is reflected in the 1789 congressional debates over which guarantees should be explicitly articulated in the Bill of Rights. I. Brant, The Bill of Rights 53–67 (1965). There was considerable debate over whether the right of assembly should be expressly mentioned. Congressman Benson of New York argued that its inclusion was necessary to assure that the right would not be infringed by the government. In response, Congressman Sedgwick of Massachusetts indicated:

"If the committee were governed by that general principle . . . they might have declared that *a man should have a right to wear his hat if he pleased* . . . but [I] would ask the gentleman whether he thought it necessary to enter these trifles in a declaration of rights, *in a Government where none of them were intended to be infringed.*" Id., at 54–55 (emphasis added).

Thus, while they did not include it in the Bill of Rights, Sedgwick and his colleagues clearly believed there to be a right in one's personal appearance. And, while they may have regarded the right as a trifle as long as it was honored, they clearly would not have so regarded it if it were infringed. . . .

To my mind, the right in one's personal appearance is inextricably bound up with the historically recognized right of "every individual to the possession and control of his own person," *Union Pacific R. Co. v. Botsford*, 141 U.S. 250, 251 (1891), and, perhaps even more fundamentally, with "the right to be let alone—the most comprehensive of rights and the right most valued by civilized men." *Olmstead v. United States, supra*, at 478 (Brandeis, J., dissenting). In an increasingly crowded society in which it is already extremely difficult to maintain one's identity and personal integrity, it would be distressing, to say the least, if the government could regulate our personal appearance unconfined by any constitutional strictures whatsoever. . . .

The Court cautions us not to view the hair-length regulation in isolation, but rather to examine it "in the context of the county's chosen mode of organization for its police force." *Ante*, at 247. While the Court's caution is well taken, one should also keep in mind, as I fear the Court does not, that what is ultimately under scrutiny is neither the overall structure of the police force nor the uniform and equipment requirements to which its members are subject, but rather the regulation which dictates acceptable hair lengths. The fact that the uniform requirement, for instance, may be rationally related to the goals of increasing police officer "identifiability" and the maintenance of esprit de corps does absolutely nothing to establish the legitimacy of the hair-length regulation. I see no connection between the regulation and the offered rationales and would accordingly affirm the judgment of the Court of Appeals.

When the government places conditions on public employment that conflict with an individual's privacy rights, the courts apply a "balancing test." As the dissenting opinion in *Kelley v. Johnson* makes clear, some members of the current Court disagree not only with the outcome of the majority's weighing process, but with the very idea that fundamental rights, such as privacy, should be "balanced" against governmental interests. The controversy over privacy as a constitutional right is grounded in very different interpretations about what rights are protected by the Constitution. While the Court in *Roe v. Wade*, 410 U.S. 113 (1973), affirmed the interpretation of privacy in *Griswold v. Connecticut*, a new conservative majority on the Court has indicated that that right may no longer be fundamental at least for women who seek abortions from public hospitals, *Webster v. Reproductive Health Services*, 492 U.S. 490 (1989).[12] The right to privacy is under attack not only in the area of abortion but in other areas directly affecting the rights of public employees—among them mandatory drug testing. The drug policies of the Reagan and Bush administrations specifically targeted public employees. Should the right of privacy prevent the government from implementing a mandatory drug screening program for public employees?

12. Citing *DeShaney v. Winnebago County Department of Social Services*, Chief Justice Rehnquist upheld provisions of a Missouri law that made it "unlawful for any public employee within the scope of his employment to perform or assist an abortion, not necessary to save the life of the mother" (Section 188.210). He wrote that "our cases have recognized that the due process clauses generally confer no affirmative right to governmental aid, even where such aid may be necessary to secure life, liberty or property interests of which the government itself may not deprive the individual."

National Treasury Employees Union et al. v. Von Raab

489 U.S. 656 (1989) 5-4
+ *Rehnquist, White, Blackmun, O'Connor, Kennedy*
– *Marshall, Brennan, Scalia, Stevens*

[In 1986, the Commissioner of the United States Customs Service announced that certain employees would be subject to a drug testing program designed to detect the presence of marijuana, cocaine, opiates, amphetamines, and phencyclidine. Anyone could be tested who sought transfer or promotion in the following positions: (1) jobs directly involving the interdiction of illegal drugs; (2) jobs requiring the carrying of firearms; and (3) jobs requiring the handling of classified materials. The National Treasury Employee Union filed suit alleging that the drug testing program violated the Fourth Amendment rights of these federal employees to be free from unreasonable government searches. The district court agreed and enjoined the drug testing program. The Court of Appeals for the Fifth Circuit reversed. The union appealed to the Supreme Court.]

Justice Kennedy delivered the opinion of the Court

I

The United States Customs Service, a bureau of the Department of the Treasury, is the federal agency responsible for processing persons, carriers, cargo, and mail into the United States, collecting revenue from imports, and enforcing customs and related laws. . . . An important responsibility of the Service is the interdiction and seizure of contraband, including illegal drugs. In 1987 alone, Customs agents seized drugs with a retail value of nearly 9 billion dollars. . . . In the routine discharge of their duties, many Customs employees have direct contact with those who traffic in drugs for profit. Drug import operations, often directed by sophisticated criminal syndicates, *United States v. Mendenhall*, 446 U.S. 544 . . . (1980) (Powell, J., concurring), may be effected by violence or its threat. As a necessary response, many Customs operatives carry and use firearms in connection with their official duties. . . .

In December 1985, respondent, the Commissioner of Customs, established a Drug Screening Task Force to explore the possibility of implementing a drug screening program within the Service. After extensive research and consultation with experts in the field, the Task Force concluded "that drug screening through urinalysis is technologically reliable, valid and accurate." Citing this conclusion, the Commissioner announced his intention to require drug tests of employees who applied for, or occupied, certain positions within the Service. The Commissioner stated his belief that "Customs is largely drugfree," but noted also that "unfortunately no segment of society is immune from the threat of illegal drug use." . . .

In May 1986, the Commissioner announced implementation of the drug testing program. Drug tests were made a condition of placement or employment for positions that meet one or more of three criteria, [see description above.] . . .

II

In *Skinner v. Railway Labor Executives' Assn.*, 103 L Ed 2d 639,109 S Ct—, decided today, we hold that federal regulations requiring employees of private railroads to produce urine samples for chemical testing implicate the Fourth Amendment, as those tests invade reasonable expectations of privacy. Our earlier cases have settled that the Fourth Amendment protects individuals from unreasonable searches conducted by the Government, even when the Government acts as an employer, . . . and, in view of our holding in *Railway Labor Executives* that urine tests are searches, it follows that the Customs Service's drug testing program must meet the reasonableness requirement of the Fourth Amendment.

While we have often emphasized, and reiterate today, that a search must be supported, as a general matter, by a warrant issued upon probable cause, . . . our decision in *Railway Labor Executives* reaffirms the longstanding principle that neither a warrant nor probable cause, nor, indeed, any measure of individualized suspicion, is an indispensable component of reasonableness in every circumstance. . . . As we note in *Railway Labor Executives*, our cases establish that where a Fourth Amendment intrusion serves special governmental needs, beyond the normal need for law enforcement, it is necessary to balance the individual's privacy expectations against the Government's interests to determine whether it is impractical to require a warrant or some level of individualized suspicion in the particular context. . . .

It is clear that the Customs Service's drug testing program is not designed to serve the ordinary needs of law enforcement. Test results may not be used in a criminal prosecution of the employee without the employee's consent. The purposes of the program are to deter drug use among those eligible for promotion to sensitive positions within the Service and to prevent the promotion of drug users to those positions. These substantial interests, no less than the Government's concern for safe rail transportation at issue in *Railway Labor Executives*, present a special need that may justify departure from the ordinary warrant and probable cause requirements.

A

Petitioners do not contend that a warrant is required by the balance of privacy and governmental interests in this context, nor could any such contention withstand scrutiny. We have recognized before that requiring the Government to procure a warrant for every work-related intrusion "would conflict with 'the common-sense realization that government offices could not function if every employment decision became a constitutional matter.' " *New Jersey v. T.L.O., supra*, at 340.

Even if Customs Service employees are more likely to be familiar with the procedures required to obtain a warrant than most other Government workers, requiring a warrant in this context would serve only to divert valuable agency resources from the Service's primary mission. The Customs Service has been entrusted with pressing responsibilities, and its mission would be compromised if it were required to seek search warrants in connection with routine, yet sensitive, employment decisions.

Furthermore, a warrant would provide little or nothing in the way of additional protection of personal privacy. A warrant serves primarily to advise the citizen that an intrusion is authorized by law and limited in its permissible scope and to interpose a neutral magistrate between the citizen and the law enforcement officer "engaged in the often competitive enterprise of ferreting out crime." *Johnson v. United States*, 333 U.S. 10 (1948). . . . Under the Customs program, every employee who seeks a transfer to a covered position knows that he must take a drug test, and is likewise aware of the procedures the Service must follow in administering the test. A covered employee is simply not subject "to the discretion of the official in the field." *Comoro, v. Municipal Court*, 387 U.S. 523 . . . (1967). The process becomes automatic when the employee elects to apply for, and thereafter pursue, a covered position. Because the Service does not make a discretionary determination to search based on a judgment that certain conditions are present, there are simply "no special facts for a neutral magistrate to evaluate." . . .

The Customs Service is our Nation's first line of defense against one of the greatest problems affecting the health and welfare of our population. We have adverted before to "the veritable national crisis in law enforcement caused by smuggling of illicit narcotics." *United States v. Montoya de Hernandez*, 473 U.S. 531 . . . (1985). . . . The record in this case confirms that, through the adroit selection of source locations, smuggling routes, and increasingly elaborate methods of concealment, drug traffickers have managed to bring into this country increasingly large quantities of illegal drugs. The record also indicates, and it is well known, that drug smugglers do not hesitate to use violence to protect their lucrative trade and avoid apprehension.

Many of the Service's employees are often exposed to this criminal element and to the controlled substances they seek to smuggle into the country. The physical safety of these employees may be threatened, and many may be tempted not only by bribes from the traffickers with whom they deal, but also by their own access to vast sources of valuable contraband seized and controlled by the Service. The Commissioner indicated below that "Customs [o]fficers have been shot, stabbed, run over, dragged by automobiles, and assaulted with blunt objects while performing their duties." . . . At least nine officers have died in the line of duty since 1974. . . .

It is readily apparent that the Government has a compelling interest in ensuring that front-line interdiction personnel are physically fit, and have unimpeachable integrity and judgment. Indeed, the Government's interest here is at least as important as its interest in searching travelers entering the country. We have long held that travelers seeking to enter the country may be stopped and required to submit to a routine search without probable cause, or even founded suspicion, "because of national self protection reasonably requiring one entering the country to identify himself as entitled to come in, and his belongings as effects which may be lawfully brought in." *Carroll v. United States*, 267 U.S. 132, . . . (1985). The public interest demands effective measures to bar drug users from positions directly involving the interdiction of illegal drugs. . . .

Against these valid public interests we must weigh the interference with individual liberty that results from requiring these classes of employees to undergo a urine test. The interference with individual privacy that results from the collection of a urine sample for subsequent chemical analysis could be substantial in some circumstances. . . . We have recognized, however, that the "operational realities of the workplace" may render entirely reasonable certain work-related intrusions by supervisors and co-workers that might be viewed as unreasonable in other contexts. . . . While these operational realities will rarely affect an employee's expectations of privacy with respect to searches of his person, or of personal effects that the employee may bring to the workplace, . . . it is plain that certain forms of public employment may diminish privacy expectations even with respect to such personal searches. Employees of the United States Mint, for example, should expect to be subject to certain routine personal searches when they leave the workplace every day. Similarly, those who join our military or intelligence services may not only be required to give what in other contexts might be viewed as extraordinary assurances of trustworthiness and probity, but also may expect intrusive inquiries into their physical fitness for those special positions. Cf. *Snepp v. United States*, 444 U.S. 507 (1980). . . .

We think Customs employees who are directly involved in the interdiction of illegal drugs or who are required to carry firearms in the line of duty likewise have a diminished expectation of privacy in respect to the intrusions occasioned by a urine test. Unlike most private citizens or government employees in general, employees involved in drug interdiction reasonably should expect effective inquiry into their fitness and probity. Much the same is true of employees who are required to carry firearms. Because successful performance of their duties depends uniquely on their judgment and dexterity, these employees cannot reasonably expect to keep from the Service personal information that bears directly on their fitness. . . .

In sum, we believe the Government has demonstrated that its compelling interests in safeguarding our borders and the public safety outweigh the privacy expectations of employees who seek to be promoted to positions that directly involve the interdiction of illegal drugs or that require the incumbent to carry a firearm. We hold that the testing of these employees is reasonable under the Fourth Amendment. . . .

It is so ordered.

Justice Marshall, with whom Justice Brennan joins, dissenting

. . . [T]he Court's abandonment of the Fourth Amendment's express requirement that searches of the person rest on probable cause is unprincipled and unjustifiable. But even if I believe that balancing analysis was appropriate under the Fourth Amendment, I would still dissent from today's judgment, for the reasons stated by Justice Scalia in his dissenting opinion. . . .

Justice Scalia, with whom Justice Stevens joins, dissenting

The issue in this case is not whether Customs Service employees can constitutionally be denied promotion, or even dismissed, for a single instance of unlawful drug use, at home or at work. They assuredly can. The issue here is what steps can constitutionally be taken to *detect* such drug use. The Government asserts it can demand that employees perform "an excretory function traditionally shielded by great privacy" . . . The Court agrees that this constitutes a search for purposes of the Fourth Amendment—and I think it obvious that it is a type of search particularly destructive of privacy and offensive to personal dignity.

Until today this Court had upheld a bodily search separate from arrest and without individualized suspicion of wrongdoing only with respect to prison inmates, relying upon the uniquely dangerous nature of that environment. See *Bell v. Wolfish*, 441 U.S. 520 . . . (1979). Today, in *Skinner*, we allow a less intrusive bodily search of railroad employees involved in train accidents. I joined the Court's

opinion there because the demonstrated frequency of drug and alcohol use by the targeted class of employees, and the demonstrated connection between such use and grave harm, rendered the search a reasonable means of protecting society. I decline to join the Court's opinion in the present case because neither frequency of use nor connection to harm is demonstrated or even likely. In my view the Customs Service rules are a kind of immolation of privacy and human dignity in symbolic opposition to drug use.

. . . While there are some absolutes in Fourth Amendment law, as soon as those have been left behind and the question comes down to whether a particular search has been "reasonable," the answer depends largely upon the social necessity that prompts the search. Thus, in upholding the administrative search of a student's purse in a school, we began with the observation (documented by an agency report to Congress) that "[m]aintaining order in the classroom has never been easy, but in recent years, school disorder has often taken particularly ugly forms: drug use and violent crime in the schools have become major social problems." *New Jersey v. T.L.O.*, 469 U.S. 325 . . . (1985). When we approved fixed checkpoints near the Mexican border to stop and search cars for illegal aliens, we observed at the outset that "the Immigration and Naturalization Service now suggests there may be as many as 10 or 12 million aliens illegally in the country," and that "[i]nterdicting the flow of illegal entrants from Mexico poses formidable law enforcement problems." *United States v. Martinez-Fuerte*, 428 U.S. 543 (1976). . . .

The Court's opinion in the present case, however, will be searched in vain for real evidence of a real problem that will be solved by urine testing of Customs Service employees. Instead, there are assurances that "[t]he Customs Service is our Nation's first line of defense against one of the greatest problems affecting the health and welfare of our population;" . . . that "[m]any of the Service's employees are often exposed to [drug smugglers] and to the controlled substances they seek to smuggle into the country"; . . . To paraphrase Churchill, all this contains much that is obviously true, and much that is relevant; unfortunately, what is obviously true is not relevant, and what is relevant is not obviously true. The only pertinent points, it seems to me, are supported by nothing but speculation, and not very plausible speculation at that. It is not apparent to me that a

Customs Service employee who uses drugs is significantly more likely to be bribed by a drug smuggler, any more than a Customs Service employee who wears diamonds is significantly more likely to be bribed by a diamond smuggler—unless, perhaps, the addiction to drugs is so severe, and requires so much money to maintain, that it would be detectable even without benefit of a urine test. Nor is it apparent to me that Customs officers who use drugs will be appreciably less "sympathetic" to their drug-interdiction mission, any more than police officers who exceed the speed limit in their private cars are appreciably less sympathetic to their mission of enforcing the traffic laws. . . . Nor, finally, is it apparent to me that urine tests will be even marginally more effective in preventing gun-carrying agents from risking "impaired perception and judgment" than is their current knowledge that, if impaired, they may be shot dead in unequal combat with unimpaired smugglers—unless, again, their addiction is so severe that no urine test is needed for detection.

What is absent in the Government's justifications—notably absent, revealingly absent, and as far as I am concerned dispositively absent—is the recitation of *even a single instance* in which any of the speculated horribles actually occurred: an instance, that is, in which the cause of bribe-taking, or of poor aim, or of unsympathetic law enforcement, or of compromise of classified information, was drug use. Although the Court points out that several employees have in the past been removed from the Service for accepting bribes and other integrity violations, and that at least nine officers have died in the line of duty since 1974, . . . 103 L Ed 2d 704, there is no indication whatever that these incidents were related to drug use by Service employees. Perhaps concrete evidence of the severity of a problem is unnecessary when it is so well known that courts can almost take judicial notice of it; but that is surely not the case here. . . .

The only plausible explanation, in my view, is what the Commissioner himself offered in the concluding sentence of his memorandum to Customs Service employees announcing the program: "Implementation of the drug screening program would set an important example in our country's struggle with this most serious threat to our national health and security." . . . Or as respondent's brief to this Court asserted: "if a law enforcement agency and its employees

do not take the law seriously, neither will the public on which the agency's effectiveness depends." . . . What better way to show that the Government is serious about its "war on drugs" than to subject its employees on the front line of that war to this invasion of their privacy and affront to their dignity? To be sure, there is only a slight chance that it will prevent some serious public harm resulting from Service employee drug use, but it will show to the world that the Service is "clean," and—most important of all—will demonstrate the determination of the Government to eliminate this scourge of our society! I think it obvious that this justification is unacceptable; that the impairment of individual liberties cannot be the means of making a point; that symbolism, even symbolism for so worthy a cause as the abolition of unlawful drugs, cannot validate an otherwise unreasonable search.

There is irony in the Government's citation, in support of its position, of Justice Brandeis's statement in *Olmstead v. United States*, 277 U.S. 438 . . . (1928) that "[f]or good or for ill, [our Government] teaches the whole people by its example." . . . Brandeis was there *dissenting* from the Court's admission of evidence obtained through an unlawful Government wiretap. He was not praising the Government's example of vigor and enthusiasm in combating crime, but condemning its example that "the end justifies the means." . . . An even more apt quotation from that famous Brandeis dissent would have been the following:

"[I]t is . . . immaterial that the intrusion was in aid of law enforcement. Experience should teach us to be most on our guard to protect liberty when the Government's purposes are beneficent. Men born to freedom are naturally alert to repel invasion of their liberty by evil-minded rulers. The greatest dangers to liberty lurk in insidious encroachment by men of zeal, well-meaning but without understanding." Id., at 479. . . .

Those who lose because of the lack of understanding that begot the present exercise in symbolism are not just the Customs Service employees, whose dignity is thus offended, but all of us—who suffer a coarsening of our national manners that ultimately give the Fourth Amendment its content, and who become subject to the administration of federal officials whose respect for our privacy can hardly be greater than the small respect they have been taught to have for their own.

Drug testing of public employees continues to pose significant questions, as seen in a recent case, *Lanier v. City of Woodburn*, 518 F.3d 1147 (9th Cir., 2008). Lanier, who had applied to be a library page in the Woodburn, Oregon, public library, challenged the municipal employer's mandatory drug testing policy for all the job applicants. The U.S. Court of Appeals for the Ninth Circuit did not declare the law facially invalid but ruled instead that, as applied in this case, the test was unreasonable and thus unconstitutional. This decision, like prior decisions by the Court, leaves it to the judiciary to determine whether particular mandatory drug testing policies are reasonable.

Another controversial issue impacting the scope of employees' privacy rights is whether the government has a right to know one's sexual orientation and whether such information constitutes grounds for discharge. According to the military's "Don't Ask, Don't Tell" policy, 10 U.S.C. § 654, homosexual activity can be a ground for discharging a member of the armed forces. Major Margaret Witt sued the Air Force, the Secretary of Defense, the Secretary of the Air Force, and her Air Force commander after she was suspended from duty as an Air Force Reserves nurse. The reason given for her suspension was that she had a homosexual relationship with a civilian woman. Major Witt alleged that the "Don't Ask, Don't Tell" policy violates substantive due process, the equal protection clause, and procedural due process. The Ninth Circuit, in a 2-1 ruling, agreed to the extent that it found applicable the "strict scrutiny" test of a law's constitutionality, rather than the less stringent "rational relationship" test, and remanded the case back to the District Court to determine the degree of governmental interest advanced by the law (*Witt v. United States Department of Air Force*, 2008). The Ninth Circuit based its reasoning on the Supreme Court's decision in *Lawrence v. Texas*, 539 U.S. 558 (2003), which held that intimate sexual conduct is a liberty protected by the Fourteenth Amendment.

Anti-Discrimination Law

Title VII of the Civil Rights Act of 1964, as amended, prohibits discrimination on the basis of color, race, religion, sex, or national origin in employment decisions.

The act affects both hiring and firing decisions. The statute itself states no concrete definition of discrimination, although it does expressly prohibit discriminating against employees or job applicants who have protested or otherwise tried to correct alleged discrimination. Thus the courts have borne the main task of formulating the specific meaning of discrimination and shaping the evidence that those alleging discrimination must prove to sustain their case. In *McDonnell Douglas Corp. v. Green* the Supreme Court stated that an individual plaintiff charging racial discrimination under Title VII must show *prima facie* (1) that he or she belongs to a racial minority; (2) that he applied and was qualified for a job the employer was trying to fill; (3) that he was rejected; and (4) that thereafter the employer continued to seek applicants with the plaintiff's qualifications.[13] *Green* involved a private corporation, but the same rules of proof apply in nearly all respects to public employers. However, as the next case, *Washington v. Davis* (1976), indicates, the standards for proving discrimination are not always the same for the public and private sector (but see Justice Brennan's dissent).

Washington v. Davis

426 U.S. 229 (1976) 7-2

+ Burger, Stewart, White, Blackmun, Powell, Rehnquist, Stevens
– Brennan, Marshall

[The Washington, D.C., Police Department administered a standardized test (Test 21) developed by a neutral third party, the United States Civil Service Commission, to all people applying to be policemen. The test, used to measure verbal ability, vocabulary, and reading skills, was also used as an examining tool by the federal government. A minimum passing grade of 40 out of 80 was required along with high school graduation and certain physical and character requirements. Davis, a rejected black applicant, brought suit claiming that the cultural bias of the test allowed whites to pass more frequently than blacks, and that the test had not been validated by showing it was a good predictor of

13. 411 U.S. 792 (1973).

on-the-job performance. The district court found for the city, here represented by Washington, D.C., mayor Walter Washington. The United States Court of Appeals for the District of Columbia Circuit reversed.]

Justice White delivered the
opinion of the Court

[T]he finding . . . of the District Court . . . warranted three conclusions: "(a) The number of black police officers, while substantial, is not proportionate to the population mix of the city. (b) A higher percentage of blacks fail the Test than whites. (c) The Test has not been validated to establish its reliability for measuring subsequent job performance." This showing was deemed sufficient to shift the burden of proof to the defendants in the action, petitioners here; but the court nevertheless concluded that on the undisputed facts respondents were not entitled to relief. The District Court relied on several factors. Since August 1969, 44% of new police force recruits had been black; that figure also represented the proportion of blacks on the total force and was roughly equivalent to 20- to 29-year-old blacks in the 50-mile radius in which the recruiting efforts of the Police Department had been constructed. It was undisputed that the Department had systematically and affirmatively sought to enroll black officers many of whom passed the test but failed to report for duty. The District Court rejected the assertion that Test 21 was culturally slanted to favor whites and was "satisfied that the undisputable facts prove the test to be reasonably and directly related to the requirements of the police recruit training program and that it is neither so designed nor operates [sic] to discriminate against otherwise qualified blacks." It was thus not necessary to show that Test 21 was not only a useful indicator of training school performance but had also been validated in terms of job performance. . . .

[The Court of Appeals] held that the statutory standards elucidated in that case were to govern the due process question tendered in this one. . . . The court went on to declare that lack of discriminatory intent in designing and administering Test 21 was irrelevant; the critical fact was rather that a far greater proportion of blacks—four times as many—failed the test than did whites. This disproportionate impact, standing alone and without regard to whether it

indicated a discriminatory purpose, was held sufficient to establish a constitutional violation, absent proof by petitioners that the test was an adequate measure of job performance in addition to being an indicator of probable success in the training program, a burden which the court ruled petitioners had failed to discharge. . . .

[W]e have never held that the constitutional standard for adjudicating claims of invidious racial discrimination is identical to the standards applicable under Title VII, and we decline to do so today. . . . [O]ur cases have not embraced the proposition that a law or other official act, without regard to whether it reflects a racially discriminatory purpose, is unconstitutional solely because it is has a racially disproportionate impact. . . .

Necessarily, an invidious discriminatory purpose may often be inferred from the totality of the relevant facts, including the fact, if it is true, that the law bears more heavily on one race than another. It is also not infrequently true that the discriminatory impact—in the jury cases for example, the total or seriously disproportionate exclusion of Negroes from jury venires—may for all practical purposes demonstrate unconstitutionality because in various circumstances the discrimination is very difficult to explain on non-racial grounds. Nevertheless, we have not held that a law, neutral on its face and serving ends otherwise within the power of government to pursue, is invalid under the Equal Protection Clause simply because it may affect a greater proportion of one race than of another. Disproportionate impact is not irrelevant, but it is not the sole touchstone of an invidious racial discrimination forbidden by the Constitution. . . .

[V]arious Courts of Appeals have held in several contexts, including public employment, that the substantially disproportionate racial impact of a statute or official practice standing alone and without regard to discriminatory purpose, suffices to prove racial discrimination violating the Equal Protection Clause absent some justification going substantially beyond what would be necessary to validate most other legislative classifications. The cases impressively demonstrate that there is another side to the issue; but, with all due respect, to the extent that those cases rested on or expressed the view that proof of discriminatory racial purpose is necessary in making out an equal protection violation, we are in disagreement. . . .

[Test 21] seeks to ascertain whether those who take it have acquired a particular level of verbal skill; and it is untenable that the Constitution prevents the Government from seeking modestly to upgrade the communicative abilities of its employees rather than to be satisfied with some lower level of competence, particularly where the job requires special ability to communicate orally and in writing. Respondents, as Negroes, could no more successfully claim that the test denied them equal protection than could white applicants who also failed. The conclusion would not be different in the face of proof that more Negroes than whites had been disqualified by Test 21. That other Negroes also failed to score well would, alone, not demonstrate that respondents individually were being denied equal protection of the laws by the application of an otherwise valid qualifying test being administered to prospective police recruits.

Nor on the facts of the case before us would the disproportionate impact of Test 21 warrant the conclusion that it is a purposeful device to discriminate against Negroes. . . . [T]he test is neutral on its face and rationally may be said to serve a purpose the Government is constitutionally empowered to pursue. Even agreeing with the District Court that the differential racial effect of Test 21 called for further inquiry, we think the District Court correctly held that the affirmative efforts of the Metropolitan Police Department to recruit black officers, the changing racial composition of the recruit classes and of the force in general, and the relationship of the test to the training program negated any inference that the Department discriminated on the basis of race or that "a police officer qualifies on the color of his skin rather than ability."

Under Title VII Congress provided that when hiring and promotion practices disqualifying substantially disproportionate numbers of blacks are challenged, discriminatory purpose need not be proved, and that it is an insufficient response to demonstrate some rational basis for the challenged practice. It is necessary, in addition, that they be "validated" in terms of job performance in any one of several ways, perhaps by ascertaining the minimum skill, ability, or potential necessary for the position at issue and determining whether the qualifying tests are appropriate for the selection of qualified applicants for the job in question. However this process proceeds, it involves a more probing

judicial review of, and less deference to, the seemingly reasonable acts of administrators and executives than is appropriate under the Constitution where special racial impact, without discriminatory purpose, is claimed. We are not disposed to adopt this more rigorous standard for the purposes of applying the Fifth and the Fourteenth Amendments in cases such as this.

A rule that a statute designed to serve neutral ends is nevertheless invalid, absent compelling justification, if in practice it benefits or burdens one race more than another *would be far reaching and* would raise serious questions about, and perhaps invalidate, a whole range of tax, welfare, public service, regulatory, and licensing statutes that may be more burdensome to the poor and to the average black than to the more affluent white.

Given that rule, such consequences would perhaps be likely to follow. However, in our view, extension of the rule beyond those areas where it is already applicable by reason of statute, such as in the field of public employment, should await legislative prescription. . . .

The judgment is reversed.

Justice Stewart joins Parts I and II of the Court's opinion

Justice Stevens, concurring [omitted]

Justice Brennan, with whom Justice Marshall joins, dissenting

. . . It is hornbook law that the Court accord deference to the construction of an administrative regulation when that construction is made by the administrative authority responsible for the regulation. *E.g., Udall v. Tallman*, 380 U.S. 1, 16 (1965). It is worthy of note, therefore, that the brief filed by the [Civil Service Commission] CSC in this case interprets the instructions in a manner directly contrary to the Court, despite the Court's claim that its result is supported by the Commissioners' "current views."

"Under Civil Service Commission regulations and current professional standards governing criterion-related test validation procedures, the job-relatedness of an entrance examination may be demonstrated by proof that scores on the examination predict properly measured success in job-relevant training (regardless of whether they predict success on the job itself).

The documentary evidence submitted in the district court demonstrates that scores on Test 21 are predictive of Recruit School

Final Averages. There is little evidence, however, concerning the relationship between the Recruit School tests and the substance of the training program, and between the substance of the training program and the post-training job of a police officer. *It cannot be determined, therefore, whether the Recruit School Final Averages are a proper measure of success in training and whether the training program is job-relevant.*" Brief for CSC 14–15 (emphasis added).

The CSC maintains that a positive correlation between scores on entrance examinations and the criterion of success in training may establish the job relatedness of an entrance test—thus relieving an employer from the burden of providing a relationship to job performance after training—but only subject to certain limitations.

"Proof that scores on an entrance examination predict scores on training school achievement tests, however, does not, by itself, satisfy the burden of demonstrating the job-relatedness of the entrance examination. There must also be evidence—the nature of which will depend on the particular circumstances of the case—showing that the achievement test scores are an appropriate measure of the trainee's mastery of the material taught in the training program and that the training program imparts to a new employee knowledge, skills, or abilities required for performance of the post-training job." *Id.,* at 24–25. . . .

The CSC's standards thus recognize that Test 21 can be validated by a correlation between Test 21 scores and recruits' averages on training examinations only if (1) the training averages predict job performance or (2) the averages are proved to measure performance in job-related training. There is no proof that the recruits' average is correlated with job performance after completion of training. . . . And although a positive relationship to the recruits' average might be sufficient to validate Test 21 if the average were proved to reflect mastery of material of the training curriculum that was in turn demonstrated to be relevant to job performance, the record is devoid of proof in this regard. First, there is no demonstration by petitioners that the training-course examinations measure comprehension of the training curriculum; indeed, these examinations do not even appear in the record. Furthermore, the Futransky study simply designated an average of 85 on the examination as a "good" performance and assumed that a recruit with such an average learned the material taught in the training course. Without any further proof of the significance of a score of 85, and there is none in the record, I cannot agree that Test 21 is predictive of "success in training."

Today's decision is also at odds with [Equal Employment Opportunity Commission] EEOC regulations issued pursuant to explicit authorization in Title VII. . . . Although the dispute in this case is not within the EEOC's jurisdiction, . . . the proper construction of Title VII nevertheless is relevant. Moreover, the 1972 extension of Title VII to public employees gave the same substantive protection to those employees as had previously been accorded in the private sector, *Morton v. Mancari,* 417 U.S. 535 . . . (1974), and it is therefore improper to maintain different standards in the public and private sectors. . . .

As with an agency's regulations, the construction of a statute by the agency charged with its administration is entitled to great deference. *Trafficante v. Metropolitan Life Ins. Co.,* 409 U.S. 205 . . . (1972). . . . The deference due the pertinent EEOC regulations is enhanced by the fact that they were neither altered nor disapproved when Congress extensively amended Title VII in 1972. . . .

The EEOC regulations require that the validity of a job qualification test be proved by "empirical data demonstrating that the test is predictive of or significantly correlated with important elements of work behavior which comprise or are relevant to the job or jobs for which candidates are being evaluated." 29 CFR § 1607.4 (c) (1975). This construction of Title VII was approved in *Albemarle,* where we quoted this provision and remarked that "[t]he message of these Guidelines is the same as that of the *Griggs* case." 442 U.S., at 431. The regulations also set forth minimum standards for validation and delineate the criteria that may be used for this purpose.

"The work behaviors or other criteria of employee adequacy which the test is intended to predict or identify must be fully described; and, additionally, in the case of rating techniques, the appraisal form(s) and instructions to the rater(s) must be included as a part of the validation evidence. Such criteria may include measures other than actual work proficiency, such as training time, supervisory ratings, regularity of attendance and tenure. Whatever criteria are used they must represent major or critical work behaviors as revealed by careful job analyses." 29 CFR § 1607.5 (b) (3) (1975).

. . . If we measure the validity of Test 21 by this standard, which I submit we are bound to do, petitioners' proof is deficient in a number of ways similar to those noted above. First, the criterion of final training examination averages does not appear to be "fully described." Although the record contains some general discussion of the training curriculum, the examinations are not in the record, and there is no other evidence completely elucidating the subject matter tested by the training examinations. Without this required description we cannot determine whether the correlation with training examination averages is sufficiently related to petitioners' need to ascertain "job-specific ability." . . . Second, the EEOC regulations do not expressly permit validation by correlation to training performance, unlike the CSC instructions. Among the specified criteria the closest to training performance is "training time." All recruits to the Metropolitan Police Department, however, go through the same training course in the same amount of time, including those who experience some difficulty. Third, the final requirement of § 1607.5 (b) (3) has not been met. There has been no job analysis establishing the significance of scores on training examinations, nor is there any other type of evidence showing that these scores are of "major or critical" importance.

Accordingly, EEOC regulations that have previously been approved by the Court set forth a construction of Title VII that is distinctly opposed to today's statutory result.

The Court also says that its conclusion is not foreclosed by *Griggs* and *Albermarle*, but today's result plainly conflicts with those cases. *Griggs* held that "[i]f an employment practice which operates to exclude Negroes cannot be shown to be *related to job performance*, the practice is prohibited." 401 U.S., at 431 (emphasis added). Once a discriminatory impact is shown, the employer carries the burden of proving that the challenged practice "bear[s] a *demonstrable relationship to successful performance of the jobs* for which it was used." *Ibid.* (emphasis added). We observed further:

"Nothing in the Act precludes the use of testing or measuring procedures; obviously they are useful. What Congress has forbidden is giving these devices and mechanisms controlling force unless they are demonstrably a reasonable measure of job performance. . . . What Congress has commanded is that any tests used must measure the person for the job and not the person in the abstract." *Id.*, at 436.

Albermarle read *Griggs* to require that a discriminatory test be validated through proof "by professionally acceptable methods" that it is " 'predictive of or significantly correlated with *important* elements of work behavior *which comprise or are relevant to the job or jobs* for which candidates are being evaluated.' " 422 U.S., at 431 (emphasis added), quoting 29 CFR § 1607.4 (c) (1975). Further, we

rejected the employer's attempts to validate a written test by proving that it was related to supervisors' job performance ratings, because there was no demonstration that the ratings accurately reflected job performance. We were unable "to determine whether the criteria *actually* considered were sufficiently related to the [employer's] legitimate interest in job-specific ability to justify a testing system with a racially discriminatory impact." 422 U.S., at 433 (emphasis in original). To me, therefore, these cases read Title VII as requiring proof of a significant relationship to job performance to establish the validity of a discriminatory test. See also *McDonnell Douglas Corp. v. Green*, 411 U.S. 792, 802, and n. 14 (1973). Petitioners do not maintain that there is a demonstrated correlation between Test 21 scores and job performance. Moreover, their validity study was unable to discern a significant positive relationship between training averages and job performance. Thus, there is no proof of a correlation—either direct or indirect—between Test 21 and performance of the job of being a police officer. . . .

White employees have challenged affirmative action plans designed to correct past racial discriminatory employment practices as violations of their Fourteenth Amendment equal protection rights. These anti-discrimination policies were dubbed "reverse discrimination" in the famous case *Regents of the University of California v. Bakke* (1978),[14] where a divided Supreme Court struck down racial quotas as unconstitutional but affirmed the use of race as one of many factors universities may consider in making admission decisions. Since the *Bakke* decision, the Court's constitutional and statutory interpretations of equal protection have given mixed messages about affirmative action programs. For example, in 1980, the Court held that government contract programs setting aside a certain percentage of contracts for minority bidders did not violate the equal protection component of the due process clause of the Fifth Amendment.[15] However, in 1989, the Court, in *City of Richmond v. Croson*,[16] appeared to back away from its earlier support for affirmative action in government contracting. The

14. 438 U.S. 265.
15. *Fullilove v. Klutznick*, 448 U.S. 448 (1980).
16. 109 S.Ct. 706.

Court ruled that Richmond violated the Fourteenth Amendment's equal protection clause because the city required that non-minority-owned prime contractors on city construction contracts must provide at least a 30 percent set-aside for minority subcontractors.

At this point in the heated controversy over affirmative action policy there is no clear federal judicial decision or legislative position on the meaning or scope of anti-employment discrimination other than "quotas are not constitutional." Organizations, such as the National Association for the Advancement of Colored People (NAACP), long involved in the struggle for discrimination-free employment, are devising means other than litigation to meet challenges to government affirmative action plans. For example, the U.S. Supreme Court granted certiorari to review an appeal by Sharon Taxman, a white public school teacher who was laid off in favor of a black teacher in *Piscataway Township Board of Education v. Sharon Taxman* (118 S.Ct. 595, 1997). Civil rights groups, fearing that the case could lead to the prohibition of affirmative action, provided money for the board to settle the case out of court before the Supreme Court could rule. The school board accepted settlement as an alternative to costly litigation, and so too did Ms. Taxman, who was primarily interested in compensation. The school board paid 30% of the settlement, while civil rights groups paid the remaining 70% of the $433,500 settlement.[17]

The politics of law in this area, be it the "law" forged through settlement or the "law" we more commonly study in court decisions, sheds light on the extent to which administrative agencies are willing to abandon their past preference for hiring white men. The text of the Administrative Procedure Act (APA), which specifically prohibits discrimination in employment, also incorporates a general government employment policy giving preference to veterans (see Appendix B). If employing veterans ranks as a "compelling state interest," should affirmative action plans also rate that distinction?

17. See Tony Mauro, "Piscataway Settlement Brings Sighs of Relief," *The Recorder*, November 26, 1997; and Amy Schroeder, "Piscataway Lawyer Wins a Settlement but Loses the Spotlight," *The American Lawyer*, January/February, 1998.

The controversies over racial discrimination, affirmative action, and reverse racial discrimination have dominated the news in this area for decades. The Constitution, through the post–Civil War amendments, speaks more specifically to the evils of racial discrimination than to other forms of discrimination. But statutory protections such as those in Title VII condemn a variety of forms of discrimination equally. Before going further, let us summarize its main requirements. To make a successful case for employment discrimination, the plaintiff must establish that the employer behaved in one or more of three distinct ways.

The first of these, *evil motive*, is in some ways the most obvious. The employer made sexist or racist or other kinds of derogatory and insulting statements against an individual or group protected by the statute. Racial slurs are obvious examples, but so are sexually harassing remarks, including same-sex remarks. When members of a protected group consistently receive worse treatment over time than other groups receive, we may also suspect an evil motive. But it is never easy in law to prove another person's motives. Proof of evil motive requires convincing testimony from those who may be reluctant to come forward.

The second and third means of establishing a violation of Title VII are more circumstantial. The second, *differential treatment*, is the charge most commonly brought. For example, a female employee is fired for being late to work too often, but male workers with similar tardiness records are not fired. Differential treatment takes place when, in similar circumstances, people in one class are treated differently from people in a separate class. Proof of differential treatment usually requires the plaintiff to present statistical information about comparative employment decisions and patterns. Such investigations can, of course, be very time-consuming and costly.

The final route to establishing a discrimination claim, *disparate impact*, is the route that the Supreme Court rejected as a matter of constitutional law in *Washington v. Davis*. In a classic 1971 case, *Griggs v. Duke Power Co.*, 401 U.S. 424, the Court described circumstances in which treating all people the same way might still lead to a violation. In this case the Court held that under Title VII, job qualifications must be proven to correlate with job performance before companies can use them in ways that disproportionately favor one group and hurt another. Thus, height and weight requirements that might discriminate against women, for example, must be shown to be job-related.

Like the civil rights movement, the women's movement has sought to eradicate discrimination against women in the workplace by using litigation and building on the antidiscrimination provisions in Title VII of the Civil Rights Act of 1964. The women's movement has specifically attacked discrimination in wages. In 1963, as a result of long and difficult negotiations in Congress, the Equal Pay Act was passed as an amendment to the Fair Labor Standards Act. It provides:

No employer having employees subject to any provisions of this section shall discriminate, within any establishment in which such employees are employed, between employees on the basis of sex by paying wages to employees in such establishment at a rate less than the rate at which he pays wages to employees of the opposite sex in such establishment for equal work on jobs the performance of which requires equal skill, effort, and responsibility, and which are performed under similar working conditions, except where such payment is made pursuant to (i) a seniority system; (ii) a merit system; (iii) a system which measures earnings by quantity or quality of production; or (iv) a differential based on any other factor other than sex: *Provided*, that an employer who is paying a wage rate differential in violation of this subsection shall not, in order to comply with the provision of this subsection, reduce the wage rate of any employee. 29 U.S.C. sec. 206(d).

Despite legislative reform, the gap in wages between men and women has not decreased significantly over the past forty years. In 1951, the median income of full-time female workers was 63.9 cents to every male dollar. By 1991, it was 69.9 cents to every male dollar, and current figures show roughly the same disparity.[18] Beginning in the early 1980s the women's movement, frustrated by the narrow scope of the Equal Pay Act, which only protects against differential pay for identical jobs, began to mobilize to achieve equal pay for comparable work in a movement called *comparable worth*.[19] The argument for comparable worth is that since 75 percent of working women are employed in jobs where more than 80 percent of the workers are female (i.e., women's jobs), efforts to redress the gross inequities between male and female wages must go beyond attacking pay differentials for identical jobs and get at the root of the problem—sex-segregated employment.

You probably can think of many "female jobs" that pay substantially less than "male jobs." In Los Angeles County female librarians employed by the county threatened to bring a comparable worth suit in the late 1980s because they were paid 20 percent less than gardeners and maintenance workers, almost all of whom were male. The union and the county resolved this conflict through negotiation. Other female workers (e.g., clerical workers) have not been as successful in labor negotiation or in the courts. In *Spaulding v. University of Washington*, 740 F.2d 686 (1984), the Ninth Circuit Court of Appeals dismissed a comparable worth claim by nursing faculty who were paid substantially less than predominant male faculty who, they alleged, were doing comparable work, such as faculty in "health services, social work, architecture, urban planning, environmental health, speech and hearing, rehabilitative medicine, and pharmacy practice."[20] The Ninth Circuit held that the nursing faculty had not presented sufficient evidence to demonstrate that the University of Washington discriminated intentionally.[21] The "disparate impact" theory, advanced by the plaintiffs in this case, and in other comparable worth suits, would require that the "plaintiff must show only disparate *effect* of facially neutral wage policies on members of a protected class."[22] Courts have been unwilling to accept the disparate impact analysis in comparable worth cases. At

18. U.S. Bureau of the Census, Current Population Reports, Series p. 60; U.S. Bureau of Labor Statistics, Department of Labor, *Employment and Earnings* (Washington, D.C., 1998). Also see Margaret A. Berger, *Litigation on Behalf of Women* (New York: Ford Foundation, 1980).

19. See Ronnie Steinberg, "The Debate on Comparable Worth," *New Politics* 1 (1986): 108.

20. 740 F.2d 686, at 696.

21. The U.S. Supreme Court denied certiorari, 105 S.Ct. 511 (1984).

22. Judith Olans Brown, Phyllis Tropper Baumann, and Elaine Millar Melnick, "Equal Pay for Jobs of Comparable Worth: An Analysis of the Rhetoric," *Harvard Civil Rights-Civil Liberties Law Review* 21 (1986): 146. Also see Janice R. Bellace, "Comparable Worth: Proving Sex-Based Discrimination," *Iowa Law Review* 69 (1984): 655.

present, then, the judiciary has not been a useful place to pursue antidiscrimination reform efforts under comparable worth theories. In his study of pay equity litigation by public employee unions, Professor Michael McCann finds that litigation is but one strategy unions have employed.[23] Contract negotiations are another area for unionized government employees to seek pay equity redress.

At the close of the millennium, the legal battle against discrimination seems far from won. For example, on April 21, 1999, the following complaint was filed in United States District Court in Seattle. We reproduce excerpts from this complaint so that you may practice applying the tools we have developed in the latter part of this chapter. What is the group that the defendant allegedly discriminates against? Might there be more than one such group in this case? What evidence below might, if it were true, make a case for evil motive? What about differential treatment or disparate impact? Do any of these allegations amount to sexual harassment? What additional facts might you need to prove, beyond those alleged below, in order to conclude that the defendant has discriminated illegally? As you analyze this case, please remember that all legal complaints present only one side of a case. This complaint is a matter of public record and we reprint it as an exercise. The accuracy of its claims can only be determined after a full adversarial legal process.

United States District Court, Western District of Washington at Seattle

DARUNEE NABADALUNG and DOLPHINE ODA, on behalf of themselves and all others similarly situated, Plaintiffs, v. THE UNIVERSITY OF WASHINGTON, an agency of the State, Defendant.

I. Introduction

1. Discrimination against female faculty is ubiquitous and persistent at institutions of higher learning throughout the United States. As a result, female faculty lag signif-

23. Michael McCann, *Rights at Work: Pay Equity Reform and the Politics of Legal Mobilization* (Chicago: University of Chicago Press, 1995).

icantly behind their male counterparts in compensation, promotion, and recognition. While equal numbers of women may now enter the academic field, gross disparities in the treatment of women become apparent as women move through (or fail to move through) the academic chain of advancement. These disparities are even greater for female faculty who are ethnic minorities.

2. A recent report by the American Association of University Professors (AAUP) notes this problem:

Substantial disparities in salary, rank, and tenure between male and female faculty persist despite the increasing proportion of women in the academic profession.

3. Sadly, as set forth in this complaint, the University of Washington, the State's leading academic institution, permits and perpetuates a system of promotion and salary practices that result in disparities in salary and rank between male and female faculty members. Such discrimination results in a statistically significant, across-the-board difference in compensation between male and female faculty members at schools within the University of Washington system. This disparity in compensation increases when pay for minority women is examined. This disparity is known to exist by the highest officials at the University of Washington. Instead of rectifying the problem, these officials have attempted to minimize or mask its significance. In terms of compensation, the disparity in compensation between male and female faculty members averages 18% on a yearly basis. For certain groups of female faculty members, such as Asian women, the disparity is even greater, averaging 27% of compensation.

4. Equal pay is just part of the problem. The promotion practices at the University of Washington perpetuate salary disparity as female faculty members are promoted less quickly than their male counterparts. As a result of unequal treatment, only 24.8% of all tenure-track faculty are women, while 60% of the lower-paid non-tenure-track faculty are women. To add insult to injury, female faculty members are often provided with less favorable working conditions, such as lab and research facilities, when compared to male faculty members. . . .

II. Parties

A. The Plaintiffs

1. Plaintiff Dr. Darunee NaBadalung is of Thai national origin, a United States citizen, and veteran of the U.S. Army Desert Storm Operation. She currently resides in King County, Washington. Dr. NaBadalung is

employed as an assistant professor at the School of Dentistry at the University of Washington. Because she was not promoted to associate professor her position will terminate June 1999.

2. Plaintiff Dr. Dolphine Oda is a full professor of Oral Pathology at the Department of Oral and Maxillofacial Surgery in the School of Dentistry at the University of Washington. She has been employed by the University since 1985. . . .

B. The Defendant

1. The University of Washington is a public agency of the state of Washington with facilities in King County and other locations within the state. . . .

B. The Plaintiffs Are Treated Unequally

1. DR. NABADALUNG

1. Dr. Darunee NaBadalung began her academic career at the University of Texas. After a few years at that institution she was hired away by the University of Washington. Despite being encouraged to accept the position, she later discovered that her starting salary was significantly below that of her male counterparts.

2. Dr. NaBadalung is one of only a handful of female, board certified prosthodontists and an accomplished maxillofacial prosthodontist. For six years she worked diligently in these specialty areas to fulfill the requirements for tenure at the school of dentistry. During those years she was compensated less than her male peers; denied timely assistance in soliciting and winning research grants; and denied the resources she needed to complete her research work. In addition, Dr. NaBadalung was given a disproportionate share of the teaching load and fewer days to conduct private practice than her male counterparts.

2. Her efforts to discuss these very real problems with the dean of the dental school were met with condescension and a dismissive attitude. Dean Paul Robertson treated her like a child stating: "I'm not your grandfather." In subsequent conversations the dean told Dr. NaBadalung he would never grant her tenure (despite the fact that he barely knew her or her work) and that she should accept a nontenure track position as a lecturer.

4. The dean also quoted unreasonably high standards, far in excess of what is normally required, for Dr. NaBadalung to achieve tenure. For example, the dean required that Dr. NaBadalung publish over 20 papers prior to a grant of tenure. But, tenure was routinely granted to male candidates with far fewer publications. In addition, the dean required that Dr. NaBadalung's research achieve international recognition, a standard applied to *full* professors, not the standard for promotion to *associate* professor.

5. Despite these difficulties Dr. NaBadalung produced a substantial body of research while successfully carrying her teaching load. As a result the senior faculty in her department and her department head recommended her for promotion and tenure. The Appointments, Promotion and Tenure Committee (APTC) denied tenure, but unanimously recommended that Dr. NaBadalung receive a one-year extension to fulfill certain requirements. . . .

6. As a result of the University's discrimination against her, Dr. NaBadalung lost wages she was entitled to. She also lost a tenured position as an associate professor and her expectations for a successful academic career. Dr. NaBadalung has been frustrated, emotionally distressed and humiliated by the treatment she received from the University's administration.

2. DR. ODA

1. Dr. Oda has received 13 Distinguished Teaching awards at the University of Washington School of Dentistry over a period of 10 years. She has twice been nominated for the University of Washington's distinguished teaching award. She has conducted extensive research and published approximately 50 manuscripts in respected medical journals as well as presenting papers and lectures nationally and internationally in the field of Oral Pathology especially in oral cancer, clinical and basic science.

2. Dr. Oda is of Assyrian ancestry. Iraq is the Nation of her birth and she has been a naturalized citizen of the United States since 1987.

3. During her time at the University, she has been treated in a discriminatory fashion. Administrators have talked down to her and humiliated her. Her concerns have been dismissed by her Dean, Ombudsman, the Vice President and the President's office, and her qualifications and performance have been ignored, unfairly criticized and discounted.

4. Dr. Robinovitch, Chair of Oral Biology, who at most may have attended one of her classes, stated that her first teaching award in 1987 was given because she was "nice" to the students not because she was a good teacher. In contrast, he stated that Dr. Tom Morton's teaching award was given to him because he was a

"good teacher." Dr. Morton is male and Caucasian. After 13 awards (by 1997), and numerous outstanding "peer review" critiques of her teaching, Dr. Robinovitch still unfairly criticized and discounted her teaching.

5. In 1991, Dr. Oda was the only board certified oral pathologist in the department, and she became Director of the Division of Oral Pathology and the Oral Pathology Biopsy Service. Board certification was required by CLIA to become the director of the Biopsy Service.

6. When she was placed in the Directorship of the Division of Oral Pathology in 1991, Dr. Thomas Morton was unhappy and promised that he would "take the directorship back" from her because he deserved it more. He was not board certified in Oral Pathology at that time, even though he could have been if he had taken the exam. After he got Board Certification in 1995, the University made him the Director.

7. In 1992, she wrote to and met with the new dean, Dr. Paul Robertson, informing him that Dr. Robinovitch, the Chair of the department, was retaliating against her for complaining about gender-based comments. Dr. Oda identified one example of discrimination being Dr. Robinovitch's refusal to pay a share of biopsy service income equal to what her male predecessor received at the time she became Director of the Biopsy Service.

8. Dr. Robinovitch threatened to "destroy her" if she was to bring a complaint to the Ombudsman stating "I am the most powerful chairman in the School of Dentistry. I will destroy you if I want to." She informed Dean Omnell and later Dean Robertson of this threat.

9. Dr. Oda did not receive appropriate responses to her requests for assistance in dealing with the hostile environment in the Department of Oral Biology created by the Department Chair, Dr. Robinovitch, and by Dr. Tom Morton, and with the knowledge and approval of Dean Robertson.

10. Department Chair Dr. Murray Robinovitch referred to her as a "hot headed Assyrian woman," "volatile Middle Eastern woman," "insatiable," and "pushy," used in ways that were serious, personal and demeaning. When she raised issues of different treatment to Dr. Robinovitch, he condescendingly referred to her legitimate concerns as "confusion" and "you do not understand." . . .

C. A Widespread Problem at the University of Washington

1. According to the University's own documents plaintiffs are one of many women discriminated against in the University system. In 1996, the President of the University requested that the provost initiate a campus-wide study of salary of all schools except the School of Medicine. That report was concluded in 1997.

2. It concluded that small but "statistically significant" differences in compensation existed between Caucasian men and other race/gender categories. The University has thus admitted that the disparity exists. To reduce the magnitude of the disparity, the report improperly attempted to explain the disparity as being caused by factors other than gender, such as rank, degree, time in job, school and other "job factors." These factors were not analyzed on a scientifically sound basis, but were utilized in a manner that minimized the disparity. . . .

One of the claims of Darunee NaBadalung and Dolphine Oda was that they represented a class—women—and discrimination against them was an example of a wider phenomenon of discrimination against women in general. Even though the trial court accepted the certification of class action, on appeal a Washington state appellate court reversed in *Oda v. Washington*, 111 Wn. App. 79 (2002). The appeals court held that "a statistical model showing gender disparities in faculty pay, without more, will not prove that the University has a discriminatory motive. Evidence of intentional discrimination in a single department will not prove a common course of intentionally discriminatory conduct that is fairly attributable to decision making by central administration." Oda and NaBadalung appealed to the Washington State Supreme Court, but the court declined to hear the case.

Discrimination in the workplace is not, of course, limited to gender or sex. There are various forms of discrimination, such as discrimination based on age and disability. We end this chapter with a summary of two recent Supreme Court cases regarding age and disability discrimination. As we indicated in chapter 11, both cases reveal that the Eleventh Amendment and the Court's tendency toward a practice of *federalism*, or deferring to the rights of states to formulate their own laws and policies, significantly limits victims of discrimination from accessing federal law to redress their claims.

Daniel Kimel, along with others similarly situated, sued Florida State University under the Age Discrimination in Employment Act of 1967. The plaintiffs claimed to have been discriminated against because the university failed to adjust their pay and this created a discrepancy with the younger employees. The case was consolidated with a lawsuit brought by a corrections officer against the Florida Department of Corrections claiming he was not promoted due to his age. The plaintiffs asked for money damages from the State. In *Kimel v. Florida Board of Regents*, 528 U.S. 62 (2000), a divided Court (5-4) held that the sovereign immunity of the states (as acknowledged in the Eleventh Amendment) prevents Congress from requiring states to pay damages for violations of the federal Age Discrimination in Employment Act (ADEA). The majority said that even though the Congress showed its clear intent to abrogate the sovereignty of states in the ADEA, the money damages awarded were not proportional to the wrong committed, thus rendering the remedy unconstitutional. The Court went on to suggest that, "age" is not a suspect category like race, and thus states can only be subject to the rational relationship test. (Does the law as implemented bear a rational relationship to the legitimate governmental interest sought to be advanced?) As long as states can put forward a reasonable/rational argument for age discrimination, they cannot be held liable under federal laws.

The following year, the Court in *Board of Trustees of the University of Alabama v. Garrett*, 531 U.S. 356 (2001), applied the same analysis in *Kimel* to the scope of states' liability in cases of discrimination on the basis of disability. Patricia Garrett was an employee of the University of Alabama system and Milton Ash was a security officer in the Alabama Youth Service Department. Both disabled according to the Americans with Disabilities Act (ADA). Alleging that they were discriminated against due to their disabilities, they sought money damages from the University of Alabama whom they argued had violated Section I of the ADA. The University of Alabama claimed that the Eleventh Amendment barred Congress from imposing money damages on states. The Court's five-member majority ruled that there must be a clear pattern of state discrimination against disabled people in order for private individuals to recover monetary damages under the ADA. In addition, the remedies sought must be proportional with the targeted violation. The Court said that there was little evidence of states consistently discriminating against disabled employees. Recognizing that disabled people were subject to discrimination, Chief Justice William Rehnquist, writing for the majority, said that this was more of a societal problem and not specifically about states. As in *Kimel*, Rehnquist argued that certain practices of discrimination by states against the disabled should be subjected to a rational relationship test. In other words, as long as the states could show that there is a rational relationship between its discrimination against disabled persons and a legitimate state interest, then the policy is constitutional under the ADA.

Administrative law decisions relating to government employment bring into focus some of the broader themes of administrative law we have studied thus far. They illustrate the fundamental tensions, so often resolved by reference to constitutional law principles, between individual liberties and the state's need to maintain order in society. They remind us that the simple opportunity for a fair hearing is among the most important rights the government can confer on its citizens. And they illuminate the recent trend in administrative (and constitutional) law toward allowing the various states to formulate their own parochial rules. Here we caution you to consider the trade-off between regional or local rules and national minimum standards that serve as a floor, not a ceiling, for states to build on.

EXERCISES AND QUESTIONS FOR FURTHER THOUGHT

1. Public employees are joining unions in increasing numbers. Even in jurisdictions that prohibit public employees from striking, union membership may give employees the benefits of more standardized and equitable grievance procedures. In such cases the collective bargaining agreement between union and management may make the union the employee's representative in a grievance procedure. But what happens if the union believes the termination was warranted and refuses to support the fired employee? Does the employee's membership in the union waive any rights to notice and hearing? See *Winston and Cummings v. U.S. Postal Service*, 585 F.2d 198 (1978).

2. Recall Ms. Horowitz, the student expelled from the University of Missouri Medical School before earning her degree. Does the fact that she was academically terminated communicate information to the public that will make it harder for her to gain admission to another medical school? On what grounds, if any, should the law offer stronger due process protections to terminated employees than terminated students?

3. For years the personnel administrator for the state of Massachusetts has granted preferences to military veterans in public sector hiring. Since the vast majority of veterans are males, does this policy constitute illegal sex discrimination? See *Personnel Administrator of Massachusetts v. Feeney*, 442 U.S. 256 (1979).

4. Do you think employers should be able to require drug and alcohol testing of public employees on their own initiative? Or should such a program be negotiated between the employee unions and the government? See *Johnson-Bateman Co.*, National Labor Relations Board, 295 NLRB No. 26 (1989), and *Minneapolis Star Tribune*, National Labor Relations Board, 295 NLRB No. 63 (1989).

5. Affirmative action employment policies are often misunderstood. Many programs seek no more than to equalize racial or sexual balance in employment where occupational tests have little or no predictive power on job performance. Is there any legal or moral objection to such programs? What principles of justice, if any, support such affirmative action policies? Reflect on the social justice implications of affirmative action with reference to the political theories of individual liberty, equality of opportunity, and the Marxist credo "from each according to his abilities, to each according to his needs."

6. Assume that the Fourth Amendment's proscription on unreasonable government searches and seizures limits mandatory drug testing to employees who work in sensitive or dangerous jobs. Would such a rule prevent the state from testing all *applicants* for these positions? Why or why not?

CHAPTER 14
PRINCIPLES AND POLITICS
IN ADMINISTRATIVE LAW

This final chapter does two things. First, it returns to the "big picture." Now that you are familiar with the many species of administrative law plants and trees, it is time to step back and look at the whole forest. We first re-emphasize that administrative law exemplifies the core political values of our liberal democratic system by regulating the government's exercise of its considerable powers while keeping abuses of that power in check—all in furtherance of what is accepted as the "public interest."

The second part of this chapter allows you to apply your developing knowledge of the field to the issues that occupy today's leading scholars of administrative law. These materials, as we have urged from the beginning, grapple with how the law can effectively minimize arbitrariness in administrative government.

SURVEYING THE TERRAIN

If we had to pick the single most important thing that students should understand in order to appreciate the importance of administrative law, it would be the message of the Old Testament's Book of Genesis. Administrative law exists because humans are imperfect. One does not need to be a believing Jew, Christian, or Muslim to see human failing all around us. Policemen brutalize innocent civilians. The National Aeronautics and Space Administration (NASA) allowed the Challenger space shuttle to take off knowing that cold temperatures at launch threatened the integrity of the O-ring seals. A fas-

cinating documentary, "Waco: The Rules of Engagement," shows infrared images of Federal Bureau of Investigation (FBI) agents shooting members of the Branch Davidian sect as they tried to escape the flames at their compound in Waco, Texas.[1] The evidence indicates that the fire was started, probably inadvertently, by the FBI, not by the Branch Davidians. Both NASA and the FBI tried to cover up these failings. All of us can recount stories about selfishness and ignorance. The point is, our political system aspires to minimize these wrongs. As we said at the beginning, from a normative standpoint administrative law seeks the maximum feasible reduction of human arbitrariness.

This book has described a number of such arbitrary decisions. Nuclear power plants were allowed to operate even when no one has yet worked out how to safely dispose of the nuclear waste it generated. Officials who knew about sexual harassment by teachers and students allowed it to continue. In spite of the potentially disastrous consequences of global warming, the Environmental Protection Agency (EPA) chose not to regulate carbon emissions from motor vehicles. The list goes on. We have also detailed the basic features of administrative law, the law that seeks to correct such decisions.

1. (Los Angeles: Fifth Estate Productions/Samford Entertainment, 1997).

How does one summarize the field of administrative law? In some ways the job is easy. The basic outlines are clear and widely accepted.

- We live in a political culture in which the "rule of law" is not just a theoretical ideal but a practical reality that requires government officials to justify their exercise of power as something more than just a means of securing personal advantage.

- We live in a political culture that values fairness to all individuals. Starting with the Declaration of Independence, the political culture in the United States has sought to promote a dignitarian view of human rights. Unlike the elaborate procedural rights guaranteed those accused of crime in the United States, a suspected thief in some parts of the Middle East might have his hand chopped off on the spot; a rhinoceros poacher in Zimbabwe might be summarily shot in the field.

- Our political culture takes the Constitution, "the supreme law of the land," seriously.

- This supreme law imposes rules of fairness that compel administrators and all other government officials to justify what they do.

- The Constitution specifically authorizes Congress to make rules governing agencies, and Congress does so with a vengeance that leaves library shelves groaning with new volumes.

- Our common law legal tradition holds that courts have the ultimate responsibility to say what the law means in concrete cases.

- The body of legal precedent created through the aggregation of those concrete cases is the heart that drives the organs of administrative law.

Yet, as you now know, once we probe more deeply into the content of administrative law's principles, rules, and cases, we find not a neatly organized system of commands but a series of contending values and principles. In the legislative-veto and line-item veto cases, for example, we see the separation-of-powers doctrine colliding with a doctrine of delegation that gives agencies nearly unfettered policy-making power. We see due process requirements laid out in detail in *Goldberg*, only to see *Mathews* and its progeny letting agencies get around the fair hearing requirements in many contexts, and dilute them in others. We see case after case in which learned judges strenuously disagree with each other about what the rules of administrative law should say and do.

Above all, we see no end to the debate about two critical questions. First, just what aspects of our lives should government regulate? One version or another of the slogan, "the era of big government is over" was uttered by Presidents Ronald Reagan, George H. W. Bush, Bill Clinton, and George W. Bush. And just as surely popular support for administrative agencies declined. That philosophy translated into deregulation in most areas, and it reduced overall funding of federal agencies. Yet Congress did not reduce agency workloads. Government agencies at all levels are responsible for more tasks than ever before. For example, while the government has gotten out of the business of regulating commercial air fares and schedules, government oversight of the tobacco industry, firearms, and storage of toxic waste is on the rise. Perhaps more importantly, government regulation of security issues has grown by leaps and bounds following the terrorist attacks of September 11, 2001.

Second, how actively should courts review and correct perceived mistakes by agencies? Courts cannot possibly "do it all," but if agencies are not threatened with the realistic possibility that a judge might review their activities, their need to justify routine decisions will vanish and the ideal of the rule of law will become a dead letter. An important subset of the question "how active should the courts be?" is whether the courts should review agency *inaction*. As we saw in *Massachusetts v. EPA*, the question is not just whether courts should correct agency mistakes, but whether they should intervene when agencies fail to act in the first place.

In short, we encounter politics, and for politics there is no neat summary. We encounter politics for all sorts of reasons. One reason is that law *is* politics. No body of law, least of all administrative law, ever develops a perfectly clear and complete and final set of rules for telling people what to do. Even in the simplest of situations—rules against running red lights, for example—cases may present unique facts to which the rule may not apply. Law is the language we use for debating what we think is just, but that debate itself doesn't end any more than, say, baseball, "ends." Law, like baseball, has moments—we can think of lawsuit "moments" as games—and these games have ends, but baseball and law start anew the next day.

Law of course differs from baseball in that people "play" law not with balls and bats and gloves but with words and arguments. One of the "rules" of the law game is that the adversaries can argue about what the law ought to mean in each case. Often, players of the law game are expected to disagree about what the rules mean and how they affect the outcome of a particular case. In arguing about what the law ought to mean, legal actors appeal to and exploit the extra-legal world of political events, relationships, and values.

When abstract legal ideals are applied in concrete situations, the fact that our society, like any, has limited resources can make those ideals difficult to implement. While using limited resources efficiently is generally valued, efficiency can result in unfairness. *Goldberg*-type hearings cost a lot more time and money than the informal "hearing" in the principal's office before the student gets suspended from school.

Administrative law seeks the "maximum feasible reduction of arbitrariness." That being its goal, administrative law aims to resolve controversies in a manner that is fair, accurate, efficient and—because ours is a democratic society—satisfactory to the litigants in the administrative process. The "administrative law game" debates how to meet this standard. Specifically, we argue that some cases and some doctrines covered earlier in this book more effectively meet our test than do others. For example:

• Judge David Bazelon's demand for "a good, hard look" at rulemaking in the area of nuclear waste appeared to be just the kind of motivation needed in the industry to finally address the health threats posed by nuclear waste. Instead, the Supreme Court's decision in *Vermont Yankee* allowed a regulatory process influenced by economic interests to let the problem worsen over time. Today, thirty years after the Supreme Court decided the case, the problem of nuclear waste is far from being solved. Even though the government proposed a permanent site for

disposal under Yucca Mountain, Nevada, scientists and public interest organizations continue to point out the grave shortcomings of this solution.

• Judges do not meet our standard when, as in the *Horowitz* case, they hide behind generalizations and abstractions. As we all know, schools and families are sometimes cooperative and sometimes rife with conflict. Judges do, on the other hand, meet our test when they do not mechanistically demand that all ten *Goldberg* ingredients be used in every hearing. Each of these cases depends on good judgment, not the legalistic, formulaic thinking of the kind illustrated in the state sovereignty cases decided at the end of the Supreme Court's 1999 term.

• Justice Marshall met our test when, in *Overton Park*, he found that the judicial review provisions in Section 7 of the Administrative Procedure Act (APA) required Secretary Volpe to justify what was, in fact, a politically expedient decision at the expense of a politically powerless group.

• Recall the "magic words" issue that comes up in the application of Section 554 of the APA. Courts meet our standard either when: (a) they "find" the magic words in the authorizing statute because the problem is one that really will benefit from holding hearings, or (b) as in the *Florida East Coast Railway* case, they do not find the magic words because adjudicatory hearings will serve no purpose.

• Justice Stevens's majority opinion in *Massachusetts v. EPA* was satisfying in pushing the Environmental Protection Agency (EPA) to articulate a reason why the agency refused to take action when scientific reports pointed to the impact of carbon emissions on global warming.

We encourage you to find other examples in this book of ways in which courts have succeeded or failed to reduce arbitrariness.

THE CURRENT ADMINISTRATIVE LAW DEBATE

We conclude this book not with pronouncements about the "correct" way to do administrative law but with a review of one of the most significant debates about administrative law today: privatization and outsourcing. As we have seen throughout the book, administrative law is about limiting the powers of the state or the bureaucracy. The goal of this body of law is, among others, to legitimize state interventions in the otherwise "free" market and make sure that public power is used in acceptable, accountable, and predictable ways. The initial success of the deregulation movement of the early 1980s, coupled with an unqualified belief in the virtues of the market following the fall of communism, however, led to calls for more deregulation and privatization during the 1990s. While the result was not a smaller state or decreased state expenditures, proponents of deregulation asserted that by outsourcing state functions to the private market, government regulation would be replaced by a self-regulating market.

Below you will read two pieces by leading administrative law scholars on the issue of privatization and outsourcing. These works do not exhaust the debate on privatization or outsourcing but they present critical perspectives on privatization rather than unreflexive endorsements. While both writers accept the inevitability of privatization, they differ about how to respond to the challenges posed by the phenomenon, and how to address what Paul Verkuil calls the "outsourcing of sovereignty."

Alfred Aman's article emphasizes how privatization and globalization have fundamentally changed the political arena. Increasingly, he argues, it is meaningless to draw sharp distinctions between the public and private. In an environment where the fundamentals of state authority are in flux, administrative law should also change, Aman writes. Focusing on the privatization of prisons in the United States, he highlights a number of important roles administrative law can play in reducing arbitrariness and increasing participation. His most important point is that in a world in which, thanks to globalization, the fundamental relationship between the state and market is changing, it would be futile to insist on traditional administrative law devices to check the use of public power. Instead, he argues, we need to come up with creative ways to make sure that those who engage in activities concerning the public are held accountable through a variety of both conventional and novel administrative law mechanisms.

In the excerpt from his book Paul Verkuil agrees that the boundaries are blurring between the public and the private, but he insists that the classical liberal framework "we the people" should be kept intact for those powers of the government he calls sovereign powers. He asks whether outsourcing of government functions to private companies might jeopardize the democratic nature of the political process. He, like Aman, is concerned with the evasion of public controls over significant public decisions in the process of outsourcing. He reminds us that the Constitution itself and the values of public law place limits on such outsourcing, and he argues that when privatization goes too far these traditional legal norms must be invoked to keep privatization in check.

Finally, we include an article about how the lack of financial regulation by the government is arguably responsible for the collapse of certain once-venerated and apparently immutable Wall Street investment banks, and for the crisis in finance capitalism generally—events taking place as the fourth edition of this book goes to press. Repeatedly compared to the Great Depression of 1929, the September 2008 crash of investment and credit banking in the United States is spreading globally and giving rise to government-funded rescue packages. On October 3, 2008, President Bush signed a "bailout plan" that would inject $700 billion into the financial system with the stated goal of saving it from collapse. When, or even if, the crisis will end is impossible to predict. Many economists foresee a recession in the year ahead. The question is: How did we get here? This article illustrates what can ensue from the mistaken belief that the financial markets can regulate themselves, and why governmental oversight is essential.

The following materials summarize and integrate virtually all of the important areas of administrative law we've touched on in the book. We are confident that you will see implicit in the articles that in administrative law one finds nothing less than an ongoing discourse about the most basic political questions of our time. These cases and materials then are not just about administrative law.

They are about fundamental questions of fairness and efficiency, and power and compassion in public life.

Privatization, Prisons, Democracy, and Human Rights: The Need to Extend the Province of Administrative Law

ALFRED C. AMAN, JR.

Indiana Journal of Global Legal Studies 12 (2005): 511

Introduction

Administrative law has an important role to play when it comes to providing democratic forums for deliberation and decisionmaking on a wide range of issues. In this paper, I will argue that domestic administrative law potentially offers a means for addressing human rights problems arising from privatization, particularly privatization in the United States dealing with prisons. As this paper will argue, creating opportunities for citizen involvement in what otherwise might be thought of as private decisionmaking processes may help prevent human rights problems before they occur. At a minimum, such an approach can create the forums and information necessary for meaningful and timely politics to develop around issues that, once privatized, can all too easily fall from public view.

. . . [A]nalyses of the relative fairness, transparency, and public participation available to citizens in what many take for granted as wholly private domains is necessary. Administrative law now no longer can remain state centric in its focus.

. . . The fusion of the market and the state in many contexts also requires a reassessment of the principles and reach of traditional administrative law.

Administrative law in the United States traditionally has been conceptualized in a state centric fashion—as a bridge between the market and the state. These two realms—markets and states—have stood for very different worlds, signaling binary approaches to obligations and constraints. Markets are said to stand for private ordering as opposed to state regulation; free markets as opposed to government bureaucracies. An important constitutionally based version of the public-private distinction derives from these differences. . . . American administrative law has followed these broad constitutional outlines. It was created primarily for public bodies. . . .

Privatization and various forms of private ordering, in general, have become more and more common as reforms, as we move from a focus on government to a study of new conceptualizations of the processes of governance. Privatization in the United States usually takes the form of giving over to the market the provision of services once provided by government. . . . Privatization subjects the activity in question to the forces of the market while freeing it from the various forms of regulation—both substantive and procedural—that apply to public bodies. This . . . usually means the Administrative Procedure Act (APA) does not apply, nor does the Freedom of Information Act (FOIA). More important, market incentives and the profit motive may too easily be substituted for the public interest as well as for primary markers of programmatic success. . . . Without a ready flow of information about the substantive success of the regulatory missions involved, the bottom line takes on more and more significance as a measure of success. . . .

Global competition, and the drive for lower taxes and lower regulatory costs that it encourages, accounts, in part, for the growth of what we might call a "nonstate public sector." This sector is one that evades the administrative law protections normally applied to a state entity, while bringing to bear the efficiencies of the market to the task at hand. Such approaches implicitly assume a zero-sum public-private game—that is, as some matters are moved from the public to the private sphere, nothing fundamental changes in what we think of as public or as private. . . . If anything, government can only be improved by the demands of the market, but the two spheres remain relatively autonomous.

But this is not the case. It is not just the recourse to the market that makes such change significant, but the change itself, located in the underlying relationship of states to markets. It is the fundamental realignment in the way states and markets interrelate and, at times, even merge—blurring and erasing the boundary between the two that requires us to examine these delegations to the market at the domestic level as part of a larger picture. . . . The cumulative effect of all of the various delegations [of state power] especially privatization, amounts to a new situation that requires that we see administrative law in a new light. The newly enlarging private sphere is not the result of simply a shift of preference for the private over the public, . . . but a new way of organizing public responsibilities and politics. Indeed, the cumulative impact of these delegations (including the privatization of social services, the deregulation of various industries, and the increased reliance on such public policy tools as school vouchers, tax credits, and faith-based initiatives), in effect, privatizes the public square, disaggregating the public and fusing concepts of citizenship with consumerism.

Such changes do not argue for a return to the past. Rather, they constitute new regulatory and procedural questions that require new solutions. Some of the new questions are: how best can nonstate actors be involved in decisionmaking processes; how can we maximize the flow of information involving these decisions; and how can we mitigate conflict of interest concerns that arise from the fusion of public and private that typify many markets and market approaches to policy issues—issues ranging from private prisons to welfare eligibility. Fundamental issues of democracy are now at stake.

. . .

The Democracy Problem

The democracy problem in globalization arises from the disjunction between global economic processes (on the one hand) and local processes of democratic participation (on the other). By disjunction I refer to the exclusion of key stakeholders . . . from the institutional processes whose outcomes affect them directly. . . . By approaching these processes as if they were only unidimensional and subject either to the rules of the market or the more traditional and hierarchical approaches of public law, we simply reify the separate worlds of markets and states, without taking into account the ways globalization is changing these worlds and their relationship to each other, and without providing room for a debate and discourse to develop that include a meaningful politics involving noneconomic values. When regulation is given over to the market or international decisionmakers, the public is no longer involved directly in decisionmaking, nor is information usually available in a form that would make public participation meaningful. . . .

This results because globalization dramatically changes the way states and markets interact, often fusing the public and private sectors in ways that can evoke a form of neocorporatism when it comes to the ways states carry out their publicly mandated goals. Rather than procedures substituting for political compromises over the substance of the underlying law involved, markets and market approaches are now used. . . . From a pragmatic point of view, markets take the place of procedures as a way of avoiding hard political choices. Markets and market approaches can cut costs in ways that politically accountable officials usually wish to avoid. . . . But such

. . . issues . . . inevitably are political in nature and would benefit from public awareness of, and input into, questions that focus not only on outcomes but the criteria used to assess. For example, who is or is not eligible for welfare, or what kinds of processes a private provider of prisons might or might not use for prisoners involved in a disciplinary proceeding.

. . . Market approaches are a part of the globally competitive landscape now. . . . To be successful, states must partner not only with other states but also with the private sector. The interconnected nature of our economies, apart from the nonterritorial nature of problems such as global warming and air pollution, requires greater cooperation among states as well as a variety of new partnerships with nonstate actors. . . . The result is a number of important changes in the ways current institutions, both domestic and international, state and nonstate, operate and interact with one another as well as a need for new understandings of the state's role in these activities. In this new context, . . . markets cannot automatically substitute more defined opportunities for democratic participation. Administrative law cannot remain the same either. It must . . . become multidimensional in its scope and reach, particularly if it is to deal effectively with the democracy deficits generated by globalization.

A new, multidimensional domestic administrative law potentially offers means for addressing the democracy deficits associated with globalization. The multidimensional aspect of a new administrative law derives from the fact that there is now both a public and a private dimension to lawmaking, and, in effect, both a vertical and a horizontal aspect to governance. . . . [N]ot to take into account the decisionmaking and norm-creating powers of the private realm leaves too many values hidden from public view, unknowable and unaccountable. [T]o deal with both the vertical and horizontal dimensions of global governance at the local level, and without automatically forcing them into a hierarchical state mode of decisionmaking, the new administrative law will have to be more focused on informational flows and democratic opportunities for participation and persuasion, and less on the procedural control of hierarchical decisionmaking power. . . .

The democracy problem generated by globalization in this broad sense is increasingly a feature of modern life in the United States and abroad. A multidimensional, domestic administrative law offers an alternate approach to the democracy problem in at least some sectors of globalization. . . .

State Centric and Denationalized Aspects of Globalization

. . . States . . . remain highly relevant to our analysis [of globalization]; however, the essence of globalization as denationalization is the recognition that along with states, nonstate actors as well as international and supranational bodies are all significant players [in the global arena]. These networks amount to governance more than government.

. . .

The essence of such a conception of [governance] and the successful exercise of power is that it depends less on hierarchy and more on the networks of actors involved. . . . Indeed, a denationalized perspective makes broad-based participation and a transparent decisionmaking process a natural part of any institution that is global in its impact. The crosscutting relations among the issues and the players require a process at least as broad as the impact of its outcomes. This is the first among my democracy criteria, to which we will return later.

A denationalized perspective on globalization highlights the need to emphasize networks and multiple decision sites and, if you will, a kind of global pluralism. Pluralism does not mean relativism in this context, but rather a decentralized system of deliberative decision-making that is interconnected by at least some common values and practices of legitimation. As a pluralist system, globalization is theoretically open. Problems of pollution, for example, are not bounded by territory, and even economic opportunities such as free trade involve a conception of markets that is not, in theory at least, limited by state jurisdictional lines.

The denationalized aspects of globalization are easily mistaken for state-centered processes. . . . The tendency to think in state centric terms—to say something is either private or public, domestic or international—cannot capture the complexity of global processes, the diversity of the global networks and players involved, and the decentered nature of the state when it does react. There is in effect a gray zone that at present cannot be captured fully either by states or (by default) by markets. This gray zone is of interest to me because it is in the areas where a more pluralistic, denationalized approach can be instituted that administrative law comes into play. . . . I believe that viewing globalization . . . as *intersecting fields* of transnational actors, both inside and outside the state sphere, yields both a richer understanding of the processes involved and a fuller account of democratic possibilities.

Globalization means that states must partner with other actors, both state and nonstate, if they are to solve problems that extend beyond their territorial reach. . . . Whether the issue is environmental pollution or the most efficient way of manufacturing and distributing automobiles, state jurisdictional lines are of ever-decreasing importance to the conceptualization and resolution of the question at hand. This does not mean that states and national interests are irrelevant. But it does mean that even when the externalities of globalization are identified, states account for only some of the actors involved. Considering globalization as denationalization facilitates understanding global lawmaking processes as inherently pluralistic, involving multiple actors representing various national and transnational networks.

With these different perceptions of globalization in mind, Part III now examines the delegations of public power to private entities in general, and then in depth, the delegation of public power to private prisons.

Delegations to the Market

A. Privatization

Privatization should be understood as a principal dynamic (i.e., both cause and effect) of globalization. It is not merely one means among many for making government more efficient or for expanding the private sector. . . . Rather, the increasing reliance on "the new governance" is indicative of a changing relationship between the market and the state. It is characterized by a fusion of public and private values, rhetoric and approaches, a fusion that is itself integral to the fusion of global and local economies. . . . The global political economy places great pressures on all entities—public and private—to be cost effective if they wish to be competitive. This encourages such delegations on the part of the state and it raises concerns over whether the cost savings that result from such public delegations to private entities occur at the expense of democratic processes, legitimacy, and individual justice. . . . This is the essence of the democracy deficit.

The democracy deficit is primarily the result of the application of a traditional conception of the public-private distinction that will likely diminish the public sector's responsibilities for transparency and accountability when private actors perform certain tasks. . . . Even in privatized contexts, private actors inevitably make policy when they carry out their delegated tasks and interpret the contracts under which they operate. A new kind of administrative law can and should be created to respond to the democracy deficit associated with privatization. It need not rely solely on traditional procedural approaches, arguably designed for governmental agencies carrying out regulatory functions. . . . It is important to emphasize that what is at stake are the values of public law—transparency, participation, fairness, and accountability, as well as the kind of democracy that can flow from all of these things. . . . It is the democracy-creating values of the APA, though not necessarily the precise procedural devices it currently employs, that need to be extended to various hybrid, public-private arrangements, if we are to ensure the legitimacy of those partnerships.

. . . The democracy problem is and should be one of the primary concerns of the new administrative law. There are, in effect, a variety of procedural responses possible to the procedural and structural questions presented by privatization. Perhaps the most common form of response is what we can call a traditional labeling approach: the actions taken are labeled either public or private. If public, a certain legal regime naturally follows with the application of the Due Process Clause; if private, another set of preordained rules may apply, including common-law approaches.

There are many problems with the labeling approach, particularly as applied to social services for the poor. Even if traditional due process protections extend to such contexts, the constitutional law that now exists may not be very effective and, in most instances, courts are increasingly reluctant to intervene. In any event, case-by-case approaches ignore the larger democratic needs that a space for politics might provide. Quite apart from the individual issues of a case, there are the larger policy issues that a purely economic discourse may ignore. However, if the private label is invoked, the resort to the common law, private remedies, and regimes may also be insufficient to deal with the public aspects of the problems involved. The emphasis is on suits based on retrospective facts, not on public participation in the creation of prospective rules. . . . There is now a need to devise responses that are sufficiently flexible to meet the demands of a world in which the relationship of markets to states is significantly different.

A new approach to administrative law is necessary—one that recognizes that global forces are not linear and that their market outcomes are not inevitable. Rather, administrative law can be a means of resisting some aspects of globalization while facilitating others. The public-private distinction need not be a source or primary cause of a domestic democracy deficit if we are willing to expand the province of administrative law, at least to the point of covering private actors carrying out public relationships. The following case study, dealing with private prisons, shows how this might be accomplished.

B. Private Prisons

"Despite its contemporary ubiquity, the prison is a relatively recent fixture in Western (indeed, every) society. Moreover, from the outset the prison was infused with private ownership and control, and with private functions, in many respects quite similar to the contemporary private prison." . . . It was not until the start of the twentieth century that it became the custom of correction agencies "to provide virtually all correctional services as governmental functions in institutions constructed and maintained at the government's expense."

The move back to private prisons began with the expansion of private services provided in prisons, which accelerated in the 1960s. These newly private services included "food preparation, vocational training, and inmate transportation." The first modern, privately operated prison was the Weaversville Intensive Treatment Unit, opened in 1976 in Pennsylvania. . . . Private prisons initially were slow to expand the number of inmates under their control. In 1987, there were only 3,100 inmates in private correctional facilities worldwide; in 1998, that number had risen to 132,000.

. . .

Use of private prisons in the United States has coincided with the widely cited rapid growth of the number of inmates: "The population grew more than 400% from less than 320,000 in 1980 to nearly 1.4 million at the end of 2002. The total population including those in jail was almost two million, with more than 1.8 million in state facilities." For comparative purposes, the U.S. houses approximately 700 prisoners per 100,000 people, while Europe averages approximately 110 per 100,000.

. . .

C. Regulating Private Prisons: Toward a Model Statute

Statutes involving the privatization of prisons vary widely from state to state in the protections they afford to the human rights of prisoners and the extent to which they involve the public at large, in a timely way, in such issues. Because "[m]ost government agencies have been satisfied with monitoring compliance with the terms of the contracts," it is imperative that statutes include human rights provisions that must be included in any private prison contract. Too often, however, there is little, if any, guidance in the applicable privatizing legislation. This is partly because decisions to privatize are often made hastily, usually in the face of budget pressures or court orders to relieve overcrowding at public facilities. Based on such realities, and given the presence of workable provisions scattered throughout state statutes in the United States, this paper suggests the establishment of a Model Privatization Code for prisons, incorporating many of these provisions found across the country. . . .

1. Privatization, Cost, Democracy, and Inequality

There is a continuing debate about whether private prisons offer any real cost benefit at all. . . . [A]s the cost-savings requirement gets larger, [however] there is an increasing danger that private prisons would need to sacrifice prisoners' rights to meet the standard.

Contrary to popular wisdom, many states operate their own prison systems incredibly frugally. Alabama's public prisons, for example, spend $1.08 per day to feed each prisoner. . . .

There are many other areas where public prisons are already run very frugally. In Alabama prisons, much of the work required to run the facility is performed by prisoners, which drastically reduces the costs of operation . . ." It is necessary to ask in privatized industries what costs have the legislators, in their statute, allowed to be lowered by the private entities, and what is the likely effect of the freedom given private companies in those provisions.

The Colorado privatization statute explicitly allows private providers to adjust worker wages and benefits: "[t]he general assembly recognizes that such contracting may result in variances from legislatively mandated pay scales and other employment practices that apply to the state personnel system." In contrast, Washington, D.C. requires a private provider to offer displaced workers a right of first refusal for jobs with the private company, and further requires that private companies comply with the government pay scale for six months. The D.C. statute restricts a private provider's ability to meet cost targets by hiring more efficient workers or changing incentive structures; any required efficiency gains must, therefore, come from the reduction of other costs. The

Colorado statute, like many others, requires that "privatization of government services not result in diminished quality in order to save money."

. . .

Part of the reason for concern about the potential for human rights abuses in private prisons is that the major rationales for the "relatively strong relationship between democratic forms of government and the protection of human rights" break down in the prison context. . . . By democracy, I refer not only to electoral democracy, but the kinds of microdemocracies that administrative law can help create by providing for a steady flow of information and public participation in privatization discussions. The dialogue such transparency can inspire places an emphasis on bargaining and compromise to resolve disputes, one that helps to further the human rights of citizens. . . . It is argued that "democracies offer their citizens the ability to remove potentially abusive leaders before violations have become too severe." Furthermore, "the civil liberties usually associated with democracies . . . enable citizens and opposition groups to publicize government abuses." These arguments lose their force in the prison context, where a defined minority of the population is stripped of both civil liberties and, often, the right to vote; prisoners are therefore excluded from the bargaining necessary to prevent oppression, and, especially in a privatized context, the general public usually is excluded from regular information about the treatment of inmates at prisons. Publicly-available information about cost and the contractual provisions is likely to replace a broader, political discourse in a privatized setting.

. . .

2. Minorities in Prison

No thorough discussion of human rights issues in connection with U.S. prisons can be complete without some mention of the disparate representation of minorities in the U.S. legal system. A discussion of one state, Alabama, with a significant private prison population is instructive. The "clientele" of many private prisons is likely to be disproportionately minority; in Alabama, 73 percent of felony defendants are minorities. While Black males are much more likely to be subjected to prison time, and therefore have to live in a private prison, they are also correspondingly less able to influence either any privatization decision or any oversight protocols. . . . [D]espite Blacks' constituting 26 percent of Alabama's population, there is not a single African-American on any of Alabama's three appellate courts: the Alabama Supreme Court, the Alabama Court of Civil Appeals, and the Alabama Court of Criminal Appeals. Not only are African-Americans underrepresented in positions of power within the judicial system, but currently over 30 percent of Black males in Alabama have lost the right to vote because of felony convictions, and "[t]he projection is that by the year 2005 the number could be as high as 40 percent." Alabama is not alone in its high disenfranchisement rate for African-American males; there are "more than 600,000 [disenfranchised felons] in Florida, not including those still in prison, on parole or on probation. More than one in four black men here may not vote."

D. Private Prisons—Transparency and Accountability

Even if adequate democratic checks existed for prison privatization decisions, most states do not subject providers to enough oversight to ensure accountability for human rights protection. States take numerous approaches to the privatization issue, subjecting private service providers to differing degrees of public accountability. Most states have statutes regarding the privatization of prisons, some allowing and encouraging them, some banning their use altogether. . . .

In order for a government to retain legitimate accountability for private prisons:

The state must retain and be able actually to exercise "step-in" rights—that is, to reclaim any privatized part of its prison system—and to do this it needs to have ongoing capacity and skill levels of its own. This can only be done if it remains a direct service provider in relation to some part, at least, of its prisoner population.

. . . For positions such as prison guards . . . the state [in order to keep the ability to step in] would have to retain a pool of public guards. Otherwise, if human rights problems developed at a private facility because of inadequate training, the state could not step-in with workers to take over security provision. . . . The Correctional Corporation of America (CCA) promised . . . [Tennessee both in 1982 and 1997] that it would be able to save $100 million per year with a completely privatized system [, an offer rejected by Tennessee]. Not only would a state lose the ability to step-in if it accepted such a proposal, but if the private provider was really able to save such a large sum of money, it would be difficult to see how a state would be able to quickly take back a prison

system. . . . The ability of a state to step-in can be ensured, at least in part, through a "contestability" process where public providers are able to bid against private providers for contracts. . . .

. . . The fact that most government oversight of private prisons concerns the monitoring of contract terms necessitates the inclusion of human rights provisions in privatization contracts. This is especially true given the increasing judicial indifference in the United States to prisoner suits, though the Supreme Court has recognized that private prisons and their employees are less immune from suit than their public sector counterparts.

One way to increase the accountability of private prison operators to the state, and thereby ensure that the state retains ultimate responsibility for prisons, is to limit the length of the privatization contract. The Supreme Court recognized this form of accountability in *Richardson v. McKnight*, where a Tennessee statute limited a contract's term to three years. The majority stated that the firm's "performance is disciplined . . . by pressure from potentially competing firms who can try to take its place." . . . Shorter contracts increase the potential frequency of public input into the process, which would ideally be encouraged before contract renewal takes place.

A problem with the Court's praise of the short term [concerns] . . . the . . . number of firms available if the private provider should fall short in its performance. Whether there is any real competitiveness in the privatized-prison industry . . . is questionable because of its oligopolistic nature. As of December 31, 1998, over 76 percent of the private prison capacity was controlled by just two companies: Wackenhut Corrections Corporation (WCC) and CCA, and CCA is a former subsidiary of WCC. . . .

In addition to the accountability-increasing feature of having a short potential contract period, Tennessee also provides that any private prison "must agree that the state may cancel the contract at any time after the first year of operation, without penalty to the state, upon giving ninety (90) days' written notice." This provision encourages the state to oversee the running of any private prison more closely, because the delegation can easily be reconsidered. Private groups who are interested in the privatization of prisons also have an incentive to monitor the private provider more closely, because at any time after the first year they can lobby the state to rescind the contract if it becomes apparent that a different provider (either public or private) would be preferable. All privatization contracts that represent the possibility of significant infringements upon human rights should contain a provision allowing the state to cancel the contract if the state believes that human rights abuses may be occurring at a facility without fearing that the private provider might be able to hold the state liable for breach of contract. . . .

Another important factor in retaining government responsibility for human rights abuses is the political accountability of the entity that actually makes the contract to privatize and what involvement other actors have in this process. [I]t is important that the participation of the public and the public's representatives be maximized as early in the process as possible. . . .

While several privatization statutes, such as Tennessee's, provide for some participation from the legislative branch in the contracting phase, few suggest any method for direct involvement from the public. One of the only states to call specifically for a public hearing does so in a statute covering all forms of government privatization. Montana requires an agency to form a privatization plan before any program can be privatized. Additionally the state provides that:

> The privatization plan must be released to the public and any affected employee organizations and must be submitted to the legislative audit committee at least 90 days prior to the proposed implementation date. At least 60 days prior to the proposed implementation date, the legislative audit committee shall conduct a public hearing on the proposed privatization plan at which public comments and testimony must be received. At least 15 days prior to the proposed implementation date, the legislative audit committee shall release to the public a summary of the results of the hearing, including any recommendations of the committee relating to the proposed privatization plan.

> . . .

. . . Public hearings produce little benefit, however, if the public is not provided with adequate information with which to make informed suggestions. Kentucky law requires the production of information necessary for the public to make informed decisions about the quality and value of privatized services[.]

. . .

Most U.S. prison privatization statutes require certification by the American Correctional Association (ACA). As Richard Harding notes, however, "[i]mportant as [ACA] standards are in maintaining a level of accountability in U.S. corrections, they are primarily processual and

formulaic. . . . Requiring certification, therefore, cannot absolve a state from responsibility for prison services touching on basic human rights such as prisoner safety. The United Kingdom and Australia do not require accreditation; the U.K. system instead relies upon government prison inspections:

. . .

By using government inspectors, the United Kingdom also maintains direct public oversight of prison conditions, a necessary element in preserving prisoner rights. Additionally, the United Kingdom—as well as Australia, Canada, and New Zealand—grant prisoners access to an ombudsman to whom prisoners can complain about violations of human rights by private prison providers. No such system is found in most U.S. systems.

Statutes that clearly specify required elements of any prison privatization contract are preferable to those that establish few (or no) concrete requirements of the private entity in such contracts. In contrast to contract provisions, statutory language is readily accessible to the public; almost all of a state's statutory law can be located, free of charge, through the state's homepage. . . .

In establishing a Model Privatization Code, it would be important to set up the basic requirements for ensuring that human rights are protected while leaving ample room for state experimentation with different procedures for enhancing the performance of private prisons. It is important to recognize that the current levels of privatization are unprecedented, and states may develop many insightful provisions to enhance the effectiveness of private prisons. Establishing a uniform code might actually aid such innovation, by enabling legislators to spend less time working out the basics of privatizing legislation, and, therefore, allowing consideration of state-specific (and other) concerns. Without some sort of guide for legislatures there is also the danger that the large private prison companies will be successful in establishing a uniform statute that represents primarily only their interests. . . .

E. The Outer Limits of Privatization and Prisons

1. Disciplinary Hearings

One of the inherent human rights problems created by the privatization of prisons is the blurred line between inmate discipline and the administering of additional prisoner punishment. Obviously, in order to run a prison effectively, the private provider must be able to assert some form of authority without clearance from a public supervisor. There is a point, however, where the discipline exacted by a private prison crosses over into punishment, and constitutional due process concerns require public oversight. In the United States many "disciplinary functions for breach of prison rules are carried out directly by the private operator." In most U.S. jurisdictions inmates can receive time off their prison sentences for "good time" served; in other words, a prisoner's sentence is reduced for behaving well behind bars. While public prisons often have an incentive to credit prisoners for "good time" because of prison overcrowding, private prisons often have the opposite incentive because they are usually paid according to their daily occupancy. Guards at CCA facilities are given the option to buy company stock, and therefore "have a vested interest in maintaining high occupancy for a protracted period of time."

These incentives have produced obvious results. "The New Mexico Corrections Department found that inmates at the [state's] CCA facility lost 'good time' eight times more frequently than prisoners in a state institution." . . . The United Kingdom retains state control over disciplinary matters: "[i]n all private prisons, disciplinary charges laid by custodial officers are adjudicated by . . . public sector officials who work on-site." . . .

2. Exporting Inmates

In the United States, it is now common for inmates to be shipped to private prisons in other states, in an effort to find the lowest cost provider. "These arrangements are not only inimical to prisoners' best interests in terms of family visits, but they also stretch the chain of accountability beyond breaking point. The state of origin of the prisoners has no standing to regulate or supervise what happens within the private prison." These transfers are often to distant states, increasing the "accountability deficit" created by these arrangements. For example, two of the largest prisoner-exporting states are the only two not within the contiguous forty-eight: Hawaii sends prisoners to Minnesota, and Alaska sends prisoners to Arizona. . . .

Much of the pressure to privatize prisons is driven by cost. While every state has seen a dramatic increase in incarceration levels, Arizona's prison population has had increases of almost 1,000 percent in the last twenty-five years. . . . "The state's prisons are built to hold 26,000 inmates. They now hold more than 30,000." . . . One issue of growing national concern—but of greater effect in Arizona—is the housing of increasing numbers of foreign national prisoners. About 10 percent of Arizona's prisoners are Mexican nationals, and state officials have estimated that housing prisoners in Mexico could possibly save over $8,000 per inmate each year. . . . This issue has been discussed in Arizona for several years, however, and it is likely that it or another state with high numbers of Mexican nationals (such as New Mexico) will experiment with a cross-border facility in the future.

Even more worrying is the emerging trend in the U.S. of "bed brokering," where private companies (such as Inmate Placement Services) find a prison bed in another state to house prisoners whom the home state cannot place. With private prisons responsible for small numbers of inmates from numerous states, there is a danger that no individual state will have enough incentive to properly oversee human rights compliance, especially where the housing state does not send any of its own prisoners to the facility. Consequently, states should be required to house, and therefore retain responsibility for, their own prisoners.

In order to protect human rights, a state must also prohibit private providers, who either house inmates in the state or accept inmates from the state within facilities found in other states, from lobbying the state on criminal sentencing laws. . . . There is no evidence that private providers attempt to either influence sentencing decisions or statute drafting in order to increase the number of prisoners, thereby increasing their potential "clients." However, as private prisons begin to saturate markets and deepen their relationships with state legislators, prudent drafting should require that all prison privatization statutes make clear that contracting prisons are prohibited from lobbying the legislature on criminal-sentencing matters. . . .

3. Privatization of Interrogation During Wartime

Privatization and the conduct of war, particularly the war in Iraq, has been a topic of great concern. Consider the current controversy surrounding Iraq and the Abu Ghraib prison. . . . When a government contracts for the regulation and administration of prisons without adequate limitations concerning what actions are acceptable, and what are beyond the scope of reason (and perhaps even unlawful), and what treaties, laws, and regulations apply, the propensity for abuse can increase considerably.

When the Abu Ghraib scandal came into the media spotlight last year, a connection between prison regulation and private firm involvement also became apparent. . . . Though the private companies hired by the U.S. Government were engaged in the interrogation of detainees and intelligence-gathering, the limited supervision given to these private contractors, and the abuse inflicted upon detainees by the employees of these firms, dramatically highlights the human rights abuses that can occur in such contexts by both public and private employees.

. . .

The investigation into the Abu Ghraib scandal has, thus far, yielded a substantial number of possible human rights violations—extending from the use of humiliation tactics (forcing detainees to stand naked, simulate sexual acts with one another, be dragged around in chains like animals, etc.) to brutality, all of which may constitute torture.

When granting government contracts to private firms for the regulation and management of prisons, certain mechanisms must be in place to ensure that human rights are upheld and abuses are kept to a minimum. Without adequate measures to guarantee that private companies are accountable to the government, the ambiguity as to who gives the orders can lead to situations like Abu Ghraib. There is a question as to whom the private contractors working at Abu Ghraib answered, if there even were persons to answer to. . . .

Two recently released reports by independent commissions . . . note various concerns and problems with the structuring of direction and command with respect to Abu Ghraib. . . . The findings of the two independent commissions support the theory that with stronger administrative safeguards and better delegation of authority, perhaps these types of violations could have been avoided.

. . . The report [that focused on the issues and concerns raised by the contracting of private firms] indicated that CACI[2] employees, hired for "numerous intelligence-related services" including "interrogator support," "screening cell support," "open source intelligence," and "special security office," among others, were able to participate in the abusive tactics, in large part because of the lack of administrative restraints. . . .

These findings . . . at a minimum, support the theory that when granting government contracts in areas as sensitive as the maintenance of prisons during wartime, where contractors have direct interaction with detainees, administrative mechanisms ensuring accountability are essential to preventing human rights violations and abuses.

. . .

Conclusion

. . .

Beyond traditional notions of electoral accountability, democracy requires the means by which issues can be drawn, information shared, and meaningful politics created. Democracy involves multiple forums for values and views to be expressed publicly on issues beyond those likely to be relevant to just an economic conception of the problems at hand. Legitimacy requires more than a process simply to check up on those in positions of responsibility to see if they are doing their job. It also involves creating the kind of information necessary to understand the issues for a real debate to ensue and for new ideas to be suggested. Administrative law can and should play an important role in making forums available to consider and assess new approaches to issues, not only those considered by public agencies but by public-private hybrids as well. The public-private distinction should not unduly shield decisionmaking processes from opportunities for participation and the articulation of values and points of view that enrich our politics and, indeed, make meaningful political discussion possible.

. . .

The province of administrative law is broad. It can and should involve the application of public law values to private actors and the creation of informal approaches to ensure a multiplicity of voices are heard and that noneconomic, as well as economic, issues are considered. In this way, human rights abuses may not only come to light, but more importantly, may never occur at all.

2. CACI International, Inc., the private firm obtained for interrogation and other intelligence-gathering purposes.

Outsourcing Sovereignty: Why Privatization of Government Functions Threatens Democracy and What We Can Do about It

PAUL R. VERKUIL (CAMBRIDGE UNIVERSITY PRESS, 2007)

From chapter 1, "Introduction and Overview— Why Outsourcing Threatens Democracy."

The government exercises sovereign powers. When those powers are delegated to outsiders, the capacity to govern is undermined. A government appointment creates a public servant who, whether through the oath, the security clearance, the desire to achieve public goals, or the psychic income of service, is different from those in the private sector. The office itself is honored. This is why many in our democratic system live in a dual reality, decrying the president, whether it be Bush or Clinton, Reagan or Roosevelt, but respecting the presidency, the office of George Washington, the first among the heroes of our Republic. Those offices that fall under the president deserve similar respect. Anyone who has served in government, from a buck private to a cabinet official, knows this feeling. And they also know that the public and private sectors have different boundaries. Outsourcing tests these boundaries. By doing so, it pushes government to justify delegations of public power to private hands.

[It is important] to show exactly when public power has been transferred. By way of introduction, consider one statistic—security clearances. These are key indicators of public responsibility, reflecting the exercise of important duties and realized only after careful investigations by federal officials. Currently over eight hundred thousand contractors have security clearances at eleven thousand government facilities. That may be more than exist on the civilian side of government. It certainly forces us to ask what it is these people do for government and whether it is something that government should be doing itself.

After many years of infatuation with the idea of privatization, the potential downsides of privatizing or contracting out governmental functions are being examined. The perceived threat is to democratic principles of accountability and process in what has been a largely unexamined shift from public to private governance. On both the national and global stage, a "democracy deficit" may be emerging. . . .

To date, strong public reactions against outsourcing sovereignty have been hard to locate. But that is changing. The recent exposé of shabby treatment and poor living conditions for wounded soldiers at Walter Reed Army Medical Center forced the resignation of the Secretary of the Army, Francis Harvey. The private contracting of support personnel and maintenance workers, something Harvey (a former chief G.E. executive) encouraged, led to a reduction in force from 300 to 60 in 2006. The House committee investigating the Walter Reed situation focused directly on the impact of outsourcing upon the performance of government functions.

In Iraq the implications of a "private military" have also been subjected to scrutiny. Ted Koppel, no isolated scholar, wrote in the op-ed pages of the *New York Times* about the "seductive . . . notion of a mercenary army." The emergence of a private military is one consequence of the privatization movement. Koppel suggested the "inevitable" next step—a defensive military force paid for by energy corporations, such as Exxon Mobil, to be deployed in countries where their interests need to be protected. He then quoted officials at Blackwater USA, a leading provider of such services: Provide a battalion or two of troops to protect oil fields in Nigeria, they responded, no problem. They are ready to take on the "Darfur account." The idea of conducting foreign policy by contract—the idea that such a duty can be delegated in the first place—is certainly an arresting one.

Noting that the Pentagon was reluctant to have private armies outside its chain of command, Koppel mentioned issues of loyalty and accountability. But Blackwater's representatives did not flinch. "We are accountable. We are transparent." After all, they said, "If we were against the U.S. government's interests we would never get another contract." Surely, this candid expression of economic interest from Blackwater and the many other private firms performing military work (which includes familiar names such as Halliburton and its subsidiary Kellogg, Brown & Root) satisfies stockholders' wishes. But it is not only stockholders whose interests must be served—it is citizens' interests as well. Blackwater and friends do not have the last word on whether they are doing too much, or whether they are transparent or accountable. This is where the government comes in.

Koppel . . . next encouraged debate on the merits of mercenary regimes. And debate he got. Six days later, a remarkable series of letters appeared in the *Times* that raised many of the policy points this book will explore. Some said as a "democratic nation," sensitive to "fueling serious human rights abuses," the "frightening prospect" of mercenaries conducting our foreign intervention is not what America is all about. One writer suggested, if the all volunteer army cannot staff the war in Iraq (or elsewhere), necessitating the use of private forces, perhaps that signals a vote against the war. Yet another writer urged congressional oversight of private military contractors and called for the restoration of compulsory military service as an obligation of citizenship and patriotism. All of the letters decried Koppel's "dubious cause." By doing so, the writers joined the issue publicly, which surely is what Koppel was hoping for.

This exchange helps to establish the theme . . . : "Outsourcing sovereignty" occurs when the idea of privatization is carried too far. In an era of national and global privatization, the temptations are great to expand it to include governmental functions inherent in sovereignty.

The *New York Times* recently published a series of articles that label contractors as the "Fourth Branch" of government. That term, coined in the 1930s to describe the independent agencies of government, has now been appropriated to cover private contractors. If the fourth branch was "headless" when composed of independent agencies, think how more so it can be when it consists of private contractors performing government services.

Privatization demonstrates efficiency principles that can improve government performance. But when privatization encourages the outsourcing of political decisions, it exceeds its limits. John Donahue reminds us that democracy is not defined by efficiency alone. Accountability is a countervailing principle of democracy. It may but need not be efficient. Indeed, as the Supreme Court has recognized, the Constitution is sometimes intentionally "inefficient." Of course, efficiency and accountability need not be in opposition—they can and do coexist. But when efficiency dominates—as is the case with outsourcing important aspects of public sector decision making—it clashes with accountability and undermines democratic values.

Moreover, although a dramatic example, the private military is in no way the exclusive setting for this problem. The urge to outsource affects many government programs, civilian as well as military. Recently, the Internal Revenue Service (IRS) decided to outsource delinquent tax collections to the private sector. The evidence was that the IRS could have done this important job itself more efficiently. Outsourcing in the face of both accountability and efficiency objections is inexplicable. It amounts to, in Paul Krugman's words, "a retreat from modern principles of government."

Outsourcing failures have been highlighted recently in the Coast Guard's decision to turn over to Lockheed Martin and Grumman the responsibility to manage its $17 billion fleet modernization program. The costs of this program now exceed $24 billion and the structural weaknesses in completed ships are rendering them unseaworthy. Many auditors and retired Coast Guard officials fault the privatization model, which "allowed the contractors at times to put their interests ahead of the Guard's." This compulsion to delegate government responsibilities has earned President Bush the title of "Outsourcer in Chief."

In both the IRS and Coast Guard examples, the outsourcing of management functions that are best performed in house undermines government performance in two ways: By utilizing second-best performers and by weakening or atrophying government's power to perform these functions in the future. Government managers cease to exist when they are not put to good use.

Some agencies, such as the Department of Defense (DOD), the Department of Energy (DOE), and the Department of Homeland Security (DHS), are outsourcing engines. The national security, public infrastructure, disaster relief, and border control missions these agencies perform are honeycombed with private contracts. And other agencies of government, when faced with personnel constraints or because of political preferences, increasingly turn to contractors to do policy formulation and implementation. The question becomes: Who is really in charge of government policy making? . . . [I]mportant work—labeled "significant" or "inherent"—is being contracted out to the detriment of democratic policy making; and . . . this trend can be moderated, if not reversed, by feasible changes in the way government operates. When the public, "We the People" under the Constitution, call this a "dubious cause," as one of Ted Koppel's responders put it, we are commanded to listen.

The "era of privatization" has unintended costs as well as intended benefits. Outsourcing can lead to corruption of our bureaucracy, at least of its politically appointed members. Political officials, who are appointed for short periods and enter service through the famous revolving door, sometimes utilize outsourcing both as a means of getting results and as a way of preserving later career opportunities.

Homeland Security seems to be the paradigm case. This multibillion-dollar agency, formed virtually overnight to meet a national security preparedness challenge, has been struggling to perform its complicated mission. More than two-thirds of the Department's most senior executives, including its first Secretary, Tom Ridge, have moved to private positions, some with companies who receive lucrative contracts from the agency. These companies are doing outsourced government work. Asa Hutchinson, a former undersecretary who ran for governor of Arkansas, allegedly had numerous private relationships with these companies, including one that sold him stock (Fortress America Acquisitions) that IPOed [initially publicly offered] for a potentially generous return. In the words of one critic, DHS itself seems to have become an IPO and "[e]veryone wants a piece of it." Ethics rules control these activities to some degree, although they too seem to have been reduced in effectiveness.

These activities reflect chronic problems with DHS itself—problems that aggressive privatization exacerbates. In agencies with big budgets such as the DHS, in which the players are inexperienced and the programs are new, officials have enormous opportunities to benefit from the outsourcing process. But outsourcing also causes demoralization costs. Civil servants may be bypassed by outsourcing decisions and their purpose and commitment are frustrated. Given the aging of our bureaucracy and difficulty in finding qualified replacements, maintaining significant functions in house is crucial to the presentation of our civil service. The Wall Street Journal puts it provocatively; Is government "outsourcing its brain"?

. . . The perspective [here] is not anti privatization. The author has long favored deregulation and the values of efficiency, and does not see government as the solution to all public problems. But it is surely the solution to some of them. The continued outsourcing of government functions has reached the point where limits on it must be addressed. There seems to be no consistent standard applied when the choice to privatize or retain government functions arises. To avoid making outsourcing the default alternative, it should be checked by public law limits. These limits must be fixed for our democracy to work.

The relationship of government to the private sector is very much in flux these days. The pressures to outsource more and more government functions are occurring at the same time as the federal bureaucracy is shrinking in alarming proportion to its oversight responsibilities, and in relationship to the size of government itself.

In these circumstances, the number of private contractors doing the work of government will inevitably accelerate to the limits of federal employees available to supervise them; and may be beyond. Contractor oversight of contractors has become a routine proposition. The Government Accountability Office (GAO) now hires contractors to review contractors who have been suspended or barred for poor performance. The surveillance of privatized activities is more difficult to achieve because of the reduction in key government personnel. A disequilibrium is occurring between those in government who should oversee and those in the private sector who need to be overseen. Accountability is lacking.

The gap is a by-product of two converging forces: the deregulation movement, which renders many government regulatory programs unnecessary, and the privatization movement, which transfers government activities to the private sector. Deregulation challenges the economic role of government over the economy. It seeks to end programs that are inefficient or counterproductive. Even after its many successes, however, "the prevailing view still holds that government regulation is overzealous and needs to be reined in." This view is not equally shared by the public or the academy, but it often drives decisions at the White House, in Congress, and even before the courts. There is no need to challenge deregulation; the need is for government officials to make all significant decisions, whether they be regulatory or deregulatory in character.

Privatization's role is different from deregulation. It accepts the need for a government activity but sees advantages in shifting its operation to private hands. In the United States, at least, privatization, unlike deregulation, is concerned less with the amount of government expenditures than with where to place responsibility for the activity. The size of government, viewed as a percentage of the Gross Domestic Product, could well grow in a privatized environment, as it has during the Bush administration. But privatization and deregulation do share a belief that the market will improve the services provided by a monopolistic bureaucracy. A cornerstone of the reinventing government movement of the Clinton-Gore administration, this commitment has become ideological under the Bush administration.

President Bush's vision of an "ownership society" tries to build public support for reducing the size of government across the board. It has been used prominently to advocate private accounts as an alternative to Social Security, but it also has become a code word that signals more generally the private sector's role in the provision of traditional government services. Privatization, in this view, is a way to pass ownership of government on to the people, or at least some of the people.

But stating a preference for private over public solutions, as the term ownership society suggests, has unintended consequences. Government has been contracting out some of its services since the post–World War II period, but its acceleration to the limits of accountability is a relatively recent phenomenon. The view that privatization provides a superior organizing principle to government monopoly puts the public sector on the defensive. It fuels the debate over whether Social Security should remain a public function or whether health care should become one. Indeed a central question arising from the privatization movement is whether the term "public sector" continues to be a viable social concept. Stated alternatively, is the public-private distinction, which has been in law and theory from the earliest times, still meaningful in an era of transcendent privatization? And if not, what replaces it?

. . . Accepting privatization . . . need not be the end of public law; instead, public law limitations should be reformulated to restrict the outsourcing of significant government functions as a way to preserve democracy.

. . .

Ultimately, the goal [should be] to balance the two positives of the private and public sectors—efficiency and accountability—in ways that confirm rather than threaten our legal and political traditions. Accountability emerges from constitutional principles, from legal standards, and from administrative practices. New formulations that embrace an invigorated conception of the public sector are also needed. [The important questions in this context are]: How can public service—the dreaded bureaucracy—be reorganized and reinvigorated to meet the challenges that privatized government presents? For years, the bureaucracy has been neglected and derided. But we have reached a point where it must be given a renewed life.

DHS [Department of Homeland Security] and FEMA's [Federal Emergency Management Agency] performance during Hurricane Katrina dramatically shows the dangers of excessive privatization. The proper balance between public and private solutions must be struck for mission oriented agencies such as DHS to work effectively. Since 2001, government has been developing a new specialty in national security and disaster relief. These enormous responsibilities are the essence inherently governmental; they cannot be shifted to the private sec-

tor. Yet contractors are expanding their roles in ways that make the shift increasingly inevitable. How did we get to the place where the proposition of who runs government admits of no easy answer?

. . .

A Note on the Meaning of Sovereignty

[Approaching] from a traditional perspective, . . . [we] view . . . sovereignty [as] the exercise of power by the state. . . .

Stephen Krasner usefully describes four kinds of sovereignty: international legal sovereignty, Westphalian sovereignty, domestic sovereignty, and interdependence sovereignty. . . . We are concerned more with definition three.

. . .

The meaning of sovereignty was much debated during the creation of the Republic. Gordon Wood teaches us that during the Constitution drafting period, anti federalists derided the notion of shared or "divided" sovereignty between the Congress and the states. They used this contradictory phrase to argue that the Supremacy Clause of the Constitution would annihilate the independent sovereignty of the states. According to Wood, James Wilson resolved the impasse by arguing that sovereignty had not been divided but remained with the People, the true Sovereign. The People then delegated powers in such proportions as she thought necessary to the states and the three branches. Wilson's concept of sovereignty triumphed when the Constitution shifted its emphasis from "We the States" to "We the People."

Akhil Amar writes that Wilson believed the Constitution only to be a private document until it was ratified by the People. The ratification process itself was "extraordinarily extended and inclusive," with ten states waiving property restrictions so as to permit a broader number of voters to participate. Once ratified, of course, this private document became public. And the unique principle of American sovereignty was established. Placing sovereignty in the People has two distinct advantages for the arguments presented here. First, it makes clear who the principal and agents are. The People is the sovereign and the Congress and president are her agents. The political branches receive delegated powers either directly or indirectly from the Constitution. Whatever powers they in turn delegate are in fact subdelegated. It is in this context that the Subdelegation Act makes perfect sense. Second, once the principal-agent relationship is established, the Constitution has a role in policing it. Thus when the Congress subdelegates to the president or the agencies or the president further delegates to private parties, the Constitution still umpires the relationships.

Thus, sovereignty is an essential force under our Constitution. When sovereign powers are delegated, it is with the permission of the People. Notions of dual sovereignty or diffused sovereignty may more accurately describe federal and state relations. But they only serve to obfuscate the question of where accountability and responsibility lie for performing the people's duties under the Constitution.

Once it is accepted where sovereignty is placed and how it is exercised, "outsourcing sovereignty" becomes a logical impossibility unless of course the people concur and the agents faithfully follow her instructions. This is not some artificial construct. The Organization Chart of the United States . . . describes the government and its three branches. Note that it places the Constitution at the top. This chart symbolizes what it means to place sovereignty in the People and similarly what it means to demand faithful accountability to the Constitution by all three branches. The People, through popular sovereignty, established the Constitution, the document under which her agents are clearly identified and properly charged.

The metaphor of the People as sovereign also permits a (hopefully forgivable) literary flourish: the opportunity to personalize the constitutional connection. Arguments expressed here are made on behalf of the People. As Lady Liberty, she for they, the citizens delegate power under the Constitution and she sets the limits on delegations of power to private hands. . . . The requirements [that each branch has to follow in delegating power to private hands, however,] establish that . . . outsourcing sovereignty, is a constitutional oxymoron.

Agency's '04 Rule Let Banks Pile up New Debt

STEPHEN LABATON

New York Times, October 3, 2008.

"We have a good deal of comfort about the capital cushions at these firms at the moment."— Christopher Cox, chairman of the Securities and Exchange Commission, March 11, 2008

As rumors swirled that Bear Stearns faced imminent collapse in early March, Christopher Cox was told by his staff that Bear Stearns had $17 billion in cash and other assets—more than enough to weather the storm.

Drained of most of its cash three days later, Bear Stearns was forced into a hastily arranged marriage with JPMorgan Chase—backed by a $29 billion taxpayer dowry.

Within six months, other lions of Wall Street would also either disappear or transform themselves to survive the financial maelstrom—Merrill Lynch sold itself to Bank of America, Lehman Brothers filed for bankruptcy protection, and Goldman Sachs and Morgan Stanley converted to commercial banks.

How could Mr. Cox have been so wrong?

Many events in Washington, on Wall Street and elsewhere around the country have led to what has been called the most serious financial crisis since the 1930s. But decisions made at a brief meeting on April 28, 2004, explain why the problems could spin out of control. The agency's failure to follow through on those decisions also explains why Washington regulators did not see what was coming.

On that bright spring afternoon, the five members of the Securities and Exchange Commission met in a basement hearing room to consider an urgent plea by the big investment banks.

They wanted an exemption for their brokerage units from an old regulation that limited the amount of debt they could take on. The exemption would unshackle billions of dollars held in reserve as a cushion against losses on their investments. Those funds could then flow up to the parent company, enabling it to invest in the fast-growing but opaque world of mortgage-backed securities; credit derivatives, a form of insurance for bond holders; and other exotic instruments.

The five investment banks led the charge, including Goldman Sachs, which was headed by Henry M. Paulson Jr. Two years later, he left to become Treasury secretary.

A lone dissenter—a software consultant and expert on risk management—weighed in from Indiana with a two-page letter to warn the commission that the move was a grave mistake. He never heard back from Washington.

One commissioner, Harvey J. Goldschmid, questioned the staff about the consequences of the proposed exemption. It would only be available for the largest firms, he was reassuringly told—those with assets greater than $5 billion.

"We've said these are the big guys," Mr. Goldschmid said, provoking nervous laughter, "but that means if anything goes wrong, it's going to be an awfully big mess."

Mr. Goldschmid, an authority on securities law from Columbia, was a behind-the-scenes adviser in 2002 to Senator Paul S. Sarbanes when he rewrote the nation's corporate laws after a wave of accounting scandals. "Do we feel secure if there are these drops in capital we really will have investor protection?" Mr. Goldschmid asked. A senior staff member said the commission would hire the best minds, including people with strong quantitative skills to parse the banks' balance sheets.

Annette L. Nazareth, the head of market regulation, reassured the commission that under the new rules, the companies for the first time could be restricted by the commission from excessively risky activity. She was later appointed a commissioner and served until January 2008.

. . .

After 55 minutes of discussion . . . the chairman, William H. Donaldson, a veteran Wall Street executive, called for a vote. It was unanimous. The decision, changing what was known as the net capital rule, was completed and published in The Federal Register a few months later.

With that, the five big independent investment firms were unleashed.

In loosening the capital rules, which are supposed to provide a buffer in turbulent times, the agency also decided to rely on the firms' own computer models for determining the riskiness of investments, essentially outsourcing the job of monitoring risk to the banks themselves.

Over the following months and years, each of the firms would take advantage of the looser rules. At Bear Stearns, the leverage ratio—a measurement of how much the firm was borrowing compared to its total assets—rose sharply, to 33 to 1. In other words, for every dollar in equity, it had $33 of debt. The ratios at the other firms also rose significantly.

The 2004 decision for the first time gave the S.E.C. a window on the banks' increasingly risky investments in mortgage-related securities.

But the agency never took true advantage of that part of the bargain. The supervisory program under Mr. Cox, who arrived at the agency a year later, was a low priority.

The commission assigned seven people to examine the parent companies—which last year controlled financial empires with combined assets of more than $4 trillion. Since March 2007, the office has not had a director. And as of last month, the office had not completed a single inspection since it was reshuffled by Mr. Cox more than a year and a half ago.

The few problems the examiners preliminarily uncovered about the riskiness of the firms' investments and their increased reliance on debt—clear signs of trouble—were all but ignored.

The commission's division of trading and markets "became aware of numerous potential red flags prior to Bear Stearns's collapse, regarding its concentration of mortgage securities, high leverage, shortcomings of risk management in mortgage-backed securities and lack of compliance with the spirit of certain" capital standards, said an inspector general's report issued last Friday. But the division "did not take actions to limit these risk factors."

Drive to Deregulate

The commission's decision effectively to outsource its oversight to the firms themselves fit squarely in the broader Washington culture of the last eight years under President Bush.

. . .

"It's a fair criticism of the Bush administration that regulators have relied on many voluntary regulatory programs," said Roderick M. Hills, a Republican who was chairman of the S.E.C. under President Gerald R. Ford. "The problem with such voluntary programs is that, as we've seen throughout history, they often don't work."

As was the case with other agencies, the commission's decision was motivated by industry complaints of excessive regulation at a time of growing competition from overseas. The 2004 decision was aimed at easing regulatory burdens that the European Union was about to impose on the foreign operations of United States investment banks.

The Europeans said they would agree not to regulate the foreign subsidiaries of the investment banks on one condition—that the commission regulate the parent companies, along with the brokerage units that the S.E.C. already oversaw.

A 1999 law, however, had left a gap that did not give the commission explicit oversight of the parent companies. To get around that problem, and in exchange for the relaxed capital rules, the banks volunteered to let the commission examine the books of their parent companies and subsidiaries.

The 2004 decision also reflected a faith that Wall Street's financial interests coincided with Washington's regulatory interests.

"We foolishly believed that the firms had a strong culture of self-preservation and responsibility and would have the discipline not to be excessively borrowing," said Professor James D. Cox, an expert on securities law and accounting at Duke School of Law (and no relationship to Christopher Cox).

"Letting the firms police themselves made sense to me because I didn't think the S.E.C. had the staff and wherewithal to impose its own standards and I foolishly thought the market would impose its own self-discipline. We've all learned a terrible lesson," he added.

In letters to the commissioners, senior executives at the five investment banks complained about what they called unnecessary regulation and oversight by both American and European authorities. A lone voice of dissent in the 2004 proceeding came from a software consultant from Valparaiso, Ind., who said the computer models run by the firms—which the regulators would be relying on—could not anticipate moments of severe market turbulence.

"With the stroke of a pen, capital requirements are removed!" the consultant, Leonard D. Bole, wrote to the commission on Jan. 22, 2004. "Has the trading environment changed sufficiently since 1997, when the current requirements were enacted, that the commission is confident that current requirements in examples such as these can be disregarded?"

He said that similar computer standards had failed to protect Long-Term Capital Management, the hedge fund that collapsed in 1998, and could not protect companies from the market plunge of October 1987.

. . .

Policing Wall Street

. . .

The [Securities and Exchanges C]ommission's most public role in policing Wall Street is its enforcement efforts. But critics say that in recent years it has failed to deter market problems. "It seems to me the enforcement effort in recent years has fallen short of what one Supreme Court justice once called the fear of the shotgun behind the door," said Arthur Levitt Jr., who was S.E.C. chairman in the Clinton administration. "With this commission, the shotgun too rarely came out from behind the door."

Christopher Cox had been a close ally of business groups in his 17 years as a House member from one of the most conservative districts in Southern California. Mr. Cox had led the effort to rewrite securities laws to make investor lawsuits harder to file. He also fought against accounting rules that would give less favorable treatment to executive stock options.

Under Mr. Cox, the commission responded to complaints by some businesses by making it more difficult for the enforcement staff to investigate and bring cases against companies. The commission has repeatedly reversed or reduced proposed settlements that companies had tentatively agreed upon. While the number of enforcement cases has risen, the number of cases involving significant players or large amounts of money has declined.

Mr. Cox dismantled a risk management office created by Mr. Donaldson that was assigned to watch for future problems. While other financial regulatory agencies criticized a blueprint by Mr. Paulson, the Treasury secretary, that proposed to reduce their stature—and that of the S.E.C.—Mr. Cox did not challenge the plan, leaving it to three former Democratic and Republican commission chairmen to complain that the blueprint would neuter the agency.

In the process, Mr. Cox has surrounded himself with conservative lawyers, economists and accountants who, before the market turmoil of recent months, had embraced a far more limited vision for the commission than many of his predecessors.

"Stakes in the Ground"

Last Friday [September 26, 2008], the commission formally ended the 2004 program, acknowledging that it had failed to anticipate the problems at Bear Stearns and the four other major investment banks.

"The last six months have made it abundantly clear that voluntary regulation does not work," Mr. Cox said.

. . .

Mr. Cox has said that the 2004 program was flawed from its inception. But former officials as well as the inspector general's report have suggested that a major reason for its failure was Mr. Cox's use of it.

"In retrospect, the tragedy is that the 2004 rule making gave us the ability to get information that would have been critical to sensible monitoring, and yet the S.E.C. didn't oversee well enough," Mr. Goldschmid said in an interview. He and Mr. Donaldson left the commission in 2005.

. . .

[Mr. Cox, in response to written questions,] said that because the commission did not have the authority to curtail the heavy borrowing at Bear Stearns and the other firms, he and the commission were powerless to stop it.

"Implementing a purely voluntary program was very difficult because the commission's regulations shouldn't be suggestions," he said. "The fact these companies could withdraw from voluntary supervision at their discretion diminished the mandate of the program and weakened its effectiveness. Experience has shown that the S.E.C. could not bootstrap itself into authority it didn't have."

But critics say that the commission could have done more, and that the agency's effectiveness comes from the tone set at the top by the chairman, or what Mr. Levitt, the longest-serving S.E.C. chairman in history, calls "stakes in the ground."

"If you go back to the chairmen in recent years, you will see that each spoke about a variety of issues that were important to them," Mr. Levitt said. "This commission placed very few stakes in the ground."

PRACTICING WHAT WE HAVE PREACHED

We will not pretend here to deliver the final word on administrative law. While we are fully committed to our definition of good administrative law as the maximum feasible reduction of arbitrariness in government, it would be impossible to state what outcome would be produced in every individual case by the conscientious application of this standard. Instead, we have chosen to end this book by giving you the opportunity to evaluate three important issues in the news. If you wish, imagine that you are yourself an administrative official or a reviewing judge. What result in cases like the following do *you* think will minimize arbitrariness?

• The Federal Trade Commission (FTC), with some very specific statutory instructions from Congress, enforced bans on radio and television advertising by casinos. For example, the FTC would decide whether a Las Vegas hotel could advertise its "high-rolling" nightlife. However, the rules permitted advertisements for state-run lotteries and advertisements for casinos owned by Indian tribes. Opponents of the casino advertising ban argued that the exceptions carved out for state lotteries and Indian casinos made the law's other prohibitions entirely arbitrary and a violation of the First Amendment. How would you decide?[3]

• The Supreme Court rules that the Americans With Disabilities Act (ADA) does not prohibit discrimination against people whose disability can be "corrected or mitigated." A person whose poor vision is corrected by eyeglasses or contact lenses, therefore, is not disabled. Suppose an agency assigned to administer the ADA rules that a paraplegic who lost both legs in the Iraq war is not disabled because he can drive a specially equipped car and get around in a battery-powered wheelchair. As a reviewing judge would you let that decision stand? Why or why not?[4]

• Consider the problem of tobacco regulation. The Food and Drug Administration (FDA) regulates many aspects of the trade in foods and drugs: "The term 'drug' means . . . articles (other than food) intended to affect the structure or function of the body." 21 U.S.C. sec. 321(g)(1)(C). After decades of debate whether tobacco is included in this definition, in 1996 the FDA determined that companies sold tobacco products with the knowledge and belief that nicotine was a drug that "affected the structure or function of the body." Nicotine is highly addictive and also functions simultaneously as a stimulant, tranquilizer, and appetite suppressant. It has been found to be approximately as addictive as heroin.

A federal trial court upheld the FDA's interpretation of the statute. But the United States Court of Appeals for the Fourth Circuit reversed on the grounds that Congress did not intend the FDA to regulate tobacco. In his dissenting opinion, Judge Hall begins by pointing out how absurd it is to conclude that the Food, Drug, and Cosmetic Act is not intended to cover a drug which all parties concede

---

3. *Greater New Orleans Broadcasting Association v. U.S.*, 527 U.S. 173 (1999).

4. See *Murphy v. United Parcel Service*, 527 U.S. 516 (1999) and *Sutton v. United Air Lines*, 527 U.S. 471 (1999).

causes the premature death of approximately 400,000 people in the United States each year. He then goes on to appeal to a basic principle of administrative law:

When reviewing an agency's construction of a statute, we must first ask "whether Congress has directly spoken to the precise question at issue." *Chevron, U.S.A., Inc. v. Natural Resources Defense Council, Inc.* . . . The usual rule is to enforce the plain language of a statute according to its terms. . . . Under a *Chevron* step-two analysis—"if the statute is silent or ambiguous with respect to the specific issue, the question is whether the agency's answer is based on a permissible construction of the statute."— we need only find that the agency construction is a reasonable one, not the best one.

Judge Hall found the FDA's interpretation of its authorizing statute valid. How would you decide?[5]

This tobacco problem provides an exceptionally fitting end to a book on administrative law and politics.[6] It takes little imagination to consider how much political power the tobacco industry has had in Congress. Might the industry wield some influence over the third branch of government as well? The Fourth Circuit is based in Richmond, Virginia, which is also home to several of America's major tobacco companies. Some might imagine that the judges on this notoriously conservative court were influenced by their belief in the virtues of the tobacco industry, especially given the majority's refusal to follow the Supreme Court's *Chevron* decision. In a deeper sense, however, this case serves as an illustration of the point with which we began both this book and this chapter— that human beings are fallible and imperfect decision makers who may at times take actions under the color of law that appear nothing short of arbitrary and capricious to those who do not share their life experiences and values. The law alone is incapable of preventing such actions. Only wise "good judgment" and a commitment to maintaining the coherence and integrity behind the law's formal rules can do so.

5. See *Brown & Williamson Tobacco Co. v. Food and Drug Administration*, 153 F.3d 155 (1998).

6. See Lynn Mather, "Theorizing about Trial Courts: Lawyers, Policymaking and Tobacco Litigation," *Law & Social Inquiry* 23 (1998): 897.

APPENDIX A
THE INFORMALITY-FORMALITY
CONTINUUM IN ADMINISTRATIVE LAW

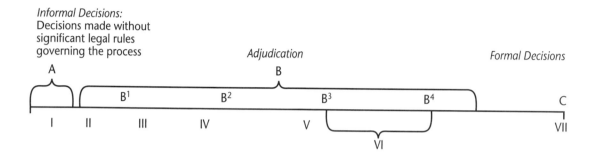

Informal Decisions:
Decisions made without significant legal rules governing the process

Adjudication

Formal Decisions

Adjudication

A. Due process adjudication where no *Goldberg* ingredients are required. Rare, but *Ingraham* (the school "spanking" case) comes close.

B. Increasing due process formality under *Goldberg*.

B^1 *Horowitz*

B^2 *Goss*

B^3 Many licensing and personnel cases

B^4 All ten *Goldberg* ingredients

C. Full adjudicatory formality under federal and state Administrative Procedure Acts.

Rulemaking

I. Classical rulemaking under *Bi-Metallic* (agencies have same discretion as legislature).

II. Negotiated Rulemaking. Rulemaking under section 561, Federal Administrative Procedure Act.

III. "Notice and Comment" rulemaking under section 553, Federal Administrative Procedure Act.

IV. Model State APA rulemaking, somewhat more formal than section 553.

V. "Hybrid" FTC rulemaking under Magnuson-Moss statute.

VI. Judicially applied due process standards in rulemaking that resembles adjudication in substance, *e.g., Sangamon Valley.*

VII. Full adjudicatory formality when statute requires hearing "on the record" in federal rulemaking (APA section 554).

APPENDIX B
FEDERAL ADMINISTRATIVE PROCEDURE ACT(1946)*
TITLE 5—GOVERNMENT ORGANIZATION AND EMPLOYEES
PART I—THE AGENCIES GENERALLY

CHAPTER 5—ADMINISTRATIVE PROCEDURE

Subchapter II—Administrative Procedure

Subchapter III—Negotiated Rulemaking Procedure

Subchapter IV—Alternative Means of Dispute Resolution in the Administrative Process

Subchapter V—Administrative Conference of the United States

* See the National Archives website for an updated version of the APA: www.archives.gov/federal-register/laws/administrative-procedure/

Subchapter II—Administrative Procedure

SHORT TITLE

The provisions of this subchapter and chapter 7 of this title were originally enacted by act June 11, 1946, ch. 324, 60 Stat. 237, popularly known as the "Administrative Procedure Act." That Act was repealed as part of the general revision of this title by Pub. L. 89-554 and its provisions incorporated into this subchapter and chapter 7 hereof.

SEC. 551. DEFINITIONS

For the purpose of this subchapter

(1)   "agency" means each authority of the Government of the United States, whether or not it is within or subject to review by another agency, but does not include—

(A)   the Congress;

(B)   the courts of the United States;

(C)   the governments of the territories or possessions of the United States;

(D)   the government of the District of Columbia; or except as to the requirements of section 552 of this title—

(E)   agencies composed of representatives of the parties or of representatives of organizations of the parties to the disputes determined by them;

(F)   courts martial and military commissions;

(G)   military authority exercised in the field in time of war or in occupied territory; or

(H)   functions conferred by sections 1738, 1739, 1743, and 1744 of title 12; chapter 2 of title 41; subchapter II of chapter 471 of title 49; or sections 1884, 1891–1902, and former section 1641 (b) (2), of title 50, appendix;

(2)   "person" includes an individual, partnership, corporation, association, or public or private organization other than an agency;

(3)   "party" includes a person or agency named or admitted as a party, or properly seeking and entitled as of right to be admitted as a party, in an agency proceeding, and a person or agency admitted by an agency as a party for limited purposes;

(4)   "rule" means the whole or a part of an agency statement of general or particular applicability and future effect designed to implement, interpret, or prescribe law or policy or describing the organization, procedure, or practice requirements of an agency and includes the approval or prescription for the future of rates, wages, corporate or financial structures or reorganizations thereof, prices, facilities, appliances, services or allowances therefor or of valuations, costs, or accounting, or practices bearing on any of the foregoing;

(5)   "rulemaking" means agency process for formulating, amending, or repealing a rule;

(6)   "order" means the whole or a part of a final disposition, whether affirmative, negative, injunctive, or declaratory in form, of an agency in a matter other than rulemaking but including licensing;

(7)   "adjudication" means agency process for the formulation of an order;

(8)   "license" includes the whole or a part of an agency permit, certificate, approval, registration, charter, membership, statutory exemption or other form of permission;

(9)   "licensing" includes agency process respecting the grant, renewal, denial, revocation, suspension, annulment, withdrawal, limitation, amendment, modification, or conditioning of a license;

(10)   "sanction" includes the whole or a part of an agency—

(A)   prohibition, requirement, limitation, or other condition affecting the freedom of a person;

(B)   withholding of relief;

(C)   imposition of penalty or fine;

(D)   destruction, taking, seizure, or withholding of property;

(E)   assessment of damages, reimbursement, restitution, compensation, costs, charges, or fees;

(F)   requirement, revocation, or suspension of a license; or

(G)   taking other compulsory or restrictive action;

(11)   "relief" includes the whole or a part of an agency—

(A)   grant of money, assistance, license, authority, exemption, exception, privilege, or remedy;

(B)   recognition of a claim, right, immunity, privilege, exemption, or exception; or

(C)   taking of other action on the application or petition of, and beneficial to, a person;

(12)   "agency proceeding" means an agency process as defined by paragraphs (5), (7), and (9) of this section;

(13)   "agency action" includes the whole or a part of an agency rule, order, license, sanction, relief, or the equivalent; or denial thereof, or failure to act; and

(14)   "ex parte communication" means an oral or written communication not on the public record with respect to which reasonable prior notice to all parties is not given, but it shall not include requests for status reports on any matter or proceeding covered by this subchapter.

SEC.   552.   PUBLIC INFORMATION; AGENCY RULES, OPINIONS, ORDERS, RECORDS, AND PROCEEDINGS

(a)   Each agency shall make available to the public information as follows:

(1)   Each agency shall separately state and currently publish in the Federal Register for the guidance of the public—

(A)   descriptions of its central and field organization and the established places at which, the employees (and in the case of a uniformed service, the members) from whom, and the methods whereby, the public may obtain information, make submittals or requests, or obtain decisions;

(B)   statements of the general course and method by which its functions are channeled and determined, including the nature and requirements of all formal and informal procedures available;

(C)   rules of procedure, descriptions of forms available or the places at which forms may be obtained, and instructions as to the scope and contents of all papers, reports, or examinations;

(D)   substantive rules of general applicability adopted as authorized by law, and statements of general policy or interpretations of general applicability formulated and adopted by the agency; and

(E)   each amendment, revision, or repeal of the foregoing.

Except to the extent that a person has actual and timely notice of the terms thereof, a person may not in any manner be required to resort to, or be adversely affected by, a matter required to be published in the Federal Register and not so published. For the purpose of this paragraph, matter reasonably available to the class of persons affected thereby is deemed published in the Federal Register when incorporated by reference therein with the approval of the Director of the Federal Register.

(2)   Each agency, in accordance with published rules, shall make available for public inspection and copying—

(A)   final opinions, including concurring and dissenting opinions, as well as orders, made in the adjudication of cases;

(B)   those statements of policy and interpretations which have been adopted by the agency and are not published in the Federal Register;

(C)   administrative staff manuals and instructions to staff that affect a member of the public;

(D)   copies of all records, regardless of form or format, which have been released to any person under paragraph (3) and which, because of the nature of their subject matter, the agency determines have become or are likely to become the subject of subsequent requests for substantially the same records; and

(E)   a general index of the records referred to under subparagraph;

unless the materials are promptly published and copies offered for sale. For records created on or after November 1, 1996, within one year after such date, each agency shall make such records available, including by computer telecommunications or, if computer telecommunications means have not been established by the agency, by other electronic means. To the extent required to prevent a clearly unwarranted invasion of personal privacy, an agency may delete identifying details when it makes available or publishes an opinion, statement of policy, interpretation, staff manual, instruction, or copies of records referred to in subparagraph (D). However, in each case the justification for the deletion shall be explained fully in writing, and the extent of such deletion shall be indicated on the portion of the record which is made available or published, unless including that indication would harm an interest protected by the exemption in subsection (b) under which the deletion is made. If technically feasible, the extent of the deletion shall be indicated at the place in the record where the deletion was made. Each agency shall also maintain and make available for pub lic inspection and copying current indexes providing identifying information for the public as to any matter issued, adopted, or promulgated after July 4, 1967, and required by this paragraph to be made available or published. Each agency shall promptly publish, quarterly or more frequently, and distribute (by sale or otherwise) copies of each index or supplements thereto unless it determines by order published in the Federal Register that the publication would be unnecessary and impracticable, in which case the agency shall nonetheless provide copies of such index on request at a cost not to exceed the direct cost of duplication. Each agency shall make the index referred to in subparagraph (E) available by computer telecommunications by December 31, 1999. A final order, opinion, statement of policy, interpretation, or staff manual or instruction that affects a member of the public may be relied on, used, or cited as precedent by an agency against a party other than an agency only if—

(i)   it has been indexed and either made available or published as provided by this paragraph; or

(ii)   the party has actual and timely notice of the terms thereof.

(3)(A) Except with respect to the records made available under paragraphs (1) and (2) of this subsection, each agency, upon any request for records which (i) reasonably describes such records and (ii) is made in accordance with published rules stating the time, place, fees (if any), and procedures to be followed, shall make the records promptly available to any person.

(B)   In making any record available to a person under this paragraph, an agency shall provide the record in any form or format requested by the person if the record is readily reproducible by the agency in that form or format. Each agency shall make reasonable efforts to maintain its records in forms or formats that are reproducible for purposes of this section.

(C)   In responding under this paragraph to a request for records, an agency shall make reasonable efforts to search for the records in electronic form or format, except when such efforts would significantly interfere with the operation of the agency's automated information system.

(D)   For purposes of this paragraph, the term "search" means to review, manually or by automated means, agency records for the purpose of locating those records which are responsive to a request.

(4) (A) (i) In order to carry out the provisions of this section, each agency shall promulgate regulations, pursuant to notice and receipt of public comment, specifying the schedule of fees applicable to the processing of requests under this section and establishing procedures and guidelines for determining when such fees should be waived or reduced. Such schedule shall conform to the guidelines which shall be promulgated, pursuant to notice and receipt of public comment, by the Director of the Office of Management and Budget and which shall provide for a uniform schedule of fees for all agencies.

(ii)   Such agency regulations shall provide that—

(I)   fees shall be limited to reasonable standard charges for document search, duplication, and review, when records are requested for commercial use;

(II)   fees shall be limited to reasonable standard charges for document duplication when records are not sought for commercial use and the request is made by an educational or noncommercial scientific institution, whose purpose is scholarly or scientific research; or a representative of the news media; and

(III)   for any request not described in (I) or (II), fees shall be limited to reasonable standard charges for document search and duplication.

(iii)   Documents shall be furnished without any charge or at a charge reduced below the fees established under clause (ii) if disclosure of the information is in the public interest because it is likely to contribute significantly to public understanding of the operations or activities of the government and is not primarily in the commercial interest of the requester.

(iv)   Fee schedules shall provide for the recovery of only the direct costs of search, duplication, or review. Review costs shall include only the direct costs incurred during the initial examination of a document for the purposes of determining whether the documents must be disclosed under this section and for the purposes of withholding any portions exempt from disclosure under this section. Review costs may not include any costs incurred in resolving issues of law or policy that may be raised in the course of processing a request under this section. No fee may be charged by any agency under this section—

(I)   if the costs of routine collection and processing of the fee are likely to equal or exceed the amount of the fee; or

(II)   for any request described in clause (ii) (II) or (III) of this subparagraph for the first two hours of search time or for the first one hundred pages of duplication.

(v)   No agency may require advance payment of any fee unless the requester has previously failed to pay fees in a timely fashion, or the agency has determined that the fee will exceed $250.

(vi)   Nothing in this subparagraph shall supersede fees chargeable under a statute specifically providing for setting the level of fees for particular types of records.

(vii)   In any action by a requester regarding the waiver of fees under this section, the court shall determine the matter de novo: Provided, That the court's review of the matter shall be limited to the record before the agency.

(B)   On complaint, the district court of the United States in the district in which the complainant resides, or has his principal place of business, or in which the agency records are situated, or in the District of Columbia, has jurisdiction to enjoin the agency from withholding agency records and to order the production of any agency records improperly withheld from the complainant. In such a case the court shall determine the matter de novo, and may examine the contents of such agency records in camera to determine whether such records or any part thereof shall be withheld under any of the exemptions set forth in subsection (b) of this section, and the burden is on the agency to sustain its action. In addition to any other matters to which a court accords substantial weight, a court shall accord substantial weight to an affidavit of an agency concerning the agency's determination as to technical feasibility under paragraph (2) (C) and subsection (b) and reproducibility under paragraph (3) (B).

(C)   Notwithstanding any other provision of law, the defendant shall serve an answer or otherwise plead to any complaint made under this subsection within thirty days after service upon the defendant of the pleading in which such complaint is made, unless the court otherwise directs for good cause shown.

((D)   Repealed. Pub. L. 98-620, title IV, Sec. 402 (2), Nov. 8, 1984, 98 Stat. 3357.)

(E)   The court may assess against the United States reasonable attorney fees and other litigation costs reasonably incurred in any case under this section in which the complainant has substantially prevailed.

(F)   Whenever the court orders the production of any agency records improperly withheld from the complainant and assesses against the United States reasonable attorney fees and other litigation costs, and the court additionally issues a written finding that the circumstances surrounding the withholding raise questions whether agency personnel acted arbitrarily or capriciously with respect to the withholding, the Special Counsel shall promptly initiate a proceeding to determine whether disciplinary action is warranted against the officer or employee who was primarily responsible for the withholding. The Special Counsel, after investigation and consideration of the evidence submitted, shall submit his findings and recommendations to the administrative authority of the agency concerned and shall send copies of the findings and recommendations to the officer or employee or his representative. The administrative authority shall take the corrective action that the Special Counsel recommends.

(G)   In the event of noncompliance with the order of the court, the district court may punish for contempt the responsible employee, and in the case of a uniformed service, the responsible member.

(5)   Each agency having more than one member shall maintain and make available for public inspection a record of the final votes of each member in every agency proceeding.

(6)(A) Each agency, upon any request for records made under paragraph (1), (2), or (3) of this subsection, shall—

(i)   determine within 20 days (excepting Saturdays, Sundays, and legal public holidays) after the receipt of any such request whether to comply with such request and shall immediately notify the person making such request of such determination and the reasons therefor, and of the right of such person to appeal to the head of the agency any adverse determination; and

(ii)   make a determination with respect to any appeal within twenty days (excepting Saturdays, Sundays, and legal public holidays) after the receipt of such appeal. If on appeal the denial of the request for records is in whole or in part upheld, the agency shall notify the person making such request of the provisions for judicial review of that determination under paragraph (4) of this subsection.

(B) (i) In unusual circumstances as specified in this subparagraph, the time limits prescribed in either clause (i) or clause (ii) of subparagraph (A) may be extended by written notice to the person making such request setting forth the unusual circumstances for such extension and the date on which a determination is expected to be dispatched. No such notice shall specify a date that would result in an extension for more than ten working days, except as provided in clause (ii) of this subparagraph.

(ii)   With respect to a request for which a written notice under clause (i) extends the time limits prescribed under clause (i) of subparagraph (A), the agency shall notify the person making the request if the request cannot be processed within the time limit specified in that clause and shall provide the person an opportunity to limit the scope of the request so that it may be processed within that time limit or an opportunity to arrange with the agency an alternative time frame for processing the request or a modified request. Refusal by the person to reasonably modify the request or arrange such an alternative time frame shall be considered as a factor in determining whether exceptional circumstances exist for purposes of subparagraph (C).

(iii)   As used in this subparagraph, "unusual circumstances" means, but only to the extent reasonably necessary to the proper processing of the particular requests—

(I)   the need to search for and collect the requested records from field facilities or other establishments that are separate from the office processing the request;

(II)   the need to search for, collect, and appropriately examine a voluminous amount of separate and distinct records which are demanded in a single request; or

(III)   the need for consultation, which shall be conducted with all practicable speed, with another agency having a substantial interest in the determination of the request or among two or more components of the agency having substantial subject-matter interest therein.

(iv)   Each agency may promulgate regulations, pursuant to notice and receipt of public comment, providing for the aggregation of certain requests by the same requestor, or by a group of requestors acting in concert, if the agency rea-sonably believes that such requests actually constitute a single request, which would otherwise satisfy the unusual circumstances specified in this subparagraph, and the requests involve clearly related matters. Multiple requests involving unrelated matters shall not be aggregated.

(C) (i) Any person making a request to any agency for records under paragraph (1), (2), or (3) of this subsection shall be deemed to have exhausted his administrative remedies with respect to such request if the agency fails to comply with the applicable time limit provisions of this paragraph. If the Government can show exceptional circumstances exist and that the agency is exercising due diligence in responding to the request, the court may retain jurisdiction and allow the agency additional time to complete its review of the records. Upon any determination by an agency to comply with a request for records, the records shall be made promptly available to such person making such request. Any notification of denial of any request for records under this subsection shall set forth the names and titles or positions of each person responsible for the denial of such request.

(ii)   For purposes of this subparagraph, the term "exceptional circumstances" does not include a delay that results from a predictable agency workload of requests under this section, unless the agency demonstrates reasonable progress in reducing its backlog of pending requests.

(iii)   Refusal by a person to reasonably modify the scope of a request or arrange an alternative time frame for processing a request (or a modified request) under clause (ii) after being given an opportunity to do so by the agency to whom the person made the request shall be considered as a factor in determining whether exceptional circumstances exist for purposes of this subparagraph.

(D) (i) Each agency may promulgate regulations, pursuant to notice and receipt of public comment, providing for multitrack processing of requests for records based on the amount of work or time (or both) involved in processing requests.

(ii)   Regulations under this subparagraph may provide a person making a request that does not qualify for the fastest multitrack processing an opportunity to limit the scope of the request in order to qualify for faster processing.

(iii)   This subparagraph shall not be considered to affect the requirement under subparagraph (C) to exercise due diligence.

(E) (i) Each agency shall promulgate regulations, pursuant to notice and receipt of public comment, providing for expedited processing of requests for records—

(I)   in cases in which the person requesting the records demonstrates a compelling need; and

(II)   in other cases determined by the agency.

(ii)   Notwithstanding clause (i), regulations under this subparagraph must ensure—

(I)   that a determination of whether to provide expedited processing shall be made, and notice of the determination shall be provided to the person making the request, within 10 days after the date of the request; and

(II)   expeditious consideration of administrative appeals of such determinations of whether to provide expedited processing.

(iii)   An agency shall process as soon as practicable any request for records to which the agency has granted expedited processing under this subparagraph. Agency action to deny or affirm denial of a request for expedited processing pursuant to this subparagraph, and failure by an agency to respond in a timely manner to such a request shall be subject to judicial review under paragraph (4), except that the judicial review shall be based on the record before the agency at the time of the determination.

(iv)   A district court of the United States shall not have jurisdiction to review an agency denial of expedited processing of a request for records after the agency has provided a complete response to the request.

(v)   For purposes of this subparagraph, the term "compelling need" means—

(I)   that a failure to obtain requested records on an expedited basis under this paragraph could reasonably be expected to pose an imminent threat to the life or physical safety of an individual; or

(II)   with respect to a request made by a person primarily engaged in disseminating information, urgency to inform the public concerning actual or alleged Federal Government activity.

(vi)   A demonstration of a compelling need by a person making a request for expedited processing shall be made by a statement certified by such person to be true and correct to the best of such person's knowledge and belief.

(F)   In denying a request for records, in whole or in part, an agency shall make a reasonable effort to estimate the volume of any requested matter the provision of which is denied, and shall provide any such estimate to the person making the request, unless providing such estimate would harm an interest protected by the exemption in subsection (b) pursuant to which the denial is made.

(b)   This section does not apply to matters that are

(1) (A) specifically authorized under criteria established by an Executive order to be kept secret in the interest of national defense or foreign policy and (B) are in fact properly classified pursuant to such Executive order;

(2)   related solely to the internal personnel rules and practices of an agency;

(3)   specifically exempted from disclosure by statute (other than section 552b of this title), provided that such statute (A) requires that the matters be withheld from the public in such a manner as to leave no discretion on the issue, or (B) establishes particular criteria for withholding or refers to particular types of matters to be withheld;

(4)   trade secrets and commercial or financial information obtained from a person and privileged or confidential;

(5)   inter-agency or intra-agency memorandums or letters which would not be available by law to a party other than an agency in litigation with the agency;

(6)   personnel and medical files and similar files the disclosure of which would constitute a clearly unwarranted invasion of personal privacy;

(7)   records or information compiled for law enforcement purposes, but only to the extent that the production of such law enforcement records or information (A) could reasonably be expected to interfere with enforcement proceedings, (B) would deprive a person of a right to a fair trial or an impartial adjudication, (C) could reasonably be expected to constitute an unwarranted invasion of personal privacy, (D) could reasonably be expected to disclose the identity of a confidential source, including a State, local, or foreign agency or authority or any private institution which furnished information on a confidential basis, and, in the case of a record or information compiled by criminal law enforcement authority in the course of a criminal investigation or by an agency conducting a lawful national security intelligence investigation, information furnished by a confidential source, (E)

would disclose techniques and procedures for law enforcement investigations or prosecutions, or would disclose guidelines for law enforcement investigations or prosecutions if such disclosure could reasonably be expected to risk circumvention of the law, or (F) could reasonably be expected to endanger the life or physical safety of any individual;

(8)   contained in or related to examination, operating, or condition reports prepared by, on behalf of, or for the use of an agency responsible for the regulation or supervision of financial institutions; or

(9)   geological and geophysical information and data, including maps, concerning wells.

Any reasonably segregable portion of a record shall be provided to any person requesting such record after deletion of the portions which are exempt under this subsection. The amount of information deleted shall be indicated on the released portion of the record, unless including that indication would harm an interest protected by the exemption in this subsection under which the deletion is made. If technically feasible, the amount of the information deleted shall be indicated at the place in the record where such deletion is made.

(c)(1) Whenever a request is made which involves access to records described in subsection (b) (7) (A) and—

(A)   the investigation or proceeding involves a possible violation of criminal law; and

(B)   there is reason to believe that (i) the subject of the investigation or proceeding is not aware of its pendency, and (ii) disclosure of the existence of the records could reasonably be expected to interfere with enforcement proceedings, the agency may, during only such time as that circumstance continues, treat the records as not subject to the requirements of this section.

(2)   Whenever informant records maintained by a criminal law enforcement agency under an informant's name or personal identifier are requested by a third party according to the informant's name or personal identifier, the agency may treat the records as not subject to the requirements of this section unless the informant's status as an informant has been officially confirmed.

(3)   Whenever a request is made that involves access to records maintained by the Federal Bureau of Investigation pertaining to foreign intelligence or counterintelligence, or

international terrorism, and the existence of the records is classified information as provided in subsection (b) (1), the Bureau may, as long as the existence of the records remains classified information, treat the records as not subject to the requirements of this section.

(d)   This section does not authorize withholding of information or limit the availability of records to the public, except as specifically stated in this section. This section is not authority to withhold information from Congress.

(e) (1) On or before February 1 of each year, each agency shall submit to the Attorney General of the United States a report, which shall cover the preceding fiscal year and which shall include—

(A)   the number of determinations made by the agency not to comply with requests for records made to such agency under subsection (a) and the reasons for each such determination;

(B) (i) the number of appeals made by persons under subsection (a) (6), the result of such appeals, and the reason for the action upon each appeal that results in a denial of information; and

(ii)   a complete list of all statutes that the agency relies upon to authorize the agency to withhold information under subsection (b)(3), a description of whether a court has upheld the decision of the agency to withhold information under each such statute, and a concise description of the scope of any information withheld;

(C)   the number of requests for records pending before the agency as of September 30 of the preceding year, and the median number of days that such requests had been pending before the agency as of that date;

(D)   the number of requests for records received by the agency and the number of requests which the agency processed;

(E)   the median number of days taken by the agency to process different types of requests;

(F)   the total amount of fees collected by the agency for processing requests; and

(G)   the number of full-time staff of the agency devoted to processing requests for records under this section, and the total amount expended by the agency for processing such requests.

(2)   Each agency shall make each such report available

to the public including by computer telecommunications, or if computer telecommunications means have not been established by the agency, by other electronic means.

(3)   The Attorney General of the United States shall make each report, which has been made available by electronic means, available at a single electronic access point. The Attorney General of the United States shall notify the Chairman and ranking minority member of the Committee on Government Reform and Oversight of the House of Representatives and the Chairman and ranking minority member of the Committees on Governmental Affairs and the Judiciary of the Senate, no later than April 1 of the year in which each such report is issued, that such reports are available by electronic means.

(4)   The Attorney General of the United States, in consultation with the Director of the Office of Management and Budget, shall develop reporting and performance guidelines in connection with reports required by this subsection by October 1, 1997, and may establish additional requirements for such reports as the Attorney General determines may be useful.

(5)   The Attorney General of the United States shall submit an annual report on or before April 1 of each calendar year which shall include for the prior calendar year a listing of the number of cases arising under this section, the exemption involved in each case, the disposition of such case, and the cost, fees, and penalties assessed under subparagraphs (E), (F), and (G) of subsection (a)(4). Such report shall also include a description of the efforts undertaken by the Department of Justice to encourage agency compliance with this section.

(f)   For purposes of this section, the term

(1)   "agency" as defined in section 551 (1) of this title includes any executive department, military department, Government corporation, Government controlled corporation, or other establishment in the executive branch of the Government (including the Executive Office of the President), or any independent regulatory agency; and

(2)   "record" and any other term used in this section in reference to information includes any information that would be an agency record subject to the requirements of this section when maintained by an agency in any format, including an electronic format.

(g)   The head of each agency shall prepare and make publicly available upon request, reference material or a guide for requesting records or information from the agency, subject to the exemptions in subsection (b), including

(1)   an index of all major information systems of the agency;

(2)   a description of major information and record locator systems maintained by the agency; and

(3)   a handbook for obtaining various types and categories of public information from the agency pursuant to chapter 35 of title 44, and under this section.

CONGRESSIONAL STATEMENT OF FINDINGS AND PURPOSE; PUBLIC ACCESS TO INFORMATION IN ELECTRONIC FORMAT

Section 2 of Pub. L. 104-231 provided that:

"(a)   Findings. The Congress finds that

"(1)   the purpose of section 552 of title 5, United States Code, popularly known as the Freedom of Information Act, is to require agencies of the Federal Government to make certain agency information available for public inspection and copying and to establish and enable enforcement of the right of any person to obtain access to the records of such agencies, subject to statutory exemptions, for any public or private purpose;

"(2)   since the enactment of the Freedom of Information Act in 1966, and the amendments enacted in 1974 and 1986, the Freedom of Information Act has been a valuable means through which any person can learn how the Federal Government operates;

"(3)   the Freedom of Information Act has led to the disclosure of waste, fraud, abuse, and wrongdoing in the Federal Government;

"(4)   the Freedom of Information Act has led to the identification of unsafe consumer products, harmful drugs, and serious health hazards;

"(5)   Government agencies increasingly use computers to conduct agency business and to store publicly valuable agency records and information; and

"(6)   Government agencies should use new technology to enhance public access to agency records and information.

"(b)   Purposes. The purposes of this Act (see Short Title of 1996 Amendment note above) are to

"(1)   foster democracy by ensuring public access to agency records and information;

"(2)   improve public access to agency records and information;

"(3)   ensure agency compliance with statutory time limits; and

"(4)   maximize the usefulness of agency records and information collected, maintained, used, retained, and disseminated by the Federal Government."

FREEDOM OF INFORMATION ACT EXEMPTION FOR CERTAIN OPEN SKIES TREATY DATA

Pub. L. 103-236, title V, Sec. 533, Apr. 30, 1994, 108 Stat. 480, provided that:

"(a)   In General. Data with respect to a foreign country collected by sensors during observation flights conducted in connection with the Treaty on Open Skies, including flights conducted prior to entry into force of the treaty, shall be exempt from disclosure under the Freedom of Information Act

"(1)   if the country has not disclosed the data to the public; and

"(2)   if the country has not, acting through the Open Skies Consultative Commission or any other diplomatic channel, authorized the United States to disclose the data to the public.

"(b)   Statutory Construction. This section constitutes a specific exemption within the meaning of section 552 (b) (3) of title 5, United States Code.

"(c)   Definitions. For the purposes of this section

"(1)   the term 'Freedom of Information Act' means the provisions of section 552 of title 5, United States Code;

"(2)   the term 'Open Skies Consultative Commission' means the commission established pursuant to Article X of the Treaty on Open Skies; and

"(3)   the term 'Treaty on Open Skies' means the Treaty on Open Skies, signed at Helsinki on March 24,1992."

CLASSIFIED NATIONAL SECURITY INFORMATION

For provisions relating to a response to a request for information under this section when the fact of its existence or nonexistence is itself classified or when it was originally classified by another agency, see Ex. Ord. No. 12958, Sec. 3.7, Apr. 17, 1995, 60 F.R. 19835, set out as a note under section 435 of Title 50. War and National Defense.

EX. ORD. NO. 12600. PREDISCLOSURE NOTIFICATION PROCEDURES FOR CONFIDENTIAL COMMERCIAL INFORMATION

Ex. Ord. No. 12600, June 23, 1987, 52 F.R. 23781, provided:

By the authority vested in me as President by the Constitution and statutes of the United States of America, and in order to provide predisclosure notification procedures under the Freedom of Information Act (5 U.S.C. 552), concerning confidential commercial information, and to make existing agency notification provisions more uniform, it is hereby ordered as follows:

Section 1. The head of each Executive department and agency subject to the Freedom of Information Act (5 U.S.C. 552) shall, to the extent permitted by law, establish procedures to notify submitters of records containing confidential commercial information as described in section 3 of this Order, when those records are requested under the Freedom of Information Act (FOIA), 5 U.S.C. 552, as amended, if after reviewing the request, the responsive records, and any appeal by the requester, the department or agency determines that it may be required to disclose the records. Such notice requires that an agency use goodfaith efforts to advise submitters of confidential commercial information of the procedures established under this Order. Further, where notification of a voluminous number of submitters is required, such notification may be accomplished by posting or publishing the notice in a place reasonably calculated to accomplish notification.

Sec. 2. For purposes of this Order, the following definitions apply:

(a)   "Confidential commercial information" means records provided to the government by a submitter that arguably contain material exempt from release under Exemption 4 of the Freedom of Information Act, 5 U.S.C. 552 (b) (4), because disclosure could reasonably be expected to cause substantial competitive harm.

(b)   "Submitter" means any person or entity who provides confidential commercial information to the government. The term "submitter" includes, but is not limited to, corporations, state governments, and foreign governments.

Sec. 3. (a) For confidential commercial information submitted prior to January 1, 1988, the head of each Executive department or agency shall, to the extent permitted by law, provide a submitter with notice pursuant to section 1 whenever:

(i)   the records are less than 10 years old and the information has been designated by the submitter as confidential commercial information; or

(ii)   the department or agency has reason to believe that disclosure of the information could reasonably be expected to cause substantial competitive harm.

(b)   For confidential commercial information submitted on or after January 1, 1988, the head of each Executive department or agency shall, to the extent permitted by law, establish procedures to permit submitters of confidential commercial information to designate, at the time the information is submitted to the Federal government or a reasonable time thereafter, any information the disclosure of which the submitter claims could reasonably be expected to cause substantial competitive harm. Such agency procedures may provide for the expiration, after a specified period of time or changes in circumstances, of designations of competitive harm made by submitters. Additionally, such procedures may permit the agency to designate specific classes of information that will be treated by the agency as if the information had been so designated by the submitter. The head of each Executive department or agency shall, to the extent permitted by law, provide the submitter notice in accordance with section 1 of this Order whenever the department or agency determines that it may be required to disclose records:

(i)   designated pursuant to this subsection; or

(ii)   the disclosure of which the department or agency has reason to believe could reasonably be expected to cause substantial competitive harm.

Sec. 4. When notification is made pursuant to section 1, each agency's procedures shall, to the extent permitted by law, afford the submitter a reasonable period of time in which the submitter or its designee may object to the disclosure of any specified portion of the information and to state all grounds upon which disclosure is opposed.

Sec. 5. Each agency shall give careful consideration to all such specified grounds for nondisclosure prior to making an administrative determination of the issue. In all instances when the agency determines to disclose the requested records, its procedures shall provide that the agency give the submitter a written statement briefly explaining why the submitter's objections are not sustained. Such statement shall, to the extent permitted by law, be provided a reasonable number of days prior to a specified disclosure date.

Sec. 6. Whenever a FOIA requester brings suit seeking to compel disclosure of confidential commercial information, each agency's procedures shall require that the submitter be promptly notified.

Sec. 7. The designation and notification procedures required by this Order shall be established by regulations, after notice and public comment. If similar procedures or regulations already exist, they should be reviewed for conformity and revised where necessary. Existing procedures or regulations need not be modified if they are in compliance with this Order.

Sec. 8. The notice requirements of this Order need not be followed if:

(a)   The agency determines that the information should not be disclosed;

(b)   The information has been published or has been officially made available to the public;

(c)   Disclosure of the information is required by law (other than 5 U.S.C. 552):

(d)   The disclosure is required by an agency rule that (1) was adopted pursuant to notice and public comment, (2) specifies narrow classes of records submitted to the agency that are to be released under the Freedom of Information Act (5 U.S.C. 552), and (3) provides in exceptional circumstances for notice when the submitter provides written justification, at the time the information is submitted or a reasonable time thereafter, that disclosure of the information could reasonably be expected to cause substantial competitive harm;

(e)   The information requested is not designated by the submitter as exempt from disclosure in accordance with agency regulations promulgated pursuant to section 7, when the submitter had an opportunity to do so at the time of submission of the information or a reasonable time thereafter, unless the agency has substantial reason to believe that disclosure of the information would result in competitive harm; or

(f)   The designation made by the submitter in accordance with agency regulations promulgated pursuant to section 7 appears obviously frivolous; except that, in such case, the agency must provide the submitter with written notice of any final administrative disclosure determination within a reasonable number of days prior to the specified disclosure date.

Sec. 9. Whenever an agency notifies a submitter that it may be required to disclose information pursuant to section 1 of this Order, the agency shall also notify the requester that notice and an opportunity to comment are being provided the submitter. Whenever an agency notifies a submitter of a final decision pursuant to section 5 of this Order, the agency shall also notify the requester.

Sec. 10. This Order is intended only to improve the internal management of the Federal government, and is not intended to create any right or benefit, substantive or procedural, enforceable at law by a party against the United States, its agencies, its officers, or any person. Ronald Reagan.

Ex. Ord. No. 13110. Nazi War Criminal Records Interagency Working Group

Ex. Ord. No. 13110, Jan. 11, 1999, 64 F.R. 2419, provided:

By the authority vested in me as President by the Constitution and the laws of the United States of America, including the Nazi War Crimes Disclosure Act (Public Law 105–246) (the "Act") (5 U.S.C. 552 note), it is hereby ordered as follows:

Section 1. Establishment of Working Group. There is hereby established the Nazi War Criminal Records Interagency Working Group (Working Group). The function of the Group shall be to locate, inventory, recommend for declassification, and make available to the public at the National Archives and Records Administration all classified Nazi war criminal records of the United States, subject to certain designated exceptions as provided in the Act. The Working Group shall coordinate with agencies and take such actions as necessary to expedite the release of such records to the public.

Sec. 2. Schedule. The Working Group should complete its work to the greatest extent possible and report to the Congress within 1 year.

Sec. 3. Membership. (a) The Working Group shall be composed of the following members:

(1)   Archivist of the United States (who shall serve as Chair of the Working Group);

(2)   Secretary of Defense;

(3)   Attorney General;

(4)   Director of Central Intelligence;

(5)   Director of the Federal Bureau of Investigation;

(6)   Director of the United States Holocaust Memorial Museum;

(7)   Historian of the Department of State; and

(8)   Three other persons appointed by the President.

(b)   The Senior Director for Records and Access Management of the National Security Council will serve as the liaison to and attend the meetings of the Working Group. Members of the Working Group who are full-time Federal officials may serve on the Working Group through designees.

Sec. 4. Administration. (a) To the extent permitted by law and subject to the availability of appropriations, the National Archives and Records Administration shall provide the Working Group with funding, administrative services, facilities, staff, and other support services necessary for the performance of the functions of the Working Group.

(b)   The Working Group shall terminate 3 years from the date of this Executive order. William J. Clinton.

SEC. 552A. RECORDS MAINTAINED ON INDIVIDU-ALS

(a)   Definitions. For purposes of this section

(1)   the term "agency" means agency as defined in section 552 (e) of this title;

(2)   the term "individual" means a citizen of the United States or an alien lawfully admitted for permanent

residence;

(3)   the term "maintain" includes maintain, collect, use, or disseminate;

(4)   the term "record" means any item, collection, or grouping of information about an individual that is maintained by an agency, including, but not limited to, his education, financial transactions, medical history, and criminal or employment history and that contains his name, or the identifying number, symbol, or other identifying particular assigned to the individual, such as a finger or voice print or a photograph;

(5)   the term "system of records" means a group of any records under the control of any agency from which information is retrieved by the name of the individual or by some identifying number, symbol, or other identifying particular assigned to the individual;

(6)   the term "statistical record" means a record in a system of records maintained for statistical research or reporting purposes only and not used in whole or in part in making any determination about an identifiable individual, except as provided by section 8 of title 13;

(7)   the term "routine use" means, with respect to the disclosure of a record, the use of such record for a purpose which is compatible with the purpose for which it was collected;

(8)   the term "matching program"

(A)   means any computerized comparison of

(i)   two or more automated systems of records or a system of records with non-Federal records for the purpose of

(I)   establishing or verifying the eligibility of, or continuing compliance with statutory and regulatory requirements by, applicants for, recipients or beneficiaries of, participants in, or providers of services with respect to, cash or in-kind assistance or payments under Federal benefit programs, or

(II)   recouping payments or delinquent debts under such Federal benefit programs, or

(ii)   two or more automated Federal personnel or payroll systems of records or a system of Federal personnel or payroll records with non-Federal records,

(B)   but does not include

(i)   matches performed to produce aggregate statistical data without any personal identifiers;

(ii)   matches performed to support any research or statistical project, the specific data of which may not be used to make decisions concerning the rights, benefits, or privileges of specific individuals;

(iii)   matches performed, by an agency (or component thereof) which performs as its principal function any activity pertaining to the enforcement of criminal laws, subsequent to the initiation of a specific criminal or civil law enforcement investigation of a named person or persons for the purpose of gathering evidence against such person or persons;

(iv)   matches of tax information (I) pursuant to section 6103 (d) of the Internal Revenue Code of 1986, (II) for purposes of tax administration as defined in section 6103 (b) (4) of such Code, (III) for the purpose of intercepting a tax refund due an individual under authority granted by section 404 (e), 464, or 1137 of the Social Security Act; or (IV) for the purpose of intercepting a tax refund due an individual under any other tax refund intercept program authorized by statute which has been determined by the Director of the Office of Management and Budget to contain verification, notice, and hearing requirements that are substantially similar to the procedures in section 1137 of the Social Security Act;

(v)   matches

(I)   using records predominantly relating to Federal personnel, that are performed for routine administrative purposes (subject to guidance provided by the Director of the Office of Management and Budget pursuant to subsection (v)); or

(II)   conducted by an agency using only records from systems of records maintained by that agency; if the purpose of the match is not to take any adverse financial, personnel, disciplinary, or other adverse action against Federal personnel;

(vi)   matches performed for foreign counterintelligence purposes or to produce background checks for security clearances of Federal personnel or Federal contractor personnel; or

(vii)   matches performed incident to a levy described in section 6103 (k) (8) of the Internal Revenue Code of 1986;

(9)   the term "recipient agency" means any agency, or contractor thereof, receiving records contained in a system

of records from a source agency for use in a matching program;

(10)   the term "non-Federal agency" means any State or local government, or agency thereof, which receives records contained in a system of records from a source agency for use in a matching program;

(11)   the term "source agency" means any agency that discloses records contained in a system of records to be used in a matching program, or any State or local government, or agency thereof, which discloses records to be used in a matching program;

(12)   the term "Federal benefit program" means any program administered or funded by the Federal Government, or by any agent or State on behalf of the Federal Government, providing cash or in-kind assistance in the form of payments, grants, loans, or loan guarantees to individuals; and

(13)   the term "Federal personnel" means officers and employees of the Government of the United States, members of the uniformed services (including members of the Reserve Components), individuals entitled to receive immediate or deferred retirement benefits under any retirement program of the Government of the United States (including survivor benefits).

(b)   Conditions of Disclosure. No agency shall disclose any record that is contained in a system of records by any means of communication to any person, or to another agency, except pursuant to a written request by, or with the prior written consent of, the individual to whom the record pertains, unless disclosure of the record would be

(1)   to those officers and employees of the agency that maintains the record who have a need for the record in the performance of their duties;

(2)   required under section 552 of this title;

(3)   for a routine use as defined in subsection (a) (7) of this section and described under subsection (e) (4) (D) of this section;

(4)   to the Bureau of the Census for purposes of planning or carrying out a census or survey or related activity pursuant to the provisions of title 13;

(5)   to a recipient who has provided the agency with advance adequate written assurance that the record will be used solely as a statistical research or reporting record, and the record is to be transferred in a form that is not individually identifiable;

(6)   to the National Archives and Records Administration as a record that has sufficient historical or other value to warrant its continued preservation by the United States Government, or for evaluation by the Archivist of the United States or the designee of the Archivist to determine whether the record has such value;

(7)   to another agency or to an instrumentality of any governmental jurisdiction within or under the control of the United States for a civil or criminal law enforcement activity if the activity is authorized by law, and of the head of the agency or instrumentality has made a written request to the agency that maintains the record specifying the particular portion desired and the law enforcement activity for which the record is sought;

(8)   to a person pursuant to a showing of compelling circumstances affecting the health or safety of an individual if upon such disclosure notification is transmitted to the last known address of such individual;

(9)   to either House of Congress, or, to the extent of matter within its jurisdiction, any committee or subcommittee thereof, any joint committee of Congress or subcommittee of any such joint committee;

(10)   to the Comptroller General, or any of his authorized representatives, in the course of the performance of the duties of the General Accounting Office;

(11)   pursuant to the order of a court of competent jurisdiction; or

(12)   to a consumer reporting agency in accordance with section 3711 (e) of title 31.

(c)   Accounting of Certain Disclosures. Each agency, with respect to each system of records under its control, shall

(1)   except for disclosures made under subsections (b) (1) or (b) (2) of this section, keep an accurate accounting of

(A)   the date, nature, and purpose of each disclosure of a record to any person or to another agency made under subsection (b) of this section; and

(B)   the name and address of the person or agency to whom the disclosure is made;

(2)   retain the accounting made under paragraph (1) of this subsection for at least five years or the life of the

record, whichever is longer, after the disclosure for which the accounting is made;

(3)   except for disclosures made under subsection (b) (7) of this section, make the accounting made under paragraph (1) of this subsection available to the individual named in the record at his request; and

(4)   inform any person or other agency about any correction or notation of dispute made by the agency in accordance with subsection (d) of this section of any record that has been disclosed to the person or agency if an accounting of the disclosure was made.

(d)   Access to Records.

Each agency that maintains a system of records shall

(1)   upon request by any individual to gain access to his record or to any information pertaining to him which is contained in the system, permit him and upon his request, a person of his own choosing to accompany him, to review the record and have a copy made of all or any portion thereof in a form comprehensible to him, except that the agency may require the individual to furnish a written statement authorizing discussion of that individual's record in the accompanying person's presence;

(2)   permit the individual to request amendment of a record pertaining to him and—

(A)   not later than 10 days (excluding Saturdays, Sundays, and legal public holidays) after the date of receipt of such request, acknowledge in writing such receipt; and

(B)   promptly, either—

(i)   make any correction of any portion thereof which the individual believes is not accurate, relevant, timely, or complete; or

(ii)   inform the individual of its refusal to amend the record in accordance with his request, the reason for the refusal, the procedures established by the agency for the individual to request a review of that refusal by the head of the agency or an officer designated by the head of the agency, and the name and business address of that official;

(3)   permit the individual who disagrees with the refusal of the agency to amend his record to request a review of such refusal, and not later than 30 days (excluding Saturdays, Sundays, and legal public holidays) from the date on which the individual requests such review, complete such review and make a final determination unless, for good

cause shown, the head of the agency extends such 30-day period; and if, after his review, the reviewing official also refuses to amend the record in accordance with the request, permit the individual to file with the agency a concise statement setting forth the reasons for his disagreement with the refusal of the agency, and notify the individual of the provisions for judicial review of the reviewing official's determination under subsection (g) (1) (A) of this section:

(4)   in any disclosure, containing information about which the individual has filed a statement of disagreement, occurring after the filing of the statement under paragraph (3) of this subsection, clearly note any portion of the record which is disputed and provide copies of the statement and, if the agency deems it appropriate, copies of a concise statement of the reasons of the agency for not making the amendments requested, to persons or other agencies to whom the disputed record has been disclosed; and

(5)   nothing in this section shall allow an individual access to any information compiled in reasonable anticipation of a civil action or proceeding.

(e)   Agency Requirements.

Each agency that maintains a system of records shall

(1)   maintain in its records only such information about an individual as is relevant and necessary to accomplish a purpose of the agency required to be accomplished by statute or by executive order of the President;

(2)   collect information to the greatest extent practicable directly from the subject individual when the information may result in adverse determinations about an individual's rights, benefits, and privileges under Federal programs;

(3)   inform each individual whom it asks to supply information on the form which it uses to collect the information or on a separate form that can be retained by the individual—

(A)   the authority (whether granted by statute, or by executive order of the President) which authorizes the solicitation of the information and whether disclosure of such information is mandatory or voluntary;

(B)   the principal purpose or purposes for which the information is intended to be used;

(C)   the routine uses which may be made of the information, as published pursuant to paragraph (4) (D) of this subsection; and

(D) the effects on him, if any, of not providing all or any part of the requested information;

(4) subject to the provisions of paragraph (11) of this subsection, publish in the Federal Register upon establishment or revision a notice of the existence and character of the system of records, which notice shall include—

(A) the name and location of the system;

(B) the categories of individuals on whom records are maintained in the system;

(C) the categories of records maintained in the system;

(D) each routine use of the records contained in the system, including the categories of users and the purpose of such use;

(E) the policies and practices of the agency regarding storage, removability, access controls, retention, and disposal of the records;

(F) the title and business address of the agency official who is responsible for the system of records;

(G) the agency procedures whereby an individual can be notified at his request if the system of records contains a record pertaining to him;

(H) the agency procedures whereby an individual can be notified at his request how he can gain access to any record pertaining to him contained in the system of records, and how he can contest its content; and

(I) the categories of sources of records in the system;

(5) maintain all records that are used by the agency in making any determination about any individual with such accuracy, relevance, timeliness, and completeness as is reasonably necessary to assure fairness to the individual in the determination;

(6) prior to disseminating any record about an individual to any person other than an agency, unless the dissemination is made pursuant to subsection (b) (2) of this section, make reasonable efforts to assure that such records are accurate, complete, timely, and relevant for agency purposes;

(7) maintain no record describing how any individual exercises rights guaranteed by the First Amendment unless expressly authorized by statute or by the individual about whom the record is maintained or unless pertinent to and within the scope of an authorized law enforcement activity;

(8) make reasonable efforts to serve notice on an individual when any record on such individual is made available to any person under compulsory legal process when such process becomes a matter of public record;

(9) establish rules of conduct for persons involved in the design, development, operation, or maintenance of any system of records, or in maintaining any record, and instruct each such person with respect to such rules and the requirements of this section, including any other rules and procedures adopted pursuant to this section and the penalties for noncompliance;

(10) establish appropriate administrative, technical, and physical safeguards to insure the security and confidentiality of records and to protect against any anticipated threats or hazards to their security or integrity, which could result in substantial harm, embarrassment, inconvenience, or unfairness to any individual on whom information is maintained;

(11) at least 30 days prior to publication of information under paragraph (4) (D) of this subsection, publish in the Federal Register notice of any new use or intended use of the information in the system, and provide an opportunity for interested persons to submit written data, views, or arguments to the agency; and

(12) if such agency is a recipient agency or a source agency in a matching program with a non-Federal agency, with respect to any establishment or revision of a matching program, at least 30 days prior to conducting such program, publish in the Federal Register notice of such establishment or revision.

(f) Agency Rules.

In order to carry out the provisions of this section, each agency that maintains a system of records shall promulgate rules, in accordance with the requirements (including general notice) of section 553 of this title, which shall

(1) establish procedures whereby an individual can be notified in response to his request if any system of records named by the individual contains a record pertaining to him;

(2) define reasonable times, places, and requirements for identifying an individual who requests his record or information pertaining to him before the agency shall make the record or information available to the individual;

(3)   establish procedures for the disclosure to an individual upon his request of his record or information pertaining to him, including special procedure, if deemed necessary, for the disclosure to an individual of medical records, including psychological records, pertaining to him;

(4)   establish procedures for reviewing a request from an individual concerning the amendment of any record or information pertaining to the individual, for making a determination on the request, for an appeal within the agency of an initial adverse agency determination, and for whatever additional means may be necessary for each individual to be able to exercise fully his rights under this section; and

(5)   establish fees to be charged, if any, to any individual for making copies of his record, excluding the cost of any search for and review of the record.

The Office of the Federal Register shall biennially compile and publish the rules promulgated under this subsection and agency notices published under subsection (e) (4) of this section in a form available to the public at low cost.

(g)   Civil Remedies.

(1)   Whenever any agency

(A)   makes a determination under subsection (d) (3) of this section not to amend an individual's record in accordance with his request, or fails to make such review in conformity with that subsection;

(B)   refuses to comply with an individual request under subsection (d) (1) of this section;

(C)   fails to maintain any record concerning any individual with such accuracy, relevance, timeliness, and completeness as is necessary to assure fairness in any determination relating to the qualifications, character, rights, or opportunities of, or benefits to the individual that may be made on the basis of such record, and consequently a determination is made which is adverse to the individual; or

(D)   fails to comply with any other provision of this section, or any rule promulgated thereunder, in such a way as to have an advese effect on an individual, the individual may bring a civil action against the agency, and the district courts of the United States shall have jurisdiction in the matters under the provisions of this subsection.

(2) (A) In any suit brought under the provisions of subsection (g) (1) (A) of this section, the court may order the agency to amend the individual's record in accordance with his request or in such other way as the court may direct. In such a case the court shall determine the matter de novo.

(B)   The court may assess against the United States reasonable attorney fees and other litigation costs reasonably incurred in any case under this paragraph in which the complainant has substantially prevailed.

(3) (A) In any suit brought under the provisions of subsection (g) (1) (B) of this section, the court may enjoin the agency from withholding the records and order the production to the complainant of any agency records improperly withheld from him. In such a case the court shall determine the matter de novo, and may examine the contents of any agency records in camera to determine whether the records or any portion thereof may be withheld under any of the exemptions set forth in subsection (k) of this section, and the burden is on the agency to sustain its action.

(B)   The court may assess against the United States reasonable attorney fees and other litigation costs reasonably incurred in any case under this paragraph in which the complainant has substantially prevailed.

(4)   In any suit brought under the provisions of subsection (g) (1) (C) or (D) of this section in which the court determines that the agency acted in a manner which was intentional or willful, the United States shall be liable to the individual in an amount equal to the sum of—

(A)   actual damages sustained by the individual as a result of the refusal or failure, but in no case shall a person entitled to recovery receive less than the sum of $1,000; and

(B)   the costs of the action together with reasonable attorney fees as determined by the court.

(5)   An action to enforce any liability created under this section may be brought in the district court of the United States in the district in which the complainant resides, or has his principal place of business, or in which the agency records are situated, or in the District of Columbia, without regard to the amount in controversy, within two years from the date on which the cause of action arises, except that where an agency has materially and willfully misrepresented any information required under this section to be disclosed to an individual and the information so misrepresented is material to establishment of the liability of the agency to the individual under this section, the action may be brought at any time within two years after discovery by

the individual of the misrepresentation. Nothing in this section shall be construed to authorize any civil action by reason of any injury sustained as the result of a disclosure of a record prior to September 27, 1975.

(h) Rights of Legal Guardians. For the purposes of this section, the parent of any minor, or the legal guardian of any individual who has been declared to be incompetent due to physical or mental incapacity or age by a court of competent jurisdiction, may act on behalf of the individual.

(i) Criminal Penalties.

(1) Any officer or employee of an agency, who by virtue of his employment or official position, has possession of, or access to, agency records which contain individually identifiable information the disclosure of which is prohibited by this section or by rules or regulations established thereunder, and who knowing that disclosure of the specific material is so prohibited, willfully discloses the material in any manner to any person or agency not entitled to receive it, shall be guilty of a misdemeanor and fined not more than $5,000.

(2) Any officer or employee of any agency who willfully maintains a system of records without meeting the notice requirements of subsection (e) (4) of this section shall be guilty of a misdemeanor and fined not more than $5,000.

(3) Any person who knowingly and willfully requests or obtains any record concerning an individual from an agency under false pretenses shall be guilty of a misdemeanor and fined not more than $5,000.

(j) General Exemptions. The head of any agency may promulgate rules, in accordance with the requirements (including general notice) of sections 553 (b) (1), (2), and (3), (c), and (e) of this title, to exempt any system of records within the agency from any part of this section except subsections (b), (c) (1) and (2), (e) (4) (A) through (F), (e) (6), (7), (9), (10), and (11), and (i) if the system of records is

(1) maintained by the Central Intelligence Agency; or

(2) maintained by an agency or component thereof which performs as its principal function any activity pertaining to the enforcement of criminal laws, including police efforts to prevent, control, or reduce crime or to apprehend criminals, and the activities of prosecutors, courts, correctional, probation, pardon, or parole authorities, and which consists of (A) information compiled for the purpose of identifying individual criminal offenders and alleged offenders and consisting only of identifying data and notations of arrests, the nature and disposition of criminal charges, sentencing, confinement, release, and parole and probation status; (B) information compiled for the purpose of a criminal investigation, including reports of informants and investigators, and associated with an identifiable individual; or (C) reports identifiable to an individual compiled at any stage of the process of enforcement of the criminal laws from arrest or indictment through release from supervision.

At the time rules are adopted under this subsection, the agency shall include in the statement required under section 553 (c) of this title, the reasons why the system of records is to be exempted from a provision of this section.

(k) Specific Exemptions. The head of any agency may promulgate rules, in accordance with the requirements (including general notice) of sections 553 (b) (1), (2), and (3), (c), and (e) of this title, to exempt any system of records within the agency from subsections (c) (3), (d), (e) (1), (e) (4) (G), (H), and (I) and (f) of this section if the system of records is

(1) subject to the provisions of section 552 (b) (1) of this title;

(2) investigatory material compiled for law enforcement purposes, other than material within the scope of subsection (j) (2) of this section: Provided, however, That if any individual is denied any right, privilege, or benefit that he would otherwise be entitled by Federal law, or for which he would otherwise be eligible, as a result of the maintenance of such material, such material shall be provided to such individual, except to the extent that the disclosure of such material would reveal the identity of a source who furnished information to the Government under an express promise that the identity of the source would be held in confidence, or, prior to the effective date of this section, under an implied promise that the identity of the source would be held in confidence;

(3) maintained in connection with providing protective services to the President of the United States or other individuals pursuant to section 3056 of title 18;

(4) required by statute to be maintained and used solely as statistical records;

(5)   investigatory material compiled solely for the purpose of determining suitability, eligibility, or qualifications for Federal civilian employment, military service, Federal contracts, or access to classified information, but only to the extent that the disclosure of such material would reveal the identity of a source who furnished information to the Government under an express promise that the identity of the source would be held in confidence, or, prior to the effective date of this section, under an implied promise that the identity of the source would be held in confidence;

(6)   testing or examination material used solely to determine individual qualifications for appointment or promotion in the Federal service the disclosure of which would compromise the objectivity or fairness of the testing or examination process, or

(7)   evaluation material used to determine potential for promotion in the armed services, but only to the extent that the disclosure of such material would reveal the identity of a source who furnished information to the Government under an express promise that the identity of the source would be held in confidence, or, prior to the effective date of this section, under an implied promise that the identity of the source would be held in confidence.

(l)   At the time rules are adopted under this subsection, the agency shall include in the statement required under section 553 (c) of this title, the reasons why the system of records is to be exempted from a provision of this section.

(1)   Archival Records. Each agency record that is accepted by the Archivist of the United States for storage, processing, and servicing in accordance with section 3103 of title 44 shall, for the purposes of this section, be considered to be maintained by the agency that deposited the record and shall be subject to the provisions of this section. The Archivist of the United States shall not disclose the record except to the agency that maintains the record, or under rules established by that agency which are not inconsistent with the provisions of this section.

(2)   Each agency record pertaining to an identifiable individual which was transferred to the National Archives of the United States as a record which has sufficient historical or other value to warrant its continued preservation by the United States Government, prior to the effective date of this section, shall, for the purposes of this section, be considered

to be maintained by the National Archives and shall not be subject to the provisions of this section, except that a statement generally describing such records (modeled after the requirements relating to records subject to subsections (e) (4) (A) through (G) of this section) shall be published in the Federal Register.

(3)   Each agency record pertaining to an identifiable individual which is transferred to the National Archives of the United States as a record which has sufficient historical or other value to warrant its continued preservation by the United States Government, on or after the effective date of this section, shall, for the purposes of this section, be considered to be maintained by the National Archives and shall be exempt from the requirements of this section except subsections (e) (4) (A) through (G) and (e) (9) of this section.

(m)   Government Contractors.

(1)   When an agency provides by a contract for the operation by or on behalf of the agency of a system of records to accomplish an agency function, the agency shall, consistent with its authority, cause the requirements of this section to be applied to such system. For purposes of subsection (i) of this section any such contractor and any employee of such contractor, if such contract is agreed to on or after the effective date of this section, shall be considered to be an employee of an agency.

(2)   A consumer reporting agency to which a record is disclosed under section 3711 (e) of title 31 shall not be considered a contractor for the purposes of this section.

(n)   Mailing Lists. An individual's name and address may not be sold or rented by an agency unless such action is specifically authorized by law. This provision shall not be construed to require the withholding of names and addresses otherwise permitted to be made public.

(o)   Matching Agreements.

(1)   No record, which is contained in a system of records, may be disclosed to a recipient agency or non-Federal agency for use in a computer matching program except pursuant to a written agreement between the source agency and the recipient agency or non-Federal agency specifying—

(A)   the purpose and legal authority for conducting the program;

(B)   the justification for the program and the anticipated results, including a specific estimate of any savings;

(C)   a description of the records that will be matched, including each data element that will be used, the approximate number of records that will be matched, and the projected starting and completion dates of the matching program;

(D)   procedures for providing individualized notice at the time of application, and notice periodically thereafter as directed by the Data Integrity Board of such agency (subject to guidance provided by the Director of the Office of Management and Budget pursuant to subsection (v)), to—

(i)   applicants for and recipients of financial assistance or payments under Federal benefit programs, and

(ii)   applicants for and holders of positions as Federal personnel, that any information provided by such applicants, recipients, holders, and individuals may be subject to verification through matching programs;

(E)   procedures for verifying information produced in such matching program as required by subsection (p);

(F)   procedures for the retention and timely destruction of identifiable records created by a recipient agency or non-Federal agency in such matching program;

(G)   procedures for ensuring the administrative, technical, and physical security of the records matched and the results of such programs;

(H)   prohibitions on duplication and redisclosure of records provided by the source agency within or outside the recipient agency or the non-Federal agency, except where required by law or essential to the conduct of the matching program;

(I)   procedures governing the use by a recipient agency or non-Federal agency of records provided in a matching program by a source agency, including procedures governing return of the records to the source agency or destruction of records used in such program;

(J)   information on assessments that have been made on the accuracy of the records that will be used in such matching program; and

(K)   that the Comptroller General may have access to all records of a recipient agency or a non-Federal agency that the Comptroller General deems necessary in order to monitor or verify compliance with the agreement.

(2)(A) A copy of each agreement entered into pursuant to paragraph (1) shall—

(i)   be transmitted to the Committee on Governmental Affairs of the Senate and the Committee on Government Operations of the House of Representatives; and

(ii)   be available upon request to the public.

(B)   No such agreement shall be effective until 30 days after the date on which such a copy is transmitted pursuant to subparagraph (A) (i).

(C)   Such an agreement shall remain in effect only for such period, not to exceed 18 months, as the Data Integrity Board of the agency determines is appropriate in light of the purposes, and length of time necessary for the conduct, of the matching program.

(D)   Within 3 months prior to the expiration of such an agreement pursuant to subparagraph (C), the Data Integrity Board of the agency may, without additional review, renew the matching agreement for a current, ongoing matching program for not more than one additional year if—

(i)   such program will be conducted without any change; and

(ii)   each party to the agreement certifies to the Board in writing that the program has been conducted in compliance with the agreement.

(p)   Verification and Opportunity to Contest Findings.

(1)   In order to protect any individual whose records are used in a matching program, no recipient agency, non-Federal agency, or source agency may suspend, terminate, reduce, or make a final denial of any financial assistance or payment under a Federal benefit program to such individual, or take other adverse action against such individual, as a result of information produced by such matching program, until—

(A)(i) the agency has independently verified the information; or

(ii)   the Data Integrity Board of the agency, or in the case of a non-Federal agency the Data Integrity Board of the source agency, determines in accordance with guidance issued by the Director of the Office of Management and Budget that—

(I)   the information is limited to identification and amount of benefits paid by the source agency under a Federal benefit program; and

(II)   there is a high degree of confidence that the information provided to the recipient agency is accurate;

(B)   the individual receives a notice from the agency containing a statement of its findings and informing the individual of the opportunity to contest such findings; and

(C)(i) the expiration of any time period established for the program by statute or regulation for the individual to respond to that notice; or

(ii)   in the case of a program for which no such period is established, the end of the 30-day period beginning on the date on which notice under subparagraph (B) is mailed or otherwise provided to the individual.

(2)   Independent verification referred to in paragraph (1) requires investigation and confirmation of specific information relating to an individual that is used as a basis for an adverse action against the individual, including where applicable investigation and confirmation of—

(A)   the amount of any asset or income involved;

(B)   whether such individual actually has or had access to such asset or income for such individual's own use; and

(C)   the period or periods when the individual actually had such asset or income.

(3)   Notwithstanding paragraph (1), an agency may take any appropriate action otherwise prohibited by such paragraph if the agency determines that the public health or public safety may be adversely affected or significantly threatened during any notice period required by such paragraph.

(q)   Sanctions.

(1)   Notwithstanding any other provision of law, no source agency may disclose any record that is contained in a system of records to a recipient agency or non-Federal agency for a matching program if such source agency has reason to believe that the requirements of subsection (p), or any matching agreement entered into pursuant to subsection (o), or both, are not being met by such recipient agency.

(2)   No source agency may renew a matching agreement unless—

(A)   the recipient agency or non-Federal agency has certified that it has complied with the provisions of that agreement; and

(B)   the source agency has no reason to believe that the certification is inaccurate.

(r)   Report on New Systems and Matching Programs. Each agency that proposes to establish or make a significant change in a system of records or a matching program shall provide adequate advance notice of any such proposal (in duplicate) to the Committee on Government Operations of the House of Representatives, the Committee on Governmental Affairs of the Senate, and the Office of Management and Budget in order to permit an evaluation of the probable or potential effect of such proposal on the privacy or other rights of individuals.

(s)   Biennial Report. The President shall biennially submit to the Speaker of the House of Representatives and the President pro tempore of the Senate a report

(1)   describing the actions of the Director of the Office of Management and Budget pursuant to section 6 of the Privacy Act of 1974 during the preceding 2 years;

(2)   describing the exercise of individual rights of access and amendment under this section during such years;

(3)   identifying changes in or additions to systems of records;

(4)   containing such other information concerning administration of this section as may be necessary or useful to the Congress in reviewing the effectiveness of this section in carrying out the purposes of the Privacy Act of 1974.

(t)   Effect of Other Laws.

(1)   No agency shall rely on any exemption contained in section 552 of this title to withhold from an individual any record which is otherwise accessible to such individual under the provisions of this section.

(2)   No agency shall rely on any exemption in this section to withhold from an individual any record which is otherwise accessible to such individual under the provisions of section 552 of this title.

(u)   Data Integrity Boards.

(1)   Every agency conducting or participating in a matching program shall establish a Data Integrity Board to oversee and coordinate among the various components of such agency the agency's implementation of this section.

(2)   Each Data Integrity Board shall consist of senior officials designated by the head of the agency, and shall include any senior official designated by the head of the agency as responsible for implementation of this section, and the inspector general of the agency, if any. The inspector

general shall not serve as chairman of the Data Integrity Board.

(3)   Each Data integrity Board—

(A)   shall review, approve, and maintain all written agreements for receipt or disclosure of agency records for matching programs to ensure compliance with subsection (o), and all relevant statutes, regulations, and guidelines;

(B)   shall review all matching programs in which the agency has participated during the year, either as a source agency or recipient agency, determine compliance with applicable laws, regulations, guidelines, and agency agreements, and assess the costs and benefits of such programs;

(C)   shall review all recurring matching programs in which the agency has participated during the year, either as a source agency or recipient agency, for continued justification for such disclosures;

(D)   shall compile an annual report, which shall be submitted to the head of the agency and the Office of Management and Budget and made available to the public on request, describing the matching activities of the agency, including—

(i)   matching programs in which the agency has participated as a source agency or recipient agency;

(ii)   matching agreements proposed under subsection (o) that were disapproved by the Board;

(iii)   any changes in membership or structure of the Board in the preceding year;

(iv)   the reasons for any waiver of the requirement in paragraph (4) of this section for completion and submission of a cost-benefit analysis prior to the approval of a matching program;

(v)   any violations of matching agreements that have been alleged or identified and any corrective action taken; and

(vi)   any other information required by the Director of the Office of Management and Budget to be included in such report;

(E)   shall serve as a clearinghouse for receiving and providing information on the accuracy, completeness, and reliability of records used in matching programs;

(F)   shall provide interpretation and guidance to agency components and personnel on the requirements of this section for matching programs;

(G)   shall review agency recordkeeping and disposal policies and practices for matching programs to assure compliance with this section; and

(H)   may review and report on any agency matching activities that are not matching programs.

(4)(A) Except as provided in subparagraphs (B) and (C), a Data Integrity Board shall not approve any written agreement for a matching program unless the agency has completed and submitted to such Board a cost-benefit analysis of the proposed program and such analysis demonstrates that the program is likely to be cost effective.

(B)   The Board may waive the requirements of subparagraph (A) of this paragraph if it determines in writing, in accordance with guidelines prescribed by the Director of the Office of Management and Budget, that a cost-benefit analysis is not required.

(C)   A cost-benefit analysis shall not be required under subparagraph (A) prior to the initial approval of a written agreement for a matching program that is specifically required by statute. Any subsequent written agreement for such a program shall not be approved by the Data Integrity Board unless the agency has submitted a cost-benefit analysis of the program as conducted under the preceding approval of such agreement.

(5)(A) If a matching agreement is disapproved by a Data Integrity Board, any party to such agreement may appeal the disapproval to the Director of the Office of Management and Budget. Timely notice of the filing of such an appeal shall be provided by the Director of the Office of Management and Budget to the Committee on Governmental Affairs of the Senate and the Committee on Government Operations of the House of Representatives.

(B)   The Director of the Office of Management and Budget may approve a matching agreement notwithstanding the disapproval of a Data Integrity Board if the Director determines that—

(i)   the matching program will be consistent with all applicable legal, regulatory, and policy requirements;

(ii)   there is adequate evidence that the matching agreement will be cost-effective; and

(iii)   the matching program is in the public interest.

(C)   The decision of the Director to approve a matching agreement shall not take effect until 30 days after it is reported to committees described in subparagraph (A).

(D)   If the Data Integrity Board and the Director of the Office of Management and Budget disapprove a matching program proposed by the inspector general of an agency, the inspector general may report the disapproval to the head of the agency and to the Congress.

(6)   In the reports required by paragraph (3)(D), agency matching activities that are not matching programs may be reported on an aggregate basis, if and to the extent necessary to protect ongoing law enforcement or counterintelligence investigations.

(v)   Office of Management and Budget Responsibilities. The Director of the Office of Management and Budget shall

(1)   develop and, after notice and opportunity for public comment, prescribe guidelines and regulations for the use of agencies in implementing the provisions of this section; and

(2)   provide continuing assistance to and oversight of the implementation of this section by agencies.

SEC. 552B. OPEN MEETINGS

(a)   For purposes of this section

(1)   the term "agency" means any agency, as defined in section 552 (e) of this title, headed by a collegial body composed of two or more individual members, a majority of whom are appointed to such position by the President with the advice and consent of the Senate, and any subdivision thereof authorized to act on behalf of the agency;

(2)   the term "meeting" means the deliberations of at least the number of individual agency members required to take action on behalf of the agency where such deliberations determine or result in the joint conduct or disposition of official agency business, but does not include deliberations required or permitted by subsection (d) or (e); and

(3)   the term "member" means an individual who belongs to a collegial body heading an agency.

(b)   Members shall not jointly conduct or dispose of agency business other than in accordance with this section. Except as provided in subsection (c), every portion of every meeting of an agency shall be open to public observation.

(c)   Except in a case where the agency finds that the public interest requires otherwise, the second sentence of

subsection (b) shall not apply to any portion of an agency meeting, and the requirements of subsections (d) and (e) shall not apply to any information pertaining to such meeting otherwise required by this section to be disclosed to the public, where the agency properly determines that such portion or portions of its meeting or the disclosure of such information is likely to—

(1)   disclose matters that are (A) specifically authorized under criteria established by an Executive order to be kept secret in the interests of national defense or foreign policy and (B) in fact properly classified pursuant to such Executive order;

(2)   relate solely to the internal personnel rules and practices of an agency;

(3)   disclose matters specifically exempted from disclosure by statute (other than section 552 of this title), provided that such statute (A) requires that the matters be withheld from the public in such a manner as to leave no discretion on the issue, or (B) establishes particular criteria for withholding or refers to particular types of matters to be withheld;

(4)   disclose trade secrets and commercial or financial information obtained from a person and privileged or confidential;

(5)   involve accusing any person of a crime, or formally censuring any person;

(6)   disclose information of a personal nature where disclosure would constitute a clearly unwarranted invasion of personal privacy;

(7)   disclose investigatory records compiled for law enforcement purposes, or information, which, if written, would be contained in such records, but only to the extent that the production of such records or information would (A) interfere with enforcement proceedings, (B) deprive a person of a right to a fair trial or an impartial adjudication, (C) constitute an unwarranted invasion of personal privacy, (D) disclose the identity of a confidential source and, in the case of a record compiled by a criminal law enforcement authority in the course of a criminal investigation, or by an agency conducting a lawful national security intelligence investigation, confidential information furnished only by the confidential source, (E) disclose investigative techniques and procedures, or (F) endanger the life or physical safety of

law enforcement personnel;

(8)   disclose information contained in or related to examination, operating, or condition reports prepared by, on behalf of, or for the use of an agency responsible for the regulation or supervision of financial institutions;

(9)   disclose information the premature disclosure of which would—

(A)   in the case of an agency that regulates currencies, securities, commodities, or financial institutions, be likely to (i) lead to significant financial speculation in currencies, securities, or commodities, or (ii) significantly endanger the stability of any financial institution; or

(B)   in the case of any agency, be likely to significantly frustrate implementation of a proposed agency action, except that subparagraph (B) shall not apply in any instance where the agency has already disclosed to the public the content or nature of its proposed action, or where the agency is required by law to make such disclosure on its own initiative prior to taking final agency action on such proposal; or

(10)   specifically concern the agency's issuance of a subpoena, or the agency's participation in a civil action or proceeding, an action in a foreign court or international tribunal, or an arbitration, or the initiation, conduct, or disposition by the agency of a particular case of formal agency adjudication pursuant to the procedures in section 554 of this title or otherwise involving a determination on the record after opportunity for a hearing.

(d)(1) Action under subsection (c) shall be taken only when a majority of the entire membership of the agency (as defined in subsection (a)(1)) votes to take such action. A separate vote of the agency members shall be taken with respect to each agency meeting a portion or portions of which are proposed to be closed to the public pursuant to subsection (c), or with respect to any information which is proposed to be withheld under subsection (c). A single vote may be taken with respect to a series of meetings, a portion or portions of which are proposed to be closed to the public, or with respect to any information concerning such series of meetings, so long as each meeting in such series involves the same particular matters and is scheduled to be held no more than thirty days after the initial meeting in such series. The vote of each agency member participating in such vote shall be recorded and no proxies shall be allowed.

(2)   Whenever any person whose interests may be directly affected by a portion of a meeting requests that the agency close such portion to the public for any of the reasons referred to in paragraph (5), (6), or (7) of subsection (c), the agency, upon request of any one of its members, shall vote by recorded vote whether to close such meeting.

(3)   Within one day of any vote taken pursuant to paragraph (1) or (2), the agency shall make publicly available a written copy of such vote reflecting the vote of each member on the question. If a portion of a meeting is to be closed to the public, the agency shall, within one day of the vote taken pursuant to paragraph (1) or (2) of this subsection, make publicly available a full written explanation of its action closing the portion together with a list of all persons expected to attend the meeting and their affiliation.

(4)   Any agency, a majority of whose meetings may properly be closed to the public pursuant to paragraph (4), (8), (9) (A), or (10) of subsection (c), or any combination thereof, may provide by regulation for the closing of such meetings or portions thereof in the event that a majority of the members of the agency votes by recorded vote at the beginning of such meeting, or portion thereof, to close the exempt portion or portions of the meeting, and a copy of such vote, reflecting the vote of each member on the question, is made available to the public. The provisions of paragraphs (1), (2), and (3) of this subsection and subsection (e) shall not apply to any portion of a meeting to which such regulations apply: Provided, That the agency shall, except to the extent that such information is exempt from disclosure under the provisions of subsection (c), provide the public with public announcement of the time, place, and subject matter of the meeting and of each portion thereof at the earliest practicable time.

(e) (1) In the case of each meeting, the agency shall make public announcement, at least one week before the meeting, of the time, place, and subject matter of the meeting, whether it is to be open or closed to the public, and the name and phone number of the official designated by the agency to respond to requests for information about the meeting. Such announcement shall be made unless a majority of the members of the agency determines by a recorded vote that agency business requires that such meeting be called at an earlier date, in which case the agency shall make public announcement of the time, place, and subject matter of such meeting, and whether open or closed to the public, at the earliest practicable time.

(2)   The time or place of a meeting may be changed following the public announcement required by paragraph (1) only if the agency publicly announces such change at the earliest practicable time. The subject matter of a meeting, or the determination of the agency to open or close a meeting, or portion of a meeting, to the public, may be changed following the public announcement required by this subsection only if (A) a majority of the entire membership of the agency determines by a recorded vote that agency business so requires and that no earlier announcement of the change was possible, and (B) the agency publicly announces such change and the vote of each member upon such change at the earliest practicable time.

(3)   Immediately following each public announcement required by this subsection, notice of the time, place, and subject matter of a meeting, whether the meeting is open or closed, any change in one of the preceding, and the name and phone number of the official designated by the agency to respond to requests for information about the meeting, shall also be submitted for publication in the Federal Register.

(f)(1) For every meeting closed pursuant to paragraphs (1) through (10) of subsection (c), the General Counsel or chief legal officer of the agency shall publicly certify that, in his or her opinion, the meeting may be closed to the public and shall state each relevant exemptive provision. A copy of such certification, together with a statement from the presiding officer of the meeting setting forth the time and place of the meeting, and the persons present, shall be retained by the agency. The agency shall maintain a complete transcript or electronic recording adequate to record fully the proceedings of each meeting, or portion of a meeting, closed to the public, except that in the case of a meeting, or portion of a meeting, closed to the public pursuant to paragraph (8), (9) (A), or (10) of subsection (c), the agency shall maintain either such a transcript or recording, or a set of minutes. Such minutes shall fully and clearly describe all matters discussed and shall provide a full and accurate summary of any actions taken, and the reasons therefor, including a description of each of the views expressed on any item and the

record of any rollcall vote (reflecting the vote of each member on the question). All documents considered in connection with any action shall be identified in such minutes.

(2)   The agency shall make promptly available to the public, in a place easily accessible to the public, the transcript, electronic recording, or minutes (as required by paragraph [1]) of the discussion of any item on the agenda, or of any item of the testimony of any witness received at the meeting, except for such item or items of such discussion or testimony as the agency determines to contain information which may be withheld under subsection (c). Copies of such transcript, or minutes, or a transcription of such recording disclosing the identity of each speaker, shall be furnished to any person at the actual cost of duplication or transcription. The agency shall maintain a complete verbatim copy of the transcript, a complete copy of the minutes, or a complete electronic recording of each meeting, or portion of a meeting, closed to the public, for a period of at least two years after such meeting, or until one year after the conclusion of any agency proceeding with respect to which the meeting or portion was held, whichever occurs later.

(g)   Each agency subject to the requirements of this section shall, within 180 days after the date of enactment of this section, following consultation with the Office of the Chairman of the Administrative Conference of the United States and published notice in the Federal Register of at least thirty days and opportunity for written comment by any person, promulgate regulations to implement the requirements of subsections (b) through (f) of this section. Any person may bring a proceeding in the United States District Court for the District of Columbia to require an agency to promulgate such regulations if such agency has not promulgated such regulations within the time period specified herein. Subject to any limitations of time provided by law any person may bring a proceeding in the United States Court of Appeals for the District of Columbia to set aside agency regulations issued pursuant to this subsection that are not in accord with the requirements of subsections (b) through (f) of this section and to require the promulgation of regulations that are in accord with such subsections.

(h)(1) The district courts of the United States shall have jurisdiction to enforce the requirements of subsections (b) through (f) of this section by declaratory judgment, injunctive relief, or other relief as may be appropriate. Such actions may be brought by any person against an agency prior to, or within sixty days after, the meeting out of which the violation of this section arises, except that if public announcement of such meeting is not initially provided by the agency in accordance with the requirements of this section, such action may be instituted pursuant to this section at any time prior to sixty days after any public announcement of such meeting. Such actions may be brought in the district court of the United States for the district in which the agency meeting is held or in which the agency in question has its headquarters, or in the District Court for the District of Columbia. In such actions a defendant shall serve his answer within thirty days after the service of the complaint. The burden is on the defendant to sustain his action. In deciding such cases the court may examine in camera any portion of the transcript, electronic recording, or minutes of a meeting closed to the public, and may take such additional evidence as it deems necessary. The court, having due regard for orderly administration and the public interest, as well as the interests of the parties, may grant such equitable relief as it deems appropriate, including granting an injunction against future violations of this section or ordering the agency to make available to the public such portion of the transcript, recording, or minutes of a meeting as is not authorized to be withheld under subsection (c) of this section.

(2)   Any Federal court otherwise authorized by law to review agency action may, at the application of any person properly participating in the proceeding pursuant to other applicable law, inquire into violations by the agency of the requirements of this section and afford such relief as it deems appropriate. Nothing in this section authorizes any Federal court having jurisdiction solely on the basis of paragraph (1) to set aside, enjoin, or invalidate any agency action (other than an action to close a meeting or to withhold information under this section) taken or discussed at any agency meeting out of which the violation of this section arose.

(i)   The court may assess against any party reasonable attorney fees and other litigation costs reasonably incurred by any other party who substantially prevails in any action brought in accordance with the provisions of subsection (g) or (h) of this section, except that costs may be assessed against the plaintiff only where the court finds that the suit was initiated by the plaintiff primarily for frivolous or dilatory purposes. In the case of assessment of costs against an agency, the costs may be assessed by the court against the United States.

(j)   Each agency subject to the requirements of this section shall annually report to the Congress regarding the following:

(1)   The changes in the policies and procedures of the agency under this section that have occurred during the preceding 1-year period.

(2)   A tabulation of the number of meetings held, the exemptions applied to close meetings, and the days of public notice provided to close meetings.

(3)   A brief description of litigation or formal complaints concerning the implementation of this section by the agency.

(4)   A brief explanation of any changes in law that have affected the responsibilities of the agency under this section.

(k)   Nothing herein expands or limits the present rights of any person under section 552 of this title, except that the exemptions set forth in subsection (c) of this section shall govern in the case of any request made pursuant to section 552 to copy or inspect the transcripts, recordings, or minutes described in subsection (f) of this section. The requirements of chapter 33 of title 44, United States Code, shall not apply to the transcripts, recordings, and minutes described in subsection (f) of this section.

(l)   This section does not constitute authority to withhold any information from Congress, and does not authorize the closing of any agency meeting or portion thereof required by any other provision of law to be open.

(m)   Nothing in this section authorizes any agency to withhold from any individual any record, including transcripts, recordings, or minutes required by this section, which is otherwise accessible to such individual under section 552a of this title.

SEC. 553. RULEMAKING

(a)   This section applies, according to the provisions thereof, except to the extent that there is involved

(1)   a military or foreign affairs function of the United States; or

(2)   a matter relating to agency management or per-

sonnel or to public property, loans, grants, benefits, or contracts.

(b)   General notice of proposed rulemaking shall be published in the Federal Register, unless persons subject thereto are named and either personally served or otherwise have actual notice thereof in accordance with law. The notice shall include—

(1)   a statement of the time, place, and nature of public rulemaking proceedings;

(2)   reference to the legal authority under which the rule is proposed; and

(3)   either the terms or substance of the proposed rule or a description of the subjects and issues involved.

Except when notice or hearing is required by statute, this subsection does not apply—

(A)   to interpretative rules, general statements of policy, or rules of agency organization, procedure, or practice; or

(B)   when the agency for good cause finds (and incorporates the finding and a brief statement of reasons therefor in the rules issued) that notice and public procedure thereon are impracticable, unnecessary, or contrary to the public interest.

(c)   After notice required by this section, the agency shall give interested persons an opportunity to participate in the rulemaking through submission of written data, views, or arguments with or without opportunity for oral presentation. After consideration of the relevant matter presented, the agency shall incorporate in the rules adopted a concise general statement of their basis and purpose. When rules are required by statute to be made on the record after opportunity for an agency hearing, sections 556 and 557 of this title apply instead of this subsection.

(d)   The required publication or service of a substantive rule shall be made not less than 30 days before its effective date, except—

(1)   a substantive rule that grants or recognizes an exemption or relieves a restriction;

(2)   interpretative rules and statements of policy; or

(3)   as otherwise provided by the agency for good cause found and published with the rule.

(e)   Each agency shall give an interested person the right to petition for the issuance, amendment, or repeal of a rule.

SEC. 554. ADJUDICATIONS

(a)   This section applies, according to the provisions thereof, in every case of adjudication required by statute to be determined on the record after opportunity for an agency hearing, except to the extent that there is involved

(1)   a matter subject to a subsequent trial of the law and the facts de novo in a court;

(2)   the selection or tenure of an employee, except administrative law judge appointed under section 3105 of this title;

(3)   proceedings in which decisions rest solely on inspections, tests, or elections;

(4)   the conduct of military or foreign affairs functions;

(5)   cases in which an agency is acting as an agent for a court; or

(6)   the certification of worker representatives.

(b)   Persons entitled to notice of an agency hearing shall be timely informed of—

(1)   the time, place, and nature of the hearing;

(2)   the legal authority and jurisdiction under which the hearing is to be held; and

(3)   the matters of fact and law asserted.

When private persons are the moving parties, other parties to the proceeding shall give prompt notice of issues controverted in fact or law; and in other instances agencies may by rule require responsive pleading. In fixing the time and place for hearings, due regard shall be had for the convenience and necessity of the parties or their representatives.

(c)   The agency shall give all interested parties opportunity for

(1)   the submission and consideration of facts, arguments, offers of settlement, or proposals of adjustment when time, the nature of the proceeding, and the public interest permit; and

(2)   to the extent that the parties are unable so to determine a controversy by consent, hearing and decision on notice and in accordance with sections 556 and 557 of this title.

(d)   The employee who presides at the reception of evidence pursuant to section 556 of this title shall make the recommended decision or initial decision required by section 557 of this title, unless he becomes unavailable to the agency. Except to the extent required for the disposition of ex parte matters as authorized by law, such an employee may not

(1)   consult a person or party on a fact in issue, unless on notice and opportunity for all parties to participate; or

(2)   be responsible to or subject to the supervision or direction of an employee or agent engaged in the performance of investigative or prosecuting functions for an agency.

An employee or agent engaged in the performance of investigative or prosecuting functions for an agency in a case may not, in that or a factually related case, participate or advise in the decision, recommended decision, or agency review pursuant to section 557 of this title, except as witness or counsel in public proceedings. This subsection does not apply

(A)   in determining applications for initial licenses;

(B)   to proceedings involving the validity or application of rates, facilities, or practices of public utilities or carriers; or

(C)   to the agency or a member or members of the body comprising the agency.

(e)   The agency, with like effect as in the case of other orders, and in its sound discretion, may issue a declaratory order to terminate a controversy or remove uncertainty.

SEC. 555. ANCILLARY MATTERS

(a)   This section applies, according to the provisions thereof, except as otherwise provided by this subchapter.

(b)   A person compelled to appear in person before an agency or representative thereof is entitled to be accompanied, represented, and advised by counsel or, if permitted by the agency, by other qualified representative. A party is entitled to appear in person or by or with counsel or other duly qualified representative in an agency proceeding. So far as the orderly conduct of public business permits, an interested person may appear before an agency or its responsible employees for the presentation, adjustment, or determination of an issue, request, or controversy in a proceeding, whether interlocutory, summary, or otherwise, or in connection with an agency function. With due regard for the con-

venience and necessity of the parties or their representatives and within a reasonable time, each agency shall proceed to conclude a matter presented to it. This subsection does not grant or deny a person who is not a lawyer the right to appear for or represent others before an agency or in an agency proceeding.

(c)   Process, requirement of a report, inspection, or other investigative act or demand may not be issued, made, or enforced except as authorized by law. A person compelled to submit data or evidence is entitled to retain or, on payment of lawfully prescribed costs, procure a copy or transcript thereof, except that in a nonpublic investigatory proceeding the witness may for good cause be limited to inspection of the official transcript of his testimony.

(d)   Agency subpoenas authorized by law shall be issued to a party on request and, when required by rules of procedure, on a statement or showing of general relevance and reasonable scope of the evidence sought. On contest, the court shall sustain the subpoena or similar process or demand to the extent that it is found to be in accordance with law. In a proceeding for enforcement, the court shall issue an order requiring the appearance of the witness or the production of the evidence or data within a reasonable time under penalty of punishment for contempt in case of contumacious failure to comply.

(e)   Prompt notice shall be given of the denial in whole or in part of a written application, petition, or other request of an interested person made in connection with any agency proceeding. Except in affirming a prior denial or when the denial is self-explanatory, the notice shall be accompanied by a brief statement of the grounds for denial.

SEC. 556. HEARINGS; PRESIDING EMPLOYEES; POWERS AND DUTIES; BURDEN OF PROOF; EVIDENCE; RECORD AS BASIS OF DECISION

(a)   This section applies, according to the provisions thereof, to hearings required by section 553 or 554 of this title to be conducted in accordance with this section.

(b)   There shall preside at the taking of evidence—

(1)   the agency;

(2)   one or more members of the body that comprises the agency; or

(3)   one or more administrative law judges appointed under section 3105 of this title.

This subchapter does not supersede the conduct of specified classes of proceedings, in whole or in part, by or before boards or other employees specially provided for by or designated under statute. The functions of presiding employees and of employees participating in decisions in accordance with section 557 of this title shall be conducted in an impartial manner. A presiding or participating employee may at any time disqualify himself. On the filing in good faith of a timely and sufficient affidavit of personal bias or other disqualification of a presiding or participating employee, the agency shall determine the matter as a part of the record and decision in the case.

(c)   Subject to published rules of the agency and within its powers, employees presiding at hearings may—

(1)   administer oaths and affirmations;

(2)   issue subpoenas authorized by law;

(3)   rule on offers of proof and receive relevant evidence;

(4)   take depositions or have depositions taken when the ends of justice would be served;

(5)   regulate the course of the hearing;

(6)   hold conferences for the settlement or simplification of the issues by consent of the parties or by the use of alternative means of dispute resolution as provided in subchapter IV of this chapter;

(7)   inform the parties as to the availability of one or more alternative means of dispute resolution, and encourage use of such methods;

(8)   require the attendance at any conference held pursuant to paragraph (6) of at least one representative of each party who has authority to negotiate concerning resolution of issues in controversy;

(9)   dispose of procedural requests or similar matters;

(10)   make or recommend decisions in accordance with section 557 of this title; and

(11)   take other action authorized by agency rule consistent with this subchapter.

(d)   Except as otherwise provided by statute, the proponent of a rule or order has the burden of proof. Any oral or documentary evidence may be received, but the agency as a matter of policy shall provide for the exclusion of irrelevant, immaterial, or unduly repetitious evidence. A sanction may not be imposed or rule or order issued except on consideration of the whole record or those parts thereof cited by a party and supported by and in accordance with the reliable, probative, and substantial evidence. The agency may, to the extent consistent with the interests of justice and the policy of the underlying statutes administered by the agency, consider a violation of section 557 (d) of this title sufficient grounds for a decision adverse to a party who has knowingly committed such violation or knowingly caused such violation to occur. A party is entitled to present his case or defense by oral or documentary evidence, to submit rebuttal evidence, and to conduct such cross-examination as may be required for a full and true disclosure of the facts. In rulemaking or determining claims for money or benefits or applications for initial licenses an agency may, when a party will not be prejudiced thereby, adopt procedures for the submission of all or part of the evidence in written form.

(e)   The transcript of testimony and exhibits, together with all papers and requests filed in the proceeding, constitutes the exclusive record for decision in accordance with section 557 of this title and, on payment of lawfully prescribed costs, shall be made available to the parties. When an agency decision rests on official notice of a material fact not appearing in the evidence in the record, a party is entitled, on timely request, to an opportunity to show the contrary.

SEC. 557. INITIAL DECISIONS; CONCLUSIVENESS; REVIEW BY AGENCY; SUBMISSIONS BY PARTIES; CONTENTS OF DECISIONS; RECORD

(a)   This section applies, according to the provisions thereof, when a hearing is required to be conducted in accordance with section 556 of this title.

(b)   When the agency did not preside at the reception of the evidence, the presiding employee or, in cases not subject to section 554 (d) of this title, an employee qualified to preside at hearings pursuant to section 556 of this title, shall initially decide the case unless the agency requires, either in specific cases or by general rule, the entire record to be certified to it for decision. When the presiding employee makes an initial decision, that decision then becomes the decision of the agency without further proceedings unless there is an appeal to, or review on motion of, the agency within time provided by rule. On appeal from or review of the initial decision, the agency has all the powers, which it would have in making the initial decision except as it may limit the issues on notice or by rule. When the agency makes the decision without having presided at the reception of the evidence, the presiding employee or an employee qualified to preside at hearings pursuant to section 556 of this title shall first recommend a decision, except that in rulemaking or determining applications for initial licenses—

(1)   instead thereof the agency may issue a tentative decision or one of its responsible employees may recommend a decision; or

(2)   this procedure may be omitted in a case in which the agency finds on the record that due and timely execution of its functions imperatively and unavoidably so requires.

(c)   Before a recommended, initial, or tentative decision, or a decision on agency review of the decision of subordinate employees, the parties are entitled to a reasonable opportunity to submit for the consideration of the employees participating in the decisions—

(1)   proposed findings and conclusions; or

(2)   exceptions to the decisions or recommended decisions of subordinate employees or to tentative agency decisions; and

(3)   supporting reasons for the exceptions or proposed findings or conclusions.

The record shall show the ruling on each finding, conclusion, or exception presented. All decisions, including initial, recommended, and tentative decisions, are a part of the record and shall include a statement of—

(A)   findings and conclusions, and the reasons or basis therefor, on all the material issues of fact, law, or discretion presented on the record; and

(B)   the appropriate rule, order, sanction, relief, or denial thereof.

(d)(1) In any agency proceeding which is subject to subsection (a) of this section, except to the extent required for the disposition of ex parte matters as authorized by law—

(A)   no interested person outside the agency shall make or knowingly cause to be made to any member of the body comprising the agency, administrative law judge, or other employee who is or may reasonably be expected to be involved in the decisional process of the proceeding, an ex parte communication relevant to the merits of the proceeding;

(B)   no member of the body comprising the agency, administrative law judge, or other employee who is or may reasonably be expected to be involved in the decisional process of the proceeding, shall make or knowingly cause to be made to any interested person outside the agency an ex parte communication relevant to the merits of the proceeding;

(C)   a member of the body comprising the agency, administrative law judge, or other employee who is or may reasonably be expected to be involved in the decisional process of such proceeding who receives, or who makes or knowingly causes to be made, a communication prohibited by this subsection shall place on the public record of the proceeding:

(i)   all such written communications;

(ii)   memoranda stating the substance of all such oral communications; and

(iii)   all written responses, and memoranda stating the substance of all oral responses, to the materials described in clauses (i) and (ii) of this subparagraph;

(D)   upon receipt of a communication knowingly made or knowingly caused to be made by a party in violation of this subsection, the agency, administrative law judge, or other employee presiding at the hearing may, to the extent consistent with the interests of justice and the policy of the underlying statutes, require the party to show cause why his claim or interest in the proceeding should not be dismissed, denied, disregarded, or otherwise adversely affected on account of such violation; and

(E)   the prohibitions of this subsection shall apply beginning at such time as the agency may designate, but in no case shall they begin to apply later than the time at which a proceeding is noticed for hearing unless the person responsible for the communication has knowledge that it will be noticed, in which case the prohibitions shall apply beginning at the time of his acquisition of such knowledge.

(2)   This subsection does not constitute authority to withhold information from Congress.

SEC. 558. IMPOSITION OF SANCTIONS; DETERMINATION OF APPLICATIONS FOR LICENSES; SUSPENSION, REVOCATION, AND EXPIRATION OF LICENSES

(a)   This section applies, according to the provisions thereof, to the exercise of a power or authority.

(b)   A sanction may not be imposed or a substantive rule or order issued except within jurisdiction delegated to the agency and as authorized by law.

(c)   When application is made for a license required by law, the agency, with due regard for the rights and privileges of all the interested parties or adversely affected persons and within a reasonable time, shall set and complete proceedings required to be conducted in accordance with sections 556 and 557 of this title or other proceedings required by law and shall make its decision. Except in cases of willfulness or those in which public health, interest, or safety requires otherwise, the withdrawal, suspension, revocation, or annulment of a license is lawful only if, before the institution of agency proceedings therefor, the licensee has been given

(1)   notice by the agency in writing of the facts or conduct which may warrant the action; and

(2)   opportunity to demonstrate or achieve compliance with all lawful requirements.

When the licensee has made timely and sufficient application for a renewal or a new license in accordance with agency rules, a license with reference to an activity of a continuing nature does not expire until the application has been finally determined by the agency.

SEC. 559. EFFECT ON OTHER LAWS; EFFECT OF SUBSEQUENT STATUTE

This subchapter, chapter 7, and sections 1305, 3105, 3344, 4301 (2) (E), 5372, and 7521 of this title, and the provisions of section 5335 (a)(B) of this title that relate to administrative law judges, do not limit or repeal additional requirements imposed by statute or otherwise recognized by law. Except as otherwise required by law, requirements or privileges relating to evidence or procedure apply equally to agencies and persons. Each agency is granted the authority necessary to comply with the requirements of this subchapter through the issuance of rules or otherwise. Subsequent statute may not be held to supersede or modify this sub-

chapter, chapter 7, sections 1305, 3105, 3344, 4301 (2) (E), 5372, or 7521 of this title, or the provisions of section 5335 (a) (B) of this title that relate to administrative law judges, except to the extent that it does so expressly.

5 USC Subchapter III—Negotiated Rulemaking Procedure

SEC. 561. PURPOSE

The purpose of this subchapter is to establish a framework for the conduct of negotiated rulemaking, consistent with section 553 of this title, to encourage agencies to use the process when it enhances the informal rulemaking process. Nothing in this subchapter should be construed as an attempt to limit innovation and experimentation with the negotiated rulemaking process or with other innovative rulemaking procedures otherwise authorized by law.

"(1)   Government regulation has increased substantially since the enactment of the Administrative Procedure Act (see Short Title note set out preceding section 551 of this title).

"(2)   Agencies currently use rulemaking procedures that may discourage the affected parties from meeting and communicating with each other, and may cause parties with different interests to assume conflicting and antagonistic positions and to engage in expensive and time-consuming litigation over agency rules.

"(3)   Adversarial rulemaking deprives the affected parties and the public of the benefits of face-to-face negotiations and cooperation in developing and reaching agreement on a rule. It also deprives them of the benefits of shared information, knowledge, expertise, and technical abilities possessed by the affected parties.

"(4)   Negotiated rulemaking, in which the parties who will be significantly affected by a rule participate in the development of the rule, can provide significant advantages over adversarial rulemaking.

"(5)   Negotiated rulemaking can increase the acceptability and improve the substance of rules, making it less likely that the affected parties will resist enforcement or challenge such rules in court. It may also shorten the amount of time needed to issue final rules.

"(6)   Agencies have the authority to establish negotiated rulemaking committees under the laws establishing such agencies and their activities and under the Federal Advisory Committee Act (5 U.S.C. App.). Several agencies have successfully used negotiated rulemaking. The process has not been widely used by other agencies, however, in part because such agencies are unfamiliar with the process or uncertain as to the authority for such rulemaking."

SEC. 562. DEFINITIONS

For the purposes of this subchapter, the term

(1)   "agency" has the same meaning as in section 551(1) of this title;

(2)   "consensus" means unanimous concurrence among the interests represented on a negotiated rulemaking committee established under this subchapter, unless such committee—

(A)   agrees to define such term to mean a general but not unanimous concurrence; or

(B)   agrees upon another specified definition;

(3)   "convener" means a person who impartially assists an agency in determining whether establishment of a negotiated rulemaking committee is feasible and appropriate in a particular rulemaking;

(4)   "facilitator" means a person who impartially aids in the discussions and negotiations among the members of a negotiated rulemaking committee to develop a proposed rule;

(5)   "interest" means, with respect to an issue or matter, multiple parties that have a similar point of view or which are likely to be affected in a similar manner;

(6)   "negotiated rulemaking" means rulemaking through the use of a negotiated rulemaking committee;

(7)   "negotiated rulemaking committee" or "committee" means an advisory committee established by an agency in accordance with this subchapter and the Federal Advisory Committee Act to consider and discuss issues for the purpose of reaching a consensus in the development of a proposed rule;

(8)   "party" has the same meaning as in section 551 (3) of this title;

(9)   "person" has the same meaning as in section 551 (2) of this title;

(10)   "rule" has the same meaning as in section 551 (4) of this title; and

(11)   "rulemaking" means "rulemaking" as that term is defined in section 551 (5) of this title.

SEC. 563. DETERMINATION OF NEED FOR NEGOTIATED RULEMAKING COMMITTEE

(a)   Determination of Need by the Agency.—An agency may establish a negotiated rulemaking committee to negotiate and develop a proposed rule, if the head of the agency determines that the use of the negotiated rulemaking procedure is in the public interest. In making such a determination, the head of the agency shall consider whether

(1)   there is a need for a rule;

(2)   there are a limited number of identifiable interests that will be significantly affected by the rule;

(3)   there is a reasonable likelihood that a committee can be convened with a balanced representation of persons who—

(A)   can adequately represent the interests identified under paragraph (2); and

(B)   are willing to negotiate in good faith to reach a consensus on the proposed rule;

(4)   there is a reasonable likelihood that a committee will reach a consensus on the proposed rule within a fixed period of time;

(5)   the negotiated rulemaking procedure will not unreasonably delay the notice of proposed rulemaking and the issuance of the final rule;

(6)   the agency has adequate resources and is willing to commit such resources, including technical assistance, to the committee; and

(7)   the agency, to the maximum extent possible consistent with the legal obligations of the agency, will use the consensus of the committee with respect to the proposed rule as the basis for the rule proposed by the agency for notice and comment.

(b)   Use of Conveners.

(1)   Purposes of conveners. —An agency may use the services of a convener to assist the agency in—

(A)   identifying persons who will be significantly affected by a proposed rule, including residents of rural areas; and

(B)   conducting discussions with such persons to identify the issues of concern to such persons, and to ascertain whether the establishment of a negotiated rulemaking committee is feasible and appropriate in the particular rulemaking.

(2)   Duties of conveners.—The convener shall report findings and may make recommendations to the agency. Upon request of the agency, the convener shall ascertain the names of persons who are willing and qualified to represent interests that will be significantly affected by the proposed rule, including residents of rural areas. The report and any recommendations of the convener shall be made available to the public upon request.

NEGOTIATED RULEMAKING COMMITTEES

Pub. L. 104-320, Sec. 11(e), Oct. 19, 1996, 110 Stat. 3874, provided that: "The Director of the Office of Management and Budget shall—

"(1)   within 180 days of the date of the enactment of this Act (Oct. 19, 1996), take appropriate action to expedite the establishment of negotiated rulemaking committees and committees established to resolve disputes under the Administrative Dispute Resolution Act (Pub. L. 101-552, see Short Title note set out under section 571 of this title), including, with respect to negotiated rulemaking committees, eliminating any redundant administrative requirements related to filing a committee charter under section 9 of the Federal Advisory Committee Act (5 U.S.C. App.) and providing public notice of such committee under section 564 of title 5, United States Code; and

"(2)   within one year of the date of the enactment of this Act, submit recommendations to Congress for any necessary legislative changes."

SEC. 564. PUBLICATION OF NOTICE; APPLICATIONS FOR MEMBERSHIP ON COMMITTEES

(a)   Publication of Notice. If, after considering the report of a convener or conducting its own assessment, an agency decides to establish a negotiated rulemaking committee, the agency shall publish in the Federal Register and, as appropriate, in trade or other specialized publications, a notice which shall include

(1)   an announcement that the agency intends to establish a negotiated rulemaking committee to negotiate and develop a proposed rule;

(2)   a description of the subject and scope of the rule to be developed, and the issues to be considered;

(3)   a list of the interests which are likely to be significantly affected by the rule;

(4)   a list of the persons proposed to represent such interests and the person or persons proposed to represent the agency;

(5)   a proposed agenda and schedule (at completing the work of the committee), including a target date for publication by the agency of a proposed rule for notice and comment;

(6)   a description of administrative support for the committee to be provided by the agency, including technical assistance;

(7)   a solicitation for comments on the proposal to establish the committee, and the proposed membership of the negotiated rulemaking committee; and

(8)   an explanation of how a person may apply or nominate another person for membership on the committee, as provided under subsection (b).

(b)   Applications for Membersrship Committee. Persons will be significantly affected by a proposed rule and who believe that their interests will not be adequately represented by any person specified in a notice under subsection (a) (4) may apply for, or nominate another person for, membership on the negotiated rulemaking committee to represent such interests with respect to the proposed rule. Each application or nomination shall include

(1)   the name of the applicant or nominee and a description of the interests such person shall represent;

(2)   evidence that the applicant or nominee is authorized to represent parties related to the interests the person proposes to represent;

(3)   a written commitment that the applicant or nominee shall actively participate in good faith in the development of the rule under consideration; and

(4)   the reasons that the persons specified in the notice under subsection (a)(4) do not adequately represent the interests of the person submitting the application or nomination.

(c) Period for Submission of Comments and Applications. The agency shall provide for a period of at least 30 calendar days for the submission of comments and applications under this section.

SEC. 565. ESTABLISHMENT OF COMMITTEE

(a) Establishment.

(1) Determination to establish committee.—If after considering comments and applications submitted under section 564, the agency determines that a negotiated rulemaking committee can adequately represent the interests that will be significantly affected by a proposed rule and that it is feasible and appropriate in the particular rulemaking, the agency may establish a negotiated rulemaking committee. In establishing and administering such a committee, the agency shall comply with the Federal Advisory Committee Act with respect to such committee, except as otherwise provided in this subchapter.

(2) Determination not to establish committee.—If after considering such comments and applications, the agency decides not to establish a negotiated rulemaking committee, the agency shall promptly publish notice of such decision and the reasons therefor in the Federal Register and, as appropriate, in trade or other specialized publications, a copy of which shall be sent to any person who applied for, or nominated another person for membership on the negotiating rulemaking committee to represent such interests with respect to the proposed rule.

(b) Membership. The agency shall limit membership on a negotiated rulemaking committee to 25 members, unless the agency head determines that a greater number of members is necessary for the functioning of the committee or to achieve balanced membership. Each committee shall include at least one person representing the agency.

(c) Administrative Support. The agency shall provide appropriate administrative support to the negotiated rulemaking committee, including technical assistance.

SEC. 566. CONDUCT OF COMMITTEE ACTIVIY

(a) Duties of Committee. Each negotiated rulemaking committee established under this subchapter shall consider the matter proposed by the agency for consideration and shall attempt to reach a consensus concerning a proposed rule with respect to such matter and any other matter the committee determines is relevant to the proposed rule.

(b) Representatives of Agency on Committee. The person or persons representing the agency on a negotiated rulemaking committee shall participate in the deliberations and activities of the committee with the same rights and responsibilities as other members of the committee, and shall be authorized to fully represent the agency in the discussions and negotiations of the committee.

(c) Selecting Facilitator. Notwithstanding section 10(e) of the Federal Advisory Committee Act, an agency may nominate either a person from the Federal Government or a person from outside the Federal Government to serve as a facilitator for the negotiations of the committee, subject to the approval of the committee by consensus. If the committee does not approve the nominee of the agency for facilitator, the agency shall submit a substitute nomination. If a committee does not approve any nominee of the agency for facilitator, the committee shall select by consensus a person to serve as facilitator. A person designated to represent the agency in substantive issues may not serve as facilitator or otherwise chair the committee.

(d) Duties of Facilitator. A facilitator approved or selected by a negotiated rulemaking committee shall

(1) chair the meetings of the committee in an impartial manner;

(2) impartially assist the members of the committee in conducting discussions and negotiations; and

(3) manage the keeping of minutes and records as required under section 10(b) and (c) of the Federal Advisory Committee Act, except that any personal notes and materials of the facilitator or of the members of a committee shall not be subject to section 552 of this title.

(e) Committee Procedures. A negotiated rulemaking committee established under this subchapter may adopt procedures for the operation of the committee. No provision of section 553 of this title shall apply to the procedures of a negotiated rulemaking committee.

(f) Report of Committee. If a committee reaches a consensus on a proposed rule, at the conclusion of negotiations the committee shall transmit to the agency that established the committee a report containing the proposed rule. If the committee does not reach a consensus on a proposed rule, the committee may transmit to the agency a report specifying any areas in which the committee reached a consensus. The committee may include in a report any other information, recommendations, or materials that the committee considers appropriate. Any committee member may include as an addendum to the report additional information, recommendations, or materials.

(g)   Records of Committee. In addition to the report required by subsection (f), a committee shall submit to the agency the records required under section 10(b) and (c) of the Federal Advisory Committee Act.

SEC. 567. TERMINATION OF COMMITTEE

A negotiated rulemaking committee shall terminate upon promulgation of the final rule under consideration, unless the committee's charter contains an earlier termination date or the agency, after consulting the committee, or the committee itself specifies an earlier termination date.

SEC. 568. SERVICES, FACILITIES, AND PAYMENT OF COMMITTEE MEMBER EXPENSES

(a)   Services of Conveners and Facilitators.

(1)   In general.—An agency may employ or enter into contracts for the services of an individual or organization to serve as a convener or facilitator for a negotiated rulemaking committee under this subchapter, or may use the services of a Government employee to act as a convener or a facilitator for such a committee.

(2)   Determination of conflicting interests.—An agency shall determine whether a person under consideration to serve as convener or facilitator of a committee under paragraph

(1)   has any financial or other interest that would preclude such person from serving in an impartial and independent manner.

(b)   Services and Facilities of Other Entities. For purposes of this subchapter, an agency may use the services and facilities of other Federal agencies and public and private agencies and instrumentalities with the consent of such agencies and instrumentalities, and with or without reimbursement to such agencies and instrumentalities, and may accept voluntary and uncompensated services without regard to the provisions of section 1342 of title 31. The Federal Mediation and Conciliation Service may provide services and facilities, with or without reimbursement, to assist agencies under this subchapter, including furnishing conveners, facilitators, and training in negotiated rulemaking.

(c)   Expenses of Committee Members. Members of a negotiated rulemaking committee shall be responsible for their own expenses of participation in such committee, except that an agency may, in accordance with section 7(d) of the Federal Advisory Committee Act, pay for a member's reasonable travel and per diem expenses, expenses to obtain technical assistance, and a reasonable rate of compensation, if

(1)   such member certifies a lack of adequate financial resources to participate in the committee; and

(2)   the agency determines that such member's participation in the committee is necessary to assure an adequate representation of the member's interest.

(d)   Status of Member as Federal Employee. A member's receipt of funds under this section or section 569 shall not conclusively determine for purposes of sections 202 through 209 of title 18 whether that member is an employee of the United States Government.

SEC. 569. ENCOURAGING NEGOTIATED RULEMAKING

(a)   The President shall designate an agency or designate or establish an interagency committee to facilitate and encourage agency use of negotiated rulemaking. An agency that is considering, planning, or conducting a negotiated rulemaking may consult with such agency or committee for information and assistance.

(b)   To carry out the purposes of this subchapter, an agency planning or conducting a negotiated rulemaking may accept, hold, administer, and utilize gifts, devises, and bequests of property, both real and personal if that agency's acceptance and use of such gifts, devises, or bequests do not create a conflict of interest. Gifts and bequests of money and proceeds from sales of other property received as gifts, devises, or bequests shall be deposited in the Treasury and shall be disbursed upon the order of the head of such agency. Property accepted pursuant to this section, and the proceeds thereof, shall be used as nearly as possible in accordance with the terms of the gifts, devises, or bequests.

SEC. 570. JUDICIAL REVIEW

Any agency action relating to establishing, assisting, or terminating a negotiated rulemaking committee under this subchapter shall not be subject to judicial review. Nothing in this section shall bar judicial review of a rule if such judicial review is otherwise provided by law. A rule which is the product of negotiated rulemaking and is subject to judicial review shall not be accorded any greater deference by a court than a rule, which is the product of other rulemaking procedures.

5 USC Subchapter IV—Alternative Means of Dispute Resolution in the Administrative Process

SEC. 571. DEFINITIONS

For the purposes of this subchapter, the term

(1)   "agency" has the same meaning as in section 551(1) of this title;

(2)   "administrative program" includes a Federal fuunction, which involves protection of the public interest and the determination of rights, privileges, and obligations of private persons through rulemaking, adjudication, licensing, or investigation, as those terms are used in subchapter II of this chapter;

(3)   "alternative means of dispute resolution" means any procedure that is used to resolve issues in controversy, including, but not limited to, conciliation, facilitation, mediation, factfinding, minitrials, arbitration, and use of ombuds, or any combination thereof;

(4)   "award" means any decision by an arbitrator resolving the issues in controversy;

(5)   "dispute resolution communication" means any oral or written communication prepared for the purposes of a dispute resolution proceeding, including any memoranda, notes or work product of the neutral, parties or nonparty participant; except that a written agreement to enter into a dispute resolution proceeding, or final written agreement or arbitral award reached as a result of a dispute resolution proceeding, is not a dispute resolution communication;

(6)   "dispute resolution proceeding" means any process in which an alternative means of dispute resolution is used to resolve an issue in controversy in which a neutral is appointed and specified parties participate;

(7)   "in confidence" means, with respect to information, that the information is provided—

(A)   with the expressed intent of the source that it not be disclosed; or

(B)   under circumstances that would create the reasonable expectation on behalf of the source that the information will not be disclosed;

(8)   "issue in controversy" means an issue which is material to a decision concerning an administrative program of an agency, and with which there is disagreement—

(A)   between an agency and persons who would be substantially affected by the decision; or

(B)   between persons who would be substantially affected by the decision;

(9)   "neutral" means an individual who, with respect to an issue in controversy, functions specifically to aid the parties in resolving the controversy;

(10)   "party" means—

(A)   for a proceeding with named parties, the same as in section 551(3) of this title; and

(B)   for a proceeding without named parties, a person who will be significantly affected by the decision in the proceeding and who participates in the proceeding;

(11)   "person" has the same meaning as in section 551(2) of this title; and

(12)   "roster" means a list of persons qualified to provide services as neutrals.

CONGRESSIONAL FINDINGS

Section 2 of Pub. L. 101-552 provided that: "The Congress finds that—

"(1)   administrative procedure, as embodied in chapter 5 of title 5, United States Code, and other statutes, is intended to offer a prompt, expert, and inexpensive means of resolving disputes as an alternative to litigation in the Federal courts;

"(2)   administrative proceedings have become increasingly formal, costly, and lengthy resulting in unnecessary expenditures of time and in a decreased likelihood of achieving consensual resolution of disputes;

"(3)   alternative means of dispute resolution have been used in the private sector for many years and, in appropriate circumstances, have yielded decisions that are faster, less expensive, and less contentious;

"(4)   such alternative means can lead to more creative, efficient, and sensible outcomes;

"(5)   such alternative means may be used advantageously in a wide variety of administrative programs;

"(6)   explicit authorization of the use of well-tested dispute resolution techniques will eliminate ambiguity of agency authority under existing law;

"(7)   Federal agencies may not only receive the benefit of techniques that were developed in the private sector, but may also take the lead in the further development and refinement of such techniques; and

"(8)   the availability of a wide range of dispute resolution procedures, and an increased understanding of the most effective use of such procedures, will enhance the operation of the Government and better serve the public."

PROMOTION OF ALTERNATIVE MEANS OF DISPUTE RESOLUTION

Section 3 of Pub. L. 101-552, as amended by Pub. L 104-320, Sec. 4(a), Oct. 19, 1996, 110 Stat. 3871, provided that:

"(a)   Promulgation of Agency Policy.—Each agency shall adopt a policy that addresses the use of alternative means of dispute resolution and case management. In developing such a policy, each agency shall—

"(1)   consult with the agency designated by, or the interagency committee designated or established by, the President under section 573 of title 5, United States Code, to facilitate and encourage agency use of alternative dispute resolution under subchapter IV of chapter 5 of such title; and

"(2)   examine alternative means of resolving disputes in connection with—

"(A)   formal and informal adjudications;

"(B)   rulemakings;

"(C)   enforcement actions;

"(D)   issuing and revoking licenses or permits;

"(E)   contract administration;

"(F)   litigation brought by or against the agency; and

"(G)   other agency actions.

"(b)   Dispute Resolution Specialists.—The head of each agency shall designate a senior official to be the dispute resolution specialist of the agency. Such official shall be responsible for the implementation of—

"(1)   the provisions of this Act (see Short Title note above) and the amendments made by this Act; and

"(2)   the agency policy developed under subsection (a).

"(c)   Training.—Each agency shall provide for training on a regular basis for the dispute resolution specialist of the agency and other employees involved in implementing the policy of the agency developed under subsection (a) Such training should encompass the theory and practice of negotiation, mediation, arbitration, or related techniques. The dispute resolution specialist shall periodically recommend to the agency head agency employees who would benefit from similar training.

"(d)   Procedures for Grants and Contracts.—

"(1)   Each agency shall review each of its standard agreements for contracts, grants, and other assistance and shall determine whether to amend any such standard agreements to authorize and encourage the use of alternative means of dispute resolution.

"(2)(A)Within 1 year after the date of the enactment of this Act (Nov. 15, 1990), the Federal Acquisition Regulation shall be amended, as necessary, to carry out this Act (see Short Title note above) and the amendments made by this Act.

"(B)   For purposes of this section, the term 'Federal Acquisition' means the single system of Government-wide procurement regulation referred to in section 6(a) of the Office of Federal Procurement Policy Act (41 U.S.C. 405 (a))."

USE OF NONATTORNEYS

Section 9 of Pub. L. 101-552 provided that:

"(a)   Representation of Parties.—Each agency, in developing a policy on the use of alternative means of dispute resolution under this Act, shall develop a policy with regard to the representation by persons other than attorneys of parties in alternative dispute resolution proceedings and shall identify any of its administrative programs with numerous claims or disputes before the agency and determine—

"(1)   the extent to which individuals are represented or assisted by attorneys or by persons who are not attorneys;

and

"(2)   whether the subject areas of the applicable proceedings or the procedures are so complex or specialized that only attorneys may adequately provide such representation or assistance.

"(b)   Representation and Assistance by Nonattorneys.—A person who is not an attorney may provide representation or assistance to any individual in a claim or dispute with an agency, if—

"(1)   such claim or dispute concerns an administrative program identified under subsection (a);

"(2)   such agency determines that the proceeding or procedure does not necessitate representation or assistance by an attorney under subsection (a) (2); and

"(3)   such person meets any requirement of the agency to provide representation or assistance in such a claim or dispute.

"(c)   Disqualification of Representation or Assistance.—Any agency that adopts regulations under subchapter IV of chapter 5 of title 5, United States Code, to permit representation or assistance by persons who are not attorneys shall review the rules of practice before such agency to—

"(1)   ensure that any rules pertaining to disqualification of attorneys from practicing before the agency shall also apply, as appropriate, to other persons who provide representation or assistance; and

"(2)   establish effective agency procedures for enforcing such rules of practice and for receiving complaints from affected persons."

SEC. 572. GENERAL AUTHORITY

(a)   An agency may use a dispute resolution proceeding for the resolution of an issue in controversy that relates to an administrative program, if the parties agree to such proceeding.

(b)   An agency shall consider not using a dispute resolution proceeding if

(1)   a definitive or authoritative resolution of the matter is required for precedential value, and such a proceeding is not likely to be accepted generally as an authoritative precedent;

(2)   the matter involves or may bear upon significant questions of Government policy that require additional procedures before a final resolution may be made, and such a proceeding would not likely serve to develop a recommended policy for the agency;

(3)   maintaining established policies is of special importance, so that variations among individual decisions are not increased and such a proceeding would not likely reach consistent results among individual decisions;

(4)   the matter significantly affects persons or organizations who are not parties to the proceeding;

(5)   a full public record of the proceeding is important, and a dispute resolution proceeding cannot provide such a record; and

(6)   the agency must maintain continuing jurisdiction over the matter with authority to alter the disposition of the matter in the light of changed circumstances, and a dispute resolution proceeding would interfere with the agency's fulfilling that requirement.

(c)   Alternative means of dispute resolution authorized under this subchapter are voluntary procedures which supplement rather than limit other available agency dispute resolution techniques.

SEC. 573. NEUTRALS

(a)   A neutral may be a permanent or temporary officer or employee of the Federal Government or any other individual who is acceptable to the parties to a dispute resolution proceeding. A neutral shall have no official, financial, or personal conflict of interest with respect to the issues in controversy, unless such interest is fully disclosed in writing to all parties and all parties agree that the neutral may serve.

(b)   A neutral who serves as a conciliator, facilitator, or mediator serves at the will of the parties.

(c)   The President shall designate an agency or designate or establish an interagency committee to facilitate and encourage agency use of dispute resolution under this subchapter. Such agency or interagency committee, in consultation with other appropriate Federal agencies and professional organizations experienced in matters concerning dispute resolution, shall

(1)   encourage and facilitate agency use of alternative means of dispute resolution; and

(2)   develop procedures that permit agencies to obtain

the services of neutrals on an expedited basis.

(d)   An agency may use the services of one or more employees of other agencies to serve as neutrals in dispute resolution proceedings. The agencies may enter into an interagency agreement that provides for the reimbursement by the user agency or the parties of the full or partial cost of the services of such an employee.

(e)   Any agency may enter into a contract with any person for services as a neutral, or for training in connection with alternative means of dispute resolution. The parties in a dispute resolution proceeding shall agree on compensation for the neutral that is fair and reasonable to the Government.

SEC. 574. CONFIDENTIALITY

(a)   Except as provided in subsections (d) and (e), a neutral in a dispute resolution proceeding shall not voluntarily disclose or through discovery or compulsory process be required to disclose any dispute resolution communication or any communication provided in confidence to the neutral, unless

(1)   all parties to the dispute resolution proceeding and the neutral consent in writing, and, if the dispute resolution communication was provided by a nonparty participant, that participant also consents in writing;

(2)   the dispute resolution communication has already been made public;

(3)   the dispute resolution communication is required by statute to be made public, but a neutral should make such communication public only if no other person is reasonably available to disclose the communication; or

(4)   a court determines that such testimony or disclosure is necessary to—

(A)   prevent a manifest injustice;

(B)   help establish a violation of law; or

(C)   prevent harm to the public health or safety, of sufficient magnitude in the particular case to outweigh the integrity of dispute resolution proceedings in general by reducing the confidence of parties in future cases that their communications will remain confidential.

(b)   A party to a dispute resolution proceeding shall not voluntarily disclose or through discovery or compulsory process be required to disclose any dispute resolution communication, unless

(1)   the communication was prepared by the party seeking disclosure;

(2)   all parties to the dispute resolution proceeding consent in writing;

(3)   the dispute resolution communication has already been made public;

(4)   the dispute resolution communication is required by statute to be made public;

(5)   a court determines that such testimony or disclosure is necessary to—

(A)   prevent a manifest injustice;

(B)   help establish a violation of law; or

(C)   prevent harm to the public health and safety, of sufficient magnitude in the particular case to outweigh the integrity of dispute resolution proceedings in general by reducing the confidence of parties in future cases that their communications will remain confidential;

(6)   the dispute resolution communication is relevant to determining the existence or meaning of an agreement or award that resulted from the dispute resolution proceeding or to the enforcement of such an agreement or award; or

(7)   except for dispute resolution communications generated by the neutral, the dispute resolution communication was provided to or was available to all parties to the dispute resolution proceeding.

(c)   Any dispute resolution communication that is disclosed in violation of subsection (a) or (b), shall not be admissible in any proceeding relating to the issues in controversy with respect to which the communication was made.

(d)(1) The parties may agree to alternative confidential procedures for disclosures by a neutral. Upon such agreement the parties shall inform the neutral before the commencement of the dispute resolution proceeding of any modifications to the provisions of subsection (a) that will govern the confidentiality of the dispute resolution proceeding. If the parties do not so inform the neutral, subsection (a) shall apply.

(2)   To qualify for the exemption established under subsection (j), an alternative confidential procedure under this subsection may not provide for less disclosure than the confidential procedures otherwise provided under this section.

(e)   If a demand for disclosure, by way of discovery

request or other legal process, is made upon a neutral regarding a dispute resolution communication, the neutral shall make reasonable efforts to notify the parties and any affected nonparty participants of the demand. Any party or affected nonparty participant who receives such notice and within 15 calendar days does not offer to defend a refusal of the neutral to disclose the requested information shall have waived any objection to such disclosure.

(f)   Nothing in this section shall prevent the discovery or admissibility of any evidence that is otherwise discoverable, merely because the evidence was presented in the course of a dispute resolution proceeding.

(g)   Subsections (a) and (b) shall have no effect on the information and data that are necessary to document an agreement reached or order issued pursuant to a dispute resolution proceeding.

(h)   Subsections (a) and (b) shall not prevent the gathering of information for research or educational purposes, in cooperation with other agencies, governmental entities, or dispute resolution programs, so long as the parties and the specific issues in controversy are not identifiable.

(i)   Subsections (a) and (b) shall not prevent use of a dispute resolution communication to resolve a dispute between the neutral in a dispute resolution proceeding and a party to or participant in such proceeding, so long as such dispute resolution communication is disclosed only to the extent necessary to resolve such dispute.

(j)   A dispute resolution communication which is between a neutral and a party and which may not be disclosed under this section shall also be exempt from disclosure under section 552 (b) (3).

SEC. 575. AUTHORIZATION OF ARBITRATION

(a)(1) Arbitration may be used as an alternative means of dispute resolution whenever all parties consent. Consent may be obtained either before or after an issue in controversy has arisen. A party may agree to—

(A)   submit only certain issues in controversy to arbitration; or

(B)   arbitration on the condition that the award must be within a range of possible outcomes.

(2)   The arbitration agreement that sets forth the subject matter submitted to the arbitrator shall be in writing.

Each such arbitration agreement shall specify a maximum award that may be issued by the arbitrator and may specify other conditions limiting the range of possible outcomes.

(3)   An agency may not require any person to consent to arbitration as a condition of entering into a contract or obtaining a benefit.

(b)   An officer or employee of an agency shall not offer to use arbitration for the resolution of issues in controversy unless such officer or employee

(1)   would otherwise have authority to enter into a settlement concerning the matter; or

(2)   is otherwise specifically authorized by the agency to consent to the use of arbitration.

(c)   Prior to using binding arbitration under this subchapter, the head of an agency, in consultation with the Attorney General and after taking into account the factors in section 572 (b), shall issue guidance on the appropriate use of binding arbitration and when an officer or employee of the agency has authority to settle an issue in controversy through binding arbitration.

SEC. 576. ENFORCEMENT OF ARBITRATION AGREEMENTS

An agreement to arbitrate a matter to which this subchapter applies is enforceable pursuant to section 4 of title 9, and no action brought to enforce such an agreement shall be dismissed nor shall relief therein be denied on the grounds that it is against the United States or that the United States is an indispensable party.

SEC. 577. ARBITRATORS

(a)   The parties to an arbitration proceeding shall be entitled to participate in the selection of the arbitrator.

(b)   The arbitrator shall be a neutral who meets the criteria of section 573 of this title.

SEC. 578. AUTHORITY OF THE ARBITRATOR

An arbitrator to whom a dispute is referred under this subchapter may

(1)   regulate the course of and conduct arbitral hearings;

(2)   administer oaths and affirmations;

(3)   compel the attendance of witnesses and produc-

tion of evidence at the hearing under the provisions of section 7 of title 9 only to the extent the agency involved is otherwise authorized by law to do so; and

(4)   make awards.

SEC. 579. ARBITRATION PROCEEDINGS

(a)   The arbitrator shall set a time and place for the hearing on the dispute and shall notify the parties not less than 5 days before the hearing.

(b)   Any party wishing a record of the hearing shall—

(1)   be responsible for the preparation of such record;

(2)   notify the other parties and the arbitrator of the preparation of such record;

(3)   furnish copies to all identified parties and the arbitrator; and

(4)   pay all costs for such record, unless the parties agree otherwise or the arbitrator determines that the costs should be apportioned.

(c) (1) The parties to the arbitration are entitled to be heard, to present evidence material to the controversy, and to cross-examine witnesses appearing at the hearing.

(2)   The arbitrator may, with the consent of the parties, conduct all or part of the hearing by telephone, television, computer, or other electronic means, if each party has an opportunity to participate.

(3)   The hearing shall be conducted expeditiously and in an informal manner.

(4)   The arbitrator may receive any oral or documentary evidence, except that irrelevant, immaterial, unduly repetitious, or privileged evidence may be excluded by the arbitrator.

(5)   The arbitrator shall interpret and apply relevant statutory and regulatory requirements, legal precedents, and policy directives.

(d)   No interested person shall make or knowingly cause to be made to the arbitrator an unauthorized ex parte communication relevant to the merits of the proceeding, unless the parties agree otherwise. If a communication is made in violation of this subsection, the arbitrator shall ensure that a memorandum of the communication is prepared and made a part of the record, and that an opportunity for rebuttal is allowed. Upon receipt of a communication made in violation of this subsection, the arbitrator may, to the extent consistent with the interests of justice and the policies underlying this subchapter, require the offending party to show cause why the claim of such party should not be resolved against such party as a result of the improper conduct.

(e)   The arbitrator shall make the award within 30 days after the close of the hearing, or the date of the filing of any briefs authorized by the arbitrator, whichever date is later, unless—

(1)   the parties agree to some other time limit; or

(2)   the agency provides by rule for some other time limit.

SEC. 580. ARBITRATION AWARDS

(a) (1) Unless the agency provides otherwise by rule, the award in an arbitration proceeding under this subchapter shall include a brief, informal discussion of the factual and legal basis for the award, but formal findings of fact or conclusions of law shall not be required.

(2)   The prevailing parties shall file the award with all relevant agencies, along with proof of service on all parties.

(b)   The award in an arbitration proceeding shall become final 30 days after it is served on all parties. Any agency that is a party to the proceeding may extend this 30-day period for an additional 30-day period by serving a notice of such extension on all other parties before the end of the first 30-day period.

(c)   A final award is binding on the parties to the arbitration proceeding, and may be enforced pursuant to sections 9 through 13 of title 9. No action brought to enforce such an award shall be dismissed nor shall relief therein be denied on the grounds that it is against the United States or that the United States is an indispensable party.

(d)   An award entered under this subchapter in an arbitration proceeding may not serve as an estoppel in any other proceeding for any issue that was resolved in the proceeding. Such an award also may not be used as precedent or otherwise be considered in any factually unrelated proceeding, whether conducted under this subchapter, by an agency, or in a court, or in any other arbitration proceeding.

SEC. 581. JUDICIAL REVIEW

(a)   Notwithstanding any other provision of law, any

person adversely affected or aggrieved by an award made in an arbitration proceeding conducted under this subchapter may bring an action for review of such award only pursuant to the provisions of sections 9 through 13 of title 9.

(b)   A decision by an agency to use or not to use a dispute resolution proceeding under this sub-chapter shall be committed to the discretion of the agency and shall not be subject to judicial review, except that arbitration shall be subject to judicial review under section 10 (b) of title 9.

SEC. 583. SUPPORT SERVICES

For the purposes of this subchapter, an agency may use (with or without reimbursement) the services and facilities of other Federal agencies, State, local, and tribal governments, public and private organizations and agencies, and individuals, with the consent of such agencies, organizations, and individuals. An agency may accept voluntary and uncompensated services for purposes of this subchapter without regard to the provisions of section 1342 of title 31.

5 USC Subchapter V Administrative Conference of the United States

TERMINATION OF ADMINISTRATIVE CONFERENCE OF UNTIED STATES

Pub. L. 104-52, title IV, Nov. 19, 1995, 109 Stat. 480, provided; "For necessary expenses of the Administrative Conference of the United States, established under subchapter V of chapter 5 of title 5, United States Code, $600,000: Provided, That these funds shall only be available for the purposes of the prompt and orderly termination of the Administrative Conference of the United States by February 1, 1996."

SEC. 591. PURPOSE

It is the purpose of this subchapter to provide suitable arrangements through which Federal agencies, assisted by outside experts, may cooperatively study mutual problems, exchange information, and develop recommendations for action by proper authorities to the end that private rights may be fully protected and regulatory activities and other Federal responsibilities may be carried out expeditiously in the public interest.

SEC. 592. DEFINITIONS

For the purpose of this subchapter—

(1)   "administrative program" includes a Federal function which involves protection of the public interest and the determination of rights, privileges, and obligations of private persons through rulemaking, adjudication, licensing, or investigation, as those terms are used in subchapter II of this chapter, except that it does not include a military or foreign affairs function of the United States;

(2)   "administrative agency" means an authority as defined by section 551 (1) of this title; and

(3)   "administrative procedure" means procedure used in carrying out an administrative program and is to be broadly construed to include any aspect of agency organization, procedure, or management that may affect the equitable consideration of public and private interests, the fairness of agency decisions, the speed of agency action, and the relationship of operating methods to later judicial review, but does not include the scope of agency responsibility as established by law or matters of substantive policy committed by law to agency discretion.

SEC. 593. ADMINISTRATIVE CONFERENCE OF THE UNITED STATES

(a)   The Administrative Conference of the United States consists of not more than 101 nor less than 75 members appointed as set forth in subsection (b) of this section.

(b)   The Conference is composed of—

(1)   a full-time Chairman appointed for a 5-year term by the President, by and with the advice and consent of the Senate. The Chairman is entitled to pay at the highest rate established by statute for the chairman of an independent regulatory board or commission, and may continue to serve until his successor is appointed and has qualified;

(2)   the chairman of each independent regulatory board or commission or an individual designated by the board or commission;

(3)   the head of each Executive department or other administrative agency which is designated by the President, or an individual designated by the head of the department or agency;

(4)   when authorized by the Council referred to in section 595 (b) of this title, one or more appointees from a board, commission, department, or agency referred to in this subsection, designated by the head thereof with, in the case of a board or commission, the approval of the board or commission;

(5)   individuals appointed by the President to membership on the Council who are not otherwise members of the Conference; and

(6)   not more than 40 other members appointed by the Chairman, with the approval of the Council, for terms of 2 years, except that the number of members appointed by the Chairman may at no time be less than one-third nor more than two-fifths of the total number of members. The Chairman shall select the members in a manner which will provide broad representation of the views of private citizens and utilize diverse experience. The members shall be members of the practicing bar, scholars in the field of administrative law or government, or others specially informed by knowledge and experience with respect to Federal administrative procedure.

(c)   Members of the Conference, except the Chairman, are not entitled to pay for service. Members appointed from outside the Federal Government are entitled to travel expenses, including per diem instead of subsistence, as authorized by section 5703 of this title for individuals serving without pay.

DEVELOPMENT OF ADMINISTRATIVE CONFERENCE

The Administrative Conference of the United States, established as a permanent body by the Administrative Conference Act, Pub. L. 88-499, Aug. 30, 1964, 78 Stat. 615, was preceded by two temporary Conferences. The first was called by President Eisenhower in 1953 and adopted a final report, which was transmitted to the President who acknowledged receipt of it on March 3, 1955. The second was established by President Kennedy by Executive Order No. 10934, Apr. 14, 1961, 26 F.R. 3233, which, by its terms, called for a final report to the President by December 31, 1962. The final report recommended a continuing Conference consisting of both government personnel and outside experts.

SEC. 594. POWERS AND DUTIES OF THE CONFERENCE

To carry out the purpose of this subchapter, the Administrative Conference of the United States may

(1)   study the efficiency, adequacy, and fairness of the administrative procedure used by administrative agencies in carrying out administrative programs, and make recommendations to administrative agencies, collectively or individually, and to the President, Congress, or the Judicial Conference of the United States, in connection therewith, as it considers appropriate;

(2)   arrange for interchange among administrative agencies of information potentially useful in improving administrative procedure;

(3)   collect information and statistics from administrative agencies and publish such reports as it considers useful for evaluating and improving administrative procedure;

(4)   enter into arrangements with any administrative agency or major organizational unit within an administrative agency pursuant to which the Conference performs any of the functions described in this section; and

(5)   provide assistance in response to requests relating to the improvement of administrative procedure in foreign countries, subject to the concurrence of the Secretary of State, the Administrator of the Agency for International Development, or the Director of the United States Information Agency, as appropriate, except that

(A)   such assistance shall be limited to the analysis of issues relating to administrative procedure, the provision of training of foreign officials in administrative procedure, and the design or improvement of administrative procedure, where the expertise of members of the Conference is indicated; and

(B)   such assistance may only be undertaken on a fully reimbursable basis, including all direct and indirect administrative costs.

Payment for services provided by the Conference pursuant to paragraph (4) shall be credited to the operating account for the Conference and shall remain available until expended.

SEC. 595. ORGANIZATION OF THE CONFERENCE

(a)   The membership of the Administrative Conference of the United States meeting in plenary session constitutes the Assembly of the Conference. The Assembly has ultimate authority over all activities of the Conference. Specifically, it has the power to

(1)   adopt such recommendations as it considers appropriate for improving administrative procedure. A member who disagrees with a recommendation adopted by the Assembly is entitled to enter a dissenting opinion and an alternate proposal in the record of the Conference proceedings, and the opinion and proposal so entered shall accompany the Conference recommendation in a publication or distribution thereof; and

(2)   adopt bylaws and regulations not inconsistent with this subchapter for carrying out the functions of the Conference, including the creation of such committees as it considers necessary for the conduct of studies and the development of recommendations for consideration by the Assembly.

(b)   The Conference includes a Council composed of the Chairman of the Conference, who is Chairman of the Council, and 10 other members appointed by the President, of whom not more than one-half shall be employees of Federal regulatory agencies or Executive departments. The President may designate a member of the Council as Vice Chairman. During the absence or incapacity of the Chairman, or when that office is vacant, the Vice Chairman shall serve as Chairman. The term of each member, except the Chairman, is 3 years. When the term of a member ends, he may continue to serve until a successor is appointed. However, the service of any member ends when a change in his employment status would make him ineligible for Council membership under the conditions of his original appointment. The Council has the power to—

(1)   determine the time and place of plenary sessions of the Conference and the agenda for the sessions. The Council shall call at least one plenary session each year;

(2)   propose bylaws and regulations, including rules of procedure and committee organization, for adoption by the Assembly;

(3)   make recommendations to the Conference or its committees on a subject germane to the purpose of the Conference;

(4)   receive and consider reports and recommendations of committees of the Conference and send them to members of the Conference with the views and recommendations of the Council;

(5)   designate a member of the Council to preside at meetings of the Council in the absence or incapacity of the Chairman and Vice Chairman;

(6)   designate such additional officers of the Conference as it considers desirable;

(7)   approve or revise the budgetary proposals of the Chairman; and

(8)   exercise such other powers as may be delegated to it by the Assembly.

(c)   The Chairman is the chief executive of the Conference. In that capacity he has the power to—

(1)   make inquiries into matters he considers important for Conference consideration, including matters proposed by individuals inside or outside the Federal Government;

(2)   be the official spokesman for the Conference in relations with the several branches and agencies of the Federal Government and with interested organizations and individuals outside the Government, including responsibility for encouraging Federal agencies to carry out the recommendations of the Conference;

(3)   request agency heads to provide information needed by the Conference, which information shall be supplied to the extent permitted by law;

(4)   recommend to the Council appropriate subjects for action by the Conference;

(5)   appoint, with the approval of the Council, members of committees authorized by the bylaws and regulations of the Conference;

(6)   prepare, for approval of the Council, estimates of the budgetary requirements of the Conference;

(7)   appoint and fix the pay of employees, define their duties and responsibilities, and direct and supervise their activities;

(8)   rent office space in the District of Columbia;

(9)   provide necessary services for the Assembly, the Council, and the committees of the Conference;

(10) organize and direct studies ordered by the Assembly or the Council, to contract for the performance of such studies with any public or private persons, firm, association, corporation, or institution under title III of the Federal Property and Administrative Services Act of 1949, as amended (41 U.S.C. 251-260), and to use from time to time, as appropriate, experts and consultants who may be employed in accordance with section 3109 of this title at rates not in excess of the maximum rate of pay for grade GS-15 as provided in section 5332 of this title;

(11) utilize, with their consent, the services and facilities of Federal agencies and of State and private agencies and instrumentalities with or without reimbursement;

(12) accept, hold, administer, and utilize gifts, devises, and bequests of property, both real and personal, for the purpose of aiding and facilitating the work of the Conference. Gifts and bequests of money and proceeds from sales of other property received as gifts, devises, or bequests shall be deposited in the Treasury and shall be disbursed upon the order of the Chairman. Property accepted pursuant to this section, and the proceeds thereof, shall be used as nearly as possible in accordance with the terms of the gifts, devises, or bequests. For purposes of Federal income, estate, or gift taxes, property accepted under this section shall be considered as a gift, devise, or bequest to the United States;

(13) accept voluntary and uncompensated services, notwithstanding the provisions of section 1342 of title 31;

(14) on request of the head of an agency, furnish assistance and advice on matters of administrative procedure;

(15) exercise such additional authority as the Council or Assembly delegates to him; and

(16) request any administrative agency to notify the Chairman of its intent to enter into any contract with any person outside the agency to study the efficiency, adequacy, or fairness of an agency proceeding (as defined in section 551 [12] of this title).

The Chairman shall preside at meetings of the Council and at each plenary session of the Conference, to which he shall make a full report concerning the affairs of the Conference since the last preceding plenary session. The Chairman, on behalf of the Conference, shall transmit to the President and Congress an annual report and such interim reports as he considers desirable.

CHAPTER 7—JUDICIAL REVIEW

SEC.

701. Application; definitions.
702. Right of review.
703. Form and venue of proceeding.
704. Actions reviewable.
705. Relief pending review.
706. Scope of review.

SEC. 701. APPLICATION; DEFINITIONS

(a) This chapter applies, according to the provisions thereof, except to the extent that—

(1) statutes preclude judicial review; or

(2) agency action is committed to agency discretion by law.

(b) For the purpose of this chapter—

(1) "agency" means each authority of the Government of the United States, whether or not it is within or subject to review by another agency, but does not include—

(A) the Congress;

(B) the courts of the United States;

(C) the governments of the territories or possessions of the United States;

(D) the government of the District of Columbia;

(E) agencies composed of representatives of the parties or of representatives of organizations of the parties to the disputes determined by them;

(F) courts martial and military commissions;

(G) military authority exercised in the field in time of war or in occupied territory; or

(H) functions conferred by sections 1738, 1739, 1743, and 1744 of title 12; chapter 2 of title 41; subchapter II of chapter 471 of title 49; or sections 1884, 1891–1902, and former section 1641 (b) (2), of title 50, appendix; and

(2) "person," "rule," "order," "license," "sanction," "relief," and "agency action" have the meanings given them by section 551 of this title.

SEC. 702. RIGHT OF REVIEW

A person suffering legal wrong because of agency action, or adversely affected or aggrieved by agency action within the meaning of a relevant statute, is entitled to judicial review thereof. An action in a court of the United States seeking relief other than money damages and stating a claim that an agency or an officer or employee thereof acted or failed to act in an official capacity or under color of legal authority shall not be dismissed nor relief therein be denied on the ground that it is against the United States or that the United States is an indispensable party. The United States may be named as a defendant in any such action, and a judgment or decree may be entered against the United States: Provided, That any mandatory or injunctive decree shall specify the Federal officer or officers (by name or by title), and their successors in office, personally responsible for compliance. Nothing herein (1) affects other limitations on judicial review or the power or duty of the court to dismiss any action or deny relief on any other appropriate legal or equitable ground; or (2) confers authority to grant relief if any other statute that grants consent to suit expressly or impliedly forbids the relief which is sought.

SEC. 703. FORM AND VENUE OF PROCEEDING

The form of proceeding for judicial review is the special statutory review proceeding relevant to the subject matter in a court specified by statute or, in the absence or inadequacy thereof, any applicable form of legal action, including actions for declaratory judgments or writs of prohibitory or mandatory injunction or habeas corpus, in a court of competent jurisdiction. If no special statutory review proceeding is applicable, the action for judicial review may be brought against the United States, the agency by its official title, or the appropriate officer. Except to the extent that prior, adequate, and exclusive opportunity for judicial review is provided by law, agency action is subject to judicial review in civil or criminal proceedings for judicial enforcement.

SEC. 704. ACTIONS REVIEWABLE

Agency action made reviewable by statute and final agency action for which there is no other adequate remedy in a court are subject to judicial review. A preliminary, procedural, or intermediate agency action or ruling not directly reviewable is subject to review on the review of the final agency action. Except as otherwise expressly required by statute, agency action otherwise final is final for the purposes of this section whether or not there has been presented or determined an application for a declaratory order, for any form of reconsideration, or, unless the agency otherwise requires by rule and provides that the action meanwhile is inoperative, for an appeal to superior agency authority.

SEC. 705. RELIEF PENDING REVIEW

When an agency finds that justice so requires, it may postpone the effective date of action taken by it, pending judicial review. On such conditions as may be required and to the extent necessary to prevent irreparable injury, the reviewing court, including the court to which a case may be taken on appeal from or on application for certiorari or other writ to a reviewing court, may issue all necessary and appropriate process to postpone the effective date of an agency action or to preserve status or rights pending conclusion of the review proceedings.

SEC. 706. SCOPE OF REVIEW

To the extent necessary to decision and when presented, the reviewing court shall decide all relevant questions of law, interpret constitutional and statutory provisions, and determine the meaning or applicability of the terms of an agency action. The reviewing court shall—

(1)   compel agency action unlawfully withheld or unreasonably delayed; and

(2)   hold unlawful and set aside agency action, findings, and conclusions found to be—

(A)   arbitrary, capricious, an abuse of discretion, or otherwise not in accordance with law;

(B)   contrary to constitutional right, power, privilege, or immunity;

(C)   in excess of statutory jurisdiction, authority, or limitations, or short of statutory right;

(D)   without observance of procedure required by law;

(E)   unsupported by substantial evidence in a case subject to sections 556 and 557 of this title or otherwise reviewed on the record of an agency hearing provided by statute; or

(F)   unwarranted by the facts to the extent that the facts are subject to trial de novo by the reviewing court.

In making the foregoing determinations, the court shall review the whole record or those parts of it cited by a party, and due account shall be taken of the rule of prejudicial error.

Part II—Civil Service Functions and Responsibilities

CHAPTER 13—SPECIAL AUTHORITY

SEC.

SEC. 1301. RULES

The Office of Personnel Management shall aid the President, as he may request, in preparing the rules he prescribes under this title for the administration of the competitive service.

SEC. 1302. REGULATIONS

(a)   The Office of Personnel Management, subject to the rules prescribed by the President under this title for the administration of the competitive service, shall prescribe regulations for, control, supervise, and preserve the records of, examinations for the competitive service.

(b)   The Office shall prescribe and enforce regulations for the administration of the provisions of this title, and Executive orders issued in furtherance thereof, that implement the Congressional policy that preference shall be given to preference eligibles in certification for appointment, and in appointment, reinstatement, reemployment, and retention, in the competitive service in Executive agencies, permanent or temporary, and in the government of the District of Columbia.

(c)   The Office shall prescribe regulations for the administration of the provisions of this title that implement the Congressional policy that preference shall be given to preference eligibles in certification for appointment, and in appointment, reinstatement, reemployment, and retention, in the excepted service in Executive agencies, permanent or temporary, and in the government of the District of Columbia.

(d)   The Office may prescribe reasonable procedure and regulations for the administration of its functions under chapter 15 of this title.

SEC. 1303. INVESTIGATIONS; REPORTS

The Office of Personnel Management, Merit Systems Protection Board, and Special Counsel may investigate and report on matters concerning—

(1)   the enforcement and effect of the rules prescribed by the President under this title for the administration of the competitive service and the regulations prescribed by the Office of Personnel Management under section 1302 (a) of this title; and

(2)   the action of an examiner, a board of examiners, and other employees concerning the execution of the provisions of this title that relate to the administration of the competitive service.

SEC. 1304. LOYALTY INVESTIGATIONS; REPORTS; REVOLVING FUND

(a)   The Office of Personnel Management shall conduct the investigations and issue the reports required by the following statutes—

(1)   sections 272b, 281b (e), and 290a of title 22;

(2)   section 1874 (c) of title 42; and

(3)   section 1203 (e) of title 6,1 District of Columbia Code.

(b)   When an investigation under subsection (a) of this section develops data indicating that the loyalty of the individual being investigated is questionable, the Office shall refer the matter to the Federal Bureau of Investigation for a full field investigation, a report of which shall be furnished to the Office for its information and appropriate action.

(c)   When the President considers it in the national interest, he may have the investigations of a group or class, which are required by subsection (a) of this section, made by the Federal Bureau of Investigation rather than the Office.

(d)   The investigation and report required by subsection (a) of this section shall be made by the Federal Bureau of Investigation rather than the Office for those specific positions which the Secretary of State certifies are of a high degree of importance or sensitivity.

(e)(1) A revolving fund is available, to the Office without fiscal year limitation, for financing investigations, training, and such other functions as the Office is authorized or required to perform on a reimbursable basis, including personnel management services performed at the request of individual agencies (which would otherwise be the responsibility of such agencies), or at the request of non-appropriated fund instrumentalities. However, the functions which may be financed in any fiscal year by the fund are restricted to those functions which are covered by the budget estimates submitted to the Congress for that fiscal year. To the maximum extent feasible, each individual activity shall be conducted generally on an actual cost basis over a reasonable period of time.

(2)   The capital of the fund consists of the aggregate of—

(A)   appropriations made to provide capital for the fund, which appropriations are hereby authorized, and

(B)   the sum of the fair and reasonable value of such supplies, equipment, and other assets as the Office from time to time transfers to the fund (including the amount of the unexpended balances of appropriations or funds relating to activities the financing of which is transferred to the fund) less the amount of related liabilities, the amount of unpaid obligations, and the value of accrued annual leave of employees, which are attributable to the activities the financing of which is transferred to the fund.

(3)   The fund shall be credited with—

(A)   advances and reimbursements from available funds of the Office or other agencies, or from other sources, for those services and supplies provided at rates estimated by the Office as adequate to recover expenses of operation (including provision for accrued annual leave of employees and depreciation of equipment); and

(B)   receipts from sales or exchanges of property, and payments for loss of or damage to property, accounted for under the fund.

(4)   Any unobligated and unexpended balances in the fund which the Office determines to be in excess of amounts needed for activities financed by the fund shall be deposited in the Treasury of the United States as miscellaneous receipts.

(5)   The Office shall prepare a business-type budget providing full disclosure of the results of operations for each of the functions performed by the Office and financed by the fund, and such budget shall be transmitted to the Congress and considered, in the manner prescribed by law for wholly owned Government corporations.

(6)   The Comptroller General of the United States shall, as a result of his periodic reviews of the activities financed by the fund, report and make such recommendations as he deems appropriate to the Committee on Governmental Affairs of the Senate and the Committee on Post Office and Civil Service of the House of Representatives.

(f)   An agency may use available appropriations to reimburse the Office or the Federal Bureau of Investigation for the cost of investigations, training, and functions performed for them under this section, or to make advances toward their cost. These advances and reimbursements shall be credited directly to the applicable appropriations of the Office or the Federal Bureau of Investigation.

(g)   This section does not affect the responsibility of the Federal Bureau of Investigation to investigate espionage, sabotage, or subversive acts.

SEC. 1305. ADMINISTRATIVE LAW JUDGES

For the purpose of sections 3105, 3344, 4301 (2) (D), and 5372 of this title and the provisions of section 5335 (a) (B) of this title that relate to administrative law judges, the Office of Personnel Management may, and for the purpose of section 7521 of this title, the Merit Systems Protection Board may investigate, prescribe regulations, appoint advisory committees as necessary, recommend legislation, subpoena witnesses and records, and pay witness fees as established for the courts of the United States.

SEC. 1306. OATHS TO WITNESSES

The Director of the Office of Personnel Management and authorized representatives of the Director may administer oaths to witnesses in matters pending before the Office.

SEC. 1307. MINUTES

The Civil Service Commission shall keep minutes of its proceedings.

Part III—Employees

CHAPTER 31—AUTHORITY FOR EMPLOYMENT

Subchapter I—Employment Authorities

SEC.

3101. General authority to employ.

3102. Employment of personal assistants for handicapped employees, including blind and deaf employees.

3103. Employment at seat of Government only for services rendered.

3104. Employment of specially qualified scientific and professional personnel.

3105. Appointment of administrative law judges.

3106. Employment of attorneys; restrictions.

3107. Employment of publicity experts; restrictions.

3108. Employment of detective agencies; restrictions.

3109. Employment of experts and consultants; temporary or intermittent.

3110. Employment of relatives; restrictions.

3111. Acceptance of volunteer service.

3112. Disabled veterans; noncompetitive appointment.

3113. Restriction on reemployment after conviction of certain crimes.

SEC. 3101. GENERAL AUTHORITY TO EMPLOY

Each Executive agency, military department, and the government of the District of Columbia may employ such number of employees of the various classes recognized by chapter 51 of this title as Congress may appropriate for from year to year.

SEC. 3102. EMPLOYMENT OF PERSONAL ASSISTANTS FOR HANDICAPPED EMPLOYEES, INCLUDING BLIND AND DEAF EMPLOYEES

(a)   For the purpose of this section—

(1)   "agency" meens—

(A)   an Executive agency; and

(B)   the Library of Congress;

(2)   "handicapped employee" means an individual employed by an agency who is blind or deaf or who otherwise qualifies as a handicapped individual within the meaning of section 501 of the Rehabilitation Act of 1973 (29 U.S.C. 794); and

(3)   "nonprofit organization" means an organization determined by the Secretary of the Treasury to be an organization described in section 501 (c) of the Internal Revenue Code of 1986 (26 U.S.C. 501 (c)), which is exempt from taxation under section 501 (a) of such Code.

(b)(1) The head of each agency may employ one or more personal assistants who the head of the agency determines are necessary to enable a handicapped employee of that agency to perform the employee's official duties and who shall serve without pay from the agency without regard to—

(A)   the provisions of this title governing appointment in the competitive service;

(B)   chapter 51 and subchapter III of chapter 53 of this title; and

(C)   section 1342 of title 31.

Such employment may include the employing of a reading assistant or assistants for a blind employee or an interpreting assistant or assistants for a deaf employee.

(2)   A personal assistant, including a reading or interpreting assistant, employed under this subsection may receive pay for services performed by the assistant from the handicapped employee or a nonprofit organization, without regard to section 209 of title 18.

(c)   The head of each agency may also employ or assign one or more personal assistants who the head of the agency determines are necessary to enable a handicapped employee of that agency to perform the employee's official duties. Such employment may include the employing of a reading assistant or assistants for a blind employee or an interpreting assistant or assistants for a deaf employee.

(d)(1) In the case of any handicapped employee (including a blind or deaf employee) traveling on official business, the head of the agency may authorize the payment to an individual to accompany or assist (or both) the handicapped employee for all or a portion of the travel period involved. Any payment under this subsection to such an individual may be made either directly to that individual or by advancement or reimbursement to the handicapped employee.

(2)   With respect to any individual paid to accompany or assist a handicapped employee under paragraph (1) of this subsection—

(A) the amount paid to that individual shall not exceed the limit or limits which the Office of Personnel Management shall prescribe by regulation to ensure that the payment does not exceed amounts (including pay and, if appropriate, travel expenses and per diem allowances) which could be paid to an employee assigned to accompany or assist the handicapped employee; and

(B) that individual shall be considered an employee, but only for purposes of chapter 81 of this title (relating to compensation for injury) and sections 2671 through 2680 of title 28 (relating to tort claims).

(e) This section may not be held or considered to prevent or limit in any way the assignment to a handicapped employee (including a blind or deaf employee) by an agency of clerical or secretarial assistance, at the expense of the agency under statutes and regulations currently applicable at the time, if that assistance normally is provided, or authorized to be provided, in that manner under currently applicable statutes and regulations.

SEC. 3103. EMPLOYMENT AT SEAT OF GOVERNMENT ONLY FOR SERVICES RENDERED

An individual may be employed in the civil service in an Executive department at the seat of Government only for services actually rendered in connection with and for the purposes of the appropriation from which he is paid. An individual who violates this section shall be removed from the service.

SEC. 3104. EMPLOYMENT OF SPECIALLY QUALIFIED SCIENTIFIC AND PROFESSIONAL PERSONNEL

(a) The Director of the Office of Personnel Management may establish, and from time to time revise, the maximum number of scientific or professional positions for carrying out research and development functions, which require the services of specially qualified personnel, which may be established outside of the General Schedule. Any such position may be established by action of the Director or, under such standards and procedures as the Office prescribes (including procedures under which the prior approval of the Director may be required), by agency action.

(b) The provisions of subsection (a) of this section shall not apply to any Senior Executive Service position (as defined in section 3132 (a) of this title).

(c) In addition to the number of positions authorized by subsection (a) of this section, the Librarian of Congress may establish, without regard to the second sentence of subsection (a) of this section, not more than 8 scientific or professional positions to carry out the research and development functions of the Library of Congress which require the services of specially qualified personnel.

SEC. 3105. APPOINTMENT OF ADMINISTRATIVE LAW JUDGES

Each agency shall appoint as many administrative law judges as are necessary for proceedings required to be conducted in accordance with sections 556 and 557 of this title. Administrative law judges shall be assigned to cases in rotation so far as practicable, and may not perform duties inconsistent with their duties and responsibilities as administrative law judges.

SEC. 3106. EMPLOYMENT OF ATTORNEYS; RESTRICTIONS

Except as otherwise authorized by law, the head of an Executive department or military department may not employ an attorney or counsel for the conduct of litigation in which the United States, an agency, or employee thereof is a party, or is interested, or for the securing of evidence therefor, but shall refer the matter to the Department of Justice. This section does not apply to the employment and payment of counsel under section 1037 of title 10.

SEC. 3107. EMPLOYMENT OF PUBLICITY EXPERTS; RESTRICTIONS

Appropriated funds may not be used to pay a publicity expert unless specifically appropriated for that purpose.

SEC. 3108. EMPLOYMENT OF DETECTIVE AGENCIES; RESTRICTIONS

An individual employed by the Pinkerton Detective Agency, or similar organization, may not be employed by the Government of the United States or the government of the District of Columbia.

SEC. 3109. EMPLOYMENT OF EXPERTS AND CONSULTANTS; TEMPORARY OR INTERMITTENT

(a)   For the purpose of this section—

(1)   "agency" has the meaning given it by section 5721 of this title; and

(2)   "appropriation" includes funds made available by statute under section 9104 of title 31.

(b)   When authorized by an appropriation or other statute, the head of an agency may procure by contract the temporary (not in excess of 1 year) or intermittent services of experts or consultants or an organization thereof, including stenographic reporting services. Services procured under this section are without regard to—

(1)   the provisions of this title governing appointment in the competitive service;

(2)   chapter 51 and subchapter III of chapter 53 of this title; and

(3)   section 5 of title 41, except in the case of stenographic reporting services by an organization.

However, an agency subject to chapter 51 and subchapter III of chapter 53 of this title may pay a rate for services under this section in excess of the daily equivalent of the highest rate payable under section 5332 of this title only when specifically authorized by the appropriation or other statute authorizing the procurement of the services.

(c)   Positions in the Senior Executive Service or the Federal Bureau of Investigation and Drug Enforcement Administration Senior Executive Service may not be filled under the authority of subsection (b) of this section.

(d)   The Office of Personnel Management shall prescribe regulations necessary for the administration of this section. Such regulations shall include—

(1)   criteria governing the circumstances in which it is appropriate to employ an expert or consultant under the provisions of this section;

(2)   criteria for setting the pay of experts and consultants under this section; and

(3)   provisions to ensure compliance with such regulations.

(e)   Each agency shall report to the Office of Personnel Management on an annual basis with respect

(1)   the number of days each expert or consultant employed by the agency during the period was so employed; and

(2)   the total amount paid by the agency to each expert and consultant for such work during the period.

SEC. 3110. EMPLOYMENT OF RELATIVES; RESTRICTIONS

(a)   For the purpose of this section—

(1)   agency means—

(A)   an Executive agency;

(B)   an office, agency, or other establishment in the legislative branch;

(C)   an office, agency, or other establishment in the judicial branch; and

(D)   the government of the District of Columbia;

(2)   "public official" means an officer (including the President and a Member of Congress), a member of the uniformed service, an employee and any other individual, in whom is vested the authority by law, or regulation, or to whom the authority has been delegated, to appoint, employ, promote, or advance individuals, or to recommend individuals for appointment, employment, promotion, or advancement in connection with employment in an agency; and

(3)   "relative" means, with respect to a public official, an individual who is related to the public official as father, mother, son, daughter, brother, sister, uncle, aunt, first cousin, nephew, niece, husband, wife, father-in-law, mother-in-law, son-in-law, daughter-in-law, brother-in-law, sister-in-law, stepfather, stepmother, stepson, stepdaughter, stepbrother, stepsister, half brother, or half sister.

(b)   A public official may not appoint, employ, promote, advance, or advocate for appointment, employment, promotion, or advancement, in or to a civilian position in the agency in which he is serving or over which he exercises jurisdiction or control any individual who is a relative of the public official. An individual may not be appointed, employed, promoted, or advanced in or to a civilian position in an agency if such appointment, employment, promotion, or advancement has been advocated by a public official, serving in or exercising jurisdiction or control over the agency, who is a relative of the individual.

(c)   An individual appointed, employed, promoted, or advanced in violation of this section is not entitled to pay, and money may not be paid from the Treasury as pay to an individual so appointed, employed, promoted, or advanced.

(d)   The Office of Personnel Management may perscribe regulations authorizing the temporary employment, in the event of emergencies resulting from natural disasters or similar unforeseen events or circumstances, of individuals whose employment would otherwise be prohibited by this section.

(e)   This section shall not be construed to prohibit the appointment of an individual who is a preference eligible in any case in which the passing over of that individual on a certificate of eligibles furnished under section 3317 (a) of this title will result in the selection for appointment of an individual who is not a preference eligible.

SEC. 3111. ACCEPTANCE OF VOLUNTEER SERVICE

(a)   For the purpose of this section, "student" means an individual who is enrolled, not less than half time, in a high school, trade school, technical or vocational institute, junior college, college, university, or comparable recognized educational institution. An individual who is a student is deemed not to have ceased to be a student during an interim between school years if the interim is not more than 5 months and if such individual shows to the satisfaction of the Office of Personnel Management that the individual has a bona fide intention of continuing to pursue a course of study or training in the same or different educational institution during the school semester (or other period into which the school year is divided) immediately after the interim.

(b)   Notwithstanding section 1342 of title 31, the head of an agency may accept, subject to regulations issued by the Office, voluntary service for the United States if the service—

(1)   is performed by a student, with the permission of the institution at which the student is enrolled, as part of an agency program established for the purpose of providing educational experiences for the student;

(2)   is to be uncompensated; and

(3)   will not be used to displace any employee.

(c) (1) Except as provided in paragraph (2), any student who provides voluntary service under subsection (b) of this section shall not be considered a Federal employee for any purpose other than for purposes of chapter 81 of this title (relating to compensation for injury) and sections 2671 through 2680 of title 28 (relating to tort claims).

(2)   In addition to being considered a Federal employee for the purposes specified in paragraph (1), any student who provides voluntary service as part of a program established under subsection (b) of this section in the Internal Revenue Service, Department of the Treasury, shall be considered an employee of the Department of the Treasury for purposes of—

(A)   section 552a of this title (relating to disclosure of records);

(B)   subsections (a) (1), (h) (1), (k) (6), and (1) (4) of section 6103 of title 26 (relating to confidentiality and disclosure of returns and return information);

(C)   sections 7213 (a) (1) and 7431 of title 26 (relating to unauthorized disclosures of returns and return information by Federal employees and other persons); and

(D)   section 7423 of title 26 (relating to suits against employees of the United States);

except that returns and return information (as defined in section 6103 (b) of title 26) shall be made available to students under such program only to the extent that the Secretary of the Treasury or his designee determines that the duties assigned to such students so require.

SEC. 3112. DISABLED VETERANS; NONCOMPETITIVE APPOINTMENT

Under such regulations as the Office of Personnel Management shall prescribe, an agency may make a noncompetitive appointment leading to conversion to career or career-conditional employment of a disabled veteran who has a compensable service-connected disability of 30 percent or more.

SEC. 3113. RESTRICTION ON REEMPLOYMENT AFTER CONVICTION OF CERTAIN CRIMES

An employee shall be separated from service and barred from reemployment in the Federal service, if—

(1)   the employee is convicted of a violation of section 201 (b) of title 18; and

(2)   such violation related to conduct prohibited under section 1010 (a) of the Controlled Substances Import and Export Act (21 U.S.C. 960 (a)).

CHAPTER 33—EXAMINATION, SELECTION, AND PLACEMENT

SEC. 3301. CIVIL SERVICE; GENERALLY

The President may—

(1)   prescribe such regulations for the admission of individuals into the civil service in the executive branch as will best promote the efficiency of that service;

(2)   ascertain the fitness of applicants as to age, health, character, knowledge, and ability for the employment sought; and

(3)   appoint and prescribe the duties of individuals to make inquiries for the purpose of this section.

SEC. 3344. DETAILS; ADMINISTRATIVE LAW JUDGES

An agency as defined by section 551 of this title, which occasionally or temporarily is insufficiently staffed with administrative law judges appointed under section 3105 of this title may use administrative law judges selected by the Office of Personnel Management from and with the consent of other agencies.

CHAPTER 53—PAY RATES AND SYSTEMS

SEC. 5372. ADMINISTRATIVE LAW JUDGES

(a)   For the purposes of this section, the term "administrative law judge" means an administrative law judge appointed under section 3105.

(b)(1) There shall be 3 levels of basic pay for administrative law judges (designated as AL-1, 2, and 3, respectively), and each such judge shall be paid at 1 of those levels, in accordance with the provisions of this section.

(2)   The Office of Personnel Management shall determine, in accordance with procedures which the Office shall by regulation prescribe, the level in which each administrative-law-judge position shall be placed and the qualifications to be required for appointment to each level.

(3)(A) Upon appointment to a position in AL-3, an administrative law judge shall be paid at rate A of AL-3, and shall be advanced successively to rates B, C, and D of that level upon completion of 52 weeks of service in the next lower rate, and to rates E and F of that level upon completion of 104 weeks of service in the next lower rate.

(B)   The Office of Personnel Management may provide for appointment of an administrative law judge in AL-3 at an advanced rate under such circumstances as the Office may determine appropriate.

(C)   The Office of Personnel Management shall prescribe regulations necessary to administer this section.

CHAPTER 75—ADVERSE ACTIONS

SEC. 7521. ACTIONS AGAINST ADMINISTRATIVE LAW JUDGES

(a)   An action may be taken against an administrative law judge appointed under section 3105 of this title by the agency in which the administrative law judge is employed only for good cause established and determined by the Merit Systems Protection Board on the record after opportunity for hearing before the Board.

(b)   The actions covered by this section are—

(1)   a removal;

(2)   a suspension;

(3)   a reduction in grade;

(4)   a reduction in pay; and

(5)   a furlough of 30 days or less; but do not include—

(A)   a suspension or removal under section 7532 of this title;

(B)   a reduction-in-force action under section 3502 of this title; or

(C)   any action initiated under section 1215 of this title.

APPENDIX C

UNIFORM LAW COMMISSIONERS' MODEL STATE ADMINISTRATIVE PROCEDURE ACT (1981)

ARTICLE I GENERAL PROVISIONS

§ 1-102. [DEFINITIONS]

As used in this Act:

(1) "Agency" means a board, commissions, department, officer, or other administrative unit of this State, including the agency head, and one or more members of the agency head or agency employees or other persons directly or indirectly purporting to act on behalf or under the authority of the agency head. The term does not include the [legislature] or the courts, [or the governor], [or the governor in the exercise of powers derived directly and exclusively from the constitution of this State]. The term does not include a political subdivision of the state or any of the administrative units of a political subdivision, but it does include a board, commission, department, officer, or other administrative unit created or appointed by joint or concerted action of an agency and one or more political subdivisions of the state or any of their units. To the extent it purports to exercise authority subject to any provision of this Act, an administrative unit otherwise qualifying as an "agency" must be treated as separate agency even if the unit is located within or subordinate to another agency.

(2) "Agency action" means:

(i) the whole or a part of a rule or an order;

(ii) the failure to issue a rule or an order; or

(iii) an agency's performance of, or failure to perform, any other duty, function, or activity, discretionary or otherwise.

(3) "Agency head" means an individual or body of individuals in whom the ultimate legal authority of the agency is vested by any provision of law.

(4) "License" means a franchise, permit, certification, approval, registration, charter, or similar form of authorization required by law.

(5) "Order" means an agency action of particular applicability that determines the legal rights, duties, privileges, immunities, or other legal interests of one or more specific persons. . . .

(6) "Party to agency proceedings," or "party" in context so indicating, means:

(i) a person to whom the agency action is specifically directed; or

(ii) a person named as a party to an agency proceeding or allowed to intervene or participate as a party in the proceeding.

(7) "Party to judicial review or civil enforcement proceedings," or "party" in context so indicating, means:

(i) a person who files a petition for judicial review or civil enforcement or

(ii) a person named as a party in a proceeding for judicial review or civil enforcement or allowed to participate as a party in the proceeding.

(8) "Person" means an individual, partnership, corporation, association, government subdivision or unit thereof, or public or private organization or entity of any character, and includes another agency.

(9) "Provision of law" means the whole or a part of the

federal or state constitution, or of any federal or state (i) statute, (ii) rule of court, (iii) executive order, or (iv) rule of an administrative agency.

(10) "Rule" means the whole or a part of an agency statement of general applicability that implements, interprets, or prescribes (i) law or policy, or (ii) the organization, procedure, or practice requirements of an agency. The term includes the amendment, repeal, or suspension of an existing rule.

(11) "Rule making" means the process for formulation and adoption of a rule.

§ 1-103. [APPLICABILITY AND RELATION TO OTHER LAW]

§ 1-104. [SUSPENSION OF ACT'S PROVISIONS WHEN NECESSARY TO AVOID LOSS OF FEDERAL FUNDS OR SERVICES] . . .

§ 1-105. [WAIVER]

Except to the extent precluded by another provision of law, a person may waive any right conferred upon that person by this Act.

§ 1-106. [INFORMAL SETTLEMENTS]

Except to the extent precluded by another provision of law, informal settlement of matters that may make unnecessary more elaborate proceedings under this Act is encouraged. Agencies shall establish by rule specific procedures to facilitate informal settlement of matters. This section does not require any party or other person to settle a matter pursuant to informal procedures.

§ 1-107. [CONVERSION OF PROCEEDINGS]

(a) At any point in an agency proceeding the presiding officer or other agency official responsible for the proceeding:

(1) may convert the proceeding to another type of agency proceeding providing for by this Act if the conversion is appropriate, is in the public interest, and does not substantially prejudice the rights of any party; and

(2) if required by any provision of law, shall convert the proceeding to another type of agency proceeding provided for by this Act.

(b) A conversion of a proceeding of one type to a proceeding of another type may be effected only upon notice to all parties to the original proceeding.

(c) If the presiding officer or other agency official responsible for the original proceeding would not have authority over the new proceeding to which it is to be converted, that officer or official, in accordance with agency rules, shall secure the appointment of a successor to preside over or be responsible for the new proceeding.

(d) To the extent feasible and consistent with the rights of parties and the requirements of this Act pertaining to the new proceeding, the record or the original agency proceeding must be used in the new agency proceeding.

(e) After a proceeding is converted from one type to another, the presiding officer or other agency official responsible for the new proceeding shall:

(1) give such additional notice to parties or other persons as is necessary to satisfy the requirements of this Act pertaining to those proceedings;

(2) dispose of the matters involved without further proceedings if sufficient proceedings have already been held to satisfy requirements of this Act pertaining to the new proceedings; and

(3) conduct or cause to be conducted any additional proceedings necessary to satisfy the requirements of this Act pertaining to those proceedings.

(f) Each agency shall adopt rules to govern the conversion of one type of proceeding to another. Those rules must include an enumeration of the factors to be considered in determining whether and under what circumstances one type of proceeding will be converted to another.

§ 1-108. [EFFECTIVE DATE]

This Act takes effect on [date] and does not govern proceedings pending on that date. This Act governs all agency proceedings, and all proceedings for judicial review or civil enforcement of agency action, commenced after that date. This Act also governs agency proceedings conducted on a remand from a court or another agency after the effective date of this Act.

§ 1-109. [SEVERABILITY]

If any provision of this Act or the application thereof to any person or circumstance is held invalid, the invalidity does not affect other provisions or applications of the Act which can be given effect without the invalid provision or application, and for this purpose the provisions of this Act are severable.

ARTICLE II PUBLIC ACCESS TO AGENCY LAW AND POLICY

§ 2-101. [ADMINISTRATIVE RULES EDITOR; PUBLICATION, COMPILATION, INDEXING, AND PUBLIC INSPECTION OF RULES]

(a)   There is created, within the executive branch, an [administrative rules editor]. The governor shall appoint the [administrative rules editor] who shall serve at the pleasure of the governor.

(b)   Subject to the provisions of this Act, the [administrative rules editor] shall prescribe a uniform numbering system, form, and style for all proposed and adopted rules caused to be published by that office, [and shall have the same editing authority with respect to the publication of rules as the [reviser of statutes] has with respect to the publication of statutes].

(c)   The [administrative rules editor] shall cause the [administrative bulletin] to be published in pamphlet form [once each week]. For purposes of calculating adherence to time requirements imposed by this Act, an issue of the [administrative bulletin] is deemed published on the later of the date indicated in that issue or the date of its mailing. The [administrative bulletin] must contain:

(1)   notices of proposed rule adoption prepared so that the text of the proposed rule shows the text of any existing rule proposed to be changed and the change proposed;

(2)   newly filed adopted rules prepared so that the text of the newly filed adopted rule shows the text of any existing rule being changed and the changes being made;

(3)   any other notices and materials designated by [law] [the administrative rules editor] for publication therein; and

(4)   an index to its contents by subject.

(d)   The [administrative rules editor] shall cause the [administrative code] to be compiled, indexed by subject, and published [in loose-leaf form]. All of the effective rules of each agency must be published and indexed in that publi-

cation. The [administrative rules editor] shall also cause [loose-leaf] supplements to the [administrative code] to be published at least every [3 months]. [The loose-leaf supplements must be in a form suitable for insertion in the appropriate places in the permanent [administrative code] compilation.]

(e)   The [administrative rules editor] may omit from the [administrative bulletin or code] any proposed or filed adopted rule the publication of which would be unduly cumbersome, expensive, or otherwise inexpedient, if:

(1)   knowledge of the rule is likely to be important to only a small class of persons;

(2)   on application to the issuing agency, the proposed or adopted rule in printed or processed form is made available at no more than its costs of reproduction; and

(3)   the [administrative bulletin or code] contains a notice stating in detail the specific subject matter of the omitted proposed or adopted rule and how a copy of the omitted material may be obtained.

(f)   The [administrative bulletin and administrative code] must be furnished to [designated officials] without charge and to all subscribers at a cost to be determined by the [administrative rules editor]. Each agency shall also make available for public inspection and copying those portions of the [administrative bulletin and administrative code] containing all rules adopted or used by the agency in the discharge of its functions, and the index to those rules.

(g)   Except as otherwise required by a provision of law, subsections, (c) through (f) do not apply to rules governed by Section 3–116, and the following provisions apply instead:

(1)   Each agency shall maintain an official, current, and dated compilation that is indexed by subject, containing all of the rules within the scope of Section 3–116. Each addition to, change in, or deletion from the official compilation must also be dated, indexed, and a record thereof kept. Except for those portions containing rules governed by Section 3–116(2), the compilation must be made available for public inspection and copying. Certified copies of the full compilation must also be furnished to the [secretary of state, the administrative rules counsel, and members of the administrative rules review committee], and be kept current by the agency at least every [30] days.

(2)   A rule subject to the requirements of this subsection may not be relied on by an agency to the detriment of any person who does not have actual, timely knowledge of the contents of the rule until the requirements of paragraph (1) are satisfied. The burden of proving that knowledge is on the agency. This provision is also inapplicable to the extent necessary to avoid imminent peril to the public health, safety, or welfare.

§ 2-102. [PUBLIC INSPECTION AND INDEXING OF AGENCY ORDERS]

(a)   In addition to other requirements imposed by any provision of law, each agency shall make all written final orders available for public inspection and copying and index them by name and subject. An agency shall delete from those orders identifying details to the extent required by any provision of law [or necessary to prevent a clearly unwarranted invasion of privacy or release of trade secrets]. In each case the justification for the deletion must be explained in writing and attached to the order.

(b)   A written final order may not be relied on as precedent by an agency to the detriment of any person until has been made available for public inspection and indexed in the manner described in subsection (a). This provision is inapplicable to any person who has actual timely knowledge of the order. The burden of proving that knowledge is on the agency.

§ 2-103. [DECLARATORY ORDERS] OMITTED

§ 2-104. [REQUIRED RULEMAKING]

In addition to other rulemaking requirements imposed by law, each agency shall:

(1)   adopt as a rule a description of the organization of the agency which states the general course and method of its operations and where and how the public may obtain information or make submissions or requests;

(2)   adopt rules of practice setting forth the nature and requirements of all formal and informal procedures available to the public, including a description of all forms and instructions that are to be used by the public in dealing with the agency; [and]

(3)   as soon as feasible and to the extent practicable, adopt rules, in addition to those otherwise required by this Act, embodying appropriate standards, principles, and procedural safeguards that the agency will apply to the law it administers [; and][.]

[(4)   as soon as feasible and to the extent practicable, adopt rules to supersede principles of law or policy lawfully declared by the agency as the basis for its decisions in particular cases.]

§ 2-105. [MODEL RULES OF PROCEDURE]

In accordance with the rulemaking requirements of this Act, the [attorney general] shall adopt model rules of procedure appropriate for use by as many agencies as possible. The model rules must deal with all general functions and duties performed in common by several agencies. Each agency shall adopt as much of the model rules as is practicable under its circumstances. To the extent an agency adopts the model rules, it shall do so in accordance with the rule-making requirements of this Act. Any agency adopting a rule of procedure that differs from the model rules shall include in the rule a finding stating the reasons why the relevant portions of the model rules were impracticable under the circumstances.

ARTICLE III RULEMAKING

Chapter i—Adoption and Effectiveness of Rules

§ 3-101. [ADVISE ON POSSIBLE RULES BEFORE NOTICE OF PROPOSED RULE ADOPTION]

(a)   In addition to seeking information by other methods, an agency, before publication of a notice of proposed rule adoption under Section 3–103, may solicit comments from the public on a subject matter of possible rulemaking under active consideration within the agency by causing notice to be published in the administrative bulletin of the subject matter and indicating where, when, and how persons may comment.

(b)   Each agency may also appoint committees to comment, before publication of a notice of proposed rule adoption under Section 3–103, on the subject matter of a possible rulemaking under active consideration within the agency. The membership of those committees must be published at least annually in the administrative bulletin.

§ 3-102. [PUBLIC RULEMAKING DOCKET]

(a)   Each agency shall maintain a current, public rulemaking docket.

(b)   The rulemaking docket [must] [may] contain a listing of the precise subject matter of each possible rule currently under active consideration within the agency for proposal under Section 3–103, the name and address of agency personnel with whom persons may communicate with respect to the matter, and an indication of the present status within the agency of that possible rule.

(c)   The rulemaking docket must list each pending rulemaking proceeding. A rulemaking proceeding is pending from the time it is commenced, by publication of a notice of proposed rule adoption, to the time it is terminated, by publication of a notice of termination or the rule becoming effective. For each rulemaking proceeding, the docket must indicate:

(1)   the subject matter of the proposed rule;

(2)   a citation to all published notices relating to the proceeding;

(3)   where written submissions on the proposed rule may be inspected;

(4)   the time during which written submissions may be made;

(5)   the names of persons who have made written requests for an opportunity to make oral presentations on the proposed rule, where those requests may be inspected, and where and when oral presentations may be made;

(6)   whether a written request for the issuance of a regulatory analysis of the proposed rule has been filed, whether that analysis has been issued, and where the written request and analysis may be inspected;

(7)   the current status of the proposed rule and any agency determinations with respect thereto;

(8)   any known timetable for agency decisions or other action in the proceeding;

(9)   the date of the rule's adoption;

(10)   the date of the rule's filing, indexing, and publication; and

(11)   when the rule will become effective.

§ 3-103. [NOTICE OF PROPOSED RULE ADOPTION]

(a)   At least 30 days before the adoption of a rule an agency shall cause notice of its contemplated action to be published in the administrative bulletin. The notice of proposed rule adoption must include;

(1)   a short explanation of the purpose of the proposed rule;

(2)   the specific legal authority authorizing the proposed rule;

(3)   subject to Section 2–101(e), the text of the proposed rule;

(4)   where, when, and how persons may present their views on the proposed rule; and

(5)   where, when, and how persons may demand an oral proceeding on the proposed rule if the notice does not already provide for one.

(b)   Within 3 days after its publication in the administrative bulletin, the agency shall cause a copy of the notice of proposed rule adoption to be mailed to each person who has made a timely request to the agency for a mailed copy of the notice. An agency may charge persons for the actual cost of providing them with mailed copies.

§ 3-104. [PUBLIC PARTICIPATION]

(a)   For at least 30 days after publication of the notice of proposed rule adoption, an agency shall afford persons the opportunity to submit in writing, argument, data, and views on the proposed rule.

(b)(1) An agency shall schedule an oral proceeding on a proposed rule if, within 20 days after the published notice of proposed rule adoption, a written request for an oral proceeding is submitted by the administrative rules review committee, the administrative rules counsel, a political subdivision, an agency, or 25 persons. At that proceeding, persons may present oral argument, data, and views on the proposed rule.

(2)   An oral proceeding on a proposed rule, if required, may not be held earlier than 20 days after notice of its location and time is published in the administrative bulletin.

(3)   The agency, a member of the agency, or another presiding officer designated by the agency, shall preside at a required oral proceeding on a proposed rule. If the agency does not preside, the presiding official shall prepare a memorandum for consideration by the agency summarizing the contents of the presentations made at the oral proceeding.

Oral proceedings must be open to the public and be recorded by stenographic or other means.

(4)   Each agency shall issue rules for the conduct of oral rulemaking proceedings. Those rules may include provisions calculated to prevent undue repetition in the oral proceedings.

§ 3-105. [REGULATORY ANALYSIS]

(a)   An agency shall issue a regulatory analysis of a proposed rule if, within 20 days after the published notice of proposed rule adoption, a written request for the analysis is filed in the office of the secretary of state by the administrative rules review committee, the governor, a political subdivision, an agency, or 300 persons signing the request. The secretary of state shall immediately forwad to the agency a certified copy of the filed request.

(b)   Except to the extent that the written request expressly waives one or more of the following, the regulatory analysis must contain: [omitted]

(c)   Each regulatory analysis must include quantification of the data to the extent practicable and must take account of both short-term and long-term consequences.

(d)   A concise summary of the regulatory analysis must be published in the administrative bulletin at least 10 days before the earliest. [omitted]

(e)   The published summary of the regulatory analysis must also indicate where persons may obtain copies of the full text of the regulatory analysis and where, when, and how persons may present their views on the proposed rule and demand an oral proceeding thereon if one is not already provided.

(f)   If the agency has made a good faith effort to comply with the requirements of subsections (a) through (f), the rule may not be invalidated on the ground that the contents of the regulatory analysis are insufficient or inaccurate.

§ 3-106. [TIME AND MANNER OF RULE ADOPTION]

(a)   An agency may not adopt a rule until the period for making written submissions and oral presentations has expired.

(b)   Within 180 days after the later of (i) the publication of the notice of proposed rule adoption, or (ii) the end of oral proceedings thereon, an agency shall adopt a rule

pursuant to the rulemaking proceeding or terminate the proceeding by publication of a notice to that effect in the [administrative bulletin].

(c)   Before the adoption of a rule, an agency shall consider the written submissions, oral submissions or any memorandum summarizing oral submissions, and any regulatory analysis, provided for by this Chapter.

(d)   Within the scope of its delegated authority, an agency may use its own experience, technical competence, specialized knowledge, and judgment in the adoption of a rule.

§ 3-107. [VARIANCE BETWEEN ADOPTED RULE AND PUBLISHED NOTICE OF PROPOSED RULE ADOPTION] OMITTED

§ 3-108. [GENERAL EXEMPTION FROM PUBLIC RULE-MAKING PROCEDURES]

(a)   To the extent an agency for good cause finds that any requirements of Sections 3–103 through 3–107 are unnecessary, impracticable, or contrary to the public interest in the process of adopting a particular rule, those requirements do not apply. The agency shall incorporate the required finding and a brief statement of its supporting reasons in each rule adopted in reliance upon this subsection.

(b)   In an action contesting a rule adopted under subsection (a), the burden is upon the agency to demonstrate that any omitted requirements of Section 3–103 through 3–107 were impracticable, unnecessary, or contrary to the public interest in the particular circumstances involved.

(c)   Within 2 years after the effective date of a rule adopted under subsection (a), the administrative rules review committee or the governor may request the agency to hold a rulemaking proceeding thereon according to the requirements of Sections 3–103 through 3–107. The request must be in writing and filed in the office of the secretary of state. The secretary of state shall immediately forward to the agency and to the administrative rules editor a certified copy of the request. Notice of the filing of the request must be published in the next issue of the administrative bulletin. The rule in question ceases to be effective 180 days after the request is filed. However, an agency, after the filing of the request, may subsequently adopt an identical rule in a rulemaking proceeding conducted pursuant to the requirements of Sections 3–103 through 3–107.

§ 3-109. [EXEMPTION FOR CERTAIN RULES]

(a)   An agency need not follow the provisions of Sections 3–103 through 3–108 in the adoption of a rule that only defines the meaning of a statute or other provision of law or precedent if the agency does not possess delegated authority to bind the courts to any extent with its definition. A rule adopted under this subsection must include a statement that it was adopted under this subsection when it is published in the administrative bulletin, and there must be an indication to that effect adjacent to the rule when it is published in the administrative code.

(b)   A reviewing court shall determine wholly de novo the validity of a rule within the scope of subsection (a) that is adopted without complying with the provisions of Sections 3–103 through 3–108.

§ 3-110. [CONCISE EXPLANATORY STATEMENT]

(a)   At the time it adopts a rule, an agency shall issue a concise explanatory statement containing:

(1)   its reasons for adopting the rule; and

(2)   an indication of any change between the text of the proposed rule contained in the published notice of proposed rule adoption and the text of the rule as finally adopted, with the reasons for any change.

(b)   Only the reasons contained in the concise explanatory statement may be used by any party as justifications for the adoption of the rule in any proceeding in which its validity is at issue.

§ 13-111. [CONTENTS, STYLE, AND FORM OF RULE] OMITTED

§ 3-112. [AGENCY RULEMAKING RECORD]

(a)   An agency shall maintain an official rulemaking record for each rule it (i) proposes by publication in the [administrative bulletin] of a notice of proposed rule adoption, or (ii) adopts. The record and materials incorporated by reference must be available for public inspection.

(b)   The agency rulemaking record must contain:

(1)   copies of all publications in the [administrative bulletin] with respect to the rule or the proceeding upon which the rule is based;

(2)   copies of any portions of the agency's public rulemaking docket containing entries relating to the rule or the proceeding upon which the rule is based;

(3)   all written petitions, requests, submissions, and comments received by the agency and all other written materials considered by the agency in connection with the formulation, proposal, or adoption of the rule or the proceeding upon which the rule is based;

(4)   any official transcript of oral presentations made in the proceeding upon which the rule is based or, if not transcribed, any tape recording or stenographic record of those presentations, and any memorandum prepared by a presiding official summarizing the contents of those presentations;

(5)   a copy of any regulatory analysis prepared for the proceeding upon which the rule is based;

(6)   a copy of the rule and explanatory statement filed in the office of the [secretary of state];

(7)   all petitions for exceptions to, amendments of, or repeal or suspension of, the rule;

(8)   a copy of any request filed pursuant to Section 3–108(c);

(9)   a copy of any objection to the rule filed by the administrative rules review committee pursuant to Section 3–204(d) and the agency's response, and

(10)   a copy of any filed executive order with respect to the rule.

(c)   Upon judicial review, the record required by this section constitutes the official agency rulemaking record with respect to a rule. Except as provided in Section 3–110(b) or otherwise required by a provision of law, the agency rulemaking record need not constitute the exclusive basis for agency action on that rule or for judicial review thereof.

§ 3-113. [INVALIDITY OF RULES NOT ADOPTED ACCORDING TO CHAPTER; TIME LIMITATION] OMITTED

§ 3-114. [FILING OF RULES] OMITTED

§ 3-115. [EFFECTIVE DATE OF RULES] OMITTED

§ 3-116. [SPECIAL PROVISION FOR CERTAIN CLASSES OF RULES] OMITTED

§ 3-117. [PETITION FOR ADOPTION OF RULE]

Any person may petition an agency requesting the adoption of a rule. Each agency shall prescribe by rule the form of the petition and the procedure for its submission, consideration, and disposition. Within [60] days after submission of a petition, the agency shall either (i) deny the petition in writing, stating its reasons therefor, (ii) initiate rulemaking proceedings in accordance with this Chapter, or (iii) if otherwise lawful, adopt a rule.

Chapter II—Review of Agency Rules

§ 3-201. [REVIEW BY AGENCY]

At least annually, each agency shall review all of its rules to determine whether any new rule should be adopted. In conducting that review, each agency shall prepare a written report summarizing its findings, its supporting reasons, and any proposed course of action. For each rule, the annual report must include, at least once every 7 years, a concise statement of:

(1)   the rule's effectiveness in achieving its objectives, including a summary of any available data supporting the conclusions reached;

(2)   criticisms of the rule received during the previous 7 years, including a summary of any petitions for waiver of the rule tendered to the agency or granted by it; and

(3)   alternative solutions to the criticisms and the reasons they were rejected or the changes made in the rule in response to those criticisms and the reasons for the changes. A copy of the annual report must be sent to the administrative rules review committee and the administrative rules counsel and be available for public inspection.

§ 3-202. [REVIEW BY GOVERNOR; ADMINISTRATIVE RULES COUNSEL]

(a)   To the extent the agency itself would have authority, the governor may rescind or suspend all or a severable portion of a rule of an agency. In exercising this authority, the governor shall act by an executive order that is subject to the provisions of this Act applicable to the adoption and effectiveness of a rule.

(b)   The Governor may summarily terminate any pending rulemaking proceeding by an executive order to that effect, stating therein the reasons for the action. The executive order must be filed in the office of the [secretary of state], which shall promptly forward a certified copy to the agency and the [administrative rules editor]. An executive order terminating a rulemaking proceeding becomes effective on [the date it is filed] and must be published in the next issue of the [administrative bulletin].

(c)   There is created within the office of the governor, an administrative rules counsel to advise the governor in the execution of the authority vested under this Article. The governor shall appoint the administrative rules counsel who shall serve at the pleasure of the governor.

§ 3-203. [ADMINISTRATIVE RULES REVIEW COMMITTEE] OMITTED

§ 3-204. [REVIEW BY THE ADMINISTRATIVE RULES REVIEW COMMITTEE] OMITTED

Article IV Adjudicative Proceedings

Chapter I—Availability of Adjudicative Proceedings; Applications; Licenses

§ 4-101. [ADJUDICATIVE PROCEEDINGS; WHEN REQUIRED; EXCEPTIONS]

(a)   An agency shall conduct an adjudicative proceeding as the process for formulating and issuing an order, unless the order is a decision:

(1)   to issue or not to issue a complaint, summons, or similar accusation;

(2)   to initiate or not to initiate an investigation, prosecution, or other proceeding before the agency, another agency, or a court; or

(3)   under Section 4–103, not to conduct an adjudicative proceeding.

(b)   This Article applies to rulemaking proceedings only to the extent that another statute expressly so requires.

§ 4-102. [ADJUDICATIVE PROCEEDINGS; COMMENCEMENT]

(a)   An agency may commence an adjudicative proceeding at any time with respect to a matter within the agency's jurisdiction.

(b)   An agency shall commence an adjudicative proceeding upon the application of any person, unless:

(1)   the agency lacks jurisdiction of the subject matter;

(2)   resolution of the matter requires the agency to exercise discretion within the scope of Section 4–101 (a);

(3)   a statute vests the agency with discretion to conduct or not to conduct an adjudicative proceeding before issuing an order to resolve the matter and, in the exercise of that discretion, the agency has determined not to conduct an adjudicative proceeding before issuing an order to resolve the matter and, in the exercise of that discretion, the agency has determined not to conduct an adjudicative proceeding;

(4)   resolution of the matter does not require the agency to issue an order that determines the applicant's legal rights, duties, privileges, immunities, or other legal interests;

(5)   the matter was not timely submitted to the agency; or

(6)   the matter was not submitted in a form substantially complying with any applicable provision of law.

(c)   An application for an agency to issue an order includes an application for the agency to conduct appropriate adjudicative proceedings, whether or not the applicant expressly requests those proceedings.

(d)   An adjudicative proceeding commences when the agency or a presiding officer:

(1)   notifies a party that a pre-hearing conference, hearing, or other state of an adjudicative proceeding will be conducted; or

(2)   begins to take action on a matter that appropriately may be determined by an adjudicative proceeding, unless this action is:

(i)   an investigation for the purpose of determining whether an adjudicative proceeding should be conducted; or

(ii)   a decision which, under Section 4–101(a), the agency may make without conducting an adjudicative proceeding.

§ 4-103. [DECISION NOT TO CONDUCT ADJUDICATIVE PROCEEDING]

If an agency decides not to conduct an adjudicative proceeding in response to an application, the agency shall furnish the applicant a copy of its decision in writing, with a brief statement of the agency's reasons and of any administrative review available to the applicant.

§ 4-104. [AGENCY ACTION ON APPLICATIONS]

(a)   Except to the extent that the time limits in this subsection are inconsistent with limits established by another statute for any stage of the proceedings, an agency shall process an application for an order, other than a declaratory order, as follows:

(1)   Within 30 days after receipt of the application, the agency shall examine the application, notify the applicant of any apparent errors or omissions, request any additional information the agency wishes to obtain and is permitted by law to require, and notify the applicant of the name, official title, mailing address and telephone number of an agency member or employee who may be contacted regarding the application.

(2)   Except in situations governed by paragraph (3), within [90] days after receipt of the application or of the response to a timely request made by the agency pursuant to paragraph (1), the agency shall:

(i)   approve or deny the application, in whole or in part, on the basis of emergency or summary adjudicative proceedings, if those proceedings are available under this Act for disposition of the matter;

(ii)   commence a formal adjudicative hearing or a conference adjudicative hearing in accordance with this Act; or

(iii)   dispose of the application in accordance with Section 4–103.

(3)   If the application pertains to subject matter that is not available when the application is filed but may be available in the future, including an application for housing or employment at a time no vacancy exists, the agency may proceed to make a determination of eligibility within the time provided in paragraph (2). If the agency determines that the applicant is eligible, the agency shall maintain the application on the agency's list of eligible applicants as provided by law and, upon request, shall notify the applicant of the status of the application.

(b)   If a timely and sufficient application has been made for renewal of a license with reference to any activity of a continuing nature, the existing license does not expire until the agency has taken final action upon the application for renewal or, if the agency's action is unfavorable, until the last day for seeking judicial review of the agency's action or a later date fixed by the reviewing court.

§ 4-105. [AGENCY ACTION AGAINST LICENSEES] OMITTED

Chapter II—Formal Adjudicative Hearing

§ 4-201. [APPLICABILITY]

An adjudicative proceeding is governed by this chapter, except as otherwise provided by:

(1)   a statute other than this Act;

(2)   a rule that adopts the procedures for the conference adjudicative hearing or summary adjudicative proceeding in accordance with the standards provided in this Act for those proceedings;

(3)   Section 4–501 pertaining to emergency adjudicative proceedings; or

(4)   Section 2–103 pertaining to declaratory proceedings.

§ 4-202. [PRESIDING OFFICER, DISQUALIFICATION, SUBSTITUTION]

(a)   The agency head, one or more members of the agency head, one or more administrative law judges assigned by the office of administrative hearings in accordance with Section 4–301 . . . in the discretion of the agency head, may be the presiding officer.

(b)   Any person serving or designated to serve along or with others as presiding officer is subject to disqualification for bias, prejudice, interest, or any other cause provided in this Act or for which a judge is or may be disqualified.

(c)   Any party may petition for the disqualification of a person promptly after receipt of notice indicating that the person will preside or promptly upon discovering facts establishing grounds for disqualification, whichever is later.

(d)   A person whose disqualification is requested shall determine whether to grant the petition, stating facts and reasons for the determination.

(e)   If a substitute is required for a person who is disqualified or becomes unavailable for any other reason, the substitute must be appointed by:

(1)   the governor, if the disqualified or unavailable person is an elected official; or

(2)   the appointing authority, if the disqualified or unavailable person is an appointed official.

(f)   Any action taken by a duly-appointed substitute for a disqualified or unavailable person is as effective as if taken by the latter.

§ 4-203. [REPRESENTATION]

(a)   Any party may participate in the hearing in person or, if the party is a corporation or other artificial person, by a duly authorized representative.

(b)   Whether or not participating in person, any party may be advised and represented at the party's own expense by counsel or, if permitted by law, other representative.

§ 4-204. [PRE-HEARING CONFERENCE—AVAILABILITY, NOTICE]

The presiding officer designated to conduct the hearing may determine, subject to the agency's rules, whether a pre-hearing conference will be conducted. If the conference is conducted:

(1)   The presiding officer shall promptly notify the agency of the determination that a pre-hearing conference will be conducted. The agency shall assign or request the office of administrative hearings to assign a presiding officer for the pre-hearing conference, exercising the same discretion as is provided by Section 4–202 concerning the selection of a presiding officer for a hearing.

(2)   The presiding officer for the pre-hearing conference shall set the time and place of the conference and give reasonable written notice to all parties and to all persons who have filed written petitions to intervene in the matter. The agency shall give notice to other persons entitled to notice under any provision of law.

(3)   The notice must include:

(i)   the names and mailing addresses of all parties and other persons to whom notice is being given by the presiding officer;

(ii)   the name, official title, mailing address, and telephone number of any counsel or employee who has been designated to appear for the agency;

(iii) the official file or other reference number, the name of the proceeding, and a general description of the subject matter;

(iv) a statement of the time, place, and nature of the pre-hearing conference;

(v) a statement of the legal authority and jurisdiction under which the pre-hearing conference and the hearing are to be held;

(vi) the name, official title, mailing address and telephone number of the presiding officer for the pre-hearing conference;

(vii) a statement that at the pre-hearing conference the proceeding, without further notice, may be converted into a conference adjudicative hearing or a summary adjudicative proceeding for disposition of the matter as provided by this Act; and

(viii) a statement that a party who fails to attend or participate in a pre-hearing conference, hearing, or other state of an adjudicative proceeding may be held in default under this Act.

(4) The notice may include any other matter that the presiding officer considers desirable to expedite the proceedings.

§ 4-205. [PRE-HEARING CONFERENCE—PROCEDURE AND PRE-HEARING ORDER]

(a) The presiding officer may conduct all or part of the pre-hearing conference by telephone, television, or other electronic means if each participant in the conference has an opportunity to participate in, to hear, and, if technically feasible, to see the entire proceeding while it is taking place.

(b) The presiding officer shall conduct the pre-hearing conference, as may be appropriate, to deal with such matters as conversion of the proceeding to another type, exploration of settlement possibilities, preparation of stipulations, clarification of issues, ruling on identity and limitation of the number of witnesses, objections to proffers of evidence, determination of the extent to which direct evidence, rebuttal evidence, or cross-examination will be presented in written form, and the extent to which telephone, television, or other electronic means will be used as a substitute for proceedings in person, order of presentation of evidence and cross-examination, rulings regarding issuance of subpoenas,

discovery orders and protective orders, and such other matters as will promote the orderly and prompt conduct of the hearings. The presiding officer shall issue a pre-hearing order incorporating the matters determined at the pre-hearing conference.

(c) If a pre-hearing conference is not held, the presiding officer for the hearing may issue a pre-hearing order, based on the pleadings, to regulate the conduct of the proceedings.

§ 4-206. [NOTICE OF HEARING]

(a) The presiding officer for the hearing shall set the time and place of the hearing and give reasonable written notice to all parties and to all persons who have filed written petitions to intervene in the matter.

(b) The notice must include a copy of any pre-hearing order rendered in the matter.

(c) To the extent not included in a pre-hearing order accompanying it, the notice must include:

(1) the names and mailing addresses of all parties and other person to whom notice is being given by the presiding officer;

(2) the name, official title, mailing address and telephone number of any counsel or employee who has been designated to appear for the agency;

(3) the official file or other reference number, the name of the proceeding, and a general description of the subject matter;

(4) a statement of the time, place, and nature of the hearing;

(5) a statement of the legal authority and jurisdiction under which the hearing is to be held;

(6) the name, official title, mailing address, and telephone number of the presiding officer;

(7) a statement of the issues involved and, to the extent known to the presiding officer, of the matters asserted by the parties; and

(8) a statement that a party who fails to attend or participate in a pre-hearing conference, hearing, or other state of an adjudicative proceeding may be held in default under this Act.

(d) The notice may include any other matters the presiding officer considers desirable to expedite the proceedings.

(e)   The agency shall give notice to persons entitled to notice under any provision of law who have not been given notice by the presiding officer. Notice under this subsection may include all types of information provided in subsections (a) through (d) or may consist of a brief statement indicating the subject matter, parties, time, place, and nature of the hearing, manner in which copies of the notice to the parties may be inspected and copied, and name and telephone number of the presiding officer.

§ 4-207. [PLEADINGS, BRIEFS, MOTIONS, SERVICE]

(a)   The presiding officer, at appropriate stages of the proceedings, shall give all parties full opportunity to file pleadings, motions, objections and offers of settlement.

(b)   The presiding officer, at appropriate stages of the proceedings, may give all parties full opportunity to file briefs, proposed findings of fact and conclusions of law, and proposed initial or final orders.

(c)   A party shall serve copies of any filed item on all parties, by mail or any means prescribed by agency rule.

§ 4-208. [DEFAULT]

(a)   If a party fails to attend or participate in a pre-hearing conference, hearing, or other stage of an adjudicative proceeding, the presiding officer may serve upon all parties written notice of a proposed default order, including a statement of the grounds.

(b)   Within 7 days after service of a proposed default order, the party against whom it was issued may file a written motion requesting that the proposed default order be vacated and stating the grounds relied upon. During the time within which a party may file a written motion under this subsection, the presiding officer may adjourn the proceedings or conduct them without the participation of the party against whom a proposed default order was issued, having due regard for the interests of justice and the orderly and prompt conduct of the proceedings.

(c)   The presiding officer shall either issue or vacate the default order promptly after expiration of the time within which the party may file a written motion under subsection (b).

§ 4-209. [INTERVENTION] OMITTED

§ 4-210. [SUBPOENAS, DISCOVERY, AND PROTECTIVE ORDERS] OMITTED

§ 4-211. [PROCEDURE AT HEARING]

At a hearing:

(1)   The presiding officer shall regulate the course of the proceedings in conformity with any pre-hearing order.

(2)   To the extent necessary for full disclosure of all relevant facts and issues, the presiding officer shall afford to all parties the opportunity to respond, present evidence and argument, conduct cross-examination, and submit rebuttal evidence, except as restricted by a limited grant of intervention or by the pre-hearing order.

(3)   The presiding officer may give nonparties an opportunity to present oral or written statements. If the presiding officer proposes to consider a statement by a nonparty, the presiding officer shall give all parties an opportunity to challenge or rebut it and, on motion of any party, the presiding officer shall require the statement to be given under oath or affirmation.

(4)   The presiding officer may conduct all or part of the hearing by telephone, television, or other electronic means, if each participant in the hearing has an opportunity to participate in, to hear, and, if technically feasible, to see the entire proceeding while it is taking place.

(5)   The presiding officer shall cause the hearing to be recorded at the agency's expense. The agency is not required, at its expense, to prepare a transcript, unless required to do so by a provision of law. Any party, at the party's expense, may cause a reporter approved by the agency to prepare a transcript from the agency's record, or cause additional recordings to be made during the hearing if the making of the additional recordings does not cause distraction or disruption.

(6)   The hearing is open to public observation, except for the parts that the presiding officer states to be closed pursuant to a provision of law expressly authorizing closure. To the extent that a hearing is conducted by telephone, television, or other electronic means, and is not closed, the availability of public observation is satisfied by giving members

of the public an opportunity, at reasonable times, to hear or inspect the agency's record, and to inspect any transcript obtained by the agency.

§ 4-212. [EVIDENCE, OFFICIAL NOTICE] OMITTED

§ 4-213. [EX PARTE COMMUNICATIONS]

(a)   Except as provided in subsection (b) or unless required for the disposition of ex parte matters specifically authorized by statute, a presiding officer serving in an adjudicative proceeding may not communicate, directly or indirectly, regarding any issue in the proceeding, while the proceeding is pending, with any party, with any person who has a direct or indirect interest in the outcome of the proceeding, or with any person who presided at a previous stage of the proceeding, without notice and opportunity for all parties to participate in the communication.

(b)   A member of a multi-member panel of presiding officers may communicate with other members of the panel regarding a matter pending before the panel, and any presiding officer may receive aid from staff assistants if the assistants do not (i) receive ex parte communications of a type that the presiding officer would be prohibited from receiving or (ii) furnish, augment, diminish, or modify the evidence in the record.

(c)   Unless required for the disposition of ex parte matters specifically authorized by statute, no party to an adjudicative proceeding, and no person who has a direct or indirect interest in the outcome of the proceeding or who presided at a previous stage of the proceeding, may communicate, directly or indirectly, in connection with any issue in that proceeding, while the proceeding is pending, with any person serving as presiding officer, without notice and opportunity for all parties to participate in the communication.

(d)   If, before serving as presiding officer in an adjudicative proceeding, a person receives an ex parte communication of a type that could not properly be received while serving, the person, promptly after starting to serve, shall disclose the communication in the manner prescribed in subsection (e).

(e)   A presiding officer who receives an ex parte communication in violation of this section shall place on the record of the pending matter all written communications received, all written responses to the communications, and a memorandum stating the substance of all oral communications received, all responses made, and the identity of each person from whom the presiding officer received an ex parte communication, and shall advise all parties that these matters have been placed on the record. Any party desiring to rebut the ex parte communication must be allowed to do so, upon requesting the opportunity for rebuttal within [10] days after notice of the communication.

(f)   If necessary to eliminate the effect of an ex parte communication received in violation of this section, a presiding officer who receives the communication may be disqualified and the portions of the record pertaining to the communication may be sealed by protective order.

(g)   The agency shall, and any party may, report any willful violation of this section to appropriate authorities for any disciplinary proceedings provided by law. In addition, each agency by rule may provide for appropriate sanctions, including default, for any violations of this section.

§ 4-214. [SEPARATION OF FUNCTIONS]

(a)   A person who has served as investigator, prosecutor or advocate in an adjudicative proceeding or in its pre-adjudicative stage may not serve as presiding officer or assist or advise a presiding officer in the same proceeding.

(b)   A person who is subject to the authority, direction, or discretion of one who has served is investigator, prosecutor, or advocate in an adjudicative proceeding or in its pre-adjudicative stage may not serve as presiding officer or assist or advise a presiding officer in the same proceeding.

(c)   A person who has participated in a determination of probable cause or other equivalent preliminary determination in an adjudicative proceeding may serve as presiding officer or assist or advise a presiding officer in the same proceeding, unless a party demonstrates grounds for disqualification in accordance with Section 4–202.

(d)   A person may serve as presiding officer at successive stages of the same adjudicative proceeding, unless a party demonstrates grounds for disqualification in accordance with Section 4–202.

§ 4-215. [FINAL ORDER, INITIAL ORDER]

(a)   If the presiding officer is the agency head, the presiding officer shall render a final order.

(b)   If the presiding officer is not the agency head, the presiding officer shall render an initial order, which becomes a final order unless reviewed in accordance with Section 4–216.

(c)   A final order or initial order must include, separately stated, findings of fact, conclusions of law, and policy reasons for the decision if it is an exercise of the agency's discretion, for all aspects of the order, including the remedy prescribed and, if applicable, the action taken on a petition for stay of effectiveness. Findings of fact, if set forth in language that is no more than mere repetition or paraphrase of the relevant provision of law, must be accompanied by a concise and explicit statement of the underlying facts of record to support the findings. If a party has submitted proposed findings of fact, the order must include a ruling on the proposed findings. The order must also include a statement of the available procedures and time limits for seeking reconsideration or other administrative relief. An initial order must include a statement of any circumstances under which the initial order, without further notice, may become a final order.

(d)   Findings of fact must be based exclusively upon the evidence of record in the adjudicative proceeding and on matters officially notice in that proceeding. Findings must be based upon the kind of evidence on which reasonably prudent persons are accustomed to rely in the conduct of their serious affairs and may be based upon such evidence even if it would be inadmissible in a civil trial. The presiding officer's experience, technical competence, and specialized knowledge may be utilized in evaluating evidence.

(e)   If a person serving or designated to serve as presiding officer becomes unavailable, for any reason, before rendition of the final order or initial order, a substitute presiding officer must be appointed as provided in Section 4–202. The substitute presiding officer shall use any existing record and may conduct any further proceedings appropriate in the interests of justice.

(f)   The presiding officer may allow the parties a designated amount of time after conclusion of the hearing for the submission of proposed findings.

(g)   A final order or initial order pursuant to this section must be rendered in writing 90 days after conclusion of the hearing or after submission of proposed findings in accordance with subsection (f) unless this period is waived or extended with the written consent of all parties for good cause shown.

(h)   The presiding officer shall cause copies of the final order or initial order to be delivered to each party and to the agency head.

§ 4-216. [REVIEW OF INITIAL ORDER; EXCEPTIONS TO REVIEWABILITY]

(a)   The agency head, upon its own motion may, and upon appeal by any party shall, review an initial order, except to the extent that:

(1)   a provision of law precludes or limits agency review of the initial order; or

(2)   the agency head, in the exercises of discretion conferred by a provision of law,

(i)   determines to review some but not all issues, or not to exercise any review,

(ii)   delegates its authority to review the initial order to one or more persons, or

(iii)   authorizes one or more persons to review the initial order, subject to further review by the agency head.

(b)   A petition for appeal from an initial order must be filed with the agency head, or with any person designated for this purpose by rule of the agency, within 10 days after rendition of the initial order. If the agency head on its own motion decides to review an initial order, the agency head shall give written notice of its intention, to review the initial order within 10 days after its rendition. The 10-day period for a party to file a petition for appeal or for the agency head to give notice of its intention to review an initial order on the agency head's own motion is tolled by the submission of a timely petition for reconsideration of the initial order pursuant to Section 4–218, and a new 10-day period starts to run upon disposition of the petition for reconsideration. If an initial order is subject both to a timely petition for reconsideration and to a petition for appeal or to review by the agency head on its own motion, the petition for reconsideration must be disposed of first, unless the agency head determines that action on the petition for reconsideration has been unreasonably delayed.

(c)   The petition for appeal must state its basis. If the agency head on its own motion gives notice of its intent to review an initial order, the agency head shall identify the issues that it intends to review.

(d)   The presiding officer for the review of an initial order shall exercise all the decision-making power that the presiding officer would have had to render a final order had the presiding officer presided over the hearing, except to the extent that the issues subject to review are limited by a provision of law or by the presiding officer upon notice to all parties.

(e)   The presiding officer shall afford each party an opportunity to present briefs and may afford each party an opportunity to present oral argument.

(f)   Before rendering a final order, the presiding officer may cause a transcript to be prepared, at the agency's expense, of such portions of the proceeding under review as the presiding officer considers necessary.

(g)   The presiding officer may render a final order disposing of the proceeding or may remand the matter for further proceedings with instructions to the persons who rendered the initial order. Upon remanding a matter, the presiding officer may order such temporary relief as is authorized and appropriate.

(h)   A final order or an order remanding the matter for further proceedings must be rendered in writing within [60] days after receipt of briefs and oral argument unless that period is waived or extended with the written consent of all parties or for good cause shown.

(i)   A final order or an order remanding the matter for further proceedings under this section must identify any difference between this order and the initial order and must include, or incorporate by express reference to the initial order, all the matters required by Section 4–215(c).

(j)   The presiding officer shall cause copies of the final order or order remanding the matter for further proceedings to be delivered to each party and to the agency head.

[SECTIONS 4–217 THROUGH 4–220 ARE OMITTED.]

§ 4-221. [AGENCY RECORD]

(a)   An agency shall maintain an official record of each adjudicative proceeding under this Chapter.

(b)   The agency record consists only of:

(1)   notices of all proceedings;

(2)   any pre-hearing order;

(3)   any motions, pleadings, briefs, petitions, requests, and intermediate rulings;

(4)   evidence received or considered;

(5)   a statement of matters officially noticed;

(6)   proffers of proof and objections and rulings thereon;

(7)   proposed findings, requested orders, and exceptions;

(8)   the record prepared for the presiding officer at the hearing, together with any transcript of all or part of the hearing considered before final disposition of the proceeding;

(9)   any final order, initial order, or order on reconsideration;

(10)   staff memoranda or data submitted to the presiding officer, unless prepared and submitted by personal assistants and not inconsistent with Section 4–213(b); and

(11)   matters placed on the record after an ex parte communication.

(c)   Except to the extent that this Act or another statute provides otherwise, the agency record constitutes the exclusive basis for agency action in adjudicative proceedings under this Chapter and for judicial review thereof.

Chapter III—Office of Administrative Hearings [omitted]

Chapter IV—Conference Adjudicative Hearing [omitted]

Chapter V—Emergency and Summary Adjudicative Proceedings [omitted]

ARTICLE V JUDICIAL REVIEW AND CIVIL ENFORCEMENT

Chapter I—Judicial Review

§ 5-101. [RELATIONSHIP BETWEEN THIS ACT AND OTHER LAW ON JUDICIAL REVIEW AND OTHER JUDICIAL REMEDIES]

This Act establishes the exclusive means of judicial review of agency action, but:

(1)   The provisions of this Act for judicial review do not apply to litigation in which the sole issue is a claim for money damages or compensation and the agency whose action is at issue does not have statutory authority to determine the claim.

(2)   Ancillary procedural matters, including intervention, class actions, consolidation, joinder, severance, transfer, protective orders, and other relief from disclosure of privileged or confidential material, are governed, to the extent not inconsistent with this Act, by other applicable law.

(3)   If the relief available under other sections of this Act is not equal or substantially equivalent to the relief otherwise available under law, the relief otherwise available and the related procedures supersede and supplement this Act to the extent necessary for their effectuation. The applicable provisions of this Act and other law must be combined to govern a single proceeding, or if the court orders, 2 or more separate proceedings, with or without transfer to other courts, but no type of relief may be sought in a combined proceeding after expiration of the time limit for doing so.

§ 5-102. [FINAL AGENCY ACTION REVIEWABLE]

(a)   A person who qualifies under this Act regarding (i) standing (Section 5–106), (ii) exhaustion of administrative remedies (Section 5–107), and (iii) time for filing the petition for review (Section 5–108), and other applicable provisions of law regarding bond, compliance, and other preconditions is entitled to judicial review of final agency action, whether or not the person has sought judicial review of any related non-final agency action.

(b)   For purposes of this section and Section 5–103:

(1)   "Final agency action" means the whole or a part of any agency action other than non-final agency action;

(2)   "Non-final agency action" means the whole or a part of an agency determination, investigation, proceeding, hearing, conference, or other process that the agency intends or is reasonably believed to intend to be preliminary, preparatory, procedural, or intermediate with regard to subsequent agency action of that agency or another agency.

[SECTIONS 5–103 THROUGH 5–115 ARE OMITTED.]

§ 5-116. [SCOPE OF REVIEW; GROUNDS FOR INVALIDITY]

(a)   Except to the extent that this Act or another statute provides otherwise:

(1)   The burden of demonstrating the invalidity of agency action is on the party asserting invalidity; and

(2)   The validity of agency action must be determined in accordance with the standards of review provided in this section, as applied to the agency action at the time it was taken.

(b)   The court shall make a separate and distinct ruling on each material issue on which the court's decision is based.

(c)   The court shall grant relief only if it determines that a person seeking judicial relief has been substantially prejudiced by any one or more of the following:

(1)   The agency action, or the statute or rule on which the agency action is based, is unconstitutional on its face or as applied.

(2)   The agency has acted beyond the jurisdiction conferred by any provision by law.

(3)   The agency has not decided all issues requiring resolution.

(4)   The agency has erroneously interpreted or applied the law.

(5)   The agency has engaged in an unlawful procedure or decision-making process, or has failed to follow prescribed procedure.

(6)   The persons taking the agency action were improperly constituted as a decision-making body, motivated by an improper purpose, or subject to disqualification.

(7)   The agency action is based on a determination of fact, made or implied by the agency, that is not supported by evidence that is substantial when viewed in light of the whole record before the court, which includes the agency record for judicial review, supplemented by any additional evidence received by the court under this Act.

(8)   The agency action is:

(i)   outside the range of discretion delegated to the agency by any provision of law;

(ii)   agency action, other than a rule, that is inconsistent with a rule of the agency; [or]

(iii)   agency action, other than a rule, that is inconsistent with the agency's prior practice unless the agency justifies the inconsistency by stating facts and reasons to demonstrate a fair and rational basis for the inconsistency. [; or][.]

(iv)   [otherwise unreasonable, arbitrary or capricious.]

§ 5-117. [TYPE OF RELIEF]

(a)   The court may award damages or compensation only to the extent expressly authorized by another provision of law.

(b)   The court may grant other appropriate relief, whether mandatory, injunctive, or declaratory, preliminary or final; temporary or permanent; equitable or legal. In granting relief, the court may order agency action required by law, order agency exercise of discretion required by law, set aside or modify agency action, enjoin or stay the effectiveness of agency action, remand the matter for further proceedings, render a declaratory judgment, or take any other action that is authorized and appropriate.

(c)   The court may also grant necessary ancillary relief to redress the effects of official action wrongfully taken or withheld, but the court may award attorney's fees or witness fees only to the extent expressly authorized by other law.

(d)   If the court sets aside or modifies agency action or remands the matter to the agency for further proceedings, the court may make any interlocutory order it finds necessary to preserve the interests of the parties and the public pending further proceedings or agency action.

§ 5-118. [REVIEW BY HIGHER COURT]

Decisions on petitions for review of agency action are reviewable by the [appellate court] as in other civil cases.

OCCUPATIONAL SAFETY
AND HEALTH ACT (1970)*

§ 651. CONGRESSIONAL STATEMENT OF FINDINGS AND DECLARATION OF PURPOSE AND POLICY

(a)   The Congress finds that personal injuries and illnesses arising out of work situations impose a substantial burden upon, and are a hindrance to, interstate commerce in terms of lost production, wage loss, medical expenses, and disability compensation payments.

(b)   The Congress declares it to be its purpose and policy, through the exercise of its power to regulate commerce among the several States and with foreign nations and to provide for the general welfare, to assure so far as possible every working man and woman in the Nation safe and healthful working conditions and to preserve our human resources—

(1)   by encouraging employers and employees in their efforts to reduce the number of occupational safety and health hazards at their places of employment, and to stimulate employers and employees to institute new and to perfect existing programs for providing safe and healthful working conditions;

(2)   by providing that employers and employees have separate but dependent responsibilities and rights with respect to achieving safe and healthful working conditions;

(3)   by authorizing the Secretary of Labor to set mandatory occupational safety and health standards applicable to businesses affecting interstate commerce, and by

creating an Occupational Safety and Health Review Commission for carrying out adjudicatory functions under this chapter

(4)   by building upon advances already made through employer and employee initiative for providing safe and healthful working conditions;

(5)   by providing for research in the field of occupational safety and health, including the psychological factors involved, and by developing innovative methods, techniques, and approaches for dealing with occupational safety and health problems;

(6)   by exploring ways to discover latent diseases establishing causal connections between diseases and work in environmental conditions, and conducting other research relating to health problems, in recognition of the fact that occupational health standards present problems often different from those involved in occupational safety;

(7)   by providing medical criteria which will assure insofar as practicable that no employee will suffer diminished health, functional capacity, or life expectancy as a result of his work experience;

(8)   by providing for training programs to increase the number and competence of personnel engaged in the field of occupational safety and health;

(9)   by providing for the development and promulgation of occupational safety and health standards;

(10)   by providing an effective enforcement program which shall include a prohibition against giving advance notice of any inspection and sanctions for any individual

*We have reprinted only the first seven sections of this Act; there are twenty-eight sections in the Act.

violating this prohibition;

(11)   by encouraging the States to assume the fullest responsibility for the administration and enforcement of their occupational safety and health laws by providing grants to the States to assist in identifying their needs and responsibilities in the area of occupational safety and health, to develop plans in accordance with the provisions of this chapter, to improve the administration and enforcement of State occupational safety and health laws, and to conduct experimental and demonstration projects in connection therewith;

(12)   by providing for appropriate reporting procedures with respect to occupational safety and health which procedures will help achieve the objectives of this chapter and accurately describe the nature of the occupational safety and health problem;

(13)   by encouraging joint labor-management efforts to reduce injuries and disease arising out of employment.

(Pub. L. 91–595, §2, Dec. 29, 1970, 84 Stat. 1590).

§ 652. DEFINITIONS

For the purposes of this chapter—

(1)   The term "Secretary" means the Secretary of Labor.

(2)   The term "Commission" means the Occupational Safety and Health Review Commission established under this chapter.

(3)   The term "commerce" means trade, traffic, commerce, transportation, or communication among the several States, or between a State and any place outside thereof, or within the District of Columbia, or a possession of the United States (other than the Trust Territory of the Pacific Islands), or between points in the same State but through a point outside thereof.

(4)   The term "person" means one or more individuals, partnerships, associations, corporations, business trusts, legal representatives, or any organized group of persons.

(5)   The term "employer" means a person engaged in a business affecting commerce who has employees, but does not include the United States or any State or political subdivision of a State.

(6)   The term "employee" means an employee of an employer who is employed in a business of his employer which affects commerce.

(7)   The term "State" includes a State of the United States, the District of Columbia, Puerto Rico, the Virgin Islands, American Samoa, Guam, and the Trust Territory of the Pacific Islands.

(8)   The term "occupational safety and health standard" means a standard which requires conditions, or the adoption or use of one or more practices, means, methods, operations, or processes, reasonably necessary or appropriate to provide safe or healthful employment and places of employment.

(9)   The term "national consensus standard" means any occupational safety and health standard or modification thereof which (1) has been adopted and promulgated by a nationally recognized standards-producing organization under procedures whereby it can be determined by the Secretary that persons interested and affected by the scope or provisions of the standard have reached substantial agreement on its adoption, (2) was formulated in a manner which afforded an opportunity for diverse views to be considered and (3) has been designated as such a standard by the Secretary, after consultation with other appropriate Federal agencies.

(10)   The term "established Federal Standard" means any operative occupational safety and health standard established by any agency of the United States and presently in effect, or contained in any Act of Congress in force on December 29, 1970.

(11)   The term "Committee" means the National Advisory Committee on Occupational Safety and Health established under this chapter.

(12)   The term "Director" means the Director of the National Institute for Occupational Safety and Health.

(13)   The term "Institute" means the National Institute for Occupational Safety and Health established under this chapter.

§ 653. GEOGRAPHIC APPLICABILITY; JUDICIAL ENFORCEMENT; APPLICABILITY TO EXISTING STANDARDS; REPORT TO CONGRESS ON DUPLICATION AND COORDINATION OF FEDERAL LAWS; WORKMEN'S

COMPENSATION LAW OR COMMON LAW OR STATUTO-RY RIGHTS, DUTIES, OR LIABILITIES OF EMPLOYERS AND EMPLOYEES UNAFFECTED

(a)   This chapter shall apply with respect to employment performed in a workplace in a State, the District of Columbia, the Commonwealth of Puerto Rico, the Virgin Islands, American Samoa, Guam, the Trust Territory of the Pacific Islands, Lake Island, Outer Continental Shelf Lands defined in the Outer Continental Shelf Lands Act [43 U.S.C. 1331 et seq.], Johnston Island, and the Canal Zone. The Secretary of the Interior shall, by regulation, provide for judicial enforcement of this chapter by the courts established for areas in which there are no United States district courts having jurisdiction.

(b)(1) Nothing in this chapter shall apply to working conditions of employees with respect to which other Federal agencies, and State agencies acting under section 2021 of title 42, exercise statutory authority to prescribe or enforce standards or regulations affecting occupational safety or health.

(2)   The safety and health standards promulgated under the Act of June 30, 1936, commonly known as the Walsh Healey Act [41 U.S.C. 35 et seq.], the Service Contract Act of 1965 [41 U.S.C. 351 et seq.], Public Law 91–54, Act of August 9, 1969, Public Law 85–742, Act of August 23, 1958, and the National Foundation on Arts and Humanities Act [20 U.S.C. 951 et seq.] are superseded on the effective date of corresponding standards, promulgated under this chapter, which are determined by the Secretary to be more effective. Standards issued under the laws listed in this paragraph and in effect on or after the effective date of this chapter shall be deemed to be occupational safety and health standards issued under this chapter, as well as under such other Acts.

(3)   The Secretary shall, within three years after the effective date of this chapter, report to the Congress his recommendations for legislation to avoid unnecessary duplication and to achieve coordination between this chapter and other Federal laws.

(4)   Nothing in this chapter shall be construed to supersede or in any manner affect any workmen's compensation law or to enlarge or diminish or affect in any other manner the common law or statutory rights, duties, or liabilities of employers and employees under any law with respect to injuries, diseases, or death of employees arising out of, or in the course of, employment. . . .

§ 654. DUTIES OF EMPLOYERS AND EMPLOYEES

(a)   Each employer—

(1)   shall furnish to each of his employees employment and a place of employment which are free from recognized hazards that are causing or are likely to cause death or serious physical harm to his employees;

(2)   shall comply with occupational safety and health standards promulgated under this chapter.

(b)   Each employee shall comply with occupational safety and health standards and all rules, regulations, and orders issued pursuant to this chapter which are applicable to his own actions and conduct . . . .

§ 655. STANDARDS

(a)   Promulgation by Secretary of national consensus standards and established Federal standards; time for promulgation; conflicting standards

Without regard to chapter 5 of title 5 or to the other subsections of this section, the Secretary shall, as soon as practicable during the period beginning with the effective date of this chapter and ending two years after such date, by rule promulgate as an occupational safety or health standard any national consensus standard, and any established Federal standard, unless he determines that the promulgation of such a standard would not result in improved safety or health for specifically designated employees. In the event of conflict among any such standards, the Secretary shall promulgate the standard which assures the greatest protection of the safety or health of the affected employees.

(b)   Procedure for promulgation, modification, or revocation of standards

The secretary may by rule promulgate, modify, or revoke any occupational safety or health standard in the following manner:

(1)   Whenever the Secretary, upon the basis of information submitted to him in writing by an interested person, a representative of any organization of employers or employees, a nationally recognized standards-producing organiza-

tion, the Secretary of Health and Human Services, the National Institute for Occupational Safety and Health, or a State or political subdivision, or on the basis of information developed by the Secretary or otherwise available to him, determines that a rule should be promulgated in order to serve the objectives of this chapter, the Secretary may request the recommendations of an advisory committee appointed under section 656 of this title. The Secretary shall provide such an advisory committee with any proposals of his own or of the Secretary of Health and Human Services, together with all pertinent factual information developed by the Secretary or the Secretary of Health and Human Services, or otherwise available, including the results of research, demonstrations, and experiments. An advisory committee shall submit to the Secretary its recommendations regarding the rule to be promulgated within ninety days from the date of its appointment or within such longer or shorter period as may be prescribed by the Secretary, but in no event for a period which is longer than two hundred and seventy days.

(2)   The Secretary shall publish a proposed rule promulgating, modifying, or revoking an occupational safety or health standard in the Federal Register and shall afford interested persons a period of thirty days after publication to submit written data or comments. Where an advisory committee is appointed and the Secretary determines that a rule should be issued, he shall publish the proposed rule within sixty days after the submission of the advisory committee's recommendations or the expiration of the period prescribed by the Secretary for such submission.

(3)   On or before the last day of the period provided for the submission of written data or comments under paragraph (2), any interested person may file with the Secretary written objections to the proposed rule, stating the grounds therefor and requesting a public hearing on such objections. Within thirty days after the last day for filing such objections, the Secretary shall publish in the Federal Register a notice specifying the occupational safety or health standard to which objections have been filed and a hearing requested, and specifying a time and place for such hearing.

(4)   Within sixty days after the expiration of the period provided for the submission of written data or comments under paragraph (2), or within sixty days after the comple-

tion of any hearing held under paragraph (3), the Secretary shall issue a rule promulgating, modifying, or revoking an occupational safety or health standard or make a determination that a rule should not be issued. Such a rule may contain a provision delaying its effective date for such period (not in excess of ninety days) as the Secretary determines may be necessary to insure that affected employers and employees will be informed of the existence of the standard and of its terms and that employers affected are given an opportunity to familiarize themselves and their employees with the existence of the requirements of the standard.

(5)   The Secretary, in promulgating standards dealing with toxic materials or harmful physical agents under this subsection, shall set the standard which most adequately assures, to the extent feasible, on the basis of the best available evidence, that no employee will suffer material impairment of health or functional capacity even if such employee has regular exposure to the hazard dealt with by such standard for the period of his working life. Development of standards under this subsection shall be based upon research, demonstrations, experiments, and such other information as may be appropriate. In addition to the attainment of the highest degree of health and safety protection for the employee, other considerations shall be the latest available scientific data in the field, the feasibility of the standards, and experience gained under this and other health and safety laws. Whenever practicable, the standard promulgated shall be expressed in terms of objective criteria and of the performance desired.

(6)(A) Any employer may apply to the Secretary for a temporary order granting a variance from a standard or any provision thereof promulgated under this section. Such temporary order shall be granted only if the employer files an application which meets the requirements of clause (B) and establishes that (i) he is unable to comply with a standard by its effective date because of unavailability of professional or technical personnel or of materials and equipment needed to come into compliance with the standard or because necessary construction or alteration of facilities cannot be completed by the effective date, (ii) he is taking all available steps to safeguard his employees against the hazards covered by the standard, and (iii) he has an effective program for coming into compliance with the standard as quickly as practicable. Any temporary order issued under this paragraph shall prescribe the practices, means, methods, operations, and processes which the employer must adopt and use while the order is in effect and state in detail his program for coming into compliance with the standard. Such a temporary order may be granted only after notice to employees and an opportunity for a hearing: *Provided*, That the Secretary may issue one interim order to be effective until a decision is made on the basis of the hearing. No temporary order may be in effect for longer than the period needed by the employer to achieve compliance with the standard or one year, whichever is shorter, except that such an order may be renewed not more than twice (I) so long as the requirements of this paragraph are met and (II) if an application for renewal is filed at least 90 days prior to the expiration date of the order. No interim renewal of an order may remain in effect for longer than 180 days.

(B)   An application for a temporary order under this paragraph (6) shall contain:

(i)   a specification of the standard or portion thereof from which the employer seeks a variance,

(ii)   a representation by the employer, supported by representations from qualified persons having first-hand knowledge of the facts represented, that he is unable to comply with the standard or portion thereof and a detailed statement of the reasons therefor,

(iii)   a statement of the steps he has taken and will take (with specific dates) to protect employees against the hazard covered by the standard,

(iv)   a statement of when he expects to be able to comply with the standard and what steps he has taken and what steps he will take (with dates specified) to come into compliance with the standard, and

(v)   a certification that he has informed his employees of the application by giving a copy thereof to their authorized representative, posting a statement giving a summary of the application and specifying where a copy may be examined at the place or places where notices to employees are normally posted, and by other appropriate means.

A description of how employees have been informed shall be contained in the certification. The information to employees shall also inform them of their right to petition the Secretary for a hearing.

(C)   The Secretary is authorized to grant a variance from any standard or portion thereof whenever he determines, or the Secretary of Health and Human Services certifies, that such variance is necessary to permit an employer to participate in an experiment approved by him or the Secretary of Health and Human Services designed to demonstrate or validate new and improved techniques to safeguard the health or safety of workers.

(7)   Any standards promulgated under this subjection shall prescribe the use of labels or other appropriate forms of warning as are necessary to insure that employees are apprised of all hazards to which they are exposed, relevant symptoms and appropriate emergency treatment, and proper conditions and precautions of safe use or exposure. Where appropriate, such standard shall also prescribe suitable protective equipment and control or technological procedures to be used in connection with such hazards and shall provide for monitoring or measuring employee exposure at such locations and intervals, and in such manner as may be necessary for the protection of employees. In addition, where appropriate, and such standard shall prescribe the type and frequency of medical examinations or other tests which shall be made available, by the employer or at his cost, to employees exposed to such hazards in order to most effectively determine whether the health of such employees is adversely affected by such exposure. In the event such medical examinations are in the nature of research, as determined by the Secretary of Health and Human Services, such examinations may be furnished at the expense of the Secretary of Health and Human Services. The results of such examinations or tests shall be furnished only to the Secretary or the Secretary of Health and Human Services, and, at the request of the employee, to his physician. The Secretary, in consultation with the Secretary of Health and Human Services, may by rule promulgated pursuant to section 553 of title 5, make appropriate modifications in the foregoing requirements relating to the use of labels or other forms of warning, monitoring or measuring, and medical examinations, as may be warranted by experience, information, or medical or technological developments acquired subsequent to the promulgation of the relevant standard.

(8)   Whenever a rule promulgated by the Secretary differs substantially from an existing national consensus stan-

dard, the Secretary shall, at the same time, publish in the Federal Register a statement of the reasons why the rule as adopted will better effectuate the purposes of this chapter than the national consensus standard.

(c)   Emergency temporary standards

(1)   The Secretary shall provide, without regard to the requirements of chapter 5 of title 5, for an emergency temporary standard to take immediate effect upon publication in the Federal Register if he determines (A) that employees are exposed to grave danger from exposure to substances or agents determined to be toxic or physically harmful or from new hazards, and (B) that such emergency standard is necessary to protect employees from such danger.

(2)   Such standard shall be effective until superseded by a standard promulgated in accordance with the procedures prescribed in paragraph (3) of this subsection.

(3)   Upon publication of such standard in the Federal Register the Secretary shall commence a proceeding in accordance with subsection (b) of this section, and the standard as published shall also serve as a proposed rule for the proceeding. The Secretary shall promulgate a standard under this paragraph no later than six months after publication of the emergency standard as provided in paragraph (2) of this subsection.

(d)   Variances from standards; procedure

Any affected employer may apply to the Secretary for a rule or order for a variance from a standard promulgated under this section. Affected employees shall be given notice of each such application and an opportunity to participate in a hearing. The Secretary shall issue such rule or order if he determines on the record, after opportunity for an inspection where appropriate and a hearing, that the proponent of the variance has demonstrated by a preponderance of the evidence that the conditions, practices, means, methods, operations, or processes used or proposed to be used by an employer will provide employment and places of employment to his employees which are as safe and healthful as those which would prevail if he complied with the standard. The rule or order so issued shall prescribe the conditions the employer must maintain, and the practices, means, methods, operations, and processes which he must adopt and utilize to the extent they differ from the standard in question. Such a rule

or order may be modified or revoked upon application by an employer, employees, or by the Secretary on his own motion, in the manner prescribed for its issuance under this subsection at any time after six months from its issuance.

(e)   Statement of reasons for Secretary's determinations; publication in Federal Register

Whenever the Secretary promulgates any standard, makes any rule, order, or decision, grants any exemption or extension of time, or compromises, mitigates, or settles any penalty assessed under this chapter, he shall include a statement of the reasons for such action, which shall be published in the Federal Register.

(f)   Judicial review

Any person may be adversely affected by a standard issue under this section may at any time prior to the sixtieth day after such standard is promulgated file a petition challenging the validity of such standard with the United States court of appeals for the circuit wherein such person resides or has his principal place of business, for a judicial review of such standard. A copy of the petition shall be forthwith transmitted by the clerk of the court to the Secretary. The filing of such petition shall not, unless otherwise ordered by the court, operate as a stay of the standard. The determinations of the Secretary shall be conclusive if supported by substantial evidence in the record considered as a whole.

(g)   Priority for establishment of standards

In determining the priority for establishing standards under this section, the Secretary shall give due regard to the urgency of the need for mandatory safety and health standards for particular industries, trades, crafts, occupations, businesses, workplaces or work environments. The Secretary shall also give due regard to the recommendations of the Secretary of Health and Human Services regarding the need for mandatory standards in determining the priority for establishing such standards.

§ 656. ADMINISTRATION

(a)   National Advisory Committee on Occupational Safety and Health; establishment; membership; appointment; Chairman; functions; meetings; compensation; secretarial and clerical personnel

(1)   There is hereby established a National Advisory Committee on Occupational Safety and Health consisting of twelve members appointed by the Secretary, four of whom are to be designated by the Secretary of Health and Human Services, without regard to the provisions of title 5 governing appointments in the competitive service, and composed of representatives of management, labor, occupational safety and occupational health professions, and of the public. The Secretary shall designate one of the public members as Chairman. The members shall be selected upon the basis of their experience and competence in the field of occupational safety and health.

(2)   The Committee shall advise, consult with, and make recommendations to the Secretary and the Secretary of Health and Human Services on matters relating to the administration of this chapter. The Committee shall hold no fewer than two meetings during each calendar year. All meetings of the Committee shall be open to the public and a transcript shall be kept and made available for public inspection.

(3)   The members of the Committee shall be compensated in accordance with the provisions of section 3109 of title 5.

(4)   The Secretary shall furnish to the Committee an executive secretary and such secretarial, clerical, and other services as are deemed necessary to the conduct of its business.

(b)   Advisory committees; appointment; duties; membership; compensation; reimbursement to member's employer; meetings; availability of records; conflict of interest

An advisory committee may be appointed by the Secretary to assist him in his standard-setting functions under section 655 of this title. Each such committee shall consist of not more than fifteen members and shall include as a member one or more designees of the Secretary of Health and Human Services, and shall include among its members an equal number of persons qualified by experience and affiliation to present the viewpoint of the employers involved, and of persons similarly qualified to present the viewpoint of the workers involved, as well as one or more representatives of health and safety agencies of the States.

An advisory committee may also include such other persons as the Secretary may appoint who are qualified by knowledge and experience to make a useful contribution to the work of such committee, including one or more representatives of professional organizations of technicians or professionals specializing in occupational safety or health, and one or more representatives of nationally recognized standards-producing organizations, but the number of persons so appointed to any such advisory committee shall not exceed the number appointed to such committee as representatives of Federal and State agencies. Persons appointed to advisory committees from private life shall be compensated in the same manner as consultants or experts under section 3109 of title 5. The Secretary shall pay to any State which is the employer of a member of such a committee who is a representative of the health or safety agency of that State, reimbursement sufficient to cover the actual cost to the State resulting from such representative's membership on such committee. Any meeting of such committee shall be open to the public and an accurate record shall be kept and made available to the public. No member of such committee (other than representatives of employers and employees) shall have an economic interest in any proposed rule.

(c)   Use of services, facilities, and personnel of Federal, State, and local agencies; reimbursement; employment of experts and consultants or organizations; renewal of contracts; compensation; travel expenses

In carrying out his responsibilities under this chapter, the Secretary is authorized to—

(1)   use, with the consent of any Federal agency, the services, facilities, and personnel of such agency, with or without reimbursement, and with the consent of any State or political subdivision, thereof, accept and use the services, facilities, and personnel of any agency of such State or subdivision with reimbursement; and

(2)   employ experts and consultants or organizations thereof as authorized by section 3109 of title 5, except that contracts for such employment may be renewed annually; compensate individuals so employed at rates not in excess of the rate specified at the time of service for grade GS-18 under section 5332 of title 5, including travel-time, and allow them

while away from their homes or regular places of business, travel expenses (including per diem in lieu of subsistence) as authorized by section 5703 of title 5 for persons in the Government service employed intermittently, while so employed.

§ 657. INSPECTIONS, INVESTIGATIONS, AND RECORD-KEEPING

(a)   Authority of Secretary to enter, inspect, and investigate places of employment; time and manner

In order to carry out the purposes of this chapter, the Secretary, upon presenting appropriate credentials to the owner, operator, or agent in charge, is authorized—

(1)   to enter without delay and at reasonable times any factory, plant, establishment, construction site, or other area, workplace or environment where work is performed by an employee of an employer; and

(2)   to inspect and investigate during regular working hours and at other reasonable times, and within reasonable limits and in a reasonable manner, any such place of employment and all pertinent conditions, structures, machines, apparatus, devices, equipment, and materials therein, and to question privately any such employer, owner, operator, agent, or employee.

(b)   Attendance and testimony of witnesses and production of evidence, enforcement of subpoena

In making his inspections and investigations under this chapter the Secretary may require the attendance and testimony of witnesses and the production of evidence under oath. Witnesses shall be paid the same fees and mileage that are paid witnesses in the courts of the United States. In case of a contumacy, failure, or refusal of any person to obey such an order, any district court of the United States or the United States courts of any territory or possession, within the jurisdiction of which such person is found, or resides or transacts business, upon the application by the Secretary, shall have jurisdiction to issue to such person an order requiring such person to appear to produce evidence if, as, and when so ordered, and to give testimony relating to the matter under investigation or in question, and any failure to obey such order of the court may be punished by said court as a contempt thereof.

(c)   Maintenance, preservation, and availability of records; issuance of regulations; scope of records; periodic inspections by employer; posting of notice by employer; notification of employee of corrective action

(1)   Each employer shall make, keep and preserve, and make available to the Secretary or the Secretary of Health and Human Services, such records regarding his activities relating to this chapter as the Secretary, in cooperation with the Secretary of Health and Human Services, may prescribe by regulation as necessary or appropriate for the enforcement of this chapter or for developing information regarding the causes and prevention of occupational accidents and illnesses. In order to carry out the provisions of this paragraph such regulations may include provisions requiring employers to conduct periodic inspections. The Secretary shall also issue regulations requiring that employers, through posting of notices or other appropriate means, keep their employees informed of their protections and obligations under this chapter, including the provisions of applicable standards.

(2)   The Secretary, in cooperation with the Secretary of Health and Human Services, shall prescribe regulations requiring employers to maintain accurate records or, and to make periodic reports on, work-related deaths, injuries and illnesses other than minor injuries requiring only first aid treatment and which do not involve medical treatment, loss of consciousness, restriction of work or motion, or transfer to another job.

(3)   The Secretary, in cooperation with the Secretary of Health and Human Services, shall issue regulations requiring employers to maintain accurate records of employees exposures to potentially toxic materials or harmful physical agents which are required to be monitored or measured under section 655 of this title. Such regulations shall provide employees or their representatives with an opportunity to observe such monitoring or measuring, and to have access to the records thereof. Such regulations shall also make appropriate provision for each employee or former employee to have access to such records as will indicate his own exposure to toxic materials or harmful physical agents. Each employer shall promptly notify any employee who has been or is being exposed to toxic materials or harmful physical

agents in concentrations or at levels which exceed those prescribed by an applicable occupational safety and health standard promulgated under section 655 of this title, and shall inform any employee who is being thus exposed of the corrective action being taken.

(d)   Obtaining of information

Any information obtained by the Secretary, the Secretary of Health and Human Services, or a State agency under this chapter shall be obtained with a minimum burden upon employers, especially those operating small businesses. Unnecessary duplication of efforts in obtaining information shall be reduced to the maximum extent feasible.

(e)   Employer and authorized employee representatives to accompany Secretary or his authorized representative on inspection of workplace; consultation with employees where no authorized employee representative is present

Subject to regulations issued by the Secretary, a representative of the employer and a representative authorized by this employees shall be given an opportunity to accompany the Secretary or his authorized representative during the physical inspection of any workplace under subsection (a) of this section for the purpose of aiding such inspection. Where there is no authorized employee representative, the Secretary or his authorized representative shall consult with a reasonable number of employees concerning matters of health and safety in the workplace.

(f)   Request for inspection by employees or representative of employees; grounds; procedure; determination of request; notification of Secretary or representative prior to or during any inspection of violations; procedure for review of refusal by representative of Secretary to issue citation for alleged violations

(1)   Any employees or representative of employees who believe that a violation of a safety or health standard exists that threatens physical harm, or that an imminent danger exists, may request an inspection by giving notice to the Secretary or his authorized representative of such violation or danger. Any such notice shall be reduced to writing,

shall set forth with reasonable particularity the grounds for the notice, and shall be signed by the employees or representative of employees, and a copy shall be provided the employer or his agent no later than at the time of inspection, except that, upon the request of the person giving such notice, his name and the names of individual employees referred to therein shall not appear in such copy or on any record published, released, or made available pursuant to subsection (g) of this section. If upon receipt of such notification the Secretary determines there are reasonable grounds to believe that such violation or danger exists, he shall make a special inspection in accordance with the provisions of this section as soon as practicable, to determine if such violation or danger exists. If the Secretary determines there are no reasonable grounds to believe that a violation or danger exists he shall notify the employees or representative of the employees in writing of such determination.

(2)   Prior to or during any inspection of a workplace, any employees or representative or employees employed in such workplace may notify the Secretary or any representative of the Secretary responsible for conducting the inspection, in writing, of any violation of this chapter which they have reason to believe exists in such workplace. The Secretary shall, by regulation establish procedures for informal review of any refusal by a representative of the Secretary to issue a citation with respect to any such alleged violation and shall furnish the employees or representative of employees requesting such review a written statement of the reasons for the Secretary's final disposition of the case.

(g)   Compilation, analysis, and publication of reports and information; rules and regulations

(1)   The Secretary and Secretary of Health and Human Services are authorized to compile, analyze, and publish, either in summary or detailed form, all reports or information obtained under this section.

(2)   The Secretary and the Secretary of Health and Human Services shall each prescribe such rules and regulations as he may deem necessary to carry out their responsibilities under this chapter, including rules and regulations dealing with the inspection of an employer's establishment.

APPENDIX E

THE CONSTITUTION OF THE UNITED STATES OF AMERICA

PREAMBLE

We the people of the United States, in order to form a more perfect union, establish justice, insure domestic tranquility, provide for the common defense, promote the general welfare, and secure the blessings of liberty to ourselves and our posterity, do ordain and establish this Constitution for the United States of America.

ARTICLE I

SECTION 1. All legislative powers herein granted shall be vested in a Congress of the United States, which shall consist of a Senate and House of Representatives.

SECTION 2. The House of Representatives shall be composed of members chosen every second year by the people of the several states, and the electors in each state shall have the qualifications requisite for electors of the most numerous branch of the state legislature.

No person shall be a Representative who shall not have attained to the age of twenty five years, and been seven years a citizen of the United States, and who shall not, when elected, be an inhabitant of that state in which he shall be chosen.

Representatives and direct taxes shall be apportioned among the several states which may be included within this union, according to their respective numbers, which shall be determined by adding to the whole number of free persons, including those bound to service for a of term of years, and excluding Indians not taxed, three fifths of all other persons. The actual enumeration shall be made within three years after the first meeting of the Congress of the United States, and within every subsequent term of ten years, in such manner as they shall by law direct. The number of Representatives shall not exceed one for every thirty thousand, but each state shall have at least one Representative; and until such enumeration shall be made, the state of New Hampshire shall be entitled to choose three, Massachusetts eight, Rhode Island and Providence Plantations one, Connecticut five, New York six, New Jersey four, Pennsylvania eight, Delaware one, Maryland six, Virginia ten, North Carolina five, South Carolina five, and Georgia three.

When vacancies happen in the Representation from any state, the executive authority thereof shall issue writs of election to fill such vacancies.

The House of Representatives shall choose their speaker and other officers; and shall have the sole power of impeachment.

SECTION 3. The Senate of the United States shall be composed of two Senators from each state, chosen by the legislature thereof, for six years; and each Senator shall have one vote.

Immediately after they shall be assembled in consequence of the first election, they shall be divided as equally as may be into three classes. The seats of the Senators of the first class shall be vacated at the expiration of the second year, of the second class at the expiration of the fourth year, and of the third class at the expiration of the sixth year, so that one third may be chosen every second year and if vacancies happen by resignation, or otherwise, during the recess of the legislature of any state, the executive thereof may make temporary appointments until the next meeting of the legislature, which shall then fill such vacancies.

No person shall be a Senator who shall not have attained to the age of thirty years, and been nine years a citizen of the United States and who shall not, when elected, be an inhabitant of that state for which he shall be chosen.

The Vice President of the United States shall be President of the Senate, but shall have no vote, unless they be equally divided.

The Senate shall choose their other officers, and also a President pro tempore, in the absence of the vice President, or when he shall exercise the office of President of the United States.

The Senate shall have the sole power to try all impeachments. When sitting for that purpose, they shall be on oath or affirmation. When the President of the United States is tried, the Chief Justice shall preside: And no person shall be convicted without the concurrence of two thirds of the members present.

Judgment in cases of impeachment shall not extend further than to removal from office, and disqualification to hold and enjoy any office of honor, trust or profit under the United States; but the party convicted shall nevertheless be liable and subject to indictment, trial, judgment and punishment, according to law.

SECTION 4. The times, places and manner of holding elections for Senators and Representatives, shall be prescribed in each state by the legislature thereof; but the Congress may at any time by law make or alter such regulations, except as to the places of choosing Senators.

The Congress shall assemble at least once in every year, and such meeting shall be on the first Monday in December, unless they shall by law appoint a different day.

SECTION 5. Each House shall be the judge of the elections, returns and qualifications of its own members, and a majority of each shall constitute a quorum to do business; but a smaller number may adjourn from day to day, and may be authorized to compel the attendance of absent members,

in such manner, and under such penalties as each House may provide.

Each House may determine the rules of its proceedings, punish its members for disorderly behavior, and with the concurrence of two thirds, expel a member.

Each House shall keep a journal of it proceedings, and from time to time publish the same, excepting such parts as may in their judgment require secrecy; and the yeas and nays of the members of either House on any question shall, at the desire of one fifth of those present, be entered on the journal.

Neither House, during the session of Congress, shall, without the consent of the other, adjourn for more than three days, nor to any other place than that in which the two Houses shall be sitting.

SECTION 6. The Senators and Representatives shall receive a compensation for their services, to be ascertained by law, and paid out of the Treasury of the United States. They shall in all cases, except treason, felony and breach of the peace, by privileged from arrest during their attendance at the session of their respective Houses, and in going to and returning from the same; and for any speech or debate in either House, they shall not be questioned in any other place.

No Senator or Representative shall, during the time for which he was elected, be appointed to any civil office under the authority of the United States, which shall have been created, or the emoluments whereof shall have been increased during such time; and no person holding any office under the United States, shall be a member of either House during his continuance in office.

SECTION 7. All bills for raising revenue shall originate in the House of Representatives; but the Senate may propose or concur with amendments as on other bills.

Every bill which shall have passed the House of Representatives and the Senate, shall, before it become a law, be presented to the President of the United States; if he approves he shall sign it, but if not he shall return it, with his objections to that House in which it shall have originated, who shall enter the objections at large on their journal, and proceed to reconsider it. If after such reconsideration two thirds of that House shall agree to pass the bill, it shall be sent, together with the objections, to the other House, by which it shall likewise be reconsidered, and if approved by two thirds of that House, it shall become a law. But in all such cases the votes of both Houses shall be determined by yeas and nays, and the names of the persons voting for and against the bill shall be entered on the journal of each House respectively. If any bill shall not be returned by the President within ten days (Sundays excepted) after it shall have been presented to him, the same shall be a law, in like manner as if he had signed it, unless the Congress by their adjournment prevent its return, in which case it shall not be a law.

Every order, resolution, or vote to which the concurrence of the Senate and House of Representatives may be necessary (except on a question of adjournment) shall be presented to the President of the United States; and before the same shall take effect, shall be approved by him, or being disapproved by him, shall be repassed by two thirds of the Senate and House of Representatives, according to the rules and limitations prescribed in the case of a bill.

SECTION 8. The Congress shall have power to lay and collect taxes, duties, imposts and excises, to pay the debts and provide for the common defense and general welfare of the United States; but all duties; imposts and excises shall be uniform throughout the United States;

To borrow money on the credit of the United States;

To regulate commerce with foreign nations, and among the several States, and with the indian tribes;

To establish a uniform rule of naturalization, and uniform laws on the subject of bankruptcies throughout the United States;

To coin money, regulate the value thereof, and of foreign coin, and fix the standard of weights and measures;

To provide for the punishment of counterfeiting the securities and current coin of the United States;

To establish post offices and post roads;

To promote the progress of science and useful arts, by securing for limited times to authors and inventors the exclusive right to their respective writings and discoveries;

To constitute tribunals inferior to the Supreme Court;

To define and punish piracies and felonies committed on the high seas, and offences against the law of nations;

To declare war, grant letters of marque and reprisal, and make rules concerning captures on land and water;

To raise and support armies, but no appropriation of money to that use shall be for a longer term than two years;

To provide and maintain a Navy;

To make rules for the government and regulation of the land and naval forces;

To provide for calling forth the militia to execute the laws of the Union, suppress insurrections and repel invasions;

To provide for organizing, arming, and disciplining, the militia, and for governing such part of them as may be employed in the service of the United States, reserving to the states respectively, the appointment of the officers, and the authority of training the militia according to the discipline prescribed by Congress;

To exercise exclusive legislation in all cases whatsoever, over such district (not exceeding ten miles square) as may, by cession of particular states, and the acceptance of Congress, become the seat of the government of the United States, and to exercise like authority over all places purchased by the consent of the legislature of the state in which the same shall be, for the erection of forts, magazines, arsenals, dockyards, and other needful buildings;—And

To make all laws which shall be necessary and proper for carrying into execution the foregoing powers, and all other powers vested by this Constitution in the government of the United States, or in any department or officer thereof.

SECTION 9. The migration or importation of such persons as any of the states now existing shall think proper to admit, shall not be prohibited by the Congress prior to the year one thousand eight hundred and eight, but a tax or duty may be imposed on such importation, not exceeding ten dollars for each person.

The privilege of the writ of habeas corpus shall not be suspended, unless when in cases of rebellion or invasion the public safety may require it.

No bill of attainder or ex post facto law shall be passed.

No capitation, or other direct, tax shall be laid, unless in proportion to the census or enumeration herein before directed to be taken.

No tax or duty shall be laid on articles exported from any state.

No preference shall be given by any regulation of commerce or revenue to the ports of one state over those of another, nor shall vessels bound to, or from, one state, be obliged to enter, clear, or pay duties in another.

No money shall be drawn from the treasury, but in consequence of appropriations made by law; and a regular statement and account of receipts and expenditures of all public money shall be published from time to time.

No title of nobility shall be granted by the United States: and no person holding any office of profit or trust under them, shall, without the consent of the Congress, accept of any present, emolument, office, or title, of any kind whatever, from any king, prince, or foreign state.

SECTION 10. No state shall enter into any treaty, alliance, or confederation; grant letters of marque and reprisal; coin money; emit bills of credit; make anything but gold and silver coin a tender in payment of debts; pass any bill of attainder, ex post facto law, or law impairing the obligation of contracts, or grant any title of nobility.

No state shall, without the consent of the Congress, lay any imposts or duties on imports or exports, except what may be absolutely necessary for executing its inspection laws: and the net produce of all duties and imposts, laid by any state on imports or exports, shall be for the use of the treasury of the United States, and all such laws shall be subject to the revision and control of the Congress.

No state shall, without the consent of Congress, lay any duty of tonnage, keep troops, or ships of war in time of peace, enter into any agreement or compact with another state, or with a foreign power, or engage in war, unless actually invaded, or in such imminent danger as will not admit of delay.

ARTICLE II

SECTION 1. The executive power shall be vested in a President of the United States of America. He shall hold his office during the term of four years, and, together with the Vice President, chosen for the same term, be elected as follows:

Each state shall appoint, in such manner as the legislature thereof may direct, a number of electors, equal to the whole number of Senators and Representatives to which the state may be entitled in the Congress; but no Senator or Representative, or person holding an office of trust of profit under the United States, shall be appointed an elector.

The electors shall meet in their respective states, and vote by ballot for two persons, of whom one at least shall not be an inhabitant of the same state with themselves. And they shall make a list of all the persons voted for, and, of the number of votes for each; which list they shall sign and certify, and transmit sealed to the seat of the government of the United States, directed to the President of the Senate. The President of the Senate shall, in the presence of the Senate and House of Representatives, open all the certificates, and the votes shall then be counted. The person having the greatest number of votes shall be the President, if such number be a majority of the whole number of electors appointed; and if there be more than one who have such majority, and have an equal number of votes, then the House of Representatives shall immediately choose by ballot one of them for President; and if no person have a majority, then from the five highest on the list the said House shall in like manner choose the President. But in choosing the President, the votes shall be taken by states, the representation from each state having one vote; a quorum for this purpose shall consist of a member or members from two thirds of the states, and a majority of all the states shall be necessary to a choice. In every case, after the choice of the President, the person having the greatest number of votes of the electors shall be the Vice President. But if there should remain two or more who have equal votes, the Senate shall choose from them by ballot the Vice President.

The Congress may determine the time of choosing the electors, and the day on which they shall give their votes; which day shall be the same throughout the United States.

No person except a natural born citizen, or a citizen of the United States, at the time of the adoption of this Constitution, shall be eligible to the office of President; neither shall any person be eligible to that office who shall not have attained to the age of thirty five years, and been fourteen years a resident within the United States.

In case of the removal of the President from office, or of his death, resignation, or inability to discharge the powers and duties of the said office, the same shall devolve on the

Vice President, and the Congress may by law provide for the case of removal, death, resignation or inability, both of the President and Vice President, declaring what officer shall then act as President, and such officer shall act accordingly, until the disability be removed, or a President shall be elected.

The President shall, at stated times, receive for his services, a compensation, which shall neither be encreased nor diminished during the period for which he shall have been elected, and he shall not receive within that period any other emolument from the United States, or any of them.

Before he enter on the execution of his office, he shall take the following oath or affirmation—"I do solemnly swear (or affirm) that I will faithfully execute the office of President of the United States, and will to the best of my ability, preserve, protect and defend the Constitution of the United States."

SECTION 2. The President shall be commander in chief of the Army, and Navy of the United States, and of the militia of the several states, when called into the actual service of the United States; he may require the opinion, in writing, of the principal officer in each of the executive departments, upon any subject relating to the duties of their respective offices, and he shall have power to grant reprieves and pardons for offences against the United States, except in cases of impeachment.

He shall have power, by and with the advice and consent of the Senate, to make treaties, provided two thirds of the Senators present concur; and he shall nominate, and by and with the advice and consent of the Senate, shall appoint ambassadors, other public ministers and consuls, judges of the Supreme Court, and all other officers of the United States, whose appointments are not herein otherwise provided for, and which shall be established by law: but the Congress may by law vest the appointment of such inferior officers, as they think proper, in the President alone, in the courts of law, or in the heads of departments.

The President shall have power to fill up all vacancies that may happen during the recess of the Senate, by granting commissions which shall expire at the end of their next session.

SECTION 3. He shall from time to time give to the Congress information of the state of the union, and recommend to their consideration such measures as he shall judge necessary and expedient; he may, on extraordinary occasions, convene both Houses, or either of them, and in case of disagreement between them, with respect to the time of adjournment, he may adjourn them to such time as he shall think proper; he shall receive Ambassadors and other public ministers; he shall take care that the laws be faithfully executed, and shall commission all the officers of the United States.

SECTION 4. The President, Vice President and all civil officers of the United States, shall be removed from office on impeachment for, and conviction of, treason, bribery, or other high crimes and misdemeanors.

ARTICLE III

SECTION 1. The judicial power of the United States, shall be vested in one Supreme Court, and in such inferior courts as the Congress may from time to time ordain and establish. The judges, both of the Supreme and inferior Courts, shall hold their offices during good behavior, and shall, at stated times, receive for their services, a compensation, which shall not be diminished during their continuance in office.

SECTION 2. The judicial power shall extend to all cases, in law and equity, arising under this Constitution, the laws of the United States, and treaties made, or which shall be made, under their authority—to all cases affecting Ambassadors, other public ministers and consuls;—to all cases of admiralty and maritime jurisdiction;—to controversies to which the United States shall be a party;—to controversies between two or more states;—between a state and citizens of another state;—between citizens of different states,—between citizens of the same state claiming lands under grants of different states,—and between a state, or the citizens thereof, and foreign states, citizens or subjects.

In all cases affecting Ambassadors, other public ministers and consuls, and those in which a state shall be party, the Supreme Court shall have original jurisdiction. In all the other cases before mentioned, the Supreme Court shall have appellate jurisdiction, both as to law and fact, with such exceptions, and under such regulations as the Congress shall make.

The trial of all crimes, except in cases of Impeachment, shall be by jury; and such trial shall be held in the state where the said crimes shall have been committed; but when not committed within any state, the trial shall be at such place or places as the Congress may by law have directed.

SECTION 3. Treason against the United States, shall consist only in levying war against them, or in adhering to their enemies, giving them aid and comfort. No person shall be convicted of treason unless on the testimony of two witnesses to the same overt act, or on confession in open court.

The Congress shall have power to declare the punishment of treason, but no attainder of treason shall work corruption of blood, or forfeiture except during the life of the person attainted.

ARTICLE IV

SECTION 1. Full faith and credit shall be given in each state to the public acts, records, and judicial proceedings of every other state. And the Congress may by general laws prescribe the manner in which such acts, records and proceedings shall be proved, and the effect thereof.

SECTION 2. The citizens of each state shall be entitled to all privileges and immunities of citizens in the several states.

A person charged in any state with treason, felony, or other crime, who shall flee from justice, and be found in another state, shall on demand of the executive authority of the state from which he fled, be delivered up, to be removed to the state having jurisdiction of the crime.

No person held to service or labor in one state under the laws thereof, escaping into another, shall, in consequence of any law or regulation therein, be discharged from such service or labour, but shall be delivered up on claim of the party to whom such service or labour may be due.

SECTION 3. New states may be admitted by the Congress into this union; but no new state shall be formed or erected within the jurisdiction of any other state; nor any state be formed by the junction of two or more states, or parts of states, without the consent of the legislatures of the states concerned as well as of the Congress.

The Congress shall have power to dispose of and make all needful rules and regulations respecting the territory or other property belonging to the United States; and nothing in this Constitution shall be so construed as to prejudice any claims of the United States, or of any particular state.

SECTION 4. The United States shall guarantee to every state in this Union a republican form of government, and shall protect each of them against Invasion, and on application of the legislature, or of the executive (when the legislature cannot be convened) against domestic violence.

ARTICLE V

The Congress, whenever two thirds of both Houses shall deem it necessary, shall propose amendments to this Constitution, or, on the application of the legislatures of two thirds of the several states, shall call a convention for proposing amendments, which, in either case, shall be valid to all Intents and purposes, as part of this Constitution, when ratified by the legislatures of three fourths of the several states, or by conventions in three fourths thereof, as the one or the other mode of ratification may be proposed by the Congress; provided that no amendment which may be made prior to the year one thousand eight hundred and eight shall in any manner affect the first and fourth clauses in the ninth section of the first article; and that no state, without its consent, shall be deprived of its equal suffrage in the Senate.

ARTICLE VI

All debts contracted and engagements entered into, before the adoption of this Constitution, shall be as valid against the United States under this Constitution, as under the confederation.

This Constitution, and the laws of the United States which shall be made in pursuance thereof; and all treaties made, or which shall be made, under the authority of the United States, shall be the supreme law of the land; and the judges in every state shall be bound thereby, anything in the Constitution or laws of any state to the contrary notwithstanding.

The Senators and Representatives before mentioned, and the members of the several state legislatures, and all executive and judicial officers, both of the United States and of the several states, shall be bound by oath or affirmation, to support this Constitution; but no religious test shall ever be required as a qualification to any office or public trust under the United States.

ARTICLE VII

The ratification of the conventions of nine states, shall be sufficient for the establishment of this Constitution between the states so ratifying the same.

Done in convention by the unanimous consent of the states present the seventeenth day of September in the year of our Lord one thousand seven hundred and eighty seven and of the Independence of the United States of America the twelfth. In witness whereof we have hereunto subscribed our names,

Go. WASHINGTON
Presid't. and deputy from Virginia

Attest
WILLIAM JACKSON
Secretary

DELWARE
Geo. Read,
Gunnung Bedford jun,
John Dickinson,
Richard Basset,
Jaco. Broom.

MASSACHUSETTS
Nathaniel Gorham,
Rufus King.

CONNECTICUT
Wm. Saml. Johnson,
Roger Sherman.

NEW YORK
Alexander Hamilton.

NEW JERSEY
Wh. Livingston,
David Brearley,
Wm. Paterson,
Jona. Dayton.

PENNSYLVANIA
B. Franklin,
Thomas Mifflin,
Robt. Morris,
Geo. Clymer,
Thos. FitzSimons,
Jared Ingersoll,
James Wilson,
Gouv. Morris

NEW HAMPSHIRE
John Langdon,
Nicholas Gilman.

MARYLAND
James McHenry,
Dan of St. Thos. Jenifer,
Danl. Carroll.

VIRGINIA
John Blair,
James Madison, Jr.

NORTH CAROLINA
Wm. Blount,
Richd. Dobbs Spaight,
Hu. Williamson.

SOUTH CAROLINA
J. Rutledge,
Charles Cotesworth Pinckney,
Charles Pinckney Pierce Butler.

GEORGIA
William Few,
Abr. Baldwin.

Articles in addition to, and amendment of the Constitution of the United States of America, proposed by Congress and ratified by the legislatures of the several states, pursuant to the fifth article of the original Constitution.

(The first ten amendments were passed by Congress on September 25, 1789, and were ratified on December 15, 1791.)

AMENDMENT I

Congress shall make no law respecting an establishment of religion, or prohibiting the free exercise thereof, or abridging the freedom of speech, or of the press; or the right of the people peaceably to assemble, and to petition the Government for a redress of grievances.

AMENDMENT II

A well regulated militia, being necessary to the security of a free state, the right of the people to keep and bear Arms, shall not be infringed.

AMENDMENT III

No soldier shall, in time of peace be quartered in any house, without the consent of the owner, nor in time of war, but in a manner to be prescribed by law.

AMENDMENT IV

The right of the people to be secure in their persons, houses, papers, and effects, against unreasonable searches and seizures, shall not be violated, and no warrants shall issue, but upon probable cause, supported by oath or affirmation, and particularly describing the place to be searched, and the persons or things to be seized.

AMENDMENT V

No person shall be held to answer for a capital, or otherwise infamous crime, unless on a presentment or indictment of a grand jury, except in cases arising in the land or naval forces, or in the militia, when in actual service in time of war or public danger; nor shall any person be subject for the same offense to be twice put in jeopardy of life or limb; nor shall be compelled in any criminal case to be a witness against himself, nor be deprived of life, liberty, or property, without due process of law; nor shall private property be taken for public use, without just compensation.

AMENDMENT VI

In all criminal prosecutions, the accused shall enjoy the right to a speedy and public trial, by an impartial jury of the state and district wherein the crime shall have been committed, which district shall have been previously ascertained by law, and to be informed of the nature and cause of the accusation; to be confronted with the witnesses against him; to have compulsory process for obtaining witnesses in his favor, and to have the assistance of counsel for his defense.

AMENDMENT VII

In suits at common law, where the value in controversy shall exceed twenty dollars, the right of trial by jury shall be preserved, and no fact tried by a jury, shall be otherwise reexamined in any court of the United States, than according to the rules of the common law.

AMENDMENT VIII

Excessive bail shall not be required, nor excessive fines imposed, nor cruel and unusual punishments inflicted.

AMENDMENT IX

The enumeration in the Constitution, of certain rights, shall not be construed to deny or disparage others retained by the people.

AMENDMENT X

The powers not delegated to the United States by the Constitution, nor prohibited by it to the states, are reserved to the states respectively, or to the people.

AMENDMENT XI

The judicial power of the United States shall not be construed to extend to any suit in law or equity, commenced or prosecuted against one of the United States by citizens of another state, or by citizens or subjects of any foreign state.

AMENDMENT XII *(RATIFIED ON JUNE 15, 1804)*

The electors shall meet in their respective states, and vote by ballot for President and Vice-President, one of whom, at least, shall not be an inhabitant of the same state with themselves; they shall name in their ballots the person voted for as President, and in distinct ballots the person voted for as Vice-President, and they shall make distinct lists of all persons voted for as President, and of all persons voted for as Vice-President, and of the number of votes for each, which lists they shall sign and certify, and transmit sealed to the seat of the government of the United States, directed to the President of the Senate;—The President of the Senate shall, in the presence of the Senate and House of Representatives, open all the certificates and the votes shall then be counted;—The person having the greatest number of votes for President, shall be the President, if such number be a majority of the whole number of electors appointed; and if no person have such majority; then from the persons having the highest numbers not exceeding three on the list of those voted for as President, the House of Representatives shall choose immediately, by ballot, the President. But in choosing the President, the votes shall be taken by states, the representation from each state having one vote; a quorum for this purpose shall consist of a member or members from two-thirds of the states, and a majority of all the states shall be necessary to a choice. And if the House of Representatives shall not choose a President whenever the right of choice shall devolve upon them, before the fourth day of March next following, then the Vice-President shall act as President, as in the case of the death or other constitutional disability of the President. The person having the greatest number of votes as Vice-President, shall be the Vice-President, if such number be a majority of the whole number of electors appointed, and if no person have a majority, then from the two highest numbers on the list, the Senate shall choose the Vice-President; a quorum for the purpose shall consist of two-thirds of the whole number of Senators, and a majority of the whole number shall be necessary to a choice. But no person constitutionally ineligible to the office of President shall be eligible to that of Vice-President of the United States.

AMENDMENT XIII

SECTION 1. Neither slavery nor involuntary servitude, except as a punishment for crime whereof the party shall have been duly convicted, shall exist within the United States, or any place subject to their jurisdiction.

SECTION 2. Congress shall have power to enforce this article by appropriate legislation.

AMENDMENT XIV

SECTION 1. All persons born or naturalized in the United States, and subject to the jurisdiction thereof, are citizens of the United States and of the state wherein they reside. No State shall make or enforce any law which shall abridge the privileges or immunities of citizens of the United States; nor shall any state deprive any person of life, liberty, or property, without due process of law; nor deny to any person within its jurisdiction the equal protection of the laws.

SECTION 2. Representatives shall be apportioned among the several states according to their respective numbers, counting the whole number of persons in each state, excluding Indians not taxed. But when the right to vote at any election for the choice of electors for President and Vice President of the United States, Representatives in Congress, the executive and judicial officers of a state, or the members of the legislature thereof, is denied to any of the male inhabitants of such state, being twenty-one years of age, and citizens of the United States, or in any way abridged, except for participation in rebellion, or other crime, the basis of representation therein shall be reduced in the proportion which the number of such male citizens shall bear to the whole number of male citizens twenty-one years of age in such state.

SECTION 3. No person shall be a Senator or Representative in Congress, or elector of President and Vice President, or hold any office, civil or military, under the United States, or under any state, who, having previously taken an oath, as a member of Congress, or as an officer of the United States, or as a member of any state legislature, or as an executive or judicial officer of any state, to support the Constitution of the United States, shall have engaged in insurrection or rebellion against the same, or given aid or comfort to the enemies thereof. But Congress may by a vote of two-thirds of each House, remove such disability.

SECTION 4. The validity of the public debt of the United States, authorized by law, including debts incurred for payment of pensions and bounties for services in suppressing insurrection or rebellion, shall not be questioned. But neither the United States nor any state shall assume or pay any debt or obligation incurred in aid of insurrection or rebellion against the United States, or any claim for the loss or emancipation of any slave, but all such debts, obligations and claims shall be held illegal and void.

SECTION 5. The Congress shall have power to enforce, by appropriate legislation, the provisions of this article.

AMENDMENT XV

SECTION 1. The right of citizens of the United States to vote shall not be denied or abridged by the United States or by any state on account of race, color, or previous condition of servitude.

SECTION 2. The Congress shall have power to enforce this article by appropriate legislation.

AMENDMENT XVI

The Congress shall have power to lay and collect taxes on incomes, from whatever source derived, without apportionment among the several states, and without regard to any census or enumeration.

AMENDMENT XVII

The Senate of the United States shall be composed of two Senators from each state, elected by the people thereof, for six years; and each Senator shall have one vote. The electors in each State shall have the qualifications requisite for electors of the most numerous branch of the state legislatures.

When vacancies happen in the representation of any state in the Senate, the executive authority of such state shall issue writs of election to fill such vacancies: provided, that the legislature of any state may empower the executive thereof to make temporary appointments until the people fill the vacancies by election as the legislature may direct.

This amendment shall not be so construed as to affect the election or term of any Senator chosen before it becomes valid as part of the Constitution.

AMENDMENT XVIII

SECTION 1. After one year from the ratification of this article the manufacture, sale, or transportation of intoxicating liquors within, the importation thereof into, or the exportation thereof from the United States and all territory subject to the jurisdiction thereof for beverage purposes is hereby prohibited.

SECTION 2. The Congress and the several states shall have concurrent power to enforce this article by appropriate legislation.

SECTION 3. This article shall be inoperative unless it shall have been ratified as an amendment to the Constitution by the legislatures of the several states, as provided in the Constitution, within seven years from the date of the submission hereof to the states by the Congress.

AMENDMENT XIX

The right of citizens of the United States to vote shall not be denied or abridged by the United States or by any state on account of sex.

Congress shall have power to enforce this article by appropriate legislation.

AMENDMENT XX

SECTION 1. The terms of the President and Vice President shall end at noon on the 20th day of January, and the terms of Senators and Representatives at noon on the 3d day of January, of the years in which such terms would have ended if this article had not been ratified; and the terms of their successors shall then begin.

SECTION 2. The Congress shall assemble at least once in every year, and such meeting shall begin at noon on the 3d day of January, unless they shall by law appoint a different day.

SECTION 3. If, at the time fixed for the beginning of the term of the President, the President elect shall have died, the Vice President elect shall become President. If a President shall not have been chosen before the time fixed for the beginning of his term, or if the President elect shall have failed to qualify, then the Vice President elect shall act as President until a President shall have qualified; and the Congress may by law provide for the case wherein neither a President elect nor a Vice President elect shall have qualified, declaring who shall then act as President, or the manner in which one who is to act shall be selected, and such person shall act accordingly until a President or Vice President shall have qualified.

SECTION 4. The Congress may by law provide for the case of the death of any of the persons from whom the House of Representatives may choose a President whenever the rights of choice shall have devolved upon them, and for the case of the death of any of the persons from whom the Senate may choose a Vice President whenever the right of choice shall have devolved upon them.

SECTION 5. Sections 1 and 2 shall take effect on the 15th day of October following the ratification of this article.

SECTION 6. This article shall be inoperative unless it shall have been ratified as an amendment to the Constitution by the legislatures of three-fourths of the several states within seven years from the date of its submission.

AMENDMENT XXI

SECTION 1. The eighteenth article of amendment to the Constitution of the United States is hereby repealed.

SECTION 2. The transportation or importation into any state, territory, or possession of the United States for delivery or use therein of intoxicating liquors, in violation of the laws thereof, is hereby prohibited.

SECTION 3. This article shall be inoperative unless it shall have been ratified as an amendment to the Constitution by conventions in the several states, as provided, in the Constitution, within seven years from the date of the submission hereof to the states by the Congress.

AMENDMENT XII

SECTION 1. No person shall be elected to the office of the President more than twice, and no person who has held the office of President, or acted as President, for more than two years of a term to which some other person was elected President shall be elected to the office of the President more than once. But this article shall not apply to any person holding the office of President when this article was proposed by the Congress, and shall not prevent any person who may be holding the office of President, or acting as President, during the term within which this article becomes operative from holding the office of President or acting as President during the remainder of such term.

SECTION 2. This article shall be inoperative unless it shall have been ratified as an amendment to the Constitution by the legislatures of three-fourths of the sever-

al states within seven years from the date of its submission to the states by the Congress.

AMENDMENT XXIII

SECTION 1. The District constituting the seat of government of the United States shall appoint in such manner as the Congress may direct:

A number of electors of President and Vice President equal to the whole number of Senators and Representatives in Congress to which the District would be entitled if it were a state, but in no event more than the least populous state; they shall be in addition to those appointed by the states, but they shall be considered, for the purposes of the election of President and Vice President, to be electors appointed by a state; and they shall meet in the District and perform such duties as provided by the twelfth article of amendment.

SECTION 2. The Congress shall have power to enforce this article by appropriate legislation.

AMENDMENT XXIV

SECTION 1. The right of citizens of the United States to vote in any primary or other election for President or Vice President, for electors for President or Vice President, or for Senator or Representative in Congress, shall not be denied or abridged by the United States or any state by reason of failure to pay any poll tax or other tax.

SECTION 2. The Congress shall have power to enforce this article by appropriate legislation.

AMENDMENT XXV

SECTION 1. In case of the removal of the President from office or of his death or resignation, the Vice President shall become President.

SECTION 2. Whenever there is a vacancy in the office of the Vice President, the President shall nominate a Vice President who shall take office upon confirmation by a majority vote of both Houses of Congress.

SECTION 3. Whenever the President transmits to the President pro tempore of the Senate and the Speaker of the House of Representatives his written declaration that he is unable to discharge the powers and duties of his office, and until he transmits to them a written declaration to the contrary, such powers and duties shall be discharged by the Vice President as Acting President.

SECTION 4. Whenever the Vice President and a majority of either the principal officers of the executive departments or of such other body as Congress may by law provide, transmit to the President pro tempore of the Senate and the Speaker of the House of Representatives their written declaration that the President is unable to discharge the powers and duties of his office, the Vice President shall immediately assume the powers and duties of the office as Acting President.

Thereafter, when the President transmits to the President pro tempore of the Senate and the Speaker of the House of Representatives his written declaration that no inability exists, he shall resume the powers and duties of his office unless the Vice President and a majority of either the principal officers of the executive department or of such other body as Congress may by law provide, transmit within four days to the President pro tempore of the Senate and the Speaker of the House of Representatives their written declaration that the President is unable to discharge the powers and duties of his office. Thereupon Congress shall decide the issue, assembling within forty-eight hours for that purpose if not in session. If the Congress, within twenty-one days after receipt of the latter written declaration, or, if Congress is not in session, within twenty-one days after Congress is required to assemble, determines by two-thirds vote of both Houses that the President is unable to discharge the powers and duties of his office, the Vice President shall continue to discharge the same as Acting President; otherwise, the President shall resume the powers and duties of his office.

AMENDMENT XXVI

SECTION 1. The right of citizens of the United States, who are eighteen years of age or older, to vote shall not be denied or abridged by the United States or by any state on account of age.

SECTION 2. The Congress shall have power to enforce this article by appropriate legislation.

AMENDMENT XXVII

No law varying the compensation for the services of Senators and Representatives shall take effect until an election of Representatives shall have intervened.

TABLE OF CASES

INDEX